BERNARD SHAW:
SELECTED PLAYS

BERNARD SHAW: SELECTED PLAYS

Preface by

REX HARRISON

Introductory Essay, "Shaw and His Plays,"

by David Bearinger

DODD, MEAD & COMPANY
New York

ISBN 0-396-07905-9
Printed in the United States of America

Contents

PREFACE
by Rex Harrison

In 1977, at the Edinburgh Festival, I gave a reading of Shaw's theatrical criticisms written for the *Saturday Review,* entitled "Our Theatre of the Nineties." These criticisms gave a clear insight into the way his mind worked, his humor, his integrity, his intelligence, and his intolerance and genuine dislike of anything that he would have called "humbug." He wrote:

> "I have frequently been accused of handling people rather recklessly, and in justice to many well known public persons, Mr. Irving, Mr. Tree, Mrs. Patrick Campbell, and even personal friends, I beg you, do not mistake my journalistic utterances for final estimates of their worth as dramatic artists. My remarks are not intended to be a series of judgements aiming at impartiality, but a siege laid at the theatre of the Nineteenth Century by an author who had to cut his way into it at the point of a pen."

This helps to account for the fact that by 1898, while he was a critic, he had written, but had been unable to get produced *The Philanderer, Mrs. Warren's Profession, Arms and the Man, Candida, Man of Destiny, You Never Can Tell, The Devil's Disciple, Cæsar and Cleopatra.* Shaw had a piercing mind and eye for truth as he saw it, but it was not very many people's truth at the turn of the century.

Shaw's plays were largely inspired by his wish to shake up the complacent attitudes towards life that were held, not only by audiences of the period, but also by the actors and playwrights. Again, he wrote:

> "The English do not know what to think until they are coached labouriously for years in the proper opinion. For ten years past with an unprecedented obstination I have been dinning into the public head that I am an extraordinary, witty, brilliant man. . . . I sometimes get quite frantic letters from people who feel they cannot stand me any longer."

He said of the leading actor of the day, Henry Irving:

> "After much striving, and if I may be allowed the expression, not a little floundering, he has at last discovered the method of heroic acting. . . . But suppose he had foregone this victory, suppose Mr. Irving had said 'I can produce studies of modern life and character.' What would have been the result of such renunciation? We should have escaped Lyceum Theatre Shakespeare and we should have had the ablest actor of the day driven by life or death necessity to create a new drama instead of galvanizing an old one."

This was of course Shaw thinking about his as yet unproduced brilliant plays—modern plays about the perils of money, of marriage, of doctors, of women's liberty, of almost everything that he felt passionate about, including the perils of the English language in a play with which I am most associated—*Pygmalion,* called in its musical version, *My Fair Lady.*

When Shaw died he divided his estate between The Dublin Art Museum, The Royal Academy of Dramatic Art, and The New Alphabet, a phonetic type of alphabet very close to his heart. Alas, the English language has not yet benefited. His belief that "every time an Englishman opens his mouth he makes some other Englishman despise him" still applies. Shaw's idealism on this subject was hard for his executors to get launched, but The Dublin Art Museum and The Royal Academy of Dramatic Art have both been very largely enriched by the musicalization of *Pygmalion.*

When I was first asked to do *My Fair Lady,* many of my friends in London, who had known and worked with Shaw, were horrified. Shaw himself was very opposed to having his works turned into musicals after *Arms and the Man* was used without his permission for an operetta called *The Chocolate Soldier.* He went so far as to state in his Will that if, after his death, anyone wanted to set his works to music, a very large percentage of every performance should go to his estate. I had great fears myself—I was very fearful that Shaw's wonderful prose would get lost or perhaps even cut if the piece did not prove an instant success. But because I was interested in the idea, I decided to do the show, making every effort to prevent a serious alteration of the text as Shaw had written it. I had the key scenes of *Pygmalion* guaranteed, and in my arrangements with the producers got firm assurances from them that these scenes could not be cut. During rehearsals I made myself very unpopular by always using Shaw's play to rehearse with, rather than the script of *My Fair Lady*.

Luckily, my fears were unfounded—Shaw worked triumphantly and it is his quality that shines through the entire evening. What other musical has ever had such scenes of literacy and prose style? I always feel that he did not get credit for being a very strong contributory factor to its success. Perhaps he would have preferred it that way! When I was playing the last scene in *My Fair Lady,* with the near-implicit suggestion that Eliza is going to stay with Higgins, I often thought of Shaw and wondered what he would have thought. The idea was anathema to him—and I absolutely understand this. He was so against the banal, the ordinary, the mundane. He thought of Higgins as an independent man, and although he, Shaw, married, his "Heroes" should not.

I had the great joy of meeting Bernard Shaw many times—mostly during the making of the film *Major Barbara* in 1940. His visits to the set were frequent and wonderful. He was a great inspiration for actors, as he had directed most of his plays himself in the early days, and had lost none of his touch. I felt very proud, as a young actor, to hear him say that he liked my acting style, and that he wanted me to play many more of his plays.

His very presence inspired hero-worship in all of us. As the late Dame Sybil Thorndike, his original St. Joan said, "G.B.S. inspired confidence in his actors. One not very good actor said to me during rehearsals, 'Mr. Shaw makes me feel as if I really were a very good actor. If he went on encouraging me, perhaps I might be!'."

One day Wendy Hiller, who was playing Major Barbara, and I were sitting puzzling over the last scene of the play, which we felt was rather "high-flown" in its language. We asked Gabriel Pascal, the producer-director, if we could ask the author for some help with it. The next time Shaw arrived at the studio we put our plea to him, and sat on either side of him, like two small children, while he painstakingly and silently read the long scene. We were agog—full of expectancy. There was a long pause. He looked up with a twinkle in his bright blue eyes and said with his strong Irish brogue "Ach! What a terrible scene!" and then repeated as if to give further emphasis, "What a terrible scene!" That was all we got!

On another occasion he came to Denham Studios all dressed up in a tweed knickerbocker suit with a Norfolk jacket and knitted tie, his white hair neatly brushed, his eye-brows bristling, his face pink and shining—he looked the picture of health. He was eighty-five. It was the day when he was to record his message to America, which was to be the frontispiece to our film when it was shown in the United States. The speech started, "Citizens of the United States of America, the whole 130 million of you, I am sending you my old plays just as you are sending us your old destroyers." It was a great treat to watch him from behind the cameras. He was a superb actor. At the opening he pretended to be writing, then looked up over his glasses, as if disturbed by the camera, took the glasses off with slight surprise, and started to speak. He was obviously very well prepared and was in full spate when I saw Gabriel Pascal talking in whispers to the cameraman. Finally Pascal reached out and tapped Shaw firmly on the knee; Shaw stopped and looked at him, irritated by the invasion of his concentration. Pascal said "Oh, I'm so sorry, G.B.S.—the camera has run out of film." Shaw just stared at Pascal. How such a terrible blunder could have been made we never found out. Of course it disturbed Shaw. He managed beautifully, nevertheless, his brain at eighty-five as lively as that of a man of forty—but it was rather nerve-wracking for us watchers. He finished,

> "As you see I am in my eighty-fifth year—I have shot my bolt—
> I have done my work. War or no war my number's up. But if
> my films are still being shown in America, my soul will go
> marching on, and that will satisfy me."

Years after *Major Barbara* was over I was supposed to have gone down to lunch with him at Ayot St. Lawrence, a thing I had quite often done. Unfortunately, on this occasion I had to send a message that I was terribly sorry but I had promised to take my eldest son out from his school in the country, and didn't want to let him down. Shaw was reported to have said "Rex is very silly. He could see his son anytime—he may never see me again." Shaw was very right. I never saw him again, and it was very sad.

There has always been a lot of talk about Shaw on his "hobbyhorses" and his "soapboxes." I don't think those are the right words. I think it was just that he was very much more engagé with social matters and against the hypocrisy of the time than other English playwrights and therefore had a problem in getting his plays produced by the established actor-managers.

Finally, however, Shaw found a home for his plays at the Royal Court Theatre in Sloane Square, where John Osborne and the other "Angry Young Men" of the 1960s expressed their feelings so brilliantly. It was a like "movement" when Shaw got some kindred spirits together in the shape of Harley Granville-Barker, the actor, and John E. Vedrenne, a superb business manager with a good company of actors, whose keynote in acting was "naturalness" and the aim "truth as opposed to effect."

Shaw directed the plays himself—and wrote *Major Barbara* especially for that Company in 1905. This put Shaw on the map and from then on he went from strength to strength.

The English speaking Theatre must always pit itself against Shaw plays, so that each generation of actors can learn about handling the subtleties and the intricate word patterns of his rhythmic prose, and also have the pleasure of meeting an unusually brilliant mind, so far ahead of his time on many topics, according to his whims, wit and humor.

Shaw and His Plays

> "I tell you that as long as I can conceive something
> better than myself I cannot be easy unless I am
> striving to bring it into existence or clearing
> the way for it. That is the law of my life. That
> is the working within me of Life's incessant aspiration. . . ."
>
> Don Juan, from
> *Man and Superman*

I

For good reason, Bernard Shaw has been called the most significant English playwright since the seventeenth century; that is, since Shakespeare. In his lifetime Shaw wrote fifty-seven plays, most of them revolutionary in their themes or execution, all more or less didactic according to his belief that "great art can never be anything else." In addition to the dramatic works he wrote influential essays, prefaces to many of his own plays, articles of music, art, and drama criticism (some of them the finest of his generation), and during his early years in London, five unsuccessful novels: in all, enough that the thirty-six-volume English edition of his *Works* is incomplete.

Both in Europe and America his wit made him famous (and notorious), arousing admiration and contempt in almost equal measure. As a self-proclaimed "professor of natural psychology," he enjoyed nothing more than lifting up the pretentious skirts of polite society. He was a merciless critic of moral and intellectual hypocrisy, a joyous iconoclast, irreverent showman, and sometimes bitter cynic. He was often contrary, and if he were alive today he could be depended upon to swiftly and surgically refute anything definitive we might try to say about him.

No literary figure of the nineteenth or twentieth century has more effectively cultivated a public persona. But underneath the sizzling electric prose and sometimes strident cynicism, the pessimism, and the antics of the intellectual clown, there was a reserve of disillusioned but courageous hopefulness, a basic shyness, and an unexpected sincerity Shaw took great pains to conceal.

II

The seven plays in this collection, while often irresistibly funny, are at bottom plays of ideas. Shaw's business, as he saw it, was to educate—not merely to entertain. Laughter, for him, was always a *means,* a device for making the pill easier to swallow, for allowing his audience to grasp and accept an idea it would otherwise reject out of hand. Very few of the institutions, public figures, moral tenets, economic classes, or polite conventions of Shaw's time managed to escape his criticism. He declared himself to be an enemy of the existing order "for good reason." He wrote:

> ". . . our laws make law impossible; our liberties destroy all freedom; our property is organized robbery; our morality is an impudent hypocrisy; our wisdom is administered by inexperienced or malexperienced dupes, our power wielded by cowards and weaklings, and our honor false in all its points."

Science, Christianity, democracy, capitalism, marriage, the family, the theatre, romantic love, the aristocracy, the poor, the middle class, and every aspect of the English character and life including Shakespeare came at one time or another under the terrible castigation of his comedy. He was rarely gentle, and he was not inclined to give quarter once he himself had sounded the call to battle: on the contrary. "It annoys me," he said, "to see people comfortable when they ought to be uncomfortable."

Needless to say, he was not always popular with his contemporaries. And without his gift of making them laugh at themselves, he might not have been tolerated—much less lionized.

Shaw's dramatic art was many-faceted, and his virtuosity not in the least limited to humor. In some of Cæsar's speeches in *Cæsar and Cleopatra,* or those of Captain Shotover in *Heartbreak House,* or in the dream scene in the last act of *Saint Joan,* there is a beautiful and touching lyric quality, as fine as anything written in dramatic form since Shakespeare's time. There is a somber, intentionally Chekhovian undercurrent throughout *Heartbreak House*. There is even horror when, in *Cæsar and Cleopatra*, Ftatateeta returns after murdering Pothinus. The savagery of this scene, like Shaw's lyrical passages, is the work of a master dramatist. Still, his most effective tool (and weapon) is always laughter.

III

On March 31, 1876, a few months before his twentieth birthday, Shaw left his native Dublin to join his mother and older sister in London. He left behind a life of "shabby-genteel" poverty and an unsuccessful father who was usually drunk. He was sure of his genius, though uncertain of the direction it would take, and he spent a good part of the next several years either looking for work (unsuccessfully), reading at the British Museum, or writing undistinguished novels without commercial success.

In September of 1882 he attended a lecture by an American economist, Henry George, on the subject "Land Nationalization and Single Tax." Immediately thereafter he read George's book *Progress and Poverty*, which in turn led to his reading of Karl Marx's *Das Kapital* and the beginning of lifelong socialist convictions.

By the mid 1880s Shaw was one of the driving forces in the newly founded Fabian Society, a group of middle-class, entirely secular London socialists who hoped to reconstruct society "in accordance with the highest moral possibilities." Like the other Fabians, he believed in the evolution of society rather than in violent revolutionary change. Like them, he called himself an atheist. When the Society published the classic *Fabian Essays in Socialism* in 1889, Shaw was its editor and major contributor.

There were at least two other important intellectual influences in Shaw's life during this time. One was the work of the Norwegian playwright Henrik Ibsen, whom Shaw would eventually place above even Shakespeare in his pantheon of writers and whose play *A Doll's House* struck to the heart of Victorian domestic morality. The other was the evolutionary ideas of Charles Darwin.

Shaw thought that Darwin's concept of natural selection was an important one, as far as it went. But he felt that it left untouched "the whole sphere of will, purpose, design, intention, even consciousness." While he called himself an atheist—was, in fact, an atheist in the popular Christian sense—Shaw was not content with the idea of a purposeless universe. Darwin stimulated his thinking about the process of "Creative Evolution," a concept which became the most important animating principle behind his work. By the time Shaw began writing plays in the 1890s, socialism, atheism, evolutionary theory, and a growing distaste for Victorian pretense and hypocrisy had begun to fuse in his mind.

IV

Candida, the first play in this collection, was Shaw's fourth play, following *Widowers' Houses,* which closed after two performances, *The Philanderer,* which no one would produce, and *Mrs. Warren's Profession,* which was banned because it dealt with prostitution.

According to Shaw himself, *Candida* was written as a reply to Ibsen's Nora in *A Doll's House,* and out of his own perception that ". . . in the real typical doll's house it is the man who is the doll." Candida is Shaw's version of the New Woman—strong-willed, independent, frank, instinctive, self-assured, decisive. In the play, she has to choose between the love of her husband, a clergyman and Christian Socialist orator named James Morell, and that of the young poet Eugene Marchbanks. Morell is hopelessly, even embarrassingly devoted to her, while Marchbanks is as ardent and exaggerated as a young poet of Romantic temperament could possibly be. Each is, in his own way, an appealing character, and the conflict between them is exploited by Shaw to the fullest extent. Furthermore each is, in his way, far more innocent than Candida herself. But the important point in this play is that Candida *chooses.* Her behavior is not predetermined by respectability. She follows her instincts—not convention or propriety. She would, she says, give her goodness and purity to Eugene as willingly as she would give her shawl "to a beggar dying of cold"—if that were the only consideration. Morell offers Candida his "strength," "honesty of purpose," "ability and industry," "authority and position." Eugene offers her his "weakness," his "desolation," and his "heart's need." On the basis of her instincts and her love—not her honor—she chooses "the weaker of the two."

V

Cæsar and Cleopatra was written in 1898, the year of Shaw's marriage to an Irish heiress named Charlotte Payne-Townshend. The marriage was his final personal resolution of a conflict which had always troubled him: it was affectionate and lifelong, but apparently celibate from beginning to end.

In the play the young Cleopatra is a fascinating study. Whereas Candida is a fully developed character almost from the moment she enters the stage, Cleopatra grows visibly from a spoiled but innocent child into a forceful woman able to command and exercise the power of a queen. But it is in Cæsar, possibly the most thoroughly appealing character Shaw ever created, that the play's real focus is found. Cæsar is practical, wise, unsentimental, clever, and fair. He can be kind or demanding, flippant or searingly direct. He is gentle with the child Cleopatra; and he knows how to make men serve him. He has self-knowledge, a well-developed sense of humor, and the authority that comes from genuine superiority. Shaw has given Cæsar no illusions, but has made him fully realistic in his expectations.

> *Cleopatra.* I have not betrayed you, Cæsar: I swear it.
> *Cæsar.* I know that. I have not trusted you.

In some ways Cæsar is as vulnerable as any man, embarrassed, for example when Cleopatra realizes he is bald. But as the following passage shows, he is set apart by the extraordinary depth of his understanding of human nature. He has just been informed by Pothinus that Cleopatra is using him for her own purposes:

> *Cæsar* (to Pothinus). Well, my friend; and is this not very natural?
> *Pothinus.* Natural! Then you do not resent this treachery?
> *Cæsar.* . . . foolish Egyptian, what have I to do with
> resentment? Do I resent the wind when it chills
> me, or the night when it makes me stumble in the
> darkness? Shall I resent youth when it turns
> from age, and ambition when it turns from servitude?
> To tell me such a story as this is but to tell me
> that the sun will rise to-morrow.

Shaw has portrayed Cæsar as a great man, endowed with superior qualities necessary to a conqueror, but, more importantly, free of the illusions and self-deceptions common to lesser men. Cæsar has no malice in him; no mercy; no generosity; and no need for forgiveness or revenge. "Having virtue," Shaw says, "he has no need of goodness."

In his perfect treatment of Rufio and Britannus in the final act, in his deeply felt but reasoned opposition to the murder of Pothinus, and in his contrasting acceptance of Ftatateeta's death at the hands of Rufio as a "natural slaying," Cæsar reveals his clear moral superiority. What is also revealed is the isolation imposed by that superiority. Saddened by the murder of his enemy Pothinus, but alone in his opposition to it, he tells Cleopatra, who set Ftatateeta to the grisly task, ". . . if one man in all the world can be found, now or forever, to know that you did wrong, that man will have either to conquer the world as I have, or be crucified by it." Cæsar's knowledge of the futility of revenge, that "murder shall breed murder," is not shared by the world. He is a lonely man who, although he has conquered the world, has found, as he confides to the sphinx in the play's first act, "no other Cæsar, no air native to me, no man . . . who can do my day's deed, and think my night's thought." His is the relationship (noted by Shaw in "The Revolutionist's Handbook") of all "accidental Supermen" to the world—men who ". . . must live as precariously as lion tamers do, taking the humor of their situation, and the dignity of their superiority, as a set-off to the horror of the one and the loneliness of the other."

Appropriately, Shaw ends the play "Hail, Cæsar!"

VI

Man and Superman was the first of Shaw's plays to be written in the twentieth century (1901–03). Among the plays in this collection, it is the most discursive, containing long passages of philosophical dialogue without much dramatic action. It also contains the famous dream episode "Don Juan in Hell," which is often staged by itself.

In this play, Shaw presents his ideas on the subjects of "Creative Evolution" and the Superman as well as the relationship of courtship, marriage, sexual instinct, and selective breeding to the higher aspirations of the race. Shaw did not care much for romantic love. He thought it was nonsense, and liked to quote the seventeenth-century French writer La Rochefoucauld, who said that very few people would fall in love if they had never read about it.

Man and Superman deals on the surface with the relations between the sexes. Jack Tanner, anarchist, revolutionary social philosopher, and author (for the purposes of this play) of "The Revolutionist's Handbook," is pursued (and captured) by the resourceful Ann Whitefield, intended by Shaw to be essentially representative of her sex. "Every woman is not Ann," he wrote, "but Ann is Everywoman."

Jack Tanner, being philosophically and personally opposed to matrimony while considering himself something of a realist with respect to women, nevertheless finds himself in the grip of a power Shaw chose to call the Life Force. When his chauffeur, 'Enry Straker (one of Shaw's most interesting minor characters) informs him of Ann's obvious designs, Tanner climbs into his motor car with 'Enry at the wheel and bolts for the Spanish Sierra. There they are robbed and taken prisoner by a band of ridiculous and supposedly dangerous brigands, giving Shaw an opportunity to lampoon his revolutionary friends (no one was safe) before getting down to business. These brigands are arguing whether anarchists or Social Democrats have the most personal courage. The anarchist among them demands a point of order in the debate and is shouted down. The three Social Democrats are not on speaking terms, and in any case have incompatible views of Social Democracy. The leader of the outlaws is a man named Mendoza. He and Tanner become friends, and after talking well into the night, they fall asleep. Tanner dreams, and the scene opens on Don Juan in Hell. Here Shaw takes the legend of Don Juan from Mozart's opera *Don Giovanni* and molds a dramatic parable through which he expresses the philosophy behind the play.

Shaw did not believe in progress (see his "Notes to *Cæsar and Cleopatra*"). He thought it was at best a convenient myth, and at worst an outright lie. But he did believe in an evolutionary process, a purposeful movement toward higher organization and greater self-awareness which is more careful and conscious than blind Darwinian evolution. He believed that, at the deepest level, the human race aspires toward the creation of the Superman (in this he was influenced by Nietzsche and by Samuel Butler). He would not define this Superman, except to say that "the proof of the Superman will be in the living." But as we have seen in the case of Cæsar, Shaw did conceive a genuinely superior being whose personal command was built on strength of character and mind, and not on the flimsier stuff of accidental privilege, political maneuvering, or profitable moral compromise.

Shaw's ideas are particularly well expressed in this play in conversations between Don Juan and the Devil in Hell, and need no restating here. But it is worth repeating that Shaw believed the sexual instinct, operating through what he called "fancy" and independent of such considerations as property, domestic compatibility, or moral propriety, is the tool of evolution. What Don Juan calls the "perfectly simple impulse of my manhood towards her womanhood," or what Tanner calls the "Life Force," is in fact the aspiration of the race to realize its full potential. Shaw saw this instinct operating with particular urgency and selectivity in women. Thus, as the dream begins to fade Doña Ana (who resembles Ann, much as Don Juan resembles Tanner) cries:

"Where can I find the Superman?"

The Devil answers:

"He is not yet created Señora."

And Ana, with the whole play pivoting around her words, cries out again:

"Not yet created! Then my work is not yet done.
(Crossing herself devoutly) I believe in the
Life to come. (Crying to the Universe) A father—
a father for the Superman!"

Back in the real world, Tanner is still in the grip of the Life Force. He resists mightily, but succumbs to Ann because (to Ann) ". . . we do the world's will, not our own. I have a frightful feeling that I shall let myself be married because it is the world's will that you should have a husband."

Shaw ends the play in "Universal laughter."

VII

Major Barbara is a firestorm of language. For that reason, it lends itself to sparkling stage production. But its basic themes are so unorthodox that it is better *read* (with its typically Shavian Preface) before it is seen.

These themes are as forcefully expressed by Andrew Undershaft, cannon maker and the "hero" of the play, as they are fully explained and defended by Shaw in the Preface. It is worth noting, however, that Shaw's unconventional ideas about the singular importance of money are not new in *Major Barbara.* Cæsar declared when he was challenged on the subject that "taxes are the chief business of a conqueror of the world." And Violet Robinson, in *Man and Superman,* cautioned her husband, Hector: "You can be as romantic as you please about love, Hector; but you mustn't be romantic about money." Undershaft's unusual conviction that poverty is the worst of all crimes and the vilest of all sins may not be shared by everyone. But what is important is the fact that Shaw's persistent demand that creeds be intellectually honest is fully met in the gospel of Andrew Undershaft. Stephen Britomart, his son, solemnly claims to know the difference between right and wrong, and is mercilessly ridiculed for his presumption. But Undershaft himself declares morality and law to be "conventions," issuing the challenge to Barbara that if her morality or religion doesn't fit the facts (as she finds that it does not) she should ". . . scrap it. Scrap it and get one that does fit."

Of particular interest in this play is its implicit challenge to social responsibility, not in the progressive altruistic sense of the reformer or Salvationist, but in the form of energetic, "unashamed" participation in the world. "Unashamed" is, after all, the Undershaft motto. And when Barbara discovers that she is, by the very fact of her being alive, connected to all the crime and corruption she would nevertheless love to escape (and would surely deny if she were less honest), she also learns that she cannot save the world with spotless purity and virtue. She has to get her hands dirty (in fact they are already stained). She and her fiancé Adolphus Cusins (who is attracted to Barbara by the operation of an "instinct"—one which is "not merciful enough to blind him to the illusions of love") soon realize that they are compelled to, in effect, "go to work"—not as a professor of Greek and a Salvation Army Major, but as the inheritors of Undershaft's cannon factory.

Undershaft freely admits that he cannot make virtue or courage or conviction. And neither can they. But they can make power for the world—power for good or evil. Once they realize that they are the accomplices of the distiller and the munitions maker, and that there is "no salvation for them through personal righteousness, but only through the redemption of the whole nation" (and, by implication, the world), the message of their responsibility becomes clear. It is Undershaft's challenge to Cusins to turn his "oughts" into "shalls."

The poet William Blake, one of the writers whose vision Shaw felt was more or less akin to his own, wrote in "The Marriage of Heaven and Hell" that "God only acts and is in existing beings and men." It remains for Barbara Undershaft, once she has gotten rid of the "bribe of Heaven," to say:

> "Let God's work be done for its own sake: the work he had to create us to do because it cannot be done except by living men and women."

The message is that no one can escape responsibility for the condition of the world or pretend that its guilt is not also on his (or her) shoulders. Thus, when Undershaft says to Cusins (triumphantly), "Six o'clock tomorrow morning, Euripides," there is a voice beneath his saying (silently), "To work!—the work of the world." It is a rare glimpse of the optimism Shaw habitually kept hidden.

VIII

Pygmalion is probably Shaw's best-known play. It is also his most straightforward. It was written in 1912, filmed in 1938 (winning an Academy Award for Shaw's screenplay), and adapted into the musical *My Fair Lady* in 1956.

Shaw had more than a casual interest in phonetics, and left a sizable portion of his estate for research into a forty-letter phonetic alphabet. In *Pygmalion,* the scientific gentleman-phonetician Henry Higgins trains a cockney flower-girl to speak and behave as a lady. Shaw considers in the play both the comic possibilities of Higgins' experiment and the repercussions of its success, seizing in the meantime every opportunity to satirize the English class structure in the genteel poverty of the Eynsford-Hills and the reluctant ascendancy of Eliza's father from the lower to the middle class.

IX

During World War I Shaw turned his dispassionate, uncompromising intellect to the subject of the war itself. In pamphlets, speeches, and polemical tracts, he was vehemently critical of certain English attitudes and aspects of his country's conduct of the war. His attitude was, on the whole, fiercely embittering to his countrymen, and he was frequently and sometimes violently denounced for his less-than-strictly patriotic views. In one pamphlet, "Common Sense About the War," which appeared in November 1914, Shaw argued that England and her allies were no less to blame than the Germans for starting the war, and called for immediate peace negotiations. Some of his speeches were censored by the newspapers; he was expelled from the Dramatists' Club, even though he was its most prominent member; and he was generally ostracized until the war was over and his attitudes were shown to have been in some cases more sensible than those of the patriots.

Heartbreak House, set in an English country house on the eve of the war, exposes the utter spiritual and moral bankruptcy of the generation responsible for the conflict. It combines brilliant comedy with the somber mood of Chekhov's *Cherry Orchard.* Its patriarchal Captain Shotover (probably the closest thing to an embodiment of Shaw himself to be found anywhere in these plays) keeps a store of dynamite to "blow up the human race if it goes too far" and is busy trying to attain the "Seventh Degree of Concentration." Shotover, with his crazy wisdom, has often been called Shaw's Lear.

This play is in many ways the summit of Shaw's achievement. Nowhere else in his work is the folly and futility of the English ruling class so mercilessly laid bare. Overall, it is the funniest of his plays, but it is also his most bitter. It is atmospheric, prophetic, with a feeling of impending darkness throughout.

In the Preface, Shaw is unusually visible. Underneath his fury at English hypocrisy, his disdain for blind patriotism, and his obvious despair at seeing that the same conditions which produced the war and the same follies that justified it were likely to continue, it is clear that the war's pain, futility and horror, and the depth of its human loss did not escape him. For a short (and rare) moment he reacts with his heart as well as with his intellect.

For the purposes of this Introduction, it is only necessary to point out that the idle, splendid people in the play are well dressed, well to do, well read, good-looking, clever, and extremely fascinating to each other; but (with the exception of Captain Shotover and, strangely enough, Hector) they are rarely wise. They represent the best of English society. But their lives are "lives of romance, sentiment, and snobbery." There is no Cæsar among them; not even an Undershaft to break the grinding futility. There is nothing to suggest the advent of the Superman—only vague feelings of impending destruction.

Ellie Dunn finds out, when she has been in Heartbreak House long enough, that the beauty of the sisters Hesione and Ariadne is too perfect to be real; Hector's intriguing and seductive stories are lies; Mangan, the "industrial Napoleon," has no money of his own and lives on "travelling expenses"; and Captain Shotover's Seventh Degree of Concentration is rum. There is nothing real about the house: it is a house "without foundations." Even the bombing raid that kills Mangan and the burglar is nothing but an interlude of excitement, a glorious experience which breaks the dullness briefly. The deaths are barely noticed at all. And with Randall, the most useless of all these useless people, playing "Keep the Home Fires Burning" on his flute, the play ends with the ladies hoping the bombers will "come again tomorrow night."

It is not difficult to understand why Shaw thought it best to withhold *Heartbreak House* from the British public until the war was over.

X

The year 1920 marked the canonization of Joan of Arc, who had been excommunicated from the Catholic Church and burned at the stake for heresy and witchcraft in 1431. In 1923 Shaw finished and produced in New York the last of his great plays, *Saint Joan.* Its success cleared the way for him to receive the Nobel Prize in 1925.

Shaw despised the dramatic conventions of villain and hero and the romance of a conflict between unmistakable good and unmistakable evil. He thought they were intellectually dishonest: "In such cheap wares," he wrote, "I do not deal." Thus, in *Saint Joan* a good part of his effort is spent taking the whitewash from the historical figure of Joan herself, showing her to be difficult, stubbornly naive, and at times practically insufferable. An equal effort is spent in removing the mud from her judges, showing them to be subject to the whole range of ordinary human failings as well as simply products of their time and of their various ecclesiastical or professional positions. Shaw argues that Joan got as fair a trial from these men as she would have gotten from any similar court in the twentieth century. He succeeds in showing how Joan's virtues—personal modesty, frankness, faith in God—aroused enmity instead of sympathy, and how these same virtues made that enmity utterly incomprehensible (and thus, even more dangerous) to her. He further succeeds in making the reasons why Joan was burnt not only intellectually comprehensible but personally understandable to the extent that you feel ". . . you might have voted for burning her yourself if you had been a member of the court that tried her": a substantial achievement.

Joan was a threat to the entire feudal system with her nationalism, and to the authority of the Catholic Church with her claims of being in direct personal touch with God. She might, we assume, have threatened one of these mighty institutions with impunity: but having threatened both, her fate was sealed. Here, with one deceptively simple stroke, Shaw symbolically unites the Church and feudal Europe against Joan:

> *Warwick* (to the bishop Cauchon). Well, if you will burn the Protestant, I will burn the Nationalist.

Shaw believed that there are forces (evolutionary forces) at work which use certain individuals for transcendent purposes. He believed that Joan was thus singled out, and that her celebrated visions were not evidence of lunacy, but merely of her own personal dramatization of the approach and action of these forces upon her. This idea is not new in *Saint Joan.* Andrew Undershaft, on the surface the least likely of Shaw's characters to be mystical, declared his cannon factory to be driven by "a Will of which I am a part." Joan heralded a new epoch—one of nationalism, Protestantism, and Reason, the decline of the Church's influence, and the breaking-up of the feudal structure. She therefore stood in powerful opposition to the world of her time. And to Shaw's mind the world could not fairly be blamed for that, or for its reaction to her.

But Joan is not Barbara Undershaft. She cries out: "Jack: the world is too wicked for me . . ." as in fact it was. Shaw's sympathy for her plight is obvious, here and throughout the play. But the deeper anguish of her situation is not shown until the epilogue, the litany of Charles's dream, when all of those—Cauchon, Dunois, the Archbishop, Warwick, De Stogumber, the Inquisitor, the soldier from Hell, the Executioner, and Charles himself—who praise Joan are nevertheless unwilling to have her back in the world. One by one they disappear from the dream, with apologies of one sort or another. Joan has been rehabilitated (she may even be canonized), but she is still not welcome.

This dream, which ends the play, contains some of Shaw's best dramatic writing. It is a scene of profound irony and touching sadness—Joan's sadness, yes, but Shaw's sadness as well. The paradox (which Cæsar understood) is that the world will continue to fear its saints and heroes until their qualities of understanding become the general condition of humanity.

And with that, Shaw, taking one last bow, leaves the stage with Joan:

> "O God that madest this beautiful earth, when will it be ready to receive thy Saints? How long, O Lord, how long?"

David Bearinger
New York
June 1980

CANDIDA:
A Mystery

Composition begun 2 October 1894; completed 7 December 1894. Published in *Plays Pleasant and Unpleasant,* 1898. Revised text in Collected Edition, 1930. Copyright reading at the Theatre Royal, South Shields, on 30 March 1895. First presented by the Independent Theatre Company at Her Majesty's Theatre, Aberdeen, on 30 July 1897, at the start of a provincial tour. Presented by the Stage Society at the Strand Theatre, London, on 1 July 1900, with the same cast except for the substitution of H. Granville Barker as Eugene Marchbanks (originally spelled Marjoribanks).

The Reverend James Mavor Morell *Charles Charrington*
Eugene Marchbanks *Courtney Thorpe*
Mr Burgess *Lionel Belmore*
The Reverend Alexander Mill *Robert Farquharson*
Miss Proserpine Garnett *Edith Craig*
Candida Morell *Janet Achurch*

Scene: The Study and General Sitting-room, St Dominic's Vicarage, Victoria Park, London. Time: October 1894.

ACT I *Morning*
ACT II *Afternoon*
ACT III *Evening*

ACT I

A fine morning in October 1894 in the north east quarter of London, a vast district miles away from the London of Mayfair and St James's, and much less narrow, squalid, fetid and airless in its slums. It is strong in unfashionable middle class life: wide-streeted; myriad-populated; well served with ugly iron urinals, Radical clubs, and tram lines carrying a perpetual stream of yellow cars; enjoying in its main thoroughfares the luxury of grass-grown "front gardens" untrodden by the foot of man save as to the path from the gate to the hall door; blighted by a callously endured monotony of miles and miles of unlovely brick houses, black iron railings, stony pavements, slated roofs, and respectably ill dressed or disreputably worse dressed people, quite accustomed to the place, and mostly plodding uninterestedly about somebody else's work. The little energy and eagerness that crop up shew themselves in cockney cupidity and business "push." Even the policemen and the chapels are not infrequent enough to break the monotony. The sun is shining cheerfully: there is no fog, and though the smoke effectually prevents anything, whether faces and hands or bricks and mortar, from looking fresh and clean, it is not hanging heavily enough to trouble a Londoner.

The desert of unattractiveness has its oasis. Near the outer end of the Hackney Road is a park of 217 acres, fenced in, not by railings, but by a wooden paling, and containing plenty of greensward, trees, a lake for bathers, flower beds which are triumphs of the admired cockney art of carpet gardening, and a sandpit, originally imported from the seaside for the delight of children, but speedily deserted on its becoming a natural vermin preserve for all the petty fauna of Kingsland, Hackney, and Hoxton. A bandstand, an unfurnished forum for religious, anti-religious, and political orators, cricket pitches, a gymnasium, and an old fashioned stone kiosk are among its attractions. Wherever the prospect is bounded by trees or rising green grounds, it is a pleasant place. Where the ground stretches flat to the grey palings, with bricks and mortar, sky signs, crowded chimneys and smoke beyond, the prospect makes it desolate and sordid.

The best view of Victoria Park is commanded by the front window of St Dominic's Parsonage, from which not a brick is visible. The parsonage is semi-detached, with a front garden and a porch. Visitors go up the flight of steps to the porch: tradespeople and members of the family go down by a door under the steps to the basement, with a breakfast room, used for all meals, in front, and the kitchen at the back. Upstairs, on the level of the hall door, is the drawingroom, with its large plate glass window looking out on the park. In this, the only sitting room that can be spared from the children and the family meals, the parson, the Reverend James Mavor Morell, does his work. He is sitting in a strong round backed revolving chair at the end of a long table, which stands across the window, so that he can cheer himself with a view of the park over his left shoulder. At the opposite end of the table, adjoining it, is a little table only half as wide as the other, with a typewriter on it. His typist is sitting at this machine, with her back to the window. The large table is littered with pamphlets, journals, letters, nests of drawers, an office diary, postage scales and the like. A spare chair for visitors having business with the parson is in the middle, turned to his end. Within reach of his hand is a stationery case, and a photograph in a frame. The wall behind him is fitted with bookshelves, on which an adept eye can measure the parson's casuistry and divinity by Maurice's Theological Essays and a complete set of Browning's poems, and the reformer's politics by a yellow backed Progress and Poverty, Fabian Essays, A Dream of John Ball, Marx's Capital, and half a dozen other literary landmarks in Socialism. Facing him on the other side of the room, near the typewriter, is the door. Further down opposite the fireplace, a bookcase stands on a cellaret, with a sofa near it. There is a generous fire burning; and the hearth, with a comfortable armchair and a black japanned flower-painted coal scuttle at one side, a miniature chair for children on the other, a varnished wooden mantelpiece, with neatly moulded shelves, tiny bits of mirror let into the panels, a travelling clock in a leather case (the inevitable wedding present), and on the wall above a large autotype of the chief figure in Titian's Assumption of the Virgin, is very inviting. Altogether the room is the room of a good housekeeper, vanquished, as far as the table is concerned, by an untidy man, but elsewhere mistress of the situation. The furniture, in its ornamental aspect, betrays the style of the advertized "drawingroom suite" of the pushing suburban furniture dealer; but there is nothing useless or pretentious in the room, money being too scarce in the house of an east end parson to be wasted on snobbish trimmings.

The Reverend James Mavor Morell is a Christian Socialist clergyman of the Church of England, and an active member of the Guild of St Matthew and the Christian Social Union. A vigorous, genial, popular man of forty, robust and goodlooking, full of energy, with pleasant, hearty, considerate manners, and a sound unaffected voice, which he uses with the clean athletic articulation of a practised orator, and with a wide range and perfect command of expression. He is a first rate clergyman, able to say what he likes to whom he likes, to lecture people without setting himself up against them, to impose his authority on them without humiliating them, and, on occasion, to interfere in their business without impertinence. His well-spring of enthusiasm and sympathetic emotion has never run dry for a moment: he still eats and sleeps heartily enough to win the daily battle between exhaustion and recuperation triumphantly. Withal, a great baby, pardonably vain of his powers and unconsciously pleased with himself. He has a healthy complexion: good forehead, with the brows somewhat blunt, and the eyes bright and eager, mouth resolute but not particularly well cut, and a substantial nose, with the mobile spreading nostrils of the dramatic orator, void, like all his features, of subtlety.

The typist, Miss Proserpine Garnett, is a brisk little woman of about 30, of the lower middle class, neatly but cheaply dressed in a black merino skirt and a blouse, notably pert and quick of speech, and not very civil in her manner, but sensitive and affectionate. She is clattering away busily at her machine whilst Morell opens the last of his morning's letters. He realizes its contents with a comic groan of despair.

PROSERPINE. Another lecture?

MORELL. Yes. The Hoxton Freedom Group want me to address them on Sunday morning [*he lays great emphasis on Sunday, this being the unreasonable part of the business*]. What are they?

PROSERPINE. Communist Anarchists, I think.

MORELL. Just like Anarchists not to know that they cant have a parson on Sunday! Tell them to come to church if they want to hear me: it will do them good. Say I can come on Mondays and Thursdays only. Have you the diary there?

PROSERPINE [*taking up the diary*] Yes.

MORELL. Have I any lecture on for next Monday?

PROSERPINE [*referring to the diary*] Tower Hamlets Radical Club.

MORELL. Well, Thursday then?
PROSERPINE. English Land Restoration League.
MORELL. What next?
PROSERPINE. Guild of St Matthew on Monday. Independent Labor Party, Greenwich Branch, on Thursday. Monday, Social-Democratic Federation, Mile End Branch. Thursday, first Confirmation class. [*Impatiently*] Oh, I'd better tell them you cant come. Theyre only half a dozen ignorant and conceited costermongers without five shillings between them.
MORELL [*amused*] Ah; but you see theyre near relatives of mine.
PROSERPINE [*staring at him*] Relatives of y o u r s!
MORELL. Yes: we have the same father—in Heaven.
PROSERPINE [*relieved*] Oh, is that all?
MORELL [*with a sadness which is a luxury to a man whose voice expresses it so finely*] Ah, you dont believe it. Everybody says it: nobody believes it: nobody. [*Briskly, getting back to business*] Well, well! Come, Miss Proserpine: cant you find a date for the costers? what about the 25th? That was vacant the day before yesterday.
PROSERPINE [*referring to diary*] Engaged. The Fabian Society.
MORELL. Bother the Fabian Society! Is the 28th gone too?
PROSERPINE. City dinner. Youre invited to dine with the Founders' Company.
MORELL. Thatll do: I'll go to the Hoxton Group of Freedom instead. [*She enters the engagement in silence, with implacable disparagement of the Hoxton Anarchists in every line of her face. Morell bursts open the cover of a copy of The Church Reformer, which has come by post, and glances through Mr Stewart Headlam's leader and the Guild of St Matthew news. These proceedings are presently enlivened by the appearance of Morell's curate, the Reverend Alexander Mill, a young gentleman gathered by Morell from the nearest University settlement, whither he had come from Oxford to give the east end of London the benefit of his university training. He is a conceitedly well intentioned, enthusiastic, immature novice, with nothing positively unbearable about him except a habit of speaking with his lips carefully closed a full half inch from each corner for the sake of a finicking articulation and a set of university vowels, this being his chief means so far of bringing his Oxford refinement (as he calls his habits) to bear on Hackney vulgarity. Morell, whom he has won over by a doglike devotion, looks up indulgently from The Church Reformer, and remarks*] Well, Lexy? Late again, as usual!

LEXY. I'm afraid so. I wish I could get up in the morning.

MORELL [*exulting in his own energy*] Ha! ha! [*Whimsically*] Watch and pray, Lexy: watch and pray.

LEXY. I know. [*Rising wittily to the occasion*] But how can I watch and pray when I am asleep? Isnt that so, Miss Prossy? [*He makes for the warmth of the fire*].

PROSERPINE [*sharply*] Miss Garnett, if you please.

LEXY. I beg your pardon. Miss Garnett.

PROSERPINE. Youve got to do all the work today.

LEXY [*on the hearth*] Why?

PROSERPINE. Never mind why. It will do you good to earn your supper before you eat it, for once in a way, as I do. Come! dont dawdle. You should have been off on your rounds half an hour ago.

LEXY [*perplexed*] Is she in earnest, Morell?

MORELL [*in the highest spirits: his eyes dancing*] Yes. *I* am going to dawdle today.

LEXY. You! You dont know how.

MORELL [*rising*] Ha! ha! Dont I? I'm going to have this morning all to myself. My wife's coming back: she's due here at 11.45.

LEXY [*surprised*] Coming back already! with the children? I thought they were to stay to the end of the month.

MORELL. So they are: she's only coming up for two days, to get some flannel things for Jimmy, and to see how we're getting on without her.

LEXY [*anxiously*] But, my dear Morell, if what Jimmy and Fluffy had was scarlatina, do you think it wise—

MORELL. Scarlatina! Rubbish! it was German measles. I brought it into the house myself from the Pycroft Street school. A parson is like a doctor, my boy: he must face infection as a soldier must face bullets. [*He claps Lexy manfully on the shoulders*]. Catch the measles if you can, Lexy: she'll nurse you; and what a piece of luck that will be for you! Eh?

LEXY [*smiling uneasily*] It's so hard to understand you about Mrs Morell—

MORELL [*tenderly*] Ah, my boy, get married: get married to a good woman; and then youll understand. Thats a foretaste of what will be best in the Kingdom of Heaven we are trying to establish on earth. That will cure you of dawdling. An honest man feels that he must pay Heaven for every hour of happiness with a good spell of hard unselfish work to make others happy. We have no more right to consume happiness without producing it than to consume wealth without producing it. Get a wife like my Candida; and youll always be in arrear with your repayment. [*He pats Lexy affectionately and moves to leave the room*].

LEXY. Oh, wait a bit: I forgot. [*Morell halts and turns with the door knob in his hand*]. Your father-in-law is coming round to see you.

Morell, surprised and not pleased, shuts the door again, with a complete change of manner.

MORELL. Mr Burgess?

LEXY. Yes. I passed him in the park, arguing with somebody. He asked me to let you know that he was coming.

MORELL [*half incredulous*] But he hasnt called here for three years. Are you sure, Lexy? Youre not joking, are you?

LEXY [*earnestly*] No sir, really.

MORELL [*thoughtfully*] Hm! Time for him to take another look at Candida before she grows out of his knowledge. [*He resigns himself to the inevitable, and goes out*].

Lexy looks after him with beaming worship. Miss Garnett, not being able to shake Lexy, relieves her feelings by worrying the typewriter.

LEXY. What a good man! What a thorough loving soul he is! [*He takes Morell's place at the table, making himself very comfortable as he takes out a cigaret*].

PROSERPINE [*impatiently, pulling the letter she has been working at off the typewriter and folding it*] Oh, a man ought to be able to be fond of his wife without making a fool of himself about her.

LEXY [*shocked*] Oh, Miss Prossy!

PROSERPINE [*snatching at the stationery case for an envelope, in which she encloses the letter as she speaks*] Candida here, and Candida there, and Candida everywhere! [*She licks the envelope*]. It's enough to drive anyone out of their s e n s e s [*thumping the envelope to make it stick*] to hear a woman raved about in that absurd manner merely because she's got good hair and a tolerable figure.

LEXY [*with reproachful gravity*] I think her extremely beautiful, Miss Garnett. [*He takes the photograph up; looks at it; and adds, with even greater impressiveness*] e x t r e m e l y beautiful. How fine her eyes are!

PROSERPINE. Her eyes are not a bit better than mine: now! [*He puts down the photograph and stares austerely at her*]. And you know very well you think me dowdy and second rate enough.

LEXY [*rising majestically*] Heaven forbid that I should think of any of God's creatures in such a way! [*He moves stiffly away from her across the room to the neighborhood of the bookcase*].

PROSERPINE [*sarcastically*] Thank you. Thats very nice and comforting.

LEXY [*saddened by her depravity*] I had no idea you had any feeling against Mrs Morell.

PROSERPINE [*indignantly*] I have no feeling against her. She's very nice, very good-hearted: I'm very fond of her, and can appreciate her real qualities far better than any man can. [*He shakes his head sadly. She rises and comes at him with intense pepperiness*]. You dont believe me? You think I'm jealous? Oh, what a knowledge of the human heart you have, Mr Lexy Mill! How well you know the weaknesses of Woman, dont you? It must be so nice to be a man and have a fine penetrating intellect instead of mere emotions like us, and to know that the reason we dont share your amorous delusions is that we're all jealous of one another! [*She abandons him with a toss of her shoulders, and crosses to the fire to warm her hands*].

LEXY. Ah, if you women only had the same clue to Man's strength that you have to his weakness, Miss Prossy, there would be no Woman Question.

PROSERPINE [*over her shoulder, as she stoops, holding her hands to the blaze*] Where did you hear Morell say that? You didnt invent it yourself: youre not clever enough.

LEXY. Thats quite true. I am not ashamed of owing him that, as I owe him so many other spiritual truths. He said it at the annual conference of the Women's Liberal Federation. Allow me to add that though they didnt appreciate it, I, a mere man, did. [*He turns to the bookcase again, hoping that this may leave her crushed*].

PROSERPINE [*putting her hair straight at a panel of mirror in the mantelpiece*] Well, when you talk to me, give me your own ideas, such as they are, and not his. You never cut a poorer figure than when you are trying to imitate him.

LEXY [*stung*] I try to follow his example, not to imitate him.

PROSERPINE [*coming at him again on her way back to her work*] Yes, you do: you i m i t a t e him. Why do you tuck your umbrella under your left arm instead of carrying it in your hand like anyone else? Why do you walk with your chin stuck out before you, hurrying along with that eager look in your eyes? you! who never get up before half past nine in the morning. Why do you say "knoaledge" in church, though you always say "knolledge" in private conversation! Bah! do you think I dont know? [*She goes back to the typewriter*]. Here! come and set about your work: weve wasted enough time for one morning. Here's a copy of the diary for today. [*She hands him a memorandum*].

LEXY [*deeply offended*] Thank you. [*He takes it and stands at the table with his back to her, reading it. She begins to transcribe her shorthand notes on the typewriter without troubling herself about his feelings*].

The door opens; and Mr Burgess enters unannounced. He is a man of sixty, made coarse and sordid by the compulsory selfishness of petty commerce, and later on softened into sluggish bumptiousness by overfeeding and commercial success. A vulgar ignorant guzzling man, offensive and contemptuous to people whose labor is cheap, respectful to wealth and rank, and quite sincere and without rancor or envy in both attitudes. The world has offered him no decently paid work except that of a sweater; and he has become, in consequence, somewhat hoggish. But he has no suspicion of this himself, and honestly regards his commercial prosperity as the inevitable and socially wholesome triumph of the ability, industry, shrewdness, and experience in business of a man who in private is easygoing, affectionate, and humorously convivial to a fault. Corporeally he is podgy, with a snoutish nose in the centre of a flat square face, a dust colored beard with a patch of grey in the centre under his chin, and small watery blue eyes with a plaintively sentimental expression, which he transfers easily to his voice by his habit of pompously intoning his sentences.

BURGESS [*stopping on the threshold, and looking round*] They told me Mr Morell was here.

PROSERPINE [*rising*] I'll fetch him for you.

BURGESS [*staring disappointedly at her*] Youre not the same young lady as hused to typewrite for him?

PROSERPINE. No.

BURGESS [*grumbling on his way to the hearth-rug*] No: she was young-er. [*Miss Garnett stares at him; then goes out, slamming the door*]. Startin on your rounds, Mr Mill?

LEXY [*folding his memorandum and pocketing it*] Yes: I must be off presently.

BURGESS [*momentously*] Dont let me detain you, Mr Mill. What I come about is p r i v a t e between me and Mr Morell.

LEXY [*huffily*] I have no intention of intruding, I am sure, Mr Burgess. G o o d morning.

BURGESS [*patronizingly*] Oh, good morning to you.

Morell returns as Lexy is making for the door.

MORELL [*to Lexy*] Off to work?

LEXY. Yes, sir.
MORELL. Take my silk handkerchief and wrap your throat up. Theres a cold wind. Away with you.

Lexy, more than consoled for Burgess's rudeness, brightens up and goes out.

BURGESS. Spoilin your korates as usu'l, James. Good mornin. When I pay a man, an' 'is livin depens on me, I keep him in 'is place.

MORELL [*rather shortly*] I always keep my curates in their places as my helpers and comrades. If you get as much work out of your clerks and warehousemen as I do out of my curates you must be getting rich pretty fast. Will you take your old chair.

He points with curt authority to the armchair beside the fireplace; then takes the spare chair from the table and sits down at an unfamiliar distance from his visitor.

BURGESS [*without moving*] Just the same as hever, James!

MORELL. When you last called—it was about three years ago, I think—you said the same thing a little more frankly. Your exact words then were "Just as big a fool as ever, James!"

BURGESS [*soothingly*] Well, praps I did; but [*with conciliatory cheerfulness*] I meant no hoffence by it. A clorgyman is privileged to be a bit of a fool, you know: it's ony becomin in 'is profession that he should. Anyhow, I come here, not to rake up hold differences, but to let bygones be bygones. [*Suddenly becoming very solemn, and approaching Morell*] James: three years ago, you done me a hil turn. You done me hout of a contrac; an when I gev you arsh words in my natral disappointment, you turned my daughrter again me. Well, Ive come to hact the part of a Kerischin. [*Offering his hand*] I forgive you, James.

MORELL [*starting up*] Confound your impudence!

BURGESS [*retreating, with almost lachrymose deprecation of this treatment*] Is that becomin language for a clorgyman, James? And you so particlar, too!

MORELL [*hotly*] No, sir: it is not becoming language for a clergyman. I used the wrong word. I should have said damn your impudence: thats what St Paul or any honest priest would have said to you. Do you think I have forgotten that tender of yours for the contract to supply clothing to the workhouse?

BURGESS [*in a paroxysm of public spirit*] I hacted in the hinterest of the ratepayers, James. It was the lowest tender: you carnt deny that.

MORELL. Yes, the lowest, because you paid worse wages than any other employer—starvation wages—aye, worse than starvation wages—to the women who made the clothing. Your wages would have driven them to the streets to keep body and soul together. [*Getting angrier and angrier*] Those women were my parishioners. I shamed the Guardians out of accepting your tender: I shamed the ratepayers out of letting them do it: I shamed everybody but you. [*Boiling over*] How dare you, sir, come here and offer to forgive me, and talk about your daughter, and—

BURGESS. Heasy, James! heasy! heasy! Dont git hinto a fluster about nothink. Ive howned I was wrong.

MORELL. Have you? I didnt hear you.

BURGESS. Of course I did. I hown it now. Come: I harsk your pardon for the letter I wrote you. Is that enough?

MORELL [*snapping his fingers*] Thats nothing. Have you raised the wages?

BURGESS [*triumphantly*] Yes.

MORELL. What!

BURGESS [*unctuously*] Ive turned a moddle hemployer. I dont hemploy no women now: theyre all sacked; and the work is done by machinery. Not a man 'as less than sixpence a *h*our; and the skilled ands gits the Trade Union rate. [*Proudly*] What ave you to say to me now?

MORELL [*overwhelmed*] Is it possible! Well, theres more joy in heaven over one sinner that repenteth!—[*Going to Burgess with an explosion of apologetic cordiality*] My dear Burgess: how splendid of you! I most heartily beg your pardon for my hard thoughts. [*Grasping his hand*] And now, dont you feel the better for the change? Come! confess! youre happier. You look happier.

BURGESS [*ruefully*] Well, praps I do. I spose I must, since you notice it. At all events, I git my contrax assepted by the County Council. [*Savagely*] They dussent ave nothink to do with me unless I paid fair wages: curse em for a parcel o meddlin fools!

MORELL [*dropping his hand, utterly discouraged*] So that was why you raised the wages! [*He sits down moodily*].

BURGESS [*severely, in spreading, mounting tones*] Woy helse should I do it? What does it lead to but drink and huppishness in workin men? [*He seats himself magisterially in the easy chair*]. It's hall very well for you, James: it gits you hinto the papers and makes a great man of you; but you never think of the arm you do, puttin money into the pockets of workin men that they dunno ow to spend, and takin it from people that might be makin a good huse on it.

MORELL [*with a heavy sigh, speaking with cold politeness*] What is your business with me this morning? I shall not pretend to believe that you are here merely out of family sentiment.
BURGESS [*obstinately*] Yes I ham: just family sentiment and nothink helse.
MORELL [*with weary calm*] I dont believe you.
BURGESS [*rising threateningly*] Dont say that to me again, James Mavor Morell.
MORELL [*unmoved*] I'll say it just as often as may be necessary to convince you that it's true. I dont believe you.
BURGESS [*collapsing into an abyss of wounded feeling*] Oh, well, if youre detormined to be hunfriendly, I spose I'd better go. [*He moves reluctantly towards the door. Morell makes no sign. He lingers*]. I didnt hexpect to find a hunforgin spirit in you, James. [*Morell still not responding, he takes a few more reluctant steps doorwards. Then he comes back, whining*]. We huseter git on well enough, spite of our different hopinions. Woy are you so changed to me? I give you my word I come here in peeorr [pure] frenliness, not wishin to be hon bad terms with my hown daughrter's usban. Come, James: be a Kerischin, and shake ands. [*He puts his hand sentimentally on Morell's shoulder*].
MORELL [*looking up at him thoughtfully*] Look here, Burgess. Do you want to be as welcome here as you were before you lost that contract?
BURGESS. I do, James. I do—*h*onest.
MORELL. Then why dont you behave as you did then?
BURGESS [*cautiously removing his hand*] Ow d'y'mean?
MORELL. I'll tell you. You thought me a young fool then.
BURGESS [*coaxingly*] No I didnt, James. I—
MORELL [*cutting him short*] Yes, you did. And I thought you an old scoundrel.
BURGESS [*most vehemently deprecating this gross self-accusation on Morell's part*] No you didnt, James. Now you do yourself a hinjustice.
MORELL. Yes I did. Well, that did not prevent our getting on very well together. God made you what I call a scoundrel as He made me what you call a fool. [*The effect of this observation on Burgess is to remove the keystone of his moral arch. He becomes bodily weak, and, with his eyes fixed on Morell in a helpless stare, puts out his hand apprehensively to balance himself, as if the floor had suddenly sloped under him. Morell proceeds, in the same tone of quiet conviction*] It was not for me to quarrel with His handiwork in the one case more than in the

other. So long as you come here honestly as a self-respecting, thorough, convinced scoundrel, justifying your scoundrelism and proud of it, you are welcome. But [*and now Morell's tone becomes formidable; and he rises and strikes the back of the chair for greater emphasis*] I wont have you here snivelling about being a model employer and a converted man when youre only an apostate with your coat turned for the sake of a County Council contract. [*He nods at him to enforce the point; then goes to the hearth-rug, where he takes up a comfortably commanding position with his back to the fire, and continues*] No: I like a man to be true to himself, even in wickedness. Come now: either take your hat and go; or else sit down and give me a good scoundrelly reason for wanting to be friends with me. [*Burgess, whose emotions have subsided sufficiently to be expressed by a dazed grin, is relieved by this concrete proposition. He ponders it for a moment, and then, slowly and very modestly, sits down in the chair Morell has just left*]. Thats right. Now out with it.

BURGESS [*chuckling in spite of himself*] Well, you orr a queer bird, James, and no mistake. But [*almost enthusiastically*] one carnt elp likin you: besides, as I said afore, of course one dont take hall a clorgyman says seriously, or the world couldnt go on. Could it now? [*He composes himself for graver discourse, and, turning his eyes on Morell, proceeds with dull seriousness*] Well, I dont mind tellin you, since it's your wish we should be free with one another, that I did think you a bit of a fool once; but I'm beginnin to think that praps I was be'ind the times a bit.

MORELL [*exultant*] Aha! Youre finding that out at last, are you?

BURGESS [*portentously*] Yes: times 'as changed mor'n I could a believed. Five yorr [year] ago, no sensible man would a thought o takin hup with your hidears. I hused to wonder you was let preach at all. Why, I know a clorgyman what 'as bin kep hout of his job for yorrs by the Bishop o London, although the pore feller's not a bit more religious than you are. But today, if hennyone was to horffer to bet me a thousan poun that youll hend by bein a bishop yourself, I dussent take the bet. [*Very impressively*] You and your crew are gittin hinfluential: I can see that. Theyll ave to give you somethink someday, if it's honly to stop your mouth. You ad the right instinc arter all, James: the line you took is the payin line in the long run for a man o your sort.

MORELL [*offering his hand with thorough decision*] Shake hands, Burgess. Now youre talking honestly. I dont think theyll make me a bishop; but if they do, I'll introduce you to the biggest jobbers I can get to come to my dinner parties.

BURGESS [*who has risen with a sheepish grin and accepted the hand of friendship*] You will ave your joke, James. Our quarrel's made up now, aint it?

A WOMAN'S VOICE. Say yes, James.

Startled, they turn quickly and find that Candida has just come in, and is looking at them with an amused maternal indulgence which is her characteristic expression. She is a woman of 33, well built, well nourished, likely, one guesses, to become matronly later on, but now quite at her best, with the double charm of youth and motherhood. Her ways are those of a woman who has found that she can always manage people by engaging their affection, and who does so frankly and instinctively without the smallest scruple. So far, she is like any other pretty woman who is just clever enough to make the most of her sexual attractions for trivially selfish ends; but Candida's serene brow, courageous eyes, and well set mouth and chin signify largeness of mind and dignity of character to ennoble her cunning in the affections. A wise-hearted observer, looking at her, would at once guess that whoever had placed the Virgin of the Assumption over her hearth did so because he fancied some spiritual resemblance between them, and yet would not suspect either her husband or herself of any such idea, or indeed of any concern with the art of Titian.

Just now she is in bonnet and mantle, carrying a strapped rug with her umbrella stuck through it, a handbag, and a supply of illustrated papers.

MORELL [*shocked at his remissness*] Candida! Why—[*he looks at his watch, and is horrified to find it so late*]. My darling! [*Hurrying to her and seizing the rug strap, pouring forth his remorseful regrets all the time*] I intended to meet you at the train. I let the time slip. [*Flinging the rug on the sofa*] I was so engrossed by—[*returning to her*] —I forgot—oh! [*He embraces her with penitent emotion*].

BURGESS [*a little shamefaced and doubtful of his reception*] How orr you, Candy? [*She, still in Morell's arms, offers him her cheek, which he kisses*]. James and me is come to a nunnerstannin. A *h*onorable unnerstannin. Ain we, James?

MORELL [*impetuously*] Oh bother your understanding! youve kept me late for Candida. [*With compassionate fervor*] My poor love: how did you manage about the luggage? How—

CANDIDA [*stopping him and disengaging herself*] There! there! there! I wasnt alone. Eugene has been down with us; and we travelled together.

MORELL [*pleased*] Eugene!

CANDIDA. Yes: he's struggling with my luggage, poor boy. Go out, dear, at once; or he'll pay for the cab; and I dont want that. [*Morell hurries out. Candida puts down her handbag; then takes off her mantle and bonnet and puts them on the sofa with the rug, chatting meanwhile*]. Well, papa: how are you getting on at home?

BURGESS. The ouse aint worth livin in since you left it, Candy. I wish youd come round and give the gurl a talkin to. Who's this Eugene thats come with you?

CANDIDA. Oh, Eugene's one of James's discoveries. He found him sleeping on the Embankment last June. Havnt you noticed our new picture [*pointing to the Virgin*]? He gave us that.

BURGESS [*incredulously*] Garn! D'you mean to tell me—your hown father!—that cab touts or such like, orf the Embankment, buys pictures like that? [*Severely*] Dont deceive me, Candy: it's a 'Igh Church picture; and James chose it hisself.

CANDIDA. Guess again. Eugene isnt a cab tout.

BURGESS. Then what is he? [*Sarcastically*] A nobleman, I spose.

CANDIDA [*nodding delightedly*] Yes. His uncle's a peer! A real live earl.

BURGESS [*not daring to believe such good news*] No!

CANDIDA. Yes. He had a seven day bill for £55 in his pocket when James found him on the Embankment. He thought he couldnt get any money for it until the seven days were up; and he was too shy to ask for credit. Oh, he's a dear boy! We are very fond of him.

BURGESS [*pretending to belittle the aristocracy, but with his eyes gleaming*] Hm! I thort you wouldnt git a hearl's nevvy visitin in Victawriar Pawrk unless he were a bit of a flat. [*Looking again at the picture*] Of course I dont old with that picture, Candy; but still it's a 'igh class fust rate work of ort: I can see that. Be sure you hintrodooce me to im, Candy. [*He looks at his watch anxiously*]. I can ony stay about two minutes.

Morell comes back with Eugene, whom Burgess contemplates moist-eyed with enthusiasm. He is a strange, shy youth of eighteen, slight, effeminate, with a delicate childish voice, and a hunted tormented expression and shrinking manner that shew the painful sensitiveness of very swift and acute apprehensiveness in youth, before the character has grown to its full strength. Miserably irresolute, he does not know where to stand or what to do. He is afraid of Burgess, and would run away into solitude if he dared; but the very intensity with which he feels a perfectly commonplace position comes from excessive nervous force; and his nostrils, mouth, and eyes betray a fiercely petulant wilfulness, as to the bent of which his brow, already lined with pity, is reassuring. He is so uncommon as to be almost unearthly; and to prosaic people there is something noxious in this unearthliness, just as to poetic people there is something angelic in it. His dress is anarchic. He wears an old blue serge jacket, unbuttoned, over a woollen lawn tennis shirt, with a silk handkerchief for a cravat, trousers matching the jacket, and brown canvas shoes. In these garments he has apparently lain in the heather and waded through the waters; and there is no evidence of his having ever brushed them.

As he catches sight of a stranger on entering, he stops, and edges along the wall on the opposite side of the room.

MORELL [*as he enters*] Come along: you can spare us quarter of an hour at all events. This is my father-in-law. Mr Burgess— Mr Marchbanks.

MARCHBANKS [*nervously backing against the bookcase*] Glad to meet you, sir.

BURGESS [*crossing to him with great heartiness, whilst Morell joins Candida at the fire*] Glad to meet you, I'm shore. Mr Morchbanks [*Forcing him to shake hands*] Ow do you find yoreself this weather? Ope you aint lettin James put no foolish ideas into your ed?

MARCHBANKS. Foolish ideas? Oh, you mean Socialism? No.

BURGESS. Thats right. [*Again looking at his watch*] Well, I must go now: theres no elp for it. Yore not comin my way, orr you, Mr Morchbanks?

MARCHBANKS. Which way is that?

BURGESS. Victawriar Pawrk Station. Theres a city train at 12.25.

MORELL. Nonsense. Eugene will stay to lunch with us, I expect.

MARCHBANKS [*anxiously excusing himself*] No—I—I

BURGESS. Well, well, I shornt press you: I bet youd rather lunch with Candy. Some night, I ope, youll come and dine with me at my club, the Freeman Founders in Nortn Folgit. Come: say you will!

MARCHBANKS. Thank you, Mr Burgess. Where is Norton Folgate? Down in Surrey, isnt it?

Burgess, inexpressibly tickled, begins to splutter with laughter.

CANDIDA [*coming to the rescue*] Youll lose your train, papa, if you dont go at once. Come back in the afternoon and tell Mr Marchbanks where to find the club.

BURGESS [*roaring with glee*] Down in Surrey! Har, har! thats not a bad one. Well, I never met a man as didnt know Nortn Folgit afore. [*Abashed at his own noisiness*] Goodbye, Mr Morchbanks: I know yore too ighbred to take my pleasantry in bad part. [*He again offers his hand*].

MARCHBANKS [*taking it with a nervous jerk*] Not at all.

BURGESS. Bye, bye, Candy. I'll look in again later on. So long, James.

MORELL. Must you go?

BURGESS. Dont stir. [*He goes out with unabated heartiness*].

MORELL. Oh, I'll see you off. [*He follows him*].

Eugene stares after them apprehensively, holding his breath until Burgess disappears.

CANDIDA [*laughing*] Well, Eugene? [*He turns with a start, and comes eagerly towards her, but stops irresolutely as he meets her amused look*]. What do you think of my father?

MARCHBANKS. I—I hardly know him yet. He seems to be a very nice old gentleman.

CANDIDA [*with gentle irony*] And youll go to the Freeman Founders to dine with him, wont you?

MARCHBANKS [*miserably, taking it quite seriously*] Yes, if it will please you.

CANDIDA [*touched*] Do you know, you are a very nice boy, Eugene, with all your queerness. If you had laughed at my father I shouldnt have minded; but I like you ever so much better for being nice to him.

MARCHBANKS. Ought I to have laughed? I noticed that he said something funny; but I am so ill at ease with strangers; and I never can see a joke. I'm very sorry. [*He sits down on the sofa, his elbows on his knees and his temples between his fists, with an expression of hopeless suffering*].

CANDIDA [*bustling him goodnaturedly*] Oh come! You great baby, you! You are worse than usual this morning. Why were you so melancholy as we came along in the cab?

MARCHBANKS. Oh, that was nothing. I was wondering how much I ought to give the cabman. I know it's utterly silly; but you dont know how dreadful such things are to me—how I shrink from having to deal with strange people. [*Quickly and reassuringly*] But it's all right. He beamed all over and touched his hat when Morell gave him two shillings. I was on the point of offering him ten.

Morell comes back with a few letters and newspapers which have come by the midday post.

CANDIDA. Oh, James dear, he was going to give the cabman ten shillings! ten shillings for a three minutes drive! Oh dear!

MORELL [*at the table, glancing through the letters*] Never mind her, Marchbanks. The overpaying instinct is a generous one: better than the underpaying instinct, and not so common.

MARCHBANKS [*relapsing into dejection*] No: cowardice, incompetence. Mrs Morell's quite right.

CANDIDA. Of course she is. [*She takes up her handbag*]. And now I must leave you to James for the present. I suppose you are too much of a poet to know the state a woman finds her house in when she's been away for three weeks. Give me my rug. [*Eugene takes the strapped rug from the couch, and gives it to her. She takes it in her left hand, having the bag in her right*]. Now hang my cloak across my arm. [*He obeys*]. Now my hat. [*He puts it into the hand which has the bag*]. Now open the door for me. [*He hurries before her and opens the door*]. Thanks. [*She goes out; and Marchbanks shuts the door*].

MORELL [*still busy at the table*] Youll stay to lunch, Marchbanks, of course.

MARCHBANKS [*scared*] I mustnt. [*He glances quickly at Morell, but at once avoids his frank look, and adds, with obvious disingenuousness*] I mean I cant.

MORELL. You mean you wont.

MARCHBANKS [*earnestly*] No: I should like to, indeed. Thank you very much. But—but—

MORELL. But—but—but—but—Bosh! If youd like to stay, stay. If youre shy, go and take a turn in the park and write poetry until half past one; and then come in and have a good feed.

MARCHBANKS. Thank you, I should like that very much. But I really mustnt. The truth is, Mrs Morell told me not to. She said she didnt think youd ask me to stay to lunch, but that I was to remember, if you did, that you didnt really want me to. [*Plaintively*] She said I'd understand; but I dont. Please dont tell her I told you.

MORELL [*drolly*] Oh, is that all? Wont my suggestion that you should take a turn in the park meet the difficulty?

MARCHBANKS. How?

MORELL [*exploding good-humoredly*] Why, you duffer—[*But this boisterousness jars himself as well as Eugene. He checks himself*]. No:

I wont put it in that way. [*He comes to Eugene with affectionate seriousness*]. My dear lad: in a happy marriage like ours, there is something very sacred in the return of the wife to her home. [*Marchbanks looks quickly at him, half anticipating his meaning*]. An old friend or a truly noble and sympathetic soul is not in the way on such occasions; but a chance visitor is. [*The hunted horrorstricken expression comes out with sudden vividness in Eugene's face as he understands. Morell, occupied with his own thoughts, goes on without noticing this*]. Candida thought I would rather not have you here; but she was wrong. I'm very fond of you, my boy; and I should like you to see for yourself what a happy thing it is to be married as I am.

MARCHBANKS. Happy! Y o u r marriage! You think that! You believe that!

MORELL [*buoyantly*] I know it, my lad. Larochefoucauld said that there are convenient marriages but no delightful ones. You dont know the comfort of seeing through and through a thundering liar and rotten cynic like that fellow. Ha! ha! Now, off with you to the park, and write your poem. Half past one, sharp, mind: we never wait for anybody.

MARCHBANKS [*wildly*] No: stop: you shant. I'll force it into the light.

MORELL [*puzzled*] Eh? Force what?

MARCHBANKS. I must speak to you. There is something that must be settled between us.

MORELL [*with a whimsical glance at his watch*] Now?

MARCHBANKS [*passionately*] Now. Before you leave this room. [*He retreats a few steps, and stands as if to bar Morell's way to the door*].

MORELL [*without moving, and gravely, perceiving now that there is something serious the matter*] I'm not going to leave it, my dear boy: I thought you were. [*Eugene, baffled by his firm tone, turns his back on him, writhing with anger. Morell goes to him and puts his hand on his shoulder strongly and kindly, disregarding his attempt to shake it off*]. Come: sit down quietly; and tell me what it is. And remember: we are friends, and need not fear that either of us will be anything but patient and kind to the other, whatever we may have to say.

MARCHBANKS [*twisting himself round on him*] Oh, I am not forgetting myself: I am only [*covering his face desperately with his hands*] full of horror. [*Then, dropping his hands, and thrusting his face forward fiercely at Morell, he goes on threateningly*] You shall see whether this is a time for patience and kindness. [*Morell, firm as a rock, looks indulgently at him*]. Dont look at me in that self-complacent way. You think yourself stronger than I am; but I shall stagger you if you have a heart in your breast.

MORELL [*powerfully confident*] Stagger me, my boy. Out with it.

MARCHBANKS. First—

MORELL. First?

MARCHBANKS. I love your wife.

Morell recoils, and, after staring at him for a moment in utter amazement, bursts into uncontrollable laughter. Eugene is taken aback, but not disconcerted; and he soon becomes indignant and contemptuous.

MORELL [*sitting down to have his laugh out*] Why, my dear child, of course you do. Everybody loves her: they cant help it. I like it. But [*looking up jocosely at him*] I say, Eugene: do you think yours is a case to be talked about? Youre under twenty: she's over thirty. Doesnt it look rather too like a case of calf love?

MARCHBANKS [*vehemently*] You dare say that of her! You think that way of the love she inspires! It is an insult to her!

MORELL [*rising quickly, in an altered tone*] To her! Eugene: take care. I have been patient. I hope to remain patient. But there are some things I wont allow. Dont force me to shew you the indulgence I should shew to a child. Be a man.

MARCHBANKS [*with a gesture as if sweeping something behind him*] Oh, let us put aside all that cant. It horrifies me when I think of the doses of it she has had to endure in all the weary years during which you have selfishly and blindly sacrificed her to minister to your self-sufficiency: y o u! [*turning on him*] who have not one thought—one sense—in common with her.

MORELL [*philosophically*] She seems to bear it pretty well. [*Looking him straight in the face*] Eugene, my boy: you are making a fool of yourself: a very great fool of yourself. Theres a piece of wholesome plain speaking for you. [*He knocks in the lesson with a nod in his old way, and posts himself on the hearth-rug, holding his hands behind him to warm them*].

MARCHBANKS. Oh, do you think I dont know all that? Do you think that the things people make fools of themselves about are any less real and true than the things they behave sensibly about? [*Morell's gaze wavers for the first time. He forgets to warm his hands, and stands listening, startled and thoughtful*]. They are more true: they are the only things that are true. You are very calm and sensible and moderate with me because you can see that I am a fool about your wife; just as no doubt that old man who was here just now is very wise over your Socialism, because he sees that y o u are a fool about it. [*Morell's perplexity deepens markedly. Eugene follows up his advantage, plying him fiercely with questions*]. Does that prove you wrong? Does your complacent superiority to me prove that *I* am wrong?

MORELL. Marchbanks: some devil is putting these words into your mouth. It is easy—terribly easy—to shake a man's faith in himself. To take advantage of that to break a man's spirit is devil's work. Take care of what you are doing. Take care.

MARCHBANKS [*ruthlessly*] I know. I'm doing it on purpose. I told you I should stagger you.

They confront one another threateningly for a moment. Then Morell recovers his dignity.

MORELL [*with noble tenderness*] Eugene: listen to me. Some day, I hope and trust, you will be a happy man like me. [*Eugene chafes intolerantly, repudiating the worth of his happiness. Morell, deeply insulted, controls himself with fine forbearance, and continues steadily with great artistic beauty of delivery*] You will be married; and you will be working with all your might and valor to make every spot on earth as happy as your own home. You will be one of the makers of the Kingdom of Heaven on earth; and—who knows?—you may be a master builder where I am only a humble journeyman; for dont think, my boy, that I cannot see in you, young as you are, promise of higher powers than I can ever pretend to. I well know that it is in the poet that the holy spirit of man—the god within him—is most godlike. It should make you tremble to think of that—to think that the heavy burthen and great gift of a poet may be laid upon you.

MARCHBANKS [*unimpressed and remorseless, his boyish crudity of assertion telling sharply against Morell's oratory*] It does not make me tremble. It is the want of it in others that makes me tremble.

MORELL [*redoubling his force of style under the stimulus of his genuine feeling and Eugene's obduracy*] Then help to kindle it in them—in me—not to extinguish it. In the future, when you are as happy as I am, I will be your true brother in the faith. I will help you to believe that God has given us a world that nothing but our own folly keeps from being a paradise. I will help you to believe that every stroke of your work is sowing happiness for the great harvest that all —even the humblest—shall one day reap. And last, but trust me, not least, I will help you to believe that your wife loves you and is happy in her home. We need such help, Marchbanks: we need it greatly and always. There are so many things to make us doubt, if once we let our understanding be troubled. Even at home, we sit as if in camp, encompassed by a hostile army of doubts. Will you play the traitor and let them in on me?

MARCHBANKS [*looking round wildly*] Is it like this for her here always? A woman, with a great soul, craving for reality, truth, freedom; and being fed on metaphors, sermons, stale perorations, mere rhetoric. Do you think a woman's soul can live on your talent for preaching?

MORELL [*stung*] Marchbanks: you make it hard for me to control myself. My talent is like yours insofar as it has any real worth at all. It is the gift of finding words for divine truth.

MARCHBANKS [*impetuously*] It's the gift of the gab, nothing more and nothing less. What has your knack of fine talking to do with the truth, any more than playing the organ has? Ive never been in your church; but Ive been to your political meetings; and Ive seen you do whats called rousing the meeting to enthusiasm: that is, you excited them until they behaved exactly as if they were drunk. And their wives looked on and saw what fools they were. Oh, it's an old story: youll find it in the Bible. I imagine King David, in his fits of enthusiasm, was very like you. [*Stabbing him with the words*] "But his wife despised him in her heart."

MORELL [*wrathfully*] Leave my house. Do you hear? [*He advances on him threateningly*].

MARCHBANKS [*shrinking back against the couch*] Let me alone. Dont touch me. [*Morell grasps him powerfully by the lappell of his coat: he cowers down on the sofa and screams passionately*] Stop, Morell: if you strike me, I'll kill myself: I wont bear it. [*Almost in hysterics*] Let me go. Take your hand away.

MORELL [*with slow emphatic scorn*] You little snivelling cowardly whelp. [*He releases him*]. Go, before you frighten yourself into a fit.

MARCHBANKS [*on the sofa, gasping, but relieved by the withdrawal of Morell's hand*] I'm not afraid of you: it's you who are afraid of me.

MORELL [*quietly, as he stands over him*] It looks like it, doesnt it?

MARCHBANKS [*with petulant vehemence*] Yes, it does. [*Morell turns away contemptuously. Eugene scrambles to his feet and follows him*]. You think because I shrink from being brutally handled—because [*with tears in his voice*] I can do nothing but cry with rage when I am met with violence—because I cant lift a heavy trunk down from the top of a cab like you—because I cant fight you for your wife as a drunken navvy would: all that makes you think I'm afraid of you. But youre wrong. If I havnt got what you call British pluck, I havnt British cowardice either: I'm not afraid of a clergyman's ideas. I'll fight your ideas. I'll rescue her from her slavery to them. I'll pit my own ideas against them. You are driving me out of the house because you darent let her choose between your ideas and mine. You are afraid to let me see her again. [*Morell, angered, turns suddenly on him. He flies to the door in involuntary dread*]. Let me alone, I say. I'm going.

MORELL [*with cold scorn*] Wait a moment: I am not going to touch you: dont be afraid. When my wife comes back she will want to know why you have gone. And when she finds that you are never going to cross our threshold again, she will want to have that explained too. Now I dont wish to distress her by telling her that you have behaved like a blackguard.

MARCHBANKS [*coming back with renewed vehemence*] You shall. You must. If you give any explanation but the true one, you are a liar and a coward. Tell her what I said; and how you were strong and manly, and shook me as a terrier shakes a rat; and how I shrank and was terrified; and how you called me a snivelling little whelp and put me out of the house. If you dont tell her, I will: I'll write it to her.

MORELL [*puzzled*] Why do you want her to know this?

MARCHBANKS [*with lyric rapture*] Because she will understand me, and know that I understand her. If you keep back one word of it from her—if you are not ready to lay the truth at her feet as I am—then you will know to the end of your days that she really belongs to me and not to you. Goodbye. [*Going*].

MORELL [*terribly disquieted*] Stop: I will not tell her.

MARCHBANKS [*turning near the door*] Either the truth or a lie you m u s t tell her, if I go.

MORELL [*temporizing*] Marchbanks: it is sometimes justifiable—

MARCHBANKS [*cutting him short*] I know: to lie. It will be useless. Goodbye, Mr Clergyman.

As he turns to the door, it opens and Candida enters in her housekeeping dress.

CANDIDA. Are you going, Eugene? [*Looking more observantly at him*] Well, dear me, just look at you, going out into the street in that state! You a r e a poet, certainly. Look at him, James! [*She takes him by the coat, and brings him forward, shewing him to Morell*]. Look at his collar! look at his tie! look at his hair! One would think somebody had been throttling you. [*Eugene instinctively tries to look round at*

Morell; but she pulls him back]. Here! Stand still. [*She buttons his collar; ties his neckerchief in a bow; and arranges his hair*]. There! Now you look so nice that I think youd better stay to lunch after all, though I told you you musnt. It will be ready in half an hour. [*She puts a final touch to the bow. He kisses her hand*]. Dont be silly.

MARCHBANKS. I want to stay, of course; unless the reverend gentleman your husband has anything to advance to the contrary.

CANDIDA. Shall he stay, James, if he promises to be a good boy and help me to lay the table?

MORELL [*shortly*] Oh yes, certainly: he had better. [*He goes to the table and pretends to busy himself with his papers there*].

MARCHBANKS [*offering his arm to Candida*] Come and lay the table [*She takes it. They go to the door together. As they pass out he adds*] I am the happiest of mortals.

MORELL. So was I—an hour ago.

ACT II

The same day later in the afternoon. The same room. The chair for visitors has been replaced at the table. Marchbanks, alone and idle, is trying to find out how the typewriter works. Hearing someone at the door, he steals guiltily away to the window and pretends to be absorbed in the view. Miss Garnett, carrying the notebook in which she takes down Morell's letters in shorthand from his dictation, sits down at the typewriter and sets to work transcribing them, much too busy to notice Eugene. When she begins the second line she stops and stares at the machine. Something wrong evidently.

PROSERPINE. Bother! Youve been meddling with my typewriter, Mr Marchbanks; and theres not the least use in your trying to look as if you hadnt.

MARCHBANKS [*timidly*] I'm very sorry, Miss Garnett. I only tried to make it write. [*Plaintively*] But it wouldnt.

PROSERPINE. Well, youve altered the spacing.

MARCHBANKS [*earnestly*] I assure you I didnt. I didnt indeed. I only turned a little wheel. It gave a sort of click.

PROSERPINE. Oh, now I understand. [*She restores the spacing, talking volubly all the time*]. I suppose you thought it was a sort of barrel-organ. Nothing to do but turn the handle, and it would write a beautiful love letter for you straight off, eh?

MARCHBANKS [*seriously*] I suppose a machine could be made to write love letters. Theyre all the same, arnt they?

PROSERPINE [*somewhat indignantly: any such discussion, except by way of pleasantry, being outside her code of manners*] How do I know? Why do you ask me?

MARCHBANKS. I beg your pardon. I thought clever people—people who can do business and write letters and that sort of thing—always had to have love affairs to keep them from going mad.

PROSERPINE [*rising outraged*] Mr Marchbanks! [*She looks severly at him, and marches majestically to the bookcase*].

MARCHBANKS [*approaching her humbly*] I hope I havnt offended you. Perhaps I shouldnt have alluded to your love affairs.

PROSERPINE [*plucking a blue book from the shelf and turning sharply on him*] I havnt any love affairs. How dare you say such a thing? The idea! [*She tucks the book under her arm, and is flouncing back to her machine when he addresses her with awakened interest and sympathy*].

MARCHBANKS. Really! Oh, then you are shy, like me.

PROSERPINE. Certainly I am not shy. What do you mean?

MARCHBANKS [*secretly*] You must be: that is the reason there are so few love affairs in the world. We all go about longing for love: it is the first need of our natures, the first prayer of our hearts; but we dare not utter our longing: we are too shy. [*Very earnestly*] Oh, Miss Garnett, what would you not give to be without fear, without shame—

PROSERPINE [*scandalized*] Well, upon my word!

MARCHBANKS [*with petulant impatience*] Ah, dont say those stupid things to me: they dont deceive me: what use are they? Why are you afraid to be your real self with me? I am just like you.

PROSERPINE. Like m e! Pray are you flattering me or flattering yourself? I dont feel quite sure which. [*She again tries to get back to her work*].

MARCHBANKS [*stopping her mysteriously*] Hush! I go about in search of love; and I find it in unmeasured stores in the bosoms of others. But when I try to ask for it, this horrible shyness strangles me; and I stand dumb, or worse than dumb, saying meaningless things: foolish lies. And I see the affection I am longing for given to dogs and cats and pet birds, because they come and ask for it. [*Almost whispering*] It must be asked for: it is like a ghost: it cannot speak unless it is first spoken to. [*At his usual pitch, but with deep melancholy*] All the love in the world is longing to speak; only it dare not, because it is shy! shy! shy! That is the world's tragedy. [*With a deep sigh he sits in the visitors' chair and buries his face in his hands*].

PROSERPINE [*amazed, but keeping her wits about her: her point of honor in encounters with strange young men*] Wicked people get over that shyness occasionally, dont they?

MARCHBANKS [*scrambling up almost fiercely*] Wicked people means people who have no love: therefore they have no shame. They have the power to ask love because they dont need it: they have the power to offer it because they have none to give. [*He collapses into his seat, and adds, mournfully*] But we, who have love, and long to mingle it with the love of others: we cannot utter a word. [*Timidly*] You find that, dont you?

PROSERPINE. Look here: if you dont stop talking like this, I'll leave the room, Mr Marchbanks: I really will. It's not proper.

She resumes her seat at the typewriter, opening the blue book and preparing to copy a passage from it.

MARCHBANKS [*hopelessly*] Nothing thats worth saying is proper. [*He rises, and wanders about the room in his lost way*]. I cant understand you, Miss Garnett. What am I to talk about?

PROSERPINE [*snubbing him*] Talk about indifferent things. Talk about the weather.

MARCHBANKS. Would you talk about indifferent things if a child were by, crying bitterly with hunger?

PROSERPINE. I suppose not.

MARCHBANKS. Well: *I* cant talk about indifferent things with my heart crying out bitterly in its hunger.

PROSERPINE. Then hold your tongue.

MARCHBANKS. Yes: that is what it always comes to. We hold our tongues. Does that stop the cry of your heart? for it does cry: doesnt it? It must, if you have a heart.

PROSERPINE [*suddenly rising with her hand pressed on her heart*] Oh, it's no use trying to work while you talk like that. [*She leaves her little table and sits on the sofa. Her feelings are keenly stirred*]. It's no business of yours whether my heart cries or not; but I have a mind to tell you, for all that.

MARCHBANKS. You neednt. I know already that it must.

PROSERPINE. But mind! if you ever say I said so, I'll deny it.

MARCHBANKS [*compassionately*] Yes, I know. And so you havnt the courage to tell him?

PROSERPINE [*bouncing up*] Him! Who?

MARCHBANKS. Whoever he is. The man you love. It might be anybody. The curate, Mr Mill, perhaps.

PROSERPINE [*with disdain*] Mr Mill!!! A fine man to break my heart about, indeed! I'd rather have you than Mr Mill.

MARCHBANKS [*recoiling*] No, really: I'm very sorry; but you mustnt think of that. I—

PROSERPINE [*testily, going to the fire-place and standing at it with her back to him*] Oh, dont be frightened: it's not you. It's not any one particular person.

MARCHBANKS. I know. You feel that you could love anybody that offered—

PROSERPINE [*turning, exasperated*] Anybody that offered! No, I do not. What do you take me for?

MARCHBANKS [*discouraged*] No use. You wont make me real answers: only those things that everybody says. [*He strays to the sofa and sits down disconsolately*].

PROSERPINE [*nettled at what she takes to be a disparagement of her manners by an aristocrat*] Oh well, if you want original conversation, youd better go and talk to yourself.

MARCHBANKS. That is what all poets do: they talk to themselves out loud; and the world overhears them. But it's horribly lonely not to hear someone else talk sometimes.

PROSERPINE. Wait until Mr Morell comes. He'll talk to you. [*Marchbanks shudders*]. Oh, you neednt make wry faces over him: he can talk better than you. [*With temper*] He'd talk your little head off. [*She is going back angrily to her place, when he, suddenly, enlightened, springs up and stops her*].

MARCHBANKS. Ah! I understand now.

PROSERPINE [*reddening*] What do you understand?

MARCHBANKS. Your secret. Tell me: is it really and truly possible for a woman to love him?

PROSERPINE [*as if this were beyond all bounds*] Well!!

MARCHBANKS [*passionately*] No: answer me. I want to know: I must know. *I* cant understand it. I can see nothing in him but words, pious resolutions, what people call goodness. You cant love that.

PROSERPINE [*attempting to snub him by an air of cool propriety*] I simply dont know what youre talking about. I dont understand you.

MARCHBANKS [*vehemently*] You do. You lie.

PROSERPINE. Oh!

MARCHBANKS. You do understand; and you know. [*Determined to have an answer*] Is it possible for a woman to love him?

PROSERPINE [*looking him straight in the face*] Yes. [*He covers his face with his hands*]. Whatever is the matter with you! [*He takes down his hands. Frightened at the tragic mask presented to her, she hurries past him at the utmost possible distance, keeping her eyes on his face until he turns from her and goes to the child's chair beside the hearth, where he sits in the deepest dejection. As she approaches the door, it opens and Burgess enters. Seeing him, she ejaculates*] Praise heaven!

here's somebody [*and feels safe enough to resume her place at the table. She puts a fresh sheet of paper into the typewriter as Burgess crosses to Eugene*].

BURGESS [*bent on taking care of the distinguished visitor*] Well: so this is the way they leave you to yoreself, Mr Morchbanks. Ive come to keep you company. [*Marchbanks looks up at him in consternation, which is quite lost on him*]. James is receivin a deppitation in the dinin room; and Candy is hupstairs heducating of a young stitcher gurl she's hinterested in. [*Condolingly*] You must find it lonesome here with no one but the typist to talk to. [*He pulls round the easy chair, and sits down*].

PROSERPINE [*highly incensed*] He'll be all right now that he has the advantage of y o u r polished conversation: thats one comfort, anyhow. [*She begins to typewrite with clattering asperity*].

BURGESS [*amazed at her audacity*] Hi was not addressin myself to you, young woman, that I'm awerr of.

PROSERPINE. Did you ever see worse manners, Mr Marchbanks?

BURGESS [*with pompous severity*] Mr Morchbanks is a gentleman, and knows his place, which is more than some people do.

PROSERPINE [*fretfully*] It's well you and I are not ladies and gentlemen: I'd talk to you pretty straight if Mr Marchbanks wasnt here. [*She pulls the letter out of the machine so crossly that it tears*]. There! now I've spoiled this letter! have to be done all over again! Oh, I cant contain myself: silly old fathead!

BURGESS [*rising, breathless with indignation*] Ho! I'm a silly ole fat'ead, am I? Ho, indeed [*gasping*]! Hall right, my gurl! Hall right. You just wait till I tell that to yore hemployer. Youll see. I'll teach you: see if I dont.

PROSERPINE [*conscious of having gone too far*] I—

BURGESS [*cutting her short*] No: youve done it now. No huse a-talkin to me. I'll let you know who I am. [*Proserpine shifts her paper carriage with a defiant bang, and disdainfully goes on with her work*]. Dont you take no notice of her, Mr Morchbanks. She's beneath it. [*He loftily sits down again*].

MARCHBANKS [*miserably nervous and disconcerted*] Hadnt we better change the subject? I—I dont think Miss Garnett meant anything.

PROSERPINE [*with intense conviction*] Oh, didnt I though, j u s t!

BURGESS. I wouldnt demean myself to take notice on her.

An electric bell rings twice.

PROSERPINE [*gathering up her note-book and papers*] Thats for me. [*She hurries out*].

BURGESS [*calling after her*] Oh, we can spare you. [*Somewhat relieved by the triumph of having the last word, and yet half inclined to try to improve on it, he looks after her for a moment; then subsides into his seat by Eugene, and addresses him very confidentially*]. Now we're alone, Mr Morchbanks, let me give you a friendly int that I wouldnt give to heverybody. Ow long ave you known my son-in-law James ere?

MARCHBANKS. I dont know. I never can remember dates. A few months, perhaps.

BURGESS. Ever notice hennythink queer about him?

MARCHBANKS. I dont think so.

BURGESS [*impressively*] No more you wouldnt. Thats the danger on it. Well, he's mad.

MARCHBANKS. Mad!

BURGESS. Mad as a Morch 'are. You take notice on him and youll see.

MARCHBANKS [*uneasily*] But surely that is only because his opinions—

BURGESS [*touching him on the knee with his forefinger, and pressing it to hold his attention*] Thats the same what I hused to think, Mr Morchbanks. Hi thought long enough that it was ony his opinions; though, mind you, hopinions becomes vurry serious things when people takes to hactin on em as e does. But thats not what I go on. [*He looks round to make sure that they are alone, and bends over to Eugene's ear*]. What do you think he sez to me this morning in this very room?

MARCHBANKS. What?

BURGESS. He sez to me—this is as sure as we're settin here now—he sez "I'm a fool," he sez; "and yore a scounderl." Me a scounderl, mind you! And then shook ands with me on it, as if it was to my credit! Do you mean to tell me as that man's sane?

MORELL [*outside, calling to Proserpine as he opens the door*] Get all their names and addresses, Miss Garnett.

PROSERPINE [*in the distance*] Yes, Mr Morell.

Morell comes in, with the deputation's documents in his hands.

BURGESS [*aside to Marchbanks*] Yorr he is. Just you keep your heye on im and see. [*Rising momentously*] I'm sorry, James, to ave to make a complaint to you. I dont want to do it; but I feel I oughter, as a matter o right and dooty.

MORELL. Whats the matter?

BURGESS. Mr Morchbanks will bear me hout: he was a witness. [*Very solemnly*] Yore young woman so far forgot herself as to call me a silly ole fat'ead.

MORELL [*with tremendous heartiness*] Oh, now, isnt that exactly like Prossy? She's so frank: she cant contain herself! Poor Prossy! Ha! ha!

BURGESS [*trembling with rage*] And do you hexpec me to put up with it from the like of er?

MORELL. Pooh, nonsense! you cant take any notice of it. Never mind. [*He goes to the cellaret and puts the papers into one of the drawers*].

BURGESS. Oh, Hi dont mind. Hi'm above it. But is it r i g h t? thats what I want to know. Is it right?

MORELL. Thats a question for the Church, not for the laity. Has it done you any harm? thats the question for you, eh? Of course it hasnt. Think no more of it. [*He dismisses the subject by going to his place at the table and setting to work at his correspondence*].

BURGESS [*aside to Marchbanks*] What did I tell you? Mad as a atter. [*He goes to the table and asks, with the sickly civility of a hungry man*] When's dinner, James?

MORELL. Not for a couple of hours yet.

BURGESS [*with plaintive resignation*] Gimme a nice book to read over the fire, will you, James: thur's a good chap.

MORELL. What sort of book? A good one?

BURGESS [*with almost a yell of remonstrance*] Nah-oo! Summat pleasant, just to pass the time. [*Morell takes an illustrated paper from the table and offers it. He accepts it humbly*]. Thank yer, James. [*He goes back to the big chair at the fire, and sits there at his ease, reading*].

MORELL [*as he writes*] Candida will come to entertain you presently. She has got rid of her pupil. She is filling the lamps.

MARCHBANKS [*starting up in the wildest consternation*] But that will soil her hands. I cant bear that, Morell: it's a shame. I'll go and fill them. [*He makes for the door*].

MORELL. Youd better not. [*Marchbanks stops irresolutely*]. She'd only set you to clean my boots, to save me the trouble of doing it myself in the morning.

BURGESS [*with grave disapproval*] Dont you keep a servant now, James?

MORELL. Yes; but she isnt a slave; and the house looks as if I kept three. That means that everyone has to lend a hand. It's not a bad plan: Prossy and I can talk business after breakfast while we're washing up. Washing up's no trouble when there are two people to do it.

MARCHBANKS [*tormentedly*] Do you think every woman is as coarse-grained as Miss Garnett?

BURGESS [*emphatically*] Thats quite right, Mr Morchbanks: thats q u i t e right. She is corsegrained.

MORELL [*quietly and significantly*] Marchbanks!

MARCHBANKS. Yes?

MORELL. How many servants does your father keep?

MARCHBANKS [*pettishly*] Oh, I dont know. [*He moves to the sofa, as if to get as far as possible from Morell's questioning, and sits down in great agony of spirit, thinking of the paraffin*].

MORELL [*very gravely*] So many that you dont know! [*More aggressively*] When theres anything coarse-grained to be done, you just ring the bell and throw it on to somebody else, eh?

MARCHBANKS. Oh, dont torture me. You dont even ring the bell. But your wife's beautiful fingers are dabbling in paraffin oil while you sit here comfortably preaching about it: everlasting preaching! preaching! words! words! words!

BURGESS [*intensely appreciating this retort*] Har, har! Devil a better! [*Radiantly*] Ad you there, James, straight.

Candida comes in, well aproned, with a reading lamp trimmed, filled, and ready for lighting. She places it on the table near Morell, ready for use.

CANDIDA [*brushing her finger tips together with a slight twitch of her nose*] If you stay with us, Eugene, I think I will hand over the lamps to you.

MARCHBANKS. I will stay on condition that you hand over all the rough work to me.

CANDIDA. Thats very gallant; but I think I should like to see how you do it first. [*Turning to Morell*] James: youve not been looking after the house properly.

MORELL. What have I done—or not done—my love?

CANDIDA [*with serious vexation*] My own particular pet scrubbing brush has been used for blackleading. [*A heart-breaking wail bursts from Marchbanks. Burgess looks round, amazed. Candida hurries to the sofa.*] Whats the matter? Are you ill, Eugene?

MARCHBANKS. No: not ill. Only horror! horror! horror! [*He bows his head on his hands*].

BURGESS [*shocked*] What! Got the orrors, Mr Morchbanks! Oh, thats bad, at your age. You must leave it off grajally.

CANDIDA [*reassured*] Nonsense, papa! It's only poetic horror, isn't it, Eugene [*petting him*]?

BURGESS [*abashed*] Oh, poetic orror, is it? I beg your pordon, I'm shore. [*He turns to the fire again, deprecating his hasty conclusion*].

CANDIDA. What is it, Eugene? the scrubbing brush? [*He shudders*] Well, there! never mind. [*She sits down beside him*]. Wouldnt you like to present me with a nice new one, with an ivory back inlaid with mother-of-pearl?

MARCHBANKS [*softly and musically, but sadly and longingly*] No, not a scrubbing brush, but a boat: a tiny shallop to sail away in, far from the world, where the marble floors are washed by the rain and dried by the sun; where the south wind dusts the beautiful green and purple carpets. Or a chariot! to carry us up into the sky, where the lamps are stars, and dont need to be filled with paraffin oil every day.

MORELL [*harshly*] And where there is nothing to do but to be idle, selfish and useless.

CANDIDA [*jarred*] Oh, James! how could you spoil it all?

MARCHBANKS [*firing up*] Yes, to be idle, selfish, and useless: that is, to be beautiful and free and happy: hasnt every man desired that with all his soul for the woman he loves? Thats my ideal: whats yours, and that of all the dreadful people who live in these hideous rows of houses? Sermons and scrubbing brushes! With you to preach the sermon and your wife to scrub.

CANDIDA [*quaintly*] He cleans the boots, Eugene. You will have to clean them to-morrow for saying that about him.

MARCHBANKS. Oh, dont talk about boots! Your feet should be beautiful on the mountains.

CANDIDA. My feet would not be beautiful on the Hackney Road without boots.

BURGESS [*scandalized*] Come, Candy! dont be vulgar. Mr Morchbanks aint accustomed to it. Youre givin him the orrors again. I mean the poetic ones.

Morell is silent. Apparently he is busy with his letters: really he is puzzling with misgiving over his new and alarming experience that the surer he is of his moral thrusts, the more swiftly and effectively Eugene parries them. To find himself beginning to fear a man whom he does not respect afflicts him bitterly.

Miss Garnett comes in with a telegram.

PROSERPINE [*handing the telegram to Morell*] Reply paid. The boy's waiting. [*To Candida, coming back to her machine and sitting down*] Maria is ready for you now in the kitchen, Mrs Morell [*Candida rises*]. The onions have come.

MARCHBANKS [*conclusively*] Onions!

CANDIDA. Yes, onions. Not even Spanish ones: nasty little red onions. You shall help me to slice them. Come along.

She catches him by the wrist and runs out, pulling him after her. Burgess rises in consternation, and stands aghast on the hearth-rug, staring after them.

BURGESS. Candy didnt oughter andle a hearl's nevvy like that. It's goin too fur with it. Lookee ere, James: do e often git taken queer like that?

MORELL [*shortly, writing a telegram*] I dont know.

BURGESS [*sentimentally*] He talks very pretty. I awlus had a turn for a bit of poetry. Candy takes arter me that-a-way. Huseter make me tell er fairy stories when she was ony a little kiddy not that igh [*indicating a stature of two feet or thereabouts*].

MORELL [*preoccupied*] Ah, indeed. [*He blots the telegram and goes out*].

PROSERPINE. Used you to make the fairy stories up out of your own head?

Burgess, not deigning to reply, strikes an attitude of the haughtiest disdain on the hearth-rug.

PROSERPINE [*calmly*] I should never have supposed you had it in you. By the way, I'd better warn you, since youve taken such a fancy to Mr Marchbanks. He's mad.

BURGESS. Mad! What! Im too!!

PROSERPINE. Mad as a March hare. He did frighten me, I can tell you, just before you came in that time. Havent you noticed the queer things he says?

BURGESS. So thats what the poetic orrors means. Blame me if it didnt come into my ed once or twyst that he was a bit horff is chump! [*He crosses the room to the door, lifting up his voice as he goes*]. Well, this is a pretty sort of asylum for a man to be in, with no one but you to take care of him!

PROSERPINE [*as he passes her*] Yes, what a dreadful thing it would be if anything happened to y o u!

BURGESS [*loftily*] Dont you haddress no remorks to me. Tell your hemployer that Ive gone into the gorden for a smoke.

PROSERPINE [*mocking*] Oh!

Before Burgess can retort, Morell comes back.

BURGESS [*sentimentally*] Goin for a turn in the gording to smoke, James.

MORELL [*brusquely*] Oh, all right, all right. [*Burgess goes out pathetically in the character of a weary old man. Morell stands at the table, turning over his papers, and adding, across to Proserpine, half humorously, half absently*] Well, Miss Prossy, why have you been calling my father-in-law names?

PROSERPINE [*blushing fiery red, and looking quickly up at him, half scared, half reproachful*] I—[*She bursts into tears*].

MORELL [*with tender gaiety, leaning across the table towards her, and consoling her*] Oh, come! come! come! Never mind, Pross: he i s a silly old fathead, isnt he?

With an explosive sob, she makes a dash at the door, and vanishes, banging it. Morell, shaking his head resignedly, sighs, and goes wearily to his chair, where he sits down and sets to work, looking old and careworn.

Candida comes in. She has finished her household work and taken off the apron. She at once notices his dejected appearance, and posts herself quietly at the visitors' chair, looking down at him attentively. She says nothing.

MORELL [*looking up, but with his pen raised ready to resume his work*] Well? Where is Eugene?

CANDIDA. Washing his hands in the scullery under the tap. He will make an excellent cook if he can only get over his dread of Maria.

MORELL [*shortly*] Ha! No doubt. [*He begins writing again*]

CANDIDA [*going nearer, and putting her hand down softly on his to stop him as she says*] Come here, dear. Let me look at you. [*He drops his pen and yields himself to her disposal. She makes him rise, and brings him a little away from the table, looking at him critically all the time*]. Turn your face to the light. [*She places him facing the window*]. My boy is not looking well. Has he been overworking?

MORELL. Nothing more than usual.

CANDIDA. He looks very pale, and grey, and wrinkled, and old. [*His melancholy deepens; and she attacks it with wilful gaiety*] Here: [*pulling him towards the easy chair*] youve done enough writing for today. Leave Prossy to finish it. Come and talk to me.

MORELL. But—

CANDIDA [*insisting*] Yes, I m u s t be talked to. [*She makes him sit down, and seats herself on the carpet beside his knee*]. Now [*patting his hand*] youre beginning to look better already. Why must you go out every night lecturing and talking? I hardly have one evening a week with you. Of course what you say is all very true; but it does no good: they dont mind what you say to them one little bit. They think they agree with you; but whats the use of their agreeing with you if they go and do just the opposite of what you tell them the moment your back is turned? Look at our congregation at St Dominic's! Why do they come to hear you talking about Christianity every Sunday? Why, just because theyve been so full of business and money-making for six days that they want to forget all about it and have a rest on the seventh; so that they can go back fresh and make money harder than ever! You positively help them at it instead of hindering them.

MORELL [*with energetic seriousness*] You know very well, Candida, that I often blow them up soundly for that. And if there is nothing in their churchgoing but rest and diversion, why dont they try something more amusing? more self-indulgent? There must be some good in the fact that they prefer St Dominic's to worse places on Sundays.

CANDIDA. Oh, the worse places arnt open; and even if they were, they darent be seen going to them. Besides, James dear, you preach so splendidly that it's as good as a play for them. Why do you think the women are so enthusiastic?

MORELL [*shocked*] Candida!

CANDIDA. Oh, *I* know. You silly boy: you think it's your Socialism and your religion; but if it were that, theyd do what you tell them instead of only coming to look at you. They all have Prossy's complaint.

MORELL. Prossy's complaint! What do you mean, Candida?

CANDIDA. Yes, Prossy, and all the other secretaries you ever had. Why does Prossy condescend to wash up the things, and to peel potatoes and abase herself in all manner of ways for six shillings a week less than she used to get in a city office? She's in love with you, James: thats the reason. Theyre all in love with you. And you are in love with preaching because you do it so beautifully. And you think it's all enthusiasm for the kingdom of Heaven on earth; and so do they. You dear silly!

MORELL. Candida: what dreadful! what soul-destroying cynicism! Are you jesting? Or—can it be?—are you jealous?

CANDIDA [*with curious thoughtfulness*] Yes, I feel a little jealous sometimes.

MORELL [*incredulously*] Of Prossy?

CANDIDA [*laughing*] No, no, no, no. Not jealous of anybody. Jealous f o r somebody else, who is not loved as he ought to be.

MORELL. Me?

CANDIDA. You! Why, youre spoiled with love and worship: you get far more than is good for you. No: I mean Eugene.

MORELL [*startled*] Eugene!

CANDIDA. It seems unfair that all the love should go to you, and none to him; although he needs it so much more than you do. [*A convulsive movement shakes him in spite of himself*] Whats the matter? Am I worrying you?

MORELL [*hastily*] Not at all. [*Looking at her with troubled intensity*] You know that I have perfect confidence in you, Candida.

CANDIDA. You vain thing! Are you so sure of your irresistible attractions?

MORELL. Candida: you are shocking me. I never thought of my attractions. I thought of your goodness, of your purity. That is what I confide in.

CANDIDA. What a nasty uncomfortable thing to say to me! Oh, you a r e a clergyman, James: a thorough clergyman!

MORELL [*turning away from her, heart-stricken*] So Eugene says.

CANDIDA [*with lively interest, leaning over to him with her arms on his knee*] Eugene's always right. He's a wonderful boy: I have grown fonder and fonder of him all the time I was away. Do you know, James, that though he has not the least suspicion of it himself, he is ready to fall madly in love with me?

MORELL [*grimly*] Oh, he has no suspicion of it himself, hasnt he?

CANDIDA. Not a bit. [*She takes her arms from his knee, and turns thoughtfully, sinking into a more restful attitude with her hands in her lap*]. Some day he will know: when he is grown up and experienced, like you. And he will know that I must have known. I wonder what he will think of me then.

MORELL. No evil, Candida. I hope and trust, no evil.

CANDIDA. [*dubiously*] That will depend.

MORELL [*bewildered*] Depend!

CANDIDA [*looking at him*] Yes: it will depend on what happens to him. [*He looks vacantly at her*]. Dont you see? It will depend on how he comes to learn what love really is. I mean on the sort of woman who will teach it to him.

MORELL [*quite at a loss*] Yes. No. I dont know what you mean.

CANDIDA [*explaining*] If he learns it from a good woman, then it will be all right: he will forgive me.

MORELL. Forgive?

CANDIDA. But suppose he learns it from a bad woman, as so many men do, especially poetic men, who imagine all women are angels! Suppose he only discovers the value of love when he has thrown it away and degraded himself in his ignorance! Will he forgive me then, do you think?

MORELL. Forgive you for what?

CANDIDA [*realizing how stupid he is, and a little disappointed, though quite tenderly so*] Dont you understand? [*He shakes his head. She turns to him again, so as to explain with the fondest intimacy*]. I mean, will he forgive me for not teaching him myself? For abandoning him to the bad women for the sake of my goodness, of my purity, as you call it? Ah, James, how little you understand me, to talk of your confidence in my goodness and purity! I would give them both to poor Eugene as willingly as I would give my shawl to a beggar dying of cold, if there were nothing else to restrain me. Put your trust in my love for you, James: for if that went, I should care very little for your sermons: mere phrases that you cheat yourself and others with every day. [*She is about to rise*].

MORELL. H i s words!

CANDIDA [*checking herself quickly in the act of getting up*] Whose words?

MORELL. Eugene's.

CANDIDA [*delighted*] He is always right. He understands you; he understands me; he understands Prossy; and you, darling, you understand nothing. [*She laughs, and kisses him to console him. He recoils as if stabbed, and springs up*].

MORELL. How can you bear to do that when—Oh, Candida [*with anguish in his voice*] I had rather you had plunged a grappling iron into my heart than given me that kiss.

CANDIDA [*amazed*] My dear: whats the matter?

MORELL [*frantically waving her off*] Dont touch me.

CANDIDA. James!!!

They are interrupted by the entrance of Marchbanks with Burgess, who stop near the door, staring.

MARCHBANKS. Is anything the matter?

MORELL [*deadly white, putting an iron constraint on himself*] Nothing but this: that either you were right this morning, or Candida is mad.

BURGESS [*in loudest protest*] What! Candy mad too! Oh, come! come! come! [*He crosses the room to the fireplace, protesting as he goes, and knocks the ashes out of his pipe on the bars*].

Morell sits down at his table desperately, leaning forward to hide his face, and interlacing his fingers rigidly to keep them steady.

CANDIDA [*to Morell, relieved and laughing*] Oh, youre only shocked! Is that all? How conventional all you unconventional people are! [*She sits gaily on the arm of the chair*].

BURGESS. Come: be'ave yourself, Candy. Whatll Mr Morchbanks think of you?

CANDIDA. This comes of James teaching me to think for myself, and never to hold back out of fear of what other people may think of me. It works beautifully as long as I think the same things as he does. But now! because I have just thought something different! look at him! Just look! [*She points to Morell, greatly amused*].

Eugene looks, and instantly presses his hand on his heart, as if some pain had shot through it. He sits down on the sofa like a man witnessing a tragedy.

BURGESS [*on the hearth-rug*] Well, James, you certnly haint as himpressive lookin as usu'l.

MORELL [*with a laugh which is half a sob*] I suppose not. I beg all your pardons: I was not conscious of making a fuss. [*Pulling himself together*] Well, well, well, well, well! [*He sets to work at his papers again with resolute cheerfulness*].

CANDIDA [*going to the sofa and sitting beside Marchbanks, still in a bantering humor*] Well, Eugene: why are you so sad? Did the onions make you cry?

MARCHBANKS [*aside to her*] It is your cruelty. I hate cruelty. It is a horrible thing to see one person make another suffer.

CANDIDA [*petting him ironically*] Poor boy! have I been cruel? Did I make it slice nasty little red onions?

MARCHBANKS [*earnestly*] Oh, stop, stop: I dont mean myself. You have made him suffer frightfully. I feel his pain in my own heart. I know that it is not your fault: it is something that must happen; but dont make light of it. I shudder when you torture him and laugh.

CANDIDA [*incredulously*] *I* torture James! Nonsense, Eugene: how you exaggerate! Silly! [*She rises and goes to the table, a little troubled*]. Dont work any more, dear. Come and talk to us.

MORELL [*affectionately but bitterly*] Ah no: *I* cant talk. I can only preach.

CANDIDA [*caressing his hand*] Well, come and preach.

BURGESS [*strongly remonstrating*] Aw no, Candy. Ang it all!

Lexy Mill comes in, anxious and important.

LEXY [*hastening to shake hands with Candida*] How do you do, Mrs Morell? So glad to see you back again.

CANDIDA. Thank you, Lexy. You know Eugene, dont you?

LEXY. Oh yes. How do you do, Marchbanks?

MARCHBANKS. Quite well, thanks.

LEXY [*to Morell*] Ive just come from the Guild of St Matthew. They are in the greatest consternation about your telegram.

CANDIDA. What did you telegraph about, James?

LEXY [*to Candida*] He was to have spoken for them tonight. Theyve taken the large hall in Mare Street and spent a lot of money on posters. Morell's telegram was to say he couldnt come. It came on them like a thunderbolt.

CANDIDA [*surprised, and beginning to suspect something wrong*] Given up an engagement to speak!

BURGESS. Fust time in his life, I'll bet. Ain it, Candy?

LEXY [*to Morell*] They decided to send an urgent telegram to you asking whether you could not change your mind. Have you received it?

MORELL [*with restrained impatience*] Yes, yes: I got it.

LEXY. It was reply paid.

MORELL. Yes, I know. I answered it. I cant go.

CANDIDA. But why, James?

MORELL [*almost fiercely*] Because I dont choose. These people forget that I am a man: they think I am a talking machine to be turned on for their pleasure every evening of my life. May I not have one night at home, with my wife, and my friends?

They are all amazed at this outburst, except Eugene. His expression remains unchanged.

CANDIDA. Oh, James, you musnt mind what I said about that. And if you dont go youll have an attack of bad conscience tomorrow.

LEXY [*intimidated, but urgent*] I know, of course, that they make the most unreasonable demands on you. But they have been telegraphing all over the place for another speaker; and they can get nobody but the President of the Agnostic League.

MORELL [*promptly*] Well, an excellent man. What better do they want?

LEXY. But he always insists so powerfully on the divorce of Socialism from Christianity. He will undo all the good we have been doing. Of course you know best; but—[*he shrugs his shoulders and wanders to the hearth beside Burgess*].

CANDIDA [*coaxingly*] Oh, d o go, James. We'll all go.

BURGESS [*grumblingly*] Look ere, Candy! I say! Lets stay at home by the fire, comfortable. He wont need to be more'n a couple-o-hour away.

CANDIDA. Youll be just as comfortable at the meeting. We'll all sit on the platform and be great people.

MARCHBANKS [*terrified*] Oh please dont let us go on the platform. No: everyone will stare at us: I couldnt. I'll sit at the back of the room.

CANDIDA. Dont be afraid. Theyll be too busy looking at James to notice you.

MORELL. Prossy's complaint, Candida! Eh?

CANDIDA [*gaily*] Yes: Prossy's complaint.

BURGESS [*mystified*] Prossy's complaint! What are you talkin about, James?

MORELL [*not heeding him, rises; goes to the door; and holds it open, calling in a commanding tone*] Miss Garnett.

PROSERPINE [*in the distance*] Yes, Mr Morell. Coming.

They all wait, except Burgess, who turns stealthily to Lexy.

BURGESS. Listen ere, Mr Mill. Whats Prossy's complaint? Whats wrong with er?

LEXY [*confidentially*] Well, I dont exactly know; but she spoke very strangely to me this morning. I'm afraid she's a little out of her mind sometimes.

BURGESS [*overwhelmed*] Why, it must be catchin! Four in the same ouse!

PROSERPINE [*appearing on the threshold*] What is it, Mr Morell?

MORELL. Telegraph to the Guild of St Matthew that I am coming.

PROSERPINE [*surprised*] Dont they expect you?

MORELL [*peremptorily*] Do as I tell you.

Proserpine, frightened, sits down at her typewriter, and obeys. Morell, now unaccountably resolute and forceful, goes across to Burgess. Candida watches his movements with growing wonder and misgiving.

MORELL. Burgess: you dont want to come.

BURGESS. Oh, dont put it like that, James. It's ony that it aint Sunday, you know.

MORELL. I'm sorry. I thought you might like to be introduced to the chairman. He's on the Works Committee of the County Council, and has some influence in the matter of contracts. [*Burgess wakes up at once*]. Youll come?

BURGESS [*with enthusiasm*] Cawrse I'll come, James. Aint it awlus a pleasure to ear you!

MORELL [*turning to Prossy*] I shall want you to take some notes at the meeting, Miss Garnett, if you have no other engagement. [*She nods, afraid to speak*]. You are coming, Lexy, I suppose?

LEXY. Certainly.

CANDIDA. We're all coming, James.

MORELL. No: you are not coming; and Eugene is not coming. You will stay here and entertain him—to celebrate your return home. [*Eugene rises, breathless*].

CANDIDA. But, James—

MORELL [*authoritatively*] I insist. You do not want to come; and he does not want to come. [*Candida is about to protest*]. Oh, dont concern yourselves: I shall have plenty of people without you: your chairs will be wanted by unconverted people who have never heard me before.

CANDIDA [*troubled*] Eugene: wouldnt you like to come?

MORELL. I should be afraid to let myself go before Eugene: he is so critical of sermons. [*Looking at him*] He knows I am afraid of him: he told me as much this morning. Well, I shall shew him how much afraid I am by leaving him here in your custody, Candida.

MARCHBANKS [*to himself, with vivid feeling*] Thats brave. Thats beautiful.

CANDIDA [*with anxious misgiving*] But—but—Is anything the matter, James? [*Greatly troubled*] I cant understand—

MORELL [*taking her tenderly in his arms and kissing her on the forehead*] Ah, I thought it was *I* who couldnt understand, dear.

ACT III

Past ten in the evening. The curtains are drawn, and the lamps lighted. The typewriter is in its case: the large table has been cleared and tidied: everything indicates that the day's work is over.

Candida and Marchbanks are sitting by the fire. The reading lamp is on the mantelshelf above Marchbanks, who is in the small chair, reading aloud. A little pile of manuscripts and a couple of volumes of poetry are on the carpet beside him. Candida is in the easy chair. The poker, a light brass one, is upright in her hand. Leaning back and looking intently at the point of it, with her feet stretched towards the blaze, she is in a waking dream, miles away from her surroundings and completely oblivious of Eugene.

MARCHBANKS [*breaking off in his recitation*] Every poet that ever lived has put that thought into a sonnet. He must: he cant help it. [*He looks to her for assent, and notices her absorption in the poker*]. Havnt you been listening? [*No response*]. Mrs Morell!

CANDIDA [*starting*] Eh?

MARCHBANKS. Havnt you been listening?

CANDIDA [*with a guilty excess of politeness*] Oh yes. It's very nice. Go on, Eugene. I'm longing to hear what happens to the angel.

MARCHBANKS [*letting the manuscript drop from his hand to the floor*] I beg your pardon for boring you.

CANDIDA. But you are not boring me, I assure you. P l e a s e go on. Do, Eugene.

MARCHBANKS. I finished the poem about the angel quarter of an hour ago. Ive read you several things since.

CANDIDA [*remorsefully*] I'm so sorry, Eugene. I think the poker must have hypnotized me. [*She puts it down*].

MARCHBANKS. It made me horribly uneasy.

CANDIDA. Why didnt you tell me? I'd have put it down at once.

MARCHBANKS. I was afraid of making you uneasy too. It looked as if it were a weapon. If I were a hero of old I should have laid my drawn sword between us. If Morell had come in he would have thought you had taken up the poker because there was no sword between us.

CANDIDA [*wondering*] What? [*With a puzzled glance at him*] I cant quite follow that. Those sonnets of yours have perfectly addled me. Why should there be a sword between us?

MARCHBANKS [*evasively*] Oh, never mind. [*He stoops to pick up the manuscript*].

CANDIDA. Put that down again, Eugene. There are limits to my appetite for poetry: even your poetry. Youve been reading to me for more than two hours, ever since James went out. I want to talk.

MARCHBANKS [*rising, scared*] No: I musnt talk. [*He looks round him in his lost way, and adds, suddenly*] I think I'll go out and take a walk in the park. [*He makes for the door*].

CANDIDA. Nonsense: it's closed long ago. Come and sit down on the hearth-rug, and talk moonshine as you usually do. I want to be amused. Dont you want to?

MARCHBANKS [*half in terror, half enraptured*] Yes.

CANDIDA. Then come along. [*She moves her chair back a little to make room*].

He hesitates; then timidly stretches himself on the hearth-rug, face upwards, and throws back his head across her knees, looking up at her.

MARCHBANKS. Oh, Ive been so miserable all the evening, because I was doing right. Now I'm doing wrong; and I'm happy.

CANDIDA [*tenderly amused at him*] Yes: I'm sure you feel a great grown-up wicked deceiver. Quite proud of yourself, arnt you?

MARCHBANKS [*raising his head quickly and turning a little to look round at her*] Take care. I'm ever so much older than you, if you only knew. [*He turns quite over on his knees, with his hands clasped and his arms on her lap, and speaks with growing impulse, his blood beginning to stir*]. May I say some wicked things to you?

CANDIDA [*without the least fear or coldness, and with perfect respect for his passion, but with a touch of her wise-hearted maternal humor*] No. But you may say anything you really and truly feel. Anything at all, no matter what it is. I am not afraid, so long as it is your real self that speaks, and not a mere attitude: a gallant attitude, or a wicked attitude, or even a poetic attitude. I put you on your honor and truth. Now say whatever you want to.

MARCHBANKS [*the eager expression vanishing utterly from his lips and nostrils as his eyes light up with pathetic spirituality*] Oh, now I cant say anything: all the words I know belong to some attitude or other—all except one.

CANDIDA. What one is that?

MARCHBANKS [*softly, losing himself in the music of the name*] Candida, Candida, Candida, Candida, Candida. I must say that now, because you have put me on my honor and truth; and I never think or feel Mrs Morell: it is always Candida.

CANDIDA. Of course. And what have you to say to Candida?

MARCHBANKS. Nothing but to repeat your name a thousand times. Dont you feel that every time is a prayer to you?

CANDIDA. Doesnt it make you happy to be able to pray?

MARCHBANKS. Yes, very happy.

CANDIDA. Well, that happiness is the answer to your prayer. Do you want anything more?

MARCHBANKS. No: I have come into heaven, where want is unknown.

Morell comes in. He halts on the threshold, and takes in the scene at a glance.

MORELL [*grave and self-contained*] I hope I dont disturb you.

Candida starts up violently, but without the smallest embarrassment, laughing at herself. Eugene, capsized by her sudden movement, recovers himself without rising, and sits on the rug hugging his ankles, also quite unembarrassed.

CANDIDA. Oh, James, how you startled me! I was so taken up with Eugene that I didnt hear your latchkey. How did the meeting go off? Did you speak well?

MORELL. I have never spoken better in my life.

CANDIDA. That was first rate! How much was the collection?

MORELL. I forgot to ask.

CANDIDA [*to Eugene*] He must have spoken splendidly, or he would never have forgotten that. [*To Morell*] Where are all the others?

MORELL. They left long before I could get away: I thought I should never escape. I believe they are having supper somewhere.

CANDIDA [*in her domestic business tone*] Oh, in that case, Maria may go to bed. I'll tell her. [*She goes out to the kitchen*].

MORELL [*looking sternly down at Marchbanks*] Well?

MARCHBANKS [*squatting grotesquely on the hearth-rug, and actually at ease with Morell: even impishly humorous*] Well?

MORELL. Have you anything to tell me?

MARCHBANKS. Only that I have been making a fool of myself here in private whilst you have been making a fool of yourself in public.

MORELL. Hardly in the same way, I think.

MARCHBANKS [*eagerly, scrambling up*] The very, very very same way. I have been playing the Good Man. Just like you. When you began your heroics about leaving me here with Candida—

MORELL [*involuntarily*] Candida!

MARCHBANKS. Oh yes: Ive got that far. But dont be afraid. Heroics are infectious: I caught the disease from you. I swore not to say a word in your absence that I would not have said a month ago in your presence.

MORELL. Did you keep your oath?

MARCHBANKS [*suddenly perching himself on the back of the easy chair*] It kept itself somehow until about ten minutes ago. Up to that moment I went on desperately reading to her—reading my own poems—anybody's poems—to stave off a conversation. I was standing outside the gate of Heaven, and refusing to go in. Oh, you cant think how heroic it was, and how uncomfortable! Then—

MORELL [*steadily controlling his suspense*] Then?

MARCHBANKS [*prosaically slipping down into a quite ordinary attitude on the seat of the chair*] Then she couldnt bear being read to any longer.

MORELL. And you approached the gate of Heaven at last?

MARCHBANKS. Yes.

MORELL. Well? [*Fiercely*] Speak, man: have you no feeling for me?

MARCHBANKS [*softly and musically*] Then she became an angel; and there was a flaming sword that turned every way, so that I couldnt go in; for I saw that that gate was really the gate of Hell.

MORELL [*triumphantly*] She repulsed you!

MARCHBANKS [*rising in wild scorn*] No, you fool: if she had done that I should never have seen that I was in Heaven already. Repulsed me! You think that would have saved us! virtuous indignation! Oh, you are not worthy to live in the same world with her. [*He turns away contemptuously to the other side of the room*].

MORELL [*who has watched him quietly without changing his place*] Do you think you make yourself more worthy by reviling me, Eugene?

MARCHBANKS. Here endeth the thousand and first lesson. Morell: I dont think much of your preaching after all: I believe I could do it better myself. The man I want to meet is the man that Candida married.

MORELL. The man that—? Do you mean me?

MARCHBANKS. I dont mean the Reverend James Mavor Morell, moralist and windbag. I mean the real man that the Reverend James must have hidden somewhere inside his black coat: the man that Candida loved. You cant make a woman like Candida love you by merely buttoning your collar at the back instead of in front.

MORELL [*boldly and steadily*] When Candida promised to marry me, I was the same moralist and windbag you now see. I wore my black coat; and my collar was buttoned behind instead of in front. Do you think she would have loved me any the better for being insincere in my profession?

MARCHBANKS [*on the sofa, hugging his ankles*] Oh, she forgave you, just as she forgives me for being a coward, and a weakling, and what you call a snivelling little whelp and all the rest of it. [*Dreamily*] A woman like that has divine insight: she loves our souls, and not our follies and vanities and illusions, nor our collars and coats, nor any other of the rags and tatters we are rolled up in. [*He reflects on this for an instant; then turns intently to question Morell*]. What I want to know is how you got past the flaming sword that stopped me.

MORELL. Perhaps because I was not interrupted at the end of ten minutes.

MARCHBANKS [*taken aback*] What!

MORELL. Man can climb to the highest summits; but he cannot dwell there long.

MARCHBANKS [*springing up*] It's false: there can he dwell for ever, and there only. It's in the other moments that he can find no rest, no sense of the silent glory of life. Where would you have me spend my moments, if not on the summits?

MORELL. In the scullery, slicing onions and filling lamps.

MARCHBANKS. Or in the pulpit, scrubbing cheap earthenware souls?

MORELL. Yes, that too. It was there that I earned my golden moment, and the right, in that moment, to ask her to love me. *I* did not take the moment on credit; nor did I use it to steal another man's happiness.

MARCHBANKS [*rather disgustedly, trotting back towards the fireplace*] I have no doubt you conducted the transaction as honestly as if you were buying a pound of cheese. [*He stops on the brink of the hearth-rug, and adds, thoughtfully, to himself, with his back turned to Morell*] I could only go to her as a beggar.

MORELL [*starting*] A beggar dying of cold! asking for her shawl!

MARCHBANKS [*turning, surprised*] Thank you for touching up my poetry. Yes, if you like: a beggar dying of cold, asking for her shawl.

MORELL [*excitedly*] And she refused. Shall I tell you why she refused? I can tell you, on her own authority. It was because of—

MARCHBANKS. She didnt refuse.

MORELL. Not!

MARCHBANKS. She offered me all I chose to ask for: her shawl, her wings, the wreath of stars on her head, the lilies in her hand, the crescent moon beneath her feet—

MORELL [*seizing him*] Out with the truth, man: my wife is my wife: I want no more of your poetic fripperies. I know well that if I have lost her love and you have gained it, no law will bind her.

MARCHBANKS [*quaintly, without fear or resistance*] Catch me by the shirt collar, Morell: she will arrange it for me afterwards as she did this morning. [*With quiet rapture*] I shall feel her hands touch me.

MORELL. You young imp, do you know how dangerous it is to say that to me? Or [*with a sudden misgiving*] has something made you brave?

MARCHBANKS. I'm not afraid now. I disliked you before: that was why I shrank from your touch. But I saw today—when she tortured you—that you love her. Since then I have been your friend: you may strangle me if you like.

MORELL [*releasing him*] Eugene: if that is not a heartless lie—if you have a spark of human feeling left in you—will you tell me what has happened during my absence?

MARCHBANKS. What happened! Why, the flaming sword [*Morell stamps with impatience*]—Well, in plain prose, I loved her so exquisitely that I wanted nothing more than the happiness of being in such love. And before I had time to come down from the highest summits, you came in.

MORELL [*suffering deeply*] So it is still unsettled. Still the misery of doubt.

MARCHBANKS. Misery! I am the happiest of men. I desire nothing now but her happiness. [*In a passion of sentiment*] Oh, Morell, let us both give her up. Why should she have to choose between a wretched little nervous disease like me, and a pig-headed parson like you? Let us go on a pilgrimage, you to the east and I to the west, in search of a worthy lover for her: some beautiful archangel with purple wings—

MORELL. Some fiddlestick! Oh, if she is mad enough to leave me for you, who will protect her? who will help her? who will work for her? who will be a father to her children? [*He sits down distractedly on the sofa, with his elbows on his knees and his head propped on his clenched fists*].

MARCHBANKS [*snapping his fingers wildly*] She does not ask those silly questions. It is she who wants somebody to protect, to help, to work for: somebody to give her children to protect, to help and to work for. Some grown up man who has become as a little child again. Oh, you fool, you fool, you triple fool! I am the man, Morell: I am the man. [*He dances about excitedly, crying*] You dont understand what a woman is. Send for her, Morell: send for her and let her choose between—[*The door opens and Candida enters. He stops as if petrified*].

CANDIDA [*amazed, on the threshold*] What on earth are you at, Eugene?

MARCHBANKS [*oddly*] James and I are having a preaching match; and he is getting the worst of it.

Candida looks quickly round at Morell. Seeing that he is distressed, she hurries down to him, greatly vexed.

CANDIDA. You have been annoying him. Now I wont have it, Eugene: do you hear? [*She puts her hand on Morell's shoulder, and quite forgets her wifely tact in her anger*]. My boy shall not be worried: I will protect him.

MORELL [*rising proudly*] Protect!

CANDIDA [*not heeding him: to Eugene*] What have you been saying?

MARCHBANKS [*appalled*] Nothing. I—

CANDIDA. Eugene! Nothing?

MARCHBANKS [*piteously*] I mean—I—I'm very sorry. I wont do it again: indeed I wont. I'll let him alone.

MORELL [*indignantly, with an aggressive movement towards Eugene*] Let me alone! You young—

CANDIDA [*stopping him*] Sh!—no: let me deal with him, James.

MARCHBANKS. Oh, youre not angry with me, are you?

CANDIDA [*severely*] Yes I am: very angry. I have a good mind to pack you out of the house.

MORELL [*taken aback by Candida's vigour, and by no means relishing the position of being rescued by her from another man*] Gently, Candida, gently. I am able to take care of myself.

CANDIDA [*petting him*] Yes, dear: of course you are. But you musnt be annoyed and made miserable.

MARCHBANKS [*almost in tears, turning to the door*] I'll go.

CANDIDA. Oh, you neednt go: I cant turn you out at this time of night. [*Vehemently*] Shame on you! For shame!

MARCHBANKS [*desperately*] But what have I done?

CANDIDA. I know what you have done: as well as if I had been here all the time. Oh, it was unworthy! You are like a child: you cannot hold your tongue.

MARCHBANKS. I would die ten times over sooner than give you a moment's pain.

CANDIDA [*with infinite contempt for this puerility*] Much good your dying would do me!

MORELL. Candida, my dear: this altercation is hardly quite seemly. It is a matter between two men; and I am the right person to settle it.

CANDIDA. Two men! Do you call that a man? [*To Eugene*] You bad boy!

MARCHBANKS [*gathering a whimsically affectionate courage from the scolding*] If I am to be scolded like a boy, I must make a boy's excuse. He began it. And he's bigger than I am.

CANDIDA [*losing confidence a little as her concern for Morell's dignity takes the alarm*] That cant be true. [*To Morell*] You didnt begin it, James, did you?

MORELL [*contemptuously*] No.

MARCHBANKS [*indignant*] Oh!

MORELL [*to Eugene*] You began it: this morning. [*Candida, instantly connecting this with his mysterious allusion in the afternoon to something told him by Eugene in the morning, looks at him with quick suspicion. Morell proceeds, with the emphasis of offended superiority*] But your other point is true. I am certainly the bigger of the two, and, I hope, the stronger, Candida. So you had better leave the matter in my hands.

CANDIDA [*again soothing him*] Yes, dear; but—[*troubled*] I dont understand about this morning.

MORELL [*gently snubbing her*] You need not understand, my dear.

CANDIDA. But James, I [*the street bell rings*]—Oh bother! Here they all come. [*She goes out to let them in*].

MARCHBANKS [*running to Morell*] Oh, Morell, isnt it dreadful? She's angry with us: she hates me. What shall I do?

MORELL [*with quaint desperation, walking up and down the middle of the room*] Eugene: my head is spinning round. I shall begin to laugh presently.

MARCHBANKS [*following him anxiously*] No, no: she'll think Ive thrown you into hysterics. Dont laugh.

Boisterous voices and laughter are heard approaching. Lexy Mill, his eyes sparkling, and his bearing denoting unwonted elevation of spirit, enters with Burgess, who is greasy and self-complacent, but has all his wits about him. Miss Garnett, with her smartest hat and jacket on, follows them; but though her eyes are brighter than before, she is evidently a prey to misgiving. She places herself with her back to her typewriting table, with one hand on it to steady herself, passing the other across her forehead as if she were a little tired and giddy. Marchbanks relapses into shyness and edges away into the corner near the window, where Morell's books are.

LEXY [*exhilarated*] Morell: I m u s t congratulate you. [*Grasping his hand*] What a noble, splendid, inspired address you gave us! You surpassed yourself.

BURGESS. So you did, James. It fair kep me awake to the lars' word. Didnt it, Miss Gornett?

PROSERPINE [*worriedly*] Oh, I wasnt minding you: I was trying to make notes. [*She takes out her note-book, and looks at her stenography, which nearly makes her cry*].

MORELL. Did I go too fast, Pross?

PROSERPINE. Much too fast. You know I cant do more than ninety words a minute. [*She relieves her feelings by throwing her note-book angrily beside her machine, ready for use next morning*].

MORELL [*soothingly*] Oh well, well, never mind, never mind, never mind. Have you all had supper?

LEXY. Mr Burgess has been kind enough to give us a really splendid supper at the Belgrave.

BURGESS [*with effusive magnanimity*] Dont mention it, Mr Mill. [*Modestly*] Youre arty welcome to my little treat.

PROSERPINE. We had champagne. I never tasted it before. I feel quite giddy.

MORELL [*surprised*] A champagne supper! That was very handsome. Was it my eloquence that produced all this extravagance?

LEXY [*rhetorically*] Your eloquence, and Mr Burgess's goodness of heart. [*With a fresh burst of exhilaration*] And what a very fine fellow the chairman is, Morell! He came to supper with us.

MORELL [*with long drawn significance, looking at Burgess*] O-o-o-h! the chairman. N o w I understand.

Burgess covers with a deprecatory cough a lively satisfaction with his own diplomatic cunning. Lexy folds his arms and leans against the head of the sofa in a high-spirited attitude after nearly losing his balance. Candida comes in with glasses, lemons, and a jug of hot water on a tray.

CANDIDA. Who will have some lemonade? You know our rules: total abstinence. [*She puts the tray on the table, and takes up the lemon squeezer, looking enquiringly round at them*].

MORELL. No use, dear. Theyve all had champagne. Pross has broken her pledge.

CANDIDA [*to Proserpine*] You dont mean to say youve been drinking champagne!

PROSERPINE [*stubbornly*] Yes I do. I'm only a beer teetotaller, not a champagne teetotaller. I dont like beer. Are there any letters for me to answer, Mr Morell?

MORELL. No more to-night.

PROSERPINE. Very well. Goodnight, everybody.

LEXY [*gallantly*] Had I not better see you home, Miss Garnett?

PROSERPINE. No thank you. I shant trust myself with anybody tonight. I wish I hadnt taken any of that stuff. [*She takes uncertain aim at the door; dashes at it; and barely escapes without disaster*].

BURGESS [*indignantly*] Stuff indeed! That gurl dunno what champagne is! Pommery and Greeno at twelve and six a bottle. She took two glasses amost straight horff.

MORELL [*anxious about her*] Go and look after her, Lexy.

LEXY [*alarmed*] But if she should really be— Suppose she began to sing in the street, or anything of that sort.

MORELL. Just so: she may. Thats why youd better see her safely home.

CANDIDA. Do, Lexy: theres a good fellow. [*She shakes his hand and pushes him gently to the door*].

LEXY. It's evidently my duty to go. I hope it may not be necessary. Goodnight, Mrs Morell. [*To the rest*] Goodnight. [*He goes. Candida shuts the door*].

BURGESS. He was gushin with hextra piety hisself arter two sips. People carnt drink like they huseter. [*Bustling across to the hearth*] Well, James: it's time to lock up. Mr Morchbanks: shall I ave the pleasure of your company for a bit o the way ome?

MARCHBANKS [*affrightedly*] Yes: I'd better go. [*He hurries towards the door; but Candida places herself before it, barring his way*].

CANDIDA [*with quiet authority*] You sit down. Youre not going yet.

MARCHBANKS [*quailing*] No: I—I didnt mean to. [*He sits down abjectly on the sofa*].

CANDIDA. Mr Marchbanks will stay the night with us, papa.

BURGESS. Oh well, I'll say goodnight. So long, James. [*He shakes hands with Morell, and goes over to Eugene*]. Make em give you a nightlight by your bed, Mr Morchbanks: itll comfort you if you wake up in the night with a touch of that complaint of yores. Goodnight.

MARCHBANKS. Thank you: I will. Goodnight, Mr Burgess. [*They shake hands. Burgess goes to the door*].

CANDIDA [*intercepting Morell, who is following Burgess*] Stay here, dear: I'll put on papa's coat for him. [*She goes out with Burgess*].

MARCHBANKS [*rising and stealing over to Morell*] Morell: theres going to be a terrible scene. Arnt you afraid?

MORELL. Not in the least.

MARCHBANKS. I never envied you your courage before. [*He puts his hand appealingly on Morell's forearm*]. Stand by me, wont you?

MORELL [*casting him off resolutely*] Each for himself, Eugene. She must choose between us now.

Candida returns. Eugene creeps back to the sofa like a guilty schoolboy.

CANDIDA [*between them, addressing Eugene*] Are you sorry?

MARCHBANKS [*earnestly*] Yes. Heartbroken.

CANDIDA. Well then, you are forgiven. Now go off to bed like a good little boy: I want to talk to James about you.

MARCHBANKS [*rising in great consternation*] Oh, I cant do that, Morell. I must be here. I'll not go away. Tell her.

CANDIDA [*her suspicions confirmed*] Tell me what? [*His eyes avoid hers furtively. She turns and mutely transfers the question to Morell*].

MORELL [*bracing himself for the catastrophe*] I have nothing to tell her, except [*here his voice deepens to a measured and mournful tenderness*] that she is my greatest treasure on earth—if she is really mine.

CANDIDA [*coldly, offended by his yielding to his orator's instinct and treating her as if she were the audience at the Guild of St Matthew*] I am sure Eugene can say no less, if that is all.

MARCHBANKS [*discouraged*] Morell: she's laughing at us.

MORELL [*with a quick touch of temper*] There is nothing to laugh at. Are you laughing at us, Candida?

CANDIDA [*with quiet anger*] Eugene is very quick-witted, James. I hope I am going to laugh; but I am not sure that I am not going to be very angry. [*She goes to the fireplace, and stands there leaning with her arm on the mantelpiece, and her foot on the fender, whilst Eugene steals to Morell and plucks him by the sleeve*].

MARCHBANKS [*whispering*] Stop, Morell. Dont let us say anything.

MORELL [*pushing Eugene away without deigning to look at him*] I hope you dont mean that as a threat, Candida.
CANDIDA [*with emphatic warning*] Take care, James. Eugene: I asked you to go. Are you going?
MORELL [*putting his foot down*] He shall not go. I wish him to remain.
MARCHBANKS. I'll go. I'll do whatever you want. [*He turns to the door*].
CANDIDA. Stop! [*He obeys*]. Didnt you hear James say he wished you to stay? James is master here. Dont you know that?
MARCHBANKS [*flushing with a young poet's rage against tyranny*] By what right is he master?
CANDIDA [*quietly*] Tell him, James.
MORELL [*taken aback*] My dear: I dont know of any right that makes me master. I assert no such right.
CANDIDA [*with infinite reproach*] You dont know! Oh, James! James! [*To Eugene, musingly*] I wonder do you understand, Eugene! [*He shakes his head helplessly, not daring to look at her*]. No: youre too young. Well, I give you leave to stay: to stay and learn. [*She comes away from the hearth and places herself between them*]. Now, James! whats the matter? Come: tell me.
MARCHBANKS [*whispering tremulously across to him*] Dont.
CANDIDA. Come. Out with it!
MORELL [*slowly*] I meant to prepare your mind carefully, Candida, so as to prevent misunderstanding.
CANDIDA. Yes, dear: I am sure you did. But never mind: I shant misunderstand.
MORELL. Well—er— [*he hesitates, unable to find the long explanation which he supposed to be available*].
CANDIDA. Well?
MORELL [*blurting it out badly*] Eugene declares that you are in love with him.
MARCHBANKS [*frantically*] No, no, no, no, never. I did not, Mrs Morell: it's not true. I said I loved you. I said I understood you, and that he couldnt. And it was not after what passed there before the fire that I spoke: it was not, on my word. It was this morning.
CANDIDA [*enlightened*] This morning!
MARCHBANKS. Yes. [*He looks at her, pleading for credence, and then adds simply*] That was what was the matter with my collar.

CANDIDA. Your collar? [*Suddenly taking in his meaning she turns to Morell, shocked*]. Oh, James: did you—[*she stops*]?

MORELL [*ashamed*] You know, Candida, that I have a temper to struggle with. And he said [*shuddering*] that you despised me in your heart.

CANDIDA [*turning quickly on Eugene*] Did you say that?

MARCHBANKS [*terrified*] No.

CANDIDA [*almost fiercely*] Then James has just told me a falsehood. Is that what you mean?

MARCHBANKS. No, no: I—I— [*desperately*] it was David's wife. And it wasnt at home: it was when she saw him dancing before all the people.

MORELL [*taking the cue with a debater's adroitness*] Dancing before all the people. Candida; and thinking he was moving their hearts by his mission when they were only suffering from—Prossy's complaint. [*She is about to protest: he raises his hand to silence her*]. Dont try to look indignant, Candida—

CANDIDA. Try!

MORELL [*continuing*] Eugene was right. As you told me a few hours after, he is always right. He said nothing that you did not say far better yourself. He is the poet, who sees everything; and I am the poor parson, who understands nothing.

CANDIDA [*remorsefully*] Do you mind what is said by a foolish boy, because I said something like it in jest?

MORELL. That foolish boy can speak with the inspiration of a child and the cunning of a serpent. He has claimed that you belong to him and not to me; and, rightly or wrongly, I have come to fear that it may be true. I will not go about tortured with doubts and suspicions. I will not live with you and keep a secret from you. I will not suffer the intolerable degradation of jealousy. We have agreed—he and I—that you shall choose between us now. I await your decision.

CANDIDA [*slowly recoiling a step, her heart hardened by his rhetoric in spite of the sincere feeling behind it*] Oh! I am to choose am I? I suppose it is quite settled that I must belong to one or the other.

MORELL [*firmly*] Quite. You must choose definitely.

MARCHBANKS [*anxiously*] Morell: you dont understand. She means that she belongs to herself.

CANDIDA [*turning on him*] I mean that, and a good deal more, Master Eugene, as you will both find out presently. And pray, my lords and masters, what have you to offer for my choice? I am up for auction, it seems. What do you bid, James?

MORELL [*reproachfully*] Cand— [*He breaks down: his eyes and throat fill with tears: the orator becomes a wounded animal*]. I cant speak—

CANDIDA [*impulsively going to him*] Ah, dearest—

MARCHBANKS [*in wild alarm*] Stop: it's not fair. You musnt shew her that you suffer, Morell. I am on the rack too; but I am not crying.

MORELL [*rallying all his forces*] Yes: you are right. It is not for pity that I am bidding. [*He disengages himself from Candida*].

CANDIDA [*retreating, chilled*] I beg your pardon, James: I did not mean to touch you. I am waiting to hear your bid.

MORELL [*with proud humility*] I have nothing to offer you but my strength for your defence, my honesty for your surety, my ability and industry for your livelihood, and my authority and position for your dignity. That is all it becomes a man to offer to a woman.

CANDIDA [*quite quietly*] And you, Eugene? What do you offer?

MARCHBANKS. My weakness. My desolation. My heart's need.

CANDIDA [*impressed*] Thats a good bid, Eugene. Now I know how to make my choice.

She pauses and looks curiously from one to the other, as if weighing them. Morell, whose lofty confidence has changed into heartbreaking dread at Eugene's bid, loses all power of concealing his anxiety. Eugene, strung to the highest tension, does not move a muscle.

MORELL [*in a suffocated voice: the appeal bursting from the depths of his anguish*] Candida!

MARCHBANKS [*aside, in a flash of contempt*] Coward!

CANDIDA [*significantly*] I give myself to the weaker of the two.

Eugene divines her meaning at once: his face whitens like steel in a furnace.

MORELL [*bowing his head with the calm of collapse*] I accept your sentence, Candida.

CANDIDA. Do y o u understand, Eugene?

MARCHBANKS. Oh, I feel I'm lost. He cannot bear the burden.

MORELL [*incredulously, raising his head and voice with comic abruptness*] Do you mean m e, Candida?

CANDIDA [*smiling a little*] Let us sit and talk comfortably over it like three friends. [*To Morell*] Sit down, dear. [*Morell, quite lost, takes the chair from the fireside: the children's chair*]. Bring me that chair,

Eugene. [*She indicates the easy chair. He fetches it silently, even with something like cold strength, and places it next Morell, a little behind him. She sits down. He takes the visitors' chair himself, and sits, inscrutable. When they are all settled she begins, throwing a spell of quietness on them by her calm, sane, tender tone*]. You remember what you told me about yourself, Eugene: how nobody has cared for you since your old nurse died: how those clever fashionable sisters and successful brothers of yours were your mother's and father's pets: how miserable you were at Eton: how your father is trying to starve you into returning to Oxford: how you have had to live without comfort or welcome or refuge: always lonely, and nearly always disliked and misunderstood, poor boy!

MARCHBANKS [*faithful to the nobility of his lot*] I had my books. I had Nature. And at last I met you.

CANDIDA. Never mind that just at present. Now I want you to look at this other boy here: my boy! spoiled from his cradle. We go once a fortnight to see his parents. You should come with us, Eugene, to see the pictures of the hero of that household. James as a baby! the most wonderful of all babies. James holding his first school prize, won at the ripe age of eight! James as the captain of his eleven! James in his first frock coat! James under all sorts of glorious circumstances! You know how strong he is (I hope he didnt hurt you): how clever he is: how happy. [*With deepening gravity*] Ask James's mother and his three sisters what it cost to save James the trouble of doing anything but be strong and clever and happy. Ask me what it costs to be James's mother and three sisters and wife and mother to his children all in one. Ask Prossy and Maria how troublesome the house is even when we have no visitors to help us to slice the onions. Ask the tradesmen who want to worry James and spoil his beautiful sermons who it is that puts them off. When there is money to give, he gives it: when there is money to refuse, I refuse it. I build a castle of comfort and indulgence and love for him, and stand sentinel always to keep little vulgar cares out. I make him master here, though he does not know it, and could not tell you a moment ago how it came to be so. [*With sweet irony*] And when he thought I might go away with you, his only anxiety was—what should become of m e ! And to tempt me to stay he offered me [*leaning forward to stroke his hair caressingly at each phrase*] h i s strength for m y defence! his industry for my livelihood! his dignity for my position! his— [*relenting*] ah, I am mixing up your beautiful cadences and spoiling them, am I not, darling? [*She lays her cheek fondly against his*].

MORELL [*quite overcome, kneeling beside her chair and embracing her with boyish ingenuousness*] It's all true, every word. What I am you have made me with the labor of your hands and the love of your heart. You are my wife, my mother, my sisters: you are the sum of all loving care to me.

CANDIDA [*in his arms, smiling, to Eugene*] Am I your mother and sisters to you, Eugene?

MARCHBANKS [*rising with a fierce gesture of disgust*] Ah, never. Out, then, into the night with me!

CANDIDA [*rising quickly*] You are not going like that, Eugene?

MARCHBANKS [*with the ring of a man's voice—no longer a boy's—in the words*] I know the hour when it strikes. I am impatient to do what must be done.

MORELL [*who has also risen*] Candida: dont let him do anything rash.

CANDIDA [*confident, smiling at Eugene*] Oh, there is no fear. He has learnt to live without happiness.

MARCHBANKS. I no longer desire happiness: life is nobler than that. Parson James: I give you my happiness with both hands: I love you because you have filled the heart of the woman I loved. Goodbye. [*He goes towards the door*].

CANDIDA. One last word. [*He stops, but without turning to her. She goes to him*]. How old are you, Eugene?

MARCHBANKS. As old as the world now. This morning I was eighteen.

CANDIDA. Eighteen! Will you, for my sake, make a little poem out of the two sentences I am going to say to you? And will you promise to repeat it to yourself whenever you think of me?

MARCHBANKS [*without moving*] Say the sentences.

CANDIDA. When I am thirty, she will be forty-five. When I am sixty, she will be seventy-five.

MARCHBANKS [*turning to her*] In a hundred years, we shall be the same age. But I have a better secret than that in my heart. Let me go now. The night outside grows impatient.

CANDIDA. Goodbye. [*She takes his face in her hands; and as he divines her intention and falls on his knees, she kisses his forehead. Then he flies out into the night. She turns to Morell, holding out her arms to him*]. Ah, James!

They embrace. But they do not know the secret in the poet's heart.

CAESAR AND CLEOPATRA:
A History

Composition begun 23 April 1898; completed 9 December 1898. Published in *Three Plays for Puritans,* 1901. Revised text & new prologue in Collected Edition, 1930. Copyright reading at the Theatre Royal, Newcastle upon Tyne, on 15 March 1899 (with Mrs Patrick Campbell as Cleopatra and Nutcombe Gould as Caesar). First presented by students of the Anna Morgan Studios for Art and Expression at the Fine Arts Building, Chicago, on 1 May 1901; repeated on 2 and 3 May. Presented in German (translation by Siegfried Trebitsch) at the Neues Theater, Berlin, on 31 March 1906. First professional performance in English presented at the New Amsterdam Theatre, New York, by Forbes Robertson's Company on 30 October 1906.

Julius Cæsar *Johnston Forbes Robertson*
Cleopatra *Gertrude Elliott*
Rufio *Percy Rhodes*
Britannus *Ian Robertson*
Lucius Septimius *Walter Ringham*
Apollodorus *A. Hylton Allen*
Ptolemy XIV *Sidney Carlisle*
Pothinus *Charles Langley*
Theodotus *S. T. Pearce*
Achillas *Halliwell Hobbes*
Belzanor *Charles Vaughan*
Bel Affris *Vernon Steel*
Ftatateeta *Adeline Bourne*
Charmian *Dorothy Paget*
Iras *Esmé Hubbard*
Also Courtiers, Soldiers, Slaves, Servants, Officials, etc.

Period–End of the XXXIII Dynasty in Egypt. The Winter of 706–7 in Rome. Christian Computation: October, 48 B.C., to March, 47 B.C.

PROLOGUE (Written in 1912)
Spoken by the God Ra in the doorway of his Temple

AN ALTERNATIVE TO THE PROLOGUE
The Courtyard of an old Syrian Palace. October, 48 B.C.

ACT I Scene 1: *The Desert. The Sphinx*
Scene 2: *The Palace. The Throne-room*

ACT II *Alexandria. Council Chamber of the Chancellors of the King's Treasury. Some Days Later*

ACT III Scene 1: *Outside the Palace. The Quay*
Scene 2: *The Pharos of Alexandria*

ACT IV Scene 1: *Cleopatra's Boudoir. Five Months Later*
Scene 2: *On the Palace Roof. The God's Answer*

ACT V *After the Campaign. The East Harbor. Cæsar's Farewell*

PROLOGUE

In the doorway of the temple of Ra in Memphis. Deep gloom. An august personage with a hawk's head is mysteriously visible by his own light in the darkness within the temple. He surveys the modern audience with great contempt; and finally speaks the following words to them.

Peace! Be silent and hearken unto me, ye quaint little islanders. Give ear, ye men with white paper on your breasts and nothing written thereon (to signify the innocency of your minds). Hear me, ye women who adorn yourselves alluringly and conceal your thoughts from your men, leading them to believe that ye deem them wondrous strong and masterful whilst in truth ye hold them in your hearts as children without judgment. Look upon my hawk's head; and know that I am Ra, who was once in Egypt a mighty god. Ye cannot kneel nor prostrate yourselves; for ye are packed in rows without freedom to move, obstructing one another's vision; neither do any of ye regard it as seemly to do ought until ye see all the rest do so too; wherefore it commonly happens that in great emergencies ye do nothing, though each telleth his fellow that something must be done. I ask you not for worship, but for silence. Let not your men speak nor your women cough; for I am come to draw you back two thousand years over the graves of sixty generations. Ye poor posterity, think not that ye are the first. Other fools before ye have seen the sun rise and set, and the moon change her shape and her hour. As they were so ye are; and yet not so great; for the pyramids my people build stand to this day; whilst the dustheaps on which ye slave, and which ye call empires, scatter in the wind even as ye pile your dead sons' bodies on them to make yet more dust.

Hearken to me then, oh ye compulsorily educated ones. Know that even as there is an old England and a new, and ye stand perplexed between the twain; so in the days when I was worshipped was there an old Rome and a new, and men standing perplexed between them. And the old Rome was poor and little, and greedy and fierce, and evil in many ways; but because its mind was little and its work was simple, it knew its own mind and did its own work; and the gods pitied it and helped it and strengthened it and shielded it; for the gods are patient with littleness. Then the old Rome, like the beggar on horseback, presumed on the favor of the gods, and said, "Lo! there is neither riches nor greatness in our littleness: the road to riches and greatness is through robbery of the poor and slaughter of the weak." So they robbed their own poor until they became great masters of that art, and knew by what laws it could be made to appear seemly and honest. And when they had squeezed their own poor dry, they robbed the poor of other lands, and added those lands to Rome until there came a new Rome, rich and huge. And I, Ra, laughed; for the minds of the Romans remained the same size whilst their dominion spread over the earth.

Now mark me, that ye may understand what ye are presently to see. Whilst the Romans still stood between the old Rome and the new, there arose among them a mighty soldier: Pompey the Great. And the way of the soldier is the way of death; but the way of the gods is the way of life; and so it comes that a god at the end of his way is wise and a soldier at the end of his way is a fool. So Pompey held by the old Rome, in which only soldiers could become great; but the gods turned to the new Rome, in which any man with wit enough could become what he would. And Pompey's friend Julius Cæsar was on the side of the gods; for he saw that Rome had passed beyond the control of the little old Romans. This Cæsar was a great talker and a politician: he bought men with words and with gold, even as ye are bought. And when they would not be satisfied with words and gold, and demanded also the glories of war, Cæsar in his middle age turned his hand to that trade; and they that were against him when he sought their welfare, bowed down before him when he became a slayer and a conqueror; for such is the nature of you mortals. And as for Pompey, the gods grew tired of his triumphs and his airs of being himself a god; for he talked of law and duty and other matters that concerned not a mere human worm. And the gods smiled on Cæsar; for he lived the life they had given him boldly, and was not forever rebuking us for our indecent ways of creation, and hiding our handiwork as a shameful thing. Ye know well what I mean; for this is one of your own sins.

And thus it fell out between the old Rome and the new, that Cæsar said, "Unless I break the law of old Rome, I cannot take my share in ruling her; and the gift of ruling that the gods gave me will perish without fruit." But Pompey said, "The law is above all; and if thou break it thou shalt die." Then said Cæsar, "I will break it: kill me who can." And he broke it. And Pompey went for him, as ye say, with a great army to slay him and uphold the old Rome. So Cæsar fled across the Adriatic sea; for the high gods had a lesson to teach him, which lesson they shall also teach you in due time if ye continue to forget them and to worship that cad among gods, Mammon. Therefore before they raised Cæsar to be master of the world, they were minded to throw him down into the dust, even beneath the feet of Pompey, and blacken his face before the nations. And Pompey they raised higher than ever, he and his laws and his high mind that aped the gods, so that his fall might be the more terrible. And Pompey followed Cæsar, and overcame him with all the majesty of old Rome, and stood over him and over the whole world even as ye stand over it with your fleet that covers thirty miles of the sea. And when Cæsar was brought down to utter nothingness, he made a last stand to die honorably, and did not despair; for he said, "Against me there is Pompey, and the old Rome, and the law and the legions: all all against me; but high above these are the gods; and Pompey is a fool." And the gods laughed and approved; and on the field of Pharsalia the impossible came to pass; the blood and iron ye pin your faith on fell before the spirit of man; for the spirit of man is the will of the gods; and Pompey's power crumbled in his hand, even as the power of imperial Spain crumbled when it was set against your fathers in the days when England was little, and knew her own mind, and had a mind to know instead of a circulation of newspapers. Wherefore look to it, lest some little people whom ye would enslave rise up and become in the hand of God the scourge of your boastings and your injustices and your lusts and stupidities.

And now, would ye know the end of Pompey, or will ye sleep while a god speaks? Heed my words well; for Pompey went where ye have gone, even to Egypt, where there was a Roman occupation even as there was but now a British one. And Cæsar pursued Pompey to Egypt: a Roman fleeing, and a Roman pursuing: dog eating dog. And the Egyptians said, "Lo: these Romans which have lent money to our kings and levied a distraint upon us with their arms, call for ever upon us to be loyal to them by betraying our own country to them. But now behold two Romes! Pompey's Rome and Cæsar's Rome! To which of the twain shall we pretend to be loyal?" So they turned in their perplexity to a soldier that had once served Pompey, and that knew the ways of Rome and was full of her lusts. And they said to him, "Lo: in thy country dog eats dog; and both dogs are coming to eat us: what counsel hast thou to give us?" And this soldier, whose name was Lucius Septimius, and whom ye shall presently see before ye, replied, "Ye shall diligently consider which is the bigger dog of the two; and ye shall kill the other dog for his sake and thereby earn his favor." And the Egyptians said, "Thy counsel is expedient; but if we kill a man outside the law we set ourselves in the place of the gods; and this we dare not do. But thou, being a Roman, art accustomed to this kind of killing; for thou hast imperial instincts. Wilt thou therefore kill the lesser dog for us?" And he said, "I will; for I have made my home in Egypt; and I desire consideration and influence among you." And they said, "We knew well thou wouldst not do it for nothing: thou shalt have thy reward." Now when Pompey came, he came alone in a little galley, putting his trust in the law and the constitution. And it was plain to the people of Egypt that Pompey was now but a very small dog. So when he set his foot on the shore he was greeted by his old comrade Lucius Septimius, who welcomed him with one hand and with the other smote off his head, and kept it as it were a pickled cabbage to make a present to Cæsar. And mankind shuddered; but the gods laughed; for Septimius was but a knife that Pompey had sharpened; and when it turned against his own throat they said that Pompey had better have made Septimius a ploughman than so brave and ready-handed a slayer. Therefore again I bid you beware, ye who would all be Pompeys if ye dared; for war is a wolf that may come to your own door.

Are ye impatient with me? Do ye crave for a story of an unchaste woman? Hath the name of Cleopatra tempted ye hither? Ye foolish ones; Cleopatra is as yet but a child that is whipped by her nurse. And what I am about to shew you for the good of your souls is how Cæsar, seeking Pompey in Egypt, found Cleopatra; and how he received that present of a pickled cabbage that was once the head of Pompey; and what things happened between the old Cæsar and the child queen before he left Egypt and battled his way back to Rome to be slain there as Pompey was slain, by men in whom the spirit of Pompey still lived. All this ye shall see; and ye shall marvel, after your ignorant manner, that men twenty centuries ago were already just such as you, and spoke and lived as ye speak and live, no worse and no better, no wiser and no sillier. And the two thousand years that have past are to me, the god Ra, but a moment; nor is this day any other than the day in which Cæsar set foot in the land of my people. And now I leave you; for ye are a dull folk, and instruction is wasted on you; and I had not spoken so much but that it is in the nature of a god to struggle for ever with the dust and the darkness, and to drag from them, by the force of his longing for the divine, more life and more light. Settle ye therefore in your seats and keep silent; for ye are about to hear a man speak, and a great man he was, as ye count greatness. And fear not that I shall speak to you again: the rest of the story must ye learn from them that lived it. Farewell; and do not presume to applaud me. [*The temple vanishes in utter darkness*].

[1912]

AN ALTERNATIVE TO THE PROLOGUE

An October night on the Syrian border of Egypt towards the end of the XXXIII Dynasty, in the years 706 by Roman computation, afterwards reckoned by Christian computation as 48 B.C. *A great radiance of silver fire, the dawn of a moonlit night, is rising in the east. The stars and the cloudless sky are our own contemporaries, nineteen and a half centuries younger than we know them; but you would not guess that from their appearance. Below them are two notable drawbacks of civilization: a palace, and soldiers. The palace, an old, low, Syrian building of whitened mud, is not so ugly as Buckingham Palace; and the officers in the courtyard are more highly civilized than modern English officers: for example, they do not dig up the corpses of their dead enemies and mutilate them, as we dug up Cromwell and the Mahdi. They are in two groups: one intent on the gambling of their captain Belzanor, a warrior of fifty, who, with his spear on the ground beside his knee, is stooping to throw dice with a sly-looking young Persian recruit; the other gathered about a guardsman who has just finished telling a naughty story (still current in English barracks) at which they are laughing uproariously. They are about a dozen in number, all highly aristocratic young Egyptian guardsmen, handsomely equipped with weapons and armor, very unEnglish in point of not being ashamed of and uncomfortable in their professional dress; on the contrary, rather ostentatiously and arrogantly warlike, as valuing themselves on their military caste.*

Belzanor is a typical veteran, tough and wilful; prompt, capable and crafty where brute force will serve; helpless and boyish when it will not: an effective sergeant, an incompetent general, a deplorable dictator. Would, if influentially connected, be employed in the two last capacities by a modern European State on the strength of his success in the first. Is rather to be pitied just now in view of the fact that Julius Cæsar is invading his country. Not knowing this, is intent on his game with the Persian, whom, as a foreigner, he considers quite capable of cheating him.

His subalterns are mostly handsome young fellows whose interest in the game and the story symbolize with tolerable completeness the main interests in life of which they are conscious. Their spears are leaning against the walls, or lying on the ground ready to their hands. The corner of the courtyard forms a triangle of which one side is the front of the palace, with a doorway, the other a wall with a gateway. The storytellers are on the palace side: the gamblers, on the gateway side. Close to the gateway, against the wall, is a stone block high enough to enable a Nubian sentinel, standing on it, to look over the wall. The yard is lighted by a torch stuck in the wall. As the laughter from the group round the storyteller dies away, the kneeling Persian, winning the throw, snatches up the stake from the ground.

BELZANOR. By Apis, Persian, thy gods are good to thee.
THE PERSIAN. Try yet again, O captain. Double or quits!
BELZANOR. No more. I am not in the vein.
THE SENTINEL [*poising his javelin as he peers over the wall*] Stand. Who goes there?

They all start, listening. A strange voice replies from without.

VOICE. The bearer of evil tidings.
BELZANOR [*calling to the sentry*] Pass him.
THE SENTINEL [*grounding his javelin*] Draw near, O bearer of evil tidings.
BELZANOR [*pocketing the dice and picking up his spear*] Let us receive this man with honor. He bears evil tidings.

The guardsmen seize their spears and gather about the gate, leaving a way through for the new comer.

PERSIAN [*rising from his knee*] Are evil tidings, then, so honorable?
BELZANOR. O barbarous Persian, hear my instruction. In Egypt the bearer of good tidings is sacrificed to the gods as a thank offering; but no god will accept the blood of the messenger of evil. When we have good tidings, we are careful to send them in the mouth of the cheapest slave we can find. Evil tidings are borne by young noblemen who desire to bring themselves into notice. [*They join the rest at the gate.*]
THE SENTINEL. Pass, O young captain; and bow thy head in the House of the Queen.
VOICE. Go anoint thy javelin with fat of swine, O Blackamoor; for before morning the Romans will make thee eat it to the very butt.

The owner of the voice, a fairhaired dandy, dressed in a different fashion from that affected by the guardsmen, but no less extrava-

gantly, comes through the gateway laughing. He is somewhat battle-stained; and his left forearm, bandaged, comes through a torn sleeve. In his right hand he carries a Roman sword in its sheath. He swaggers down the courtyard, the Persian on his right, Belzanor on his left, and the guardsmen crowding down behind him.

BELZANOR. Who are thou that laughest in the House of Cleopatra the Queen, and in the teeth of Belzanor, the captain of her guard?

THE NEW COMER. I am Bel Affris, descended from the gods.

BELZANOR [*ceremoniously*] Hail, cousin!

ALL [*except the Persian*] Hail, cousin!

PERSIAN. All the Queen's guards are descended from the gods, O stranger, save myself. I am Persian, and descended from many kings.

BEL AFFRIS [*to the guardsmen*] Hail, cousins! [*To the Persian, condescendingly*] Hail, mortal!

BELZANOR. You have been in battle, Bel Affris; and you are a soldier among soldiers. You will not let the Queen's women have the first of your tidings.

BEL AFFRIS. I have no tidings, except that we shall have our throats cut presently, women, soldiers, and all.

PERSIAN [*to Belzanor*] I told you so.

THE SENTINEL [*who has been listening*] Woe, alas!

BEL AFFRIS [*calling to him*] Peace, peace, poor Ethiop: destiny is with the gods who painted thee black. [*To Belzanor*] What has this mortal [*indicating the Persian*] told you?

BELZANOR. He says that the Roman Julius Cæsar, who has landed on our shores with a handful of followers, will make himself master of Egypt. He is afraid of the Roman soldiers. [*The guardsmen laugh with boisterous scorn*]. Peasants, brought up to scare crows and follow the plough! Sons of smiths and millers and tanners! And we nobles, consecrated to arms, descended from the gods!

PERSIAN. Belzanor: the gods are not always good to their poor relations.

BELZANOR [*hotly, to the Persian*] Man to man, are we worse than the slaves of Cæsar?

BEL AFFRIS [*stepping between them*] Listen, cousin. Man to man, we Egyptians are as gods above the Romans.

THE GUARDSMEN [*exultantly*] Aha!

BEL AFFRIS. But this Cæsar does not pit man against man: he throws a legion at you where you are weakest as he throws a stone from a catapult; and that legion is as a man with one head, a thousand arms, and no religion. I have fought against them; and I know.

BELZANOR [*derisively*] Were you frightened, cousin?

The guardsmen roar with laughter, their eyes sparkling at the wit of their captain.

BEL AFFRIS. No, cousin; but I was beaten. They were frightened (perhaps); but they scattered us like chaff.

The guardsmen, much damped, utter a growl of contemptuous disgust.

BELZANOR. Could you not die?

BEL AFFRIS. No: that was too easy to be worthy of a descendant of the gods. Besides, there was no time: all was over in a moment. The attack came just where we least expected it.

BELZANOR. That shews that the Romans are cowards.

BEL AFFRIS. They care nothing about cowardice, these Romans: they fight to win. The pride and honor of war are nothing to them.

PERSIAN. Tell us the tale of the battle. What befell?

THE GUARDSMEN [*gathering eagerly round Bel Affris*] Ay: the tale of the battle.

BEL AFFRIS. Know then, that I am a novice in the guard of the temple of Ra in Memphis, serving neither Cleopatra nor her brother Ptolemy, but only the high gods. We went a journey to inquire of Ptolemy why he had driven Cleopatra into Syria, and how we of Egypt should deal with the Roman Pompey, newly come to our shores after his defeat by Cæsar at Pharsalia. What, think ye, did we learn? Even that Cæsar is coming also in hot pursuit of his foe, and that Ptolemy has slain Pompey, whose severed head he holds in readiness to present to the conqueror. [*Sensation among the guardsmen*]. Nay, more: we found that Cæsar is already come; for we had not made half a day's journey on our way back when we came upon a city rabble flying from his legions, whose landing they had gone out to withstand.

BELZANOR. And ye, the temple guard! did ye not withstand these legions?

BEL AFFRIS. What man could, that we did. But there came the sound of a trumpet whose voice was as the cursing of a black mountain. Then saw we a moving wall of shields coming towards us. You know how the heart burns when you charge a fortified wall; but how if the fortified wall were to charge y o u?

THE PERSIAN [*exulting in having told them so*] Did I not say it?

BEL AFFRIS. When the wall came nigh, it changed into a line of men—

common fellows enough, with helmets, leather tunics, and breastplates. Every man of them flung his javelin: the one that came my way drove through my shield as through a papyrus—lo there! [*he points to the bandage on his left arm*] and would have gone through my neck had I not stooped. They were charging at the double then, and were upon us with short swords almost as soon as their javelins. When a man is close to you with such a sword, you can do nothing with our weapons: they are all too long.

THE PERSIAN. What did you do?

BEL AFFRIS. Doubled my fist and smote my Roman on the sharpness of his jaw. He was but mortal after all: he lay down in a stupor: and I took his sword and laid it on. [*Drawing the sword*] Lo! a Roman sword with Roman blood on it!

THE GUARDSMEN [*approvingly*] Good! [*They take the sword and hand it round, examining it curiously*].

THE PERSIAN. And your men?

BEL AFFRIS. Fled. Scattered like sheep.

BELZANOR [*furiously*] The cowardly slaves! Leaving the descendants of the gods to be butchered!

BEL AFFRIS [*with acid coolness*] The descendants of the gods did not stay to be butchered, cousin. The battle was not to the strong; but the race was to the swift. The Romans who have no chariots, sent a cloud of horsemen in pursuit, and slew multitudes. Then our high priest's captain rallied a dozen descendants of the gods and exhorted us to die fighting. I said to myself: surely it is safer to stand than to lose my breath and be stabbed in the back; so I joined our captain and stood. Then the Romans treated us with respect; for no man attacks a lion when the field is full of sheep, except for the pride and honor of war, of which these Romans know nothing. So we escaped with our lives; and I am come to warn you that you must open your gates to Cæsar; for his advance guard is scarce an hour behind me; and not an Egyptian warrior is left standing between you and his legions.

THE SENTINEL. Woe, alas! [*He throws down his javelin and flies into the palace.*]

BELZANOR. Nail him to the door, quick! [*The guardsmen rush for him with their spears; but he is too quick for them*]. Now this news will run through the palace like fire through stubble.

BEL AFFRIS. What shall we do to save the women from the Romans?

BELZANOR. Why not kill them?

PERSIAN. Because we should have to pay blood money for some of them. Better let the Romans kill them: it is cheaper.
BELZANOR [*awestruck at his brain power*] O subtle one! O serpent!
BEL AFFRIS. But your Queen?
BELZANOR. True: we must carry off Cleopatra.
BEL AFFRIS. Will ye not await her command?
BELZANOR. Command! a girl of sixteen! Not we. At Memphis ye deem her a Queen: here we know better. I will take her on the crupper of my horse. When we soldiers have carried her out of Cæsar's reach, then the priests and the nurses and the rest of them can pretend she is a queen again, and put their commands into her mouth.
PERSIAN. Listen to me, Belzanor.
BELZANOR. Speak, O subtle beyond thy years.
THE PERSIAN. Cleopatra's brother Ptolemy is at war with her. Let us sell her to him.
THE GUARDSMEN. O subtle one! O serpent!
BELZANOR. We dare not. We are descended from the gods; but Cleopatra is descended from the river Nile; and the lands of our fathers will grow no grain if the Nile rises not to water them. Without our father's gifts we should live the lives of dogs.
PERSIAN. It is true: the Queen's guard cannot live on its pay. But hear me further, O ye kinsmen of Osiris.
THE GUARDSMEN. Speak, O subtle one. Hear the serpent begotten!
PERSIAN. Have I heretofore spoken truly to you of Cæsar, when you thought I mocked you?
GUARDSMEN. Truly, truly.
BELZANOR [*reluctantly admitting it*] So Bel Affris says.
PERSIAN. Hear more of him, then. This Cæsar is a great lover of women: he makes them his friends and counsellors.
BELZANOR. Faugh! This rule of women will be the ruin of Egypt.
THE PERSIAN. Let it rather be the ruin of Rome! Cæsar grows old now: he is past fifty and full of labors and battles. He is too old for the young women; and the old women are too wise to worship him.
BEL AFFRIS. Take heed, Persian. Cæsar is by this time almost within earshot.
PERSIAN. Cleopatra is not yet a woman: neither is she wise. But she already troubles men's wisdom.
BELZANOR. Ay: that is because she is descended from the river Nile and a black kitten of the sacred White Cat. What then?
PERSIAN. Why, sell her secretly to Ptolemy, and then offer ourselves to

Cæsar as volunteers to fight for the overthrow of her brother and the rescue of our Queen, the Great Granddaughter of the Nile.

THE GUARDSMEN. O serpent!

PERSIAN. He will listen to us if we come with her picture in our mouths. He will conquer and kill her brother, and reign in Egypt with Cleopatra for his Queen. And we shall be her guard.

GUARDSMEN. O subtlest of all the serpents! O admiration! O wisdom!

BEL AFFRIS. He will also have arrived before you have done talking, O word spinner.

BELZANOR. That is true. [*An affrighted uproar in the palace interrupts him*]. Quick: the flight has begun: guard the door. [*They rush to the door and form a cordon before it with their spears. A mob of women-servants and nurses surges out. Those in front recoil from the spears, screaming to those behind to keep back. Belzanor's voice dominates the disturbance as he shouts*] Back there. In again, unprofitable cattle.

THE GUARDSMEN. Back, unprofitable cattle.

BELZANOR. Send us out Ftatateeta, the Queen's chief nurse.

THE WOMEN [*calling into the palace*] Ftatateeta, Ftatateeta. Come, come. Speak to Belzanor.

A WOMAN. Oh, keep back. You are thrusting me on the spearheads.

A huge grim woman, her face covered with a network of tiny wrinkles, and her eyes old, large, and wise; sinewy handed, very tall, very strong; with the mouth of a bloodhound and the jaws of a bulldog, appears on the threshold. She is dressed like a person of consequence in the palace, and confronts the guardsmen insolently.

FTATATEETA. Make way for the Queen's chief nurse.

BELZANOR [*with solemn arrogance*] Ftatateeta: I am Belzanor, the captain of the Queen's guard, descended from the gods.

FTATATEETA [*retorting his arrogance with interest*] Belzanor: I am Ftatateeta, the Queen's chief nurse; and your divine ancestors were proud to be painted on the wall in the pyramids of the kings whom my fathers served.

The women laugh triumphantly.

BELZANOR [*with grim humor*] Ftatateeta: daughter of a long-tongued, swivel-eyed chameleon, the Romans are at hand. [*A cry of terror from the women: they would fly but for the spears*]. Not even the descendants of the gods can resist them; for they have each man seven arms, each carrying seven spears. The blood in their veins is boiling quicksilver; and their wives become mothers in three hours, and are slain and eaten the next day.

A shudder of horror from the women. Ftatateeta, despising them and scorning the soldiers, pushes her way through the crowd and confronts the spear points undismayed.

FTATATEETA. Then fly and save yourselves, O cowardly sons of the cheap clay gods that are sold to fish porters; and leave us to shift for ourselves.

BELZANOR. Not until you have first done our bidding, O terror of manhood. Bring out Cleopatra the Queen to us; and then go whither you will.

FTATATEETA [*with a derisive laugh*] Now I know why the gods have taken her out of our hands. [*The guardsmen start and look at one another*]. Know, thou foolish soldier, that the Queen has been missing since an hour past sundown.

BELZANOR [*furiously*] Hag: you have hidden her to sell to Cæsar or her brother. [*He grasps her by the left wrist, and drags her, helped by a few of the guard, to the middle of the courtyard, where, as they fling her on her knees, he draws a murderous looking knife*]. Where is she? Where is she? or—[*he threatens to cut her throat*].

FTATATEETA [*savagely*] Touch me, dog; and the Nile will not rise on your fields for seven times seven years of famine.

BELZANOR [*frightened but desperate*] I will sacrifice: I will pay. Or stay. [*To the Persian*] You, O subtle one: your father's lands lie far from the Nile. Slay her.

PERSIAN [*threatening her with his knife*] Persia has but one god; yet he loves the blood of old women. Where is Cleopatra?

FTATATEETA. Persian: as Osiris lives, I do not know. I chid her for bringing evil days upon us by talking to the sacred cats of the priests, and carrying them in her arms. I told her she would be left alone here when the Romans came as a punishment for her disobedience. And now she is gone—run away—hidden. I speak the truth. I call Osiris to witness—

THE WOMEN [*protesting officiously*] She speaks the truth, Belzanor.

BELZANOR. You have frightened the child: she is hiding. Search—quick—into the palace—search every corner.

The guards, led by Belzanor, shoulder their way into the palace through the flying crowd of women, who escape through the courtyard gate.

FTATATEETA [*screaming*] Sacrilege! Men in the Queen's chambers! Sa—[*her voice dies away as the Persian puts his knife to her throat*].

BEL AFFRIS [*laying a hand on Ftatateeta's left shoulder*] Forbear her yet a moment, Persian. [*To Ftatateeta, very significantly*] Mother: your gods are asleep or away hunting; and the sword is at your throat. Bring us to where the Queen is hid, and you shall live.

FTATATEETA [*contemptuously*] Who shall stay the sword in the hand of a fool, if the high gods put it there? Listen to me, ye young men without understanding. Cleopatra fears me; but she fears the Romans more. There is but one power greater in her eyes than the wrath of the Queen's nurse and the cruelty of Cæsar; and that is the power of the Sphinx that sits in the desert watching the way to the sea. What she would have it know, she tells into the ears of the sacred cats; and on her birthday she sacrifices to it and decks it with poppies. Go ye therefore into the desert and seek Cleopatra in the shadow of the Sphinx; and on your heads see to it that no harm comes to her.

BEL AFFRIS [*to the Persian*] May we believe this, O subtle one?

PERSIAN. Which way come the Romans?

BEL AFFRIS. Over the desert, from the sea, by this very Sphinx.

PERSIAN [*to Ftatateeta*] O mother of guile! O aspic's tongue! You have made up this tale so that we two may go into the desert and perish on the spears of the Romans. [*Lifting his knife*] Taste death.

FTATATEETA. Not from thee, baby. [*She snatches his ankle from under him and flies stooping along the palace wall, vanishing in the darkness within its precinct. Bel Affris roars with laughter as the Persian tumbles. The guardsmen rush out of the palace with Belzanor and a mob of fugitives, mostly carrying bundles*].

PERSIAN. Have you found Cleopatra?

BELZANOR. She is gone. We have searched every corner.

THE NUBIAN SENTINEL [*appearing at the door of the palace*] Woe! Alas! Fly, fly!

BELZANOR. What is the matter now?

THE NUBIAN SENTINEL. The sacred white cat has been stolen.

ALL. Woe! woe! [*General panic. They all fly with cries of consternation. The torch is thrown down and extinguished in the rush. The noise of the fugitives dies away. Darkness and dead silence*].

ACT I

The same darkness into which the temple of Ra and the Syrian palace vanished. The same silence. Suspense. Then the blackness and stillness break softly into silver mist and strange airs as the windswept harp of Memnon plays at the dawning of the moon. It rises full over the desert; and a vast horizon comes into relief, broken by a huge shape which soon reveals itself in the spreading radiance as a Sphinx pedestalled on the sands. The light still clears, until the upraised eyes of the image are distinguished looking straight forward and upward in infinite fearless vigil, and a mass of color between its great paws defines itself as a heap of red poppies on which a girl lies motionless, her silken vest heaving gently and regularly with the breathing of a dreamless sleeper, and her braided hair glittering in a shaft of moonlight like a bird's wing.

Suddenly there comes from afar a vaguely fearful sound (it might be the bellow of a Minotaur softened by great distance) and Memnon's music stops. Silence: then a few faint high-ringing trumpet notes. Then silence again. Then a man comes from the south with stealing steps, ravished by the mystery of the night, all wonder, and halts, lost in contemplation, opposite the left flank of the Sphinx, whose bosom, with its burden, is hidden from him by its massive shoulder.

THE MAN. Hail, Sphinx: salutation from Julius Cæsar! I have wandered in many lands, seeking the lost regions from which my birth into this world exiled me, and the company of creatures such as I myself. I have found flocks and pastures, men and cities, but no other Cæsar, no air native to me, no man kindred to me, none who can do my day's deed, and think my night's thought. In the little world yonder, Sphinx, my place is as high as yours in this great desert; only I wander, and you sit still; I conquer, and you endure; I work and wonder, you watch and wait; I look up and am dazzled, look down and am darkened, look round and am puzzled, whilst your eyes never turn from looking out—out of the world—to the lost region—the home from which we have strayed. Sphinx, you and I, strangers to the race of men, are no strangers to one another: have I not been conscious of you and of this place since I was born? Rome is a madman's dream: this is my Reality. These starry lamps of yours I have seen from afar in Gaul, in Britain, in Spain, in Thessaly, signalling great secrets to some eternal sentinel below, whose post I never could find. And here at last is their sentinel—an image of the constant and immortal part of my life, silent, full of thoughts, alone in the silver desert. Sphinx, Sphinx: I have climbed mountains at night to hear in the distance the stealthy footfall of the winds that chase your sands in forbidden play—our invisible children, O Sphinx, laughing in whispers. My way hither was the way of destiny; for I am he of whose genius you are the symbol: part brute, part woman, and part god—nothing of man in me at all. Have I read your riddle, Sphinx?

THE GIRL [*who has wakened, and peeped cautiously from her nest to see who is speaking*] Old gentleman.

CÆSAR [*starting violently, and clutching his sword*] Immortal gods!

THE GIRL. Old gentleman: dont run away.

CÆSAR [*stupefied*] "Old gentleman: dont run away"!!! This! to Julius Cæsar!

THE GIRL [*urgently*] Old gentleman.

CÆSAR. Sphinx: you presume on your centuries. I am younger than you, though your voice is but a girl's voice as yet.

THE GIRL. Climb up here, quickly; or the Romans will come and eat you.

CÆSAR [*running forward past the Sphinx's shoulder, and seeing her*] A child at its breast! a divine child!

THE GIRL. Come up quickly. You must get up at its side and creep round.

CÆSAR [*amazed*] Who are you?

THE GIRL. Cleopatra, Queen of Egypt.

CÆSAR. Queen of the Gypsies, you mean.

CLEOPATRA. You must not be disrespectful to me, or the Sphinx will let the Romans eat you. Come up. It is quite cosy here.

CÆSAR [*to himself*] What a dream! What a magnificent dream! Only let me not wake, and I will conquer ten continents to pay for dreaming it out to the end. [*He climbs to the Sphinx's flank, and presently reappears to her on the pedestal, stepping round its right shoulder*].

CLEOPATRA. Take care. Thats right. Now sit down: you may have its other paw. [*She seats herself comfortably on its left paw*]. It is very powerful and will protect us; but [*shivering, and with plaintive loneliness*] it would not take any notice of me or keep me company. I am glad you have come: I was very lonely. Did you happen to see a white cat anywhere?

CÆSAR [*sitting slowly down on the right paw in extreme wonderment*] Have you lost one?

CLEOPATRA. Yes: the sacred white cat: is it not dreadful? I brought him here to sacrifice him to the Sphinx; but when we got a little way from the city a black cat called him, and he jumped out of my arms and ran away to it. Do you think that the black cat can have been my great-great-great-grandmother?

CÆSAR [*staring at her*] Your great-great-great-grandmother! Well, why not? Nothing would surprise me on this night of nights.

CLEOPATRA. I think it must have been. My great-grandmother's great-grandmother was a black kitten of the sacred white cat; and the river Nile made her his seventh wife. That is why my hair is so wavy. And I always want to be let do as I like, no matter whether it is the will of the gods or not: that is because my blood is made with Nile water.

CÆSAR. What are you doing here at this time of night? Do you live here?

CLEOPATRA. Of course not: I am the Queen; and I shall live in the palace at Alexandria when I have killed my brother, who drove me out of it. When I am old enough I shall do just what I like. I shall be able to poison the slaves and see them wriggle, and pretend to Ftatateeta that she is going to be put into the fiery furnace.

CÆSAR. Hm! Meanwhile why are you not at home and in bed?

CLEOPATRA. Because the Romans are coming to eat us all. You are not at home and in bed either.

CÆSAR [*with conviction*] Yes I am. I live in a tent; and I am now in that tent, fast asleep and dreaming. Do you suppose that I believe you are real, you impossible little dream witch?

CLEOPATRA [*giggling and leaning trustfully towards him*] You are a funny old gentleman. I like you.

CÆSAR. Ah, that spoils the dream. Why dont you dream that I am young?

CLEOPATRA. I wish you were; only I think I should be more afraid of you. I like men, especially young men with round strong arms; but I am afraid of them. You are old and rather thin and stringy; but you have a nice voice; and I like to have somebody to talk to, though I think you are a little mad. It is the moon that makes you talk to yourself in that silly way.

CÆSAR. What! you heard that, did you? I was saying my prayers to the great Sphinx.

CLEOPATRA. But this isnt the great Sphinx.

CÆSAR [*much disappointed, looking up at the statue*] What!

CLEOPATRA. This is only a dear little kitten of a Sphinx. Why, the great Sphinx is so big that it has a temple between its paws. This is my pet Sphinx. Tell me: do you think the Romans have any sorcerers who would take us away from the Sphinx by magic?

CÆSAR Why? Are you afraid of the Romans?

CLEOPATRA [*very seriously*] Oh, they would eat us if they caught us. They are barbarians. Their chief is called Julius Cæsar. His father was a tiger and his mother a burning mountain; and his nose is like an elephant's trunk. [*Cæsar involuntarily rubs his nose*]. They all have long noses, and ivory tusks, and little tails, and seven arms with a hundred arrows in each; and they live on human flesh.

CÆSAR. Would you like me to shew you a real Roman?

CLEOPATRA [*terrified*] No. You are frightening me.

CÆSAR. No matter: this is only a dream—

CLEOPATRA [*excitedly*] It is not a dream: it is not a dream. See, see. [*She plucks a pin from her hair and jabs it repeatedly into his arm*].

CÆSAR. Ffff—Stop [*Wrathfully*] How dare you?

CLEOPATRA [*abashed*] You said you were dreaming. [*Whimpering*] I only wanted to shew you—

CÆSAR [*gently*] Come, come: dont cry. A queen mustnt cry. [*He rubs his arm, wondering at the reality of the smart*]. Am I awake? [*He strikes his hand against the Sphinx to test its solidity. It feels so real that he begins to be alarmed, and says perplexedly*] Yes, I—[*quite panicstricken*] no: impossible: madness, madness! [*Desperately*] Back to camp—to camp. [*He rises to spring down from the pedestal*].

CLEOPATRA [*flinging her arms in terror round him*] No: you shant leave me. No, no, no: dont go. I'm afraid—afraid of the Romans.

CÆSAR [*as the conviction that he is really awake forces itself on him*] Cleopatra: can you see my face well?

CLEOPATRA. Yes. It is so white in the moonlight.

CÆSAR. Are you sure it is the moonlight that makes me look whiter than an Egyptian? [*Grimly*] Do you notice that I have a rather long nose?

CLEOPATRA [*recoiling, paralysed by a terrible suspicion*] Oh!

CÆSAR. It is a Roman nose, Cleopatra.

CLEOPATRA. Ah! [*With a piercing scream she springs up; darts round the left shoulder of the Sphinx; scrambles down to the sand; and falls on her knees in frantic supplication, shrieking*] Bite him in two, Sphinx: bite him in two. I meant to sacrifice the white cat—I did indeed—I [*Cæsar, who has slipped down from the pedestal, touches her on the shoulder*]—Ah! [*She buries her head in her arms*].

CÆSAR. Cleopatra: shall I teach you a way to prevent Cæsar from eating you?

CLEOPATRA [*clinging to him piteously*] Oh do, do, do. I will steal Ftatateeta's jewels and give them to you. I will make the river Nile water your lands twice a year.

CÆSAR. Peace, peace, my child. Your gods are afraid of the Romans: you see the Sphinx dare not bite me, nor prevent me carrying you off to Julius Cæsar.

CLEOPATRA [*in pleading murmurings*] You wont, you wont. You said you wouldnt.

CÆSAR. Cæsar never eats women.

CLEOPATRA [*springing up full of hope*] What!

CÆSAR [*impressively*] But he eats girls [*she relapses*] and cats. Now you are a silly little girl; and you are descended from the black kitten. You are both a girl and a cat.

CLEOPATRA [*trembling*] And will he eat m e?

CÆSAR. Yes; unless you make him believe that you are a woman.

CLEOPATRA. Oh, you must get a sorcerer to make a woman of me. Are you a sorcerer?

CÆSAR. Perhaps. But it will take a long time; and this very night you must stand face to face with Cæsar in the palace of your fathers.

CLEOPATRA. No, no. I darent.

CÆSAR. Whatever dread may be in your soul—however terrible Cæsar may be to you—you must confront him as a brave woman and a great queen; and you must feel no fear. If your hand shakes: if your voice quavers; then—night and death! [*She moans*]. But if he thinks you worthy to rule, he will set you on the throne by his side and make you the real ruler of Egypt.

CLEOPATRA [*despairingly*] No: he will find me out: he will find me out.

CÆSAR [*rather mournfully*] He is easily deceived by women. Their eyes dazzle him; and he sees them not as they are, but as he wishes them to appear to him.

CLEOPATRA [*hopefully*] Then we will cheat him. I will put on Ftatateeta's head-dress; and he will think me quite an old woman.

CÆSAR. If you do that he will eat you at one mouthful.

CLEOPATRA. But I will give him a cake with my magic opal and seven hairs of the white cat baked in it; and—

CÆSAR [*abruptly*] Pah! you are a little fool. He will eat your cake and you too. [*He turns contemptuously from her*].

CLEOPATRA [*running after him and clinging to him*] Oh please, p l e a s e! I will do whatever you tell me. I will be good. I will be your slave. [*Again the terrible bellowing note sounds across the desert, now closer at hand. It is the bucina, the Roman war trumpet*].

CÆSAR. Hark!

CLEOPATRA [*trembling*] What was that?

CÆSAR. Cæsar's voice.

CLEOPATRA [*pulling at his hand*] Let us run away. Come. Oh, come.

CÆSAR. You are safe with me until you stand on your throne to receive Cæsar. Now lead me thither.

CLEOPATRA [*only too glad to get away*] I will, I will. [*Again the bucina*]. Oh come, come, come: the gods are angry. Do you feel the earth shaking?

CÆSAR. It is the tread of Cæsar's legions.

CLEOPATRA [*drawing him away*] This way, quickly. And let us look for the white cat as we go. It is he that has turned you into a Roman.

CÆSAR. Incorrigible, oh, incorrigible! Away! [*He follows her, the bucina sounding louder as they steal across the desert. The moonlight wanes: the horizon again shews black against the sky, broken only by the fantastic silhouette of the Sphinx. The sky itself vanishes in darkness, from which there is no relief until the gleam of a distant torch falls on great Egyptian pillars supporting the roof of a majestic corridor. At the further end of this corridor a Nubian slave appears carrying the torch. Cæsar, still led by Cleopatra, follows him. They come down the corridor, Cæsar peering keenly about at the strange architecture, and at the pillar shadows between which, as the passing torch makes them hurry noiselessly backwards, figures of men with wings and hawks' heads, and vast black marble cats, seem to flit in and out of ambush. Further along, the wall turns a corner and makes a spacious transept in which Cæsar sees, on his right, a throne, and behind the throne a door. On each side of the throne is a slender pillar with a lamp on it*].

CÆSAR. What place is this?

CLEOPATRA. This is where I sit on the throne when I am allowed to wear my crown and robes. [*The slave holds his torch to shew the throne*].
CÆSAR. Order the slave to light the lamps.
CLEOPATRA [*shyly*] Do you think I may?
CÆSAR. Of course. You are the Queen. [*She hesitates*]. Go on.
CLEOPATRA [*timidly, to the slave*] Light all the lamps.
FTATATEETA [*suddenly coming from behind the throne*] Stop. [*The slave stops. She turns sternly to Cleopatra, who quails like a naughty child*]. Who is this you have with you; and how dare you order the lamps to be lighted without my permission? [*Cleopatra is dumb with apprehension*].
CÆSAR. Who is she?
CLEOPATRA. Ftatateeta.
FTATATEETA [*arrogantly*] Chief nurse to—
CÆSAR [*cutting her short*] I speak to the Queen. Be silent. [*To Cleopatra*] Is this how your servants know their places? Send her away; and do you [*to the slave*] do as the Queen has bidden. [*The slave lights the lamps. Meanwhile Cleopatra stands hesitating, afraid of Ftatateeta*]. You are the Queen: send her away.
CLEOPATRA [*cajoling*] Ftatateeta, dear: you must go away—just for a little.
CÆSAR. You are not commanding her to go away: you are begging her. You are no Queen. You will be eaten. Farewell. [*He turns to go*].
CLEOPATRA [*clutching him*] No, no, no. Dont leave me.
CÆSAR. A Roman does not stay with queens who are afraid of their slaves.
CLEOPATRA. I am not afraid. Indeed I am not afraid.
FTATATEETA. We shall see who is afraid here. [*Menacingly*] Cleopatra—
CÆSAR. On your knees, woman: am I also a child that you dare trifle with me? [*He points to the floor at Cleopatra's feet. Ftatateeta, half cowed, half savage, hesitates. Cæsar calls to the Nubian*] Slave. [*The Nubian comes to him*] Can you cut off a head? [*The Nubian nods and grins ecstatically, showing all his teeth. Cæsar takes his sword by the scabbard, ready to offer the hilt to the Nubian, and turns again to Ftatateeta, repeating his gesture*]. Have you remembered yourself, mistress?

Ftatateeta, crushed, kneels before Cleopatra, who can hardly believe her eyes.

FTATATEETA [*hoarsely*] O Queen, forget not thy servant in the days of thy greatness.

CLEOPATRA [*blazing with excitement*] Go. Begone. Go away. *Ftatateeta rises with stooped head, and moves backwards towards the door. Cleopatra watches her submission eagerly, almost clapping her hands, which are trembling. Suddenly she cries*] Give me something to beat her with. [*She snatches a snake-skin from the throne and dashes after Ftatateeta, whirling it like a scourge in the air. Cæsar makes a bound and manages to catch her and hold her while Ftatateeta escapes*].

CÆSAR. You scratch, kitten, do you?

CLEOPATRA [*breaking from him*] I will beat somebody. I will beat him. [*She attacks the slave*]. There, there, there! [*The slave flies for his life up the corridor and vanishes. She throws the snake-skin away and jumps on the step of the throne with her arms waving, crying*] I am a real Queen at last—a real, real Queen! Cleopatra the Queen! [*Cæsar shakes his head dubiously, the advantage of the change seeming open to question from the point of view of the general welfare of Egypt. She turns and looks at him exultantly. Then she jumps down from the steps, runs to him, and flings her arms round him rapturously, crying*] Oh, I love you for making me a Queen.

CÆSAR. But queens love only kings.

CLEOPATRA. I will make all the men I love kings. I will make you a king. I will have many young kings, with round, strong arms; and when I am tired of them I will whip them to death; but you shall always be my king: my nice, kind, wise, good old king.

CÆSAR. Oh, my wrinkles, my wrinkles! And my child's heart! You will be the most dangerous of all Cæsar's conquests.

CLEOPATRA [*appalled*] Cæsar! I forgot Cæsar. [*Anxiously*] You will tell him that I am a Queen, will you not?—a real Queen. Listen! [*stealthily coaxing him*]: let us run away and hide until Cæsar is gone.

CÆSAR. If you fear Cæsar, you are no true queen; and though you were to hide beneath a pyramid, he would go straight to it and lift it with one hand. And then—! [*he chops his teeth together*].

CLEOPATRA [*trembling*] Oh!

CÆSAR. Be afraid if you dare. [*The note of the bucina resounds again in the distance. She moans with fear. Cæsar exults in it, exclaiming*] Aha! Cæsar approaches the throne of Cleopatra. Come: take your place. [*He takes her hand and leads her to the throne. She is too downcast to speak*]. Ho, there, Teetatota. How do you call your slaves?

CLEOPATRA [*spiritlessly, as she sinks on the throne and cowers there, shaking*] Clap your hands.

He claps his hands. Ftatateeta returns.

CÆSAR. Bring the Queen's robes, and her crown, and her women; and prepare her.

CLEOPATRA [*eagerly—recovering herself a little*] Yes, the crown, Ftatateeta: I shall wear the crown.

FTATATEETA. For whom must the Queen put on her state?

CÆSAR. For a citizen of Rome. A king of kings, Totateeta.

CLEOPATRA [*stamping at her*] How dare you ask questions? Go and do as you are told. [*Ftatateeta goes out with a grim smile. Cleopatra goes on eagerly, to Cæsar*] Cæsar will know that I am a Queen when he sees my crown and robes, will he not?

CÆSAR. No. How shall he know that you are not a slave dressed up in the Queen's ornaments?

CLEOPATRA. You must tell him.

CÆSAR. He will not ask me. He will know Cleopatra by her pride, her courage, her majesty, and her beauty. [*She looks very doubtful*] Are you trembling?

CLEOPATRA [*shivering with dread*] No, I—I—[*in a very sickly voice*] No.

Ftatateeta and three women come in with the regalia.

FTATATEETA. Of all the Queen's women, these three alone are left. The rest are fled. [*They begin to deck Cleopatra, who submits, pale and motionless*].

CÆSAR. Good, good. Three are enough. Poor Cæsar generally has to dress himself.

FTATATEETA [*contemptuously*] The queen of Egypt is not a Roman barbarian. [*To Cleopatra*] Be brave, my nursling. Hold up your head before this stranger.

CÆSAR [*admiring Cleopatra, and placing the crown on her head*] Is it sweet or bitter to be a Queen, Cleopatra?

CLEOPATRA. Bitter.

CÆSAR. Cast out fear; and you will conquer Cæsar. Tota: are the Romans at hand?

FTATATEETA. They are at hand; and the guard has fled.

THE WOMEN [*wailing subduedly*] Woe to us!

The Nubian comes running down the hall.

NUBIAN. The Romans are in the courtyard. [*He bolts through the door. With a shriek, the women fly after him. Ftatateeta's jaw expresses savage resolution: she does not budge. Cleopatra can hardly restrain herself from following them. Cæsar grips her wrist, and looks steadfastly at her. She stands like a martyr*].

CÆSAR. The Queen must face Cæsar alone. Answer "So be it."

CLEOPATRA [*white*] So be it.

CÆSAR [*releasing her*] Good.

A tramp and tumult of armed men is heard. Cleopatra's terror increases. The bucina sounds close at hand, followed by a formidable clangor of trumpets. This is too much for Cleopatra: she utters a cry and darts towards the door. Ftatateeta stops her ruthlessly.

FTATATEETA. You are my nursling. You have said "So be it"; and if you die for it, you must make the Queen's word good. [*She hands Cleopatra to Cæsar, who takes her back, almost beside herself with apprehension, to the throne*].

CÆSAR. Now, if you quail—! [*He seats himself on the throne*].

She stands on the step, all but unconscious, waiting for death. The Roman soldiers troop in tumultuously through the corridor, headed by their ensign with his eagle, and their bucinator, a burly fellow with his instrument coiled round his body, its brazen bell shaped like the head of a howling wolf. When they reach the transept, they stare in amazement at the throne; dress into ordered rank opposite it; draw their swords and lift them in the air with a shout of Hail, Cæsar. *Cleopatra turns and stares wildly at Cæsar; grasps the situation; and, with a great sob of relief, falls into his arms.*

ACT II

Alexandria. A hall on the first floor of the Palace, ending in a loggia approached by two steps. Through the arches of the loggia the Mediterranean can be seen, bright in the morning sun. The clean lofty walls, painted with a procession of the Egyptian theocracy, presented in profile as flat ornament, and the absence of mirrors, sham perspectives, stuffy upholstery and textiles, make the place handsome, wholesome, simple and cool, or, as a rich English manufacturer would express it, poor, bare, ridiculous and unhomely. For Tottenham Court Road civilization is to this Egyptian civilization as glass bead and tattoo civilization is to Tottenham Court Road.

The young king Ptolemy Dionysus (aged ten) is at the top of the steps, on his way in through the loggia, led by his guardian Pothinus, who has him by the hand. The court is assembled to receive him. It is made up of men and women (some of the women being officials) of various complexions and races, mostly Egyptian; some of them, comparatively fair, from lower Egypt, some, much darker, from upper Egypt; with a few Greeks and Jews. Prominent in a group on Ptolemy's right hand is Theodotus, Ptolemy's tutor. Another group, on Ptolemy's left is headed by Achillas, the general of Ptolemy's troops. Theodotus is a little old man, whose features are as cramped and wizened as his limbs, except his tall straight forehead, which occupies more space than all the rest of his face. He maintains an air of magpie keenness and profundity, listening to what the others say with the sarcastic vigilance of a philosopher listening to the exercises of his disciples. Achillas is a tall handsome man of thirty-five, with a fine black beard curled like the coat of a poodle. Apparently not a clever man, but distinguished and dignified. Pothinus is a vigorous man of fifty, a eunuch, passionate, energetic and quick witted, but of common mind and character; impatient and unable to control his temper. He has fine tawny hair, like fur. Ptolemy, the King, looks much older than an English boy of ten; but he has the childish air, the habit of being in leading strings, the mixture of impotence and petulance, the appearance of being excessively washed, combed and dressed by other hands, which is exhibited by court-bred princes of all ages.

All receive the King with reverences. He comes down the steps to a chair of state which stands a little to his right, the only seat in the hall. Taking his place before it, he looks nervously for instructions to Pothinus, who places himself at his left hand.

POTHINUS. The king of Egypt has a word to speak.

THEODOTUS [*in a squeak which he makes impressive by sheer self-opinionativeness*] Peace for the King's word!

PTOLEMY [*without any vocal inflexions: he is evidently repeating a lesson*] Take notice of this all of you. I am the first-born son of Auletes the Flute Blower who was your King. My sister Berenice drove him from his throne and reigned in his stead but—but—[*he hesitates*]—

POTHINUS [*stealthily prompting*]—but the gods would not suffer—

PTOLEMY. Yes—the gods would not suffer—not suffer—[*He stops; then, crestfallen*] I forget what the gods would not suffer.

THEODOTUS. Let Pothinus, the King's guardian, speak for the King.

POTHINUS [*suppressing his impatience with difficulty*] The King wished to say that the gods would not suffer the impiety of his sister to go unpunished.

PTOLEMY [*hastily*] Yes: I remember the rest of it. [*He resumes his monotone*]. Therefore the gods sent a stranger one Mark Antony a Roman captain of horsemen across the sands of the desert and he set my father again upon the throne. And my father took Berenice my sister and struck her head off. And now that my father is dead yet another of his daughters my sister Cleopatra would snatch the kingdom from me and reign in my place. But the gods would not suffer—[*Pothinus coughs admonitorily*]—the gods—the gods would not suffer—

POTHINUS [*prompting*]—will not maintain—

PTOLEMY. Oh yes—will not maintain such iniquity they will give her head to the axe even as her sister's. But with the help of the witch Ftatateeta she hath cast a spell on the Roman Julius Cæsar to make him uphold her false pretence to rule in Egypt. Take notice then that I will not suffer—that I will not suffer—[*pettishly to Pothinus*] What is it that I will not suffer?

POTHINUS [*suddenly exploding with all the force and emphasis of political passion*] The King will not suffer a foreigner to take from him the throne of our Egypt. [*A shout of applause*]. Tell the King, Achillas, how many soldiers and horsemen follow the Roman?

THEODOTUS. Let the King's general speak!

ACHILLAS. But two Roman legions, O King. Three thousand soldiers and scarce a thousand horsemen.

The court breaks into derisive laughter; and a great chattering begins, amid which Rufio, a Roman officer, appears in the loggia. He is a burly, black-bearded man of middle age, very blunt, prompt and rough, with small clear eyes, and plump nose and cheeks, which, however, like the rest of his flesh, are in ironhard condition.

RUFIO [*from the steps*] Peace, ho! [*The laughter and chatter cease abruptly*]. Cæsar approaches.

THEODOTUS [*with much presence of mind*] The King permits the Roman commander to enter!

Cæsar, plainly dressed, but wearing an oak wreath to conceal his baldness, enters from the loggia, attended by Britannus, his secretary, a Briton, about forty, tall, solemn, and already slightly bald, with a heavy, drooping, hazel-colored moustache trained so as to lose its ends in a pair of trim whiskers. He is carefully dressed in blue, with portfolio, inkhorn, and reed pen at his girdle. His serious air and sense of the importance of the business in hand is in marked contrast to the kindly interest of Cæsar, who looks at the scene, which is new to him, with the frank curiosity of a child, and then turns to the king's chair: Britannus and Rufio posting themselves near the steps at the other side.

CÆSAR [*looking at Pothinus and Ptolemy*] Which is the King? the man or the boy?

POTHINUS. I am Pothinus, the guardian of my lord the King.

CÆSAR [*patting Ptolemy kindly on the shoulder*] So you are the King. Dull work at your age, eh? [*To Pothinus*] Your servant, Pothinus. [*He turns away unconcernedly and comes slowly along the middle of the hall, looking from side to side at the courtiers until he reaches Achillas*]. And this gentleman?

THEODOTUS. Achillas, the King's general.

CÆSAR [*to Achillas, very friendly*] A general, eh? I am a general myself. But I began too old, too old. Health and many victories, Achillas!

ACHILLAS. As the gods will, Cæsar.

CÆSAR [*turning to Theodotus*] And you, sir, are—?

THEODOTUS. Theodotus, the King's tutor.

CÆSAR. You teach men how to be kings, Theodotus. That is very clever of you. [*Looking at the gods on the walls as he turns away from Theodotus and goes up again to Pothinus*] And this place?

POTHINUS. The council chamber of the chancellors of the King's treasury, Cæsar.

CÆSAR. Ah! that reminds me. I want some money.

POTHINUS. The King's treasury is poor, Cæsar.

CÆSAR. Yes: I notice that there is but one chair in it.

RUFIO [*shouting gruffly*] Bring a chair there, some of you, for Cæsar.

PTOLEMY [*rising shyly to offer his chair*] Cæsar—

CÆSAR [*kindly*] No, no, my boy: that is your chair of state. Sit down.

He makes Ptolemy sit down again. Meanwhile Rufio, looking about him, sees in the nearest corner an image of the god Ra, represented as a seated man with the head of a hawk. Before the image is a bronze tripod, about as large as a three-legged stool, with a stick of incense burning on it. Rufio, with Roman resourcefulness and indifference to foreign superstitions, promptly seizes the tripod; shakes off the incense; blows away the ash; and dumps it down behind Cæsar, nearly in the middle of the hall.

RUFIO. Sit on that, Cæsar.

A shiver runs through the court, followed by a hissing whisper of Sacrilege!

CÆSAR [*seating himself*] Now, Pothinus, to business. I am badly in want of money.

BRITANNUS [*disapproving of these informal expressions*] My master would say that there is a lawful debt due to Rome by Egypt, contracted by the King's deceased father to the Triumvirate; and that it is Cæsar's duty to his country to require immediate payment.

CÆSAR [*blandly*] Ah, I forgot. I have not made my companions known here. Pothinus: this is Britannus, my secretary. He is an islander from the western end of the world, a day's voyage from Gaul. [*Britannus bows stiffly*]. This gentleman is Rufio, my comrade in arms. [*Rufio nods*]. Pothinus: I want 1,600 talents.

The courtiers, appalled, murmur loudly, and Theodotus and Achillas appeal mutely to one another against so monstrous a demand.

POTHINUS [*aghast*] Forty million sesterces! Impossible. There is not so much money in the King's treasury.

CÆSAR [*encouragingly*] Only sixteen hundred talents, Pothinus. Why count it in sesterces? A sestertius is only worth a loaf of bread.

POTHINUS. And a talent is worth a racehorse. I say it is impossible. We have been at strife here, because the King's sister Cleopatra falsely claims his throne. The King's taxes have not been collected for a whole year.

CÆSAR. Yes they have, Pothinus. My officers have been collecting them all morning. [*Renewed whisper and sensation, not without some stifled laughter, among the courtiers*].

RUFIO [*bluntly*] You must pay, Pothinus. Why waste words? You are getting off cheaply enough.

POTHINUS [*bitterly*] Is it possible that Cæsar, the conqueror of the world, has time to occupy himself with such a trifle as our taxes?

CÆSAR. My friend: taxes are the chief business of a conqueror of the world.

POTHINUS. Then take warning, Cæsar. This day, the treasures of the temple and the gold of the King's treasury shall be sent to the mint to be melted down for our ransom in the sight of the people. They shall see us sitting under bare walls and drinking from wooden cups. And their wrath be on your head, Cæsar, if you force us to this sacrilege!

CÆSAR. Do not fear, Pothinus: the people know how well wine tastes in wooden cups. In return for your bounty, I will settle this dispute about the throne for you, if you will. What say you?

POTHINUS. If I say no, will that hinder you?

RUFIO [*defiantly*] No.

CÆSAR. You say the matter has been at issue for a year, Pothinus. May I have ten minutes at it?

POTHINUS. You will do your pleasure, doubtless.

CÆSAR. Good! But first, let us have Cleopatra here.

THEODOTUS. She is not in Alexandria: she is fled into Syria.

CÆSAR. I think not. [*To Rufio*] Call Totateeta.

RUFIO [*Calling*] Ho there, Teetatota.

Ftatateeta enters the loggia, and stands arrogantly at the top of the steps.

FTATATEETA. Who pronounces the name of Ftatateeta, the Queen's chief nurse?

CÆSAR. Nobody can pronounce it, Tota, except yourself. Where is your mistress?

Cleopatra, who is hiding behind Ftatateeta, peeps out at them laughing. Cæsar rises.

CÆSAR. Will the Queen favor us with her presence for a moment?

CLEOPATRA [*pushing Ftatateeta aside and standing haughtily on the brink of the steps*] Am I to behave like a Queen?

CÆSAR. Yes.

Cleopatra immediately comes down to the chair of state; seizes Ptolemy; drags him out of his seat; then takes his place in the chair.

Ftatateeta seats herself on the step of the loggia, and sits there, watching the scene with sibylline intensity.

PTOLEMY [*mortified, and struggling with his tears*] Cæsar: this is how she treats me always. If I am a king why is she allowed to take everything from me?

CLEOPATRA. You are not to be King, you little crybaby. You are to be eaten by the Romans.

CÆSAR [*touched by Ptolemy's distress*] Come here, my boy, and stand by me.

Ptolemy goes over to Cæsar, who, resuming his seat on the tripod, takes the boy's hand to encourage him. Cleopatra, furiously jealous, rises and glares at them.

CLEOPATRA [*with flaming cheeks*] Take your throne: I dont want it. [*She flings away from the chair, and approaches Ptolemy, who shrinks from her*]. Go this instant and sit down in your place.

CÆSAR. Go, Ptolemy. Always take a throne when it is offered to you.

RUFIO. I hope you will have the good sense to follow your own advice when we return to Rome, Cæsar.

Ptolemy slowly goes back to the throne, giving Cleopatra a wide berth, in evident fear of her hands. She takes his place beside Cæsar.

CÆSAR. Pothinus—

CLEOPATRA [*interrupting him*] Are you not going to speak to me?

CÆSAR. Be quiet. Open your mouth again before I give you leave; and you shall be eaten.

CLEOPATRA. I am not afraid. A queen must not be afraid. Eat my husband there, if you like: h e is afraid.

CÆSAR [*starting*] Your husband! What do you mean?

CLEOPATRA [*pointing to Ptolemy*] That little thing.

The two Romans and the Briton stare at one another in amazement.

THEODOTUS. Cæsar: you are a stranger here, and not conversant with our laws. The kings and queens of Egypt may not marry except with their own royal blood. Ptolemy and Cleopatra are born king and consort just as they are born brother and sister.

BRITANNUS [*shocked*] Cæsar: this is not proper.

THEODOTUS [*outraged*] How!

CÆSAR [*recovering his self-possession*] Pardon him, Theodotus: he is a barbarian, and thinks that the customs of his tribe and island are the laws of nature.

BRITANNUS. On the contrary, Cæsar, it is these Egyptians who are barbarians; and you do wrong to encourage them. I say it is a scandal.

CÆSAR. Scandal or not, my friend, it opens the gate of peace. [*He addresses Pothinus seriously*]. Pothinus: hear what I propose.

RUFIO. Hear Cæsar there.

CÆSAR. Ptolemy and Cleopatra shall reign jointly in Egypt.

ACHILLAS. What of the King's younger brother and Cleopatra's younger sister?

RUFIO [*explaining*] There is another little Ptolemy, Cæsar: so they tell me.

CÆSAR. Well, the little Ptolemy can marry the other sister; and we will make them both a present of Cyprus.

POTHINUS [*impatiently*] Cyprus is of no use to anybody.

CÆSAR. No matter: you shall have it for the sake of peace.

BRITANNUS [*unconsciously anticipating a later statesman*] Peace with honor, Pothinus.

POTHINUS [*mutinously*] Cæsar: be honest. The money you demand is the price of our freedom. Take it; and leave us to settle our own affairs.

THE BOLDER COURTIERS [*encouraged by Pothinus's tone and Cæsar's quietness*] Yes, yes. Egypt for the Egyptians!

The conference now becomes an altercation, the Egyptians becoming more and more heated. Cæsar remains unruffled; but Rufio grows fiercer and doggeder, and Britannus haughtily indignant.

RUFIO [*contemptuously*] Egypt for the Egyptians! Do you forget that there is a Roman army of occupation here, left by Aulus Gabinius when he set up your toy king for you?

ACHILLAS [*suddenly asserting himself*] And now under my command. *I* am the Roman general here, Cæsar.

CÆSAR [*tickled by the humor of the situation*] And also the Egyptian general, eh?

POTHINUS [*triumphantly*] That is so, Cæsar.

CÆSAR [*to Achillas*] So you can make war on the Egyptians in the name of Rome, and on the Romans—on m e, if necessary—in the name of Egypt?

ACHILLAS. That is so, Cæsar.

CÆSAR. And which side are you on at present, if I may presume to ask, general?

ACHILLAS. On the side of the right and of the gods.

CÆSAR. Hm! How many men have you?

ACHILLAS. That will appear when I take the field.

RUFIO [*truculently*] Are your men Romans? If not, it matters not how many there are, provided you are no stronger than 500 to ten.

POTHINUS. It is useless to try to bluff us, Rufio. Cæsar has been defeated before and may be defeated again. A few weeks ago Cæsar was flying for his life before Pompey: a few months hence he may be flying for his life before Cato and Juba of Numidia, the African King.

ACHILLAS [*following up Pothinus's speech menacingly*] What can you do with 4,000 men?

THEODOTUS [*following up Achillas's speech with a raucous squeak*] And without money? Away with you.

ALL THE COURTIERS [*shouting fiercely and crowding towards Cæsar*] Away with you. Egypt for the Egyptians! Begone.

Rufio bites his beard, too angry to speak. Cæsar sits as comfortably as if he were at breakfast, and the cat were clamoring for a piece of Finnan-haddie.

CLEOPATRA. Why do you let them talk to you like that, Cæsar? Are you afraid?

CÆSAR. Why, my dear, what they say is quite true.

CLEOPATRA. But if you go away, I shall not be Queen.

CÆSAR. I shall not go away until you are Queen.

POTHINUS. Achillas: if you are not a fool, you will take that girl whilst she is under your hand.

RUFIO [*daring them*] Why not take Cæsar as well, Achillas?

POTHINUS [*retorting the defiance with interest*] Well said, Rufio. Why not?

RUFIO. Try, Achillas. [*Calling*] Guard there.

The loggia immediately fills with Cæsar's soldiers, who stand, sword in hand, at the top of the steps, waiting the word to charge from their centurion, who carries a cudgel. For a moment the Egyptians face them proudly: then they retire sullenly to their former places.

BRITANNUS. You are Cæsar's prisoners, all of you.

CÆSAR [*benevolently*] Oh no, no, no. By no means. Cæsar's guests, gentlemen.

CLEOPATRA. Wont you cut their heads off?

CÆSAR. What! Cut off your brother's head?

CLEOPATRA. Why not? He would cut off mine, if he got the chance. Wouldnt you, Ptolemy?

PTOLEMY [*pale and obstinate*] I would. I will too, when I grow up.

Cleopatra is rent by a struggle between her newly-acquired dignity as a queen, and a strong impulse to put out her tongue at him. She takes no part in the scene which follows, but watches it with curiosity and wonder, fidgeting with the restlessness of a child, and sitting down on Cæsar's tripod when he rises.

POTHINUS. Cæsar: if you attempt to detain us—

RUFIO. He will succeed, Egyptian: make up your mind to that. We hold the palace, the beach, and the eastern harbor. The road to Rome is open; and you shall travel it if Cæsar chooses.

CÆSAR [*courteously*] I could do no less, Pothinus, to secure the retreat of my own soldiers. I am accountable for every life among them. But you are free to go. So are all here, and in the palace.

RUFIO [*aghast at this clemency*] What! Renegades and all?

CÆSAR [*softening the expression*] Roman army of occupation and all, Rufio.

POTHINUS [*bewildered*] But—but—but—

CÆSAR. Well, my friend?

POTHINUS. You are turning us out of our own palace into the streets; and you tell us with a grand air that we are free to go! It is for you to go.

CÆSAR. Your friends are in the street, Pothinus. You will be safer there.

POTHINUS. This is a trick. I am the king's guardian: I refuse to stir. I stand on my right here. Where is your right?

CÆSAR. It is in Rufio's scabbard, Pothinus. I may not be able to keep it there if you wait too long.

Sensation.

POTHINUS [*bitterly*] And this is Roman justice!

THEODOTUS. But not Roman gratitude, I hope.

CÆSAR. Gratitude! Am I in your debt for any service, gentlemen?

THEODOTUS. Is Cæsar's life of so little account to him that he forgets that we have saved it?

CÆSAR. My life! Is that all?

THEODOTUS. Your life. Your laurels. Your future.

POTHINUS. It is true. I can call a witness to prove that but for us, the Roman army of occupation, led by the greatest soldier in the world, would now have Cæsar at its mercy. [*Calling through the loggia*] Ho, there, Lucius Septimius [*Cæsar starts, deeply moved*]: if my voice can reach you, come forth and testify before Cæsar.

CÆSAR [*shrinking*] No, no.

THEODOTUS. Yes, I say. Let the military tribune bear witness.

Lucius Septimius, a clean shaven, trim athlete of about 40, with symmetrical features, resolute mouth, and handsome, thin Roman nose, in the dress of a Roman officer, comes in through the loggia and confronts Cæsar, who hides his face with his robe for a moment; then, mastering himself, drops it, and confronts the tribune with dignity.

POTHINUS. Bear witness, Lucius Septimius. Cæsar came hither in pursuit of his foe. Did we shelter his foe?

LUCIUS. As Pompey's foot touched the Egyptian shore, his head fell by the stroke of my sword.

THEODOTUS [*with viperish relish*] Under the eyes of his wife and child! Remember that, Cæsar! They saw it from the ship he had just left. We have given you a full and sweet measure of vengeance.

CÆSAR [*with horror*] Vengeance!

POTHINUS. Our first gift to you, as your galley came into the roadstead, was the head of your rival for the empire of the world. Bear witness, Lucius Septimius: is it not so?

LUCIUS. It is so. With this hand, that slew Pompey, I placed his head at the feet of Cæsar.

CÆSAR. Murderer! So would you have slain Cæsar, had Pompey been victorious at Pharsalia.

LUCIUS. Woe to the vanquished, Cæsar! When I served Pompey, I slew as good men as he, only because he conquered them. His turn came at last.

THEODOTUS [*flatteringly*] The deed was not yours, Cæsar, but ours—nay, mine; for it was done by my counsel. Thanks to us, you keep your reputation for clemency, and have your vengeance too.

CÆSAR. Vengeance! Vengeance!! Oh, if I could stoop to vengeance, what would I not exact from you as the price of this murdered man's blood? [*They shrink back, appalled and disconcerted*]. Was he not my son-in-law, my ancient friend, for 20 years the master of great Rome, for 30 years the compeller of victory? Did not I, as a Roman, share his glory? Was the Fate that forced us to fight for the mastery of the world, of our making? Am I Julius Cæsar, or am I a wolf, that you fling to me the grey head of the old soldier, the laurelled conqueror, the mighty Roman, treacherously struck down by this callous ruffian, and then claim my gratitude for it! [*To Lucius Septimius*] Begone: you fill me with horror.

LUCIUS [*cold and undaunted*] Pshaw! You have seen severed heads before, Cæsar, and severed right hands too, I think; some thousands of them, in Gaul, after you vanquished Vercingetorix. Did you spare him, with all your clemency? Was that vengeance?

CÆSAR. No, by the gods! would that it had been! Vengeance at least is human. No, I say: those severed right hands, and the brave Vercingetorix basely strangled in a vault beneath the Capitol, were [*with shuddering satire*] a wise severity, a necessary protection to the commonwealth, a duty of statesmanship—follies and fictions ten times bloodier than honest vengeance! What a fool was I then! To think that men's lives should be at the mercy of such fools! [*Humbly*] Lucius Septimius, pardon me: why should the slayer of Vercingetorix rebuke the slayer of Pompey? You are free to go with the rest. Or stay if you will: I will find a place for you in my service.

LUCIUS. The odds are against you, Cæsar. I go. [*He turns to go out through the loggia*].

RUFIO [*full of wrath at seeing his prey escaping*] That means that he is a Republican.

LUCIUS [*turning defiantly on the loggia steps*] And what are you?

RUFIO. A Cæsarian, like all Cæsar's soldiers.

CÆSAR [*courteously*] Lucius: believe me, Cæsar is no Cæsarian. Were Rome a true republic, then were Cæsar the first of Republicans. But you have made your choice. Farewell.

LUCIUS. Farewell. Come, Achillas, whilst there is yet time.

Cæsar, seeing that Rufio's temper threatens to get the worse of him, puts his hand on his shoulder and brings him down the hall out of harm's way, Britannus accompanying them and posting himself on Cæsar's right hand. This movement brings the three in a little group to the place occupied by Achillas, who moves haughtily away and joins Theodotus on the other side. Lucius Septimius goes out through the soldiers in the loggia. Pothinus, Theodotus and Achillas follow him with the courtiers, very mistrustful of the soldiers, who close up in their rear and go out after them, keeping them moving without much ceremony. The King is left in his chair, piteous, obstinate, with twitching face and fingers. During these movements Rufio maintains an energetic grumbling, as follows:—

RUFIO [*as Lucius departs*] Do you suppose he would let us go if he had our heads in his hands?

CÆSAR. I have no right to suppose that his ways are any baser than mine.

RUFIO. Psha!

CÆSAR. Rufio: if I take Lucius Septimius for my model, and become exactly like him, ceasing to be Cæsar, will you serve me still?

BRITANNUS. Cæsar: this is not good sense. Your duty to Rome demands that her enemies should be prevented from doing further mischief.

[*Cæsar, whose delight in the moral eye-to-business of his British secretary is inexhaustible, smiles indulgently*].

RUFIO. It is no use talking to him, Britannus: you may save your breath to cool your porridge. But mark this, Cæsar. Clemency is very well for you; but what is it for your soldiers, who have to fight tomorrow the men you spared yesterday? You may give what orders you please; but I tell you that your next victory will be a massacre, thanks to your clemency. *I*, for one, will take no prisoners. I will kill my enemies in the field; and then you can preach as much clemency as you please: I shall never have to fight them again. And now, with your leave, I will see these gentry off the premises. [*He turns to go*].

CÆSAR [*turning also and seeing Ptolemy*] What! have they left the boy alone! Oh shame, shame!

RUFIO [*taking Ptolemy's hand and making him rise*] Come, your majesty!

PTOLEMY [*to Cæsar, drawing away his hand from Rufio*] Is he turning me out of my palace?

RUFIO [*grimly*] You are welcome to stay if you wish.

CÆSAR [*kindly*] Go, my boy. I will not harm you; but you will be safer away, among your friends. Here you are in the lion's mouth.

PTOLEMY [*turning to go*] It is not the lion I fear, but [*looking at Rufio*] the jackal. [*He goes out through the loggia*].

CÆSAR [*laughing approvingly*] Brave boy!

CLEOPATRA [*jealous of Cæsar's approbation, calling after Ptolemy*] Little silly. You think that very clever.

CÆSAR. Britannus: attend the King. Give him in charge to that Pothinus fellow. [*Britannus goes out after Ptolemy*].

RUFIO [*pointing to Cleopatra*] And this piece of goods? What is to be done with h e r? However, I suppose I may leave that to you. [*He goes out through the loggia*].

CLEOPATRA [*flushing suddenly and turning on Cæsar*] Did you mean me to go with the rest?

CÆSAR [*a little preoccupied, goes with a sigh to Ptolemy's chair, whilst she waits for his answer with red cheeks and clenched fists*] You are free to do just as you please, Cleopatra.

CLEOPATRA. Then you do not care whether I stay or not?

CÆSAR [*smiling*] Of course I had rather you stayed.

CLEOPATRA. Much, m u c h rather?

CÆSAR [*nodding*] Much, much rather.

CLEOPATRA. Then I consent to stay, because I am asked. But I do not want to, mind.

CÆSAR. That is quite understood. [*Calling*] Totateeta.

Ftatateeta, still seated, turns her eyes on him with a sinister expression, but does not move.

CLEOPATRA [*with a splutter of laughter*] Her name is not Totateeta: it is Ftatateeta. [*Calling*] Ftatateeta. [*Ftatateeta instantly rises and comes to Cleopatra*].

CÆSAR [*stumbling over the name*] Tfatafeeta will forgive the erring tongue of a Roman. Tota: the Queen will hold her state here in Alexandria. Engage women to attend upon her; and do all that is needful.

FTATATEETA. Am I then the mistress of the Queen's household?

CLEOPATRA [*sharply*] No: *I* am the mistress of the Queen's household. Go and do as you are told, or I will have you thrown into the Nile this very afternoon, to poison the poor crocodiles.

CÆSAR [*shocked*] Oh no, no.

CLEOPATRA. Oh yes, yes. You are very sentimental, Cæsar; but you are clever; and if you do as I tell you, you will soon learn to govern.

Cæsar, quite dumbfounded by this impertinence, turns in his chair and stares at her.

Ftatateeta, smiling grimly, and shewing a splendid set of teeth, goes, leaving them alone together.

CÆSAR. Cleopatra: I really think I must eat you, after all.

CLEOPATRA [*kneeling beside him and looking at him with eager interest, half real, half affected to shew how intelligent she is*] You must not talk to me now as if I were a child.

CÆSAR. You have been growing up since the sphinx introduced us the other night; and you think you know more than I do already.

CLEOPATRA [*taken down, and anxious to justify herself*] No: that would be very silly of me: of course I know that. But—[*suddenly*] are you angry with me?

CÆSAR. No.

CLEOPATRA [*only half believing him*] Then why are you so thoughtful?

CÆSAR [*rising*] I have work to do, Cleopatra.

CLEOPATRA [*drawing back*] Work! [*Offended*] You are tired of talking to me; and that is your excuse to get away from me.

CÆSAR [*sitting down again to appease her*] Well, well: another minute. But then—work!

CLEOPATRA. Work! what nonsense! You must remember that you are a king now: I have made you one. Kings dont work.

CÆSAR. Oh! Who told you that, little kitten? Eh?

CLEOPATRA. My father was King of Egypt; and he never worked. But he was a great king, and cut off my sister's head because she rebelled against him and took the throne from him.

CÆSAR. Well; and how did he get his throne back again?

CLEOPATRA [*eagerly, her eyes lighting up*] I will tell you. A beautiful young man, with strong round arms, came over the desert with many horsemen, and slew my sister's husband and gave my father back his throne. [*Wistfully*] I was only twelve then. Oh, I wish he would come again, now that I am queen. I would make him my husband.

CÆSAR. It might be managed, perhaps; for it was I who sent that beautiful young man to help your father.

CLEOPATRA [*enraptured*] You know him!

CÆSAR [*nodding*] I do.

CLEOPATRA. Has he come with you? [*Cæsar shakes his head: she is cruelly disappointed*]. Oh, I wish he had, I wish he had. If only I were a little older; so that he might not think me a mere kitten, as you do! But perhaps that is because you are old. He is many many years younger than you, is he not?

CÆSAR [*as if swallowing a pill*] He is somewhat younger.

CLEOPATRA. Would he be my husband, do you think, if I asked him?

CÆSAR. Very likely.

CLEOPATRA. But I should not like to ask him. Could you not persuade him to ask me—without knowing that I wanted him to?

CÆSAR [*touched by her innocence of the beautiful young man's character*] My poor child!

CLEOPATRA. Why do you say that as if you were sorry for me? Does he love anyone else?

CÆSAR. I am afraid so.

CLEOPATRA [*tearfully*] Then I shall not be his first love.

CÆSAR. Not quite the first. He is greatly admired by women.

CLEOPATRA. I wish I could be the first. But if he loves me, I will make him kill all the rest. Tell me: is he still beautiful? Do his strong round arms shine in the sun like marble?

CÆSAR. He is in excellent condition—considering how much he eats and drinks.

CLEOPATRA. Oh, you must not say common, earthly things about him; for I love him. He is a god.

CÆSAR. He is a great captain of horsemen, and swifter of foot than any other Roman.

CLEOPATRA. What is his real name?

CÆSAR [*puzzled*] His real name?

CLEOPATRA. Yes. I always call him Horus, because Horus is the most beautiful of our gods. But I want to know his real name.

CÆSAR. His name is Mark Antony.

CLEOPATRA [*musically*] Mark Antony, Mark Antony, Mark Antony! What a beautiful name! [*She throws her arms around Cæsar's neck*]. Oh, how I love you for sending him to help my father! Did you love my father very much?

CÆSAR. No, my child; but your father, as you say, never worked. I always work. So when he lost his crown he had to promise me 16,000 talents to get it back for him.

CLEOPATRA. Did he ever pay you?

CÆSAR. Not in full.

CLEOPATRA. He was quite right: it was too dear. The whole world is not worth 16,000 talents.

CÆSAR. That is perhaps true, Cleopatra. Those Egyptians who work paid as much of it as he could drag from them. The rest is still due. But as I most likely shall not get it, I must go back to my work. So you must run away for a little and send my secretary to me.

CLEOPATRA [*coaxing*] No: I want to stay and hear you talk about Mark Antony.

CÆSAR. But if I do not get to work, Pothinus and the rest of them will cut us off from the harbor; and then the way from Rome will be blocked.

CLEOPATRA. No matter: I dont want you to go back to Rome.

CÆSAR. But you want Mark Antony to come from it.

CLEOPATRA [*springing up*] Oh yes, yes, yes: I forgot. Go quickly and work, Cæsar; and keep the way over the sea open for my Mark Antony. [*She runs out through the loggia, kissing her hand to Mark Antony across the sea*].

CÆSAR [*going briskly up the middle of the hall to the loggia steps*] Ho, Britannus. [*He is startled by the entry of a wounded Roman soldier, who confronts him from the upper step*]. What now?

SOLDIER [*pointing to his bandaged head*] This, Cæsar; and two of my comrades killed in the market place.

CÆSAR [*quiet, but attending*] Ay. Why?

SOLDIER. There is an army come to Alexandria, calling itself the Roman army.

CÆSAR. The Roman army of occupation. Ay?

SOLDIER. Commanded by one Achillas.

CÆSAR. Well?

SOLDIER. The citizens rose against us when the army entered the gates. I was with two others in the market place when the news came. They set upon us. I cut my way out; and here I am.

CÆSAR. Good. I am glad to see you alive. [*Rufio enters the loggia hastily, passing behind the soldier to look out through one of the arches at the quay beneath*]. Rufio: we are besieged.

RUFIO. What! Already?

CÆSAR. Now or tomorrow: what does it matter? We s h a l l be besieged.

Britannus runs in.

BRITANNUS. Cæsar—

CÆSAR [*anticipating him*] Yes: I know. [*Rufio and Britannus come down the hall from the loggia at opposite sides, past Cæsar, who waits for a moment near the step to say to the soldier*] Comrade: give the word to turn out on the beach and stand by the boats. Get your wound attended to. Go. [*The soldier hurries out. Cæsar comes down the hall between Rufio and Britannus*] Rufio: we have some ships in the west harbor. Burn them.

RUFIO [*staring*] Burn them!!

CÆSAR. Take every boat we have in the east harbor, and seize the Pharos—that island with the lighthouse. Leave half our men behind to hold the beach and the quay outside this palace: that is the way home.

RUFIO [*disapproving strongly*] Are we to give up the city?

CÆSAR. We have not got it, Rufio. This palace we have; and—what is that building next door?

RUFIO. The theatre.

CÆSAR. We will have that too: it commands the strand. For the rest, Egypt for the Egyptians!

RUFIO. Well you know best, I suppose. Is that all?

CÆSAR. That is all. Are those ships burnt yet?

RUFIO. Be easy: I shall waste no more time. [*He runs out*].

BRITANNUS. Cæsar: Pothinus demands speech of you. In my opinion he needs a lesson. His manner is most insolent.

CÆSAR. Where is he?

BRITANNUS. He waits without.

CÆSAR. Ho there! admit Pothinus.

Pothinus appears in the loggia, and comes down the hall very haughtily to Cæsar's left hand.

CÆSAR. Well, Pothinus?

POTHINUS. I have brought you our ultimatum, Cæsar.

CÆSAR. Ultimatum! The door was open: you should have gone out through it before you declared war. You are my prisoner now. [*He goes to the chair and loosens his toga*].

POTHINUS [*scornfully*] I your prisoner! Do you know that you are in Alexandria, and that King Ptolemy, with an army outnumbering your little troop a hundred to one, is in possession of Alexandria?

CÆSAR [*unconcernedly taking off his toga and throwing it on the chair*] Well, my friend, get out if you can. And tell your friends not to kill any more Romans in the market place. Otherwise my soldiers, who do not share my celebrated clemency, will probably kill you. Britannus: pass the word to the guard; and fetch my armor. [*Britannus runs out. Rufio returns*]. Well?

RUFIO [*pointing from the loggia to a cloud of smoke drifting over the harbor*] See there! [*Pothinus runs eagerly up the steps to look out*].

CÆSAR. What, ablaze already! Impossible!

RUFIO. Yes, five good ships, and a barge laden with oil grappled to each. But it is not my doing: the Egyptians have saved me the trouble. They have captured the west harbor.

CÆSAR [*anxiously*] And the east harbor? The lighthouse, Rufio?

RUFIO [*with a sudden splutter of raging ill usage, coming down to Cæsar and scolding him*] Can I embark a legion in five minutes? The first cohort is already on the beach. We can do no more. If you want faster work, come and do it yourself.

CÆSAR [*soothing him*] Good, good. Patience, Rufio, patience.

RUFIO. Patience! Who is impatient here, you or I? Would I be here, if I could not oversee them from that balcony?

CÆSAR. Forgive me, Rufio; and [*anxiously*] hurry them as much as—

He is interrupted by an outcry as of an old man in the extremity of misfortune. It draws near rapidly; and Theodotus rushes in, tearing his hair, and squeaking the most lamentable exclamations. Rufio steps back to stare at him, amazed at his frantic condition. Pothinus turns to listen.

THEODOTUS [*on the steps, with uplifted arms*] Horror unspeakable! Woe, alas! Help!

RUFIO. What now?

CÆSAR [*frowning*] Who is slain?

THEODOTUS. Slain! Oh, worse than the death of ten thousand men! Loss irreparable to mankind!

RUFIO. What has happened, man?

THEODOTUS [*rushing down the hall between them*] The fire has spread from your ships. The first of the seven wonders of the world perishes. The library of Alexandria is in flames.

RUFIO. Psha! [*Quite relieved, he goes up to the loggia and watches the preparations of the troops on the beach*].

CÆSAR. Is that all?

THEODOTUS [*unable to believe his senses*] All! Cæsar: will you go down to posterity as a barbarous soldier too ignorant to know the value of books?

CÆSAR. Theodotus: I am an author myself; and I tell you it is better that the Egyptians should live their lives than dream them away with the help of books.

THEODOTUS [*kneeling, with genuine literary emotion: the passion of the pedant*] Cæsar: once in ten generations of men, the world gains an immortal book.

CÆSAR [*inflexible*] If it did not flatter mankind, the common executioner would burn it.

THEODOTUS. Without history, death will lay you beside your meanest soldier.

CÆSAR. Death will do that in any case. I ask no better grave.

THEODOTUS. What is burning there is the memory of mankind.

CÆSAR. A shameful memory. Let it burn.

THEODOTUS [*wildly*] Will you destroy the past?

CÆSAR. Ay, and build the future with its ruins. [*Theodotus, in despair, strikes himself on the temples with his fists*]. But harken, Theodotus, teacher of kings: you who valued Pompey's head no more than a shepherd values an onion, and who now kneel to me, with tears in your old eyes, to plead for a few sheepskins scrawled with errors. I cannot spare you a man or a bucket of water just now; but you shall pass freely out of the palace. Now, away with you to Achillas; and borrow his legions to put out the fire. [*He hurries him to the steps*].

POTHINUS [*significantly*] You understand, Theodotus: I remain a prisoner.

THEODOTUS. A prisoner!

CÆSAR. Will you stay to talk whilst the memory of mankind is burning? [*Calling through the loggia*] Ho there! Pass Theodotus out. [*To Theodotus*] Away with you.

THEODOTUS [*To Pothinus*] I must go to save the library. [*He hurries out*].

CÆSAR. Follow him to the gate, Pothinus. Bid him urge your people to kill no more of my soldiers, for your sake.

POTHINUS. My life will cost you dear if you take it, Cæsar. [*He goes out after Theodotus*].

Rufio, absorbed in watching the embarkation, does not notice the departure of the two Egyptians.

RUFIO [*shouting from the loggia to the beach*] All ready, there?

A CENTURION [*from below*] All ready. We wait for Cæsar.

CÆSAR. Tell them Cæsar is coming—the rogues! [*Calling*] Britannicus. [*This magniloquent version of his secretary's name is one of Cæsar's jokes. In later years it would have meant, quite seriously and officially, Conqueror of Britain*].

RUFIO [*calling down*] Push off, all except the longboat. Stand by it to embark, Cæsar's guard there. [*He leaves the balcony and comes down into the hall*]. Where are those Egyptians? Is this more clemency? Have you let them go?

CÆSAR [*chuckling*] I have let Theodotus go to save the library. We must respect literature, Rufio.

RUFIO [*raging*] Folly on folly's head! I believe if you could bring back all the dead of Spain, Gaul, and Thessaly to life, you would do it that we might have the trouble of fighting them over again.

CÆSAR. Might not the gods destroy the world if their only thought were to be at peace next year? [*Rufio, out of all patience, turns away in anger. Cæsar suddenly grips his sleeve, and adds slyly in his ear*] Besides, my friend: every Egyptian we imprison means imprisoning two Roman soldiers to guard him. Eh?

RUFIO. Agh! I might have known there was some fox's trick behind your fine talking. [*He gets away from Cæsar with an ill-humored shrug, and goes to the balcony for another look at the preparations; finally goes out*].

CÆSAR. Is Britannus asleep? I sent him for my armor an hour ago. [*Calling*] Britannicus, thou British islander. Britannicus!

Cleopatra runs in through the loggia with Cæsar's helmet and sword, snatched from Britannus, who follows her with a cuirass and greaves. They come down to Cæsar, she to his left hand, Britannus to his right.

CLEOPATRA. I am going to dress you, Cæsar. Sit down. [*He obeys*]. These Roman helmets are so becoming! [*She takes off his wreath*]. Oh! [*She bursts out laughing at him*].

CÆSAR. What are you laughing at?

CLEOPATRA. Youre bald [*beginning with a big B, and ending with a splutter*].

CÆSAR [*almost annoyed*] Cleopatra! [*He rises, for the convenience of Britannus, who puts the cuirass on him*].

CLEOPATRA. So that is why you wear the wreath—to hide it.

BRITANNUS. Peace, Egyptian: they are the bays of the conqueror. [*He buckles the cuirass*].

CLEOPATRA. Peace, thou: islander! [*To Cæsar*] You should rub your head with strong spirits of sugar, Cæsar. That will make it grow.

CÆSAR [*with a wry face*] Cleopatra: do you like to be reminded that you are very young?

CLEOPATRA [*pouting*] No.

CÆSAR [*sitting down again, and setting out his leg for Britannus, who kneels to put on his greaves*] Neither do I like to be reminded that I am—middle aged. Let me give you ten of my superfluous years. That will make you 26, and leave me only—no matter. Is it a bargain?

CLEOPATRA. Agreed. 26, mind. [*She puts the helmet on him*]. Oh! How nice! You look only about 50 in it!

BRITANNUS [*looking up severely at Cleopatra*] You must not speak in this manner to Cæsar.

CLEOPATRA. Is it true that when Cæsar caught you on that island, you were painted all over blue?

BRITANNUS. Blue is the color worn by all Britons of good standing. In war we stain our bodies blue; so that though our enemies may strip us of our clothes and our lives, they cannot strip us of our respectability. [*He rises*].

CLEOPATRA [*with Cæsar's sword*] Let me hang this on. Now you look spendid. Have they made any statues of you in Rome?

CÆSAR. Yes, many statues.

CLEOPATRA. You must send for one and give it to me.

RUFIO [*coming back into the loggia, more impatient than ever*] Now Cæsar: have you done talking? The moment your foot is aboard there will be no holding our men back: the boats will race one another for the lighthouse.

CÆSAR [*drawing his sword and trying the edge*] Is this well set today, Britannicus? At Pharsalia it was as blunt as a barrel-hoop.

BRITANNUS. It will split one of the Egyptian's hairs today, Cæsar. I have set it myself.

CLEOPATRA [*suddenly throwing her arms in terror round Cæsar*] Oh, you are not really going into battle to be killed?

CÆSAR. No, Cleopatra. No man goes to battle to be killed.

CLEOPATRA. But they do get killed. My sister's husband was killed in battle. You must not go. Let him go [*pointing to Rufio. They all laugh at her*]. Oh please, please dont go. What will happen to me if you never come back?

CÆSAR [*gravely*] Are you afraid?

CLEOPATRA [*shrinking*] No.

CÆSAR [*with quiet authority*] Go to the balcony; and you shall see us take the Pharos. You must learn to look on battles. Go. [*She goes, downcast, and looks out from the balcony*]. That is well. Now, Rufio. March.

CLEOPATRA [*suddenly clapping her hands*] Oh, you will not be able to go!

CÆSAR. Why? What now?

CLEOPATRA. They are drying up the harbor with buckets—a multitude of soldiers—over there [*pointing out across the sea to her left*]—they are dipping up the water.

RUFIO [*hastening to look*] It is true. The Egyptian army! Crawling over the edge of the west harbor like locusts. [*With sudden anger he strides down to Cæsar*]. This is your accursed clemency, Cæsar. Theodotus has brought them.

CÆSAR [*delighted at his own cleverness*] I meant him to, Rufio. They have come to put out the fire. The library will keep them busy whilst we seize the lighthouse. Eh? [*He rushes out buoyantly through the loggia, followed by Britannus*].

RUFIO [*disgustedly*] More foxing! Agh! [*He rushes off. A shout from the soldiers announces the appearance of Cæsar below*].

CENTURION [*below*] All aboard. Give way there. [*Another shout*].

CLEOPATRA [*waving her scarf through the loggia arch*] Goodbye, goodbye, dear Cæsar. Come back safe. Goodbye!

ACT III

The edge of the quay in front of the palace, looking out west over the east harbor of Alexandria to Pharos island, just off the end of which, and connected with it by a narrow mole, is the famous lighthouse, a gigantic square tower of white marble diminishing in size storey by storey to the top, on which stands a cresset beacon. The island is joined to the main land by the Heptastadium, a great mole or causeway five miles long bounding the harbor on the south.

In the middle of the quay a Roman sentinel stands on guard, pilum in hand, looking out to the lighthouse with strained attention, his left hand shading his eyes. The pilum is a stout wooden shaft 4½ feet long, with an iron spit about three feet long fixed to it. The sentinel is so absorbed that he does not notice the approach from the north end of the quay of four Egyptian market porters carrying rolls of carpet, preceded by Ftatateeta and Apollodorus the Sicilian. Apollodorus is a dashing young man of about 24, handsome and debonair, dressed with deliberate æstheticism in the most delicate purples and dove greys, with ornaments of bronze, oxydized silver, and stones of jade and agate. His sword, designed as carefully as a medieval cross, has a blued blade shewing through an openwork scabbard of purple leather and filagree. The porters, conducted by Ftatateeta, pass along the quay behind the sentinel to the steps of the palace, where they put down their bales and squat on the ground. Apollodorus does not pass along with them: he halts, amused by the preoccupation of the sentinel.

APOLLODORUS [*calling to the sentinel*] Who goes there, eh?

SENTINEL [*starting violently and turning with his pilum at the charge, revealing himself as a small, wiry, sandy-haired, conscientious young man with an elderly face*] Whats this? Stand. Who are you?

APOLLODORUS. I am Apollodorus the Sicilian. Why, man, what are you dreaming of? Since I came through the lines beyond the theatre there, I have brought my caravan past three sentinels, all so busy staring at the lighthouse that not one of them challenged me. Is this Roman discipline?

SENTINEL. We are not here to watch the land but the sea. Cæsar has just landed on the Pharos. [*Looking at Ftatateeta*] What have you here? Who is this piece of Egyptian crockery?

FTATATEETA. Apollodorus: rebuke this Roman dog; and bid him bridle his tongue in the presence of Ftatateeta, the mistress of the Queen's household.

APOLLODORUS. My friend: this is a great lady, who stands high with Cæsar.

SENTINEL [*not at all impressed, pointing to the carpets*] And what is all this truck?

APOLLODORUS. Carpets for the furnishing of the Queen's apartments in the palace. I have picked them from the best carpets in the world; and the Queen shall choose the best of my choosing.

SENTINEL. So you are the carpet merchant?

APOLLODORUS [*hurt*] My friend: I am a patrician.

SENTINEL. A patrician! A patrician keeping a shop instead of following arms!

APOLLODORUS. I do not keep a shop. Mine is a temple of the arts. I am a worshipper of beauty. My calling is to choose beautiful things for beautiful queens. My motto is Art for Art's sake.

SENTINEL. That is not the password.

APOLLODORUS. It is a universal password.

SENTINEL. I know nothing about universal passwords. Either give me the password for the day or get back to your shop.

Ftatateeta, roused by his hostile tone, steals towards the edge of the quay with the step of a panther, and gets behind him.

APOLLODORUS. How if I do neither?

SENTINEL. Then I will drive this pilum through you.

APOLLODORUS. At your service, my friend. [*He draws his sword, and springs to his guard with unruffled grace*].

FTATATEETA [*suddenly seizing the sentinel's arms from behind*] Thrust your knife into the dog's throat, Apollodorus. [*The chivalrous Apollodorus laughingly shakes his head; breaks ground away from the sentinel towards the palace; and lowers his point*].

SENTINEL [*struggling vainly*] Curse on you! Let me go. Help ho!

FTATATEETA [*lifting him from the ground*] Stab the little Roman reptile. Spit him on your sword.

A couple of Roman soldiers, with a centurion, come running along the edge of the quay from the north end. They rescue their comrade, and throw off Ftatateeta, who is sent reeling away on the left hand of the sentinel.

CENTURION [*an unattractive man of fifty, short in his speech and manners, with a vinewood cudgel in his hand*] How now? What is all this?

FTATATEETA [*to Apollodorus*] Why did you not stab him? There was time?

APOLLODORUS. Centurion: I am here by order of the Queen to—

CENTURION [*interrupting him*] The Queen! Yes, yes: [*to the sentinel*] pass him in. Pass all these bazaar people in to the Queen, with their goods. But mind you pass no one out that you have not passed in—not even the Queen herself.

SENTINEL. This old woman is dangerous: she is as strong as three men. She wanted the merchant to stab me.

APOLLODORUS. Centurion: I am not a merchant. I am a patrician and a votary of art.

CENTURION. Is the woman your wife?

APOLLODORUS [*horrified*] No no! [*Correcting himself politely*] Not that the lady is not a striking figure in her own way. But [*emphatically*] she is n o t my wife.

FTATATEETA [*to the centurion*] Roman: I am Ftatateeta, the mistress of the Queen's household.

CENTURION. Keep your hands off our men, mistress; or I will have you pitched into the harbor, though you were as strong as ten men. [*To his men*] To your posts: march! [*He returns with his men the way they came*].

FTATATEETA [*looking malignantly after him*] We shall see whom Isis loves best: her servant Ftatateeta or a dog of a Roman.

SENTINEL [*to Apollodorus, with a wave of his pilum towards the palace*] Pass in there; and keep your distance. [*Turning to Ftatateeta*] Come within a yard of me, you old crocodile; and I will give you this [*the pilum*] in your jaws.

CLEOPATRA [*calling from the palace*] Ftatateeta, Ftatateeta.

FTATATEETA [*looking up, scandalized*] Go from the window, go from the window. There are men here.

CLEOPATRA. I am coming down.

FTATATEETA [*distracted*] No, no. What are you dreaming of? O ye gods, ye gods! Apollodorus: bid your men pick up your bales; and in with me quickly.

APOLLODORUS. Obey the mistress of the Queen's household.

FTATATEETA [*impatiently, as the porters stoop to lift the bales*] Quick, quick: she will be out upon us. [*Cleopatra comes from the palace and runs across the quay to Ftatateeta*]. Oh that ever I was born!

CLEOPATRA [*eagerly*] Ftatateeta: I have thought of something. I want a boat—at once.

FTATATEETA. A boat! No, no: you cannot. Apollodorus: speak to the Queen.

APOLLODORUS [*gallantly*] Beautiful queen: I am Apollodorus the Sicilian, your servant, from the bazaar. I have brought you the three most beautiful Persian carpets in the world to choose from.

CLEOPATRA. I have no time for carpets today. Get me a boat.

FTATATEETA. What whim is this? You cannot go on the water except in the royal barge.

APOLLODORUS. Royalty, Ftatateeta, lies not in the barge but in the Queen. [*To Cleopatra*] The touch of your majesty's foot on the gunwale of the meanest boat in the harbor will make it royal. [*He turns to the harbor and calls seaward*] Ho there, boatman! Pull in to the steps.

CLEOPATRA. Apollodorus: you are my perfect knight; and I will always buy my carpets through you. [*Apollodorus bows joyously. An oar appears above the quay; and the boatman, a bullet-headed, vivacious, grinning fellow, burnt almost black by the sun, comes up a flight of steps from the water on the sentinel's right, oar in hand, and waits at the top*]. Can you row, Apollodorus?

APOLLODORUS. My oars shall be your majesty's wings. Whither shall I row my Queen?

CLEOPATRA. To the lighthouse. Come. [*She makes for the steps*].

SENTINEL [*opposing her with his pilum at the charge*] Stand. You cannot pass.

CLEOPATRA [*flushing angrily*] How dare you? Do you know that I am the Queen?

SENTINEL. I have my orders. You cannot pass.

CLEOPATRA. I will make Cæsar have you killed if you do not obey me.

SENTINEL. He will do worse to me if I disobey my officer. Stand back.

CLEOPATRA. Ftatateeta: strangle him.

SENTINEL [*alarmed—looking apprehensively at Ftatateeta, and brandishing his pilum*] Keep off, there.

CLEOPATRA [*running to Apollodorus*] Apollodorus: make your slaves help us.

APOLLODORUS. I shall not need their help, lady. [*He draws his sword*].

Now, soldier: choose which weapon you will defend yourself with. Shall it be sword against pilum, or sword against sword?

SENTINEL. Roman against Sicilian, curse you. Take that. [*He hurls his pilum at Apollodorus, who drops expertly on one knee. The pilum passes whizzing over his head and falls harmless. Apollodorus, with a cry of triumph, springs up and attacks the sentinel, who draws his sword and defends himself, crying*] Ho there, guard. Help!

Cleopatra, half frightened, half delighted, takes refuge near the palace, where the porters are squatting among the bales. The boatman, alarmed, hurries down the steps out of harm's way, but stops, with his head just visible above the edge of the quay, to watch the fight. The sentinel is handicapped by his fear of an attack in the rear from Ftatateeta. His swordsmanship, which is of a rough and ready sort, is heavily taxed, as he has occasionally to strike at her to keep her off between a blow and a guard with Apollodorus. The centurion returns with several soldiers. Apollodorus springs back towards Cleopatra as this reinforcement confronts him.

CENTURION [*coming to the sentinel's right hand*] What is this? What now?

SENTINEL [*panting*] I could do well enough by myself if it werent for the old woman. Keep her off me: that is all the help I need.

CENTURION. Make your report, soldier. What has happened?

FTATATEETA. Centurion: he would have slain the Queen.

SENTINEL [*bluntly*] I would, sooner than let her pass. She wanted to take boat, and go—so she said—to the lighthouse. I stopped her, as I was ordered to; and she set this fellow on me. [*He goes to pick up his pilum and returns to his place with it*].

CENTURION [*turning to Cleopatra*] Cleopatra: I am loth to offend you; but without Cæsar's express order we dare not let you pass beyond the Roman lines.

APOLLODORUS. Well, Centurion; and has not the lighthouse been within the Roman lines since Cæsar landed there?

CLEOPATRA. Yes, yes. Answer that, if you can.

CENTURION [*to Apollodorus*] As for you, Apollodorus, you may thank the gods that you are not nailed to the palace door with a pilum for your meddling.

APOLLODORUS [*urbanely*] My military friend, I was not born to be slain by so ugly a weapon. When I fall, it will be [*holding up his sword*] by this white queen of arms, the only weapon fit for an artist. And now that you are convinced that we do not want to go beyond the lines, let me finish killing your sentinel and depart with the Queen.

CENTURION [*as the sentinel makes an angry demonstration*] Peace there. Cleopatra: I must abide by my orders, and not by the subtleties of this Sicilian. You must withdraw into the palace and examine your carpets there.

CLEOPATRA [*pouting*] I will not: I am the Queen. Cæsar does not speak to me as you do. Have Cæsar's centurions changed manners with his scullions?

CENTURION [*sulkily*] I do my duty. That is enough for me.

APOLLODORUS. Majesty: when a stupid man is doing something he is ashamed of, he always declares that it is his duty.

CENTURION [*angry*] Apollodorus—

APOLLODORUS [*interrupting him with defiant elegance*] I will make amends for that insult with my sword at fitting time and place. Who says artist, says duellist. [*To Cleopatra*] Hear my counsel, star of the east. Until word comes to these soldiers from Cæsar himself, you are a prisoner. Let me go to him with a message from you, and a present; and before the sun has stooped half way to the arms of the sea, I will bring you back Cæsar's order of release.

CENTURION [*sneering at him*] And you will sell the Queen the present, no doubt.

APOLLODORUS. Centurion: the Queen shall have from me, without payment, as the unforced tribute of Sicilian taste to Egyptian beauty, the richest of these carpets for her present to Cæsar.

CLEOPATRA [*exultantly, to the centurion*] Now you see what an ignorant common creature you are!

CENTURION [*curtly*] Well, a fool and his wares are soon parted. [*He turns to his men*]. Two more men to this post here? and see that no one leaves the palace but this man and his merchandize. If he draws his sword again inside the lines, kill him. To your posts. March.

He goes out, leaving two auxiliary sentinels with the other.

APOLLODORUS [*with polite goodfellowship*] My friends: will you not enter the palace and bury our quarrel in a bowl of wine? [*He takes out his purse, jingling the coins in it*]. The Queen has presents for you all.

SENTINEL [*very sulky*] You heard our orders. Get about your business.

FIRST AUXILIARY. Yes: you ought to know better. Off with you.

SECOND AUXILIARY [*looking longingly at the purse—this sentinel is a *hooknosed man, unlike his comrade, who is squab faced*] Do not tantalize a poor man.

APOLLODORUS [*to Cleopatra*] Pearl of Queens: the centurion is at hand; and the Roman soldier is incorruptible when his officer is looking. I must carry your word to Cæsar.

CLEOPATRA [*who has been meditating among the carpets*] Are these carpets very heavy?

APOLLODORUS. It matters not how heavy. There are plenty of porters.

CLEOPATRA. How do they put the carpets into boats? Do they throw them down?

APOLLODORUS. Not into small boats, majesty. It would sink them.

CLEOPATRA. Not into that man's boat, for instance? [*pointing to the boatman*].

APOLLODORUS. No. Too small.

CLEOPATRA. But you can take a carpet to Cæsar in it if I send one?

APOLLODORUS. Assuredly.

CLEOPATRA. And you will have it carried gently down the steps and take great care of it?

APOLLODORUS. Depend on me.

CLEOPATRA. Great, g r e a t care?

APOLLODORUS. More than of my own body.

CLEOPATRA. You will promise me not to let the porters drop it or throw it about?

APOLLODORUS. Place the most delicate glass goblet in the palace in the heart of the roll, Queen; and if it be broken, my head shall pay for it.

CLEOPATRA. Good. Come, Ftatateeta. [*Ftatateeta comes to her. Apollodorus offers to squire them into the palace*]. No, Apollodorus, you must not come. I will choose a carpet for myself. You must wait here. [*She runs into the palace*].

APOLLODORUS [*to the porters*] Follow this lady [*indicating Ftatateeta*] and obey her.

The porters rise and take up their bales.

FTATATEETA [*addressing the porters as if they were vermin*] This way. And take your shoes off before you put your feet on those stairs.

She goes in, followed by the porters with the carpets. Meanwhile Apollodorus goes to the edge of the quay and looks out over the harbor. The sentinels keep their eyes on him malignantly.

APOLLODORUS [*addressing the sentinel*] My friend—

SENTINEL [*rudely*] Silence there.

FIRST AUXILIARY. Shut your muzzle, you.

SECOND AUXILIARY [*in a half whisper, glancing apprehensively towards the north end of the quay*] Cant you wait a bit?

APOLLODORUS. Patience, worthy three-headed donkey. [*They mutter ferociously; but he is not at all intimidated*]. Listen: were you set here to watch me, or to watch the Egyptians?

SENTINEL. We know our duty.

APOLLODORUS. Then why dont you do it? There is something going on over there [*pointing southwestward to the mole*].

SENTINEL [*sulkily*] I do not need to be told what to do by the likes of you.

APOLLODORUS. Blockhead. [*He begins shouting*] Ho there, Centurion, Hoiho!

SENTINEL. Curse your meddling. [*Shouting*] Hoiho! Alarm! Alarm!

FIRST AND SECOND AUXILIARIES. Alarm! alarm! Hoiho!

The Centurion comes running in with his guard.

CENTURION. What now? Has the old woman attacked you again? [*Seeing Apollodorus*] Are you here still?

APOLLODORUS [*pointing as before*] See there. The Egyptians are moving. They are going to recapture the Pharos. They will attack by sea and land: by land along the great mole; by sea from the west harbor. Stir yourselves, my military friends: the hunt is up. [*A clangor of trumpets from several points along the quay*]. Aha! I told you so.

CENTURION [*quickly*] The two extra men pass the alarm to the south posts. One man keep guard here. The rest with me—quick.

The two auxiliary sentinels run off to the south. The centurion and his guard run off northward; and immediately afterwards the bucina sounds. The four porters come from the palace carrying a carpet, followed by Ftatateeta.

SENTINEL [*handling his pilum apprehensively*] You again! [*The porters stop*].

FTATATEETA. Peace, Roman fellow: you are now single-handed. Apollodorus: this carpet is Cleopatra's present to Cæsar. It has rolled up in it ten precious goblets of the thinnest Iberian crystal, and a hundred eggs of the sacred blue pigeon. On your honor, let not one of them be broken.

APOLLODORUS. On my head be it! [*To the porters*] Into the boat with them carefully.

The porters carry the carpet to the steps.

FIRST PORTER [*looking down at the boat*] Beware what you do, sir.

Those eggs of which the lady speaks must weigh more than a pound apiece. This boat is too small for such a load.

BOATMAN [*excitedly rushing up the steps*] Oh thou injurious porter! Oh thou unnatural son of a she-camel! [*To Apollodorus*] My boat, sir, hath often carried five men. Shall it not carry your lordship and a bale of pigeon's eggs? [*To the porter*] Thou mangey dromedary, the gods shall punish thee for this envious wickedness.

FIRST PORTER [*stolidly*] I cannot quit this bale now to beat thee; but another day I will lie in wait for thee.

APOLLODORUS [*going between them*] Peace there. If the boat were but a single plank, I would get to Cæsar on it.

FTATATEETA [*anxiously*] In the name of the gods, Apollodorus, run no risks with that bale.

APOLLODORUS. Fear not, thou venerable grotesque: I guess its great worth. [*To the porters*] Down with it, I say; and gently; or ye shall eat nothing but stick for ten days.

The boatman goes down the steps, followed by the porters with the bale: Ftatateeta and Apollodorus watching from the edge.

APOLLODORUS. Gently, my sons, my children—[*with sudden alarm*] gently, ye dogs. Lay it level in the stern—so—tis well.

FTATATEETA [*screaming down at one of the porters*] Do not step on it, do not step on it. Oh thou brute beast!

FIRST PORTER [*ascending*] Be not excited, mistress: all is well.

FTATATEETA [*panting*] All well! Oh, thou hast given my heart a turn! [*She clutches her side, gasping*].

The four porters have now come up and are waiting at the stairhead to be paid.

APOLLODORUS. Here, ye hungry ones. [*He gives money to the first porter, who holds it in his hand to shew to the others. They crowd greedily to see how much it is, quite prepared, after the Eastern fashion, to protest to heaven against their patron's stinginess. But his liberality overpowers them*].

FIRST PORTER. O bounteous prince!

SECOND PORTER. O lord of the bazaar!

THIRD PORTER. O favored of the gods!

FOURTH PORTER. O father to all the porters of the market!

SENTINEL [*enviously, threatening them fiercely with his pilum*] Hence, dogs: off. Out of this. [*They fly before him northward along the quay*].

APOLLODORUS. Farewell, Ftatateeta. I shall be at the lighthouse before the Egyptians. [*He descends the steps*].

FTATATEETA. The gods speed thee and protect my nursling!

The sentry returns from chasing the porters and looks down at the boat, standing near the stairhead lest Ftatateeta should attempt to escape.

APOLLODORUS [*from beneath, as the boat moves off*] Farewell, valiant pilum pitcher.

SENTINEL. Farewell, shopkeeper.

APOLLODORUS. Ha, ha! Pull, thou brave boatman, pull. Soho-o-o-o-o! [*He begins to sing in barcarolle measure to the rhythm of the oars*]

> My heart, my heart, spread out thy wings:
> Shake off thy heavy load of love—

Give me the oars, O son of a snail.

SENTINEL [*threatening Ftatateeta*] Now mistress: back to your henhouse. In with you.

FTATATEETA [*falling on her knees and stretching her hands over the waters*] Gods of the seas, bear her safely to the shore!

SENTINEL. Bear w h o safely? What do you mean?

FTATATEETA [*looking darkly at him*] Gods of Egypt and of Vengeance, let this Roman fool be beaten like a dog by his captain for suffering her to be taken over the waters.

SENTINEL. Accursed one: is she then in the boat? [*He calls over the sea*] Hoiho, there, boatman! Hoiho!

APOLLODORUS [*singing in the distance*]

> My heart, my heart, be whole and free:
> Love is thine only enemy.

Meanwhile Rufio, the morning's fighting done, sits munching dates on a faggot of brushwood outside the door of the lighthouse, which towers gigantic to the clouds on his left. His helmet, full of dates, is between his knees; and a leathern bottle of wine is by his side. Behind him the great stone pedestal of the lighthouse is shut in from the open sea by a low stone parapet, with a couple of steps in the middle to the broad coping. A huge chain with a hook hangs down from the lighthouse crane above his head. Faggots like the one he sits on lie beneath it ready to be drawn up to feed the beacon.

Cæsar is standing on the step at the parapet looking out anxiously, evidently ill at ease. Britannus comes out of the lighthouse door.

RUFIO. Well, my British islander. Have you been up to the top?

BRITANNUS. I have. I reckon it at 200 feet high.

RUFIO. Anybody up there?

BRITANNUS. One elderly Tyrian to work the crane; and his son, a well conducted youth of 14.

RUFIO [*looking at the chain*] What! An old man and a boy work that! Twenty men, you mean.

BRITANNUS. Two only, I assure you. They have counterweights, and a machine with boiling water in it which I do not understand: it is not of British design. They use it to haul up barrels of oil and faggots to burn in the brazier on the roof.

RUFIO. But—

BRITANNUS. Excuse me: I came down because there are messengers coming along the mole to us from the island. I must see what their business is. [*He hurries out past the lighthouse*].

CÆSAR [*coming away from the parapet, shivering and out of sorts*] Rufio: this has been a mad expedition. We shall be beaten. I wish I knew how our men are getting on with that barricade across the great mole.

RUFIO [*angrily*] Must I leave my food and go starving to bring you a report?

CÆSAR [*soothing him nervously*] No, Rufio, no. Eat, my son, eat. [*He takes another turn, Rufio chewing dates meanwhile*]. The Egyptians cannot be such fools as not to storm the barricade and swoop down on us here before it is finished. It is the first time I have ever run an avoidable risk. I should not have come to Egypt.

RUFIO. An hour ago you were all for victory.

CÆSAR [*apologetically*] Yes: I was a fool—rash, Rufio—boyish.

RUFIO. Boyish! Not a bit of it. Here [*offering him a handful of dates*].

CÆSAR. What are these for?

RUFIO. To eat. Thats whats the matter with you. When a man comes to your age, he runs down before his midday meal. Eat and drink; and then have another look at our chances.

CÆSAR [*taking the dates*] My age! [*He shakes his head and bites a date*]. Yes, Rufio: I am an old man—worn out now—true, quite true. [*He gives way to melancholy contemplation, and eats another date*]. Achillas is still in his prime: Ptolemy is a boy. [*He eats another date, and plucks up a little*]. Well, every dog has his day; and I have had mine: I cannot complain. [*With sudden cheerfulness*] These dates are not bad, Rufio. [*Britannus returns, greatly excited, with a leathern bag. Cæsar is himself again in a moment*]. What now?

BRITANNUS [*triumphantly*] Our brave Rhodian mariners have captured a treasure. There! [*He throws the bag down at Cæsar's feet*]. Our enemies are delivered into our hands.

CÆSAR. In that bag?

BRITANNUS. Wait till you hear, Cæsar. This bag contains all the letters which have passed between Pompey's party and the army of occupation here.

CÆSAR. Well?

BRITANNUS [*impatient of Cæsar's slowness to grasp the situation*] Well, we shall now know who your foes are. The name of every man who has plotted against you since you crossed the Rubicon may be in these papers, for all we know.

CÆSAR. Put them in the fire.

BRITANNUS. Put them—[*he gasps*]!!!!

CÆSAR. In the fire. Would you have me waste the next three years of my life in proscribing and condemning men who will be my friends when I have proved that my friendship is worth more than Pompey's was—than Cato's is. O incorrigible British islander: am I a bull dog, to seek quarrels merely to shew how stubborn my jaws are?

BRITANNUS. But your honor—the honor of Rome—

CÆSAR. I do not make human sacrifices to my honor, as your Druids do. Since you will not burn these, at least I can drown them. [*He picks up the bag and throws it over the parapet into the sea*].

BRITANNUS. Cæsar: this is mere eccentricity. Are traitors to be allowed to go free for the sake of a paradox?

RUFIO [*rising*] Cæsar: when the islander has finished preaching, call me again. I am going to have a look at the boiling water machine. [*He goes into the lighthouse*].

BRITANNUS [*with genuine feeling*] O Cæsar, my great master, if I could but persuade you to regard life seriously, as men do in my country!

CÆSAR. Do they truly do so, Britannus?

BRITANNUS. Have you not been there? Have you not seen them? What Briton speaks as you do in your moments of levity? What Briton neglects to attend the services at the sacred grove? What Briton wears clothes of many colors as you do, instead of plain blue, as all solid, well esteemed men should? These are moral questions with us.

CÆSAR. Well, well, my friend: some day I shall settle down and have a blue toga, perhaps. Meanwhile, I must get on as best I can in my flippant Roman way. [*Apollodorus comes past the lighthouse*]. What now?

BRITANNUS [*turning quickly, and challenging the stranger with official haughtiness*] What is this? Who are you? How did you come here?

APOLLODORUS. Calm yourself, my friend: I am not going to eat you. I have come by boat, from Alexandria, with precious gifts for Cæsar.

CÆSAR. From Alexandria!

BRITANNUS [*severely*] That is Cæsar, sir.

RUFIO [*appearing at the lighthouse door*] Whats the matter now?

APOLLODORUS. Hail, great Cæsar! I am Apollodorus the Sicilian, an artist.

BRITANNUS. An artist! Why have they admitted this vagabond?

CÆSAR. Peace, man. Apollodorus is a famous patrician amateur.

BRITANNUS [*disconcerted*] I crave the gentleman's pardon. [*To Cæsar*] I understood him to say that he was a professional. [*Somewhat out of countenance, he allows Apollodorus to approach Cæsar, changing places with him. Rufio, after looking Apollodorus up and down with marked disparagement, goes to the other side of the platform*].

CÆSAR. You are welcome, Apollodorus. What is your business?

APOLLODORUS. First, to deliver to you a present from the Queen of Queens.

CÆSAR. Who is that?

APOLLODORUS. Cleopatra of Egypt.

CÆSAR [*taking him into his confidence in his most winning manner*] Apollodorus: this is no time for playing with presents. Pray you, go back to the Queen, and tell her that if all goes well I shall return to the palace this evening.

APOLLODORUS. Cæsar: I cannot return. As I approached the lighthouse, some fool threw a great leathern bag into the sea. It broke the nose of my boat; and I had hardly time to get myself and my charge to the shore before the poor little cockleshell sank.

CÆSAR. I am sorry, Apollodorus. The fool shall be rebuked. Well, well: what have you brought me? The Queen will be hurt if I do not look at it.

RUFIO. Have we time to waste on this trumpery? The Queen is only a child.

CÆSAR. Just so: that is why we must not disappoint her. What is the present, Apollodorus?

APOLLODORUS. Cæsar: it is a Persian carpet—a beauty! And in it are—so I am told—pigeons' eggs and crystal goblets and fragile precious things. I dare not for my head have it carried up that narrow ladder from the causeway.

RUFIO. Swing it up by the crane, then. We will send the eggs to the cook; drink our wine from the goblets; and the carpet will make a bed for Cæsar.

APOLLODORUS. The crane! Cæsar: I have sworn to tender this bale of carpet as I tender my own life.

CÆSAR [*cheerfully*] Then let them swing you up at the same time; and if the chain breaks, you and the pigeons' eggs will perish together. [*He goes to the chain and looks up along it, examining it curiously*].

APOLLODORUS [*to Britannus*] Is Cæsar serious?

BRITANNUS. His manner is frivolous because he is an Italian; but he means what he says.

APOLLODORUS. Serious or not, he spake well. Give me a squad of soldiers to work the crane.

BRITANNUS. Leave the crane to me. Go and await the descent of the chain.

APOLLODORUS. Good. You will presently see me there [*turning to them all and pointing with an eloquent gesture to the sky above the parapet*] rising like the sun with my treasure.

He goes back the way he came. Britannus goes into the lighthouse.

RUFIO [*ill-humoredly*] Are you really going to wait here for this foolery, Cæsar?

CÆSAR [*backing away from the crane as it gives signs of working*] Why not?

RUFIO. The Egyptians will let you know why not if they have the sense to make a rush from the shore end of the mole before our barricade is finished. And here we are waiting like children to see a carpet full of pigeons' eggs.

The chain rattles, and is drawn up high enough to clear the parapet. It then swings round out of sight behind the lighthouse.

CÆSAR. Fear not, my son Rufio. When the first Egyptian takes his first step along the mole, the alarm will sound; and we two will reach the barricade from our end before the Egyptians reach it from their end—we two, Rufio: I, the old man, and you, his biggest boy. And the old man will be there first. So peace; and give me some more dates.

APOLLODORUS [*from the causeway below*] Soho, haul away. So-ho-o-o-o! [*The chain is drawn up and comes round again from behind the lighthouse. Apollodorus is swinging in the air with his bale of carpet at the end of it. He breaks into song as he soars above the parapet*]

Aloft, aloft, behold the blue
That never shone in woman's eyes—

Easy there: stop her. [*He ceases to rise*]. Further round! [*The chain comes forward above the platform*].

RUFIO [*calling up*] Lower away there. [*The chain and its load begin to descend*].

APOLLODORUS [*calling up*] Gently—slowly—mind the eggs.

RUFIO [*calling up*] Easy there—slowly—slowly.

Apollodorus and the bale are deposited safely on the flags in the middle of the platform. Rufio and Cæsar help Apollodorus to cast off the chain from the bale.

RUFIO. Haul up.

The chain rises clear of their heads with a rattle. Britannus comes from the lighthouse and helps them to uncord the carpet.

APOLLODORUS [*when the cords are loose*] Stand off, my friends: let Cæsar see. [*He throws the carpet open*].

RUFIO. Nothing but a heap of shawls. Where are the pigeons' eggs?

APOLLODORUS. Approach, Cæsar; and search for them among the shawls.

RUFIO [*drawing his sword*] Ha, treachery! Keep back, Cæsar: I saw the shawl move: there is something alive there.

BRITANNUS [*drawing his sword*] It is a serpent.

APOLLODORUS. Dares Cæsar thrust his hand into the sack where the serpent moves?

RUFIO [*turning on him*] Treacherous dog—

CÆSAR. Peace. Put up your swords. Apollodorus: your serpent seems to breathe very regularly. [*He thrusts his hand under the shawls and draws out a bare arm*]. This is a pretty little snake.

RUFIO [*drawing out the other arm*] Let us have the rest of you.

They pull Cleopatra up by the wrists into a sitting position. Britannus, scandalized, sheathes his sword with a drive of protest.

CLEOPATRA [*gasping*] Oh, I'm smothered. Oh, Cæsar, a man stood on me in the boat; and a great sack of something fell upon me out of the sky; and then the boat sank; and then I was swung up into the air and bumped down.

CÆSAR [*petting her as she rises and takes refuge on his breast*] Well, never mind: here you are safe and sound at last.

RUFIO. Ay; and now that she is here, what are we to do with her?

BRITANNUS. She cannot stay here, Cæsar, without the companionship of some matron.

CLEOPATRA [*jealously, to Cæsar, who is obviously perplexed*] Arnt you glad to see me?

CÆSAR. Yes, yes; *I* am very glad. But Rufio is very angry; and Britannus is shocked.

CLEOPATRA [*contemptuously*] You can have their heads cut off, can you not?

CÆSAR. They would not be so useful with their heads cut off as they are now, my sea bird.

RUFIO [*to Cleopatra*] We shall have to go away presently and cut some of your Egyptians' heads off. How will you like being left here with the chance of being captured by that little brother of yours if we are beaten?

CLEOPATRA. But you mustnt leave me alone. Cæsar: you will not leave me alone, will you?

RUFIO. What! not when the trumpet sounds and all our lives depend on Cæsar's being at the barricade before the Egyptians reach it? Eh?

CLEOPATRA. Let them lose their lives: they are only soldiers.

CÆSAR [*gravely*] Cleopatra: when that trumpet sounds, we must take every man his life in his hand, and throw it in the face of Death. And of my soldiers who have trusted me there is not one whose hand I shall not hold more sacred than your head. [*Cleopatra is overwhelmed. Her eyes fill with tears*]. Apollodorus: you must take her back to the palace.

APOLLODORUS. Am I a dolphin, Cæsar, to cross the seas with young ladies on my back? My boat is sunk: all yours are either at the barricade or have returned to the city. I will hail one if I can: that is all I can do. [*He goes back to the causeway*].

CLEOPATRA [*struggling with her tears*] It does not matter. I will not go back. Nobody cares for me.

CÆSAR. Cleopatra—

CLEOPATRA. You want me to be killed.

CÆSAR [*still more gravely*] My poor child: your life matters little here to anyone but yourself. [*She gives way altogether at this, casting herself down on the faggots weeping. Suddenly a great tumult is heard in the distance, bucinas and trumpets sounding through a storm of shout-*

ing. Britannus rushes to the parapet and looks along the mole. Cæsar and Rufio turn to one another with quick intelligence].

CÆSAR. Come, Rufio.

CLEOPATRA [*scrambling to her knees and clinging to him*] No no. Do not leave me, Cæsar [*He snatches his skirt from her clutch*]. Oh!

BRITANNUS [*from the parapet*] Cæsar: we are cut off. The Egyptians have landed from the west harbor between us and the barricade!!!

RUFIO [*running to see*] Curses! It is true. We are caught like rats in a trap.

CÆSAR [*ruthfully*] Rufio, Rufio: my men at the barricade are between the sea party and the shore party. I have murdered them.

RUFIO [*coming back from the parapet to Cæsar's right hand*] Ay: that comes of fooling with this girl here.

APOLLODORUS [*coming up quickly from the causeway*] Look over the parapet, Cæsar.

CÆSAR. We have looked, my friend. We must defend ourselves here.

APOLLODORUS. I have thrown the ladder into the sea. They cannot get in without it.

RUFIO. Ay; and we cannot get out. Have you thought of that?

APOLLODORUS. Not get out! Why not? You have ships in the east harbor.

BRITANNUS [*hopefully, at the parapet*] The Rhodian galleys are standing in towards us already. [*Cæsar quickly joins Britannus at the parapet*].

RUFIO [*to Apollodorus, impatiently*] And by what road are we to walk to the galleys, pray?

APOLLODORUS [*with gay, defiant rhetoric*] By the road that leads everywhere—the diamond path of the sun and moon. Have you never seen the child's shadow play of The Broken Bridge? "Ducks and geese with ease get over"—eh? [*He throws away his cloak and cap, and binds his sword on his back*].

RUFIO. What are you talking about?

APOLLODORUS. I will shew you. [*Calling to Britannus*] How far off is the nearest galley?

BRITANNUS. Fifty fathom.

CÆSAR. No, no: they are further off than they seem in this clear air to your British eyes. Nearly quarter of a mile, Apollodorus.

APOLLODORUS. Good. Defend yourselves here until I send you a boat from that galley.

RUFIO. Have you wings, perhaps?

APOLLODORUS. Water wings, soldier. Behold!

He runs up the steps between Cæsar and Britannus to the coping of the parapet; springs into the air; and plunges head foremost into the sea.

CÆSAR [*like a schoolboy—wildly excited*] Bravo, bravo! [*Throwing off his cloak*] By Jupiter, I will do that too.

RUFIO [*seizing him*] You are mad. You shall not.

CÆSAR. Why not? Can I not swim as well as he?

RUFIO [*frantic*] Can an old fool dive and swim like a young one? He is twenty-five and you are fifty.

CÆSAR [*breaking loose from Rufio*] Old!!!

BRITANNUS [*shocked*] Rufio: you forget yourself.

CÆSAR. I will race you to the galley for a week's pay, father Rufio.

CLEOPATRA. But me! me!! me!!! what is to become of me?

CÆSAR. I will carry you on my back to the galley like a dolphin. Rufio: when you see me rise to the surface, throw her in: I will answer for her. And then in with you after her, both of you.

CLEOPATRA. No, no, NO. I shall be drowned.

BRITANNUS. Cæsar: I am a man and a Briton, not a fish. I must have a boat. I cannot swim.

CLEOPATRA. Neither can I.

CÆSAR [*to Britannus*] Stay here, then, alone, until I recapture the lighthouse: I will not forget you. Now, Rufio.

RUFIO. You have made up your mind to this folly?

CÆSAR. The Egyptians have made it up for me. What else is there to do? And mind where you jump: I do not want to get your fourteen stone in the small of my back as I come up. [*He runs up the steps and stands on the coping*].

BRITANNUS [*anxiously*] One last word, Cæsar. Do not let yourself be seen in the fashionable part of Alexandria until you have changed your clothes.

CÆSAR [*calling over the sea*] Ho, Apollodorus: [*he points skyward and quotes the barcaolle*]

The white upon the blue above—

APOLLODORUS [*swimming in the distance*]

Is purple on the green below—

CÆSAR [*exultantly*] Aha! [*He plunges into the sea*].

CLEOPATRA [*running excitedly to the steps*] Oh, let me see. He will be drowned [*Rufio seizes her*]—Ah—ah—ah—ah! [*He pitches her screaming into the sea. Rufio and Britannus roar with laughter*].

RUFIO [*looking down after her*] He has got her. [*To Britannus*] Hold the fort, Briton. Cæsar will not forget you. [*He springs off*].

BRITANNUS [*running to the steps to watch them as they swim*] All safe, Rufio?

RUFIO [*swimming*] All safe.

CÆSAR [*swimming further off*] Take refuge up there by the beacon; and pile the fuel on the trap door, Britannus.

BRITANNUS [*calling in reply*] I will first do so, and then commend myself to my country's gods. [*A sound of cheering from the sea. Britannus gives full vent to his excitement*]. The boat has reached him: Hip, hip, hip, hurrah!

ACT IV

Cleopatra's sousing in the east harbor of Alexandria was in October 48 B.C. *In March 47 she is passing the afternoon in her boudoir in the palace, among a bevy of her ladies, listening to a slave girl who is playing the harp in the middle of the room. The harpist's master, an old musician, with a lined face, prominent brows, white beard, moustache and eyebrows twisted and horned at the ends, and a consciously keen and pretentious expression, is squatting on the floor close to her on her right, watching her performance. Ftatateeta is in attendance near the door, in front of a group of female slaves. Except the harp player all are seated: Cleopatra in a chair opposite the door on the other side of the room; the rest on the ground. Cleopatra's ladies are all young, the most conspicuous being Charmian and Iras, her favorites. Charmian is a hatchet faced, terra cotta colored little goblin, swift in her movements, and neatly finished at the hands and feet. Iras is a plump, goodnatured creature, rather fatuous, with a profusion of red hair, and a tendency to giggle on the slightest provocation.*

CLEOPATRA. Can I—

FTATATEETA [*insolently, to the player*] Peace, thou! The Queen speaks. [*The player stops*].

CLEOPATRA [*to the old musician*] I want to learn to play the harp with my own hands. Cæsar loves music. Can you teach me?

MUSICIAN. Assuredly I and no one else can teach the queen. Have I not discovered the lost method of the ancient Egyptians, who could make a pyramid tremble by touching a bass string? All the other teachers are quacks: I have exposed them repeatedly.

CLEOPATRA. Good: you shall teach me. How long will it take?

MUSICIAN. Not very long: only four years. Your Majesty must first become proficient in the philosophy of Pythagoras.

CLEOPATRA. Has she [*indicating the slave*] become proficient in the philosophy of Pythagoras?

MUSICIAN. Oh, she is but a slave. She learns as a dog learns.

CLEOPATRA. Well, then, I will learn as a dog learns; for she plays better than you. You shall give me a lesson every day for a fortnight. [*The musician hastily scrambles to his feet and bows profoundly*]. After that, whenever I strike a false note you shall be flogged; and if I strike so many that there is not time to flog you, you shall be thrown into the Nile to feed the crocodiles. Give the girl a piece of gold; and send them away.

MUSICIAN [*much taken aback*] But true art will not be thus forced.

FTATATEETA [*pushing him out*] What is this? Answering the Queen, forsooth. Out with you.

He is pushed out by Ftatateeta, the girl following with her harp, amid the laughter of the ladies and slaves.

CLEOPATRA. Now, can any of you amuse me? Have you any stories or any news?

IRAS. Ftatateeta–

CLEOPATRA. Oh, Ftatateeta, Ftatateeta, always Ftatateeta. Some new tale to set me against her.

IRAS. No: this time Ftatateeta has been virtuous. [*All the ladies laugh –not the slaves*]. Pothinus has been trying to bribe her to let him speak with you.

CLEOPATRA [*wrathfully*] Ha! you all sell audiences with me, as if I saw whom you please, and not whom I please. I should like to know how much of her gold piece that harp girl will have to give up before she leaves the palace.

IRAS. We can easily find out that for you.

The ladies laugh.

CLEOPATRA [*frowning*] You laugh; but take care, take care. I will find out some day how to make myself served as Cæsar is served.

CHARMIAN. Old hooknose! [*They laugh again*].

CLEOPATRA [*revolted*] Silence. Charmian: do not you be a silly little Egyptian fool. Do you know why I allow you all to chatter impertinently just as you please, instead of treating you as Ftatateeta would treat you if she were Queen?

CHARMIAN. Because you try to imitate Cæsar in everything; and he lets everybody say what they please to him.

CLEOPATRA. No; but because I asked him one day why he did so; and he said "Let your women talk; and you will learn something from them." What have I to learn from them? I said, "What they are," said he; and oh! you should have seen his eye as he said it. You would have curled up, you shallow things. [*They laugh. She turns fiercely on Iras*]. At whom are you laughing–at me or at Cæsar?

IRAS. At Cæsar.

CLEOPATRA. If you were not a fool, you would laugh at me; and if you were not a coward you would not be afraid to tell me so. [*Ftatateeta returns*]. Ftatateeta: they tell me that Pothinus has offered you a bribe to admit him to my presence.

FTATATEETA [*protesting*] Now by my father's gods—

CLEOPATRA [*cutting her short despotically*] Have I not told you not to deny things? You would spend the day calling your father's gods to witness to your virtues if I let you. Go take the bribe; and bring in Pothinus. [*Ftatateeta is about to reply*]. Dont answer me. Go.

Ftatateeta goes out; and Cleopatra rises and begins to prowl to and fro between her chair and the door, meditating. All rise and stand.

IRAS [*as she reluctantly rises*] Heigho! I wish Cæsar were back in Rome.

CLEOPATRA [*threateningly*] It will be a bad day for you all when he goes. Oh, if I were not ashamed to let him see that I am as cruel at heart as my father, I would make you repent that speech! Why do you wish him away?

CHARMIAN. He makes you so terribly prosy and serious and learned and philosophical. It is worse than being religious, at our ages. [*The ladies laugh*].

CLEOPATRA. Cease that endless cackling, will you. Hold your tongues.

CHARMIAN [*with mock resignation*] Well, well: we must try to live up to Cæsar.

They laugh again. Cleopatra rages silently as she continues to prowl to and fro. Ftatateeta comes back with Pothinus, who halts on the threshold.

FTATATEETA [*at the door*] Pothinus craves the ear of the—

CLEOPATRA. There, there: that will do: let him come in. [*She resumes her seat. All sit down except Pothinus, who advances to the middle of the room. Ftatateeta takes her former place.*] Well, Pothinus, what is the latest news from your rebel friends?

POTHINUS [*haughtily*] I am no friend of rebellion. And a prisoner does not receive news.

CLEOPATRA. You are no more a prisoner than I am—than Cæsar is. These six months we have been besieged in this palace by my subjects. You are allowed to walk on the beach among the soldiers. Can I go further myself, or can Cæsar?

POTHINUS. You are but a child, Cleopatra, and do not understand these matters.

The ladies laugh. Cleopatra looks inscrutably at him.

CHARMIAN. I see you do not know the latest news, Pothinus.

POTHINUS. What is that?

CHARMIAN. That Cleopatra is no longer a child. Shall I tell you how to grow much older, and much, m u c h wiser in one day?

POTHINUS. I should prefer to grow wiser without growing older.

CHARMIAN. Well, go up to the top of the lighthouse; and get somebody to take you by the hair and throw you into the sea. [*The ladies laugh*].

CLEOPATRA. She is right, Pothinus: you will come to the shore with much conceit washed out of you. [*The ladies laugh. Cleopatra rises impatiently*]. Begone, all of you. I will speak with Pothinus alone. Drive them out, Ftatateeta. [*They run out laughing. Ftatateeta shuts the door on them*]. What are you waiting for?

FTATATEETA. It is not meet that the Queen remain alone with—

CLEOPATRA [*interrupting her*] Ftatateeta: must I sacrifice you to your father's gods to teach you that *I* am Queen of Egypt, and not you?

FTATATEETA [*indignantly*] You are like the rest of them. You want to be what these Romans call a New Woman. [*She goes out, banging the door*].

CLEOPATRA [*sitting down again*] Now, Pothinus: why did you bribe Ftatateeta to bring you hither?

POTHINUS [*studying her gravely*] Cleopatra: what they tell me is true. You are changed.

CLEOPATRA. Do you speak with Cæsar every day for six months: and y o u will be changed.

POTHINUS. It is the common talk that you are infatuated with this old man?

CLEOPATRA. Infatuated? What does that mean? Made foolish, is it not? Oh no: I wish I were.

POTHINUS. You wish you were made foolish! How so?

CLEOPATRA. When I was foolish, I did what I liked, except when Ftatateeta beat me; and even then I cheated her and did it by stealth. Now that Cæsar has made me wise, it is no use my liking or disliking: I do what must be done, and have no time to attend to myself. That is not happiness; but it is greatness. If Cæsar were gone, I think I could govern the Egyptians; for what Cæsar is to me, I am to the fools around me.

POTHINUS [*looking hard at her*] Cleopatra: this may be the vanity of youth.

CLEOPATRA. No, no: it is not that I am so clever, but that the others are so stupid.

POTHINUS [*musingly*] Truly, that is the great secret.

CLEOPATRA. Well, now tell me what you came to say?

POTHINUS [*embarrassed*] I! Nothing.

CLEOPATRA. Nothing!

POTHINUS. At least—to beg for my liberty: that is all.

CLEOPATRA. For that you would have knelt to Cæsar. No, Pothinus, you came with some plan that depended on Cleopatra being a little nursery kitten. Now that Cleopatra is a Queen, the plan is upset.

POTHINUS [*bowing his head submissively*] It is so.

CLEOPATRA [*exultant*] Aha!

POTHINUS [*raising his eyes keenly to hers*] Is Cleopatra then indeed a Queen, and no longer Cæsar's prisoner and slave?

CLEOPATRA. Pothinus: we are all Cæsar's slaves—all we in this land of Egypt—whether we will or no. And she who is wise enough to know this will reign when Cæsar departs.

POTHINUS. You harp on Cæsar's departure.

CLEOPATRA. What if I do?

POTHINUS. Does he not love you?

CLEOPATRA. Love me! Pothinus: Cæsar loves no one. Who are those we love? Only those whom we do not hate: all people are strangers and enemies to us except those we love. But it is not so with Cæsar. He has no hatred in him: he makes friends with everyone as he does with dogs and children. His kindness to me is a wonder: neither mother, father, nor nurse have ever taken so much care for me, or thrown open their thoughts to me so freely.

POTHINUS. Well: is not this love?

CLEOPATRA. What! when he will do as much for the first girl he meets on his way back to Rome? Ask his slave, Britannus: he has been just as good to him. Nay, ask his very horse! His kindness is not for anything in m e: it is in his own nature.

POTHINUS. But how can you be sure that he does not love you as men love women?

CLEOPATRA. Because I cannot make him jealous. I have tried.

POTHINUS. Hm! Perhaps I should have asked, then, do you love h i m?

CLEOPATRA. Can one love a god? Besides, I love another Roman: one whom I saw long before Cæsar—no god, but a man—one who can love and hate—one whom I can hurt and who would hurt me.

POTHINUS. Does Cæsar know this?

CLEOPATRA. Yes.

POTHINUS. And he is not angry?

CLEOPATRA. He promises to send him to Egypt to please me!

POTHINUS. I do not understand this man.

CLEOPATRA [*with superb contempt*] You understand Cæsar! How could you? [*Proudly*] I do—by instinct.

POTHINUS [*deferentially, after a moment's thought*] Your Majesty caused me to be admitted today. What message has the Queen for me?

CLEOPATRA. This. You think that by making my brother king, you will rule in Egypt, because you are his guardian and he is a little silly.

POTHINUS. The Queen is pleased to say so.

CLEOPATRA. The Queen is pleased to say this also. That Cæsar will eat up you, and Achillas, and my brother, as a cat eats up mice; and that he will put on this land of Egypt as a shepherd puts on his garment. And when he has done that, he will return to Rome, and leave Cleopatra here as his viceroy.

POTHINUS [*breaking out wrathfully*] That he shall never do. We have a thousand men to his ten; and we will drive him and his beggarly legions into the sea.

CLEOPATRA [*with scorn, getting up to go*] You rant like any common fellow. Go, then and marshal your thousands; and make haste; for Mithridates of Pergamos is at hand with reinforcements for Cæsar. Cæsar has held you at bay with two legions: we shall see what he will do with twenty.

POTHINUS. Cleopatra—

CLEOPATRA. Enough, enough: Cæsar has spoiled me for talking to weak things like you. [*She goes out. Pothinus, with a gesture of rage, is following, when Ftatateeta enters and stops him.*]

POTHINUS. Let me go forth from this hateful place.

FTATATEETA. What angers you?

POTHINUS. The curse of all the gods of Egypt be upon her! She has sold her country to the Roman, that she may buy it back from him with her kisses.

FTATATEETA. Fool: did she not tell you that she would have Cæsar gone?

POTHINUS. You listened?

FTATATEETA. I took care that some honest woman should be at hand whilst you were with her.

POTHINUS. Now by the gods—

FTATATEETA. Enough of your gods! Cæsar's gods are all powerful here. It is no use y o u coming to Cleopatra: you are only an Egyptian. She will not listen to any of her own race: she treats us all as children.

POTHINUS. May she perish for it!

FTATATEETA [*balefully*] May your tongue wither for that wish! Go! send for Lucius Septimius, the slayer of Pompey. He is a Roman: may be she will listen to him. Begone!

POTHINUS [*darkly*] I know to whom I must go now.

FTATATEETA [*suspiciously*] To whom, then?

POTHINUS. To a greater Roman than Lucius. And mark this, mistress. You thought, before Cæsar came, that Egypt should presently be ruled by you and your crew in the name of Cleopatra. I set myself against it—

FTATATEETA [*interrupting him—wrangling*] Ay; that it might be ruled by you and y o u r crew in the name of Ptolemy.

POTHINUS. Better me, or even you, than a woman with a Roman heart; and that is what Cleopatra is now become. Whilst I live, she shall never rule. So guide yourself accordingly. [*He goes out*].

It is by this time drawing on to dinner time. The table is laid on the roof of the palace; and thither Rufio is now climbing, ushered by a majestic palace official, wand of office in hand, and followed by a slave carrying an inlaid stool. After many stairs they emerge at last into a massive colonnade on the roof. Light curtains are drawn between the columns on the north and east to soften the westering sun. The official leads Rufio to one of these shaded sections. A cord for pulling the curtains apart hangs down between the pillars.

THE OFFICIAL [*bowing*] The Roman commander will await Cæsar here.

The slave sets down the stool near the southernmost column, and slips out through the curtains.

RUFIO [*sitting down, a little blown*] Pouf! That was a climb. How high have we come?

THE OFFICIAL. We are on the palace roof, O Beloved of Victory!

RUFIO. Good! the Beloved of Victory has no more stairs to get up.

A second official enters from the opposite end, walking backwards.

THE SECOND OFFICIAL. Cæsar approaches.

Cæsar, fresh from the bath, clad in a new tunic of purple silk, comes in, beaming and festive, followed by two slaves carrying a light couch, which is hardly more than an elaborately designed bench. They place it near the northmost of the two curtained columns. When this is done they slip out through the curtains; and the two officials, formally bowing, follow them. Rufio rises to receive Cæsar.

CÆSAR [*coming over to him*] Why, Rufio! [*Surveying his dress with an air of admiring astonishment*] A new baldrick! A new golden pommel to your sword! And you have had your hair cut! But not your beard—? impossible! [*He sniffs at Rufio's beard*]. Yes, perfumed, by Jupiter Olympus!

RUFIO [*growling*] Well: is it to please myself?

CÆSAR [*affectionately*] No, my son Rufio, but to please me—to celebrate my birthday.

RUFIO [*contemptuously*] Your birthday! You always have a birthday when there is a pretty girl to be flattered or an ambassador to be conciliated. We had seven of them in ten months last year.

CÆSAR [*contritely*] It is true, Rufio! I shall never break myself of these petty deceits.

RUFIO. Who is to dine with us—besides Cleopatra?

CÆSAR. Apollodorus the Sicilian.

RUFIO. That popinjay!

CÆSAR. Come! the popinjay is an amusing dog—tells a story; sings a song; and saves us the trouble of flattering the Queen. What does she care for old politicians and camp-fed bears like us? No: Apollodorus is good company, Rufio, good company.

RUFIO. Well, he can swim a bit and fence a bit: he might be worse, if he only knew how to hold his tongue.

CÆSAR. The gods forbid he should ever learn! Oh, this military life! this tedious, brutal life of action! That is the worst of us Romans: we are mere doers and drudgers: a swarm of bees turned into men. Give me a good talker—one with wit and imagination enough to live without continually doing something!

RUFIO. Ay! a nice time he would have of it with you when dinner was over! Have you noticed that I am before my time?

CÆSAR. Aha! I thought that meant something. What is it?

RUFIO. Can we be overheard here?

CÆSAR. Our privacy invites eavesdropping. I can remedy that. [*He claps his hands twice. The curtains are drawn, revealing the roof garden with a banqueting table set across in the middle for four persons, one at each end, and two side by side. The side next Cæsar and Rufio is blocked with golden wine vessels and basins. A gorgeous majordomo is superintending the laying of the table by a staff of slaves. The colonnade goes round the garden at both sides to the further end, where a gap in it, like a great gateway, leaves the view open to the sky beyond the western edge of the roof, except in the middle, where a life size image of Ra, seated on a huge plinth, towers up, with hawk head and crown of asp and disk. His altar, which stands at his feet, is a single white stone.*] Now everybody can see us, nobody will think of listening to us. [*He sits down on the bench left by the two slaves*].

RUFIO [*sitting down on his stool*] Pothinus wants to speak to you. I advise you to see him: there is some plotting going on here among the women.

CÆSAR. Who is Pothinus?

RUFIO. The fellow with hair like squirrel's fur—the little King's bear leader, whom you kept prisoner.

CÆSAR [*annoyed*] And has he not escaped?

RUFIO. No.

CÆSAR [*rising imperiously*] Why not? You have been guarding this man instead of watching the enemy. Have I not told you always to let prisoners escape unless there are special orders to the contrary? Are there not enough mouths to be fed without him?

RUFIO. Yes; and if you would have a little sense and let me cut his throat, you would save his rations. Anyhow, he w o n t escape. Three sentries have told him they would put a pilum through him if they saw him again. What more can they do? He prefers to stay and spy on us. So would I if I had to do with generals subject to fits of clemency.

CÆSAR [*resuming his seat, argued down*] Hm! And so he wants to see me.

RUFIO. Ay. I have brought him with me. He is waiting there [*jerking his thumb over his shoulder*] under guard.

CÆSAR. And you want me to see him?

RUFIO [*obstinately*] I dont want anything. I daresay you will do what you like. Dont put it on to me.

CÆSAR [*with an air of doing it expressly to indulge Rufio*] Well, well: let us have him.

RUFIO [*calling*] Ho there, guard! Release you man and send him up. [*Beckoning*]. Come along!

Pothinus enters and stops mistrustfully between the two, looking from one to the other.

CÆSAR [*graciously*] Ah, Pothinus! You are welcome. And what is the news this afternoon?

POTHINUS. Cæsar: I come to warn you of a danger, and to make you an offer.

CÆSAR. Never mind the danger. Make the offer.

RUFIO. Never mind the offer. Whats the danger?

POTHINUS. Cæsar: you think that Cleopatra is devoted to you.

CÆSAR [*gravely*] My friend: I already know what I think. Come to your offer.

POTHINUS. I will deal plainly. I know not by what strange gods you have been enabled to defend a palace and a few yards of beach against a city and an army. Since we cut you off from Lake Mareotis, and you dug wells in the salt sea sand and brought up buckets of fresh water from them, we have known that your gods are irresistible, and that you are a worker of miracles. I no longer threaten you—

RUFIO [*sarcastically*] Very handsome of you, indeed.

POTHINUS. So be it: you are the master. Our gods sent the north west winds to keep you in our hands; but you have been too strong for them.

CÆSAR [*gently urging him to come to the point*] Yes, yes, my friend. But what then?

RUFIO. Spit it out, man. What have you to say?

POTHINUS. I have to say that you have a traitress in your camp. Cleopatra—

THE MAJOR-DOMO [*at the table, announcing*] The Queen! [*Cæsar and Rufio rise*].

RUFIO [*aside to Pothinus*] You should have spat it out sooner, you fool. Now it is too late.

Cleopatra, in gorgeous raiment, enters in state through the gap in the colonnade, and comes down past the image of Ra and past the table to Cæsar. Her retinue, headed by Ftatateeta, joins the staff at the table. Cæsar gives Cleopatra his seat, which she takes.

CLEOPATRA [*quickly, seeing Pothinus*] What is h e doing here?

CÆSAR [*seating himself beside her, in the most amiable of tempers*] Just going to tell me something about you. You shall hear it. Proceed, Pothinus.

POTHINUS [*disconcerted*] Cæsar—[*he stammers*].

CÆSAR. Well, out with it.

POTHINUS. What I have to say is for your ear, not for the Queen's.

CLEOPATRA [*with subdued ferocity*] There are means of making you speak. Take care.

POTHINUS [*defiantly*] Cæsar does not employ those means.

CÆSAR. My friend: when a man has anything to tell in this world, the difficulty is not to make him tell it, but to prevent him from telling it too often. Let me celebrate my birthday by setting you free. Farewell: we shall not meet again.

CLEOPATRA [*angrily*] Cæsar: this mercy is foolish.

POTHINUS [*to Cæsar*] Will you not give me a private audience? Your life may depend on it. [*Cæsar rises loftily*].

RUFIO [*aside to Pothinus*] Ass! Now we shall have some heroics.

CÆSAR [*oratorically*] Pothinus—

RUFIO [*interrupting him*] Cæsar: the dinner will spoil if you begin preaching your favorite sermon about life and death.

CLEOPATRA [*priggishly*] Peace, Rufio. I desire to hear Cæsar.

RUFIO [*bluntly*] Your Majesty has heard it before. You repeated it to Apollodorus last week; and he thought it was all your own. [*Cæsar's dignity collapses. Much tickled, he sits down again and looks roguishly at Cleopatra, who is furious. Rufio calls as before*] Ho there, guard! Pass the prisoner out. He is released. [*To Pothinus*] Now off with you. You have lost your chance.

POTHINUS [*his temper overcoming his prudence*] I will speak.

CÆSAR [*to Cleopatra*] You see. Torture would not have wrung a word from him.

POTHINUS. Cæsar: you have taught Cleopatra the arts by which the Romans govern the world.

CÆSAR. Alas! they cannot even govern themselves. What then?

POTHINUS. What then? Are you so besotted with her beauty that you do not see that she is impatient to reign in Egypt alone, and that her heart is set on your departure?

CLEOPATRA [*rising*] Liar!

CÆSAR [*shocked*] What! Protestations! Contradictions!

CLEOPATRA [*ashamed, but trembling with suppressed rage*] No. I do not deign to contradict. Let him talk. [*She sits down again*].

POTHINUS. From her own lips I have heard it. You are to be her catspaw: you are to tear the crown from her brother's head and set it on her own, delivering us all into her hand—delivering yourself also. And then Cæsar can return to Rome, or depart through the gate of death, which is nearer and surer.

CÆSAR [*calmly*] Well, my friend; and is not this very natural?

POTHINUS [*astonished*] Natural! Then you do not resent treachery?

CÆSAR. Resent! O thou foolish Egyptian, what have I to do with resentment? Do I resent the wind when it chills me, or the night when it makes me stumble in the darkness? Shall I resent youth when it turns from age, and ambition when it turns from servitude? To tell me such a story as this is but to tell me that the sun will rise tomorrow.

CLEOPATRA [*unable to contain herself*] But it is false—false. I swear it.

CÆSAR. It is true, though you swore it a thousand times, and believed all you swore. [*She is convulsed with emotion. To screen her, he rises and takes Pothinus to Rufio, saying*] Come, Rufio: let us see Pothinus past the guard. I have a word to say to him. [*Aside to them*] We must give the Queen a moment to recover herself. [*Aloud*] Come. [*He takes Pothinus and Rufio out with him, conversing with them meanwhile*]. Tell your friends, Pothinus, that they must not think I am opposed to a reasonable settlement of the country's affairs—[*They pass out of hearing*].

CLEOPATRA [*in a stifled whisper*] Ftatateeta, Ftatateeta.

FTATATEETA [*hurrying to her from the table and petting her*] Peace, child: be comforted—

CLEOPATRA [*interrupting her*] Can they hear us?

FTATATEETA. No, dear heart, no.

CLEOPATRA. Listen to me. If he leaves the Palace alive, never see my face again.

FTATATEETA. He? Poth—

CLEOPATRA [*striking her on the mouth*] Strike his life out as I strike his name from your lips. Dash him down from the wall. Break him on the stones. Kill, kill, k i l l him.

FTATATEETA [*shewing all her teeth*] The dog shall perish.

CLEOPATRA. Fail in this, and you go out from before me for ever.

FTATATEETA [*resolutely*] So be it. You shall not see my face until his eyes are darkened.

Cæsar comes back, with Apollodorus, exquisitely dressed, and Rufio.

CLEOPATRA [*to Ftatateeta*] Come soon—soon. [*Ftatateeta turns her meaning eyes for a moment on her mistress; then goes grimly away past Ra and out. Cleopatra runs like a gazelle to Cæsar*] So you have come back to me, Cæsar. [*Caressingly*] I thought you were angry. Welcome, Apollodorus. [*She gives him her hand to kiss, with her other arm about Cæsar*].

APOLLODORUS. Cleopatra grows more womanly beautiful from week to week.

CLEOPATRA. Truth, Apollodorus?

APOLLODORUS. Far, far short of the truth! Friend Rufio threw a pearl into the sea: Cæsar fished up a diamond.

CÆSAR. Cæsar fished up a touch of rheumatism, my friend. Come: to dinner! to dinner! [*They move towards the table*].

CLEOPATRA [*skipping like a young fawn*] Yes, to dinner. I have ordered s u c h a dinner for you, Cæsar!

CÆSAR. Ay? What are we to have?

CLEOPATRA. Peacocks' brains.

CÆSAR [*as if his mouth watered*] Peacocks' brains, Apollodorus!

APOLLODORUS. Not for me. I prefer nightingales' tongues. [*He goes to one of the two covers set side by side*].

CLEOPATRA. Roast boar, Rufio!

RUFIO [*gluttonously*] Good! [*He goes to the seat next Apollodorus, on his left*].

CÆSAR [*looking at his seat, which is at the end of the table, to Ra's left hand*] What has become of my leathern cushion?

CLEOPATRA [*at the opposite end*] I have got new ones for you.

THE MAJOR-DOMO. These cushions, Cæsar, are of Maltese gauze, stuffed with rose leaves.

CÆSAR. Rose leaves! Am I a caterpillar? [*He throws the cushions away and seats himself on the leather mattress underneath*].

CLEOPATRA. What a shame! My new cushions!

THE MAJOR-DOMO [*at Cæsar's elbow*] What shall we serve to whet Cæsar's appetite?

CÆSAR. What have you got?

THE MAJOR-DOMO. Sea hedgehogs, black and white sea acorns, sea nettles, beccaficoes, purple shellfish—

CÆSAR. Any oysters?

THE MAJOR-DOMO. Assuredly.

CÆSAR. B r i t i s h oysters?

THE MAJOR-DOMO [*assenting*] British oysters, Cæsar.

CÆSAR. Oysters, then. [*The Major-Domo signs to a slave at each order; and the slave goes out to execute it*]. I have been in Britain—that western land of romance—the last piece of earth on the edge of the ocean that surrounds the world. I went there in search of its famous pearls. The British pearl was a fable; but in searching for it I found the British oyster.

APOLLODORUS. All posterity will bless you for it. [*To the Major-Domo*] Sea hedgehogs for me.

RUFIO. Is there nothing solid to begin with?

THE MAJOR-DOMO. Fieldfares with asparagus—

CLEOPATRA [*interrupting*] Fattened fowls! have some fattened fowls, Rufio.

RUFIO. Ay, that will do.

CLEOPATRA [*greedily*] Fieldfares for me.

THE MAJOR-DOMO. Cæsar will deign to choose his wine? Sicilian, Lesbian, Chian—

RUFIO [*contemptuously*] All Greek.

APOLLODORUS. Who would drink Roman wine when he could get Greek. Try the Lesbian, Cæsar.

CÆSAR. Bring me my barley water.

RUFIO [*with intense disgust*] Ugh! Bring me my Falernian. [*The Falernian is presently brought to him*].

CLEOPATRA [*pouting*] It is waste of time giving you dinners, Cæsar. My scullions would not condescend to your diet.

CÆSAR [*relenting*] Well, well: let us try the Lesbian. [*The Major-Domo fills Cæsar's goblet; then Cleopatra's and Apollodorus's*]. But when I return to Rome, I will make laws against these extravagances. I will even get the laws carried out.

CLEOPATRA [*coaxingly*] Never mind. Today you are to be like other people: idle, luxurious, and kind. [*She stretches her hand to him along the table*].

CÆSAR. Well, for once I will sacrifice my comfort—[*kissing her hand*] there! [*He takes a draught of wine*]. Now are you satisfied?

CLEOPATRA. And you no longer believe that I long for your departure for Rome?

CÆSAR. I no longer believe anything. My brains are asleep. Besides, who knows whether I shall return to Rome?

RUFIO [*alarmed*] How? Eh? What?

CÆSAR. What has Rome to shew me that I have not seen already? One year of Rome is like another, except that I grow older, whilst the crowd in the Appian Way is always the same age.

APOLLODORUS. It is no better here in Egypt. The old men, when they are tired of life, say "We have seen everything except the source of the Nile."

CÆSAR [*his imagination catching fire*] And why not see that? Cleopatra: will you come with me and track the flood to its cradle in the heart of the regions of mystery? Shall we leave Rome behind us—Rome, that has achieved greatness only to learn how greatness destroys nations of men who are not great! Shall I make you a new kingdom, and build you a holy city there in the great unknown?

CLEOPATRA [*rapturously*] Yes, yes. You shall.
RUFIO. Ay: now he will conquer Africa with two legions before we come to the roast boar.
APOLLODORUS. Come: no scoffing. This is a noble scheme: in it Cæsar is no longer merely the conquering soldier, but the creative poet-artist. Let us name the holy city, and consecrate it with Lesbian wine.
CÆSAR. Cleopatra shall name it herself.
CLEOPATRA. It shall be called Cæsar's Gift to his Beloved.
APOLLODORUS. No, no. Something vaster than that—something universal, like the starry firmament.
CÆSAR [*prosaically*] Why not simply The Cradle of the Nile?
CLEOPATRA. No: the Nile is my ancestor; and he is a god. Oh! I have thought of something. The Nile shall name it himself. Let us call upon him. [*To the Major-Domo*] Send for him. [*The three men stare at one another; but the Major-Domo goes out as if he had received the most matter-of-fact order*]. And [*to the retinue*] away with you all.

The retinue withdraws, making obeisance.

A priest enters, carrying a miniature sphinx with a tiny tripod before it. A morsel of incense is smoking in the tripod. The priest comes to the table and places the image in the middle of it. The light begins to change to the magenta purple of the Egyptian sunset, as if the god had brought a strange colored shadow with him. The three men are determined not to be impressed; but they feel curious in spite of themselves.

CÆSAR. What hocus-pocus is this?
CLEOPATRA. You shall see. And it is n o t hocus-pocus. To do it properly, we should kill something to please him; but perhaps he will answer Cæsar without that if we spill some wine to him.
APOLLODORUS [*turning his head to look up over his shoulder at Ra*] Why not appeal to our hawkheaded friend here?
CLEOPATRA [*nervously*] Sh! He will hear you and be angry.
RUFIO [*phlegmatically*] The source of the Nile is out of his district, I expect.
CLEOPATRA. No: I will have my city named by nobody but my dear little sphinx, because it was in its arms that Cæsar found me asleep. [*She languishes at Cæsar then turns curtly to the priest*]. Go. I am a priestess, and have power to take your charge from you. [*The priest makes a reverence and goes out*]. Now let us call on the Nile all together. Perhaps he will rap on the table.

CÆSAR. What! table rapping! Are such superstitions still believed in this year 707 of the Republic?

CLEOPATRA. It is no superstition: our priests learn lots of things from the tables. Is it not so, Apollodorus?

APOLLODORUS. Yes: I profess myself a converted man. When Cleopatra is priestess, Apollodorus is devotee. Propose the conjuration.

CLEOPATRA. You must say with me "Send us thy voice, Father Nile."

ALL FOUR [*holding their glasses together before the idol*] Send us thy voice, Father Nile.

The death cry of a man in mortal terror and agony answers them. Appalled, the men set down their glasses, and listen. Silence. The purple deepens in the sky. Cæsar, glancing at Cleopatra, catches her pouring out her wine before the god, with gleaming eyes, and mute assurances of gratitude and worship. Apollodorus springs up and runs to the edge of the roof to peer down and listen.

CÆSAR [*looking piercingly at Cleopatra*] What was that?

CLEOPATRA [*petulantly*] Nothing. They are beating some slave.

CÆSAR. Nothing.

RUFIO. A man with a knife in him, I'll swear.

CÆSAR [*rising*] A murder!

APOLLODORUS [*at the back, waving his hand for silence*] S-sh! Silence. Did you hear that?

CÆSAR. Another cry?

APOLLODORUS [*returning to the table*] No, a thud. Something fell on the beach, I think.

RUFIO [*grimly, as he rises*] Something with bones in it, eh?

CÆSAR [*shuddering*] Hush, hush, Rufio. [*He leaves the table and returns to the colonnade: Rufio following at his left elbow, and Apollodorus at the other side*].

CLEOPATRA [*still in her place at the table*] Will you leave me, Cæsar? Apollodorus: are you going?

APOLLODORUS. Faith, dearest Queen, my appetite is gone.

CÆSAR. Go down to the courtyard, Apollodorus; and find out what has happened.

Apollodorus nods and goes out, making for the staircase by which Rufio ascended.

CLEOPATRA. Your soldiers have killed somebody, perhaps. What does it matter?

The murmur of a crowd rises from the beach below. Cæsar and Rufio look at one another.

CÆSAR. This must be seen to. [*He is about to follow Apollodorus when Rufio stops him with a hand on his arm as Ftatateeta comes back by the far end of the roof, with dragging steps, a drowsy satiety in her eyes and in the corners of the bloodhound lips. For a moment Cæsar suspects that she is drunk with wine. Not so Rufio: he knows well the red vintage that has inebriated her*].

RUFIO [*in a low tone*] There is some mischief between those two.

FTATATEETA. The Queen looks again on the face of her servant.

Cleopatra looks at her for a moment with an exultant reflection of her murderous expression. Then she flings her arms round her; kisses her repeatedly and savagely; and tears off her jewels and heaps them on her. The two men turn from the spectacle to look at one another. Ftatateeta drags herself sleepily to the altar; kneels before Ra; and remains there in prayer. Cæsar goes to Cleopatra, leaving Rufio in the colonnade.

CÆSAR [*with searching earnestness*] Cleopatra: what has happened?

CLEOPATRA [*in mortal dread of him, but with her utmost cajolery*] Nothing, dearest Cæsar. [*With sickly sweetness, her voice almost failing*] Nothing. I am innocent. [*She approaches him affectionately*] Dear Cæsar: are you angry with me? Why do you look at me so? I have been here with you all the time. How can I know what has happened?

CÆSAR [*reflectively*] That is true.

CLEOPATRA [*greatly relieved, trying to caress him*] Of course it is true. [*He does not respond to the caress*] You know it is true, Rufio.

The murmur without suddenly swells to a roar and subsides.

RUFIO. I shall know presently. [*He makes for the altar in the burly trot that serves him for a stride, and touches Ftatateeta on the shoulder*]. Now, mistress: I shall want you. [*He orders her, with a gesture, to go before him*].

FTATATEETA [*rising and glowering at him*] My place is with the Queen.

CLEOPATRA. She has done no harm, Rufio.

CÆSAR [*to Rufio*] Let her stay.

RUFIO [*sitting down on the altar*] Very well. Then my place is here too; and you can see what is the matter for yourself. The city is in a pretty uproar, it seems.

CÆSAR [*with grave displeasure*] Rufio: there is a time for obedience.

RUFIO. And there is a time for obstinacy. [*He folds his arms doggedly*].

CÆSAR [*to Cleopatra*] Send her away.

CLEOPATRA [*whining in her eagerness to propitiate him*] Yes, I will. I will do whatever you ask me, Cæsar, always, because I love you. Ftatateeta: go away.

FTATATEETA. The Queen's word is my will. I shall be at hand for the Queen's call. [*She goes out past Ra, as she came*].

RUFIO [*following her*] Remember, Cæsar, your bodyguard also is within call. [*He follows her out*].

Cleopatra, presuming upon Cæsar's submission to Rufio, leaves the table and sits down on the bench in the colonnade.

CLEOPATRA. Why do you allow Rufio to treat you so? You should teach him his place.

CÆSAR. Teach him to be my enemy, and to hide his thoughts from me as you are now hiding yours.

CLEOPATRA [*her fears returning*] Why do you say that, Cæsar? Indeed, indeed, I am not hiding anything. You are wrong to treat me like this. [*She stifles a sob*]. I am only a child; and you turn into stone because you think some one has been killed. I cannot bear it. [*She purposely breaks down and weeps. He looks at her with profound sadness and complete coldness. She looks up to see what effect she is producing. Seeing that he is unmoved, she sits up, pretending to struggle with her emotion and to put it bravely away*]. But there: I know you hate tears: you shall not be troubled with them. I know you are not angry, but only sad; only I am so silly, I cannot help being hurt when you speak coldly. Of course you are quite right: it is dreadful to think of anyone being killed or even hurt; and I hope nothing really serious has—[*her voice dies away under his contemptuous penetration*].

CÆSAR. What has frightened you into this? What have you done? [*A trumpet sounds on the beach below*]. Aha! that sounds like the answer.

CLEOPATRA [*sinking back trembling on the bench and covering her face with her hands*] I have not betrayed you, Cæsar: I swear it.

CÆSAR. I know that. I have not trusted you. [*He turns from her, and is about to go out when Apollodorus and Britannus drag in Lucius Septimius to him. Rufio follows. Cæsar shudders*]. Again, Pompey's murderer!

RUFIO. The town has gone mad, I think. They are for tearing the palace down and driving us into the sea straight away. We laid hold of this renegade in clearing them out of the courtyard.

CÆSAR. Release him. [*They let go his arms*]. What has offended the citizens, Lucius Septimius?
LUCIUS. What did you expect, Cæsar? Pothinus was a favorite of theirs.
CÆSAR. What has happened to Pothinus? I set him free, here, not half an hour ago. Did they not pass him out?
LUCIUS. Ay, through the gallery arch sixty feet above ground, with three inches of steel in his ribs. He is as dead as Pompey. We are quits now, as to killing—you and I.
CÆSAR [*shocked*] Assassinated!—our prisoner, our guest! [*He turns reproachfully on Rufio*] Rufio—
RUFIO [*emphatically—anticipating the question*] Whoever did it was a wise man and a friend of yours [*Cleopatra is greatly emboldened*]; but none of us had a hand in it. So it is no use to frown at me. [*Cæsar turns and looks at Cleopatra*].
CLEOPATRA [*violently—rising*] He was slain by order of the Queen of Egypt. I am not Julius Cæsar the dreamer, who allows every slave to insult him. Rufio has said I did well: now the others shall judge me too. [*She turns to the others*]. This Pothinus sought to make me conspire with him to betray Cæsar to Achillas and Ptolemy. I refused; and he cursed me and came privily to Cæsar to accuse me of his own treachery. I caught him in the act; and he insulted me—me, the Queen! to my face. Cæsar would not avenge me: he spoke him fair and set him free. Was I right to avenge myself? Speak, Lucius.
LUCIUS. I do not gainsay it. But you will get little thanks from Cæsar for it.
CLEOPATRA. Speak, Apollodorus. Was I wrong?
APOLLODORUS. I have only one word of blame, most beautiful. You should have called upon me, your knight; and in fair duel I should have slain the slanderer.
CLEOPATRA [*passionately*] I will be judged by your very slave, Cæsar. Britannus: speak. Was I wrong?
BRITANNUS. Were treachery, falsehood, and disloyalty left unpunished, society must become like an arena full of wild beasts, tearing one another to pieces. Cæsar is in the wrong.
CÆSAR [*with quiet bitterness*] And so the verdict is against me, it seems.
CLEOPATRA [*vehemently*] Listen to me, Cæsar. If one man in all Alexandria can be found to say that I did wrong, I swear to have myself crucified on the door of the palace by my own slaves.

CÆSAR. If one man in all the world can be found, now or forever, to know that you did wrong, that man will have either to conquer the world as I have, or be crucified by it. [*The uproar in the streets again reaches them*]. Do you hear? These knockers at your gate are also believers in vengeance and in stabbing. You have slain their leader: it is right that they shall slay you. If you doubt it, ask your four counsellors here. And then in the name of that right [*he emphasizes the word with great scorn*] shall I not slay them for murdering their Queen, and be slain in my turn by their countrymen as the invader of their fatherland? Can Rome do less then than slay these slayers, too, to shew the world how Rome avenges her sons and her honor. And so, to the end of history, murder shall breed murder, always in the name of right and honor and peace, until the gods are tired of blood and create a race that can understand. [*Fierce uproar. Cleopatra becomes white with terror*] Hearken, you who must not be insulted. Go near enough to catch their words: you will find them bitterer than the tongue of Pothinus. [*Loftily, wrapping himself up in an impenetrable dignity*] Let the Queen of Egypt now give her orders for vengeance, and take her measures for defence; for she has renounced Cæsar. [*He turns to go*].

CLEOPATRA [*terrified, running to him and falling on her knees*] You will not desert me, Cæsar. You will defend the palace.

CÆSAR. You have taken the powers of life and death upon you. I am only a dreamer.

CLEOPATRA. But they will kill me.

CÆSAR. And why not?

CLEOPATRA. In pity—

CÆSAR. Pity! What! has it come to this so suddenly, that nothing can save you now but pity? Did it save Pothinus?

She rises, wringing her hands, and goes back to the bench in despair. Apollodorus shews his sympathy with her by quietly posting himself behind the bench. The sky has by this time become the most vivid purple, and soon begins to change to a glowing pale orange, against which the colonnade and the great image shew darklier and darklier.

RUFIO. Cæsar: enough of preaching. The enemy is at the gate.

CÆSAR [*turning on him and giving way to his wrath*] Ay; and what has held him baffled at the gate all these months? Was it my folly, as you deem it, or your wisdom? In this Egyptian Red Sea of blood, whose hand has held all your heads above the waves? [*Turning on*

Cleopatra] And yet, when Cæsar says to such an one, "Friend, go free," you, clinging for your little life to my sword, dare steal out and stab him in the back? And you, soldiers and gentlemen, and honest servants as you forget that you are, applaud this assassination, and say "Cæsar is in the wrong." By the gods, I am tempted to open my hand and let you all sink into the flood.

CLEOPATRA [*with a ray of cunning hope*] But, Cæsar, if you do, you will perish yourself.

Cæsar's eyes blaze.

RUFIO [*greatly alarmed*] Now, by great Jove, you filthy little Egyptian rat, that is the very word to make him walk out alone into the city and leave us here to be cut to pieces. [*Desperately, to Cæsar*] Will you desert us because we are a parcel of fools? I mean no harm by killing: I do it as a dog kills a cat, by instinct. We are all dogs at your heels; but we have served you faithfully.

CÆSAR [*relenting*] Alas, Rufio, my son, my son: as dogs we are like to perish now in the streets.

APOLLODORUS [*at his post behind Cleopatra's seat*] Cæsar: what you say has an Olympian ring in it: it must be right; for it is fine art. But I am still on the side of Cleopatra. If we must die, she shall not want the devotion of a man's heart nor the strength of a man's arm.

CLEOPATRA [*sobbing*] But I dont want to die.

CÆSAR [*sadly*] Oh, ignoble, ignoble!

LUCIUS [*coming forward between Cæsar and Cleopatra*] Hearken to me, Cæsar. It may be ignoble; but I also mean to live as long as I can.

CÆSAR. Well, my friend, you are likely to outlive Cæsar. Is it any magic of mine, think you, that has kept your army and this whole city at bay for so long? Yesterday, what quarrel had they with me that they should risk their lives against me? But today we have flung them down their hero, murdered; and now every man of them is set upon clearing out this nest of assassins—for such we are and no more. Take courage then; and sharpen your sword. Pompey's head has fallen; and Cæsar's head is ripe.

APOLLODORUS. Does Cæsar despair?

CÆSAR [*with infinite pride*] He who has never hoped can never despair. Cæsar, in good or bad fortune, looks his fate in the face.

LUCIUS. Look it in the face, then; and it will smile as it always has on Cæsar.

CÆSAR [*with involuntary haughtiness*] Do you presume to encourage me?

LUCIUS. I offer you my services. I will change sides if you will have me.

CÆSAR [*suddenly coming down to earth again, and looking sharply at him, divining that there is something behind the offer*] What! At this point?

LUCIUS [*firmly*] At this point.

RUFIO. Do you suppose Cæsar is mad, to trust you?

LUCIUS. I do not ask him to trust me until he is victorious. I ask for my life, and for a command in Cæsar's army. And since Cæsar is a fair dealer, I will pay in advance.

CÆSAR. Pay! How?

LUCIUS. With a piece of good news for you.

Cæsar divines the news in a flash.

RUFIO. What news?

CÆSAR [*with an elate and buoyant energy which makes Cleopatra sit up and stare*] What news! What news, did you say, my son Rufio? The relief has arrived: what other news remains for us? Is it not so, Lucius Septimius? Mithridates of Pergamos is on the march.

LUCIUS. He has taken Pelusium.

CÆSAR [*delighted*] Lucius Septimius: you are henceforth my officer. Rufio: the Egyptians must have sent every soldier from the city to prevent Mithridates crossing the Nile. There is nothing in the streets now but mob—mob!

LUCIUS. It is so. Mithridates is marching by the great road to Memphis to cross above the Delta. Achillas will fight him there.

CÆSAR [*all audacity*] Achillas shall fight Cæsar there. See, Rufio. [*He runs to the table; snatches a napkin; and draws a plan on it with his finger dipped in wine, whilst Rufio and Lucius Septimius crowd about him to watch, all looking closely, for the light is now almost gone*]. Here is the palace [*pointing to his plan*]: here is the theatre. You [*to Rufio*] take twenty men and pretend to go by t h a t street [*pointing it out*]; and whilst they are stoning you, out go the cohorts by this and this. My streets are right, are they, Lucius?

LUCIUS. Ay, that is the fig market—

CÆSAR [*too much excited to listen to him*] I saw them the day we arrived. Good! [*He throws the napkin on the table, and comes down again into the colonnade*]. Away, Britannus: tell Petronius that within an hour half our forces must take ship for the western lake. See to my horse and armor. [*Britannus runs out.*] With the rest, *I* shall march round the lake and up the Nile to meet Mithridates. Away, Lucius;

and give the word. [*Lucius hurries out after Britannus.*] Apollodorus: lend me your sword and your right arm for this campaign.

APOLLODORUS. Ay, and my heart and life to boot.

CÆSAR [*grasping his hand*] I accept both. [*Mighty handshake*]. Are you ready for work?

APOLLODORUS. Ready for Art—the Art of War [*he rushes out after Lucius, totally forgetting Cleopatra*].

RUFIO. Come! this is something like business.

CÆSAR [*buoyantly*] Is it not, my only son? [*He claps his hands. The slaves hurry in to the table*]. No more of this mawkish revelling: away with all this stuff: shut it out of my sight and be off with you. [*The slaves begin to remove the table; and the curtains are drawn, shutting in the colonnade*]. You understand about the streets, Rufio?

RUFIO. Ay, I think I do. I will get through them, at all events.

The bucina sounds busily in the courtyard beneath.

CÆSAR. Come, then: we must talk to the troops and hearten them. You down to the beach: I to the courtyard. [*He makes for the staircase*].

CLEOPATRA [*rising from her seat, where she has been quite neglected all this time, and stretching out her hands timidly to him*] Cæsar.

CÆSAR [*turning*] Eh?

CLEOPATRA. Have you forgotten me?

CÆSAR [*indulgently*] I am busy now, my child, busy. When I return your affairs shall be settled. Farewell; and be good and patient.

He goes, preoccupied and quite indifferent. She stands with clenched fists, in speechless rage and humiliation.

RUFIO. That game is played and lost, Cleopatra. The woman always gets the worst of it.

CLEOPATRA [*haughtily*] Go. Follow your master.

RUFIO [*in her ear, with rough familiarity*] A word first. Tell your executioner that if Pothinus had been properly killed—in the throat—he would not have called out. Your man bungled his work.

CLEOPATRA [*enigmatically*] How do you know it was a man?

RUFIO [*startled, and puzzled*] It was not you: you were with us when it happened. [*She turns her back scornfully on him. He shakes his head, and draws the curtains to go out. It is now a magnificent moonlit night. The table has been removed. Ftatateeta is seen in the light of the moon and stars, again in prayer before the white altar-stone of Ra. Rufio starts; closes the curtains again softly; and says in a low voice to Cleopatra*] Was it she? with her own hand?

CLEOPATRA [*threateningly*] Whoever it was, let my enemies beware of her. Look to it, Rufio, you who dare make the Queen of Egypt a fool before Cæsar.

RUFIO [*looking grimly at her*] I will look to it, Cleopatra. [*He nods in confirmation of the promise, and slips out through the curtains, loosening his sword in its sheath as he goes*].

ROMAN SOLDIERS [*in the courtyard below*] Hail, Cæsar! Hail, hail!

Cleopatra listens. The bucina sounds again, followed by several trumpets.

CLEOPATRA [*wringing her hands and calling*] Ftatateeta. Ftatateeta. It is dark; and I am alone. Come to me. [*Silence*] Ftatateeta. [*Louder*] Ftatateeta. [*Silence. In a panic she snatches the cord and pulls the curtains apart*].

Ftatateeta is lying dead on the altar of Ra, with her throat cut. Her blood deluges the white stone.

ACT V

High noon. Festival and military pageant on the esplanade before the palace. In the east harbor Cæsar's galley, so gorgeously decorated that it seems to be rigged with flowers, is alongside the quay, close to the steps Apollodorus descended when he embarked with the carpet. A Roman guard is posted there in charge of a gangway, whence a red floorcloth is laid down the middle of the esplanade, turning off to the north opposite the central gate in the palace front, which shuts in the esplanade on the south side. The broad steps of the gate, crowded with Cleopatra's ladies, all in their gayest attire, are like a flower garden. The façade is lined by her guard, officered by the same gallants to whom Bel Affris announced the coming of Cæsar six months before in the old palace on the Syrian border. The north side is lined by Roman soldiers, with the townsfolk on tiptoe behind them, peering over their heads at the cleared esplanade, in which the officers stroll about, chatting. Among these are Belzanor and the Persian; also the centurion, vinewood cudgel in hand, battle worn, thick-booted, and much outshone, both socially and decoratively, by the Egyptian officers.

Apollodorus makes his way through the townsfolk and calls to the officers from behind the Roman line.

APOLLODORUS. Hullo! May I pass?

CENTURION. Pass Apollodorus the Sicilian there! [*The soldiers let him through*].

BELZANOR. Is Cæsar at hand?

APOLLODORUS. Not yet. He is still in the market place. I could not stand any more of the roaring of the soldiers! After half an hour of the enthusiasm of an army, one feels the need of a little sea air.

PERSIAN. Tell us the news. Hath he slain the priests?

APOLLODORUS. Not he. They met him in the market place with ashes on their heads and their gods in their hands. They placed the gods at his feet. The only one that was worth looking at was Apis: a miracle of gold and ivory work. By my advice he offered the chief priest two talents for it.

BELZANOR [*appalled*] Apis the all-knowing for two talents! What said the chief Priest?

APOLLODORUS. He invoked the mercy of Apis, and asked for five.

BELZANOR. There will be famine and tempest in the land for this.

PERSIAN. Pooh! Why did not Apis cause Cæsar to be vanquished by Achillas? Any fresh news from the war, Apollodorus?

APOLLODORUS. The little King Ptolemy was drowned.

BELZANOR. Drowned! How?

APOLLODORUS. With the rest of them. Cæsar attacked them from three sides at once and swept them into the Nile. Ptolemy's barge sank.

BELZANOR. A marvellous man, this Cæsar! Will he come soon, think you?

APOLLODORUS. He was settling the Jewish question when I left.

A flourish of trumpets from the north, and commotion among the townsfolk, announces the approach of Cæsar.

PERSIAN. He has made short work of them. Here he comes. [*He hurries to his post in front of the Egyptian lines*].

BELZANOR [*following him*] Ho there! Cæsar comes.

The soldiers stand at attention, and dress their lines. Apollodorus goes to the Egyptian line.

CENTURION [*hurrying to the gangway guard*] Attention there! Cæsar comes.

Cæsar arrives in state with Rufio: Britannus following. The soldiers receive him with enthusiastic shouting.

CÆSAR. I see my ship awaits me. The hour of Cæsar's farewell to Egypt has arrived. And now, Rufio, what remains to be done before I go?

RUFIO [*at his left hand*] You have not yet appointed a Roman governor for this province.

CÆSAR [*looking whimsically at him, but speaking with perfect gravity*] What say you to Mithridates of Pergamos, my reliever and rescuer, the great son of Eupator?

RUFIO. Why, that you will want him elsewhere. Do you forget that you have some three or four armies to conquer on your way home?

CÆSAR. Indeed! Well, what say you to yourself?

RUFIO [*incredulously*] I! I a governor! What are you dreaming of? Do you not know that I am only the son of a freedman?

CÆSAR [*affectionately*] Has not Cæsar called you his son? [*Calling to the whole assembly*] Peace awhile there; and hear me.

THE ROMAN SOLDIERS. Hear Cæsar.

CÆSAR. Hear the service, quality, rank and name of the Roman governor. By service, Cæsar's shield; by quality, Cæsar's friend; by rank, a Roman soldier. [*The Roman soldiers give a triumphant shout*]. By name, Rufio [*They shout again*].

RUFIO [*kissing Cæsar's hand*] Ay: I am Cæsar's shield; but of what use shall I be when I am no longer on Cæsar's arm? Well, no matter— [*He becomes husky, and turns away to recover himself*].

CÆSAR. Where is that British Islander of mine?

BRITANNUS [*coming forward on Cæsar's right hand*] Here, Cæsar.

CÆSAR. Who bade you, pray, thrust yourself into the battle of the Delta, uttering the barbarous cries of your native land, and affirming yourself a match for any four of the Egyptians, to whom you applied unseemly epithets?

BRITANNUS. Cæsar: I ask you to excuse the language that escaped me in the heat of the moment.

CÆSAR. And how did you, who cannot swim, cross the canal with us when we stormed the camp?

BRITANNUS. Cæsar: I clung to the tail of your horse.

CÆSAR. These are not the deeds of a slave, Britannicus, but of a free man.

BRITANNUS. Cæsar: I was born free.

CÆSAR. But they call you Cæsar's slave.

BRITANNUS. Only as Cæsar's slave have I found real freedom.

CÆSAR [*moved*] Well said. Ungrateful that I am, I was about to set you free; but now I will not part from you for a million talents. [*He claps him friendly on the shoulder. Britannus, gratified, but a trifle shamefaced, takes his hand and kisses it sheepishly*].

BELZANOR [*to the Persian*] This Roman knows how to make men serve him.

PERSIAN. Ay: men too humble to become dangerous rivals to him.

BELZANOR. O subtle one! O cynic!

CÆSAR [*seeing Apollodorus in the Egyptian corner, and calling to him*] Apollodorus: I leave the art of Egypt in your charge. Remember: Rome loves art and will encourage it ungrudgingly.

APOLLODORUS. I understand, Cæsar. Rome will produce no art itself; but it will buy up and take away whatever the other nations produce.

CÆSAR. What! Rome produce no art! Is peace not an art? is war not an art? is government not an art? is civilization not an art? All these we give you in exchange for a few ornaments. You will have the best of the bargain. [*Turning to Rufio*] And now, what else have I to do before I embark? [*Trying to recollect*] There is something I cannot remember: what c a n it be? Well, well: it must remain undone: we must not waste this favorable wind. Farewell Rufio.

RUFIO. Cæsar: I am loth to let you go to Rome without your shield. There are too many daggers there.

CÆSAR. It matters not: I shall finish my life's work on my way back; and then I shall have lived long enough. Besides: I have always disliked the idea of dying: I had rather be killed. Farewell.

RUFIO [*with a sigh, raising his hands and giving Cæsar up as incorrigible*] Farewell. [*They shake hands*].

CÆSAR [*waving his hand to Apollodorus*] Farewell, Apollodorus, and my friends, all of you. Aboard!

The gangway is run out from the quay to the ship. As Cæsar moves towards it, Cleopatra, cold and tragic, cunningly dressed in black, without ornaments or decoration of any kind, and thus making a striking figure among the brilliantly dressed bevy of ladies as she passes through it, comes from the palace and stands on the steps. Cæsar does not see her until she speaks.

CLEOPATRA. Has Cleopatra no part in this leave-taking?

CÆSAR [*enlightened*] Ah, I k n e w there was something. [*To Rufio*] How could you let me forget her, Rufio? [*Hastening to her*] Had I gone without seeing you, I should never have forgiven myself. [*He takes her hands, and brings her into the middle of the esplanade. She submits stonily*]. Is this mourning for me?

CLEOPATRA. No.

CÆSAR [*remorsefully*] Ah, that was thoughtless of me! It is for your brother.

CLEOPATRA. No.

CÆSAR. For whom, then?

CLEOPATRA. Ask the Roman governor whom you have left us.

CÆSAR. Rufio?

CLEOPATRA. Yes: Rufio. [*She points at him with deadly scorn*]. He who is to rule here in Cæsar's name, in Cæsar's way, according to Cæsar's boasted laws of life.

CÆSAR [*dubiously*] He is to rule as he can, Cleopatra. He has taken the work upon him, and will do it in his own way.

CLEOPATRA. Not in your way, then?

CÆSAR [*puzzled*] What do you mean by my way?

CLEOPATRA. Without punishment. Without revenge. Without judgment.

CÆSAR [*approvingly*] Ay: that is the right way, the great way, the only possible way in the end. [*To Rufio*] Believe it, Rufio, if you can.

RUFIO. Why, I believe it, Cæsar. You have convinced me of it long ago. But look you. You are sailing for Numidia today. Now tell me: if you meet a hungry lion there, you will not punish it for wanting to eat you?

CÆSAR [*wondering what he is driving at*] No.

RUFIO. Nor revenge upon it the blood of those it has already eaten.

CÆSAR. No.

RUFIO. Nor judge it for its guiltiness.

CÆSAR. No.

RUFIO. What, then, will you do to save your life from it?

CÆSAR [*promptly*] Kill it, man, without malice, just as it would kill me. What does this parable of the lion mean?

RUFIO. Why, Cleopatra had a tigress that killed men at her bidding. I thought she might bid it kill you some day. Well, had I not been Cæsar's pupil, what pious things might I not have done to that tigress! I might have punished it. I might have revenged Pothinus on it.

CÆSAR [*interjects*] Pothinus!

RUFIO [*continuing*] I might have judged it. But I put all these follies behind me; and, without malice, only cut its throat. And that is why Cleopatra comes to you in mourning.

CLEOPATRA [*vehemently*] He has shed the blood of my servant Ftatateeta. On your head be it as upon his, Cæsar, if you hold him free of it.

CÆSAR [*energetically*] On my head be it, then; for it was well done. Rufio: had you set yourself in the seat of judge, and with hateful ceremonies and appeals to the gods handed that woman over to some hired executioner to be slain before the people in the name of justice, never again would I have touched your hand without a shudder. But this was natural slaying: I feel no horror at it.

Rufio, satisfied, nods at Cleopatra, mutely inviting her to mark that.

CLEOPATRA [*pettish and childish in her impotence*] No: not when a Roman slays an Egyptian. All the world will now see how unjust and corrupt Cæsar is.

CÆSAR [*taking her hands coaxingly*] Come: do not be angry with me.

I am sorry for that Poor Totateeta. [*She laughs in spite of herself*]. Aha! you are laughing. Does that mean reconciliation?

CLEOPATRA [*angry with herself for laughing*] No, no, NO!! But it is so ridiculous to hear you call her Totateeta.

CÆSAR. What! As much a child as ever, Cleopatra! Have I not made a woman of you after all?

CLEOPATRA. Oh, it is you who are a great baby: you make me seem silly because you will not behave seriously. But you have treated me badly; and I do not forgive you.

CÆSAR. Bid me farewell.

CLEOPATRA. I will not.

CÆSAR [*coaxing*] I will send you a beautiful present from Rome.

CLEOPATRA [*proudly*] Beauty from Rome to Egypt indeed! What can Rome give m e that Egypt cannot give me?

APOLLODORUS. That is true, Cæsar. If the present is to be really beautiful, I shall have to buy it for you in Alexandria.

CÆSAR. You are forgetting the treasures for which Rome is most famous, my friend. You cannot buy t h e m in Alexandria.

APOLLODORUS. What are they, Cæsar?

CÆSAR. Her sons. Come, Cleopatra: forgive me and bid me farewell; and I will send you a man, Roman from head to heel and Roman of the noblest; not old and ripe for the knife; not lean in the arms and cold in the heart; not hiding a bald head under his conqueror's laurels; not stooped with the weight of the world on his shoulders; but brisk and fresh, strong and young, hoping in the morning, fighting in the day, and revelling in the evening. Will you take such an one in exchange for Cæsar?

CLEOPATRA [*palpitating*] His name, his name?

CÆSAR. Shall it be Mark Antony? [*She throws herself into his arms*].

RUFIO. You are a bad hand at a bargain, mistress, if you will swop Cæsar for Antony.

CÆSAR. So now you are satisfied.

CLEOPATRA. You will not forget.

CÆSAR. I will not forget. Farewell: I do not think we shall meet again. Farewell. [*He kisses her on the forehead. She is much affected and begins to sniff. He embarks*].

THE ROMAN SOLDIERS [*as he sets his foot on the gangway*] Hail, Cæsar; and farewell!

He reaches the ship and returns Rufio's wave of the hand.

APOLLODORUS [*to Cleopatra*] No tears, dearest Queen: they stab your servant to the heart. He will return some day.

CLEOPATRA. I hope not. But I cant help crying, all the same. [*She waves her handkerchief to Cæsar; and the ship begins to move*].

THE ROMAN SOLDIERS [*drawing their swords and raising them in the air*] Hail, Cæsar!

Notes to Cæsar and Cleopatra

Contents

CLEOPATRA'S CURE FOR BALDNESS

For the sake of conciseness in a hurried situation I have made Cleopatra recommend rum. This, I am afraid, is an anachronism: the only real one in the play. To balance it, I give a couple of the remedies she actually believed in. They are quoted by Galen from Cleopatra's book on Cosmetic.

"For bald patches, powder red sulphuret of arsenic and take it up with oak gum, as much as it will bear. Put on a rag and apply, having soaped the place well first. I have mixed the above with a foam of nitre, and it worked well."

Several other receipts follow, ending with: "The following is the best of all, acting for fallen hairs, when applied with oil or pomatum; acts for falling off of eyelashes or for people getting bald all over. It is wonderful. Of domestic mice burnt, one part; of vine rag burnt, one part; of horse's teeth burnt, one part; of bear's grease one; of deer's marrow one; of reed bark one. To be pounded when dry, and mixed with plenty of honey til it gets the consistency of honey; then the bear's grease and marrow to be mixed (when melted), the medicine to be put in a brass flask, and the bald part rubbed til it sprouts."

Concerning these ingredients, my fellow-dramatist Gilbert Murray, who, as a Professor of Greek, has applied to classical antiquity the methods of high scholarship (my own method is pure divination), writes to me as follows: "Some of this I dont understand, and possibly Galen did not, as he quotes your heroine's own language. Foam of nitre is, I think, something like soapsuds. Reed bark is an odd expression. It might mean the outside membrane of a reed: I do not know what it ought to be called. In the burnt mice receipt I take it that you first mixed the solid powders with honey, and then added the grease. I expect Cleopatra preferred it because in most of the others you have to lacerate the skin, prick it, or rub it til it bleeds. I do not know what vine rag is. I translate literally."

APPARENT ANACHRONISMS

The only way to write a play which shall convey to the general public an impression of antiquity is to make the characters speak blank verse and abstain from reference to steam, telegraphy, or any of the material conditions of their existence. The more ignorant men are, the more convinced are they that their little parish and their little chapel is an apex to which civilization and philosophy has painfully struggled up the pyramid of time from a desert of savagery. Savagery, they think, became barbarism; barbarism became ancient civilization; ancient civilization became Pauline Christianity; Pauline Christianity became Roman Catholicism; Roman Catholicism became the Dark Ages; and the Dark Ages were finally enlightened by the Protestant instincts of the English race. The whole process is summed up as Progress with a capital P. And any elderly gentleman of Progressive temperament will testify that the improvement since he was a boy is enormous.

Now if we count the generations of Progressive elderly gentlemen since, say, Plato, and add together the successive enormous improvements to which each of them has testified, it will strike us at once as an unaccountable fact that the world, instead of having been improved in 67 generations out of all recognition, presents, on the whole, a rather less dignified appearance in Ibsen's Enemy of the People than in Plato's Republic. And in truth, the period of time covered by history is far too short to allow of any perceptible progress in the popular sense of Evolution of the Human Species. The notion that there has been any such Progress since Cæsar's time (less than 20 centuries) is too absurd for discussion. All the savagery, barbarism, dark ages and the rest of it of which we have any record as existing in the past, exists at the present moment. A British carpenter or stone-mason may point out that he gets twice as much money for his labor as his father did in the same trade, and that his suburban house, with its bath, its cottage piano, its drawing room suite, and its album of photographs, would have shamed the plainness of his grandmother's. But the descendants of feudal barons, living in squalid lodgings on a salary of fifteen shillings a week instead of in castles on princely revenues, do not congratulate the world on the change. Such changes, in fact, are not to the point. It has been known, as far back as our records go, that man running wild in the woods is different from man kennelled in a city slum; that a dog seems to understand a shepherd better than a hewer of wood and drawer of water can understand an astronomer; and that breeding, gentle nurture, and luxurious food and shelter will produce a kind of man with whom the common laborer is socially incompatible. The same thing is true of horses and dogs. Now there is clearly room for great changes in the world by increasing the percentage of individuals who are carefully bred and gently nurtured, even to finally making the most of every man and woman born. But that possibility existed in the days of the Hittites as much as it does today. It does not give the slightest real support to the common assumption that the civilized contemporaries of the Hittites were unlike their civilized descendants today.

This would appear the tritest commonplace if it were not that the ordinary citizen's ignorance of the past combines with his idealization of the present to mislead and flatter him. Our latest book on the new railway across Asia describes the dulness of the Siberian farmer and the vulgar pursepride of the Siberian man of business without the least consciousness that the string of contemptuous instances given might have been saved by writing simply "Farmers and provincial plutocrats in Siberia are exactly what they are in England." The latest professor descanting on the civilization of the Western Empire in the fifth century feels bound to assume, in the teeth of his own researches, that the Christian was one sort of animal and the Pagan another. It might as well be assumed as indeed it generally is assumed by implication, that a murder committed with a poisoned arrow is different from a murder committed with a Mauser rifle. All such notions are illusions. Go back to the first syllable of recorded time, and there you will find your Christian and your Pagan, your yokel and your poet, helot and hero, Don Quixote and Sancho, Tamino and Papageno, Newton and bushman unable to count eleven, all alive and contemporaneous, and all convinced that they are the heirs of all the ages and the privileged recipients of THE truth (all others damnable heresies), just as you have them today, flourishing in countries each of which is the bravest and best that ever sprang at Heaven's command from out the azure main.

Again, there is the illusion of "increased command over Nature," meaning that cotton is cheap and that ten miles of country road on a bicycle have replaced four on foot. But even if man's increased command over Nature included any increased command over himself (the only sort of command relevant to his evolution into a higher being), the fact remains that it is only by running away from the increased command over Nature to country places where Nature is still in primitive command over Man that he can recover from the effects of the smoke, the stench, the foul air, the overcrowding, the racket, the ugliness, the dirt which the cheap cotton costs us. If manufacturing activity means Progress, the town must be more advanced than the country; and the field laborers and village artisans of today must be much less changed from the servants of Job than the proletariat of modern London from the proletariat of Cæsar's Rome. Yet the cockney proletarian is so inferior to the village laborer that it is only by steady recruiting from the country that London is kept alive. This does not seem as if the change since Job's time were Progress in the popular sense: quite the reverse. The common stock of discoveries in physics has accumulated a little: that is all.

One more illustration. Is the Englishman prepared to admit that the American is his superior as a human being? I ask this question because the scarcity of labor in America relatively to the demand for it has led to a development of machinery there, and a consequent "increase of command over Nature" which makes many of our English methods appear almost medieval to the up-to-date Chicagoan. This means that the American has an advantage over the Englishman of exactly the same nature that the Englishman has over the contemporaries of Cicero. Is the Englishman prepared to draw the same conclusion in both cases? I think not. The American, of course, will draw it cheerfully; but I must then ask him whether, since a modern negro has a greater "command over Nature" than Washington had, we are also to accept the conclusion, involved in his former one, that humanity has progressed from Washington to the *fin de siècle* negro.

Finally, I would point out that if life is crowned by its success and devotion in industrial organization and ingenuity, we had better worship the ant and the bee (as moralists urge us to do in our childhood), and humble ourselves before the arrogance of the birds of Aristophanes.

My reason then for ignoring the popular conception of Progress in Cæsar and Cleopatra is that there is no reason to suppose that any Progress has taken place since their time. But even if I shared the popular delusion, I do not see that I could have made any essential difference in the play. I can only imitate humanity as I know it. Nobody knows whether Shakespear thought that ancient Athenian joiners, weavers, or bellows menders were any different from Elizabethan ones; but it is quite certain that he could not have made them so, unless, indeed, he had played the literary man and made Quince say, not "Is all our company here?" but "Bottom: was not that Socrates that passed us at the Piræus with Glaucon and Polemarchus on his way to the house of Kephalus?" And so on.

CLEOPATRA

Cleopatra was only sixteen when Cæsar went to Egypt; but in Egypt sixteen is a riper age than it is in England. The childishness I have ascribed to her, as far as it is childishness of character and not lack of experience, is not a matter of years. It may be observed in our own climate at the present day in many women of fifty. It is a mistake to suppose that the difference between wisdom and folly has anything to do with the difference between physical age and physical youth. Some women are younger at seventy than most women at seventeen.

It must be borne in mind, too, that Cleopatra was a queen, and was therefore not the typical Greek-cultured, educated Egyptian lady of her time. To represent her by any such type would be as absurd as to represent George IV by a type founded on the attainments of Sir Isaac Newton. It is true that an ordinarily well educated Alexandrian girl of her time would no more have believed bogey stories about the Romans than the daughter of a modern Oxford professor would believe them about the Germans (though, by the way, it is possible to talk great nonsense at Oxford about foreigners when we are at war with them). But I do not feel bound to believe that Cleopatra was well educated. Her father, the illustrious Flute Blower, was not at all a parent of the Oxford professor type. And Cleopatra was a chip of the old block.

BRITANNUS

I find among those who have read this play in manuscript a strong conviction that an ancient Briton could not possibly have been like a modern one. I see no reason to adopt this curious view. It is true that the Roman and Norman conquests must have for a time disturbed the normal British type produced by the climate. But Britannus, born before these events, represents the unadulterated Briton who fought Cæsar and impressed Roman observers much as we should expect the ancestors of Mr Podsnap to impress the cultivated Italians of their time.

I am told that it is not scientific to treat national character as a product of climate. This only shews the wide difference between common knowledge and the intellectual game called science. We have men of exactly the same stock and speaking the same language, growing in Great Britain, in Ireland, and in America. The result is three of the most distinctly marked nationalities under the sun. Racial characteristics are quite another matter. The difference between a Jew and a Gentile has nothing to do with the difference between an Englishman and a German. The characteristics of Britannus are local characteristics, not race characteristics. In an ancient Briton they would, I take it, be exaggerated, since modern Britain, disforested, drained, urbanified and consequently cosmopolized, is presumably less characteristically British than Cæsar's Britain.

And again I ask does anyone who, in the light of a competent knowledge of his own age, has studied history from contemporary documents, believe that 67 generations of promiscuous marriage have made any appreciable difference in the human fauna of these isles? Certainly I do not.

JULIUS CÆSAR

As to Cæsar himself, I have purposely avoided the usual anachronism of going to Cæsar's books, and concluding that the style is the man.

That is only true of authors who have the specific literary genius, and have practised long enough to attain complete self-expression in letters. It is not true even on these conditions in an age when literature is conceived as a game of style, and not as a vehicle of self-expression by the author. Now Cæsar was an amateur stylist writing books of travel and campaign histories in a style so impersonal that the authenticity of the later volumes is disputed. They reveal some of his qualities just as the Voyage of a Naturalist Round the World reveals some of Darwin's, without expressing his private personality. An Englishman reading them would say that Cæsar was a man of great common sense and good taste, meaning thereby a man without originality or moral courage.

In exhibiting Cæsar as a much more various person than the historian of the Gallic wars, I hope I have not been too much imposed on by the dramatic illusion to which all great men owe part of their reputation and some the whole of it. I admit that reputations gained in war are specially questionable. Able civilians taking up the profession of arms, like Cæsar and Cromwell, in middle age, have snatched all its laurels from opponent commanders bred to it, apparently because capable persons engaged in military pursuits are so scarce that the existence of two of them at the same time in the same hemisphere is extremely rare. The capacity of any conqueror is therefore more likely than not to be an illusion produced by the incapacity of his adversary. At all events, Cæsar might have won his battles without being wiser than Charles XII or Nelson or Joan of Arc, who were, like most modern "self-made" millionaires, half-witted geniuses, enjoying the worship accorded by all races to certain forms of insanity. But Cæsar's victories were only advertisements for an eminence that would never have become popular without them. Cæsar is greater off the battle field than on it. Nelson off his quarter-deck was so quaintly out of the question that when his head was injured at the battle of the Nile, and his conduct became for some years openly scandalous, the difference was not important enough to be noticed. It may, however, be said that peace hath her illusory reputations no less than war. And it is certainly true that in civil life mere capacity for work—the power of killing a dozen secretaries under you, so to speak, as a life-or-death courier kills horses—enables men with common ideas and superstitions to distance all competitors in the strife of political ambition. It was this power of work that astonished Cicero as the most prodigious of Cæsar's gifts, as it astonished later observers in Napoleon before it wore him out. How if Cæsar were nothing but a Nelson and a Gladstone combined! a prodigy of vitality without any special quality of mind! nay, with ideas that were worn out before he was born, as Nelson's and Gladstone's were! I have considered that possibility too, and rejected it. I cannot cite all the stories about Cæsar which seem to me to shew that he was genuinely original; but let me at least point out that I have been careful to attribute nothing but originality to him. Originality gives a man an air of frankness, generosity and magnanimity by enabling him to estimate the value of truth, money, or success in any particular instance quite independently of convention and moral generalization. He therefore will not, in the ordinary Treasury bench fashion, tell a lie which everybody knows to be a lie (and consequently expects him as a matter of good taste to tell). His lies are not found out: they pass for candors. He understands the paradox of money, and gives it away when he can get most for it: in other words, when its value is least, which is just when a common man tries hardest to get it. He knows that the real moment of success is not the moment apparent to the crowd. Hence, in order to produce an impression of complete disinterestedness and magnanimity, he has only to act with entire selfishness; and this is perhaps the only sense in which a man can be said to be *naturally* great. It is in this sense that I have represented Cæsar as great. Having virtue, he has no need of goodness. He is neither forgiving, frank, nor generous, because a man who is too great to resent has nothing to forgive; a man who says things that other people are afraid to say need be no more frank than Bismarck was; and there is no generosity in giving things you do not want to people of whom you intend to make use. This distinction between virtue and goodness is not understood in England: hence the poverty of our drama in heroes. Our stage attempts at them are mere goody-goodies. Goodness, in its popular British sense of self-denial, implies that man is vicious by nature, and that supreme goodness is supreme martyrdom. Not sharing that pious opinion, I have not given countenance to it in any of my plays. In this I follow the precedent of the ancient myths, which represent the hero as vanquishing his enemies, not in fair fight, but with enchanted sword, superequine horse and magical invulnerability, the possession of which, from the vulgar moralistic point of view, robs his exploits of any merit whatever.

As to Cæsar's sense of humor, there is no more reason to assume that he lacked it than to assume that he was deaf or blind. It is said that on the occasion of his assassination by a conspiracy of moralists (it is always your moralist who makes assassination a duty, on the scaffold or off it), he defended himself until the good Brutus struck him, when he exclaimed "What! you too, Brutus!" and disdained further fight. If this be true, he must have been an incorrigible comedian. But even if we waive this story, or accept the traditional sentimental interpretation of it, there is still abundant evidence of his lightheartedness and adventurousness. Indeed it is clear from his whole history that what has been called his ambition was an instinct for exploration. He had much more of Columbus and Franklin in him than of Henry V.

However, nobody need deny Cæsar a share, at least, of the qualities I have attributed to him. All men, much more Julius Cæsars, possess all qualities in some degree. The really interesting question is whether I am right in assuming that the way to produce an impression of greatness is by exhibiting a man, not as mortifying his nature by doing his duty, in the manner which our system of putting little men into great positions (not having enough great men in our influential families to go round) forces us to inculcate, but as simply doing what he naturally wants to do. For this raises the question whether our world has not been wrong in its moral theory for the last 2,500 years or so. It must be a constant puzzle to many of us that the Christian era, so excellent in its intentions, should have been practically such a very discreditable episode in the history of the race. I doubt if this is altogether due to the vulgar and sanguinary sensationalism of our religious legends, with their substitution of gross physical torments and public executions for the passion of humanity. Islam, substituting voluptuousness for torment (a merely superficial difference, it is true), has done no better. It may have been the failure of Christianity to emancipate itself from expiatory theories of moral responsibility, guilt, innocence, reward, punishment, and the rest of it, that baffled its intention of changing the world. But these are bound up in all philosophies of creation as opposed to cosmism. They may therefore be regarded as the price we pay for popular religion.

MAN AND SUPERMAN:
A Comedy and a Philosophy

Composition begun in 1901 (scenario for the play begun 2 July 1901 and completed 8 October 1901); completed June 1902. Published 1903. Revised text in Collected Edition, 1930. Copyright reading at the Victoria Hall (Bijou Theatre), London, on 29 June 1903. First presented (without Act III, which includes the *Don Juan in Hell* dream scene) by the Stage Society at the Royal Court Theatre, London, for two performances on 21 May 1905. *Don Juan in Hell* first presented as a one-act play at the Royal Court Theatre, London, on 4 June 1907 for 8 matinées.

Roebuck Ramsden *Charles Goodhart*
Parlormaid *Hazel Thompson*
Octavius Robinson *Lewis Casson*
John Tanner *Granville Barker*
Ann Whitefield *Lillah McCarthy*
Mrs Whitefield *Florence Haydon*
Miss Ramsden *Agnes Thomas*
Violet Robinson *Sarah Brooke*
Henry Straker *Edmund Gwenn*
Hector Malone *Hubert Harben*
Mr Malone *J. D. Beveridge*
Mendoza
Anarchist
Duval
Rowdy Social-Democrat
Sulky Social-Democrat
Goatherd
An Officer
(omitted from 1905 production)

Don Juan in Hell (1907 cast)

Don Juan *Robert Loraine*
Doña Ana de Ulloa *Lillah McCarthy*
The Statue *Michael Sherbrooke*
The Devil *Norman McKinnel*

Period—The Present

ACT I *Portland Place, London. Roebuck Ramsden's Study*

ACT II *Richmond. The Avenue to Mrs Whitefield's House*

ACT III Scene 1: *Evening in the Sierra Nevada*
Scene 2: *Beyond Space, Beyond Time*
Scene 3: *Early Morning in the Sierra Nevada*

ACT IV *Granada. The Villa Garden*

Epistle Dedicatory

TO ARTHUR BINGHAM WALKLEY

My dear Walkley

You once asked me why I did not write a Don Juan play. The levity with which you assumed this frightful responsibility has probably by this time enabled you to forget it; but the day of reckoning has arrived: here is your play! I say your play, because *qui facit per alium facit per se.* Its profits, like its labor, belong to me: its morals, its manners, its philosophy, its influence on the young, are for you to justify. You were of mature age when you made the suggestion; and you knew your man. It is hardly fifteen years since, as twin pioneers of the New Journalism of that time, we two, cradled in the same new sheets, began an epoch in the criticism of the theatre and the opera house by making it the pretext for a propaganda of our own views of life. So you cannot plead ignorance of the character of the force you set in motion. You meant me to épater le bourgeois; and if he protests, I hereby refer him to you as the accountable party.

I warn you that if you attempt to repudiate your responsibility, I shall suspect you of finding the play too decorous for your taste. The fifteen years have made me older and graver. In you I can detect no such becoming change. Your levities and audacities are like the loves and comforts prayed for by Desdemona: they increase, even as your days do grow. No mere pioneering journal dares meddle with them now: the stately Times itself is alone sufficiently above suspicion to act as your chaperone; and even the Times must sometimes thank its stars that new plays are not produced every day, since after each such event its gravity is compromised, its platitude turned to epigram, its portentousness to wit, its propriety to elegance, and even its decorum into naughtiness by criticisms which the traditions of the paper do not allow you to sign at the end, but which you take care to sign with the most extravagant flourishes between the lines. I am not sure that this is not a portent of Revolution. In eighteenth century France the end was at hand when men bought the Encyclopedia and found Diderot there. When I buy The Times and find you there, my prophetic ear catches a rattle of twentieth century tumbrils.

However, that is not my present anxiety. The question is, will you not be disappointed with a Don Juan play in which not one of that hero's *mille e tre* adventures is brought upon the stage? To propitiate you, let me explain myself. You will retort that I never do anything else: it is your favorite jibe at me that what I call drama is nothing but explanation. But you must not expect me to adopt your inexplicable, fantastic, petulant, fastidious ways: you must take me as I am, a reasonable, patient, consistent, apologetic, laborious person, with the temperament of a schoolmaster and the pursuits of a vestryman. No doubt that literary knack of mine which happens to amuse the British public distracts attention from my character; but the character is there none the less, solid as bricks. I have a conscience; and conscience is always anxiously explanatory. You, on the contrary, feel that a man who discusses his conscience is much like a woman who discusses her modesty. The only moral force you condescend to parade is the force of your wit: the only demand you make in public is the demand of your artistic temperament for symmetry, elegance, style, grace, refinement, and the cleanliness which comes next to godliness if not before it. But my conscience is the genuine pulpit article: it annoys me to see people comfortable when they ought to be uncomfortable; and I insist on making them think in order to bring them to conviction of sin. If you dont like my preaching you must lump it. I really cannot help it.

In the preface to my Plays for Puritans I explained the predicament of our contemporary English drama, forced to deal almost exclusively with cases of sexual attraction, and yet forbidden to exhibit the incidents of that attraction or even to discuss its nature. Your suggestion that I should write a Don Juan play was virtually a challenge to me to treat this subject myself dramatically. The challenge was difficult enough to be worth accepting, because, when you come to think of it, though we have plenty of dramas with heroes and heroines who are in love and must accordingly marry or perish at the end of the play, or about people whose relations with one another have been complicated by the marriage laws, not to mention the looser sort of plays which trade on the tradition that illicit love affairs are at once vicious and delightful, we have no modern English plays in which the natural attraction of the sexes for one another is made the mainspring of the action. That is why we insist on beauty in our performers, differing herein from the countries our friend William Archer holds up as examples of seriousness to our childish theatres. There the Juliets and Isoldes, the Romeos and Tristans, might be our mothers and fathers. Not so the English actress. The heroine she impersonates is not allowed to discuss the elemental relations of men and women: all her romantic twaddle about novelet-made love, all her purely legal dilemmas as to whether she was married or "betrayed," quite miss our hearts and worry our minds. To console ourselves we must just look at her. We do so; and her beauty feeds our starving emotions. Sometimes we grumble ungallantly at the lady because she does not act as well as she looks. But in a drama which, with all its preoccupation with sex, is really void of sexual interest, good looks are more desired than histrionic skill.

Let me press this point on you, since you are too clever to raise the fool's cry of paradox whenever I take hold of a stick by the right instead of the wrong end. Why are our occasional attempts to deal with the sex problem on the stage so repulsive and dreary that even those who are most determined that sex questions shall be held open and their discussion kept free, cannot pretend to relish these joyless attempts at social sanitation? Is it not because at bottom they are utterly sexless? What is the usual formula for such plays? A woman has, on some past occasion, been brought into conflict with the law which regulates the relations of the sexes. A man, by falling in love with her, or marrying her, is brought into conflict with the social convention which discountenances the woman. Now the conflicts of individuals with law and convention can be dramatized like all other human conflicts; but they are purely judicial; and the fact that we are much more curious about the suppressed relations between the man and the woman than about the relations between both and our courts of law and private juries of matrons, produces that sensation of evasion, of dissatisfaction, of fundamental irrelevance, of shallowness, of useless disagreeableness, of total failure to edify and partial failure to interest, which is as familiar to you in the theatres as it was to me when I, too, frequented those uncomfortable buildings, and found our popular playwrights in the mind to (as they thought) emulate Ibsen.

I take it that when you asked me for a Don Juan play you did not want that sort of thing. Nobody does: the successes such plays sometimes obtain are due to the incidental conventional melodrama with which the experienced popular author instinctively saves himself from failure. But what did you want? Owing to your unfortunate habit—you now, I hope, feel its inconvenience—of not explaining yourself, I have had to discover this for myself. First, then, I have had to ask myself, what is a Don Juan? Vulgarly, a libertine. But your dislike of vulgarity is pushed to the length of a defect (universality of character is impossible without a share of vulgarity); and even if you could acquire the taste, you would find yourself overfed from ordinary sources without troubling me. So I took it that you demanded a Don Juan in the philosophic sense.

Philosophically, Don Juan is a man who, though gifted enough to be exceptionally capable of distinguishing between good and evil, follows his own instincts without regard to the common, statute, or canon law; and therefore, whilst gaining the ardent sympathy of our rebellious instincts (which are flattered by the brilliancies with which Don Juan associates them) finds himself in mortal conflict with existing institutions, and defends himself by fraud and force as unscrupulously as a farmer defends his crops by the same means against vermin. The prototypic Don Juan, invented early in the XVI century by a Spanish monk, was presented, according to the ideas of that time, as the enemy of God, the approach of whose vengeance is felt throughout the drama, growing in menace from minute to minute. No anxiety is caused on Don Juan's account by any minor antagonist: he easily eludes the police, temporal and spiritual; and when an indignant father seeks private redress with the sword, Don Juan kills him without an effort. Not until the slain father returns from heaven as the agent of God, in the form of his own statue, does he prevail against his slayer and cast him into hell. The moral is a monkish one: repent and reform now; for tomorrow it may be too late. This is really the only point on which Don Juan is sceptical; for he is a devout believer in an ultimate hell, and risks damnation only because, as he is young, it seems so far off that repentance can be postponed until he has amused himself to his heart's content.

But the lesson intended by an author is hardly ever the lesson the world chooses to learn from his book. What attracts and impresses us in El Burlador de Sevilla is not the immediate urgency of repentance, but the heroism of daring to be the enemy of God. From Prometheus to my own Devil's Disciple, such enemies have always been popular. Don Juan became such a pet that the world could not bear his damnation. It reconciled him sentimentally to God in a second version, and clamored for his canonization for a whole century, thus treating him as English journalism has treated that comic foe of the gods, Punch. Molière's Don Juan casts back to the original in point of impenitence; but in piety he falls off greatly. True, he also proposes to repent; but in what terms! "Oui, ma foi! il faut s'amender. Encore vingt ou trente ans de cette vie-ci, et puis nous songerons à nous." After Molière comes the artist-enchanter, the master beloved by masters, Mozart, revealing the hero's spirit in magical harmonies, elfin tones, and elate darting rhythms as of summer lightning made audible. Here you have freedom in love and in morality mocking exquisitely at slavery to them, and interesting you, attracting you, tempting you, inexplicably forcing you to range the hero with his enemy the statue on a transcendent plane, leaving the prudish daughter and her priggish lover on a crockery shelf below to live piously ever after.

After these completed works Byron's fragment does not count for much philosophically. Our vagabond libertines are no more interesting from that point of view than the sailor who has a wife in every port; and Byron's hero is, after all, only a vagabond libertine. And he is dumb: he does not discuss himself with a Sganarelle-Leporello or with the fathers or brothers of his mistresses: he does not even, like Casanova, tell his own story. In fact he is not a true Don Juan at all; for he is no more an enemy of God than any romantic and adventurous young sower of wild oats. Had you and I been in his place at his age, who knows whether we might not have done as he did, unless indeed your fastidiousness had saved you from the empress Catherine. Byron was as little of a philosopher as Peter the Great: both were instances of that rare and useful, but unedifying variation, an energetic genius born without the prejudices or superstitions of his contemporaries. The resultant unscrupulous freedom of thought made Byron a bolder poet than Wordsworth just as it made Peter a bolder king than George III; but as it was, after all, only a negative qualification, it did not prevent Peter from being an appalling blackguard and an arrant poltroon, nor did it enable Byron to become a religious force like Shelley. Let us, then, leave Byron's Don Juan out of account. Mozart's is the last of the true Don Juans; for by the time he was of age, his cousin Faust had, in the hands of Goethe, taken his place and carried both his warfare and his reconciliation with the gods far beyond mere lovemaking into politics, high art, schemes for reclaiming new continents from the ocean, and recognition of an eternal womanly principle in the universe. Goethe's Faust and Mozart's Don Juan were the last words of the XVIII century on the subject; and by the time the polite critics of the XIX century, ignoring William Blake as superficially as the XVIII had ignored Hogarth or the XVII Bunyan, had got past the Dickens-Macaulay Dumas-Guizot stage and the Stendhal-Meredith-Turgenieff stage, and were confronted with philosophic fiction by such pens as Ibsen's and Tolstoy's, Don Juan had changed his sex and become Doña Juana, breaking out of the Doll's House and asserting herself as an individual instead of a mere item in a moral pageant.

Now it is all very well for you at the beginning of the XX century to ask me for a Don Juan play; but you will see from the foregoing survey that Don Juan is a full century out of date for you and for me; and if there are millions of less literate people who are still in the eighteenth century, have they not Molière and Mozart, upon whose art no human hand can improve? You would laugh at me if at this time of day I dealt in duels and ghosts and "womanly" women. As to mere libertinism, you would be the first to remind me that the Festin de Pierre of Molière is not a play for amorists, and that one bar of the voluptuous sentimentality of Gounod or Bizet would appear as a licentious stain on the score of Don Giovanni. Even the more abstract parts of the Don Juan play are dilapidated past use: for instance, Don Juan's supernatural antagonist hurled those who refuse to repent into lakes of burning brimstone, there to be tormented by devils with horns and tails. Of that antagonist, and of that conception of repentance, how much is left that could be used in a play by me dedicated to you? On the other hand, those forces of middle class public opinion which hardly existed for a Spanish nobleman in the days of the first Don Juan, are now triumphant everywhere. Civilized society is one huge bourgeoisie: no nobleman dares now shock his greengrocer. The women, "marchesane, principesse, cameriere, cittadine" and all, are become equally dangerous: the sex is aggressive, powerful: when women are wronged they do not group themselves pathetically to sing "Protegga il giusto cielo": they grasp formidable legal and social weapons, and retaliate. Political parties are wrecked and public careers undone by a single indiscretion. A man had better have all the statues in London to supper with him, ugly as they are, than be brought to the bar of the Nonconformist Conscience by Donna Elvira. Excommunication has become almost as serious a business as it was in the tenth century.

As a result, Man is no longer, like Don Juan, victor in the duel of sex. Whether he has ever really been may be doubted: at all events the enormous superiority of Woman's natural position in this matter is telling with greater and greater force. As to pulling the Nonconformist Conscience by the beard as Don Juan plucked the beard of the Commandant's statue in the convent of San Francisco, that is out of the question nowadays: prudence and good manners alike forbid it to a hero with any mind. Besides, it is Don Juan's own beard that is in danger of plucking. Far from relapsing into hypocrisy, as Sganarelle feared, he has unexpectedly discovered a moral in his immorality. The growing recognition of his new point of view is heaping responsibility on him. His former jests he has had to take as seriously as I have had to take some of the jests of Mr W. S. Gilbert. His scepticism, once his least tolerated quality, has now triumphed so completely that he can no longer assert himself by witty negations, and must, to save himself from cipherdom, find an affirmative position. His thousand and three affairs of gallantry, after becoming, at most, two immature intrigues leading to sordid and prolonged complications and humiliations, have been discarded altogether as unworthy of his philosophic dignity and compromising to his newly acknowledged position as the founder of a school. Instead of pretending to read Ovid he does actually read Schopenhauer and Nietzsche, studies Westermarck, and is concerned for the future of the race instead of for the freedom of his own instincts. Thus his profligacy and his dare-devil airs have gone the way of his sword and mandoline into the rag shop of anachronisms and superstitions. In fact, he is now more Hamlet than Don Juan; for though the lines put into the actor's mouth to indicate to the pit that Hamlet is a philosopher are for the most part mere harmonious platitude which, with a little debasement of the word-music, would be properer to Pecksniff, yet if you separate the real hero, inarticulate and unintelligible to himself except in flashes of inspiration, from the performer who has to talk at any cost through five acts; and if you also do what you must always do in Shakespear's tragedies: that is, dissect out the absurd sensational incidents and physical violences of the borrowed story from the genuine Shakespearian tissue, you will get a true Promethean foe of the gods, whose instinctive attitude towards women much resembles that to which Don Juan is now driven. From this point of view Hamlet was a developed Don Juan whom Shakespear palmed off as a reputable man just as he palmed poor Macbeth off as a murderer. Today the palming off is no longer necessary (at least on your plane and mine) because Don Juanism is no longer misunderstood as mere Casanovism. Don Juan himself is almost ascetic in his desire to avoid that misunderstanding; and so my attempt to bring him up to date by launching him as a modern Englishman into a modern English environment has produced a figure superficially quite unlike the hero of Mozart.

And yet I have not the heart to disappoint you wholly of another glimpse of the Mozartian *dissoluto punito* and his antagonist the statue. I feel sure you would like to know more of that statue—to draw him out when he is off duty, so to speak. To gratify you, I have resorted to the trick of the strolling theatrical manager who advertizes the pantomime of Sinbad the Sailor with a stock of second-hand picture posters designed for Ali Baba. He simply thrusts a few oil jars into the valley of diamonds, and so fulfils the promise held out by the hoardings to the public eye. I have adapted this easy device to our occasion by thrusting into my perfectly modern three-act play a totally extraneous act in which my hero, enchanted by the air of the Sierra, has a dream in which his Mozartian ancestor appears and philosophizes at great length in a Shavio-Socratic dialogue with the lady, the statue, and the devil.

But this pleasantry is not the essence of the play. Over this essence I have no control. You propound a certain social substance, sexual attraction to wit, for dramatic distillation; and I distil it for you. I do not adulterate the product with aphrodisiacs nor dilute it with romance and water; for I am merely executing your commission, not producing a popular play for the market. You must therefore (unless, like most wise men, you read the play first and the preface afterwards) prepare yourself to face a trumpery story of modern London life, a life in which, as you know, the ordinary man's main business is to get means to keep up the position and habits of a gentleman, and the ordinary woman's business is to get married. In 9,999 cases out of 10,000, you can count on their doing nothing, whether noble or base, that conflicts with these ends; and that assurance is what you rely on as their religion, their morality, their principles, their patriotism, their reputation, their honor and so forth.

On the whole, this is a sensible and satisfactory foundation for society. Money means nourishment and marriage means children; and that men should put nourishment first and women children first is, broadly speaking, the law of Nature and not the dictate of personal ambition. The secret of the prosaic man's success, such as it is, is the simplicity with which he pursues these ends: the secret of the artistic man's failure, such as that is, is the versatility with which he strays in all directions after secondary ideals. The artist is either a poet or a scallawag: as poet, he cannot see, as the prosaic man does, that chivalry is at bottom only romantic suicide: as scallawag, he cannot see that it does not pay to spunge and beg and lie and brag and neglect his person. Therefore do not misunderstand my plain statement of the fundamental constitution of London society as an Irishman's reproach to your nation. From the day I first set foot on this foreign soil I knew the value of the prosaic qualities of which Irishmen teach Englishmen to be ashamed as well as I knew the vanity of the poetic qualities of which Englishmen teach Irishmen to be proud. For the Irishman instinctively disparages the quality which makes the Englishman dangerous to him; and the Englishman instinctively flatters the fault that makes the Irishman harmless and amusing to him. What is wrong with the prosaic Englishman is what is wrong with the prosaic men of all countries: stupidity. The vitality which places nourishment and children first, heaven and hell a somewhat remote second, and the health of society as an organic whole nowhere, may muddle successfully through the comparatively tribal stages of gregariousness; but in nineteenth century nations and twentieth century commonwealths the resolve of every man to be rich at all costs, and of every woman to be married at all costs, must, without a highly scientific social organization, produce a ruinous development of poverty, celibacy, prostitution, infant mortality, adult degeneracy, and everything that wise men most dread. In short, there is no future for men, however brimming with crude vitality, who are neither intelligent nor politically educated enough to be Socialists. So do not misunderstand me in the other direction either: if I appreciate the vital qualities of the Englishman as I appreciate the vital qualities of the bee, I do not guarantee the Englishmen against being, like the bee (or the Canaanite) smoked out and unloaded of his honey by beings inferior to himself in simple acquisitiveness, combativeness, and fecundity, but superior to him in imagination and cunning.

The Don Juan play, however, is to deal with sexual attraction, and not with nutrition, and to deal with it in a society in which the serious business of sex is left by men to women, as the serious business of nutrition is left by women to men. That the men, to protect themselves against a too aggressive prosecution of the women's business, have set up a feeble romantic convention that the initiative in sex business must always come from the man, is true; but the pretence is so shallow that even in the theatre, that last sanctuary of unreality, it imposes only on the inexperienced. In Shakespear's plays the woman always takes the initiative. In his problem plays and his popular plays alike the love interest is the interest of seeing the woman hunt the man down. She may do it by charming him, like Rosalind, or by stratagem, like Mariana; but in every case the relation between the woman and the man is the same: she is the pursuer and contriver, he the pursued and disposed of. When she is baffled, like Ophelia, she goes mad and commits suicide; and the man goes straight from her funeral to a fencing match. No doubt Nature, with very young creatures, may save the woman the trouble of scheming: Prospero knows that he has only to throw Ferdinand and Miranda together and they will mate like a pair of doves; and there is no need for Perdita to capture Florizel as the lady doctor in All's Well That Ends Well (an early Ibsenite heroine) captures Bertram. But the mature cases all illustrate the Shakespearian law. The one apparent exception, Petruchio, is not a real one: he is most carefully characterized as a purely commercial matrimonial adventurer. Once he is assured that Katharine has money, he undertakes to marry her before he has seen her. In real life we find not only Petruchios, but Mantalinis and Dobbins who pursue women with appeals to their pity or jealousy or vanity, or cling to them in a romantically infatuated way. Such effeminates do not count in the world scheme: even Bunsby dropping like a fascinated bird into the jaws of Mrs MacStinger is by comparison a true tragic object of pity and terror. I find in my own plays that Woman, projecting herself dramatically by my hands (a process over which I assure you I have no more real control than I have over my wife), behaves just as Woman did in the plays of Shakespear.

And so your Don Juan has come to birth as a stage projection of the tragi-comic love chase of the man by the woman; and my Don Juan is the quarry instead of the huntsman. Yet he is a true Don Juan, with a sense of reality that disables convention, defying to the last the fate which finally overtakes him. The woman's need of him to enable her to carry on Nature's most urgent work, does not prevail against him until his resistance gathers her energy to a climax at which she dares to throw away her customary exploitations of the conventional affectionate and dutiful poses, and claim him by natural right for a purpose that far transcends their mortal personal purposes.

Among the friends to whom I have read this play in manuscript are some of our own sex who are shocked at the "unscrupulousness," meaning the utter disregard of masculine fastidiousness, with which the woman pursues her purpose. It does not occur to them that if women were as fastidious as men, morally or physically, there would be an end of the race. Is there anything meaner than to throw necessary work upon other people and then disparage it as unworthy and indelicate. We laugh at the haughty American nation because it makes the negro clean its boots and then proves the moral and physical inferiority of the negro by the fact that he is a shoeblack; but we ourselves throw the whole drudgery of creation on one sex, and then imply that no female of any womanliness or delicacy would initiate any effort in that direction. There are no limits to male hypocrisy in this matter. No doubt there are moments when man's sexual immunities are made acutely humiliating to him. When the terrible moment of birth arrives, its supreme importance and its superhuman effort and peril, in which the father has no part, dwarf him into the meanest insignificance: he slinks out of the way of the humblest petticoat, happy if he be poor enough to be pushed out of the house to outface his ignominy by drunken rejoicings. But when the crisis is over he takes his revenge, swaggering as the breadwinner, and speaking of Woman's "sphere" with condescension, even with chivalry, as if the kitchen and the nursery were less important than the office in the city. When his swagger is exhausted he drivels into erotic poetry or sentimental uxoriousness; and the Tennysonian King Arthur posing at Guinevere becomes Don Quixote grovelling before Dulcinea. You must admit that here Nature beats Comedy out of the field: the wildest hominist or feminist farce is insipid after the most commonplace "slice of life." The pretence that women do not take the initiative is part of the farce. Why, the whole world is strewn with snares, traps, gins, and pitfalls for the capture of men by women. Give women the vote, and in five years there will be a crushing tax on bachelors. Men, on the other hand, attach penalties to marriage, depriving women of property, of the franchise, of the free use of their limbs, of that ancient symbol of immortality, the right to make oneself at home in the house of God by taking off the hat, of everything that he can force Woman to dispense with without compelling himself to dispense with her. All in vain. Woman must marry because the race must perish without her travail: if the risk of death and the certainty of pain, danger, and unutterable discomforts cannot deter her, slavery and swaddled ankles will not. And yet we assume that the force that carries women through all these perils and hardships, stops abashed before the primnesses of our behavior for young ladies. It is assumed that the woman must wait, motionless, until she is wooed. Nay, she often does wait motionless. That is how the spider waits for the fly. But the spider spins her web. And if the fly, like my hero, shews a strength that promises to extricate him, how swiftly does she abandon her pretence of passiveness, and openly fling coil after coil about him until he is secured for ever!

If the really impressive books and other art-works of the world were produced by ordinary men, they would express more fear of women's pursuit than love of their illusory beauty. But ordinary men cannot produce really impressive art-works. Those who can are men of genius: that is, men selected by Nature to carry on the work of building up an intellectual consciousness of her own instinctive purpose. Accordingly, we observe in the man of genius all the unscrupulousness and all the "self-sacrifice" (the two things are the same) of Woman. He will risk the stake and the cross; starve, when necessary, in a garret all his life; study women and live on their work and care as Darwin studied worms and lived upon sheep; work his nerves into rags without payment, a sublime altruist in his disregard of himself, an atrocious egotist in his disregard of others. Here Woman meets a purpose as impersonal, as irresistible as her own; and the clash is sometimes tragic. When it is complicated by the genius being a woman, then the game is one for a king of critics: your George Sand becomes a mother to gain experience for the novelist and to develop her, and gobbles up men of genius, Chopins, Mussets and the like, as mere hors d'œuvres.

I state the extreme case, of course; but what is true of the great man who incarnates the philosophic consciousness of Life and the woman who incarnates its fecundity, is true in some degree of all geniuses and all women. Hence it is that the world's books get written, its pictures painted, its statues modelled, its symphonies composed, by people who are free from the otherwise universal dominion of the tyranny of sex. Which leads us to the conclusion, astonishing to the vulgar, that art, instead of being before all things the expression of the normal sexual situation, is really the only department in which sex is a superseded and secondary power, with its consciousness so confused and its purpose so perverted, that its ideas are mere fantasy to common men. Whether the artist becomes poet or philosopher, moralist or founder of a religion, his sexual doctrine is nothing but a barren special pleading for pleasure, excitement, and knowledge when he is young, and for contemplative tranquillity when he is old and satiated. Romance and Asceticism, Amorism and Puritanism are equally unreal in the great Philistine world. The world shewn us in books, whether the books be confessed epics or professed gospels, or in codes, or in political orations, or in philosophic systems, is not the main world at all: it is only the self-consciousness of certain abnormal people who have the specific artistic talent and temperament. A serious matter this for you and me, because the man whose consciousness does not correspond to that of the majority is a madman; and the old habit of worshipping madmen is giving way to the new habit of locking them up. And since what we call education and culture is for the most part nothing but the substitution of reading for experience, of literature for life, of the obsolete fictitious for the contemporary real, education, as you no doubt observed at Oxford, destroys, by supplantation, every mind that is not strong enough to see through the imposture and to use the great Masters of Arts as what they really are and no more: that is, patentees of highly questionable methods of thinking, and manufacturers of highly questionable, and for the majority but half valid representations of life. The schoolboy who uses his Homer to throw at his fellow's head makes perhaps the safest and most rational use of him; and I observe with reassurance that you occasionally do the same, in your prime, with your Aristotle.

Fortunately for us, whose minds have been so overwhelmingly sophisticated by literature, what produces all these treatises and poems and scriptures of one sort or another is the struggle of Life to become divinely conscious of itself instead of blindly stumbling hither and thither in the line of least resistance. Hence there is a driving towards truth in all books on matters where the writer, though exceptionally gifted, is normally constituted, and has no private axe to grind. Copernicus had no motive for misleading his fellowmen as to the place of the sun in the solar system: he looked for it as honestly as a shepherd seeks his path in a mist. But Copernicus would not have written love stories scientifically. When it comes to sex relations, the man of genius does not share the common man's danger of capture, nor the woman of genius the common woman's overwhelming specialization. And that is why our scriptures and other art works, when they deal with love, turn from honest attempts at science in physics to romantic nonsense, erotic ecstasy, or the stern asceticism of satiety ("the road of excess leads to the palace of wisdom" said William Blake; for "you never know what is enough unless you know what is more than enough").

There is a political aspect of this sex question which is too big for my comedy, and too momentous to be passed over without culpable frivolity. It is impossible to demonstrate that the initiative in sex transactions remains with Woman, and has been confirmed to her, so far, more and more by the suppression of rapine and discouragement of importunity, without being driven to very serious reflections on the fact that this initiative is politically the most important of all the initiatives, because our political experiment of democracy, the last refuge of cheap misgovernment, will ruin us if our citizens are ill bred.

When we two were born, this country was still dominated by a selected class bred by political marriages. The commercial class had not then completed the first twentyfive years of its new share of political power; and it was itself selected by money qualification, and bred, if not by political marriage, at least by a pretty rigorous class marriage. Aristocracy and plutocracy still furnish the figureheads of politics; but they are now dependent on the votes of the promiscuously bred masses. And this, if you please, at the very moment when the political problem, having suddenly ceased to mean a very limited and occasional interference, mostly by way of jobbing public appointments, in the mismanagement of a tight but parochial little island, with occasional meaningless prosecution of dynastic wars, has become the industrial reorganization of Britain, the construction of a practically international Commonwealth, and the partition of the whole of Africa and perhaps the whole of Asia by the civilized Powers. Can you believe that the people whose conceptions of society and conduct, whose power of attention and scope of interest, are measured by the British theatre as you know it today, can either handle this colossal task themselves, or understand and support the sort of mind and character that is (at least comparatively) capable of handling it? For remember: what our voters are in the pit and gallery they are also in the polling booth. We are all now under what Burke called "the hoofs of the swinish multitude." Burke's language gave great offence because the implied exceptions to its universal application made it a class insult; and it certainly was not for the pot to call the kettle black. The aristocracy he defended, in spite of the political marriages by which it tried to secure breeding for itself, had its mind undertrained by silly schoolmasters and governesses, its character corrupted by gratuitous luxury, its self-respect adulterated to complete spuriousness by flattery and flunkeyism. It is no better today and never will be any better: our very peasants have something morally hardier in them that culminates occasionally in a Bunyan, a Burns, or a Carlyle. But observe, this aristocracy, which was overpowered from 1832 to 1885 by the middle class, has come back to power by the votes of "the swinish multitude." Tom Paine has triumphed over Edmund Burke; and the swine are now courted electors. How many of their own class have these electors sent to parliament? Hardly a dozen out of 670, and these only under the persuasion of conspicuous personal qualifications and popular eloquence. The multitude thus pronounces judgment on its own units: it admits itself unfit to govern, and will vote only for a man morphologically and generically transfigured by palatial residence and equipage, by transcendent tailoring, by the glamor of aristocratic kinship. Well, we two know these transfigured persons, these college passmen, these well groomed monocular Algys and Bobbies, these cricketers to whom age brings golf instead of wisdom, these plutocratic products of "the nail and sarspan business as he got his money by." Do you know whether to laugh or cry at the notion that they, poor devils! will drive a team of continents as they drive a four-in-hand; turn a jostling anarchy of casual trade and speculation into an ordered productivity; and federate our colonies into a world-Power of the first magnitude? Give these people the most perfect political constitution and the soundest political program that benevolent omniscience can devise for them, and they will interpret it into mere fashionable folly or canting charity as infallibly as a savage converts the philosophical theology of a Scotch missionary into crude African idolatry.

I do not know whether you have any illusions left on the subject of education, progress, and so forth. I have none. Any pamphleteer can shew the way to better things; but when there is no will there is no way. My nurse was fond of remarking that you cannot make a silk purse out of a sow's ear; and the more I see of the efforts of our churches and universities and literary sages to raise the mass above its own level, the more convinced I am that my nurse was right. Progress can do nothing but make the most of us all as we are, and that most would clearly not be enough even if those who are already raised out of the lowest abysses would allow the others a chance. The bubble of Heredity has been pricked: the certainty that acquirements are negligible as elements in practical heredity has demolished the hopes of the educationists as well as the terrors of the degeneracy mongers; and we know now that there is no hereditary "governing class" any more than a hereditary hooliganism. We must either breed political capacity or be ruined by Democracy, which was forced on us by the failure of the older alternatives. Yet if Despotism failed only for want of a capable benevolent despot, what chance has Democracy, which requires a whole population of capable voters: that is, of political critics who, if they cannot govern in person for lack of spare energy or specific talent for administration, can at least recognize and appreciate capacity and benevolence in others, and so govern through capably benevolent representatives? Where are such voters to be found today? Nowhere. Plutocratic inbreeding has produced a weakness of character that is too timid to face the full stringency of a thoroughly competitive struggle for existence and too lazy and petty to organize the commonwealth co-operatively. Being cowards, we defeat natural selection under cover of philanthropy: being sluggards, we neglect artificial selection under cover of delicacy and morality.

Yet we must get an electorate of capable critics or collapse as Rome and Egypt collapsed. At this moment the Roman decadent phase of *panem et circenses* is being inaugurated under our eyes. Our newspapers and melodramas are blustering about our imperial destiny; but our eyes and hearts turn eagerly to the American millionaire. As his hand goes down to his pocket, our fingers go up to the brims of our hats by instinct. Our ideal prosperity is not the prosperity of the industrial north, but the prosperity of the Isle of Wight, of Folkestone and Ramsgate, of Nice and Monte Carlo. That is the only prosperity you see on the stage, where the workers are all footmen, parlourmaids, comic lodging-letters, and fashionable professional men, whilst the heroes and heroines are miraculously provided with unlimited dividends and eat gratuitously, like the knights in Don Quixote's books of chivalry. The city papers prate of the competition of Bombay with Manchester and the like. The real competition is the competition of Regent Street with the Rue de Rivoli, of Brighton and the south coast with the Riviera, for the spending money of the American Trusts. What is all this growing love of pageantry, this effusive loyalty, this officious rising and uncovering at a wave from a flag or a blast from a brass band? Imperialism? Not a bit of it. Obsequiousness, servility, cupidity roused by the prevailing smell of money. When Mr Carnegie rattled his millions in his pockets all England became one rapacious cringe. Only, when Rhodes (who had probably been reading my Socialism for Millionaires) left word that no idler was to inherit his estate, the bent backs straightened mistrustfully for a moment. Could it be that the Diamond King was no gentleman after all? However, it was easy to ignore a rich man's solecism. The ungentlemanly clause was not mentioned again; and the backs soon bowed themselves back into their natural shape.

But I hear you asking me in alarm whether I have actually put all this tub thumping into a Don Juan comedy. I have not. I have only made my Don Juan a political pamphleteer, and given you his pamphlet in full by way of appendix. You will find it at the end of the book. I am sorry to say that it is a common practice with romancers to announce their hero as a man of extraordinary genius, and then leave his works entirely to the reader's imagination; so that at the end of the book you whisper to yourself ruefully that but for the author's solemn preliminary assurance you should hardly have given the gentleman credit for ordinary good sense. You cannot accuse me of this pitiable barrenness, this feeble evasion. I not only tell you that my hero wrote a revolutionists' handbook: I give you the handbook at full length for your edification if you care to read it. And in that handbook you will find the politics of the sex question as I conceive Don Juan's descendant to understand them. Not that I disclaim the fullest responsibility for his opinions and for those of all my characters, pleasant and unpleasant. They are all right from their several points of view; and their points of view are, for the dramatic moment, mine also. This may puzzle the people who believe that there is such a thing as an absolutely right point of view, usually their own. It may seem to them that nobody who doubts this can be in a state of grace. However that may be, it is certainly true that nobody who agrees with them can possibly be a dramatist, or indeed anything else that turns upon a knowledge of mankind. Hence it has been pointed out that Shakespear had no conscience. Neither have I, in that sense.

You may, however, remind me that this digression of mine into politics was preceded by a very convincing demonstration that the artist never catches the point of view of the common man on the question of sex, because he is not in the same predicament. I first prove that anything I write on the relation of the sexes is sure to be misleading; and then I proceed to write a Don Juan play. Well, if you insist on asking me why I behave in this absurd way, I can only reply that you asked me to, and that in any case my treatment of the subject may be valid for the artist, amusing to the amateur, and at least intelligible and therefore possibly suggestive to the Philistine. Every man who records his illusions is providing data for the genuinely scientific psychology which the world still waits for. I plank down my view of the existing relations of men to women in the most highly civilized society for what it is worth. It is a view like any other view and no more, neither true nor false, but, I hope, a way of looking at the subject which throws into the familiar order of cause and effect a sufficient body of fact and experience to be interesting to you, if not to the play-going public of London. I have certainly shewn little consideration for that public in this enterprise; but I know that it has the friendliest disposition towards you and me as far as it has any consciousness of our existence, and quite understands that what I write for you must pass at a considerable height over its simple romantic head. It will take my books as read and my genius for granted, trusting me to put forth work of such quality as shall bear out its verdict. So we may disport ourselves on our own plane to the top of our bent; and if any gentleman points out that neither this epistle dedicatory nor the dream of Don Juan in the third act of the ensuing comedy is suitable for immediate production at a popular theatre we need not contradict him. Napoleon provided Talma with a pit of kings, with what effect on Talma's acting is not recorded. As for me, what I have always wanted is a pit of philosophers; and this is a play for such a pit.

I should make formal acknowledgement to the authors whom I have pillaged in the following pages if I could recollect them all. The theft of the brigand-poetaster from Sir Arthur Conan Doyle is deliberate; and the metamorphosis of Leporello into Enry Straker, motor engineer and New Man, is an intentional dramatic sketch of the contemporary embryo of Mr H. G. Wells's anticipation of the efficient engineering class which will, he hopes, finally sweep the jabberers out of the way of civilization. Mr Barrie has also, whilst I am correcting my proofs, delighted London with a servant who knows more than his masters. The conception of Mendoza Limited I trace back to a certain West Indian colonial secretary, who, at a period when he and I and Mr Sidney Webb were sowing our political wild oats as a sort of Fabian Three Musketeers, without any prevision of the surprising respectability of the crop that followed, recommended Webb, the encyclopedic and inexhaustible, to form himself into a company for the benefit of the shareholders. Octavius I take over unaltered from Mozart; and I hereby authorize any actor who impersonates him, to sing "Dalla sua pace" (if he can) at any convenient moment during the representation. Ann was suggested to me by the fifteenth century Dutch morality called Everyman, which Mr William Poel has lately resuscitated so triumphantly. I trust he will work that vein further, and recognize that Elizabethan Renascence fustian is no more bearable after medieval poesy than Scribe after Ibsen. As I sat watching Everyman at the Charterhouse, I said to myself Why not Everywoman? Ann was the result: every woman is not Ann; but Ann is Everywoman.

That the author of Everyman was no mere artist, but an artist-philosopher, and that the artist-philosophers are the only sort of artists I take quite seriously, will be no news to you. Even Plato and Boswell, as the dramatists who invented Socrates and Dr Johnson, impress me more deeply than the romantic playwrights. Ever since, as a boy, I first breathed the air of the transcendental regions at a performance of Mozart's Zauberflöte, I have been proof against the garish splendors and alcoholic excitements of the ordinary stage combinations of Tappertitian romance with the police intelligence. Bunyan, Blake, Hogarth, and Turner (these four apart and above all the English classics), Goethe, Shelley, Schopenhauer, Wagner, Ibsen, Morris, Tolstoy, and Nietzsche are among the writers whose peculiar sense of the world I recognize as more or less akin to my own. Mark the word peculiar. I read Dickens and Shakespear without shame or stint; but their pregnant observations and demonstrations of life are not coordinated into any philosophy or religion: on the contrary, Dickens's sentimental assumptions are violently contradicted by his observations; and Shakespear's pessimism is only his wounded humanity. Both have the specific genius of the fictionist and the common sympathies of human feeling and thought in preeminent degree. They are often saner and shrewder than the philosophers just as Sancho-Panza was often saner and shrewder than Don Quixote. They clear away vast masses of oppressive gravity by their sense of the ridiculous, which is at bottom a combination of sound moral judgment with lighthearted good humor. But they are concerned with the diversities of the world instead of with its unities: they are so irreligious that they exploit popular religion for professional purposes without delicacy or scruple (for example, Sydney Carton and the ghost in Hamlet!): they are anarchical, and cannot balance their exposures of Angelo and Dogberry, Sir Leicester Dedlock and Mr Tite Barnacle, with any portrait of a prophet or a worthy leader: they have no constructive ideas: they regard those who have them as dangerous fanatics: in all their fictions there is no leading thought or inspiration for which any man could conceivably risk the spoiling of his hat in a shower, much less his life. Both are alike forced to borrow motives for the more strenuous actions of their personages from the common stockpot of melodramatic plots; so that Hamlet has to be stimulated by the prejudices of a policeman and Macbeth by the cupidities of a bushranger. Dickens, without the excuse of having to manufacture motives for Hamlets and Macbeths, superfluously punts his crew down the stream of his monthly parts by mechanical devices which I leave you to describe, my own memory being quite baffled by the simplest question as to Monks in Oliver Twist, or the long lost parentage of Smike, or the relations between the Dorrit and Clennam families so inopportunely discovered by Monsieur Rigaud Blandois. The truth is, the world was to Shakespear a great "stage of fools" on which he was utterly bewildered. He could see no sort of sense in living at all; and Dickens saved himself from the despair of the dream in The Chimes by taking the world for granted and busying himself with its details. Neither of them could do anything with a serious positive character: they could place a human figure before you with perfect verisimilitude; but when the moment came for making it live and move, they found, unless it made them laugh, that they had a puppet on their hands, and had to invent some artificial external stimulus to make it work. This is what is the matter with Hamlet all through: he has no will except in his bursts of temper. Foolish Bardolaters make a virtue of this after their fashion: they declare that the play is the tragedy of irresolution; but all Shakespear's projections of the deepest humanity he knew have the same defect: their characters and manners are lifelike; but their actions are forced on them from without, and the external force is grotesquely inappropriate except when it is quite conventional, as in the case of Henry V. Falstaff is more vivid than any of these serious reflective characters, because he is self-acting: his motives are his own appetites and instincts and humors. Richard III, too, is delightful as the whimsical comedian who stops a funeral to make love to the corpse's son's widow; but when, in the next act, he is replaced by a stage villain who smothers babies and offs with people's heads, we are revolted at the imposture and repudiate the changeling. Faulconbridge, Coriolanus, Leontes are admirable descriptions of instinctive temperaments: indeed the play of Coriolanus is the greatest of Shakespear's comedies; but description is not philosophy; and comedy neither compromises the author nor reveals him. He must be judged by those characters into which he puts what he knows of himself, his Hamlets and Macbeths and Lears and Prosperos. If these characters are agonizing in a void about factitious melodramatic murders and revenges and the like, whilst the comic characters walk with their feet on solid ground, vivid and amusing, you know that the author has much to shew and nothing to teach. The comparison between Falstaff and Prospero is like the comparison between Micawber and David Copperfield. At the end of the book you know Micawber, whereas you only know what has happened to David, and are not interested enough in him to wonder what his politics or religion might be if anything so stupendous as a religious or political idea, or a general idea of any sort, were to occur to him. He is tolerable as a child; but he never becomes a man, and might be left out of his own biography altogether but for his usefulness as a stage confidant, a Horatio or "Charles his friend": what they call on the stage a feeder.

Now you cannot say this of the works of the artist-philosophers. You cannot say it, for instance, of The Pilgrim's Progress. Put your Shakespearian hero and coward, Henry V and Pistol or Parolles, beside Mr Valiant and Mr Fearing, and you have a sudden revelation of the abyss that lies between the fashionable author who could see nothing in the world but personal aims and the tragedy of their disappointment or the comedy of their incongruity, and the field preacher who achieved virtue and courage by identifying himself with the purpose of the world as he understood it. The contrast is enormous: Bunyan's coward stirs your blood more than Shakespear's hero, who actually leaves you cold and secretly hostile. You suddenly see that Shakespear, with all his flashes and divinations, never understood virtue and courage, never conceived how any man who was not a fool could, like Bunyan's hero, look back from the brink of the river of death over the strife and labor of his pilgrimage, and say "yet do I not repent me"; or, with the panache of a millionaire, bequeath "my sword to him that shall succeed me in my pilgrimage, and my courage and skill to him that can get it." This is the true joy in life, the being used for a purpose recognized by yourself as a mighty one; the being thoroughly worn out before you are thrown on the scrap heap; the being a force of Nature instead of a feverish selfish little clod of ailments and grievances complaining that the world will not devote itself to making you happy. And also the only real tragedy in life is the being used by personally minded men for purposes which you recognize to be base. All the rest is at worst mere misfortune or mortality: this alone is misery, slavery, hell on earth; and the revolt against it is the only force that offers a man's work to the poor artist, whom our personally minded rich people would so willingly employ as pandar, buffoon, beauty monger, sentimentalizer and the like.

It may seem a long step from Bunyan to Nietzsche; but the difference between their conclusions is merely formal. Bunyan's perception that righteousness is filthy rags, his scorn for Mr Legality in the village of Morality, his defiance of the Church as the supplanter of religion, his insistence on courage as the virtue of virtues, his estimate of the career of the conventionally respectable and sensible Worldly Wiseman as no better at bottom than the life and death of Mr Badman: all this, expressed by Bunyan in the terms of a tinker's theology, is what Nietzsche has expressed in terms of post-Darwin, post-Schopenhauer philosophy; Wagner in terms of polytheistic mythology; and Ibsen in terms of mid-XIX century Parisian dramaturgy. Nothing is new in these matters except their novelties: for instance, it is a novelty to call Justification by Faith "Wille," and Justification by Works "Vorstellung." The sole use of the novelty is that you and I buy and read Schopenhauer's treatise on Will and Representation when we should not dream of buying a set of sermons on Faith versus Works. At bottom the controversy is the same, and the dramatic results are the same. Bunyan makes no attempt to present his pilgrims as more sensible or better conducted than Mr Worldly Wiseman. Mr W. W.'s worst enemies, Mr Embezzler, Mr Never-go-to-Church-on-Sunday, Mr Bad Form, Mr Murderer, Mr Burglar, Mr Co-respondent, Mr Blackmailer, Mr Cad, Mr Drunkard, Mr Labor Agitator and so forth, can read the Pilgrim's Progress without finding a word said against them; whereas the respectable people who snub them and put them in prison, such as Mr W. W. himself and his young friend Civility; Formalist and Hypocrisy; Wildhead, Inconsiderate, and Pragmatick (who were clearly young university men of good family and high feeding); that brisk lad Ignorance, Talkative, By-ends of Fairspeech and his mother-in-law Lady Feigning, and other reputable gentlemen and citizens, catch it very severely. Even Little Faith, though he gets to heaven at last, is given to understand that it served him right to be mobbed by the brothers Faint Heart, Mistrust, and Guilt, all three recognized members of respectable society and veritable pillars of the law. The whole allegory is a consistent attack on morality and respectability, without a word that one can remember against vice and crime. Exactly what is complained of in Nietzsche and Ibsen, is it not? And also exactly what would be complained of in all the literature which is great enough and old enough to have attained canonical rank, officially or unofficially, were it not that books are admitted to the canon by a compact which confesses their greatness in consideration of abrogating their meaning; so that the reverend rector can agree with the prophet Micah as to his inspired style without being committed to any complicity in Micah's furiously Radical opinions. Why, even I, as I force myself, pen in hand, into recognition and civility, find all the force of my onslaught destroyed by a simple policy of nonresistance. In vain do I redouble the violence of the language in which I proclaim my heterodoxies. I rail at the theistic credulity of Voltaire, the amoristic superstition of Shelley, the revival of tribal sooth-saying and idolatrous rites which Huxley called Science and mistook for an advance on the Pentateuch, no less than at the welter of ecclesiastical and professional humbug which saves the face of the stupid system of violence and robbery which we call Law and Industry. Even atheists reproach me with infidelity and anarchists with nihilism because I cannot endure their moral tirades. And yet, instead of exclaiming "Send this inconceivable Satanist to the stake," the respectable newspapers pith me by announcing "another book by this brilliant and thoughtful writer." And the ordinary citizen, knowing that an author who is well spoken of by a respectable newspaper must be all right, reads me, as he reads Micah, with undisturbed edification from his own point of view. It is narrated that in the eighteenseventies an old lady, a very devout Methodist, moved from Colchester to a house in the neighborhood of the City Road, in London, where, mistaking the Hall of Science for a chapel, she sat at the feet of Charles Bradlaugh for many years, entranced by his eloquence, without questioning his orthodoxy or moulting a feather of her faith. I fear I shall be defrauded of my just martyrdom in the same way.

However, I am digressing, as a man with a grievance always does. And after all, the main thing in determining the artistic quality of a book is not the opinions it propagates, but the fact that the writer has opinions. The old lady from Colchester was right to sun her simple soul in the energetic radiance of Bradlaugh's genuine beliefs and disbeliefs rather than in the chill of such mere painting of light and heat as elocution and convention can achieve. My contempt for *belles lettres*, and for amateurs who become the heroes of the fanciers of literary virtuosity, is not founded on any illusion of mine as to the permanence of those forms of thought (call them opinions) by which I strive to communicate my bent to my fellows. To younger men they are already outmoded; for though they have no more lost their logic than an eighteenth century pastel has lost its drawing or its color, yet, like the pastel, they grow indefinably shabby, and will grow shabbier until they cease to count at all, when my books will either perish, or, if the world is still poor enough to want them, will have to stand, with Bunyan's, by quite amorphous qualities of temper and energy. With this conviction I cannot be a bellettrist. No doubt I must recognize, as even the Ancient Mariner did, that I must tell my story entertainingly if I am to hold the wedding guest spellbound in spite of the siren sounds of the loud bassoon. But "for art's sake" alone I would not face the toil of writing a single sentence. I know that there are men who, having nothing to say and nothing to write, are nevertheless so in love with oratory and with literature that they delight in repeating as much as they can understand of what others have said or written aforetime. I know that the leisurely tricks which their want of conviction leaves them free to play with the diluted and misapprehended message supply them with a pleasant parlor game which they call style. I can pity their dotage and even sympathize with their fancy. But a true original style is never achieved for its own sake: a man may pay from a shilling to a guinea, according to his means, to see, hear, or read another man's act of genius; but he will not pay with his whole life and soul to become a mere virtuoso in literature, exhibiting an accomplishment which will not even make money for him, like fiddle playing. Effectiveness of assertion is the Alpha and Omega of style. He who has nothing to assert has no style and can have none: he who has something to assert will go as far in power of style as its momentousness and his conviction will carry him. Disprove his assertion after it is made, yet its style remains. Darwin has no more destroyed the style of Job nor of Handel than Martin Luther destroyed the style of Giotto. All the assertions get disproved sooner or later; and so we find the world full of a magnificent débris of artistic fossils, with the matter-of-fact credibility gone clean out of them, but the form still splendid. And that is why the old masters play the deuce with our mere susceptibles. Your Royal Academician thinks he can get the style of Giotto without Giotto's beliefs, and correct his perspective into the bargain. Your man of letters thinks he can get Bunyan's or Shakespear's style without Bunyan's conviction or Shakespear's apprehension, especially if he takes care not to split his infinitives. And so with your Doctors of Music, who, with their collections of discords duly prepared and resolved or retarded or anticipated in the manner of the great composers, think they can learn the art of Palestrina from Cherubini's treatise. All this academic art is far worse than the trade in sham antique furniture; for the man who sells me an oaken chest which he swears was made in the XIII century, though as a matter of fact he made it himself only yesterday, at least does not pretend that there are any modern ideas in it; whereas your academic copier of fossils offers them to you as the latest outpouring of the human spirit, and, worst of all, kidnaps young people as pupils and persuades them that his limitations are rules, his observances dexterities, his timidities good taste, and his emptinesses purities. And when he declares that art should not be didactic, all the people who have nothing to teach and all the people who dont want to learn agree with him emphatically.

I pride myself on not being one of these susceptibles. If you study the electric light with which I supply you in that Bumbledonian public capacity of mine over which you make merry from time to time, you will find that your house contains a great quantity of highly susceptible copper wire which gorges itself with electricity and gives you no light whatever. But here and there occurs a scrap of intensely insusceptible, intensely resistant material; and that stubborn scrap grapples with the current and will not let it through until it has made itself useful to you as those two vital qualities of literature, light and heat. Now if I am to be no mere copper wire amateur but a luminous author, I must also be a most intensely refractory person, liable to go out and to go wrong at inconvenient moments, and with incendiary possibilities. These are the faults of my qualities; and I assure you that I sometimes dislike myself so much that when some irritable reviewer chances at that moment to pitch into me with zest, I feel unspeakably relieved and obliged. But I never dream of reforming, knowing that I must take myself as I am and get what work I can out of myself. All this you will understand; for there is community of material between us: we are both critics of life as well as of art; and you have perhaps said to yourself when I have passed your windows "There, but for the grace of God, go I." An awful and chastening reflection, which shall be the closing cadence of this immoderately long letter from yours faithfully,

G. BERNARD SHAW

WOKING, 1903

P.S.—Amid unprecedented critical cerebration over this book of ours —alas! that your own voice should be dedicated to silence!—I find myself warned to prepare a new edition. I take the opportunity to correct a slip or two. You may have noticed (nobody else has, by the way) that I fitted you with a quotation from Othello, and then unconsciously referred it to A Winter's Tale. I correct this with regret; for half its appropriateness goes with Florizel and Perdita: still, one must not trifle with Shakespear; so I have given Desdemona back her property.

On the whole, the book has done very well. The strong critics are impressed; the weak intimidated; the connoisseurs tickled by my literary bravura (put in to please you): the humorists alone, oddly enough, sermonize me, scared out of their profession into the quaintest tumults of conscience. Not all my reviewers have understood me: like Englishmen in France, confidently uttering their own island diphthongs as good French vowels, many of them offer, as samples of the Shavian philosophy, the likest article from their own stock. Others are the victims of association of ideas: they call me Pessimist because my remarks wound their self-complacency, and Renegade because I would have my mob all Cæsars instead of Toms, Dicks, and Harrys. Worst of all, I have been accused of preaching a Final Ethical Superman: no other, in fact, than our old friend the Just Man made Perfect! This misunderstanding is so galling that I lay down my pen without another word lest I should be tempted to make the postscript longer even than the letter.

POSTSCRIPT 1933. The evolutionary theme of the third act of *Man and Superman* was resumed by me twenty years later in the preface to *Back to Methuselah,* where it is developed as the basis of the religion of the near future.

A Foreword to the Popular Edition of "Man and Superman"

I have a special reason for making this book more widely accessible than it can be, even in these days of free libraries, at the customary price of my books. It is described on the title page as "A Comedy and a Philosophy." It might have been called a religion as well; for the vision of hell in the third act, which has never been performed on the stage except as a separate work, is expressly intended to be a revelation of the modern religion of evolution.

Putting it roughly and briefly, the discovery and vogue of evolution, from 1790 to 1830, made an end, for the pioneers of thought, of XVIII century rationalist atheism and deism on the one hand, and, on the other, of what may be called Garden-of-Edenism. In the middle of the XIX century the discovery by Darwin and Wallace of Natural Selection, which might have had as its sub-title "The revelation of a method by which all the appearances of intelligent design in the universe may have been produced by pure accident," practically destroyed religion in cultured Europe for a whole generation, in spite of Darwin's and Wallace's own reservations and the urgent warnings and fierce criticisms of Samuel Butler. With the beginning of the present century the return swing of the pendulum has inaugurated a counterfashion of saying that Natural Selection, instead of accounting for everything, accounts for nothing. That it accounts for nothing in any religious sense is of course true; for it leaves untouched the whole sphere of will, purpose, design, intention, even consciousness; and a religion is nothing but a common view of the nature of will, the purpose of life, the design of organism, and the intention of evolution. Such a common view has been gradually detaching itself from the welter of negation provoked by the extremely debased forms of religion which have masqueraded as Christianity in England during the period of petty commercialism from which we are emerging. The time has come for an attempt to formulate this common view as a modern religion, and to provide it with a body of doctrine, a poesy, and a political and industrial system. Shelley and Wagner made notable attempts to provide it with materials for a Bible; and I, with later lights of science to guide me than either of these prophets had, have made a further attempt in this Man and Superman. As I have not been sparing of such lighter qualities as I could endow the book with for the sake of those who ask nothing from a play but an agreeable pastime, I think it well to affirm plainly that the third act, however fantastic its legendary framework may appear, is a careful attempt to write a new Book of Genesis for the Bible of the Evolutionists; and as it is recognized that no matter how highly priced other works of art may be, Bibles must be cheap, I have consented to the issue of this edition at the lowest price possible in the book market to-day.

G.B.S.

22nd March, 1911

ACT I

Roebuck Ramsden is in his study, opening the morning's letters. The study, handsomely and solidly furnished, proclaims the man of means. Not a speck of dust is visible: it is clear that there are at least two housemaids and a parlormaid downstairs, and a housekeeper upstairs who does not let them spare elbow-grease. Even the top of Roebuck's head is polished: on a sunshiny day he could heliograph his orders to distant camps by merely nodding. In no other respect, however, does he suggest the military man. It is in active civil life that men get his broad air of importance, his dignified expectation of deference, his determinate mouth disarmed and refined since the hour of his success by the withdrawal of opposition and the concession of comfort and precedence and power. He is more than a highly respectable man: he is marked out as a president of highly respectable men, a chairman among directors, an alderman among councillors, a mayor among aldermen. Four tufts of iron-grey hair, which will soon be as white as isinglass, and are in other respects not at all unlike it, grow in two symmetrical pairs above his ears and at the angles of his spreading jaws. He wears a black frock coat, a white waistcoat (it is bright spring weather), and trousers, neither black nor perceptibly blue, of one of those indefinitely mixed hues which the modern clothier has produced to harmonize with the religions of respectable men. He has not been out of doors yet today; so he still wears his slippers, his boots being ready for him on the hearthrug. Surmising that he has no valet, and seeing that he has no secretary with a shorthand notebook and a typewriter, one meditates on how little our great burgess domesticity has been disturbed by new fashions and methods, or by the enterprise of the railway and hotel companies which sell you a Saturday to Monday of life at Folkestone as a real gentleman for two guineas, first class fares both ways included.

How old is Roebuck? The question is important on the threshold of a drama of ideas; for under such circumstances everything depends on whether his adolescence belonged to the sixties or to the eighties. He was born, as a matter of fact, in 1839, and was a Unitarian and Free Trader from his boyhood, and an Evolutionist from the publication of the Origin of Species. Consequently he has always classed himself as an advanced thinker and fearlessly outspoken reformer.

Sitting at his writing table, he has on his right the windows giving on Portland Place. Through these, as through a proscenium, the curious spectator may contemplate his profile as well as the blinds will permit. On his left is the inner wall, with a stately bookcase, and the door not quite in the middle, but somewhat further from him. Against the wall opposite him are two busts on pillars: one, to his left, of John Bright; the other, to his right, of Mr Herbert Spencer. Between them hang an engraved portrait of Richard Cobden; enlarged photographs of Martineau, Huxley, and George Eliot; autotypes of allegories by Mr G. F. Watts (for Roebuck believes in the fine arts with all the earnestness of a man who does not understand them), and an impression of Dupont's engraving of Delaroche's Beaux Arts hemicycle, representing the great men of all ages. On the wall behind him, above the mantelshelf, is a family portrait of impenetrable obscurity.

A chair stands near the writing table for the convenience of business visitors. Two other chairs are against the wall between the busts.

A parlormaid enters with a visitor's card. Roebuck takes it, and nods, pleased. Evidently a welcome caller.

RAMSDEN. Shew him in.

The parlormaid goes out and returns with the visitor.

THE MAID. Mr Robinson.

Mr Robinson is really an uncommonly nice looking young fellow. He must, one thinks, be the jeune premier; for it is not in reason to suppose that a second such attractive male figure should appear in one story. The slim, shapely frame, the elegant suit of new mourning, the small head and regular features, the pretty little moustache, the frank clear eyes, the wholesome bloom on the youthful complexion, the well brushed glossy hair, not curly, but of fine texture and good dark color, the arch of good nature in the eyebrows, the erect forehead and neatly pointed chin, all announce the man who will love and suffer later on. And that he will not do so without sympathy is guaranteed by an engaging sincerity and eager modest serviceableness which stamp him as a man of amiable nature. The moment he appears, Ramsden's face expands into fatherly liking and welcome, an expression which drops into one of decorous grief as the young man approaches him with sor-

row in his face as well as in his black clothes. Ramsden seems to know the nature of the bereavement. As the visitor advances silently to the writing table, the old man rises and shakes his hand across it without a word: a long, affectionate shake which tells the story of a recent sorrow common to both.

RAMSDEN [*concluding the handshake and cheering up*] Well, well, Octavius, it's the common lot. We must all face it some day. Sit down.

Octavius takes the visitor's chair. Ramsden replaces himself in his own.

OCTAVIUS. Yes: we must face it, Mr Ramsden. But I owed him a great deal. He did everything for me that my father could have done if he had lived.

RAMSDEN. He had no son of his own, you see.

OCTAVIUS. But he had daughters; and yet he was as good to my sister as to me. And his death was so sudden! I always intended to thank him—to let him know that I had not taken all his care of me as a matter of course, as any boy takes his father's care. But I waited for an opportunity; and now he is dead—dropped without a moment's warning. He will never know what I felt. [*He takes out his handkerchief and cries unaffectedly*].

RAMSDEN. How do we know that, Octavius? He may know it: we cannot tell. Come! dont grieve. [*Octavius masters himself and puts up his handkerchief*]. Thats right. Now let me tell you something to console you. The last time I saw him—it was in this very room—he said to me: "Tavy is a generous lad and the soul of honor; and when I see how little consideration other men get from their sons, I realize how much better than a son he's been to me." There! Doesnt that do you good?

OCTAVIUS. Mr Ramsden: he used to say to me that he had met only one man in the world who was the soul of honor, and that was Roebuck Ramsden.

RAMSDEN. Oh, that was his partiality: we were very old friends, you know. But there was something else he used to say about you. I wonder whether I ought to tell you or not!

OCTAVIUS. You know best.

RAMSDEN. It was something about his daughter.

OCTAVIUS [*eagerly*] About Ann! Oh, do tell me that, Mr Ramsden.

RAMSDEN. Well, he said he was glad, after all, you were not his son, because he thought that someday Annie and you—[*Octavius blushes vividly*]. Well, perhaps I shouldnt have told you. But he was in earnest.

OCTAVIUS. Oh, if only I thought I had a chance! You know, Mr Ramsden, I don't care about money or about what people call position; and I cant bring myself to take an interest in the business of struggling for them. Well, Ann has a most exquisite nature; but she is so accustomed to be in the thick of that sort of thing that she thinks a man's character incomplete if he is not ambitious. She knows that if she married me she would have to reason herself out of being ashamed of me for not being a big success of some kind.

RAMSDEN [*getting up and planting himself with his back to the fireplace*] Nonsense, my boy, nonsense! Youre too modest. What does she know about the real value of men at her age? [*More seriously*] Besides, she's a wonderfully dutiful girl. Her father's wish would be sacred to her. Do you know that since she grew up to years of discretion, I dont believe she has ever once given her own wish as a reason for doing anything or not doing it. It's always "Father wishes me to," or "Mother wouldnt like it." It's really almost a fault in her. I have often told her she must learn to think for herself.

OCTAVIUS [*shaking his head*] I couldnt ask her to marry me because her father wished it, Mr. Ramsden.

RAMSDEN. Well, perhaps not. No: of course not. I see that. No: you certainly couldnt. But when you win her on your own merits, it will be a great happiness to her to fulfil her father's desire as well as her own. Eh? Come! youll ask her, wont you?

OCTAVIUS [*with sad gaiety*] At all events I promise you I shall never ask anyone else.

RAMSDEN. Oh, you shant need to. She'll accept you, my boy—although [*here he suddenly becomes very serious indeed*] you have one great drawback.

OCTAVIUS [*anxiously*] What drawback is that, Mr Ramsden? I should rather say which of my many drawbacks?

RAMSDEN. I'll tell you, Octavius. [*He takes from the table a book bound in red cloth*]. I have in my hand a copy of the most infamous, the most scandalous, the most mischievous, the most blackguardly book that ever escaped burning at the hands of the common hangman. I have not read it: I would not soil my mind with such filth; but I have read what the papers say of it. The title is quite enough for me.

[*He reads it*]. The Revolutionist's Handbook and Pocket Companion. By John Tanner, M.I.R.C., Member of the Idle Rich Class.

OCTAVIUS [*smiling*] But Jack—

RAMSDEN [*testily*] For goodness' sake, dont call him Jack under my roof [*he throws the book violently down on the table. Then, somewhat relieved, he comes past the table to Octavius, and addresses him at close quarters with impressive gravity*]. Now, Octavius, I know that my dead friend was right when he said you were a generous lad. I know that this man was your school-fellow, and that you feel bound to stand by him because there was a boyish friendship between you. But I ask you to consider the altered circumstances. You were treated as a son in my friend's house. You lived there; and your friends could not be turned from the door. This man Tanner was in and out there on your account almost from his childhood. He addresses Annie by her Christian name as freely as you do. Well, while her father was alive, that was her father's business, not mine. This man Tanner was only a boy to him: his opinions were something to be laughed at, like a man's hat on a child's head. But now Tanner is a grown man and Annie a grown woman. And her father is gone. We dont as yet know the exact terms of his will; but he often talked it over with me; and I have no more doubt than I have that youre sitting there that the will appoints me Annie's trustee and guardian. [*Forcibly*] Now I tell you, once for all, I cant and I wont have Annie placed in such a position that she must, out of regard for you, suffer the intimacy of this fellow Tanner. It's not fair: it's not right: it's not kind. What are you going to do about it?

OCTAVIUS. But Ann herself has told Jack that whatever his opinions are, he will always be welcome because he knew her dear father.

RAMSDEN [*out of patience*] That girl's mad about her duty to her parents. [*He starts off like a goaded ox in the direction of John Bright, in whose expression there is no sympathy for him. As he speaks he fumes down to Herbert Spencer, who receives him still more coldly*]. Excuse me, Octavius; but there are limits to social toleration. You know that I am not a bigoted or prejudiced man. You know that I am plain Roebuck Ramsden when other men who have done less have got handles to their names, because I have stood for equality and liberty of conscience while they were truckling to the Church and to the aristocracy. Whitefield and I lost chance after chance through our advanced opinions. But I draw the line at Anarchism and Free Love and that sort of thing. If I am to be Annie's guardian, she will have to learn that she has a duty to me. I wont have it: I will n o t have it. She must forbid John Tanner the house; and so must you.

The parlormaid returns.

OCTAVIUS. But—

RAMSDEN [*calling his attention to the servant*] Ssh! Well?

THE MAID. Mr Tanner wishes to see you, sir.

RAMSDEN. Mr Tanner!

OCTAVIUS. Jack!

RAMSDEN. How dare Mr Tanner call on me! Say I cannot see him.

OCTAVIUS [*hurt*] I am sorry you are turning my friend from your door like that.

THE MAID [*calmly*] He's not at the door, sir. He's upstairs in the drawing room with Miss Ramsden. He came with Mrs Whitefield and Miss Ann and Miss Robinson, sir.

Ramsden's feelings are beyond words.

OCTAVIUS [*grinning*] Thats very like Jack, Mr Ramsden. You must see him, even if it's only to turn him out.

RAMSDEN [*hammering out his words with suppressed fury*] Go upstairs and ask Mr Tanner to be good enough to step down here. [*The parlormaid goes out; and Ramsden returns to the fireplace, as to a fortified position*]. I must say that of all the confounded pieces of impertinence—well, if these are Anarchist manners, I hope you like them. And Annie with him! Annie! A— [*he chokes*].

OCTAVIUS. Yes: thats what surprises me. He's so desperately afraid of Ann. There must be something the matter.

Mr John Tanner suddenly opens the door and enters. He is too young to be described simply as a big man with a beard. But it is already plain that middle life will find him in that category. He has still some of the slimness of youth; but youthfulness is not the effect he aims at: his frock coat would befit a prime minister; and a certain high chested carriage of the shoulders, a lofty pose of the head, and the Olympian majesty with which a mane, or rather a huge wisp, of hazel colored hair is thrown back from an imposing brow, suggest Jupiter rather than Apollo. He is prodigiously fluent of speech, restless, excitable (mark the snorting nostril and the restless blue eye, just the thirty-secondth of an inch too wide open), possibly a little mad. He is carefully dressed, not from the vanity that cannot resist finery, but from a sense of the importance of everything he does which leads him to make as much of paying a call as other men do of getting married or laying a foundation stone. A sensitive, susceptible, exaggerative, earnest man: a megalomaniac, who would be lost without a sense of humor.

Just at present the sense of humor is in abeyance. To say that he is excited is nothing: all his moods are phases of excitement. He is now in the panic-stricken phase; and he walks straight up to Ramsden as if with the fixed intention of shooting him on his own hearthrug. But what he pulls from his breast pocket is not a pistol, but a foolscap document which he thrusts under the indignant nose of Ramsden as he exclaims

TANNER. Ramsden: do you know what that is?

RAMSDEN [*loftily*] No, sir.

TANNER. It's a copy of Whitefield's will. Ann got it this morning.

RAMSDEN. When you say Ann, you mean, I presume, Miss Whitefield.

TANNER. I mean our Ann, your Ann, Tavy's Ann, and now, Heaven help me, m y Ann!

OCTAVIUS [*rising, very pale*] What do you mean?

TANNER. Mean! [*He holds up the will*]. Do you know who is appointed Ann's guardian by this will?

RAMSDEN [*coolly*] I believe I am.

TANNER. You! You and I, man. I! I!! I!!! Both of us! [*He flings the will down on the writing table*].

RAMSDEN. You! Impossible.

TANNER. It's only too hideously true. [*He throws himself into Octavius's chair*]. Ramsden: get me out of it somehow. You dont know Ann as well as I do. She'll commit every crime a respectable woman can; and she'll justify every one of them by saying that it was the wish of her guardians. She'll put everything on us; and we shall have no more control over her than a couple of mice over a cat.

OCTAVIUS. Jack: I wish you wouldnt talk like that about Ann.

TANNER. This chap's in love with her: thats another complication. Well, she'll either jilt him and say I didnt approve of him, or marry him and say you ordered her to. I tell you, this is the most staggering blow that has ever fallen on a man of my age and temperament.

RAMSDEN. Let me see that will, sir. [*He goes to the writing table and picks it up*]. I cannot believe that my old friend Whitefield would have shewn such a want of confidence in me as to associate me with— [*His countenance falls as he reads*].

TANNER. It's all my own doing: thats the horrible irony of it. He told me one day that you were to be Ann's guardian; and like a fool I began arguing with him about the folly of leaving a young woman under the control of an old man with obsolete ideas.

RAMSDEN [*stupended*] My ideas obsolete!!!!!!!

TANNER. Totally. I had just finished an essay called Down with Government by the Greyhaired; and I was full of arguments and illustrations. I said the proper thing was to combine the experience of an old hand with the vitality of a young one. Hang me if he didnt take me at my word and alter his will—it's dated only a fortnight after that conversation—appointing me as joint guardian with you!

RAMSDEN [*pale and determined*] I shall refuse to act.

TANNER. Whats the good of that? Ive been refusing all the way from Richmond; but Ann keeps on saying that of course she's only an orphan; and that she cant expect the people who were glad to come to the house in her father's time to trouble much about her now. Thats the latest game. An orphan! It's like hearing an ironclad talk about being at the mercy of the wind and waves.

OCTAVIUS. This is not fair, Jack. She is an orphan. And you ought to stand by her.

TANNER. Stand by her! What danger is she in? She has the law on her side; she has popular sentiment on her side; she has plenty of money and no conscience. All she wants with me is to load up all her moral responsibilities on me, and do as she likes at the expense of my character. I cant control her; and she can compromise me as much as she likes. I might as well be her husband.

RAMSDEN. You can refuse to accept the guardianship. *I* shall certainly refuse to hold it jointly with you.

TANNER. Yes; and what will she say to that? what does she say to it? Just that her father's wishes are sacred to her, and that she shall always look up to me as her guardian whether I care to face the responsibility or not. Refuse! You might as well refuse to accept the embraces of a boa constrictor when once it gets round your neck.

OCTAVIUS. This sort of talk is not kind to me, Jack.

TANNER [*rising and going to Octavius to console him, but still lamenting*] If he wanted a young guardian, why didnt he appoint Tavy?

RAMSDEN. Ah! why indeed?

OCTAVIUS. I will tell you. He sounded me about it; but I refused the trust because I loved her. I had no right to let myself be forced on her as a guardian by her father. He spoke to her about it; and she said I was right. You know I love her, Mr Ramsden; and Jack knows it too.

If Jack loved a woman, I would not compare her to a boa constrictor in his presence, however much I might dislike her [*he sits down between the busts and turns his face to the wall*].

RAMSDEN. I do not believe that Whitefield was in his right senses when he made that will. You have admitted that he made it under your influence.

TANNER. You ought to be pretty well obliged to me for my influence. He leaves you two thousand five hundred for your trouble. He leaves Tavy a dowry for his sister and five thousand for himself.

OCTAVIUS [*his tears flowing afresh*] Oh, I cant take it. He was too good to us.

TANNER. You wont get it, my boy, if Ramsden upsets the will.

RAMSDEN. Ha! I see. You have got me in a cleft stick.

TANNER. He leaves m e nothing but the charge of Ann's morals, on the ground that I have already more money than is good for me. That shews that he had his wits about him, doesnt it?

RAMSDEN [*grimly*] I admit that.

OCTAVIUS [*rising and coming from his refuge by the wall*] Mr Ramsden: I think you are prejudiced against Jack. He is a man of honor, and incapable of abusing—

TANNER. Dont, Tavy: youll make me ill. I am not a man of honor: I am a man struck down by a dead hand. Tavy: you must marry her after all and take her off my hands. And I had set my heart on saving you from her!

OCTAVIUS. Oh, Jack, you talk of saving me from my highest happiness.

TANNER. Yes, a lifetime of happiness. If it were only the first half hour's happiness, Tavy, I would buy it for you with my last penny. But a lifetime of happiness! No man alive could bear it: it would be hell on earth.

RAMSDEN [*violently*] Stuff, sir. Talk sense; or else go and waste someone else's time: I have something better to do than listen to your fooleries [*he positively kicks his way to his table and resumes his seat*].

TANNER. You hear him, Tavy! Not an idea in his head later than eighteensixty. We cant leave Ann with no other guardian to turn to.

RAMSDEN. I am proud of your contempt for my character and opinions, sir. Your own are set forth in that book, I believe.

TANNER [*eagerly going to the table*] What! Youve got my book! What do you think of it?

RAMSDEN. Do you suppose I would read such a book, sir?

TANNER. Then why did you buy it?

RAMSDEN. I did not buy it, sir. It has been sent me by some foolish lady who seems to admire your views. I was about to dispose of it when Octavius interrupted me. I shall do so now, with your permission. [*He throws the book into the waste-paper basket with such vehemence that Tanner recoils under the impression that it is being thrown at his head*].

TANNER. You have no more manners than I have myself. However, that saves ceremony between us. [*He sits down again*]. What do you intend to do about this will?

OCTAVIUS. May I make a suggestion?

RAMSDEN. Certainly, Octavius.

OCTAVIUS. Arnt we forgetting that Ann herself may have some wishes in this matter?

RAMSDEN. I quite intend that Annie's wishes shall be consulted in every reasonable way. But she is only a woman, and a young and inexperienced woman at that.

TANNER. Ramsden: I begin to pity you.

RAMSDEN [*hotly*] I dont want to know how you feel towards me, Mr Tanner.

TANNER. Ann will do just exactly what she likes. And whats more, she'll force us to advise her to do it; and she'll put the blame on us if it turns out badly. So, as Tavy is longing to see her—

OCTAVIUS [*shyly*] I am not, Jack.

TANNER. You lie, Tavy: you are. So lets have her down from the drawing room and ask her what she intends us to do. Off with you, Tavy, and fetch her. [*Tavy turns to go*]. And dont be long; for the strained relations between myself and Ramsden will make the interval rather painful. [*Ramsden compresses his lips, but says nothing*].

OCTAVIUS. Never mind him, Mr Ramsden. He's not serious. [*He goes out*].

RAMSDEN [*very deliberately*] Mr Tanner: you are the most impudent person I have ever met.

TANNER [*seriously*] I know it, Ramsden. Yet even I cannot wholly conquer shame. We live in an atmosphere of shame. We are ashamed of everything that is real about us; ashamed of ourselves, of our relatives, of our incomes, of our accents, of our opinions, of our experience, just as we are ashamed of our naked skins. Good Lord, my dear Ramsden, we are ashamed to walk, ashamed to ride in an omnibus, ashamed to hire a hansom instead of keeping a carriage, ashamed of keeping one horse instead of two and a groom-gardener instead of a coachman and footman. The more things a man is ashamed of, the more respectable he is. Why, youre ashamed to buy my book, ashamed to read it: the only thing youre not ashamed of is to judge me for it without having read it; and even that only means that youre ashamed to have heterodox opinions. Look at the effect I produce because my fairy godmother withheld from me this gift of shame. I have every possible virtue that a man can have except—

RAMSDEN. I am glad you think so well of yourself.

TANNER. All you mean by that is that you think I ought to be ashamed of talking about my virtues. You dont mean that I havnt got them: you know perfectly well that I am as sober and honest a citizen as yourself, as truthful personally, and much more truthful politically and morally.

RAMSDEN [*touched on his most sensitive point*] I deny that. I will not allow you or any man to treat me as if I were a mere member of the British public. I detest its prejudices; I scorn its narrowness; I demand the right to think for myself. You pose as an advanced man. Let me tell you that I was an advanced man before you were born.

TANNER. I knew it was a long time ago.

RAMSDEN. I am as advanced as ever I was. I defy you to prove that I have ever hauled down the flag. I am m o r e advanced than ever I was. I grow more advanced every day.

TANNER. More advanced in years, Polonius.

RAMSDEN. Polonius! So you are Hamlet, I suppose.

TANNER. No: I am only the most impudent person youve ever met. Thats your notion of a thoroughly bad character. When you want to give me a piece of your mind, you ask yourself, as a just and upright man, what is the worst you can fairly say of me. Thief, liar, forger, adulterer, perjurer, glutton, drunkard? Not one of these names fit me. You have to fall back on my deficiency in shame. Well, I admit it. I even congratulate myself; for if I were ashamed of my real self, I should cut as stupid a figure as any of the rest of you. Cultivate a little impudence, Ramsden; and you will become quite a remarkable man.

RAMSDEN. I have no—

TANNER. You have no desire for that sort of notoriety. Bless you, I knew that answer would come as well as I know that a box of matches will come out of an automatic machine when I put a penny in the slot: you would be ashamed to say anything else.

The crushing retort for which Mr Ramsden has been visibly collect-

ing his forces is lost for ever; for at this point Octavius returns with Miss Ann Whitefield and her mother; and Ramsden springs up and hurries to the door to receive them. Whether Ann is good-looking or not depends upon your taste; also and perhaps chiefly on your age and sex. To Octavius she is an enchantingly beautiful woman, in whose presence the world becomes transfigured, and the puny limits of individual consciousness are suddenly made infinite by a mystic memory of the whole life of the race to its beginnings in the east, or even back to the paradise from which it fell. She is to him the reality of romance, the inner good sense of nonsense, the unveiling of his eyes, the freeing of his soul, the abolition of time, place, and circumstance, the etherealization of his blood into rapturous rivers of the very water of life itself, the revelation of all the mysteries and the sanctification of all the dogmas. To her mother she is, to put it as moderately as possible, nothing whatever of the kind. Not that Octavius's admiration is in any way ridiculous or discreditable. Ann is a well formed creature, as far as that goes; and she is perfectly ladylike, graceful, and comely, with ensnaring eyes and hair. Besides, instead of making herself an eyesore, like her mother, she has devised a mourning costume of black and violet silk which does honor to her late father and reveals the family tradition of brave unconventionality by which Ramsden sets such store.

But all this is beside the point as an explanation of Ann's charm. Turn up her nose, give a cast to her eye, replace her black and violet confection by the apron and feathers of a flower girl, strike all the aitches out of her speech, and Ann would still make men dream. Vitality is as common as humanity; but, like humanity, it sometimes rises to genius; and Ann is one of the vital geniuses. Not at all, if you please, an oversexed person: that is a vital defect, not a true excess. She is a perfectly respectable, perfectly self-controlled woman, and looks it; though her pose is fashionably frank and impulsive. She inspires confidence as a person who will do nothing she does not mean to do; also some fear, perhaps, as a woman who will probably do everything she means to do without taking more account of other people than may be necessary and what she calls right. In short, what the weaker of her own sex sometimes call a cat.

Nothing can be more decorous than her entry and her reception by Ramsden, whom she kisses. The late Mr Whitefield would be gratified almost to impatience by the long faces of the men (except Tanner, who is fidgety), the silent handgrasps, the sympathetic placing of chairs, the sniffing of the widow, and the liquid eye of the daughter, whose heart, apparently, will not let her control her tongue to speech. Ramsden and Octavius take the two chairs from the wall, and place them for the two ladies; but Ann comes to Tanner and takes his chair, which he offers with a brusque gesture, subsequently relieving his irritation by sitting down on the corner of the writing table with studied indecorum. Octavius gives Mrs Whitefield a chair next Ann, and himself takes the vacant one which Ramsden has placed under the nose of the effigy of Mr Herbert Spencer.

Mrs Whitefield, by the way, is a little woman, whose faded flaxen hair looks like straw on an egg. She has an expression of muddled shrewdness, a squeak of protest in her voice, and an odd air of continually elbowing away some larger person who is crushing her into a corner. One guesses her as one of those women who are conscious of being treated as silly and negligible, and who, without having strength enough to assert themselves effectually, at any rate never submit to their fate. There is a touch of chivalry in Octavius's scrupulous attention to her, even whilst his whole soul is absorbed by Ann.

Ramsden goes solemnly back to his magisterial seat at the writing table, ignoring Tanner, and opens the proceedings.

RAMSDEN. I am sorry, Annie, to force business on you at a sad time like the present. But your poor dear father's will has raised a very serious question. You have read it, I believe?

Ann assents with a nod and a catch of her breath, too much affected to speak.

I must say I am surprised to find Mr Tanner named as joint guardian and trustee with myself of you and Rhoda. [*A pause. They all look portentous; but they have nothing to say. Ramsden, a little ruffled by the lack of any response, continues*] I dont know that I can consent to act under such conditions. Mr Tanner has, I understand, some objection also; but I do not profess to understand its nature: he will no doubt speak for himself. But we are agreed that we can decide nothing until we know your views. I am afraid I shall have to ask you to choose between my sole guardianship and that of Mr Tanner; for I fear it is impossible for us to undertake a joint arrangement.

ANN [*in a low musical voice*] Mamma—

MRS WHITEFIELD [*hastily*] Now, Ann, I do beg you not to put it on me. I have no opinion on the subject; and if I had, it would probably not be attended to. I am quite content with whatever you three think best.

Tanner turns his head and looks fixedly at Ramsden, who angrily refuses to receive this mute communication.

ANN [*resuming in the same gentle voice, ignoring her mother's bad taste*] Mamma knows that she is not strong enough to bear the whole responsibility for me and Rhoda without some help and advice. Rhoda must have a guardian; and though I am older, I do not think any young unmarried woman should be left quite to her own guidance. I hope you agree with me, Granny?

TANNER [*starting*] Granny! Do you intend to call your guardians Granny?

ANN. Dont be foolish, Jack. Mr Ramsden has always been Grandpapa Roebuck to me: I am Granny's Annie; and he is Annie's Granny. I christened him so when I first learned to speak.

RAMSDEN [*sarcastically*] I hope you are satisfied, Mr Tanner. Go on, Annie: I quite agree with you.

ANN. Well, if I am to have a guardian, can I set aside anybody whom my dear father appointed for me?

RAMSDEN [*biting his lip*] You approve of your father's choice, then?

ANN. It is not for me to approve or disapprove. I accept it. My father loved me and knew best what was good for me.

RAMSDEN. Of course I understand your feelings, Annie. It is what I should have expected of you; and it does you credit. But it does not settle the question so completely as you think. Let me put a case to you. Suppose you were to discover that I had been guilty of some disgraceful action—that I was not the man your poor dear father took me for! Would you still consider it right that I should be Rhoda's guardian?

ANN. I cant imagine you doing anything disgraceful, Granny.

TANNER [*to Ramsden*] You havnt done anything of the sort, have you?

RAMSDEN [*indignantly*] No, sir.

MRS WHITEFIELD [*placidly*] Well, then, why suppose it?

ANN. You see, Granny, Mamma would not like me to suppose it.

RAMSDEN [*much perplexed*] You are both so full of natural and affectionate feeling in these family matters that it is very hard to put the situation fairly before you.

TANNER. Besides, my friend, you are not putting the situation fairly before them.

RAMSDEN [*sulkily*] Put it yourself, then.

TANNER. I will. Ann: Ramsden thinks I am not fit to be your guardian; and I quite agree with him. He considers that if your father had read my book, he wouldnt have appointed me. That book is the disgraceful action he has been talking about. He thinks it's your duty for Rhoda's sake to ask him to act alone and to make me withdraw. Say the word; and I will.

ANN. But I havnt read your book, Jack.

TANNER [*diving at the waste-paper basket and fishing the book out for her*] Then read it at once and decide.

RAMSDEN [*vehemently*] If I am to be your guardian, I positively forbid you to read that book, Annie. [*He smites the table with his fist and rises*].

ANN. Of course not if you dont wish it. [*She puts the book on the table*].

TANNER. If one guardian is to forbid you to read the other guardian's book, how are we to settle it? Suppose I order you to read it! What about your duty to me?

ANN [*gently*] I am sure you would never purposely force me into a painful dilemma, Jack.

RAMSDEN [*irritably*] Yes, yes, Annie: this is all very well, and, as I said, quite natural and becoming. But you must make a choice one way or the other. We are as much in a dilemma as you.

ANN. I feel that I am too young, too inexperienced, to decide. My father's wishes are sacred to me.

MRS WHITEFIELD. If you two men wont carry them out I must say it is rather hard that you should put the responsibility on Ann. It seems to me that people are always putting things on other people in this world.

RAMSDEN. I am sorry you take it in that way.

ANN [*touchingly*] Do you refuse to accept me as your ward, Granny?

RAMSDEN. No: I never said that. I greatly object to act with Mr Tanner: thats all.

MRS WHITEFIELD. Why? What's the matter with poor Jack?

TANNER. My views are too advanced for him.

RAMSDEN [*indignantly*] They are not. I deny it.

ANN. Of course not. What nonsense! Nobody is more advanced than Granny. I am sure it is Jack himself who has made all the difficulty. Come, Jack! be kind to me in my sorrow. You dont refuse to accept me as your ward, do you?

TANNER [*gloomily*] No. I let myself in for it; so I suppose I must face it. [*He turns away to the bookcase, and stands there, moodily studying the titles of the volumes*].

ANN [*rising and expanding with subdued but gushing delight*] Then we are all agreed; and my dear father's will is to be carried out. You dont know what a joy that is to me and to my mother! [*She goes to Ramsden and presses both his hands, saying*] And I shall have my dear Granny to help and advise me. [*She casts a glance at Tanner over her shoulder*]. And Jack the Giant Killer. [*She goes past her mother to Octavius*] And Jack's inseparable friend Ricky-ticky-tavy [*he blushes and looks inexpressibly foolish*].

MRS WHITEFIELD [*rising and shaking her widow's weeds straight*] Now that you are Ann's guardian, Mr Ramsden, I wish you would speak to her about her habit of giving people nicknames. They cant be expected to like it. [*She moves towards the door*].

ANN. How can you say such a thing, Mamma! [*Glowing with affectionate remorse*] Oh, I wonder can you be right! H a v e I been inconsiderate! [*She turns to Octavius, who is sitting astride his chair with his elbows on the back of it. Putting her hand on his forehead she turns his face up suddenly*]. Do you want to be treated like a grown-up man? Must I call you Mr Robinson in future?

OCTAVIUS [*earnestly*] Oh please call me Ricky-ticky-tavy. "Mr Robinson" would hurt me cruelly.

ANN [*laughs and pats his cheek with her finger; then comes back to Ramsden*]. You know I'm beginning to think that Granny is rather a piece of impertinence. But I never dreamt of its hurting you.

RAMSDEN [*breezily, as he pats her affectionately on the back*] My dear Annie, nonsense. I insist on Granny. I wont answer to any other name than Annie's Granny.

ANN [*gratefully*] You all spoil me, except Jack.

TANNER [*over his shoulder, from the bookcase*] I think you ought to call me Mr Tanner.

ANN [*gently*] No you dont, Jack. Thats like the things you say on purpose to shock people: those who know you pay no attention to them. But, if you like, I'll call you after your famous ancestor Don Juan.

RAMSDEN. Don Juan!

ANN [*innocently*] Oh, is there any harm in it? I didn't know. Then I certainly wont call you that. May I call you Jack until I can think of something else?

TANNER. Oh, for Heaven's sake dont try to invent anything worse. I capitulate. I consent to Jack. I embrace Jack. Here endeth my first and last attempt to assert my authority.

ANN. You see, Mamma, they all really like to have pet names.

MRS WHITEFIELD. Well, I think you might at least drop them until we are out of mourning.

ANN [*reproachfully, stricken to the soul*] Oh, how could you remind me, mother? [*She hastily leaves the room to conceal her emotion*].

MRS WHITEFIELD. Of course. My fault as usual! [*She follows Ann*].

TANNER [*coming from the bookcase*] Ramsden: we're beaten—smashed—nonentitized, like her mother.

RAMSDEN. Stuff, sir. [*He follows Mrs Whitefield out of the room*].

TANNER [*left alone with Octavius, stares whimsically at him*] Tavy: do you want to count for something in the world?

OCTAVIUS. I want to count for something as a poet: I want to write a great play.

TANNER. With Ann as the heroine?

OCTAVIUS. Yes: I confess it.

TANNER. Take care, Tavy. The play with Ann as the heroine is all right; but if youre not very careful, by Heaven she'll marry you.

OCTAVIUS [*sighing*] No such luck, Jack!

TANNER. Why, man, your head is in the lioness's mouth: you are half swallowed already—in three bites—Bite One, Ricky; Bite Two, Ticky; Bite Three, Tavy; and down you go.

OCTAVIUS. She is the same to everybody, Jack: you know her ways.

TANNER. Yes: she breaks everybody's back with the stroke of her paw; but the question is, which of us will she eat? My own opinion is that she means to eat you.

OCTAVIUS [*rising, pettishly*] It's horrible to talk like that about her when she is upstairs crying for her father. But I do so want her to eat me that I can bear your brutalities because they give me hope.

TANNER. Tavy: thats the devilish side of a woman's fascination: she makes you will your own destruction.

OCTAVIUS. But it's not destruction: it's fulfilment.

TANNER. Yes, of her purpose; and that purpose is neither her happiness nor yours, but Nature's. Vitality in a woman is a blind fury of creation. She sacrifices herself to it: do you think she will hesitate to sacrifice you?

OCTAVIUS. Why, it is just because she is self-sacrificing that she will not sacrifice those she loves.

TANNER. That is the profoundest of mistakes, Tavy. It is the self-sacrificing women that sacrifice others most recklessly. Because they are unselfish, they are kind in little things. Because they have a purpose which is not their own purpose, but that of the whole universe, a man is nothing to them but an instrument of that purpose.

OCTAVIUS. Dont be ungenerous, Jack. They take the tenderest care of us.

TANNER. Yes, as a soldier takes care of his rifle or a musician of his violin. But do they allow us any purpose or freedom of our own? Will they lend us to one another? Can the strongest man escape from them when once he is appropriated? They tremble when we are in danger, and weep when we die; but the tears are not for us, but for a father wasted, a son's breeding thrown away. They accuse us of treating them as a mere means to our pleasure; but how can so feeble and transient a folly as a man's selfish pleasure enslave a woman as the whole purpose of Nature embodied in a woman can enslave a man?

OCTAVIUS. What matter, if the slavery makes us happy?

TANNER. No matter at all if you have no purpose of your own, and are, like most men, a mere breadwinner. But you, Tavy, are an artist: that is, you have a purpose as absorbing and as unscrupulous as a woman's purpose.

OCTAVIUS. Not unscrupulous.

TANNER. Quite unscrupulous. The true artist will let his wife starve, his children go barefoot, his mother drudge for his living at seventy, sooner than work at anything but his art. To women he is half vivisector, half vampire. He gets into intimate relations with them to study them, to strip the mask of convention from them, to surprise their inmost secrets, knowing that they have the power to rouse his deepest creative energies, to rescue him from his cold reason, to make him see visions and dream dreams, to inspire him, as he calls it. He persuades women that they may do this for their own purpose whilst he really means them to do it for his. He steals the mother's milk and blackens it to make printer's ink to scoff at her and glorify ideal women with. He pretends to spare her the pangs of child-bearing so that he may have for himself the tenderness and fostering that belong of right to her children. Since marriage began, the great artist has been known as a bad husband. But he is worse: he is a child-robber, a blood-sucker, a hypocrite, and a cheat. Perish the race and wither a thousand women if only the sacrifice of them enable him to act Hamlet better, to paint a finer picture, to write a deeper poem, a greater play, a profounder philosophy! For mark you, Tavy, the artist's work is to shew us ourselves as we really are. Our minds are nothing but this knowledge of ourselves; and he who adds a jot to such knowledge creates new mind as surely as any woman creates new men. In the rage of that creation he is as ruthless as the woman, as dangerous to her as she to him, and as horribly fascinating. Of all human struggles there is none so treacherous and remorseless as the struggle between the artist man and the mother woman. Which shall use up the other? that is the issue between them. And it is all the deadlier because, in your romanticist cant, they love one another.

OCTAVIUS. Even if it were so—and I dont admit it for a moment—it is out of the deadliest struggles that we get the noblest characters.

TANNER. Remember that the next time you meet a grizzly bear or a Bengal tiger, Tavy.

OCTAVIUS. I meant where there is love, Jack.

TANNER. Oh, the tiger will love you. There is no love sincerer than the love of food. I think Ann loves you that way: she patted your cheek as if it were a nicely underdone chop.

OCTAVIUS. You know, Jack, I should have to run away from you if I did not make it a fixed rule not to mind anything you say. You come out with perfectly revolting things sometimes.

Ramsden returns, followed by Ann. They come in quickly, with their former leisurely air of decorous grief changed to one of genuine concern, and, on Ramsden's part, of worry. He comes between the two men, intending to address Octavius, but pulls himself up abruptly as he sees Tanner.

RAMSDEN. I hardly expected to find you still here, Mr Tanner.

TANNER. Am I in the way? Good morning, fellow guardian [*he goes towards the door*].

ANN. Stop, Jack. Granny: he must know, sooner or later.

RAMSDEN. Octavius: I have a very serious piece of news for you. It is of the most private and delicate nature—of the most painful nature too, I am sorry to say. Do you wish Mr Tanner to be present whilst I explain?

OCTAVIUS [*turning pale*] I have no secrets from Jack.

RAMSDEN. Before you decide that finally, let me say that the news concerns your sister, and that it is t e r r i b l e news.

OCTAVIUS. Violet! What has happened? Is she—dead?

RAMSDEN. I am not sure that it is not even worse than that.

OCTAVIUS. Is she badly hurt? Has there been an accident?

RAMSDEN. No: nothing of that sort.

TANNER. Ann: will *you* have the common humanity to tell us what the matter is?

ANN [*half whispering*] I cant. Violet has done something dreadful. We shall have to get her away somewhere. [*She flutters to the writing table and sits in Ramsden's chair, leaving the three men to fight it out between them*].

OCTAVIUS [*enlightened*] Is *that* what you meant, Mr Ramsden?

RAMSDEN. Yes. [*Octavius sinks upon a chair, crushed*]. I am afraid there is no doubt that Violet did not really go to Eastbourne three weeks ago when we thought she was with the Parry Whitefields. And she called on a strange doctor yesterday with a wedding ring on her finger. Mrs Parry Whitefield met her there by chance; and so the whole thing came out.

OCTAVIUS [*rising with his fists clenched*] Who is the scoundrel?

ANN. She wont tell us.

OCTAVIUS [*collapsing into the chair again*] What a frightful thing!

TANNER [*with angry sarcasm*] Dreadful. Appalling. Worse than death, as Ramsden says. [*He comes to Octavius*]. What would you not give, Tavy, to turn it into a railway accident, with all her bones broken, or something equally respectable and deserving of sympathy?

OCTAVIUS. Dont be brutal, Jack.

TANNER. Brutal! Good Heavens, man, what are you crying for? Here is a woman we all supposed to be making bad water color sketches, practising Grieg and Brahms, gadding about to concerts and parties, wasting her life and her money. We suddenly learn that she has turned from these sillinesses to the fulfilment of her highest purpose and greatest function—to increase, multiply, and replenish the earth. And instead of admiring her courage and rejoicing in her instinct; instead of crowning the completed womanhood and raising the triumphal strain of "Unto us a child is born: unto us a son is given", here you are—you who have been as merry as grigs in your mourning for the dead—all pulling long faces and looking as ashamed and disgraced as if the girl had committed the vilest of crimes.

RAMSDEN [*roaring with rage*] I will not have these abominations uttered in my house [*he smites the writing table with his fist*].

TANNER. Look here: if you insult me again I'll take you at your word and leave your house. Ann: where is Violet now?

ANN. Why? Are you going to her?

TANNER. Of course I am going to her. She wants help; she wants money; she wants respect and congratulation; she wants every chance for her child. She does not seem likely to get it from you: she shall from me. Where is she?

ANN. Dont be so headstrong, Jack. She's upstairs.

TANNER. What! Under Ramsden's sacred roof! Go and do your miserable duty, Ramsden. Hunt her out into the street. Cleanse your threshold from her contamination. Vindicate the purity of your English home. I'll go for a cab.

ANN [*alarmed*] Oh, Granny, you mustnt do that.

OCTAVIUS [*broken-heartedly, rising*] I'll take her away, Mr Ramsden. She had no right to come to your house.

RAMSDEN [*indignantly*] But I am only too anxious to help her. [*Turning on Tanner*] How dare you, sir, impute such monstrous intentions to me? I protest against it. I am ready to put down my last penny to save her from being driven to run to you for protection.

TANNER [*subsiding*] It's all right, then. He's not going to act up to his principles. It's agreed that we all stand by Violet.

OCTAVIUS. But who is the man? He can make reparation by marrying her; and he shall, or he shall answer for it to me.

RAMSDEN. He shall, Octavius. There you speak like a man.

TANNER. Then you dont think him a scoundrel, after all?

OCTAVIUS. Not a scoundrel! He is a heartless scoundrel.

RAMSDEN. A damned scoundrel. I beg your pardon, Annie; but I can say no less.

TANNER. So we are to marry your sister to a damned scoundrel by way of reforming her character! On my soul, I think you are all mad.

ANN. Dont be absurd, Jack. Of course you are quite right, Tavy; but we dont know who he is: Violet wont tell us.

TANNER. What on earth does it matter who he is? He's done his part; and Violet must do the rest.

RAMSDEN [*beside himself*] Stuff! lunacy! There is a rascal in our midst, a libertine, a villain worse than a murderer; and we are not to learn who he is! In our ignorance we are to shake him by the hand; to introduce him into our homes; to trust our daughters with him; to— to—

ANN [*coaxingly*] There, Granny, dont talk so loud. It's most shocking: we must all admit that; but if Violet wont tell us, what can we do? Nothing. Simply nothing.

RAMSDEN. Hmph! I'm not so sure of that. If any man has paid Violet any special attention, we can easily find that out. If there is any man of notoriously loose principles among us—

TANNER. Ahem!

RAMSDEN [*raising his voice*] Yes, sir, I repeat, if there is any man of notoriously loose principles among us—

TANNER. Or any man notoriously lacking in self-control.

RAMSDEN [*aghast*] Do you dare to suggest that *I* am capable of such an act?

TANNER. My dear Ramsden, this is an act of which every man is capable. That is what comes of getting at cross purposes with Nature. The suspicion you have just flung at me clings to us all. It's a sort of mud that sticks to the judge's ermine or the cardinal's robe as fast as to the rags of the tramp. Come, Tavy! dont look so bewildered: it might have been me: it might have been Ramsden; just as it might have been anybody. If it had, what could we do but lie and protest—as Ramsden is going to protest.

RAMSDEN [*choking*] I—I—I—

TANNER. Guilt itself could not stammer more confusedly. And yet you know perfectly well he's innocent, Tavy.

RAMSDEN [*exhausted*] I am glad you admit that, sir. I admit, myself, that there is an element of truth in what you say, grossly as you may distort it to gratify your malicious humor. I hope, Octavius, no suspicion of me is possible in your mind.

OCTAVIUS. Of you! No, not for a moment.

TANNER [*drily*] I think he suspects me just a little.

OCTAVIUS. Jack: you couldnt—you wouldnt—

TANNER. Why not?

OCTAVIUS [*appalled*] Why not!

TANNER. Oh, well, I'll tell you why not. First, you would feel bound to quarrel with me. Second, Violet doesnt like me. Third, if I had the honor of being the father of Violet's child, I should boast of it instead of denying it. So be easy: our friendship is not in danger.

OCTAVIUS. I should have put away the suspicion with horror if only you would think and feel naturally about it. I beg your pardon.

TANNER. My pardon! nonsense! And now lets sit down and have a family council. [*He sits down. The rest follow his example, more or less under protest*]. Violet is going to do the State a service; consequently she must be packed abroad like a criminal until it's over. Whats happening upstairs?

ANN. Violet is in the housekeeper's room—by herself, of course.

TANNER. Why not in the drawing room?

ANN. Dont be absurd, Jack. Miss Ramsden is in the drawing room with my mother, considering what to do.

TANNER. Oh! the housekeeper's room is the pententiary, I suppose; and the prisoner is waiting to be brought before her judges. The old cats!

ANN. Oh, Jack!

RAMSDEN. You are at present a guest beneath the roof of one of the old cats, sir. My sister is the mistress of this house.

TANNER. She would put me in the housekeeper's room, too, if she dared, Ramsden. However, I withdraw cats. Cats would have more sense. Ann: as your guardian, I order you to go to Violet at once and be particularly kind to her.

ANN. I h a v e seen her, Jack. And I am sorry to say I am afraid she is going to be rather obstinate about going abroad. I think Tavy ought to speak to her about it.

OCTAVIUS. How can I speak to her about such a thing [*he breaks down*]?

ANN. Dont break down, Ricky. Try to bear it for all our sakes.

RAMSDEN. Life is not all plays and poems, Octavius. Come! face it like a man.

TANNER [*chafing again*] Poor dear brother! Poor dear friends of the family! Poor dear Tabbies and Grimalkins! Poor dear everybody except the woman who is going to risk her life to create another life! Tavy: dont you be a selfish ass. Away with you and talk to Violet; and bring her down here if she cares to come. [*Octavius rises*]. Tell her we'll stand by her.

RAMSDEN [*rising*] No, sir—

TANNER [*rising also and interrupting him*] Oh, we understand: it's against your conscience; but still youll do it.

OCTAVIUS. I assure you all, on my word, I never meant to be selfish. It's so hard to know what to do when one wishes earnestly to do right.

TANNER. My dear Tavy, your pious English habit of regarding the world as a moral gymnasium built expressly to strengthen your character in, occasionally leads you to think about your own confounded principles when you should be thinking about other people's necessities. The need of the present hour is a happy mother and a healthy baby. Bend your energies on that; and you will see your way clearly enough.

Octavius, much perplexed, goes out.

RAMSDEN [*facing Tanner impressively*] And Morality, sir? What is to become of that?

TANNER. Meaning a weeping Magdalen and an innocent child branded with her shame. Not in our circle, thank you. Morality can go to its father the devil.

RAMSDEN. I thought so, sir. Morality sent to the devil to please our libertines, male and female. That is to be the future of England, is it?

TANNER. Oh, England will survive your disapproval. Meanwhile, I understand that you agree with me as to the practical course we are to take?

RAMSDEN. Not in your spirit, sir. Not for your reasons.

TANNER. You can explain that if anybody calls you to account, here or hereafter. [*He turns away, and plants himself in front of Mr Herbert Spencer, at whom he stares gloomily*].

ANN [*rising and coming to Ramsden*] Granny: hadnt you better go up to the drawing room and tell them what we intend to do?

RAMSDEN [*looking pointedly at Tanner*] I hardly like to leave you alone with this gentleman. Will you not come with me?

ANN. Miss Ramsden would not like to speak about it before me, Granny. I ought not to be present.

RAMSDEN. You are right: I should have thought of that. You are a good girl, Annie.

He pats her on the shoulder. She looks up at him with beaming eyes; and he goes out, much moved. Having disposed of him, she looks at Tanner. His back being turned to her, she gives a moment's attention to her personal appearance, then softly goes to him and speaks almost into his ear.

ANN. Jack [*he turns with a start*]: are you glad that you are my guardian? You dont mind being made responsible for me, I hope.

TANNER. The latest addition to your collection of scapegoats, eh?

ANN. Oh, that stupid old joke of yours about me! Do please drop it. Why do you say things that you know must pain me? I do my best to please you, Jack: I suppose I may tell you so now that you are my guardian. You will make me so unhappy if you refuse to be friends with me.

TANNER [*studying her as gloomily as he studied the bust*] You need not go begging for my regard. How unreal our moral judgments are! You seem to me to have absolutely no conscience—only hypocrisy; and you cant see the difference—yet there is a sort of fascination about you. I always attend to you, somehow. I should miss you if I lost you.

ANN [*tranquilly slipping her arm into his and walking about with him*] But isnt that only natural, Jack? We have known each other since we were children. Do you remember—

TANNER [*abruptly breaking loose*] Stop! I remember e v e r y t h i n g.

ANN. Oh, I daresay we were often very silly; but—

TANNER. I wont have it, Ann. I am no more that schoolboy now than I am the dotard of ninety I shall grow into if I live long enough. It is over: let me forget it.

ANN. Wasnt it a happy time? [*She attempts to take his arm again*].

TANNER. Sit down and behave yourself. [*He makes her sit down in the chair next the writing table*]. No doubt it was a happy time for you. You were a good girl and never compromised yourself. And yet the wickedest child that ever was slapped could hardly have had a better time. I can understand the success with which you bullied the other girls: your virtue imposed on them. But tell me this: did you ever know a good boy?

ANN. Of course. All boys are foolish sometimes; but Tavy was always a really good boy.

TANNER [*struck by this*] Yes: youre right. For some reason you never tempted Tavy.

ANN. Tempted! Jack!

TANNER. Yes, my dear Lady Mephistopheles, tempted. You were insatiably curious as to what a boy might be capable of, and diabolically clever at getting through his guard and surprising his inmost secrets.

ANN. What nonsense! All because you used to tell me long stories of the wicked things you had done—silly boy's tricks! And you call such things inmost secrets! Boys' secrets are just like men's; and you know what t h e y are!

TANNER [*obstinately*] No I dont. What are they, pray?

ANN. Why, the things they tell everybody, of course.

TANNER. Now I swear I told you things I told no one else. You lured me into a compact by which we were to have no secrets from one another. We were to tell one another everything. I didnt notice that you never told me anything.

ANN. You didnt want to talk about me, Jack. You wanted to talk about yourself.

TANNER. Ah, true, horribly true. But what a devil of a child you must have been to know that weakness and to play on it for the satisfaction of your own curiosity! I wanted to brag to you, to make myself interesting. And I found myself doing all sorts of mischievous things simply to have something to tell you about. I fought with boys I didnt hate; I lied about things I might just as well have told the truth about; I stole things I didnt want; I kissed little girls I didnt care for. It was all bravado: passionless and therefore unreal.

ANN. I never told of you, Jack.

TANNER. No; but if you had wanted to stop me you would have told of me. You wanted me to go on.

ANN [*flashing out*] Oh, thats not true: it's n o t true, Jack. I never wanted you to do those dull, disappointing, brutal, stupid, vulgar things. I always hoped that it would be something really heroic at last. [*Recovering herself*] Excuse me, Jack; but the things you did were never a bit like the things I wanted you to do. They often gave me great uneasiness; but I could not tell of you and get you into trouble. And you were only a boy. I knew you would grow out of them. Perhaps I was wrong.

TANNER [*sardonically*] Do not give way to remorse, Ann. At least nineteen twentieths of the exploits I confessed to you were pure lies. I soon noticed that you didnt like the true stories.

ANN. Of course I knew that some of the things couldnt have happened. But—

TANNER. You are going to remind me that some of the most disgraceful ones did.

ANN [*fondly, to his great terror*] I dont want to remind you of anything. But I knew the people they happened to, and heard about them.

TANNER. Yes; but even the true stories were touched up for telling. A sensitive boy's humiliations may be very good fun for ordinary thick-skinned grown-ups; but to the boy himself they are so acute, so ignominious, that he cannot confess them—cannot but deny them passionately. However, perhaps it was as well for me that I romanced a bit; for, on the one occasion when I told you the truth, you threatened to tell of me.

ANN. Oh, never. Never once.

TANNER. Yes, you did. Do you remember a dark-eyed girl named Rachel Rosetree? [*Ann's brows contract for an instant involuntarily*]. I got up a love affair with her; and we met one night in the garden and walked about very uncomfortably with our arms round one another, and kissed at parting, and were most conscientiously romantic. If that love affair had gone on, it would have bored me to death; but it didnt go on; for the next thing that happened was that Rachel cut me because she found out that I had told you. How did she find it out? From you. You went to her and held the guilty secret over her head, leading her a life of abject terror and humiliation by threatening to tell on her.

ANN. And a very good thing for her, too. It was my duty to stop her misconduct; and she is thankful to me for it now.

TANNER. Is she?

ANN. She ought to be, at all events.

TANNER. It was not your duty to stop *my* misconduct, I suppose.

ANN. I did stop it by stopping her.

TANNER. Are you sure of that? You stopped my telling you about my adventures; but how do you know that you stopped the adventures?

ANN. Do you mean to say that you went on in the same way with other girls?

TANNER. No. I had enough of that sort of romantic tomfoolery with Rachel.

ANN [*unconvinced*] Then why did you break off our confidences and become quite strange to me?

TANNER [*enigmatically*] It happened just then that I got something that I wanted to keep all to myself instead of sharing it with you.

ANN. I am sure I shouldnt have asked for any of it if you had grudged it.

TANNER. It wasnt a box of sweets, Ann. It was something youd never have let me call my own.

ANN [*incredulously*] What?

TANNER. My soul.

ANN. Oh, do be sensible, Jack. You know youre talking nonsense.

TANNER. The most solemn earnest, Ann. You didnt notice at that time that you were getting a soul too. But you were. It was not for nothing that you suddenly found you had a moral duty to chastise and reform Rachel. Up to that time you had traded pretty extensively in being a good child; but you had never set up a sense of duty to others. Well, I set one up too. Up to that time I had played the boy buccaneer with no more conscience than a fox in a poultry farm. But now I began to have scruples, to feel obligations, to find that veracity and honor were no longer goody-goody expressions in the mouths of grown-up people, but compelling principle in myself.

ANN [*quietly*] Yes, I suppose youre right. You were beginning to be a man, and I to be a woman.

TANNER. Are you sure it was not that we were beginning to be something more? What does the beginning of manhood and womanhood mean in most people's mouths? You know: it means the beginning of love. But love began long before that for me. Love played its part in the earliest dreams and follies and romances I can remember—may I say the earliest follies and romances we can remember?—though we did not understand it at the time. No: the change that came to me was the birth in me of moral passion; and I declare that according to my experience moral passion is the only real passion.

ANN. All passions ought to be moral, Jack.

TANNER. Ought! Do you think that anything is strong enough to impose oughts on a passion except a stronger passion still?

ANN. Our moral sense controls passion, Jack. Dont be stupid.

TANNER. Our moral sense! And is that not a passion? Is the devil to have all the passions as well as all the good tunes? If it were not a passion—if it were not the mightiest of the passions, all the other passions would sweep it away like a leaf before a hurricane. It is the birth of that passion that turns a child into a man.

ANN. There are other passions, Jack. Very strong ones.

TANNER. All the other passions were in me before; but they were idle and aimless—mere childish greedinesses and cruelties, curiosities and fancies, habits and superstitions, grotesque and ridiculous to the mature intelligence. When they suddenly began to shine like newly lit flames it was by no light of their own, but by the radiance of the dawning moral passion. That passion dignified them, gave them conscience and meaning, found them a mob of appetites and organized them into an army of purposes and principles. My soul was born of that passion.

ANN. I noticed that you got more sense. You were a dreadfully destructive boy before that.

TANNER. Destructive! Stuff! I was only mischievous.

ANN. Oh, Jack, you were very destructive. You ruined all the young fir trees by chopping off their leaders with a wooden sword. You broke all the cucumber frames with your catapult. You set fire to the common: the police arrested Tavy for it because he ran away when he couldnt stop you. You—

TANNER. Pooh! pooh! pooh! these were battles, bombardments, stratagems to save our scalps from the red Indians. You have no imagination, Ann. I am ten times more destructive now than I was then. The moral passion has taken my destructiveness in hand and directed it to moral ends. I have become a reformer, and, like all reformers, an iconoclast. I no longer break cucumber frames and burn gorse bushes: I shatter creeds and demolish idols.

ANN [*bored*] I am afraid I am too feminine to see any sense in destruction. Destruction can only destroy.

TANNER. Yes. That is why it is so useful. Construction cumbers the ground with institutions made by busybodies. Destruction clears it and gives us breathing space and liberty.

ANN. It's no use, Jack. No woman will agree with you there.

TANNER. Thats because you confuse construction and destruction with creation and murder. Theyre quite different: I adore creation and abhor murder. Yes: I adore it in tree and flower, in bird and beast, even in you. [*A flush of interest and delight suddenly chases the growing perplexity and boredom from her face*]. It was the creative instinct that led you to attach me to you by bonds that have left their mark on me to this day. Yes, Ann: the old childish compact between us was an unconscious love compact—

ANN. Jack!

TANNER. Oh, dont be alarmed—

ANN. I am not alarmed.

TANNER [*whimsically*] Then you ought to be: where are your principles?

ANN. Jack: are you serious or are you not?

TANNER. Do you mean about the moral passion?

ANN. No, no: the other one. [*Confused*] Oh! you are so silly: one never knows how to take you.

TANNER. You must take me quite seriously. I am your guardian; and it is my duty to improve your mind.

ANN. The love compact is over, then, is it? I suppose you grew tired of me?

TANNER. No; but the moral passion made our childish relations impossible. A jealous sense of my new individuality arose in me—

ANN. You hated to be treated as a boy any longer. Poor Jack!

TANNER. Yes, because to be treated as a boy was to be taken on the old footing. I had become a new person; and those who knew the old person laughed at me. The only man who behaved sensibly was my tailor: he took my measure anew every time he saw me, whilst all the rest went on with their old measurements and expected them to fit me.

ANN. You became frightfully self-conscious.

TANNER. When you go to heaven, Ann, you will be frightfully conscious of your wings for the first year or so. When you meet your relatives there, and they persist in treating you as if you were still a mortal, you will not be able to bear them. You will try to get into a circle which has never known you except as an angel.

ANN. So it was only your vanity that made you run away from us after all?

TANNER. Yes, only my vanity, as you call it.

ANN. You need not have kept away from m e on that account.

TANNER. From you above all others. You fought harder than anybody against my emancipation.

ANN [*earnestly*] Oh, how wrong you are! I would have done anything for you.

TANNER. Anything except let me get loose from you. Even then you had acquired by instinct that damnable woman's trick of heaping obligations on a man, of placing yourself so entirely and helplessly at his mercy that at last he dare not take a step without running to you for leave. I know a poor wretch whose one desire in life is to run away from his wife. She prevents him by threatening to throw herself in front of the engine of the train he leaves her in. That is what all women do. If we try to go where you do not want us to go there is no law to prevent us; but when we take the first step your breasts are under our foot as it descends: your bodies are under our wheels as we start. No woman shall ever enslave me in that way.

ANN. But, Jack, you cannot get through life without considering other people a little.

TANNER. Ay; but what other people? It is this consideration of other people—or rather this cowardly fear of them which we call consideration—that makes us the sentimental slaves we are. To consider you, as you call it, is to substitute your will for my own. How if it be a baser will than mine? Are women taught better than men or worse? Are mobs of voters taught better than statesmen or worse? Worse, of course, in both cases. And then what sort of world are you going to get, with its public men considering its voting mobs, and its private men considering their wives? What does Church and State mean nowadays? The Woman and the Ratepayer.

ANN [*placidly*] I am so glad you understand politics, Jack: it will be most useful to you if you go into parliament [*he collapses like a pricked bladder*]. But I am sorry you thought my influence a bad one.

TANNER. I dont say it was a bad one. But bad or good, I didnt choose to be cut to your measure. And I wont be cut to it.

ANN. Nobody wants you to, Jack. I assure you—really on my word—I dont mind your queer opinions one little bit. You know we have all been brought up to have advanced opinions. Why do you persist in thinking me so narrow minded?

TANNER. Thats the danger of it. I know you dont mind, because youve found out that it doesnt matter. The boa constrictor doesnt mind the opinions of a stag one little bit when once she has got her coils round it.

ANN [*rising in sudden enlightenment*] O-o-o-o-oh! now I understand why you warned Tavy that I am a boa constrictor. Granny told me. [*She laughs and throws her boa round his neck*]. Doesnt it feel nice and soft, Jack?

TANNER [*in the toils*] You scandalous woman, will you throw away even your hypocrisy?

ANN. I am never hypocritical with you, Jack. Are you angry? [*She withdraws the boa and throws it on a chair*]. Perhaps I shouldnt have done that.

TANNER [*contemptuously*] Pooh, prudery! Why should you not, if it amuses you?

ANN [*shyly*] Well, because—because I suppose what you really meant by the boa constrictor was t h i s [*she puts her arms round his neck*].

TANNER [*staring at her*] Magnificent audacity! [*She laughs and pats his cheeks*]. Now just to think that if I mentioned this episode not a soul would believe me except the people who would cut me for telling, whilst if you accused me of it nobody would believe my denial!

ANN [*taking her arms away with perfect dignity*] You are incorrigible, Jack. But you should not jest about our affection for one another. Nobody could possibly misunderstand it. You do not misunderstand it, I hope.

TANNER. My blood interprets for me, Ann. Poor Ricky Ticky Tavy!

ANN [*looking quickly at him as if this were a new light*] Surely you are not so absurd as to be jealous of Tavy.

TANNER. Jealous! Why should I be? But I dont wonder at your grip of him. I feel the coils tightening round my very self, though you are only playing with me.

ANN. Do you think I have designs on Tavy?

TANNER. I know you have.

ANN [*earnestly*] Take care, Jack. You may make Tavy very unhappy if you mislead him about me.

TANNER. Never fear: he will not escape you.

ANN. I wonder are you really a clever man!

TANNER. Why this sudden misgiving on the subject?

ANN. You seem to understand all the things I dont understand; but you are a perfect baby in the things I do understand.

TANNER. I understand how Tavy feels for you, Ann: you may depend on that, at all events.

ANN. And you think you understand how I feel for Tavy, dont you?

TANNER. I know only too well what is going to happen to poor Tavy.

ANN. I should laugh at you, Jack, if it were not for poor papa's death. Mind! Tavy will be very unhappy.

TANNER. Yes; but he wont know it, poor devil. He is a thousand times too good for you. Thats why he is going to make the mistake of his life about you.

ANN. I think men make more mistakes by being too clever than by being too good [*she sits down, with a trace of contempt for the whole male sex in the elegant carriage of her shoulders*].

TANNER. Oh, I know you dont care very much about Tavy. But there is always one who kisses and one who only allows the kiss. Tavy will kiss; and you will only turn the cheek. And you will throw him over if anybody better turns up.

ANN [*offended*] You have no right to say such things, Jack. They are not true, and not delicate. If you and Tavy choose to be stupid about me, that is not my fault.

TANNER [*remorsefully*] Forgive my brutalities, Ann. They are levelled at this wicked world, not at you. [*She looks up at him, pleased and forgiving. He becomes cautious at once*]. All the same, I wish Ramsden would come back. I never feel safe with you: there is a devilish charm—or no: not a charm, a subtle interest [*she laughs*]—Just so: you know it; and you triumph in it. Openly and shamelessly triumph in it!

ANN. What a shocking flirt you are, Jack!

TANNER. A flirt!! I!!!

ANN. Yes, a flirt. You are always abusing and offending people; but you never really mean to let go your hold of them.

TANNER. I will ring the bell. This conversation has already gone further than I intended.

Ramsden and Octavius come back with Miss Ramsden, a hard-headed old maiden lady in a plain brown silk gown, with enough rings, chains, and brooches to shew that her plainness of dress is a matter of principle, not of poverty. She comes into the room very determinedly: the two men, perplexed and downcast, following her. Ann rises and goes eagerly to meet her. Tanner retreats to the wall between the busts and pretends to study the pictures. Ramsden goes to his table as usual; and Octavius clings to the neighborhood of Tanner.

MISS RAMSDEN [*almost pushing Ann aside as she comes to Mrs Whitefield's chair and plants herself there resolutely*] I wash my hands of the whole affair.

OCTAVIUS [*very wretched*] I know you wish me to take Violet away, Miss Ramsden. I will. [*He turns irresolutely to the door*].

RAMSDEN. No, no—

MISS RAMSDEN. What is the use of saying no, Roebuck? Octavius knows that I would not turn any truly contrite and repentant woman from your doors. But when a woman is not only wicked, but intends to go on being wicked, she and I part company.

ANN. Oh, Miss Ramsden, what do you mean? What has Violet said?

RAMSDEN. Violet is certainly very obstinate. She wont leave London. I dont understand her.

MISS RAMSDEN. I do. It's as plain as the nose on your face, Roebuck, that she wont go because she doesnt want to be separated from this man, whoever he is.

ANN. Oh, surely, surely! Octavius: did y o u speak to her?

OCTAVIUS. She wont tell us anything. She wont make any arrangement until she has consulted somebody. It cant be anybody else than the scoundrel who has betrayed her.

TANNER [*to Octavius*] Well, let her consult him. He will be glad enough to have her sent abroad. Where is the difficulty?

MISS RAMSDEN [*taking the answer out of Octavius's mouth*] The difficulty, Mr. Jack, is that when I offered to help her I didn't offer to become her accomplice in her wickedness. She either pledges her word never to see that man again, or else she finds some new friends; and the sooner the better.

The parlormaid appears at the door. Ann hastily resumes her seat, and looks as unconcerned as possible. Octavius instinctively imitates her.

THE MAID. The cab is at the door, maam.

MISS RAMSDEN. What cab?

THE MAID. For Miss Robinson.

MISS RAMSDEN. Oh! [*Recovering herself*] All right. [*The maid withdraws*]. She has sent for a cab.

TANNER. *I* wanted to send for that cab half an hour ago.

MISS RAMSDEN. I am glad she understands the position she has placed herself in.

RAMSDEN. I dont like her going away in this fashion, Susan. We had better not do anything harsh.

OCTAVIUS. No: thank you again and again; but Miss Ramsden is quite right. Violet cannot expect to stay.

ANN. Hadnt you better go with her, Tavy?

OCTAVIUS. She wont have me.

MISS RAMSDEN. Of course she wont. She's going straight to that man.

TANNER. As a natural result of her virtuous reception here.

RAMSDEN [*much troubled*] There, Susan! You hear! and theres some truth in it. I wish you could reconcile it with your principles to be a little patient with this poor girl. She's very young; and theres a time for everything.

MISS RAMSDEN. Oh, she will get all the sympathy she wants from the men. I'm surprised at you, Roebuck.

TANNER. So am I, Ramsden, most favorably.

Violet appears at the door. She is as impenitent and self-possessed a young lady as one would desire to see among the best behaved of her sex. Her small head and tiny resolute mouth and chin; her haughty crispness of speech and trimness of carriage; the ruthless elegance of her equipment, which includes a very smart hat with a dead bird in it, mark a personality which is as formidable as it is exquisitely pretty. She is not a siren, like Ann: admiration comes to her without any compulsion or even interest on her part; besides, there is some fun in Ann, but in this woman none, perhaps no mercy either: if anything restrains her, it is intelligence and pride, not compassion. Her voice might be the voice of a schoolmistress addressing a class of girls who had disgraced themselves, as she proceeds with complete composure and some disgust to say what she has come to say.

VIOLET. I have only looked in to tell Miss Ramsden that she will find her birthday present to me, the filagree bracelet, in the housekeeper's room.

TANNER. Do come in, Violet; and talk to us sensibly.

VIOLET. Thank you: I have had quite enough of the family conversation this morning. So has your mother, Ann: she has gone home crying. But at all events, I have found out what some of my pretended friends are worth. Goodbye.

TANNER. No, no: one moment. I have something to say which I beg you to hear. [*She looks at him without the slightest curiosity, but waits, apparently as much to finish getting her glove on as to hear what he has to say*]. I am altogether on your side in this matter. I congratulate you, with the sincerest respect, on having the courage to do what you have done. You are entirely in the right; and the family is entirely in the wrong.

Sensation. Ann and Miss Ramsden rise and turn towards the two. Violet, more surprised than any of the others, forgets her glove, and comes forward into the middle of the room, both puzzled and displeased. Octavius alone does not move nor raise his head: he is overwhelmed with shame.

ANN [*pleading to Tanner to be sensible*] Jack!

MISS RAMSDEN [*outraged*] Well, I must say!

VIOLET [*sharply to Tanner*] Who told you?

TANNER. Why, Ramsden and Tavy of course. Why should they not?

VIOLET. But they dont know.

TANNER. Dont know what?

VIOLET. They dont know that I am in the right, I mean.

TANNER. Oh, they know it in their hearts, though they think themselves bound to blame you by their silly superstitions about morality and propriety and so forth. But I know, and the whole world really knows, though it dare not say so, that you were right to follow your instinct; that vitality and bravery are the greatest qualities a woman can have, and motherhood her solemn initiation into womanhood; and that the fact of your not being legally married matters not one scrap either to your own worth or to our real regard for you.

VIOLET [*flushing with indignation*] Oh! You think me a wicked woman, like the rest. You think I have not only been vile, but that I share your abominable opinions. Miss Ramsden: I have borne your hard words because I knew you would be sorry for them when you found out the truth. But I wont bear such a horrible insult as to be complimented by Jack on being one of the wretches of whom he approves. I have kept my marriage a secret for my husband's sake. But now I claim my right as a married woman not to be insulted.

OCTAVIUS [*raising his head with inexpressible relief*] You are married!

VIOLET. Yes; and I think you might have guessed it. What business had you all to take it for granted that I had no right to wear my wedding ring? Not one of you even asked me: I cannot forget that.

TANNER [*in ruins*] I am utterly crushed. I meant well. I apologize—abjectly apologize.

VIOLET. I hope you will be more careful in future about the things you say. Of course one does not take them seriously; but they are very disagreeable, and rather in bad taste, I think.

TANNER [*bowing to the storm*] I have no defence: I shall know better in future than to take any woman's part. We have all disgraced ourselves in your eyes, I am afraid, except Ann. S h e befriended you. For Ann's sake, forgive us.

VIOLET. Yes: Ann has been kind; but then Ann knew.

TANNER [*with a desperate gesture*] Oh!!! Unfathomable deceit! Double crossed!

MISS RAMSDEN [*stiffly*] And who, pray, is the gentleman who does not acknowledge his wife?

VIOLET [*promptly*] That is my business, Miss Ramsden, and not yours. I have my reasons for keeping my marriage a secret for the present.

RAMSDEN. All I can say is that we are extremely sorry, Violet. I am shocked to think of how we have treated you.

OCTAVIUS [*awkwardly*] I beg your pardon, Violet. I can say no more.

MISS RAMSDEN [*still loath to surrender*] Of course what you say puts a very different complexion on the matter. All the same, I owe it to myself—

VIOLET [*cutting her short*] You owe m e an apology, Miss Ramsden: thats what you owe both to yourself and to me. If you were a married woman you would not like sitting in the housekeeper's room and being treated like a naughty child by young girls and old ladies without any serious duties and responsibilities.

TANNER. Dont hit us when we're down, Violet. We seem to have made fools of ourselves; but really it was you who made fools of us.

VIOLET. It was no business of yours, Jack, in any case.

TANNER. No business of mine! Why, Ramsden as good as accused me of being the unknown gentleman.

Ramsden makes a frantic demonstration; but Violet's cool keen anger extinguishes it.

VIOLET. You! Oh, how infamous! how abominable! how disgracefully you have all been talking about me! If my husband knew it he would

never let me speak to any of you again. [*To Ramsden*] I think you might have spared me that, at least.
RAMSDEN. But I assure you I never—at least it is a monstrous perversion of something I said that—
MISS RAMSDEN. You neednt apologize, Roebuck. She brought it all on herself. It is for her to apologize for having deceived us.
VIOLET. I can make allowances for you, Miss Ramsden: you cannot understand how I feel on this subject, though I should have expected rather better taste from people of greater experience. However, I quite feel that you have placed yourselves in a very painful position; and the most truly considerate thing for me to do is to go at once. Good morning.

She goes, leaving them staring.

MISS RAMSDEN. Well, I must say!
RAMSDEN [*plaintively*] I dont think she is quite fair to us.
TANNER. You must cower before the wedding ring like the rest of us, Ramsden. The cup of our ignominy is full.

ACT II

On the carriage drive in the park of a country house near Richmond an open touring car has broken down. It stands in front of a clump of trees round which the drive sweeps to the house, which is partly visible through them: indeed Tanner, standing in the drive with his back to us, could get an unobstructed view of the west corner of the house on his left were he not far too much interested in a pair of supine legs in dungaree overalls which protrude from beneath the machine. He is watching them intently with bent back and hands supported on his knees. His leathern overcoat and peaked cap proclaim him one of the dismounted passengers.

THE LEGS. Aha! I got him.
TANNER. All right now?
THE LEGS. Aw rawt nah.

Tanner stoops and takes the legs by the ankles, drawing their owner forth like a wheelbarrow, walking on his hands, with a hammer in his mouth. He is a young man in a neat suit of blue serge, clean shaven, dark eyed, square fingered, with short well brushed black hair and rather irregular sceptically turned eye-brows. When he is manipulating the car his movements are swift and sudden, yet attentive and deliberate. With Tanner and Tanner's friends his manner is not in the least deferential, but cool and reticent, keeping them quite effectually at a distance whilst giving them no excuse for complaining of him. Nevertheless he has a vigilant eye on them always, and that, too, rather cynically, like a man who knows the world well from its seamy side. He speaks slowly and with a touch of sarcasm; and as he does not at all affect the gentleman in his speech, it may be inferred that his smart appearance is a mark of respect to himself and his own class, not to that which employs him.

He now gets into the car to stow away his tools and divest himself of his overalls. Tanner takes off his leathern overcoat and pitches it into the car with a sigh of relief, glad to be rid of it. The chauffeur, noting this, tosses his head contemptuously, and surveys his employer sardonically.

THE CHAUFFEUR. Had enough of it, eh?

TANNER. I may as well walk to the house and stretch my legs and calm my nerves a little. [*Looking at his watch*] I suppose you know that we have come from Hyde Park Corner to Richmond in twenty-one minutes.

THE CHAUFFEUR. I'd ha done it under fifteen if I'd had a clear road all the way.

TANNER. Why do you do it? Is it for love of sport or for the fun of terrifying your unfortunate employer?

THE CHAUFFEUR. What are you afraid of?

TANNER. The police, and breaking my neck.

THE CHAUFFEUR. Well, if you like easy going, you can take a bus, you know. It's cheaper. You pay me to save your time and give you the value of what you paid for the car. [*He sits down calmly*].

TANNER. I am the slave of that car and of you too. I dream of the accursed thing at night.

THE CHAUFFEUR. Youll get over that all right. If youre going up to the house, may I ask how long youre goin to stay? Because if you mean to put in the whole morning in there talkin to the ladies, I'll put the car in the garage and make myself agreeable with a view to lunching here. If not, I'll keep the car on the go about here till you come.

TANNER. Better wait here. We shant be long. Theres a young American gentleman, a Mr Malone, who is driving Mr Robinson down in his new American steam car.

THE CHAUFFEUR [*springing up and coming hastily out of the car to Tanner*] American steam car! Wot! racin us dahn from London!

TANNER. Perhaps theyre here already.

THE CHAUFFEUR. If I'd known it! [*With deep reproach*] Why didnt you tell me, Mr Tanner?

TANNER. Because Ive been told that this car is capable of 84 miles an hour; and I already know what y o u are capable of when there is a rival car on the road. No, Henry: there are things it is not good for you to know; and this was one of them. However, cheer up: we are going to have a day after your own heart. The American is to take Mr Robinson and his sister and Miss Whitefield. We are to take Miss Rhoda.

THE CHAUFFEUR [*consoled and musing on another matter*] Thats Miss Whitefield's sister, isnt it?

TANNER. Yes.

THE CHAUFFEUR. And Miss Whitefield herself is goin in the other car? Not with you?

TANNER. Why the devil should she come with me? Mr Robinson will be in the other car. [*The Chauffeur looks at Tanner with cool incredulity, and turns to the car, whistling a popular air softly to himself. Tanner, a little annoyed, is about to pursue the subject when he hears the footsteps of Octavius on the gravel. Octavius is coming from the house, dressed for motoring, but without his overcoat*]. Weve lost the race, thank Heaven: heres Mr Robinson. Well, Tavy, is the steam car a success?

OCTAVIUS. I think so. We came from Hyde Park Corner here in seventeen minutes. [*The Chauffeur, furious, kicks the car with a groan of vexation*]. How long were you?

TANNER. Oh, about three quarters of an hour or so.

THE CHAUFFEUR [*remonstrating*] Now, now, Mr Tanner, come now! We could ha done it easy under fifteen.

TANNER. By the way, let me introduce you. Mr Octavius Robinson: Mr Enry Straker.

STRAKER. Pleased to meet you, sir. Mr Tanner is gittin at you with is Enry Straker, you know. You call it Henery. But I dont mind, bless you!

TANNER. You think it's simply bad taste in me to chaff him, Tavy. But youre wrong. This man takes more trouble to drop his aitches than ever his father did to pick them up. It's a mark of caste to him. I have never met anybody more swollen with the pride of class than Enry is.

STRAKER. Easy, easy! A little moderation, Mr Tanner.

TANNER. A little moderation, Tavy, you observe. Y o u would tell me to draw it mild. But this chap has been educated. Whats more, he knows that we havnt. What was that Board School of yours, Straker?

STRAKER. Sherbrooke Road.

TANNER. Sherbrooke Road! Would any of us say Rugby! Harrow! Eton! in that tone of intellectual snobbery? Sherbrooke Road is a place where boys learn something: Eton is a boy farm where we are sent because we are nuisances at home, and because in after life, whenever a Duke is mentioned, we can claim him as an old schoolfellow.

STRAKER. You dont know nothing about it, Mr Tanner. It's not the Board School that does it: it's the Polytechnic.

TANNER. His university, Octavius. Not Oxford, Cambridge, Durham,

Dublin, or Glasgow. Not even those Nonconformist holes in Wales. No, Tavy. Regent Street! Chelsea! the Borough!—I dont know half their confounded names: these are his universities, not mere shops for selling class limitations like ours. You despise Oxford, Enry, dont you?

STRAKER. No, I dont. Very nice sort of place, Oxford, I should think, for people that like that sort of place. They teach you to be a gentleman there. In the Polytechnic they teach you to be an engineer or such like. See?

TANNER. Sarcasm, Tavy, sarcasm! Oh, if you could only see into Enry's soul, the depth of his contempt for a gentleman, the arrogance of his pride in being an engineer, would appal you. He positively likes the car to break down because it brings out my gentlemanly helplessness and his workmanlike skill and resource.

STRAKER. Never you mind him, Mr Robinson. He likes to talk. We know him, dont we?

OCTAVIUS [*earnestly*] But theres a great truth at the bottom of what he says. I believe most intensely in the dignity of labor.

STRAKER [*unimpressed*] Thats because you never done any, Mr Robinson. My business is to do away with labor. Youll get more out of me and a machine than you will out of twenty laborers, and not so much to drink either.

TANNER. For Heaven's sake, Tavy, dont start him on political economy. He knows all about it; and we dont. Youre only a poetic Socialist, Tavy: he's a scientific one.

STRAKER [*unperturbed*] Yes. Well, this conversation is very improvin; but Ive got to look after the car; and you two want to talk about your ladies. *I* know. [*He pretends to busy himself about the car, but presently saunters off to indulge in a cigaret*].

TANNER. Thats a very momentous social phenomenon.

OCTAVIUS. What is?

TANNER. Straker is. Here have we literary and cultured persons been for years setting up a cry of the New Woman whenever some unusually old fashioned female came along, and never noticing the advent of the New Man. Straker's the New Man.

OCTAVIUS. I see nothing new about him, except your way of chaffing him. But I dont want to talk about him just now. I want to speak to you about Ann.

TANNER. Straker knew even that. He learnt it at the Polytechnic, probably. Well, what about Ann? Have you proposed to her?

OCTAVIUS [*self-reproachfully*] I was brute enough to do so last night.

TANNER. Brute enough! What do you mean?

OCTAVIUS [*dithyrambically*] Jack: we men are all coarse: we never understand how exquisite a woman's sensibilities are. How could I have done such a thing!

TANNER. Done what, you maudlin idiot?

OCTAVIUS. Yes, I a m an idiot. Jack: if you had heard her voice! if you had seen her tears! I have lain awake all night thinking of them. If she had reproached me, I could have borne it better.

TANNER. Tears! thats dangerous. What did she say?

OCTAVIUS. She asked me how she could think of anything now but her dear father. She stifled a sob—[*he breaks down*].

TANNER [*patting him on the back*] Bear it like a man, Tavy, even if you feel it like an ass. It's the old game: she's not tired of playing with you yet.

OCTAVIUS [*impatiently*] Oh, dont be a fool, Jack. Do you suppose this eternal shallow cynicism of yours has any real bearing on a nature like hers?

TANNER. Hm! Did she say anything else?

OCTAVIUS. Yes; and that is why I expose myself and her to your ridicule by telling you what passed.

TANNER [*remorsefully*] No, dear Tavy, not ridicule, on my honor! However, no matter. Go on.

OCTAVIUS. Her sense of duty is so devout, so perfect, so—

TANNER. Yes: I know. Go on.

OCTAVIUS. You see, under this new arrangement, you and Ramsden are her guardians; and she considers that all her duty to her father is now transferred to you. She said she thought I ought to have spoken to you both in the first instance. Of course she is right; but somehow it seems rather absurd that I am to come to you and formally ask to be received as a suitor for your ward's hand.

TANNER. I am glad that love has not totally extinguished your sense of humor, Tavy.

OCTAVIUS. That answer wont satisfy her.

TANNER. My official answer is, obviously, Bless you, my children: may you be happy!

OCTAVIUS. I wish you would stop playing the fool about this. If it is not serious to you, it is to me, and to her.

TANNER. You know very well that she is as free to choose as you are.

OCTAVIUS. She does not think so.

TANNER. Oh, doesnt she! j u s t! However, say what you want me to do?

OCTAVIUS. I want you to tell her sincerely and earnestly what you think about me. I want you to tell her that you can trust her to me—that is, if you feel you can.

TANNER. I have no doubt that I can trust her to you. What worries me is the idea of trusting you to her. Have you read Maeterlinck's book about the bee?

OCTAVIUS [*keeping his temper with difficulty*] I am not discussing literature at present.

TANNER. Be just a little patient with me. *I* am not discussing literature: the book about the bee is natural history. It's an awful lesson to mankind. You think that you are Ann's suitor; that you are the pursuer and she the pursued; that it is your part to woo, to persuade, to prevail, to overcome. Fool: it is you who are the pursued, the marked down quarry, the destined prey. You need not sit looking longingly at the bait through the wires of the trap: the door is open, and will remain so until it shuts behind you for ever.

OCTAVIUS. I wish I could believe that, vilely as you put it.

TANNER. Why, man, what other work has she in life but to get a husband? It is a woman's business to get married as soon as possible, and a man's to keep unmarried as long as he can. You have your poems and your tragedies to work at: Ann has nothing.

OCTAVIUS. I cannot write without inspiration. And nobody can give me that except Ann.

TANNER. Well, hadnt you better get it from her at a safe distance? Petrarch didnt see half as much of Laura, nor Dante of Beatrice, as you see of Ann now; and yet they wrote first-rate poetry—at least so I'm told. They never exposed their idolatry to the test of domestic familiarity; and it lasted them to their graves. Marry Ann; and at the end of a week youll find no more inspiration in her than in a plate of muffins.

OCTAVIUS. You think I shall tire of her!

TANNER. Not at all: you dont get tired of muffins. But you dont find inspiration in them; and you wont in her when she ceases to be a poet's dream and becomes a solid eleven stone wife. Youll be forced to dream about somebody else; and then there will be a row.

OCTAVIUS. This sort of talk is no use, Jack. You dont understand. You have never been in love.

TANNER. I! I have never been out of it. Why, I am in love even with Ann. But I am neither the slave of love nor its dupe. Go to the bee, thou poet: consider her ways and be wise. By Heaven, Tavy, if women could do without our work, and we ate their children's bread instead of making it, they would kill us as the spider kills her mate or as the bees kill the drone. And they would be right if we were good for nothing but love.

OCTAVIUS. Ah, if we were only good enough for Love! There is nothing like Love: there is nothing else but Love: without it the world would be a dream of sordid horror.

TANNER. And this—t h i s is the man who asks me to give him the hand of my ward! Tavy: I believe we were changed in our cradles, and that you are the real descendant of Don Juan.

OCTAVIUS. I beg you not to say anything like that to Ann.

TANNER. Dont be afraid. She has marked you for her own; and nothing will stop her now. You are doomed. [*Straker comes back with a newspaper*]. Here comes the New Man, demoralizing himself with a halfpenny paper as usual.

STRAKER. Now would you believe it, Mr Robinson, when we're out motoring we take in two papers: the Times for him, the Leader or the Echo for me. And do you think I ever see my paper? Not much. He grabs the Leader and leaves me to stodge myself with his Times.

OCTAVIUS. Are there no winners in the Times?

TANNER. Enry dont old with bettin, Tavy. Motor records are his weakness. Whats the latest?

STRAKER. Paris to Biskra at forty mile an hour average, not countin the Mediterranean.

TANNER. How many killed?

STRAKER. Two silly sheep. What does it matter? Sheep dont cost such a lot: they were glad to ave the price without the trouble o sellin em to the butcher. All the same, d'y'see, therell be a clamor agin it presently; and then the French Government'll stop it; an our chance'll be gone, see? Thats what makes me fairly mad: Mr Tanner wont do a good run while he can.

TANNER. Tavy: do you remember my uncle James?

OCTAVIUS. Yes. Why?

TANNER. Uncle James had a first rate cook: he couldnt digest anything except what she cooked. Well, the poor man was shy and hated society. But his cook was proud of her skill, and wanted to serve up dinners to princes and ambassadors. To prevent her from leaving him, that poor old man had to give a big dinner twice a month, and suffer agonies of awkwardness. Now here am I; and here is this chap Enry Straker, the New Man. I loathe travelling; but I rather like Enry. He cares for nothing but tearing along in a leather coat and goggles, with two inches of dust all over him, at sixty miles an hour and the risk of his life and mine. Except, of course, when he is lying on his back in the mud under the machine trying to find out where it has given way. Well, if I dont give him a thousand mile run at least once a fortnight I shall lose him. He will give me the sack and go to some American millionaire; and I shall have to put up with a nice respectful groom-gardener-amateur, who will touch his hat and know his place. I am Enry's slave, just as Uncle James was his cook's slave.

STRAKER [*exasperated*] Garn! I wish I had a car that would go as fast as you can talk, Mr Tanner. What I say is that you lose money by a motor car unless you keep it workin. Might as well ave a pram and a nussmaid to wheel you in it as that car and me if you dont git the last inch out of us both.

TANNER [*soothingly*] All right, Henry, all right. We'll go out for half an hour presently.

STRAKER [*in disgust*] Arf an ahr! [*He returns to his machine; seats himself in it; and turns up a fresh page of his paper in search of more news*].

OCTAVIUS. Oh, that reminds me. I have a note for you from Rhoda. [*He gives Tanner a note*].

TANNER [*opening it*] I rather think Rhoda is heading for a row with Ann. As a rule there is only one person an English girl hates more than she hates her eldest sister; and thats her mother. But Rhoda positively prefers her mother to Ann. She—[*indignantly*] Oh, I say!

OCTAVIUS. Whats the matter?

TANNER. Rhoda was to have come with me for a ride in the motor car. She says Ann has forbidden her to go out with me.

Straker suddenly begins whistling his favorite air with remarkable deliberation. Surprised by this burst of larklike melody, and jarred by a sardonic note in its cheerfulness, they turn and look inquiringly at him. But he is busy with his paper; and nothing comes of their movement.

OCTAVIUS [*recovering himself*] Does she give any reason?

TANNER. Reason! An insult is not a reason. Ann forbids her to be alone with me on any occasion. Says I am not a fit person for a young girl to be with. What do you think of your paragon now?

OCTAVIUS. You must remember that she has a very heavy responsibility now that her father is dead. Mrs Whitefield is too weak to control Rhoda.

TANNER [*staring at him*] In short, you agree with Ann.

OCTAVIUS. No; but I think I understand her. You must admit that your views are hardly suited for the formation of a young girl's mind and character.

TANNER. I admit nothing of the sort. I admit that the formation of a young lady's mind and character usually consists in telling her lies; but I object to the particular lie that I am in the habit of abusing the confidence of girls.

OCTAVIUS. Ann doesnt say that, Jack.

TANNER. What else does she mean?

STRAKER [*catching sight of Ann coming from the house*] Miss Whitefield, gentlemen. [*He dismounts and strolls away down the avenue with the air of a man who knows he is no longer wanted*].

ANN [*coming between Octavius and Tanner*] Good morning, Jack. I have come to tell you that poor Rhoda has got one of her headaches and cannot go out with you today in the car. It is a cruel disappointment to her, poor child!

TANNER. What do you say now, Tavy?

OCTAVIUS. Surely you cannot misunderstand, Jack. Ann is shewing you the kindest consideration, even at the cost of deceiving you.

ANN. What do you mean?

TANNER. Would you like to cure Rhoda's headache, Ann?

ANN. Of course.

TANNER. Then tell her what you said just now; and add that you arrived about two minutes after I had received her letter and read it.

ANN. Rhoda has written to you!

TANNER. With full particulars.

OCTAVIUS. Never mind him, Ann. You were right—quite right. Ann was only doing her duty, Jack; and you know it. Doing it in the kindest way, too.

ANN [*going to Octavius*] How kind you are, Tavy! How helpful! How well you understand!

Octavius beams.

TANNER. Ay: tighten the coils. You love her, Tavy, dont you?

OCTAVIUS. She knows I do.

ANN. Hush. For shame, Tavy!

TANNER. Oh, I give you leave. I am your guardian; and I commit you to Tavy's care for the next hour. I am off for a turn in the car.

ANN. No, Jack. I must speak to you about Rhoda. Ricky: will you go back to the house and entertain your American friend. He's rather on

Mamma's hands so early in the morning. She wants to finish her housekeeping.

OCTAVIUS. I fly, dearest Ann [*he kisses her hand*].

ANN [*tenderly*] Ricky Ticky Tavy!

He looks at her with an eloquent blush, and runs off.

TANNER [*bluntly*] Now look here, Ann. This time youve landed yourself; and if Tavy were not in love with you past all salvation he'd have found out what an incorrigible liar you are.

ANN. You misunderstand, Jack. I didnt dare tell Tavy the truth.

TANNER. No: your daring is generally in the opposite direction. What the devil do you mean by telling Rhoda that I am too vicious to associate with her? How can I ever have any human or decent relations with her again, now that you have poisoned her mind in that abominable way?

ANN. I know you are incapable of behaving badly—

TANNER. Then why did you lie to her?

ANN. I had to.

TANNER. Had to!

ANN. Mother made me.

TANNER [*his eye flashing*] Ha! I might have known it. The mother! Always the mother!

ANN. It was that dreadful book of yours. You know how timid mother is. All timid women are conventional: we m u s t be conventional, Jack, or we are so cruelly, so vilely misunderstood. Even you, who are a man, cannot say what you think without being misunderstood and vilified—yes: I admit it: I have had to vilify you. Do you want to have poor Rhoda misunderstood and vilified in the same way? Would it be right for mother to let her expose herself to such treatment before she is old enough to judge for herself?

TANNER. In short, the way to avoid misunderstanding is for everybody to lie and slander and insinuate and pretend as hard as they can. That is what obeying your mother comes to.

ANN. I love my mother, Jack.

TANNER [*working himself up into a sociological rage*] Is that any reason why you are not to call your soul your own? Oh, I protest against this vile abjection of youth to age! Look at fashionable society as you know it. What does it pretend to be? An exquisite dance of nymphs. What i s it? A horrible procession of wretched girls, each in the claws of a cynical, cunning, avaricious, disillusioned, ignorantly experienced, foul-minded old woman whom she calls mother, and whose duty it is to corrupt her mind and sell her to the highest bidder. Why do these unhappy slaves marry anybody, however old and vile, sooner than not marry at all? Because marriage is their only means of escape from these decrepit fiends who hide their selfish ambitions, their jealous hatreds of the young rivals who have supplanted them, under the mask of maternal duty and family affection. Such things are abominable: the voice of nature proclaims for the daughter a father's care and for the son a mother's. The law for father and son and mother and daughter is not the law of love: it is the law of revolution, of emancipation, of final supersession of the old and worn-out by the young and capable. I tell you, the first duty of manhood and womanhood is a Declaration of Independence: the man who pleads his father's authority is no man: the woman who pleads her mother's authority is unfit to bear citizens to a free people.

ANN [*watching him with quiet curiosity*] I suppose you will go in seriously for politics some day, Jack.

TANNER [*heavily let down*] Eh? What? Wh—? [*Collecting his scattered wits*] What has that got to do with what I have been saying?

ANN. You talk so well.

TANNER. Talk! Talk! It means nothing to you but talk. Well, go back to your mother, and help her to poison Rhoda's imagination as she has poisoned yours. It is the tame elephants who enjoy capturing the wild ones.

ANN. I am getting on. Yesterday I was a boa constrictor: today I am an elephant.

TANNER. Yes. So pack your trunk and begone: I have no more to say to you.

ANN. You are so utterly unreasonable and impracticable. What c a n I do?

TANNER. Do! Break your chains. Go your way according to your own conscience and not according to your mother's. Get your mind clean and vigorous; and learn to enjoy a fast ride in a motor car instead of seeing nothing in it but an excuse for a detestable intrigue. Come with me to Marseilles and across to Algiers and to Biskra, at sixty miles an hour. Come right down to the Cape if you like. That will be a Declaration of Independence with a vengeance. You can write a book about it afterwards. That will finish your mother and make a woman of you.

ANN [*thoughtfully*] I dont think there would be any harm in that, Jack. You are my guardian: you stand in my father's place, by his own wish. Nobody could say a word against our travelling together. It would be delightful: thank you a thousand times, Jack. I'll come.

TANNER [*aghast*] Youll come!!!
ANN. Of course.
TANNER. But—[*he stops, utterly appalled; then resumes feebly*] No: look here, Ann: if theres no harm in it theres no point in doing it.
ANN. How absurd you are! You dont want to compromise me, do you?
TANNER. Yes: thats the whole sense of my proposal.
ANN. You are talking the greatest nonsense; and you know it. You would never do anything to hurt me.
TANNER. Well, if you dont want to be compromised, dont come.
ANN [*with simple earnestness*] Yes, I will come, Jack, since you wish it. You are my guardian; and I think we ought to see more of one another and come to know one another better. [*Gratefully*] It's very thoughtful and very kind of you, Jack, to offer me this lovely holiday, especially after what I said about Rhoda. You really are good—much better than you think. When do we start?
TANNER. But—

The conversation is interrupted by the arrival of Mrs Whitefield from the house. She is accompanied by the American gentleman, and followed by Ramsden and Octavius.

Hector Malone is an Eastern American; but he is not at all ashamed of his nationality. This makes English people of fashion think well of him, as of a young fellow who is manly enough to confess to an obvious disadvantage without any attempt to conceal or extenuate it. They feel that he ought not to be made to suffer for what is clearly not his fault, and make a point of being specially kind to him. His chivalrous manners to women, and his elevated moral sentiments, being both gratuitous and unusual, strike them as perhaps a little unfortunate; and though they find his vein of easy humor rather amusing when it has ceased to puzzle them (as it does at first), they have had to make him understand that he really must not tell anecdotes unless they are strictly personal and scandalous, and also that oratory is an accomplishment which belongs to a cruder stage of civilization than that in which his migration has landed him. On these points Hector is not quite convinced: he still thinks that the British are apt to make merits of their stupidities, and to represent their various incapacities as points of good breeding. English life seems to him to suffer from a lack of edifying rhetoric (which he calls moral tone); English behavior to shew a want of respect for womanhood; English pronunciation to fail very vulgarly in tackling such words as world, girl, bird, etc.; English society to be plain spoken to an extent which stretches occasionally to intolerable coarseness; and English intercourse to need enlivening by games and stories and other pastimes; so he does not feel called upon to acquire these defects after taking great pains to cultivate himself in a first rate manner before venturing across the Atlantic. To this culture he finds English people either totally indifferent, as they very commonly are to all culture, or else politely evasive, the truth being that Hector's culture is nothing but a state of saturation with our literary exports of thirty years ago, reimported by him to be unpacked at a moment's notice and hurled at the head of English literature, science, and art, at every conversational opportunity. The dismay set up by these sallies encourages him in his belief that he is helping to educate England. When he finds people chattering harmlessly about Anatole France and Nietzsche, he devastates them with Matthew Arnold, the Autocrat of the Breakfast Table, and even Macaulay; and as he is devoutly religious at bottom, he first leads the unwary, by humorous irreverence, to leave popular theology out of account in discussing moral questions with him, and then scatters them in confusion by demanding whether the carrying out of his ideals of conduct was not the manifest object of God Almighty in creating honest men and pure women. The engaging freshness of his personality and the dumbfoundering staleness of his culture make it extremely difficult to decide whether he is worth knowing; for whilst his company is undeniably pleasant and enlivening, there is intellectually nothing new to be got out of him, especially as he despises politics, and is careful not to talk commercial shop, in which department he is probably much in advance of his English capitalist friends. He gets on best with romantic Christians of the amoristic sect: hence the friendship which has sprung up between him and Octavius.

In appearance Hector is a neatly built young man of twenty-four, with a short, smartly trimmed black beard, clear, well shaped eyes, and an ingratiating vivacity of expression. He is, from the fashionable point of view, faultlessly dressed. As he comes along the drive from the house with Mrs Whitefield he is sedulously making himself agreeable and entertaining, and thereby placing on her slender wit a burden it is unable to bear. An Englishman would let her alone, accepting boredom and indifference as their common lot; and the poor lady wants to be either let alone or let prattle about the things that interest her.

Ramsden strolls over to inspect the motor car. Octavius joins Hector.

ANN [*pouncing on her mother joyously*] Oh, mamma, what do you think! Jack is going to take me to Nice in his motor car. Isnt it lovely? I am the happiest person in London.

TANNER [*desperately*] Mrs Whitefield objects. I am sure she objects. Doesnt she, Ramsden?

RAMSDEN. I should think it very likely indeed.

ANN. You dont object, do you, mother?

MRS WHITEFIELD. *I* object! Why should I? I think it will do you good, Ann. [*Trotting over to Tanner*] I meant to ask you to take Rhoda out for a run occasionally: she is too much in the house; but it will do when you come back.

TANNER. Abyss beneath abyss of perfidy!

ANN [*hastily, to distract attention from this outburst*] Oh, I forgot: you have not met Mr Malone. Mr Tanner, my guardian: Mr Hector Malone.

HECTOR. Pleased to meet you, Mr Tanner. I should like to suggest an extension of the travelling party to Nice, if I may.

ANN. Oh, we're all coming. Thats understood, isnt it?

HECTOR. I also am the mawdest possessor of a motor car. If Miss Rawbnsn will allow me the privilege of taking her, my car is at her service.

OCTAVIUS. Violet!

General constraint.

ANN [*subduedly*] Come, mother: we must leave them to talk over the arrangements. I must see to my travelling kit.

Mrs Whitefield looks bewildered; but Ann draws her discreetly away; and they disappear round the corner towards the house.

HECTOR. I think I may go so far as to say that I can depend on Miss Rawbnsn's consent.

Continued embarrassment.

OCTAVIUS. I'm afraid we must leave Violet behind. There are circumstances which make it impossible for her to come on such an expedition.

HECTOR [*amused and not at all convinced*] Too American, eh? Must the young lady have a chaperone?

OCTAVIUS. It's not that, Malone—at least not altogether.

HECTOR. Indeed! May I ask what other objection applies?

TANNER [*impatiently*] Oh, tell him, tell him. We shall never be able to keep the secret unless everybody knows what it is. Mr Malone: if you go to Nice with Violet, you go with another man's wife. She is married.

HECTOR [*thunderstruck*] You dont tell me so!

TANNER. We do. In confidence.

RAMSDEN [*with an air of importance, lest Malone should suspect a misalliance*] Her marriage has not yet been made known: she desires that it shall not be mentioned for the present.

HECTOR. I shall respect the lady's wishes. Would it be indiscreet to ask who her husband is, in case I should have an opportunity of cawnsulting him about this trip?

TANNER. We dont know who he is.

HECTOR [*retiring into his shell in a very marked manner*] In that case, I have no more to say.

They become more embarrassed than ever.

OCTAVIUS. You must think this very strange.

HECTOR. A little singular. Pardn mee for saying so.

RAMSDEN [*half apologetic, half huffy*] The young lady was married secretly; and her husband has forbidden her, it seems, to declare his name. It is only right to tell you, since you are interested in Miss—er —in Violet.

OCTAVIUS [*sympathetically*] I hope this is not a disappointment to you.

HECTOR [*softened, coming out of his shell again*] Well: it is a blow. I can hardly understand how a man can leave his wife in such a position. Surely it's not customary. It's not manly. It's not considerate.

OCTAVIUS. We feel that, as you may imagine, pretty deeply.

RAMSDEN [*testily*] It is some young fool who has not enough experience to know what mystifications of this kind lead to.

HECTOR [*with strong symptoms of moral repugnance*] I hope so. A man need be very young and pretty foolish too to be excused for such conduct. You take a very lenient view, Mr Ramsden. Too lenient to my mind. Surely marriage should ennoble a man.

TANNER [*sardonically*] Ha!

HECTOR. Am I to gather from that cachinnation that you dont agree with me, Mr Tanner?

TANNER [*drily*] Get married and try. You may find it delightful for a while: you certainly wont find it ennobling. The greatest common measure of a man and a woman is not necessarily greater than the man's single measure.

HECTOR. Well, we think in America that a woman's morl number is higher than a man's, and that the purer nature of a woman lifts a man right out of himself, and makes him better than he was.

OCTAVIUS [*with conviction*] So it does.

TANNER. No wonder American women prefer to live in Europe! It's more comfortable than standing all their lives on an altar to be worshipped. Anyhow, Violet's husband has not been ennobled. So whats to be done?

HECTOR [*shaking his head*] I cant dismiss that man's cawnduct as lightly as you do, Mr Tanner. However, I'll say no more. Whoever he is, he's Miss Rawbnsn's husband; and I should be glad for her sake to think better of him.

OCTAVIUS [*touched; for he divines a secret sorrow*] I'm very sorry, Malone. Very sorry.

HECTOR [*gratefully*] Youre a good fellow, Rawbnsn. Thank you.

TANNER. Talk about something else. Violet's coming from the house.

HECTOR. I should esteem it a very great favor, gentlemen, if you would take the opportunity to let me have a few words with the lady alone. I shall have to cry off this trip; and it's rather a dullicate—

RAMSDEN [*glad to escape*] Say no more. Come, Tanner. Come, Tavy. [*He strolls away into the park with Octavius and Tanner, past the motor car*].

Violet comes down the avenue to Hector.

VIOLET. Are they looking?

HECTOR. No.

She kisses him.

VIOLET. Have you been telling lies for my sake?

HECTOR. Lying! Lying hardly describes it. I overdo it. I get carried away in an ecstasy of mendacity. Violet: I wish youd let me own up.

VIOLET [*instantly becoming serious and resolute*] No, no, Hector: you promised me not to.

HECTOR. I'll keep my prawmis until you release me from it. But I feel mean, lying to those men, and denying my wife. Just dastardly.

VIOLET. I wish your father were not so unreasonable.

HECTOR. He's not unreasonable. He's right from his point of view. He has a prejudice against the English middle class.

VIOLET. It's too ridiculous. You know how I dislike saying such things to you, Hector; but if I were to—oh, well, no matter.

HECTOR. I know. If you were to marry the son of an English manufacturer of awffice furniture, your friends would consider it a misalliance. And here's my silly old dad, who is the biggest awffice furniture man in the world, would shew me the door for marrying the most perfect lady in England merely because she has no handle to her name. Of course it's just absurd. But I tell you, Violet, I dont like deceiving him. I feel as if I was stealing his money. Why wont you let me own up?

VIOLET. We cant afford it. You can be as romantic as you please about love, Hector; but you mustnt be romantic about money.

HECTOR [*divided between his uxoriousness and his habitual elevation of moral sentiment*] Thats very English. [*Appealing to her impulsively*] Violet: dad's bound to find us out someday.

VIOLET. Oh yes, later on of course. But dont lets go over this everytime we meet, dear. You promised—

HECTOR. All right, all right, I—

VIOLET [*not to be silenced*] It is I and not you who suffer by this concealment; and as to facing a struggle and poverty and all that sort of thing I simply will not do it. It's too silly.

HECTOR. You shall not. I'll sort of borrow the money from my dad until I get on my own feet; and then I can own up and pay up at the same time.

VIOLET [*alarmed and indignant*] Do you mean to work? Do you want to spoil our marriage?

HECTOR. Well, I don't mean to let marriage spoil my character. Your friend Mr Tanner has got the laugh on me a bit already about that; and—

VIOLET. The beast! I hate Jack Tanner.

HECTOR [*magnanimously*] Oh, h e e' s all right: he only needs the love of a good woman to ennoble him. Besides, he's proposed a motoring trip to Nice; and I'm going to take you.

VIOLET. How jolly!

HECTOR. Yes; but how are we going to manage? You see, theyve warned me off going with you, so to speak. Theyve told me in cawnfidnce that youre married. Thats just the most overwhelming cawnfidnce Ive ever been honored with.

Tanner returns with Straker, who goes to his car.

TANNER. Your car is a great success, Mr Malone. Your engineer is showing it off to Mr Ramsden.

HECTOR [*eagerly—forgetting himself*] Lets come, Vi.

VIOLET [*coldly, warning him with her eyes*] I beg your pardon, Mr Malone: I did not quite catch—

HECTOR [*recollecting himself*] I ask to be allowed the pleasure of shewing you my little American steam car, Miss Rawbnsn.

VIOLET. I shall be very pleased. [*They go off together down the avenue*].

TANNER. About this trip, Straker.

STRAKER [*preoccupied with the car*] Yes?

TANNER. Miss Whitefield is supposed to be coming with me.

STRAKER. So I gather.
TANNER. Mr Robinson is to be one of the party.
STRAKER. Yes.
TANNER. Well, if you can manage so as to be a good deal occupied with me, and leave Mr Robinson a good deal occupied with Miss Whitefield, he will be deeply grateful to you.
STRAKER [*looking round at him*] Evidently.
TANNER. "Evidently"! Your grandfather would have simply winked.
STRAKER. My grandfather would have touched his at.
TANNER. And I should have given your good nice respectful grandfather a sovereign.
STRAKER. Five shillings, more likely. [*He leaves the car and approaches Tanner*]. What about the lady's views?
TANNER. She is just as willing to be left to Mr Robinson as Mr Robinson is to be left to her. [*Straker looks at his principal with cool scepticism; then turns to the car whistling his favorite air*]. Stop that aggravating noise. What do you mean by it? [*Straker calmly resumes the melody and finishes it. Tanner politely hears it out before he again addresses Straker, this time with elaborate seriousness*]. Enry: I have ever been a warm advocate of the spread of music among the masses; but I object to your obliging the company whenever Miss Whitefield's name is mentioned. You did it this morning, too.
STRAKER [*obstinately*] It's not a bit o use. Mr Robinson may as well give it up first as last.
TANNER. Why?
STRAKER. Garn! You know why. Course it's not my business; but you neednt start kiddin me about it.
TANNER. I am not kidding. I dont know why.
STRAKER [*cheerfully sulky*] Oh, very well. All right. It aint my business.
TANNER [*impressively*] I trust, Enry, that, as between employer and engineer, I shall always know how to keep my proper distance, and not intrude my private affairs on you. Even our business arrangements are subject to the approval of your Trade Union. But dont abuse your advantages. Let me remind you that Voltaire said that what was too silly to be said could be sung.
STRAKER. It wasnt Voltaire: it was Bow Mar Shay.
TANNER. I stand corrected: Beaumarchais of course. Now you seem to think that what is too delicate to be said can be whistled. Unfortunately your whistling, though melodious, is unintelligible. Come! theres nobody listening: neither my genteel relatives nor the secretary

of your confounded Union. As man to man, Enry, why do you think that my friend has no chance with Miss Whitefield?

STRAKER. Cause she's arter summun else.

TANNER. Bosh! who else?

STRAKER. You.

TANNER. Me!!!

STRAKER. Mean to tell me you didnt know? Oh, come, Mr Tanner!

TANNER [*in fierce earnest*] Are you playing the fool, or do you mean it?

STRAKER [*with a flash of temper*] I'm not playin no fool. [*More coolly*] Why, it's as plain as the nose on your face. If you aint spotted that, you dont know much about these sort of things. [*Serene again*] Ex-cuse me, you know, Mr Tanner; but you asked me as man to man; and I told you as man to man.

TANNER [*wildly appealing to the heavens*] Then I–*I* am the bee, the spider, the marked down victim, the destined prey.

STRAKER. I dunno about the bee and the spider. But the marked down victim, thats what you are and no mistake; and a jolly good job for you, too, I should say.

TANNER [*momentously*] Henry Straker: the golden moment of your life has arrived.

STRAKER. What d'y' mean?

TANNER. That record to Biskra.

STRAKER [*eagerly*] Yes?

TANNER. Break it.

STRAKER [*rising to the height of his destiny*] D'y'mean it?

TANNER. I do.

STRAKER. When?

TANNER. Now. Is that machine ready to start?

STRAKER [*quailing*] But you cant–

TANNER [*cutting him short by getting into the car*] Off we go. First to the bank for money; then to my rooms for my kit; then to your rooms for your kit; then break the record from London to Dover or Folkestone; then across the channel and away like mad to Marseilles, Gibraltar, Genoa, any port from which we can sail to a Mahometan country where men are protected from women.

STRAKER. Garn! youre kiddin.

TANNER [*resolutely*] Stay behind then. If you wont come I'll do it alone. [*He starts the motor*].

STRAKER [*running after him*] Here! Mister! arf a mo! steady on! [*he scrambles in as the car plunges forward*].

ACT III

Evening in the Sierra Nevada. Rolling slopes of brown with olive trees instead of apple trees in the cultivated patches, and occasional prickly pears instead of gorse and bracken in the wilds. Higher up, tall stone peaks and precipices, all handsome and distinguished. No wild nature here: rather a most aristocratic mountain landscape made by a fastidious artist-creator. No vulgar profusion of vegetation: even a touch of aridity in the frequent patches of stones: Spanish magnificence and Spanish economy everywhere.

Not very far north of a spot at which the high road over one of the passes crosses a tunnel on the railway from Malaga to Granada, is one of the mountain amphitheatres of the Sierra. Looking at it from the wide end of the horse-shoe, one sees, a little to the right, in the face of the cliff, a romantic cave which is really an abandoned quarry, and towards the left a little hill, commanding a view of the road, which skirts the amphitheatre on the left, maintaining its higher level on embankments and an occasional stone arch. On the hill, watching the road, is a man who is either a Spaniard or a Scotchman. Probably a Spaniard, since he wears the dress of a Spanish goatherd and seems at home in the Sierra Nevada, but very like a Scotchman for all that. In the hollow, on the slope leading to the quarry-cave, are about a dozen men who, as they recline at their ease round a heap of smouldering white ashes of dead leaf and brushwood, have an air of being conscious of themselves as picturesque scoundrels honoring the Sierra by using it as an effective pictorial background. As a matter of artistic fact they are not picturesque; and the mountains tolerate them as lions tolerate lice. An English policeman or Poor Law Guardian would recognize them as a selected band of tramps and ablebodied paupers.

This description of them is not wholly contemptuous. Whoever has intelligently observed the tramp, or visited the ablebodied ward of a workhouse, will admit that our social failures are not all drunkards and weaklings. Some of them are men who do not fit the class they were born into. Precisely the same qualities that make the educated gentleman an artist may make an uneducated manual laborer an ablebodied pauper. There are men who fall helplessly into the workhouse because they are good for nothing; but there are also men who are there because they are strongminded enough to disregard the social convention (obviously not a disinterested one on the part of the ratepayer) which bids a man live by heavy and badly paid drudgery when he has the alternative of walking into the workhouse, announcing himself as a destitute person, and legally compelling the Guardians to feed, clothe, and house him better than he could feed, clothe, and house himself without great exertion. When a man who is born a poet refuses a stool in a stockbroker's office, and starves in a garret, spunging on a poor landlady or on his friends and relatives sooner than work against his grain; or when a lady, because she is a lady, will face any extremity of parasitic dependence rather than take a situation as cook or parlormaid, we make large allowances for them. To such allowances the ablebodied pauper, and his nomadic variant the tramp, are equally entitled.

Further, the imaginative man, if his life is to be tolerable to him, must have leisure to tell himself stories, and a position which lends itself to imaginative decoration. The ranks of unskilled labor offer no such positions. We misuse our laborers horribly; and when a man refuses to be misused, we have no right to say that he is refusing honest work. Let us be frank in this matter before we go on with our play; so that we may enjoy it without hypocrisy. If we were reasoning, farsighted people, four fifths of us would go straight to the Guardians for relief, and knock the whole social system to pieces with most beneficial reconstructive results. The reason we do not do this is because we work like bees or ants, by instinct or habit, not reasoning about the matter at all. Therefore when a man comes along who can and does reason, and who, applying the Kantian test to his conduct, can truly say to us, If everybody did as I do, the world would be compelled to reform itself industrially, and abolish slavery and squalor, which exist only because everybody does as you do, let us honor that man and seriously consider the advisability of following his example. Such a man is the ablebodied, ableminded pauper. Were he a gentleman doing his best to get a pension or a sinecure instead of sweeping a crossing, nobody would blame him for deciding that so long as the alternative lies between living mainly at the expense of the community and allowing the community to live mainly at his, it would be folly to accept what is to him personally the greater of the two evils.

We may therefore contemplate the tramps of the Sierra without prejudice, admitting cheerfully that our objects—briefly, to be gentle-

men of fortune—are much the same as theirs, and the difference in our position and methods merely accidental. One or two of them, perhaps, it would be wiser to kill without malice in a friendly and frank manner; for there are bipeds, just as there are quadrupeds, who are too dangerous to be left unchained and unmuzzled; and these cannot fairly expect to have other men's lives wasted in the work of watching them. But as society has not the courage to kill them, and, when it catches them, simply wreaks on them some superstitious expiatory rites of torture and degradation, and then lets them loose with heightened qualifications for mischief, it is just as well that they are at large in the Sierra, and in the hands of a chief who looks as if he might possibly, on provocation, order them to be shot.

This chief, seated in the centre of the group on a squared block of stone from the quarry, is a tall strong man, with a striking cockatoo nose, glossy black hair, pointed beard, upturned moustache, and a Mephistophelean affectation which is fairly imposing, perhaps because the scenery admits of a larger swagger than Piccadilly, perhaps because of a certain sentimentality in the man which gives him that touch of grace which alone can excuse deliberate picturesqueness. His eyes and mouth are by no means rascally; he has a fine voice and a ready wit; and whether he is really the strongest man in the party or not, he looks it. He is certainly the best fed, the best dressed, and the best trained. The fact that he speaks English is not unexpected, in spite of the Spanish landscape; for with the exception of one man who might be guessed as a bullfighter ruined by drink, and one unmistakeable Frenchman, they are all cockney or American; therefore, in a land of cloaks and sombreros, they mostly wear seedy overcoats, woollen mufflers, hard hemispherical hats, and dirty brown gloves. Only a very few dress after their leader, whose broad sombrero with a cock's feather in the band, and voluminous cloak descending to his high boots, are as un-English as possible. None of them are armed; and the ungloved ones keep their hands in their pockets because it is their national belief that it must be dangerously cold in the open air with the night coming on. (It is as warm an evening as any reasonable man could desire).

Except the bullfighting inebriate there is only one person in the company who looks more than, say, thirty-three. He is a small man with reddish whiskers, weak eyes, and the anxious look of a small tradesman in difficulties. He wears the only tall hat visible: it shines in the sunset with the sticky glow of some sixpenny patent hat reviver, often applied and constantly tending to produce a worse state of the original surface than the ruin it was applied to remedy. He has a collar and cuffs of celluloid; and his brown Chesterfield overcoat, with velvet collar, is still presentable. He is pre-eminently the respectable man of the party, and is certainly over forty, possibly over fifty. He is the corner man on the leader's right, opposite three men in scarlet ties on his left. One of these three is the Frenchman. Of the remaining two, who are both English, one is argumentative, solemn, and obstinate; the other rowdy and mischievous.

The chief, with a magnificent fling of the end of his cloak across his left shoulder, rises to address them. The applause which greets him shews that he is a favorite orator.

THE CHIEF. Friends and fellow brigands. I have a proposal to make to this meeting. We have now spent three evenings in discussing the question Have Anarchists or Social-Democrats the most personal courage? We have gone into the principles of Anarchism and Social-Democracy at great length. The cause of Anarchy has been ably represented by our one Anarchist, who doesnt know what Anarchism means [*laughter*]—

THE ANARCHIST [*rising*] A point of order, Mendoza—

MENDOZA [*forcibly*] No, by thunder: your last point of order took half an hour. Besides, Anarchists dont believe in order.

THE ANARCHIST [*mild, polite but persistent: he is, in fact, the respectable looking elderly man in the celluloid collar and cuffs*] That is a vulgar error. I can prove—

MENDOZA. Order, order.

THE OTHERS [*shouting*] Order, order. Sit down. Chair! Shut up.

The Anarchist is suppressed.

MENDOZA. On the other hand we have three Social-Democrats among us. They are not on speaking terms; and they have put before us three distinct and incompatible views of Social-Democracy.

THE THREE MEN IN SCARLET TIES. 1. Mr Chairman, I protest. A personal explanation. 2. It's a lie. I never said so. Be fair, Mendoza. 3. Je demande la parole. C'est absolument faux. C'est faux! faux!! faux!!! Assas-s-s-s-sin!!!!!!

MENDOZA. Order, order.

THE OTHERS. Order, order, order! Chair!

The Social-Democrats are suppressed.

MENDOZA. Now, we tolerate all opinions here. But after all, comrades, the vast majority of us are neither Anarchists nor Socialists, but gentlemen and Christians.

THE MAJORITY [*shouting assent*] Hear, hear! So we are. Right.

THE ROWDY SOCIAL-DEMOCRAT [*smarting under suppression*] You aint no Christian. Youre a Sheeny, you are.

MENDOZA [*with crushing magnanimity*] My friend: *I* am an exception to all rules. It is true that I have the honor to be a Jew; and when the Zionists need a leader to reassemble our race on its historic soil of Palestine, Mendoza will not be the last to volunteer [*sympathetic applause*—Hear, hear, *&c.*]. But I am not a slave to any superstition. I have swallowed all the formulas, even that of Socialism; though, in a sense, once a Socialist, always a Socialist.

THE SOCIAL-DEMOCRATS. Hear, hear!

MENDOZA. But I am well aware that the ordinary man—even the ordinary brigand, who can scarcely be called an ordinary man [Hear, hear!]—is not a philosopher. Common sense is good enough for him; and in our business affairs common sense is good enough for me. Well, what is our business here in the Sierra Nevada, chosen by the Moors as the fairest spot in Spain? Is it to discuss abstruse questions of political economy? No: it is to hold up motorcars and secure a more equitable distribution of wealth.

THE SULKY SOCIAL-DEMOCRAT. All made by labor, mind you.

MENDOZA [*urbanely*] Undoubtedly. All made by labor, and on its way to be squandered by wealthy vagabonds in the dens of vice that disfigure the sunny shores of the Mediterranean. We intercept that wealth. We restore it to circulation among the class that produced it and that chiefly needs it: the working class. We do this at the risk of our lives and liberties, by the exercise of the virtues of courage, endurance, foresight, and abstinence—especially abstinence. I myself have eaten nothing but prickly pears and broiled rabbit for three days.

THE SULKY SOCIAL-DEMOCRAT [*stubbornly*] No more aint we.

MENDOZA [*indignantly*] Have I taken more than my share?

THE SULKY SOCIAL-DEMOCRAT [*unmoved*] Why should you?

THE ANARCHIST. Why should he not? To each according to his needs: from each according to his means.

THE FRENCHMAN [*shaking his fist at the Anarchist*] Fumiste!

MENDOZA [*diplomatically*] I agree with both of you.

THE GENUINELY ENGLISH BRIGANDS. Hear, hear! Bravo Mendoza!

MENDOZA. What I say is, let us treat one another as gentlemen, and strive to excel in personal courage only when we take the field.

THE ROWDY SOCIAL-DEMOCRAT [*derisively*] Shikespear.

A whistle comes from the goatherd on the hill. He springs up and points excitedly forward along the road to the north.

THE GOATHERD. Automobile! Automobile! [*He rushes down the hill and joins the rest, who all scramble to their feet*].

MENDOZA [*in ringing tones*] To arms! Who has the gun?

THE SULKY SOCIAL-DEMOCRAT [*handing a rifle to Mendoza*] Here.

MENDOZA. Have the nails been strewn in the road?

THE ROWDY SOCIAL-DEMOCRAT. Two ahnces of em.

MENDOZA. Good! [*To the Frenchman*] With me, Duval. If the nails fail, puncture their tires with a bullet. [*He gives the rifle to Duval, who follows him up the hill. Mendoza produces an opera glass. The others hurry across to the road and disappear to the north*].

MENDOZA [*on the hill, using his glass*] Two only, a capitalist and his chauffeur. They look English.

DUVAL. Angliche! Aoh yess. Cochons! [*Handling the rifle*] Faut tirer, n'est-ce-pas?

MENDOZA. No: the nails have gone home. Their tire is down: they stop.

DUVAL [*shouting to the others*] Fondez sur eux, nom de Dieu!

MENDOZA [*rebuking his excitement*] Du calme, Duval: keep your hair on. They take it quietly. Let us descend and receive them.

Mendoza descends, passing behind the fire and coming forward, whilst Tanner and Straker, in their motoring goggles, leather coats, and caps, are led in from the road by the brigands.

TANNER. Is this the gentleman you describe as your boss? Does he speak English?

THE ROWDY SOCIAL-DEMOCRAT. Course e daz. Y' downt suppowz we Hinglishmen luts ahrselves be bossed by a bloomin Spenniard, do you?

MENDOZA [*with dignity*] Allow me to introduce myself: Mendoza, President of the League of the Sierra! [*Posing loftily*] I am a brigand: I live by robbing the rich.

TANNER [*promptly*] I am a gentleman: I live by robbing the poor. Shake hands.

THE ENGLISH SOCIAL-DEMOCRATS. Hear, hear!

General laughter and good humor. Tanner and Mendoza shake hands. The Brigands drop into their former places.

STRAKER. Ere! where do I come in?

TANNER [*introducing*] My friend and chauffeur.

THE SULKY SOCIAL-DEMOCRAT [*suspiciously*] Well, which is he? friend or show-foor? It makes all the difference, you know.

MENDOZA [*explaining*] We should expect ransom for a friend. A professional chauffeur is free of the mountains. He even takes a trifling percentage of his principal's ransom if he will honor us by accepting it.

STRAKER. I see. Just to encourage me to come this way again. Well, I'll think about it.

DUVAL [*impulsively rushing across to Straker*] Mon frère! [*He embraces him rapturously and kisses him on both cheeks*].

STRAKER [*disgusted*] Ere, git aht: dont be silly. Who are you, pray?

DUVAL. Duval: Social-Democrat.

STRAKER. Oh, youre a Social-Democrat, are you?

THE ANARCHIST. He means that he has sold out to the parliamentary humbugs and the bourgeoisie. Compromise! that is his faith.

DUVAL [*furiously*] I understand what he say. He say Bourgeois. He say Compromise. Jamais de la vie! Misérable menteur—

STRAKER. See here, Captain Mendoza, ah mach o this sort o thing do you put up with here? Are we avin a pleasure trip in the mountains, or are we at a Socialist meetin?

THE MAJORITY. Hear, hear! Shut up. Chuck it. Sit down, &c. &c. [*The Social-Democrats and the Anarchist are hustled into the background. Straker, after superintending this proceeding with satisfaction, places himself on Mendoza's left, Tanner being on his right*].

MENDOZA. Can we offer you anything? Broiled rabbit and prickly pears—

TANNER. Thank you: we have dined.

MENDOZA [*to his followers*] Gentlemen: business is over for the day. Go as you please until morning.

The Brigands disperse into groups lazily. Some go into the cave. Others sit down or lie down to sleep in the open. A few produce a pack of cards and move off towards the road; for it is now starlight; and they know that motor cars have lamps which can be turned to account for lighting a card party.

STRAKER [*calling after them*] Dont none of you go fooling with that car, d'ye hear?

MENDOZA. No fear, Monsieur le Chauffeur. The first one we captured cured us of that.

STRAKER [*interested*] What did it do?

MENDOZA. It carried three brave comrades of ours, who did not know how to stop it, into Granada, and capsized them opposite the police station. Since then we never touch one without sending for the chauffeur. Shall we chat at our ease?

TANNER. By all means.

Tanner, Mendoza, and Straker sit down on the turf by the fire. Mendoza delicately waives his presidential dignity, of which the right to sit on the squared stone block is the appanage, by sitting on the ground like his guests, and using the stone only as a support for his back.

MENDOZA. It is the custom in Spain always to put off business until tomorrow. In fact, you have arrived out of office hours. However, if you would prefer to settle the question of ransom at once, I am at your service.

TANNER. Tomorrow will do for me. I am rich enough to pay anything in reason.

MENDOZA [*respectfully, much struck by this admission*] You are a remarkable man, sir. Our guests usually describe themselves as miserably poor.

TANNER. Pooh! Miserably poor people dont own motor cars.

MENDOZA. Precisely what we say to them.

TANNER. Treat us well: we shall not prove ungrateful.

STRAKER. No prickly pears and broiled rabbits, you know. Dont tell me you cant do us a bit better than that if you like.

MENDOZA. Wine, kids, milk, cheese, and bread can be procured for ready money.

STRAKER [*graciously*] Now youre talkin.

TANNER. Are you all Socialists here, may I ask?

MENDOZA [*repudiating this humiliating misconception*] Oh no, no, no: nothing of the kind, I assure you. We naturally have modern views as to the injustice of the existing distribution of wealth: otherwise we should lose our self-respect. But nothing that you could take exception to, except two or three faddists.

TANNER. I had no intention of suggesting anything discreditable. In fact, I am a bit of a Socialist myself.

STRAKER [*drily*] Most rich men are, I notice.

MENDOZA. Quite so. It has reached us, I admit. It is in the air of the century.

STRAKER. Socialism must be lookin up a bit if your chaps are taking to it.

MENDOZA. That is true, sir. A movement which is confined to philosophers and honest men can never exercise any real political influence: there are too few of them. Until a movement shews itself capable of spreading among brigands, it can never hope for a political majority.

TANNER. But are your brigands any less honest than ordinary citizens?

MENDOZA. Sir: I will be frank with you. Brigandage is abnormal. Abnormal professions attract two classes: those who are not good enough for ordinary bourgeois life and those who are too good for it. We are dregs and scum, sir: the dregs very filthy, the scum very superior.

STRAKER. Take care! some o the dregs'll hear you.

MENDOZA. It does not matter: each brigand thinks himself scum, and likes to hear the others called dregs.

TANNER. Come! you are a wit. [*Mendoza inclines his head, flattered*]. May one ask you a blunt question?

MENDOZA. As blunt as you please.

TANNER. How does it pay a man of your talent to shepherd such a flock as this on broiled rabbit and prickly pears? I have seen men less gifted, and I'll swear less honest, supping at the Savoy on foie gras and champagne.

MENDOZA. Pooh! they have all had their turn at the broiled rabbit, just as I shall have my turn at the Savoy. Indeed, I have had a turn there already—as waiter.

TANNER. A waiter! You astonish me!

MENDOZA [*reflectively*] Yes: I, Mendoza of the Sierra, was a waiter. Hence, perhaps, my cosmopolitanism. [*With sudden intensity*] Shall I tell you the story of my life?

STRAKER [*apprehensively*] If it aint too long, old chap—

TANNER [*interrupting him*] Tsh-sh: you are a Philistine, Henry: you have no romance in you. [*To Mendoza*] You interest me extremely, President. Never mind Henry: he can go to sleep.

MENDOZA. The woman I loved—

STRAKER. Oh, this is a love story, is it? Right you are. Go on: I was only afraid you were going to talk about yourself.

MENDOZA. Myself! I have thrown myself away for her sake: that is why I am here. No matter: I count the world well lost for her. She had, I pledge you my word, the most magnificent head of hair I ever saw. She had humor; she had intellect; she could cook to perfection; and her highly strung temperament made her uncertain, incalculable, variable, capricious, cruel, in a word, enchanting.

STRAKER. A six shillin novel sort o woman, all but the cookin. Er name was Lady Gladys Plantagenet, wasnt it?

MENDOZA. No, sir: she was not an earl's daughter. Photography, reproduced by the half-tone process, has made me familiar with the appearance of the daughters of the English peerage; and I can honestly say that I would have sold the lot, faces, dowries, clothes, titles, and all, for a smile from this woman. Yet she was a woman of the people, a worker: otherwise—let me reciprocate your bluntness—I should have scorned her.

TANNER. Very properly. And did she respond to your love?

MENDOZA. Should I be here if she did? She objected to marry a Jew.

TANNER. On religious grounds?

MENDOZA. No: she was a freethinker. She said that every Jew considers in his heart that English people are dirty in their habits.

TANNER [*surprised*] Dirty!

MENDOZA. It shewed her extraordinary knowledge of the world; for it is undoubtedly true. Our elaborate sanitary code makes us unduly contemptuous of the Gentile.

TANNER. Did you ever hear that, Henry?

STRAKER. Ive heard my sister say so. She was cook in a Jewish family once.

MENDOZA. I could not deny it; neither could I eradicate the impression it made on her mind. I could have got round any other objection; but no woman can stand a suspicion of indelicacy as to her person. My entreaties were in vain: she always retorted that she wasnt good enough for me, and recommended me to marry an accursed barmaid named Rebecca Lazarus, whom I loathed. I talked of suicide: she offered me a packet of beetle poison to do it with. I hinted at murder: she went into hysterics; and as I am a living man I went to America so that she might sleep without dreaming that I was stealing upstairs to cut her throat. In America I went out west and fell in with a man who was wanted by the police for holding up trains. It was he who had the idea of holding up motor cars in the South of Europe: a welcome idea to a desperate and disappointed man. He gave me some valuable introductions to capitalists of the right sort. I formed a syndicate; and the present enterprise is the result. I became leader, as the Jew always becomes leader, by his brains and imagination. But with all my pride of race I would give everything I possess to be an Englishman. I am like a boy: I cut her name on the trees and her initials on the sod.

When I am alone I lie down and tear my wretched hair and cry Louisa—

STRAKER [*startled*] Louisa!

MENDOZA. It is her name—Louisa—Louisa Straker—

TANNER. Straker!

STRAKER [*scrambling up on his knees most indignantly*] Look here: Louisa Straker is my sister, see? Wot do you mean by gassin about her like this? Wotshe got to do with you?

MENDOZA. A dramatic coincidence! You are Enry, her favorite brother!

STRAKER. Oo are you callin Enry? What call have you to take a liberty with my name or with hers? For two pins I'd punch your fat edd, so I would.

MENDOZA [*with grandiose calm*] If I let you do it, will you promise to brag of it afterwards to her? She will be reminded of her Mendoza: that is all I desire.

TANNER. This is genuine devotion, Henry. You should respect it.

STRAKER [*fiercely*] Funk, more likely.

MENDOZA [*springing to his feet*] Funk! Young man: I come of a famous family of fighters; and as your sister well knows, you would have as much chance against me as a perambulator against your motor car.

STRAKER [*secretly daunted, but rising from his knees with an air of reckless pugnacity*] I aint afraid of you. With your Louisa! Louisa! Miss Straker is good enough for you, I should think.

MENDOZA. I wish you could persuade her to think so.

STRAKER [*exasperated*] Here—

TANNER [*rising quickly and interposing*] Oh come, Henry: even if you could fight the President you cant fight the whole League of the Sierra. Sit down again and be friendly. A cat may look at a king; and even a President of brigands may look at your sister. All this family pride is really very old fashioned.

STRAKER [*subdued, but grumbling*] Let him look at her. But wot does he mean by makin out that she ever looked at im? [*Reluctantly resuming his couch on the turf*] Ear him talk, one ud think she was keepin company with him. [*He turns his back on them and composes himself to sleep*].

MENDOZA [*to Tanner, becoming more confidential as he finds himself virtually alone with a sympathetic listener in the still starlight of the mountains, for all the rest are asleep by this time*] It was just so with her, sir. Her intellect reached forward into the twentieth century: her social prejudices and family affections reached back into the dark ages. Ah, sir, how the words of Shakespear seem to fit every crisis in our emotions!

> I loved Louisa: 40,000 brothers
> Could not with all their quantity of love
> Make up my sum.

And so on. I forget the rest. Call it madness if you will—infatuation. I am an able man, a strong man: in ten years I should have owned a first-class hotel. I met her; and—you see!—I am a brigand, an outcast. Even Shakespear cannot do justice to what I feel for Louisa. Let me read you some lines that I have written about her myself. However slight their literary merit may be, they express what I feel better than any casual words can. [*He produces a packet of hotel bills, scrawled with manuscript, and kneels at the fire to decipher them, poking it with a stick to make it glow*].

TANNER [*slapping him rudely on the shoulder*] Put them in the fire, President.

MENDOZA [*startled*] Eh?

TANNER. You are sacrificing your career to a monomania.

MENDOZA. I know it.

TANNER. No you dont. No man would commit such a crime against himself if he really knew what he was doing. How can you look round at these august hills, look up at this divine sky, taste this finely tempered air, and then talk like a literary hack on a second floor in Bloomsbury?

MENDOZA [*shaking his head*] The Sierra is no better than Bloomsbury when once the novelty has worn off. Besides, these mountains make you dream of women—of women with magnificent hair.

TANNER. Of Louisa, in short. They will not make me dream of women, my friend: I am heartwhole.

MENDOZA. Do not boast until morning, sir. This is a strange country for dreams.

TANNER. Well, we shall see. Goodnight. [*He lies down and composes himself to sleep*].

Mendoza, with a sigh, follows his example; and for a few moments there is peace in the Sierra. Then Mendoza sits up suddenly and says pleadingly to Tanner—

MENDOZA. Just allow me to read a few lines before you go to sleep. I should really like your opinion of them.

TANNER [*drowsily*] Go on. I am listening.

MENDOZA. I saw thee first in Whitsun week
Louisa, Louisa—

TANNER [*rousing himself*] My dear President, Louisa is a very pretty name; but it really doesnt rhyme well to Whitsun week.

MENDOZA. Of course not. Louisa is not the rhyme, but the refrain.

TANNER [*subsiding*] Ah, the refrain. I beg your pardon. Go on.

MENDOZA. Perhaps you do not care for that one: I think you will like this better. [*He recites, in rich soft tones, and in slow time*]

Louisa, I love thee.
I love thee, Louisa.
Louisa, Louisa, Louisa, I love thee.
One name and one phrase make my music, Louisa.
Louisa, Louisa, Louisa, I love thee.

Mendoza thy lover,
Thy lover, Mendoza,
Mendoza adoringly lives for Louisa.
Theres nothing but that in the world for Mendoza.
Louisa, Louisa, Mendoza adores thee.

[*Affected*] There is no merit in producing beautiful lines upon such a name. Louisa is an exquisite name, is it not?

TANNER [*all but asleep, responds with faint groan*].

MENDOZA. O wert thou, Louisa,
The wife of Mendoza,
Mendoza's Louisa, Louisa Mendoza,
How blest were the life of Louisa's Mendoza!
How painless his longing of love for Louisa!

That is real poetry—from the heart—from the heart of hearts. Dont you think it will move her?

No answer.

[*Resignedly*] Asleep, as usual. Doggrel to all the world: heavenly music to me! Idiot that I am to wear my heart on my sleeve! [*He composes himself to sleep, murmuring*] Louisa, I love thee; I love thee, Louisa; Louisa, Louisa, Louisa, I—

Straker snores; rolls over on his side; and relapses into sleep. Stillness settles on the Sierra; and the darkness deepens. The fire has again buried itself in white ash and ceased to glow. The peaks shew unfathomably dark against the starry firmament; but now the stars dim and vanish; and the sky seems to steal away out of the universe. Instead of the Sierra there is nothing: omnipresent nothing. No sky, no peaks, no light, no sound, no time nor space, utter void. Then somewhere the beginning of a pallor, and with it a faint throbbing buzz as of a ghostly violoncello palpitating on the same note endlessly. A couple of ghostly violins presently take advantage of this bass

and therewith the pallor reveals a man in the void, an incorporeal but visible man, seated, absurdly enough, on nothing. For a moment he raises his head as the music passes him by. Then, with a heavy sigh, he droops in utter dejection; and the violins, discouraged, retrace their melody in despair and at last give it up, extinguished by wailings from uncanny wind instruments, thus:—

It is all very odd. One recognizes the Mozartian strain; and on this hint, and by the aid of certain sparkles of violet light in the pallor, the man's costume explains itself as that of a Spanish nobleman of the XV-XVI century. Don Juan, of course; but where? why? how? Besides, in the brief lifting of his face, now hidden by his hat brim, there was a curious suggestion of Tanner. A more critical, fastidious, handsome face, paler and colder, without Tanner's impetuous credulity and enthusiasm, and without a touch of his modern plutocratic vulgarity, but still a resemblance, even an identity. The name too: Don Juan Tenorio, John Tanner. Where on earth—or elsewhere—have we got to from the XX century and the Sierra?

Another pallor in the void, this time not violet, but a disagreeable smoky yellow. With it, the whisper of a ghostly clarinet turning this tune into infinite sadness:

The yellowish pallor moves: there is an old crone wandering in the void, bent and toothless; draped, as well as one can guess, in the coarse brown frock of some religious order. She wanders and wanders in her slow hopeless way, much as a wasp flies in its rapid busy way, until she blunders against the thing she seeks: companionship. With a sob of relief the poor old creature clutches at the presence of the man and addresses him in her dry unlovely voice, which can still express pride and resolution as well as suffering.

THE OLD WOMAN. Excuse me; but I am so lonely; and this place is so awful.

DON JUAN. A new comer?

THE OLD WOMAN. Yes: I suppose I died this morning. I confessed; I had extreme unction; I was in bed with my family about me and my eyes fixed on the cross. Then it grew dark; and when the light came back it was this light by which I walk seeing nothing. I have wandered for hours in horrible loneliness.

DON JUAN [*sighing*] Ah! you have not yet lost the sense of time. One soon does, in eternity.

THE OLD WOMAN. Where are we?

DON JUAN. In Hell.

THE OLD WOMAN [*proudly*] Hell! I in Hell! How dare you?

DON JUAN [*unimpressed*] Why not, Señora?

THE OLD WOMAN. You do not know to whom you are speaking. I am a lady, and a faithful daughter of the Church.

DON JUAN. I do not doubt it.

THE OLD WOMAN. But how then can I be in Hell? Purgatory, perhaps: I have not been perfect: who has? But Hell! oh, you are lying.

DON JUAN. Hell, Señora, I assure you; Hell at its best: that is, its most solitary—though perhaps you would prefer company.

THE OLD WOMAN. But I have sincerely repented; I have confessed—

DON JUAN. How much?

THE OLD WOMAN. More sins than I really committed. I loved confession.

DON JUAN. Ah, that is perhaps as bad as confessing too little. At all events, Señora, whether by oversight or intention, you are certainly damned, like myself; and there is nothing for it now but to make the best of it.

THE OLD WOMAN [*indignantly*] Oh! and I might have been so much wickeder! All my good deeds wasted! It is unjust.

DON JUAN. No: you were fully and clearly warned. For your bad deeds, vicarious atonement, mercy without justice. For your good deeds, justice without mercy. We have many good people here.

THE OLD WOMAN. Were you a good man?

DON JUAN. I was a murderer.

THE OLD WOMAN. A murderer! Oh, how dare they send me to herd with murderers! I was not as bad as that: I was a good woman. There is some mistake: where can I have it set right?

DON JUAN. I do not know whether mistakes can be corrected here. Probably they will not admit a mistake even if they have made one.

THE OLD WOMAN. But whom can I ask?

DON JUAN. I should ask the Devil, Señora: he understands the ways of this place, which is more than I ever could.

THE OLD WOMAN. The Devil! *I* speak to the Devil!

DON JUAN. In Hell, Señora, the Devil is the leader of the best society.

THE OLD WOMAN. I tell you, wretch, I know I am not in Hell.

DON JUAN. How do you know?

THE OLD WOMAN. Because I feel no pain.

DON JUAN. Oh, then there is no mistake: you are intentionally damned.

THE OLD WOMAN. Why do you say that?

DON JUAN. Because Hell, Señora, is a place for the wicked. The wicked are quite comfortable in it: it was made for them. You tell me you feel no pain. I conclude you are one of those for whom Hell exists.

THE OLD WOMAN. Do y o u feel no pain?

DON JUAN. I am not one of the wicked, Señora; therefore it bores me, bores me beyond description, beyond belief.

THE OLD WOMAN. Not one of the wicked! You said you were a murderer.

DON JUAN. Only a duel. I ran my sword through an old man who was trying to run his through me.

THE OLD WOMAN. If you were a gentleman, that was not a murder.

DON JUAN. The old man called it murder, because he was, he said, defending his daughter's honor. By this he meant that because I foolishly fell in love with her and told her so, she screamed; and he tried to assassinate me after calling me insulting names.

THE OLD WOMAN. You were like all men. Libertines and murderers all, all, all!

DON JUAN. And yet we meet here, dear lady.

THE OLD WOMAN. Listen to me. My father was slain by just such a wretch as you, in just such a duel, for just such a cause. I screamed: it was my duty. My father drew on my assailant: his honor demanded it. He fell: that was the reward of honor. I am here: In Hell, you tell me: that is the reward of duty. Is there justice in Heaven?

DON JUAN. No; but there is justice in Hell: Heaven is far above such idle human personalities. You will be welcome in Hell, Señora. Hell is the home of honor, duty, justice, and the rest of the seven deadly virtues. All the wickedness on earth is done in their name: where else but in Hell should they have their reward? Have I not told you that the truly damned are those who are happy in Hell?

THE OLD WOMAN. And are you happy here?

DON JUAN [*springing to his feet*] No; and that is the enigma on which I ponder in darkness. Why am I here? I, who repudiated all duty, trampled honor underfoot, and laughed at justice!

THE OLD WOMAN. Oh, what do I care why you are here? Why am *I* here? I, who sacrificed all my inclinations to womanly virtue and propriety!

DON JUAN. Patience, lady: you will be perfectly happy and at home here. As saith the poet, "Hell is a city much like Seville."

THE OLD WOMAN. Happy! here! where I am nothing! where I am nobody!

DON JUAN. Not at all: you are a lady; and wherever ladies are is Hell. Do not be surprised or terrified: you will find everything here that a lady can desire, including devils who will serve you from sheer love of servitude, and magnify your importance for the sake of dignifying their service—the best of servants.

THE OLD WOMAN. My servants will be devils!

DON JUAN. Have you ever had servants who were not devils?

THE OLD WOMAN. Never: they were devils, perfect devils, all of them. But that is only a manner of speaking. I thought you meant that my servants here would be real devils.

DON JUAN. No more real devils than you will be a real lady. Nothing is real here. That is the horror of damnation.

THE OLD WOMAN. Oh, this is all madness. This is worse than fire and the worm.

DON JUAN. For you, perhaps, there are consolations. For instance: how old were you when you changed from time to eternity?

THE OLD WOMAN. Do not ask me how old I w a s—as if I were a thing of the past. I a m 77.

DON JUAN. A ripe age, Señora. But in Hell old age is not tolerated. It is too real. Here we worship Love and Beauty. Our souls being entirely damned, we cultivate our hearts. As lady of 77, you would not have a single acquaintance in Hell.

THE OLD WOMAN. How can I help my age, man?

DON JUAN. You forget that you have left your age behind you in the realm of time. You are no more 77 than you are 7 or 17 or 27.

THE OLD WOMAN. Nonsense!

DON JUAN. Consider, Señora: was not this true even when you lived on earth? When you were 70, were you really older underneath your wrinkles and your grey hairs than when you were 30?

THE OLD WOMAN. No, younger: at 30 I was a fool. But of what use is it to feel younger and look older?

DON JUAN. You see, Señora, the look was only an illusion. Your wrinkles lied, just as the plump smooth skin of many a stupid girl of 17, with heavy spirits and decrepit ideas, lies about her age? Well, here we have no bodies: we see each other as bodies only because we learnt to think about one another under that aspect when we were alive; and we still think in that way, knowing no other. But we can appear to one another at what age we choose. You have but to will any of your old looks back, and back they will come.

THE OLD WOMAN. It cannot be true.

DON JUAN. Try.

THE OLD WOMAN. Seventeen!

DON JUAN. Stop. Before you decide, I had better tell you that these things are a matter of fashion. Occasionally we have a rage for 17; but it does not last long. Just at present the fashionable age is 40—or say 37; but there are signs of a change. If you were at all good-looking at 27, I should suggest your trying that, and setting a new fashion.

THE OLD WOMAN. I do not believe a word you are saying. However, 27 be it. [*Whisk! the old woman becomes a young one, magnificently attired, and so handsome that in the radiance into which her dull yellow halo has suddenly lightened one might almost mistake her for Ann Whitefield*].

DON JUAN. Doña Ana de Ulloa!

ANA. What? You know me!

DON JUAN. And you forget me!

ANA. I cannot see your face. [*He raises his hat*]. Don Juan Tenorio! Monster! You who slew my father! even here you pursue me.

DON JUAN. I protest I do not pursue you. Allow me to withdraw [*going*].

ANA [*seizing his arm*] You shall not leave me alone in this dreadful place.

DON JUAN. Provided my staying be not interpreted as pursuit.

ANA [*releasing him*] You may well wonder how I can endure your presence. My dear, dear father!

DON JUAN. Would you like to see him?

ANA. My father here!!!

DON JUAN. No: he is in Heaven.

ANA. I knew it. My noble father! He is looking down on us now. What must he feel to see his daughter in this place, and in conversation with his murderer!

DON JUAN. By the way, if we should meet him—

ANA. How can we meet him? He is in Heaven.

DON JUAN. He condescends to look in upon us here from time to time. Heaven bores him. So let me warn you that if you meet him he will be mortally offended if you speak of me as his murderer! He maintains that he was a much better swordsman than I, and that if his foot had not slipped he would have killed me. No doubt he is right: I was not a good fencer. I never dispute the point; so we are excellent friends.

ANA. It is no dishonor to a soldier to be proud of his skill in arms.

DON JUAN. You would rather not meet him, probably.

ANA. How dare you say that?

DON JUAN. Oh, that is the usual feeling here. You may remember that on earth—though of course we never confessed it—the death of anyone we knew, even those we liked best, was always mingled with a certain satisfaction at being finally done with them.

ANA. Monster! Never, never.

DON JUAN [*placidly*] I see you recognize the feeling. Yes: a funeral was always a festivity in black, especially the funeral of a relative. At all events, family ties are rarely kept up here. Your father is quite accustomed to this: he will not expect any devotion from you.

ANA. Wretch: I wore mourning for him all my life.

DON JUAN. Yes: it became you. But a life of mourning is one thing: an eternity of it quite another. Besides, here you are as dead as he. Can anything be more ridiculous than one dead person mourning for another? Do not look shocked, my dear Ana; and do not be alarmed: there is plenty of humbug in Hell (indeed there is hardly anything else); but the humbug of death and age and change is dropped because here we are all dead and all eternal. You will pick up our ways soon.

ANA. And will all the men call me their dear Ana?

DON JUAN. No. That was a slip of the tongue. I beg your pardon.

ANA [*almost tenderly*] Juan: did you really love me when you behaved so disgracefully to me?

DON JUAN [*impatiently*] Oh, I beg you not to begin talking about love. Here they talk of nothing else but love: its beauty, its holiness, its spirituality, its devil knows what!—excuse me; but it does so bore me. They dont know what theyre talking about: I do. They think they have achieved the perfection of love because they have no bodies. Sheer imaginative debauchery! Faugh!

ANA. Has even death failed to refine your soul, Juan? Has the terrible judgment of which my father's statue was the minister taught you no reverence?

DON JUAN. How is that very flattering statue, by the way? Does it still come to supper with naughty people and cast them into this bottomless pit?

ANA. It has been a great expense to me. The boys in the monastery school would not let it alone: the mischievous ones broke it; and the studious ones wrote their names on it. Three new noses in two years, and fingers without end. I had to leave it to its fate at last; and now I fear it is shockingly mutilated. My poor father!

DON JUAN. Hush! Listen! [*Two great chords rolling on syncopated waves of sound break forth: D minor and its dominant: a sound of dreadful joy to all musicians*]. Ha! Mozart's statue music. It is your father. You had better disappear until I prepare him. [*She vanishes*].

From the void comes a living statue of white marble, designed to represent a majestic old man. But he waives his majesty with infinite grace; walks with a feather-like step; and makes every wrinkle in his war worn visage brim over with holiday joyousness. To his sculptor he owes a perfectly trained figure, which he carries erect and trim; and the ends of his moustache curl up, elastic as watchsprings, giving him an air which, but for its Spanish dignity, would be called jaunty. He is on the pleasantest terms with Don Juan. His voice, save for a much more distinguished intonation, is so like the voice of Roebuck Rams-

den that it calls attention to the fact that they are not unlike one another in spite of their very different fashions of shaving.

DON JUAN. Ah, here you are, my friend. Why dont you learn to sing the splendid music Mozart has written for you?

THE STATUE. Unluckily he has written it for a bass voice. Mine is a counter tenor. Well: have you repented yet?

DON JUAN. I have too much consideration for you to repent, Don Gonzalo. If I did, you would have no excuse for coming from Heaven to argue with me.

THE STATUE. True. Remain obdurate, my boy. I wish I had killed you, as I should have done but for an accident. Then I should have come here; and you would have had a statue and a reputation for piety to live up to. Any news?

DON JUAN. Yes: your daughter is dead.

THE STATUE [*puzzled*] My daughter? [*Recollecting*] Oh! the one you were taken with. Let me see: what was her name?

DON JUAN. Ana.

THE STATUE. To be sure: Ana. A goodlooking girl, if I recollect aright. Have you warned Whatshisname? her husband.

DON JUAN. My friend Ottavio? No: I have not seen him since Ana arrived.

Ana comes indignantly to light.

ANA. What does this mean? Ottavio here and your friend! And you, father, have forgotten my name. You are indeed turned to stone.

THE STATUE. My dear: I am so much more admired in marble than I ever was in my own person that I have retained the shape the sculptor gave me. He was one of the first men of his day: you must acknowledge that.

ANA. Father! Vanity! personal vanity! from you!

THE STATUE. Ah, you outlived that weakness, my daughter: you must be nearly 80 by this time. I was cut off (by an accident) in my 64th year, and am considerably your junior in consequence. Besides, my child, in this place, what our libertine friend here would call the farce of parental wisdom is dropped. Regard me, I beg, as a fellow creature, not as a father.

ANA. You speak as this villain speaks.

THE STATUE. Juan is a sound thinker, Ana. A bad fencer, but a sound thinker.

ANA [*horror creeping upon her*] I begin to understand. These are devils, mocking me. I had better pray.

THE STATUE [*consoling her*] No, no, no, my child: do not pray. If you do, you will throw away the main advantage of this place. Written over the gate here are the words "Leave every hope behind, ye who enter." Only think what a relief that is! For what is hope? A form of moral responsibility. Here there is no hope, and consequently no duty, no work, nothing to be gained by praying, nothing to be lost by doing what you like. Hell, in short, is a place where you have nothing to do but amuse yourself. [*Don Juan sighs deeply*]. You sigh, friend Juan; but if you dwelt in Heaven, as I do, you would realize your advantages.

DON JUAN. You are in good spirits today, Commander. You are positively brilliant. What is the matter?

THE STATUE. I have come to a momentous decision, my boy. But first, where is our friend the Devil? I must consult him in the matter. And Ana would like to make his acquaintance, no doubt.

ANA. You are preparing some torment for me.

DON JUAN. All that is superstition, Ana. Reassure yourself. Remember: the devil is not so black as he is painted.

THE STATUE. Let us give him a call.

At the wave of the statue's hand the great chords roll out again: but this time Mozart's music gets grotesquely adulterated with Gounod's. A scarlet halo begins to glow; and into it the Devil rises, very Mephistophelean, and not at all unlike Mendoza, though not so interesting. He looks older; is getting prematurely bald; and, in spite of an effusion of goodnature and friendliness, is peevish and sensitive when his advances are not reciprocated. He does not inspire much confidence in his powers of hard work or endurance, and is, on the whole, a disagreeably self-indulgent looking person; but he is clever and plausible, though perceptibly less well bred than the two other men, and enormously less vital than the woman.

THE DEVIL [*heartily*] Have I the pleasure of again receiving a visit from the illustrious Commander of Calatrava? [*Coldly*] Don Juan, your servant. [*Politely*] And a strange lady? My respects, Señora.

ANA. Are you—

THE DEVIL [*bowing*] Lucifer, at your service.

ANA. I shall go mad.

THE DEVIL [*gallantly*] Ah, Señora, do not be anxious. You come to us from earth, full of the prejudices and terrors of that priest-ridden place. You have heard me ill spoken of; and yet, believe me, I have hosts of friends there.

ANA. Yes: you reign in their hearts.

THE DEVIL [*shaking his head*] You flatter me, Señora; but you are mistaken. It is true that the world cannot get on without me; but it never gives me credit for that: in its heart it mistrusts and hates me. Its sympathies are all with misery, with poverty, with starvation of the body and of the heart. I call on it to sympathize with joy, with love, with happiness, with beauty—

DON JUAN [*nauseated*] Excuse me: I am going. You know I cannot stand this.

THE DEVIL [*angrily*] Yes: I know that you are no friend of mine.

THE STATUE. What harm is he doing you, Juan? It seems to me that he was talking excellent sense when you interrupted him.

THE DEVIL [*warmly patting the statue's hand*] Thank you, my friend: thank you. You have always understood me: he has always disparaged and avoided me.

DON JUAN. I have treated you with perfect courtesy.

THE DEVIL. Courtesy! What is courtesy? I care nothing for mere courtesy. Give me warmth of heart, true sincerity, the bond of sympathy with love and joy—

DON JUAN. You are making me ill.

THE DEVIL. There! [*Appealing to the statue*] You hear, sir! Oh, by what irony of fate was this cold selfish egotist sent to my kingdom, and you taken to the icy mansions of the sky!

THE STATUE. I cant complain. I was a hypocrite; and it served me right to be sent to Heaven.

THE DEVIL. Why, sir, do you not join us, and leave a sphere for which your temperament is too sympathetic, your heart too warm, your capacity for enjoyment too generous?

THE STATUE. I have this day resolved to do so. In future, excellent Son of the Morning, I am yours. I have left Heaven for ever.

THE DEVIL [*again touching the marble hand*] Ah, what an honor! what a triumph for our cause! Thank you, thank you. And now, my friend—I may call you so at last—could you not persuade h i m to take the place you have left vacant above?

THE STATUE [*shaking his head*] I cannot conscientiously recommend anybody with whom I am on friendly terms to deliberately make himself dull and uncomfortable.

THE DEVIL. Of course not; but are you sure h e would be uncomfortable? Of course you know best: you brought him here originally; and we had the greatest hopes of him. His sentiments were in the best taste of our best people. You remember how he sang? [*He begins to sing in a nasal operatic baritone, tremulous from an eternity of misuse in the French manner*]

Vivan le femmine!
Viva il buon vino!

THE STATUE [*taking up the tune an octave higher in his counter tenor*]

Sostegno e gloria
D'umanità.

THE DEVIL. Precisely. Well, he never sings for us now.

DON JUAN. Do you complain of that? Hell is full of musical amateurs: music is the brandy of the damned. May not one lost soul be permitted to abstain?

THE DEVIL. You dare blaspheme against the sublimest of the arts!

DON JUAN [*with cold disgust*] You talk like a hysterical woman fawning on a fiddler.

THE DEVIL. I am not angry. I merely pity you. You have no soul; and you are unconscious of all that you lose. Now you, Señor Commander, are a born musician. How well you sing! Mozart would be delighted if he were still here; but he moped and went to Heaven. Curious how these clever men, whom you would have supposed born to be popular here, have turned out social failures, like Don Juan!

DON JUAN. I am really very sorry to be a social failure.

THE DEVIL. Not that we dont admire your intellect, you know. We do. But I look at the matter from your own point of view. You dont get on with us. The place doesn't suit you. The truth is, you have—I wont say no heart; for we know that beneath all your affected cynicism you have a warm one—

DON JUAN [*shrinking*] Dont, please dont.

THE DEVIL [*nettled*] Well, youve no capacity for enjoyment. Will that satisfy you?

DON JUAN. It is a somewhat less insufferable form of cant than the other. But if youll allow me, I'll take refuge, as usual, in solitude.

THE DEVIL. Why not take refuge in Heaven? Thats the proper place for you. [*To Ana*] Come, Señora! could you not persuade him for his own good to try change of air?

ANA. But can he go to Heaven if he wants to?

THE DEVIL. Whats to prevent him?

ANA. Can anybody—can *I* go to Heaven if I want to?

THE DEVIL [*rather contemptuously*] Certainly, if your taste lies that way.

ANA. But why doesnt everybody go to Heaven, then?

THE STATUE [*chuckling*] I can tell you that, my dear. It's because Heaven is the most angelically dull place in all creation: thats why.

THE DEVIL. His excellency the Commander puts it with military bluntness; but the strain of living in Heaven is intolerable. There is a notion that I was turned out of it; but as a matter of fact nothing could have induced me to stay there. I simply left it and organized this place.

THE STATUE. I dont wonder at it. Nobody could stand an eternity of Heaven.

THE DEVIL. Oh, it suits some people. Let us be just, Commander: it is a question of temperament. I dont admire the heavenly temperament: I dont understand it: I dont know that I particularly want to understand it; but it takes all sorts to make a universe. There is no accounting for tastes: there are people who like it. I think Don Juan would like it.

DON JUAN. But—pardon my frankness—could you really go back there if you desired to; or are the grapes sour?

THE DEVIL. Back there! I often go back there. Have you never read the book of Job? Have you any canonical authority for assuming that there is any barrier between our circle and the other one?

ANA. But surely there is a great gulf fixed.

THE DEVIL. Dear lady: a parable must not be taken literally. The gulf is the difference between the angelic and the diabolic temperament. What more impassable gulf could you have? Think of what you have seen on earth. There is no physical gulf between the philosopher's class room and the bull ring; but the bull fighters do not come to the class room for all that. Have you ever been in the country where I have the largest following? England. There they have great racecourses, and also concert rooms where they play the classical compositions of his Excellency's friend Mozart. Those who go to the racecourses can stay away from them and go to the classical concerts instead if they like: there is no law against it; for Englishmen never will be slaves: they are free to do whatever the Government and public opinion allow them to do. And the classical concert is admitted to be a higher, more cultivated, poetic, intellectual, ennobling place than the racecourse. But do the lovers of racing desert their sport and flock to the concert room? Not they. They would suffer there all the weariness the Commander has suffered in Heaven. There is the great gulf of the parable between the two places. A mere physical gulf they could bridge; or at least I could bridge it for them (the earth is full of Devil's Bridges); but the gulf of dislike is impassable and eternal. And that is the only gulf that separates my friends here from those who are invidiously called the blest.

ANA. I shall go to Heaven at once.

THE STATUE. My child: one word of warning first. Let me complete my friend Lucifer's similitude of the classical concert. At every one of these concerts in England you will find rows of weary people who are there, not because they really like classical music, but because they think they ought to like it. Well, there is the same thing in Heaven. A number of people sit there in glory, not because they are happy, but because they think they owe it to their position to be in Heaven. They are almost all English.

THE DEVIL. Yes: the Southerners give it up and join me just as you have done. But the English really do not seem to know when they are thoroughly miserable. An Englishman thinks he is moral when he is only uncomfortable.

THE STATUE. In short, my daughter, if you go to Heaven without being naturally qualified for it, you will not enjoy yourself there.

ANA. And who dares say that I am not naturally qualified for it? The most distinguished princes of the Church have never questioned it. I owe it to myself to leave this place at once.

THE DEVIL [*offended*] As you please, Señora. I should have expected better taste from you.

ANA. Father: I shall expect you to come with me. You cannot stay here. What will people say?

THE STATUE. People! Why, the best people are here—princes of the Church and all. So few go to Heaven, and so many come here, that the blest, once called a heavenly host, are a continually dwindling minority. The saints, the fathers, the elect of long ago are the cranks, the faddists, the outsiders of today.

THE DEVIL. It is true. From the beginning of my career I knew that I should win in the long run by sheer weight of public opinion, in spite of the long campaign of misrepresentation and calumny against me. At bottom the universe is a constitutional one; and with such a majority as mine I cannot be kept permanently out of office.

DON JUAN. I think, Ana, you had better stay here.

ANA [*jealously*] You do not want me to go with you.

DON JUAN. Surely you do not want to enter Heaven in the company of a reprobate like me.

ANA. All souls are equally precious. You repent, do you not?

DON JUAN. My dear Ana, you are silly. Do you suppose Heaven is like earth, where people persuade themselves that what is done can be undone by repentance; that what is spoken can be unspoken by withdrawing it; that what is true can be annihilated by a general agreement to give it the lie? No: Heaven is the home of the masters of reality: that is why I am going thither.

ANA. Thank you: I am going to Heaven for happiness. I have had quite enough of reality on earth.

DON JUAN. Then you must stay here; for Hell is the home of the unreal and of the seekers for happiness. It is the only refuge from Heaven, which is, as I tell you, the home of the masters of reality, and from earth, which is the home of the slaves of reality. The earth is a nursery in which men and women play at being heroes and heroines, saints and sinners; but they are dragged down from their fool's paradise by their bodies: hunger and cold and thirst, age and decay and disease, death above all, make them slaves of reality: thrice a day meals must be eaten and digested: thrice a century a new generation must be engendered: ages of faith, of romance, and of science are all driven at last to have but one prayer "Make me a healthy animal." But here you escape this tyranny of the flesh; for here you are not an animal at all: you are a ghost, an appearance, an illusion, a convention, deathless, ageless: in a word, bodiless. There are no social questions here, no political questions, no religious questions, best of all, perhaps, no sanitary questions. Here you call your appearance beauty, your emotions love, your sentiments heroism, your aspirations virtue, just as you did on earth; but here there are no hard facts to contradict you, no ironic contrast of your needs with your pretensions, no human comedy, nothing but a perpetual romance, a universal melodrama. As our German friend put it in his poem, "the poetically nonsensical here is good sense; and the Eternal Feminine draws us ever upward and on"—without getting us a step farther. And yet you want to leave this paradise!

ANA. But if Hell be so beautiful as this, how glorious must Heaven be!

The Devil the Statue and Don Juan all begin to speak at once in violent protest; then stop, abashed.

DON JUAN. I beg your pardon.

THE DEVIL. Not at all. I interrupted you.

THE STATUE. You were going to say something.

DON JUAN. After you, gentlemen.

THE DEVIL [*to Don Juan*] You have been so eloquent on the advantages of my dominions that I leave you to do equal justice to the drawbacks of the alternative establishment.

DON JUAN. In Heaven, as I picture it, dear lady, you live and work instead of playing and pretending. You face things as they are; you escape nothing but glamor; and your steadfastness and your peril are your glory. If the play still goes on here and on earth, and all the world is a stage, Heaven is at least behind the scenes. But Heaven cannot be described by metaphor. Thither I shall go presently, because there I hope to escape at last from lies and from the tedious, vulgar pursuit of happiness, to spend my eons in contemplation—

THE STATUE. Ugh!

DON JUAN. Señor Commander: I do not blame your disgust: a picture gallery is a dull place for a blind man. But even as you enjoy the contemplation of such romantic mirages as beauty and pleasure; so would I enjoy the contemplation of that which interests me above all things: namely, Life: the force that ever strives to attain greater power of contemplating itself. What made this brain of mine, do you think? Not the need to move my limbs; for a rat with half my brains moves as well as I. Not merely the need to do, but the need to know what I do, lest in my blind efforts to live I should be slaying myself.

THE STATUE. You would have slain yourself in your blind efforts to fence but for my foot slipping, my friend.

DON JUAN. Audacious ribald: your laughter will finish in hideous boredom before morning.

THE STATUE. Ha ha! Do you remember how I frightened you when I said something like that to you from my pedestal in Seville? It sounds rather flat without my trombones.

DON JUAN. They tell me it generally sounds flat with them, Commander.

ANA. Oh, do not interrupt with these frivolities, father. Is there nothing in Heaven but contemplation, Juan?

DON JUAN. In the Heaven I seek, no other joy. But there is the work of helping Life in its struggle upward. Think of how it wastes and scatters itself, how it raises up obstacles to itself and destroys itself in its ignorance and blindness. It needs a brain, this irresistible force, lest in its ignorance it should resist itself. What a piece of work is man! says the poet. Yes; but what a blunderer! Here is the highest miracle of organization yet attained by life, the most intensely alive thing that exists, the most conscious of all the organisms; and yet, how wretched are his brains! Stupidity made sordid and cruel by the realities learnt from toil and poverty: Imagination resolved to starve sooner than face these realities, piling up illusions to hide them, and calling itself cleverness, genius! And each accusing the other of its own defect: Stupidity accusing Imagination of folly, and Imagination accusing Stupidity of ignorance: whereas, alas! Stupidity has all the knowledge, and Imagination all the intelligence.

THE DEVIL. And a pretty kettle of fish they make of it between them. Did I not say, when I was arranging that affair of Faust's, that all Man's reason has done for him is to make him beastlier than any beast. One splendid body is worth the brains of a hundred dyspeptic, flatulent philosophers.

DON JUAN. You forget that brainless magnificence of body has been tried. Things immeasurably greater than man in every respect but brain have existed and perished. The megatherium, the ichthyosaurus have paced the earth with seven-league steps and hidden the day with cloud vast wings. Where are they now? Fossils in museums, and so few and imperfect at that, that a knuckle bone or a tooth of one of them is prized beyond the lives of a thousand soldiers. These things lived and wanted to live; but for lack of brains they did not know how to carry out their purpose, and so destroyed themselves.

THE DEVIL. And is Man any the less destroying himself for all this boasted brain of his? Have you walked up and down upon the earth lately? I have; and I have examined Man's wonderful inventions. And I tell you that in the arts of life man invents nothing; but in the arts of death he outdoes Nature herself, and produces by chemistry and machinery all the slaughter of plague, pestilence, and famine. The peasant I tempt today eats and drinks what was eaten and drunk by the peasants of ten thousand years ago; and the house he lives in has not altered as much in a thousand centuries as the fashion of a lady's bonnet in a score of weeks. But when he goes out to slay, he carries a marvel of mechanism that lets loose at the touch of his finger all the hidden molecular energies, and leaves the javelin, the arrow, the blowpipe of his fathers far behind. In the arts of peace Man is a bungler. I have seen his cotton factories and the like, with machinery that a greedy dog could have invented if it had wanted money instead of food. I know his clumsy typewriters and bungling locomotives and tedious bicycles: they are toys compared to the Maxim gun, the submarine torpedo boat. There is nothing in Man's industrial machinery but his greed and sloth: his heart is in his weapons. This marvellous force of Life of which you boast is a force of Death: Man measures his strength by his destructiveness. What is his religion? An excuse for hating me. What is his law? An excuse for hanging y o u. What is his morality? Gentility! An excuse for consuming without producing. What is his art? An excuse for gloating over pictures of slaughter. What are his politics? Either the worship of a despot because a despot can kill, or parliamentary cockfighting. I spent an evening lately in a certain celebrated legislature, and heard the pot lecturing the kettle for its blackness, and ministers answering questions. When I left I chalked up on the door the old nursery saying "Ask no questions and you will be told no lies." I bought a sixpenny family magazine, and found it full of pictures of young men shooting and stabbing one another. I saw a man die: he was a London bricklayer's laborer with seven children. He left seventeen pounds club money; and his wife spent it all on his funeral and went into the workhouse with the children next day. She would not have spent sevenpence on her children's schooling: the law had to force her to let them be taught gratuitously; but on death she spent all she had. Their imagination glows, their energies rise up at the idea of death, these people: they love it; and the more horrible it is the more they enjoy it. Hell is a place far above their comprehension: they derive their notion of it from two of the greatest fools that ever lived, an Italian and an Englishman. The Italian described it as a place of mud, frost, filth, fire, and venomous serpents: all torture. This ass, when he was not lying about me, was maundering about some woman whom he saw once in the street. The Englishman described me as being expelled from Heaven by cannons and gunpowder; and to this day every Briton believes that the whole of his silly story is in the Bible. What else he says I do not know; for it is all in a long poem which neither I nor anyone else ever succeeded in wading through. It is the same in everything. The highest form of literature is the tragedy, a play in which everybody is murdered at the end. In the old chronicles you read of earthquakes and pestilences, and are told that these shewed the power and majesty of God and the littleness of Man. Nowadays the chronicles describe battles. In a battle two bodies of men shoot at one another with bullets and explosive shells until one body runs away, when the others chase the fugitives on horseback and cut them to pieces as they fly. And this, the chronicle concludes, shews the greatness and majesty of empires, and the littleness of the vanquished. Over such battles the people run about the streets yelling with delight, and egg their Governments on to spend hundreds of millions of money in the slaughter, whilst the strongest Ministers dare not spend an extra penny in the pound against the poverty and pestilence through which they themselves daily walk. I could give you a thousand instances; but they all come to the same thing: the power that governs the earth is not the power of Life but of Death; and the inner need that has nerved Life to the effort of organizing itself into the human being is not the need for higher life but for a more efficient engine of destruction. The plague, the famine, the earthquake, the tempest were too spasmodic in their action; the tiger and crocodile were too easily satiated and not cruel enough: something more constantly, more ruthlessly, more ingeniously destructive was needed; and that something was Man, the inventor of the rack, the stake, the gallows, the electric chair; of sword and gun and poison gas: above all, of justice, duty, patriotism, and all the other isms by which even those who are clever enough to be humanely disposed are persuaded to become the most destructive of all the destroyers.

DON JUAN. Pshaw! all this is old. Your weak side, my diabolic friend, is that you have always been a gull: you take Man at his own valuation. Nothing would flatter him more than your opinion of him. He loves to think of himself as bold and bad. He is neither one nor the other: he is only a coward. Call him tyrant, murderer, pirate, bully; and he will adore you, and swagger about with the consciousness of having the blood of the old sea kings in his veins. Call him liar and thief; and he will only take an action against you for libel. But call him coward; and he will go mad with rage: he will face death to outface that stinging truth. Man gives every reason for his conduct save one, every excuse for his crimes save one, every plea for his safety save one; and that one is his cowardice. Yet all his civilization is founded on his cowardice, on his abject tameness, which he calls his respectability. There are limits to what a mule or an ass will stand; but Man will suffer himself to be degraded until his vileness becomes so loathsome to his oppressors that they themselves are forced to reform it.

THE DEVIL. Precisely. And these are the creatures in whom you discover what you call a Life Force!

DON JUAN. Yes; for now comes the most surprising part of the whole business.

THE STATUE. Whats that?

DON JUAN. Why, that you can make any of these cowards brave by simply putting an idea into his head.
THE STATUE. Stuff! As an old soldier I admit the cowardice: it's as universal as sea sickness, and matters just as little. But that about putting an idea into a man's head is stuff and nonsense. In a battle all you need to make you fight is a little hot blood and the knowledge that it's more dangerous to lose than to win.
DON JUAN. That is perhaps why battles are so useless. But men never really overcome fear until they imagine they are fighting to further a universal purpose—fighting for an idea, as they call it. Why was the Crusader braver than the pirate? Because he fought, not for himself, but for the Cross. What force was it that met him with a valor as reckless as his own? The force of men who fought, not for themselves, but for Islam. They took Spain from us though we were fighting for our very hearths and homes; but when we, too, fought for that mighty idea, a Catholic Church, we swept them back to Africa.
THE DEVIL [*ironically*] What! you a Catholic, Señor Don Juan! A devotee! My congratulations.
THE STATUE [*seriously*] Come, come! as a soldier, I can listen to nothing against the Church.
DON JUAN. Have no fear, Commander: this idea of a Catholic Church will survive Islam, will survive the Cross, will survive even that vulgar pageant of incompetent schoolboyish gladiators which you call the Army.
THE STATUE. Juan: you will force me to call you to account for this.
DON JUAN. Useless: I cannot fence. Every idea for which Man will die will be a Catholic idea. When the Spaniard learns at last that he is no better than the Saracen, and his prophet no better than Mahomet, he will arise, more Catholic than ever, and die on a barricade across the filthy slum he starves in, for universal liberty and equality.
THE STATUE. Bosh!
DON JUAN. What you call bosh is the only thing men dare die for. Later on, Liberty will not be Catholic enough: men will die for human perfection, to which they will sacrifice all their liberty gladly.
THE DEVIL. Ay: they will never be at a loss for an excuse for killing one another.
DON JUAN. What of that? It is not death that matters, but the fear of death. It is not killing and dying that degrades us, but base living, and accepting the wages and profits of degradation. Better ten dead men than one live slave or his master. Men shall yet rise up, father against

son and brother against brother, and kill one another for the great Catholic idea of abolishing slavery.

THE DEVIL. Yes, when the Liberty and Equality of which you prate shall have made free white Christians cheaper in the labor market than black heathen slaves sold by auction at the block.

DON JUAN. Never fear! the white laborer shall have his turn too. But I am not now defending the illusory forms the great ideas take. I am giving you examples of the fact that this creature Man, who in his own selfish affairs is a coward to the backbone, will fight for an idea like a hero. He may be abject as a citizen; but he is dangerous as a fanatic. He can only be enslaved whilst he is spiritually weak enough to listen to reason. I tell you, gentlemen, if you can shew a man a piece of what he now calls God's work to do, and what he will later on call by many new names, you can make him entirely reckless of the consequences to himself personally.

ANA. Yes: he shirks all his responsibilities, and leaves his wife to grapple with them.

THE STATUE. Well said, daughter. Do not let him talk you out of your common sense.

THE DEVIL. Alas! Señor Commander, now that we have got on to the subject of Woman, he will talk more than ever. However, I confess it is for me the one supremely interesting subject.

DON JUAN. To a woman, Señora, man's duties and responsibilities begin and end with the task of getting bread for her children. To her, Man is only a means to the end of getting children and rearing them.

ANA. Is that your idea of a woman's mind? I call it cynical and disgusting animalism.

DON JUAN. Pardon me, Ana: I said nothing about a woman's whole mind. I spoke of her view of Man as a separate sex. It is no more cynical than her view of herself as above all things a Mother. Sexually, Woman is Nature's contrivance for perpetuating its highest achievement. Sexually, Man is Woman's contrivance for fulfilling Nature's behest in the most economical way. She knows by instinct that far back in the evolutional process she invented him, differentiated him, created him in order to produce something better than the single-sexed process can produce. Whilst he fulfils the purpose for which she made him, he is welcome to his dreams, his follies, his ideals, his heroisms, provided that the keystone of them all is the worship of woman, of motherhood, of the family, of the hearth. But how rash and dangerous it was to invent a separate creature whose sole function was her own impregnation! For mark what has happened. First Man has multiplied on her hands until there are as many men as women; so that she has been unable to employ for her purposes more than a fraction of the immense energy she has left at his disposal by saving him the exhausting labor of gestation. This superfluous energy has gone to his brain and to his muscle. He has become too strong to be controlled by her bodily, and too imaginative and mentally vigorous to be content with mere self-reproduction. He has created civilization without consulting her, taking her domestic labor for granted as the foundation of it.

ANA. That is true, at all events.

THE DEVIL. Yes; and this civilization! what is it, after all?

DON JUAN. After all, an excellent peg to hang your cynical commonplaces on; but before all, it is an attempt on Man's part to make himself something more than the mere instrument of Woman's purpose. So far, the result of Life's continual effort not only to maintain itself, but to achieve higher and higher organization and completer self-consciousness, is only, at best, a doubtful campaign between its forces and those of Death and Degeneration. The battles in this campaign are mere blunders, mostly won, like actual military battles, in spite of the commanders.

THE STATUE. That is a dig at me. No matter: go on, go on.

DON JUAN. It is a dig at a much higher power than you, Commander. Still, you must have noticed in your profession that even a stupid general can win battles when the enemy's general is a little stupider.

THE STATUE [*very seriously*] Most true, Juan, most true. Some donkeys have amazing luck.

DON JUAN. Well, the Life Force is stupid; but it is not so stupid as the forces of Death and Degeneration. Besides, these are in its pay all the time. And so Life wins, after a fashion. What mere copiousness of fecundity can supply and mere greed preserve, we possess. The survival of whatever form of civilization can produce the best rifle and the best fed riflemen is assured.

THE DEVIL. Exactly! the survival, not of the most effective means of Life but of the most effective means of Death. You always come back to my point, in spite of your wrigglings and evasions and sophistries, not to mention the intolerable length of your speeches.

DON JUAN. Oh, come! who began making long speeches? However, if I overtax your intellect, you can leave us and seek the society of love and beauty and the rest of your favorite boredoms.

THE DEVIL [*much offended*] This is not fair, Don Juan, and not civil. I am also on the intellectual plane. Nobody can appreciate it more than I do. I am arguing fairly with you, and, I think, successfully refuting you. Let us go on for another hour if you like.

DON JUAN. Good: let us.

THE STATUE. Not that I see any prospect of your coming to any point in particular, Juan. Still, since in this place, instead of merely killing time we have to kill eternity, go ahead by all means.

DON JUAN [*somewhat impatiently*] My point, you marble-headed old masterpiece, is only a step ahead of you. Are we agreed that Life is a force which has made innumerable experiments in organizing itself; that the mammoth and the man, the mouse and the megatherium, the flies and the fleas and the Fathers of the Church, are all more or less successful attempts to build up that raw force into higher and higher individuals, the ideal individual being omnipotent, omniscient, infallible, and withal completely, unilludedly self-conscious: in short, a god?

THE DEVIL. I agree, for the sake of argument.

THE STATUE. I agree, for the sake of avoiding argument.

ANA. I most emphatically disagree as regards the Fathers of the Church; and I must beg you not to drag them into the argument.

DON JUAN. I did so purely for the sake of alliteration, Ana; and I shall make no further allusion to them. And now, since we are, with that exception, agreed so far, will you not agree with me further that Life has not measured the success of its attempts at godhead by the beauty or bodily perfection of the result, since in both these respects the birds, as our friend Aristophanes long ago pointed out, are so extraordinarily superior, with their power of flight and their lovely plumage, and, may I add, the touching poetry of their loves and nestings, that it is inconceivable that Life, having once produced them, should, if love and beauty were her object, start off on another line and labor at the clumsy elephant and the hideous ape, whose grandchildren we are?

ANA. Aristophanes was a heathen; and you, Juan, I am afraid, are very little better.

THE DEVIL. You conclude, then, that Life was driving at clumsiness and ugliness?

DON JUAN. No, perverse devil that you are, a thousand times no. Life was driving at brains—at its darling object: an organ by which it can attain not only self-consciousness but self-understanding.

THE STATUE. This is metaphysics, Juan. Why the devil should—[*to The Devil*] I beg your pardon.

THE DEVIL. Pray dont mention it. I have always regarded the use of my name to secure additional emphasis as a high compliment to me. It is quite at your service, Commander.

THE STATUE. Thank you: thats very good of you. Even in Heaven, I never quite got out of my old military habits of speech. What I was going to ask Juan was why Life should bother itself about getting a brain. Why should it want to understand itself? Why not be content to enjoy itself?

DON JUAN. Without a brain, Commander, you would enjoy yourself without knowing it, and so lose all the fun.

THE STATUE. True, most true. But I am quite content with brain enough to know that I'm enjoying myself. I dont want to understand why. In fact, I'd rather not. My experience is that one's pleasures dont bear thinking about.

DON JUAN. That is why intellect is so unpopular. But to Life, the force behind the Man, intellect is a necessity, because without it he blunders into death. Just as Life, after ages of struggle, evolved that wonderful bodily organ the eye, so that the living organism could see where it was going and what was coming to help or threaten it, and thus avoid a thousand dangers that formerly slew it, so it is evolving today a mind's eye that shall see, not the physical world, but the purpose of Life, and thereby enable the individual to work for that purpose instead of thwarting and baffling it by setting up shortsighted personal aims as at present. Even as it is, only one sort of man has ever been happy, has ever been universally respected among all the conflicts of interests and illusions.

THE STATUE. You mean the military man.

DON JUAN. Commander: I do n o t mean the military man. When the military man approaches, the world locks up its spoons and packs off its womankind. No: I sing, not arms and the hero, but the philosophic man: he who seeks in contemplation to discover the inner will of the world, in invention to discover the means of fulfilling that will, and in action to do that will by the so-discovered means. Of all other sorts of men I declare myself tired. They are tedious failures. When I was on earth, professors of all sorts prowled round me feeling for an unhealthy spot in me on which they could fasten. The doctors of medicine bade me consider what I must do to save my body, and offered me quack cures for imaginary diseases. I replied that I was not a hypochondriac; so they called me Ignoramus and went their way. The doctors of divinity bade me consider what I must do to save my soul;

but I was not a spiritual hypochondriac any more than a bodily one, and would not trouble myself about that either; so they called me Atheist and went their way. After them came the politician, who said there was only one purpose in nature, and that was to get him into parliament. I told him I did not care whether he got into parliament or not; so he called me Mugwump and went his way. Then came the romantic man, the Artist, with his love songs and his paintings and his poems; and with him I had great delight for many years, and some profit; for I cultivated my senses for his sake; and his songs taught me to hear better, his paintings to see better, and his poems to feel more deeply. But he led me at last into the worship of Woman.

ANA. Juan!

DON JUAN. Yes: I came to believe that in her voice was all the music of the song, in her face all the beauty of the painting, and in her soul all the emotion of the poem.

ANA. And you were disappointed, I suppose. Well, was it her fault that you attributed all these perfections to her?

DON JUAN. Yes, partly. For with a wonderful instinctive cunning, she kept silent and allowed me to glorify her: to mistake my own visions, thoughts, and feelings for hers. Now my friend the romantic man was often too poor or too timid to approach those women who were beautiful or refined enough to seem to realize his ideal; and so he went to his grave believing in his dream. But I was more favored by nature and circumstance. I was of noble birth and rich; and when my person did not please, my conversation flattered, though I generally found myself fortunate in both.

THE STATUE. Coxcomb!

DON JUAN. Yes; but even my coxcombry pleased. Well, I found that when I had touched a woman's imagination, she would allow me to persuade myself that she loved me; but when my suit was granted she never said "I am happy: my love is satisfied": she always said, first, "At last, the barriers are down," and second, "When will you come again?"

ANA. That is exactly what men say.

DON JUAN. I protest I never said it. But all women say it. Well, these two speeches always alarmed me; for the first meant that the lady's impulse had been solely to throw down my fortifications and gain my citadel; and the second openly announced that henceforth she regarded me as her property, and counted my time as already wholly at her disposal.

THE DEVIL. That is where your want of heart came in.

THE STATUE [*shaking his head*] You shouldnt repeat what a woman says, Juan.

ANA [*severely*] It should be sacred to you.

THE STATUE. Still, they certainly do say it. I never minded the barriers; but there was always a slight shock about the other, unless one was very hard hit indeed.

DON JUAN. Then the lady, who had been happy and idle enough before, became anxious, preoccupied with me, always intriguing, conspiring, pursuing, watching, waiting, bent wholly on making sure of her prey: I being the prey, you understand. Now this was not what I had bargained for. It may have been very proper and very natural; but it was not music, painting, poetry, and joy incarnated in a beautiful woman. I ran away from it. I ran away from it very often: in fact I became famous for running away from it.

ANA. Infamous, you mean.

DON JUAN. I did not run away from you. Do you blame me for running away from the others?

ANA. Nonsense, man. You are talking to a woman of 77 now. If you had had the chance, you would have run away from me too—if I had let you. You would not have found it so easy with me as with some of the others. If men will not be faithful to their home and their duties, they must be made to be. I daresay you all want to marry lovely incarnations of music and painting and poetry. Well, you cant have them, because they dont exist. If flesh and blood is not good enough for you you must go without: thats all. Women have to put up with flesh-and-blood husbands—and little enough of that too, sometimes; and you will have to put up with flesh-and-blood wives. [*The Devil looks dubious. The Statue makes a wry face*]. I see you dont like that, any of you; but it's true, for all that; so if you dont like it you can lump it.

DON JUAN. My dear lady, you have put my whole case against romance into a few sentences. That is just why I turned my back on the romantic man with the artist nature, as he called his infatuation. I thanked him for teaching me to use my eyes and ears; but I told him that his beauty worshipping and happiness hunting and woman idealizing was not worth a dump as a philosophy of life; so he called me Philistine and went his way.

ANA. It seems that Woman taught you something, too, with all her defects.

DON JUAN. She did more: she interpreted all the other teaching for me.

Ah, my friends, when the barriers were down for the first time, what an astounding illumination! I had been prepared for infatuation, for intoxication, for all the illusions of love's young dream; and lo! never was my perception clearer, nor my criticism more ruthless. The most jealous rival of my mistress never saw every blemish in her more keenly than I. I was not duped: I took her without chloroform.

ANA. But you did take her.

DON JUAN. That was the revelation. Up to that moment I had never lost the sense of being my own master; never consciously taken a single step until my reason had examined and approved it. I had come to believe that I was a purely rational creature: a thinker! I said, with the foolish philosopher, "I think; therefore I am." It was Woman who taught me to say "I am; therefore I think." And also "I would think more; therefore I must be more."

THE STATUE. This is extremely abstract and metaphysical, Juan. If you would stick to the concrete, and put your discoveries in the form of entertaining anecdotes about your adventures with women, your conversation would be easier to follow.

DON JUAN. Bah! what need I add? Do you not understand that when I stood face to face with Woman, every fibre in my clear critical brain warned me to spare her and save myself. My morals said No. My conscience said No. My chivalry and pity for her said No. My prudent regard for myself said No. My ear, practised on a thousand songs and symphonies; my eye, exercised on a thousand paintings; tore her voice, her features, her color to shreds. I caught all those tell-tale resemblances to her father and mother by which I knew what she would be like in thirty years' time. I noted the gleam of gold from a dead tooth in the laughing mouth: I made curious observations of the strange odors of the chemistry of the nerves. The visions of my romantic reveries, in which I had trod the plains of Heaven with a deathless, ageless creature of coral and ivory, deserted me in that supreme hour. I remembered them and desperately strove to recover their illusion; but they now seemed the emptiest of inventions: my judgment was not to be corrupted: my brain still said No on every issue. And whilst I was in the act of framing my excuse to the lady, Life seized me and threw me into her arms as a sailor throws a scrap of fish into the mouth of a seabird.

THE STATUE. You might as well have gone without thinking such a lot about it, Juan. You are like all the clever men; you have more brains than is good for you.

THE DEVIL. And were you not the happier for the experience, Señor Don Juan?

DON JUAN. The happier, no: the wiser, yes. That moment introduced me for the first time to myself, and, through myself, to the world. I saw then how useless it is to attempt to impose conditions on the irresistible force of Life; to preach prudence, careful selection, virtue, honor, chastity—

ANA. Don Juan: a word against chastity is an insult to me.

DON JUAN. I say nothing against your chastity, Señora, since it took the form of a husband and twelve children. What more could you have done had you been the most abandoned of women?

ANA. I could have had twelve husbands and no children: thats what I could have done, Juan. And let me tell you that that would have made all the difference to the earth which I replenished.

THE STATUE. Bravo Ana! Juan: you are floored, quelled, annihilated.

DON JUAN. No: for though that difference is the true essential difference—Doña Ana has, I admit, gone straight to the real point—yet it is not a difference of love or chastity, or even constancy; for twelve children by twelve different husbands would have replenished the earth perhaps more effectively. Suppose my friend Ottavio had died when you were thirty, you would never have remained a widow: you were too beautiful. Suppose the successor of Ottavio had died when you were forty, you would still have been irresistible; and a woman who marries twice marries three times if she becomes free to do so. Twelve lawful children borne by one highly respectable lady to three different fathers is not impossible nor condemned by public opinion. That such a lady may be more law abiding than the poor girl whom we used to spurn into the gutter for bearing one unlawful infant is no doubt true; but dare you say she is less self-indulgent?

ANA. She is more virtuous: that is enough for me.

DON JUAN. In that case, what is virtue but the Trade Unionism of the married? Let us face the facts, dear Ana. The Life Force respects marriage only because marriage is a contrivance of its own to secure the greatest number of children and the closest care of them. For honor, chastity, and all the rest of your moral figments it cares not a rap. Marriage is the most licentious of human institutions—

ANA. Juan!

THE STATUE [*protesting*] Really!—

DON JUAN [*determinedly*] I say the most licentious of human institutions: that is the secret of its popularity. And a woman seeking a husband is the most unscrupulous of all the beasts of prey. The confusion of marriage with morality has done more to destroy the conscience of the human race than any other single error. Come, Ana! do not look shocked: you know better than any of us that marriage is a mantrap baited with simulated accomplishments and delusive idealizations. When your sainted mother, by dint of scoldings and punishments, forced you to learn how to play half a dozen pieces on the spinet—which she hated as much as you did—had she any other purpose than to delude your suitors into the belief that your husband would have in his home an angel who would fill it with melody, or at least play him to sleep after dinner? You married my friend Ottavio: well, did you ever open the spinet from the hour when the Church united him to you?

ANA. You are a fool, Juan. A young married woman has something else to do than sit at the spinet without any support for her back; so she gets out of the habit of playing.

DON JUAN. Not if she loves music. No: believe me, she only throws away the bait when the bird is in the net.

ANA [*bitterly*] And men, I suppose, never throw off the mask when their bird is in the net. The husband never becomes negligent, selfish, brutal—oh, never!

DON JUAN. What do these recriminations prove, Ana? Only that the hero is as gross an imposture as the heroine.

ANA. It is all nonsense: most marriages are perfectly comfortable.

DON JUAN. "Perfectly" is a strong expression, Ana. What you mean is that sensible people make the best of one another. Send me to the galleys and chain me to the felon whose number happens to be next before mine; and I must accept the inevitable and make the best of the companionship. Many such companionships, they tell me, are touchingly affectionate; and most are at least tolerably friendly. But that does not make a chain a desirable ornament nor the galleys an abode of bliss. Those who talk most about the blessings of marriage and the constancy of its vows are the very people who declare that if the chain were broken and the prisoners left free to choose, the whole social fabric would fly asunder. You cannot have the argument both ways. If the prisoner is happy, why lock him in? If he is not, why pretend that he is?

ANA. At all events, let me take an old woman's privilege again, and tell you flatly that marriage peoples the world and debauchery does not.

DON JUAN. How if a time come when this shall cease to be true? Do you not know that where there is a will there is a way? that whatever Man really wishes to do he will finally discover a means of doing? Well, you have done your best, you virtuous ladies, and others of your way of thinking, to bend Man's mind wholly towards honorable love as the highest good, and to understand by honorable love romance and beauty and happiness in the possession of beautiful, refined, delicate, affectionate women. You have taught women to value their own youth, health, shapeliness, and refinement above all things. Well, what place have squalling babies and household cares in this exquisite paradise of the senses and emotions? Is it not the inevitable end of it all that the human will shall say to the human brain: Invent me a means by which I can have love, beauty, romance, emotion, passion, without their wretched penalties, their expenses, their worries, their trials, their illnesses and agonies and risks of death, their retinue of servants and nurses and doctors and schoolmasters.

THE DEVIL. All this, Señor Don Juan, is realized here in my realm.

DON JUAN. Yes, at the cost of death. Man will not take it at that price: he demands the romantic delights of your Hell whilst he is still on earth. Well, the means will be found: the brain will not fail when the will is in earnest. The day is coming when great nations will find their numbers dwindling from census to census; when the six roomed villa will rise in price above the family mansion; when the viciously reckless poor and the stupidly pious rich will delay the extinction of the race only by degrading it; whilst the boldly prudent, the thriftily selfish and ambitious, the imaginative and poetic, the lovers of money and solid comfort, the worshippers of success, of art, and of love, will all oppose to the Force of Life the device of sterility.

THE STATUE. That is all very eloquent, my young friend; but if you had lived to Ana's age, or even to mine, you would have learned that the people who get rid of the fear of poverty and children and all the other family troubles, and devote themselves to having a good time of it, only leave their minds free for the fear of old age and ugliness and impotence and death. The childless laborer is more tormented by his wife's idleness and her constant demands for amusement and distraction than he could be by twenty children; and his wife is more wretched than he. I have had my share of vanity; for as a young man I was admired by women; and as a statue I am praised by art critics. But I confess that had I found nothing to do in the world but wallow in these delights I should have cut my throat. When I married Ana's mother—or perhaps, to be strictly correct, I should rather say when I at last gave in and allowed Ana's mother to marry me—I knew that I was planting thorns in my pillow, and that marriage for me, a swaggering young officer thitherto unvanquished, meant defeat and capture.

ANA [*scandalized*] Father!

THE STATUE. I am sorry to shock you, my love; but since Juan has stripped every rag of decency from the discussion I may as well tell the frozen truth.

ANA. Hmf! I suppose I was one of the thorns.

THE STATUE. By no means: you were often a rose. You see, your mother had most of the trouble you gave.

DON JUAN. Then may I ask, Commander, why you have left Heaven to come here and wallow, as you express it, in sentimental beatitudes which you confess would once have driven you to cut your throat?

THE STATUE [*struck by this*] Egad, thats true.

THE DEVIL [*alarmed*] What! You are going back from your word! [*To Don Juan*] And all y o u r philosophizing has been nothing but a mask for proselytizing! [*To the Statue*] Have you forgotten already the hideous dulness from which I am offering you a refuge here? [*To Don Juan*] And does your demonstration of the approaching sterilization and extinction of mankind lead to anything better than making the most of those pleasures of art and love which you yourself admit refined you, elevated you, developed you?

DON JUAN. I never demonstrated the extinction of mankind. Life cannot will its own extinction either in its blind amorphous state or in any of the forms into which it has organized itself. I had not finished when His Excellency interrupted me.

THE STATUE. I begin to doubt whether you ever will finish, my friend. You are extremely fond of hearing yourself talk.

DON JUAN. True; but since you have endured so much, you may as well endure to the end. Long before this sterilization which I described becomes more than a clearly foreseen possibility, the reaction will begin. The great central purpose of breeding the race: ay, breeding it to heights now deemed superhuman: that purpose which is now hidden in a mephitic cloud of love and romance and prudery and fastidiousness, will break through into clear sunlight as a purpose no longer to be confused with the gratification of personal fancies, the impossible realization of boys' and girls' dreams of bliss, or the need of older people for companionship or money. The plain-spoken marriage services of the vernacular Churches will no longer be abbreviated and half suppressed as indelicate. The sober decency, earnestness, and authority of their declaration of the real purpose of marriage will be honored and accepted, whilst their romantic vowings and pledgings and until-death-do-us-partings and the like will be expunged as unbearable frivolities. Do my sex the justice to admit, Señora, that we have always recognized that the sex relation is not a personal or friendly relation at all.

ANA. Not a personal or friendly relation! What relation is more personal? more sacred? more holy?

DON JUAN. Sacred and holy, if you like, Ana, but not personally friendly. Your relation to God is sacred and holy: dare you call it personally friendly? In the sex relation the universal creative energy, of which the parties are both the helpless agents, overrides and sweeps away all personal considerations, and dispenses with all personal relations. The pair may be utter strangers to one another, speaking different languages, differing in race and color, in age and disposition, with no bond between them but a possibility of that fecundity for the sake of which the Life Force throws them into one another's arms at the exchange of a glance. Do we not recognize this by allowing marriages to be made by parents without consulting the woman? Have you not often expressed your disgust at the immorality of the English nation, in which women and men of noble birth become acquainted and court each other like peasants? And how much does even the peasant know of his bride or she of him before he engages himself? Why, you would not make a man your lawyer or your family doctor on so slight an acquaintance as you would fall in love with and marry him!

ANA. Yes, Juan: we know the libertine's philosophy. Always ignore the consequences to the woman.

DON JUAN. The consequences, yes: they justify her fierce grip of the man. But surely you do not call that attachment a sentimental one. As well call the policeman's attachment to his prisoner a love relation.

ANA. You see you have to confess that marriage is necessary, though, according to you, love is the slightest of all human relations.

DON JUAN. How do you know that it is not the greatest of all human relations? far too great to be a personal matter. Could your father have served his country if he had refused to kill any enemy of Spain unless he personally hated him? Can a woman serve her country if she refuses to marry any man she does not personally love? You know it is not so: the woman of noble birth marries as the man of noble birth fights, on political and family grounds, not on personal ones.

THE STATUE [*impressed*] A very clever point that, Juan: I must think it over. You are really full of ideas. How did you come to think of this one?

DON JUAN. I learnt it by experience. When I was on earth, and made those proposals to ladies which, though universally condemned, have made me so interesting a hero of legend, I was not infrequently met in some such way as this. The lady would say that she would countenance my advances, provided they were honourable. On inquiring what that proviso meant, I found that it meant that I proposed to get possession of her property if she had any, or to undertake her support for life if she had not; that I desired her continual companionship, counsel, and conversation to the end of my days, and would take a most solemn oath to be always enraptured by them above all, that I would turn my back on all other women for ever for her sake. I did not object to these conditions because they were exorbitant and inhuman: it was their extraordinary irrelevance that prostrated me. I invariably replied with perfect frankness that I had never dreamt of any of these things; that unless the lady's character and intellect were equal or superior to my own, her conversation must degrade and her counsel mislead me; that her constant companionship might, for all I knew, become intolerably tedious to me; that I could not answer for my feelings for a week in advance, much less to the end of my life; that to cut me off from all natural and unconstrained intercourse with half my fellowcreatures would narrow and warp me if I submitted to it, and, if not, would bring me under the curse of clandestinity; that, finally, my proposals to her were wholly unconnected with any of these matters, and were the outcome of a perfectly simple impulse of my manhood towards her womanhood.

ANA. You mean that it was an immoral impulse.

DON JUAN. Nature, my dear lady, is what you call immoral. I blush for it; but I cannot help it. Nature is a pandar, Time a wrecker, and Death a murderer. I have always preferred to stand up to those facts and build institutions on their recognition. You prefer to propitiate the three devils by proclaiming their chastity, their thrift, and their loving kindness; and to base your institutions on these flatteries. Is it any wonder that the institutions do not work smoothly?

THE STATUE. What used the ladies to say, Juan?

DON JUAN. Oh, come! Confidence for confidence. First tell me what you used to say to the ladies.

THE STATUE. I! Oh, I swore that I would be faithful to the death; that I should die if they refused me; that no woman could ever be to me what she was—

ANA. She! Who?

THE STATUE. Whoever it happened to be at the time, my dear. I had certain things I always said. One of them was that even when I was eighty, one white hair of the woman I loved would make me tremble more than the thickest gold tress from the most beautiful young head. Another was that I could not bear the thought of anyone else being the mother of my children.

DON JUAN [*revolted*] You old rascal!

THE STATUE [*stoutly*] Not a bit; for I really believed it with all my soul at the moment. I had a heart: not like you. And it was this sincerity that made me successful.

DON JUAN. Sincerity! To be fool enough to believe a ramping, stamping, thumping lie: that is what you call sincerity! To be so greedy for a woman that you deceive yourself in your eagerness to deceive her: sincerity, you call it!

THE STATUE. Oh damn your sophistries! I was a man in love, not a lawyer. And the women loved me for it, bless them!

DON JUAN. They made you think so. What will you say when I tell you that though I played the lawyer so callously, they made me think so too? I also had my moments of infatuation in which I gushed nonsense and believed it. Sometimes the desire to give pleasure by saying beautiful things so rose in me on the flood of emotion that I said them recklessly. At other times I argued against myself with a devilish coldness that drew tears. But I found it just as hard to escape when I was cruel as when I was kind. When the lady's instinct was set on me, there was nothing for it but lifelong servitude or flight.

ANA. You dare boast, before me and my father, that every woman found you irresistible.

DON JUAN. Am I boasting? It seems to me that I cut the most pitiable of figures. Besides, I said "when the lady's instinct was set on me." It was not always so; and then, heavens! what transports of virtuous indignation! what overwhelming defiance to the dastardly seducer! what scenes of Imogen and Iachimo!

ANA. I made no scenes. I simply called my father.

DON JUAN. And he came, sword in hand, to vindicate outraged honor and morality by murdering me.

THE STATUE. Murdering! What do you mean? Did I kill you or did you kill me?

DON JUAN. Which of us was the better fencer?

THE STATUE. I was.

DON JUAN. Of course you were. And yet you, the hero of those scandalous adventures you have just been relating to us, *you* had the effrontery to pose as the avenger of outraged morality and condemn me to death! You would have slain me but for an accident.

THE STATUE. I was expected to, Juan. That is how things were arranged on earth. I was not a social reformer; and I always did what it was customary for a gentleman to do.

DON JUAN. That may account for your attacking me, but not for the revolting hypocrisy of your subsequent proceedings as a statue.

THE STATUE. That all came of my going to Heaven.

THE DEVIL. I still fail to see, Señor Don Juan, that these episodes in your earthly career and in that of the Señor Commander in any way discredit my view of life. Here, I repeat, you have all that you sought without anything that you shrank from.

DON JUAN. On the contrary, here I have everything that disappointed me without anything that I have not already tried and found wanting. I tell you that as long as I can conceive something better than myself I cannot be easy unless I am striving to bring it into existence or clearing the way for it. That is the law of my life. That is the working within me of Life's incessant aspiration to higher organization, wider, deeper, intenser self-consciousness, and clearer self-understanding. It was the supremacy of this purpose that reduced love for me to the mere pleasure of a moment, art for me to the mere schooling of my faculties, religion for me to a mere excuse for laziness, since it had set up a God who looked at the world and saw it was good, against the instinct in me that looked through my eyes at the world and saw that it could be improved. I tell you that in the pursuit of my own pleasure, my own health, my own fortune, I have never known happiness. It was not love for Woman that delivered me into her hands: it was fatigue, exhaustion. When I was a child, and bruised my head against a stone, I ran to the nearest woman and cried away my pain against her apron. When I grew up, and bruised my soul against the brutalities and stupidities with which I had to strive, I did again just what I had done as a child. I have enjoyed, too, my rests, my recuperations, my breathing times, my very prostrations after strife; but rather would I be dragged through all the circles of the foolish Italian's Inferno than through the pleasures of Europe. That is what has made this place of eternal pleasures so deadly to me. It is the absence of this instinct in you that makes you that strange monster called a Devil. It is the success with which you have diverted the attention of men from their real purpose, which in one degree or another is the same as mine, to yours, that has earned you the name of The Tempter. It is the fact that they are doing your will, or rather drifting with your want of will, instead of doing their own, that makes them the uncomfortable, false, restless, artificial, petulant, wretched creatures they are.

THE DEVIL [*mortified*] Señor Don Juan: you are uncivil to my friends.

DON JUAN. Pooh! Why should I be civil to them or to you? In this Palace of Lies a truth or two will not hurt you. Your friends are all the dullest dogs I know. They are not beautiful: they are only decorated. They are not clean: they are only shaved and starched. They are not dignified: they are only fashionably dressed. They are not educated: they are only college passmen. They are not religious: they are only pew-renters. They are not moral: they are only conventional. They are not virtuous: they are only cowardly. They are not even vicious: they are only "frail." They are not artistic: they are only lascivious. They are not prosperous: they are only rich. They are not loyal, they are only servile; not dutiful, only sheepish; not public spirited, only patriotic; not courageous, only quarrelsome; not determined, only obstinate; not masterful, only domineering; not self-controlled, only obtuse; not self-respecting, only vain; not kind, only sentimental; not social, only gregarious; not considerate, only polite; not intelligent, only opinionated; not progressive, only factious; not imaginative, only superstitious; not just, only vindictive; not generous, only propitiatory; not disciplined, only cowed; and not truthful at all: liars every one of them, to the very backbone of their souls.

THE STATUE. Your flow of words is simply amazing, Juan. How I wish I could have talked like that to my soldiers.

THE DEVIL. It is mere talk, though. It has all been said before; but what change has it ever made? What notice has the world ever taken of it?

DON JUAN. Yes, it is mere talk. But why is it mere talk? Because, my friend, beauty, purity, respectability, religion, morality, art, patriotism, bravery, and the rest are nothing but words which I or anyone else can turn inside out like a glove. Were they realities, you would have to plead guilty to my indictment; but fortunately for your self-respect, my diabolical friend, they are not realities. As you say, they are mere words, useful for duping barbarians into adopting civilization, or the civilized poor into submitting to be robbed and enslaved. That is the family secret of the governing caste; and if we who are of that caste aimed at more Life for the world instead of at more power and luxury for our miserable selves, that secret would make us great. Now, since I, being a nobleman, am in the secret too, think how tedious to me must be your unending cant about all these moralistic figments, and how squalidly disastrous your sacrifice of your lives to them! If you even believed in your moral game enough to play it fairly, it would be interesting to watch; but you dont: you cheat at every trick; and if your opponent outcheats you, you upset the table and try to murder him.

THE DEVIL. On earth there may be some truth in this, because the people are uneducated and cannot appreciate my religion of love and beauty; but here—

DON JUAN. Oh yes: I know. Here there is nothing but love and beauty. Ugh! it is like sitting for all eternity at the first act of a fashionable play, before the complications begin. Never in my worst moments of superstitious terror on earth did I dream that Hell was so horrible. I live, like a hairdresser, in the continual contemplation of beauty, toying with silken tresses. I breathe an atmosphere of sweetness, like a confectioner's shopboy. Commander: a r e there any beautiful women in Heaven?

THE STATUE. None. Absolutely none. All dowdies. Not two pennorth of jewellery among a dozen of them. They might be men of fifty.

DON JUAN. I am impatient to get there. Is the word beauty ever mentioned; and are there any artistic people?

THE STATUE. I give you my word they wont admire a fine statue even when it walks past them.

DON JUAN. I go.

THE DEVIL. Don Juan: shall I be frank with you?

DON JUAN. Were you not so before?

THE DEVIL. As far as I went, yes. But I will now go further, and confess to you that men get tired of everything, of Heaven no less than of Hell; and that all history is nothing but a record of the oscillations of the world between these two extremes. An epoch is but a swing of the pendulum; and each generation thinks the world is progressing because it is always moving. But when you are as old as I am; when you have a thousand times wearied of Heaven, like myself and the Commander, and a thousand times wearied of Hell, as you are wearied now, you will no longer imagine that every swing from Heaven to Hell is an emancipation, every swing from Hell to Heaven an evolution. Where you now see reform, progress, fulfilment of upward tendency, continual ascent by Man on the stepping stones of his dead selves to higher things, you will see nothing but an infinite comedy of illusion. You will discover the profound truth of the saying of my friend Koheleth, that there is nothing new under the sun. Vanitas vanitatum—

DON JUAN [*out of all patience*] By Heaven, this is worse than your cant about love and beauty. Clever dolt that you are, is a man no better than a worm, or a dog than a wolf, because he gets tired of everything? Shall he give up eating because he destroys his appetite in the act of gratifying it? Is a field idle when it is fallow? Can the Commander expend his hellish energy here without accumulating heavenly energy for his next term of blessedness? Granted that the great Life Force has hit on the device of the clockmaker's pendulum, and uses the earth for its bob; that the history of each oscillation, which seems so novel to us the actors, is but the history of the last oscillation repeated; nay more, that in the unthinkable infinitude of time the sun throws off the earth and catches it again a thousand times as a circus rider throws up a ball, and that our agelong epochs are but the moments between the toss and the catch, has the colossal mechanism no purpose?

THE DEVIL. None, my friend. You think because you have a purpose, Nature must have one. You might as well expect it to have fingers and toes because you have them.

DON JUAN. But I should not have them if they served no purpose. And I, my friend, am as much a part of Nature as my own finger is a part of me. If my finger is the organ by which I grasp the sword and the mandoline, my brain is the organ by which Nature strives to understand itself. My dog's brain serves only my dog's purposes; but my own brain labors at a knowledge which does nothing for me personally but make my body bitter to me and my decay and death a calamity. Were I not possessed with a purpose beyond my own I had better be a ploughman than a philosopher; for the ploughman lives as long as the philosopher, eats more, sleeps better, and rejoices in the wife of his bosom with less misgiving. This is because the philosopher is in the grip of the Life Force. This Life Force says to him "I have done a thousand wonderful things unconsciously by merely willing to live and following the line of least resistance: now I want to know myself and my destination, and choose my path; so I have made a special brain—a philosopher's brain—to grasp this knowledge for me as the husbandman's hand grasps the plough for me. And this" says the Life Force to the philosopher "must thou strive to do for me until thou diest, when I will make another brain and another philosopher to carry on the work."

THE DEVIL. What is the use of knowing?

DON JUAN. Why, to be able to choose the line of greatest advantage instead of yielding in the direction of the least resistance. Does a ship sail to its destination no better than a log drifts nowhither? The philosopher is Nature's pilot. And there you have our difference: to be in Hell is to drift: to be in Heaven is to steer.

THE DEVIL. On the rocks, most likely.

DON JUAN. Pooh! which ship goes oftenest on the rocks or to the bottom? the drifting ship or the ship with a pilot on board?

THE DEVIL. Well, well, go your way, Señor Don Juan. I prefer to be my own master and not the tool of any blundering universal force. I know that beauty is good to look at; that music is good to hear; that love is good to feel; and that they are all good to think about and talk about. I know that to be well exercised in these sensations, emotions, and studies is to be a refined and cultivated being. Whatever they may say of me in churches on earth, I know that it is universally admitted in good society that the Prince of Darkness is a gentleman; and that is enough for me. As to your Life Force, which you think irresistible, it is the most resistible thing in the world for a person of any character. But if you are naturally vulgar and credulous, as all reformers are, it will thrust you first into religion, where you will sprinkle water on babies to save their souls from m e; then it will drive you from religion into science, where you will snatch the babies from the water sprinkling and inoculate them with disease to save them from catching it accidentally; then you will take to politics, where you will become the catspaw of corrupt functionaries and the henchman of ambitious humbugs; and the end will be despair and decrepitude, broken nerve and shattered hopes, vain regrets for that worst and silliest of wastes and sacrifices, the waste and sacrifice of the power of enjoyment: in a word, the punishment of the fool who pursues the better before he has secured the good.

DON JUAN. But at least I shall not be bored. The service of the Life Force has that advantage, at all events. So fare you well, Señor Satan.

THE DEVIL [*amiably*] Fare you well, Don Juan. I shall often think of our interesting chats about things in general. I wish you every happiness: Heaven, as I said before, suits some people. But if you should change your mind, do not forget that the gates are always open here to the repentant prodigal. If you feel at any time that warmth of heart, sincere unforced affection, innocent enjoyment, and warm, breathing, palpitating reality—

DON JUAN. Why not say flesh and blood at once, though we have left those two greasy commonplaces behind us?

THE DEVIL [*angrily*] You throw my friendly farewell back in my teeth, then, Don Juan?

DON JUAN. By no means. But though there is much to be learnt from a cynical devil, I really cannot stand a sentimental one. Señor Commander: you know the way to the frontier of Hell and Heaven. Be good enough to direct me.

THE STATUE. Oh, the frontier is only the difference between two ways of looking at things. Any road will take you across it if you really want to get there.

DON JUAN. Good. [*Saluting Doña Ana*] Señora: your servant.

ANA. But I am going with you.

DON JUAN. I can find my own way to Heaven, Ana; not yours [*he vanishes*].

ANA. How annoying!

THE STATUE [*calling after him*] Bon voyage, Juan! [*He wafts a final blast of his great rolling chords after him as a parting salute. A faint echo of the first ghostly melody comes back in acknowledgment*]. Ah! there he goes. [*Puffing a long breath out through his lips*] Whew! How he does talk! Theyll never stand it in Heaven.

THE DEVIL [*gloomily*] His going is a political defeat. I cannot keep these Life Worshippers: they all go. This is the greatest loss I have had since that Dutch painter went: a fellow who would paint a hag of 70 with as much enjoyment as a Venus of 20.

THE STATUE. I remember: he came to Heaven. Rembrandt.

THE DEVIL. Ay, Rembrandt. There is something unnatural about these fellows. Do not listen to their gospel, Señor Commander: it is dangerous. Beware of the pursuit of the Superhuman: it leads to an indiscriminate contempt for the Human. To a man, horses and dogs and cats are mere species, outside the moral world. Well, to the Superman, men and women are a mere species too, also outside the moral world. This Don Juan was kind to women and courteous to men as your daughter here was kind to her pet cats and dogs; but such kindness is a denial of the exclusively human character of the soul.

THE STATUE. And who the deuce is the Superman?

THE DEVIL. Oh, the latest fashion among the Life Force fanatics. Did you not meet in Heaven, among the new arrivals, that German Polish madman? what was his name? Nietzsche?

THE STATUE. Never heard of him.

THE DEVIL. Well, he came here first, before he recovered his wits. I had some hopes of him; but he was a confirmed Life Force worshipper. It was he who raked up the Superman, who is as old as Prometheus; and the 20th century will run after this newest of the old crazes when it gets tired of the world, the flesh, and your humble servant.

THE STATUE. Superman is a good cry; and a good cry is half the battle. I should like to see this Nietzsche.

THE DEVIL. Unfortunately he met Wagner here, and had a quarrel with him.

THE STATUE. Quite right, too. Mozart for me!

THE DEVIL. Oh, it was not about music. Wagner once drifted into Life Force worship, and invented a Superman called Siegfried. But he came to his senses afterwards. So when they met here, Nietzsche denounced him as a renegade; and Wagner wrote a pamphlet to prove that Nietzsche was a Jew; and it ended in Nietzsche's going to Heaven in a huff. And a good riddance too. And now, my friend, let us hasten to my palace and celebrate your arrival with a grand musical service.

THE STATUE. With pleasure: youre most kind.

THE DEVIL. This way, Commander. We go down the old trap [*he places himself on the grave trap*].

THE STATUE. Good. [*Reflectively*] All the same, the Superman is a fine conception. There is something statuesque about it. [*He places himself on the grave trap beside The Devil. It begins to descend slowly. Red glow from the abyss*]. Ah, this reminds me of old times.

THE DEVIL. And me also.

ANA. Stop! [*The trap stops*].

THE DEVIL. You, Señora, cannot come this way. You will have an apotheosis. But you will be at the palace before us.

ANA. That is not what I stopped you for. Tell me: where can I find the Superman?

THE DEVIL. He is not yet created, Señora.

THE STATUE. And never will be, probably. Let us proceed: the red fire will make me sneeze. [*They descend*].

ANA. Not yet created! Then my work is not yet done. [*Crossing herself devoutly*] I believe in the Life to Come. [*Crying to the universe*] A father! a father for the Superman!

She vanishes into the void; and again there is nothing; all existence seems suspended infinitely. Then, vaguely, there is a live human voice crying somewhere. One sees, with a shock, a mountain peak shewing faintly against a lighter background. The sky has returned from afar; and we suddenly remember where we were. The cry becomes distinct and urgent: it says Automobile, Automobile. *The complete reality comes back with a rush: in a moment it is full morning in the Sierra; and the brigands are scrambling to their feet and making for the road as the goatherd runs down from the hill, warning them of the approach of another motor. Tanner and Mendoza rise amazedly and stare at one another with scattered wits. Straker sits up to yawn for a moment before he gets on his feet, making it a point of honor not to shew any undue interest in the excitement of the bandits. Mendoza gives a quick look to see that his followers are attending to the alarm; then exchanges a private word with Tanner.*

MENDOZA. Did you dream?

TANNER. Damnably. Did you?

MENDOZA. Yes. I forget what. You were in it.

TANNER. So were you. Amazing!

MENDOZA. I warned you. [*A shot is heard from the road*]. Dolts! they will play with that gun. [*The brigands come running back scared*]. Who fired that shot? [*to Duval*] was it you?

DUVAL [*breathless*] I have not shoot. Dey shoot first.

ANARCHIST. I told you to begin by abolishing the State. Now we are all lost.

THE ROWDY SOCIAL-DEMOCRAT [*stampeding across the amphitheatre*] Run, everybody.

MENDOZA [*collaring him; throwing him on his back; and drawing a knife*] I stab the man who stirs. [*He blocks the way. The stampede is checked*]. What has happened?

THE SULKY SOCIAL-DEMOCRAT. A motor—

THE ANARCHIST. Three men—

DUVAL. Deux femmes—

MENDOZA. Three men and two women! Why have you not brought them here? Are you afraid of them?

THE ROWDY ONE [*getting up*] Thyve a hescort. Ow, de-ooh luts ook it, Mendowza.

THE SULKY ONE. Two armored cars full o soldiers at the ed o the valley.

ANARCHIST. The shot was fired in the air. It was a signal.

Straker whistles his favorite air, which falls on the ears of the brigands like a funeral march.

TANNER. It is not an escort, but an expedition to capture you. We were advised to wait for it; but I was in a hurry.

THE ROWDY ONE [*in an agony of apprehension*] And Ow my good Lord, ere we are, wytin for em! Luts tike to the mahntns.

MENDOZA. Idiot, what do you know about the mountains? Are you a Spaniard? You would be given up by the first shepherd you met. Besides, we are already within range of their rifles.

THE ROWDY ONE. Bat—

MENDOZA. Silence. Leave this to me. [*To Tanner*] Comrade: you will not betray us.

STRAKER. Oo are you callin comrade?

MENDOZA. Last night the advantage was with me. The robber of the poor was at the mercy of the robber of the rich. You offered your hand: I took it.

TANNER. I bring no charge against you, comrade. We have spent a pleasant evening with you: that is all.

STRAKER. I gev my and to nobody, see?

MENDOZA [*turning on him impressively*] Young man: if I am tried, I shall plead guilty, and explain what drove me from England, home, and duty. Do you wish to have the respectable name of Straker dragged through the mud of a Spanish criminal court? The police will search me. They will find Louisa's portrait. It will be published in the illustrated papers. You blench. It will be your doing, remember.

STRAKER [*with baffled rage*] I dont care about the court. It's avin our name mixed up with yours that I object to, you blackmailin swine, you.

MENDOZA. Language unworthy of Louisa's brother! But no matter: you are muzzled: that is enough for us. [*He turns to face his own men, who back uneasily across the amphitheatre towards the cave to take refuge behind him as a fresh party, muffled for motoring, comes from the road in riotous spirits. Ann, who makes straight for Tanner, comes first; then Violet, helped over the rough ground by Hector holding her right hand and Ramsden her left. Mendoza goes to his presidential block and seats himself calmly with his rank and file grouped behind him, and his Staff consisting of Duval and the Anarchist on his right and the two Social-Democrats on his left, supporting him in flank*].

ANN. It's Jack!

TANNER. Caught!

HECTOR. Why, certainly it is. I said it was you, Tanner. Weve just been stopped by a puncture: the road is full of nails.

VIOLET. What are you doing here with all these men?

ANN. Why did you leave us without a word of warning?

HECTOR. I wawnt that bunch of roses, Miss Whitefield. [*To Tanner*] When we found you were gone, Miss Whitefield bet me a bunch of roses my car would not overtake yours before you reached Monte Carlo.

TANNER. But this is not the road to Monte Carlo.

HECTOR. No matter. Miss Whitefield tracked you at every stopping place: she is a regular Sherlock Holmes.

TANNER. The Life Force! I am lost.

OCTAVIUS [*bounding gaily down from the road into the amphitheatre, and coming between Tanner and Straker*] I am so glad you are safe, old chap. We were afraid you had been captured by brigands.

RAMSDEN [*who has been staring at Mendoza*] I seem to remember the face of your friend here. [*Mendoza rises politely and advances with a smile between Ann and Ramsden*].

HECTOR. Why, so do I.

OCTAVIUS. I know you perfectly well, sir; but I cant think where I have met you.

MENDOZA [*to Violet*] Do you remember me, madam?

VIOLET. Oh, quite well; but I am so stupid about names.

MENDOZA. It was at the Savoy Hotel. [*To Hector*] You, sir, used to come with this lady [*Violet*] to lunch. [*To Octavius*] You, sir, often brought this lady [*Ann*] and her mother to dinner on your way to the Lyceum Theatre [*To Ramsden*] You, sir, used to come to supper, with [*dropping his voice to a confidential but perfectly audible whisper*] several different ladies.

RAMSDEN [*angrily*] Well, what is that to you, pray?

OCTAVIUS. Why, Violet, I thought you hardly knew one another before this trip, you and Malone!

VIOLET [*vexed*] I suppose this person was the manager.

MENDOZA. The waiter, madam. I have a grateful recollection of you all. I gathered from the bountiful way in which you treated me that you all enjoyed your visits very much.
VIOLET. What impertinence! [*She turns her back on him, and goes up the hill with Hector*].
RAMSDEN. That will do, my friend. You do not expect these ladies to treat you as an acquaintance, I suppose, because you have waited on them at table.
MENDOZA. Pardon me: it was you who claimed my acquaintance. The ladies followed your example. However, this display of the unfortunate manners of your class closes the incident. For the future, you will please address me with the respect due to a stranger and fellow traveller. [*He turns haughtily away and resumes his presidential seat*].
TANNER. There! I have found one man on my journey capable of reasonable conversation; and you all instinctively insult him. Even the New Man is as bad as any of you. Enry: you have behaved just like a miserable gentleman.
STRAKER. Gentleman! Not me.
RAMSDEN. Really, Tanner, this tone—
ANN. Dont mind him, Granny: you ought to know him by this time [*she takes his arm and coaxes him away to the hill to join Violet and Hector. Octavius follows her, doglike*].
VIOLET [*calling from the hill*] Here are the soldiers. They are getting out of their motors.
DUVAL [*panicstricken*] Oh, nom de Dieu!
THE ANARCHIST. Fools: the State is about to crush you because you spared it at the prompting of the political hangers-on of the bourgeoisie.
THE SULKY SOCIAL-DEMOCRAT [*argumentative to the last*] On the contrary, only by capturing the State machine—
THE ANARCHIST. It is going to capture y o u.
THE ROWDY SOCIAL-DEMOCRAT [*his anguish culminating*] Ow, chack it. Wot are we ere for? W o t are we wytin for?
MENDOZA [*between his teeth*] Go on. Talk politics, you idiots: nothing sounds more respectable. Keep it up, I tell you.

The soldiers line the road, commanding the amphitheatre with their rifles. The brigands, struggling with an overwhelming impulse to hide behind one another, look as unconcerned as they can. Mendoza rises superbly, with undaunted front. The officer in command steps down from the road into the amphitheatre; looks hard at the brigands; and then inquiringly at Tanner.

THE OFFICER. Who are these men, Señor Ingles?

TANNER. My escort.

Mendoza, with a Mephistophelean smile, bows profoundly. An irrepressible grin runs from face to face among the brigands. They touch their hats, except the Anarchist, who defies the State with folded arms.

ACT IV

The garden of a villa in Granada. Whoever wishes to know what it is like must go to Granada to see. One may prosaically specify a group of hills dotted with villas, the Alhambra on the top of one of the hills, and a considerable town in the valley, approached by dusty white roads in which the children, no matter what they are doing or thinking about, automatically whine for halfpence and reach out little clutching brown palms for them; but there is nothing in this description except the Alhambra, the begging, and the color of the roads, that does not fit Surrey as well as Spain. The difference is that the Surrey hills are comparatively small and ugly, and should properly be called the Surrey Protuberances; but these Spanish hills are of mountain stock: the amenity which conceals their size does not compromise their dignity.

This particular garden is on a hill opposite the Alhambra; and the villa is as expensive and pretentious as a villa must be if it is to be let furnished by the week to opulent American and English visitors. If we stand on the lawn at the foot of the garden and look uphill, our horizon is the stone balustrade of a flagged platform on the edge of infinite space at the top of the hill. Between us and this platform is a flower garden with a circular basin and fountain in the centre, surrounded by geometrical flower beds, gravel paths, and clipped yew trees in the genteelest order. The garden is higher than our lawn; so we reach it by a few steps in the middle of its embankment. The platform is higher again than the garden, from which we mount a couple more steps to look over the balustrade at a fine view of the town up the valley and of the hills that stretch away beyond it to where, in the remotest distance, they become mountains. On our left is the villa, accessible by steps from the left hand corner of the garden. Returning from the platform through the garden and down again to the lawn (a movement which leaves the villa behind us on our right) we find evidence of literary interests on the part of the tenants in the fact that there is no tennis net nor set of croquet hoops, but, on our left, a little iron garden table with books on it, mostly yellow-backed, and a chair beside it. A chair on the right has also a couple of open books upon it.

There are no newspapers, a circumstance which, with the absence of games, might lead an intelligent spectator to the most far reaching conclusions as to the sort of people who live in the villa. Such speculations are checked, however, on this delightfully fine afternoon, by the appearance at a little gate in a paling on our left, of Henry Straker in his professional costume. He opens the gate for an elderly gentleman, and follows him on to the lawn.

This elderly gentleman defies the Spanish sun in a black frock coat, tall silk hat, trousers in which narrow stripes of dark grey and lilac blend into a highly respectable color, and a black necktie tied into a bow over spotless linen. Probably therefore a man whose social position needs constant and scrupulous affirmation without regard to climate: one who would dress thus for the middle of the Sahara or the top of Mont Blanc. And since he has not the stamp of the class which accepts as its life-mission the advertizing and maintenance of first rate tailoring and millinery, he looks vulgar in his finery, though in a working dress of any kind he would look dignified enough. He is a bullet cheeked man with a red complexion, stubbly hair, smallish eyes, a hard mouth that folds down at the corners, and a dogged chin. The looseness of skin that comes with age has attacked his throat and the laps of his cheeks; but he is still hard as an apple above the mouth; so that the upper half of his face looks younger than the lower. He has the self-confidence of one who has made money, and something of the truculence of one who has made it in a brutalizing struggle, his civility having under it a perceptible menace that he has other methods in reserve if necessary. Withal, a man to be rather pitied when he is not to be feared; for there is something pathetic about him at times, as if the huge commercial machine which has worked him into his frock coat had allowed him very little of his own way and left his affections hungry and baffled. At the first word that falls from him it is clear that he is an Irishman whose native intonation has clung to him through many changes of place and rank. One can only guess that the original material of his speech was perhaps the surly Kerry brogue; but the degradation of speech that occurs in London, Glasgow, Dublin, and big cities generally has been at work on it so long that nobody but an arrant cockney would dream of calling it a brogue now; for its music is almost gone, though its surliness is still perceptible. Straker, being a very obvious cockney, inspires him with implacable contempt, as a stupid Englishman who cannot even speak his own language properly. Straker, on the other hand, regards the old gentleman's accent as a joke thoughtfully provided by Providence expressly for the amusement of the British race, and treats him normally with the indulgence due to an inferior and unlucky species, but occasionally with indignant alarm when the old gentleman shews signs of intending his Irish nonsense to be taken seriously.

STRAKER. I'll go tell the young lady. She said youd prefer to stay here [*he turns to go up through the garden to the villa*].

THE IRISHMAN [*who has been looking round him with lively curiosity*] The young lady? Thats Miss Violet, eh?

STRAKER [*stopping on the steps with sudden suspicion*] Well, you know, dont you?

THE IRISHMAN. Do I?

STRAKER [*his temper rising*] Well, do you or dont you?

THE IRISHMAN. What business is that of yours?

Straker, now highly indignant, comes back from the steps and confronts the visitor.

STRAKER. I'll tell you what business it is of mine. Miss Robinson—

THE IRISHMAN [*interrupting*] Oh, her name is Robinson, is it? Thank you.

STRAKER. Why, you dont know even her name?

THE IRISHMAN. Yes I do, now that youve told me.

STRAKER [*after a moment of stupefaction at the old man's readiness in repartee*] Look here: what do you mean by gittin into my car and lettin me bring you here if youre not the person I took that note to?

THE IRISHMAN. Who else did you take it to, pray?

STRAKER. I took it to Mr Ector Malone, at Miss Robinson's request, see? Miss Robinson is not my principal: I took it to oblige her. I know Mr Malone; and he aint you, not by a long chalk. At the hotel they told me that your name is Ector Malone—

MALONE. *H*ector Malone.

STRAKER [*with calm superiority*] Hector in your own country: thats what comes o livin in provincial places like Ireland and America. Over here youre Ector: if you avnt noticed it before you soon will.

The growing strain of the conversation is here relieved by Violet, who has sallied from the villa and through the garden to the steps, which she now descends, coming very opportunely between Malone and Straker.

VIOLET [*to Straker*] Did you take my message?

STRAKER. Yes, miss. I took it to the hotel and sent it up, expecting to see young Mr Malone. Then out walks this gent, and says it's all right and he'll come with me. So as the hotel people said he was Mr Ector Malone, I fetched him. And now he goes back on what he said. But if he isnt the gentleman you meant, say the word: it's easy enough to fetch him back again.

MALONE. I should esteem it a great favor if I might have a short conversation with you, madam. I am Hector's father, as this bright Britisher would have guessed in the course of another hour or so.

STRAKER [*coolly defiant*] No, not in another year or so. When weve ad you as long to polish up as weve ad im, perhaps youll begin to look a little bit up to is mark. At present you fall a long way short. Youve got too many aitches, for one thing. [*To Violet, amiably*] All right, Miss: you want to talk to him: I shant intrude. [*He nods affably to Malone and goes out through the little gate in the paling*].

VIOLET [*very civilly*] I am so sorry, Mr Malone, if that man has been rude to you. But what can we do? He is our chauffeur.

MALONE. Your hwat?

VIOLET. The driver of our automobile. He can drive a motor car at seventy miles an hour, and mend it when it breaks down. We are dependent on our motor cars; and our motor cars are dependent on him; so of course we are dependent on him.

MALONE. Ive noticed, madam, that every thousand dollars an Englishman gets seems to add one to the number of people he's dependent on. However, you neednt apologize for your man: I made him talk on purpose. By doing so I learnt that youre stayin here in Grannida with a party of English, including my son Hector.

VIOLET [*conversationally*] Yes. We intended to go to Nice; but we had to follow a rather eccentric member of our party who started first and came here. Wont you sit down? [*She clears the nearest chair of the two books on it*].

MALONE [*impressed by this attention*] Thank you. [*He sits down, examining her curiously as she goes to the iron table to put down the books. When she turns to him again, he says*] Miss Robinson, I believe?

VIOLET [*sitting down*] Yes.

MALONE [*taking a letter from his pocket*] Your note to Hector runs as follows [*Violet is unable to repress a start. He pauses quietly to take out and put on his spectacles, which have gold rims*]: "Dearest: they have all gone to the Alhambra for the afternoon. I have shammed headache and have the garden all to myself. Jump into Jack's motor: Straker will rattle you here in a jiffy. Quick, quick, quick. Your loving Violet." [*He looks at her; but by this time she has recovered herself, and meets his spectacles with perfect composure. He continues slowly*] Now I dont know on hwat terms young people associate in English society; but in America that note would be considered to imply a very considerable degree of affectionate intimacy between the parties.

VIOLET. Yes: I know your son very well, Mr Malone. Have you any objection?

MALONE [*somewhat taken aback*] No, no objection exactly. Provided it is understood that my son is altogether dependent on me, and that I have to be consulted in any important step he may propose to take.

VIOLET. I am sure you would not be unreasonable with him, Mr Malone.

MALONE. I hope not, Miss Robinson; but at your age you might think many things unreasonable that dont seem so to me.

VIOLET [*with a little shrug*] Oh, well, I suppose theres no use our playing at cross purposes, Mr Malone. Hector wants to marry me.

MALONE. I inferred from your note that he might. Well, Miss Robinson, he is his own master; but if he marries you he shall not have a rap from me. [*He takes off his spectacles and pockets them with the note*].

VIOLET [*with some severity*] That is not very complimentary to me, Mr Malone.

MALONE. I say nothing against you, Miss Robinson: I daresay you are an amiable and excellent young lady. But I have other views for Hector.

VIOLET. Hector may not have other views for himself, Mr Malone.

MALONE. Possibly not. Then he does without me: thats all. I daresay you are prepared for that. When a young lady writes to a young man to come to her quick, quick, quick, money seems nothing and love seems everything.

VIOLET [*sharply*] I beg your pardon, Mr Malone: I do not think anything so foolish. Hector must have money.

MALONE [*staggered*] Oh, very well, very well. No doubt he can work for it.

VIOLET. What is the use of having money if you have to work for it? [*She rises impatiently*]. It's all nonsense, Mr Malone: you m u s t enable your son to keep up his position. It is his right.

MALONE [*grimly*] I should not advise you to marry him on the strength of that right, Miss Robinson.

Violet, who has almost lost her temper, controls herself with an effort; unclenches her fingers; and resumes her seat with studied tranquillity and reasonableness.

VIOLET. What objection have you to me, pray? My social position is as good as Hector's, to say the least. He admits it.

MALONE [*shrewdly*] You tell him so from time to time, eh? Hector's social position in England, Miss Robinson, is just what I choose to buy for him. I have made him a fair offer. Let him pick out the most historic house, castle, or abbey that England contains. The very day he tells me he wants it for a wife worthy of its traditions, I buy it for him, and give him the means of keeping it up.

VIOLET. What do you mean by a wife worthy of its traditions? Cannot any well bred woman keep such a house for him?

MALONE. No: she must be born to it.

VIOLET. Hector was not born to it, was he?

MALONE. His granmother was a barefooted Irish girl that nursed me by a turf fire. Let him marry another such, and I will not stint her marriage portion. Let him raise himself socially with my money or raise somebody else: so long as there is a social profit somewhere, I'll regard my expenditure as justified. But there must be a profit for someone. A marriage with you would leave things just where they are.

VIOLET. Many of my relations would object very much to my marrying the grandson of a common woman, Mr Malone. That may be prejudice; but so is your desire to have him marry a title prejudice.

MALONE [*rising, and approaching her with a scrutiny in which there is a good deal of reluctant respect*] You seem a pretty straightforward downright sort of a young woman.

VIOLET. I do not see why I should be made miserably poor because I cannot make profits for you. Why do you want to make Hector unhappy?

MALONE. He will get over it all right enough. Men thrive better on disappointments in love than on disappointments in money. I daresay you think that sordid; but I know what I'm talking about. Me father died of starvation in Ireland in the black 47. Maybe youve heard of it.

VIOLET. The Famine?

MALONE [*with smouldering passion*] No, the starvation. When a country is full o food, and exporting it, there can be no famine. Me father was starved dead; and I was starved out to America in me mother's arms. English rule drove me and mine out of Ireland. Well, you can keep Ireland. Me and me like are coming back to buy England; and we'll buy the best of it. I want no middle class properties and no middle class women for Hector. Thats straightforward, isnt it, like yourself?

VIOLET [*icily pitying his sentimentality*] Really, Mr Malone, I am astonished to hear a man of your age and good sense talking in that romantic way. Do you suppose English noblemen will sell their places to you for the asking?

MALONE. I have the refusal of two of the oldest family mansions in England. One historic owner cant afford to keep all the rooms dusted: the other cant afford the death duties. What do you say now?

VIOLET. Of course it is very scandalous; but surely you know that the Government will sooner or later put a stop to all these Socialistic attacks on property.

MALONE [*grinning*] D'y'think they'll be able to get that done before I buy the house—or rather the abbey? Theyre both abbeys.

VIOLET [*putting that aside rather impatiently*] Oh, well, let us talk sense, Mr Malone. You must feel that we havnt been talking sense so far.

MALONE. I cant say I do. I mean all I say.

VIOLET. Then you dont know Hector as I do. He is romantic and faddy—he gets it from you, I fancy—and he wants a certain sort of wife to take care of him. Not a faddy sort of person, you know.

MALONE. Somebody like you, perhaps?

VIOLET [*quietly*] Well, yes. But you cannot very well ask me to undertake this with absolutely no means of keeping up his position.

MALONE [*alarmed*] Stop a bit, stop a bit. Where are we getting to? I'm not aware that I'm asking you to undertake anything.

VIOLET. Of course, Mr Malone, you can make it very difficult for me to speak to you if you choose to misunderstand me.

MALONE [*half bewildered*] I dont wish to take any unfair advantage; but we seem to have got off the straight track somehow.

Straker, with the air of a man who has been making haste, opens the little gate, and admits Hector, who, snorting with indignation, comes upon the lawn, and is making for his father when Violet, greatly dismayed, springs up and intercepts him. Straker does not wait; at least he does not remain visibly within earshot.

VIOLET. Oh, how unlucky! Now please, Hector, say nothing. Go away until I have finished speaking to your father.

HECTOR [*inexorably*] No, Violet: I mean to have this thing out, right away. [*He puts her aside; passes her by; and faces his father, whose cheeks darken as his Irish blood begins to simmer*]. Dad: youve not played this hand straight.

MALONE. Hwat d'y'mean?

HECTOR. Youve opened a letter addressed to me. Youve impersonated me and stolen a march on this lady. Thats disawnerable.

MALONE [*threateningly*] Now you take care what youre saying, Hector. Take care, I tell you.

HECTOR. I have taken care. I am taking care. I'm taking care of my honor and my position in English society.

MALONE [*hotly*] Your position has been got by my money: do you know that?

HECTOR. Well, youve just spoiled it all by opening that letter. A letter from an English lady, not addressed to you—a cawnfidential letter! a dullicate letter! a private letter! opened by my father! Thats a sort of thing a man cant struggle against in England. The sooner we go back together the better. [*He appeals mutely to the heavens to witness the shame and anguish of two outcasts*].

VIOLET [*snubbing him with an instinctive dislike for scene making*] Dont be unreasonable, Hector. It was quite natural for Mr Malone to open my letter: his name was on the envelope.

MALONE. There! Youve no common sense, Hector. I thank you, Miss Robinson.

HECTOR. I thank you, too. It's very kind of you. My father knows no better.

MALONE [*furiously clenching his fists*] Hector—

HECTOR [*with undaunted moral force*] Oh, it's no use hectoring me. A private letter's a private letter, dad: you cant get over that.

MALONE [*raising his voice*] I wont be talked back to by you, d'y'hear?

VIOLET. Ssh! please, p l e a s e. Here they all come.

Father and son, checked, glare mutely at one another as Tanner comes in through the little gate with Ramsden, followed by Octavius and Ann.

VIOLET. Back already!

TANNER. The Alhambra is not open this afternoon.

VIOLET. What a sell!

Tanner passes on, and presently finds himself between Hector and a strange elder, both apparently on the verge of personal combat. He looks from one to the other for an explanation. They sulkily avoid his eye, and nurse their wrath in silence.

RAMSDEN. Is it wise for you to be out in the sunshine with such a headache, Violet?

TANNER. Have you recovered too, Malone?

VIOLET. Oh, I forgot. We have not all met before. Mr Malone: wont you introduce your father?

HECTOR [*with Roman firmness*] No, I will not. He is no father of mine.

MALONE [*very angry*] You disown your dad before your English friends, do you?

VIOLET. Oh, please dont make a scene.

Ann and Octavius, lingering near the gate, exchange an astonished glance, and discreetly withdraw up the steps to the garden, where they can enjoy the disturbance without intruding. On their way to the steps Ann sends a little grimace of mute sympathy to Violet, who is standing with her back to the little table, looking on in helpless annoyance as her husband soars to higher and higher moral eminences without the least regard to the old man's millions.

HECTOR. I'm very sorry, Miss Rawbnsn; but I'm contending for a principle. I am a son, and, I hope, a dutiful one; but before everything I'm a Mahn!!! And when dad treats my private letters as his own, and takes it on himself to say that I shant marry you if I am happy and fortunate enough to gain your consent, then I just snap my fingers and go my own way.

TANNER. Marry Violet!

RAMSDEN. Are you in your senses?

TANNER. Do you forget what we told you?

HECTOR [*recklessly*] I dont care what you told me.

RAMSDEN [*scandalized*] Tut tut, sir! Monstrous! [*he flings away towards the gate, his elbows quivering with indignation*].

TANNER. Another madman! These men in love should be locked up. [*He gives Hector up as hopeless, and turns away towards the garden; but Malone, taking offence in a new direction, follows him and compels him, by the aggressiveness of his tone, to stop*].

MALONE. I dont understand this. Is Hector not good enough for this lady, pray?

TANNER. My dear sir, the lady is married already. Hector knows it; and yet he persists in his infatuation. Take him home and lock him up.

MALONE [*bitterly*] So this is the highborn social tone Ive spoilt be me ignorant, uncultivated behavior! Makin love to a married woman!

[*He comes angrily between Hector and Violet, and almost bawls into Hector's left ear*] Youve picked up that habit of the British aristocracy, have you?

HECTOR. Thats all right. Dont you trouble yourself about that. I'll answer for the morality of what I'm doing.

TANNER [*coming forward to Hector's right hand with flashing eyes*] Well said, Malone! You also see that mere marriage laws are not morality! I agree with you; but unfortunately Violet does not.

MALONE. I take leave to doubt that, sir. [*Turning on Violet*] Let me tell you, Mrs Robinson, or whatever your right name is, you had no right to send that letter to my son when you were the wife of another man.

HECTOR [*outraged*] This is the last straw. Dad: you have insulted my wife.

MALONE. Your wife!

TANNER. You the missing husband! Another moral impostor! [*He smites his brow, and collapses into Malone's chair*].

MALONE. Youve married without my consent!

RAMSDEN. You have deliberately humbugged us, sir!

HECTOR. Here: I have had just about enough of being badgered. Violet and I are married: thats the long and the short of it. Now what have you got to say—any of you?

MALONE. I know what Ive got to say. She's married a beggar.

HECTOR. No: she's married a Worker [*his American pronunciation imparts an overwhelming intensity to this simple and unpopular word*]. I start to earn my own living this very afternoon.

MALONE [*sneering angrily*] Yes: youre very plucky now, because you got your remittance from me yesterday or this morning, I reckon. Wait! it's spent. You wont be so full of cheek then.

HECTOR [*producing a letter from his pocketbook*] Here it is [*thrusting it on his father*]. Now you just take your remittance and yourself out of my life. I'm done with remittances; and I'm done with you. I dont sell the privilege of insulting my wife for a thousand dollars.

MALONE [*deeply wounded and full of concern*] Hector: you dont know what poverty is.

HECTOR [*fervidly*] Well, I wawnt to know what it is. I wawnt'be a Mahn. Violet: you come along with me, to your own home: I'll see you through.

OCTAVIUS [*jumping down from the garden to the lawn and running to Hector's left hand*] I hope youll shake hands with me before you go,

Hector. I admire and respect you more than I can say. [*He is affected almost to tears as they shake hands*].

VIOLET [*also almost in tears, but of vexation*] Oh, dont be an idiot, Tavy. Hector's about as fit to become a workman as you are.

TANNER [*rising from his chair on the other side of Hector*] Never fear: theres no question of his becoming a navvy, Mrs Malone. [*To Hector*] Theres really no difficulty about capital to start with. Treat me as a friend: draw on me.

OCTAVIUS [*impulsively*] Or on me.

MALONE [*with fierce jealousy*] Who wants your durty money? Who should he draw on but his own father? [*Tanner and Octavius recoil, Octavius rather hurt, Tanner consoled by the solution of the money difficulty. Violet looks up hopefully*]. Hector: dont be rash, my boy. I'm sorry for what I said: I never meant to insult Violet: I take it all back. She's just the wife you want: there!

HECTOR [*patting him on the shoulder*] Well, thats all right, dad. Say no more: we're friends again. Only, I take no money from anybody.

MALONE [*pleading abjectly*] Dont be hard on me, Hector. I'd rather you quarrelled and took the money than made friends and starved. You dont know what the world is: I do.

HECTOR. No, no, NO. Thats fixed: thats not going to change. [*He passes his father inexorably by, and goes to Violet*]. Come, Mrs Malone: youve got to move to the hotel with me, and take your proper place before the world.

VIOLET. But I must go in, dear, and tell Davis to pack. Wont you go on and make them give you a room overlooking the garden for me? I'll join you in half an hour.

HECTOR. Very well. Youll dine with us, Dad, wont you?

MALONE [*eager to conciliate him*] Yes, yes.

HECTOR. See you all later. [*He waves his hand to Ann, who has now been joined by Tanner, Octavius, and Ramsden in the garden, and goes out through the little gate, leaving his father and Violet together on the lawn*].

MALONE. Youll try to bring him to his senses, Violet: I know you will.

VIOLET. I had no idea he could be so headstrong. If he goes on like that, what can I do?

MALONE. Dont be discurridged: domestic pressure may be slow; but it's sure. Youll wear him down. Promise me you will.

VIOLET. I will do my best. Of course I think it's the greatest nonsense deliberately making us poor like that.

MALONE. Of course it is.

VIOLET [*after a moment's reflection*] You had better give me the remittance. He will want it for his hotel bill. I'll see whether I can induce him to accept it. Not now, of course, but presently.

MALONE [*eagerly*] Yes, yes, yes: thats just the thing [*he hands her the thousand dollar bill, and adds cunningly*] Y'understand that this is only a bachelor allowance.

VIOLET [*coolly*] Oh, quite. [*She takes it*]. Thank you. By the way, Mr Malone, those two houses you mentioned—the abbeys.

MALONE. Yes?

VIOLET. Dont take one of them until Ive seen it. One never knows what may be wrong with these places.

MALONE. I wont. I'll do nothing without consulting you, never fear.

VIOLET [*politely, but without a ray of gratitude*] Thanks: that will be much the best way. [*She goes calmly back to the villa, escorted obsequiously by Malone to the upper end of the garden*].

TANNER [*drawing Ramsden's attention to Malone's cringing attitude as he takes leave of Violet*] And that poor devil is a billionaire! one of the master spirits of the age! Led in a string like a pug dog by the first girl who takes the trouble to despise him! I wonder will it ever come to that with me. [*He comes down to the lawn*].

RAMSDEN [*following him*] The sooner the better for you.

MALONE [*slapping his hands as he returns through the garden*] That'll be a grand woman for Hector. I wouldnt exchange her for ten duchesses. [*He descends to the lawn and comes between Tanner and Ramsden*].

RAMSDEN [*very civil to the billionaire*] It's an unexpected pleasure to find you in this corner of the world, Mr Malone. Have you come to buy up the Alhambra?

MALONE. Well, I dont say I mightnt. I think I could do better with it than the Spanish government. But thats not what I came about. To tell you the truth, about a month ago I overheard a deal between two men over a bundle of shares. They differed about the price: they were young and greedy, and didnt know that if the shares were worth what was bid for them they must be worth what was asked, the margin being too small to be of any account, you see. To amuse meself, I cut in and bought the shares. Well, to this day I havnt found out what the business is. The office is in this town; and the name is Mendoza, Limited. Now whether Mendoza's a mine, or a steamboat line, or a bank, or a patent article—

TANNER. He's a man. I know him: his principles are thoroughly commercial. Let us take you round the town in our motor, Mr Malone, and call on him on the way.

MALONE. If youll be so kind, yes. And may I ask who—

TANNER. Mr Roebuck Ramsden, a very old friend of your daughter-in-law.

MALONE. Happy to meet you, Mr Ramsden.

RAMSDEN. Thank you. Mr Tanner is also one of our circle.

MALONE. Glad to know you also, Mr Tanner.

TANNER. Thanks. [*Malone and Ramsden go out very amicably through the little gate. Tanner calls to Octavius, who is wandering in the garden with Ann*] Tavy! [*Tavy comes to the steps, Tanner whispers loudly to him*] Violet's father-in-law is a financier of brigands. [*Tanner hurries away to overtake Malone and Ramsden. Ann strolls to the steps with an idle impulse to torment Octavius*].

ANN. Wont you go with them, Tavy?

OCTAVIUS [*tears suddenly flushing his eyes*] You cut me to the heart, Ann, by wanting me to go [*he comes down on the lawn to hide his face from her. She follows him caressingly*].

ANN. Poor Ricky Ticky Tavy! Poor heart!

OCTAVIUS. It belongs to you, Ann. Forgive me: I must speak of it. I love you. You know I love you.

ANN. Whats the good, Tavy? You know that my mother is determined that I shall marry Jack.

OCTAVIUS [*amazed*] Jack!

ANN. It seems absurd, doesnt it?

OCTAVIUS [*with growing resentment*] Do you mean to say that Jack has been playing with me all this time? That he has been urging me not to marry you because he intends to marry you himself?

ANN [*alarmed*] No, no: you mustnt lead him to believe that I said that. I dont for a moment think that Jack knows his own mind. But it's clear from my father's will that he wished me to marry Jack. And my mother is set on it.

OCTAVIUS. But you are not bound to sacrifice yourself always to the wishes of your parents.

ANN. My father loved me. My mother loves me. Surely their wishes are a better guide than my own selfishness.

OCTAVIUS. Oh, I know how unselfish you are, Ann. But believe me—though I know I am speaking in my own interest—there is another side to this question. Is it fair to Jack to marry him if you do not love him? Is it fair to destroy my happiness as well as your own if you can bring yourself to love me?

ANN [*looking at him with a faint impulse of pity*] Tavy, my dear, you are a nice creature—a good boy.

OCTAVIUS [*humiliated*] Is that all?

ANN [*mischievously in spite of her pity*] Thats a great deal, I assure you. You would always worship the ground I trod on, wouldnt you?

OCTAVIUS. I do. It sounds ridiculous; but it's no exaggeration. I do; and I always shall.

ANN. Always is a long word, Tavy. You see, I shall have to live up always to your idea of my divinity; and I dont think I could do that if we were married. But if I marry Jack, youll never be disillusioned—at least not until I grow too old.

OCTAVIUS. I too shall grow old, Ann. And when I am eighty, one white hair of the woman I love will make me tremble more than the thickest gold tress from the most beautiful young head.

ANN [*quite touched*] Oh, thats poetry, Tavy, real poetry. It gives me that strange sudden sense of an echo from a former existence which always seems to me such a striking proof that we have immortal souls.

OCTAVIUS. Do you believe that it is true?

ANN. Tavy: if it is to come true, you must lose me as well as love me.

OCTAVIUS. Oh! [*he hastily sits down at the little table and covers his face with his hands*].

ANN [*with conviction*] Tavy: I wouldnt for worlds destroy your illusions. I can neither take you nor let you go. I can see exactly what will suit you. You must be a sentimental old bachelor for my sake.

OCTAVIUS [*desperately*] Ann: I'll kill myself.

ANN. Oh no, you wont: that wouldnt be kind. You wont have a bad time. You will be very nice to women; and you will go a good deal to the opera. A broken heart is a very pleasant complaint for a man in London if he has a comfortable income.

OCTAVIUS [*considerably cooled, but believing that he is only recovering his self-control*] I know you mean to be kind, Ann. Jack has persuaded you that cynicism is a good tonic for me. [*He rises with quiet dignity*].

ANN [*studying him slyly*] You see, I'm disillusionizing you already. Thats what I dread.

OCTAVIUS. You do not dread disillusionizing Jack.

ANN [*her face lighting up with mischievous ecstasy—whispering*] I cant: he has no illusions about me. I shall surprise Jack the other way.

Getting over an unfavorable impression is ever so much easier than living up to an ideal. Oh, I shall enrapture Jack sometimes!

OCTAVIUS [*resuming the calm phase of despair, and beginning to enjoy his broken heart and delicate attitude without knowing it*] I dont doubt that. You will enrapture him always. And he—the fool!—thinks you would make him wretched.

ANN. Yes: thats the difficulty, so far.

OCTAVIUS [*heroically*] Shall *I* tell him that you love him?

ANN [*quickly*] Oh no: he'd run away again.

OCTAVIUS [*shocked*] Ann: would you marry an unwilling man?

ANN. What a queer creature you are, Tavy! Theres no such thing as a willing man when you really go for him. [*She laughs naughtily*]. I'm shocking you, I suppose. But you know you are really getting a sort of satisfaction already in being out of danger yourself.

OCTAVIUS [*startled*] Satisfaction! [*Reproachfully*] You say that to me!

ANN. Well, if it were really agony, would you ask for more of it?

OCTAVIUS. H a v e I asked for more of it?

ANN. You have offered to tell Jack that I love him. Thats self-sacrifice, I suppose; but there must be some satisfaction in it. Perhaps it's because youre a poet. You are like the bird that presses its breast against the sharp thorn to make itself sing.

OCTAVIUS. It's quite simple. I love you; and want you to be happy. You dont love me; so I cant make you happy myself; but I can help another man to do it.

ANN. Yes: it seems quite simple. But I doubt if we ever know why we do things. The only really simple thing is to go straight for what you want and grab it. I suppose I dont love you, Tavy; but sometimes I feel as if I should like to make a man of you somehow. You are very foolish about women.

OCTAVIUS [*almost coldly*] I am content to be what I am in that respect.

ANN. Then you must keep away from them, and only dream about them. I wouldnt marry you for worlds, Tavy.

OCTAVIUS. I have no hope, Ann: I accept my ill luck. But I dont think you quite know how much it hurts.

ANN. You are so softhearted! It's queer that you should be so different from Violet. Violet's as hard as nails.

OCTAVIUS. Oh no. I am sure Violet is thoroughly womanly at heart.

ANN [*with some impatience*] Why do you say that? Is it unwomanly to be thoughtful and businesslike and sensible? Do you want Violet to be an idiot—or something worse, like me?

OCTAVIUS. Something worse—like *you*! What do you mean, Ann?

ANN. Oh well, I dont mean that, of course. But I have a great respect for Violet. She gets her own way always.

OCTAVIUS [*sighing*] So do you.

ANN. Yes; but somehow she gets it without coaxing—without having to make people sentimental about her.

OCTAVIUS [*with brotherly callousness*] Nobody could get very sentimental about Violet, I think, pretty as she is.

ANN. Oh yes they could, if she made them.

OCTAVIUS. But surely no really nice woman would deliberately practise on men's instincts in that way.

ANN [*throwing up her hands*] Oh, Tavy, Tavy, Ricky Ticky Tavy, heaven help the woman who marries you!

OCTAVIUS [*his passion reviving at the name*] Oh why, why, why do you say that? Dont torment me. I dont understand.

ANN. Suppose she were to tell fibs, and lay snares for men?

OCTAVIUS. Do you think *I* could marry such a woman—I, who have known and loved *you*?

ANN. Hm! Well, at all events, she wouldnt let you if she were wise. So thats settled. And now I cant talk any more. Say you forgive me, and that the subject is closed.

OCTAVIUS. I have nothing to forgive; and the subject is closed. And if the wound is open at least you shall never see it bleed.

ANN. Poetic to the last, Tavy. Goodbye, dear. [*She pats his cheek; has an impulse to kiss him and then another impulse of distaste which prevents her; finally runs away through the garden and into the villa*].

Octavius again takes refuge at the table, bowing his head on his arms and sobbing softly. Mrs Whitefield, who has been pottering round the Granada shops, and has a net full of little parcels in her hand, comes in through the gate and sees him.

MRS WHITEFIELD [*running to him and lifting his head*] Whats the matter, Tavy? Are you ill?

OCTAVIUS. No, nothing, nothing.

MRS WHITEFIELD [*still holding his head, anxiously*] But youre crying. Is it about Violet's marriage?

OCTAVIUS. No, no. Who told you about Violet?

MRS WHITEFIELD [*restoring the head to its owner*] I met Roebuck and that awful old Irishman. Are you sure youre not ill? Whats the matter?

OCTAVIUS [*affectionately*] It's nothing. Only a man's broken heart. Doesnt that sound ridiculous?

MRS WHITEFIELD. But what is it all about? Has Ann being doing anything to you?

OCTAVIUS. It's not Ann's fault. And dont think for a moment that I blame y o u.

MRS WHITEFIELD [*startled*] For what?

OCTAVIUS [*pressing her hand consolingly*] For nothing. I said I didnt blame you.

MRS WHITEFIELD. But I havnt done anything. Whats the matter?

OCTAVIUS [*smiling sadly*] Cant you guess? I daresay you are right to prefer Jack to me as a husband for Ann; but I love Ann; and it hurts rather. [*He rises and moves away from her towards the middle of the lawn*].

MRS WHITEFIELD [*following him hastily*] Does Ann say that I want her to marry Jack?

OCTAVIUS. Yes: she has told me.

MRS WHITEFIELD [*thoughtfully*] Then I'm very sorry for you, Tavy. It's only her way of saying s h e wants to marry Jack. Little she cares what *I* say or what *I* want!

OCTAVIUS. But she would not say it unless she believed it. Surely you dont suspect Ann of—of d e c e i t!!

MRS WHITEFIELD. Well, never mind, Tavy. I dont know which is best for a young man: to know too little, like you, or too much, like Jack.

Tanner returns.

TANNER. Well, Ive disposed of old Malone. Ive introduced him to Mendoza, Limited; and left the two brigands together to talk it out. Hullo, Tavy! anything wrong?

OCTAVIUS. I must go wash my face, I see. [*To Mrs Whitefield*] Tell him what you wish. [*To Tanner*] You may take it from me, Jack, that Ann approves of it.

TANNER [*puzzled by his manner*] Approves of what?

OCTAVIUS. Of what Mrs Whitefield wishes. [*He goes his way with sad dignity to the villa*].

TANNER [*to Mrs Whitefield*] This is very mysterious. What is it you wish? It shall be done, whatever it is.

MRS WHITEFIELD [*with snivelling gratitude*] Thank you, Jack. [*She sits down. Tanner brings the other chair from the table and sits close to her with his elbows on his knees, giving her his whole attention*]. I dont know why it is that other people's children are so nice to me, and that my own have so little consideration for me. It's no wonder I dont seem able to care for Ann and Rhoda as I do for you and Tavy and Violet. It's a very queer world. It used to be so straightforward and simple; and now nobody seems to think and feel as they ought. Nothing has been right since that speech that Professor Tyndall made at Belfast.

TANNER. Yes: life is more complicated than we used to think. But what am I to do for you?

MRS WHITEFIELD. Thats just what I want to tell you. Of course youll marry Ann whether I like it or not—

TANNER [*starting*] It seems to me that I shall presently be married to Ann whether I like it myself or not.

MRS WHITEFIELD [*peacefully*] Oh, very likely you will: you know what she is when she has set her mind on anything. But dont put it on me: thats all I ask. Tavy has just let out that she's been saying that I am making her marry you; and the poor boy is breaking his heart about it; for he is in love with her himself, though what he sees in her so wonderful, goodness knows: *I* dont. It's no use telling Tavy that Ann puts things into people's heads by telling them that I want them when the thought of them never crossed my mind. It only sets Tavy against me. But you know better than that. So if you marry her, dont put the blame on me.

TANNER [*emphatically*] I havnt the slightest intention of marrying her.

MRS WHITEFIELD [*slyly*] She'd suit you better than Tavy. She'd meet her match in you, Jack. I'd like to see her meet her match.

TANNER. No man is a match for a woman, except with a poker and a pair of hobnailed boots. Not always even then. Anyhow, *I* cant take the poker to her. I should be a mere slave.

MRS WHITEFIELD. No: she's afraid of you. At all events, you would tell her the truth about herself. She wouldnt be able to slip out of it as she does with me.

TANNER. Everybody would call me a brute if I told Ann the truth about herself in terms of her own moral code. To begin with, Ann says things that are not strictly true.

MRS WHITEFIELD. I'm glad somebody sees she is not an angel.

TANNER. In short—to put it as a husband would put it when exasperated to the point of speaking out—she is a liar. And since she has plunged Tavy head over ears in love with her without any intention of marrying him, she is a coquette, according to the standard definition of a coquette as a woman who rouses passions she has no intention of gratifying. And as she has now reduced you to the point of being willing to sacrifice me at the altar for the mere satisfaction of getting me to call her a liar to her face, I may conclude that she is a bully as well. She cant bully men as she bullies women; so she habitually and unscrupulously uses her personal fascination to make men give her whatever she wants. That makes her almost something for which I know no polite name.

MRS WHITEFIELD [*in mild expostulation*] Well, you cant expect perfection, Jack.

TANNER. I dont. But what annoys me is that Ann does. I know perfectly well that all this about her being a liar and a bully and a coquette and so forth is a trumped-up moral indictment which might be brought against anybody. We all lie; we all bully as much as we dare; we all bid for admiration without the least intention of earning it; we all get as much rent as we can out of our powers of fascination. If Ann would admit this I shouldnt quarrel with her. But she wont. If she has children she'll take advantage of their telling lies to amuse herself by whacking them. If another woman makes eyes at me, she'll refuse to know a coquette. She will do just what she likes herself whilst insisting on everybody else doing what the conventional code prescribes. In short, I can stand everything except her confounded hypocrisy. Thats what beats me.

MRS WHITEFIELD [*carried away by the relief of hearing her own opinion so eloquently expressed*] Oh, she i s a hypocrite. She is: she is. Isnt she?

TANNER. Then why do you want to marry me to her?

MRS WHITEFIELD [*querulously*] There now! put it on me, of course. I never thought of it until Tavy told me she said I did. But, you know, I'm very fond of Tavy: he's a sort of son to me; and I dont want him to be trampled on and made wretched.

TANNER. Whereas I dont matter, I suppose.

MRS WHITEFIELD. Oh, you are different, somehow: you are able to take care of yourself. Youd serve her out. And anyhow, she must marry somebody.

TANNER. Aha! there speaks the life instinct. You detest her; but you feel that you must get her married.

MRS WHITEFIELD [*rising, shocked*] Do you mean that I detest my own daughter! Surely you dont believe me to be so wicked and unnatural as that, merely because I see her faults.

TANNER [*cynically*] You love her, then?

MRS WHITEFIELD. Why, of course I do. What queer things you say, Jack! We cant help loving our own blood relations.

TANNER. Well, perhaps it saves unpleasantness to say so. But for my part, I suspect that the tables of consanguinity have a natural basis in a natural repugnance [*he rises*].

MRS WHITEFIELD. You shouldnt say things like that, Jack. I hope you wont tell Ann that I have been speaking to you. I only wanted to set myself right with you and Tavy. I couldnt sit mumchance and have everything put on me.

TANNER [*politely*] Quite so.

MRS WHITEFIELD [*dissatisfied*] And now Ive only made matters worse. Tavy's angry with me because I dont worship Ann. And when it's been put into my head that Ann ought to marry you, what can I say except that it would serve her right?

TANNER. Thank you.

MRS WHITEFIELD. Now dont be silly and twist what I say into something I dont mean. I ought to have fair play—

Ann comes from the villa, followed presently by Violet, who is dressed for driving.

ANN [*coming to her mother's right hand with threatening suavity*] Well, mamma darling, you seem to be having a delightful chat with Jack. We can hear you all over the place.

MRS WHITEFIELD [*appalled*] Have you overheard—

TANNER. Never fear: Ann is only—well, we were discussing that habit of hers just now. She hasnt heard a word.

MRS WHITEFIELD [*stoutly*] I dont care whether she has or not: I have a right to say what I please.

VIOLET [*arriving on the lawn and coming between Mrs Whitefield and Tanner*] Ive come to say goodbye. I'm off for my honeymoon.

MRS WHITEFIELD [*crying*] Oh, dont say that, Violet. And no wedding, no breakfast, no clothes, nor anything.

VIOLET [*petting her*] It wont be for long.

MRS WHITEFIELD. Dont let him take you to America. Promise me that you wont.

VIOLET [*very decidedly*] I should think not, indeed. Dont cry, dear: I'm only going to the hotel.

MRS WHITEFIELD. But going in that dress, with your luggage, makes one realize—[*she chokes, and then breaks out again*] How I wish you were m y daughter, Violet!

VIOLET [*soothing her*] There, there: so I am. Ann will be jealous.

MRS WHITEFIELD. Ann doesnt care a bit for me.

ANN. Fie, mother! Come, now: you mustnt cry any more: you know Violet doesnt like it [*Mrs Whitefield dries her eyes, and subsides*].

VIOLET. Goodbye, Jack.

TANNER. Goodbye, Violet.

VIOLET. The sooner you get married too the better. You will be much less misunderstood.

TANNER [*restively*] I quite expect to get married in the course of the afternoon. You all seem to have set your minds on it.

VIOLET. You might do worse. [*To Mrs Whitefield: putting her arm round her*] Let me take you to the hotel with me: the drive will do you good. Come in and get a wrap. [*She takes her towards the villa*].

MRS WHITEFIELD [*as they go up through the garden*] I dont know what I shall do when you are gone, with no one but Ann in the house; and she always occupied with the men! It's not to be expected that your husband will care to be bothered with an old woman like me. Oh, you neednt tell me: politeness is all very well; but I know what people think–[*She talks herself and Violet out of sight and hearing*].

Ann, alone with Tanner, watches him and waits. He makes an irresolute movement towards the gate; but some magnetism in her draws him to her, a broken man.

ANN. Violet is quite right. You ought to get married.

TANNER [*explosively*] Ann: I will not marry you. Do you hear? I wont, wont, wont, wont, WONT marry you.

ANN [*placidly*] Well, nobody axd you, sir she said, sir she said, sir she said. So thats settled.

TANNER. Yes, nobody has asked me; but everybody treats the thing as settled. It's in the air. When we meet, the others go away on absurd pretexts to leave us alone together. Ramsden no longer scowls at me: his eye beams, as if he were already giving you away to me in church. Tavy refers me to your mother and gives me his blessing. Straker openly treats you as his future employer: it was he who first told me of it.

ANN. Was that why you ran away?

TANNER. Yes, only to be stopped by a lovesick brigand and run down like a truant schoolboy.

ANN. Well, if you dont want to be married, you neednt be [*she turns away from him and sits down, much at her ease*].

TANNER [*following her*] Does any man want to be hanged? Yet men let themselves be hanged without a struggle for life, though they could at least give the chaplain a black eye. We do the world's will, not our own. I have a frightful feeling that I shall let myself be married because it is the world's will that you should have a husband.

ANN. I daresay I shall, someday.

TANNER. But why me? me of all men! Marriage is to me apostasy, profanation of the sanctuary of my soul, violation of my manhood, sale of my birthright, shameful surrender, ignominious capitulation, acceptance of defeat. I shall decay like a thing that has served its purpose and is done with; I shall change from a man with a future to a man with a past; I shall see in the greasy eyes of all the other husbands their relief at the arrival of a new prisoner to share their ignominy. The young men will scorn me as one who has sold out: to the women I, who have always been an enigma and a possibility, shall be merely somebody else's property—and damaged goods at that: a secondhand man at best.

ANN. Well, your wife can put on a cap and make herself ugly to keep you in countenance, like my grandmother.

TANNER. So that she may make her triumph more insolent by publicly throwing away the bait the moment the trap snaps on the victim!

ANN. After all, though, what difference would it make? Beauty is all very well at first sight; but who ever looks at it when it has been in the house three days? I thought our pictures very lovely when papa bought them; but I havnt looked at them for years. You never bother about my looks: you are too well used to me. I might be the umbrella stand.

TANNER. You lie, you vampire: you lie.

ANN. Flatterer. Why are you trying to fascinate me, Jack, if you dont want to marry me?

TANNER. The Life Force. I am in the grip of the Life Force.

ANN. I dont understand in the least: it sounds like the Life Guards.

TANNER. Why dont you marry Tavy? He is willing. Can you not be satisfied unless your prey struggles?

ANN [*turning to him as if to let him into a secret*] Tavy will never marry. Havnt you noticed that that sort of man never marries?

TANNER. What! a man who idolizes women! who sees nothing in nature but romantic scenery for love duets! Tavy, the chivalrous, the faithful, the tenderhearted and true! Tavy, never marry! Why, he was born to be swept up by the first pair of blue eyes he meets in the street.

ANN. Yes, I know. All the same, Jack, men like that always live in comfortable bachelor lodgings with broken hearts, and are adored by their landladies, and never get married. Men like you always get married.

TANNER [*smiting his brow*] How frightfully, horribly true! It has been staring me in the face all my life; and I never saw it before.
ANN. Oh, it's the same with women. The poetic temperament's a very nice temperament, very amiable, very harmless and poetic, I daresay; but it's an old maid's temperament.
TANNER. Barren. The Life Force passes it by.
ANN. If thats what you mean by the Life Force, yes.
TANNER. You dont care for Tavy?
ANN [*looking round carefully to make sure that Tavy is not within earshot*] No.
TANNER. And you do care for me?
ANN [*rising quietly and shaking her finger at him*] Now, Jack! Behave yourself.
TANNER. Infamous, abandoned woman! Devil!
ANN. Boa-constrictor! Elephant!
TANNER. Hypocrite!
ANN [*softly*] I must be, for my future husband's sake.
TANNER. For mine! [*Correcting himself savagely*] I mean for his.
ANN [*ignoring the correction*] Yes, for yours. You had better marry what you call a hypocrite, Jack. Women who are not hypocrites go about in rational dress and are insulted and get into all sorts of hot water. And then their husbands get dragged in too, and live in continual dread of fresh complications. Wouldnt you prefer a wife you could depend on?
TANNER. No: a thousand times no: hot water is the revolutionist's element. You clean men as you clean milk-pails, by scalding them.
ANN. Cold water has its uses too. It's healthy.
TANNER [*despairingly*] Oh, you are witty: at the supreme moment the Life Force endows you with every quality. Well, I too can be a hypocrite. Your father's will appointed me your guardian, not your suitor. I shall be faithful to my trust.
ANN [*in low siren tones*] He asked me who I would have as my guardian before he made that will. I chose you!
TANNER. The will is yours then! The trap was laid from the beginning.
ANN [*concentrating all her magic*] From the beginning—from our childhood—for both of us—by the Life Force.
TANNER. I will not marry you. I will not marry you.
ANN. Oh, you will, you will.
TANNER. I tell you, no, no, no.
ANN. I tell you, yes, yes, yes.
TANNER. No

ANN [*coaxing—imploring—almost exhausted*] Yes. Before it is too late for repentance. Yes.

TANNER [*struck by the echo from the past*] When did all this happen to me before? Are we two dreaming?

ANN [*suddenly losing her courage, with an anguish that she does not conceal*] No. We are awake; and you have said no: that is all.

TANNER [*brutally*] Well?

ANN. Well, I made a mistake: you do not love me.

TANNER [*seizing her in his arms*] It is false: I love you. The Life Force enchants me: I have the whole world in my arms when I clasp you. But I am fighting for my freedom, for my honor, for my self, one and indivisible.

ANN. Your happiness will be worth them all.

TANNER. You would sell freedom and honor and self for happiness?

ANN. It will not be all happiness for me. Perhaps death.

TANNER [*groaning*] Oh, that clutch holds and hurts. What have you grasped in me? Is there a father's heart as well as a mother's?

ANN. Take care, Jack: if anyone comes while we are like this, you will have to marry me.

TANNER. If we two stood now on the edge of a precipice, I would hold you tight and jump.

ANN [*panting, failing more and more under the strain*] Jack: let me go. I have dared so frightfully—it is lasting longer than I thought. Let me go: I cant bear it.

TANNER. Nor I. Let it kill us.

ANN. Yes: I dont care. I am at the end of my forces. I dont care. I think I am going to faint.

At this moment Violet and Octavius come from the villa with Mrs Whitefield, who is wrapped up for driving. Simultaneously Malone and Ramsden, followed by Mendoza and Straker, come in through the little gate in the paling. Tanner shamefacedly releases Ann, who raises her hand giddily to her forehead.

MALONE. Take care. Something's the matter with the lady.

RAMSDEN. What does this mean?

VIOLET [*running between Ann and Tanner*] Are you ill?

ANN [*reeling, with a supreme effort*] I have promised to marry Jack. [*She swoons. Violet kneels by her and chafes her hand. Tanner runs round to her other hand, and tries to lift her head. Octavius goes to Violet's assistance, but does not know what to do. Mrs Whitefield hurries back into the villa. Octavius, Malone, and Ramsden run to Ann and crowd round her, stooping to assist. Straker coolly comes to Ann's feet, and Mendoza to her head, both upright and self-possessed*].

STRAKER. Now then, ladies and gentlemen: she dont want a crowd round her: she wants air—all the air she can git. If you please, gents— [*Malone and Ramsden allow him to drive them gently past Ann and up the lawn towards the garden, where Octavius, who has already become conscious of his uselessness, joins them. Straker, following them up, pauses for a moment to instruct Tanner*]. Dont lift er ed, Mr Tanner: let it go flat so's the blood can run back into it.

MENDOZA. He is right, Mr Tanner. Trust to the air of the Sierra. [*He withdraws delicately to the garden steps*].

TANNER [*rising*] I yield to your superior knowledge of physiology, Henry. [*He withdraws to the corner of the lawn; and Octavius immediately hurries down to him*].

TAVY [*aside to Tanner, grasping his hand*] Jack: be very happy.

TANNER [*aside to Tavy*] I never asked her. It is a trap for me. [*He goes up the lawn towards the garden. Octavius remains petrified*].

MENDOZA [*intercepting Mrs Whitefield, who comes from the villa with a glass of brandy*] What is this, madam [*he takes it from her*]?

MRS WHITEFIELD. A little brandy.

MENDOZA. The worst thing you could give her. Allow me. [*He swallows it*]. Trust to the air of the Sierra, madam.

For a moment the men all forget Ann and stare at Mendoza.

ANN [*in Violet's ear, clutching her round the neck*] Violet: did Jack say anything when I fainted?

VIOLET. No.

ANN. Ah! [*with a sigh of intense relief she relapses*].

MRS WHITEFIELD. Oh, she's fainted again.

They are about to rush back to her; but Mendoza stops them with a warning gesture.

ANN [*supine*] No, I havnt. I'm quite happy.

TANNER [*suddenly walking determinedly to her, and snatching her hand from Violet to feel her pulse*] Why, her pulse is positively bounding. Come! get up. What nonsense! Up with you. [*He hauls her up summarily*].

ANN. Yes: I feel strong enough now. But you very nearly killed me, Jack, for all that.

MALONE. A rough wooer, eh? Theyre the best sort, Miss Whitefield. I congratulate Mr Tanner; and I hope to meet you and him as frequent guests at the abbey.

ANN. Thank you. [*She goes past Malone to Octavius*] Ricky Ticky Tavy: congratulate me. [*Aside to him*] I want to make you cry for the last time.

TAVY [*steadfastly*] No more tears. I am happy in your happiness. And I believe in you in spite of everything.

RAMSDEN [*coming between Malone and Tanner*] You are a happy man, Jack Tanner. I envy you.

MENDOZA [*advancing between Violet and Tanner*] Sir: there are two tragedies in life. One is to lose your heart's desire. The other is to gain it. Mine and yours, sir.

TANNER. Mr Mendoza: I have no heart's desires. Ramsden: it is very easy for you to call me a happy man: you are only a spectator. I am one of the principals; and I know better. Ann: stop tempting Tavy, and come back to me.

ANN [*complying*] You are absurd, Jack. [*She takes his proffered arm*].

TANNER [*continuing*] I solemnly say that I am not a happy man. Ann l o o k s happy; but she is only triumphant, successful, victorious. That is not happiness, but the price for which the strong sell their happiness. What we have both done this afternoon is to renounce happiness, renounce freedom, renounce tranquillity, above all, renounce the romantic possibilities of an unknown future, for the cares of a household and a family. I beg that no man may seize the occasion to get half drunk and utter imbecile speeches and coarse pleasantries at my expense. We propose to furnish our own house according to our own taste; and I hereby give notice that the seven or eight travelling clocks, the four or five dressing cases, the carvers and fish slices, the copies of Patmore's Angel In The House in extra morocco, and the other articles you are preparing to heap upon us, will be instantly sold, and the proceeds devoted to circulating free copies of the Revolutionist's Handbook. The wedding will take place three days after our return to England, by special licence, at the office of the district superintendent registrar, in the presence of my solicitor and his clerk, who, like his clients, will be in ordinary walking dress—

VIOLET [*with intense conviction*] You a r e a brute, Jack.

ANN [*looking at him with fond pride and caressing his arm*] Never mind her, dear. Go on talking.

TANNER. Talking!

Universal laughter.

The Revolutionist's Handbook and Pocket Companion

BY

JOHN TANNER,
M.I.R.C.

(*Member of the Idle Rich Class*)

Preface to
The Revolutionist's Handbook

"No one can contemplate the present condition of the masses of the people without desiring something like a revolution for the better." *Sir Robert Giffen.* Essays in Finance, vol. ii. p. 393.

FOREWORD

A REVOLUTIONIST is one who desires to discard the existing social order and try another.

The constitution of England is revolutionary. To a Russian or Anglo-Indian bureaucrat, a general election is as much a revolution as a referendum or plebiscite in which the people fight instead of voting. The French Revolution overthrew one set of rulers and substituted another with different interests and different views. That is what a general election enables the people to do in England every seven years if they choose. Revolution is therefore a national institution in England; and its advocacy by an Englishman needs no apology.

Every man is a revolutionist concerning the thing he understands. For example, every person who has mastered a profession is a sceptic concerning it, and consequently a revolutionist.

Every genuine religious person is a heretic and therefore a revolutionist.

All who achieve real distinction in life begin as revolutionists. The most distinguished persons become more revolutionary as they grow older, though they are commonly supposed to become more conservative owing to their loss of faith in conventional methods of reform.

Any person under the age of thirty, who, having any knowledge of the existing social order, is not a revolutionist, is an inferior.

AND YET

Revolutions have never lightened the burden of tyranny: they have only shifted it to another shoulder.

JOHN TANNER

The Revolutionist's Handbook

Contents

I. ON GOOD BREEDING

If there were no God, said the eighteenth century Deist, it would be necessary to invent Him. Now this XVIII century god was *deus ex machina,* the god who helped those who could not help themselves, the god of the lazy and incapable. The nineteenth century decided that there is indeed no such god; and now Man must take in hand all the work that he used to shirk with an idle prayer. He must, in effect, change himself into the political Providence which he formerly conceived as god; and such change is not only possible, but the only sort of change that is real. The mere transfiguration of institutions, as from military and priestly dominance to commercial and scientific dominance, from commercial dominance to proletarian democracy, from slavery to serfdom, from serfdom to capitalism, from monarchy to republicanism, from polytheism to monotheism, from monotheism to atheism, from atheism to pantheistic humanitarianism, from general illiteracy to general literacy, from romance to realism, from realism to mysticism, from metaphysics to physics, are all but changes from

Tweedledum to Tweedledee: *plus ça change, plus c'est la même chose*. But the changes from the crab apple to the pippin, from the wolf and fox to the house dog, from the charger of Henry V to the brewer's draught horse and the racehorse, are real; for here Man has played the god, subduing Nature to his intention, and ennobling or debasing Life for a set purpose. And what can be done with a wolf can be done with a man. If such monsters as the tramp and the gentleman can appear as mere by-products of Man's individual greed and folly, what might we not hope for as a main product of his universal aspiration?

This is no new conclusion. The despair of institutions, and the inexorable "ye must be born again," with Mrs Poyser's stipulation, "and born different," recurs in every generation. The cry for the Superman did not begin with Nietzsche, nor will it end with his vogue. But it has always been silenced by the same question: what kind of person is this Superman to be? You ask, not for a super-apple, but for an eatable apple; not for a super-horse, but for a horse of greater draught or velocity. Neither is it of any use to ask for a Superman: you must furnish a specification of the sort of man you want. Unfortunately you do not know what sort of man you want. Some sort of good-looking philosopher-athlete, with a handsome healthy woman for his mate, perhaps.

Vague as this is, it is a great advance on the popular demand for a perfect gentleman and a perfect lady. And, after all, no market demand in the world takes the form of exact technical specification of the article required. Excellent poultry and potatoes are produced to satisfy the demand of housewives who do not know the technical differences between a tuber and a chicken. They will tell you that the proof of the pudding is in the eating; and they are right. The proof of the Superman will be in the living; and we shall find out how to produce him by the old method of trial and error, and not by waiting for a completely convincing prescription of his ingredients.

Certain common and obvious mistakes may be ruled out from the beginning. For example, we agree that we want superior mind; but we need not fall into the football club folly of counting on this as a product of superior body. Yet if we recoil so far as to conclude that superior mind consists in being the dupe of our ethical classifications of virtues and vices, in short, of conventional morality, we shall fall out of the frying-pan of the football club into the fire of the Sunday School. If we must choose between a race of athletes and a race of "good" men, let us have the athletes: better Samson and Milo than Calvin and Robespierre. But neither alternative is worth changing for: Samson is no more a Superman than Calvin. What then are we to do?

II. PROPERTY AND MARRIAGE

Let us hurry over the obstacles set up by property and marriage. Revolutionists make too much of them. No doubt it is easy to demonstrate that property will destroy society unless society destroys it. No doubt, also, property has hitherto held its own and destroyed all the empires. But that was because the superficial objection to it (that it distributes social wealth and the social labor burden in a grotesquely inequitable manner) did not threaten the existence of the race, but only the individual happiness of its units, and finally the maintenance of some irrelevant political form or other, such as a nation, an empire, or the like. Now as happiness never matters to Nature, as she neither recognizes flags and frontiers nor cares a straw whether the economic system adopted by a society is feudal, capitalistic, or collectivist, provided it keeps the race afoot (the hive and the anthill being as acceptable to her as Utopia), the demonstrations of Socialists, though irrefutable, will never make any serious impression on property. The knell of that overrated institution will not sound until it is felt to conflict with some more vital matter than mere personal inequities in industrial economy. No such conflict was perceived whilst society had not yet grown beyond national communities too small and simple to overtax Man's limited political capacity disastrously. But we have now reached the stage of international organization. Man's political capacity and magnanimity are clearly beaten by the vastness and complexity of the problems forced on him. And it is at this anxious moment that he finds, when he looks upward for a mightier mind to help him, that the heavens are empty. He will presently see that his discarded formula that Man is the Temple of the Holy Ghost happens to be precisely true, and that it is only through his own brain and hand that this Holy Ghost, formally the most nebulous person in the Trinity, and now become its sole survivor as it has always been its real Unity, can help him in any way. And so, if the Superman is to come, he must be born of Woman by Man's intentional and well-considered contrivance. Conviction of this will smash everything that opposes it. Even Property and Marriage, which laugh at the laborer's petty complaint that he is defrauded of "surplus value," and at the domestic miseries of the slaves of the wedding ring, will themselves be laughed aside as the lightest of trifles if they cross this conception when it becomes a fully realized vital purpose of the race.

That they must cross it becomes obvious the moment we acknowledge the futility of breeding men for special qualities as we breed cocks for game, greyhounds for speed, or sheep for mutton. What is really important in Man is the part of him that we do not yet understand. Of much of it we are not even conscious, just as we are not normally conscious of keeping up our circulation by our heart-pump, though if we neglect it we die. We are therefore driven to the conclusion that when we have carried selection as far as we can by rejecting from the list of eligible parents all persons who are uninteresting, unpromising, or blemished without any set-off, we shall still have to trust to the guidance of fancy (*alias* Voice of Nature), both in the breeders and the parents, for that superiority in the unconscious self which will be the true characteristic of the Superman.

At this point we perceive the importance of giving fancy the widest possible field. To cut humanity up into small cliques, and effectively limit the selection of the individual to his own clique, is to postpone the Superman for eons, if not for ever. Not only should every person be nourished and trained as a possible parent, but there should be no possibility of such an obstacle to natural selection as the objection of a countess to a navvy or of a duke to a charwoman. Equality is essential to good breeding; and equality, as all economists know, is incompatible with property.

Besides, equality is an essential condition of bad breeding also; and bad breeding is indispensable to the weeding out of the human race. When the conception of heredity took hold of the scientific imagination in the middle of last century, its devotees announced that it was a crime to marry the lunatic to the lunatic or the consumptive to the consumptive. But pray are we to try to correct our diseased stocks by infecting our healthy stocks with them? Clearly the attraction which disease has for diseased people is beneficial to the race. If two really unhealthy people get married, they will, as likely as not, have a great number of children who will all die before they reach maturity. This is a far more satisfactory arrangement than the tragedy of a union between a healthy and an unhealthy person. Though more costly than sterilization of the unhealthy, it has the enormous advantage that in the event of our notions of health and unhealth being erroneous (which to some extent they most certainly are), the error will be corrected by experience instead of confirmed by evasion.

One fact must be faced resolutely, in spite of the shrieks of the romantic. There is no evidence that the best citizens are the offspring of congenial marriages, or that a conflict of temperament is not a highly important part of what breeders call crossing. On the contrary, it is quite sufficiently probable that good results may be obtained from parents who would be extremely unsuitable companions and partners, to make it certain that the experiment of mating them will sooner or later be tried purposely almost as often as it is now tried accidentally. But mating such couples must clearly not involve marrying them. In conjugation two complementary persons may supply one another's deficiencies: in the domestic partnership of marriage they only feel them and suffer from them. Thus the son of a robust, cheerful, eupeptic British country squire, with the tastes and range of his class, and of a clever, imaginative, intellectual, highly civilized Jewess, might be very superior to both his parents; but it is not likely that the Jewess would find the squire an interesting companion, or his habits, his friends, his place and mode of life congenial to her. Therefore marriage, whilst it is made an indispensable condition of mating, will delay the advent of the Superman as effectually as Property, and will be modified by the impulse towards him just as effectually.

The practical abrogation of Property and Marriage as they exist at present will occur without being much noticed. To the mass of men, the intelligent abolition of property would mean nothing except an increase in the quantity of food, clothing, housing, and comfort at their personal disposal, as well as a greater control over their time and circumstances. Very few persons now make any distinction between virtually complete property and property held on such highly developed public conditions as to place its income on the same footing as that of a propertyless clergyman, officer, or civil servant. A landed proprietor may still drive men and women off his land, demolish their dwellings, and replace them with sheep or deer; and in the unregulated trades the private trader may still spunge on the regulated trades and sacrifice the life and health of the nation as lawlessly as the Manchester cotton manufacturers did at the beginning of last century. But though the Factory Code on the one hand, and Trade Union organization on the other, have, within the lifetime of men still living, converted the old unrestricted property of the cotton manufacturer in his mill and the cotton spinner in his labor into a mere permission to trade or work on stringent public or collective conditions, imposed in the interest of the general welfare without any regard for individual hard cases, people in Lancashire still speak of their "property" in the old terms, meaning nothing more by it than the things a thief can be punished for stealing. The total abolition of property, and the conversion of every citizen into a salaried functionary in the public service, would leave much more than 99 per cent of the nation quite unconscious of any greater change than now takes place when the son of a shipowner goes into the navy. They would still call their watches and umbrellas and back gardens their property.

Marriage also will persist as a name attached to a general custom long after the custom itself will have altered. For example, modern English marriage, as modified by divorce and by Married Women's Property Acts, differs more from early XIX century marriage than Byron's marriage did from Shakespear's. At the present moment marriage in England differs not only from marriage in France, but from marriage in Scotland. Marriage as modified by the divorce laws in South Dakota would be called mere promiscuity in Clapham. Yet the Americans, far from taking a profligate and cynical view of marriage, do homage to its ideals with a seriousness that seems old fashioned in Clapham. Neither in England nor America would a proposal to abolish marriage be tolerated for a moment; and yet nothing is more certain than that in both countries the progressive modification of the marriage contract will be continued until it is no more onerous nor irrevocable than any ordinary commercial deed of partnership. Were even this dispensed with, people would still call themselves husbands and wives; describe their companionships as marriages; and be for the most part unconscious that they were any less married than Henry VIII. For though a glance at the legal conditions of marriage in different Christian countries shews that marriage varies legally from frontier to frontier, domesticity varies so little that most people believe their own marriage laws to be universal. Consequently here again, as in the case of Property, the absolute confidence of the public in the stability of the institution's name, makes it all the easier to alter its substance.

However, it cannot be denied that one of the changes in public opinion demanded by the need for the Superman is a very unexpected one. It is nothing less than the dissolution of the present necessary association of marriage with conjugation, which most unmarried people regard as the very diagnostic of marriage. They are wrong, of course:

it would be quite as near the truth to say that conjugation is the one purely accidental and incidental condition of marriage. Conjugation is essential to nothing but the propagation of the race; and the moment that paramount need is provided for otherwise than by marriage, conjugation, from Nature's creative point of view, ceases to be essential in marriage. But marriage does not thereupon cease to be so economical, convenient, and comfortable, that the Superman might safely bribe the matrimonomaniacs by offering to revive all the old inhuman stringency and irrevocability of marriage, to abolish divorce, to confirm the horrible bond which still chains decent people to drunkards, criminals, and wasters, provided only the complete extrication of conjugation from it were conceded to him. For if people could form domestic companionships on no easier terms than these, they would still marry. The Roman Catholic, forbidden by his Church to avail himself of the divorce laws, marries as freely as the South Dakotan Presbyterians who can change partners with a facility that scandalizes the old world; and were his Church to dare a further step towards Christianity and enjoin celibacy on its laity as well as on its clergy, marriages would still be contracted for the sake of domesticity by perfectly obedient sons and daughters of the Church. One need not further pursue these hypotheses: they are only suggested here to help the reader to analyse marriage into its two functions of regulating conjugation and supplying a form of domesticity. These two functions are quite separable; and domesticity is the only one of the two which is essential to the existence of marriage, because conjugation without domesticity is not marriage at all, whereas domesticity without conjugation is still marriage: in fact it is necessarily the actual condition of all fertile marriages during a great part of their duration, and of some marriages during the whole of it.

Taking it, then, that Property and Marriage, by destroying Equality and thus hampering sexual selection with irrelevant conditions, are hostile to the evolution of the Superman, it is easy to understand why the only generally known modern experiment in breeding the human race took place in a community which discarded both institutions.

III. THE PERFECTIONIST EXPERIMENT AT ONEIDA CREEK

In 1848 the Oneida Community was founded in America to carry out a resolution arrived at by a handful of Perfectionist Communists "that we will devote ourselves exclusively to the establishment of the Kingdom of God." Though the American nation declared that this sort of thing was not to be tolerated in a Christian country, the Oneida Community held its own for over thirty years, during which period it seems to have produced healthier children and done and suffered less evil than any Joint Stock Company on record. It was, however, a highly selected community; for a genuine communist (roughly definable as an intensely proud person who proposes to enrich the common fund instead of to spunge on it) is superior to an ordinary joint stock capitalist precisely as an ordinary joint stock capitalist is superior to a pirate. Further, the Perfectionists were mightily shepherded by their chief Noyes, one of those chance attempts at the Superman which occur from time to time in spite of the interference of Man's blundering institutions. The existence of Noyes simplified the breeding problem for the Communists, the question as to what sort of man they should strive to breed being settled at once by the obvious desirability of breeding another Noyes.

But an experiment conducted by a handful of people, who, after thirty years of immunity from the unintentional child slaughter that goes on by ignorant parents in private homes, numbered only 300, could do very little except prove that Communists, under the guidance of a Superman "devoted exclusively to the establishment of the Kingdom of God," and caring no more for property and marriage than a Camberwell minister cares for Hindoo Caste or Suttee, might make a much better job of their lives than ordinary folk under the harrow of both these institutions. Yet their Superman himself admitted that this apparent success was only part of the abnormal phenomenon of his own occurrence; for when he came to the end of his powers through age, he himself guided and organized the voluntary relapse of the communists into marriage, capitalism, and customary private life, thus admitting that the real social solution was not what a casual Superman could persuade a picked company to do for him, but what a whole community of Supermen would do spontaneously. If Noyes had had to organize, not a few dozen Perfectionists, but the whole United States, America would have beaten him as completely as England beat Oliver Cromwell, France Napoleon, or Rome Julius Cæsar. Cromwell learnt by bitter experience that God himself cannot raise a people above its own level, and that even though you stir a nation to sacrifice all its appetites to its conscience, the result will still depend wholly on what sort of conscience the nation has got. Napoleon seems to have ended by regarding mankind as a troublesome pack of hounds only worth keeping for the sport of hunting with them. Cæsar's capacity for fighting without hatred or resentment was defeated by the determination of his soldiers to kill their enemies in the field instead of taking them prisoners to be spared by Cæsar; and his civil supremacy was purchased by colossal bribery of the citizens of Rome. What great rulers cannot do, codes and religions cannot do. Man reads his own nature into every ordinance: if you devise a superhuman commandment so cunningly that it cannot be misinterpreted in terms of his will, he will denounce it as seditious blasphemy, or else disregard it as either crazy or totally unintelligible. Parliaments and synods may tinker as much as they please with their codes and creeds as circumstances alter the balance of classes and their interests; and, as a result of the tinkering, there may be an occasional illusion of moral evolution, as when the victory of the commercial caste over the military caste leads to the substitution of social boycotting and pecuniary damages for duelling. At certain moments there may even be a considerable material advance, as when the conquest of political power by the working class produces a better distribution of wealth through the simple action of the selfishness of the new masters; but all this is mere readjustment and reformation: until the heart and mind of the people is changed the very greatest man will no more dare to govern on the assumption that all are as great as he than a drover dare leave his flock to find its way through the streets as he himself would. Until there is an England in which every man is a Cromwell, a France in which every man is a Napoleon, a Rome in which every man is a Cæsar, a Germany in which every man is a Luther plus a Goethe, the world will be no more improved by its heroes than a Brixton villa is improved by the pyramid of Cheops. The production of such nations is the only real change possible to us.

IV. MAN'S OBJECTION TO HIS OWN IMPROVEMENT

But would such a change be tolerated if Man must rise above himself to desire it? It would, through his misconception of its nature. Man does desire an ideal Superman with such energy as he can spare from his nutrition, and has in every age magnified the best living substitute for it he can find. His least incompetent general is set up as an Alexander; his king is the first gentleman in the world; his Pope is a saint. He is never without an array of human idols who are all nothing but sham Supermen. That the real Superman will snap his superfingers at all Man's present trumpery ideals of right, duty, honor, justice, religion, even decency, and accept moral obligations beyond present human endurance, is a thing that contemporary Man does not foresee: in fact he does not notice it when our casual Supermen do it in his very face. He actually does it himself every day without kowing it. He will therefore make no objection to the production of a race of what he calls Great Men or Heroes, because he will imagine them, not as true Supermen, but as himself endowed with infinite brains, infinite courage, and infinite money.

The most troublesome opposition will arise from the general fear of mankind that any interference with our conjugal customs will be an interference with our pleasures and our romance. This fear, by putting on airs of offended morality, has always intimidated people who have not measured its essential weakness; but it will prevail with those degenerates only in whom the instinct of fertility has faded into a mere itching for pleasure. The modern devices for combining pleasure with sterility, now universally known and accessible, enable these persons to weed themselves out of the race, a process already vigorously at work; and the consequent survival of the intelligently fertile means the survival of the partizans of the Superman; for what is proposed is nothing but the replacement of the old unintelligent, inevitable, almost unconscious fertility by an intelligently controlled, conscious fertility, and the elimination of the mere voluptuary from the evolutionary process.* Even if this selective agency had not been invented, the purpose of the race would still shatter the opposition of individual instincts. Not only do the bees and the ants satisfy their reproductive and parental instincts vicariously; but marriage itself successfully imposes celibacy on millions of unmarried normal

* The part played in evolution by the voluptuary will be the same as that already played by the glutton. The glutton, as the man with the strongest motive for nourishing himself, will always take more pains than his fellows to get food. When food is so difficult to get that only great exertions can secure a sufficient supply of it, the glutton's appetite develops his cunning and enterprise to the utmost; and he becomes not only the best fed but the ablest man in the community. But in more hospitable climates, or where the social organization of the food supply makes it easy for a man to overeat, then the glutton eats himself out of health and finally out of existence. All other voluptuaries prosper and perish in the same way; and this is why the survival of the fittest means finally the survival of the self-controlled, because they alone can adapt themselves to the perpetual shifting of conditions produced by industrial progress.

men and women. In short, the individual instinct in this matter, overwhelming as it is thoughtlessly supposed to be, is really a finally negligible one.

V. THE POLITICAL NEED FOR THE SUPERMAN

The need for the Superman is, in its most imperative aspect, a political one. We have been driven to Proletarian Democracy by the failure of all the alternative systems; for these depended on the existence of Supermen acting as despots or oligarchs; and not only were these Supermen not always or even often forthcoming at the right moment and in an eligible social position, but when they were forthcoming they could not, except for a short time and by morally suicidal coercive methods, impose superhumanity on those whom they governed; so, by mere force of "human nature," government by consent of the governed has supplanted the old plan of governing the citizen as a public-schoolboy is governed.

Now we have yet to see the man who, having any practical experience of Proletarian Democracy, has any belief in its capacity for solving great political problems, or even for doing ordinary parochial work intelligently and economically. Only under despotisms and oligarchies has the Radical faith in "universal suffrage" as a political panacea arisen. It withers the moment it is exposed to practical trial, because Democracy cannot rise above the level of the human material of which its voters are made. Switzerland seems happy in comparison with Russia; but if Russia were as small as Switzerland, and had her social problems simplified in the same way by impregnable natural fortifications and a population educated by the same variety and intimacy of international intercourse, there might be little to choose between them. At all events Australia and Canada, which are virtually protected democratic republics, and France and the United States, which are avowedly independent democratic republics, are neither healthy, wealthy, nor wise; and they would be worse instead of better if their popular ministers were not experts in the art of dodging popular enthusiasms and duping popular ignorance. The politician who once had to learn how to flatter Kings has now to learn how to fascinate, amuse, coax, humbug, frighten, or otherwise strike the fancy of the electorate; and though in advanced modern States, where the artizan is better educated than the King, it takes a much bigger man to be a successful demagogue than to be a successful courtier, yet he who holds popular convictions with prodigious energy is the man for the mob, whilst the frailer sceptic who is cautiously feeling his way towards the next century has no chance unless he happens by accident to have the specific artistic talent of the mountebank as well, in which case it is as a mountebank that he catches votes, and not as a meliorist. Consequently the demagogue, though he professes (and fails) to readjust matters in the interests of the majority of the electors, yet stereotypes mediocrity, organizes intolerance, disparages exhibitions of uncommon qualities, and glorifies conspicuous exhibitions of common ones. He manages a small job well: he muddles rhetorically through a large one. When a great political movement takes place, it is not consciously led nor organized: the unconscious self in mankind breaks its way through the problem as an elephant breaks through a jungle; and the politicians make speeches about whatever happens in the process which, with the best intentions, they do all in their power to prevent. Finally, when social aggregation arrives at a point demanding international organization before the demagogues and electorates have learnt how to manage even a country parish properly much less internationalize Constantinople, the whole political business goes to smash; and presently we have Ruins of Empires, New Zealanders sitting on a broken arch of London Bridge, and so forth.

To that recurrent catastrophe we shall certainly come again unless we can have a Democracy of Supermen; and the production of such a Democracy is the only change that is now hopeful enough to nerve us to the effort that Revolution demands.

VI. PRUDERY EXPLAINED

Why the bees should pamper their mothers whilst we pamper only our operatic prima donnas is a question worth reflecting on. Our notion of treating a mother is, not to increase her supply of food, but to cut it off by forbidding her to work in a factory for a month after her confinement. Everything that can make birth a misfortune to the parents as well as a danger to the mother is conscientiously done. When a great French writer, Emile Zola, alarmed at the sterilization of his nation, wrote an eloquent and powerful book to restore the prestige of parentage, it was at once assumed in England that a work of this character, with such a title as Fecundity, was too abominable to be translated, and that any attempt to deal with the relations of the sexes from any other than the voluptury or romantic point of view must be sternly put down. Now if this assumption were really founded on public opinion, it would indicate an attitude of disgust and resentment towards the Life Force that could only arise in a diseased and moribund community in which Ibsen's Hedda Gabler would be the typical woman. But it has no vital foundation at all. The prudery of the newspapers is, like the prudery of the dinner table, a mere difficulty of education and language. We are not taught to think decently on these subjects, and consequently we have no language for them except indecent language. We therefore have to declare them unfit for public discussion, because the only terms in which we can conduct the discussion are unfit for public use. Physiologists, who have a technical vocabulary at their disposal, find no difficulty; and masters of language who think decently can write popular stories like Zola's Fecundity or Tolstoy's Resurrection without giving the smallest offence to readers who can also think decently. But the ordinary modern journalist, who has never discussed such matters except in ribaldry, cannot write a simple comment on a divorce case without a conscious shamefulness or a furtive facetiousness that makes it impossible to read the comment aloud in company. All this ribaldry and prudery (the two are the same) does not mean that people do not feel decently on the subject: on the contrary, it is just the depth and seriousness of our feeling that makes its desecration by vile language and coarse humor intolerable; so that at last we cannot bear to have it spoken of at all because only one in a thousand can speak of it without wounding our self-respect, especially the self-respect of women. Add to the horrors of popular language the horrors of popular poverty. In crowded populations poverty destroys the possibility of cleanliness; and in the absence of cleanliness many of the natural conditions of life become offensive and noxious, with the result that at last the association of uncleanliness with these natural conditions becomes so overpowering that among civilized people (that is, people massed in the labyrinths of slums we call cities), half their bodily life becomes a guilty secret, unmentionable except to the doctor in emergencies; and Hedda Gabler shoots herself because maternity is so unladylike. In short, popular prudery is only a mere incident of popular squalor: the subjects which it taboos remain the most interesting and earnest of subjects in spite of it.

VII. PROGRESS AN ILLUSION

Unfortunately the earnest people get drawn off the track of evolution by the illusion of progress. Any Socialist can convince us easily that the difference between Man as he is and Man as he might become, without further evolution, under millennial conditions of nutrition, environment, and training, is enormous. He can shew that inequality and iniquitous distribution of wealth and allotment of labor have arisen through an unscientific economic system, and that Man, faulty as he is, no more intended to establish any such ordered disorder than a moth intends to be burnt when it flies into a candle flame. He can shew that the difference between the grace and strength of the acrobat and the bent back of the rheumatic field laborer is a difference produced by conditions, not by nature. He can shew that many of the most detestable human vices are not radical, but are mere reactions of our institutions on our very virtues. The Anarchist, the Fabian, the Salvationist, the Vegetarian, the doctor, the lawyer, the parson, the professor of ethics, the gymnast, the soldier, the sportsman, the inventor, the political program-maker, all have some prescription for bettering us; and almost all their remedies are physically possible and aimed at admitted evils. To them the limit of progress is, at worst, the completion of all the suggested reforms and the levelling up of all men to the point attained already by the most highly nourished and cultivated in mind and body.

Here, then, as it seems to them, is an enormous field for the energy of the reformer. Here are many noble goals attainable by many of those paths up the Hill Difficulty along which great spirits love to aspire. Unhappily, the hill will never be climbed by Man as we know him. It need not be denied that if we all struggled bravely to the end of the reformers' paths we should improve the world prodigiously. But there is no more hope in that If than in the equally plausible assurance that if the sky falls we shall all catch larks. We are not going to tread those paths: we have not sufficient energy. We do not desire the end enough: indeed in most cases we do not effectively desire it at all. Ask any man would he like to be a better man; and he will say yes, most piously. Ask him would he like to have a million of money; and he will say yes, most sincerely. But the pious citizen who would like to be a better man goes on behaving just as he did before. And the tramp who would like the million does not take the trouble to earn ten shillings: multitudes of men and women, all eager to accept a legacy of a million, live and die without having ever possessed five pounds at one time, although beggars have died in rags on mattresses stuffed with gold which they accumulated because they desired it enough to nerve them to get it and keep it. The economists who discovered that demand created supply soon had to limit the proposition to "effective demand," which turned out, in the final analysis, to mean nothing more than supply itself; and this holds good in politics, morals, and all other departments as well: the actual supply is the measure of the effective demand; and the mere aspirations and professions produce nothing. No community has ever yet passed beyond the initial phases in which its pugnacity and fanaticism enabled it to found a nation, and its cupidity to establish and develop a commercial civilization. Even these stages have never been attained by public spirit, but always by intolerant wilfulness and brute force. Take the Reform Bill of 1832 as an example of a conflict between two sections of educated Englishmen concerning a political measure which was as obviously necessary and inevitable as any political measure has ever been or is ever likely to be. It was not passed until the gentlemen of Birmingham had made arrangements to cut the throats of the gentlemen of St. James's parish in due military form. It would not have been passed to this day if there had been no force behind it except the logic and public conscience of the Utilitarians. A despotic ruler with as much sense as Queen Elizabeth would have done better than the mob of grown-up Eton boys who governed us then by privilege, and who, since the introduction of practically Manhood Suffrage in 1884, now govern us at the request of proletarian Democracy.

At the present time we have, instead of the Utilitarians, the Fabian Society, with its peaceful, constitutional, moral, economical policy of Socialism, which needs nothing for its bloodless and benevolent realization except that the English people shall understand it and approve of it. But why are the Fabians well spoken of in circles where thirty years ago the word Socialist was understood as equivalent to cutthroat and incendiary? Not because the English have the smallest intention of studying or adopting the Fabian policy, but because they believe that the Fabians, by eliminating the element of intimidation from the Socialist agitation, have drawn the teeth of insurgent poverty and saved the existing order from the only method of attack it really fears. Of course, if the nation adopted the Fabian policy, it would be carried out by brute force exactly as our present property system is. It would become the law; and those who resisted it would be fined, sold up, knocked on the head by policemen, thrown into prison, and in the last resort "executed" just as they are when they break the present law. But as our proprietary class has no fear of that conversion taking place, whereas it does fear sporadic cut-throats and gunpowder plots, and strives with all its might to hide the fact that there is no moral difference whatever between the methods by which it enforces its proprietary rights and the method by which the dynamitard asserts his conception of natural human right, the Fabian Society is patted on the back just as the Christian Social Union is, whilst the Socialist who says bluntly that a Social revolution can be made only as all other revolutions have been made, by the people who want it killing, coercing, and intimidating the people who dont want it, is denounced as a misleader of the people, and imprisoned with hard labor to shew him how much sincerity there is in the objection of his captors to physical force.

Are we then to repudiate Fabian methods, and return to those of the barricader, or adopt those of the dynamitard and the assassin? On the contrary, we are to recognize that both are fundamentally futile. It seems easy for the dynamitard to say "Have you not just admitted that nothing is ever conceded except to physical force? Did not Gladstone admit that the Irish Church was disestablished, not by the spirit of Liberalism, but by the explosion which wrecked Clerkenwell prison?" Well, we need not foolishly and timidly deny it. Let it be fully granted. Let us grant, further, that all this lies in the nature of things; that the most ardent Socialist, if he owns property, can by no means do otherwise than Conservative proprietors until property is forcibly abolished by the whole nation; nay, that ballots and parliamentary divisions, in spite of their vain ceremony of discussion, differ from battles only as the bloodless surrender of an outnumbered force in the field differs from Waterloo or Trafalgar. I make a present of all these admissions to the Fenian who collects money from thoughtless Irishmen in America to blow up Dublin Castle; to the detective who persuades foolish young workmen to order bombs from the nearest ironmonger and then delivers them up to penal servitude; to our military and naval commanders who believe, not in preaching, but in an ultimatum backed by plenty of lyddite; and, generally, to all whom it may concern. But of what use is it to substitute the way of the reckless and bloodyminded for the way of the cautious and humane? Is England any the better for the wreck of Clerkenwell prison, or Ireland for the disestablishment of the Irish Church? Is there the smallest reason to suppose that the nation which sheepishly let Charles and Laud and Strafford coerce it, gained anything because it afterwards, still more sheepishly, let a few strongminded Puritans, inflamed by the masterpieces of Jewish revolutionary literature, cut off the heads of the three? Suppose the Gunpowder plot had succeeded, and set a Fawkes dynasty permanently on the throne, would it have made any difference to the present state of the nation? The guillotine was used in France up to the limit of human endurance, both on Girondins and Jacobins. Fouquier Tinville followed Marie Antoinette to the scaffold; and Marie Antoinette might have asked the crowd, just as pointedly as Fouquier did, whether their bread would be any cheaper when her head was off. And what came of it all? The Imperial France of the Rougon Macquart family, and the Republican France of the Panama scandal and the Dreyfus case. Was the difference worth the guillotining of all those unlucky ladies and gentlemen, useless and mischievous as many of them were? Would any sane man guillotine a mouse to bring about such a result? Turn to Republican America. America has no Star Chamber, and no feudal barons. But it has Trusts; and it has millionaires whose factories, fenced in by live electric wires and defended by Pinkerton retainers with magazine rifles, would have made a Radical of Reginald Front de Bœuf. Would Washington or Franklin have lifted a finger in the cause of American Independence if they had foreseen its reality?

No: what Cæsar, Cromwell, and Napoleon could not do with all the physical force and moral prestige of the State in their mighty hands, cannot be done by enthusiastic criminals and lunatics. Even the Jews, who, from Moses to Marx and Lassalle, have inspired all the revolutions, have had to confess that, after all, the dog will return to his vomit and the sow that was washed to her wallowing in the mire; and we may as well make up our minds that Man will return to his idols and his cupidities, in spite of all "movements" and all revolutions, until his nature is changed. Until then, his early successes in building commercial civilizations (and such civilizations, Good Heavens!) are but preliminaries to the inevitable later stage, now threatening us, in which the passions which built the civilization become fatal instead of productive, just as the same qualities which make the lion king in the forest ensure his destruction when he enters a city. Nothing can save society then except the clear head and the wide purpose: war and competition, potent instruments of selection and evolution in one epoch, become ruinous instruments of degeneration in the next. In the breeding of animals and plants, varieties which have arisen by selection through many generations relapse precipitously into the wild type in a generation or two when selection ceases; and in the same way a civilization in which lusty pugnacity and greed have ceased to act as selective agents and have begun to obstruct and destroy, rushes downwards and backwards with a suddenness that enables an observer to see with consternation the upward steps of many centuries retraced in a single lifetime. This has often occurred even within the period covered by history; and in every instance the turning point has been reached long before the attainment, or even the general advocacy on paper, of the levelling-up of the mass to the highest point attainable by the best nourished and cultivated normal individuals.

We must therefore frankly give up the notion that Man as he exists is capable of net progress. There will always be an illusion of progress, because wherever we are conscious of an evil we remedy it, and therefore always seem to ourselves to be progressing, forgetting that most of the evils we see are the effects, finally become acute, of long-unnoticed retrogressions; that our compromising remedies seldom fully recover the lost ground; above all, that on the lines along which we are degenerating, good has become evil in our eyes, and is being undone in the name of progress precisely as evil is undone and replaced by good on the lines which we are evolving. This is indeed the Illusion of Illusions; for it gives us infallible and appalling assurance that if our political ruin is to come, it will be effected by ardent reformers and supported by enthusiastic patriots as a series of necessary steps in our progress. Let the Reformer, the Progressive, the Meliorist then reconsider himself and his eternal ifs and ans which never become pots and pans. Whilst Man remains what he is, there can be no progress beyond the point already attained and fallen headlong from at every attempt at civilization; and since even that point is but a pinnacle to which a few people cling in giddy terror above an abyss of squalor, mere progress should no longer charm us.

VIII. THE CONCEIT OF CIVILIZATION

After all, the progress illusion is not so very subtle. We begin by reading the satires of our fathers' contemporaries; and we conclude (usually quite ignorantly) that the abuses exposed by them are things of the past. We see also that reforms of crying evils are frequently produced by the sectional shifting of political power from oppressors to oppressed. The poor man is given a vote by the Liberals in the hope that he will cast it for his emancipators. The hope is not fulfilled; but the lifelong imprisonment of penniless men for debt ceases; Factory Acts are passed to mitigate sweating; schooling is made free and compulsory; sanitary bylaws are multiplied; public steps are taken to house the masses decently; the barefooted get boots; rags become rare; and bathrooms and pianos, smart weeds and starched collars, reach numbers of people who once, as "the unsoaped," played the Jew's harp or the accordion in moleskins and belchers. Some of these changes are gains: some of them are losses. Some of them are not changes at all: all of them are merely the changes that money makes. Still, they produce an illusion of bustling progress; and the reading class infers from them that the abuses of the early Victorian period no longer exist except as amusing pages in the novels of Dickens. But the moment we look for a reform due to character and not to money, to statesmanship and not to interest or mutiny, we are disillusioned. For example, we remembered the maladministration and incompetence revealed by the Crimean War as part of a bygone state of things until the South African war shewed that the nation and the War Office, like those poor Bourbons who have been so impudently blamed for a universal characteristic, had learnt nothing and forgotten nothing. We had hardly recovered from the fruitless irritation of this discovery when it transpired that the officers' mess of our most select regiment included a flogging club presided over by the senior subaltern. The disclosure provoked some disgust at the details of this schoolboyish debauchery, but no surprise at the apparent absence of any conception of manly honor and virtue, of personal courage and self-respect, in the front rank of our chivalry. In civil affairs we had assumed that the sycophancy and idolatry which encouraged Charles I to undervalue the Puritan revolt of the XVII century had been long outgrown; but it has needed nothing but favorable circumstances to revive, with added abjectness to compensate for its lost piety. We have relapsed into disputes about transubstantiation at the very moment when the discovery of the wide prevalence of theophagy as a tribal custom has deprived us of the last excuse for believing that our official religious rites differ in essentials from those of barbarians. The Christian doctrine of the uselessness of punishment and the wickedness of revenge has not, in spite of its simple common sense, found a single convert among the nations: Christianity means nothing to the masses but a sensational public execution which is made an excuse for other executions. In its name we take ten years of a thief's life minute by minute in the slow misery and degradation of modern reformed imprisonment with as little remorse as Laud and his Star Chamber clipped the ears of Bastwick and Burton. We dug up and mutilated the remains of the Madhi the other day exactly as we dug up and mutilated the remains of Cromwell two centuries ago. We have demanded the decapitation of the Chinese Boxer princes as any Tartar would have done; and our military and naval expeditions to kill, burn, and destroy tribes and villages for knocking an Englishman on the head are so common a part of our Imperial routine that the last dozen of them has not called forth as much pity as can be counted on by any lady criminal. The judicial use of torture to extort confession is supposed to be a relic of darker ages; but whilst these pages are being written an English judge has sentenced a forger to twenty years penal servitude with an open declaration that the sentence will be carried out in full unless he confesses where he has hidden the notes he forged. And no comment whatever is made either on this or on a telegram from the seat of war in Somaliland mentioning that certain information has been given by a prisoner of war "under punishment." Even if these reports are false, the fact that they are accepted without protest as indicating a natural and proper course of public conduct shews that we are still as ready to resort to torture as Bacon was. As to vindictive cruelty, an incident in the South African war, when the relatives and friends of a prisoner were forced to witness his execution, betrayed a baseness of temper and character which hardly leaves us the right to plume ourselves on our superiority to Edward III at the surrender of Calais. And the democratic American officer indulges in torture in the Philippines just as the aristocratic English officer did in South Africa. The incidents of the white invasion of Africa in search of ivory, gold, diamonds, and sport, have proved that the modern European is the same beast of prey that formerly marched to the conquest of new worlds under Alexander, Antony, and Pizarro. Parliaments and vestries are just what they were when Cromwell suppressed them and Dickens derided them. The democratic politician remains exactly as Plato described him; the physician is still the credulous impostor and petulant scientific coxcomb whom Molière ridiculed; the schoolmaster remains at best a pedantic child farmer and at worst a flagellomaniac; arbitrations are more dreaded by honest men than lawsuits; the philanthropist is still a parasite on misery as the doctor is on disease; the miracles of priestcraft are none the less fraudulent and mischievous because they are now called scientific experiments and conducted by professors; witchcraft, in the modern form of patent medicines and prophylactic inoculations, is rampant; the landowner who is no longer powerful enough to set the mantrap of Rhampsinitis improves on it by barbed wire; the modern gentleman who is too lazy to daub his face with vermilion as a symbol of bravery employs a laundress to daub his shirt with starch as a symbol of cleanliness; we shake our heads at the dirt of the middle ages in cities made grimy with soot and foul and disgusting with shameless tobacco smoking; holy water, in its latest form of disinfectant fluid, is more widely used and believed in than ever; public authorities deliberately go through incantations with burning sulphur (which they know to be useless) because the people believe in it as devoutly as the Italian peasant believes in the liquefaction of the blood of St Januarius; and straightforward public lying has reached gigantic developments, there being nothing to choose in this respect between the pickpocket at the police station and the minister on the treasury bench, the editor in the newspaper office, the city magnate advertizing bicycle tires that do not side-slip, the clergyman subscribing the thirty-nine articles, and the vivisector who pledges his knightly honor that no animal operated on in the physiological laboratory suffers the slightest pain. Hypocrisy is at its worse; for we not only persecute bigotedly but sincerely in the name of the curemongering witchcraft we do believe in, but callously and hypocritically in the name of the Evangelical creed that our rulers privately smile at as the Italian patricians of the fifth century smiled at Jupiter and Venus. Sport is, as it has always been, murderous excitement: the impulse to slaughter is universal; and museums are set up throughout the country to encourage little children and elderly gentlemen to make collections of corpses preserved in alcohol, and to steal birds' eggs and keep them as the red Indian used to keep scalps. Coercion with the lash is as natural to an Englishman as it was to Solomon spoiling Rehoboam: indeed, the comparison is unfair to the Jews in view of the facts that the Mosaic law forbade more than forty lashes in the name of humanity, and that floggings of a thousand lashes were inflicted on English soldiers in the XVIII and XIX centuries, and would be inflicted still but for the change in the balance of political power between the military caste and the commercial classes and the proletariat. In spite of that change, flogging is still an institution in the public school, in the military prison, on the training ship, and in that school of littleness called the home. The lascivious clamor of the flagellomaniac for more of it, constant as the clamor for more insolence, more war, and lower rates, is tolerated and even gratified because, having no moral ends in view, we have sense enough to see that nothing but brute coercion can impose our selfish will on others. Cowardice is universal: patriotism, public opinion, parental duty, discipline, religion, morality, are only fine names for intimidation; and cruelty, gluttony, and credulity keep cowardice in countenance. We cut the throat of a calf and hang it up by the heels to bleed to death so that our veal cutlet may be white; we nail geese to a board and cram them with food because we like the taste of liver disease; we tear birds to pieces to decorate our women's hats; we mutilate domestic animals for no reason at all except to follow an instinctively cruel fashion; and we connive at the most abominable tortures in the hope of discovering some magical cure for our own diseases by them.

Now please observe that these are not exceptional developments of our admitted vices, deplored and prayed against by all good men. Not a word has been said here of the excesses of our Neros, of whom we have the full usual percentage. With the exception of the few military examples, which are mentioned mainly to shew that the education and standing of a gentleman, reinforced by the strongest conventions of honor, *esprit de corps,* publicity and responsibility, afford no better guarantees of conduct than the passions of a mob, the illustrations given above are commonplaces taken from the daily practices of our best citizens, vehemently defended in our newspapers and in our pulpits. The very humanitarians who abhor them are stirred to murder by them: the dagger of Brutus and Ravaillac is still active in the hands of Caserio and Luccheni; and the pistol has come to its aid in the hands of Guiteau and Czolgosz. Our remedies are still limited to endurance or assassination; and the assassin is still judicially assassinated on the principle that two blacks make a white. The only novelty is in our methods: through the discovery of dynamite the overloaded musket of Hamilton of Bothwellhaugh has been superseded by the bomb; but Ravachol's heart burns just as Hamilton's did. The world will not bear thinking of to those who know what it is, even with the largest discount for the restraints of poverty on the poor and cowardice on the rich.

All that can be said for us is that people must and do live and let live up to a certain point. Even the horse, with his docked tail and bitted jaw, finds his slavery mitigated by the fact that a total disregard of his need for food and rest would put his master to the expense of buying a new horse every second day; for you cannot work a horse to death and then pick up another one for nothing, as you can a laborer. But this natural check on inconsiderate selfishness is itself checked, partly by our shortsightedness, and partly by deliberate calculation; so that beside the man who, to his own loss, will shorten his horse's life in mere stinginess, we have the tramway company which discovers actuarially that though a horse may live from 24 to 40 years, yet it pays better to work him to death in 4 and then replace him by a fresh victim. And human slavery, which has reached its worst recorded point within our own time in the form of free wage labor, has encountered the same personal and commercial limits to both its aggravation and its mitigation. Now that the freedom of wage labor has produced a scarcity of it, as in South Africa, the leading English newspaper and the leading English weekly review have openly and without apology demanded a return to compulsory labor: that is, to the methods by which, as we believe, the Egyptians built the pyramids. We know now that the crusade against chattel slavery in the XIX century succeeded solely because chattel slavery was neither the most effective nor the least humane method of labor exploitation; and the world is now feeling its way towards a still more effective system which shall abolish the freedom of the worker without again making his exploiter responsible for him.

Still, there is always some mitigation: there is the fear of revolt; and there are the effects of kindliness and affection. Let it be repeated therefore that no indictment is here laid against the world on the score of what its criminals and monsters do. The fires of Smithfield and of the Inquisition were lighted by earnestly pious people, who were kind and good as kindness and goodness go. And when a negro is dipped in kerosine and set on fire in America at the present time, he is not a good man lynched by ruffians: he is a criminal lynched by crowds of respectable, charitable, virtuously indignant, high-minded citizens, who, though they act outside the law, are at least more merciful than the American legislators and judges who not so long ago condemned men to solitary confinement for periods, not of five months, as our own practice is, but of five years and more. The things that our moral monsters do may be left out of account with St Bartholomew massacres and other momentary outbursts of social disorder. Judge us by the admitted and respected practice of our most reputable circles; and, if you know the facts and are strong enough to look them in the face, you must admit that unless we are replaced by a more highly evolved animal—in short, by the Superman—the world must remain a den of dangerous animals among whom our few accidental supermen, our Shakespears, Goethes, Shelleys and their like, must live as precariously as lion tamers do, taking the humor of their situation, and the dignity of their superiority, as a set-off to the horror of the one and the loneliness of the other.

IX. THE VERDICT OF HISTORY

It may be said that though the wild beast breaks out of Man and casts him back momentarily into barbarism under the excitement of war and crime, yet his normal life is higher than the normal life of his forefathers. This view is very acceptable to Englishmen, who always lean sincerely to virtue's side as long as it costs them nothing either in money or in thought. They feel deeply the injustice of foreigners, who allow them no credit for this conditional highmindedness. But there is no reason to suppose that our ancestors were less capable of it than we are. To all such claims for the existence of a progressive moral evolution operating visibly from grandfather to grandson, there is the conclusive reply that a thousand years of such evolution would have produced enormous social changes, of which the historical evidence would be overwhelming. But not Macaulay himself, the most confident of Whig meliorists, can produce any such evidence that will bear cross-examination. Compare our conduct and our codes with those mentioned contemporarily in such ancient scriptures and classics as have come down to us, and you will find no jot of ground for the belief that any moral progress whatever has been made in historic time, in spite of all the romantic attempts of historians to reconstruct the past on that assumption. Within that time it has happened to nations as to private families and individuals that they have flourished and decayed, repented and hardened their hearts, submitted and protested, acted and reacted, oscillated between natural and artificial sanitation (the oldest house in the world, unearthed the other day in Crete, has quite modern sanitary arrangements), and rung a thousand changes on the different scales of income and pressure of population, firmly believing all the time that mankind was advancing by leaps and bounds because men were constantly busy. And the mere chapter of accidents has left a small accumulation of chance discoveries, such as the wheel, the arch, the safety pin, gunpowder, the magnet, the Voltaic pile and so forth: things which, unlike the gospels and philosophic treatises of the sages, can be usefully understood and applied by common men; so that steam locomotion is possible without a nation of Stephensons, although national Christianity is impossible without a nation of Christs. But does any man seriously believe that the *chauffeur* who drives a motor car from Paris to Berlin is a more highly evolved man than the charioteer of Achilles, or that a modern Prime Minister is a more enlightened ruler then Cæsar because he rides a tricycle, writes his dispatches by the electric light, and instructs his stockbroker through the telephone?

Enough, then, of this goose-cackle about Progress: Man, as he is, never will nor can add a cubit to his stature by any of its quackeries, political, scientific, educational, religious, or artistic. What is likely to happen when this conviction gets into the minds of the men whose present faith in these illusions is the cement of our social system, can be imagined only by those who know how suddenly a civilization which has long ceased to think (or in the old phrase, to watch and pray) can fall to pieces when the vulgar belief in its hypocrisies and impostures can no longer hold out against its failures and scandals. When religious and ethical formulæ become so obsolete that no man of strong mind can believe them, they have also reached the point at which no man of high character will profess them; and from that moment until they are formally disestablished, they stand at the door of every profession and every public office to keep out every able man who is not a sophist or a liar. A nation which revises its parish councils once in three years, but will not revise its articles of religion once in three hundred, even when those articles avowedly began as a political compromise dictated by Mr Facing-Both-Ways, is a nation that needs remaking.

Our only hope, then, is in evolution. We must replace the man by the superman. It is frightful for the citizen, as the years pass him, to see his own contemporaries so exactly reproduced by the younger generation, that his companions of thirty years ago have their counterparts in every city crowd, where he has to check himself repeatedly in the act of saluting as an old friend some young man to whom he is only an elderly stranger. All hope of advance dies in his bosom as he watches them: he knows that they will do just what their fathers did, and that the few voices which will still, as always before, exhort them to do something else and be something better, might as well spare their breath to cool their porridge (if they can get any). Men like Ruskin and Carlyle will preach to Smith and Brown for the sake of preaching, just as St Francis preached to the birds and St Anthony to the fishes. But Smith and Brown, like the fishes and birds, remain as they are; and poets who plan Utopias and prove that nothing is necessary for their realization but that Man should will them, perceive at last, like Richard Wagner, that the fact to be faced is that Man does not effectively will them. And he never will until he becomes Superman.

And so we arrive at the end of the Socialist's dream of "the socialization of the means of production and exchange," of the Positivist's dream of moralizing the capitalist, and of the ethical professor's, legislator's, educator's dream of putting commandments and codes and lessons and examination marks on a man as harness is put on a horse, ermine on a judge, pipeclay on a soldier, or a wig on an actor, and pretending that his nature has been changed. The only fundamental and possible Socialism is the socialization of the selective breeding of Man: in other terms, of humane evolution. We must eliminate the Yahoo, or his vote will wreck the commonwealth.

X. THE METHOD

As to the method, what can be said as yet except that where there is a will, there is a way? If there be no will, we are lost. That is a possibility for our crazy little empire, if not for the universe; and as such possibilities are not to be entertained without despair, we must, whilst we survive, proceed on the assumption that we have still energy enough to not only will to live, but to will to live better. That may mean that we must establish a State Department of Evolution, with a seat in the Cabinet for its chief, and a revenue to defray the cost of direct State experiments, and provide inducements to private persons to achieve successful results. It may mean a private society or a chartered company for the improvement of human live stock. But for the present it is far more likely to mean a blatant repudiation of such proposals as indecent and immoral, with, nevertheless, a general secret pushing of the human will in the repudiated direction; so that all sorts of institutions and public authorities will under some pretext or other feel their way furtively towards the Superman. Mr Graham Wallas has already ventured to suggest, as Chairman of the School Management Committee of the London School Board, that the accepted policy of the Sterilization of the Schoolmistress, however administratively convenient, is open to criticism from the national stock-breeding point of view; and this is as good an example as any of the way in which the drift towards the Superman may operate in spite of all our hypocrisies. One thing at least is clear to begin with. If a woman can, by careful selection of a father, and nourishment of herself, produce a citizen with efficient senses, sound organs, and a good digestion, she should clearly be secured a sufficient reward for that natural service to make her willing to undertake and repeat it. Whether she be financed in the undertaking by herself, or by the father, or by a speculative capitalist, or by a new department of, say, the Royal Dublin Society, or (as at present) by the War Office maintaining her "on the strength" and authorizing a particular soldier to marry her, or by a local authority under a by-law directing that women may under certain circumstances have a year's leave of absence on full salary, or by the central government, does not matter provided the result be satisfactory.

It is a melancholy fact that as the vast majority of women and their husbands have, under existing circumstances, not enough nourishment, no capital, no credit, and no knowledge of science or business, they would, if the State would pay for birth as it now pays for death, be exploited by joint stock companies for dividends, just as they are in ordinary industries. Even a joint stock human stud farm (piously disguised as a reformed Foundling Hospital or something of that sort) might well, under proper inspection and regulation, produce better results than our present reliance on promiscuous marriage. It may be objected that when an ordinary contractor produces stores for sale to the Government, and the Government rejects them as not up to the required standard, the condemned goods are either sold for what they will fetch or else scrapped: that is, treated as waste material; whereas if the goods consisted of human beings, all that could be done would be to let them loose or send them to the nearest workhouse. But there is nothing new in private enterprise throwing its human refuse on the cheap labor market and the workhouse; and the refuse of the new industry would presumably be better bred than the staple product of ordinary poverty. In our present happy-go-lucky industrial disorder, all the human products, successful or not, would have to be thrown on the labor market; but the unsuccessful ones would not entitle the company to a bounty and so would be a dead loss to it. The practical commercial difficulty would be the uncertainty and the cost in time and money of the first experiments. Purely commercial capital would not touch such heroic operations during the experimental stage; and in any case the strength of mind needed for so momentous a new departure could not be fairly expected from the Stock Exchange. It will have to be handled by statesmen with character enough to tell our democracy and plutocracy that statecraft does not consist in flattering their follies or applying their suburban standards of propriety to the affairs of four continents. The matter must be taken up either by the State or by some organization strong enough to impose respect upon the State.

The novelty of any such experiment, however, is only in the scale of it. In one conspicuous case, that of royalty, the State does already select the parents on purely political grounds; and in the peerage, though the heir to a dukedom is legally free to marry a dairymaid, yet the social pressure on him to confine his choice to politically and socially eligible mates is so overwhelming that he is really no more free to marry the dairymaid than George IV was to marry Mrs Fitzherbert; and such a marriage could only occur as a result of extraordinary strength of character on the part of the dairymaid acting upon extraordinary weakness on the part of the duke. Let those who think the whole conception of intelligent breeding absurd and scandalous ask themselves why George IV was not allowed to choose his own wife whilst any tinker could marry whom he pleased? Simply because it did not matter a rap politically whom the tinker married, whereas it mattered very much whom the king married. The way in which all considerations of the king's personal rights, of the claims of the heart, of the sanctity of the marriage oath, and of romantic morality crumpled up before this political need shews how negligible all these apparently irresistible prejudices are when they come into conflict with the demand for quality in our rulers. We learn the same lesson from the case of the soldier, whose marriage, when it is permitted at all, is despotically controlled with a view solely to military efficiency.

Well, nowadays it is not the King that rules, but the tinker. Dynastic wars are no longer feared, dynastic alliances no longer valued. Marriages in royal families are becoming rapidly less political, and more popular, domestic, and romantic. If all the kings in Europe were made as free tomorrow as King Cophetua, nobody but their aunts and chamberlains would feel a moment's anxiety as to the consequences. On the other hand a sense of the social importance of the tinker's marriage has been steadily growing. We have made a public matter of his wife's health in the month after her confinement. We have taken the minds of his children out of his hands and put them into those of our State schoolmaster. We shall presently make their bodily nourishment independent of him. But they are still riff-raff; and to hand the country over to riff-raff is national suicide, since riff-raff can neither govern nor will let anyone else govern except the highest bidder of bread and circuses. There is no public enthusiast alive of twenty years' practical democratic experience who believes in the political adequacy of the electorate or of the bodies it elects. The overthrow of the aristocrat has created the necessity for the Superman.

Englishmen hate Liberty and Equality too much to understand them. But every Englishman loves and desires a pedigree. And in that he is right. King Demos must be bred like all other Kings; and with Must there is no arguing. It is idle for an individual writer to carry so great a matter further in a pamphlet. A conference on the subject is the next step needed. It will be attended by men and women who, no longer believing that they can live for ever, are seeking for some immortal work into which they can build the best of themselves before their refuse is thrown into that arch dust destructor, the cremation furnace.

Maxims for Revolutionists

THE GOLDEN RULE

Do not do unto others as you would that they should do unto you. Their tastes may not be the same.

Never resist temptation: prove all things: hold fast that which is good.

Do not love your neighbor as yourself. If you are on good terms with yourself it is an impertinence: if on bad, an injury.

The golden rule is that there are no golden rules.

IDOLATRY

The art of government is the organization of idolatry. The bureaucracy consists of functionaries; the aristocracy, of idols; the democracy, of idolaters.

The populace cannot understand the bureaucracy: it can only worship the national idols.

The savage bows down to idols of wood and stone: the civilized man to idols of flesh and blood.

A limited monarchy is a device for combining the inertia of a wooden idol with the credibility of a flesh and blood one.

When the wooden idol does not answer the peasant's prayer, he beats it: when the flesh and blood idol does not satisfy the civilized man, he cuts its head off.

He who slays a king and he who dies for him are alike idolaters.

ROYALTY

Kings are not born: they are made by artificial hallucination. When the process is interrupted by adversity at a critical age, as in the case of Charles II, the subject becomes sane and never completely recovers his kingliness.

The Court is the servant's hall of the sovereign.

Vulgarity in a king flatters the majority of the nation.

The flunkeyism propagated by the throne is the price we pay for its political convenience.

DEMOCRACY

If the lesser mind could measure the greater as a footrule can measure a pyramid, there would be finality in universal suffrage. As it is, the political problem remains unsolved.

Democracy substitutes election by the incompetent many for appointment by the corrupt few.

Democratic republics can no more dispense with national idols than monarchies with public functionaries.

Government presents only one problem: the discovery of a trustworthy anthropometric method.

IMPERIALISM

Excess of insularity makes a Briton an Imperialist.

Excess of local self-assertion makes a colonist an Imperialist.

A colonial Imperialist is one who raises colonial troops, equips a colonial squadron, claims a Federal Parliament sending its measures to the Throne instead of to the Colonial Office, and, being finally brought by this means into insoluble conflict with the insular British Imperialist, "cuts the painter" and breaks up the Empire.

LIBERTY AND EQUALITY

He who confuses political liberty with freedom and political equality with similarity has never thought for five minutes about either.

Nothing can be unconditional: consequently nothing can be free.

Liberty means responsibility. That is why most men dread it.

The duke inquires contemptuously whether his gamekeeper is the equal of the Astronomer Royal; but he insists that they shall both be hanged equally if they murder him.

The notion that the colonel need be a better man than the private is as confused as the notion that the keystone need be stronger than the coping stone.

Where equality is undisputed, so also is subordination.

Equality is fundamental in every department of social organization.

The relation of superior to inferior excludes good manners.

EDUCATION

When a man teaches something he does not know to somebody else who has no aptitude for it, and gives him a certificate of proficiency, the latter has completed the education of a gentleman.

A fool's brain digests philosophy into folly, science into superstition, and art into pedantry. Hence University education.

The best brought-up children are those who have seen their parents as they are. Hypocrisy is not the parent's first duty.

The vilest abortionist is he who attempts to mould a child's character.

At the University every great treatise is postponed until its author attains impartial judgment and perfect knowledge. If a horse could wait as long for its shoes and would pay for them in advance, our blacksmiths would all be college dons.

He who can, does. He who cannot, teaches.

A learned man is an idler who kills time with study. Beware of his false knowledge: it is more dangerous than ignorance.

Activity is the only road to knowledge.

Every fool believes what his teachers tell him, and calls his credulity science or morality as confidently as his father called it divine revelation.

No man fully capable of his own language ever masters another.

No man can be a pure specialist without being in the strict sense an idiot.

Do not give your children moral and religious instruction unless you are quite sure they will not take it too seriously. Better be the mother of Henri Quatre and Nell Gwynne than of Robespierre and Queen Mary Tudor.

MARRIAGE

Marriage is popular because it combines the maximum of temptation with the maximum of opportunity.

Marriage is the only legal contract which abrogates as between the parties all the laws that safeguard the particular relation to which it refers.

The essential function of marriage is the continuance of the race, as stated in the Book of Common Prayer.

The accidental function of marriage is the gratification of the amoristic sentiment of mankind.

The artificial sterilization of marriage makes it possible for marriage to fulfil its accidental function whilst neglecting its essential one.

The most revolutionary invention of the XIX century was the artificial sterilization of marriage.

Any marriage system which condemns a majority of the population to celibacy will be violently wrecked on the pretext that it outrages morality.

Polygamy, when tried under modern democratic conditions, as by the Mormons, is wrecked by the revolt of the mass of inferior men who are condemned to celibacy by it; for the maternal instinct leads a woman to prefer a tenth share in a first rate man to the exclusive possession of a third rate one. Polyandry has not been tried under these conditions.

The minimum of national celibacy (ascertained by dividing the number of males in the community by the number of females, and taking the quotient as the number of wives or husbands permitted to each person) is secured in England (where the quotient is 1) by the institution of monogamy.

The modern sentimental term for the national minimum of celibacy is Purity.

Marriage, or any other form of promiscuous amoristic monogamy, is fatal to large States because it puts its ban on the deliberate breeding of man as a political animal.

CRIME AND PUNISHMENT

All scoundrelism is summed up in the phrase "Que Messieurs les Assassins commencent!"

The man who has graduated from the flogging block at Eton to the bench from which he sentences the garotter to be flogged is the same social product as the garotter who has been kicked by his father and cuffed by his mother until he has grown strong enough to throttle and rob the rich citizen whose money he desires.

Imprisonment is as irrevocable as death.

Criminals do not die by the hands of the law. They die by the hands of other men.

The assassin Czolgosz made President McKinley a hero by assassinating him. The United States of America made Czolgosz a hero by the same process.

Assassination on the scaffold is the worst form of assassination, because there it is invested with the approval of society.

It is the deed that teaches, not the name we give it. Murder and capital punishment are not opposites that cancel one another, but similars that breed their kind.

Crime is only the retail department of what, in wholesale, we call penal law.

When a man wants to murder a tiger he calls it sport: when the tiger wants to murder him he calls it ferocity. The distinction between Crime and Justice is no greater.

Whilst we have prisons it matters little which of us occupy the cells.

The most anxious man in a prison is the governor.

It is not necessary to replace a guillotined criminal: it is necessary to replace a guillotined social system.

TITLES

Titles distinguish the mediocre, embarrass the superior, and are disgraced by the inferior.

Great men refuse titles because they are jealous of them.

HONOR

There are no perfectly honorable men; but every true man has one main point of honor and a few minor ones.

You cannot believe in honor until you have achieved it. Better keep yourself clean and bright: you are the window through which you must see the world.

Your word can never be as good as your bond, because your memory can never be as trustworthy as your honor.

PROPERTY

Property, said Proudhon, is theft. This is the only perfect truism that has been uttered on the subject.

SERVANTS

When domestic servants are treated as human beings it is not worth while to keep them.

The relation of master and servant is advantageous only to masters who do not scruple to abuse their authority, and to servants who do not scruple to abuse their trust.

The perfect servant, when his master makes humane advances to him, feels that his existence is threatened, and hastens to change his place.

Masters and servants are both tyrannical; but the masters are the more dependent of the two.

A man enjoys what he uses, not what his servants use.

Man is the only animal which esteems itself rich in proportion to the number and voracity of its parasites.

Ladies and gentlemen are permitted to have friends in the kennel, but not in the kitchen.

Domestic servants, by making spoiled children of their masters, are forced to intimidate them in order to be able to live with them.

In a slave state, the slaves rule: in Mayfair, the tradesman rules.

HOW TO BEAT CHILDREN

If you strike a child, take care that you strike it in anger, even at the risk of maiming it for life. A blow in cold blood neither can nor should be forgiven.

If you beat children for pleasure, avow your object frankly, and play the game according to the rules, as a foxhunter does, and you will do comparatively little harm. No foxhunter is such a cad as to pretend that he hunts the fox to teach it not to steal chickens, or that he suffers more acutely than the fox at the death. Remember that even in childbeating there is the sportsman's way and the cad's way.

RELIGION

Beware of the man whose god is in the skies.

What a man believes may be ascertained, not from his creed, but from the assumptions on which he habitually acts.

VIRTUES AND VICES

No specific virtue or vice in a man implies the existence of any other specific virtue or vice in him, however closely the imagination may associate them.

Virtue consists, not in abstaining from vice, but in not desiring it.

Self-denial is not a virtue: it is only the effect of prudence on rascality.

Obedience simulates subordination as fear of the police simulates honesty.

Disobedience, the rarest and most courageous of the virtues, is seldom distinguished from neglect, the laziest and commonest of the vices.

Vice is waste of life. Poverty, obedience, and celibacy are the canonical vices.

Economy is the art of making the most of life.

The love of economy is the root of all virtue.

FAIRPLAY

The love of fairplay is a spectator's virtue, not a principal's.

GREATNESS

Greatness is only one of the sensations of littleness.

In heaven an angel is nobody in particular.

Greatness is the secular name for Divinity: both mean simply what lies beyond us.

If a great man could make us understand him, we should hang him.

We admit that when the divinity we worshipped made itself visible and comprehensible we crucified it.

To a mathematician the eleventh means only a single unit: to the bushman who cannot count further than his ten fingers it is an incalculable myriad.

The difference between the shallowest routineer and the deepest thinker appears, to the latter, trifling; to the former, infinite.

In a stupid nation the man of genius becomes a god: everybody worships him and nobody does his will.

BEAUTY AND HAPPINESS, ART AND RICHES

Happiness and Beauty are by-products.

Folly is the direct pursuit of Happiness and Beauty.

Riches and Art are spurious receipts for the production of Happiness and Beauty.

He who desires a lifetime of happiness with a beautiful woman desires to enjoy the taste of wine by keeping his mouth always full of it.

The most intolerable pain is produced by prolonging the keenest pleasure.

The man with toothache thinks everyone happy whose teeth are sound. The poverty stricken man makes the same mistake about the rich man.

The more a man possesses over and above what he uses, the more careworn he becomes.

The tyranny that forbids you to make the road with pick and shovel is worse than that which prevents you from lolling along it in a carriage and pair.

In an ugly and unhappy world the richest man can purchase nothing but ugliness and unhappiness.

In his efforts to escape from ugliness and unhappiness the rich man intensifies both. Every new yard of West End creates a new acre of East End.

The XIX century was the Age of Faith in Fine Art. The results are before us.

THE PERFECT GENTLEMAN

The fatal reservation of the gentleman is that he sacrifices everything to his honor except his gentility.

A gentleman of our days is one who has money enough to do what every fool would do if he could afford it: that is, consume without producing.

The true diagnostic of modern gentility is parasitism.

No elaboration of physical or moral accomplishment can atone for the sin of parasitism.

A modern gentleman is necessarily the enemy of his country. Even in war he does not fight to defend it, but to prevent his power of preying on it from passing to a foreigner. Such combatants are patriots in the same sense as two dogs fighting for a bone are lovers of animals.

The North American Indian was a type of the sportsman warrior gentleman. The Periclean Athenian was a type of the intellectually and artistically cultivated gentleman. Both were political failures. The modern gentleman, without the hardihood of the one or the culture of the other, has the appetite of both put together. He will not succeed where they failed.

He who believes in education, criminal law, and sport, needs only property to make him a perfect modern gentleman.

MODERATION

Moderation is never applauded for its own sake.

A moderately honest man with a moderately faithful wife, moderate drinkers both, in a moderately healthy house: that is the true middle class unit.

THE UNCONSCIOUS SELF

The unconscious self is the real genius. Your breathing goes wrong the moment your conscious self meddles with it.

Except during the nine months before he draws his first breath, no man manages his affairs as well as a tree does.

REASON

The reasonable man adapts himself to the world: the unreasonable one persists in trying to adapt the world to himself. Therefore all progress depends on the unreasonable man.

The man who listens to Reason is lost: Reason enslaves all whose minds are not strong enough to master her.

DECENCY

Decency is Indecency's Conspiracy of Silence.

EXPERIENCE

Men are wise in proportion, not to their experience, but to their capacity for experience.

If we could learn from mere experience, the stones of London would be wiser than its wisest men.

TIME'S REVENGES

Those whom we called brutes had their revenge when Darwin shewed us that they are our cousins.

The thieves had their revenge when Marx convicted the bourgeoisie of theft.

GOOD INTENTIONS

Hell is paved with good intentions, not with bad ones.

All men mean well.

NATURAL RIGHTS

The Master of Arts, by proving that no man has any natural rights, compels himself to take his own for granted.

The right to live is abused whenever it is not constantly challenged.

FAUTE DE MIEUX

In my childhood I demurred to the description of a certain young lady as "the pretty Miss So and So." My aunt rebuked me by saying "Remember always that the least plain sister is the family beauty."

No age or condition is without its heroes. The least incapable general in a nation is its Cæsar, the least imbecile statesman its Solon, the least confused thinker its Socrates, the least commonplace poet its Shakespear.

CHARITY

Charity is the most mischievous sort of pruriency.

Those who minister to poverty and disease are accomplices in the two worst of all the crimes.

He who gives money he has not earned is generous with other people's labor.

Every genuinely benevolent person loathes almsgiving and mendicity.

FAME

Life levels all men: death reveals the eminent.

DISCIPLINE

Mutiny Acts are needed only by officers who command without authority. Divine right needs no whip.

WOMEN IN THE HOME

Home is the girl's prison and the woman's workhouse.

CIVILIZATION

Civilization is a disease produced by the practice of building societies with rotten material.

Those who admire modern civilization usually identify it with the steam engine and the electric telegraph.

Those who understand the steam engine and the electric telegraph spend their lives in trying to replace them with something better.

The imagination cannot conceive a viler criminal than he who should build another London like the present one, nor a greater benefactor than he who should destroy it.

GAMBLING

The most popular method of distributing wealth is the method of the roulette table.

The roulette table pays nobody except him that keeps it. Nevertheless a passion for gaming is common, though a passion for keeping roulette tables is unknown.

Gambling promises the poor what Property performs for the rich: that is why the bishops dare not denounce it fundamentally.

THE SOCIAL QUESTION

Do not waste your time on Social Questions. What is the matter with the poor is Poverty: what is the matter with the rich is Uselessness.

STRAY SAYINGS

We are told that when Jehovah created the world he saw that it was good. What would he say now?

The conversion of a savage to Christianity is the conversion of Christianity to savagery.

No man dares say so much of what he thinks as to appear to himself an extremist.

Mens sana in corpore sano is a foolish saying. The sound body is a product of the sound mind.

Decadence can find agents only when it wears the mask of progress.

In moments of progress the noble succeed, because things are going their way: in moments of decadence the base succeed for the same reason: hence the world is never without the exhilaration of contemporary success.

The reformer for whom the world is not good enough finds himself shoulder to shoulder with him that is not good enough for the world.

Every man over forty is a scoundrel.

Youth, which is forgiven everything, forgives itself nothing: age, which forgives itself everything, is forgiven nothing.

When we learn to sing that Britons never will be masters we shall make an end of slavery.

Do not mistake your objection to defeat for an objection to fighting, your objection to being a slave for an objection to slavery, your objection to not being as rich as your neighbor for an objection to poverty. The cowardly, the insubordinate, and the envious share your objections.

Take care to get what you like or you will be forced to like what you get. Where there is no ventilation fresh air is declared unwholesome. Where there is no religion hypocrisy becomes good taste. Where there is no knowledge ignorance calls itself science.

If the wicked flourish and the fittest survive, Nature must be the God of rascals.

If history repeats itself, and the unexpected always happens, how incapable must Man be of learning from experience!

Compassion is the fellow-feeling of the unsound.

Those who understand evil pardon it: those who resent it destroy it.

Acquired notions of propriety are stronger than natural instincts. It is easier to recruit for monasteries and convents than to induce an Arab woman to uncover her mouth in public, or a British officer to walk through Bond Street in a golfing cap on an afternoon in May.

It is dangerous to be sincere unless you are also stupid.

The Chinese tame fowls by clipping their wings, and women by deforming their feet. A petticoat round the ankles serves equally well.

Political Economy and Social Economy are amusing intellectual games; but Vital Economy is the Philosopher's Stone.

When a heretic wishes to avoid martyrdom he speaks of "Orthodoxy, True and False" and demonstrates that the True is his heresy.

Beware of the man who does not return your blow: he neither forgives you nor allows you to forgive yourself.

If you injure your neighbour, better not do it by halves.

Sentimentality is the error of supposing that quarter can be given or taken in moral conflicts.

Two starving men cannot be twice as hungry as one; but two rascals can be ten times as vicious as one.

Make your cross your crutch; but when you see another man do it, beware of him.

SELF-SACRIFICE

Self-sacrifice enables us to sacrifice other people without blushing.

If you begin by sacrificing yourself to those you love, you will end by hating those to whom you have sacrificed yourself.

MAJOR BARBARA:
A Discussion

Composition begun 22 March 1905; completed 8 September 1905. Published in *John Bull's Other Island and Major Barbara: also How he Lied to Her Husband*, 1907. Revised text in Collected Edition, 1930. First presented at the Royal Court Theatre, London, on 28 November 1905, for six matinées.

Lady Britomart Undershaft *Rosina Filippi*
Stephen Undershaft *Hubert Harben*
Morrison *C. L. Delph*
Barbara Undershaft *Annie Russell*
Sarah Undershaft *Hazel Thompson*
Charles Lomax *Dawson Millward*
Adolphus Cusins *Granville Barker*
Andrew Undershaft *Louis Calvert*
Rummy Mitchens *Clare Greet*
Snobby Price *Arthur Laceby*
Jenny Hill *Dorothy Minto*
Peter Shirley *Fred Cremlin*
Bill Walker *Oswald Yorke*
Mrs Baines *E. Wynne-Matthison*
Bilton *Edmund Gwenn*

Period—Three successive days in January 1906

ACT I *The Library in Lady Britomart Undershaft's House in Wilton Crescent, London*

ACT II *The West Ham Shelter of the Salvation Army*

ACT III Scene 1: *The Library at Wilton Crescent*

Scene 2: *Among the High-explosive Sheds at the Arsenal of Messrs Undershaft and Lazarus, near the Model Town of Perivale St Andrews*

N.B. The Euripidean verses in the second act of Major Barbara are not by me, nor even directly by Euripides. They are by Professor Gilbert Murray, whose English version of The Bacchæ came into our dramatic literature with all the impulsive power of an original work shortly before Major Barbara was begun. The play, indeed, stands indebted to him in more ways than one.

G.B.S.

Preface

Contents

FIRST AID TO CRITICS

Before dealing with the deeper aspects of Major Barbara, let me, for the credit of English literature, make a protest against an unpatriotic habit into which many of my critics have fallen. Whenever my view strikes them as being at all outside the range of, say, an ordinary suburban churchwarden, they conclude that I am echoing Schopenhauer, Nietzsche, Ibsen, Strindberg, Tolstoy, or some other heresiarch in northern or eastern Europe.

I confess there is something flattering in this simple faith in my accomplishment as a linguist and my erudition as a philosopher. But I cannot countenance the assumption that life and literature are so poor in these islands that we must go abroad for all dramatic material that is not common and all ideas that are not superficial. I therefore venture to put my critics in possession of certain facts concerning my contact with modern ideas.

About half a century ago, an Irish novelist, Charles Lever, wrote a story entitled A Day's Ride: A Life's Romance. It was published by Charles Dickens in Household Words, and proved so strange to the public taste that Dickens pressed Lever to make short work of it. I read scraps of this novel when I was a child; and it made an enduring impression on me. The hero was a very romantic hero, trying to live bravely, chivalrously, and powerfully by dint of mere romance-fed imagination, without courage, without means, without knowledge, without skill, without anything real except his bodily appetites. Even in my childhood I found in this poor devil's unsuccessful encounters with the facts of life, a poignant quality that romantic fiction lacked. The book, in spite of its first failure, is not dead: I saw its title the other day in the catalogue of Tauchnitz.

Now why is it that when I also deal in the tragicomic irony of the conflict between real life and the romantic imagination, critics never affiliate me to my countryman and immediate forerunner, Charles Lever, whilst they confidently derive me from a Norwegian author of whose language I do not know three words, and of whom I knew nothing until years after the Shavian *Anschauung* was already unequivocally declared in books full of what came, ten years later, to be perfunctorily labelled Ibsenism? I was not Ibsenist even at second hand; for Lever, though he may have read Henri Beyle, *alias* Stendhal, certainly never read Ibsen. Of the books that made Lever popular, such as Charles O'Malley and Harry Lorrequer, I know nothing but the names and some of the illustrations. But the story of the day's ride and life's romance of Potts (claiming alliance with Pozzo di Borgo) caught me and fascinated me as something strange and significant, though I already knew all about Alnaschar and Don Quixote and Simon Tappertit and many another romantic hero mocked by reality. From the plays of Aristophanes to the tales of Stevenson that mockery has been made familiar to all who are properly saturated with letters.

Where, then, was the novelty in Lever's tale? Partly, I think, in a new seriousness in dealing with Potts's disease. Formerly, the contrast between madness and sanity was deemed comic: Hogarth shews us how fashionable people went in parties to Bedlam to laugh at the lunatics. I myself have had a village idiot exhibited to me as something irresistibly funny. On the stage the madman was once a regular comic figure: that was how Hamlet got his opportunity before Shakespear touched him. The originality of Shakespear's version lay in his taking the lunatic sympathetically and seriously, and thereby making an advance towards the eastern consciousness of the fact that lunacy may be inspiration in disguise, since a man who has more brains than his fellows necessarily appears as mad to them as one who has less. But Shakespear did not do for Pistol and Parolles what he did for Hamlet. The particular sort of madman they represented, the romantic make-believer, lay outside the pale of sympathy in literature: he was pitilessly despised and ridiculed here as he was in the east under the name of Alnaschar, and was doomed to be, centuries later, under the name of Simon Tappertit. When Cervantes relented over Don Quixote, and Dickens relented over Pickwick, they did not become impartial: they simply changed sides, and became friends and apologists where they had formerly been mockers.

In Lever's story there is a real change of attitude. There is no relenting towards Potts: he never gains our affections like Don Quixote and Pickwick: he has not even the infatuate courage of Tappertit. But we dare not laugh at him, because, somehow, we recognize ourselves in Potts. We may, some of us, have enough nerve, enough muscle, enough luck, enough tact or skill or address or knowledge to carry things off better than he did; to impose on the people who saw through him; to fascinate Katinka (who cut Potts so ruthlessly at the end of the story); but for all that, we know that Potts plays an enormous part in ourselves and in the world, and that the social problem is not a problem of story-book heroes of the older pattern, but a problem of Pottses, and of how to make men of them. To fall back on my old phrase, we have the feeling—one that Alnaschar, Pistol, Parolles, and Tappertit never gave us—that Potts is a piece of really scientific natural history as distinguished from funny story telling. His author is not throwing a stone at a creature of another and inferior order, but making a confession, with the effect that the stone hits each of us full in the conscience and causes our self-esteem to smart very sorely. Hence the failure of Lever's book to please the readers of Household Words. That pain in the self-esteem nowadays causes critics to raise a cry of Ibsenism. I therefore assure them that the sensation first came to me from Lever and may have come to him from Beyle, or at least out of the Stendhalian atmosphere. I exclude the hypothesis of complete originality on Lever's part, because a man can no more be completely original in that sense than a tree can grow out of air.

Another mistake as to my literary ancestry is made whenever I violate the romantic convention that all women are angels when they are not devils; that they are better looking than men; that their part in courtship is entirely passive; and that the human female form is the most beautiful object in nature. Schopenhauer wrote a splenetic essay which, as it is neither polite nor profound, was probably intended to knock this nonsense violently on the head. A sentence denouncing the idolized form as ugly has been largely quoted. The English critics have read that sentence; and I must here affirm, with as much gentleness as the implication will bear, that it has yet to be proved that they have dipped any deeper. At all events, whenever an English playwright represents a young and marriageable woman as being anything but a romantic heroine, he is disposed of without further thought as an echo of Schopenhauer. My own case is a specially hard one, because, when I implore the critics who are obsessed with the Schopenhauerian formula to remember that playwrights, like sculptors, study their figures from life, and not from philosophic essays, they reply passionately that I am not a playwright and that my stage figures do not live. But even so, I may and do ask them why, if they must give the credit of my plays to a philosopher, they do not give it to an English philosopher? Long before I ever read a word by Schopenhauer, or even knew whether he was a philosopher or a chemist, the Socialist revival of the eighteen-eighties brought me into contact, both literary and personal, with Ernest Belfort Bax, an English Socialist and philosophic essayist, whose handling of modern feminism would provoke romantic protests from Schopenhauer himself, or even Strindberg. As a matter of fact I hardly noticed Schopenhauer's disparagements of women when they came under my notice later on, so thoroughly had Bax familiarized me with the homoist attitude, and forced me to recognize the extent to which public opinion, and consequently legislation and jurisprudence, is corrupted by feminist sentiment.

Belfort Bax's essays were not confined to the Feminist question. He was a ruthless critic of current morality. Other writers have gained sympathy for dramatic criminals by eliciting the alleged "soul of goodness in things evil"; but Bax would propound some quite undramatic and apparently shabby violation of our commercial law and morality, and not merely defend it with the most disconcerting ingenuity, but actually prove it to be a positive duty that nothing but the certainty of police persecution should prevent every right-minded man from at once doing on principle. The Socialists were naturally shocked, being for the most part morbidly moral people; but at all events they were saved later on from the delusion that nobody but Nietzsche had ever challenged our mercanto-Christian morality. I first heard the name of Nietzsche from a German mathematician, Miss Borchardt, who had read my Quintessence of Ibsenism, and told me that she saw what I had been reading: namely, Nietzsche's Jenseits von Gut und Böse. Which I protest I had never seen, and could not have read with any comfort, for want of the necessary German, if I had seen it.

Nietzsche, like Schopenhauer, is the victim in England of a single much quoted sentence containing the phrase "big blonde beast." On the strength of this alliteration it is assumed that Nietzsche gained his European reputation by a senseless glorification of selfish bullying as the rule of life, just as it is assumed, on the strength of the single word Superman (Übermensch) borrowed by me from Nietzsche, that I look for the salvation of society to the despotism of a single Napoleonic Superman, in spite of my careful demonstration of the folly of that outworn infatuation. But even the less recklessly superficial critics seem to believe that the modern objection to Christianity as a pernicious slave-morality was first put forward by Nietzsche. It was familiar to me before I ever heard of Nietzsche. The late Captain Wilson, author of several queer pamphlets, propagandist of a metaphysical system called Comprehensionism, and inventor of the term "Crosstianity" to distinguish the retrograde element in Christendom, was wont thirty years ago, in the discussions of the Dialectical Society, to protest earnestly against the beatitudes of the Sermon on the Mount as excuses for cowardice and servility, as destructive of our will, and consequently of our honor and manhood. Now it is true that Captain Wilson's moral criticism of Christianity was not a historical theory of it, like Nietzsche's; but this objection cannot be made to Stuart-Glennie, the successor of Buckle as a philosophic historian, who devoted his life to the elaboration and propagation of his theory that Christianity is part of an epoch (or rather an aberration, since it began as recently as 6000 B.C. and is already collapsing) produced by the necessity in which the numerically inferior white races found themselves to impose their domination on the colored races by priestcraft, making a virtue and a popular religion of drudgery and submissiveness in this world not only as a means of achieving saintliness of character but of securing a reward in heaven. Here was the slave-morality view formulated by a Scotch philosopher of my acquaintance long before we all began chattering about Nietzsche.

As Stuart-Glennie traced the evolution of society to the conflict of races, his theory made some sensation among Socialists—that is, among the only people who were seriously thinking about historical evolution at all—by its collision with the class-conflict theory of Karl Marx. Nietzsche, as I gather, regarded the slave-morality as having been invented and imposed on the world by slaves making a virtue of necessity and a religion of their servitude. Stuart-Glennie regarded the slave-morality as an invention of the superior white race to subjugate the minds of the inferior races whom they wished to exploit, and who would have destroyed them by force of numbers if their minds had not been subjugated. As this process is in operation still, and can be studied at first hand not only in our Church schools and in the struggle between our modern proprietary classes and the proletariat, but in the part played by Christian missionaries in reconciling the black races of Africa to their subjugation by European Capitalism, we can judge for ourselves whether the initiative came from above or below. My object here is not to argue the historical point, but simply to make our theatre critics ashamed of their habit of treating Britain as an intellectual void, and assuming that every philosophical idea, every historic theory, every criticism of our moral, religious and juridical institutions, must necessarily be either a foreign import, or else a fantastic sally (in rather questionable taste) totally unrelated to the existing body of thought. I urge them to remember that this body of thought is the slowest of growths and the rarest of blossomings, and that if there be such a thing on the philosophic plane as a matter of course, it is that no individual can make more than a minute contribution to it. In fact, their conception of clever persons parthenogenetically bringing forth complete original cosmogonies by dint of sheer "brilliancy" is part of that ignorant credulity which is the despair of the honest philosopher, and the opportunity of the religious impostor.

THE GOSPEL OF ST ANDREW UNDERSHAFT

It is this credulity that drives me to help my critics out with Major Barbara by telling them what to say about it. In the millionaire Undershaft I have represented a man who has become intellectually and spiritually as well as practically conscious of the irresistible natural truth which we all abhor and repudiate: to wit, that the greatest of our evils, and the worst of our crimes is poverty, and that our first duty, to which every other consideration should be sacrificed, is not to be poor. "Poor but honest," "the respectable poor," and such phrases are as intolerable and as immoral as "drunken but amiable," "fraudulent but a good after-dinner speaker," "splendidly criminal," or the like. Security, the chief pretence of civilization, cannot exist where the worst of dangers, the danger of poverty, hangs over everyone's head, and where the alleged protection of our persons from violence is only an accidental result of the existence of a police force whose real business is to force the poor man to see his children starve whilst idle people overfeed pet dogs with the money that might feed and clothe them.

It is exceedingly difficult to make people realize that an evil is an evil. For instance, we seize a man and deliberately do him a malicious injury: say, imprison him for years. One would not suppose that it needed any exceptional clearness of wit to recognize in this an act of diabolical cruelty. But in England such a recognition provokes a stare of surprise, followed by an explanation that the outrage is punishment or justice or something else that is all right, or perhaps by a heated attempt to argue that we should all be robbed and murdered in our beds if such stupid villainies as sentences of imprisonment were not committed daily. It is useless to argue that even if this were true, which it is not, the alternative to adding crimes of our own to the crimes from which we suffer is not helpless submission. Chickenpox is an evil; but if I were to declare that we must either submit to it or else repress it sternly by seizing everyone who suffers from it and punishing them by inoculation with smallpox, I should be laughed at; for though nobody could deny that the result would be to prevent chickenpox to some extent by making people avoid it much more carefully, and to effect a further apparent prevention by making them conceal it very anxiously, yet people would have sense enough to see that the deliberate propagation of smallpox was a creation of evil, and must therefore be ruled out in favor of purely humane and hygienic measures. Yet in the precisely parallel case of a man breaking into my house and stealing my wife's diamonds I am expected as a matter of course to steal ten years of his life, torturing him all the time. If he tries to defeat that monstrous retaliation by shooting me, my survivors hang him. The net result suggested by the police statistics is that we inflict atrocious injuries on the burglars we catch in order to make the rest take effectual precautions against detection; so that instead of saving our wives' diamonds from burglary we only greatly decrease our chances of ever getting them back, and increase our chances of being shot by the robber if we are unlucky enough to disturb him at his work.

But the thoughtless wickedness with which we scatter sentences of imprisonment, torture in the solitary cell and on the plank bed, and flogging, on moral invalids and energetic rebels, is as nothing compared to the silly levity with which we tolerate poverty as if it were either a wholesome tonic for lazy people or else a virtue to be embraced as St Francis embraced it. If a man is indolent, let him be poor. If he is drunken, let him be poor. If he is not a gentleman, let him be poor. If he is addicted to the fine arts or to pure science instead of to trade and finance, let him be poor. If he chooses to spend his urban eighteen shillings a week or his agricultural thirteen shillings a week on his beer and his family instead of saving it up for his old age, let him be poor. Let nothing be done for "the undeserving": let him be poor. Serve him right! Also—somewhat inconsistently—blessed are the poor!

Now what does this Let Him Be Poor mean? It means let him be weak. Let him be ignorant. Let him become a nucleus of disease. Let him be a standing exhibition and example of ugliness and dirt. Let him have rickety children. Let him be cheap, and drag his fellows down to his own price by selling himself to do their work. Let his habitations turn our cities into poisonous congeries of slums. Let his daughters infect our young men with the diseases of the streets, and his sons revenge him by turning the nation's manhood into scrofula, cowardice, cruelty, hypocrisy, political imbecility, and all the other fruits of oppression and malnutrition. Let the underserving become still less deserving; and let the deserving lay up for himself, not treasures in heaven, but horrors in hell upon earth. This being so, is it really wise to let him be poor? Would he not do ten times less harm as a prosperous burglar, incendiary, ravisher or murderer, to the utmost limits of humanity's comparatively negligible impulses in these directions? Suppose we were to abolish all penalties for such activities, and decide that poverty is the one thing we will not tolerate—that every adult with less than, say, £365 a year, shall be painlessly but inexorably killed, and every hungry half naked child forcibly fattened and clothed, would not that be an enormous improvement on our existing system, which has already destroyed so many civilizations, and is visibly destroying ours in the same way?

Is there any radicle of such legislation in our parliamentary system? Well, there are two measures just sprouting in the political soil, which may conceivably grow to something valuable. One is the institution of a Legal Minimum Wage. The other, Old Age Pensions. But there is a better plan than either of these. Some time ago I mentioned the subject of Universal Old Age Pensions to my fellow Socialist Cobden-Sanderson, famous as an artist-craftsman in book-binding and printing. "Why not Universal Pensions for Life?" said Cobden-Sanderson. In saying this, he solved the industrial problem at a stroke. At present we say callously to each citizen "If you want money, earn it" as if his having or not having it were a matter that concerned himself alone. We do not even secure for him the opportunity of earning it: on the contrary, we allow our industry to be organized in open dependence on the maintenance of "a reserve army of unemployed" for the sake of "elasticity." The sensible course would be Cobden-Sanderson's: that is, to give every man enough to live well on, so as to guarantee the community against the possibility of a case of the malignant disease of poverty, and then (necessarily) to see that he earned it.

Undershaft, the hero of Major Barbara, is simply a man who, having grasped the fact that poverty is a crime, knows that when society offered him the alternative of poverty or a lucrative trade in death and destruction, it offered him, not a choice between opulent villainy and humble virtue, but between energetic enterprise and cowardly infamy. His conduct stands the Kantian test, which Peter Shirley's does not. Peter Shirley is what we call the honest poor man. Undershaft is what we call the wicked rich one: Shirley is Lazarus, Undershaft Dives. Well, the misery of the world is due to the fact that the great mass of men act and believe as Peter Shirley acts and believes. If they acted and believed as Undershaft acts and believes, the immediate result would be a revolution of incalculable beneficence. To be wealthy, says Undershaft, is with me a point of honor for which I am prepared to kill at the risk of my own life. This preparedness is, as he says, the final test of sincerity. Like Froissart's medieval hero, who saw that "to rob and pill was a good life" he is not the dupe of that public sentiment against killing which is propagated and endowed by people who would otherwise be killed themselves, or of the mouth-honor paid to poverty and obedience by rich and insubordinate do-nothings who want to rob the poor without courage and command them without superiority. Froissart's knight, in placing the achievement of a good life before all the other duties—which indeed are not duties at all when they conflict with it, but plain wickednesses—behaved bravely, admirably, and, in the final analysis, public-spiritedly. Medieval society, on the other hand, behaved very badly indeed in organizing itself so stupidly that a good life could be achieved by robbing and pilling. If the knight's contemporaries had been all as resolute as he, robbing and pilling would have been the shortest way to the gallows, just as, if we were all as resolute and clearsighted as Undershaft, an attempt to live by means of what is called "an independent income" would be the shortest way to the lethal chamber. But as, thanks to our political imbecility and personal cowardice (fruits of poverty, both), the best imitation of a good life now procurable is life on an independent income, all sensible people aim at securing such an income, and are, of course, careful to legalize and moralize both it and all the actions and sentiments which lead to it and support it as an institution. What else can they do? They know, of course, that they are rich because others are poor. But they cannot help that: it is for the poor to repudiate poverty when they have had enough of it. The thing can be done easily enough: the demonstrations to the contrary made by the economists, jurists, moralists and sentimentalists hired by the rich to defend them, or even doing the work gratuitously out of sheer folly and abjectness, impose only on those who want to be imposed on.

The reason why the independent income-tax payers are not solid in defence of their position is that since we are not medieval rovers through a sparsely populated country, the poverty of those we rob prevents our having the good life for which we sacrifice them. Rich men or aristocrats with a developed sense of life—men like Ruskin and William Morris and Kropotkin—have enormous social appetites and very fastidious personal ones. They are not content with handsome houses: they want handsome cities. They are not content with bediamonded wives and blooming daughters: they complain because the charwoman is badly dressed, because the laundress smells of gin, because the sempstress is anemic, because every man they meet is not a friend and every woman not a romance. They turn up their noses at their neighbor's drains, and are made ill by the architecture of their neighbor's houses. Trade patterns made to suit vulgar people do not please them (and they can get nothing else): they cannot sleep nor sit at ease upon "slaughtered" cabinet makers' furniture. The very air is not good enough for them: there is too much factory smoke in it. They even demand abstract conditions: justice, honor, a noble moral atmosphere, a mystic nexus to replace the cash nexus. Finally they declare that though to rob and pill with your own hand on horseback and in steel coat may have been a good life, to rob and pill by the hands of the policeman, the bailiff, and the soldier, and to underpay them meanly for doing it, is not a good life, but rather fatal to all possibility of even a tolerable one. They call on the poor to revolt, and, finding the poor shocked at their ungentlemanliness, despairingly revile the proletariat for its "damned wantlessness" (*verdammte Bedürfnislosigkeit*).

So far, however, their attack on society has lacked simplicity. The poor do not share their tastes nor understand their art-criticisms. They do not want the simple life, nor the esthetic life; on the contrary, they want very much to wallow in all the costly vulgarities from which the elect souls among the rich turn away with loathing. It is by surfeit and not by abstinence that they will be cured of their hankering after unwholesome sweets. What they do dislike and despise and are ashamed of is poverty. To ask them to fight for the difference between the Christmas number of the Illustrated London News and the Kelmscott Chaucer is silly: they prefer the News. The difference between a stock-broker's cheap and dirty starched white shirt and collar and the comparatively costly and carefully dyed blue shirt of William Morris is a difference so disgraceful to Morris in their eyes that if they fought on the subject at all, they would fight in defence of the starch. "Cease to be slaves, in order that you may become cranks" is not a very inspiring call to arms; nor is it really improved by substituting saints for cranks. Both terms denote men of genius; and the common man does not want to live the life of a man of genius: he would much rather live the life of a pet collie if that were the only alternative. But he does want more money. Whatever else he may be vague about, he is clear about that. He may or may not prefer Major Barbara to the Drury Lane pantomime; but he always prefers five hundred pounds to five hundred shillings.

Now to deplore this preference as sordid, and teach children that it is sinful to desire money, is to strain towards the extreme possible limit of impudence in lying and corruption in hypocrisy. The universal regard for money is the one hopeful fact in our civilization, the one sound spot in our social conscience. Money is the most important thing in the world. It represents health, strength, honor, generosity and beauty as conspicuously and undeniably as the want of it represents illness, weakness, disgrace, meanness and ugliness. Not the least of its virtues is that it destroys base people as certainly as it fortifies and dignifies noble people. It is only when it is cheapened to worthlessness for some and made impossibly dear to others, that it becomes a curse. In short, it is a curse only in such foolish social conditions that life itself is a curse. For the two things are inseparable: money is the counter that enables life to be distributed socially: it *is* life as truly as sovereigns and bank notes are money. The first duty of every citizen is to insist on having money on reasonable terms; and this demand is not complied with by giving four men three shillings each for ten or twelve hours' drudgery and one man a thousand pounds for nothing. The crying need of the nation is not for better morals, cheaper bread, temperance, liberty, culture, redemption of fallen sisters and erring brothers, nor the grace, love and fellowship of the Trinity, but simply for enough money. And the evil to be attacked is not sin, suffering, greed, priestcraft, kingcraft, demagogy, monopoly, ignorance, drink, war, pestilence, nor any other of the scapegoats which reformers sacrifice, but simply poverty.

Once take your eyes from the ends of the earth and fix them on this truth just under your nose; and Andrew Undershaft's views will not perplex you in the least. Unless indeed his constant sense that he is only the instrument of a Will or Life Force which uses him for purposes wider than his own, may puzzle you. If so, that is because you are walking either in artificial Darwinian darkness, or in mere stupidity. All genuinely religious people have that consciousness. To them Undershaft the Mystic will be quite intelligible, and his perfect comprehension of his daughter the Salvationist and her lover the Euripidean republican natural and inevitable. That, however, is not new, even on the stage. What is new, as far as I know, is that article in Undershaft's religion which recognizes in Money the first need and in poverty the vilest sin of man and society.

This dramatic conception has not, of course, been attained *per saltum.* Nor has it been borrowed from Nietzsche or from any man born beyond the Channel. The late Samuel Butler, in his own department the greatest English writer of the latter half of the XIX century, steadily inculcated the necessity and morality of a conscientious Laodiceanism in religion and of an earnest and constant sense of the importance of money. It drives one almost to despair of English literature when one sees so extraordinary a study of English life as Butler's posthumous Way of All Flesh making so little impression that when, some years later, I produce plays in which Butler's extraordinarily fresh, free and future-piercing suggestions have an obvious share, I am met with nothing but vague cacklings about Ibsen and Nietzsche, and am only too thankful that they are not about Alfred de Musset and Georges Sand. Really, the English do not deserve to have great men. They allowed Butler to die practically unknown, whilst I, a comparatively insignificant Irish journalist, was leading them by the nose into an advertisement of me which has made my own life a burden. In Sicily there is a Via Samuele Butler. When an English tourist sees it, he either asks "Who the devil was Samuele Butler?" or wonders why the Sicilians should perpetuate the memory of the author of Hudibras.

Well, it cannot be denied that the English are only too anxious to recognize a man of genius if somebody will kindly point him out to them. Having pointed myself out in this manner with some success, I now point out Samuel Butler, and trust that in consequence I shall hear a little less in future of the novelty and foreign origin of the ideas which are now making their way into the English theatre through plays written by Socialists. There are living men whose originality and power are as obvious as Butler's and when they die that fact will be discovered. Meanwhile I recommend them to insist on their own merits as an important part of their own business.

THE SALVATION ARMY

When Major Barbara was produced in London, the second act was reported in an important northern newspaper as a withering attack on the Salvation Army, and the despairing ejaculation of Barbara deplored by a London daily as a tasteless blasphemy. And they were set right, not by the professed critics of the theatre, but by religious and philosophical publicists like Sir Oliver Lodge and Dr Stanton Coit, and strenuous Nonconformist journalists like William Stead, who not only understood the act as well as the Salvationists themselves, but also saw it in its relation to the religious life of the nation, a life which seems to lie not only outside the sympathy of many of our theatre critics, but actually outside their knowledge of society. Indeed nothing could be more ironically curious than the confrontation Major Barbara effected of the theatre enthusiasts with the religious enthusiasts. On the one hand was the playgoer, always seeking pleasure, paying exorbitantly for it, suffering unbearable discomforts for it, and hardly ever getting it. On the other hand was the Salvationist, repudiating gaiety and courting effort and sacrifice, yet always in the wildest spirits, laughing, joking, singing, rejoicing, drumming, and tambourining: his life flying by in a flash of excitement, and his death arriving as a climax of triumph. And, if you please, the playgoer despising the Salvationist as a joyless person, shut out from the heaven of the theatre, self-condemned to a life of hideous gloom; and the Salvationist mourning over the playgoer as over a prodigal with vine leaves in his hair, careering outrageously to hell amid the popping of champagne corks and the ribald laughter of sirens! Could misunderstanding be more complete, or sympathy worse misplaced?

Fortunately, the Salvationists are more accessible to the religious character of the drama than the playgoers to the gay energy and artistic fertility of religion. They can see, when it is pointed out to them, that a theatre, as a place where two or three are gathered together, takes from that divine presence an inalienable sanctity of which the grossest and profanest farce can no more deprive it than a hypocritical sermon by a snobbish bishop can desecrate Westminster Abbey. But in our professional playgoers this indispensable preliminary conception of sanctity seems wanting. They talk of actors as mimes and mummers, and, I fear, think of dramatic authors as liars and pandars, whose main business is the voluptuous soothing of the tired city speculator when what he calls the serious business of the day is over. Passion, the life of drama, means nothing to them but primitive sexual excitement: such phrases as "impassioned poetry" or "passionate love of truth" have fallen quite out of their vocabulary and been replaced by "passional crime" and the like. They assume, as far as I can gather, that people in whom passion has a larger scope are passionless and therefore uninteresting. Consequently they come to think of religious people as people who are not interesting and not amusing. And so, when Barbara cuts the regular Salvation Army jokes, and snatches a kiss from her lover across his drum, the devotees of the theatre think they ought to appear shocked, and conclude that the whole play is an elaborate mockery of the Army. And then either hypocritically rebuke me for mocking, or foolishly take part in the supposed mockery!

Even the handful of mentally competent critics got into difficulties over my demonstration of the economic deadlock in which the Salvation Army finds itself. Some of them thought that the Army would not have taken money from a distiller and a cannon founder: others thought it should not have taken it: all assumed more or less definitely that it reduced itself to absurdity or hypocrisy by taking it. On the first point the reply of the Army itself was prompt and conclusive. As one of its officers said, they would take money from the devil himself and be only too glad to get it out of his hands and into God's. They gratefully acknowledged that publicans not only give them money but allow them to collect it in the bar—sometimes even when there is a Salvation meeting outside preaching teetotalism. In fact, they questioned the verisimilitude of the play, not because Mrs Baines took the money, but because Barbara refused it.

On the point that the Army ought not to take such money, its justification is obvious. It must take the money because it cannot exist without money, and there is no other money to be had. Practically all the spare money in the country consists of a mass of rent, interest, and profit, every penny of which is bound up with crime, drink, prostitution, disease, and all the evil fruits of poverty, as inextricably as with enterprise, wealth, commercial probity, and national prosperity. The notion that you can earmark certain coins as tainted is an unpractical individualist superstition. None the less the fact that all our money is tainted gives a very severe shock to earnest young souls when some dramatic instance of the taint first makes them conscious of it. When an enthusiastic young clergyman of the Established Church first realizes that the Ecclesiastical Commissioners receive the rents of sporting public houses, brothels, and sweating dens; or that the most generous contributor at his last charity sermon was an employer trading in female labor cheapened by prostitution as unscrupulously as a hotel keeper trades in waiters' labor cheapened by tips, or commissionaires' labor cheapened by pensions; or that the only patron who can afford to rebuild his church or his schools or give his boys' brigade a gymnasium or a library is the son-in-law of a Chicago meat King, that young clergyman has, like Barbara, a very bad quarter hour. But he cannot help himself by refusing to accept money from anybody except sweet old ladies with independent incomes and gentle and lovely ways of life. He has only to follow up the income of the sweet ladies to its industrial source, and there he will find Mrs Warren's profession and the poisonous canned meat and all the rest of it. His own stipend has the same root. He must either share the world's guilt or go to another planet. He must save the world's honor if he is to save his own. That is what all the Churches find just as the Salvation Army and Barbara find it in the play. Her discovery that she is her father's accomplice; that the Salvation Army is the accomplice of the distiller and the dynamite maker; that they can no more escape one another than they can escape the air they breathe; that there is no salvation for them through personal righteousness, but only through the redemption of the whole nation from its vicious, lazy, competitive anarchy: this discovery has been made by everyone except the Pharisees and (apparently) the professional playgoers, who still wear their Tom Hood shirts and underpay their washerwomen without the slightest misgiving as to the elevation of their private characters, the purity of their private atmospheres, and their right to repudiate as foreign to themselves the coarse depravity of the garret and the slum. Not that they mean any harm: they only desire to be, in their little private way, what they call gentlemen. They do not understand Barbara's lesson because they have not, like her, learnt it by taking their part in the larger life of the nation.

BARBARA'S RETURN TO THE COLORS

Barbara's return to the colors may yet provide a subject for the dramatic historian of the future. To go back to the Salvation Army with the knowledge that even the Salvationists themselves are not saved yet; that poverty is not blessed, but a most damnable sin; and that when General Booth chose Blood and Fire for the emblem of Salvation instead of the Cross, he was perhaps better inspired than he knew: such knowledge, for the daughter of Andrew Undershaft, will clearly lead to something hopefuller than distributing bread and treacle at the expense of Bodger.

It is a very significant thing, this instinctive choice of the military form of organization, this substitution of the drum for the organ, by the Salvation Army. Does it not suggest that the Salvationists divine that they must actually fight the devil instead of merely praying at him? At present, it is true, they have not quite ascertained his correct address. When they do, they may give a very rude shock to that sense of security which he has gained from his experience of the fact that hard words, even when uttered by eloquent essayists and lecturers, or carried unanimously at enthusiastic public meetings on the motion of eminent reformers, break no bones. It has been said that the French Revolution was the work of Voltaire, Rousseau and the Encyclopedists. It seems to me to have been the work of men who had observed that virtuous indignation, caustic criticism, conclusive argument and instructive pamphleteering, even when done by the most earnest and witty literary geniuses, were as useless as praying, things going steadily from bad to worse whilst the Social Contract and the pamphlets of Voltaire were at the height of their vogue. Eventually, as we know, perfectly respectable citizens and earnest philanthropists connived at the September massacres because hard experience had convinced them that if they contented themselves wth appeals to humanity and patriotism, the aristocracy, though it would read their appeals with the greatest enjoyment and appreciation, flattering and admiring the writers, would none the less continue to conspire with foreign monarchists to undo the revolution and restore the old system with every circumstance of savage vengeance and ruthless repression of popular liberties.

The nineteenth century saw the same lesson repeated in England. It had its Utilitarians, its Christian Socialists, its Fabians (still extant): it had Bentham, Mill, Dickens, Ruskin, Carlyle, Butler, Henry George, and Morris. And the end of all their efforts is the Chicago described by Mr Upton Sinclair and the London in which the people who pay to be amused by my dramatic representation of Peter Shirley turned out to starve at forty because there are younger slaves to be had for his wages, do not take, and have not the slightest intention of taking, any effective step to organize society in such a way as to make that everyday infamy impossible. I, who have preached and pamphleteered like any Encyclopedist, have to confess that my methods are no use, and would be no use if I were Voltaire, Rousseau, Bentham, Marx, Mill, Dickens, Carlyle, Ruskin, Butler, and Morris all rolled into one, with Euripides, More, Montaigne, Molière, Beaumarchais, Swift, Goethe, Ibsen, Tolstoy, Jesus and the prophets all thrown in (as indeed in some sort I actually am, standing as I do on all their shoulders). The problem being to make heroes out of cowards, we paper apostles and artist-magicians have succeeded only in giving cowards all the sensations of heroes whilst they tolerate every abomination, accept every plunder, and submit to every oppression. Christianity, in making a merit of such submission, has marked only that depth in the abyss at which the very sense of shame is lost. The Christian has been like Dickens' doctor in the debtor's prison, who tells the newcomer of its ineffable peace and security: no duns; no tyrannical collector of rates, taxes, and rent; no importunate hopes nor exacting duties; nothing but the rest and safety of having no farther to fall.

Yet in the poorest corner of this soul-destroying Christendom vitality suddenly begins to germinate again. Joyousness, a sacred gift long dethroned by the hellish laughter of derision and obscenity, rises like a flood miraculously out of the fetid dust and mud of the slums; rousing marches and impetuous dithyrambs rise to the heavens from people among whom the depressing noise called "sacred music" is a standing joke; a flag with Blood and Fire on it is unfurled, not in murderous rancor, but because fire is beautiful and blood a vital and splendid red; Fear, which we flatter by calling Self, vanishes; and transfigured men and women carry their gospel through a transfigured world, calling their leader General, themselves captains and brigadiers, and their whole body an Army: praying, but praying only for refreshment, for strength to fight, and for needful MONEY (a notable sign, that); preaching, but not preaching submission; daring ill-usage and abuse, but not putting up with more of it than is inevitable; and practising what the world will let them practise, including soap and water, color and music. There is danger in such activity; and where there is danger there is hope. Our present security is nothing, and can be nothing, but evil made irresistible.

WEAKNESSES OF THE SALVATION ARMY

For the present, however, it is not my business to flatter the Salvation Army. Rather must I point out to it that it has almost as many weaknesses as the Church of England itself. It is building up a business organization which will compel it eventually to see that its present staff of enthusiast-commanders shall be succeeded by a bureaucracy of men of business who will be no better than bishops, and perhaps a good deal more unscrupulous. That has always happened sooner or later to great orders founded by saints; and the order founded by St William Booth is not exempt from the same danger. It is even more dependent than the Church on rich people who would cut off supplies at once if it began to preach that indispensable revolt against poverty which must also be a revolt against riches. It is hampered by a heavy contingent of pious elders who are not really Salvationists at all, but Evangelicals of the old school. It still, as Commissioner Howard affirms, "sticks to Moses," which is flat nonsense at this time of day if the Commissioner means, as I am afraid he does, that the Book of Genesis contains a trustworthy scientific account of the origin of species, and that the god to whom Jephthah sacrificed his daughter is any less obviously a tribal idol than Dagon or Chemosh.

Further, there is still too much other-worldliness about the Army. Like Frederick's grenadier, the Salvationist wants to live for ever (the most monstrous way of crying for the moon); and though it is evident to anyone who has ever heard General Booth and his best officers that they would work as hard for human salvation as they do at present if they believed that death would be the end of them individually, they and their followers have a bad habit of talking as if the Salvationists were heroically enduring a very bad time on earth as an investment which will bring them in dividends later on in the form, not of a better life to come for the whole world, but of an eternity spent by themselves personally in a sort of bliss which would bore any active person to a second death. Surely the truth is that the Salvationists are unusually happy people. And is it not the very diagnostic of true salvation that it shall overcome the fear of death? Now the man who has come to believe that there is no such thing as death, the change so called being merely the transition to an exquisitely happy and utterly careless life, has not overcome the fear of death at all: on the contrary, it has overcome him so completely that he refuses to die on any terms whatever. I do not call a Salvationist really saved until he is ready to lie down cheerfully on the scrap heap, having paid scot and lot and something over, and let his eternal life pass on to renew its youth in the battalions of the future.

Then there is the nasty lying habit called confession, which the Army encourages because it lends itself to dramatic oratory, with plenty of thrilling incident. For my part, when I hear a convert relating the violences and oaths and blasphemies he was guilty of before he was saved, making out that he was a very terrible fellow then and is the most contrite and chastened of Christians now, I believe him no more than I believe the millionaire who says he came up to London or Chicago as a boy with only three halfpence in his pocket. Salvationists have said to me that Barbara in my play would never have been taken in by so transparent a humbug as Snobby Price; and certainly I do not think Snobby could have taken in any experienced Salvationist on a point on which the Salvationist did not wish to be taken in. But on the point of conversion all Salvationists wish to be taken in; for the more obvious the sinner the more obvious the miracle of his conversion. When you advertize a converted burglar or reclaimed drunkard as one of the attractions at an experience meeting, your burglar can hardly have been too burglarious or your drunkard too drunken. As long as such attractions are relied on, you will have your Snobbies claiming to have beaten their mothers when they were as a matter of prosaic fact habitually beaten by them, and your Rummies of the tamest respectability pretending to a past of reckless and dazzling vice. Even when confessions are sincerely autobiographic we should beware of assuming that the impulse to make them was pious or that the interest of the hearers is wholesome. As well might we assume that the poor people who insist on shewing disgusting ulcers to district visitors are convinced hygienists, or that the curiosity which sometimes welcomes such exhibitions is a pleasant and creditable one. One is often tempted to suggest that those who pester our police superintendents with confessions of murder might very wisely be taken at their word and executed, except in the few cases in which a real murderer is seeking to be relieved of his guilt by confession and expiation. For though I am not, I hope, an unmerciful person, I do not think that the inexorability of the deed once done should be disguised by any ritual, whether in the confessional or on the scaffold.

And here my disagreement with the Salvation Army, and with all propagandists of the Cross (which I loathe as I loathe all gibbets) becomes deep indeed. Forgiveness, absolution, atonement, are figments: punishment is only a pretence of cancelling one crime by another; and you can no more have forgiveness without vindictiveness than you can have a cure without a disease. You will never get a high morality from people who conceive that their misdeeds are revocable and pardonable, or in a society where absolution and expiation are officially provided for us all. The demand may be very real; but the supply is spurious. Thus Bill Walker, in my play, having assaulted the Salvation Lass, presently finds himself overwhelmed with an intolerable conviction of sin under the skilled treatment of Barbara. Straightway he begins to try to unassault the lass and deruffianize his deed, first by getting punished for it in kind, and, when that relief is denied him, by fining himself a pound to compensate the girl. He is foiled both ways. He finds the Salvation Army as inexorable as fact itself. It will not punish him: it will not take his money. It will not tolerate a redeemed ruffian: it leaves him no means of salvation except ceasing to be a ruffian. In doing this, the Salvation Army instinctively grasps the central truth of Christianity and discards its central superstition: that central truth being the vanity of revenge and punishment, and that central superstition the salvation of the world by the gibbet.

For, be it noted, Bill has assaulted an old and starving woman also; and for this worse offence he feels no remorse whatever, because she makes it clear that her malice is as great as his own. "Let her have the law of me, as she said she would," says Bill: "what I done to her is no more on what you might call my conscience than sticking a pig." This shews a perfectly natural and wholesome state of mind on his part. The old woman, like the law she threatens him with, is perfectly ready to play the game of retaliation with him: to rob him if he steals, to flog him if he strikes, to murder him if he kills. By example and precept the law and public opinion teach him to impose his will on others by anger, violence, and cruelty, and to wipe off the moral score by punishment. That is sound Crosstianity. But this Crosstianity has got entangled with something which Barbara calls Christianity, and which unexpectedly causes her to refuse to play the hangman's game of Satan casting out Satan. She refuses to prosecute a drunken ruffian; she converses on equal terms with a blackguard to whom no lady should be seen speaking in the public street: in short she imitates Christ. Bill's conscience reacts to this just as naturally as it does to the old woman's threats. He is placed in a position of unbearable moral inferiority, and strives by every means in his power to escape from it, whilst he is still quite ready to meet the abuse of the old woman by attempting to smash a mug on her face. And that is the triumphant justification of Barbara's Christianity as against our system of judicial punishment and the vindictive villain-thrashings and "poetic justice" of the romantic stage.

For the credit of literature it must be pointed out that the situation is only partly novel. Victor Hugo long ago gave us the epic of the convict and the bishop's candlesticks, of the Crosstian policeman annihilated by his encounter with the Christian Valjean. But Bill Walker is not, like Valjean, romantically changed from a demon into an angel. There are millions of Bill Walkers in all classes of society today; and the point which I, as a professor of natural psychology, desire to demonstrate, is that Bill, without any change in his character or circumstances whatsoever, will react one way to one sort of treatment and another way to another.

In proof I might point to the sensational object lesson provided by our commercial millionaires today. They begin as brigands: merciless, unscrupulous, dealing out ruin and death and slavery to their competitors and employees, and facing desperately the worst that their competitors can do to them. The history of the English factories, the American Trusts, the exploitation of African gold, diamonds, ivory and rubber, outdoes in villainy the worst that has ever been imagined of the buccaneers of the Spanish Main. Captain Kidd would have marooned a modern Trust magnate for conduct unworthy of a gentleman of fortune. The law every day seizes on unsuccessful scoundrels of this type and punishes them with a cruelty worse than their own, with the result that they come out of the torture house more dangerous than they went in, and renew their evil doing (nobody will employ them at anything else) until they are again seized, again tormented, and again let loose, with the same result.

But the successful scoundrel is dealt with very differently, and very Christianly. He is not only forgiven: he is idolized, respected, made much of, all but worshipped. Society returns him good for evil in the most extravagant overmeasure. And with what result? He begins to idolize himself, to respect himself, to live up to the treatment he receives. He preaches sermons; he writes books of the most edifying advice to young men, and actually persuades himself that he got on by taking his own advice; he endows educational institutions, he supports charities; he dies finally in the odor of sanctity, leaving a will which is a monument of public spirit and bounty. And all this without any change in his character. The spots of the leopard and the stripes of the tiger are as brilliant as ever; but the conduct of the world towards him has changed; and his conduct has changed accordingly. You have only to reverse your attitude towards him—to lay hands on his property, revile him, assault him, and he will be a brigand again in a moment, as ready to crush you as you are to crush him, and quite as full of pretentious moral reasons for doing it.

In short, when Major Barbara says that there are no scoundrels, she is right: there are no absolute scoundrels, though there are impracticable people of whom I shall treat presently. Every reasonable man (and woman) is a potential scoundrel and a potential good citizen. What a man is depends on his character; but what he does, and what we think of what he does, depends on his circumstances. The characteristics that ruin a man in one class make him eminent in another. The characters that behave differently in different circumstances behave alike in similar circumstances. Take a common English character like that of Bill Walker. We meet Bill everywhere: on the judicial bench, on the episcopal bench, in the Privy Council, at the War Office and Admiralty, as well as in the Old Bailey dock or in the ranks of casual unskilled labor. And the morality of Bill's characteristics varies with these various circumstances. The faults of the burglar are the qualities of the financier: the manners and habits of a duke would cost a city clerk his situation. In short, though character is independent of circumstances, conduct is not; and our moral judgments of character are not: both are circumstantial. Take any condition of life in which the circumstances are for a mass of men practically alike: felony, the House of Lords, the factory, the stables, the gipsy encampment or where you please! In spite of diversity of character and temperament, the conduct and morals of the individuals in each group are as predictable and as alike in the main as if they were a flock of sheep, morals being mostly only social habits and circumstantial necessities. Strong people know this and count upon it. In nothing have the masterminds of the world been distinguished from the ordinary suburban season-ticket holder more than in their straightforward perception of the fact that mankind is practically a single species, and not a menagerie of gentlemen and bounders, villains and heroes, cowards and daredevils, peers and peasants, grocers and aristocrats, artisans and laborers, washerwomen and duchesses, in which all the grades of income and caste represent distinct animals who must not be introduced to one another or intermarry. Napoleon constructing a galaxy of generals and courtiers, and even of monarchs, out of his collection of social nobodies: Julius Cæsar appointing as governor of Egypt the son of a freedman—one who but a short time before would have been legally disqualified for the post even of a private soldier in the Roman army; Louis XI making his barber his privy councillor: all these had in their different ways a firm hold of the scientific fact of human equality, expressed by Barbara in the Christian formula that all men are children of one father. A man who believes that men are naturally divided into upper and lower and middle classes morally is making exactly the same mistake as the man who believes that they are naturally divided in the same way socially. And just as our persistent attempts to found political institutions on a basis of social inequality have always produced long periods of destructive friction relieved from time to time by violent explosions of revolution; so the attempt—will Americans please note—to found moral institutions on a basis of moral inequality can lead to nothing but unnatural Reigns of the Saints relieved by licentious Restorations; to Americans who have made divorce a public institution turning the face of Europe into one huge sardonic smile by refusing to stay in the same hotel with a Russian man of genius who has changed wives without the sanction of South Dakota; to grotesque hypocrisy, cruel persecution, and final utter confusion of conventions and compliances with benevolence and respectability. It is quite useless to declare that all men are born free if you deny that they are born good. Guarantee a man's goodness and his liberty will take care of itself. To guarantee his freedom on condition that you approve of his moral character is formally to abolish all freedom whatsoever, as every man's liberty is at the mercy of a moral indictment which any fool can trump up against everyone who violates custom, whether as a prophet or as a rascal. This is the lesson Democracy has to learn before it can become anything but the most oppressive of all the priesthoods.

Let us now return to Bill Walker and his case of conscience against the Salvation Army. Major Barbara, not being a modern Tetzel, or the treasurer of a hospital, refuses to sell absolution to Bill for a sovereign. Unfortunately, what the Army can afford to refuse in the case of Bill Walker, it cannot refuse in the case of Bodger. Bodger is master of the situation because he holds the purse strings. "Strive as you will," says Bodger, in effect: "me you cannot do without. You cannot save Bill Walker without my money." And the Army answers, quite rightly under the circumstances, "We will take money from the devil himself sooner than abandon the work of Salvation." So Bodger pays his conscience-money and gets the absolution that is refused to Bill. In real life Bill would perhaps never know this. But I, the dramatist whose business it is to shew the connexion between things that seem apart and unrelated in the haphazard order of events in real life, have contrived to make it known to Bill, with the result that the Salvation Army loses its hold of him at once.

But Bill may not be lost, for all that. He is still in the grip of the facts and of his own conscience, and may find his taste for blackguardism permanently spoiled. Still, I cannot guarantee that happy ending. Walk through the poorer quarters of our cities on Sunday when the men are not working, but resting and chewing the cud of their reflections. You will find one expression common to every mature face: the expression of cynicism. The discovery made by Bill Walker about the Salvation Army has been made by everyone there. They have found that every man has his price; and they have been foolishly or corruptly taught to mistrust and despise him for that necessary and salutary condition of social existence. When they learn that General Booth, too, has his price, they do not admire him because it is a high one, and admit the need of organizing society so that he shall get it in an honorable way: they conclude that his character is unsound and that all religious men are hypocrites and allies of their sweaters and oppressors. They know that the large subscriptions which help to support the Army are endowments, not of religion, but of the wicked doctrine of docility in poverty and humility under oppression; and they are rent by the most agonizing of all the doubts of the soul, the doubt whether their true salvation must not come from their most abhorrent passions, from murder, envy, greed, stubbornness, rage, and terrorism, rather than from public spirit, reasonableness, humanity, generosity, tenderness, delicacy, pity and kindness. The confirmation of that doubt, at which our newspapers have been working so hard for years past, is the morality of militarism; and the justification of militarism is that circumstances may at any time make it the true morality of the moment. It is by producing such moments that we produce violent and sanguinary revolutions, such as the one now in progress in Russia and the one which Capitalism in England and America is daily and diligently provoking.

At such moments it becomes the duty of the Churches to evoke all the powers of destruction against the existing order. But if they do this, the existing order must forcibly suppress them. Churches are suffered to exist only on condition that they preach submission to the State as at present capitalistically organized. The Church of England itself is compelled to add to the thirtysix articles in which it formulates its religious tenets, three more in which it apologetically protests that the moment any of these articles comes in conflict with the State it is to be entirely renounced, abjured, violated, abrogated and abhorred, the policeman being a much more important person than any of the Persons of the Trinity. And this is why no tolerated Church nor Salvation Army can ever win the entire confidence of the poor. It must be on the side of the police and the military, no matter what it believes or disbelieves; and as the police and the military are the instruments by which the rich rob and oppress the poor (on legal and moral principles made for the purpose), it is not possible to be on the side of the poor and of the police at the same time. Indeed the religious bodies, as the almoners of the rich, become a sort of auxiliary police, taking off the insurrectionary edge of poverty with coals and blankets, bread and treacle, and soothing and cheering the victims with hopes of immense and inexpensive happiness in another world when the process of working them to premature death in the service of the rich is complete in this.

CHRISTIANITY AND ANARCHISM

Such is the false position from which neither the Salvation Army nor the Church of England nor any other religious organization whatever can escape except through a reconstitution of society. Nor can they merely endure the State passively, washing their hands of its sins. The

State is constantly forcing the consciences of men by violence and cruelty. Not content with exacting money from us for the maintenance of its soldiers and policemen, its gaolers and executioners, it forces us to take an active personal part in its proceedings on pain of becoming ourselves the victims of its violence. As I write these lines, a sensational example is given to the world. A royal marriage has been celebrated, first by sacrament in a cathedral, and then by a bullfight having for its main amusement the spectacle of horses gored and disembowelled by the bull, after which, when the bull is so exhausted as to be no longer dangerous, he is killed by a cautious matador. But the ironic contrast between the bullfight and the sacrament of marriage does not move anyone. Another contrast—that between the splendor, the happiness, the atmosphere of kindly admiration surrounding the young couple, and the price paid for it under our abominable social arrangements in the misery, squalor and degradation of millions of other young couples—is drawn at the same moment by a novelist, Mr Upton Sinclair, who chips a corner of the veneering from the huge meat packing industries of Chicago, and shews it to us as a sample of what is going on all over the world underneath the top layer of prosperous plutocracy. One man is sufficiently moved by that contrast to pay his own life as the price of one terrible blow at the responsible parties. His poverty has left him ignorant enough to be duped by the pretence that the innocent young bride and bridegroom, put forth and crowned by plutocracy as the heads of a State in which they have less personal power than any policeman, and less influence than any Chairman of a Trust, are responsible. At them accordingly he launches his sixpennorth of fulminate, missing his mark, but scattering the bowels of as many horses as any bull in the arena, and slaying twentythree persons, besides wounding ninetynine. And of all these, the horses alone are innocent of the guilt he is avenging: had he blown all Madrid to atoms with every adult person in it, not one could have escaped the charge of being an accessory, before, at, and after the fact, to poverty and prostitution, to such wholesale massacre of infants as Herod never dreamt of, to plague, pestilence and famine, battle, murder and lingering death—perhaps not one who had not helped, through example, precept, connivance, and even clamor, to teach the dynamiter his well-learnt gospel of hatred and vengeance, by approving every day of sentences of years of imprisonment so infernal in their unnatural stupidity and panic-stricken cruelty, that their advocates can disavow neither the dagger nor the bomb without stripping the mask of justice and humanity from themselves also.

Be it noted that at this very moment there appears the biography of one of our dukes, who, being a Scot, could argue about politics, and therefore stood out as a great brain among our aristocrats. And what, if you please, was his grace's favorite historical episode, which he declared he never read without intense satisfaction? Why, the young General Bonapart's pounding of the Paris mob to pieces in 1795, called in playful approval by our respectable classes "the whiff of grapeshot," though Napoleon, to do him justice, took a deeper view of it, and would fain have had it forgotten. And since the Duke of Argyll was not a demon, but a man of like passions with ourselves, by no means rancorous or cruel as men go, who can doubt that all over the world proletarians of the ducal kidney are now revelling in "the whiff of dynamite" (the flavor of the joke seems to evaporate a little, does it not?) because it was aimed at the class they hate even as our argute duke hated what he called the mob.

In such an atmosphere there can be only one sequel to the Madrid explosion. All Europe burns to emulate it. Vengeance! More blood! Tear "the Anarchist beast" to shreds. Drag him to the scaffold. Imprison him for life. Let all civilized States band together to drive his like off the face of the earth; and if any State refuses to join, make war on it. This time the leading London newspaper, anti-Liberal and therefore anti-Russian in politics, does not say "Serve you right" to the victims, as it did, in effect, when Bobrikoff, and De Plehve, and Grand Duke Sergius, were in the same manner unofficially fulminated into fragments. No: fulminate our rivals in Asia by all means, ye brave Russian revolutionaries; but to aim at an English princess! monstrous! hideous! hound down the wretch to his doom; and observe, please, that we are a civilized and merciful people, and, however much we may regret it, must not treat him as Ravaillac and Damiens were treated. And meanwhile, since we have not yet caught him, let us soothe our quivering nerves with the bullfight, and comment in a courtly way on the unfailing tact and good taste of the ladies of our royal houses, who, though presumably of full normal natural tenderness, have been so effectually broken in to fashionable routine that they can be taken to see the horses slaughtered as helplessly as they could no doubt be taken to a gladiator show, if that happened to be the mode just now.

Strangely enough, in the midst of this raging fire of malice, the one man who still has faith in the kindness and intelligence of human nature is the fulminator, now a hunted wretch, with nothing, apparently, to secure his triumph over all the prisons and scaffolds of infuriate Europe except the revolver in his pocket and his readiness to discharge it at a moment's notice into his own or any other head. Think of him setting out to find a gentleman and a Christian in the multitude of human wolves howling for his blood. Think also of this: that at the very first essay he finds what he seeks, a veritable grandee of Spain, a noble, high-thinking, unterrified, malice-void soul, in the guise—of all masquerades in the world!—of a modern editor. The Anarchist wolf, flying from the wolves of plutocracy, throws himself on the honor of the man. The man, not being a wolf (nor a London editor), and therefore not having enough sympathy with his exploit to be made bloodthirsty by it, does not throw him back to the pursuing wolves—gives him, instead, what help he can to escape, and sends him off acquainted at last with a force that goes deeper than dynamite, though you cannot buy so much of it for sixpence. That righteous and honorable high human deed is not wasted on Europe, let us hope, though it benefits the fugitive wolf only for a moment. The plutocratic wolves presently smell him out. The fugitive shoots the unlucky wolf whose nose is nearest; shoots himself; and then convinces the world, by his photograph, that he was no monstrous freak of reversion to the tiger, but a good looking young man with nothing abnormal about him except his appalling courage and resolution (that is why the terrified shriek Coward at him): one to whom murdering a happy young couple on their wedding morning would have been an unthinkably unnatural abomination under rational and kindly human circumstances.

Then comes the climax of irony and blind stupidity. The wolves, balked of their meal of fellow-wolf, turn on the man, and proceed to torture him, after their manner, by imprisonment, for refusing to fasten his teeth in the throat of the dynamiter and hold him down until they came to finish him.

Thus, you see, a man may not be a gentleman nowadays even if he wishes to. As to being a Christian, he is allowed some latitude in that matter, because, I repeat, Christianity has two faces. Popular Christianity has for its emblem a gibbet, for its chief sensation a sanguinary execution after torture, for its central mystery an insane vengeance bought off by a trumpery expiation. But there is a nobler and profounder Christianity which affirms the sacred mystery of Equality, and forbids the glaring futility and folly of vengeance, often politely called punishment or justice. The gibbet part of Christianity is tolerated. The other is criminal felony. Connoisseurs in irony are well aware of the fact that the only editor in England who denounces punishment as radically wrong, also repudiates Christianity; calls his paper The Freethinker; and has been imprisoned for "bad taste" under the law against blasphemy.

SANE CONCLUSIONS

And now I must ask the excited reader not to lose his head on one side or the other, but to draw a sane moral from these grim absurdities. It is not good sense to propose that laws against crime should apply to principals only and not to accessories whose consent, counsel, or silence may secure impunity to the principal. If you institute punishment as part of the law, you must punish people for refusing to punish. If you have a police, part of its duty must be to compel everybody to assist the police. No doubt if your laws are unjust, and your policemen agents of oppression, the result will be an unbearable violation of the private consciences of citizens. But that cannot be helped: the remedy is, not to license everybody to thwart the law if they please, but to make laws that will command the public assent, and not to deal cruelly and stupidly with law-breakers. Everybody disapproves of burglars; but the modern burglar, when caught and overpowered by a householder, usually appeals, and often, let us hope, with success, to his captor not to deliver him over to the useless horrors of penal servitude. In other cases the lawbreaker escapes because those who could give him up do not consider his breach of the law a guilty action. Sometimes, even, private tribunals are formed in opposition to the official tribunals; and these private tribunals employ assassins as executioners, as was done, for example, by Mahomet before he had established his power officially, and by the Ribbon lodges of Ireland in their long struggle with the landlords. Under such circumstances, the assassin goes free although everybody in the district knows who he is and what he has done. They do not betray him, partly because they justify him exactly as the regular Government justifies its official executioner, and partly because they would themselves be assassinated if they betrayed him: another method learnt from the official government. Given a tribunal, employing a slayer who has no personal quarrel with the slain; and there is clearly no moral difference between official and unofficial killing.

In short, all men are anarchists with regard to laws which are against their consciences, either in the preamble or in the penalty. In London our worst anarchists are the magistrates, because many of them are so old and ignorant that when they are called upon to administer any law that is based on ideas or knowledge less than half a century old, they disagree with it, and being mere ordinary homebred private Englishmen without any respect for law in the abstract, naïvely set the example of violating it. In this instance the man lags behind the law; but when the law lags behind the man, he becomes equally an anarchist. When some huge change in social conditions, such as the industrial revolution of the eighteenth and nineteenth centuries, throws our legal and industrial institutions out of date, Anarchism becomes almost a religion. The whole force of the most energetic geniuses of the time in philosophy, economics, and art, concentrates itself on demonstrations and reminders that morality and law are only conventions, fallible and continually obsolescing. Tragedies in which the heroes are bandits, and comedies in which law-abiding and conventionally moral folk are compelled to satirize themselves by outraging the conscience of the spectators every time they do their duty, appear simultaneously with economic treatises entitled "What is Property? Theft!" and with histories of "The Conflict between Religion and Science."

Now this is not a healthy state of things. The advantages of living in society are proportionate, not to the freedom of the individual from a code, but to the complexity and subtlety of the code he is prepared not only to accept but to uphold as a matter of such vital importance that a lawbreaker at large is hardly to be tolerated on any plea. Such an attitude becomes impossible when the only men who can make themselves heard and remembered throughout the world spend all their energy in raising our gorge against current law, current morality, current respectability, and legal property. The ordinary man, uneducated in social theory even when he is schooled in Latin verse, cannot be set against all the laws of his country and yet persuaded to regard law in the abstract as vitally necessary to society. Once he is brought to repudiate the laws and institutions he knows, he will repudiate the very conception of law and the very groundwork of institutions, ridiculing human rights, extolling brainless methods as "historical," and tolerating nothing except pure empiricism in conduct, with dynamite as the basis of politics and vivisection as the basis of science. That is hideous; but what is to be done? Here am I, for instance, by class a respectable man, by common sense a hater of waste and disorder, by intellectual constitution legally minded to the verge of pedantry, and by temperament apprehensive and economically disposed to the limit of old-maidishness; yet I am, and have always been, and shall now always be, a revolutionary writer, because our laws make law impossible; our liberties destroy all freedom; our property is organized robbery; our morality is an impudent hypocrisy; our wisdom is administered by inexperienced or malexperienced dupes, our power wielded by cowards and weaklings, and our honor false in all its points. I am an enemy of the existing order for good reasons; but that does not make my attacks any less encouraging or helpful to people who are its enemies for bad reasons. The existing order may shriek that if I tell the truth about it, some foolish person may drive it to become still worse by trying to assassinate it. I cannot help that, even if I could see what worse it could do than it is already doing. And the disadvantage of that worst even from its own point of view is that society, with all its prisons and bayonets and whips and ostracisms and starvations, is powerless in the face of the Anarchist who is prepared to sacrifice his own life in the battle with it. Our natural safety from the cheap and devastating explosives which every Russian student can make, and every Russian grenadier has learnt to handle in Manchuria, lies in the fact that brave and resolute men, when they are rascals, will not risk their skins for the good of humanity, and, when they are not, are sympathetic enough to care for humanity, abhorring murder, and never committing it until their consciences are outraged beyond endurance. The remedy is, then, simply not to outrage their consciences.

Do not be afraid that they will not make allowances. All men make very large allowances indeed before they stake their own lives in a war to the death with society. Nobody demands or expects the millennium. But there are two things that must be set right, or we shall perish, like Rome, of soul atrophy disguised as empire.

The first is, that the daily ceremony of dividing the wealth of the country among its inhabitants shall be so conducted that no crumb shall, save as a criminal's ration, go to any able-bodied adults who are not producing by their personal exertions not only a full equivalent for what they take, but a surplus sufficient to provide for their superannuation and pay back the debt due for their nurture.

The second is that the deliberate infliction of malicious injuries which now goes on under the name of punishment be abandoned; so that the thief, the ruffian, the gambler, and the beggar, may without inhumanity be handed over to the law, and made to understand that a State which is too humane to punish will also be too thrifty to waste the life of honest men in watching or restraining dishonest ones. That is why we do not imprison dogs. We even take our chance of their first bite. But if a dog delights to bark and bite, it goes to the lethal chamber. That seems to me sensible. To allow the dog to expiate his bite by a period of torment, and then let him loose in a much more savage condition (for the chain makes a dog savage) to bite again and expiate again, having meanwhile spent a great deal of human life and happiness in the task of chaining and feeding and tormenting him, seems to me idiotic and superstitious. Yet that is what we do to men who bark and bite and steal. It would be far more sensible to put up with their vices, as we put up with their illnesses, until they give more trouble than they are worth, at which point we should, with many apologies and expressions of sympathy, and some generosity in complying with their last wishes, place them in the lethal chamber and get rid of them. Under no circumstances should they be allowed to expiate their misdeeds by a manufactured penalty, to subscribe to a charity, or to compensate the victims. If there is to be no punishment there can be no forgiveness. We shall never have real moral responsibility until everyone knows that his deeds are irrevocable, and that his life depends on his usefulness. Hitherto, alas! humanity has never dared face these hard facts. We frantically scatter conscience money and invent systems of conscience banking, with expiatory penalties, atonements, redemptions, salvations, hospital subscription lists and what not, to enable us to contract-out of the moral code. Not content with the old scapegoat and sacrificial lamb, we deify human saviors, and pray to miraculous virgin intercessors. We attribute mercy to the inexorable; soothe our consciences after committing murder by throwing ourselves on the bosom of divine love; and shrink even from our own gallows because we are forced to admit that it, at least, is irrevocable—as if one hour of imprisonment were not as irrevocable as any execution!

If a man cannot look evil in the face without illusion, he will never know what it really is, or combat it effectually. The few men who have been able (relatively) to do this have been called cynics, and have sometimes had an abnormal share of evil in themselves, corresponding to the abnormal strength of their minds; but they have never done mischief unless they intended to do it. That is why great scoundrels have been beneficent rulers whilst amiable and privately harmless monarchs have ruined their countries by trusting to the hocus-pocus of innocence and guilt, reward and punishment, virtuous indignation and pardon, instead of standing up to the facts without either malice or mercy. Major Barbara stands up to Bill Walker in that way, with the result that the ruffian who cannot get hated, has to hate himself. To relieve this agony he tries to get punished; but the Salvationist whom he tries to provoke is as merciless as Barbara, and only prays for him. Then he tries to pay, but can get nobody to take his money. His doom is the doom of Cain, who, failing to find either a savior, a policeman, or an almoner to help him to pretend that his brother's blood no longer cried from the ground, had to live and die a murderer. Cain took care not to commit another murder, unlike our railway shareholders (I am one) who kill and maim shunters by hundreds to save the cost of automatic couplings, and make atonement by annual subscriptions to deserving charities. Had Cain been allowed to pay off his score, he might possibly have killed Adam and Eve for the mere sake of a second luxurious reconciliation with God afterwards. Bodger, you may depend on it, will go on to the end of his life poisoning people with bad whisky, because he can always depend on the Salvation Army or the Church of England to negotiate a redemption for him in consideration of a trifling percentage of his profits.

There is a third condition too, which must be fulfilled before the great teachers of the world will cease to scoff at its religions. Creeds must become intellectually honest. At present there is not a single credible established religion in the world. That is perhaps the most stupendous fact in the whole world-situation. This play of mine, Major Barbara, is, I hope, both true and inspired; but whoever says that it all happened, and that faith in it and understanding of it consist in believing that it is a record of an actual occurrence, is, to speak according to Scripture, a fool and a liar, and is hereby solemnly denounced and cursed as such by me, the author, to all posterity.

London, June 1906

POSTSCRIPT 1933. In spite of the emphasis laid both in this preface and in the play on the fact that poverty is an infectious pestilence to be prevented at all costs, the lazy habit still prevails of tolerating it not only as an inevitable misfortune to be charitably patronized and relieved, but as a useful punishment for all sorts of misconduct and inefficiency that are not expressly punishable by law. Until we have a general vital hatred of poverty, and a determination to "liquidate" the underfed either by feeding them or killing them, we shall not tackle the poverty question seriously. Long ago I proposed to eradicate the dangerous disease of hunger among children by placing good bread on public supply like drinking water. No Government nor municipality has yet taken up that very sensible proposal.

ACT I

It is after dinner in January 1906, in the library in Lady Britomart Undershaft's house in Wilton Crescent. A large and comfortable settee is in the middle of the room, upholstered in dark leather. A person sitting on it (it is vacant at present) would have, on his right, Lady Britomart's writing table, with the lady herself busy at it; a smaller writing table behind him on his left; the door behind him on Lady Britomart's side; and a window with a window seat directly on his left. Near the window is an armchair.

Lady Britomart is a woman of fifty or thereabouts, well dressed and yet careless of her dress, well bred and quite reckless of her breeding, well mannered and yet appallingly outspoken and indifferent to the opinion of her interlocutors, amiable and yet peremptory, arbitrary, and high-tempered to the last bearable degree, and withal a very typical managing matron of the upper class, treated as a naughty child until she grew into a scolding mother, and finally settling down with plenty of practical ability and worldly experience, limited in the oddest way with domestic and class limitations, conceiving the universe exactly as if it were a large house in Wilton Crescent, though handling her corner of it very effectively on that assumption, and being quite enlightened and liberal as to the books in the library, the pictures on the walls, the music in the portfolios, and the articles in the papers.

Her son, Stephen, comes in. He is a gravely correct young man under 25, taking himself very seriously, but still in some awe of his mother, from childish habit and bachelor shyness rather than from any weakness of character.

STEPHEN. Whats the matter?

LADY BRITOMART. Presently, Stephen.

Stephen submissively walks to the settee and sits down. He takes up a Liberal weekly called The Speaker.

LADY BRITOMART. Dont begin to read, Stephen. I shall require all your attention.

STEPHEN. It was only while I was waiting—

LADY BRITOMART. Dont make excuses, Stephen. [*He puts down The Speaker*]. Now! [*She finishes her writing; rises; comes to the settee*]. I have not kept you waiting v e r y long, I think.

STEPHEN. Not at all, mother.

LADY BRITOMART. Bring me my cushion. [*He takes the cushion from the chair at the desk and arranges it for her as she sits down on the settee*]. Sit down. [*He sits down and fingers his tie nervously*]. Dont fiddle with your tie, Stephen: there is nothing the matter with it.

STEPHEN. I beg your pardon. [*He fiddles with his watch chain instead*].

LADY BRITOMART. Now are you attending to me, Stephen?

STEPHEN. Of course, mother.

LADY BRITOMART. No: it's n o t of course. I want something much more than your everyday matter-of-course attention. I am going to speak to you very seriously, Stephen. I wish you would let that chain alone.

STEPHEN [*hastily relinquishing the chain*] Have I done anything to annoy you, mother? If so, it was quite unintentional.

LADY BRITOMART [*astonished*] Nonsense! [*With some remorse*] My poor boy, did you think I was angry with you?

STEPHEN. What is it, then, mother? You are making me very uneasy.

LADY BRITOMART [*squaring herself at him rather aggressively*] Stephen: may I ask how soon you intend to realize that you are a grown-up man, and that I am only a woman?

STEPHEN [*amazed*] Only a—

LADY BRITOMART. Dont repeat my words, please: it is a most aggravating habit. You must learn to face life seriously, Stephen. I really cannot bear the whole burden of our family affairs any longer. You must advise me: you must assume the responsibility.

STEPHEN. I!

LADY BRITOMART. Yes, you, of course. You were 24 last June. Youve been at Harrow and Cambridge. Youve been to India and Japan. You must know a lot of things, now; unless you have wasted your time most scandalously. Well, a d v i s e me.

STEPHEN [*much perplexed*] You know I have never interfered in the household—

LADY BRITOMART. No: I should think not. I dont want you to order the dinner.

STEPHEN. I mean in our family affairs.

LADY BRITOMART. Well, you must interfere now; for they are getting quite beyond me.

STEPHEN [*troubled*] I have thought sometimes that perhaps I ought; but really, mother, I know so little about them; and what I do know is so painful! it is so impossible to mention some things to you– [*he stops, ashamed*].

LADY BRITOMART. I suppose you mean your father.

STEPHEN [*almost inaudibly*] Yes.

LADY BRITOMART. My dear: we cant go on all our lives not mentioning him. Of course you were quite right not to open the subject until I asked you to; but you are old enough now to be taken into my confidence, and to help me to deal with him about the girls.

STEPHEN. But the girls are all right. They are engaged.

LADY BRITOMART [*complacently*] Yes: I have made a very good match for Sarah. Charles Lomax will be a millionaire at 35. But that is ten years ahead; and in the meantime his trustees cannot under the terms of his father's will allow him more than £800 a year.

STEPHEN. But the will says also that if he increases his income by his own exertions, they may double the increase.

LADY BRITOMART. Charles Lomax's exertions are much more likely to decrease his income than to increase it. Sarah will have to find at least another £800 a year for the next ten years; and even then they will be as poor as church mice. And what about Barbara? I thought Barbara was going to make the most brilliant career of all of you. And what does she do? Joins the Salvation Army; discharges her maid; lives on a pound a week; and walks in one evening with a professor of Greek whom she has picked up in the street, and who pretends to be a Salvationist, and actually plays the big drum for her in public because he has fallen head over ears in love with her.

STEPHEN. I was certainly rather taken aback when I heard they were engaged. Cusins is a very nice fellow, certainly: nobody would ever guess that he was born in Australia; but–

LADY BRITOMART. Oh, Adolphus Cusins will make a very good husband. After all, nobody can say a word against Greek: it stamps a man at once as an educated gentleman. And my family, thank Heaven, is not a pig-headed Tory one. We are Whigs, and believe in liberty. Let snobbish people say what they please: Barbara shall marry, not the man they like, but the man *I* like.

STEPHEN. Of course I was thinking only of his income. However, he is not likely to be extravagant.

LADY BRITOMART. Dont be too sure of that, Stephen. I know your quiet, simple, refined, poetic people like Adolphus: quite content with the best of everything! They cost more than your extravagant people, who are always as mean as they are second rate. No: Barbara will need at least £2000 a year. You see it means two additional households. Besides, my dear, y o u must marry soon. I dont approve of the present fashion of philandering bachelors and late marriages; and I am trying to arrange something for you.

STEPHEN. It's very good of you, mother; but perhaps I had better arrange that for myself.

LADY BRITOMART. Nonsense! you are much too young to begin matchmaking: you would be taken in by some pretty little nobody. Of course I dont mean that you are not to be consulted: you know that as well as I do. [*Stephen closes his lips and is silent*]. Now dont sulk, Stephen.

STEPHEN. I am not sulking, mother. What has all this got to do with—with—with my father?

LADY BRITOMART. My dear Stephen: where is the money to come from? It is easy enough for you and the other children to live on my income as long as we are in the same house; but I cant keep four families in four separate houses. You know how poor my father is: he has barely seven thousand a year now; and really, if he were not the Earl of Stevenage, he would have to give up society. He can do nothing for us. He says, naturally enough, that it is absurd that he should be asked to provide for the children of a man who is rolling in money. You see, Stephen, your father must be fabulously wealthy, because there is always a war going on somewhere.

STEPHEN. You need not remind me of that, mother. I have hardly ever opened a newspaper in my life without seeing our name in it. The Undershaft torpedo! The Undershaft quick firers! The Undershaft ten inch! the Undershaft disappearing rampart gun! the Undershaft submarine! and now the Undershaft aerial battleship! At Harrow they called me the Woolwich Infant. At Cambridge it was the same. A little brute at King's who was always trying to get up revivals, spoilt my Bible—your first birthday present to me—by writing under my name, "Son and heir to Undershaft and Lazarus, Death and Destruction Dealers: address, Christendom and Judea." But that was not so bad as the way I was kowtowed to everywhere because my father was making millions by selling cannons.

LADY BRITOMART. It is not only the cannons, but the war loans that

Lazarus arranges under cover of giving credit for the cannons. You know, Stephen, it's perfectly scandalous. Those two men, Andrew Undershaft and Lazarus, positively have Europe under their thumbs. That is why your father is able to behave as he does. He is above the law. Do you think Bismarck or Gladstone or Disraeli could have openly defied every social and moral obligation all their lives as your father has? They simply wouldnt have dared. I asked Gladstone to take it up. I asked The Times to take it up. I asked the Lord Chamberlain to take it up. But it was just like asking them to declare war on the Sultan. They w o u l d n t. They said they couldnt touch him. I believe they were afraid.

STEPHEN. What could they do? He does not actually break the law.

LADY BRITOMART. Not break the law! He is always breaking the law. He broke the law when he was born: his parents were not married.

STEPHEN. Mother! Is that true?

LADY BRITOMART. Of course it's true: that was why we separated.

STEPHEN. He married without letting you know this!

LADY BRITOMART [*rather taken aback by this inference*] Oh no. To do Andrew justice, that was not the sort of thing he did. Besides, you know the Undershaft motto: Unashamed. Everybody knew.

STEPHEN. But you said that was why you separated.

LADY BRITOMART. Yes, because he was not content with being a foundling himself: he wanted to disinherit you for another foundling. That was what I couldnt stand.

STEPHEN [*ashamed*] Do you mean for—for—for—

LADY BRITOMART. Dont stammer, Stephen. Speak distinctly.

STEPHEN. But this is so frightful to me, mother. To have to speak to you about such things!

LADY BRITOMART. It's not pleasant for me, either, especially if you are still so childish that you must make it worse by a display of embarrassment. It is only in the middle classes, Stephen, that people get into a state of dumb helpless horror when they find that there are wicked people in the world. In our class, we have to decide what is to be done with wicked people; and nothing should disturb our self-possession. Now ask your question properly.

STEPHEN. Mother: have you no consideration for me? For Heaven's sake either treat me as a child, as you always do, and tell me nothing at all; or tell me everything and let me take it as best I can.

LADY BRITOMART. Treat you as a child! What do you mean? It is most unkind and ungrateful of you to say such a thing. You know I have never treated any of you as children. I have always made you my companions and friends, and allowed you perfect freedom to do and say whatever you liked, so long as you liked what I could approve of.

STEPHEN [*desperately*] I daresay we have been the very imperfect children of a very perfect mother; but I do beg you to let me alone for once, and tell me about this horrible business of my father wanting to set me aside for another son.

LADY BRITOMART [*amazed*] Another son! I never said anything of the kind. I never dreamt of such a thing. This is what comes of interrupting me.

STEPHEN. But you said—

LADY BRITOMART [*cutting him short*] Now be a good boy, Stephen, and listen to me patiently. The Undershafts are descended from a foundling in the parish of St Andrew Undershaft in the city. That was long ago, in the reign of James the First. Well, this foundling was adopted by an armorer and gun-maker. In the course of time the foundling succeeded to the business; and from some notion of gratitude, or some vow or something, he adopted another foundling, and left the business to him. And that foundling did the same. Ever since that, the cannon business has always been left to an adopted foundling named Andrew Undershaft.

STEPHEN. But did they never marry? Were there no legitimate sons?

LADY BRITOMART. Oh yes: they married just as your father did; and they were rich enough to buy land for their own children and leave them well provided for. But they always adopted and trained some foundling to succeed them in the business; and of course they always quarrelled with their wives furiously over it. Your father was adopted in that way; and he pretends to consider himself bound to keep up the tradition and adopt somebody to leave the business to. Of course I was not going to stand that. There may have been some reason for it when the Undershafts could only marry women in their own class, whose sons were not fit to govern great estates. But there could be no excuse for passing over my son.

STEPHEN [*dubiously*] I am afraid I should make a poor hand of managing a cannon foundry.

LADY BRITOMART. Nonsense! you could easily get a manager and pay him a salary.

STEPHEN. My father evidently had no great opinion of my capacity.

LADY BRITOMART. Stuff, child! you were only a baby: it had nothing to do with your capacity. Andrew did it on principle, just as he did every perverse and wicked thing on principle. When my father remonstrated, Andrew actually told him to his face that history tells us of only two successful institutions: one the Undershaft firm, and the other the Roman Empire under the Antonines. That was because the Antonine emperors all adopted their successors. Such rubbish! The Stevenages are as good as the Antonines, I hope; and you are a Stevenage. But that was Andrew all over. There you have the man! Always clever and unanswerable when he was defending nonsense and wickedness: always awkward and sullen when he had to behave sensibly and decently!

STEPHEN. Then it was on my account that your home life was broken up, mother. I am sorry.

LADY BRITOMART. Well, dear, there were other differences. I really cannot bear an immoral man. I am not a Pharisee, I hope; and I should not have minded his merely d o i n g wrong things: we are none of us perfect. But your father didnt exactly d o wrong things: he said them and thought them: that was what was so dreadful. He really had a sort of religion of wrongness. Just as one doesnt mind men practising immorality so long as they own that they are in the wrong by preaching morality; so I couldnt forgive Andrew for preaching immorality while he practised morality. You would all have grown up without principles, without any knowledge of right and wrong, if he had been in the house. You know, my dear, your father was a very attractive man in some ways. Children did not dislike him; and he took advantage of it to put the wickedest ideas into their heads, and make them quite unmanageable. I did not dislike him myself: very far from it; but nothing can bridge over moral disagreement.

STEPHEN. All this simply bewilders me, mother. People may differ about matters of opinion, or even about religion; but how can they differ about right and wrong? Right is right; and wrong is wrong; and if a man cannot distinguish them properly, he is either a fool or a rascal: thats all.

LADY BRITOMART [*touched*] Thats my own boy [*she pats his cheek*]! Your father never could answer that: he used to laugh and get out of it under cover of some affectionate nonsense. And now that you understand the situation, what do you advise me to do?

STEPHEN. Well, what c a n you do?

LADY BRITOMART. I must get the money somehow.

STEPHEN. We cannot take money from him. I had rather go and live in some cheap place like Bedford Square or even Hampstead than take a farthing of his money.

LADY BRITOMART. But after all, Stephen, our present income comes from Andrew.

STEPHEN [*shocked*] I never knew that.

LADY BRITOMART. Well, you surely didnt suppose your grandfather had anything to give me. The Stevenages could not do everything for you. We gave you social position. Andrew had to contribute s o m e t h i n g. He had a very good bargain, I think.

STEPHEN [*bitterly*] We are utterly dependent on him and his cannons, then?

LADY BRITOMART. Certainly not: the money is settled. But he provided it. So you see it is not a question of taking money from him or not: it is simply a question of how much. I dont want any more for myself.

STEPHEN. Nor do I.

LADY BRITOMART. But Sarah does; and Barbara does. That is, Charles Lomax and Adolphus Cusins will cost them more. So I must put my pride in my pocket and ask for it, I suppose. That is your advice, Stephen, is it not?

STEPHEN. No.

LADY BRITOMART [*sharply*] Stephen!

STEPHEN. Of course if you are determined—

LADY BRITOMART. I am not determined: I ask your advice; and I am waiting for it. I will not have all the responsibility thrown on my shoulders.

STEPHEN [*obstinately*] I would die sooner than ask him for another penny.

LADY BRITOMART [*resignedly*] You mean that *I* must ask him. Very well, Stephen: it shall be as you wish. You will be glad to know that your grandfather concurs. But he thinks I ought to ask Andrew to come here and see the girls. After all, he must have some natural affection for them.

STEPHEN. Ask him here!!!

LADY BRITOMART. Do n o t repeat my words, Stephen. Where else can I ask him?

STEPHEN. I never expected you to ask him at all.

LADY BRITOMART. Now dont tease, Stephen. Come! you see that it is necessary that he should pay us a visit, dont you?

STEPHEN [*reluctantly*] I suppose so, if the girls cannot do without his money.

LADY BRITOMART. Thank you, Stephen: I knew you would give me the right advice when it was properly explained to you. I have asked your father to come this evening. [*Stephen bounds from his seat*] Dont jump, Stephen: it fidgets me.

STEPHEN [*in utter consternation*] Do you mean to say that my father is coming here tonight—that he may be here at any moment?

LADY BRITOMART [*looking at her watch*] I said nine. [*He gasps. She rises*]. Ring the bell, please. [*Stephen goes to the smaller writing table; presses a button on it; and sits at it with his elbows on the table and his head in his hands, outwitted and overwhelmed*]. It is ten minutes to nine yet: and I have to prepare the girls. I asked Charles Lomax and Adolphus to dinner on purpose that they might be here. Andrew had better see them in case he should cherish any delusions as to their being capable of supporting their wives. [*The butler enters: Lady Britomart goes behind the settee to speak to him*]. Morrison: go up to the drawing room and tell everybody to come down here at once. [*Morrison withdraws. Lady Britomart turns to Stephen*]. Now remember, Stephen: I shall need all your countenance and authority. [*He rises and tries to recover some vestige of these attributes*]. Give me a chair, dear. [*He pushes a chair forward from the wall to where she stands, near the smaller writing table. She sits down; and he goes to the armchair, into which he throws himself*]. I dont know how Barbara will take it. Ever since they made her a major in the Salvation Army she has developed a propensity to have her own way and order people about which quite cows me sometimes. It's not ladylike: I'm sure I dont know where she picked it up. Anyhow, Barbara shant bully me; but still it's just as well that your father should be here before she has time to refuse to meet him or make a fuss. Dont look nervous, Stephen: it will only encourage Barbara to make difficulties. *I* am nervous enough, goodness knows: but I dont shew it.

Sarah and Barbara come in with their respective young men, Charles Lomax and Adolphus Cusins. Sarah is slender, bored, and mundane. Barbara is robuster, jollier, much more energetic. Sarah is fashionably dressed: Barbara is in Salvation Army uniform. Lomax, a young man about town, is like many other young men about town. He is afflicted with a frivolous sense of humor which plunges him at the most inopportune moments into paroxysms of imperfectly suppressed laughter. Cusins is a spectacled student, slight, thin haired, and sweet voiced, with a more complex form of Lomax's complaint. His sense of humor is intellectual and subtle, and is complicated by an appalling temper. The lifelong struggle of a benevolent temperament and a high conscience against impulses of inhuman ridicule and fierce impatience has set up a chronic strain which has visibly wrecked his constitution. He is a most implacable, determined, tenacious, intolerant person who by mere force of character presents himself as—and indeed actually is—considerate, gentle, explanatory, even mild and apologetic, capable possibly of murder, but not of cruelty or coarseness. By the operation of some instinct which is not merciful enough to blind him with the illusions of love, he is obstinately bent on marrying Barbara. Lomax likes Sarah and thinks it will be rather a lark to marry her. Consequently he has not attempted to resist Lady Britomart's arrangements to that end.

All four look as if they had been having a good deal of fun in the drawing room. The girls enter first, leaving the swains outside. Sarah comes to the settee. Barbara comes in after her and stops at the door.

BARBARA. Are Cholly and Dolly to come in?

LADY BRITOMART [*forcibly*] Barbara: I will not have Charles called Cholly: the vulgarity of it positively makes me ill.

BARBARA. It's all right, mother: Cholly is quite correct nowadays. Are they to come in?

LADY BRITOMART. Yes, if they will behave themselves.

BARBARA [*through the door*] Come in, Dolly; and behave yourself.

Barbara comes to her mother's writing table. Cusins enters smiling, and wanders towards Lady Britomart.

SARAH [*calling*] Come in, Cholly. [*Lomax enters, controlling his features very imperfectly, and places himself vaguely between Sarah and Barbara*].

LADY BRITOMART [*peremptorily*] Sit down, all of you. [*They sit. Cusins crosses to the window and seats himself there. Lomax takes a chair. Barbara sits at the writing table and Sarah on the settee*]. I dont in the least know what you are laughing at, Adolphus. I am surprised at you, though I expected nothing better from Charles Lomax.

CUSINS [*in a remarkably gentle voice*] Barbara has been trying to teach me the West Ham Salvation March.

LADY BRITOMART. I see nothing to laugh at in that; nor should you if you are really converted.

CUSINS [*sweetly*] You were not present. It was really funny, I believe.

LOMAX. Ripping.

LADY BRITOMART. Be quiet, Charles. Now listen to me, children. Your father is coming here this evening.

General stupefaction. Lomax, Sarah, and Barbara rise; Sarah scared, and Barbara amused and expectant.

LOMAX [*remonstrating*] Oh I say!

LADY BRITOMART. You are not called on to say anything, Charles.

SARAH. Are you serious, mother?

LADY BRITOMART. Of course I am serious. It is on your account, Sarah, and also on Charles's. [*Silence. Sarah sits, with a shrug. Charles looks painfully unworthy*]. I hope you are not going to object, Barbara.

BARBARA. I! why should I? My father has a soul to be saved like anybody else. He's quite welcome as far as I am concerned. [*She sits on the table, and softly whistles "Onward Christian Soldiers"*].

LOMAX [*still remonstrant*] But really, dont you know! Oh I say!

LADY BRITOMART [*frigidly*] What do you wish to convey, Charles?

LOMAX. Well, you must admit that this is a bit thick.

LADY BRITOMART [*turning with ominous suavity to Cusins*] Adolphus: you are a professor of Greek. Can you translate Charles Lomax's remarks into reputable English for us?

CUSINS [*cautiously*] If I may say so, Lady Brit, I think Charles has rather happily expressed what we all feel. Homer, speaking of Autolycus, uses the same phrase. *πυχινὸν δόμον ἐλθεῖν* means a bit thick.

LOMAX [*handsomely*] Not that I mind, you know, if Sarah dont. [*He sits*].

LADY BRITOMART [*crushingly*] Thank you. Have I y o u r permission, Adolphus, to invite my own husband to my own house?

CUSINS [*gallantly*] You have my unhesitating support in everything you do.

LADY BRITOMART. Tush! Sarah: have you nothing to say?

SARAH. Do you mean that he is coming regularly to live here?

LADY BRITOMART. Certainly not. The spare room is ready for him if he likes to stay for a day or two and see a little more of you; but there are limits.

SARAH. Well, he cant eat us, I suppose. *I* dont mind.

LOMAX [*chuckling*] I wonder how the old man will take it.

LADY BRITOMART. Much as the old woman will, no doubt, Charles.

LOMAX [*abashed*] I didnt mean—at least—

LADY BRITOMART. You didnt t h i n k, Charles. You never do; and the result is, you never mean anything. And now please attend to me, children. Your father will be quite a stranger to us.

LOMAX. I suppose he hasnt seen Sarah since she was a little kid.

LADY BRITOMART. Not since she was a little kid, Charles, as you express it with that elegance of diction and refinement of thought that seem never to desert you. Accordingly—er—[*impatiently*] Now I have forgotten what I was going to say. That comes of your provoking me to be sarcastic, Charles. Adolphus: you will kindly tell me where I was.

CUSINS [*sweetly*] You were saying that as Mr Undershaft has not seen his children since they were babies, he will form his opinion of the way you have brought them up from their behavior tonight, and that therefore you wish us all to be particularly careful to conduct ourselves well, especially Charles.

LADY BRITOMART [*with emphatic approval*] Precisely.

LOMAX. Look here, Dolly: Lady Brit didnt say that.

LADY BRITOMART [*vehemently*] I did, Charles. Adolphus's recollection is perfectly correct. It is most important that you should be good; and I do beg you for once not to pair off into opposite corners and giggle and whisper while I am speaking to your father.

BARBARA. All right, mother. We'll do you credit. [*She comes off the table, and sits in her chair with ladylike elegance*].

LADY BRITOMART. Remember, Charles, that Sarah will want to feel proud of you instead of ashamed of you.

LOMAX. Oh I say! theres nothing to be exactly proud of, dont you know.

LADY BRITOMART. Well, try and look as if there was.

Morrison, pale and dismayed, breaks into the room in unconcealed disorder.

MORRISON. Might I speak a word to you, my lady?

LADY BRITOMART. Nonsense! Shew him up.

MORRISON. Yes, my lady. [*He goes*].

LOMAX. Does Morrison know who it is?

LADY BRITOMART. Of course. Morrison has always been with us.

LOMAX. It must be a regular corker for him, dont you know.

LADY BRITOMART. Is this a moment to get on my nerves, Charles, with your outrageous expressions?

LOMAX. But this is something out of the ordinary, really—

MORRISON [*at the door*] The—er—Mr Undershaft. [*He retreats in confusion*].

Andrew Undershaft comes in. All rise. Lady Britomart meets him in the middle of the room behind the settee.

Andrew is, on the surface, a stoutish, easygoing elderly man, with kindly patient manners, and an engaging simplicity of character. But he has a watchful, deliberate, waiting, listening face, and formidable reserves of power, both bodily and mental, in his capacious chest and long head. His gentleness is partly that of a strong man who has learnt by experience that his natural grip hurts ordinary people unless he handles them very carefully, and partly the mellowness of age and success. He is also a little shy in his present very delicate situation.

LADY BRITOMART. Good evening, Andrew.

UNDERSHAFT. How d'ye do, my dear.

LADY BRITOMART. You look a good deal older.

UNDERSHAFT [*apologetically*] I am somewhat older. [*Taking her hand with a touch of courtship*] Time has stood still with you.

LADY BRITOMART [*throwing away his hand*] Rubbish! This is your family.

UNDERSHAFT [*surprised*] Is it so large? I am sorry to say my memory is failing very badly in some things. [*He offers his hand with paternal kindness to Lomax*].

LOMAX [*jerkily shaking his hand*] Ahdedoo.

UNDERSHAFT. I can see you are my eldest. I am very glad to meet you again, my boy.

LOMAX [*remonstrating*] No, but look here dont you know– [*Overcome*] Oh I say!

LADY BRITOMART [*recovering from momentary speechlessness*] Andrew: do you mean to say that you dont remember how many children you have?

UNDERSHAFT. Well, I am afraid I–. They have grown so much–er. Am I making any ridiculous mistake? I may as well confess: I recollect only one son. But so many things have happened since, of course–er–

LADY BRITOMART [*decisively*] Andrew: you are talking nonsense. Of course you have only one son.

UNDERSHAFT. Perhaps you will be good enough to introduce me, my dear.

LADY BRITOMART. That is Charles Lomax, who is engaged to Sarah.

UNDERSHAFT. My dear sir, I beg your pardon.

LOMAX. Notatall. Delighted, I assure you.

LADY BRITOMART. This is Stephen.

UNDERSHAFT [*bowing*] Happy to make your acquaintance, Mr Stephen. Then [*going to Cusins*] *you* must be my son. [*Taking Cusins' hands in his*] How are you, my young friend? [*To Lady Britomart*] He is very like you, my love.

CUSINS. You flatter me, Mr Undershaft, My name is Cusins: engaged to Barbara. [*Very explicitly*] That is Major Barbara Undershaft, of the Salvation Army. That is Sarah, your second daughter. This is Stephen Undershaft, your son.

UNDERSHAFT. My dear Stephen, I b e g your pardon.

STEPHEN. Not at all.

UNDERSHAFT. Mr Cusins: I am much indebted to you for explaining so precisely. [*Turning to Sarah*] Barbara, my dear—

SARAH [*prompting him*] Sarah.

UNDERSHAFT. Sarah, of course. [*They shake hands. He goes over to Barbara*] Barbara—I am right this time, I hope?

BARBARA. Quite right. [*They shake hands*].

LADY BRITOMART [*resuming command*] Sit down, all of you. Sit down, Andrew. [*She comes forward and sits on the settee. Cusins also brings his chair forward on her left. Barbara and Stephen resume their seats. Lomax gives his chair to Sarah and goes for another*].

UNDERSHAFT. Thank you, my love.

LOMAX [*conversationally, as he brings a chair forward between the writing table and the settee, and offers it to Undershaft*] Takes you some time to find out exactly where you are, dont it?

UNDERSHAFT [*accepting the chair, but remaining standing*] That is not what embarrasses me, Mr Lomax. My difficulty is that if I play the part of a father, I shall produce the effect of an intrusive stranger; and if I play the part of a discreet stranger, I may appear a callous father.

LADY BRITOMART. There is no need for you to play any part at all, Andrew. You had much better be sincere and natural.

UNDERSHAFT [*submissively*] Yes, my dear: I daresay that will be best. [*He sits down comfortably*]. Well, here I am. Now what can I do for you all?

LADY BRITOMART. You need not do anything, Andrew. You are one of the family. You can sit with us and enjoy yourself.

A painfully conscious pause. Barbara makes a face at Lomax, whose too long suppressed mirth immediately explodes in agonized neighings.

LADY BRITOMART [*outraged*] Charles Lomax: if you can behave yourself, behave yourself. If not, leave the room.

LOMAX. I'm awfully sorry, Lady Brit; but really you know, upon my soul! [*He sits on the settee between Lady Britomart and Undershaft, quite overcome*].

BARBARA. Why dont you laugh if you want to, Cholly? It's good for your inside.

LADY BRITOMART. Barbara: you have had the education of a lady. Please let your father see that; and dont talk like a street girl.

UNDERSHAFT. Never mind me, my dear. As you know, I am not a gentleman; and I was never educated.

LOMAX [*encouragingly*] Nobody'd know it, I assure you. You look all right, you know.

CUSINS. Let me advise you to study Greek, Mr Undershaft. Greek scholars are privileged men. Few of them know Greek; and none of them know anything else; but their position is unchallengeable. Other languages are the qualifications of waiters and commercial travellers: Greek is to a man of position what the hallmark is to silver.

BARBARA. Dolly: dont be insincere. Cholly: fetch your concertina and play something for us.

LOMAX [*jumps up eagerly, but checks himself to remark doubtfully to Undershaft*] Perhaps that sort of thing isnt in your line, eh?

UNDERSHAFT. I am particularly fond of music.

LOMAX [*delighted*] Are you? Then I'll get it. [*He goes upstairs for the instrument*].

UNDERSHAFT. Do you play, Barbara?

BARBARA. Only the tambourine. But Cholly's teaching me the concertina.

UNDERSHAFT. Is Cholly also a member of the Salvation Army?

BARBARA. No: he says it's bad form to be a dissenter. But I dont despair of Cholly. I made him come yesterday to a meeting at the dock gates, and take the collection in his hat.

UNDERSHAFT [*looks whimsically at his wife*]!!

LADY BRITOMART. It is not my doing, Andrew. Barbara is old enough to take her own way. She has no father to advise her.

BARBARA. Oh yes she has. There are no orphans in the Salvation Army.

UNDERSHAFT. Your father there has a great many children and plenty of experience, eh?

BARBARA [*looking at him with quick interest and nodding*] Just so. How did y o u come to understand that? [*Lomax is heard at the door trying the concertina*].

LADY BRITOMART. Come in, Charles. Play us something at once.

LOMAX. Righto! [*He sits down in his former place, and preludes*].

UNDERSHAFT. One moment, Mr Lomax. I am rather interested in the Salvation Army. Its motto might be my own: Blood and Fire.

LOMAX [*shocked*] But not your sort of blood and fire, you know.

UNDERSHAFT. My sort of blood cleanses: my sort of fire purifies.

BARBARA. So do ours. Come down tomorrow to my shelter—the West Ham shelter—and see what we're doing. We're going to march to a great meeting in the Assembly Hall at Mile End. Come and see the shelter and then march with us: it will do you a lot of good. Can you play anything?

UNDERSHAFT. In my youth I earned pennies, and even shillings occasionally, in the streets and in public parlors by my natural talent for stepdancing. Later on, I became a member of the Undershaft orchestral society, and performed passably on the tenor trombone.

LOMAX [*scandalized—putting down the concertina*] Oh I say!

BARBARA. Many a sinner has played himself into heaven on the trombone, thanks to the Army.

LOMAX [*to Barbara, still rather shocked*] Yes; but what about the cannon business, dont you know? [*To Undershaft*] Getting into heaven is not exactly in your line, is it?

LADY BRITOMART. Charles!!!

LOMAX. Well; but it stands to reason, dont it? The cannon business may be necessary and all that: we cant get on without cannons; but it isnt right, you know. On the other hand, there may be a certain amount of tosh about the Salvation Army—I belong to the Established Church myself—but still you cant deny that it's religion; and you cant go against religion, can you? At least unless youre downright immoral, dont you know.

UNDERSHAFT. You hardly appreciate my position, Mr Lomax—

LOMAX [*hastily*] I'm not saying anything against you personally—

UNDERSHAFT. Quite so, quite so. But consider for a moment. Here I am, a profiteer in mutilation and murder. I find myself in a specially amiable humor just now because, this morning, down at the foundry, we blew twenty-seven dummy soldiers into fragments with a gun which formerly destroyed only thirteen.

LOMAX [*leniently*] Well, the more destructive war becomes, the sooner it will be abolished, eh?

UNDERSHAFT. Not at all. The more destructive war becomes the more fascinating we find it. No, Mr Lomax: I am obliged to you for making the usual excuse for my trade; but I am not ashamed of it. I am not one of those men who keep their morals and their business in watertight compartments. All the spare money my trade rivals spend on hospitals, cathedrals, and other receptacles for conscience money, I devote to experiments and researches in improved methods of destroying life and property. I have always done so; and I always shall. Therefore your Christmas card moralities of peace on earth and goodwill among men are of no use to me. Your Christianity, which enjoins you to resist not evil, and to turn the other cheek, would make *me* a bankrupt. *My* morality—*my* religion—must have a place for cannons and torpedoes in it.

STEPHEN [*coldly—almost sullenly*] You speak as if there were half a dozen moralities and religions to choose from, instead of one true morality and one true religion.

UNDERSHAFT. For me there is only one true morality; but it might not fit you, as you do not manufacture aerial battleships. There is only one true morality for every man; but every man has not the same true morality.

LOMAX [*overtaxed*] Would you mind saying that again? I didnt quite follow it.

CUSINS. It's quite simple. As Euripides says, one man's meat is another man's poison morally as well as physically.

UNDERSHAFT. Precisely.

LOMAX. Oh, *that*! Yes, yes, yes. True. True.

STEPHEN. In other words, some men are honest and some are scoundrels.

BARBARA. Bosh! There are no scoundrels.

UNDERSHAFT. Indeed? Are there any good men?

BARBARA. No. Not one. There are neither good men nor scoundrels: there are just children of one Father; and the sooner they stop calling one another names the better. You neednt talk to me: I know them. Ive had scores of them through my hands: scoundrels, criminals, infidels, philanthropists, missionaries, county councillors, all sorts. Theyre all just the same sort of sinner; and theres the same salvation ready for them all.

UNDERSHAFT. May I ask have you ever saved a maker of cannons?

BARBARA. No. Will you let me try?

UNDERSHAFT. Well, I will make a bargain with you. If I go to see you tomorrow in your Salvation Shelter, will you come the day after to see me in my cannon works?

BARBARA. Take care. It may end in your giving up the cannons for the sake of the Salvation Army.

UNDERSHAFT. Are you sure it will not end in your giving up the Salvation Army for the sake of the cannons?

BARBARA. I will take my chance of that.

UNDERSHAFT. And I will take my chance of the other. [*They shake hands on it*]. Where is your shelter?

BARBARA. In West Ham. At the sign of the cross. Ask anybody in Canning Town. Where are your works?

UNDERSHAFT. In Perivale St Andrews. At the sign of the sword. Ask anybody in Europe.

LOMAX. Hadnt I better play something?

BARBARA. Yes. Give us Onward, Christian Soldiers.

LOMAX. Well, thats rather a strong order to begin with, dont you know. Suppose I sing Thourt passing hence, my brother. It's much the same tune.

BARBARA. It's too melancholy. You get saved, Cholly; and youll pass hence, my brother, without making such a fuss about it.

LADY BRITOMART. Really, Barbara, you go on as if religion were a pleasant subject. Do have some sense of propriety.

UNDERSHAFT. I do not find it an unpleasant subject, my dear. It is the only one that capable people really care for.

LADY BRITOMART [*looking at her watch*] Well, if you are determined to have it, I insist on having it in a proper and respectable way. Charles: ring for prayers.

General amazement. Stephen rises in dismay.

LOMAX [*rising*] Oh I say!

UNDERSHAFT [*rising*] I am afraid I must be going.

LADY BRITOMART. You cannot go now, Andrew: it would be most improper. Sit down. What will the servants think?

UNDERSHAFT. My dear: I have conscientious scruples. May I suggest a compromise? If Barbara will conduct a little service in the drawing room, with Mr Lomax as organist, I will attend it willingly. I will even take part, if a trombone can be procured.

LADY BRITOMART. Dont mock, Andrew.

UNDERSHAFT [*shocked—to Barbara*] You dont think I am mocking, my love, I hope.

BARBARA. No, of course not; and it wouldnt matter if you were: half the Army came to their first meeting for a lark. [*Rising*] Come along. [*She throws her arm round her father and sweeps him out, calling to the others from the threshold*] Come, Dolly. Come, Cholly.

Cusins rises.

LADY BRITOMART. I will not be disobeyed by everybody. Adolphus: sit down. [*He does not*]. Charles: you may go. You are not fit for prayers: you cannot keep your countenance.

LOMAX. Oh I say! [*He goes out*].

LADY BRITOMART [*continuing*] But you, Adolphus, can behave yourself if you choose to. I insist on your staying.

CUSINS. My dear Lady Brit: there are things in the family prayer book that I couldnt bear to hear you say.

LADY BRITOMART. What things, pray?

CUSINS. Well, you would have to say before all the servants that we have done things we ought not to have done, and left undone things we ought to have done, and that there is no health in us. I cannot bear to hear you doing yourself such an injustice, and Barbara such an injustice. As for myself, I flatly deny it: I have done my best. I shouldnt dare to marry Barbara—I couldnt look you in the face—if it were true. So I must go to the drawing room.

LADY BRITOMART [*offended*] Well, go. [*He starts for the door*]. And remember this, Adolphus [*he turns to listen*]: I have a very strong suspicion that you went to the Salvation Army to worship Barbara and nothing else. And I quite appreciate the very clever way in which you systematically humbug me. I have found you out. Take care Barbara doesnt. Thats all.

CUSINS [*with unruffled sweetness*] Dont tell on me. [*He steals out*].

LADY BRITOMART. Sarah: if you want to go, go. Anything's better than to sit there as if you wished you were a thousand miles away.

SARAH [*languidly*] Very well, mamma. [*She goes*].

Lady Britomart, with a sudden flounce, gives way to a little gust of tears.

STEPHEN [*going to her*] Mother: whats the matter?

LADY BRITOMART [*swishing away her tears with her handkerchief*] Nothing! Foolishness. You can go with him, too, if you like, and leave me with the servants.

STEPHEN. Oh, you mustnt think that, mother. I—I dont like him.

LADY BRITOMART. The others do. That is the injustice of a woman's lot. A woman has to bring up her children; and that means to restrain them, to deny them things they want, to set them tasks, to punish them when they do wrong, to do all the unpleasant things. And the father, who has nothing to do but pet them and spoil them, comes in when all her work is done and steals their affection from her.

STEPHEN. He has not stolen our affection from you. It is only curiosity.

LADY BRITOMART [*violently*] I wont be consoled, Stephen. There is nothing the matter with me. [*She rises and goes towards the door*].

STEPHEN. Where are you going, mother?

LADY BRITOMART. To the drawing room, of course [*She goes out. Onward, Christian Soldiers, on the concertina, with tambourine accompaniment, is heard when the door opens*]. Are you coming, Stephen?

STEPHEN. No. Certainly not. [*She goes. He sits down on the settee, with compressed lips and an expression of strong dislike*].

ACT II

The yard of the West Ham shelter of the Salvation Army is a cold place on a January morning. The building itself, an old warehouse, is newly whitewashed. Its gabled end projects into the yard in the middle, with a door on the ground floor, and another in the loft above it without any balcony or ladder, but with a pulley rigged over it for hoisting sacks. Those who come from this central gable end into the yard have the gateway leading to the street on their left, with a stone horse-trough just beyond it, and, on the right, a penthouse shielding a table from the weather. There are forms at the table; and on them are seated a man and a woman, both much down on their luck, finishing a meal of bread (one thick slice each, with margarine and golden syrup) and diluted milk.

The man, a workman out of employment, is young, agile, a talker, a poser, sharp enough to be capable of anything in reason except honesty or altruistic considerations of any kind. The woman is a commonplace old bundle of poverty and hard-worn humanity. She looks sixty and is probably forty-five. If they were rich people, gloved and muffed and well wrapped up in furs and overcoats, they would be numbed and miserable; for it is a grindingly cold raw January day; and a glance at the background of grimy warehouses and leaden sky visible over the whitewashed walls of the yard would drive any idle rich person straight to the Mediterranean. But these two, being no more troubled with visions of the Mediterranean than of the moon, and being compelled to keep more of their clothes in the pawnship, and less on their persons, in winter than in summer, are not depressed by the cold: rather are they stung into vivacity, to which their meal has just now given an almost jolly turn. The man takes a pull at his mug, and then gets up and moves about the yard with his hands deep in his pockets, occasionally breaking into a stepdance.

THE WOMAN. Feel better arter your meal, sir?

THE MAN. No. Call that a meal! Good enough for you, praps; but wot is it to me, an intelligent workin man.

THE WOMAN. Workin man! Wot are you?

THE MAN. Painter.

THE WOMAN [*sceptically*] Yus, I dessay.

THE MAN. Yus, you dessay! I know. Every loafer that cant do nothink calls isself a painter. Well, I'm a real painter: grainer, finisher, thirty-eight bob a week when I can get it.

THE WOMAN. Then why dont you go and get it?

THE MAN. I'll tell you why. Fust: I'm intelligent—fffff! it's rotten cold here [*he dances a step or two*]—yes: intelligent beyond the station o life into which it has pleased the capitalists to call me; and they dont like a man that sees through em. Second, an intelligent bein needs a doo share of appiness; so I drink somethink cruel when I get the chawnce. Third, I stand by my class and do as little as I can so's to leave arf the job for me fellow workers. Fourth, I'm fly enough to know wots inside the law and wots outside it; and inside it I do as the capitalists do: pinch wot I can lay me ands on. In a proper state of society I am sober, industrious and honest: in Rome, so to speak, I do as the Romans do. Wots the consequence? When trade is bad—and it's rotten bad just now—and the employers az to sack arf their men, they generally start on me.

THE WOMAN. Whats your name?

THE MAN. Price. Bronterre O'Brien Price. Usually called Snobby Price, for short.

THE WOMAN. Snobby's a carpenter, aint it? You said you was a painter.

PRICE. Not that kind of snob, but the genteel sort. I'm too uppish, owing to my intelligence, and my father being a Chartist and a reading, thinking man: a stationer, too. I'm none of your common hewers of wood and drawers of water; and dont you forget it. [*He returns to his seat at the table, and takes up his mug*]. Wots y o u r name?

THE WOMAN. Rummy Mitchens, sir.

PRICE [*quaffing the remains of his milk to her*] Your elth, Miss Mitchens.

RUMMY [*correcting him*] Missis Mitchens.

PRICE. Wot! Oh Rummy, Rummy! Respectable married woman, Rummy, gittin rescued by the Salvation Army by pretendin to be a bad un. Same old game!

RUMMY. What am I to do? I cant starve. Them Salvation lasses is dear good girls; but the better you are, the worse they likes to think you were before they rescued you. Why shouldnt they av a bit o credit, poor loves? theyre worn to rags by their work. And where would they get the money to rescue us if we was to let on we're no worse than other people? You know what ladies and gentlemen are.

PRICE. Thievin swine! Wish I ad their job, Rummy, all the same. Wot does Rummy stand for? Pet name praps?

RUMMY. Short for Romola.

PRICE. For wot!?

RUMMY. Romola. It was out of a new book. Somebody me mother wanted me to grow up like.

PRICE. We're companions in misfortune, Rummy. Both on us got names that nobody cawnt pronounce. Consequently I'm Snobby and youre Rummy because Bill and Sally wasnt good enough for our parents. Such is life!

RUMMY. Who saved you, Mr Price? Was it Major Barbara?

PRICE. No: I come here on my own. I'm going to be Bronterre O'Brien Price, the converted painter. I know wot they like. I'll tell em how I blasphemed and gambled and wopped my poor old mother—

RUMMY [*shocked*] Used you to beat your mother?

PRICE. Not likely. She used to beat me. No matter: you come and listen to the converted painter, and youll hear how she was a pious woman that taught me me prayers at er knee, an how I used to come home drunk and drag her out o bed be er snow white airs, an lam into er with the poker.

RUMMY. Thats whats so unfair to us women. Your confessions is just as big lies as ours: you dont tell what you really done no more than us; but you men can tell your lies right out at the meetins and be made much of for it; while the sort o confessions we az to make az to be wispered to one lady at a time. It aint right, spite of all their piety.

PRICE. Right! Do you spose the Army'd be allowed if it went and did right? Not much. It combs our air and makes us good little blokes to be robbed and put upon. But I'll play the game as good as any of em. I'll see somebody struck by lightnin, or hear a voice sayin "Snobby Price: where will you spend eternity?" I'll av a time of it, I tell you.

RUMMY. You wont be let drink, though.

PRICE. I'll take it out in gorspellin, then. I dont want to drink if I can get fun enough any other way.

Jenny Hill, a pale, overwrought, pretty Salvation lass of 18, comes in through the yard gate, leading Peter Shirley, a half hardened, half worn-out elderly man, weak with hunger.

JENNY [*supporting him*] Come! pluck up. I'll get you something to eat. Youll be all right then.

PRICE [*rising and hurrying officiously to take the old man off Jenny's hands*] Poor old man! Cheer up, brother: youll find rest and peace and appiness ere. Hurry up with the food, miss: e's fair done. [*Jenny hurries into the shelter*]. Ere, buck up, daddy! she's fetchin y'a thick slice o breadn treacle an a mug o skyblue. [*He seats him at the corner of the table*].

RUMMY [*gaily*] Keep up your old art! Never say die!

SHIRLEY. I'm not an old man. I'm only 46. I'm as good as ever I was. The grey patch come in my hair before I was thirty. All it wants is three pennorth o hair dye: am I to be turned on the streets to starve for it? Holy God! Ive worked ten to twelve hours a day since I was thirteen, and paid my way all through; and now am I to be thrown into the gutter and my job given to a young man that can do it no better than me because Ive black hair that goes white at the first change?

PRICE [*cheerfully*] No good jawrin about it. Youre ony a jumped-up, jerked-off, orspittle-turned-out incurable of an ole workin man: who cares about you? Eh? Make the thievin swine give you a meal: theyve stole many a one from you. Get a bit o your own back. [*Jenny returns with the usual meal*]. There you are, brother. Awsk a blessin an tuck that into you.

SHIRLEY [*looking at it ravenously but not touching it, and crying like a child*] I never took anything before.

JENNY [*petting him*] Come, come! the Lord sends it to you: he wasnt above taking bread from his friends; and why should you be? Besides, when we find you a job you can pay us for it if you like.

SHIRLEY [*eagerly*] Yes, yes: thats true. I can pay you back: it's only a loan. [*Shivering*] Oh Lord! oh Lord! [*He turns to the table and attacks the meal ravenously*].

JENNY. Well, Rummy, are you more comfortable now?

RUMMY. God bless you, lovey! youve fed my body and saved my soul, havnt you? [*Jenny, touched, kisses her*]. Sit down and rest a bit: you must be ready to drop.

JENNY. Ive been going hard since morning. But theres more work than we can do. I mustnt stop.

RUMMY. Try a prayer for just two minutes. Youll work all the better after.

JENNY [*her eyes lighting up*] Oh isnt it wonderful how a few minutes prayer revives you! I was quite light-headed at twelve o'clock, I was so tired; but Major Barbara just sent me to pray for five minutes; and

I was able to go on as if I had only just begun. [*To Price*] Did you have a piece of bread?

PRICE [*with unction*] Yes, miss; but Ive got the piece that I value more; and thats the peace that passeth hall hannerstennin.

RUMMY [*fervently*] Glory Hallelujah!

Bill Walker, a rough customer of about 25, appears at the yard gate and looks malevolently at Jenny.

JENNY. That makes me so happy. When you say that, I feel wicked for loitering here. I must get to work again.

She is hurrying to the shelter, when the new-comer moves quickly up to the door and intercepts her. His manner is so threatening that she retreats as he comes at her truculently, driving her down the yard.

BILL. Aw knaow you. Youre the one that took awy maw girl. Youre the one that set er agen me. Well, I'm gowin to ev er aht. Not that Aw care a carse for er or you: see? Bat Aw'll let er knaow; and Aw'll let you knaow. Aw'm gowing to give her a doin thatll teach er to cat awy from me. Nah in wiv you and tell er to cam aht afore Aw cam in and kick er aht. Tell er Bill Walker wants er. She'll knaow wot thet means; and if she keeps me witin itll be worse. You stop to jawr beck at me; and Aw'll stawt on you: d'ye eah? Theres your wy. In you gow. [*He takes her by the arm and slings her towards the door of the shelter. She falls on her hand and knee. Rummy helps her up again*].

PRICE [*rising, and venturing irresolutely towards Bill*] Easy there, mate. She aint doin you no arm.

BILL. Oo are you callin mite? [*Standing over him threateningly*] Youre gowin to stend ap for er, aw yer? Put ap your ends.

RUMMY [*running indignantly to scold him*] Oh, you great brute—[*He instantly swings his left hand back against her face. She screams and reels back to the trough, where she sits down, covering her bruised face with her hands and rocking herself and moaning with pain*]

JENNY [*going to her*] Oh, God forgive you! How could you strike an old woman like that?

BILL [*seizing her by the hair so violently that she also screams, and tearing her away from the old woman*] You Gawd forgimme again an Aw'll Gawd forgive you one on the jawr thetll stop you pryin for a week. [*Holding her and turning fiercely on Price*] Ev you ennything to sy agen it?

PRICE [*intimidated*] No, matey: she aint anything to do with me.

BILL. Good job for you! Aw'd pat two meals into you and fawt you with one finger arter, you stawvved cur. [*To Jenny*] Nah are you gowin to fetch aht Mog Ebbijen; or em Aw to knock your fice off you and fetch her meself?

JENNY [*writhing in his grasp*] Oh please someone go in and tell Major Barbara—[*she screams again as he wrenches her head down; and Price and Rummy flee into the shelter*].

BILL. You want to gow in and tell your Mijor of me, do you?

JENNY. Oh please dont drag my hair. Let me go.

BILL. Do you or downt you? [*She stifles a scream*]. Yus or nao?

JENNY. God give me strength—

BILL [*striking her with his fist in the face*] Gow an shaow her thet, and tell her if she wants one lawk it to cam and interfere with me. [*Jenny, crying with pain, goes into the shed. He goes to the form and addresses the old man*]. Eah: finish your mess; an git aht o maw wy.

SHIRLEY [*springing up and facing him fiercely, with the mug in his hand*] You take a liberty with me, and I'll smash you over the face with the mug and cut your eye out. Aint you satisfied—young whelps like you—with takin the bread out o the mouths of your elders that have brought you up and slaved for you, but you must come shovin and cheekin and bullyin in here, where the bread of charity is sickenin in our stummicks?

BILL [*contemptuously, but backing a little*] Wot good are you, you aold palsy mag? Wot good are you?

SHIRLEY. As good as you and better. I'll do a day's work agen you or any fat young soaker of your age. Go and take my job at Horrockses, where I worked for ten year. They want young men there: they cant afford to keep men over forty-five. Theyre very sorry—give you a character and happy to help you to get anything suited to your years—sure a steady man wont be long out of a job. Well, let em try y o u. Theyll find the differ. What do y o u know? Not as much as how to beeyave yourself—layin your dirty fist across the mouth of a respectable woman!

BILL. Downt provowk me to ly it acrost yours: d'ye eah?

SHIRLEY [*with blighting contempt*] Yes: you like an old man to hit, dont you, when youve finished with the women. I aint seen you hit a young one yet.

BILL [*stung*] You loy, you aold soupkitchener, you. There was a yang menn eah. Did Aw offer to itt him or did Aw not?

SHIRLEY. Was he starvin or was he not? Was he a man or only a cross-eyed thief an a loafer? Would you hit my son-in-law's brother?

BILL. Oo's ee?

SHIRLEY. Todger Fairmile o Balls Pond. Him that won £20 off the Japanese wrastler at the music hall by standin out 17 minutes 4 seconds agen him.

BILL [*sullenly*] Aw'm nao music awl wrastler. Ken he box?

SHIRLEY. Yes: an you cant.

BILL. Wot! Aw cawnt, cawnt Aw? Wots thet you sy [*threatening him*]?

SHIRLEY [*not budging an inch*] Will you box Todger Fairmile if I put him on to you? Say the word.

BILL [*subsiding with a slouch*] Aw'll stend ap to enny menn alawv, if he was ten Todger Fairmawls. But Aw dont set ap to be a perfeshnal.

SHIRLEY [*looking down on him with unfathomable disdain*] You box! Slap an old woman with the back o your hand! You hadnt even the sense to hit her where a magistrate couldnt see the mark of it, you silly young lump of conceit and ignorance. Hit a girl in the jaw and ony make her cry! If Todger Fairmile'd done it, she wouldnt a got up inside o ten minutes, no more than you would if he got on to you. Yah! I'd set about you myself if I had a week's feedin in me instead o two months' starvation. [*He turns his back on him and sits down moodily at the table*].

BILL [*following him and stooping over him to drive the taunt in*] You loy! youve the bread and treacle in you that you cam eah to beg.

SHIRLEY [*bursting into tears*] Oh God! it's true: I'm only an old pauper on the scrap heap. [*Furiously*] But youll come to it yourself; and then youll know. Youll come to it sooner than a teetotaller like me, fillin yourself with gin at this hour o the mornin!

BILL. Aw'm nao gin drinker, you oald lawr; bat wen Aw want to give my girl a bloomin good awdin Aw lawk to ev a bit o devil in me: see? An eah Aw emm, talkin to a rotten aold blawter like you sted o givin her wot for. [*Working himself into a rage*] Aw'm gowin in there to fetch her aht. [*He makes vengefully for the shelter door*].

SHIRLEY. Youre goin to the station on a stretcher, more likely; and theyll take the gin and the devil out of you there when they get you inside. You mind what youre about: the major here is the Earl o Stevenage's granddaughter.

BILL [*checked*] Garn!

SHIRLEY. Youll see.

BILL [*his resolution oozing*] Well, Aw aint dan nathin to er.

SHIRLEY. Spose she said you did! who'd believe you?

BILL [*very uneasy, skulking back to the corner of the penthouse*]

Gawd! theres no jastice in this cantry. To think wot them people can do! Aw'm as good as er.

SHIRLEY. Tell her so. It's just what a fool like you would do.

Barbara, brisk and businesslike, comes from the shelter with a note book, and addresses herself to Shirley. Bill, cowed, sits down in the corner on a form, and turns his back on them.

BARBARA. Good morning.

SHIRLEY [*standing up and taking off his hat*] Good morning, miss.

BARBARA. Sit down: make yourself at home. [*He hesitates; but she puts a friendly hand on his shoulder and makes him obey.*] Now then! since youve made friends with us, we want to know all about you. Names and addresses and trades.

SHIRLEY. Peter Shirley. Fitter. Chucked out two months ago because I was too old.

BARBARA [*not at all surprised*] Youd pass still. Why didnt you dye your hair?

SHIRLEY. I did. Me age come out at a coroner's inquest on me daughter.

BARBARA. Steady?

SHIRLEY. Teetotaller. Never out of a job before. Good worker. And sent to the knackers like an old horse!

BARBARA. No matter: if you did your part God will do his.

SHIRLEY [*suddenly stubborn*] My religion's no concern of anybody but myself.

BARBARA [*guessing*] *I* know. Secularist?

SHIRLEY [*hotly*] Did I offer to deny it?

BARBARA. Why should you? My own father's a Secularist, I think. Our Father—yours and mine—fulfils himself in many ways; and I daresay he knew what he was about when he made a Secularist of you. So buck up, Peter! we can always find a job for a steady man like you. [*Shirley, disarmed and a little bewildered, touches his hat. She turns from him to Bill*]. Whats y o u r name?

BILL [*insolently*] Wots thet to you?

BARBARA [*calmly making a note*] Afraid to give his name. Any trade?

BILL. Oo's afride to give is nime? [*Doggedly, with a sense of heroically defying the House of Lords in the person of Lord Stevenage*] If you want to bring a chawge agen me, bring it. [*She waits, unruffled*]. Moy nime's Bill Walker.

BARBARA [*as if the name were familiar: trying to remember how*] Bill Walker? [*Recollecting*] Oh, I know: youre the man that Jenny Hill was praying for inside just now. [*She enters his name in her note book*].

BILL. Oo's Jenny Ill? And wot call as she to pry for me?

BARBARA. I dont know. Perhaps it was you that cut her lip.

BILL [*defiantly*] Yus, it w a s me that cat her lip. Aw aint afride o y o u.

BARBARA. How could you be, since youre not afraid of God? Youre a brave man, Mr Walker. It takes some pluck to do o u r work here; but none of us dare lift our hand against a girl like that, for fear of her father in heaven.

BILL [*sullenly*] I want nan o your kentin jawr. I spowse you think Aw cam eah to beg from you, like this demmiged lot eah. Not me. Aw downt want your bread and scripe and ketlep. Aw dont blieve in your Gawd, no more than you do yourself.

BARBARA [*sunnily apologetic and ladylike, as on a new footing with him*] Oh, I beg your pardon for putting your name down, Mr Walker. I didnt understand. I'll strike it out.

BILL [*taking this as a slight, and deeply wounded by it*] Eah! you let maw nime alown. Aint it good enaff to be in your book?

BARBARA [*considering*] Well, you see, theres no use putting down your name unless I can do something for you, is there? Whats your trade?

BILL [*still smarting*] Thets nao concern o yours.

BARBARA. Just so. [*Very businesslike*] I'll put you down as [*writing*] the man who—struck—poor little Jenny Hill—in the mouth.

BILL [*rising threateningly*] See eah. Awve ed enaff o this.

BARBARA [*quite sunny and fearless*] What did you come to us for?

BILL. Aw cam for maw gel, see? Aw cam to tike her aht o this and to brike er jawr for er.

BARBARA [*complacently*] You see I was right about your trade. [*Bill, on the point of retorting furiously, finds himself, to his great shame and terror, in danger of crying instead. He sits down again suddenly*]. Whats her name?

BILL [*dogged*] Er nime's Mog Ebbijem: thets wot her nime is.

BARBARA. Mog Habbijam! Oh, she's gone to Canning Town, to our barracks there.

BILL [*fortified by his resentment of Mog's perfidy*] Is she? [*Vindictively*] Then Aw'm gowin to Kennintahn arter her. [*He crosses to the gate; hesitates; finally comes back at Barbara*]. Are you loyin to me to git shat o me?

BARBARA. I dont want to get shut of you. I want to keep you here and save your soul. Youd better stay: youre going to have a bad time today, Bill.

BILL. Oo's gowin to give it to me? Y o u, preps?

BARBARA. Someone you dont believe in. But youll be glad afterwards.

BILL [*slinking off*] Aw'll gow to Kennintahn to be aht o reach o your tangue. [*Suddenly turning on her with intense malice*] And if Aw downt fawnd Mog there, Aw'll cam beck and do two years for you, selp me Gawd if Aw downt!

BARBARA [*a shade kindlier, if possible*] It's no use, Bill. She's got another bloke.

BILL. Wot!

BARBARA. One of her own converts. He fell in love with her when he saw her with her soul saved, and her face clean, and her hair washed.

BILL [*surprised*] Wottud she wash it for, the carroty slat? It's red.

BARBARA. It's quite lovely now, because she wears a new look in her eyes with it. It's a pity youre too late. The new bloke has put your nose out of joint, Bill.

BILL. Aw'll put his nowse aht o joint for him. Not that Aw care a carse for er, mawnd thet. But Aw'll teach her to drop me as if Aw was dirt. And Aw'll teach him to meddle with maw judy. Wots iz bleedin nime?

BARBARA. Sergeant Todger Fairmile.

SHIRLEY [*rising with grim joy*] I'll go with him, miss. I want to see them two meet. I'll take him to the infirmary when it's over.

BILL [*to Shirley, with undissembled misgiving*] Is thet im you was speakin on?

SHIRLEY. Thats him.

BILL. Im that wrastled in the music awl?

SHIRLEY. The competitions at the National Sportin Club was worth nigh a hundred a year to him. He's gev em up now for religion; so he's a bit fresh for want of the exercise he was accustomed to. He'll be glad to see you. Come along.

BILL. Wots is wight?

SHIRLEY. Thirteen four. [*Bill's last hope expires*].

BARBARA. Go and talk to him, Bill. He'll convert you.

SHIRLEY. He'll convert your head into a mashed potato.

BILL [*sullenly*] Aw aint afride of im. Aw aint afride of ennybody Bat e can lick me. She's dan me. [*He sits down moodily on the edge of the horse trough*].

SHIRLEY. You aint goin. I thought not. [*He resumes his seat*].

BARBARA [*calling*] Jenny!

JENNY [*appearing at the shelter door with a plaster on the corner of her mouth*] Yes, Major.

BARBARA. Send Rummy Mitchens out to clear away here.

JENNY. I think she's afraid.

BARBARA [*her resemblance to her mother flashing out for a moment*] Nonsense! she must do as she's told.

JENNY [*calling into the shelter*] Rummy: the Major says you must come.

Jenny comes to Barbara, purposely keeping on the side next Bill, lest he should suppose that she shrank from him or bore malice.

BARBARA. Poor little Jenny! Are you tired? [*Looking at the wounded cheek*] Does it hurt?

JENNY. No: it's all right now. It was nothing.

BARBARA [*critically*] It was as hard as he could hit, I expect. Poor Bill! You dont feel angry with him, do you?

JENNY. Oh no, no, no: indeed I dont, Major, bless his poor heart! [*Barbara kisses her; and she runs away merrily into the shelter. Bill writhes with an agonizing return of his new and alarming symptoms, but says nothing. Rummy Mitchens comes from the shelter*].

BARBARA [*going to meet Rummy*] Now Rummy, bustle. Take in those mugs and plates to be washed; and throw the crumbs about for the birds.

Rummy takes the three plates and mugs; but Shirley takes back his mug from her, as there is still some milk left in it.

RUMMY. There aint any crumbs. This aint a time to waste good bread on birds.

PRICE [*appearing at the shelter door*] Gentleman come to see the shelter, Major. Says he's your father.

BARBARA. All right. Coming [*Snobby goes back into the shelter, followed by Barbara*].

RUMMY [*stealing across to Bill and addressing him in a subdued voice, but with intense conviction*] I'd av the lor of you, you flat eared pignosed potwalloper, if she'd let me. Youre no gentleman, to hit a lady in the face. [*Bill, with greater things moving in him, takes no notice*].

SHIRLEY [*following her*] Here! in with you and dont get yourself into more trouble by talking.

RUMMY [*with hauteur*] I aint ad the pleasure o being hintroduced to you, as I can remember. [*She goes into the shelter with the plates*].

SHIRLEY. Thats the—

BILL [*savagely*] Downt you talk to me, d'ye eah? You lea me alown, or Aw'll do you a mischief. Aw'm not dirt under y o u r feet, ennywy.

SHIRLEY [*calmly*] Dont you be afeerd. You aint such prime company that you need expect to be sought after. [*He is about to go into the shelter when Barbara comes out, with Undershaft on her right*].

BARBARA. Oh, there you are, Mr Shirley! [*Between them*] This is my father: I told you he was a Secularist, didnt I? Perhaps youll be able to comfort one another.

UNDERSHAFT [*startled*] A Secularist! Not the least in the world: on the contrary, a confirmed mystic.

BARBARA. Sorry, I'm sure. By the way, papa, what is your religion? in case I have to introduce you again.

UNDERSHAFT. My religion? Well, my dear, I am a Millionaire. That is my religion.

BARBARA. Then I'm afraid you and Mr Shirley wont be able to comfort one another after all. Youre not a Millionaire, are you, Peter?

SHIRLEY. No; and proud of it.

UNDERSHAFT [*gravely*] Poverty, my friend, is not a thing to be proud of.

SHIRLEY [*angrily*] Who made your millions for you? Me and my like. Whats kep us poor? Keepin you rich. I wouldnt have your conscience, not for all your income.

UNDERSHAFT. I wouldnt have your income, not for all your conscience, Mr Shirley. [*He goes to the penthouse and sits down on a form*].

BARBARA [*stopping Shirley adroitly as he is about to retort*] You wouldnt think he was my father, would you, Peter? Will you go into the shelter and lend the lasses a hand for a while: we're worked off our feet.

SHIRLEY [*bitterly*] Yes: I'm in their debt for a meal, aint I?

BARBARA. Oh, not because youre in their debt, but for love of them, Peter, for love of them. [*He cannot understand, and is rather scandalized*] There! dont stare at me. In with you; and give that conscience of yours a holiday [*bustling him into the shelter*].

SHIRLEY [*as he goes in*] Ah! it's a pity you never was trained to use your reason, miss. Youd have been a very taking lecturer on Secularism.

Barbara turns to her father.

UNDERSHAFT. Never mind me, my dear. Go about your work; and let me watch it for a while.

BARBARA. All right.

UNDERSHAFT. For instance, whats the matter with that outpatient over there?

BARBARA [*looking at Bill, whose attitude has never changed, and whose expression of brooding wrath has deepened*] Oh, we shall cure him in no time. Just watch [*She goes over to Bill and waits. He glances up at her and casts his eyes down again, uneasy, but grimmer than ever*]. It w o u l d be nice to just stamp on Mog Habbijam's face, wouldnt it, Bill?

BILL [*starting up from the trough in consternation*] It's a loy: Aw never said so. [*She shakes her head*]. Oo taold you wot was in moy mawnd?

BARBARA. Only your new friend.

BILL. Wot new friend?

BARBARA. The devil, Bill. When he gets round people they get miserable, just like you.

BILL [*with a heartbreaking attempt at devil-may-care cheerfulness*] Aw aint miserable. [*He sits down again, and stretches his legs in an attempt to seem indifferent*].

BARBARA. Well, if youre happy, why dont you look happy, as we do?

BILL [*his legs curling back in spite of him*] Aw'm eppy enaff, Aw tell you. Woy cawnt you lea me alown? Wot ev I dan to y o u? Aw aint smashed y o u r fice, ev Aw?

BARBARA [*softly: wooing his soul*] It's not me thats getting at you, Bill.

BILL. Oo else is it?

BARBARA. Somebody that doesnt intend you to smash women's faces, I suppose. Somebody or something that wants to make a man of you.

BILL [*blustering*] Mike a menn o m e. Aint Aw a menn? eh? Oo sez Aw'm not a menn?

BARBARA. Theres a man in you somewhere, I suppose. But why did he let you hit poor little Jenny Hill? That wasnt very manly of him, was it?

BILL [*tormented*] Ev dan wiv it, Aw tell you. Chack it. Aw'm sick o your Jenny Ill and er silly little fice.

BARBARA. Then why do you keep thinking about it? Why does it keep coming up against you in your mind? Youre not getting converted, are you?

BILL [*with conviction*] Not M E. Not lawkly.

BARBARA. Thats right, Bill. Hold out against it. Put out your strength. Dont lets get you cheap. Todger Fairmile said he wrestled for three nights against his salvation harder than he ever wrestled with the Jap at the music hall. He gave in to the Jap when his arm was going to break. But he didnt give in to his salvation until his heart was going to break. Perhaps youll escape that. You havnt any heart, have you?

BILL. Wot d'ye mean? Woy aint Aw got a awt the sime as ennybody else?

BARBARA. A man with a heart wouldnt have bashed poor little Jenny's face, would he?

BILL [*almost crying*] Ow, will you lea me alown? Ev Aw ever offered to meddle with you, that you cam neggin and provowkin me lawk this? [*He writhes convulsively from his eyes to his toes*].

BARBARA [*with a steady soothing hand on his arm and a gentle voice that never lets him go*] It's your soul thats hurting you, Bill, and not me. Weve been through it all ourselves. Come with us, Bill. [*He looks wildly round*]. To brave manhood on earth and eternal glory in heaven. [*He is on the point of breaking down*]. Come. [*A drum is heard in the shelter; and Bill, with a gasp, escapes from the spell as Barbara turns quickly. Adolphus enters from the shelter with a big drum*]. Oh! there you are, Dolly. Let me introduce a new friend of mine, Mr Bill Walker. This is my bloke, Bill: Mr Cusins. [*Cusins salutes with his drumstick*].

BILL. Gowin to merry im?

BARBARA. Yes.

BILL [*fervently*] Gawd elp im! Gaw-aw-aw-awd elp im!

BARBARA. Why? Do you think he wont be happy with me?

BILL. Awve aony ed to stend it for a mawnin: e'll ev to stend it for a lawftawm.

CUSINS. That is a frightful reflection, Mr Walker. But I cant tear myself away from her.

BILL. Well, Aw ken. [*To Barbara*] Eah! do you knaow where Aw'm gowin to, and wot Aw'm gowin to do?

BARBARA. Yes: youre going to heaven; and youre coming back here before the week's out to tell me so.

BILL. You loy. Aw'm gowin to Kennintahn, to spit in Todger Fairmawl's eye. Aw beshed Jenny Ill's fice; an nar Aw'll git me aown fice beshed and cam beck and shaow it to er. Ee'll itt me ardern Aw itt er. Thatll mike us square. [*To Adolphus*] Is thet fair or is it not? Youre a genlmn: you oughter knaow.

BARBARA. Two black eyes wont make one white one, Bill.

BILL. Aw didnt awst you. Cawnt you never keep your mahth shat? Oy awst the genlmn.

CUSINS [*reflectively*] Yes: I think youre right, Mr Walker. Yes: I should do it. It's curious: it's exactly what an ancient Greek would have done.

BARBARA. But what good will it do?

CUSINS. Well, it will give Mr Fairmile some exercise; and it will satisfy Mr Walker's soul.

BILL. Rot! there aint nao sach a thing as a saoul. Ah kin you tell wevver Awve a saoul or not? You never seen it.

BARBARA. Ive seen it hurting you when you went against it.

BILL [*with compressed aggravation*] If you was maw gel and took the word aht o me mahth lawk thet, Aw'd give you sathink youd feel urtin, Aw would. [*To Adolphus*] You tike maw tip, mite. Stop er jawr; or youll doy afoah your tawn [*With intense expression*] Wore aht: thets wot youll be: wore aht. [*He goes away through the gate*].

CUSINS [*looking after him*] I wonder!

BARBARA. Dolly! [*indignant, in her mother's manner*].

CUSINS. Yes, my dear, it's very wearing to be in love with you. If it lasts, I quite think I shall die young.

BARBARA. Should you mind?

CUSINS. Not at all. [*He is suddenly softened, and kisses her over the drum, evidently not for the first time, as people cannot kiss over a big drum without practice. Undershaft coughs*].

BARBARA. It's all right, papa, weve not forgotten you. Dolly: explain the place to papa: I havnt time. [*She goes busily into the shelter*].

Undershaft and Adolphus now have the yard to themselves. Undershaft, seated on a form, and still keenly attentive, looks hard at Adolphus. Adolphus looks hard at him.

UNDERSHAFT. I fancy you guess something of what is in my mind, Mr Cusins. [*Cusins flourishes his drumsticks as if in the act of beating a lively rataplan, but makes no sound.* Exactly so. But suppose Barbara finds you out!

CUSINS. You know, I do not admit that I am imposing on Barbara. I am quite genuinely interested in the views of the Salvation Army. The fact is, I am a sort of collector of religions; and the curious thing is that I find I can believe them all. By the way, have you any religion?

UNDERSHAFT. Yes.

CUSINS. Anything out of the common?

UNDERSHAFT. Only that there are two things necessary to Salvation.

CUSINS [*disappointed, but polite*] Ah, the Church Catechism. Charles Lomax also belongs to the Established Church.

UNDERSHAFT. The two things are—

CUSINS. Baptism and—

UNDERSHAFT. No. Money and gunpowder.

CUSINS [*surprised, but interested*] That is the general opinion of our governing classes. The novelty is in hearing any man confess it.

UNDERSHAFT. Just so.

CUSINS. Excuse me: is there any place in your religion for honor, justice, truth, love, mercy and so forth?

UNDERSHAFT. Yes: they are the graces and luxuries of a rich, strong, and safe life.

CUSINS. Suppose one is forced to choose between them and money or gunpowder?

UNDERSHAFT. Choose money a n d gunpowder; for without enough of both you cannot afford the others.

CUSINS. That is your religion?

UNDERSHAFT. Yes.

The cadence of this reply makes a full close in the conversation. Cusins twists his face dubiously and contemplates Undershaft. Undershaft contemplates him.

CUSINS. Barbara wont stand that. You will have to choose between your religion and Barbara.

UNDERSHAFT. So will you, my friend. She will find out that that drum of yours is hollow.

CUSINS. Father Undershaft: you are mistaken: I am a sincere Salvationist. You do not understand the Salvation Army. It is the army of joy, of love, of courage: it has banished the fear and remorse and despair of the old hell-ridden evangelical sects: it marches to fight the devil with trumpet and drum, with music and dancing, with banner and palm, as becomes a sally from heaven by its happy garrison. It picks the waster out of the public house and makes a man of him: it finds a worm wriggling in a back kitchen, and lo! a woman! Men and women of rank too, sons and daughters of the Highest. It takes the poor professor of Greek, the most artificial and self-suppressed of human creatures, from his meal of roots, and lets loose the rhapsodist in him; reveals the true worship of Dionysos to him; sends him down the public street drumming dithyrambs [*he plays a thundering flourish on the drum*].

UNDERSHAFT. You will alarm the shelter.

CUSINS. Oh, they are accustomed to these sudden ecstasies. However, if the drum worries you—[*he pockets the drumsticks; unhooks the drum; and stands it on the ground opposite the gateway*].

UNDERSHAFT. Thank you.

CUSINS. You remember what Euripides says about your money and gunpowder?

UNDERSHAFT. No.

CUSINS [*declaiming*]

One and another
In money and guns may outpass his brother;
And men in their millions float and flow
And seethe with a million hopes as leaven;
And they win their will; or they miss their will;
And their hopes are dead or are pined for still;
But whoe'er can know
As the long days go
That to live is happy, has found h i s heaven.

My translation: what do you think of it?

UNDERSHAFT. I think, my friend, that if you wish to know, as the long days go, that to live is happy, you must first acquire money enough for a decent life, and power enough to be your own master.

CUSINS. You are damnably discouraging. [*He resumes his declamation*].

Is it so hard a thing to see
That the spirit of God—whate'er it be—
The law that abides and changes not, ages long,
The Eternal and Nature-born: t h e s e things be strong?
What else is Wisdom? What of Man's endeavor,
Or God's high grace so lovely and so great?
To stand from fear set free? to breathe and wait?
To hold a hand uplifted over Fate?
And shall not Barbara be loved for ever?

UNDERSHAFT. Euripides mentions Barbara, does he?

CUSINS. It is a fair translation. The word means Loveliness.

UNDERSHAFT. May I ask—as Barbara's father—how much a year she is to be loved for ever on?

CUSINS. As Barbara's father, that is more your affair than mine. I can feed her by teaching Greek: that is about all.

UNDERSHAFT. Do you consider it a good match for her?

CUSINS [*with polite obstinacy*] Mr Undershaft: I am in many ways a weak, timid, ineffectual person; and my health is far from satisfactory. But whenever I feel that I must have anything, I get it, sooner or later. I feel that way about Barbara. I dont like marriage: I feel intensely afraid of it; and I dont know what I shall do with Barbara or what she will do with me. But I feel that I and nobody else must marry her. Please regard that as settled.—Not that I wish to be arbitrary; but why should I waste your time in discussing what is inevitable?

UNDERSHAFT. You mean that you will stick at nothing: not even the conversion of the Salvation Army to the worship of Dionysos.

CUSINS. The business of the Salvation Army is to save, not to wrangle about the name of the pathfinder. Dionysos or another: what does it matter?

UNDERSHAFT [*rising and approaching him*] Professor Cusins: you are a young man after my own heart.

CUSINS. Mr Undershaft: you are, as far as I am able to gather, a most infernal old rascal; but you appeal very strongly to my sense of ironic humor.

Undershaft mutely offers his hand. They shake.

UNDERSHAFT [*suddenly concentrating himself*] And now to business.

CUSINS. Pardon me. We are discussing religion. Why go back to such an uninteresting and unimportant subject as business?

UNDERSHAFT. Religion is our business at present, because it is through religion alone that we can win Barbara.

CUSINS. Have you, too, fallen in love with Barbara?

UNDERSHAFT. Yes, with a father's love.

CUSINS. A father's love for a grown-up daughter is the most dangerous of all infatuations. I apologize for mentioning my own pale, coy, mistrustful fancy in the same breath with it.

UNDERSHAFT. Keep to the point. We have to win her; and we are neither of us Methodists.

CUSINS. That doesnt matter. The power Barbara wields here—the power that wields Barbara herself—is not Calvinism, not Presbyterianism, not Methodism—

UNDERSHAFT. Not Greek Paganism either, eh?

CUSINS. I admit that. Barbara is quite original in her religion.

UNDERSHAFT [*triumphantly*] Aha! Barbara Undershaft would be. Her inspiration comes from within herself.

CUSINS. How do you suppose it got there?

UNDERSHAFT [*in towering excitement*] It is the Undershaft inheritance. I shall hand on my torch to my daughter. She shall make my converts and preach my gospel—

CUSINS. What! Money and gunpowder!

UNDERSHAFT. Yes, money and gunpowder. Freedom and power. Command of life and command of death.

CUSINS [*urbanely: trying to bring him down to earth*] This is extremely interesting, Mr Undershaft. Of course you know that you are mad.

UNDERSHAFT [*with redoubled force*] And you?

CUSINS. Oh, mad as a hatter. You are welcome to my secret since I have discovered yours. But I am astonished. Can a madman make cannons?

UNDERSHAFT. Would anyone else than a madman make them? And now [*with surging energy*] question for question. Can a sane man translate Euripides?

CUSINS. No.

UNDERSHAFT [*seizing him by the shoulder*] Can a sane woman make a man of a waster or a woman of a worm?

CUSINS [*reeling before the storm*] Father Colossus—Mammoth Millionaire—

UNDERSHAFT [*pressing him*] Are there two mad people or three in this Salvation shelter today?

CUSINS. You mean Barbara is as mad as we are?

UNDERSHAFT [*pushing him lightly off and resuming his equanimity suddenly and completely*] Pooh, Professor! let us call things by their proper names. I am a millionaire; you are a poet; Barbara is a savior of souls. What have we three to do with the common mob of slaves and idolaters? [*He sits down again with a shrug of contempt for the mob*].

CUSINS. Take care! Barbara is in love with the common people. So am I. Have you never felt the romance of that love?

UNDERSHAFT [*cold and sardonic*] Have you ever been in love with Poverty, like St Francis? Have you ever been in love with Dirt, like St Simeon! Have you ever been in love with disease and suffering, like our nurses and philanthropists? Such passions are not virtues, but the most unnatural of all the vices. This love of the common people may please an earl's granddaughter and a university professor; but I have been a common man and a poor man; and it has no romance for me. Leave it to the poor to pretend that poverty is a blessing: leave it to the coward to make a religion of his cowardice by preaching humility: we know better than that. We three must stand together above the common people: how else can we help their children to climb up beside us? Barbara must belong to us, not to the Salvation Army.

CUSINS. Well, I can only say that if you think you will get her away from the Salvation Army by talking to her as you have been talking to me, you dont know Barbara.

UNDERSHAFT. My friend: I never ask for what I can buy.

CUSINS [*in a white fury*] Do I understand you to imply that you can buy Barbara?

UNDERSHAFT. No; but I can buy the Salvation Army.

CUSINS. Quite impossible.

UNDERSHAFT. You shall see. All religious organizations exist by selling themselves to the rich.

CUSINS. Not the Army. That is the Church of the poor.

UNDERSHAFT. All the more reason for buying it.

CUSINS. I dont think you quite know what the Army does for the poor.

UNDERSHAFT. Oh yes I do. It draws their teeth: that is enough for me as a man of business.

CUSINS. Nonsense! It makes them sober—

UNDERSHAFT. I prefer sober workmen. The profits are larger.

CUSINS—honest—

UNDERSHAFT. Honest workmen are the most economical.

CUSINS—attached to their homes—

UNDERSHAFT. So much the better: they will put up with anything sooner than change their shop.

CUSINS—happy—

UNDERSHAFT. An invaluable safeguard against revolution.

CUSINS—unselfish—

UNDERSHAFT. Indifferent to their own interests, which suits me exactly.

CUSINS—with their thoughts on heavenly things—

UNDERSHAFT [*rising*] And not on Trade Unionism nor Socialism. Excellent.

CUSINS [*revolted*] You really are an infernal old rascal.

UNDERSHAFT [*indicating Peter Shirley, who has just come from the shelter and strolled dejectedly down the yard between them*] And this is an honest man!

SHIRLEY. Yes; and what av I got by it? [*he passes on bitterly and sits on the form, in the corner of the penthouse*].

Snobby Price, beaming sanctimoniously, and Jenny Hill, with a tam-

bourine full of coppers, come from the shelter and go to the drum, on which Jenny begins to count the money.

UNDERSHAFT [*replying to Shirley*] Oh, your employers must have got a good deal by it from first to last. [*He sits on the table, with one foot on the side form. Cusins, overwhelmed, sits down on the same form nearer the shelter. Barbara comes from the shelter to the middle of the yard. She is excited and a little overwrought*].

BARBARA. Weve just had a splendid experience meeting at the other gate in Cripps's lane. Ive hardly ever seen them so much moved as they were by your confession, Mr Price.

PRICE. I could almost be glad of my past wickedness if I could believe that it would elp to keep hathers stright.

BARBARA. So it will, Snobby. How much, Jenny?

JENNY. Four and tenpence, Major.

BARBARA. Oh Snobby, if you had given your poor mother just one more kick, we should have got the whole five shillings!

PRICE. If she heard you say that, miss, she'd be sorry I didnt. But I'm glad. Oh what a joy it will be to her when she hears I'm saved!

UNDERSHAFT. Shall I contribute the odd twopence, Barbara? The millionaire's mite, eh? [*He takes a couple of pennies from his pocket*].

BARBARA. How did you make that twopence?

UNDERSHAFT. As usual. By selling cannons, torpedoes, submarines, and my new patent Grand Duke hand grenade.

BARBARA. Put it back in your pocket. You cant buy your salvation here for twopence: you must work it out.

UNDERSHAFT. Is twopence not enough? I can afford a little more, if you press me.

BARBARA. Two million millions would not be enough. There is bad blood on your hands; and nothing but good blood can cleanse them. Money is no use. Take it away. [*She turns to Cusins*]. Dolly: you must write another letter for me to the papers. [*He makes a wry face*]. Yes: I know you dont like it; but it must be done. The starvation this winter is beating us: everybody is unemployed. The General says we must close this shelter if we cant get more money. I force the collections at the meetings until I am ashamed: dont I, Snobby?

PRICE. It's a fair treat to see you work it, miss. The way you got them up from three-and-six to four-and-ten with that hymn, penny by penny and verse by verse, was a caution. Not a Cheap Jack on Mile End Waste could touch you at it.

BARBARA. Yes; but I wish we could do without it. I am getting at last to think more of the collection than of the people's souls. And what are those hatfuls of pence and halfpence? We want thousands! tens of thousands! hundreds of thousands! I want to convert people, not to be always begging for the Army in a way I'd die sooner than beg for myself.

UNDERSHAFT [*in profound irony*] Genuine unselfishness is capable of anything, my dear.

BARBARA [*unsuspectingly, as she turns away to take the money from the drum and put it in a cashbag she carries*] Yes, isnt it? [*Undershaft looks sardonically at Cusins*].

CUSINS [*aside to Undershaft*] Mephistopheles! Machiavelli!

BARBARA [*tears coming into her eyes as she ties the bag and pockets it*] How are we to feed them? I cant talk religion to a man with bodily hunger in his eyes. [*Almost breaking down*] It's frightful.

JENNY [*running to her*] Major, dear—

BARBARA [*rebounding*] No: dont comfort me. It will be all right. We shall get the money.

UNDERSHAFT. How?

JENNY. By praying for it, of course. Mrs Baines says she prayed for it last night; and she has never prayed for it in vain: never once. [*She goes to the gate and looks out into the street*].

BARBARA [*who has dried her eyes and regained her composure*] By the way, dad, Mrs Baines has come to march with us to our big meeting this afternoon; and she is very anxious to meet you, for some reason or other. Perhaps she'll convert you.

UNDERSHAFT. I shall be delighted, my dear.

JENNY [*at the gate: excitedly*] Major! Major! heres that man back again.

BARBARA. What man?

JENNY. The man that hit me. Oh, I hope he's coming back to join us.

Bill Walker, with frost on his jacket, comes through the gate, his hands deep in his pockets and his chin sunk between his shoulders, like a cleaned-out gambler. He halts between Barbara and the drum.

BARBARA. Hullo, Bill! Back already!

BILL [*nagging at her*] Bin talkin ever sence, ev you?

BARBARA. Pretty nearly. Well, has Todger paid you out for poor Jenny's jaw?

BILL. Nao e aint.

BARBARA. I thought your jacket looked a bit snowy.

BILL. Sao it is snaowy. You want to knaow where the snaow cam from, downt you?

BARBARA. Yes.

BILL. Well, it cam from orf the grahnd in Pawkinses Corner in Kennintahn. It got rabbed orf be maw shaoulders: see?

BARBARA. Pity you didnt rub some off with your knees, Bill! That would have done you a lot of good.

BILL [*with sour mirthless humor*] Aw was sivin anather menn's knees at the tawm. E was kneelin on moy ed, e was.

JENNY. Who was kneeling on your head?

BILL. Todger was. E was pryin for me: pryin camfortable wiv me as a cawpet. Sow was Mog. Sao was the aol bloomin meetin. Mog she sez "Ow Lawd brike is stabborn sperrit; bat downt urt is dear art." Thet was wot she said. "Downt urt is dear art"! An er blowk—thirteen stun four!—kneelin wiv all is wight on me. Fanny, aint it?

JENNY. Oh no. We're so sorry, Mr Walker.

BARBARA [*enjoying it frankly*] Nonsense! of course it's funny. Served you right, Bill! You must have done something to him first.

BILL [*doggedly*] Aw did wot Aw said Aw'd do. Aw spit in is eye. E looks ap at the skoy and sez, "Ow that Aw should be fahnd worthy to be spit upon for the gospel's sike!" e sez; an Mog sez "Glaory Allelloolier!"; an then e called me Braddher, an dahned me as if Aw was a kid and e was me mather worshin me a Setterda nawt. Aw ednt jast nao shaow wiv im at all. Arf the street pryed; an the tather arf larfed fit to split theirselves. [*To Barbara*] There! are you settisfawd nah?

BARBARA [*her eyes dancing*] Wish I'd been there, Bill.

BILL. Yus: youd a got in a hextra bit o talk on me, wouldnt you?

JENNY. I'm so sorry, Mr Walker.

BILL [*fiercely*] Downt you gow bein sorry for me: youve no call. Listen eah. Aw browk your jawr.

JENNY. No, it didnt hurt me: indeed it didnt, except for a moment. It was only that I was frightened.

BILL. Aw downt want to be forgive be you, or be ennybody. Wot Aw did Aw'll py for. Aw trawd to gat me aown jawr browk to settisfaw you—

JENNY [*distressed*] Oh no—

BILL [*impatiently*] Tell y' Aw did: cawnt you listen to wots being taold you? All Aw got be it was bein mide a sawt of in the pablic street for me pines. Well, if Aw cawnt settisfaw you one wy, Aw ken anather. Listen eah! Aw ed two quid sived agen the frost; an Awve a pahnd of it left. A mite o mawn last week ed words with the judy e's gowin to merry. E give er wot-for; an e's bin fawnd fifteen bob. E ed a rawt to itt er cause they was gowin to be merrid; but Aw ednt nao rawt to itt you; sao put anather fawv bob on an call it a pahnd's worth. [*He produces a sovereign*]. Eahs the manney. Tike it; and lets ev no more o your forgivin an pryin and your Mijor jawrin me. Let wot Aw dan be dan an pide for; and let there be a end of it.

JENNY. Oh, I couldnt take it, Mr Walker. But if you would give a shilling or two to poor Rummy Mitchens! you really did hurt her; and she's old.

BILL [*contemptuously*] Not lawkly. Aw'd give her anather as soon as look at er. Let her ev the lawr o me as she threatened! She aint forgiven me: not mach. Wot Aw dan to er is not on me mawnd—wot she [*indicating Barbara*] mawt call on me conscience—no more than stickin a pig. It's this Christian gime o yours that Aw wownt ev plyed agen me: this bloomin forgivin an neggin an jawrin that mikes a menn thet sore that iz lawf's a burdn to im. Aw wownt ev it, Aw tell you; sao tike your manney and stop thraowin your silly beshed fice hap agen me.

JENNY. Major: may I take a little of it for the Army?

BARBARA. No: the Army is not to be bought. We want your soul, Bill; and we'll take nothing less.

BILL [*bitterly*] Aw knaow. Me an maw few shillins is not good enaff for you. Youre a earl's grendorter, you are. Nathink less than a anderd pahnd for you.

UNDERSHAFT. Come, Barbara! you could do a great deal of good with a hundred pounds. If you will set this gentleman's mind at ease by taking his pound, I will give the other ninety-nine.

Bill, dazed by such opulence, instinctively touches his cap.

BARBARA. Oh, youre too extravagant, papa. Bill offers twenty pieces of silver. All you need offer is the other ten. That will make the standard price to buy anybody who's for sale. I'm not; and the Army's not. [*To Bill*] Youll never have another quiet moment, Bill, until you come round to us. You cant stand out against your salvation.

BILL [*sullenly*] Aw cawnt stend aht agen music awl wrastlers and awtful tangued women. Awve offered to py. Aw can do no more. Tike it or leave it. There it is. [*He throws the sovereign on the drum, and sits down on the horse-trough. The coin fascinates Snobby Price, who takes an early opportunity of dropping his cap on it*].

Mrs Baines comes from the shelter. She is dressed as a Salvation Army Commissioner. She is an earnest looking woman of about 40, with a caressing, urgent voice, and an appealing manner.

BARBARA. This is my father, Mrs Baines. [*Undershaft comes from the table, taking off his hat with marked civility*]. Try what you can do with him. He wont listen to me, because he remembers what a fool I was when I was a baby. [*She leaves them together and chats with Jenny*].

MRS BAINES. Have you been shewn over the shelter, Mr Undershaft? You know the work we're doing, of course.

UNDERSHAFT [*very civilly*] The whole nation knows it, Mrs Baines.

MRS BAINES. No, sir: the whole nation does not know it, or we should not be crippled as we are for want of money to carry our work through the length and breadth of the land. Let me tell you that there would have been rioting this winter in London but for us.

UNDERSHAFT. You really think so?

MRS BAINES. I know it. I remember 1886, when you rich gentlemen hardened your hearts against the cry of the poor. They broke the windows of your clubs in Pall Mall.

UNDERSHAFT [*gleaming with approval of their method*] And the Mansion House Fund went up next day from thirty thousand pounds to seventy-nine thousand! I remember quite well.

MRS BAINES. Well, wont you help me to get at the people? They wont break windows then. Come here, Price. Let me shew you to this gentleman [*Price comes to be inspected*]. Do you remember the window breaking?

PRICE. My ole father thought it was the revolution, maam.

MRS BAINES. Would you break windows now?

PRICE. Oh no, maam. The windows of eaven av bin opened to me. I know now that the rich man is a sinner like myself.

RUMMY [*appearing above at the loft door*] Snobby Price!

SNOBBY. Wot is it?

RUMMY. Your mother's askin for you at the other gate in Cripps's Lane. She's heard about your confession [*Price turns pale*].

MRS BAINES. Go, Mr Price; and pray with her.

JENNY. You can go through the shelter, Snobby.

PRICE [*to Mrs Baines*] I couldnt face her now, maam, with all the weight of my sins fresh on me. Tell her she'll find her son at ome, waitin for her in prayer. [*He skulks off through the gate, incidentally stealing the sovereign on his way out by picking up his cap from the drum*].

MRS BAINES [*with swimming eyes*] You see how we take the anger and the bitterness against you out of their hearts, Mr Undershaft.

UNDERSHAFT. It is certainly most convenient and gratifying to all large employers of labor, Mrs Baines.

MRS BAINES. Barbara: Jenny: I have good news: most wonderful news. [*Jenny runs to her*]. My prayers have been answered. I told you they would, Jenny, didnt I?

JENNY. Yes, yes.

BARBARA [*moving nearer to the drum*] Have we got money enough to keep the shelter open?

MRS BAINES. I hope we shall have enough to keep all the shelters open. Lord Saxmundham has promised us five thousand pounds—

BARBARA. Hooray!

JENNY. Glory!

MRS BAINES.—if—

BARBARA. "If!" If what?

MRS BAINES.—if five other gentlemen will give a thousand each to make it up to ten thousand.

BARBARA. Who is Lord Saxmundham? I never heard of him.

UNDERSHAFT [*who has pricked up his ears at the peer's name, and is now watching Barbara curiously*] A new creation, my dear. You have heard of Sir Horace Bodger?

BARBARA. Bodger! Do you mean the distiller? Bodger's whisky!

UNDERSHAFT. That is the man. He is one of the greatest of our public benefactors. He restored the cathedral at Hakington. They made him a baronet for that. He gave half a million to the funds of his party: they made him a baron for that.

SHIRLEY. What will they give him for the five thousand?

UNDERSHAFT. There is nothing left to give him. So the five thousand, I should think is to save his soul.

MRS BAINES. Heaven grant it may! Oh Mr Undershaft, you have some very rich friends. Cant you help us towards the other five thousand? We are going to hold a great meeting this afternoon at the Assembly Hall in the Mile End Road. If I could only announce that one gentleman had come forward to support Lord Saxmundham, others would follow. Dont you know somebody? couldnt you? wouldnt you? [*her eyes fill with tears*] oh, think of those poor people, Mr Undershaft: think of how much it means to them, and how little to a great man like you.

UNDERSHAFT [*sardonically gallant*] Mrs Baines: you are irresistible. I cant disappoint you; and I cant deny myself the satisfaction of making Bodger pay up. You shall have your five thousand pounds.

MRS BAINES. Thank God!

UNDERSHAFT. You dont thank me?

MRS BAINES. Oh sir, dont try to be cynical: dont be ashamed of being a good man. The Lord will bless you abundantly; and our prayers will be like a strong fortification round you all the days of your life. [*With a touch of caution*] You will let me have the cheque to shew at the meeting, wont you? Jenny: go in and fetch a pen and ink. [*Jenny runs to the shelter door*].

UNDERSHAFT. Do not disturb Miss Hill: I have a fountain pen [*Jenny halts. He sits at the table and writes the cheque. Cusins rises to make room for him. They all watch him silently*].

BILL [*cynically, aside to Barbara, his voice and accent horribly debased*] Wot prawce selvytion nah?

BARBARA. Stop. [*Undershaft stops writing: they all turn to her in surprise*]. Mrs Baines: are you really going to take this money?

MRS BAINES [*astonished*] Why not, dear?

BARBARA. Why not! Do you know what my father is? Have you forgotten that Lord Saxmundham is Bodger the whisky man? Do you remember how we implored the County Council to stop him from writing Bodger's Whisky in letters of fire against the sky; so that the poor drink-ruined creatures on the Embankment could not wake up from their snatches of sleep without being reminded of their deadly thirst by that wicked sky sign? Do you know that the worst thing I have had to fight here is not the devil, but Bodger, Bodger, Bodger, with his whisky, his distilleries, and his tied houses? Are you going to make our shelter another tied house for him, and ask me to keep it?

BILL. Rotten dranken whisky it is too.

MRS BAINES. Dear Barbara: Lord Saxmundham has a soul to be saved like any of us. If heaven has found the way to make a good use of his money, are we to set ourselves up against the answer to our prayers?

BARBARA. I know he has a soul to be saved. Let him come down here; and I'll do my best to help him to his salvation. But he wants to send his cheque down to buy us, and go on being as wicked as ever.

UNDERSHAFT [*with a reasonableness which Cusins alone perceives to be ironical*] My dear Barbara: alcohol is a very necessary article. It heals the sick—

BARBARA. It does nothing of the sort.

UNDERSHAFT. Well, it assists the doctor: that is perhaps a less questionable way of putting it. It makes life bearable to millions of people who could not endure their existence if they were quite sober. It enables Parliament to do things at eleven at night that no sane person would do at eleven in the morning. Is it Bodger's fault that this inestimable gift is deplorably abused by less than one per cent of the poor? [*He turns again to the table; signs the cheque; and crosses it*].

MRS BAINES. Barbara: will there be less drinking or more if all those poor souls we are saving come tomorrow and find the doors of our shelters shut in their faces? Lord Saxmundham gives us the money to stop drinking—to take his own business from him.

CUSINS [*impishly*] Pure self-sacrifice on Bodger's part, clearly! Bless dear Bodger! [*Barbara almost breaks down as Adolphus, too, fails her*].

UNDERSHAFT [*tearing out the cheque and pocketing the book as he rises and goes past Cusins to Mrs Baines*] I also, Mrs Baines, may claim a little disinterestedness. Think of my business! think of the widows and orphans! the men and lads torn to pieces with shrapnel and poisoned with lyddite! [*Mrs Baines shrinks; but he goes on remorselessly*] the oceans of blood, not one drop of which is shed in a really just cause! the ravaged crops! the peaceful peasants forced, women and men, to till their fields under the fire of opposing armies on pain of starvation! the bad blood of the fierce little cowards at home who egg on others to fight for the gratification of their national vanity! All this makes money for me: I am never richer, never busier than when the papers are full of it. Well, it is your work to preach peace on earth and goodwill to men. [*Mrs Baines's face lights up again*]. Every convert you make is a vote against war. [*Her lips move in prayer*]. Yet I give you this money to help you to hasten my own commercial ruin. [*He gives her the cheque*].

CUSINS [*mounting the form in an ecstasy of mischief*] The millennium will be inaugurated by the unselfishness of Undershaft and Bodger. Oh be joyful! [*He takes the drum-sticks from his pocket and flourishes them*].

MRS BAINES [*taking the cheque*] The longer I live the more proof I see that there is an Infinite Goodness that turns everything to the work of salvation sooner or later. Who would have thought that any good could have come out of war and drink? And yet their profits are brought today to the feet of salvation to do its blessed work. [*She is affected to tears*].

JENNY [*running to Mrs Baines and throwing her arms around her*] Oh dear! how blessed, how glorious it all is!

CUSINS [*in a convulsion of irony*] Let us seize this unspeakable moment. Let us march to the great meeting at once. Excuse me just an instant. [*He rushes into the shelter. Jenny takes her tambourine from the drum head*].

MRS BAINES. Mr Undershaft: have you ever seen a thousand people fall on their knees with one impulse and pray? Come with us to the meeting. Barbara shall tell them that the Army is saved, and saved through you.

CUSINS [*returning impetuously from the shelter with a flag and a trombone, and coming between Mrs Baines and Undershaft*] You shall carry the flag down the first street, Mrs Baines [*he gives her the flag*]. Mr Undershaft is a gifted trombonist: he shall intone an Olympian diapason to the West Ham Salvation March. [*Aside to Undershaft, as he forces the trombone on him*] Blow, Machiavelli, blow.

UNDERSHAFT [*aside to him, as he takes the trombone*] The trumpet in Zion! [*Cusins rushes to the drum, which he takes up and puts on. Undershaft continues, aloud*] I will do my best. I could vamp a bass if I knew the tune.

CUSINS. It is a wedding chorus from one of Donizetti's operas; but we have converted it. We convert everything to good here, including Bodger. You remember the chorus. "For thee immense rejoicing–immenso giubilo–immenso giubilo." [*With drum obbligato*] Rum tum ti tum tum, tum tum ti ta–

BARBARA. Dolly: you are breaking my heart.

CUSINS. What is a broken heart more or less here? Dionysos Undershaft has descended. I am possessed.

MRS BAINES. Come, Barbara: I must have my dear Major to carry the flag with me.

JENNY. Yes, yes, Major darling.

CUSINS [*snatches the tambourine out of Jenny's hand and mutely offers it to Barbara*].

BARBARA [*coming forward a little as she puts the offer behind her with a shudder, whilst Cusins recklessly tosses the tambourine back to Jenny and goes to the gate*] I cant come.

JENNY. Not come!

MRS BAINES [*with tears in her eyes*] Barbara: do you think I am wrong to take the money?
BARBARA [*impulsively going to her and kissing her*] No, no: God help you, dear, you must; you are saving the Army. Go; and may you have a great meeting!
JENNY. But arnt you coming?
BARBARA. No. [*She begins taking off the silver S brooch from her collar*].
MRS BAINES. Barbara: what are you doing?
JENNY. Why are you taking your badge off? You cant be going to leave us, Major.
BARBARA [*quietly*] Father: come here.
UNDERSHAFT [*coming to her*] My dear! [*Seeing that she is going to pin the badge on his collar, he retreats to the penthouse in some alarm*].
BARBARA [*following him*] Dont be frightened. [*She pins the badge on and steps back towards the table, shewing him to the others*] There! It's not much for £5000, is it?
MRS BAINES. Barbara: if you wont come and pray with us, promise me you will pray for us.
BARBARA. I cant pray now. Perhaps I shall never pray again.
MRS BAINES. Barbara!
JENNY. Major!
BARBARA [*almost delirious*] I cant bear any more. Quick march!
CUSINS [*calling to the procession in the street outside*] Off we go. Play up, there! Immenso giubilo. [*He gives the time with his drum; and the band strikes up the march, which rapidly becomes more distant as the procession moves briskly away*].
MRS BAINES. I must go, dear. Youre overworked: you will be all right tomorrow. We'll never lose you. Now Jenny: step out with the old flag. Blood and Fire! [*She marches out through the gate with her flag*].
JENNY. Glory Hallelujah! [*flourishing her tambourine and marching*]
UNDERSHAFT [*to Cusins, as he marches out past him easing the slide of his trombone*] "My ducats and my daughter"!
CUSINS [*following him out*] Money and gunpowder!
BARBARA. Drunkenness and Murder! My God: why hast thou forsaken me?

She sinks on the form with her face buried in her hands. The march passes away into silence. Bill Walker steals across to her.

BILL [*taunting*] Wot prawce selvytion nah?

SHIRLEY. Dont you hit her when she's down.

BILL. She itt me wen aw wiz dahn. Waw shouldnt Aw git a bit o me aown beck?

BARBARA [*raising her head*] I didnt take your money, Bill. [*She crosses the yard to the gate and turns her back on the two men to hide her face from them*].

BILL [*sneering after her*] Naow, it warnt enaff for you. [*Turning to the drum, he misses the money*] Ellow! If you aint took it sammun else ez. Weres it gorn? Bly me if Jenny Ill didnt tike it arter all!

RUMMY [*screaming at him from the loft*] You lie, you dirty blackguard! Snobby Price pinched it off the drum when he took up his cap. I was up here all the time an see im do it.

BILL. Wot! Stowl maw manney! Waw didnt you call thief on him, you silly aold macker you?

RUMMY. To serve you aht for ittin me acrost the fice. It's cost y'pahnd, that az. [*Raising a pæan of squalid triumph*] I done you. I'm even with you. Ive ad it aht o y—[*Bill snatches up Shirley's mug and hurls it at her. She slams the loft door and vanishes. The mug smashes against the door and falls in fragments*].

BILL [*beginning to chuckle*] Tell us, aol menn, wot o'clock this mawnin was it wen im as they call Snobby Prawce was sived?

BARBARA [*turning to him more composedly, and with unspoiled sweetness*] About half past twelve, Bill. And he pinched your pound at a quarter to two. *I* know. Well, you cant afford to lose it. I'll send it to you.

BILL [*his voice and accent suddenly improving*] Not if Aw wiz to stawve for it. Aw aint to be bought.

SHIRLEY. Aint you? Youd sell yourself to the devil for a pint o beer; ony there aint no devil to make the offer.

BILL [*unshamed*] Sao Aw would, mite, and often ev, cheerful. But she cawnt baw me. [*Approaching Barbara*] You wanted maw saoul, did you? Well, you aint got it.

BARBARA. I nearly got it, Bill. But weve sold it back to you for ten thousand pounds.

SHIRLEY. And dear at the money!

BARBARA. No, Peter: it was worth more than money.

BILL [*salvationproof*] It's nao good: you cawnt get rahnd me nah. Aw downt blieve in it; and Awve seen tody that Aw was rawt. [*Going*]

Sao long, aol soupkitchener! Ta, ta, Mijor Earl's Grendorter! [*Turning at the gate*] Wot prawce selvytion nah? Snobby Prawce! Ha! ha!

BARBARA [*offering her hand*] Goodbye, Bill.

BILL [*taken aback, half plucks his cap off; then shoves it on again defiantly*] Git aht. [*Barbara drops her hand, discouraged. He has a twinge of remorse*]. But thets aw rawt, you knaow. Nathink pasnl. Naow mellice. Sao long, Judy. [*He goes*].

BARBARA. No malice. So long, Bill.

SHIRLEY [*shaking his head*] You make too much of him, miss, in your innocence.

BARBARA [*going to him*] Peter: I'm like you now. Cleaned out, and lost my job.

SHIRLEY. Youve youth an hope. Thats two better than me.

BARBARA. I'll get you a job, Peter. Thats hope for you: the youth will have to be enough for me. [*She counts her money*]. I have just enough left for two teas at Lockharts, a Rowton doss for you, and my tram and bus home. [*He frowns and rises with offended pride. She takes his arm*]. Dont be proud, Peter: it's sharing between friends. And promise me youll talk to me and not let me cry. [*She draws him towards the gate*].

SHIRLEY. Well, I'm not accustomed to talk to the like of you—

BARBARA [*urgently*] Yes, yes: you must talk to me. Tell me about Tom Paine's books and Bradlaugh's lectures. Come along.

SHIRLEY. Ah, if you would only read Tom Paine in the proper spirit, miss! [*They go out through the gate together*].

ACT III

Next day after lunch Lady Britomart is writing in the library in Wilton Crescent. Sarah is reading in the armchair near the window. Barbara, in ordinary fashionable dress, pale and brooding, is on the settee. Charles Lomax enters. He starts on seeing Barbara fashionably attired and in low spirits.

LOMAX. Youve left off your uniform!

Barbara says nothing; but an expression of pain passes over her face.

LADY BRITOMART [*warning him in low tones to be careful*] Charles!

LOMAX [*much concerned, coming behind the settee and bending sympathetically over Barbara*] I'm awfully sorry, Barbara. You know I helped you all I could with the concertina and so forth. [*Momentously*] Still, I have never shut my eyes to the fact that there is a certain amount of tosh about the Salvation Army. Now the claims of the Church of England—

LADY BRITOMART. Thats enough, Charles. Speak of something suited to your mental capacity.

LOMAX. But surely the Church of England is suited to all our capacities.

BARBARA [*pressing his hand*] Thank you for your sympathy, Cholly. Now go and spoon with Sarah.

LOMAX [*dragging a chair from the writing table and seating himself affectionately by Sarah's side*] How is my ownest today?

SARAH. I wish you wouldnt tell Cholly to do things, Barbara. He always comes straight and does them. Cholly: we're going to the works this afternoon.

LOMAX. What works?

SARAH. The cannon works.

LOMAX. What? your governor's shop!

SARAH. Yes.

LOMAX. Oh I say!

Cusins enters in poor condition. He also starts visibly when he sees Barbara without her uniform.

BARBARA. I expected you this morning, Dolly. Didnt you guess that?

CUSINS [*sitting down beside her*] I'm sorry. I have only just breakfasted.

SARAH. But weve just finished lunch.

BARBARA. Have you had one of your bad nights?

CUSINS. No: I had rather a good night: in fact, one of the most remarkable nights I have ever passed.

BARBARA. The meeting?

CUSINS. No: after the meeting.

LADY BRITOMART. You should have gone to bed after the meeting. What were you doing?

CUSINS. Drinking.

LADY BRITOMART. Adolphus!
SARAH. Dolly!
BARBARA. Dolly!
LOMAX. Oh I say!

LADY BRITOMART. What were you drinking, may I ask?

CUSINS. A most devilish kind of Spanish burgundy, warranted free from added alcohol: a Temperance burgundy in fact. Its richness in natural alcohol made any addition superfluous.

BARBARA. Are you joking, Dolly?

CUSINS [*patiently*] No. I have been making a night of it with the nominal head of this household: that is all.

LADY BRITOMART. Andrew made you drunk!

CUSINS. No: he only provided the wine. I think it was Dionysos who made me drunk. [*To Barbara*] I told you I was possessed.

LADY BRITOMART. Youre not sober yet. Go home to bed at once.

CUSINS. I have never before ventured to reproach you, Lady Brit; but how could you marry the Prince of Darkness?

LADY BRITOMART. It was much more excusable to marry him than to get drunk with him. That is a new accomplishment of Andrew's, by the way. He usent to drink.

CUSINS. He doesnt now. He only sat there and completed the wreck of my moral basis, the rout of my convictions, the purchase of my soul. He cares for you, Barbara. That is what makes him so dangerous to me.

BARBARA. That has nothing to do with it, Dolly. There are larger loves and diviner dreams than the fireside ones. You know that, dont you?

CUSINS. Yes: that is our understanding. I know it. I hold to it. Unless he can win me on that holier ground he may amuse me for a while; but he can get no deeper hold, strong as he is.

BARBARA. Keep to that; and the end will be right. Now tell me what happened at the meeting?

CUSINS. It was an amazing meeting. Mrs Baines almost died of emotion. Jenny Hill simply gibbered with hysteria. The Prince of Darkness played his trombone like a madman: its brazen roarings were like the laughter of the damned. 117 conversions took place then and there. They prayed with the most touching sincerity and gratitude for Bodger, and for the anonymous donor of the £5000. Your father would not let his name be given.

LOMAX. That was rather fine of the old man, you know. Most chaps would have wanted the advertisement.

CUSINS. He said all the charitable institutions would be down on him like kites on a battle-field if he gave his name.

LADY BRITOMART. Thats Andrew all over. He never does a proper thing without giving an improper reason for it.

CUSINS. He convinced me that I have all my life been doing improper things for proper reasons.

LADY BRITOMART. Adolphus: now that Barbara has left the Salvation Army, you had better leave it too. I will not have you playing that drum in the streets.

CUSINS. Your orders are already obeyed, Lady Brit.

BARBARA. Dolly: were you ever really in earnest about it? Would you have joined if you had never seen me?

CUSINS [*disingenuously*] Well—er—well, possibly, as a collector of religions—

LOMAX [*Cunningly*] Not as a drummer, though, you know. You are a very clearheaded brainy chap, Dolly; and it must have been apparent to you that there is a certain amount of tosh about—

LADY BRITOMART. Charles: if you must drivel, drivel like a grown-up man and not like a schoolboy.

LOMAX [*out of countenance*] Well, drivel is drivel, dont you know, whatever a man's age.

LADY BRITOMART. In good society in England, Charles, men drivel at all ages by repeating silly formulas with an air of wisdom. Schoolboys make their own formulas out of slang, like you. When they reach your age, and get political private secretaryships and things of that sort, they drop slang and get their formulas out of The Spectator or The

Times. You had better confine yourself to The Times. You will find that there is a certain amount of tosh about The Times; but at least its language is reputable.

LOMAX [*overwhelmed*] You are so awfully strongminded, Lady Brit—

LADY BRITOMART. Rubbish! [*Morrison comes in*]. What is it?

MORRISON. If you please, my lady, Mr Undershaft has just drove up to the door.

LADY BRITOMART. Well, let him in. [*Morrison hesitates*]. Whats the matter with you?

MORRISON. Shall I announce him, my lady; or is he at home here, so to speak, my lady?

LADY BRITOMART. Announce him.

MORRISON. Thank you, my lady. You wont mind my asking, I hope. The occasion is in a manner of speaking new to me.

LADY BRITOMART. Quite right. Go and let him in.

MORRISON. Thank you, my lady. [*He withdraws*].

LADY BRITOMART. Children: go and get ready. [*Sarah and Barbara go upstairs for their out-of-door wraps*]. Charles: go and tell Stephen to come down here in five minutes: you will find him in the drawing room. [*Charles goes*]. Adolphus: tell them to send round the carriage in about fifteen minutes. [*Adolphus goes*].

MORRISON [*at the door*] Mr Undershaft.

Undershaft comes in. Morrison goes out.

UNDERSHAFT. Alone! How fortunate!

LADY BRITOMART [*rising*] Dont be sentimental, Andrew. Sit down. [*She sits on the settee: he sits beside her, on her left. She comes to the point before he has time to breathe*]. Sarah must have £800 a year until Charles Lomax comes into his property. Barbara will need more, and need it permanently, because Adolphus hasnt any property.

UNDERSHAFT [*resignedly*] Yes, my dear: I will see to it. Anything else? for yourself, for instance?

LADY BRITOMART. I want to talk to you about Stephen.

UNDERSHAFT [*rather wearily*] Dont, my dear. Stephen doesnt interest me.

LADY BRITOMART. He does interest me. He is our son.

UNDERSHAFT. Do you really think so? He has induced us to bring him into the world; but he chose his parents very incongruously, I think. I see nothing of myself in him, and less of you.

LADY BRITOMART. Andrew: Stephen is an excellent son, and a most steady, capable, highminded young man. You are simply trying to find an excuse for disinheriting him.

UNDERSHAFT. My dear Biddy: the Undershaft tradition disinherits him. It would be dishonest of me to leave the cannon foundry to my son.

LADY BRITOMART. It would be most unnatural and improper of you to leave it to anyone else, Andrew. Do you suppose this wicked and immoral tradition can be kept up for ever? Do you pretend that Stephen could not carry on the foundry just as well as all the other sons of the big business houses?

UNDERSHAFT. Yes: he could learn the office routine without understanding the business, like all the other sons; and the firm would go on by its own momentum until the real Undershaft—probably an Italian or a German—would invent a new method and cut him out.

LADY BRITOMART. There is nothing that any Italian or German could do that Stephen could not do. And Stephen at least has breeding.

UNDERSHAFT. The son of a foundling! Nonsense!

LADY BRITOMART. My son, Andrew! And even you may have good blood in your veins for all you know.

UNDERSHAFT. True. Probably I have. That is another argument in favor of a foundling.

LADY BRITOMART. Andrew: dont be aggravating. And dont be wicked. At present you are both.

UNDERSHAFT. This conversation is part of the Undershaft tradition, Biddy. Every Undershaft's wife has treated him to it ever since the house was founded. It is mere waste of breath. If the tradition be ever broken it will be for an abler man than Stephen.

LADY BRITOMART [*pouting*] Then go away.

UNDERSHAFT [*deprecatory*] Go away!

LADY BRITOMART. Yes: go away. If you will do nothing for Stephen, you are not wanted here. Go to your foundling, whoever he is; and look after h i m.

UNDERSHAFT. The fact is, Biddy—

LADY BRITOMART. Dont call me Biddy. I dont call you Andy.

UNDERSHAFT. I will not call my wife Britomart: it is not good sense. Seriously, my love, the Undershaft tradition has landed me in a difficulty. I am getting on in years; and my partner Lazarus has at last made a stand and insisted that the succession must be settled one way or the other; and of course he is quite right. You see, I havnt found a fit successor yet.

LADY BRITOMART [*obstinately*] There is Stephen.

UNDERSHAFT. Thats just it: all the foundlings I can find are exactly like Stephen.

LADY BRITOMART. Andrew!!

UNDERSHAFT. I want a man with no relations and no schooling: that is, a man who would be out of the running altogether if he were not a strong man. And I cant find him. Every blessed foundling nowadays is snapped up in his infancy by Barnardo homes, or School Board Officers, or Boards of Guardians; and if he shews the least ability he is fastened on by schoolmasters; trained to win scholarships like a racehorse; crammed with secondhand ideas; drilled and disciplined in docility and what they call good taste; and lamed for life so that he is fit for nothing but teaching. If you want to keep the foundry in the family, you had better find an eligible foundling and marry him to Barbara.

LADY BRITOMART. Ah! Barbara! Your pet! You would sacrifice Stephen to Barbara.

UNDERSHAFT. Cheerfully. And you, my dear, would boil Barbara to make soup for Stephen.

LADY BRITOMART. Andrew: this is not a question of our likings and dislikings: it is a question of duty. It is your duty to make Stephen your successor.

UNDERSHAFT. Just as much as it is your duty to submit to your husband. Come, Biddy! these tricks of the governing class are of no use with me. I am one of the governing class myself; and it is waste of time giving tracts to a missionary. I have the power in this matter; and I am not to be humbugged into using it for your purposes.

LADY BRITOMART. Andrew: you can talk my head off; but you cant change wrong into right. And your tie is all on one side. Put it straight.

UNDERSHAFT [*disconcerted*] It wont stay unless it's pinned [*he fumbles at it with childish grimaces*]—

Stephen comes in.

STEPHEN [*at the door*] I beg your pardon [*about to retire*].

LADY BRITOMART. No: come in, Stephen. [*Stephen comes forward to his mother's writing table*].

UNDERSHAFT [*not very cordially*] Good afternoon.

STEPHEN [*coldly*] Good afternoon.

UNDERSHAFT [*to Lady Britomart*] He knows all about the tradition, I suppose?

LADY BRITOMART. Yes. [*To Stephen*] It is what I told you last night, Stephen.
UNDERSHAFT [*sulkily*] I understand you want to come into the cannon business.
STEPHEN. *I* go into trade! Certainly not.
UNDERSHAFT [*opening his eyes, greatly eased in mind and manner*] Oh! in that case—
LADY BRITOMART. Cannons are not trade, Stephen. They are enterprise.
STEPHEN. I have no intention of becoming a man of business in any sense. I have no capacity for business and no taste for it. I intend to devote myself to politics.
UNDERSHAFT [*rising*] My dear boy: this is an immense relief to me. And I trust it may prove an equally good thing for the country. I was afraid you would consider yourself disparaged and slighted [*He moves towards Stephen as if to shake hands with him*].
LADY BRITOMART [*rising and interposing*] Stephen: I cannot allow you to throw away an enormous property like this.
STEPHEN [*stiffly*] Mother: there must be an end of treating me as a child, if you please. [*Lady Britomart recoils, deeply wounded by his tone*]. Until last night I did not take your attitude seriously, because I did not think you meant it seriously. But I find now that you left me in the dark as to matters which you should have explained to me years ago. I am extremely hurt and offended. Any further discussion of my intentions had better take place with my father, as between one man and another.
LADY BRITOMART. Stephen! [*She sits down again, her eyes filling with tears*].
UNDERSHAFT [*with grave compassion*] You see, my dear, it is only the big men who can be treated as children.
STEPHEN. I am sorry, mother, that you have forced me—
UNDERSHAFT [*stopping him*] Yes, yes, yes, yes: thats all right, Stephen. She wont interfere with you any more: your independence is achieved: you have won your latchkey. Dont rub it in; and above all, dont apologize. [*He resumes his seat*]. Now what about your future, as between one man and another—I beg your pardon, Biddy: as between two men and a woman.
LADY BRITOMART [*who has pulled herself together strongly*] I quite understand, Stephen. By all means go your own way if you feel strong

enough. [*Stephen sits down magisterially in the chair at the writing table with an air of affirming his majority*].

UNDERSHAFT. It is settled that you do not ask for the succession to the cannon business.

STEPHEN. I hope it is settled that I repudiate the cannon business.

UNDERSHAFT. Come, come! dont be so devilishly sulky: it's boyish. Freedom should be generous. Besides, I owe you a fair start in life in exchange for disinheriting you. You cant become prime minister all at once. Havnt you a turn for something? What about literature, art, and so forth?

STEPHEN. I have nothing of the artist about me, either in faculty or character, thank Heaven.

UNDERSHAFT. A philosopher, perhaps? Eh?

STEPHEN. I make no such ridiculous pretension.

UNDERSHAFT. Just so. Well, there is the army, the navy, the Church, the Bar. The Bar requires some ability. What about the Bar?

STEPHEN. I have not studied law. And I am afraid I have not the necessary push—I believe that is the name barristers give to their vulgarity—for success in pleading.

UNDERSHAFT. Rather a difficult case, Stephen. Hardly anything left but the stage, is there? [*Stephen makes an impatient movement*]. Well, come! is there a n y t h i n g you know or care for?

STEPHEN [*rising and looking at him steadily*] I know the difference between right and wrong.

UNDERSHAFT [*hugely tickled*] You dont say so! What! no capacity for business, no knowledge of law, no sympathy with art, no pretension to philosophy; only a simple knowledge of the secret that has puzzled all the philosophers, baffled all the lawyers, muddled all the men of business, and ruined most of the artists: the secret of right and wrong. Why, man, youre a genius, a master of masters, a god! At twentyfour, too!

STEPHEN [*keeping his temper with difficulty*] You are pleased to be facetious. I pretend to nothing more than any honorable English gentleman claims as his birthright [*he sits down angrily*].

UNDERSHAFT. Oh, thats everybody's birthright. Look at poor little Jenny Hill, the Salvation lassie! she would think you were laughing at her if you asked her to stand up in the street and teach grammar or geography or mathematics or even drawing room dancing; but it never occurs to her to doubt that she can teach morals and religion. You are all alike, you respectable people. You cant tell me the bursting strain of a ten-inch gun, which is a very simple matter; but you all think you can tell me the bursting strain of a man under temptation. You darent handle high explosives; but youre all ready to handle honesty and truth and justice and the whole duty of man, and kill one another at that game. What a country! What a world!

LADY BRITOMART [*uneasily*] What do you think he had better do, Andrew?

UNDERSHAFT. Oh, just what he wants to do. He knows nothing and he thinks he knows everything. That points clearly to a political career. Get him a private secretaryship to someone who can get him an Under Secretaryship; and then leave him alone. He will find his natural and proper place in the end on the Treasury Bench.

STEPHEN [*springing up again*] I am sorry, sir, that you force me to forget the respect due to you as my father. I am an Englishman and I will not hear the Government of my country insulted. [*He thrusts his hands in his pockets, and walks angrily across to the window*].

UNDERSHAFT [*with a touch of brutality*] The government of your country! *I* am the government of your country: I, and Lazarus. Do you suppose that you and half a dozen amateurs like you, sitting in a row in that foolish gabble shop, can govern Undershaft and Lazarus? No, my friend: you will do what pays u s. You will make war when it suits us, and keep peace when it doesnt. You will find out that trade requires certain measures when we have decided on those measures. When I want anything to keep my dividends up, you will discover that my want is a national need. When other people want something to keep my dividends down, you will call out the police and military. And in return you shall have the support and applause of my newspapers, and the delight of imagining that you are a great statesman. Government of your country! Be off with you, my boy, and play with your caucuses and leading articles and historic parties and great leaders and burning questions and the rest of your toys. *I* am going back to my counting-house to pay the piper and call the tune.

STEPHEN [*actually smiling, and putting his hand on his father's shoulder with indulgent patronage*] Really, my dear father, it is impossible to be angry with you. You dont know how absurd all this sounds to m e. You are properly proud of having been industrious enough to make money; and it is greatly to your credit that you have made so much of it. But it has kept you in circles where you are valued for your money and deferred to for it, instead of in the doubtless very old-fashioned and behind-the-times public school and university where I formed my habits of mind. It is natural for you to think that money governs England; but you must allow me to think I know better.

UNDERSHAFT. And what d o e s govern England, pray?

STEPHEN. Character, father, character.

UNDERSHAFT. Whose character? Yours or mine?

STEPHEN. Neither yours nor mine, father, but the best elements in the English national character.

UNDERSHAFT. Stephen: Ive found your profession for you. Youre a born journalist. I'll start you with a high-toned weekly review. There!

Before Stephen can reply Sarah, Barbara, Lomax, and Cusins come in ready for walking. Barbara crosses the room to the window and looks out. Cusins drifts amiably to the armchair. Lomax remains near the door, whilst Sarah comes to her mother.

Stephen goes to the smaller writing table and busies himself with his letters.

SARAH. Go and get ready, mamma: the carriage is waiting. [*Lady Britomart leaves the room*].

UNDERSHAFT [*to Sarah*] Good day, my dear. Good afternoon, Mr Lomax.

LOMAX [*vaguely*] Ahdedoo.

UNDERSHAFT [*to Cusins*] Quite well after last night, Euripides, eh?

CUSINS. As well as can be expected.

UNDERSHAFT. Thats right. [*To Barbara*] So you are coming to see my death and devastation factory, Barbara?

BARBARA [*at the window*] You came yesterday to see my salvation factory. I promised you a return visit.

LOMAX [*coming forward between Sarah and Undershaft*] Youll find it awfully interesting. Ive been through the Woolwich Arsenal; and it gives you a ripping feeling of security, you know, to think of the lot of beggars we could kill if it came to fighting. [*To Undershaft, with sudden solemnity*] Still, it must be rather an awful reflection for you, from the religious point of view as it were. Youre getting on, you know, and all that.

SARAH. You dont mind Cholly's imbecility, papa, do you?

LOMAX [*much taken aback*] Oh I s a y!

UNDERSHAFT. Mr Lomax looks at the matter in a very proper spirit, my dear.

LOMAX. Just so. Thats all I meant, I assure you.

SARAH. Are you coming, Stephen?

STEPHEN. Well, I am rather busy—er—[*Magnanimously*] Oh well, yes: I'll come. That is, if there is room for me.
UNDERSHAFT. I can take two with me in a little motor I am experimenting with for field use. You wont mind its being rather unfashionable. It's not painted yet; but it's bullet proof.
LOMAX [*appalled at the prospect of confronting Wilton Crescent in an unpainted motor*] Oh I s a y!
SARAH. The carriage for me, thank you. Barbara doesnt mind what she's seen in.
LOMAX. I say, Dolly, old chap: do you really mind the car being a guy? Because of course if you do I'll go in it. Still—
CUSINS. I prefer it.
LOMAX. Thanks awfully, old man. Come, my ownest. [*He hurries out to secure his seat in the carriage. Sarah follows him*].
CUSINS [*moodily walking across to Lady Britomart's writing table*] Why are we two coming to this Works Department of Hell? that is what I ask myself.
BARBARA. I have always thought of it as a sort of pit where lost creatures with blackened faces stirred up smoky fires and were driven and tormented by my father. Is it like that, dad?
UNDERSHAFT [*scandalized*] My dear! It is a spotlessly clean and beautiful hillside town.
CUSINS. With a Methodist chapel? Oh d o say theres a Methodist chapel.
UNDERSHAFT. There are two: a Primitive one and a sophisticated one. There is even an Ethical Society; but it is not much patronized, as my men are all strongly religious. In the High Explosives Sheds they object to the presence of Agnostics as unsafe.
CUSINS. And yet they dont object to you!
BARBARA. Do they obey all your orders?
UNDERSHAFT. I never give them any orders. When I speak to one of them it is "Well, Jones, is baby doing well? and has Mrs Jones made a good recovery?" "Nicely, thank you, sir." And thats all.
CUSINS. But Jones has to be kept in order. How do you maintain discipline among your men?
UNDERSHAFT. I dont. They do. You see, the one thing Jones wont stand is any rebellion from the man under him, or any assertion of social equality between the wife of the man with 4 shillings a week less than himself, and Mrs Jones! Of course they all rebel against me, theoret-

ically. Practically, every man of them keeps the man just below him in his place. I never meddle with them. I never bully them. I dont even bully Lazarus. I say that certain things are to be done; but I dont order anybody to do them. I dont say, mind you, that there is no ordering about and snubbing and even bullying. The men snub the boys and order them about; the carmen snub the sweepers; the artisans snub the unskilled laborers; the foremen drive and bully both the laborers and artisans; the assistant engineers find fault with the foremen; the chief engineers drop on the assistants; the departmental managers worry the chiefs; and the clerks have tall hats and hymnbooks and keep up the social tone by refusing to associate on equal terms with anybody. The result is a colossal profit, which comes to me.

CUSINS [*revolted*] You really are a—well, what I was saying yesterday.

BARBARA. What was he saying yesterday?

UNDERSHAFT. Never mind, my dear. He thinks I have made you unhappy. Have I?

BARBARA. Do you think I can be happy in this vulgar silly dress? I! who have worn the uniform. Do you understand what you have done to me? Yesterday I had a man's soul in my hand. I set him in the way of life with his face to salvation. But when we took your money he turned back to drunkenness and derision. [*With intense conviction*] I will never forgive you that. If I had a child, and you destroyed its body with your explosives—if you murdered Dolly with your horrible guns—I could forgive you if my forgiveness would open the gates of heaven to you. But to take a human soul from me, and turn it into the soul of a wolf! that is worse than any murder.

UNDERSHAFT. Does my daughter despair so easily? Can you strike a man to the heart and leave no mark on him?

BARBARA [*her face lighting up*] Oh, you are right: he can never be lost now: where was my faith?

CUSINS. Oh, clever clever devil!

BARBARA. You may be a devil; but God speaks through you sometimes. [*She takes her father's hands and kisses them*]. You have given me back my happiness: I feel it deep down now, though my spirit is troubled.

UNDERSHAFT. You have learnt something. That always feels at first as if you had lost something.

BARBARA. Well, take me to the factory of death; and let me learn something more. There must be some truth or other behind all this frightful irony. Come, Dolly. [*She goes out*].

CUSINS. My guardian angel! [*To Undershaft*] Avaunt! [*He follows Barbara*].

STEPHEN [*quietly, at the writing table*] You must not mind Cusins, father. He is a very amiable good fellow; but he is a Greek scholar and naturally a little eccentric.

UNDERSHAFT. Ah, quite so. Thank you, Stephen. Thank you. [*He goes out*].

Stephen smiles patronizingly; buttons his coat responsibly; and crosses the room to the door. Lady Britomart, dressed for out-of-doors, opens it before he reaches it. She looks round for the others; looks at Stephen; and turns to go without a word.

STEPHEN [*embarrassed*] Mother—

LADY BRITOMART. Dont be apologetic, Stephen. And dont forget that you have outgrown your mother. [*She goes out*].

Perivale St Andrews lies between two Middlesex hills, half climbing the northern one. It is an almost smokeless town of white walls, roofs of narrow green slates or red tiles, tall trees, domes, campaniles, and slender chimney shafts, beautifully situated and beautiful in itself. The best view of it is obtained from the crest of a slope about half a mile to the east, where the high explosives are dealt with. The foundry lies hidden in the depths between, the tops of its chimneys sprouting like huge skittles into the middle distance. Across the crest runs an emplacement of concrete, with a firestep, and a parapet which suggests a fortification, because there is a huge cannon of the obsolete Woolwich Infant pattern peering across it at the town. The cannon is mounted on an experimental gun carriage: possibly the original model of the Undershaft disappearing rampart gun alluded to by Stephen. The firestep, being a convenient place to sit, is furnished here and there with straw disc cushions; and at one place there is the additional luxury of a fur rug.

Barbara is standing on the firestep, looking over the parapet towards the town. On her right is the cannon; on her left the end of a shed raised on piles, with a ladder of three or four steps up to the door, which opens outwards and has a little wooden landing at the threshold, with a fire bucket in the corner of the landing. Several dummy soldiers more or less mutilated, with straw protruding from their gashes, have been shoved out of the way under the landing. A few others are nearly upright against the shed; and one has fallen forward and lies, like a grotesque corpse, on the emplacement. The parapet stops short of the shed, leaving a gap which is the beginning of the path down the hill through the foundry to the town. The rug is on the firestep near this gap. Down on the emplacement behind the cannon is a trolley carrying a huge conical bombshell with a red band painted on it. Further to the right is the door of an office, which, like the sheds, is of the lightest possible construction.

Cusins arrives by the path from the town.

BARBARA. Well?

CUSINS. Not a ray of hope. Everything perfect! wonderful! real! It only needs a cathedral to be a heavenly city instead of a hellish one.

BARBARA. Have you found out whether they have done anything for old Peter Shirley?

CUSINS. They have found him a job as gatekeeper and timekeeper. He's frightfully miserable. He calls the time-keeping brainwork, and says he isnt used to it; and his gate lodge is so splendid that he's ashamed to use the rooms, and skulks in the scullery.

BARBARA. Poor Peter!

Stephen arrives from the town. He carries a fieldglass.

STEPHEN [*enthusiastically*] Have you two seen the place? Why did you leave us?

CUSINS. I wanted to see everything I was not intended to see; and Barbara wanted to make the men talk.

STEPHEN. Have you found anything discreditable?

CUSINS. No. They call him Dandy Andy and are proud of his being a cunning old rascal; but it's all horribly, frightfully, immorally, unanswerably perfect.

Sarah arrives.

SARAH. Heavens! what a place! [*She crosses to the trolley*]. Did you see the nursing home!? [*She sits down on the shell*].

STEPHEN. Did you see the libraries and schools!?

SARAH. Did you see the ball room and the banqueting chamber in the Town Hall!?

STEPHEN. Have you gone into the insurance fund, the pension fund, the building society, the various applications of co-operation!?

Undershaft comes from the office, with a sheaf of telegrams in his hand.

UNDERSHAFT. Well, have you seen everything? I'm sorry I was called away. [*Indicating the telegrams*] Good news from Manchuria.

STEPHEN. Another Japanese victory?

UNDERSHAFT. Oh, I dont know. Which side wins does not concern us here. No: the good news is that the aerial battleship is a tremendous success. At the first trial it has wiped out a fort with three hundred soldiers in it.

CUSINS [*from the platform*] Dummy soldiers?

UNDERSHAFT [*striding across to Stephen and kicking the prostrate dummy brutally out of his way*] No: the real thing.

Cusins and Barbara exchange glances. Then Cusins sits on the step and buries his face in his hands. Barbara gravely lays her hand on his shoulder. He looks up at her in whimsical desperation.

UNDERSHAFT. Well, Stephen, what do you think of the place?

STEPHEN. Oh, magnificent. A perfect triumph of modern industry. Frankly, my dear father, I have been a fool: I had no idea of what it all meant: of the wonderful forethought, the power of organization, the administrative capacity, the financial genius, the colossal capital it represents. I have been repeating to myself as I came through your streets "Peace hath her victories no less renowned than War." I have only one misgiving about it all.

UNDERSHAFT. Out with it.

STEPHEN. Well, I cannot help thinking that all this provision for every want of your workmen may sap their independence and weaken their sense of responsibility. And greatly as we enjoyed our tea at that splendid restaurant—how they gave us all that luxury and cake and jam and cream for threepence I really cannot imagine!—still you must remember that restaurants break up home life. Look at the continent, for instance! Are you sure so much pampering is really good for the men's characters?

UNDERSHAFT. Well you see, my dear boy, when you are organizing civilization you have to make up your mind whether trouble and anxiety are good things or not. If you decide that they are, then, I take it, you simply dont organize civilization; and there you are, with trouble and anxiety enough to make us all angels! But if you decide the other way, you may as well go through with it. However, Stephen, our characters are safe here. A sufficient dose of anxiety is always provided by the fact that we may be blown to smithereens at any moment.

SARAH. By the way, papa, where do you make the explosives?

UNDERSHAFT. In separate little sheds, like that one. When one of them blows up, it costs very little; and only the people quite close to it are killed.

Stephen, who is quite close to it, looks at it rather scaredly, and moves away quickly to the cannon. At the same moment the door of the shed is thrown abruptly open; and a foreman in overalls and list slippers comes out on the little landing and holds the door for Lomax, who appears in the doorway.

LOMAX [*with studied coolness*] My good fellow: you neednt get into a state of nerves. Nothing's going to happen to you; and I suppose it wouldnt be the end of the world if anything did. A little bit of British pluck is what y o u want, old chap. [*He descends and strolls across to Sarah*].

UNDERSHAFT [*to the foreman*] Anything wrong, Bilton?

BILTON [*with ironic calm*] Gentleman walked into the high explosives shed and lit a cigaret, sir: thats all.

UNDERSHAFT. Ah, quite so. [*Going over to Lomax*] Do you happen to remember what you did with the match?

LOMAX. Oh come! I'm not a fool. I took jolly good care to blow it out before I chucked it away.

BILTON. The top of it was red hot inside, sir.

LOMAX. Well, suppose it was! I didn't chuck it into any of y o u r messes.

UNDERSHAFT. Think no more of it, Mr Lomax. By the way, would you mind lending me your matches.

LOMAX [*offering his box*] Certainly.

UNDERSHAFT. Thanks. [*He pockets the matches*].

LOMAX [*lecturing to the company generally*] You know, these high explosives dont go off like gunpowder, except when theyre in a gun. When theyre spread loose, you can put a match to them without the least risk; they just burn quietly like a bit of paper. [*Warming to the scientific interest of the subject*] Did you know that, Undershaft? Have you ever tried?

UNDERSHAFT. Not on a large scale, Mr Lomax. Bilton will give you a sample of gun cotton when you are leaving if you ask him. You can experiment with it at home. [*Bilton looks puzzled*].

SARAH. Bilton will do nothing of the sort, papa. I suppose it's your business to blow up the Russians and Japs; but you might really stop short of blowing up poor Cholly. [*Bilton gives it up and retires into the shed*].

LOMAX. My ownest, there is no danger. [*He sits beside her on the shell*].

Lady Britomart arrives from the town with a bouquet.

LADY BRITOMART [*impetuously*] Andrew: you shouldnt have let me see this place.

UNDERSHAFT. Why, my dear?

LADY BRITOMART. Never mind why: you shouldnt have: thats all. To think of all that [*indicating the town*] being yours! and that you have kept it to yourself all these years!

UNDERSHAFT. It does not belong to me. I belong to it. It is the Undershaft inheritance.

LADY BRITOMART. It is not. Your ridiculous cannons and that noisy banging foundry may be the Undershaft inheritance; but all that plate and linen, all that furniture and those houses and orchards and gardens belong to us. They belong to m e: they are not a man's business. I wont give them up. You must be out of your senses to throw them all away; and if you persist in such folly, I will call in a doctor.

UNDERSHAFT [*stooping to smell the bouquet*] Where did you get the flowers, my dear?

LADY BRITOMART. Your men presented them to me in your William Morris Labor Church.

CUSINS. Oh! It needed only that. A Labor Church! [*he mounts the firestep distractedly, and leans with his elbows on the parapet, turning his back to them*].

LADY BRITOMART. Yes, with Morris's words in mosaic letters ten feet high round the dome. NO MAN IS GOOD ENOUGH TO BE ANOTHER MAN'S MASTER. The cynicism of it!

UNDERSHAFT. It shocked the men at first, I am afraid. But now they take no more notice of it than of the ten commandments in church.

LADY BRITOMART. Andrew: you are trying to put me off the subject of the inheritance by profane jokes. Well, you shant. I dont ask it any longer for Stephen: he has inherited far too much of your perversity to be fit for it. But Barbara has rights as well as Stephen. Why should not Adolphus succeed to the inheritance? I could manage the town for him; and he can look after the cannons, if they are really necessary.

UNDERSHAFT. I should ask nothing better if Adolphus were a foundling. He is exactly the sort of new blood that is wanted in English business. But he's not a foundling; and theres an end of it. [*He makes for the office door*].

CUSINS [*turning to them*] Not quite. [*They all turn and stare at him*]. I think—Mind! I am not committing myself in any way as to my future course—but I t h i n k the foundling difficulty can be got over. [*He jumps down to the emplacement*].

UNDERSHAFT [*coming back to him*] What do you mean?

CUSINS. Well, I have something to say which is in the nature of a confession.

SARAH.
LADY BRITOMART.
BARBARA.
STEPHEN. } Confession!

LOMAX. Oh I say!

CUSINS. Yes, a confession. Listen, all. Until I met Barbara I thought myself in the main an honorable, truthful man, because I wanted the approval of my conscience more than I wanted anything else. But the moment I saw Barbara, I wanted her far more than the approval of my conscience.

LADY BRITOMART. Adolphus!

CUSINS. It is true. You accused me yourself, Lady Brit, of joining the Army to worship Barbara; and so I did. She bought my soul like a flower at a street corner; but she bought it for herself.

UNDERSHAFT. What! Not for Dionysos or another?

CUSINS. Dionysos and all the others are in herself. I adored what was divine in her, and was therefore a true worshipper. But I was romantic about her too. I thought she was a woman of the people, and that a marriage with a professor of Greek would be far beyond the wildest social ambitions of her rank.

LADY BRITOMART. Adolphus!!

LOMAX. Oh I s a y!!!

CUSINS. When I learnt the horrible truth—

LADY BRITOMART. What do you mean by the horrible truth, pray?

CUSINS. That she was enormously rich; that her grandfather was an earl; that her father was the Prince of Darkness—

UNDERSHAFT. Chut!

CUSINS.—and that I was only an adventurer trying to catch a rich wife, then I stooped to deceive her about my birth.

BARBARA [*rising*] Dolly!

LADY BRITOMART. Your birth! Now Adolphus, dont dare to make up a wicked story for the sake of these wretched cannons. Remember: I have seen photographs of your parents; and the Agent General for South Western Australia knows them personally and has assured me that they are most respectable married people.

CUSINS. So they are in Australia; but here they are outcasts. Their marriage is legal in Australia, but not in England. My mother is my father's deceased wife's sister; and in this island I am consequently a foundling. [*Sensation*].

BARBARA. Silly! [*She climbs to the cannon, and leans, listening, in the angle it makes with the parapet*].

CUSINS. Is the subterfuge good enough, Machiavelli?

UNDERSHAFT [*thoughtfully*] Biddy: this may be a way out of the difficulty.

LADY BRITOMART. Stuff! A man cant make cannons any the better for being his own cousin instead of his proper self [*she sits down on the rug with a bounce that expresses her downright contempt for their casuistry*].

UNDERSHAFT [*to Cusins*] You are an educated man. That is against the tradition.

CUSINS. Once in ten thousand times it happens that the schoolboy is a born master of what they try to teach him. Greek has not destroyed my mind: it has nourished it. Besides, I did not learn it at an English public school.

UNDERSHAFT. Hm! Well, I cannot afford to be too particular: you have cornered the foundling market. Let it pass. You are eligible, Euripides: you are eligible.

BARBARA. Dolly: yesterday morning, when Stephen told us all about the tradition, you became very silent; and you have been strange and excited ever since. Were you thinking of your birth then?

CUSINS. When the finger of Destiny suddenly points at a man in the middle of his breakfast, it makes him thoughtful.

UNDERSHAFT. Aha! You have had your eye on the business, my young friend, have you?

CUSINS. Take care! There is an abyss of moral horror between me and your accursed aerial battleships.

UNDERSHAFT. Never mind the abyss for the present. Let us settle the practical details and leave your final decision open. You know that you will have to change your name. Do you object to that?

CUSINS. Would any man named Adolphus—any man called Dolly!—object to be called something else?

UNDERSHAFT. Good. Now, as to money! I propose to treat you handsomely from the beginning. You shall start at a thousand a year.

CUSINS [*with sudden heat, his spectacles twinkling with mischief*] A thousand! You dare offer a miserable thousand to the son-in-law of a millionaire! No, by Heavens, Machiavelli! you shall not cheat me. You cannot do without me; and I can do without you. I must have two thousand five hundred a year for two years. At the end of that time, if I am a failure, I go. But if I am a success, and stay on, you must give me the other five thousand.

UNDERSHAFT. What other five thousand?

CUSINS. To make the two years up to five thousand a year. The two thousand five hundred is only half pay in case I should turn out a failure. The third year I must have ten per cent on the profits.

UNDERSHAFT [*taken aback*] Ten per cent! Why, man, do you know what my profits are?

CUSINS. Enormous, I hope: otherwise I shall require twentyfive per cent.

UNDERSHAFT. But, Mr Cusins, this is a serious matter of business. You are not bringing any capital into the concern.

CUSINS. What! no capital! Is my mastery of Greek no capital? Is my access to the subtlest thought, the loftiest poetry yet attained by humanity, no capital? My character! my intellect! my life! my career! what Barbara calls my soul! are these no capital? Say another word; and I double my salary.

UNDERSHAFT. Be reasonable—

CUSINS [*peremptorily*] Mr Undershaft: you have my terms. Take them or leave them.

UNDERSHAFT [*recovering himself*] Very well. I note your terms; and I offer you half.

CUSINS [*disgusted*] Half!

UNDERSHAFT [*firmly*] Half.

CUSINS. You call yourself a gentleman; and you offer me half!!

UNDERSHAFT. I do not call myself a gentleman; but I offer you half.

CUSINS. This to your future partner! your successor! your son-in-law!

BARBARA. You are selling your own soul, Dolly, not mine. Leave me out of the bargain, please.

UNDERSHAFT. Come! I will go a step further for Barbara's sake. I will give you three fifths; but that is my last word.

CUSINS. Done!

LOMAX. Done in the eye! Why, *I* get only eight hundred, you know.

CUSINS. By the way, Mac, I am a classical scholar, not an arithmetical one. Is three fifths more than half or less?

UNDERSHAFT. More, of course.

CUSINS. I would have taken two hundred and fifty. How you can succeed in business when you are willing to pay all that money to a University don who is obviously not worth a junior clerk's wages!—well! What will Lazarus say?

UNDERSHAFT. Lazarus is a gentle romantic Jew who cares for nothing but string quartets and stalls at fashionable theatres. He will be blamed for your rapacity in money matters, poor fellow! as he has hitherto been blamed for mine. You are a shark of the first order, Euripides. So much the better for the firm!

BARBARA. Is the bargain closed, Dolly? Does your soul belong to him now?

CUSINS. No: the price is settled: that is all. The real tug of war is still to come. What about the moral question?

LADY BRITOMART. There is no moral question in the matter at all, Adolphus. You must simply sell cannons and weapons to people whose cause is right and just, and refuse them to foreigners and criminals.

UNDERSHAFT [*determinedly*] No: none of that. You must keep the true faith of an Armorer, or you dont come in here.

CUSINS. What on earth is the true faith of an Armorer?

UNDERSHAFT. To give arms to all men who offer an honest price for them, without respect of persons or principles: to aristocrat and republican, to Nihilist and Tsar, to Capitalist and Socialist, to Protestant and Catholic, to burglar and policeman, to black man, white man and yellow man, to all sorts and conditions, all nationalities, all faiths, all follies, all causes and all crimes. The first Undershaft wrote up in his shop IF GOD GAVE THE HAND, LET NOT MAN WITHHOLD THE SWORD. The second wrote up ALL HAVE THE RIGHT TO FIGHT: NONE HAVE THE RIGHT TO JUDGE. The third wrote up TO MAN THE WEAPON: TO HEAVEN THE VICTORY. The fourth had no literary turn; so he did not write up anything; but he sold cannons to Napoleon under the nose of George the Third. The fifth wrote up PEACE SHALL NOT PREVAIL SAVE WITH A SWORD IN HER HAND. The sixth, my master, was the best of all. He wrote up NOTHING IS EVER DONE IN THIS WORLD UNTIL MEN ARE PREPARED TO KILL ONE ANOTHER IF IT IS NOT DONE. After that, there was nothing left for the seventh to say. So he wrote up, simply, UNASHAMED.

CUSINS. My good Machiavelli, I shall certainly write something up on the wall; only, as I shall write it in Greek, you wont be able to read it. But as to your Armorer's faith, if I take my neck out of the noose of my own morality I am not going to put it into the noose of yours. I shall sell cannons to whom I please and refuse them to whom I please. So there!

UNDERSHAFT. From the moment when you become Andrew Undershaft, you will never do as you please again. Dont come here lusting for power, young man.

CUSINS. If power were my aim I should not come here for it. You have no power.

UNDERSHAFT. None of my own, certainly.

CUSINS. I have more power than you, more will. You do not drive this place: it drives you. And what drives the place?

UNDERSHAFT [*enigmatically*] A will of which I am a part.

BARBARA [*startled*] Father! Do you know what you are saying; or are you laying a snare for my soul?

CUSINS. Dont listen to his metaphysics, Barbara. The place is driven by the most rascally part of society, the money hunters, the pleasure hunters, the military promotion hunters; and he is their slave.

UNDERSHAFT. Not necessarily. Remember the Armorer's Faith. I will take an order from a good man as cheerfully as from a bad one. If you good people prefer preaching and shirking to buying my weapons and fighting the rascals, dont blame me. I can make cannons: I cannot make courage and conviction. Bah! you tire me, Euripides, with your morality mongering. Ask Barbara: she understands. [*He suddenly reaches up and takes Barbara's hands, looking powerfully into her eyes*] Tell him, my love, what power really means.

BARBARA [*hypnotized*] Before I joined the Salvation Army, I was in my own power; and the consequence was that I never knew what to do with myself. When I joined it, I had not time enough for all the things I had to do.

UNDERSHAFT [*approvingly*] Just so. And why was that, do you suppose?

BARBARA. Yesterday I should have said, because I was in the power of God. [*She resumes her self-possession, withdrawing her hands from his with a power equal to his own*]. But you came and shewed me that I was in the power of Bodger and Undershaft. Today I feel—oh! how can I put it into words? Sarah: do you remember the earthquake at Cannes, when we were little children?—how little the surprise of the first shock mattered compared to the dread and horror of waiting for the second? That is how I feel in this place today. I stood on the rock I thought eternal: and without a word of warning it reeled and crumbled under me. I was safe with an infinite wisdom watching me, an army marching to Salvation with me; and in a moment, at a stroke of your pen in a cheque book, I stood alone; and the heavens were empty. That was the first shock of the earthquake: I am waiting for the second.

UNDERSHAFT. Come, come, my daughter! dont make too much of your little tinpot tragedy. What do we do here when we spend years of work and thought and thousands of pounds of solid cash on a new gun or an aerial battleship that turns out just a hairsbreadth wrong after all? Scrap it. Scrap it without wasting another hour or another pound on it. Well, you have made for yourself something that you call a morality or a religion or what not. It doesnt fit the facts. Well, scrap it. Scrap it and get one that does fit. That is what is wrong with the world at present. It scraps its obsolete steam engines and dynamos; but it wont scrap its old prejudices and its old moralities and its old religions and its old political constitutions. Whats the result? In machinery it does very well; but in morals and religion and politics it is working at a loss that brings it nearer bankruptcy every year. Dont persist in that folly. If your old religion broke down yesterday, get a newer and a better one for tomorrow.

BARBARA. Oh how gladly I would take a better one to my soul! But you offer me a worse one. [*Turning on him with sudden vehemence*]. Justify yourself: shew me some light through the darkness of this dreadful place, with its beautifully clean workshops, and respectable workmen, and model homes.

UNDERSHAFT. Cleanliness and respectability do not need justification, Barbara: they justify themselves. I see no darkness here, no dreadfulness. In your Salvation shelter I saw poverty, misery, cold and hunger. You gave them bread and treacle and dreams of heaven. I give from thirty shillings a week to twelve thousand a year. They find their own dreams; but I look after the drainage.

BARBARA. And their souls?

UNDERSHAFT. I save their souls just as I saved yours.

BARBARA [*revolted*] You saved my soul! What do you mean?

UNDERSHAFT. I fed you and clothed you and housed you. I took care that you should have money enough to live handsomely—more than enough; so that you could be wasteful, careless, generous. That saved your soul from the seven deadly sins.

BARBARA [*bewildered*] The seven deadly sins!

UNDERSHAFT. Yes, the deadly seven. [*Counting on his fingers*] Food, clothing, firing, rent, taxes, respectability and children. Nothing can lift those seven millstones from Man's neck but money; and the spirit cannot soar until the millstones are lifted. I lifted them from your spirit. I enabled Barbara to become Major Barbara; and I saved her from the crime of poverty.

CUSINS. Do you call poverty a crime?

UNDERSHAFT. The worst of crimes. All the other crimes are virtues beside it: all the other dishonors are chivalry itself by comparison. Poverty blights whole cities; spreads horrible pestilences; strikes dead the very souls of all who come within sight, sound, or smell of it. What you call crime is nothing: a murder here and a theft there, a blow now and a curse then: what do they matter? they are only the accidents and illnesses of life: there are not fifty genuine professional criminals in London. But there are millions of poor people, abject people, dirty people, ill fed, ill clothed people. They poison us morally and physically: they kill the happiness of society: they force us to do away with our own liberties and to organize unnatural cruelties for fear they should rise against us and drag us down into their abyss. Only fools fear crime: we all fear poverty. Pah! [*turning on Barbara*] you talk of your half-saved ruffian in West Ham: you accuse me of dragging his soul back to perdition. Well, bring him to me here; and I will drag his soul back again to salvation for you. Not by words and dreams; but by thirtyeight shillings a week, a sound house in a handsome street, and a permanent job. In three weeks he will have a fancy waistcoat; in three months a tall hat and a chapel sitting; before the end of the year he will shake hands with a duchess at a Primrose League meeting, and join the Conservative Party.

BARBARA. And will he be the better for that?

UNDERSHAFT. You know he will. Dont be a hypocrite, Barbara. He will be better fed, better housed, better clothed, better behaved; and his children will be pounds heavier and bigger. That will be better than an American cloth mattress in a shelter, chopping firewood, eating bread and treacle, and being forced to kneel down from time to time to thank heaven for it: knee drill, I think you call it. It is cheap work converting starving men with a Bible in one hand and a slice of bread in the other. I will undertake to convert West Ham to Mahometanism on the same terms. Try your hand on my men: their souls are hungry because their bodies are full.

BARBARA. And leave the east end to starve?

UNDERSHAFT [*his energetic tone dropping into one of bitter and brooding remembrance*] I was an east ender. I moralized and starved until one day I swore that I would be a full-fed free man at all costs; that nothing should stop me except a bullet, neither reason nor morals nor the lives of other men. I said "Thou shalt starve ere I starve"; and with that word I became free and great. I was a dangerous man until I had my will: now I am a useful, beneficent, kindly person. That is the history of most self-made millionaires, I fancy. When it is the history of every Englishman we shall have an England worth living in.

LADY BRITOMART. Stop making speeches, Andrew. This is not the place for them.

UNDERSHAFT [*punctured*] My dear: I have no other means of conveying my ideas.

LADY BRITOMART. Your ideas are nonsense. You got on because you were selfish and unscrupulous.

UNDERSHAFT. Not at all. I had the strongest scruples about poverty and starvation. Your moralists are quite unscrupulous about both: they make virtues of them. I had rather be a thief than a pauper. I had rather be a murderer than a slave. I dont want to be either; but if you force the alternative on me, then, by Heaven, I'll choose the braver and more moral one. I hate poverty and slavery worse than any other crimes whatsoever. And let me tell you this. Poverty and slavery have stood up for centuries to your sermons and leading articles: they will not stand up to my machine guns. Dont preach at them: dont reason with them. Kill them.

BARBARA. Killing. Is that your remedy for everything?

UNDERSHAFT. It is the final test of conviction, the only lever strong enough to overturn a social system, the only way of saying Must. Let six hundred and seventy fools loose in the streets; and three policemen can scatter them. But huddle them together in a certain house in Westminster; and let them go through certain ceremonies and call themselves certain names until at last they get the courage to kill; and your six hundred and seventy fools become a government. Your pious mob fills up ballot papers and imagines it is governing its masters; but the ballot paper that really governs is the paper that has a bullet wrapped up in it.

CUSINS. That is perhaps why, like most intelligent people, I never vote.

UNDERSHAFT. Vote! Bah! When you vote, you only change the names of the cabinet. When you shoot, you pull down governments, inaugurate new epochs, abolish old orders and set up new. Is that historically true, Mr Learned Man, or is it not?

CUSINS. It is historically true. I loathe having to admit it. I repudiate your sentiments. I abhor your nature. I defy you in every possible way. Still, it is true. But it ought not to be true.

UNDERSHAFT. Ought! ought! ought! ought! ought! Are you going to spend your life saying ought, like the rest of our moralists? Turn your oughts into shalls, man. Come and make explosives with me. Whatever can blow men up can blow society up. The history of the world is the history of those who had courage enough to embrace this truth. Have you the courage to embrace it, Barbara?

LADY BRITOMART. Barbara: I positively forbid you to listen to your father's abominable wickedness. And you, Adolphus, ought to know better than to go about saying that wrong things are true. What does it matter whether they are true if they are wrong?

UNDERSHAFT. What does it matter whether they are wrong if they are true?

LADY BRITOMART [*rising*] Children: come home instantly. Andrew: I am exceedingly sorry I allowed you to call on us. You are wickeder than ever. Come at once.

BARBARA [*shaking her head*] It's no use running away from wicked people, mamma.

LADY BRITOMART. It is every use. It shews your disapprobation of them.

BARBARA. It does not save them.

LADY BRITOMART. I can see that you are going to disobey me. Sarah: are you coming home or are you not?

SARAH. I daresay it's very wicked of papa to make cannons; but I dont think I shall cut him on that account.

LOMAX [*pouring oil on the troubled waters*] The fact is, you know, there is a certain amount of tosh about this notion of wickedness. It doesnt work. You must look at facts. Not that I would say a word in favor of anything wrong; but then, you see, all sorts of chaps are always doing all sorts of things; and we have to fit them in somehow, dont you know. What I mean is that you cant go cutting everybody; and thats about what it comes to. [*Their rapt attention to his eloquence makes him nervous*]. Perhaps I dont make myself clear.

LADY BRITOMART. You are lucidity itself, Charles. Because Andrew is successful and has plenty of money to give to Sarah, you will flatter him and encourage him in his wickedness.

LOMAX [*unruffled*] Well, where the carcase is, there will the eagles be gathered, dont you know. [*To Undershaft*] Eh? What?

UNDERSHAFT. Precisely. By the way, m a y I call you Charles?

LOMAX. Delighted. Cholly is the usual ticket.

UNDERSHAFT [*to Lady Britomart*] Biddy—

LADY BRITOMART [*violently*] Dont dare call me Biddy. Charles Lomax: you are a fool. Adolphus Cusins: you are a Jesuit. Stephen: you are a prig. Barbara: you are a lunatic. Andrew: you are a vulgar tradesman. Now you all know my opinion; and my conscience is clear, at all events [*she sits down with a vehemence that the rug fortunately softens*].

UNDERSHAFT. My dear: you are the incarnation of morality. [*She snorts*]. Your conscience is clear and your duty done when you have called everybody names. Come, Euripides! it is getting late; and we all want to go home. Make up your mind.

CUSINS. Understand this, you old demon—

LADY BRITOMART. Adolphus!

UNDERSHAFT. Let him alone, Biddy. Proceed, Euripides.

CUSINS. You have me in a horrible dilemma. I want Barbara.

UNDERSHAFT. Like all young men, you greatly exaggerate the difference between one young woman and another.

BARBARA. Quite true, Dolly.

CUSINS. I also want to avoid being a rascal.

UNDERSHAFT [*with biting contempt*] You lust for personal righteousness, for self-approval, for what you call a good conscience, for what Barbara calls salvation, for what I call patronizing people who are not so lucky as yourself.

CUSINS. I do not: all the poet in me recoils from being a good man. But there are things in me that I must reckon with. Pity—

UNDERSHAFT. Pity! The scavenger of misery.

CUSINS. Well, love.

UNDERSHAFT. I know. You love the needy and the outcast: you love the oppressed races, the negro, the Indian ryot, the underdog everywhere. Do you love the Japanese? Do you love the French? Do you love the English?

CUSINS. No. Every true Englishman detests the English. We are the wickedest nation on earth; and our success is a moral horror.

UNDERSHAFT. That is what comes of your gospel of love, is it?

CUSINS. May I not love even my father-in-law?

UNDERSHAFT. Who wants your love, man? By what right do you take the liberty of offering it to me? I will have your due heed and respect, or I will kill you. But your love! Damn your impertinence!

CUSINS [*grinning*] I may not be able to control my affections, Mac.

UNDERSHAFT. You are fencing, Euripides. You are weakening: your grip is slipping. Come! try your last weapon. Pity and love have broken in your hand: forgiveness is still left.

CUSINS. No: forgiveness is a beggar's refuge. I am with you there: we must pay our debts.

UNDERSHAFT. Well said. Come! you will suit me. Remember the words of Plato.

CUSINS [*starting*] Plato! You dare quote Plato to me!

UNDERSHAFT. Plato says, my friend, that society cannot be saved until either the Professors of Greek take to making gunpowder, or else the makers of gunpowder become Professors of Greek.

CUSINS. Oh, tempter, cunning tempter!

UNDERSHAFT. Come! choose, man, choose.

CUSINS. But perhaps Barbara will not marry me if I make the wrong choice.

BARBARA. Perhaps not.

CUSINS [*desperately perplexed*] You hear!

BARBARA. Father: do you love nobody?

UNDERSHAFT. I love my best friend.

LADY BRITOMART. And who is that, pray?

UNDERSHAFT. My bravest enemy. That is the man who keeps me up to the mark.

CUSINS. You know, the creature is really a sort of poet in his way. Suppose he is a great man, after all!

UNDERSHAFT. Suppose you stop talking and make up your mind, my young friend.

CUSINS. But you are driving me against my nature. I hate war.

UNDERSHAFT. Hatred is the coward's revenge for being intimidated. Dare you make war on war? Here are the means: my friend Mr Lomax is sitting on them.

LOMAX [*springing up*] Oh I say! You dont mean that this thing is loaded, do you? My ownest: come off it.

SARAH [*sitting placidly on the shell*] If I am to be blown up, the more thoroughly it is done the better. Dont fuss, Cholly.

LOMAX [*to Undershaft, strongly remonstrant*] Your own daughter, you know!

UNDERSHAFT. So I see. [*To Cusins*] Well, my friend, may we expect you here at six tomorrow morning?

CUSINS [*firmly*] Not on any account. I will see the whole establishment blown up with its own dynamite before I will get up at five. My hours are healthy, rational hours: eleven to five.

UNDERSHAFT. Come when you please: before a week you will come at six and stay until I turn you out for the sake of your health. [*Calling*] Bilton! [*He turns to Lady Britomart, who rises*]. My dear: let us leave these two young people to themselves for a moment. [*Bilton comes from the shed*]. I am going to take you through the gun cotton shed.

BILTON [*Barring the way*] You cant take anything explosive in here, sir.

LADY BRITOMART. What do you mean? Are you alluding to me?

BILTON [*unmoved*] No, maam. Mr Undershaft has the other gentleman's matches in his pocket.

LADY BRITOMART [*abruptly*] Oh! I beg your pardon. [*She goes into the shed*].

UNDERSHAFT. Quite right, Bilton, quite right: here you are. [*He gives Bilton the box of matches*]. Come, Stephen. Come, Charles. Bring Sarah. [*He passes into the shed*].

Bilton opens the box and deliberately drops the matches into the fire-bucket.

LOMAX. Oh! I say [*Bilton hands him the empty box*]. Infernal nonsense! Pure scientific ignorance! [*He goes in*].

SARAH. Am I all right, Bilton?

BILTON. Youll have to put on list slippers, miss: thats all. Weve got em inside. [*She goes in*].

STEPHEN [*very seriously to Cusins*] Dolly, old fellow, think. Think before you decide. Do you feel that you are a sufficiently practical man? It is a huge undertaking, an enormous responsibility. All this mass of business will be Greek to you.

CUSINS. Oh, I think it will be much less difficult than Greek.

STEPHEN. Well, I just want to say this before I leave you to yourselves. Dont let anything I have said about right and wrong prejudice you against this great chance in life. I have satisfied myself that the business is one of the highest character and a credit to our country. [*Emotionally*] I am very proud of my father. I—[*Unable to proceed, he presses Cusins' hand and goes hastily into the shed, followed by Bilton*].

Barbara and Cusins, left alone together, look at one another silently.

CUSINS. Barbara: I am going to accept this offer.

BARBARA. I thought you would.

CUSINS. You understand, dont you, that I had to decide without consulting you. If I had thrown the burden of the choice on you, you would sooner or later have despised me for it.

BARBARA. Yes: I did not want you to sell your soul for me any more than for this inheritance.

CUSINS. It is not the sale of my soul that troubles me: I have sold it too often to care about that. I have sold it for a professorship. I have sold it for an income. I have sold it to escape being imprisoned for refusing to pay taxes for hangmen's ropes and unjust wars and things that I abhor. What is all human conduct but the daily and hourly sale of our souls for trifles? What I am now selling it for is neither money nor position nor comfort, but for reality and for power.

BARBARA. You know that you will have no power, and that he has none.

CUSINS. I know. It is not for myself alone. I want to make power for the world.

BARBARA. I want to make power for the world too; but it must be spiritual power.

CUSINS. I think all power is spiritual: these cannons will not go off by themselves. I have tried to make spiritual power by teaching Greek. But the world can never be really touched by a dead language and a dead civilization. The people must have power; and the people cannot have Greek. Now the power that is made here can be wielded by all men.

BARBARA. Power to burn women's houses down and kill their sons and tear their husbands to pieces.

CUSINS. You cannot have power for good without having power for evil too. Even mother's milk nourishes murderers as well as heroes. This power which only tears men's bodies to pieces has never been so horribly abused as the intellectual power, the imaginative power, the poetic, religious power that can enslave men's souls. As a teacher of Greek I gave the intellectual man weapons against the common man. I now want to give the common man weapons against the intellectual man. I love the common people. I want to arm them against the lawyers, the doctors, the priests, the literary men, the professors, the artists, and the politicians, who, once in authority, are more disastrous and tyrannical than all the fools, rascals, and impostors. I want a power simple enough for common men to use, yet strong enough to force the intellectual oligarchy to use its genius for the general good.

BARBARA. Is there no higher power than that [*pointing to the shell*]?

CUSINS. Yes: but that power can destroy the higher powers just as a tiger can destroy a man: there Man must master that power first. I admitted this when the Turks and Greeks were last at war. My best pupil went out to fight for Hellas. My parting gift to him was not a copy of Plato's Republic, but a revolver and a hundred Undershaft cartridges. The blood of every Turk he shot—if he shot any—is on my head as well as on Undershaft's. That act committed me to this place for ever. Your father's challenge has beaten me. Dare I make war on war? I dare. I must. I will. And now, is it all over between us?

BARBARA [*touched by his evident dread of her answer*] Silly baby Dolly! How could it be!

CUSINS [*overjoyed*] Then you—you—you—Oh for my drum! [*He flourishes imaginary drumsticks*].

BARBARA [*angered by his levity*] Take care, Dolly, take care. Oh, if only I could get away from you and from father and from it all! if I could have the wings of a dove and fly away to heaven!

CUSINS. And leave m e!

BARBARA. Yes, you, and all the other naughty mischievous children of men. But I cant. I was happy in the Salvation Army for a moment. I escaped from the world into a paradise of enthusiasm and prayer and soul saving; but the moment our money ran short, it all came back to Bodger: it was he who saved our people: he, and the Prince of Darkness, my papa. Undershaft and Bodger: their hands stretch everywhere: when we feed a starving fellow creature, it is with their bread, because there is no other bread; when we tend the sick, it is in the hospitals they endow; if we turn from the churches they build, we must kneel on the stones of the streets they pave. As long as that lasts, there is no getting away from them. Turning our backs on Bodger and Undershaft is turning our backs on life.

CUSINS. I thought you were determined to turn your back on the wicked side of life.

BARBARA. There is no wicked side: life is all one. And I never wanted to shirk my share in whatever evil must be endured, whether it be sin or suffering. I wish I could cure you of middle-class ideas, Dolly.

CUSINS [*gasping*] Middle cl—! A snub! A social snub to m e! from the daughter of a foundling!

BARBARA. That is why I have no class, Dolly: I come straight out of the heart of the whole people. If I were middle-class I should turn my back on my father's business; and we should both live in an artistic drawing room, with you reading the reviews in one corner, and I in the other at the piano, playing Schumann: both very superior persons, and neither of us a bit of use. Sooner than that, I would sweep out the guncotton shed, or be one of Bodger's barmaids. Do you know what would have happened if you had refused papa's offer?

CUSINS. I wonder!

BARBARA. I should have given you up and married the man who accepted it. After all, my dear old mother has more sense than any of you. I felt like her when I saw this place—felt that I must have it—that never, never, never could I let it go; only she thought it was the houses and the kitchen ranges and the linen and china, when it was really all the human souls to be saved: not weak souls in starved bodies, sobbing with gratitude for a scrap of bread and treacle, but fullfed quarrelsome, snobbish, uppish creatures, all standing on their little rights and dignities, and thinking that my father ought to be greatly obliged to them for making so much money for him—and so he ought. That is where salvation is really wanted. My father shall never throw it in my teeth again that my converts were bribed with bread. [*She is transfigured*]. I have got rid of the bribe of bread. I have got rid of the bribe of heaven. Let God's work be done for its own sake: the work he had to create us to do because it cannot be done except by living men and women. When I die, let him be in my debt, not I in his; and let me forgive him as becomes a woman of my rank.

CUSINS. Then the way of life lies through the factory of death?

BARBARA. Yes, through the raising of hell to heaven and of man to God, through the unveiling of an eternal light in the Valley of The Shadow. [*Seizing him with both hands*] Oh, did you think my courage would never come back? did you believe that I was a deserter? that I, who have stood in the streets, and taken my people to my heart, and talked of the holiest and greatest things with them, could ever turn back and chatter foolishly to fashionable people about nothing in a drawing room? Never, never, never, never: Major Barbara will die with the colors. Oh! and I have my dear little Dolly boy still; and he has found me my place and my work. Glory Hallelujah! [*She kisses him*].

CUSINS. My dearest: consider my delicate health. I cannot stand as much happiness as you can.

BARBARA. Yes: it is not easy work being in love with me, is it? But it's good for you. [*She runs to the shed, and calls, childlike*] Mamma! Mamma! [*Bilton comes out of the shed, followed by Undershaft*]. I want Mamma.

UNDERSHAFT. She is taking off her list slippers, dear. [*He passes on to Cusins*]. Well? What does she say?
CUSINS. She has gone right up into the skies.
LADY BRITOMART [*coming from the shed and stopping on the steps, obstructing Sarah, who follows with Lomax. Barbara clutches like a baby at her mother's skirt*] Barbara: when will you learn to be independent and to act and think for yourself? I know as well as possible what that cry of "Mamma, Mamma," means. Always running to me!
SARAH [*touching Lady Britomart's ribs with her finger tips and imitating a bicycle horn*] Pip! pip!
LADY BRITOMART [*highly indignant*] How dare you say Pip! pip! to me, Sarah? You are both very naughty children. What do you want, Barbara?
BARBARA. I want a house in the village to live in with Dolly. [*Dragging at the skirt*] Come and tell me which one to take.
UNDERSHAFT [*to Cusins*] Six o'clock tomorrow morning, Euripides.

PYGMALION:
A Romance in Five Acts

Composition begun 7 March 1912; completed early June 1912. First published in German translation, 1913. Published in *Everybody's Magazine* (New York), November 1914, and in *Nash's Magazine,* November-December 1914. First collected in *Androcles and the Lion, Overruled, Pygmalion,* 1916. Revised 1941 for separate printing of *Pygmalion* in Standard Edition text, also incorporating several revised sequences from the film scenario. This revision was followed for the Penguin Books edition later in 1941. First presented in German at the Hofburg Theater, Vienna, on 16 October 1913. First presented in English at His Majesty's Theatre, London, on 11 April 1914.

Clara Eynsford-Hill *Margaret Bussé*
Mrs Eynsford-Hill *Carlotta Addison*
A Bystander *Roy Byford*
Freddy Eynsford-Hill *Algernon Greig*
Eliza Doolittle *Mrs Patrick Campbell*
Colonel Pickering *Philip Merivale*
Henry Higgins *Herbert Tree*
A Sarcastic Bystander *Alexander Sarner*
Mrs Pearce *Geraldine Olliffe*
Alfred Doolittle *Edmund Gurney*
Mrs Higgins *Rosamond Mayne-Young*
Parlormaid *Irene Delisse*

Period—The Present

ACT I *The Portico of St Paul's, Covent Garden. 11.15 p.m.*

ACT II *Professor Higgins's Phonetic Laboratory, Wimpole Street. Next day. 11 a.m.*

ACT III *The Drawing Room in Mrs Higgins's Flat on Chelsea Embankment. Several Months Later. At-Home Day*

ACT IV *The Same as Act 2. Several Months Later. Midnight*

ACT V *The Same as Act 3. The Following Morning*

Preface

A PROFESSOR OF PHONETICS

As will be seen later on, Pygmalion needs, not a preface, but a sequel, which I have supplied in its due place.

The English have no respect for their language, and will not teach their children to speak it. They cannot spell it because they have nothing to spell it with but an old foreign alphabet of which only the consonants—and not all of them—have any agreed speech value. Consequently no man can teach himself what it should sound like from reading it; and it is impossible for an Englishman to open his mouth without making some other Englishman despise him. Most European languages are now accessible in black and white to foreigners: English and French are not thus accessible even to Englishmen and Frenchmen. The reformer we need most today is an energetic phonetic enthusiast: that is why I have made such a one the hero of a popular play.

There have been heroes of that kind crying in the wilderness for many years past. When I became interested in the subject towards the end of the eighteen-seventies, the illustrious Alexander Melville Bell, the inventor of Visible Speech, had emigrated to Canada, where his son invented the telephone; but Alexander J. Ellis was still a London patriarch, with an impressive head always covered by a velvet skull cap, for which he would apologize to public meetings in a very courtly manner. He and Tito Pagliardini, another phonetic veteran, were men whom it was impossible to dislike. Henry Sweet, then a young man, lacked their sweetness of character: he was about as conciliatory to conventional mortals as Ibsen or Samuel Butler. His great ability as a phonetician (he was, I think, the best of them all at his job) would have entitled him to high official recognition, and perhaps enabled him to popularize his subject, but for his Satanic contempt for all academic dignitaries and persons in general who thought more of Greek than of phonetics. Once, in the days when the Imperial Institute rose in South Kensington, and Joseph Chamberlain was booming the Empire, I induced the editor of a leading monthly review to commission an article from Sweet on the imperial importance of his subject. When it arrived, it contained nothing but a savagely derisive attack on a professor of language and literature whose chair Sweet regarded as proper to a phonetic expert only. The article, being libellous, had to be returned as impossible; and I had to renounce my dream of dragging its author into the limelight. When I met him afterwards, for the first time for many years, I found to my astonishment that he, who had been a quite tolerably presentable young man, had actually managed by sheer scorn to alter his personal appearance until he had become a sort of walking repudiation of Oxford and all its traditions. It must have been largely in his own despite that he was squeezed into something called a Readership of phonetics there. The future of phonetics rests probably with his pupils, who all swore by him; but nothing could bring the man himself into any sort of compliance with the university to which he nevertheless clung by divine right in an intensely Oxonian way. I daresay his papers, if he has left any, include some satires that may be published without too destructive results fifty years hence. He was, I believe, not in the least an ill-natured man: very much the opposite, I should say; but he would not suffer fools gladly; and to him all scholars who were not rabid phoneticians were fools.

Those who knew him will recognize in my third act the allusion to the Current Shorthand in which he used to write postcards. It may be acquired from a four and sixpenny manual published by the Clarendon Press. The postcards which Mrs Higgins describes are such as I have received from Sweet. I would decipher a sound which a cockney would represent by *zerr*, and a Frenchman by *seu*, and then write demanding with some heat what on earth it meant. Sweet, with boundless contempt for my stupidity, would reply that it not only meant but obviously was the word Result, as no other word containing that sound, and capable of making sense with the context, existed in any language spoken on earth. That less expert mortals should require fuller indications was beyond Sweet's patience. Therefore, though the whole point of his Current Shorthand is that it can express every sound in the language perfectly, vowels as well as consonants, and that your hand has to make no stroke except the easy and current ones with which you write m, n, and u, l, p, and q, scribbling them at whatever angle comes easiest to you, his unfortunate determination to make this remarkable and quite legible script serve also as a shorthand reduced it in his own practice to the most inscrutable of cryptograms. His true objective was the provision of a full, accurate, legible script for our language; but he was led past that by his contempt for the popular Pitman system of shorthand, which he called the Pitfall system. The triumph of Pitman was a triumph of business organization: there was a weekly paper to persuade you to learn Pitman: there were cheap textbooks and exercise books and transcripts of speeches for you to copy, and schools where experienced teachers coached you up to the necessary proficiency. Sweet could not organize his market in that fashion. He might as well have been the Sybil who tore up the leaves of prophecy that nobody would attend to. The four and sixpenny manual, mostly in his lithographed handwriting, that was never vulgarly advertized, many perhaps some day be taken up by a syndicate and pushed upon the public as The Times pushed the Encyclopædia Britannica; but until then it will certainly not prevail against Pitman. I have bought three copies of it during my lifetime; and I am informed by the publishers that its cloistered existence is still a steady and healthy one. I actually learned the system two several times; and yet the shorthand in which I am writing these lines is Pitman's. And the reason is, that my secretary cannot transcribe Sweet, having been perforce taught in the schools of Pitman. In America I could use the commercially organized Gregg shorthand, which has taken a hint from Sweet by making its letters writable (current, Sweet would have called them) instead of having to be geometrically drawn like Pitman's; but all these systems, including Sweet's, are spoilt by making them available for verbatim reporting, in which complete and exact spelling and word division are impossible. A complete and exact phonetic script is neither practicable nor necessary for ordinary use; but if we enlarge our alphabet to the Russian size, and make our spelling as phonetic as Spanish, the advance will be prodigious.

Pygmalion Higgins is not a portrait of Sweet, to whom the adventure of Eliza Doolittle would have been impossible; still, as will be seen, there are touches of Sweet in the play. With Higgins's physique and temperament Sweet might have set the Thames on fire. As it was, he impressed himself professionally on Europe to an extent that made his comparative personal obscurity, and the failure of Oxford to do justice to his eminence, a puzzle to foreign specialists in his subject. I do not blame Oxford, because I think Oxford is quite right in demanding a certain social amenity from its nurslings (heaven knows it is not exorbitant in its requirements!); for although I well know how hard it is for a man of genius with a seriously underrated subject to maintain serene and kindly relations with the men who underrate it, and who keep all the best places for less important subjects which they profess without originality and sometimes without much capacity for them, still, if he overwhelms them with wrath and disdain, he cannot expect them to heap honors on him.

Of the later generations of phoneticians I know little. Among them towered Robert Bridges, to whom perhaps Higgins may owe his Miltonic sympathies, though here again I must disclaim all portraiture. But if the play makes the public aware that there are such people as phoneticians, and that they are among the most important people in England at present, it will serve its turn.

I wish to boast that Pygmalion has been an extremely successful play, both on stage and screen, all over Europe and North America as well as at home. It is so intensely and deliberately didactic, and its subject is esteemed so dry, that I delight in throwing it at the heads of the wiseacres who repeat the parrot cry that art should never be didactic. It goes to prove my contention that great art can never be anything else.

Finally, and for the encouragement of people troubled with accents that cut them off from all high employment, I may add that the change wrought by Professor Higgins in the flower-girl is neither impossible nor uncommon. The modern concierge's daughter who fulfils her ambition by playing the Queen of Spain in Ruy Blas at the Théâtre Français is only one of many thousands of men and women who have sloughed off their native dialects and acquired a new tongue. Our West End shop assistants and domestic servants are bilingual. But the thing has to be done scientifically, or the last state of the aspirant may be worse than the first. An honest slum dialect is more tolerable than the attempts of phonetically untaught persons to imitate the plutocracy. Ambitious flower-girls who read this play must not imagine that they can pass themselves off as fine ladies by untutored imitation. They must learn their alphabet over again, and different, from a phonetic expert. Imitation will only make them ridiculous.

ACT I

London at 11.15 p.m. Torrents of heavy summer rain. Cab whistles blowing frantically in all directions. Pedestrians running for shelter into the portico of St Paul's church (not Wren's cathedral but Inigo Jones's church in Covent Garden vegetable market), among them a lady and her daughter in evening dress. All are peering out gloomily at the rain, except one man with his back turned to the rest, wholly preoccupied with a notebook in which he is writing.

The church clock strikes the first quarter.

THE DAUGHTER [*in the space between the central pillars, close to the one on her left*] I'm getting chilled to the bone. What can Freddy be doing all this time? He's been gone twenty minutes.

THE MOTHER [*on her daughter's right*] Not so long. But he ought to have got us a cab by this.

A BYSTANDER [*on the lady's right*] He wont get no cab not until half-past eleven, missus, when they come back after dropping their theatre fares.

THE MOTHER. But we must have a cab. We cant stand here until half-past eleven. It's too bad.

THE BYSTANDER. Well, it aint my fault, missus.

THE DAUGHTER. If Freddy had a bit of gumption, he would have got one at the theatre door.

THE MOTHER. What could he have done, poor boy?

THE DAUGHTER. Other people got cabs. Why couldnt he?

Freddy rushes in out of the rain from the Southampton Street side, and comes between them closing a dripping umbrella. He is a young man of twenty, in evening dress, very wet round the ankles.

THE DAUGHTER. Well, havnt you got a cab?

FREDDY. Theres not one to be had for love or money.

THE MOTHER. Oh, Freddy, there must be one. You cant have tried.

THE DAUGHTER. It's too tiresome. Do you expect us to go and get one ourselves?

FREDDY. I tell you theyre all engaged. The rain was so sudden: nobody was prepared; and everybody had to take a cab. Ive been to Charing Cross one way and nearly to Ludgate Circus the other; and they were all engaged.

THE MOTHER. Did you try Trafalgar Square?

FREDDY. There wasnt one at Trafalgar Square.

THE DAUGHTER. Did you try?

FREDDY. I tried as far as Charing Cross Station. Did you expect me to walk to Hammersmith?

THE DAUGHTER. You havnt tried at all.

THE MOTHER. You really are very helpless, Freddy. Go again; and dont come back until you have found a cab.

FREDDY. I shall simply get soaked for nothing.

THE DAUGHTER. And what about us? Are we to stay here all night in this draught, with next to nothing on? You selfish pig—

FREDDY. Oh, very well: I'll go, I'll go. [*He opens his umbrella and dashes off Strandwards, but comes into collision with a flower girl who is hurrying in for shelter, knocking her basket out of her hands. A blinding flash of lightning, followed instantly by a rattling peal of thunder, orchestrates the incident*].

THE FLOWER GIRL. Nah then, Freddy: look wh' y' gowin, deah.

FREDDY. Sorry [*he rushes off*].

THE FLOWER GIRL [*picking up her scattered flowers and replacing them in the basket*] Theres menners f' yer! Tə-oo banches o voylets trod into the mad. [*She sits down on the plinth of the column, sorting her flowers, on the lady's right. She is not at all a romantic figure. She is perhaps eighteen, perhaps twenty, hardly older. She wears a little sailor hat of black straw that has long been exposed to the dust and soot of London and has seldom if ever been brushed. Her hair needs washing rather badly: its mousy color can hardly be natural. She wears a shoddy black coat that reaches nearly to her knees and is shaped to her waist. She has a brown skirt with a coarse apron. Her boots are much the worse for wear. She is no doubt as clean as she can afford to be; but compared to the ladies she is very dirty. Her features are no worse than theirs; but their condition leaves something to be desired; and she needs the services of a dentist*].

THE MOTHER. How do you know that my son's name is Freddy, pray?

THE FLOWER GIRL. Ow, eez, yə-ooa san, is e? Wal, fewd dan y' də-ooty bawmz a mather should, eed now bettern to spawl a pore gel's flahrzn than ran awy athaht pyin. Will ye-oo py me f'them? [*Here, with apol-*

ogies, this desperate attempt to represent her dialect without a phonetic alphabet must be abandoned as unintelligible outside London].

THE DAUGHTER. Do nothing of the sort, mother. The idea!

THE MOTHER. Please allow me, Clara. Have you any pennies?

THE DAUGHTER. No. Ive nothing smaller than sixpence.

THE FLOWER GIRL [*hopefully*] I can give you change for a tanner, kind lady.

THE MOTHER [*to Clara*] Give it to me. [*Clara parts reluctantly*]. Now [*to the girl*] This is for your flowers.

THE FLOWER GIRL. Thank you kindly, lady.

THE DAUGHTER. Make her give you the change. These things are only a penny a bunch.

THE MOTHER. Do hold your tongue, Clara. [*To the girl*] You can keep the change.

THE FLOWER GIRL. Oh, thank you, lady.

THE MOTHER. Now tell me how you know that young gentleman's name.

THE FLOWER GIRL. I didnt.

THE MOTHER. I heard you call him by it. Dont try to deceive me.

THE FLOWER GIRL [*protesting*] Who's trying to deceive you? I called him Freddy or Charlie same as you might yourself if you was talking to a stranger and wished to be pleasant.

THE DAUGHTER. Sixpence thrown away! Really, mamma, you might have spared Freddy t h a t. [*She retreats in disgust behind the pillar*].

An elderly gentleman of the amiable military type rushes into the shelter, and closes a dripping umbrella. He is in the same plight as Freddy, very wet about the ankles. He is in evening dress, with a light overcoat. He takes the place left vacant by the daughter.

THE GENTLEMAN. Phew!

THE MOTHER [*to the gentleman*] Oh sir, is there any sign of its stopping?

THE GENTLEMAN. I'm afraid not. It started worse than ever about two minutes ago [*he goes to the plinth beside the flower girl; puts up his foot on it; and stoops to turn down his trouser ends*].

THE MOTHER. Oh dear! [*She retires sadly and joins her daughter*].

THE FLOWER GIRL [*taking advantage of the military gentleman's proximity to establish friendly relations with him*] If it's worse, it's a sign it's nearly over. So cheer up, Captain; and buy a flower off a poor girl.

THE GENTLEMAN. I'm sorry. I havnt any change.

THE FLOWER GIRL. I can give you change, Captain.

THE GENTLEMAN. For a sovereign? Ive nothing less.

THE FLOWER GIRL. Garn! Oh do buy a flower off me, Captain. I can change half-a-crown. Take this for tuppence.

THE GENTLEMAN. Now dont be troublesome: theres a good girl. [*Trying his pockets*] I really havnt any change—Stop: heres three hapence, if thats any use to you [*he retreats to the other pillar*].

THE FLOWER GIRL [*disappointed, but thinking three halfpence better than nothing*] Thank you, sir.

THE BYSTANDER [*to the girl*] You be careful: give him a flower for it. Theres a bloke here behind taking down every blessed word youre saying. [*All turn to the man who is taking notes*].

THE FLOWER GIRL [*springing up terrified*] I aint done nothing wrong by speaking to the gentleman. Ive a right to sell flowers if I keep off the kerb. [*Hysterically*] I'm a respectable girl: so help me, I never spoke to him except to ask him to buy a flower off me.

General hubbub, mostly sympathetic to the flower girl, but deprecating her excessive sensibility. Cries of Dont start hollerin. Who's hurting you? Nobody's going to touch you. Whats the good of fussing? Steady on. Easy easy, etc., *come from the elderly staid spectators, who pat her comfortingly. Less patient ones bid her shut her head, or ask her roughly what is wrong with her. A remoter group, not knowing what the matter is, crowd in and increase the noise with question and answer:* Whats the row? What-she do? Where is he? A tec taking her down. What! him? Yes: him over there: Took money off the gentleman, etc.

THE FLOWER GIRL [*breaking through them to the gentleman, crying wildly*] Oh, sir, dont let him charge me. You dunno what it means to me. Theyll take away my character and drive me on the streets for speaking to gentlemen. They—

THE NOTE TAKER [*coming forward on her right, the rest crowding after him*] There! there! there! there! who's hurting you, you silly girl? What do you take me for?

THE BYSTANDER. It's aw rawt: e's a genleman: look at his bə-oots. [*Explaining to the note taker*] She thought you was a copper's nark, sir.

THE NOTE TAKER [*with quick interest*] Whats a copper's nark?

THE BYSTANDER [*inapt at definition*] It's a—well, it's a copper's nark, as you might say. What else would you call it? A sort of informer.

THE FLOWER GIRL [*still hysterical*] I take my Bible oath I never said a word—

THE NOTE TAKER [*overbearing but good-humored*] Oh, shut up, shut up. Do I look like a policeman?

THE FLOWER GIRL [*far from reassured*] Then what did you take down my words for? How do I know whether you took me down right? You just shew me what youve wrote about me. [*The note taker opens his book and holds it steadily under her nose, though the pressure of the mob trying to read it over his shoulders would upset a weaker man*]. Whats that? That aint proper writing. I cant read that.

THE NOTE TAKER. I can. [*Reads, reproducing her pronunciation exactly*] "Cheer ap, Keptin; n' baw ya flahr orf a pore gel."

THE FLOWER GIRL [*much distressed*] It's because I called him Captain. I meant no harm. [*To the gentleman*] Oh, sir, dont let him lay a charge agen me for a word like that. You—

THE GENTLEMAN. Charge! I make no charge. [*To the note taker*] Really, sir, if you are a detective, you need not begin protecting me against molestation by young women until I ask you. Anybody could see that the girl meant no harm.

THE BYSTANDERS GENERALLY [*demonstrating against police espionage*] Course they could. What business is it of yours? You mind your own affairs. He wants promotion, he does. Taking down people's words! Girl never said a word to him. What harm if she did? Nice thing a girl cant shelter from the rain without being insulted, etc., etc., etc. [*She is conducted by the more sympathetic demonstrators back to her plinth, where she resumes her seat and struggles with her emotion*].

THE BYSTANDER. He aint a tec. He's a blooming busybody: thats what he is. I tell you, look at his bə-oots.

THE NOTE TAKER [*turning on him genially*] And how are all your people down at Selsey?

THE BYSTANDER [*suspiciously*] Who told you my people come from Selsey?

THE NOTE TAKER. Never you mind. They did. [*To the girl*] How do you come to be up so far east? You were born in Lisson Grove.

THE FLOWER GIRL [*appalled*] Oh, what harm is there in my leaving Lisson Grove? It wasnt fit for a pig to live in; and I had to pay four-and-six a week [*In tears*] Oh, boo—hoo—oo—

THE NOTE TAKER. Live where you like; but stop that noise.

THE GENTLEMAN [*to the girl*] Come, come! he cant touch you: you have a right to live where you please.

A SARCASTIC BYSTANDER [*thrusting himself between the note taker and the gentleman*] Park Lane, for instance. I'd like to go into the Housing Question with you, I would.

THE FLOWER GIRL [*subsiding into a brooding melancholy over her basket, and talking very low-spiritedly to herself*] I'm a good girl, I am.

THE SARCASTIC BYSTANDER [*not attending to her*] Do you know where *I* come from?

THE NOTE TAKER [*promptly*] Hoxton.

Titterings. Popular interest in the note taker's performance increases.

THE SARCASTIC ONE [*amazed*] Well, who said I didnt? Bly me! you know everything, you do.

THE FLOWER GIRL [*still nursing her sense of injury*] Aint no call to meddle with me, he aint.

THE BYSTANDER [*to her*] Of course he aint. Dont you stand it from him. [*To the note taker*] See here: what call have you to know about people what never offered to meddle with you?

THE FLOWER GIRL. Let him say what he likes. I dont want to have no truck with him.

THE BYSTANDER. You take us for dirt under your feet, dont you? Catch you taking liberties with a gentleman!

THE SARCASTIC BYSTANDER. Yes: tell him where he come from if you want to go fortune-telling.

THE NOTE TAKER. Cheltenham, Harrow, Cambridge, and India.

THE GENTLEMAN. Quite right.

Great laughter. Reaction in the note taker's favor. Exclamations of He knows all about it. Told him proper. Hear him tell the toff where he come from? etc.

THE GENTLEMAN. May I ask, sir, do you do this for your living at a music hall?

THE NOTE TAKER. I've thought of that. Perhaps I shall some day.

The rain has stopped; and the persons on the outside of the crowd begin to drop off.

THE FLOWER GIRL [*resenting the reaction*] He's no gentleman, he aint, to interfere with a poor girl.

THE DAUGHTER [*out of patience, pushing her way rudely to the front and displacing the gentleman, who politely retires to the other side of the pillar*] What on earth is Freddy doing? I shall get pneumownia if I stay in this draught any longer.

THE NOTE TAKER [*to himself, hastily making a note of her pronunciation of "monia"*] Earlscourt.

THE DAUGHTER [*violently*] Will you please keep your impertinent remarks to yourself.

THE NOTE TAKER. Did I say that out loud? I didnt mean to. I beg your pardon. Your mother's Epsom, unmistakeably.

THE MOTHER [*advancing between her daughter and the note taker*] How very curious! I was brought up in Largelady Park, near Epsom.

THE NOTE TAKER [*uproariously amused*] Ha! ha! What a devil of a name! Excuse me. [*To the daughter*] You want a cab, do you?

THE DAUGHTER. Dont dare speak to me.

THE MOTHER. Oh please, please, Clara. [*Her daughter repudiates her with an angry shrug and retires haughtily*]. We should be so grateful to you, sir, if you found us a cab. [*The note taker produces a whistle*]. Oh, thank you. [*She joins her daughter*].

The note taker blows a piercing blast.

THE SARCASTIC BYSTANDER. There! I knowed he was a plainclothes copper.

THE BYSTANDER. That aint a police whistle: thats a sporting whistle.

THE FLOWER GIRL [*still preoccupied with her wounded feelings*] He's no right to take away my character. My character is the same to me as any lady's.

THE NOTE TAKER. I dont know whether youve noticed it; but the rain stopped about two minutes ago.

THE BYSTANDER. So it has. Why didnt you say so before? and us losing our time listening to your silliness! [*He walks off towards the Strand*].

THE SARCASTIC BYSTANDER. I can tell where you come from. You come from Anwell. Go back there.

THE NOTE TAKER [*helpfully*] *H*anwell.

THE SARCASTIC BYSTANDER [*affecting great distinction of speech*] Thenk you, teacher. Haw haw! So long [*he touches his hat with mock respect and strolls off*].

THE FLOWER GIRL. Frightening people like that! How would he like it himself?

THE MOTHER. It's quite fine now, Clara. We can walk to a motor bus. Come. [*She gathers her skirts above her ankles and hurries off towards the Strand*].

THE DAUGHTER. But the cab—[*her mother is out of hearing*]. Oh, how tiresome! [*She follows angrily*].

All the rest have gone except the note taker, the gentleman, and the flower girl, who sits arranging her basket, and still pitying herself in murmurs.

THE FLOWER GIRL. Poor girl! Hard enough for her to live without being worrited and chivied.

THE GENTLEMAN [*returning to his former place on the note taker's left*] How do you do it, if I may ask?

THE NOTE TAKER. Simply phonetics. The science of speech. Thats my profession: also my hobby. Happy is the man who can make a living by his hobby! You can spot an Irishman or a Yorkshireman by his brogue. *I* can place any man within six miles. I can place him within two miles in London. Sometimes within two streets.

THE FLOWER GIRL. Ought to be ashamed of himself, unmanly coward!

THE GENTLEMAN. But is there a living in that?

THE NOTE TAKER. Oh yes. Quite a fat one. This is an age of upstarts. Men begin in Kentish Town with £80 a year, and end in Park Lane with a hundred thousand. They want to drop Kentish Town; but they give themselves away every time they open their mouths. Now I can teach them—

THE FLOWER GIRL. Let him mind his own business and leave a poor girl—

THE NOTE TAKER [*explosively*] Woman: cease this detestable boohooing instantly; or else seek the shelter of some other place of worship.

THE FLOWER GIRL [*with feeble defiance*] Ive a right to be here if I like, same as you.

THE NOTE TAKER. A woman who utters such depressing and disgusting sounds has no right to be anywhere—no right to live. Remember that you are a human being with a soul and the divine gift of articulate speech: that your native language is the language of Shakespear and Milton and The Bible; and dont sit there crooning like a bilious pigeon.

THE FLOWER GIRL [*quite overwhelmed, looking up at him in mingled wonder and deprecation without daring to raise her head*] Ah-ah-ah-ow-ow-ow-oo!

THE NOTE TAKER [*whipping out his book*] Heavens! what a sound! [*He writes; then holds out the book and reads, reproducing her vowels exactly*] Ah-ah-ah-ow-ow-ow-oo!

THE FLOWER GIRL [*tickled by the performance, and laughing in spite of herself*] Garn!

THE NOTE TAKER. You see this creature with her kerbstone English: the

English that will keep her in the gutter to the end of her days. Well, sir, in three months I could pass that girl off as a duchess at an ambassador's garden party. I could even get her a place as lady's maid or shop assistant, which requires better English.

THE FLOWER GIRL. What's that you say?

THE NOTE TAKER. Yes, you squashed cabbage leaf, you disgrace to the noble architecture of these columns, you incarnate insult to the English language: I could pass you off as the Queen of Sheba. [*To the Gentleman*] Can you believe that?

THE GENTLEMAN. Of course I can. I am myself a student of Indian dialects; and—

THE NOTE TAKER [*eagerly*] Are you? Do you know Colonel Pickering, the author of Spoken Sanscrit?

THE GENTLEMAN. I a m Colonel Pickering. Who are you?

THE NOTE TAKER. Henry Higgins, author of Higgins's Universal Alphabet.

PICKERING [*with enthusiasm*] I came from India to meet you.

HIGGINS. I was going to India to meet you.

PICKERING. Where do you live?

HIGGINS. 27A Wimpole Street. Come and see me tomorrow.

PICKERING. I'm at the Carlton. Come with me now and lets have a jaw over some supper.

HIGGINS. Right you are.

THE FLOWER GIRL [*to Pickering, as he passes her*] Buy a flower, kind gentleman. I'm short for my lodging.

PICKERING. I really havnt any change. I'm sorry [*he goes away*].

HIGGINS [*shocked at the girl's mendacity*] Liar. You said you could change half-a-crown.

THE FLOWER GIRL [*rising in desperation*] You ought to be stuffed with nails, you ought. [*Flinging the basket at his feet*] Take the whole blooming basket for sixpence.

The church clock strikes the second quarter.

HIGGINS [*hearing in it the voice of God, rebuking him for his Pharisaic want of charity to the poor girl*] A reminder. [*He raises his hat solemnly; then throws a handful of money into the basket and follows Pickering*].

THE FLOWER GIRL [*picking up a half-crown*] Ah-ow-ooh! [*Picking up a couple of florins*] Aaah-ow-ooh! [*Picking up several coins*] Aaaaaah-ow-ooh! [*Picking up a half-sovereign*] Aaaaaaaaaaah-ow-ooh!!!

FREDDY [*springing out of a taxicab*] Got one at last. Hallo! [*To the girl*] Where are the two ladies that were here?

THE FLOWER GIRL. They walked to the bus when the rain stopped.

FREDDY. And left me with a cab on my hands! Damnation!

THE FLOWER GIRL [*with grandeur*] Never mind, young man. I'm going home in a taxi. [*She sails off to the cab. The driver puts his hand behind him and holds the door firmly shut against her. Quite understanding his mistrust, she shews him her handful of money*]. A taxi fare aint no object to me, Charlie. [*He grins and opens the door*]. Here. What about the basket?

THE TAXIMAN. Give it here. Tuppence extra.

LIZA. No: I dont want nobody to see it. [*She crushes it into the cab and gets in, continuing the conversation through the window*] Goodbye, Freddy.

FREDDY [*dazedly raising his hat*] Goodbye.

TAXIMAN. Where to?

LIZA. Bucknam Pellis [Buckingham Palace].

TAXIMAN. What d'ye mean—Bucknam Pellis?

LIZA. Dont you know where it is? In the Green Park, where the King lives. Goodbye, Freddy. Dont let me keep you standing there. Goodbye.

FREDDY. Goodbye. [*He goes*].

TAXIMAN. Here? Whats this about Bucknam Pellis? What business have you at Bucknam Pellis?

LIZA. Of course I havnt none. But I wasnt going to let him know that. You drive me home.

TAXIMAN. And wheres home?

LIZA. Angel Court, Drury Lane, next Meiklejohn's oil shop.

TAXIMAN. That sounds more like it, Judy. [*He drives off*].

★ ★ ★ ★ ★

Let us follow the taxi to the entrance to Angel Court, a narrow little archway between two shops, one of them Meiklejohn's oil shop. When it stops there, Eliza gets out, dragging her basket with her.

LIZA. How much?

TAXIMAN [*indicating the taximeter*] Cant you read? A shilling.

LIZA. A shilling for two minutes!!

TAXIMAN. Two minutes or ten: it's all the same.

LIZA. Well, I dont call it right.

TAXIMAN. Ever been in a taxi before?

LIZA [*with dignity*] Hundreds and thousands of times, young man.

TAXIMAN [*laughing at her*] Good for you, Judy. Keep the shilling, darling, with best love from all at home. Good luck! [*He drives off*].

LIZA [*humiliated*] Impidence!

She picks up the basket and trudges up the alley with it to her lodging: a small room with very old wall paper hanging loose in the damp places. A broken pane in the window is mended with paper. A portrait of a popular actor and a fashion plate of ladies' dresses, all wildly beyond poor Eliza's means, both torn from newspapers, are pinned up on the wall. A birdcage hangs in the window; but its tenant died long ago: it remains as a memorial only.

These are the only visible luxuries: the rest is the irreducible minimum of poverty's needs: a wretched bed heaped with all sorts of coverings that have any warmth in them, a draped packing case with a basin and jug on it and a little looking glass over it, a chair and table, the refuse of some suburban kitchen, and an American alarum clock on the shelf above the unused fireplace: the whole lighted with a gas lamp with a penny in the slot meter. Rent: four shillings a week.

Here Eliza, chronically weary, but too excited to go to bed, sits, counting her new riches and dreaming and planning what to do with them, until the gas goes out, when she enjoys for the first time the sensation of being able to put in another penny without grudging it. This prodigal mood does not extinguish her gnawing sense of the need for economy sufficiently to prevent her from calculating that she can dream and plan in bed more cheaply and warmly than sitting up without a fire. So she takes off her shawl and skirt and adds them to the miscellaneous bedclothes. Then she kicks off her shoes and gets into bed without any further change.

ACT II

Next day at 11 a.m. Higgins's laboratory in Wimpole Street. It is a room on the first floor, looking on the street, and was meant for the drawing room. The double doors are in the middle of the back wall; and persons entering find in the corner to their right two tall file cabinets at right angles to one another against the walls. In this corner stands a flat writing-table, on which are a phonograph, a laryngoscope, a row of tiny organ pipes with a bellows, a set of lamp chimneys for singing flames with burners attached to a gas plug in the wall by an indiarubber tube, several tuning-forks of different sizes, a life-size image of half a human head, shewing in section the vocal organs, and a box containing a supply of wax cylinders for the phonograph.

Further down the room, on the same side, is a fireplace, with a comfortable leather-covered easy-chair at the side of the hearth nearest the door, and a coal-scuttle. There is a clock on the mantel-piece. Between the fireplace and the phonograph table is a stand for newspapers.

On the other side of the central door, to the left of the visitor, is a cabinet of shallow drawers. On it is a telephone and the telephone directory. The corner beyond, and most of the side wall, is occupied by a grand piano, with the keyboard at the end furthest from the door, and a bench for the player extending the full length of the keyboard. On the piano is a dessert dish heaped with fruit and sweets, mostly chocolates.

The middle of the room is clear. Besides the easy-chair, the piano bench, and two chairs at the phonograph table, there is one stray chair. It stands near the fireplace. On the walls, engravings: mostly Piranesis and mezzotint portraits. No paintings.

Pickering is seated at the table, putting down some cards and a tuning-fork which he has been using. Higgins is standing up near him,. closing two or three file drawers which are hanging out. He appears in the morning light as a robust, vital, appetizing sort of man of forty or thereabouts, dressed in a professional-looking black frock-coat with a white linen collar and black silk tie. He is of the energetic, scientific type, heartily, even violently interested in everything that can be stud-

ied as a scientific subject, and careless about himself and other people, including their feelings. He is, in fact, but for his years and size, rather like a very impetuous baby "taking notice" eagerly and loudly, and requiring almost as much watching to keep him out of unintended mischief. His manner varies from genial bullying when he is in a good humor to stormy petulance when anything goes wrong; but he is so entirely frank and void of malice that he remains likeable even in his least reasonable moments.

HIGGINS [*as he shuts the last drawer*] Well, I think thats the whole show.

PICKERING. It's really amazing. I havnt taken half of it in, you know.

HIGGINS. Would you like to go over any of it again?

PICKERING [*rising and coming to the fireplace, where he plants himself with his back to the fire*] No, thank you: not now. I'm quite done up for this morning.

HIGGINS [*following him, and standing beside him on his left*] Tired of listening to sounds?

PICKERING. Yes. It's a fearful strain. I rather fancied myself because I can pronounce twenty-four distinct vowel sounds; but your hundred and thirty beat me. I cant hear a bit of difference between most of them.

HIGGINS [*chuckling, and going over to the piano to eat sweets*] Oh, that comes with practice. You hear no difference at first; but you keep on listening, and presently you find theyre all as different as A from B. [*Mrs Pearce looks in: she is Higgins's housekeeper*]. Whats the matter?

MRS PEARCE [*hesitating, evidently perplexed*] A young woman asks to see you, sir.

HIGGINS. A young woman! What does she want?

MRS PEARCE. Well, sir, she says youll be glad to see her when you know what she's come about. She's quite a common girl, sir. Very common indeed. I should have sent her away, only I thought perhaps you wanted her to talk into your machines. I hope Ive not done wrong; but really you see such queer people sometimes—youll excuse me, I'm sure, sir—

HIGGINS. Oh, thats all right, Mrs Pearce. Has she an interesting accent?

MRS PEARCE. Oh, something dreadful, sir, really. I dont know how you can take an interest in it.

HIGGINS [*to Pickering*] Lets have her up. Shew her up, Mrs Pearce [*he rushes across to his working table and picks out a cylinder to use on the phonograph*].

MRS PEARCE [*only half resigned to it*] Very well, sir. It's for you to say. [*She goes downstairs*].

HIGGINS. This is rather a bit of luck. I'll shew you how I make records. We'll set her talking; and I'll take it down first in Bell's Visible Speech; then in broad Romic; and then we'll get her on the phonograph so that you can turn her on as often as you like with the written transcript before you.

MRS PEARCE [*returning*] This is the young woman, sir.

The flower girl enters in state. She has a hat with three ostrich feathers, orange, sky-blue, and red. She has a nearly clean apron, and the shoddy coat has been tidied a little. The pathos of this deplorable figure, with its innocent vanity and consequential air, touches Pickering, who has already straightened himself in the presence of Mrs Pearce. But as to Higgins, the only distinction he makes between men and women is that when he is neither bullying nor exclaiming to the heavens against some feather-weight cross, he coaxes women as a child coaxes its nurse when it wants to get anything out of her.

HIGGINS [*brusquely, recognizing her with unconcealed disappointment, and at once, babylike, making an intolerable grievance of it*] Why, this is the girl I jotted down last night. She's no use: Ive got all the records I want of the Lisson Grove lingo; and I'm not going to waste another cylinder on it. [*To the girl*] Be off with you: I dont want you.

THE FLOWER GIRL. Dont you be so saucy. You aint heard what I come for yet. [*To Mrs Pearce, who is waiting at the door for further instructions*] Did you tell him I come in a taxi?

MRS PEARCE. Nonsense, girl! what do you think a gentleman like Mr Higgins cares what you came in?

THE FLOWER GIRL. Oh, we a r e proud! He aint above giving lessons, not him: I heard him say so. Well, I aint come here to ask for any compliment; and if my money's not good enough I can go elsewhere.

HIGGINS. Good enough for what?

THE FLOWER GIRL. Good enough for yə-oo. Now you know, dont you? I'm come to have lessons, I am. And to pay for em tə-oo: make no mistake.

HIGGINS [*stupent*] Well!!! [*Recovering his breath with a gasp*] What do you expect me to say to you?

THE FLOWER GIRL. Well, if you was a gentleman, you might ask me to sit down, I think. Dont I tell you I'm bringing you business?

HIGGINS. Pickering: shall we ask this baggage to sit down, or shall we throw her out of the window?

THE FLOWER GIRL [*running away in terror to the piano, where she turns at bay*] Ah-ah-oh-ow-ow-ow-oo! [*Wounded and whimpering*] I wont be called a baggage when Ive offered to pay like any lady.

Motionless, the two men stare at her from the other side of the room, amazed.

PICKERING [*gently*] But what is it you want?

THE FLOWER GIRL. I want to be a lady in a flower shop stead of sellin at the corner of Tottenham Court Road. But they wont take me unless I can talk more genteel. He said he could teach me. Well, here I am ready to pay him—not asking any favor—and he treats me zif I was dirt.

MRS PEARCE. How can you be such a foolish ignorant girl as to think you could afford to pay Mr Higgins?

THE FLOWER GIRL. Why shouldnt I? I know what lessons cost as well as you do; and I'm ready to pay.

HIGGINS. How much?

THE FLOWER GIRL [*coming back to him, triumphant*] Now youre talking! I thought youd come off it when you saw a chance of getting back a bit of what you chucked at me last night. [*Confidentially*] Youd had a drop in, hadnt you?

HIGGINS [*peremptorily*] Sit down.

THE FLOWER GIRL. Oh, if youre going to make a compliment of it—

HIGGINS [*thundering at her*] Sit down.

MRS PEARCE [*severely*] Sit down, girl. Do as youre told.

THE FLOWER GIRL. Ah-ah-ah-ow-ow-oo! [*She stands, half rebellious, half bewildered*].

PICKERING [*very courteous*] Wont you sit down? [*He places the stray chair near the hearthrug between himself and Higgins*].

LIZA [*coyly*] Dont mind if I do. [*She sits down. Pickering returns to the hearthrug*].

HIGGINS. Whats your name?

THE FLOWER GIRL. Liza Doolittle.

HIGGINS [*declaiming gravely*]

Eliza, Elizabeth, Betsy and Bess,
They went to the woods to get a bird's nes':

PICKERING. They found a nest with four eggs in it:
HIGGINS. They took one apiece, and left three in it.

They laugh heartily at their own fun.

LIZA. Oh, dont be silly.

MRS PEARCE [*placing herself behind Eliza's chair*] You mustnt speak to the gentleman like that.

LIZA. Well, why wont he speak sensible to me?

HIGGINS. Come back to business. How much do you propose to pay me for the lessons?

LIZA. Oh, I know whats right. A lady friend of mine gets French lessons for eighteenpence an hour from a real French gentleman. Well, you wouldnt have the face to ask me the same for teaching me my own language as you would for French; so I wont give more than a shilling. Take it or leave it.

HIGGINS [*walking up and down the room, rattling his keys and his cash in his pockets*] You know, Pickering, if you consider a shilling, not as a simple shilling, but as a percentage of this girl's income, it works out as fully equivalent to sixty or seventy guineas from a millionaire.

PICKERING. How so?

HIGGINS. Figure it out. A millionaire has about £150 a day. She earns about half-a-crown.

LIZA [*haughtily*] Who told you I only—

HIGGINS [*continuing*] She offers me two-fifths of her day's income for a lesson. Two-fifths of a millionaire's income for a day would be somewhere about £60. It's handsome. By George, it's enormous! it's the biggest offer I ever had.

LIZA [*rising, terrified*] Sixty pounds! What are you talking about? I never offered you sixty pounds. Where would I get—

HIGGINS. Hold your tongue.

LIZA [*weeping*] But I aint got sixty pounds. Oh—

MRS PEARCE. Dont cry, you silly girl. Sit down. Nobody is going to touch your money.

HIGGINS. Somebody is going to touch you, with a broomstick, if you dont stop snivelling. Sit down.

LIZA [*obeying slowly*] Ah-ah-ah-ow-oo-o! One would think you was my father.

HIGGINS. If I decide to teach you, I'll be worse than two fathers to you. Here [*he offers her his silk handkerchief*]!

LIZA. Whats this for?

HIGGINS. To wipe your eyes. To wipe any part of your face that feels moist. Remember: thats your handkerchief; and thats your sleeve. Dont mistake the one for the other if you wish to become a lady in a shop.

Liza, utterly bewildered, stares helplessly at him.

MRS PEARCE. It's no use talking to her like that, Mr Higgins: she doesnt understand you. Besides, youre quite wrong: she doesnt do it that way at all [*she takes the handkerchief*].

LIZA [*snatching it*] Here! You give me that handkerchief. He gev it to me, not to you.

PICKERING [*laughing*] He did. I think it must be regarded as her property, Mrs Pearce.

MRS PEARCE [*resigning herself*] Serve you right, Mr Higgins.

PICKERING. Higgins: I'm interested. What about the ambassador's garden party? I'll say youre the greatest teacher alive if you make that good. I'll bet you all the expenses of the experiment you cant do it. And I'll pay for the lessons.

LIZA. Oh, you are real good. Thank you, Captain.

HIGGINS [*tempted, looking at her*] It's almost irresistible. She's so deliciously low—so horribly dirty—

LIZA [*protesting extremely*] Ah-ah-ah-ah-ow-ow-oo-oo!!! I aint dirty: I washed my face and hands afore I come, I did.

PICKERING. Youre certainly not going to turn her head with flattery, Higgins.

MRS PEARCE [*uneasy*] Oh, dont say that, sir: theres more ways than one of turning a girl's head; and nobody can do it better than Mr Higgins, though he may not always mean it. I do hope, sir, you wont encourage him to do anything foolish.

HIGGINS [*becoming excited as the idea grows on him*] What is life but a series of inspired follies? The difficulty is to find them to do. Never lose a chance: it doesnt come every day. I shall make a duchess of this draggletailed guttersnipe.

LIZA [*strongly deprecating this view of her*] Ah-ah-ah-ow-ow-oo!

HIGGINS [*carried away*] Yes: in six months—in three if she has a good ear and a quick tongue—I'll take her anywhere and pass her off as anything. We'll start today: now! this moment! Take her away and clean her, Mrs Pearce. Monkey Brand, if it wont come off any other way. Is there a good fire in the kitchen?

MRS PEARCE [*protesting*] Yes; but—

HIGGINS [*storming on*] Take all her clothes off and burn them. Ring up Whiteley or somebody for new ones. Wrap her up in brown paper til they come.

LIZA. Youre no gentleman, youre not, to talk of such things. I'm a good girl, I am; and I know what the like of you are, I do.

HIGGINS. We want none of your Lisson Grove prudery here, young woman. You've got to learn to behave like a duchess. Take her away, Mrs Pearce. If she gives you any trouble, wallop her.

LIZA [*springing up and running between Pickering and Mrs Pearce for protection*] No! I'll call the police, I will.

MRS PEARCE. But Ive no place to put her.

HIGGINS. Put her in the dustbin.

LIZA. Ah-ah-ah-ow-ow-oo!

PICKERING. Oh come, Higgins! be reasonable.

MRS PEARCE [*resolutely*] You must be reasonable, Mr Higgins: really you must. You cant walk over everybody like this.

Higgins, thus scolded, subsides. The hurricane is succeeded by a zephyr of amiable surprise.

HIGGINS [*with professional exquisiteness of modulation*] *I* walk over everybody! My dear Mrs Pearce, my dear Pickering, I never had the slightest intention of walking over anyone. All I propose is that we should be kind to this poor girl. We must help her to prepare and fit herself for her new station in life. If I did not express myself clearly it was because I did not wish to hurt her delicacy, or yours.

Liza, reassured, steals back to her chair.

MRS PEARCE [*to Pickering*] Well, did you ever hear anything like that, sir?

PICKERING [*laughing heartily*] Never, Mrs Pearce: never.

HIGGINS [*patiently*] Whats the matter?

MRS PEARCE. Well, the matter is, sir, that you cant take a girl up like that as if you were picking up a pebble on the beach.

HIGGINS. Why not?

MRS PEARCE. Why not! But you dont know anything about her. What about her parents? She may be married.

LIZA. Garn!

HIGGINS. There! As the girl very properly says, Garn! Married indeed! Dont you know that a woman of that class looks a worn out drudge of fifty a year after she's married?

LIZA. Whood marry m e?

HIGGINS [*suddenly resorting to the most thrillingly beautiful low tones in his best elocutionary style*] By George, Eliza, the streets will be strewn with the bodies of men shooting themselves for your sake before Ive done with you.

MRS PEARCE. Nonsense, sir. You mustnt talk like that to her.

LIZA [*rising and squaring herself determinedly*] I'm going away. He's off his chump, he is. I dont want no balmies teaching me.

HIGGINS [*wounded in his tenderest point by her insensibility to his elocution*] Oh, indeed! I'm mad, am I? Very well, Mrs Pearce: you neednt order the new clothes for her. Throw her out.

LIZA [*whimpering*] Nah-ow. You got no right to touch me.

MRS PEARCE. You see now what comes of being saucy. [*Indicating the door*] This way, please.

LIZA [*almost in tears*] I didnt want no clothes. I wouldnt have taken them [*she throws away the handkerchief*]. I can buy my own clothes.

HIGGINS [*deftly retrieving the handkerchief and intercepting her on her reluctant way to the door*] Youre an ungrateful wicked girl. This is my return for offering to take you out of the gutter and dress you beautifully and make a lady of you.

MRS PEARCE. Stop, Mr Higgins. I wont allow it. It's you that are wicked. Go home to your parents, girl; and tell them to take better care of you.

LIZA. I aint got no parents. They told me I was big enough to earn my own living and turned me out.

MRS PEARCE. Wheres your mother?

LIZA. I aint got no mother. Her that turned me out was my sixth stepmother. But I done without them. And I'm a good girl, I am.

HIGGINS. Very well, then, what on earth is all this fuss about? The girl doesnt belong to anybody—is no use of anybody but me. [*He goes to Mrs Pearce and begins coaxing*]. You can adopt her, Mrs Pearce: I'm sure a daughter would be a great amusement to you. Now dont make any more fuss. Take her downstairs; and—

MRS PEARCE. But whats to become of her? Is she to be paid anything? Do be sensible, sir.

HIGGINS. Oh, pay her whatever is necessary: put it down in the housekeeping book. [*Impatiently*] What on earth will she want with money? She'll have her food and her clothes. She'll only drink if you give her money.

LIZA [*turning on him*] Oh you a r e a brute. It's a lie: nobody ever saw the sign of liquor on me. [*To Pickering*] Oh, sir: youre a gentleman: dont let him speak to me like that.

PICKERING [*in good-humored remonstrance*] Does it occur to you, Higgins, that the girl has some feelings?

HIGGINS [*looking critically at her*] Oh no, I dont think so. Not any feelings that we need bother about. [*Cheerily*] Have you, Eliza?

LIZA. I got my feelings same as anyone else.

HIGGINS [*to Pickering, reflectively*] You see the difficulty?

PICKERING. Eh? What difficulty?

HIGGINS. To get her to talk grammar. The mere pronunciation is easy enough.

LIZA. I dont want to talk grammar. I want to talk like a lady in a flower-shop.

MRS PEARCE. Will you please keep to the point, Mr Higgins. I want to know on what terms the girl is to be here. Is she to have any wages? And what is to become of her when youve finished your teaching? You must look ahead a little.

HIGGINS [*impatiently*] Whats to become of her if I leave her in the gutter? Tell me that, Mrs Pearce.

MRS PEARCE. Thats her own business, not yours, Mr Higgins.

HIGGINS. Well, when Ive done with her, we can throw her back into the gutter; and then it will be her own business again; so thats all right.

LIZA. Oh, youve no feeling heart in you: you dont care for nothing but yourself. [*She rises and takes the floor resolutely*]. Here! Ive had enough of this. I'm going [*making for the door*]. You ought to be ashamed of yourself, you ought.

HIGGINS [*snatching a chocolate cream from the piano, his eyes suddenly beginning to twinkle with mischief*] Have some chocolates, Eliza.

LIZA [*halting, tempted*] How do I know what might be in them? Ive heard of girls being drugged by the like of you.

Higgins whips out his penknife; cuts a chocolate in two; puts one half into his mouth and bolts it; and offers her the other half.

HIGGINS. Pledge of good faith, Eliza. I eat one half: you eat the other. [*Liza opens her mouth to retort: he pops the half chocolate into it*]. You shall have boxes of them, barrels of them, every day. You shall live on them. Eh?

LIZA [*who has disposed of the chocolate after being nearly choked by it*] I wouldnt have ate it, only I'm too ladylike to take it out of my mouth.

HIGGINS. Listen, Eliza. I think you said you came in a taxi.

LIZA. Well, what if I did? Ive as good a right to take a taxi as anyone else.

HIGGINS. You have, Eliza; and in future you shall have as many taxis as you want. You shall go up and down and round the town in a taxi every day. Think of that, Eliza.

MRS PEARCE. Mr Higgins: youre tempting the girl. It's not right. She should think of the future.

HIGGINS. At her age! Nonsense! Time enough to think of the future when you havnt any future to think of. No, Eliza: do as this lady does: think of other people's futures; but never think of your own. Think of chocolates, and taxis, and gold, and diamonds.

LIZA. No: I dont want no gold and no diamonds. I'm a good girl, I am. [*She sits down again, with an attempt at dignity*].

HIGGINS. You shall remain so, Eliza, under the care of Mrs Pearce. And you shall marry an officer in the Guards, with a beautiful moustache: the son of a marquis, who will disinherit him for marrying you, but will relent when he sees your beauty and goodness—

PICKERING. Excuse me, Higgins; but I really must interfere. Mrs Pearce is quite right. If this girl is to put herself in your hands for six months for an experiment in teaching, she must understand thoroughly what she's doing.

HIGGINS. How can she? She's incapable of understanding anything. Besides, do any of us understand what we are doing? If we did, would we ever do it?

PICKERING. Very clever, Higgins; but not to the present point. [*To Eliza*] Miss Doolittle—

LIZA [*overwhelmed*] Ah-ah-ow-oo!

HIGGINS. There! Thats all youll get out of Eliza. Ah-ah-ow-oo! No use explaining. As a military man you ought to know that. Give her her orders: thats enough for her. Eliza: you are to live here for the next six months, learning how to speak beautifully, like a lady in a florist's shop. If youre good and do whatever youre told, you shall sleep in a proper bedroom, and have lots to eat, and money to buy chocolates and take rides in taxis. If youre naughty and idle you will sleep in the back kitchen among the black beetles, and be walloped by Mrs Pearce with a broomstick. At the end of six months you shall go to Buckingham Palace in a carriage, beautifully dressed. If the King finds out youre not a lady, you will be taken by the police to the Tower of London, where your head will be cut off as a warning to other presumptuous flower girls. If you are not found out, you shall have a present of seven-and-sixpence to start life with as a lady in a shop. If you refuse this offer you will be a most ungrateful wicked girl; and the angels will weep for you. [*To Pickering*] Now are you satisfied, Pickering? [*To Mrs Pearce*] Can I put it more plainly and fairly, Mrs Pearce?

MRS PEARCE [*patiently*] I think youd better let me speak to the girl properly in private. I dont know that I can take charge of her or consent to the arrangement at all. Of course I know you dont mean her any harm; but when you get what you call interested in people's accents, you never think or care what may happen to them or you. Come with me, Eliza.

HIGGINS. Thats all right. Thank you, Mrs Pearce. Bundle her off to the bathroom.

LIZA [*rising reluctantly and suspiciously*] Youre a great bully, you are. I wont stay here if I dont like. I wont let nobody wallop me. I never asked to go to Bucknam Palace, I didnt. I was never in trouble with the police, not me. I'm a good girl—

MRS PEARCE. Dont answer back, girl. You dont understand the gentleman. Come with me. [*She leads the way to the door, and holds it open for Eliza*].

LIZA [*as she goes out*] Well, what I say is right. I wont go near the King, not if I'm going to have my head cut off. If I'd known what I was letting myself in for, I wouldnt have come here. I always been a good girl; and I never offered to say a word to him; and I dont owe him nothing; and I dont care; and I wont be put upon; and I have my feelings the same as anyone else—

Mrs. Pearce shuts the door; and Eliza's plaints are no longer audible.

★ ★ ★ ★ ★

Eliza is taken upstairs to the third floor greatly to her surprise; for she expected to be taken down to the scullery. There Mrs Pearce opens a door and takes her into a spare bedroom.

MRS PEARCE. I will have to put you here. This will be your bedroom.

LIZA. O-h, I couldnt sleep here, missus. It's too good for the likes of me. I should be afraid to touch anything. I aint a duchess yet, you know.

MRS PEARCE. You have got to make yourself as clean as the room: then you wont be afraid of it. And you must call me Mrs Pearce, not missus. [*She throws open the door of the dressingroom, now modernized as a bathroom*].

LIZA. Gawd! whats this? Is this where you wash clothes? Funny sort of copper I call it.

MRS PEARCE. It is not a copper. This is where we wash ourselves, Eliza, and where I am going to wash you.

LIZA. You expect me to get into that and wet myself all over! Not me. I should catch my death. I knew a woman did it every Saturday night; and she died of it.

MRS PEARCE. Mr Higgins has the gentlemen's bathroom downstairs; and he has a bath every morning, in cold water.

LIZA. Ugh! He's made of iron, that man.

MRS PEARCE. If you are to sit with him and the Colonel and be taught you will have to do the same. They wont like the smell of you if you dont. But you can have the water as hot as you like. There are two taps: hot and cold.

LIZA [*weeping*] I couldnt. I dursnt. Its not natural: it would kill me. Ive never had a bath in my life: not what youd call a proper one.

MRS PEARCE. Well, dont you want to be clean and sweet and decent, like a lady? You know you cant be a nice girl inside if youre a dirty slut outside.

LIZA. Boohoo!!!!

MRS PEARCE. Now stop crying and go back into your room and take off all your clothes. Then wrap yourself in this [*Taking down a gown from its peg and handing it to her*] and come back to me. I will get the bath ready.

LIZA [*all tears*] I cant. I wont. I'm not used to it. Ive never took off all my clothes before. It's not right: it's not decent.

MRS PEARCE. Nonsense, child. Dont you take off all your clothes every night when you go to bed?

LIZA [*amazed*] No. Why should I? I should catch my death. Of course I take off my skirt.

MRS PEARCE. Do you mean that you sleep in the underclothes you wear in the daytime?

LIZA. What else have I to sleep in?

MRS PEARCE. You will never do that again as long as you live here. I will get you a proper nightdress.

LIZA. Do you mean change into cold things and lie awake shivering half the night? You want to kill me, you do.

MRS PEARCE. I want to change you from a frowzy slut to a clean respectable girl fit to sit with the gentlemen in the study. Are you going to trust me and do what I tell you or be thrown out and sent back to your flower basket?

LIZA. But you dont know what the cold is to me. You dont know how I dread it.

MRS PEARCE. Your bed wont be cold here: I will put a hot water bottle in it. [*Pushing her into the bedroom*] Off with you and undress.

LIZA. Oh, if only I'd a known what a dreadful thing it is to be clean I'd never have come. I didnt know when I was well off. I–[*Mrs Pearce pushes her through the door, but leaves it partly open lest her prisoner should take to flight*].

Mrs Pearce puts on a pair of white rubber sleeves, and fills the bath, mixing hot and cold, and testing the result with the bath thermometer. She perfumes it with a handful of bath salts and adds a palmful of mustard. She then takes a formidable looking long handled scrubbing brush and soaps it profusely with a ball of scented soap.

Eliza comes back with nothing on but the bath gown huddled tightly round her, a piteous spectacle of abject terror.

MRS PEARCE. Now come along. Take that thing off.

LIZA. Oh I couldnt, Mrs Pearce: I reely couldnt. I never done such a thing.

MRS PEARCE. Nonsense. Here: step in and tell me whether it's hot enough for you.

LIZA. Ah-oo! Ah-hoo! It's too hot.

MRS PEARCE [*deftly snatching the gown away and throwing Eliza down on her back*] It wont hurt you. [*She sets to work with the scrubbing brush*].

Eliza's screams are heartrending.

★ ★ ★ ★ ★

Meanwhile the Colonel has been having it out with Higgins about Eliza. Pickering has come from the hearth to the chair and seated himself astride of it with his arms on the back to cross-examine him.

PICKERING. Excuse the straight question, Higgins. Are you a man of good character where women are concerned?

HIGGINS [*moodily*] Have you ever met a man of good character where women are concerned?

PICKERING. Yes: very frequently.

HIGGINS [*dogmatically, lifting himself on his hands to the level of the piano, and sitting on it with a bounce*] Well, I havnt. I find that the moment I let a woman make friends with me, she becomes jealous, exacting, suspicious, and a damned nuisance. I find that the moment I let myself make friends with a woman, I become selfish and tyrannical. Women upset everything. When you let them into your life, you find that the woman is driving at one thing and youre driving at another.

PICKERING. At what, for example?

HIGGINS [*coming off the piano restlessly*] Oh, Lord knows! I suppose the woman wants to live her own life; and the man wants to live his; and each tries to drag the other on to the wrong track. One wants to go north and the other south; and the result is that both have to go east, though they both hate the east wind. [*He sits down on the bench at the keyboard*]. So here I am, a confirmed old bachelor, and likely to remain so.

PICKERING [*rising and standing over him gravely*] Come, Higgins! You know what I mean. If I'm to be in this business I shall feel responsible for that girl. I hope it's understood that no advantage is to be taken of her position.

HIGGINS. What! That thing! Sacred, I assure you. [*Rising to explain*] You see, she'll be a pupil; and teaching would be impossible unless pupils were sacred. Ive taught scores of American millionairesses how to speak English: the best looking women in the world. I'm seasoned. They might as well be blocks of wood. *I* might as well be a block of wood. It's—

Mrs Pearce opens the door. She has Eliza's hat in her hand. Pickering retires to the easy-chair at the hearth and sits down.

HIGGINS [*eagerly*] Well, Mrs Pearce: is it all right?

MRS PEARCE [*at the door*] I just wish to trouble you with a word, if I may, Mr Higgins.

HIGGINS. Yes, certainly. Come in. [*She comes forward*]. Dont burn that, Mrs Pearce. I'll keep it as a curiosity. [*He takes the hat*].

MRS PEARCE. Handle it carefully, sir, p l e a s e. I had to promise her not to burn it; but I had better put it in the oven for a while.

HIGGINS [*putting it down hastily on the piano*] Oh! thank you. Well, what have you to say to me?

PICKERING. Am I in the way?

MRS PEARCE. Not at all, sir. Mr. Higgins: will you please be very particular what you say before the girl?

HIGGINS [*sternly*] Of course. I'm always particular about what I say. Why do you say this to me?

MRS PEARCE [*unmoved*] No, sir: youre not at all particular when youve mislaid anything or when you get a little impatient. Now it doesnt matter before me: I'm used to it. But you really must not swear before the girl.

HIGGINS [*indignantly*] *I* swear! [*Most emphatically*] I never swear. I detest the habit. What the devil do you mean?

MRS PEARCE [*stolidly*] Thats what I mean, sir. You swear a great deal too much. I dont mind your damning and blasting, and what the devil and where the devil and who the devil—

HIGGINS. Mrs Pearce: this language from your lips! Really!

MRS PEARCE [*not to be put off*]—but there is a certain word I must ask you not to use. The girl used it herself when she began to enjoy the bath. It begins with the same letter as bath. She knows no better: she learnt it at her mother's knee. But she must not hear it from your lips.

HIGGINS [*loftily*] I cannot charge myself with having ever uttered it, Mrs Pearce. [*She looks at him steadfastly. He adds, hiding an uneasy conscience with a judicial air*] Except perhaps in a moment of extreme and justifiable excitement.

MRS PEARCE. Only this morning, sir, you applied it to your boots, to the butter, and to the brown bread.

HIGGINS. Oh, that! Mere alliteration, Mrs Pearce, natural to a poet.

MRS PEARCE. Well, sir, whatever you choose to call it, I beg you not to let the girl hear you repeat it.

HIGGINS. Oh, very well, very well. Is that all?

MRS PEARCE. No, sir. We shall have to be very particular with this girl as to personal cleanliness.

HIGGINS. Certainly. Quite right. Most important.

MRS PEARCE. I mean not to be slovenly about her dress or untidy in leaving things about.

HIGGINS [*going to her solemnly*] Just so. I intended to call your attention to that. [*He passes on to Pickering, who is enjoying the conversation immensely*]. It is these little things that matter, Pickering. Take care of the pence and the pounds will take care of themselves is as true of personal habits as of money. [*He comes to anchor on the hearthrug, with the air of a man in an unassailable position*].

MRS PEARCE. Yes, sir. Then might I ask you not to come down to breakfast in your dressing-gown, or at any rate not to use it as a napkin to the extent you do, sir. And if you would be so good as not to eat everything off the same plate, and to remember not to put the porridge saucepan out of your hand on the clean tablecloth, it would be a better example to the girl. You know you nearly choked yourself with a fishbone in the jam only last week.

HIGGINS [*routed from the hearthrug and drifting back to the piano*] I may do these things sometimes in absence of mind; but surely I dont do them habitually. [*Angrily*] By the way: my dressing-gown smells most damnably of benzine.

MRS PEARCE. No doubt it does, Mr Higgins. But if you will wipe your fingers—

HIGGINS [*yelling*] Oh very well, very well: I'll wipe them in my hair in future.

MRS PEARCE. I hope youre not offended, Mr Higgins.

HIGGINS [*shocked at finding himself thought capable of an unamiable sentiment*] Not at all, not at all. Youre quite right, Mrs Pearce: I shall be particularly careful before the girl. Is that all?

MRS PEARCE. No, sir. Might she use some of those Japanese dresses you brought from abroad? I really cant put her back into her old things.

HIGGINS. Certainly. Anything you like. Is t h a t all?

MRS PEARCE. Thank you, sir. Thats all. [*She goes out*].

HIGGINS. You know, Pickering, that woman has the most extraordinary ideas about me. Here I am, a shy, diffident sort of man. Ive never been able to feel really grown-up and tremendous, like other chaps. And yet she's firmly persuaded that I'm an arbitrary overbearing bossing kind of person. I cant account for it.

Mrs Pearce returns.

MRS PEARCE. If you please, sir, the trouble's beginning already. Theres a dustman downstairs, Alfred Doolittle, wants to see you. He says you have his daughter here.

PICKERING [*rising*] Phew! I say!

HIGGINS [*promptly*] Send the blackguard up.

MRS PEARCE. Oh, very well, sir. [*She goes out*].

PICKERING. He may not be a blackguard, Higgins.

HIGGINS. Nonsense. Of course he's a blackguard.

PICKERING. Whether he is or not, I'm afraid we shall have some trouble with him.

HIGGINS [*confidently*] Oh no: I think not. If theres any trouble he shall have it with me, not I with him. And we are sure to get something interesting out of him.

PICKERING. About the girl?

HIGGINS. No. I mean his dialect.

PICKERING. Oh!

MRS PEARCE [*at the door*] Doolittle, sir. [*She admits Doolittle and retires*].

Alfred Doolittle is an elderly but vigorous dustman, clad in the costume of his profession, including a hat with a back brim covering his neck and shoulders. He has well marked and rather interesting features, and seems equally free from fear and conscience. He has a remarkably expressive voice, the result of a habit of giving vent to his feelings without reserve. His present pose is that of wounded honor and stern resolution.

DOOLITTLE [*at the door, uncertain which of the two gentlemen is his man*] Professor Iggins?

HIGGINS. Here. Good morning. Sit down.

DOOLITTLE. Morning, Governor. [*He sits down magisterially*] I come about a very serious matter, Governor.

HIGGINS [*to Pickering*] Brought up in Hounslow. Mother Welsh, I should think. [*Doolittle opens his mouth, amazed. Higgins continues*] What do you want, Doolittle?

DOOLITTLE [*menacingly*] I want my daughter: thats what I want. See?

HIGGINS. Of course you do. Youre her father, arnt you? You dont suppose anyone else wants her, do you? I'm glad to see you have some spark of family feeling left. She's upstairs. Take her away at once.

DOOLITTLE [*rising, fearfully taken aback*] What!

HIGGINS. Take her away. Do you suppose I'm going to keep your daughter for you?

DOOLITTLE [*remonstrating*] Now, now, look here, Governor. Is this reasonable? Is it fairity to take advantage of a man like this? The girl belongs to me. You got her. Where do I come in? [*He sits down again*].

HIGGINS. Your daughter had the audacity to come to my house and ask me to teach her how to speak properly so that she could get a place in a flower-shop. This gentleman and my housekeeper have been here all the time. [*Bullying him*] How dare you come here and attempt to blackmail me? You sent her here on purpose.

DOOLITTLE [*protesting*] No, Governor.

HIGGINS. You must have. How else could you possibly know that she is here?

DOOLITTLE. Dont take a man up like that, Governor.

HIGGINS. The police shall take you up. This is a plant—a plot to extort money by threats. I shall telephone for the police [*he goes resolutely to the telephone and opens the directory*].

DOOLITTLE. Have I asked you for a brass farthing? I leave it to the gentleman here: have I said a word about money?

HIGGINS [*throwing the book aside and marching down on Doolittle with a poser*] What else did you come for?

DOOLITTLE [*sweetly*] Well, what w o u l d a man come for? Be human, Governor.

HIGGINS [*disarmed*] Alfred: did you put her up to it?

DOOLITTLE. So help me, Governor, I never did. I take my Bible oath I aint seen the girl these two months past.

HIGGINS. Then how did you know she was here?

DOOLITTLE [*"most musical, most melancholy"*] I'll tell you, Governor, if youll only let me get a word in. I'm willing to tell you. I'm wanting to tell you. I'm waiting to tell you.

HIGGINS. Pickering: this chap has a certain natural gift of rhetoric. Observe the rhythm of his native woodnotes wild. "I'm willing to tell you: I'm wanting to tell you: I'm waiting to tell you." Sentimental rhetoric! thats the Welsh strain in him. It also accounts for his mendacity and dishonesty.

PICKERING. Oh, p l e a s e, Higgins: I'm west country myself. [*To Doolittle*] How did you know the girl was here if you didnt send her?

DOOLITTLE. It was like this, Governor. The girl took a boy in the taxi to give him a jaunt. Son of her landlady, he is. He hung about on the chance of her giving him another ride home. Well, she sent him back for her luggage when she heard you was willing for her to stop here. I met the boy at the corner of Long Acre and Endell Street.

HIGGINS. Public house. Yes?

DOOLITTLE. The poor man's club, Governor: why shouldnt I?

PICKERING. Do let him tell his story, Higgins.

DOOLITTLE. He told me what was up. And I ask you, what was my feelings and my duty as a father? I says to the boy, "You bring me the luggage," I says—

PICKERING. Why didnt you go for it yourself?

DOOLITTLE. Landlady wouldnt have trusted me with it, Governor. She's that kind of woman: y o u know. I had to give the boy a penny afore h e trusted me with it, the little swine. I brought it to her just to oblige you like, and make myself agreeable. Thats all.

HIGGINS. How much luggage?

DOOLITTLE. Musical instrument, Governor. A few pictures, a trifle of jewelry, and a bird-cage. She said she didnt want no clothes. What was I to think from that, Governor? I ask you as a parent what was I to think?

HIGGINS. So you came to rescue her from worse than death, eh?

DOOLITTLE [*appreciatively: relieved at being so well understood*] Just so, Governor. Thats right.

PICKERING. But why did you bring her luggage if you intended to take her away?

DOOLITTLE. Have I said a word about taking her away? Have I now?

HIGGINS [*determinedly*] Youre going to take her away, double quick. [*He crosses to the hearth and rings the bell*].

DOOLITTLE [*rising*] No, Governor. Dont say that. I'm not the man to stand in my girl's light. Heres a career opening for her, as you might say; and—

Mrs Pearce opens the door and awaits orders.

HIGGINS. Mrs Pearce: this is Eliza's father. He has come to take her away. Give her to him. [*He goes back to the piano, with an air of washing his hands of the whole affair*].

DOOLITTLE. No. This is a misunderstanding. Listen here—

MRS PEARCE. He cant take her away, Mr Higgins: how can he? You told me to burn her clothes.

DOOLITTLE. Thats right. I cant carry the girl through the streets like a blooming monkey, can I? I put it to you.

HIGGINS. You have put it to me that you want your daughter. Take your daughter. If she has no clothes go out and buy her some.

DOOLITTLE [*desperate*] Wheres the clothes she come in? Did I burn them or did your missus here?

MRS PEARCE. I am the housekeeper, if you please. I have sent for some clothes for your girl. When they come you can take her away. You can wait in the kitchen. This way, please.

Doolittle, much troubled, accompanies her to the door; then hesitates; finally turns confidentially to Higgins.

DOOLITTLE. Listen here, Governor. You and me is men of the world aint we?

HIGGINS. Oh! Men of the world, are we? Youd better go, Mrs Pearce.

MRS PEARCE. I think so, indeed, sir. [*She goes, with dignity*].

PICKERING. The floor is yours, Mr Doolittle.

DOOLITTLE [*to Pickering*] I thank you, Governor. [*To Higgins, who takes refuge on the piano bench, a little overwhelmed by the proximity of his visitor; for Doolittle has a professional flavor of dust about him*]. Well, the truth is, Ive taken a sort of fancy to you, Governor; and if you want the girl, I'm not so set on having her back home again but what I might be open to an arrangement. Regarded in the light of a young woman, she's a fine handsome girl. As a daughter she's not worth her keep; and so I tell you straight. All I ask is my rights as a father; and youre the last man alive to expect me to let her go for nothing; for I can see youre one of the straight sort, Governor. Well, whats a five-pound note to you? and whats Eliza to me? [*He turns to his chair and sits down judicially*].

PICKERING. I think you ought to know, Doolittle, that Mr Higgins's intentions are entirely honorable.

DOOLITTLE. Course they are, Governor. If I thought they wasnt, I'd ask fifty.

HIGGINS [*revolted*] Do you mean to say that you would sell your daughter for £50?

DOOLITTLE. Not in a general way I wouldnt; but to oblige a gentleman like you I'd do a good deal, I do assure you.

PICKERING. Have you no morals, man?

DOOLITTLE [*unabashed*] Cant afford them, Governor. Neither could you if you was as poor as me. Not that I mean any harm, you know. But if Liza is going to have a bit out of this, why not me too?

HIGGINS [*troubled*] I dont know what to do, Pickering. There can be no question that as a matter of morals it's a positive crime to give this chap a farthing. And yet I feel a sort of rough justice in his claim.

DOOLITTLE. Thats it, Governor. Thats all I say. A father's heart, as it were.

PICKERING. Well, I know the feeling; but really it seems hardly right—

DOOLITTLE. Dont say that, Governor. Dont look at it that way. What am I, Governors both? I ask you, what a m I? I'm one of the undeserving poor: thats what I am. Think of what that means to a man. It means that he's up agen middle class morality all the time. If theres anything going, and I put in for a bit of it, it's always the same story: "Youre undeserving; so you cant have it." But my needs is as great as the most deserving widow's that ever got money out of six different charities in one week for the death of the same husband. I dont need less than a deserving man: I need more. I dont eat less hearty than him; and I drink a lot more. I want a bit of amusement, cause I'm a thinking man. I want cheerfulness and a song and a band when I feel low. Well, they charge me just the same for everything as they charge the deserving. What is middle class morality? Just an excuse for never giving me anything. Therefore, I ask you, as two gentlemen, not to play that game on me. I'm playing straight with you. I aint pretending to be deserving. I'm undeserving; and I mean to go on being undeserving. I like it; and thats the truth. Will you take advantage of a man's nature to do him out of the price of his own daughter what he's brought up and fed and clothed by the sweat of his brow until she's growed big enough to be interesting to you two gentlemen? Is five pounds unreasonable? I put it to you; and I leave it to you.

HIGGINS [*rising, and going over to Pickering*] Pickering: if we were to take this man in hand for three months, he could choose between a seat in the Cabinet and a popular pulpit in Wales.

PICKERING. What do you say to that, Doolittle?

DOOLITTLE. Not me, Governor, thank you kindly. Ive heard all the preachers and all the prime ministers—for I'm a thinking man and game for politics or religion or social reform same as all the other amusements—and I tell you it's a dog's life any way you look at it. Undeserving poverty is my line. Taking one station in society with another, it's—it's—well, it's the only one that has any ginger in it, to my taste.

HIGGINS. I suppose we must give him a fiver.

PICKERING. He'll make a bad use of it, I'm afraid.

DOOLITTLE. Not me, Governor, so help me I wont. Dont you be afraid that I'll save it and spare it and live idle on it. There wont be a penny of it left by Monday: I'll have to go to work same as if I'd never had it. It wont pauperize me, you bet. Just one good spree for myself and the missus, giving pleasure to ourselves and employment to others, and satisfaction to you to think it's not been throwed away. You couldnt spend it better.

HIGGINS [*taking out his pocket book and coming between Doolittle and the piano*] This is irresistible. Lets give him ten. [*He offers two notes to the dustman*].

DOOLITTLE. No, Governor. She wouldnt have the heart to spend ten; and perhaps I shouldnt neither. Ten pounds is a lot of money: it makes a man feel prudent like; and then goodbye to happiness. You give me what I ask you, Governor: not a penny more, and not a penny less.

PICKERING. Why dont you marry that missus of yours? I rather draw the line at encouraging that sort of immorality.

DOOLITTLE. Tell her so, Governor: tell her so. *I'm* willing. It's me that suffers by it. Ive no hold on her. I got to be agreeable to her. I got to give her presents. I got to buy her clothes something sinful. I'm a slave to that woman, Governor, just because I'm not her lawful husband. And she knows it too. Catch her marrying me! Take my advice, Governor: marry Eliza while she's young and dont know no better. If you dont youll be sorry for it after. If you do, s h e ' l l be sorry for it after; but better her than you, because youre a man, and she's only a woman and dont know how to be happy anyhow.

HIGGINS. Pickering: if we listen to this man another minute, we shall have no convictions left. [*To Doolittle*] Five pounds I think you said.

DOOLITTLE. Thank you kindly, Governor.

HIGGINS. Youre sure you wont take ten?

DOOLITTLE. Not now. Another time, Governor.

HIGGINS [*handing him a five-pound note*] Here you are.

DOOLITTLE. Thank you, Governor. Good morning. [*He hurries to the door, anxious to get away with his booty. When he opens it he is confronted with a dainty and exquisitely clean young Japanese lady in a simple blue cotton kimono printed cunningly with small white jasmine blossoms. Mrs Pearce is with her. He gets out of her way deferentially and apologizes*]. Beg pardon, miss.

THE JAPANESE LADY. Garn! Dont you know your own daughter?

DOOLITTLE	*exclaiming*	Bly me! it's Eliza!
HIGGINS	*simul-*	Whats that? This!
PICKERING	*taneously*	By Jove!

LIZA. Dont I look silly?

HIGGINS. Silly?

MRS PEARCE [*at the door*] Now, Mr Higgins, please dont say anything to make the girl conceited about herself.

HIGGINS [*conscientiously*] Oh! Quite right, Mrs Pearce. [*To Eliza*] Yes: damned silly.

MRS PEARCE. Please, sir.

HIGGINS [*correcting himself*] I mean extremely silly.

LIZA. I should look all right with my hat on. [*She takes up her hat; puts it on; and walks across the room to the fireplace with a fashionable air*].

HIGGINS. A new fashion, by George! And it ought to look horrible!

DOOLITTLE [*with fatherly pride*] Well, I never thought she'd clean up as good looking as that, Governor. She's a credit to me, aint she?

LIZA. I tell you, it's easy to clean up here. Hot and cold water on tap, just as much as you like, there is. Woolly towels, there is; and a towel horse so hot, it burns your fingers. Soft brushes to scrub yourself, and a wooden bowl of soap smelling like primroses. Now I know why ladies is so clean. Washing's a treat for them. Wish they could see what it is for the like of me!

HIGGINS. I'm glad the bathroom met with your approval.

LIZA. It didnt: not all of it; and I dont care who hears me say it. Mrs Pearce knows.

HIGGINS. What was wrong, Mrs Pearce?

MRS PEARCE [*blandly*] Oh, nothing, sir. It doesnt matter.

LIZA. I had a good mind to break it. I didnt know which way to look. But I hung a towel over it, I did.

HIGGINS. Over what?

MRS PEARCE. Over the looking-glass, sir.

HIGGINS. Doolittle: you have brought your daughter up too strictly.

DOOLITTLE. Me! I never brought her up at all, except to give her a lick of a strap now and again. Dont put it on me, Governor. She aint accustomed to it, you see: thats all. But she'll soon pick up your free-and-easy ways.

LIZA. I'm a good girl, I am; and I wont pick up no free-and-easy ways.

HIGGINS. Eliza: if you say again that youre a good girl, your father shall take you home.

LIZA. Not him. You dont know my father. All he come here for was to touch you for some money to get drunk on.

DOOLITTLE. Well, what else would I want money for? To put into the plate in church, I suppose. [*She puts out her tongue at him. He is so incensed by this that Pickering presently finds it necessary to step between them*] Dont you give me none of your lip; and dont let me hear you giving this gentleman any of it neither, or youll hear from me about it. See?

HIGGINS. Have you any further advice to give her before you go, Doolittle? Your blessing, for instance.

DOOLITTLE. No, Governor: I aint such a mug as to put up my children to all I know myself. Hard enough to hold them in without that. If you want Eliza's mind improved, Governor, you do it yourself with a strap. So long, gentlemen. [*He turns to go*].

HIGGINS [*impressively*] Stop. Youll come regularly to see your daughter. It's your duty, you know. My brother is a clergyman; and he could help you in your talks with her.

DOOLITTLE [*evasively*] Certainly, I'll come, Governor. Not just this week, because I have a job at a distance. But later on you may depend on me. Afternoon, gentlemen. Afternoon, maam. [*He touches his hat to Mrs Pearce, who disdains the salutation and goes out. He winks at Higgins, thinking him probably a fellow sufferer from Mrs Pearce's difficult disposition, and follows her*].

LIZA. Dont you believe the old liar. He'd as soon you set a bulldog on him as a clergyman. You wont see him again in a hurry.

HIGGINS. I dont want to, Eliza. Do you?

LIZA. Not me. I dont want never to see him again, I dont. He's a disgrace to me, he is, collecting dust, instead of working at his trade.

PICKERING. What is his trade, Eliza?

LIZA. Talking money out of other people's pockets into his own. His proper trade's a navvy; and he works at it sometimes too—for exercise—and earns good money at it. Aint you going to call me Miss Doolittle any more?

PICKERING. I beg your pardon, Miss Doolittle. It was a slip of the tongue.

LIZA. Oh, I dont mind; only it sounded so genteel. I s h o u l d just like to take a taxi to the corner of Tottenham Court road and get out there and tell it to wait for me, just to put the girls in their place a bit. I wouldnt speak to them, you know.

PICKERING. Better wait til we get you something really fashionable.

HIGGINS. Besides, you shouldnt cut your old friends now that you have risen in the world. Thats what we call snobbery.

LIZA. You dont call the like of them my friends now, I should hope. Theyve took it out of me often enough with their ridicule when they had the chance; and now I mean to get a bit of my own back. But if I'm to have fashionable clothes, I'll wait. I should like to have some. Mrs Pearce says youre going to give me some to wear in bed at night different to what I wear in the daytime; but it do seem a waste of money when you could get something to shew. Besides, I never could fancy changing into cold things on a winter night.

MRS PEARCE [*coming back*] Now, Eliza. The new things have come for you to try on.

LIZA. Ah-ow-oo-ooh! [*She rushes out*].

MRS PEARCE [*following her*] Oh, dont rush about like that, girl. [*She shuts the door behind her*].

HIGGINS. Pickering: we have taken on a stiff job.

PICKERING [*with conviction*] Higgins: we have.

★ ★ ★ ★ ★

There seems to be some curiosity as to what Higgins's lessons to Eliza were like. Well, here is a sample: the first one.

Picture Eliza, in her new clothes, and feeling her inside put out of step by a lunch, dinner, and breakfast of a kind to which it is unaccustomed, seated with Higgins and the Colonel in the study, feeling like a hospital out-patient at a first encounter with the doctors.

Higgins, constitutionally unable to sit still, discomposes her still more by striding restlessly about. But for the reassuring presence and quietude of her friend the Colonel she would run for her life, even back to Drury Lane.

HIGGINS. Say your alphabet.

LIZA. I know my alphabet. Do you think I know nothing? I dont need to be taught like a child.

HIGGINS [*thundering*] Say your alphabet.

PICKERING. Say it, Miss Doolittle. You will understand presently. Do what he tells you; and let him teach you in his own way.

LIZA. Oh well, if you put it like that—Ahyee, bəyee, cəyee, dəyee—

HIGGINS [*with the roar of a wounded lion*] Stop. Listen to this, Pickering. This is what we pay for as elementary education. This unfortunate animal has been locked up for nine years in school at our expense to teach her to speak and read the language of Shakespear and Milton. And the result is Ahyee, Bə-yee, Cə-yee, Də-yee. [*To Eliza*] Say A, B, C, D.

LIZA [*almost in tears*] But I'm sayin it. Ahyee, Bəyee, Cə-yee—

HIGGINS. Stop. Say a cup of tea.

LIZA. A cappətə-ee.

HIGGINS. Put your tongue forward until it squeezes against the top of your lower teeth. Now say cup.

LIZA. C-c-c—I cant. C-Cup.

PICKERING. Good. Splendid, Miss Doolittle.

HIGGINS. By Jupiter, she's done it at the first shot. Pickering: we shall make a duchess of her. [*To Eliza*] Now do you think you could possibly say tea? Not tə-yee, mind: if you ever say bə-yee cə-yee də-yee again you shall be dragged round the room three times by the hair of your head. [*Fortissimo*] T, T, T, T.

LIZA [*weeping*] I cant hear no difference cep that it sounds more genteel-like when you say it.

HIGGINS. Well, if you can hear that difference, what the devil are you crying for? Pickering: give her a chocolate.

PICKERING. No, no. Never mind crying a little, Miss Doolittle: you are doing very well; and the lessons wont hurt. I promise you I wont let him drag you round the room by your hair.

HIGGINS. Be off with you to Mrs Pearce and tell her about it. Think about it. Try to do it by yourself: and keep your tongue well forward in your mouth instead of trying to roll it up and swallow it. Another lesson at half-past four this afternoon. Away with you.

Eliza, still sobbing, rushes from the room.

And that is the sort of ordeal poor Eliza has to go through for months before we meet her again on her first appearance in London society of the professional class.

ACT III

It is Mrs Higgins's at-home day. Nobody has yet arrived. Her drawing room, in a flat on Chelsea Embankment, has three windows looking on the river; and the ceiling is not so lofty as it would be in an older house of the same pretension. The windows are open, giving access to a balcony with flowers in pots. If you stand with your face to the windows, you have the fireplace on your left and the door in the right-hand wall close to the corner nearest the windows.

Mrs Higgins was brought up on Morris and Burne Jones; and her room, which is very unlike her son's room in Wimpole Street, is not crowded with furniture and little tables and nicknacks. In the middle of the room there is a big ottoman; and this, with the carpet, the Morris wall-papers, and the Morris chintz window curtains and brocade covers of the ottoman and its cushions, supply all the ornament, and are much too handsome to be hidden by odds and ends of useless things. A few good oil-paintings from the exhibitions in the Grosvenor Gallery thirty years ago (the Burne Jones, not the Whistler side of them) are on the walls. The only landscape is a Cecil Lawson on the scale of a Rubens. There is a portrait of Mrs Higgins as she was when she defied fashion in her youth in one of the beautiful Rossettian costumes which, when caricatured by people who did not understand, led to the absurdities of popular estheticism in the eighteen-seventies.

In the corner diagonally opposite the door Mrs Higgins, now over sixty and long past taking the trouble to dress out of the fashion, sits writing at an elegantly simple writing-table with a bell button within reach of her hand. There is a Chippendale chair further back in the room between her and the window nearest her side. At the other side of the room, further forward, is an Elizabethan chair roughly carved in the taste of Inigo Jones. On the same side a piano in a decorated case. The corner between the fireplace and the window is occupied by a divan cushioned in Morris chintz.

It is between four and five in the afternoon.

The door is opened violently; and Higgins enters with his hat on.

MRS HIGGINS [*dismayed*] Henry! [*Scolding him*] What are you doing here today? It is my at-home day: you promised not to come. [*As he bends to kiss her, she takes his hat off, and presents it to him*].

HIGGINS. Oh bother! [*He throws the hat down on the table.*]

MRS HIGGINS. Go home at once.

HIGGINS [*kissing her*] I know, mother. I came on purpose.

MRS HIGGINS. But you mustnt. I'm serious, Henry. You offend all my friends: they stop coming whenever they meet you.

HIGGINS. Nonsense! I know I have no small talk; but people dont mind. [*He sits on the settee*].

MRS HIGGINS. Oh! dont they? Small talk indeed! What about your large talk? Really, dear, you mustnt stay.

HIGGINS. I must. Ive a job for you. A phonetic job.

MRS HIGGINS. No use, dear. I'm sorry; but I cant get round your vowels; and though I like to get pretty postcards in your patent shorthand, I always have to read the copies in ordinary writing you so thoughtfully send me.

HIGGINS. Well, this isnt a phonetic job.

MRS HIGGINS. You said it was.

HIGGINS. Not your part of it. Ive picked up a girl.

MRS HIGGINS. Does that mean that some girl has picked y o u up?

HIGGINS. Not at all. I dont mean a love affair.

MRS HIGGINS. What a pity!

HIGGINS. Why?

MRS HIGGINS. Well, you never fall in love with anyone under forty-five. When will you discover that there are some rather nice-looking young women about?

HIGGINS. Oh, I cant be bothered with young women. My idea of a lovable woman is somebody as like you as possible. I shall never get into the way of seriously liking young women: some habits lie too deep to be changed. [*Rising abruptly and walking about, jingling his money and his keys in his trouser pockets*] Besides, theyre all idiots.

MRS HIGGINS. Do you know what you would do if you really loved me, Henry?

HIGGINS. Oh bother! What? Marry, I suppose.

MRS HIGGINS. No. Stop fidgeting and take your hands out of your pockets. [*With a gesture of despair, he obeys and sits down again*]. Thats a good boy. Now tell me about the girl.

HIGGINS. She's coming to see you.

MRS HIGGINS. I dont remember asking her.

HIGGINS. You didnt. *I* asked her. If youd known her you wouldnt have asked her.
MRS HIGGINS. Indeed! Why?
HIGGINS. Well, it's like this. She's a common flower girl. I picked her off the kerbstone.
MRS HIGGINS. And invited her to my at-home!
HIGGINS [*rising and coming to her to coax her*] Oh, thatll be all right. Ive taught her to speak properly; and she has strict orders as to her behavior. She's to keep to two subjects: the weather and everybody's health—Fine day and How do you do, you know—and not to let herself go on things in general. That will be safe.
MRS HIGGINS. Safe! To talk about our health! about our insides! perhaps about our outsides! How could you be so silly, Henry?
HIGGINS [*impatiently*] Well, she must talk about something. [*He controls himself and sits down again*]. Oh, she'll be all right: dont you fuss. Pickering is in it with me. Ive a sort of bet on that I'll pass her off as a duchess in six months. I started on her some months ago; and she's getting on like a house on fire. I shall win my bet. She has a quick ear; and she's been easier to teach than my middle-class pupils because she's had to learn a complete new language. She talks English almost as you talk French.
MRS HIGGINS. Thats satisfactory, at all events.
HIGGINS. Well, it is and it isnt.
MRS HIGGINS. What does that mean?
HIGGINS. You see, Ive got her pronunciation all right; but you have to consider not only h o w a girl pronounces, but w h a t she pronounces; and thats where—

They are interrupted by the parlor-maid, announcing guests.

THE PARLOR-MAID. Mrs and Miss Eynsford Hill. [*She withdraws*].
HIGGINS. Oh Lord! [*He rises; snatches his hat from the table; and makes for the door; but before he reaches it his mother introduces him*].

Mrs and Miss Eynsford Hill are the mother and daughter who sheltered from the rain in Covent Garden. The mother is well bred, quiet, and has the habitual anxiety of straitened means. The daughter has acquired a gay air of being very much at home in society: the bravado of genteel poverty.

MRS EYNSFORD HILL [*to Mrs Higgins*] How do you do? [*They shake hands*].
MISS EYNSFORD HILL. How d'you do? [*She shakes*].

MRS HIGGINS [*introducing*] My son Henry.

MRS EYNSFORD HILL. Your celebrated son! I have so longed to meet you, Professor Higgins.

HIGGINS [*glumly, making no movement in her direction*] Delighted. [*He backs against the piano and bows brusquely*].

MRS EYNSFORD HILL [*going to him with confident familiarity*] How do you do?

HIGGINS [*staring at her*] Ive seen you before somewhere. I havnt the ghost of a notion where; but Ive heard your voice. [*Drearily*] It doesnt matter. Youd better sit down.

MRS HIGGINS. I'm sorry to say that my celebrated son has no manners. You mustnt mind him.

MISS EYNSFORD HILL [*gaily*] I dont. [*She sits in the Elizabethan chair*].

MRS EYNSFORD HILL [*a little bewildered*] Not at all. [*She sits on the ottoman between her daughter and Mrs Higgins, who has turned her chair away from the writing-table*].

HIGGINS. Oh, have I been rude? I didnt mean to be.

He goes to the central window, through which, with his back to the company, he contemplates the river and the flowers in Battersea Park on the opposite bank as if they were a frozen desert.

The parlor-maid returns, ushering in Pickering.

THE PARLOR-MAID. Colonel Pickering. [*She withdraws*].

PICKERING. How do you do, Mrs Higgins?

MRS HIGGINS. So glad youve come. Do you know Mrs Eynsford Hill—Miss Eynsford Hill? [*Exchange of bows. The Colonel brings the Chippendale chair a little forward between Mrs Hill and Mrs Higgins, and sits down*].

PICKERING. Has Henry told you what weve come for?

HIGGINS [*over his shoulder*] We were interrupted: damn it!

MRS HIGGINS. Oh Henry, Henry, really!

MRS EYNSFORD HILL [*half rising*] Are we in the way?

MRS HIGGINS [*rising and making her sit down again*] No, no. You couldnt have come more fortunately: we want you to meet a friend of ours.

HIGGINS [*turning hopefully*] Yes, by George! We want two or three people. Youll do as well as anybody else.

The parlor-maid returns, ushering Freddy.

THE PARLOR-MAID. Mr Eynsford Hill.

HIGGINS [*almost audibly, past endurance*] God of Heaven! another of them.

FREDDY [*shaking hands with Mrs Higgins*] Ahdedo?

MRS HIGGINS. Very good of you to come. [*Introducing*] Colonel Pickering.

FREDDY [*bowing*] Ahdedo?

MRS HIGGINS. I dont think you know my son, Professor Higgins.

FREDDY [*going to Higgins*] Ahdedo?

HIGGINS [*looking at him much as if he were a pickpocket*] I'll take my oath Ive met you before somewhere. Where was it?

FREDDY. I dont think so.

HIGGINS [*resignedly*] It dont matter, anyhow. Sit down.

He shakes Freddy's hand, and almost slings him on to the ottoman with his face to the windows; then comes round to the other side of it.

HIGGINS. Well, here we are, anyhow! [*He sits down on the ottoman next Mrs Eynsford Hill on her left*]. And now what the devil are we going to talk about until Eliza comes?

MRS HIGGINS. Henry: you are the life and soul of the Royal Society's soirées; but really youre rather trying on more commonplace occasions.

HIGGINS. Am I? Very sorry. [*Beaming suddenly*] I suppose I am, you know. [*Uproariously*] Ha, ha!

MISS EYNSFORD HILL [*who considers Higgins quite eligible matrimonially*] I sympathize. *I* havnt any small talk. If people would only be frank and say what they really think!

HIGGINS [*relapsing into gloom*] Lord forbid!

MRS EYNSFORD HILL [*taking up her daughter's cue*] But why?

HIGGINS. What they think they ought to think is bad enough, Lord knows; but what they really think would break up the whole show. Do you suppose it would be really agreeable if I were to come out now with what *I* really think?

MISS EYNSFORD HILL [*gaily*] Is it so very cynical?

HIGGINS. Cynical! Who the dickens said it was cynical? I mean it wouldnt be decent.

MRS EYNSFORD HILL [*seriously*] Oh! I'm sure you dont mean that, Mr Higgins.

HIGGINS. You see, we're all savages, more or less. We're supposed to be civilized and cultured—to know all about poetry and philosophy and art and science, and so on; but how many of us know even the meanings of these names? [*To Miss Hill*] What do you know of poetry? [*To Mrs Hill*] What do *you* know of science? [*Indicating Freddy*] What does *he* know of art or science or anything else? What the devil do you imagine I know of philosophy?

MRS HIGGINS [*warningly*] Or of manners, Henry?

THE PARLOR-MAID [*opening the door*] Miss Doolittle. [*She withdraws*].

HIGGINS [*rising hastily and running to Mrs Higgins*] Here she is, mother. [*He stands on tiptoe and makes signs over his mother's head to Eliza to indicate to her which lady is her hostess*].

Eliza, who is exquisitely dressed, produces an impression of such remarkable distinction and beauty as she enters that they all rise, quite fluttered. Guided by Higgins's signals, she comes to Mrs Higgins with studied grace.

LIZA [*speaking with pedantic correctness of pronunciation and great beauty of tone*] How do you do, Mrs Higgins? [*She gasps slightly in making sure of the H in Higgins, but is quite successful*]. Mr Higgins told me I might come.

MRS HIGGINS [*cordially*] Quite right: I'm very glad indeed to see you.

PICKERING. How do you do, Miss Doolittle?

LIZA [*shaking hands with him*] Colonel Pickering, is it not?

MRS EYNSFORD HILL. I feel sure we have met before, Miss Doolittle. I remember your eyes.

LIZA. How do you do? [*She sits down on the ottoman gracefully in the place just left vacant by Higgins*].

MRS EYNSFORD HILL [*introducing*] My daughter Clara.

LIZA. How do you do?

CLARA [*impulsively*] How do you do? [*She sits down on the ottoman beside Eliza, devouring her with her eyes*].

FREDDY [*coming to their side of the ottoman*] Ive certainly had the pleasure.

MRS EYNSFORD HILL [*introducing*] My son Freddy.

LIZA. How do you do?

Freddy bows and sits down in the Elizabethan chair, infatuated.

HIGGINS [*suddenly*] By George, yes: it all comes back to me! [*They stare at him*]. Covent Garden! [*Lamentably*] What a damned thing!

MRS HIGGINS. Henry, please! [*He is about to sit on the edge of the table*] Dont sit on my writing-table: youll break it.

HIGGINS [*sulkily*] Sorry.

He goes to the divan, stumbling into the fender and over the fire-irons on his way; extricating himself with muttered imprecations; and finishing his disastrous journey by throwing himself so impatiently on the divan that he almost breaks it. Mrs Higgins looks at him, but controls herself and says nothing.

A long and painful pause ensues.

MRS HIGGINS [*at last, conversationally*] Will it rain, do you think?

LIZA. The shallow depression in the west of these islands is likely to move slowly in an easterly direction. There are no indications of any great change in the barometrical situation.

FREDDY. Ha! ha! how awfully funny!

LIZA. What is wrong with that, young man? I bet I got it right.

FREDDY. Killing!

MRS EYNSFORD HILL. I'm sure I hope it wont turn cold. Theres so much influenza about. It runs right through our whole family regularly every spring.

LIZA [*darkly*] My aunt died of influenza: so they said.

MRS EYNSFORD HILL [*clicks her tongue sympathetically*] !!!

LIZA [*in the same tragic tone*] But it's my belief they done the old woman in.

MRS HIGGINS [*puzzled*] Done her in?

LIZA. Y-e-e-e-es, Lord love you! Why should she die of influenza? She come through diphtheria right enough the year before. I saw her with my own eyes. Fairly blue with it, she was. They all thought she was dead; but my father he kept ladling gin down her throat til she came to so sudden that she bit the bowl off the spoon.

MRS EYNSFORD HILL [*startled*] Dear me!

LIZA [*piling up the indictment*] What call would a woman with that strength in her have to die of influenza? What become of her new straw hat that should have come to me? Somebody pinched it; and what I say is, them as pinched it done her in.

MRS EYNSFORD HILL. What does doing her in mean?

HIGGINS [*hastily*] Oh, thats the new small talk. To do a person in means to kill them.

MRS EYNSFORD HILL [*to Eliza, horrified*] You surely dont believe that your aunt was killed?

LIZA. Do I not! Them she lived with would have killed her for a hat-pin, let alone a hat.

MRS EYNSFORD HILL. But it cant have been right for your father to pour spirits down her throat like that. It might have killed her.

LIZA. Not her. Gin was mother's milk to her. Besides, he'd poured so much down his own throat that he knew the good of it.

MRS EYNSFORD HILL. Do you mean that he drank?

LIZA. Drank! My word! Something chronic.

MRS EYNSFORD HILL. How dreadful for you!

LIZA. Not a bit. It never did him no harm what I could see. But then he did not keep it up regular. [*Cheerfully*] On the burst, as you might say, from time to time. And always more agreeable when he had a drop in. When he was out of work, my mother used to give him fourpence and tell him to go out and not come back until he'd drunk himself cheerful and loving-like. Theres lots of women has to make their husbands drunk to make them fit to live with. [*Now quite at her ease*] You see, it's like this. If a man has a bit of a conscience, it always takes him when he's sober; and then it makes him low-spirited. A drop of booze just takes that off and makes him happy. [*To Freddy, who is in convulsions of suppressed laughter*] Here! what are you sniggering at?

FREDDY. The new small talk. You do it so awfully well.

LIZA. If I was doing it proper, what was you laughing at? [*To Higgins*] Have I said anything I oughtnt?

MRS HIGGINS [*interposing*] Not at all, Miss Doolittle.

LIZA. Well, thats a mercy, anyhow. [*Expansively*] What I always say is—

HIGGINS [*rising and looking at his watch*] Ahem!

LIZA [*looking round at him; taking the hint; and rising*] Well: I must go. [*They all rise. Freddy goes to the door*]. So pleased to have met you. Goodbye. [*She shakes hands with Mrs Higgins*].

MRS HIGGINS. Goodbye.

LIZA. Goodbye, Colonel Pickering.

PICKERING. Goodbye, Miss Doolittle. [*They shake hands*].

LIZA [*nodding to the others*] Goodbye, all.

FREDDY [*opening the door for her*] Are you walking across the Park, Miss Doolittle? If so—

LIZA [*with perfectly elegant diction*] Walk! Not bloody likely. [*Sensation*]. I am going in a taxi. [*She goes out*].

Pickering gasps and sits down. Freddy goes out on the balcony to catch another glimpse of Eliza.

MRS EYNSFORD HILL [*suffering from shock*] Well, I really cant get used to the new ways.

CLARA [*throwing herself discontentedly into the Elizabethan chair*] Oh, it's all right, mamma, quite right. People will think we never go anywhere or see anybody if you are so old-fashioned.

MRS EYNSFORD HILL. I daresay I am very old-fashioned; but I do hope you wont begin using that expression, Clara. I have got accustomed to hear you talking about men as rotters, and calling everything filthy and beastly; though I do think it horrible and unladylike. But this last is really too much. Dont you think so, Colonel Pickering?

PICKERING. Dont ask me. Ive been away in India for several years; and manners have changed so much that I sometimes dont know whether I'm at a respectable dinner-table or in a ship's forecastle.

CLARA. It's all a matter of habit. Theres no right or wrong in it. Nobody means anything by it. And it's so quaint, and gives such a smart emphasis to things that are not in themselves very witty. I find the new small talk delightful and quite innocent.

MRS EYNSFORD HILL [*rising*] Well, after that, I think it's time for us to go.

Pickering and Higgins rise.

CLARA [*rising*] Oh yes: we have three at-homes to go to still. Goodbye, Mrs Higgins. Goodbye, Colonel Pickering. Goodbye, Professor Higgins.

HIGGINS [*coming grimly at her from the divan, and accompanying her to the door*] Goodbye. Be sure you try on that small talk at the three at-homes. Dont be nervous about it. Pitch it in strong.

CLARA [*all smiles*] I will. Goodbye. Such nonsense, all this early Victorian prudery!

HIGGINS [*tempting her*] Such damned nonsense!

CLARA. Such bloody nonsense!

MRS EYNSFORD HILL [*convulsively*] Clara!

CLARA. Ha! ha! [*She goes out radiant, conscious of being thoroughly up to date, and is heard descending the stairs in a stream of silvery laughter*].

FREDDY [*to the heavens at large*] Well, I ask you–[*He gives it up, and comes to Mrs Higgins*]. Goodbye.

MRS HIGGINS [*shaking hands*] Goodbye. Would you like to meet Miss Doolittle again?

FREDDY [*eagerly*] Yes, I should, most awfully.

MRS HIGGINS. Well, you know my days.

FREDDY. Yes, Thanks awfully. Goodbye. [*He goes out*].

MRS EYNSFORD HILL. Goodbye, Mr Higgins.

HIGGINS. Goodbye. Goodbye.

MRS EYNSFORD HILL [*to Pickering*] It's no use. I shall never be able to bring myself to use that word.

PICKERING. Dont. It's not compulsory, you know. Youll get on quite well without it.

MRS EYNSFORD HILL. Only, Clara is so down on me if I am not positively reeking with the latest slang. Goodbye.

PICKERING. Goodbye [*They shake hands*].

MRS EYNSFORD HILL [*to Mrs Higgins*] You mustnt mind Clara. [*Pickering, catching from her lowered tone that this is not meant for him to hear, discreetly joins Higgins at the window*]. We're so poor! and she gets so few parties, poor child! She doesnt quite know. [*Mrs Higgins, seeing that her eyes are moist, takes her hand sympathetically and goes with her to the door*]. But the boy is nice. Dont you think so?

MRS HIGGINS. Oh, quite nice. I shall always be delighted to see him.

MRS EYNSFORD HILL. Thank you, dear. Goodbye. [*She goes out*].

HIGGINS [*eagerly*] Well? Is Eliza presentable [*he swoops on his mother and drags her to the ottoman, where she sits down in Eliza's place with her son on her left*]?

Pickering returns to his chair on her right.

MRS HIGGINS. You silly boy, of course she's not presentable. She's a triumph of your art and of her dressmaker's; but if you suppose for a moment that she doesnt give herself away in every sentence she utters, you must be perfectly cracked about her.

PICKERING. But dont you think something might be done? I mean something to eliminate the sanguinary element from her conversation.

MRS HIGGINS. Not as long as she is in Henry's hands.

HIGGINS [*aggrieved*] Do you mean that my language is improper?

MRS HIGGINS. No, dearest: it would be quite proper—say on a canal barge; but it would not be proper for her at a garden party.

HIGGINS [*deeply injured*] Well I must say—

PICKERING [*interrupting him*] Come, Higgins: you must learn to know yourself. I havnt heard such language as yours since we used to review the volunteers in Hyde Park twenty years ago.

HIGGINS [*sulkily*] Oh, well, if you say so, I suppose I dont always talk like a bishop.

MRS HIGGINS [*quieting Henry with a touch*] Colonel Pickering: will you tell me what is the exact state of things in Wimpole Street?

PICKERING [*cheerfully: as if this completely changed the subject*] Well, I have come to live there with Henry. We work together at my Indian Dialects; and we think it more convenient—

MRS HIGGINS. Quite so. I know all about that: it's an excellent arrangement. But where does this girl live?

HIGGINS. With us, of course. Where *should* she live?

MRS HIGGINS. But on what terms? Is she a servant? If not, what is she?

PICKERING [*slowly*] I think I know what you mean, Mrs Higgins.

HIGGINS. Well, dash me if *I* do! Ive had to work at the girl every day for months to get her to her present pitch. Besides, she's useful. She knows where my things are, and remembers my appointments and so forth.

MRS HIGGINS. How does your housekeeper get on with her?

HIGGINS. Mrs Pearce? Oh, she's jolly glad to get so much taken off her hands; for before Eliza came, *she* used to have to find things and remind me of my appointments. But she's got some silly bee in her bonnet about Eliza. She keeps saying "You dont think, sir": doesnt she, Pick?

PICKERING. Yes: thats the formula. "You dont think, sir." Thats the end of every conversation about Eliza.

HIGGINS. As if I ever stop thinking about the girl and her confounded vowels and consonants. I'm worn out, thinking about her, and watching her lips and her teeth and her tongue, not to mention her soul, which is the quaintest of the lot.

MRS HIGGINS. You certainly are a pretty pair of babies, playing with your live doll.

HIGGINS. Playing! The hardest job I ever tackled: make no mistake about that, mother. But you have no idea how frightfully interesting it is to take a human being and change her into a quite different human being by creating a new speech for her. It's filling up the deepest gulf that separates class from class and soul from soul.

PICKERING [*drawing his chair closer to Mrs Higgins and bending over to her eagerly*] Yes: it's enormously interesting. I assure you, Mrs Higgins, we take Eliza very seriously. Every week—every day almost—there is some new change. [*Closer again*] We keep records of every stage—dozens of gramophone disks and photographs—

HIGGINS [*assailing her at the other ear*] Yes, by George: it's the most absorbing experiment I ever tackled. She regularly fills our lives up: doesnt she, Pick?

PICKERING. We're always talking Eliza.

HIGGINS. Teaching Eliza.

PICKERING. Dressing Eliza.

MRS HIGGINS. What!

HIGGINS. Inventing new Elizas.

HIGGINS. [*speaking together*]	You know, she has the most extraordinary quickness of ear:
PICKERING.	I assure you, my dear Mrs Higgins, that girl
HIGGINS.	just like a parrot. Ive tried her with every
PICKERING.	is a genius. She can play the piano quite beautifully.
HIGGINS.	possible sort of sound that a human being can make
PICKERING.	We have taken her to classical concerts and to music
HIGGINS.	Continental dialects, African dialects, Hottentot
PICKERING.	halls; and it's all the same to her: she plays everything
HIGGINS.	clicks, things it took me years to get hold of; and
PICKERING.	she hears right off when she comes home, whether it's
HIGGINS.	she picks them up like a shot, right away, as if she had
PICKERING.	Beethoven and Brahms or Lehar and Lionel Monckton;
HIGGINS.	been at it all her life.
PICKERING.	though six months ago, she'd never as much as touched a piano—

MRS HIGGINS [*putting her fingers in her ears, as they are by this time shouting one another down with an intolerable noise*] Sh-sh-sh—sh! [*They stop*].

PICKERING. I beg your pardon. [*He draws his chair back apologetically*].

HIGGINS. Sorry. When Pickering starts shouting nobody can get a word in edgeways.

MRS HIGGINS. Be quiet, Henry. Colonel Pickering: dont you realize that when Eliza walked into Wimpole Street, something walked in with her?

PICKERING. Her father did. But Henry soon got rid of him.

MRS HIGGINS. It would have been more to the point if her mother had. But as her mother didnt something else did.

PICKERING. But what?

MRS HIGGINS [*unconsciously dating herself by the word*] A problem.

PICKERING. Oh, I see. The problem of how to pass her off as a lady.

HIGGINS. I'll solve that problem. Ive half solved it already.

MRS HIGGINS. No, you two infinitely stupid male creatures: the problem of what is to be done with her afterwards.

HIGGINS. I dont see anything in that. She can go her own way, with all the advantages I have given her.

MRS HIGGINS. The advantages of that poor woman who was here just now! The manners and habits that disqualify a fine lady from earning her own living without giving her a fine lady's income! Is that what you mean?

PICKERING [*indulgently, being rather bored*] Oh, that will be all right, Mrs Higgins. [*He rises to go*].

HIGGINS [*rising also*] We'll find her some light employment.

PICKERING. She's happy enough. Dont you worry about her. Goodbye. [*He shakes hands as if he were consoling a frightened child, and makes for the door*].

HIGGINS. Anyhow, theres no good bothering now. The thing's done. Goodbye, mother. [*He kisses her, and follows Pickering*].

PICKERING [*turning for a final consolation*] There are plenty of openings. We'll do whats right. Goodbye.

HIGGINS [*to Pickering as they go out together*] Lets take her to the Shakespear exhibition at Earls Court.

PICKERING. Yes: lets. Her remarks will be delicious.

HIGGINS. She'll mimic all the people for us when we get home.

PICKERING. Ripping. [*Both are heard laughing as they go downstairs*].

MRS HIGGINS [*rises with an impatient bounce, and returns to her work at the writing-table. She sweeps a litter of disarranged papers out of her way; snatches a sheet of paper from her stationery case; and tries resolutely to write. At the third line she gives it up; flings down her pen; grips the table angrily and exclaims*] Oh, men! men!! men!!!

★ ★ ★ ★ ★

Clearly Eliza will not pass as a duchess yet; and Higgins's bet remains unwon. But the six months are not yet exhausted; and just in time Eliza does actually pass as a princess. For a glimpse of how she did it imagine an Embassy in London one summer evening after dark. The hall door has an awning and a carpet across the sidewalk to the kerb, because a grand reception is in progress. A small crowd is lined up to see the guests arrive.

A Rolls-Royce car drives up. Pickering in evening dress, with medals and orders, alights, and hands out Eliza, in opera cloak, evening dress, diamonds, fan, flowers and all accessories. Higgins follows. The car drives off; and the three go up the steps and into the house, the door opening for them as they approach.

Inside the house they find themselves in a spacious hall from which the grand staircase rises. On the left are the arrangements for the gentlemen's cloaks. The male guests are depositing their hats and wraps there.

On the right is a door leading to the ladies' cloakroom. Ladies are going in cloaked and coming out in splendor. Pickering whispers to Eliza and points out the ladies' room. She goes into it. Higgins and Pickering take off their overcoats and take tickets for them from the attendant.

One of the guests, occupied in the same way, has his back turned. Having taken his ticket, he turns round and reveals himself as an important looking young man with an astonishingly hairy face. He has an enormous moustache, flowing out into luxuriant whiskers. Waves of hair cluster on his brow. His hair is cropped closely at the back, and glows with oil. Otherwise he is very smart. He wears several worthless orders. He is evidently a foreigner, guessable as a whiskered Pandour from Hungary; but in spite of the ferocity of his moustache he is amiable and genially voluble.

Recognizing Higgins, he flings his arms wide apart and approaches him enthusiastically.

WHISKERS. Maestro, maestro [*he embraces Higgins and kisses him on both cheeks*]. You remember me?

HIGGINS. No I dont. Who the devil are you?

WHISKERS. I am your pupil: your first pupil, your best and greatest pupil. I am little Nepommuck, the marvellous boy. I have made your name famous throughout Europe. You teach me phonetic. You cannot forget ME.

HIGGINS. Why dont you shave?

NEPOMMUCK. I have not your imposing appearance, your chin, your brow. Nobody notice me when I shave. Now I am famous: they call me Hairy Faced Dick.

HIGGINS. And what are you doing here among all these swells?

NEPOMMUCK. I am interpreter. I speak 32 languages. I am indispensable at these international parties. You are great cockney specialist: you place a man anywhere in London the moment he open his mouth. I place any man in Europe.

A footman hurries down the grand staircase and comes to Nepommuck.

FOOTMAN. You are wanted upstairs. Her Excellency cannot understand the Greek gentleman.

NEPOMMUCK. Thank you, yes, immediately.

The footman goes and is lost in the crowd.

NEPOMMUCK [*to Higgins*] This Greek diplomatist pretends he cannot speak nor understand English. He cannot deceive me. He is the son of a Clerkenwell watchmaker. He speaks English so villainously that he dare not utter a word of it without betraying his origin. I help him to pretend; but I make him pay through the nose. I make them all pay. Ha Ha! [*He hurries upstairs*].

PICKERING. Is this fellow really an expert? Can he find out Eliza and blackmail her?

HIGGINS. We shall see. If he finds her out I lose my bet.

Eliza comes from the cloakroom and joins them.

PICKERING. Well, Eliza, now for it. Are you ready?

LIZA. Are you nervous, Colonel?

PICKERING. Frightfully. I feel exactly as I felt before my first battle. It's the first time that frightens.

LIZA. It is not the first time for me, Colonel. I have done this fifty times—hundreds of times—in my little piggery in Angel Court in my day-dreams. I am in a dream now. Promise me not to let Professor Higgins wake me; for if he does I shall forget everything and talk as I used to in Drury Lane.

PICKERING. Not a word, Higgins. [*To Eliza*] Now, ready?

LIZA. Ready.

PICKERING. Go.

They mount the stairs, Higgins last. Pickering whispers to the footman on the first landing.

FIRST LANDING FOOTMAN. Miss Doolittle, Colonel Pickering, Professor Higgins.

SECOND LANDING FOOTMAN. Miss Doolittle, Colonel Pickering, Professor Higgins.

At the top of the staircase the Ambassador and his wife, with Nepommuck at her elbow, are receiving.

HOSTESS [*taking Eliza's hand*] How d'ye do?

HOST [*same play*] How d'ye do? How d'ye do, Pickering?
LIZA [*with a beautiful gravity that awes her hostess*] How do you do? [*She passes on to the drawing room*].
HOSTESS. Is that your adopted daughter, Colonel Pickering? She will make a sensation.
PICKERING. Most kind of you to invite her for me. [*He passes on*].
HOSTESS [*to Nepommuck*] Find out all about her.
NEPOMMUCK [*bowing*] Excellency–[*he goes into the crowd*].
HOST. How d'ye do, Higgins? You have a rival here tonight. He introduced himself as your pupil. Is he any good?
HIGGINS. He can learn a language in a fortnight–knows dozens of them. A sure mark of a fool. As a phonetician, no good whatever.
HOSTESS. How d'ye do, Professor?
HIGGINS. How do you do? Fearful bore for you this sort of thing. Forgive my part in it. [*He passes on*].

In the drawing room and its suite of salons the reception is in full swing. Eliza passes through. She is so intent on her ordeal that she walks like a somnambulist in a desert instead of a débutante in a fashionable crowd. They stop talking to look at her, admiring her dress, her jewels, and her strangely attractive self. Some of the younger ones at the back stand on their chairs to see.

The Host and Hostess come in from the staircase and mingle with their guests. Higgins, gloomy and contemptuous of the whole business, comes into the group where they are chatting.

HOSTESS. Ah, here is Professor Higgins: he will tell us. Tell us all about the wonderful young lady, Professor.
HIGGINS [*almost morosely*] What wonderful young lady?
HOSTESS. You know very well. They tell me there has been nothing like her in London since people stood on their chairs to look at Mrs Langtry.

Nepommuck joins the group, full of news.

HOSTESS. Ah, here you are at last, Nepommuck. Have you found out all about the Doolittle lady?
NEPOMMUCK. I have found out all about her. She is a fraud.
HOSTESS. A fraud! Oh no.
NEPOMMUCK. YES, yes. She cannot deceive me. Her name cannot be Doolittle.
HIGGINS. Why?
NEPOMMUCK. Because Doolittle is an English name. And she is not English.

HOSTESS. Oh, nonsense! She speaks English perfectly.
NEPOMMUCK. Too perfectly. Can you shew me any English woman who speaks English as it should be spoken? Only foreigners who have been taught to speak it speak it well.
HOSTESS. Certainly she terrified me by the way she said How d'ye do. I had a schoolmistress who talked like that; and I was mortally afraid of her. But if she is not English what is she?
NEPOMMUCK. Hungarian.
ALL THE REST. Hungarian!
NEPOMMUCK. Hungarian. And of royal blood. I am Hungarian. My blood is royal.
HIGGINS. Did you speak to her in Hungarian?
NEPOMMUCK. I did. She was very clever. She said "Please speak to me in English: I do not understand French." French! She pretends not to know the difference between Hungarian and French. Impossible: she knows both.
HIGGINS. And the blood royal? How did you find that out?
NEPOMMUCK. Instinct, maestro, instinct. Only the Magyar races can produce that air of the divine right, those resolute eyes. She is a princess.
HOST. What do you say, Professor?
HIGGINS. I say an ordinary London girl out of the gutter and taught to speak by an expert. I place her in Drury Lane.
NEPOMMUCK. Ha ha ha! Oh, maestro, maestro, you are mad on the subject of cockney dialects. The London gutter is the whole world for you.
HIGGINS [*to the Hostess*] What does your Excellency say?
HOSTESS. Oh, of course I agree with Nepommuck. She must be a princess at least.
HOST. Not necessarily legitimate, of course. Morganatic perhaps. But that is undoubtedly her class.
HIGGINS. I stick to my opinion.
HOSTESS. Oh, you are incorrigible.

The group breaks up, leaving Higgins isolated. Pickering joins him.

PICKERING. Where is Eliza? We must keep an eye on her.

Eliza joins them.

LIZA. I dont think I can bear much more. The people all stare so at me. An old lady has just told me that I speak exactly like Queen Victoria. I am sorry if I have lost your bet. I have done my best; but nothing can make me the same as these people.

PICKERING. You have not lost it, my dear. You have won it ten times over.

HIGGINS. Let us get out of this. I have had enough of chattering to these fools.

PICKERING. Eliza is tired; and I am hungry. Let us clear out and have supper somewhere.

ACT IV

The Wimpole Street laboratory. Midnight. Nobody in the room. The clock on the mantelpiece strikes twelve. The fire is not alight: it is a summer night.

Presently Higgins and Pickering are heard on the stairs.

HIGGINS [*calling down to Pickering*] I say, Pick: lock up, will you? I shant be going out again.

PICKERING. Right. Can Mrs Pearce go to bed? We dont want anything more, do we?

HIGGINS. Lord, no!

Eliza opens the door and is seen on the lighted landing in all the finery in which she has just won Higgins's bet for him. She comes to the hearth, and switches on the electric lights there. She is tired: her pallor contrasts strongly with her dark eyes and hair; and her expression is almost tragic. She takes off her cloak; puts her fan and gloves on the piano; and sits down on the bench, brooding and silent. Higgins, in evening dress, with overcoat and hat, comes in, carrying a smoking jacket which he has picked up downstairs. He takes off the hat and overcoat; throws them carelessly on the newspaper stand; disposes of his coat in the same way; puts on the smoking jacket; and throws himself wearily into the easy-chair at the hearth. Pickering, similarly attired, comes in. He also takes off his hat and overcoat, and is about to throw them on Higgins's when he hesitates.

PICKERING. I say: Mrs Pearce will row if we leave these things lying about in the drawing room.

HIGGINS. Oh, chuck them over the bannisters into the hall. She'll find them there in the morning and put them away all right. She'll think we were drunk.

PICKERING. We are, slightly. Are there any letters?

HIGGINS. I didnt look. [*Pickering takes the overcoats and hats and goes downstairs. Higgins begins half singing half yawning an air from La Fanciulla del Golden West. Suddenly he stops and exclaims*] I wonder where the devil my slippers are!

Eliza looks at him darkly; then rises suddenly and leaves the room.

Higgins yawns again, and resumes his song.

Pickering returns, with the contents of the letter-box in his hand.

PICKERING. Only circulars, and this coroneted billet-doux for you. [*He throws the circulars into the fender, and posts himself on the hearthrug, with his back to the grate*].

HIGGINS [*glancing at the billet-doux*] Money-lender. [*He throws the letter after the circulars*].

Eliza returns with a pair of large down-at-heel slippers. She places them on the carpet before Higgins, and sits as before without a word.

HIGGINS [*yawning again*] Oh Lord! What an evening! What a crew! What a silly tomfoolery! [*He raises his shoe to unlace it, and catches sight of the slippers. He stops unlacing and looks at them as if they had appeared there of their own accord*]. Oh! theyre there, are they?

PICKERING [*stretching himself*] Well, I feel a bit tired. It's been a long day. The garden party, a dinner party, and the reception! Rather too much of a good thing. But youve won your bet, Higgins. Eliza did the trick, and something to spare, eh?

HIGGINS [*fervently*] Thank God it's over!

Eliza flinches violently; but they take no notice of her; and she recovers herself and sits stonily as before.

PICKERING. Were you nervous at the garden party? *I* was. Eliza didnt seem a bit nervous.

HIGGINS. Oh, she wasnt nervous. I knew she'd be all right. No: it's the strain of putting the job through all these months that has told on me. It was interesting enough at first, while we were at the phonetics; but after that I got deadly sick of it. If I hadnt backed myself to do it I should have chucked the whole thing up two months ago. It was a silly notion: the whole thing has been a bore.

PICKERING. Oh come! the garden party was frightfully exciting. My heart began beating like anything.

HIGGINS. Yes, for the first three minutes. But when I saw we were going to win hands down, I felt like a bear in a cage, hanging about doing nothing. The dinner was worse: sitting gorging there for over an hour, with nobody but a damned fool of a fashionable woman to talk to! I tell you, Pickering, never again for me. No more artificial duchesses. The whole thing has been simple purgatory.

PICKERING. Youve never been broken in properly to the social routine. [*Strolling over to the piano*] I rather enjoy dipping into it occasionally myself: it makes me feel young again. Anyhow, it was a great success: an immense success. I was quite frightened once or twice because Eliza was doing it so well. You see, lots of the real people cant do it at all: theyre such fools that they think style comes by nature to people in their position; and so they never learn. Theres always something professional about doing a thing superlatively well.

HIGGINS. Yes: thats what drives me mad: the silly people dont know their own silly business. [*Rising*] However, it's over and done with; and now I can go to bed at last without dreading tomorrow.

Eliza's beauty becomes murderous.

PICKERING. I think I shall turn in too. Still, it's been a great occasion: a triumph for you. Goodnight. [*He goes*].

HIGGINS [*following him*] Goodnight. [*Over his shoulder, at the door*] Put out the lights, Eliza; and tell Mrs Pearce not to make coffee for me in the morning: I'll take tea. [*He goes out*].

Eliza tries to control herself and feel indifferent as she rises and walks across to the hearth to switch off the lights. By the time she gets there she is on the point of screaming. She sits down in Higgins's chair and holds on hard to the arms. Finally she gives way and flings herself furiously on the floor, raging.

HIGGINS [*in despairing wrath outside*] What the devil have I done with my slippers? [*He appears at the door*].

LIZA [*snatching up the slippers, and hurling them at him one after the other with all her force*] There are your slippers. And there. Take your slippers; and may you never have a day's luck with them!

HIGGINS [*astounded*] What on earth—! [*He comes to her*]. Whats the matter? Get up. [*He pulls her up*]. Anything wrong?

LIZA [*breathless*] Nothing wrong—with y o u. Ive won your bet for you, havnt I? Thats enough for you. *I* dont matter, I suppose.

HIGGINS. Y o u won my bet! You! Presumptuous insect! *I* won it. What did you throw those slippers at me for?

LIZA. Because I wanted to smash your face. I'd like to kill you, you selfish brute. Why didnt you leave me where you picked me out of—in the gutter? You thank God it's all over, and that now you can throw me back again there, do you? [*She crisps her fingers frantically*].

HIGGINS [*looking at her in cool wonder*] The creature is nervous, after all.

LIZA [*gives a suffocated scream of fury, and instinctively darts her nails at his face*]!!

HIGGINS [*catching her wrists*] Ah! would you? Claws in, you cat.

How dare you shew your temper to me? Sit down and be quiet. [*He throws her roughly into the easy-chair*].

LIZA [*crushed by superior strength and weight*] Whats to become of me? Whats to become of me?

HIGGINS. How the devil do I know whats to become of you? What does it matter what becomes of you?

LIZA. You dont care. I know you dont care. You wouldnt care if I was dead. I'm nothing to you—not so much as them slippers.

HIGGINS [*thundering*] T h o s e slippers.

LIZA [*with bitter submission*] Those slippers. I didnt think it made any difference now.

A pause. Eliza hopeless and crushed. Higgins a little uneasy.

HIGGINS [*in his loftiest manner*] Why have you begun going on like this? May I ask whether you complain of your treatment here?

LIZA. No.

HIGGINS. Has anybody behaved badly to you? Colonel Pickering? Mrs Pearce? Any of the servants?

LIZA. No.

HIGGINS. I presume you dont pretend that *I* have treated you badly?

LIZA. No.

HIGGINS. I am glad to hear it. [*He moderates his tone*]. Perhaps youre tired after the strain of the day. Will you have a glass of champagne? [*He moves towards the door*].

LIZA. No. [*Recollecting her manners*] Thank you.

HIGGINS [*good-humored again*] This has been coming on you for some days. I suppose it was natural for you to be anxious about the garden party. But thats all over now. [*He pats her kindly on the shoulder. She writhes*]. Theres nothing more to worry about.

LIZA. No. Nothing more for y o u to worry about. [*She suddenly rises and gets away from him by going to the piano bench, where she sits and hides her face*]. Oh God! I wish I was dead.

HIGGINS [*staring after her in sincere surprise*] Why? In heaven's name, why? [*Reasonably, going to her*] Listen to me, Eliza. All this irritation is purely subjective.

LIZA. I dont understand. I'm too ignorant.

HIGGINS. It's only imagination. Low spirits and nothing else. Nobody's hurting you. Nothing's wrong. You go to bed like a good girl and sleep it off. Have a little cry and say your prayers: that will make you comfortable.

LIZA. I heard your prayers. "Thank God it's all over!"

HIGGINS [*impatiently*] Well, d o n t you thank God it's all over? Now you are free and can do what you like.

LIZA [*pulling herself together in desperation*] What am I fit for? What have you left me fit for? Where am I to go? What am I to do? Whats to become of me?

HIGGINS [*enlightened, but not at all impressed*] Oh, thats whats worrying you, is it? [*He thrusts his hands into his pockets, and walks about in his usual manner, rattling the contents of his pockets, as if condescending to a trivial subject out of pure kindness*]. I shouldnt bother about it if I were you. I should imagine you wont have much difficulty in settling yourself somewhere or other, though I hadnt quite realized that you were going away. [*She looks quickly at him: he does not look at her, but examines the dessert stand on the piano and decides that he will eat an apple*]. You might marry, you know. [*He bites a large piece out of the apple and munches it noisily*]. You see, Eliza, all men are not confirmed old bachelors like me and the Colonel. Most men are the marrying sort (poor devils!); and youre not bad-looking: it's quite a pleasure to look at you sometimes—not now, of course, because youre crying and looking as ugly as the very devil; but when youre all right and quite yourself, youre what I should call attractive. That is, to the people in the marrying line, you understand. You go to bed and have a good nice rest; and then get up and look at yourself in the glass; and you wont feel so cheap.

Eliza again looks at him, speechless, and does not stir.

The look is quite lost on him: he eats his apple with a dreamy expression of happiness, as it is quite a good one.

HIGGINS [*a genial afterthought occuring to him*] I daresay my mother could find some chap or other who would do very well.

LIZA. We were above that at the corner of Tottenham Court Road.

HIGGINS [*waking up*] What do you mean?

LIZA. I sold flowers. I didnt sell myself. Now youve made a lady of me I'm not fit to sell anything else. I wish youd left me where you found me.

HIGGINS [*slinging the core of the apple decisively into the grate*] Tosh, Eliza. Dont you insult human relations by dragging all this cant about buying and selling into it. You neednt marry the fellow if you dont like him.

LIZA. What else am I to do?

HIGGINS. Oh, lots of things. What about your old idea of a florist's shop? Pickering could set you up in one: he has lots of money.

[*Chuckling*] He'll have to pay for all those togs you have been wearing today; and that, with the hire of the jewellery, will make a big hole in two hundred pounds. Why, six months ago you would have thought it the millennium to have a flower shop of your own. Come! youll be all right. I must clear off to bed: I'm devilish sleepy. By the way, I came down for something: I forget what it was.

LIZA. Your slippers.

HIGGINS. Oh yes, of course. You shied them at me. [*He picks them up, and is going out when she rises and speaks to him*].

LIZA. Before you go, sir—

HIGGINS [*dropping the slippers in his surprise at her calling him Sir*] Eh?

LIZA. Do my clothes belong to me or to Colonel Pickering?

HIGGINS [*coming back into the room as if her question were the very climax of unreason*] What the devil use would they be to Pickering?

LIZA. He might want them for the next girl you pick up to experiment on.

HIGGINS [*shocked and hurt*] Is t h a t the way you feel towards us?

LIZA. I dont want to hear anything more about that. All I want to know is whether anything belongs to me. My own clothes were burnt.

HIGGINS. But what does it matter? Why need you start bothering about that in the middle of the night?

LIZA. I want to know what I may take away with me. I dont want to be accused of stealing.

HIGGINS [*now deeply wounded*] Stealing! You shouldnt have said that, Eliza. That shews a want of feeling.

LIZA. I'm sorry. I'm only a common ignorant girl; and in my station I have to be careful. There cant be any feelings between the like of you and the like of me. Please will you tell me what belongs to me and what doesnt?

HIGGINS [*very sulky*] You may take the whole damned houseful if you like. Except the jewels. Theyre hired. Will that satisfy you? [*He turns on his heel and is about to go in extreme dudgeon*].

LIZA [*drinking in his emotion like nectar, and nagging him to provoke a further supply*] Stop, please. [*She takes off her jewels*]. Will you take these to your room and keep them safe? I dont want to run the risk of their being missing.

HIGGINS [*furious*] Hand them over. [*She puts them into his hands*]. If these belonged to me instead of to the jeweller, I'd ram them down your ungrateful throat. [*He perfunctorily thrusts them into his *pockets unconsciously decorating himself with the protruding ends of the chains*].

LIZA [*taking a ring off*] This ring isnt thc jeweller's: it's the one you bought me in Brighton. I dont want it now. [*Higgins dashes the ring violently into the fireplace, and turns on her so threateningly that she crouches over the piano with her hands over her face, and exclaims*] Dont you hit me.

HIGGINS. Hit you! You infamous creature, how dare you accuse me of such a thing? It is you who have hit me. You have wounded me to the heart.

LIZA [*thrilling with hidden joy*] I'm glad. Ive got a little of my own back, anyhow.

HIGGINS [*with dignity, in his finest professional style*] You have caused me to lose my temper: a thing that has hardly ever happened to me before. I prefer to say nothing more tonight. I am going to bed.

LIZA [*pertly*] Youd better leave a note for Mrs Pearce about the coffee; for she wont be told by me.

HIGGINS [*formally*] Damn Mrs Pearce; and damn the coffee; and damn you; and [*wildly*] damn my own folly in having lavished my hard-earned knowledge and the treasure of my regard and intimacy on a heartless guttersnipe. [*He goes out with impressive decorum, and spills it by slamming the door savagely*].

Eliza goes down on her knees on the hearthrug to look for the ring When she finds it she considers for a moment what to do with it. Finally she flings it down on the dessert stand and goes upstairs in a tearing rage.

★ ★ ★ ★ ★

The furniture of Eliza's room has been increased by a big wardrobe and a sumptuous dressing-table. She comes in and switches on the electric light. She goes to the wardrobe; opens it; and pulls out a walking dress, a hat, and a pair of shoes, which she throws on the bed. She takes off her evening dress and shoes; then takes a padded hanger from the wardrobe; adjusts it carefully in the evening dress; and hangs it in the wardrobe, which she shuts with a slam. She puts on her walking shoes, her walking dress, and hat. She takes her wrist watch from the dressing-table and fastens it on. She pulls on her gloves; takes her vanity bag; and looks into it to see that her purse is there before hanging it on her wrist. She makes for the door. Every movement expresses her furious resolution.

She takes a last look at herself in the glass.

She suddenly puts out her tongue at herself; then leaves the room, switching off the electric light at the door.

Meanwhile, in the street outside, Freddy Eynsford Hill, lovelorn, is gazing up at the second floor, in which one of the windows is still lighted.

The light goes out.

FREDDY. Goodnight, darling, darling, darling.

Eliza comes out, giving the door a considerable bang behind her.

LIZA. Whatever are you doing here?

FREDDY. Nothing. I spend most of my nights here. It's the only place where I'm happy. Dont laugh at me, Miss Doolittle.

LIZA. Dont you call me Miss Doolittle, do you hear? Liza's good enough for me. [*She breaks down and grabs him by the shoulders*] Freddy: you dont think I'm a heartless guttersnipe, do you?

FREDDY. Oh no, no, darling: how can you imagine such a thing? You are the loveliest, dearest—

He loses all self-control and smothers her with kisses. She, hungry for comfort, responds. They stand there in one another's arms.

An elderly police constable arrives.

CONSTABLE [*scandalized*] Now then! Now then!! Now then!!!

They release one another hastily.

FREDDY. Sorry, constable. Weve only just become engaged.

They run away.

The constable shakes his head, reflecting on his own courtship and on the vanity of human hopes. He moves off in the opposite direction with slow professional steps.

The flight of the lovers takes them to Cavendish Square. There they halt to consider their next move.

LIZA [*out of breath*] He didnt half give me a fright, that copper. But you answered him proper.

FREDDY. I hope I havnt taken you out of your way. Where were you going?

LIZA. To the river.

FREDDY. What for?

LIZA. To make a hole in it.

FREDDY [*horrified*] Eliza, darling. What do you mean? What's the matter?

LIZA. Never mind. It doesnt matter now. There's nobody in the world now but you and me, is there?

FREDDY. Not a soul.

They indulge in another embrace, and are again surprised by a much younger constable.

SECOND CONSTABLE. Now then, you two! What's this? Where do you think you are? Move along here, double quick.

FREDDY. As you say, sir, double quick.

They run away again, and are in Hanover Square before they stop for another conference.

FREDDY. I had no idea the police were so devilishly prudish.

LIZA. It's their business to hunt girls off the streets.

FREDDY. We must go somewhere. We cant wander about the streets all night.

LIZA. Cant we? I think it'd be lovely to wander about for ever.

FREDDY. Oh, darling.

They embrace again, oblivious of the arrival of a crawling taxi. It stops.

TAXIMAN. Can I drive you and the lady anywhere, sir?

They start asunder.

LIZA. Oh, Freddy, a taxi. The very thing.

FREDDY. But, damn it, Ive no money.

LIZA. I have plenty. The Colonel thinks you should never go out without ten pounds in your pocket. Listen. We'll drive about all night; and in the morning I'll call on old Mrs Higgins and ask her what I ought to do. I'll tell you all about it in the cab. And the police wont touch us there.

FREDDY. Righto! Ripping. [*To the Taximan*] Wimbledon Common. [*They drive off*].

ACT V

Mrs Higgins's drawing room. She is at her writing-table as before. The parlormaid comes in.

THE PARLORMAID [*at the door*] Mr Henry, maam, is downstairs with Colonel Pickering.

MRS HIGGINS. Well, shew them up.

THE PARLORMAID. Theyre using the telephone, maam. Telephoning to the police, I think.

MRS HIGGINS. What!

THE PARLORMAID [*coming further in and lowering her voice*] Mr Henry is in a state, maam. I thought I'd better tell you.

MRS HIGGINS. If you had told me that Mr Henry was not in a state it would have been more surprising. Tell them to come up when theyve finished with the police. I suppose he's lost something.

THE PARLORMAID. Yes, maam [*going*].

MRS HIGGINS. Go upstairs and tell Miss Doolittle that Mr Henry and the Colonel are here. Ask her not to come down til I send for her.

THE PARLORMAID. Yes, maam.

Higgins bursts in. He is, as the parlormaid has said, in a state.

HIGGINS. Look here, mother: heres a confounded thing!

MRS HIGGINS. Yes, dear. Good morning. [*He checks his impatience and kisses her, whilst the parlormaid goes out*]. What is it?

HIGGINS. Eliza's bolted.

MRS HIGGINS [*calmly continuing her writing*] You must have frightened her.

HIGGINS. Frightened her! nonsense! She was left last night, as usual, to turn out the lights and all that; and instead of going to bed she changed her clothes and went right off: her bed wasnt slept in. She came in a cab for her things before seven this morning; and that fool Mrs Pearce let her have them without telling me a word about it. What am I to do?

MRS HIGGINS. Do without, I'm afraid, Henry. The girl has a perfect right to leave if she chooses.

HIGGINS [*wandering distractedly across the room*] But I cant find anything. I dont know what appointments Ive got. I'm–[*Pickering comes in. Mrs Higgins puts down her pen and turns away from the writing-table*].

PICKERING [*shaking hands*] Good morning, Mrs Higgins. Has Henry told you? [*He sits down on the ottoman*].

HIGGINS. What does that ass of an inspector say? Have you offered a reward?

MRS HIGGINS [*rising in indignant amazement*] You dont mean to say you have set the police after Eliza.

HIGGINS. Of course. What are the police for? What else could we do? [*He sits in the Elizabethan chair*].

PICKERING. The inspector made a lot of difficulties. I really think he suspected us of some improper purpose.

MRS HIGGINS. Well, of course he did. What right have you to go to the police and give the girl's name as if she were a thief, or a lost umbrella, or something? Really! [*She sits down again, deeply vexed*].

HIGGINS. But we want to find her.

PICKERING. We cant let her go like this, you know, Mrs Higgins. What were we to do?

MRS HIGGINS. You have no more sense, either of you, than two children. Why–

The parlormaid comes in and breaks off the conversation.

THE PARLORMAID. Mr Henry: a gentleman wants to see you very particular. He's been sent on from Wimpole Street.

HIGGINS. Oh, bother! I cant see anyone now. Who is it?

THE PARLORMAID. A Mr Doolittle, sir.

PICKERING. Doolittle! Do you mean the dustman?

THE PARLORMAID. Dustman! Oh no, sir: a gentleman.

HIGGINS [*springing up excitedly*] By George, Pick, it's some relative of hers that she's gone to. Somebody we know nothing about. [*To the parlormaid*] Send him up, quick.

THE PARLORMAID. Yes, sir. [*She goes*].

HIGGINS [*eagerly, going to his mother*] Genteel relatives! now we shall hear something. [*He sits down in the Chippendale chair*].

MRS HIGGINS. Do you know any of her people?

PICKERING. Only her father: the fellow we told you about.

THE PARLORMAID [*announcing*] Mr Doolittle. [*She withdraws*].

Doolittle enters. He is resplendently dressed as for a fashionable wedding, and might, in fact, be the bridegroom. A flower in his but-

tonhole, a dazzling silk hat, and patent leather shoes complete the effect. He is too concerned with the business he has come on to notice Mrs Higgins. He walks straight to Higgins, and accosts him with vehement reproach.

DOOLITTLE [*indicating his own person*] See here! Do you see this? You done this.

HIGGINS. Done what, man?

DOOLITTLE. This, I tell you. Look at it. Look at this hat. Look at this coat.

PICKERING. Has Eliza been buying you clothes?

DOOLITTLE. Eliza! not she. Why would she buy me clothes?

MRS HIGGINS. Good morning, Mr Doolittle. Wont you sit down?

DOOLITTLE [*taken aback as he becomes conscious that he has forgotten his hostess*] Asking your pardon, maam. [*He approaches her and shakes her proffered hand*]. Thank you. [*He sits down on the ottoman, on Pickering's right*]. I am that full of what has happened to me that I cant think of anything else.

HIGGINS. What the dickens has happened to you?

DOOLITTLE. I shouldnt mind if it had only happened to me: anything might happen to anybody and nobody to blame but Providence, as you might say. But this is something that you done to me: yes, you, Enry Iggins.

HIGGINS. Have you found Eliza?

DOOLITTLE. Have you lost her?

HIGGINS. Yes.

DOOLITTLE. You have all the luck, you have. I aint found her; but she'll find me quick enough now after what you done to me.

MRS HIGGINS. But what has my son done to you, Mr Doolittle?

DOOLITTLE. Done to me! Ruined me. Destroyed my happiness. Tied me up and delivered me into the hands of middle class morality.

HIGGINS [*rising intolerantly and standing over Doolittle*] Youre raving. Youre drunk. Youre mad. I gave you five pounds. After that I had two conversations with you, at half-a-crown an hour. Ive never seen you since.

DOOLITTLE. Oh! Drunk am I? Mad am I? Tell me this. Did you or did you not write a letter to an old blighter in America that was giving five millions to found Moral Reform Societies all over the world, and that wanted you to invent a universal language for him?

HIGGINS. What! Ezra D. Wannafeller! He's dead. [*He sits down again carelessly*].

DOOLITTLE. Yes: he's dead; and I'm done for. Now did you or did you not write a letter to him to say that the most original moralist at present in England, to the best of your knowledge, was Alfred Doolittle, a common dustman?

HIGGINS. Oh, after your first visit I remember making some silly joke of the kind.

DOOLITTLE. Ah! you may well call it a silly joke. It put the lid on me right enough. Just give him the chance he wanted to shew that Americans is not like us: that they reckonize and respect merit in every class of life, however humble. Them words is in his blooming will, in which, Henry Higgins, thanks to your silly joking, he leaves me a share in his Predigested Cheese Trust worth three thousand a year on condition that I lecture for his Wannafeller Moral Reform World League as often as they ask me up to six times a year.

HIGGINS. The devil he does! Whew! [*Brightening suddenly*] What a lark!

PICKERING. A safe thing for you, Doolittle. They wont ask you twice.

DOOLITTLE. It aint the lecturing I mind. I'll lecture them blue in the face, I will, and not turn a hair. It's making a gentleman of me that I object to. Who asked him to make a gentleman of me? I was happy. I was free. I touched pretty nigh everybody for money when I wanted it, same as I touched you, Enry Iggins. Now I am worrited; tied neck and heels; and everybody touches m e for money. It's a fine thing for you, says my solicitor. Is it? says I. You mean it's a good thing for you, I says. When I was a poor man and had a solicitor once when they found a pram in the dust cart, he got me off, and got shut of me and got me shut of him as quick as he could. Same with the doctors: used to shove me out of the hospital before I could hardly stand on my legs, and nothing to pay. Now they finds out that I'm not a healthy man and cant live unless they looks after me twice a day. In the house I'm not let do a hand's turn for myself: somebody else must do it and touch me for it. A year ago I hadnt a relative in the world except two or three that wouldnt speak to me. Now Ive fifty, and not a decent week's wages among the lot of them. I have to live for others and not for myself: thats middle class morality. You talk of losing Eliza. Dont you be anxious: I bet she's on my doorstep by this: she that could support herself easy by selling flowers if I wasnt respectable. And the next one to touch me will be you, Enry Iggins. I'll have to learn to speak middle class language from you, instead of speaking proper

English. Thats where youll come in; and I daresay thats what you done it for.

MRS HIGGINS. But, my dear Mr Doolittle, you need not suffer all this if you are really in earnest. Nobody can force you to accept this bequest. You can repudiate it. Isnt that so, Colonel Pickering?

PICKERING. I believe so.

DOOLITTLE [*softening his manner in deference to her sex*] Thats the tragedy of it, maam. It's easy to say chuck it; but I havnt the nerve. Which of us has? We're all intimidated. Intimidated, maam: thats what we are. What is there for me if I chuck it but the workhouse in my old age? I have to dye my hair already to keep my job as a dustman. If I was one of the deserving poor, and had put by a bit, I could chuck it; but then why should I, acause the deserving poor might as well be millionaires for all the happiness they ever has. They dont know what happiness is. But I, as one of the undeserving poor, have nothing between me and the pauper's uniform but this here blasted three thousand a year that shoves me into the middle class. (Excuse the expression, maam; youd use it yourself if you had my provocation.) Theyve got you every way you turn: it's a choice between the Skilly of the workhouse and the Char Bydis of the middle class; and I havnt the nerve for the workhouse. Intimidated: thats what I am. Broke. Bought up. Happier men than me will call for my dust, and touch me for their tip; and I'll look on helpless, and envy them. And thats what your son has brought me to. [*He is overcome by emotion*].

MRS HIGGINS. Well, I'm very glad youre not going to do anything foolish, Mr Doolittle. For this solves the problem of Eliza's future. You can provide for her now.

DOOLITTLE [*with melancholy resignation*] Yes, maam: I'm expected to provide for everyone now, out of three thousand a year.

HIGGINS [*jumping up*] Nonsense! he cant provide for her. He shant provide for her. She doesnt belong to him. I paid him five pounds for her. Doolittle: either youre an honest man or a rogue.

DOOLITTLE [*tolerantly*] A little of both, Henry, like the rest of us: a little of both.

HIGGINS. Well, you took that money for the girl; and you have no right to take her as well.

MRS HIGGINS. Henry: dont be absurd. If you want to know where Eliza is, she is upstairs.

HIGGINS [*amazed*] Upstairs!!! Then I shall jolly soon fetch her downstairs. [*He makes resolutely for the door*].

MRS HIGGINS [*rising and following him*] Be quiet, Henry. Sit down.
HIGGINS. I—
MRS HIGGINS. Sit down, dear; and listen to me.
HIGGINS. Oh very well, very well, very well. [*He throws himself ungraciously on the ottoman, with his face towards the windows*]. But I think you might have told us this half an hour ago.
MRS HIGGINS. Eliza came to me this morning. She told me of the brutal way you two treated her.
HIGGINS [*bounding up again*] What!
PICKERING [*rising also*] My dear Mrs Higgins, she's been telling you stories. We didnt treat her brutally. We hardly said a word to her; and we parted on particularly good terms. [*Turning to Higgins*] Higgins: did you bully her after I went to bed?
HIGGINS. Just the other way about. She threw my slippers in my face. She behaved in the most outrageous way. I never gave her the slightest provocation. The slippers came bang into my face the moment I entered the room—before I had uttered a word. And used perfectly awful language.
PICKERING [*astonished*] But why? What did we do to her?
MRS HIGGINS. I think I know pretty well what you did. The girl is naturally rather affectionate, I think. Isnt she, Mr Doolittle?
DOOLITTLE. Very tender-hearted, maam. Takes after me.
MRS HIGGINS. Just so. She had become attached to you both. She worked very hard for you, Henry. I dont think you quite realize what anything in the nature of brain work means to a girl of her class. Well, it seems that when the great day of trial came, and she did this wonderful thing for you without making a single mistake, you two sat there and never said a word to her, but talked together of how glad you were that it was all over and how you had been bored with the whole thing. And then you were surprised because she threw your slippers at you! *I* should have thrown the fire-irons at you.
HIGGINS. We said nothing except that we were tired and wanted to go to bed. Did we, Pick?
PICKERING [*shrugging his shoulders*] That was all.
MRS HIGGINS [*ironically*] Quite sure?
PICKERING. Absolutely. Really, that was all.
MRS HIGGINS. You didnt thank her, or pet her, or admire her, or tell her how splendid she'd been.
HIGGINS [*impatiently*] But she knew all about that. We didnt make speeches to her, if thats what you mean.

PICKERING [*conscience stricken*] Perhaps we were a little inconsiderate. Is she very angry?

MRS HIGGINS [*returning to her place at the writing-table*] Well, I'm afraid she wont go back to Wimpole Street, especially now that Mr Doolittle is able to keep up the position you have thrust on her; but she says she is quite willing to meet you on friendly terms and to let bygones be bygones.

HIGGINS [*furious*] Is she, by George? Ho!

MRS HIGGINS. If you promise to behave yourself, Henry, I'll ask her to come down. If not, go home; for you have taken up quite enough of my time.

HIGGINS. Oh, all right. Very well. Pick: you behave yourself. Let us put on our best Sunday manners for this creature that we picked out of the mud. [*He flings himself sulkily into the Elizabethan chair*].

DOOLITTLE [*remonstrating*] Now, now, Enry Iggins! Have some consideration for my feelings as a middle class man.

MRS HIGGINS. Remember your promise, Henry. [*She presses the bell-button on the writing-table*]. Mr Doolittle: will you be so good as to step out on the balcony for a moment. I dont want Eliza to have the shock of your news until she has made it up with these two gentlemen. Would you mind?

DOOLITTLE. As you wish, lady. Anything to help Henry to keep her off my hands. [*He disappears through the window*].

The parlormaid answers the bell. Pickering sits down in Doolittle's place.

MRS HIGGINS. Ask Miss Doolittle to come down, please.

THE PARLORMAID. Yes, maam. [*She goes out*].

MRS HIGGINS. Now, Henry: be good.

HIGGINS. I am behaving myself perfectly.

PICKERING. He is doing his best, Mrs Higgins.

A pause. Higgins throws back his head; stretches out his legs; and begins to whistle.

MRS HIGGINS. Henry, dearest, you dont look at all nice in that attitude.

HIGGINS [*pulling himself together*] I was not trying to look nice, mother.

MRS HIGGINS. It doesnt matter, dear. I only wanted to make you speak.

HIGGINS. Why?

MRS HIGGINS. Because you cant speak and whistle at the same time.

Higgins groans. Another very trying pause.

HIGGINS [*springing up, out of patience*] Where the devil is that girl? Are we to wait here all day?

Eliza enters, sunny, self-possessed, and giving a staggeringly convincing exhibition of ease of manner. She carries a little work-basket, and is very much at home. Pickering is too much taken aback to rise.

LIZA. How do you do, Professor Higgins? Are you quite well?

HIGGINS [*choking*] Am I—[*He can say no more*].

LIZA. But of course you are: you are never ill. So glad to see you again, Colonel Pickering. [*He rises hastily; and they shake hands*]. Quite chilly this morning, isnt it? [*She sits down on his left. He sits beside her*].

HIGGINS. Dont you dare try this game on me. I taught it to you; and it doesnt take me in. Get up and come home; and dont be a fool.

Eliza takes a piece of needlework from her basket, and begins to stitch at it, without taking the least notice of this outburst.

MRS HIGGINS. Very nicely put, indeed, Henry. No woman could resist such an invitation.

HIGGINS. You let her alone, mother. Let her speak for herself. You will jolly soon see whether she has an idea that I havnt put into her head or a word that I havnt put into her mouth. I tell you I have created this thing out of the squashed cabbage leaves of Covent Garden; and now she pretends to play the fine lady with me.

MRS HIGGINS [*placidly*] Yes, dear; but youll sit down, wont you?

Higgins sits down again, savagely.

LIZA [*to Pickering, taking no apparent notice of Higgins, and working away deftly*] Will y o u drop me altogether now that the experiment is over, Colonel Pickering?

PICKERING. Oh dont. You mustnt think of it as an experiment. It shocks me, somehow.

LIZA. Oh, I'm only a squashed cabbage leaf—

PICKERING [*impulsively*] No.

LIZA [*continuing quietly*]—but I owe so much to you that I should be very unhappy if you forgot me.

PICKERING. It's very kind of you to say so, Miss Doolittle.

LIZA. It's not because you paid for my dresses. I know you are generous to everybody with money. But it was from you that I learnt really nice manners; and that is what makes one a lady, isnt it? You see it was so very difficult for me with the example of Professor Higgins always before me. I was brought up to be just like him, unable to control myself, and using bad language on the slightest provocation. And I should never have known that ladies and gentlemen didnt behave like that if you hadnt been there.

HIGGINS. Well!!

PICKERING. Oh, thats only his way, you know. He doesnt mean it.

LIZA. Oh, *I* didnt mean it either, when I was a flower girl. It was only my way. But you see I did it; and thats what makes the difference after all.

PICKERING. No doubt. Still, he taught you to speak; and I couldnt have done that, you know.

LIZA [*trivially*] Of course: that is his profession.

HIGGINS. Damnation!

LIZA [*continuing*] It was just like learning to dance in the fashionable way: there was nothing more than that in it. But do you know what began my real education?

PICKERING. What?

LIZA [*stopping her work for a moment*] Your calling me Miss Doolittle that day when I first came to Wimpole Street. That was the beginning of self-respect for me. [*She resumes her stitching*]. And there were a hundred little things you never noticed, because they came naturally to you. Things about standing up and taking off your hat and opening doors—

PICKERING. Oh, that was nothing.

LIZA. Yes: things that shewed you thought and felt about me as if I were something better than a scullery-maid; though of course I know you would have been just the same to a scullery-maid if she had been let into the drawing room. You never took off your boots in the dining room when I was there.

PICKERING. You mustnt mind that. Higgins takes off his boots all over the place.

LIZA. I know. I am not blaming him. It is his way, isnt it? But it made such a difference to me that you didnt do it. You see, really and truly, apart from the things anyone can pick up (the dressing and the proper way of speaking, and so on), the difference between a lady and a flower girl is not how she behaves, but how she's treated. I shall always be a flower girl to Professor Higgins, because he always treats me as a flower girl, and always will; but I know I can be a lady to you, because you always treat me as a lady, and always will.

MRS HIGGINS. Please dont grind your teeth, Henry.

PICKERING. Well, this is really very nice of you, Miss Doolittle.

LIZA. I should like you to call me Eliza, now, if you would.

PICKERING. Thank you. Eliza, of course.

LIZA. And I should like Professor Higgins to call me Miss Doolittle.

HIGGINS. I'll see you damned first.

MRS HIGGINS. Henry! Henry!

PICKERING [*laughing*] Why dont you slang back at him? Dont stand it. It would do him a lot of good.

LIZA. I cant. I could have done it once; but now I cant go back to it. You told me, you know, that when a child is brought to a foreign country, it picks up the language in a few weeks, and forgets its own. Well, I am a child in your country. I have forgotten my own language, and can speak nothing but yours. Thats the real break-off with the corner of Tottenham Court Road. Leaving Wimpole Street finishes it.

PICKERING [*much alarmed*] Oh! but youre coming back to Wimpole Street, arnt you? Youll forgive Higgins?

HIGGINS [*rising*] Forgive! Will she, by George! Let her go. Let her find out how she can get on without us. She will relapse into the gutter in three weeks without me at her elbow.

Doolittle appears at the centre window. With a look of dignified reproach at Higgins, he comes slowly and silently to his daughter, who, with her back to the window, is unconscious of his approach.

PICKERING. He's incorrigible, Eliza. You wont relapse, will you?

LIZA. No: not now. Never again. I have learnt my lesson. I dont believe I could utter one of the old sounds if I tried. [*Doolittle touches her on her left shoulder. She drops her work, losing her self-possession utterly at the spectacle of her father's splendor*] A-a-a-a-a-ah-ow-ooh!

HIGGINS [*with a crow of triumph*] Aha! Just so. A-a-a-a-ahowooh! A-a-a-a-ahowooh! A-a-a-a-ahowooh! Victory! Victory! [*He throws himself on the divan, folding his arms, and spraddling arrogantly*].

DOOLITTLE. Can you blame the girl? Dont look at me like that, Eliza. It aint my fault. Ive come into some money.

LIZA. You must have touched a millionaire this time, dad.

DOOLITTLE. I have. But I'm dressed something special today. I'm going to St George's, Hanover Square. Your stepmother is going to marry me.

LIZA [*angrily*] Youre going to let yourself down to marry that low common woman!

PICKERING [*quietly*] He ought to, Eliza. [*To Doolittle*] Why has she changed her mind?

DOOLITTLE [*sadly*] Intimidated, Governor. Intimidated. Middle class morality claims its victim. Wont you put on your hat, Liza, and come and see me turned off?

LIZA. If the Colonel says I must, I–I'll [*almost sobbing*] I'll demean myself. And get insulted for my pains, like enough.

DOOLITTLE. Dont be afraid: she never comes to words with anyone now, poor woman! respectability has broke all the spirit out of her.

PICKERING [*squeezing Eliza's elbow gently*] Be kind to them, Eliza. Make the best of it.

LIZA [*forcing a little smile for him through her vexation*] Oh well, just to shew theres no ill feeling. I'll be back in a moment. [*She goes out*].

DOOLITTLE [*sitting down beside Pickering*] I feel uncommon nervous about the ceremony, Colonel. I wish youd come and see me through it.

PICKERING. But youve been through it before, man. You were married to Eliza's mother.

DOOLITTLE. Who told you that, Colonel?

PICKERING. Well, nobody told me. But I concluded–naturally–

DOOLITTLE. No: that aint the natural way, Colonel: it's only the middle class way. My way was always the undeserving way. But dont say nothing to Eliza. She dont know: I always had a delicacy about telling her.

PICKERING. Quite right. We'll leave it so, if you dont mind.

DOOLITTLE. And youll come to the church, Colonel, and put me through straight?

PICKERING. With pleasure. As far as a bachelor can.

MRS HIGGINS. May I come, Mr Doolittle? I should be very sorry to miss your wedding.

DOOLITTLE. I should indeed be honored by your condescension, maam; and my poor old woman would take it as a tremenjous compliment. She's been very low, thinking of the happy days that are no more.

MRS HIGGINS [*rising*] I'll order the carriage and get ready. [*The men rise, except Higgins*]. I shant be more than fifteen minutes. [*As she goes to the door Eliza comes in, hatted and buttoning her gloves*]. I'm going to the church to see your father married, Eliza. You had better come in the brougham with me. Colonel Pickering can go on with the bridegroom.

Mrs Higgins goes out. Eliza comes to the middle of the room between the centre window and the ottoman. Pickering joins her.

DOOLITTLE. Bridegroom! What a word! It makes a man realize his position, somehow. [*He takes up his hat and goes towards the door*].

PICKERING. Before I go, Eliza, do forgive Higgins and come back to us.

LIZA. I dont think dad would allow me. Would you, dad?

DOOLITTLE [*sad but magnanimous*] They played you off very cunning, Eliza, them two sportsmen. It if had been only one of them, you could have nailed him. But you see, there was two; and one of them chaperoned the other, as you might say. [*To Pickering*] It was artful of you, Colonel; but I bear no malice: I should have done the same myself. I been the victim of one woman after another all my life; and I dont grudge you two getting the better of Eliza. I shant interfere. It's time for us to go, Colonel. So long, Henry. See you in St George's, Eliza. [*He goes out*].

PICKERING [*coaxing*] Do stay with us, Eliza. [*He follows Doolittle*].

Eliza goes out on the balcony to avoid being alone with Higgins. He rises and joins her there. She immediately comes back into the room and makes for the door; but he goes along the balcony quickly and gets his back to the door before she reaches it.

HIGGINS. Well, Eliza, youve had a bit of your own back, as you call it. Have you had enough? and are you going to be reasonable? Or do you want any more?

LIZA. You want me back only to pick up your slippers and put up with your tempers and fetch and carry for you.

HIGGINS. I havnt said I wanted you back at all.

LIZA. Oh, indeed. Then what are we talking about?

HIGGINS. About you, not about me. If you come back I shall treat you just as I have always treated you. I cant change my nature; and I dont intend to change my manners. My manners are exactly the same as Colonel Pickering's.

LIZA. Thats not true. He treats a flower girl as if she was a duchess.

HIGGINS. And I treat a duchess as if she was a flower girl.

LIZA. I see. [*She turns away composedly, and sits on the ottoman, facing the window*]. The same to everybody.

HIGGINS. Just so.

LIZA. Like father.

HIGGINS [*grinning, a little taken down*] Without accepting the comparison at all points, Eliza, it's quite true that your father is not a snob, and that he will be quite at home in any station of life to which his eccentric destiny may call him. [*Seriously*] The great secret, Eliza, is not having bad manners or good manners or any other particular sort of manners, but having the same manner for all human souls: in short, behaving as if you were in Heaven, where there are no third-class carriages, and one soul is as good as another.

LIZA. Amen. You are a born preacher.

HIGGINS [*irritated*] The question is not whether I treat you rudely, but whether you ever heard me treat anyone else better.

LIZA [*with sudden sincerity*] I dont care how you treat me. I dont mind your swearing at me. I shouldnt mind a black eye: Ive had one before this. But [*standing up and facing him*] I wont be passed over.

HIGGINS. Then get out of my way; for I wont stop for you. You talk about me as if I were a motor bus.

LIZA. So you are a motor bus: all bounce and go, and no consideration for anyone. But I can do without you: dont think I cant.

HIGGINS. I know you can. I told you you could.

LIZA [*wounded, getting away from him to the other side of the ottoman with her face to the hearth*] I know you did, you brute. You wanted to get rid of me.

HIGGINS. Liar.

LIZA. Thank you. [*She sits down with dignity*].

HIGGINS. You never asked yourself, I suppose, whether *I* could do without y o u.

LIZA [*earnestly*] Dont you try to get round me. Youll h a v e to do without me.

HIGGINS [*arrogant*] I can do without anybody. I have my own soul: my own spark of divine fire. But [*with sudden humility*] I shall miss you, Eliza. [*He sits down near her on the ottoman*]. I have learnt something from your idiotic notions: I confess that humbly and gratefully. And I have grown accustomed to your voice and appearance. I like them, rather.

LIZA. Well, you have both of them on your gramophone and in your book of photographs. When you feel lonely without me, you can turn the machine on. It's got no feelings to hurt.

HIGGINS. I cant turn your soul on. Leave me those feelings; and you can take away the voice and the face. They are not you.

LIZA. Oh, you a r e a devil. You can twist the heart in a girl as easy as some could twist her arms to hurt her. Mrs Pearce warned me. Time and again she has wanted to leave you; and you always got round her at the last minute. And you dont care a bit for her. And you dont care a bit for me.

HIGGINS. I care for life, for humanity; and you are a part of it that has come my way and been built into my house. What more can you or anyone ask?

LIZA. I wont care for anybody that doesnt care for me.

HIGGINS. Commercial principles, Eliza. Like [*reproducing her Covent Garden pronunciation with professional exactness*] s'yollin voylets [selling violets], isn't it?

LIZA. Dont sneer at me. It's mean to sneer at me.

HIGGINS. I have never sneered in my life. Sneering doesnt become either the human face or the human soul. I am expressing my righteous contempt for Commercialism. I dont and wont trade in affection. You call me a brute because you couldnt buy a claim on me by fetching my slippers and finding my spectacles. You were a fool: I think a woman fetching a man's slippers is a disgusting sight: did I ever fetch y o u r slippers? I think a good deal more of you for throwing them in my face. No use slaving for me and then saying you want to be cared for: who cares for a slave? If you come back, come back for the sake of good fellowship; for youll get nothing else. Youve had a thousand times as much out of me as I have out of you; and if you dare to set up your little dog's tricks of fetching and carrying slippers against my creation of a Duchess Eliza, I'll slam the door in your silly face.

LIZA. What did you do it for if you didnt care for me?

HIGGINS [*heartily*] Why, because it was my job.

LIZA. You never thought of the trouble it would make for me.

HIGGINS. Would the world ever have been made if its maker had been afraid of making trouble? Making life means making trouble. Theres only one way of escaping trouble; and thats killing things. Cowards, you notice, are always shrieking to have troublesome people killed.

LIZA. I'm no preacher: I dont notice things like that. I notice that you dont notice me.

HIGGINS [*jumping up and walking about intolerantly*] Eliza: youre an idiot. I waste the treasures of my Miltonic mind by spreading them before you. Once for all, understand that I go my way and do my work without caring twopence what happens to either of us. I am not intimidated, like your father and your stepmother. So you can come back or go to the devil: which you please.

LIZA. What am I to come back for?

HIGGINS [*bouncing up on his knees on the ottoman and leaning over it to her*] For the fun of it. Thats why I took you on.

LIZA [*with averted face*] And you may throw me out tomorrow if I dont do everything you want me to?
HIGGINS. Yes; and you may walk out tomorrow if I dont do everything you want me to.
LIZA. And live with my stepmother?
HIGGINS. Yes, or sell flowers.
LIZA. Oh! if I only could go back to my flower basket! I should be independent of both you and father and all the world! Why did you take my independence from me? Why did I give it up? I'm a slave now, for all my fine clothes.
HIGGINS. Not a bit. I'll adopt you as my daughter and settle money on you if you like. Or would you rather marry Pickering?
LIZA [*looking fiercely round at him*] I wouldnt marry you if you asked me; and youre nearer my age than what he is.
HIGGINS [*gently*] Than he is: not "than what he is."
LIZA [*losing her temper and rising*] I'll talk as I like. Youre not my teacher now.
HIGGINS [*reflectively*] I dont suppose Pickering would, though. He's as confirmed an old bachelor as I am.
LIZA. Thats not what I want; and dont you think it. Ive always had chaps enough wanting me that way. Freddy Hill writes to me twice and three times a day, sheets and sheets.
HIGGINS [*disagreeably surprised*] Damn his impudence! [*He recoils and finds himself sitting on his heels*].
LIZA. He has a right to if he likes, poor lad. And he does love me.
HIGGINS [*getting off the ottoman*] You have no right to encourage him.
LIZA. Every girl has a right to be loved.
HIGGINS. What! By fools like that?
LIZA. Freddy's not a fool. And if he's weak and poor and wants me, may be he'd make me happier than my betters that bully me and dont want me.
HIGGINS. Can he make anything of you? Thats the point.
LIZA. Perhaps I could make something of him. But I never thought of us making anything of one another; and you never think of anything else. I only want to be natural.
HIGGINS. In short, you want me to be as infatuated about you as Freddy? Is that it?
LIZA. No I dont. Thats not the sort of feeling I want from you. And

dont you be too sure of yourself or of me. I could have been a bad girl if I'd liked. Ive seen more of some things than you, for all your learning. Girls like me can drag gentlemen down to make love to them easy enough. And they wish each other dead the next minute.

HIGGINS. Of course they do. Then what in thunder are we quarrelling about?

LIZA [*much troubled*] I want a little kindness. I know I'm a common ignorant girl, and you a book-learned gentleman; but I'm not dirt under your feet. What I done [*correcting herself*] what I did was not for the dresses and the taxis: I did it because we were pleasant together and I come—came—to care for you; not to want you to make love to me, and not forgetting the difference between us, but more friendly like.

HIGGINS. Well, of course. Thats just how I feel. And how Pickering feels. Eliza: youre a fool.

LIZA. Thats not a proper answer to give me [*she sinks on the chair at the writing-table in tears*].

HIGGINS. It's all youll get until you stop being a common idiot. If youre going to be a lady, youll have to give up feeling neglected if the men you know dont spend half their time snivelling over you and the other half giving you black eyes. If you cant stand the coldness of my sort of life, and the strain of it, go back to the gutter. Work til youre more a brute than a human being; and then cuddle and squabble and drink til you fall asleep. Oh, it's a fine life, the life of the gutter. It's real: it's warm: it's violent: you can feel it through the thickest skin: you can taste it and smell it without any training or any work. Not like Science and Literature and Classical Music and Philosophy and Art. You find me cold, unfeeling, selfish, dont you? Very well: be off with you to the sort of people you like. Marry some sentimental hog or other with lots of money, and a thick pair of lips to kiss you with and a thick pair of boots to kick you with. If you cant appreciate what youve got, youd better get what you can appreciate.

LIZA [*desperate*] Oh, you a r e a cruel tyrant. I cant talk to you: you turn everything against me: I'm always in the wrong. But you know very well all the time that youre nothing but a bully. You know I cant go back to the gutter, as you call it, and that I have no real friends in the world but you and the Colonel. You know well I couldnt bear to live with a low common man after you two; and it's wicked and cruel of you to insult me by pretending I could. You think I must go back to Wimpole Street because I have nowhere else to go but father's. But dont you be too sure that you have me under your feet to be trampled on and talked down. I'll marry Freddy, I will, as soon as I'm able to support him.

HIGGINS [*thunderstruck*] Freddy!!! that young fool! That poor devil who couldnt get a job as an errand boy even if he had the guts to try for it! Woman: do you not understand that I have made you a consort for a king?

LIZA. Freddy loves me: that makes him king enough for me. I dont want him to work: he wasnt brought up to it as I was. I'll go and be a teacher.

HIGGINS. Whatll you teach, in heaven's name?

LIZA. What you taught me. I'll teach phonetics.

HIGGINS. Ha! ha! ha!

LIZA. I'll offer myself as an assistant to that hairy-faced Hungarian.

HIGGINS [*rising in a fury*] What! That impostor! that humbug! that toadying ignoramus! Teach him my methods! my discoveries! You take one step in his direction and I'll wring your neck. [*He lays hands on her*]. Do you hear?

LIZA [*defiantly non-resistant*] Wring away. What do I care? I knew youd strike me some day. [*He lets her go, stamping with rage at having forgotten himself, and recoils so hastily that he stumbles back into his seat on the ottoman*]. Aha! Now I know how to deal with you. What a fool I was not to think of it before! You cant take away the knowledge you gave me. You said I had a finer ear than you. And I can be civil and kind to people, which is more than you can. Aha! [*Purposely dropping her aitches to annoy him*] Thats done you, Enry Iggins, it az. Now I dont care that [*snapping her fingers*] for your bullying and your big talk. I'll advertize it in the papers that your duchess is only a flower girl that you taught, and that she'll teach anybody to be a duchess just the same in six months for a thousand guineas. Oh, when I think of myself crawling under your feet and being trampled on and called names, when all the time I had only to lift up my finger to be as good as you, I could just kick myself.

HIGGINS [*wondering at her*] You damned impudent slut, you! But it's better than snivelling; better than fetching slippers and finding spectacles, isnt it? [*Rising*] By George, Eliza, I said I'd make a woman of you; and I have. I like you like this.

LIZA. Yes: you turn round and make up to me now that I'm not afraid of you, and can do without you.

HIGGINS. Of course I do, you little fool. Five minutes ago you were like a millstone round my neck. Now youre a tower of strength: a consort battleship. You and I and Pickering will be three old bachelors together instead of only two men and a silly girl.

Mrs Higgins returns, dressed for the wedding. Eliza instantly becomes cool and elegant.

MRS HIGGINS. The carriage is waiting, Eliza. Are you ready?

LIZA. Quite. Is the Professor coming?

MRS HIGGINS. Certainly not. He cant behave himself in church. He makes remarks out loud all the time on the clergyman's pronunciation.

LIZA. Then I shall not see you again, Professor. Goodbye. [*She goes to the door*].

MRS HIGGINS [*coming to Higgins*] Goodbye, dear.

HIGGINS. Goodbye, mother. [*He is about to kiss her, when he recollects something*]. Oh, by the way, Eliza, order a ham and a Stilton cheese, will you? And buy me a pair of reindeer gloves, number eights, and a tie to match that new suit of mine. You can choose the color. [*His cheerful, careless, vigorous voice shews that he is incorrigible*].

LIZA [*disdainfully*] Number eights are too small for you if you want them lined with lamb's wool. You have three new ties that you have forgotten in the drawer of your washstand. Colonel Pickering prefers double Gloucester to Stilton; and you dont notice the difference. I telephoned Mrs Pearce this morning not to forget the ham. What you are to do without me I cannot imagine. [*She sweeps out*].

MRS HIGGINS. I'm afraid youve spoilt that girl, Henry. I should be uneasy about you and her if she were less fond of Colonel Pickering.

HIGGINS. Pickering! Nonsense: she's going to marry Freddy. Ha ha! Freddy! Freddy!! Ha ha ha ha ha!!!!! [*He roars with laughter as the play ends*].

★ ★ ★ ★ ★

The rest of the story need not be shewn in action, and indeed, would hardly need telling if our imaginations were not so enfeebled by their lazy dependence on the ready-mades and reach-me-downs of the ragshop in which Romance keeps its stock of "happy endings" to misfit all stories. Now, the history of Eliza Doolittle, though called a romance because the transfiguration it records seems exceedingly improbable, is common enough. Such transfigurations have been achieved by hundreds of resolutely ambitious young women since Nell Gwynne set them the example by playing queens and fascinating kings in the theatre in which she began by selling oranges. Nevertheless, people in all directions have assumed, for no other reason than that she became the heroine of a romance, that she must have married the hero of it. This is unbearable, not only because her little drama, if acted on such a thoughtless assumption, must be spoiled, but because the true sequel is patent to anyone with a sense of human nature in general, and of feminine instinct in particular.

Eliza, in telling Higgins she would not marry him if he asked her, was not coquetting: she was announcing a well-considered decision. When a bachelor interests, and dominates, and teaches, and becomes important to a spinster, as Higgins with Eliza, she always, if she has character enough to be capable of it, considers very seriously indeed whether she will play for becoming that bachelor's wife, especially if he is so little interested in marriage that a determined and devoted woman might capture him if she set herself resolutely to do it. Her decision will depend a good deal on whether she is really free to choose; and that, again, will depend on her age and income. If she is at the end of her youth, and has no security for her livelihood, she will marry him because she must marry anybody who will provide for her. But at Eliza's age a good-looking girl does not feel that pressure: she feels free to pick and choose. She is therefore guided by her instinct in the matter. Eliza's instinct tells her not to marry Higgins. It does not tell her to give him up. It is not in the slightest doubt as to his remaining one of the strongest personal interests in her life. It would be very sorely strained if there was another woman likely to supplant her with him. But as she feels sure of him on that last point, she has no doubt at all as to her course, and would not have any, even if the difference of twenty years in age, which seems so great to youth, did not exist between them.

As our own instincts are not appealed to by her conclusion, let us see whether we cannot discover some reason in it. When Higgins excused his indifference to young women on the ground that they had an irresistible rival in his mother, he gave the clue to his inveterate old-bachelordom. The case is uncommon only to the extent that remarkable mothers are uncommon. If an imaginative boy has a sufficiently rich mother who has intelligence, personal grace, dignity of character without harshness, and a cultivated sense of the best art of her time to enable her to make her house beautiful, she sets a standard for him against which very few women can struggle, besides effecting for him a disengagement of his affections, his sense of beauty, and his idealism from his specifically sexual impulses. This makes him a standing puzzle to the huge number of uncultivated people who have been brought up in tasteless homes by commonplace or disagreeable parents, and to whom, consequently, literature, painting, sculpture, music, and affectionate personal relations come as modes of sex if they come at all. The word passion means nothing else to them; and that Higgins could have a passion for phonetics and idealize his mother instead of Eliza, would seem to them absurd and unnatural. Nevertheless, when we look round and see that hardly anyone is too ugly or disagreeable to find a wife or a husband if he or she wants one, whilst many old maids and bachelors are above the average in quality and culture, we cannot help suspecting that the disentanglement of sex from the associations with which it is so commonly confused, a disentanglement which persons of genius achieve by sheer intellectual analysis, is sometimes produced or aided by parental fascination.

Now, though Eliza was incapable of thus explaining to herself Higgins's formidable powers of resistance to the charm that prostrated Freddy at the first glance, she was instinctively aware that she could never obtain a complete grip of him, or come between him and his mother (the first necessity of the married woman). To put it shortly, she knew that for some mysterious reason he had not the makings of a married man in him, according to her conception of a husband as one to whom she would be his nearest and fondest and warmest interest. Even had there been no mother-rival, she would still have refused to accept an interest in herself that was secondary to philosophic interests. Had Mrs Higgins died, there would still have been Milton and the Universal Alphabet. Landor's remark that to those who have the greatest power of loving, love is a secondary affair, would not have recommended Landor to Eliza. Put that along with her resentment of Higgins's domineering superiority, and her mistrust of his coaxing cleverness in getting round her and evading her wrath when he had gone too far with his impetuous bullying, and you will see that Eliza's instinct had good grounds for warning her not to marry her Pygmalion.

And now, whom did Eliza marry? For if Higgins was a predestinate old bachelor, she was most certainly not a predestinate old maid. Well, that can be told very shortly to those who have not guessed it from the indications she has herself given them.

Almost immediately after Eliza is stung into proclaiming her considered determination not to marry Higgins, she mentions the fact that young Mr Frederick Eynsford Hill is pouring out his love for her daily through the post. Now Freddy is young, practically twenty years younger than Higgins: he is a gentleman (or, as Eliza would qualify him, a toff), and speaks like one. He is nicely dressed, is treated by the Colonel as an equal, loves her unaffectedly, and is not her master, nor ever likely to dominate her in spite of his advantage of social standing. Eliza has no use for the foolish romantic tradition that all women love to be mastered, if not actually bullied and beaten. "When you go to women" says Nietzsche "take your whip with you." Sensible despots have never confined that precaution to women: they have taken their whips with them when they have dealt with men, and been slavishly idealized by the men over whom they have flourished the whip much more than by women. No doubt there are slavish women as well as slavish men; and women, like men, admire those that are stronger than themselves. But to admire a strong person and to live under that strong person's thumb are two different things. The weak may not be admired and hero-worshipped; but they are by no means disliked or shunned; and they never seem to have the least difficulty in marrying people who are too good for them. They may fail in emergencies; but life is not one long emergency: it is mostly a string of situations for which no exceptional strength is needed, and with which even rather weak people can cope if they have a stronger partner to help them out. Accordingly, it is a truth everywhere in evidence that strong people, masculine or feminine, not only do not marry stronger people, but do not shew any preference for them in selecting their friends. When a lion meets another with a louder roar "the first lion thinks the last a bore." The man or woman who feels strong enough for two, seeks for every other quality in a partner than strength.

The converse is also true. Weak people want to marry strong people who do not frighten them too much; and this often leads them to make the mistake we describe metaphorically as "biting off more than they can chew." They want too much for too little; and when the bargain is unreasonable beyond all bearing, the union becomes impossible: it ends in the weaker party being either discarded or borne as a cross, which is worse. People who are not only weak, but silly or obtuse as well, are often in these difficulties.

This being the state of human affairs, what is Eliza fairly sure to do when she is placed between Freddy and Higgins? Will she look forward to a lifetime of fetching Higgins's slippers or to a lifetime of

Freddy fetching hers? There can be no doubt about the answer. Unless Freddy is biologically repulsive to her, and Higgins biologically attractive to a degree that overwhelms all her other instincts, she will, if she marries either of them, marry Freddy.

And that is just what Eliza did.

Complications ensued; but they were economic, not romantic. Freddy had no money and no occupation. His mother's jointure, a last relic of the opulence of Largelady Park, had enabled her to struggle along in Earlscourt with an air of gentility, but not to procure any serious secondary education for her children, much less give the boy a profession. A clerkship at thirty shillings a week was beneath Freddy's dignity, and extremely distasteful to him besides. His prospects consisted of a hope that if he kept up appearances somebody would do something for him. The something appeared vaguely to his imagination as a private secretaryship or a sinecure of some sort. To his mother it perhaps appeared as a marriage to some lady of means who could not resist her boy's niceness. Fancy her feelings when he married a flower girl who had become disclassed under extraordinary circumstances which were now notorious!

It is true that Eliza's situation did not seem wholly ineligible. Her father, though formerly a dustman, and now fantastically disclassed, had become extremely popular in the smartest society by a social talent which triumphed over every prejudice and every disadvantage. Rejected by the middle class, which he loathed, he had shot up at once into the highest circles by his wit, his dustmanship (which he carried like a banner), and his Nietzschean transcendence of good and evil. At intimate ducal dinners he sat on the right hand of the Duchess; and in country houses he smoked in the pantry and was made much of by the butler when he was not feeding in the dining room and being consulted by cabinet ministers. But he found it almost as hard to do all this on four thousand a year as Mrs Eynsford Hill to live in Earlscourt on an income so pitiably smaller that I have not the heart to disclose its exact figure. He absolutely refused to add the last straw to his burden by contributing to Eliza's support.

Thus Freddy and Eliza, now Mr and Mrs Eynsford Hill, would have spent a penniless honeymoon but for a wedding present of £500 from the Colonel to Eliza. It lasted a long time because Freddy did not know how to spend money, never having had any to spend, and Eliza, socially trained by a pair of old bachelors, wore her clothes as long as they held together and looked pretty, without the least regard to their being many months out of fashion. Still, £500 will not last two young people for ever; and they both knew, and Eliza felt as well, that they must shift for themselves in the end. She could quarter herself on Wimpole Street because it had come to be her home; but she was quite aware that she ought not to quarter Freddy there, and that it would not be good for his character if she did.

Not that the Wimpole Street bachelors objected. When she consulted them, Higgins declined to be bothered about her housing problem when that solution was so simple. Eliza's desire to have Freddy in the house with her seemed of no more importance than if she had wanted an extra piece of bedroom furniture. Pleas as to Freddy's character, and the moral obligation on him to earn his own living, were lost on Higgins. He denied that Freddy had any character, and declared that if he tried to do any useful work some competent person would have the trouble of undoing it: a procedure involving a net loss to the community, and great unhappiness to Freddy himself, who was obviously intended by Nature for such light work as amusing Eliza, which, Higgins declared, was a much more useful and honorable occupation than working in the city. When Eliza referred again to her project of teaching phonetics, Higgins abated not a jot of his violent opposition to it. He said she was not within ten years of being qualified to meddle with his pet subject; and as it was evident that the Colonel agreed with him, she felt she could not go against them in this grave matter, and that she had no right, without Higgins's consent, to exploit the knowledge he had given her; for his knowledge seemed to her as much his private property as his watch: Eliza was no communist. Besides, she was superstitiously devoted to them both, more entirely and frankly after her marriage than before it.

It was the Colonel who finally solved the problem, which had cost him much perplexed cogitation. He one day asked Eliza, rather shyly, whether she had quite given up her notion of keeping a flower shop. She replied that she had thought of it, but had put it out of her head, because the Colonel had said, that day at Mrs Higgins's, that it would never do. The Colonel confessed that when he said that, he had not quite recovered from the dazzling impression of the day before. They broke the matter to Higgins that evening. The sole comment vouchsafed by him very nearly led to a serious quarrel with Eliza. It was to the effect that she would have in Freddy an ideal errand boy.

Freddy himself was next sounded on the subject. He said he had been thinking of a shop himself; though it had presented itself to his pennilessness as a small place in which Eliza should sell tobacco at one counter whilst he sold newspapers at the opposite one. But he agreed that it would be extraordinarily jolly to go early every morning with Eliza to Covent Garden and buy flowers on the scene of their first meeting: a sentiment which earned him many kisses from his wife. He added that he had always been afraid to propose anything of the sort, because Clara would make an awful row about a step that must damage her matrimonial chances, and his mother could not be expected to like it after clinging for so many years to that step of the social ladder on which retail trade is impossible.

This difficulty was removed by an event highly unexpected by Freddy's mother. Clara, in the course of her incursions into those artistic circles which were the highest within her reach, discovered that her conversational qualifications were expected to include a grounding in the novels of Mr H. G. Wells. She borrowed them in various directions so energetically that she swallowed them all within two months. The result was a conversion of a kind quite common today. A modern Acts of the Apostles would fill fifty whole Bibles if anyone were capable of writing it.

Poor Clara, who appeared to Higgins and his mother as a disagreeable and ridiculous person, and to her own mother as in some inexplicable way a social failure, had never seen herself in either light; for, though to some extent ridiculed and mimicked in West Kensington like everybody else there, she was accepted as a rational and normal—or shall we say inevitable?—sort of human being. At worst they called her The Pusher; but to them no more than to herself had it ever occurred that she was pushing the air, and pushing it in a wrong direction. Still, she was not happy. She was growing desperate. Her one asset, the fact that her mother was what the Epsom greengrocer called a carriage lady, had no exchange value, apparently. It had prevented her from getting educated, because the only education she could have afforded was education with the Earlscourt greengrocer's daughter. It had led her to seek the society of her mother's class; and that class simply would not have her, because she was much poorer than the greengrocer, and, far from being able to afford a maid, could not afford even a housemaid, and had to scrape along at home with an illiberally treated general servant. Under such circumstances nothing could give her an air of being a genuine product of Largelady Park. And yet its tradition made her regard a marriage with anyone within her reach as an unbearable humiliation. Commercial people and professional people in a small way were odious to her. She ran after painters and novelists; but she did not charm them; and her bold attempts to pick up and practise artistic and literary talk irritated them. She was, in short, an utter failure, an ignorant, incompetent, pretentious, unwelcome, penniless, useless little snob; and though she did not admit these disqualifications (for nobody ever faces unpleasant truths of this kind until the possibility of a way out dawns on them) she felt their effects too keenly to be satisfied with her position.

Clara had a startling eyeopener when, on being suddenly wakened to enthusiasm by a girl of her own age who dazzled her and produced in her a gushing desire to take her for a model, and gain her friendship, she discovered that this exquisite apparition had graduated from the gutter in a few months time. It shook her so violently, that when Mr H. G. Wells lifted her on the point of his puissant pen, and placed her at the angle of view from which the life she was leading and the society to which she clung appeared in its true relation to real human needs and worthy social structure, he effected a conversion and a conviction of sin comparable to the most sensational feats of General Booth or Gypsy Smith. Clara's snobbery went bang. Life suddenly began to move with her. Without knowing how or why, she began to make friends and enemies. Some of the acquaintances to whom she had been a tedious or indifferent or ridiculous affliction, dropped her: others became cordial. To her amazement she found that some "quite nice" people were saturated with Wells, and that this accessibility to ideas was the secret of their niceness. People she had thought deeply religious, and had tried to conciliate on that tack with disastrous results, suddenly took an interest in her, and revealed a hostility to conventional religion which she had never conceived possible except among the most desperate characters. They made her read Galsworthy; and Galsworthy exposed the vanity of Largelady Park and finished her. It exasperated her to think that the dungeon in which she had languished for so many unhappy years had been unlocked all the time, and that the impulses she had so carefully struggled with and stifled for the sake of keeping well with society, were precisely those by which alone she could have come into any sort of sincere human contact. In the radiance of these discoveries, and the tumult of their reaction, she made a fool of herself as freely and conspicuously as when she so rashly adopted Eliza's expletive in Mrs Higgins's drawing room; for the new-born Wellsian had to find her bearings almost as ridiculously as a baby; but nobody hates a baby for its ineptitudes, or thinks the worse of it for trying to eat the matches; and Clara lost no friends by her follies. They laughed at her to her face this time; and she had to defend herself and fight it out as best she could.

When Freddy paid a visit to Earlscourt (which he never did when he could possibly help it) to make the desolating announcement that he and his Eliza were thinking of blackening the Largelady scutcheon by opening a shop, he found the little household already convulsed by a prior announcement from Clara that she also was going to work in an old furniture shop in Dover Street, which had been started by a fellow Wellsian. This appointment Clara owed, after all, to her old social accomplishment of Push. She had made up her mind that, cost what it might, she would see Mr Wells in the flesh; and she had achieved her end at a garden party. She had better luck than so rash an enterprise deserved. Mr Wells came up to her expectations. Age had not withered him, nor could custom stale his infinite variety in half an hour. His pleasant neatness and compactness, his small hands and feet, his teeming ready brain, his unaffected accessibility, and a certain fine apprehensiveness which stamped him as susceptible from his topmost hair to his tipmost toe, proved irresistible. Clara talked of nothing else for weeks and weeks afterwards. And as she happened to talk to the lady of the furniture shop, and that lady also desired above all things to know Mr Wells and sell pretty things to him, she offered Clara a job on the chance of achieving that end through her.

And so it came about that Eliza's luck held, and the expected opposition to the flower shop melted away. The shop is in the arcade of a railway station not very far from the Victoria and Albert Museum; and if you live in that neighborhood you may go there any day and buy a buttonhole from Eliza.

Now here is a last opportunity for romance. Would you not like to be assured that the shop was an immense success, thanks to Eliza's charms and her early business experience in Covent Garden? Alas! the truth is the truth: the shop did not pay for a long time, simply because Eliza and her Freddy did not know how to keep it. True, Eliza had not to begin at the very beginning: she knew the names and prices of the cheaper flowers; and her elation was unbounded when she found that Freddy, like all youths educated at cheap, pretentious, and thoroughly inefficient schools, knew a little Latin. It was very little, but enough to make him appear to her a Porson or Bentley, and to put him at ease with botanical nomenclature. Unfortunately he knew nothing else; and Eliza, though she could count money up to eighteen shillings or so, and had acquired a certain familiarity with the language of Milton from her struggles to qualify herself for winning Higgins's bet, could not write out a bill without utterly disgracing the establishment. Freddy's power of stating in Latin that Balbus built a wall and that Gaul was divided into three parts did not carry with it the slightest knowledge of accounts or business: Colonel Pickering had to explain to him what a cheque book and a bank account meant. And the pair were by no means easily teachable. Freddy backed up Eliza in her obstinate refusal to believe that they could save money by engaging a bookkeeper with some knowledge of the business. How, they argued, could you possibly save money by going to extra expense when you already could not make both ends meet? But the Colonel, after making the ends meet over and over again, at last gently insisted; and Eliza, humbled to the dust by having to beg from him so often, and stung by the uproarious derision of Higgins, to whom the notion of Freddy succeeding at anything was a joke that never palled, grasped the fact that business, like phonetics, has to be learned.

On the piteous spectacle of the pair spending their evenings in shorthand schools and polytechnic classes, learning bookkeeping and typewriting with incipient junior clerks, male and female, from the elementary schools, let me not dwell. There were even classes at the London School of Economics, and a humble personal appeal to the director of that institution to recommend a course bearing on the flower business. He, being a humorist, explained to them the method of the celebrated Dickensian essay on Chinese Metaphysics by the gentleman who read an article on China and an article on Metaphysics and combined the information. He suggested that they should combine the London School with Kew Gardens. Eliza, to whom the procedure of the Dickensian gentleman seemed perfectly correct (as in fact it was) and not in the least funny (which was only her ignorance), took the advice with entire gravity. But the effort that cost her the deepest humiliation was a request to Higgins, whose pet artistic fancy, next to Milton's verse, was caligraphy, and who himself wrote a most beautiful Italian hand, that he would teach her to write. He declared that she was congenitally incapable of forming a single letter worthy of the least of Milton's words; but she persisted; and again he suddenly threw himself into the task of teaching her with a combination of stormy intensity, concentrated patience, and occasional bursts of interesting disquisition on the beauty and nobility, the august mission and destiny, of human handwriting. Eliza ended by acquiring an extremely uncommercial script which was a positive extension of her personal beauty, and spending three times as much on stationery as anyone else because certain qualities and shapes of paper became indispensable to her. She could not even address an envelope in the usual way because it made the margins all wrong.

Their commercial schooldays were a period of disgrace and despair for the young couple. They seemed to be learning nothing about flower shops. At last they gave it up as hopeless, and shook the dust of the shorthand schools, and the polytechnics, and the London School of Economics from their feet for ever. Besides, the business was in some mysterious way beginning to take care of itself. They had somehow forgotten their objections to employing other people. They came to the conclusion that their own way was the best, and that they had really a remarkable talent for business. The Colonel, who had been compelled for some years to keep a sufficient sum on current account at his bankers to make up their deficits, found that the provision was unnecessary: the young people were prospering. It is true that there was not quite fair play between them and their competitors in trade. Their week-ends in the country cost them nothing, and saved them the price of their Sunday dinners; for the motor car was the Colonel's; and he and Higgins paid the hotel bills. Mr F. Hill, florist and greengrocer (they soon discovered that there was money in asparagus; and asparagus led to other vegetables), had an air which stamped the business as classy; and in private life he was still Frederick Eynsford Hill, Esquire. Not that there was any swank about him: nobody but Eliza knew that he had been christened Frederick Challoner. Eliza herself swanked like anything.

That is all. That is how it has turned out. It is astonishing how much Eliza still manages to meddle in the housekeeping at Wimpole Street in spite of the shop and her own family. And it is notable that though she never nags her husband, and frankly loves the Colonel as if she were his favorite daughter, she has never got out of the habit of nagging Higgins that was established on the fatal night when she won his bet for him. She snaps his head off on the faintest provocation, or on none. He no longer dares to tease her by assuming an abysmal inferiority of Freddy's mind to his own. He storms and bullies and derides; but she stands up to him so ruthlessly that the Colonel has to ask her from time to time to be kinder to Higgins; and it is the only request of his that brings a mulish expression into her face. Nothing but some emergency or calamity great enough to break down all likes and dislikes, and throw them both back on their common humanity—and may they be spared any such trial!—will ever alter this. She knows that Higgins does not need her, just as her father did not need her. The very scrupulousness with which he told her that day that he had become used to having her there, and dependent on her for all sorts of little services, and that he should miss her if she went away (it would never have occurred to Freddy or the Colonel to say anything of the sort) deepens her inner certainty that she is "no more to him than them slippers"; yet she has a sense, too, that his indifference is deeper than the infatuation of commoner souls. She is immensely interested in him. She has even secret mischievous moments in which she wishes she could get him alone, on a desert island, away from all ties and with nobody else in the world to consider, and just drag him off his pedestal and see him making love like any common man. We all have private imaginations of that sort. But when it comes to business, to the life that she really leads as distinguished from the life of dreams and fancies, she likes Freddy and she likes the Colonel; and she does not like Higgins and Mr Doolittle. Galatea never does quite like Pygmalion: his relation to her is too godlike to be altogether agreeable.

THE END

HEARTBREAK HOUSE:
A Fantasia in the Russian Manner on English Themes

Composition begun 4 March 1916; completed May 1917. (Shaw stated on several occasions that the play was begun before the war, but all surviving evidence contradicts this.) Published in *Heartbreak House, Great Catherine, & Playlets of the War,* 1919. First presented by the Theatre Guild at the Garrick Theatre, New York, on 10 November 1920.

Ellie Dunn *Elizabeth Risdon*
Nurse Guinness *Helen Westley*
Captain Shotover *Albert Perry*
Lady Utterword *Lucile Watson*
Hesione Hushabye *Effie Shannon*
Mazzini Dunn *Erskine Sanford*
Hector Hushabye ("Marcus Darnley") *Fred Eric*
Alfred "Boss" Mangan *Dudley Digges*
Randall Utterword *Ralph Roeder*
The Burglar (Billy Dunn) *Henry Travers*

Period—Late September

ACT I *Captain Shotover's Villa in Sussex—the Poop. Evening*

ACT II *The Same. After Dinner*

ACT III *The Garden, astern of the Poop. Night*

Heartbreak House and Horseback Hall

Contents

WHERE HEARTBREAK HOUSE STANDS

Heartbreak House is not merely the name of the play which follows this preface. It is cultured, leisured Europe before the war. When the play was begun not a shot had been fired; and only the professional diplomatists and the very few amateurs whose hobby is foreign policy even knew that the guns were loaded. A Russian playwright, Tchekov, had produced four fascinating dramatic studies of Heartbreak House, of which three, The Cherry Orchard, Uncle Vanya, and The Seagull, had been performed in England. Tolstoy, in his Fruits of Enlightenment, had shewn us through it in his most ferociously contemptuous manner. Tolstoy did not waste any sympathy on it: it was to him the house in which Europe was stifling its soul; and he knew that our utter enervation and futilization in that overheated drawingroom atmosphere was delivering the world over to the control of ignorant and soulless cunning and energy, with the frightful consequences which have now overtaken it. Tolstoy was no pessimist: he was not disposed to leave the house standing if he could bring it down about the ears of its pretty and amiable voluptuaries; and he wielded the pickaxe with a will. He treated the case of the inmates as one of opium poisoning, to be dealt with by seizing the patients roughly and exercising them violently until they were broad awake. Tchekov, more of a fatalist, had no faith in these charming people extricating themselves. They would, he thought, be sold up and sent adrift by the bailiffs; therefore he had no scruple in exploiting and even flattering their charm.

THE INHABITANTS

Tchekov's plays, being less lucrative than swings and roundabouts, got no further in England, where theatres are only ordinary commercial affairs, than a couple of performances by the Stage Society. We stared and said, "How Russian!" They did not strike me in that way. Just as

Ibsen's intensely Norwegian plays exactly fitted every middle and professional class suburb in Europe, these intensely Russian plays fitted all the country houses in Europe in which the pleasures of music, art, literature, and the theatre had supplanted hunting, shooting, fishing, flirting, eating, and drinking. The same nice people, the same utter futility. The nice people could read; some of them could write; and they were the only repositories of culture who had social opportunities of contact with our politicians, administrators, and newspaper proprietors, or any chance of sharing or influencing their activities. But they shrank from that contact. They hated politics. They did not wish to realize Utopia for the common people: they wished to realize their favourite fictions and poems in their own lives; and, when they could, they lived without scruple on incomes which they did nothing to earn. The women in their girlhood made themselves look like variety theatre stars, and settled down later into the types of beauty imagined by the previous generation of painters. They took the only part of our society in which there was leisure for high culture, and made it an economic, political, and, as far as practicable, a moral vacuum; and as Nature, abhorring the vacuum, immediately filled it up with sex and with all sorts of refined pleasures, it was a very delightful place at its best for moments of relaxation. In other moments it was disastrous. For prime ministers and their like, it was a veritable Capua.

HORSEBACK HALL

But where were our front benchers to nest if not here? The alternative to Heartbreak House was Horseback Hall, consisting of a prison for horses with an annex for the ladies and gentlemen who rode them, hunted them, talked about them, bought them and sold them, and gave nine-tenths of their lives to them, dividing the other tenth between charity, church-going (as a substitute for religion), and conservative electioneering (as a substitute for politics). It is true that the two establishments got mixed at the edges. Exiles from the library, the music room, and the picture gallery would be found languishing among the stables, miserably discontented; and hardy horsewomen who slept at the first chord of Schumann were born, horribly misplaced, into the garden of Klingsor; but sometimes one came upon horsebreakers and heartbreakers who could make the best of both worlds. As a rule, however, the two were apart and knew little of one another; so the prime minister folk had to choose between barbarism and Capua. And of the two atmospheres it is hard to say which was the more fatal to statesmanship.

REVOLUTION ON THE SHELF

Heartbreak House was quite familiar with revolutionary ideas on paper. It aimed at being advanced and freethinking, and hardly ever went to church or kept the Sabbath except by a little extra fun at week-ends. When you spent a Friday to Tuesday in it you found on the shelf in your bedroom not only the books of poets and novelists, but of revolutionary biologists and even economists. Without at least a few plays by myself and Mr Granville Barker, and a few stories by Mr H. G. Wells, Mr Arnold Bennett, and Mr John Galsworthy, the house would have been out of the movement. You would find Blake among the poets, and beside him Bergson, Butler, Scott Haldane, the poems of Meredith and Thomas Hardy, and, generally speaking, all the literary implements for forming the mind of the perfect modern Socialist and Creative Evolutionist. It was a curious experience to spend Sunday in dipping into these books, and on Monday morning to read in the daily paper that the country had just been brought to the verge of anarchy because a new Home Secretary or chief of police, without an idea in his head that his great-grandmother might not have had to apologize for, had refused to "recognize" some powerful Trade Union, just as a gondola might refuse to recognize a 20,000-ton liner.

In short, power and culture were in separate compartments. The barbarians were not only literally in the saddle, but on the front bench in the House of Commons, with nobody to correct their incredible ignorance of modern thought and political science but upstarts from the counting-house, who had spent their lives furnishing their pockets instead of their minds. Both, however, were practised in dealing with money and with men, as far as acquiring the one and exploiting the other went; and although this is as undesirable an expertness as that of the medieval robber baron, it qualifies men to keep an estate or a business going in its old routine without necessarily understanding it, just as Bond Street tradesmen and domestic servants keep fashionable society going without any instruction in sociology.

THE CHERRY ORCHARD

The Heartbreak people neither could nor would do anything of the sort. With their heads as full of the Anticipations of Mr H. G. Wells as the heads of our actual rulers were empty even of the anticipations of Erasmus or Sir Thomas More, they refused the drudgery of politics, and would have made a very poor job of it if they had changed their minds. Not that they would have been allowed to meddle anyhow, as only through the accident of being a hereditary peer can anyone in these days of Votes for Everybody get into parliament if handicapped by a serious modern cultural equipment; but if they had, their habit of living in a vacuum would have left them helpless and ineffective in public affairs. Even in private life they were often helpless wasters of their inheritance, like the people in Tchekov's Cherry Orchard. Even those who lived within their incomes were really kept going by their solicitors and agents, being unable to manage an estate or run a business without continual prompting from those who have to learn how to do such things or starve.

From what is called Democracy no corrective to this state of things could be hoped. It is said that every people has the Government it deserves. It is more to the point that every Government has the electorate it deserves; for the orators of the front bench can edify or debauch an ignorant electorate at will. Thus our democracy moves in a vicious circle of reciprocal worthiness and unworthiness.

NATURE'S LONG CREDITS

Nature's way of dealing with unhealthy conditions is unfortunately not one that compels us to conduct a solvent hygiene on a cash basis. She demoralizes us with long credits and reckless overdrafts, and then pulls us up cruelly with catastrophic bankruptcies. Take, for example, common domestic sanitation. A whole city generation may neglect it utterly and scandalously, if not with absolute impunity, yet without any evil consequences that anyone thinks of tracing to it. In a hospital two generations of medical students may tolerate dirt and carelessness, and then go out into general practice to spread the doctine that fresh air is a fad, and sanitation an imposture set up to make profits for plumbers. Then suddenly Nature takes her revenge. She strikes at the city with a pestilence and at the hospital with an epidemic of hospital gangrene, slaughtering right and left until the innocent young have paid for the guilty old, and the account is balanced. And then she goes to sleep again and gives another period of credit, with the same result.

This is what has just happened in our political hygiene. Political science has been as recklessly neglected by Governments and electorates during my lifetime as sanitary science was in the days of Charles the Second. In international relations diplomacy has been a boyishly lawless affair of family intrigues, commercial and territorial brigandage, torpors of pseudo-goodnature produced by laziness, and spasms of ferocious activity produced by terror. But in these islands we muddled through. Nature gave us a longer credit than she gave to France or Germany or Russia. To British centenarians who died in their beds in 1914, any dread of having to hide underground in London from the shells of an enemy seemed more remote and fantastic than a dread of the appearance of a colony of cobras and rattlesnakes in Kensington Gardens. In the prophetic works of Charles Dickens we were warned against many evils which have since come to pass; but of the evil of being slaughtered by a foreign foe on our own doorsteps there was no shadow. Nature gave us a very long credit; and we abused it to the utmost. But when she struck at last she struck with a vengeance. For four years she smote our firstborn and heaped on us plagues of which Egypt never dreamed. They were all as preventible as the great Plague of London, and came solely because they had not been prevented. They were not undone by winning the war. The earth is still bursting with the dead bodies of the victors.

THE WICKED HALF CENTURY

It is difficult to say whether indifference and neglect are worse than false doctrine; but Heartbreak House and Horseback Hall unfortunately suffered from both. For half a century before the war civilization had been going to the devil very precipitately under the influence of a pseudo-science as disastrous as the blackest Calvinism.

Calvinism taught that as we are predestinately saved or damned, nothing that we do can alter our destiny. Still, as Calvinism gave the individual no clue as to whether he had drawn a lucky number or an unlucky one, it left him a fairly strong interest in encouraging his hopes of salvation and allaying his fear of damnation by behaving as one of the elect might be expected to behave rather than as one of the reprobate. But in the middle of the XIX century naturalists and physicists assured the world, in the name of Science, that salvation and damnation are all nonsense, and that predestination is the central truth of religion, inasmuch as human beings are produced by their environment, their sins and good deeds being only a series of chemical and mechanical reactions over which they have no control. Such figments as mind, choice, purpose, conscience, will, and so forth, are, they taught, mere illusions, produced because they are useful in the continual struggle of the human machine to maintain its environment in a favourable condition, a process incidentally involving the ruthless destruction or subjection of its competitors for the supply (assumed to be limited) of subsistence available. We taught Prussia this religion; and Prussia bettered our instruction so effectively that we presently found ourselves confronted with the necessity of destroying Prussia to prevent Prussia destroying us. And that has just ended in each destroying the other to an extent doubtfully reparable in our time.

It may be asked how so imbecile and dangerous a creed ever came to be accepted by intelligent beings. I will answer that question more fully in my next volume of plays, which will be entirely devoted to the subject. For the present I will only say that there were better reasons than the obvious one that such sham science as this opened a scientific career to very stupid men, and all the other careers to shameless rascals, provided they were industrious enough. It is true that this motive operated very powerfully; but when the new departure in scientific doctrine which is associated with the name of the great naturalist Charles Darwin began, it was not only a reaction against a barbarous pseudo-evangelical teleology intolerably obstructive to all scientific progress, but was accompanied, as it happened, by discoveries of extraordinary interest in physics, chemistry, and that lifeless method of evolution which its investigators called Natural Selection. Howbeit, there was only one result possible in the ethical sphere, and that was the banishment of conscience from human affairs, or, as Samuel Butler vehemently put it, "of mind from the universe."

HYPOCHONDRIA

Now Heartbreak House, with Butler and Bergson and Scott Haldane alongside Blake and the other major poets on its shelves (to say nothing of Wagner and the tone poets), was not so completely blinded by the doltish materialism of the laboratories as the uncultured world outside. But being an idle house it was a hypochondriacal house, always running after cures. It would stop eating meat, not on valid Shelleyan grounds, but in order to get rid of a bogey called Uric Acid; and it would actually let you pull all its teeth out to exorcize another demon named Pyorrhea. It was superstitious, and addicted to table-rapping, materialization séances, clairvoyance, palmistry, crystal-gazing and the like to such an extent that it may be doubted whether ever before in the history of the world did soothsayers, astrologers, and unregistered therapeutic specialists of all sorts flourish as they did during this half century of the drift to the abyss. The registered doctors and surgeons were hard put to it to compete with the unregistered. They were not clever enough to appeal to the imagination and sociability of the Heartbreakers by the arts of the actor, the orator, the poet, the winning conversationalist. They had to fall back coarsely on the terror of infection and death. They prescribed inoculations and operations. Whatever part of a human being could be cut out without necessarily killing him they cut out; and he often died (unnecessarily of course) in consequence. From such trifles as uvulas and tonsils they went on to ovaries and appendices until at last no one's inside was safe. They explained that the human intestine was too long, and that nothing could make a child of Adam healthy except short circuiting the pylorus by cutting a length out of the lower intestine and fastening it directly to the stomach. As their mechanist theory taught them that medicine was the business of the chemist's laboratory, and surgery of the carpenter's shop, and also that Science (by which they meant their practices) was so important that no consideration for the interests of any individual creature, whether frog or philosopher, much less the vulgar commonplaces of sentimental ethics, could weigh for a moment against the remotest off-chance of an addition to the body of scientific knowledge, they operated and vivisected and inoculated and lied on a stupendous scale, clamoring for and actually acquiring such legal powers over the bodies of their fellow-citizens as neither king, pope, nor parliament dare ever have claimed. The Inquisition itself was a Liberal institution compared to the General Medical Council.

THOSE WHO DO NOT KNOW HOW TO LIVE MUST MAKE A MERIT OF DYING

Heartbreak House was far too lazy and shallow to extricate itself from this palace of evil enchantment. It rhapsodized about love; but it believed in cruelty. It was afraid of the cruel people; and it saw that cruelty was at least effective. Cruelty did things that made money, whereas Love did nothing but prove the soundness of Larochefoucauld's saying that very few people would fall in love if they had never read about it. Heartbreak House, in short, did not know how to live, at which point all that was left to it was the boast that at least it knew how to die: a melancholy accomplishment which the outbreak of war presently gave it practically unlimited opportunities of displaying. Thus were the firstborn of Heartbreak House smitten; and the young, the innocent, the hopeful expiated the folly and worthlessness of their elders.

WAR DELIRIUM

Only those who have lived through a first-rate war, not in the field, but at home, and kept their heads, can possibly understand the bitterness of Shakespear and Swift, who both went through this experience. The horror of Peer Gynt in the madhouse, when the lunatics, exalted by illusions of splendid talent and visions of a dawning millennium, crowned him as their emperor, was tame in comparison. I do not know whether anyone really kept his head completely except those who had to keep it because they had to conduct the war at first hand. I should not have kept my own (as far as I did keep it) if I had not at once understood that as a scribe and speaker I too was under the most serious public obligation to keep my grip on realities; but this did not save me from a considerable degree of hyperaesthesia. There were of course some happy people to whom the war meant nothing: all political and general matters lying outside their little circle of interest. But the ordinary war-conscious civilian went mad, the main symptom being a conviction that the whole order of nature had been reversed. All foods, he felt, must now be adulterated. All schools must be closed. No advertisements must be sent to the newspapers, of which new editions must appear and be bought up every ten minutes. Travelling must be stopped, or, that being impossible, greatly hindered. All pretences about fine art and culture and the like must be flung off as an intolerable affectation; and the picture galleries and museums and schools at once occupied by war workers. The British Museum itself was saved only by a hairsbreadth. The sincerity of all this, and of much more which would not be believed if I chronicled it, may be established by one conclusive instance of the general craziness. Men were seized with the illusion that they could win the war by giving away money. And they not only subscribed millions to Funds of all sorts with no discoverable object, and to ridiculous voluntary organizations for doing what was plainly the business of the civil and military authorities, but actually handed out money to any thief in the street who had the presence of mind to pretend that he (or she) was "collecting" it for the annihilation of the enemy. Swindlers were emboldened to take offices; label themselves Anti-Enemy Leagues; and simply pocket the money that was heaped on them. Attractively dressed young women found that they had nothing to do but parade the streets, collecting-box in hand, and live gloriously on the profits. Many months elapsed before, as a first sign of returning sanity, the police swept an Anti-Enemy secretary into prison *pour encourager les autres,* and the passionate penny collecting of the Flag Days was brought under some sort of regulation.

MADNESS IN COURT

The demoralization did not spare the Law Courts. Soldiers were acquitted, even on fully proved indictments for wilful murder, until at last the judges and magistrates had to announce that what was called the Unwritten Law, which meant simply that a soldier could do what he liked with impunity in civil life, was not the law of the land, and that a Victoria Cross did not carry with it a perpetual plenary indulgence. Unfortunately the insanity of the juries and magistrates did not always manifest itself in indulgence. No person unlucky enough to be charged with any sort of conduct, however reasonable and salutary, that did not smack of war delirium had the slightest chance of acquittal. There were in the country, too, a certain number of people who had conscientious objections to war as criminal or unchristian. The Act of Parliament introducing Compulsory Military Service thoughtlessly exempted these persons, merely requiring them to prove the genuineness of their convictions. Those who did so were very ill-advised from the point of view of their own personal interest; for they were persecuted with savage logicality in spite of the law; whilst those who made no pretence of having any objection to war at all, and had not only had military training in Officers' Training Corps, but had proclaimed on public occasions that they were perfectly ready to engage in civil war on behalf of their political opinions, were allowed the benefit of the Act on the ground that they did not approve of this particular war. For the Christians there was no mercy. In cases where the evidence as to their being killed by ill treatment was so unequivocal that the verdict would certainly have been one of wilful murder had the prejudice of the coroner's jury been on the other side, their tormentors were gratuitously declared to be blameless. There was only one virtue, pugnacity: only one vice, pacifism. That is an essential condition of war; but the Government had not the courage to legislate accordingly; and its law was set aside for Lynch law.

The climax of legal lawlessness was reached in France. The greatest Socialist statesman in Europe, Jaurès, was shot and killed by a gentleman who resented his efforts to avert the war. M. Clemenceau was shot by another gentleman of less popular opinions, and happily came off no worse than having to spend a precautionary couple of days in bed. The slayer of Jaurès was recklessly acquitted: the would-be slayer of M. Clemenceau was carefully found guilty. There is no reason to doubt that the same thing would have happened in England if the war had begun with a successful attempt to assassinate Keir Hardie, and ended with an unsuccessful one to assassinate Mr Lloyd George.

THE LONG ARM OF WAR

The pestilence which is the usual accompaniment of war was called influenza. Whether it was really a war pestilence or not was made doubtful by the fact that it did its worst in places remote from the battlefields, notably on the west coast of North America and in India. But the moral pestilence, which was unquestionably a war pestilence, reproduced this phenomenon. One would have supposed that the war fever would have raged most furiously in the countries actually under fire, and that the others would be more reasonable. Belgium and Flanders, where over large districts literally not one stone was left upon another as the opposed armies drove each other back and forward over it after terrific preliminary bombardments, might have been pardoned for relieving their feelings more emphatically than by shrugging their shoulders and saying "C'est la guerre." England, inviolate for so many centuries that the swoop of war on her homesteads had long ceased to be more credible than a return of the Flood, could hardly be expected to keep her temper sweet when she knew at last what it was to hide in cellars and underground railway stations, or lie quaking in bed, whilst bombs crashed, houses crumbled, and aircraft guns distributed shrapnel on friend and foe alike until certain shop windows in London, formerly full of fashionable hats, were filled with steel helmets. Slain and mutilated women and children, and burnt and wrecked dwellings, excuse a good deal of violent language, and produce a wrath on which many suns go down before it is appeased. Yet it was in the United States of America, where nobody slept the worse for the war, that the war fever went beyond all sense and reason. In European Courts there was vindictive illegality: in American Courts there was raving lunacy. It is not for me to chronicle the extravagances of an Ally: let some candid American do that. I can only say that to us sitting in our gardens in England, with the guns in France making themselves felt by a throb in the air as unmistakeable as an audible sound, or with tightening hearts studying the phases of the moon in London in their bearing on the chances whether our houses would be standing or ourselves alive next morning, the newspaper accounts of the sentences American Courts were passing on young girls and old men alike for the expression of opinions which were being uttered amid thundering applause before huge audiences in England, and the more private records of the methods by which the American War Loans were raised, were so amazing that they would put the guns and the possibilities of a raid clean out of our heads for the moment.

THE RABID WATCHDOGS OF LIBERTY

Not content with these rancorous abuses of the existing law, the war maniacs made a frantic rush to abolish all constitutional guarantees of liberty and well-being. The ordinary law was superseded by Acts under which newspapers were seized and their printing machinery destroyed by simple police raids *à la Russe,* and persons arrested and shot without any pretence of trial by jury or publicity of procedure or evidence. Though it was urgently necessary that production should be increased by the most scientific organization and economy of labor, and though no fact was better established than that excessive duration and intensity of toil reduces production heavily instead of increasing it, the factory laws were suspended, and men and women recklessly overworked until the loss of their efficiency became too glaring to be ignored. Remonstrances and warnings were met either with an accusation of pro-Germanism or the formula, "Remember that we are at war now." I have said that men assumed that war had reversed the order of nature, and that all was lost unless we did the exact opposite of everything we had found necessary and beneficial in peace. But the truth was worse than that. The war did not change men's minds in any such impossible way. What really happened was that the impact of physical death and destruction, the one reality that every fool can understand, tore off the masks of education, art, science, and religion from our ignorance and barbarism, and left us glorying grotesquely in the licence suddenly accorded to our vilest passions and most abject terrors. Ever since Thucydides wrote his history, it has been on record that when the angel of death sounds his trumpet the pretences of civilization are blown from men's heads into the mud like hats in a gust of wind. But when this scripture was fulfilled among us, the shock was not the less appalling because a few students of Greek history were not surprised by it. Indeed these students threw themselves into the orgy as shamelessly as the illiterate. The Christian priest joining in the war dance without even throwing off his cassock first, and the respectable school governor expelling the German professor with insult and bodily violence, and declaring that no English child should ever again be taught the language of Luther and Goethe, were kept in countenance by the most impudent repudiations of every decency of civilization and every lesson of political experience on the part of the very persons who, as university professors, historians, philosophers, and men of science, were the accredited custodians of culture. It was crudely natural, and perhaps necessary for recruiting purposes, that German militarism and German dynastic ambition should be painted by journalists and recruiters in black and red as European dangers (as in fact they are), leaving it to be inferred that our own militarism and our own political constitution are millennially democratic (which they certainly are not); but when it came to frantic denunciations of German chemistry, German biology, German poetry, German music, German literature, German philosophy, and even German engineering, as malignant abominations standing towards British and French chemistry and so forth in the relation of heaven to hell, it was clear that the utterers of such barbarous ravings had never really understood or cared for the arts and sciences they professed and were profaning, and were only the appallingly degenerate descendants of the men of the seventeenth and eighteenth centuries who, recognizing no national frontiers in the great realm of the human mind, kept the European comity of that realm loftily and even ostentatiously above the rancors of the battle-field. Tearing the Garter from the Kaiser's leg, striking the German dukes from the roll of our peerage, changing the King's illustrious and historically appropriate surname for that of a traditionless locality, was not a very dignified business; but the erasure of German names from the British rolls of science and learning was a confession that in England the little respect paid to science and learning is only an affectation which hides a savage contempt for both. One felt that the figure of St George and the Dragon on our coinage should be replaced by that of the soldier driving his spear through Archimedes. But by that time there was no coinage: only paper money in which ten shillings called itself a pound as confidently as the people who were disgracing their country called themselves patriots.

THE SUFFERINGS OF THE SANE

The mental distress of living amid the obscene din of all these carmagnoles and corobberies was not the only burden that lay on sane people during the war. There was also the emotional strain, complicated by the offended economic sense, produced by the casualty lists. The stupid, the selfish, the narrow-minded, the callous and unimaginative were spared a great deal. "Blood and destruction shall be so in use that mothers shall but smile when they behold their infants quartered by the hands of war," was a Shakespearean prophecy that very nearly came true; for when nearly every house had a slaughtered son to mourn, we should all have gone quite out of our senses if we had taken our own and our friends' bereavements at their peace value. It became necessary to give them a false value; to proclaim the young life worthily and gloriously sacrificed to redeem the liberty of mankind, instead of to expiate the heedlessness and folly of their fathers, and expiate it in vain. We had even to assume that the parents and not the children had made the sacrifice, until at last the comic papers were driven to satirize fat old men, sitting comfortably in club chairs, and boasting of the sons they had "given" to their country.

No one grudged these anodynes to acute personal grief; but they only embittered those who knew that the young men were having their teeth set on edge because their parents had eaten sour political grapes. Then think of the young men themselves! Many of them had no illusions about the policy that led to the war: they went clear-sighted to a horribly repugnant duty. Men essentially gentle and essentially wise, with really valuable work in hand, laid it down voluntarily and spent months forming fours in the barrack yard, and stabbing sacks of straw in the public eye, so that they might go out to kill and maim men as gentle as themselves. These men, who were perhaps, as a class, our most efficient soldiers (Frederick Keeling, for example), were not duped for a moment by the hypocritical melodrama that consoled and stimulated the others. They left their creative work to drudge at destruction, exactly as they would have left it to take their turn at the pumps in a sinking ship. They did not, like some of the conscientious objectors, hold back because the ship had been neglected by its officers and scuttled by its wreckers. The ship had to be saved, even if Newton had to leave his fluxions and Michael Angelo his marbles to save it; so they threw away the tools of their beneficent and ennobling trades, and took up the bloodstained bayonet and the murderous bomb, forcing themselves to pervert their divine instinct for perfect artistic execution to the effective handling of these diabolical things, and their economic faculty for organization to the contriving of ruin and slaughter. For it gave an ironic edge to their tragedy that the very talents they were forced to prostitute made the prostitution not only effective, but even interesting; so that some of them were rapidly promoted, and found themselves actually becoming artists in war, with a growing relish for it, like Napoleon and all the other scourges of mankind, in spite of themselves. For many of them there was not even this consolation. They "stuck it," and hated it, to the end.

EVIL IN THE THRONE OF GOOD

This distress of the gentle was so acute that those who shared it in civil life, without having to shed blood with their own hands, or witness destruction with their own eyes, hardly care to obtrude their own woes. Nevertheless, even when sitting at home in safety, it was not easy for those who had to write and speak about the war to throw away their highest conscience, and deliberately work to a standard of inevitable evil instead of to the ideal of life more abundant. I can answer for at least one person who found the change from the wisdom of Jesus and St Francis to the morals of Richard III and the madness of Don Quixote extremely irksome. But that change had to be made; and we are all the worse for it, except those for whom it was not really a change at all, but only a relief from hypocrisy.

Think, too, of those who, though they had neither to write nor to fight, and had no children of their own to lose, yet knew the inestimable loss to the world of four years of the life of a generation wasted on destruction. Hardly one of the epoch-making works of the human mind might not have been aborted or destroyed by taking their authors away from their natural work for four critical years. Not only were Shakespears and Platos being killed outright; but many of the best harvests of the survivors had to be sown in the barren soil of the trenches. And this was no mere British consideration. To the truly civilized man, to the good European, the slaughter of the German youth was as disastrous as the slaughter of the English. Fools exulted in "German losses." They were our losses as well. Imagine exulting in the death of Beethoven because Bill Sikes dealt him his death blow!

STRAINING AT THE GNAT AND SWALLOWING THE CAMEL

But most people could not comprehend these sorrows. There was a frivolous exultation in death for its own sake, which was at bottom an inability to realize that the deaths were real deaths and not stage ones. Again and again, when an air raider dropped a bomb which tore a child and its mother limb from limb, the people who saw it, though they had been reading with great cheerfulness of thousands of such happenings day after day in their newspapers, suddenly burst into furious imprecations on "the Huns" as murderers, and shrieked for savage and satisfying vengeance. At such moments it became clear that the deaths they had not seen meant no more to them than the mimic deaths of the cinema screen. Sometimes it was not necessary that death should be actually witnessed: it had only to take place under circumstances of sufficient novelty and proximity to bring it home almost as sensationally and effectively as if it had been actually visible.

For example, in the spring of 1915 there was an appalling slaughter of our young soldiers at Neuve Chapelle and at the Gallipoli landing. I will not go so far as to say that our civilians were delighted to have such exciting news to read at breakfast. But I cannot pretend that I noticed either in the papers, or in general intercourse, any feeling beyond the usual one that the cinema show at the front was going splendidly, and that our boys were the bravest of the brave. Suddenly there came the news that an Atlantic liner, the Lusitania, had been torpedoed, and that several well-known first class passengers, including a famous theatrical manager and the author of a popular farce, had been drowned, among others. The others included Sir Hugh Lane; but as he had only laid the country under great obligations in the sphere of the fine arts, no great stress was laid on that loss.

Immediately an amazing frenzy swept through the country. Men who up to that time had kept their heads now lost them utterly. "Killing saloon passengers! What next?" was the essence of the whole agitation; but it is far too trivial a phrase to convey the faintest notion of the rage which possessed us. To me, with my mind full of the hideous cost of Neuve Chapelle, Ypres, and the Gallipoli landing, the fuss about the Lusitania seemed almost a heartless impertinence, though I was well acquainted personally with the three best-known victims, and understood, better perhaps than most people, the misfortune of the death of Lane. I even found a grim satisfaction, very intelligible to all soldiers, in the fact that the civilians who found the war such splendid British sport should get a sharp taste of what it was to the actual combatants. I expressed my impatience very freely, and found that my very straightforward and natural feeling in the matter was received as a monstrous and heartless paradox. When I asked those who gaped at me whether they had anything to say about the holocaust of Festubert, they gaped wider than before, having totally forgotten it, or rather, having never realized it. They were not heartless any more than I was; but the big catastrophe was too big for them to grasp, and the little one had been just the right size for them. I was not surprised. Have I not seen a public body for just the same reason pass a vote for £30,000 without a word, and then spend three special meetings, prolonged into the night, over an item of seven shillings for refreshments?

LITTLE MINDS AND BIG BATTLES

Nobody will be able to understand the vagaries of public feeling during the war unless they bear constantly in mind that the war in its entire magnitude did not exist for the average civilian. He could not conceive even a battle, much less a campaign. To the suburbs the war was nothing but a suburban squabble. To the miner and navvy it was only a series of bayonet fights between German champions and English ones. The enormity of it was quite beyond most of us. Its episodes had to be reduced to the dimensions of a railway accident or a shipwreck before it could produce any effect on our minds at all. To us the ridiculous bombardments of Scarborough and Ramsgate were colossal tragedies, and the battle of Jutland a mere ballad. The words "after thorough artillery preparation" in the news from the front meant nothing to us; but when our seaside trippers learned that an elderly gentleman at breakfast in a week-end marine hotel had been interrupted by a bomb dropping into his egg-cup, their wrath and horror knew no bounds. They declared that this would put a new spirit into the army, and had no suspicion that the soldiers in the trenches roared with laughter over it for days, and told each other that it would do the blighters at home good to have a taste of what the army was up against. Sometimes the smallness of view was pathetic. A man would work at home regardless of the call "to make the world safe for democracy." His brother would be killed at the front. Immediately he would throw up his work and take up the war as a family blood feud against the Germans. Sometimes it was comic. A wounded man, entitled to his discharge, would return to the trenches with a grim determination to find the Hun who had wounded him and pay him out for it.

It is impossible to estimate what proportion of us, in khaki or out of it, grasped the war and its political antecedents as a whole in the light of any philosophy of history or knowledge of what war is. I doubt whether it was as high as our proportion of higher mathematicians.

But there can be no doubt that it was prodigiously outnumbered by the comparatively ignorant and childish. Remember that these people had to be stimulated to make the sacrifices demanded by the war, and that this could not be done by appeals to a knowledge which they did not possess, and a comprehension of which they were incapable. When the armistice at last set me free to tell the truth about the war at the following general election, a soldier said to a candidate whom I was supporting "If I had known all that in 1914, they would never have got me into khaki." And that, of course, was precisely why it had been necessary to stuff him with a romance that any diplomatist would have laughed at. Thus the natural confusion of ignorance was increased by a deliberately propagated confusion of nursery bogey stories and melodramatic nonsense, which at last overreached itself and made it impossible to stop the war before we had not only achieved the triumph of vanquishing the German army and thereby overthrowing its militarist monarchy, but made the very serious mistake of ruining the centre of Europe, a thing that no sane European State could afford to do.

THE DUMB CAPABLES AND THE NOISY INCAPABLES

Confronted with this picture of insensate delusion and folly, the critical reader will immediately counterplead that England all this time was conducting a war which involved the organization of several millions of fighting men and of the workers who were supplying them with provisions, munitions, and transport, and that this could not have been done by a mob of hysterical ranters. This is fortunately true. To pass from the newspaper offices and political platforms and club fenders and suburban drawing-rooms to the Army and the munition factories was to pass from Bedlam to the busiest and sanest of workaday worlds. It was to rediscover England, and find solid ground for the faith of those who still believed in her. But a necessary condition of this efficiency was that those who were efficient should give all their time to their business and leave the rabble raving to its hearts' content. Indeed the raving was useful to the efficient, because, as it was always wide of the mark, it often distracted attention very conveniently from operations that would have been defeated or hindered by publicity. A precept which I endeavored vainly to popularize early in the war, "If you have anything to do go and do it: if not, for heaven's sake get out of the way," was only half carried out. Certainly the capable people went and did it; but the incapables would by no means get out of the way: they fussed and bawled and were only prevented from getting very seriously into the way by the blessed fact that they never knew where the way was. Thus whilst all the efficiency of England was silent and invisible, all its imbecility was deafening the heavens with its clamor and blotting out the sun with its dust. It was also unfortunately intimidating the Government by its blusterings into using the irresistible powers of the State to intimidate the sensible people, thus enabling a despicable minority of would-be lynchers to set up a reign of terror which could at any time have been broken by a single stern word from a responsible minister. But our ministers had not that sort of courage: neither Heartbreak House nor Horseback Hall had bred it, much less the suburbs. When matters at last came to the looting of shops by criminals under patriotic pretexts, it was the police force and not the Government that put its foot down. There was even one deplorable moment, during the submarine scare, in which the Government yielded to a childish cry for the maltreatment of naval prisoners of war, and, to our great disgrace, was forced by the enemy to behave itself. And yet behind all this public blundering and misconduct and futile mischief, the effective England was carrying on with the most formidable capacity and activity. The ostensible England was making the empire sick with its incontinences, its ignorances, its ferocities, its panics, and its endless and intolerable blarings of Allied national anthems in season and out. The esoteric England was proceeding irresistibly to the conquest of Europe.

THE PRACTICAL BUSINESS MEN

From the beginning the useless people set up a shriek for "practical business men." By this they meant men who had become rich by placing their personal interests before those of the country, and measuring the success of every activity by the pecuniary profit it brought to them and to those on whom they depended for their supplies of capital. The pitiable failure of some conspicuous samples from the first batch we tried of these poor devils helped to give the whole public side of the war an air of monstrous and hopeless farce. They proved not only that they were useless for public work, but that in a well-ordered nation they would never have been allowed to control private enterprise.

HOW THE FOOLS SHOUTED THE WISE MEN DOWN

Thus, like a fertile country flooded with mud, England shewed no sign of her greatness in the days when she was putting forth all her strength to save herself from the worst consequences of her littleness. Most of the men of action, occupied to the last hour of their time with urgent practical work, had to leave to idler people, or to professional rhetoricians, the presentation of the war to the reason and imagination of the country and the world in speeches, poems, manifestos, picture posters, and newspaper articles. I have had the privilege of hearing some of our ablest commanders talking about their work; and I have shared the common lot of reading the accounts of that work given to the world by the newspapers. No two experiences could be more different. But in the end the talkers obtained a dangerous ascendancy over the rank and file of the men of action; for though the great men of action are always inveterate talkers and often very clever writers, and therefore cannot have their minds formed for them by others, the average man of action, like the average fighter with the bayonet, can give no account of himself in words even to himself, and is apt to pick up and accept what he reads about himself and other people in the papers, except when the writer is rash enough to commit himself on technical points. It was not uncommon during the war to hear a soldier, or a civilian engaged on war work, describing events within his own experience that reduced to utter absurdity the ravings and maunderings of his daily paper, and yet echo the opinions of that paper like a parrot. Thus, to escape from the prevailing confusion and folly, it was not enough to seek the company of the ordinary man of action: one had to get into contact with the master spirits. This was a privilege which only a handful of people could enjoy. For the unprivileged citizen there was no escape. To him the whole country seemed mad, futile, silly, incompetent, with no hope of victory except the hope that the enemy might be just as mad. Only by very resolute reflection and reasoning could he reassure himself that if there was nothing more solid beneath these appalling appearances the war could not possibly have gone on for a single day without a total breakdown of its organization.

THE MAD ELECTION

Happy were the fools and the thoughtless men of action in those days. The worst of it was that the fools were very strongly represented in parliament, as fools not only elect fools, but can persuade men of action to elect them too. The election that immediately followed the armistice was perhaps the maddest that has ever taken place. Soldiers who had done voluntary and heroic service in the field were defeated by persons who had apparently never run a risk or spent a farthing that they could avoid, and who even had in the course of the election to apologize publicly for bawling Pacifist or Pro-German at their opponent. Party leaders seek such followers, who can always be depended on to walk tamely into the lobby at the party whip's orders, provided the leader will make their seats safe for them by the process which was called, in derisive reference to the war rationing system, "giving them the coupon." Other incidents were so grotesque that I cannot mention them without enabling the reader to identify the parties, which would not be fair, as they were no more to blame than thousands of others who must necessarily be nameless. The general result was patently absurd; and the electorate, disgusted at its own work, instantly recoiled to the opposite extreme, and cast out all the coupon candidates at the earliest bye-elections by equally silly majorities. But the mischief of the general election could not be undone; and the Government had not only to pretend to abuse its European victory as it had promised, but actually to do it by starving the enemies who had thrown down their arms. It had, in short, won the election by pledging itself to be thriftlessly wicked, cruel, and vindictive; and it did not find it as easy to escape from this pledge as it had from nobler ones. The end, as I write, is not yet; but it is clear that this thoughtless savagery will recoil on the heads of the Allies so severely that we shall be forced by the sternest necessity to take up our share of healing the Europe we have wounded almost to death instead of attempting to complete her destruction.

THE YAHOO AND THE ANGRY APE

Contemplating this picture of a state of mankind so recent that no denial of its truth is possible, one understands Shakespear comparing Man to an angry ape, Swift describing him as a Yahoo rebuked by the superior virtue of the horse, and Wellington declaring that the British can behave themselves neither in victory nor defeat. Yet none of the three had seen war as we have seen it. Shakespear blamed great men, saying that "Could great men thunder as Jove himself does Jove would ne'er be quiet; for every pelting petty officer would use his heaven for thunder: nothing but thunder." What would Shakespear have said if he had seen something far more destructive than thunder in the hand of every village laborer, and found on the Messines Ridge the craters of the nineteen volcanoes that were let loose there at the touch of a finger that might have been a child's finger without the result being a whit less ruinous? Shakespear may have seen a Stratford cottage struck by one of Jove's thunderbolts, and have helped to extinguish the lighted thatch and clear away the bits of the broken chimney. What would he have said if he had seen Ypres as it is now, or returned to Stratford, as French peasants are returning to their homes today, to find the old familiar signpost inscribed "To Stratford, 1 mile," and at the end of the mile nothing but some holes in the ground and a fragment of a broken churn here and there? Would not the spectacle of the angry ape endowed with powers of destruction that Jove never pretended to, have beggared even his command of words?

And yet, what is there to say except that war puts a strain on human nature that breaks down the better half of it, and makes the worse half a diabolical virtue? Better for us if it broke it down altogether; for then the warlike way out of our difficulties would be barred to us, and we should take greater care not to get into them. In truth, it is, as Byron said, "not difficult to die," and enormously difficult to live: that explains why, at bottom, peace is not only better than war, but infinitely more arduous. Did any hero of the war face the glorious risk of death more bravely than the traitor Bolo faced the ignominious certainty of it? Bolo taught us all how to die: can we say that he taught us all how to live? Hardly a week passes now without some soldier who braved death in the field so recklessly that he was decorated or specially commended for it, being haled before our magistrates for having failed to resist the paltriest temptations of peace, with no better excuse than the old one that "a man must live." Strange that one who, sooner than do honest work, will sell his honor for a bottle of wine, a visit to the theatre, and an hour with a strange woman, all obtained by passing a worthless cheque, could yet stake his life on the most desperate chances of the battle-field! Does it not seem as if, after all, the glory of death were cheaper than the glory of life? If it is not easier to attain, why do so many more men attain it? At all events it is clear that the kingdom of the Prince of Peace has not yet become the kingdom of this world. His attempts at invasion have been resisted far more fiercely than the Kaiser's. Successful as that resistance has been, it has piled up a sort of National Debt that is not the less oppressive because we have no figures for it and do not intend to pay it. A blockade that cuts off "the grace of our Lord" is in the long run less bearable than the blockades which merely cut off raw materials; and against that blockade our Armada is impotent. In the blockader's house, he has assured us, there are many mansions; but I am afraid they do not include either Heartbreak House or Horseback Hall.

PLAGUE ON BOTH YOUR HOUSES!

Meanwhile the Bolshevist picks and petards are at work on the foundations of both buildings; and though the Bolshevists may be buried in the ruins, their deaths will not save the edifices. Unfortunately they can be built again. Like Doubting Castle, they have been demolished many times by successive Greathearts, and rebuilt by Simple, Sloth, and Presumption, by Feeble Mind and Much Afraid, and by all the jurymen of Vanity Fair. Another generation of "secondary education" at our ancient public schools and the cheaper institutions that ape them will be quite sufficient to keep the two going until the next war.

For the instruction of that generation I leave these pages as a record of what civilian life was during the war: a matter on which history is usually silent. Fortunately it was a very short war. It is true that the people who thought it could not last more than six months were very signally refuted by the event. As Sir Douglas Haig has pointed out, its Waterloos lasted months instead of hours. But there would have been nothing surprising in its lasting thirty years. If it had not been for the fact that the blockade achieved the amazing feat of starving out Europe, which it could not possibly have done had Europe been properly organized for war, or even for peace, the war would have lasted until the belligerents were so tired of it that they could no longer be compelled to compel themselves to go on with it. Considering its magnitude, the war of 1914–18 will certainly be classed as the shortest in history. The end came so suddenly that the combatants literally stumbled over it; and yet it came a full year later than it should have come if the belligerents had not been far too afraid of one another to face the situation sensibly. Germany, having failed to provide for the war she began, failed again to surrender before she was dangerously exhausted. Her opponents, equally improvident, went as much too close to bankruptcy as Germany to starvation. It was a bluff at which both were bluffed. And, with the usual irony of war, it remains doubtful whether Germany and Russia, the defeated, will not be the gainers; for the victors are already busy fastening on themselves the chains they have struck from the limbs of the vanquished.

HOW THE THEATRE FARED

Let us now contract our view rather violently from the European theatre of war to the theatre in which the fights are sham fights, and the slain, rising the moment the curtain has fallen, go comfortably home to supper after washing off their rosepink wounds. It is nearly twenty years since I was last obliged to introduce a play in the form of a book for lack of an opportunity of presenting it in its proper mode by a performance in a theatre. The war has thrown me back on this expedient. Heartbreak House has not yet reached the stage. I have withheld it because the war has completely upset the economic conditions which formerly enabled serious drama to pay its way in London. The change is not in the theatres nor in the management of them, nor in the authors and actors, but in the audiences. For four years the London theatres were crowded every night with thousands of soldiers on leave from the front. These soldiers were not seasoned London playgoers. A childish experience of my own gave me a clue to their condition. When I was a small boy I was taken to the opera. I did not then know what an opera was, though I could whistle a good deal of opera music. I had seen in my mother's album photographs of all the great opera singers, mostly in evening dress. In the theatre I found myself before a gilded balcony filled with persons in evening dress whom I took to be the opera singers. I picked out one massive dark lady as Alboni, and wondered how soon she would stand up and sing. I was puzzled by the fact that I was made to sit with my back to the singers instead of facing them. When the curtain went up, my astonishment and delight were unbounded.

THE SOLDIER AT THE THEATRE FRONT

In 1915 I saw in the theatres men in khaki in just the same predicament. To everyone who had my clue to their state of mind it was evident that they had never been in a theatre before and did not know what it was. At one of our great variety theatres I sat beside a young officer, not at all a rough specimen, who, even when the curtain rose and enlightened him as to the place where he had to look for his entertainment, found the dramatic part of it utterly incomprehensible. He did not know how to play his part of the game. He could understand the people on the stage singing and dancing and performing gymnastic feats. He not only understood but intensely enjoyed an artist who imitated cocks crowing and pigs squeaking. But the people who pretended that they were somebody else, and that the painted picture behind them was real, bewildered him. In his presence I realized how very sophisticated the natural man has to become before the conventions of the theatre can be easily acceptable, or the purpose of the drama obvious to him.

Well, from the moment when the routine of leave for our soldiers was established, such novices, accompanied by damsels (called flappers) often as innocent as themselves, crowded the theatres to the doors. It was hardly possible at first to find stuff crude enough to nurse them on. The best music-hall comedians ransacked their memories for the oldest quips and the most childish antics to avoid carrying the military spectators out of their depth. I believe that this was a mistake as far as the novices were concerned. Shakespear, or the dramatized histories of George Barnwell, Maria Martin, or the Demon Barber of Fleet Street, would probably have been quite popular with them. But the novices were only a minority after all. The cultivated soldier, who in time of peace would look at nothing theatrical except the most advanced post-Ibsen plays in the most artistic settings, found himself, to his own astonishment, thirsting for silly jokes, dances, and brainlessly sensuous exhibitions of pretty girls. The author of some of the most grimly serious plays of our time told me that after enduring the trenches for months without a glimpse of the female of his species, it gave him an entirely innocent but delightful pleasure merely to see a flapper. The reaction from the battle-field produced a condition of hyperaesthesia in which all the theatrical values were altered. Trivial things gained intensity and stale things novelty. The actor, instead of having to coax his audiences out of the boredom which had driven them to the theatre in an ill humor to seek some sort of distraction, had only to exploit the bliss of smiling men who were no longer under fire and under military discipline, but actually clean and comfortable and in a mood to be pleased with anything and everything that a bevy of pretty girls and a funny man, or even a bevy of girls pretending to be pretty and a man pretending to be funny, could do for them.

Then could be seen every night in the theatres old-fashioned farcical comedies, in which a bedroom, with four doors on each side and a practicable window in the middle, was understood to resemble exactly the bedroom in the flats beneath and above, all three inhabited by couples consumed with jealousy. When these people came home drunk at night; mistook their neighbor's flats for their own; and in due course got into the wrong beds, it was not only the novices who found the resulting complications and scandals exquisitely ingenious and amusing, nor their equally verdant flappers who could not help squealing in a manner that astonished the oldest performers when the gentleman who had just come in drunk through the window pretended to undress, and allowed glimpses of his naked person to be descried from time to time. Men who had just read the news that Charles Wyndham was dying, and were thereby sadly reminded of Pink Dominos and the torrent of farcical comedies that followed it in his heyday until every trick of that trade had become so stale that the laughter they provoked turned to loathing: these veterans also, when they returned from the field, were as much pleased by what they knew to be stale and foolish as the novices by what they thought fresh and clever.

COMMERCE IN THE THEATRE

Wellington said that an army moves on its belly. So does a London theatre. Before a man acts he must eat. Before he performs plays he must pay rent. In London we have no theatres for the welfare of the people: they are all for the sole purpose of producing the utmost obtainable rent for the proprietor. If the twin flats and twin beds produce a guinea more than Shakespear, out goes Shakespear, and in come the twin flats and the twin beds. If the brainless bevy of pretty girls and the funny man outbid Mozart, out goes Mozart.

UNSER SHAKESPEAR

Before the war an effort was made to remedy this by establishing a national theatre in celebration of the tercentenary of the death of Shakespear. A committee was formed; and all sorts of illustrious and influential persons lent their names to a grand appeal to our national culture. My play, The Dark Lady of The Sonnets, was one of the incidents of that appeal. After some years of effort the result was a single handsome subscription from a German gentleman. Like the celebrated swearer in the anecdote when the cart containing all his household goods lost its tailboard at the top of the hill and let its contents roll in ruin to the bottom, I can only say, "I cannot do justice to this situation," and let it pass without another word.

THE HIGHER DRAMA PUT OUT OF ACTION

The effect of the war on the London theatres may now be imagined. The beds and the bevies drove every higher form of art out of it. Rents went up to an unprecedented figure. At the same time prices doubled everywhere except at the theatre pay-boxes, and raised the expenses of management to such a degree that unless the houses were quite full every night, profit was impossible. Even bare solvency could not be attained without a very wide popularity. Now what had made serious drama possible to a limited extent before the war was that a play could pay its way even if the theatre were only half full until Saturday and three-quarters full then. A manager who was an enthusiast and a desperately hard worker, with an occasional grant-in-aid from an artistically disposed millionaire, and a due proportion of those rare and happy accidents by which plays of the higher sort turn out to be potboilers as well, could hold out for some years, by which time a relay might arrive in the person of another enthusiast. Thus and not otherwise occurred that remarkable revival of the British drama at the beginning of the century which made my own career as a playwright possible in England. In America I had already established myself, not as part of the ordinary theatre system, but in association with the exceptional genius of Richard Mansfield. In Germany and Austria I had no difficulty: the system of publicly aided theatres there, Court and Municipal, kept drama of the kind I dealt in alive; so that I was indebted to the Emperor of Austria for magnificent productions of my works at a time when the sole official attention paid me by the British Court was the announcement to the English-speaking world that certain plays of mine were unfit for public performance, a substantial set-off against this being that the British Court, in the course of its private playgoing, paid no regard to the bad character given me by the chief officer of its household.

Howbeit, the fact that my plays effected a lodgment on the London stage, and were presently followed by the plays of Granville Barker, Gilbert Murray, John Masefield, St John Hankin, Laurence Housman, Arnold Bennett, John Galsworthy, John Drinkwater, and others which would in the XIX century have stood rather less chance of production at a London theatre than the Dialogues of Plato, not to mention revivals of the ancient Athenian drama, and a restoration to the stage of Shakespear's plays as he wrote them, was made economically possible solely by a supply of theatres which could hold nearly twice as much money as it cost to rent and maintain them. In such theatres work appealing to a relatively small class of cultivated persons, and therefore attracting only from half to three-quarters as many spectators as the more popular pastimes, could nevertheless keep going in the hands of young adventurers who were doing it for its own sake, and had not yet been forced by advancing age and responsibilities to consider the commercial value of their time and energy too closely. The war struck this foundation away in the manner I have just described. The expenses of running the cheapest west-end theatres rose to a sum which exceeded by twenty-five per cent the utmost that the higher drama can, as an ascertained matter of fact, be depended on to draw. Thus the higher drama, which has never really been a commercially sound speculation, now became an impossible one. Accordingly, attempts are being made to provide a refuge for it in suburban theatres in London and repertory theatres in the provinces. But at the moment when the army has at last disgorged the survivors of the gallant band of dramatic pioneers whom it swallowed, they find that the economic conditions which formerly made their work no worse than precarious now put it out of the question altogether, as far as the west end of London is concerned.

CHURCH AND THEATRE

I do not suppose many people care particularly. We are not brought up to care; and a sense of the national importance of the theatre is not born in mankind: the natural man, like so many of the soldiers at the beginning of the war, does not know what a theatre is. But please note that all these soldiers who did not know what a theatre was, knew what a church was. And they had been taught to respect churches. Nobody had ever warned them against a church as a place where frivolous women paraded in their best clothes; where stories of improper females like Potiphar's wife, and erotic poetry like the Song of Songs, were read aloud; where the sensuous and sentimental music of Schubert, Mendelssohn, Gounod, and Brahms was more popular than severe music by greater composers; where the prettiest sort of pretty pictures of pretty saints assailed the imagination and senses through stained-glass windows; and where sculpture and architecture came to the help of painting. Nobody ever reminded them that these things had sometimes produced such developments of erotic idolatry that men who were not only enthusiastic amateurs of literature, painting, and music, but famous practitioners of them, had actually exulted when mobs and even regular troops under express command had mutilated church statues, smashed church windows, wrecked church organs, and torn up the sheets from which the church music was read and sung. When they saw broken statues in churches, they were told that this was the work of wicked godless rioters, instead of, as it was, the work partly of zealots bent on driving the world, the flesh, and the devil out of the temple, and partly of insurgent men who had become intolerably poor because the temple had become a den of thieves. But all the sins and perversions that were so carefully hidden from them in the history of the Church were laid on the shoulders of the Theatre: that stuffy, uncomfortable place of penance in which we suffer so much inconvenience on the slenderest chance of gaining a scrap of food for our starving souls. When the Germans bombed the Cathedral of Rheims the world rang with the horror of the sacrilege. When they bombed the Little Theatre in the Adelphi, and narrowly missed bombing two writers of plays who lived within a few yards of it, the fact was not even mentioned in the papers. In point of appeal to the senses no theatre ever built could touch the fane at Rheims: no actress could rival its Virgin in beauty, nor any operatic tenor look otherwise than a fool beside its David. Its picture glass was glorious even to those who had seen the glass of Chartres. It was wonderful in its very grotesques: who would look at the Blondin Donkey after seeing its leviathans? In spite of the Adam-Adelphian decoration on which Miss Kingston had lavished so much taste and care, the Little Theatre was in comparison with Rheims the gloomiest of little conventicles: indeed the cathedral must, from the Puritan point of view, have debauched a million voluptuaries for every one whom the Little Theatre had sent home thoughtful to a chaste bed after Mr Chesterton's Magic or Brieux's *Les Avariés*. Perhaps that is the real reason why the Church is lauded and the Theatre reviled. Whether or no, the fact remains that the lady to whose public spirit and sense of the national value of the theatre I owed the first regular public performance of a play of mine had to conceal her action as if it had been a crime, whereas if she had given the money to the Church she would have worn a halo for it. And I admit, as I have always done, that this state of things may have been a very sensible one. I have asked Londoners again and again why they pay half a guinea to go to a theatre when they can go to St Paul's or Westminster Abbey for nothing. Their only possible reply is that they want to see something new and possibly something wicked; but the theatres mostly disappoint both hopes. If ever a revolution makes me Dictator, I shall establish a heavy charge for admission to our churches. But everyone who pays at the church door shall receive a ticket entitling him or her to free admission to one performance at any theatre he or she prefers. Thus shall the sensuous charms of the church service be made to subsidize the sterner virtue of the drama.

THE NEXT PHASE

The present situation will not last. Although the newspaper I read at breakfast this morning before writing these words contains a calculation that no less than twenty-three wars are at present being waged to confirm the peace, England is no longer in khaki; and a violent reaction is setting in against the crude theatrical fare of the four terrible years. Soon the rents of theatres will once more be fixed on the assumption that they cannot always be full, nor even on the average half full week in and week out. Prices will change. The higher drama will be at no greater disadvantage than it was before the war; and it may benefit, first, by the fact that many of us have been torn from the fools' paradise in which the theatre formerly traded, and thrust upon the sternest realities and necessities until we have lost both faith in and patience with the theatrical pretences that had no root either in reality or necessity; second, by the startling change made by the war in the distribution of income. It seems only the other day that a millionaire was a man with £50,000 a year. Today, when he has paid his income tax and super tax, and insured his life for the amount of his death duties, he is lucky if his net income is £10,000, though his nominal property remains the same. And this is the result of a Budget which is called "a respite for the rich." At the other end of the scale millions of persons have had regular incomes for the first time in their lives; and their men have been regularly clothed, fed, lodged, and taught to make up their minds that certain things have to be done, also for the first time in their lives. Hundreds of thousands of women have been taken out of their domestic cages and tasted both discipline and independence. The thoughtless and snobbish middle classes have been pulled up short by the very unpleasant experience of being ruined to an unprecedented extent. We have all had a tremendous jolt; and although the widespread notion that the shock of the war would automatically make a new heaven and a new earth, and that the dog would never go back to his vomit nor the sow to her wallowing in the mire, is already seen to be a delusion, yet we are far more conscious of our condition than we were, and far less disposed to submit to it. Revolution, lately only a sensational chapter in history or a demagogic claptrap, is now a possibility so imminent that hardly by trying to suppress it in other countries by arms and defamation, and calling the process anti-Bolshevism, can our Government stave it off at home.

Perhaps the most tragic figure of the day is the American President who was once a historian. In those days it became his task to tell us how, after that great war in America which was more clearly than any other war of our time a war for an idea, the conquerors, confronted with a heroic task of reconstruction, turned recreant, and spent fifteen years in abusing their victory under cover of pretending to accomplish the task they were doing what they could to make impossible. Alas!

Hegel was right when he said that we learn from history that men never learn anything from history. With what anguish of mind the President sees that we, the new conquerors, forgetting everything we professed to fight for, are sitting down with watering mouths to a good square meal of ten years revenge upon and humiliation of our prostrate foe, can only be guessed by those who know, as he does, how hopeless is remonstrance, and how happy Lincoln was in perishing from the earth before his inspired messages became scraps of paper. He knows well that from the Peace Conference will come, in spite of his utmost, no edict on which he will be able, like Lincoln, to invoke "the considerate judgment of mankind, and the gracious favor of Almighty God." He led his people to destroy the militarism of Zabern; and the army they rescued is busy in Cologne imprisoning every German who does not salute a British officer; whilst the Government at home, asked whether it approves, replies that it does not propose even to discontinue this Zabernism when the Peace is concluded, but in effect looks forward to making Germans salute British officers until the end of the world. That is what war makes of men and women. It will wear off; and the worst it threatens is already proving impracticable; but before the humble and contrite heart ceases to be despised, the President and I, being of the same age, will be dotards. In the meantime there is, for him, another history to write; for me, another comedy to stage. Perhaps, after all, that is what wars are for, and what historians and playwrights are for. If men will not learn until their lessons are written in blood, why, blood they must have, their own for preference.

THE EPHEMERAL THRONES AND THE ETERNAL THEATRE

To the theatre it will not matter. Whatever Bastilles fall, the theatre will stand. Apostolic Hapsburg has collapsed; All Highest Hohenzollern languishes in Holland, threatened with trial on a capital charge of fighting for his country against England; Imperial Romanoff, said to have perished miserably by a more summary method of murder, is perhaps alive or perhaps dead: nobody cares more than if he had been a peasant; the lord of Hellas is level with his lackeys in republican Switzerland; Prime Ministers and Commanders-in-Chief have passed from a brief glory as Solons and Caesars into failure and obscurity as closely on one another's heels as the descendants of Banquo; but Euripides and Aristophanes, Shakespear and Molière, Goethe and Ibsen remain fixed in their everlasting seats.

HOW WAR MUZZLES THE DRAMATIC POET

As for myself, why, it may be asked, did I not write two plays about the war instead of two pamphlets on it? The answer is significant. You cannot make war on war and on your neighbor at the same time. War cannot bear the terrible castigation of comedy, the ruthless light of laughter that glares on the stage. When men are heroically dying for their country, it is not the time to shew their lovers and wives and fathers and mothers how they are being sacrificed to the blunders of boobies, the cupidity of capitalists, the ambition of conquerors, the electioneering of demagogues, the Pharisaism of patriots, the lusts and lies and rancors and bloodthirsts that love war because it opens their prison doors, and sets them in the thrones of power and popularity. For unless these things are mercilessly exposed they will hide under the mantle of the ideals on the stage just as they do in real life.

And though there may be better things to reveal, it may not, and indeed cannot, be militarily expedient to reveal them whilst the issue is still in the balance. Truth telling is not compatible with the defence of the realm. We are just now reading the revelations of our generals and admirals, unmuzzled at last by the armistice. During the war, General A, in his moving despatches from the field, told how General B had covered himself with deathless glory in such and such a battle. He now tells us that General B came within an ace of losing us the war by disobeying his orders on that occasion, and fighting instead of running away as he ought to have done. An excellent subject for comedy now that the war is over, no doubt; but if General A had let this out at the time, what would have been the effect on General B's soldiers? And had the stage made known what the Prime Minister and the Secretary of State for War who overruled General A thought of him, and what he thought of them, as now revealed in raging controversy, what would have been the effect on the nation? That is why comedy, though sorely tempted, had to be loyally silent; for the art of the dramatic poet knows no patriotism; recognizes no obligation but truth to natural history; cares not whether Germany or England perish; is ready to cry with Brynhild, "Lass' uns verderben, lachend zu grunde geh'n" sooner than deceive or be deceived; and thus becomes in time of war a greater military danger than poison, steel, or trinitrotoluene. That is why I had to withhold Heartbreak House from the footlights during the war; for the Germans might on any night have turned the last act from play into earnest, and even then might not have waited for their cues.

June 1919.

ACT I

The hilly country in the middle of the north edge of Sussex, looking very pleasant on a fine evening at the end of September, is seen through the windows of a room which has been built so as to resemble the after part of an old-fashioned high-pooped ship with a stern gallery; for the windows are ship built with heavy timbering, and run right across the room as continuously as the stability of the wall allows. A row of lockers under the windows provides an unupholstered window-seat interrupted by twin glass doors, respectively halfway between the stern post and the sides. Another door strains the illusion a little by being apparently in the ship's port side, and yet leading, not to the open sea, but to the entrance hall of the house. Between this door and the stern gallery are bookshelves. There are electric light switches beside the door leading to the hall and the glass doors in the stern gallery. Against the starboard wall is a carpenter's bench. The vice has a board in its jaws; and the floor is littered with shavings, overflowing from a waste-paper basket. A couple of planes and a centrebit are on the bench. In the same wall, between the bench and the windows, is a narrow doorway with a half door, above which a glimpse of the room beyond shews that it is a shelved pantry with bottles and kitchen crockery.

On the starboard side, but close to the middle, is a plain oak drawing-table with drawing-board, T-square, straightedges, set squares, mathematical instruments, saucers of water color, a tumbler of discolored water, Indian ink, pencils, and brushes on it. The drawing-board is set so that the draughtsman's chair has the window on its left hand. On the floor at the end of the table, on his right, is a ship's fire bucket. On the port side of the room, near the bookshelves, is a sofa with its back to the windows. It is a sturdy mahogany article, oddly upholstered in sailcloth, including the bolster, with a couple of blankets hanging over the back. Between the sofa and the drawing-table is a big wicker chair, with broad arms and a low sloping back, with its back to the light. A small but stout table of teak, with a round top and gate legs, stands against the port wall between the door and the bookcase. It is the only article in the room that suggests (not at all convincingly) a woman's hand in the furnishing. The uncarpeted floor of narrow boards is caulked and holystoned like a deck.

The garden to which the glass doors lead dips to the south before the landscape rises again to the hills. Emerging from the hollow is the cupola of an observatory. Between the observatory and the house is a flagstaff on a little esplanade, with a hammock on the east side and a long garden seat on the west.

A young lady, gloved and hatted, with a dust coat on, is sitting in the window-seat with her body twisted to enable her to look out at the view. One hand props her chin: the other hangs down with a volume of the Temple Shakespear in it, and her finger stuck in the page she has been reading.

A clock strikes six.

The young lady turns and looks at her watch. She rises with an air of one who waits and is almost at the end of her patience. She is a pretty girl, slender, fair, and intelligent looking, nicely but not expensively dressed, evidently not a smart idler.

With a sigh of weary resignation she comes to the draughtsman's chair; sits down; and begins to read Shakespear. Presently the book sinks to her lap; her eyes close; and she dozes into a slumber.

An elderly womanservant comes in from the hall with three unopened bottles of rum on a tray. She passes through and disappears in the pantry without noticing the young lady. She places the bottles on the shelf and fills her tray with empty bottles. As she returns with these, the young lady lets her book drop, awakening herself, and startling the womanservant so that she all but lets the tray fall.

THE WOMANSERVANT. God bless us! [*The young lady picks up the book and places it on the table*]. Sorry to wake you, miss, I'm sure; but you are a stranger to me. What might you be waiting here for now?

THE YOUNG LADY. Waiting for somebody to shew some signs of knowing that I have been invited here.

THE WOMANSERVANT. Oh, youre invited, are you? And has nobody come? Dear! dear!

THE YOUNG LADY. A wild-looking old gentleman came and looked in at the window; and I heard him calling out "Nurse: there is a young and attractive female waiting in the poop. Go and see what she wants." Are you the nurse?

THE WOMANSERVANT. Yes, miss; I'm Nurse Guinness. That was old

Captain Shotover, Mrs Hushabye's father. I heard him roaring; but I thought it was for something else. I suppose it was Mrs Hushabye that invited you, ducky?

THE YOUNG LADY. I understood her to do so. But really I think I'd better go.

NURSE GUINNESS. Oh, dont think of such a thing, miss. If Mrs Hushabye has forgotten all about it, it will be a pleasant surprise for her to see you, wont it?

THE YOUNG LADY. It has been a very unpleasant surprise to me to find that nobody expects me.

NURSE GUINNESS. Youll get used to it, miss: this house is full of surprises for them that dont know our ways.

CAPTAIN SHOTOVER [*looking in from the hall suddenly: an ancient but still hardy man with an immense white beard, in a reefer jacket with a whistle hanging from his neck*] Nurse: there is a hold-all and a handbag on the front steps for everybody to fall over. Also a tennis racquet. Who the devil left them there?

THE YOUNG LADY. They are mine, I'm afraid.

THE CAPTAIN [*advancing to the drawing-table*] Nurse: who is this misguided and unfortunate young lady?

NURSE GUINNESS. She says Miss Hessy invited her, sir.

THE CAPTAIN. And had she no friend, no parents, to warn her against my daughter's invitations? This is a pretty sort of house, by heavens! A young and attractive lady is invited here. Her luggage is left on the steps for hours; and she herself is deposited in the poop and abandoned, tired and starving. This is our hospitality. These are our manners. No room ready. No hot water. No welcoming hostess. Our visitor is to sleep in the toolshed, and to wash in the duckpond.

NURSE GUINNESS. Now it's all right, Captain: I'll get the lady some tea; and her room shall be ready before she has finished it. [*To the young lady*] Take off your hat, ducky; and make yourself at home [*she goes to the door leading to the hall*].

THE CAPTAIN [*as she passes him*] Ducky! Do you suppose, woman, that because this young lady has been insulted and neglected, you have the right to address her as you address my wretched children, whom you have brought up in ignorance of the commonest decencies of social intercourse?

NURSE GUINNESS. Never mind him, doty. [*Quite unconcerned, she goes out into the hall on her way to the kitchen*].

THE CAPTAIN. Madam: will you favor me with your name? [*He sits down in the big wicker chair*].

THE YOUNG LADY. My name is Ellie Dunn.

THE CAPTAIN. Dunn! I had a boatswain whose name was Dunn. He was originally a pirate in China. He set up as a ship's chandler with stores which I have every reason to believe he stole from me. No doubt he became rich. Are you his daughter?

ELLIE [*indignant*] No: certainly not. I am proud to be able to say that though my father has not been a successful man, nobody has ever had one word to say against him. I think my father is the best man I have ever known.

THE CAPTAIN. He must be greatly changed. Has he attained the seventh degree of concentration?

ELLIE. I dont understand.

THE CAPTAIN. But how could he, with a daughter? I, madam, have two daughters. One of them is Hesione Hushabye, who invited you here. I keep this house: she upsets it. I desire to attain the seventh degree of concentration: she invites visitors and leaves me to entertain them. [*Nurse Guinness returns with the tea-tray, which she places on the teak table*]. I have a second daughter who is, thank God, in a remote part of the Empire with her numskull of a husband. As a child she thought the figure-head of my ship, the Dauntless, the most beautiful thing on earth. He resembled it. He had the same expression: wooden yet enterprising. She married him, and will never set foot in this house again.

NURSE GUINNESS [*carrying the table, with the tea-things on it, to Ellie's side*] Indeed you never were more mistaken. She is in England this very moment. You have been told three times this week that she is coming home for a year for her health. And very glad you should be to see your own daughter again after all these years.

THE CAPTAIN. I am not glad. The natural term of the affection of the human animal for its offspring is six years. My daughter Ariadne was born when I was forty-six. I am now eighty-eight. If she comes, I am not at home. If she wants anything, let her take it. If she asks for me, let her be informed that I am extremely old, and have totally forgotten her.

NURSE GUINNESS. Thats no talk to offer to a young lady. Here, ducky, have some tea; and dont listen to him [*she pours out a cup of tea*].

THE CAPTAIN [*rising wrathfully*] Now before high heaven they have given this innocent child Indian tea: the stuff they tan their own leather insides with. [*He seizes the cup and the tea-pot and empties both into the leathern bucket*].

ELLIE [*almost in tears*] Oh, please! I am so tired. I should have been glad of anything.

NURSE GUINNESS. Oh, what a thing to do! The poor lamb is ready to drop.

THE CAPTAIN. You shall have some of my tea. Do not touch that fly-blown cake: nobody eats it here except the dogs. [*He disappears into the pantry*].

NURSE GUINNESS. Theres a man for you! They say he sold himself to the devil in Zanzibar before he was a captain; and the older he grows the more I believe them.

A WOMAN'S VOICE [*in the hall*] Is anyone at home? Hesione! Nurse! Papa! Do come, somebody; and take in my luggage.

Thumping heard, as of an umbrella, on the wainscot.

NURSE GUINNESS. My gracious! It's Miss Addie, Lady Utterword, Mrs Hushabye's sister: the one I told the Captain about. [*Calling*] Coming, Miss, coming.

She carries the table back to its place by the door, and is hurrying out when she is intercepted by Lady Utterword, who bursts in much flustered. Lady Utterword, a blonde, is very handsome, very well dressed, and so precipitate in speech and action that the first impression (erroneous) is one of comic silliness.

LADY UTTERWORD. Oh, is that you, Nurse? How are you? You dont look a day older. Is nobody at home? Where is Hesione? Doesnt she expect me? Where are the servants? Whose luggage is that on the steps? Where's Papa? Is everybody asleep? [*Seeing Ellie*] Oh! I beg your pardon. I suppose you are one of my nieces. [*Approaching her with outstretched arms*] Come and kiss your aunt, darling.

ELLIE. I'm only a visitor. It is my luggage on the steps.

NURSE GUINNESS. I'll go get you some fresh tea, ducky. [*She takes up the tray*].

ELLIE. But the old gentleman said he would make some himself.

NURSE GUINNESS. Bless you! he's forgotten what he went for already. His mind wanders from one thing to another.

LADY UTTERWORD. Papa, I suppose?

NURSE GUINNESS. Yes, Miss.

LADY UTTERWORD [*vehemently*] Dont be silly nurse. Dont call me Miss.

NURSE GUINNESS [*placidly*] No, lovey [*she goes out with the tea-tray*].

LADY UTTERWORD [*sitting down with a flounce on the sofa*] I know what you must feel. Oh, this house, this house! I come back to it after twenty-three years; and it is just the same: the luggage lying on the steps, the servants spoilt and impossible, nobody at home to receive anybody, no regular meals, nobody ever hungry because they are always gnawing bread and butter or munching apples, and, what is worse, the same disorder in ideas, in talk, in feeling. When I was a child I was used to it: I had never known anything better, though I was unhappy, and longed all the time—oh, how I longed!—to be respectable, to be a lady, to live as others did, not to have to think of everything for myself. I married at nineteen to escape from it. My husband is Sir Hastings Utterword, who has been governor of all the crown colonies in succession. I have always been the mistress of Government House. I have been so happy: I had forgotten that people could live like this. I wanted to see my father, my sister, my nephews and nieces (one ought to, you know), and I was looking forward to it. And now the state of the house! the way I'm received! the casual impudence of that woman Guinness, our old nurse! really Hesione might at least have been here: s o m e preparation might have been made for me. You must excuse my going on in this way; but I am really very much hurt and annoyed and disillusioned: and if I had realized it was to be like this, I wouldnt have come. I have a great mind to go away without another word [*she is on the point of weeping*].

ELLIE [*also very miserable*] Nobody has been here to receive me either. I thought I ought to go away too. But how can I, Lady Utterword? My luggage is on the steps; and the station fly has gone.

The Captain emerges from the pantry with a tray of Chinese lacquer and a very fine tea-set on it. He rests it provisionally on the end of the table; snatches away the drawing-board, which he stands on the floor against the table legs; and puts the tray in the space thus cleared. Ellie pours out a cup greedily.

THE CAPTAIN. Your tea, young lady. What! another lady! I must fetch another cup [*he makes for the pantry*].

LADY UTTERWORD [*rising from the sofa, suffused with emotion*] Papa! Dont you know me? I'm your daughter.

THE CAPTAIN. Nonsense! my daughter's upstairs asleep. [*He vanishes through the half door*].

Lady Utterword retires to the window to conceal her tears.

ELLIE [*going to her with the cup*] Dont be so distressed. Have this cup of tea. He is very old and very strange: he has been just like that to me. I know how dreadful it must be: my own father is all the world to me. Oh, I'm sure he didnt mean it.

The Captain returns with another cup.

THE CAPTAIN. Now we are complete. [*He places it on the tray*].

LADY UTTERWORD [*hysterically*] Papa: you cant have forgotten me. I am Ariadne. I'm little Paddy Patkins. Wont you kiss me? [*She goes to him and throws her arms round his neck*].

THE CAPTAIN [*woodenly enduring her embrace*] How can you be Ariadne? You are a middle-aged woman: well preserved, madam, but no longer young.

LADY UTTERWORD. But think of all the years and years I have been away, Papa. I have had to grow old, like other people.

THE CAPTAIN [*disengaging himself*] You should grow out of kissing strange men: they may be striving to attain the seventh degree of concentration.

LADY UTTERWORD. But I'm your daughter. You havnt seen me for years.

THE CAPTAIN. So much the worse! When our relatives are at home, we have to think of all their good points or it would be impossible to endure them. But when they are away, we console ourselves for their absence by dwelling on their vices. That is how I have come to think my absent daughter Ariadne a perfect fiend; so do not try to ingratiate yourself here by impersonating her [*he walks firmly away to the other side of the room*].

LADY UTTERWORD. Ingratiating myself indeed! [*With dignity*] Very well, papa. [*She sits down at the drawing-table and pours out tea for herself*].

THE CAPTAIN. I am neglecting my social duties. You remember Dunn? Billy Dunn?

LADY UTTERWORD. Do you mean that villainous sailor who robbed you?

THE CAPTAIN [*introducing Ellie*] His daughter. [*He sits down on the sofa*].

ELLIE [*protesting*] No—

Nurse Guinness returns with fresh tea.

THE CAPTAIN. Take that hogwash away. Do you hear?

NURSE. Youve actually remembered about the tea! [*To Ellie*] O, miss, he didnt forget you after all! You h a v e made an impression.

THE CAPTAIN [*gloomily*] Youth! beauty! novelty! They are badly wanted in this house. I am excessively old. Hesione is only moderately young. Her children are not youthful.

LADY UTTERWORD. How can children be expected to be youthful in this house? Almost before we could speak we were filled with notions that might have been all very well for pagan philosophers of fifty, but were certainly quite unfit for respectable people of any age.

NURSE. You were always for respectability, Miss Addy.

LADY UTTERWORD. Nurse: will you please remember that I am Lady Utterword, and not Miss Addy, nor lovey, nor darling, nor doty? Do you hear?

NURSE. Yes, ducky: all right. I'll tell them all they must call you my lady. [*She takes her tray out with undisturbed placidity*].

LADY UTTERWORD. What comfort? what sense is there in having servants with no manners?

ELLIE [*rising and coming to the table to put down her empty cup*] Lady Utterword: do you think Mrs Hushabye really expects me?

LADY UTTERWORD. Oh, dont ask me. You can see for yourself that Ive just arrived; her only sister, after twenty-three years absence! and it seems that *I* am not expected.

THE CAPTAIN. What does it matter whether the young lady is expected or not? She is welcome. There are beds: there is food. I'll find a room for her myself [*he makes for the door*].

ELLIE [*following him to stop him*] Oh please– [*he goes out*]. Lady Utterword: I dont know what to do. Your father persists in believing that my father is some sailor who robbed him.

LADY UTTERWORD. You had better pretend not to notice it. My father is a very clever man; but he always forgot things; and now that he is old, of course he is worse. And I must warn you that it is sometimes very hard to feel quite sure that he really forgets.

Mrs Hushabye bursts into the room tempestuously, and embraces Ellie. She is a couple of years older than Lady Utterword, and even better looking. She has magnificent black hair, eyes like the fishpools of Heshbon, and a nobly modelled neck, short at the back and low between her shoulders in front. Unlike her sister she is uncorseted and dressed anyhow in a rich robe of black pile that shews off her white skin and statuesque contour.

MRS HUSHABYE. Ellie, my darling, my pettikins [*kissing her*]: how long have you been here? Ive been at home all the time: I was putting flowers and things in your room; and when I just sat down for a moment to try how comfortable the armchair was I went off to sleep. Papa woke me and told me you were here. Fancy your finding no one, and being neglected and abandoned. [*Kissing her again*], My poor love! [*She deposits Ellie on the sofa. Meanwhile Ariadne has left the table and come over to claim her share of attention*]. Oh! youve brought someone with you. Introduce me.

LADY UTTERWORD. Hesione: is it possible that you dont know me?

MRS HUSHABYE [*conventionally*] Of course I remember your face quite well. Where have we met?

LADY UTTERWORD. Didnt Papa tell you I was here? Oh! this is really too much. [*She throws herself sulkily into the big chair*].

MRS HUSHABYE. Papa!

LADY UTTERWORD. Yes: Papa. O u r papa, you unfeeling wretch. [*Rising angrily*] I'll go straight to a hotel.

MRS HUSHABYE [*seizing her by the shoulders*] My goodness gracious goodness, you dont mean to say that youre Addy!

LADY UTTERWORD. I certainly am Addy; and I dont think I can be so changed that you would not have recognized me if you had any real affection for me. And papa didnt think me even worth mentioning!

MRS HUSHABYE. What a lark! Sit down [*she pushes her back into the chair instead of kissing her, and posts herself behind it*]. You d o look a swell. Youre much handsomer than you used to be. Youve made the acquaintance of Ellie, of course. She is going to marry a perfect hog of a millionaire for the sake of her father, who is as poor as a church mouse; and you must help me to stop her.

ELLIE. Oh p l e a s e, Hesione.

MRS HUSHABYE. My pettikins, the man's coming here today with your father to begin persecuting you; and everybody will see the state of the case in ten minutes; so whats the use of making a secret of it?

ELLIE. He is not a hog, Hesione. You dont know how wonderfully good he was to my father, and how deeply grateful I am to him.

MRS HUSHABYE [*to Lady Utterword*] Her father is a very remarkable man, Addy. His name is Mazzini Dunn. Mazzini was a celebrity of some kind who knew Ellie's grandparents. They were both poets, like the Brownings; and when her father came into the world Mazzini said "Another soldier born for freedom!" So they christened him Mazzini; and he has been fighting for freedom in his quiet way ever since. Thats why he is so poor.

ELLIE. I am proud of his poverty.

MRS HUSHABYE. Of course you are, pettikins. Why not leave him in it, and marry someone you love?

LADY UTTERWORD [*rising suddenly and explosively*] Hesione: are you going to kiss me or are you not?

MRS HUSHABYE. What do you want to be kissed for?

LADY UTTERWORD. I dont want to be kissed; but I do want you to behave properly and decently. We are sisters. We have been separated for twenty three years. You ought to kiss me.

MRS HUSHABYE. Tomorrow morning, dear, before you make up. I hate the smell of powder.

LADY UTTERWORD. Oh! you unfeeling–[*she is interrupted by the return of the captain*].

THE CAPTAIN [*to Ellie*] Your room is ready. [*Ellie rises*]. The sheets were damp; but I have changed them [*he makes for the garden door on the port side*].

LADY UTTERWORD. Oh! What about my sheets?

THE CAPTAIN [*halting at the door*] Take my advice: air them; or take them off and sleep in blankets. You shall sleep in Ariadne's old room.

LADY UTTERWORD. Indeed I shall do nothing of the sort. That little hole! I am entitled to the best spare room.

THE CAPTAIN [*continuing unmoved*] She married a numskull. She told me she would marry anyone to get away from home.

LADY UTTERWORD. You are pretending not to know me on purpose. I will leave the house.

Mazzini Dunn enters from the hall. He is a little elderly man with bulging credulous eyes and earnest manners. He is dressed in a blue serge jacket suit with an unbuttoned mackintosh over it, and carries a soft black hat of clerical cut.

ELLIE. At last! Captain Shotover: here is my father.

THE CAPTAIN. This! Nonsense! not a bit like him [*he goes away through the garden, shutting the door sharply behind him*].

LADY UTTERWORD. I will not be ignored and pretended to be somebody else. I will have it out with papa now, this instant. [*To Mazzini*] Excuse me. [*She follows the Captain out, making a hasty bow to Mazzini, who returns it*].

MRS HUSHABYE [*hospitably, shaking hands*] How good of you to come, Mr Dunn! You dont mind papa, do you? He is as mad as a hatter, you know, but quite harmless, and extremely clever. You will have some delightful talks with him.

MAZZINI. I hope so. [*To Ellie*] So here you are, Ellie, dear. [*He draws her arm affectionately through his*]. I must thank you, Mrs Hushabye, for your kindness to my daughter. I'm afraid she would have had no holiday if you had not invited her.

MRS HUSHABYE. Not at all. Very nice of her to come and attract young people to the house for us.

MAZZINI [*smiling*] I'm afraid Ellie is not interested in young men, Mrs Hushabye. Her taste is on the graver, solider side.

MRS HUSHABYE [*with a sudden rather hard brightness in her manner*] Wont you take off your overcoat, Mr Dunn? You will find a cupboard for coats and hats and things in the corner of the hall.

MAZZINI [*hastily releasing Ellie*] Yes—thank you—I had better—[*he goes out*].

MRS HUSHABYE [*emphatically*] The old brute!

ELLIE. Who?

MRS HUSHABYE. Who! Him. He. It [*pointing after Mazzini*]. "Graver, solider tastes," indeed!

ELLIE [*aghast*] You dont mean that you were speaking like that of my father!

MRS HUSHABYE. I was. You know I was.

ELLIE [*with dignity*] I will leave your house at once. [*She turns to the door*].

MRS HUSHABYE. If you attempt it, I'll tell your father why.

ELLIE [*turning again*] Oh! How can you treat a visitor like this, Mrs Hushabye?

MRS HUSHABYE. I thought you were going to call me Hesione.

ELLIE. Certainly not now?

MRS HUSHABYE. Very well: I'll tell your father.

ELLIE [*distressed*] Oh!

MRS HUSHABYE. If you turn a hair—if you take his part against me and against your own heart for a moment, I'll give that born soldier of freedom a piece of my mind that will stand him on his selfish old head for a week.

ELLIE. Hesione! My father selfish! How little you know—

She is interrupted by Mazzini, who returns, excited and perspiring.

MAZZINI. Ellie: Mangan has come: I thought youd like to know. Excuse me, Mrs Hushabye: the strange old gentleman—

MRS HUSHABYE. Papa. Quite so.

MAZZINI. Oh, I beg your pardon: of course: I was a little confused by his manner. He is making Mangan help him with something in the garden; and he wants me too—

A powerful whistle is heard.

THE CAPTAIN'S VOICE. Bosun ahoy! [*the whistle is repeated*].

MAZZINI [*flustered*] Oh dear! I believe he is whistling for me [*He hurries out*].

MRS HUSHABYE. Now my father is a wonderful man if you like.

ELLIE. Hesione: listen to me. You dont understand. My father and Mr Mangan were boys together. Mr Ma—

MRS HUSHABYE. I dont care what they were: we must sit down if you are going to begin as far back as that [*She snatches at Ellie's waist, and makes her sit down on the sofa beside her*]. Now, pettikins: tell me all about Mr Mangan. They call him Boss Mangan, dont they? He is a Napoleon of industry and disgustingly rich, isnt he? Why isnt your father rich?

ELLIE. My poor father should never have been in business. His parents were poets; and they gave him the noblest ideas; but they could not afford to give him a profession.

MRS HUSHABYE. Fancy your grandparents, with their eyes in fine frenzy rolling! And so your poor father had to go into business. Hasnt he succeeded in it?

ELLIE. He always used to say he could succeed if he only had some capital. He fought his way along, to keep a roof over our heads and bring us up well; but it was always a struggle: always the same difficulty of not having capital enough. I dont know how to describe it to you.

MRS HUSHABYE. Poor Ellie! I know. Pulling the devil by the tail.

ELLIE [*hurt*] Oh no. Not like that. It was at least dignified.

MRS HUSHABYE. That made it all the harder, didnt it? *I* shouldnt have pulled the devil by the tail with dignity. I should have pulled hard— [*between her teeth*] h a r d. Well? Go on.

ELLIE. At last it seemed that all our troubles were at an end. Mr Mangan did an extraordinarily noble thing out of pure friendship for my father and respect for his character. He asked him how much capital he wanted, and gave it to him. I dont mean that he lent it to him, or that he invested it in his business. He just simply made him a present of it. Wasnt that splendid of him?

MRS HUSHABYE. On condition that you married him?

ELLIE. Oh no, no, no. This was when I was a child. He had never even seen me: he never came to our house. It was absolutely disinterested. Pure generosity.

MRS HUSHABYE. Oh! I beg the gentleman's pardon. Well, what became of the money?

ELLIE. We all got new clothes and moved into another house. And I went to another school for two years.

MRS HUSHABYE. Only two years?

ELLIE. That was all; for at the end of two years my father was utterly ruined.

MRS HUSHABYE. How?

ELLIE. I dont know. I never could understand. But it was dreadful. When we were poor my father had never been in debt. But when he launched out into business on a large scale, he had to incur liabilities. When the business went into liquidation he owed more money than Mr Mangan had given him.

MRS HUSHABYE. Bit off more than he could chew, I suppose.

ELLIE. I think you are a little unfeeling about it.

MRS HUSHABYE. My pettikins: you mustnt mind my way of talking. I was quite as sensitive and particular as you once; but I have picked up so much slang from the children that I am really hardly presentable. I suppose your father had no head for business, and made a mess of it.

ELLIE. Oh, that just shews how entirely you are mistaken about him. The business turned out a great success. It now pays forty-four per cent after deducting the excess profits tax.

MRS HUSHABYE. Then why arnt you rolling in money?

ELLIE. I dont know. It seems very unfair to me. You see, my father was made bankrupt. It nearly broke his heart, because he had persuaded several of his friends to put money into the business. He was sure it would succeed; and events proved that he was quite right. But they all lost their money. It was dreadful. I dont know what we should have done but for Mr Mangan.

MRS HUSHABYE. What! Did the Boss come to the rescue again, after all his money being thrown away?

ELLIE. He did indeed, and never uttered a reproach to my father. He bought what was left of the business—the buildings and the machinery and things—from the official trustee for enough money to enable my father to pay six and eightpence in the pound and get his discharge. Everyone pitied papa so much, and saw so plainly that he was an honorable man, that they let him off at six-and-eightpence instead of ten shillings. Then Mr Mangan started a company to take up the business, and made my father a manager in it to save us from starvation; for I wasnt earning anything then.

MRS HUSHABYE. Quite a romance. And when did the Boss develop the tender passion?

ELLIE. Oh, that was years after, quite lately. He took the chair one night at a sort of people's concert. I was singing there. As an amateur, you know: half a guinea for expenses and three songs with three encores. He was so pleased with my singing that he asked might he walk home with me. I never saw anyone so taken aback as he was when I took him home and introduced him to my father: his own manager. It was then that my father told me how nobly he had behaved. Of course it was considered a great chance for me, as he is so rich. And—and—we drifted into a sort of understanding—I suppose I should call it an engagement—[*she is distressed and cannot go on*].

MRS HUSHABYE [*rising and marching about*] You may have drifted into it; but you will bounce out of it, my pettikins, if I am to have anything to do with it.

ELLIE [*hopelessly*] No: it's no use. I am bound in honor and gratitude. I will go through with it.

MRS HUSHABYE [*behind the sofa, scolding down at her*] You know, of course, that it's not honorable or grateful to marry a man you dont love. Do you love this Mangan man?

ELLIE. Yes. At least—

MRS HUSHABYE. I dont want to know about "the least": I want to know the worst. Girls of your age fall in love with all sorts of impossible people, especially old people.

ELLIE. I like Mr Mangan very much; and I shall always be—

MRS HUSHABYE [*impatiently completing the sentence and prancing away intolerantly to starboard*]—grateful to him for his kindness to dear father. I know. Anybody else?

ELLIE. What do you mean?

MRS HUSHABYE. Anybody else? Are you in love with anybody else?

ELLIE. Of course not.

MRS HUSHABYE. Humph! [*The book on the drawing-table catches her eye. She picks it up, and evidently finds the title very unexpected. She looks at Ellie, and asks, quaintly*] Quite sure youre not in love with an actor?

ELLIE. No, no. Why? What put such a thing into your head?

MRS HUSHABYE. This is yours, isnt it? Why else should you be reading Othello?

ELLIE. My father taught me to love Shakespear.

MRS HUSHABYE [*flinging the book down on the table*] Really! your father does seem to be about the limit.

ELLIE [*naïvely*] Do you never read Shakespear, Hesione? That seems to me so extraordinary. I like Othello.

MRS HUSHABYE. Do you indeed? He was jealous, wasnt he?
ELLIE. Oh, not that. I think all the part about jealousy is horrible. But dont you think it must have been a wonderful experience for Desdemona, brought up so quietly at home, to meet a man who had been out in the world doing all sorts of brave things and having terrible adventures, and yet finding something in her that made him love to sit and talk with her and tell her about them?
MRS HUSHABYE. Thats your idea of romance, is it?
ELLIE. Not romance, exactly. It might really happen.

Ellie's eyes shew that she is not arguing, but in a daydream. Mrs Hushabye, watching her inquisitively, goes deliberately back to the sofa and resumes her seat beside her.

MRS HUSHABYE. Ellie darling: have you noticed that some of those stories that Othello told Desdemona couldnt have happened?
ELLIE. Oh no. Shakespear thought they could have happened.
MRS HUSHABYE. Hm! Desdemona thought they could have happened. But they didnt.
ELLIE. Why do you look so enigmatic about it? You are such a sphinx: I never know what you mean.
MRS HUSHABYE. Desdemona would have found him out if she had lived, you know. I wonder was that why he strangled her!
ELLIE. Othello was not telling lies.
MRS HUSHABYE. How do you know?
ELLIE. Shakespear would have said if he was. Hesione: there are men who have done wonderful things: men like Othello, only, of course, white, and very handsome, and—
MRS HUSHABYE. Ah! Now we're coming to it. Tell me all about him. I knew there must be somebody, or youd never have been so miserable about Mangan: youd have thought it quite a lark to marry him.
ELLIE [*blushing vividly*] Hesione: you are dreadful. But I dont want to make a secret of it, though of course I dont tell everybody. Besides, I dont know him.
MRS HUSHABYE. Dont know him! What does that mean?
ELLIE. Well, of course I know him to speak to.
MRS HUSHABYE. But you want to know him ever so much more intimately, eh?
ELLIE. No no: I know him quite—almost intimately.
MRS HUSHABYE. You dont know him; and you know him almost intimately. How lucid!

ELLIE. I mean that he does not call on us. I—I got into conversation with him by chance at a concert.

MRS HUSHABYE. You seem to have rather a gay time at your concerts, Ellie.

ELLIE. Not at all: we talk to everyone in the greenroom waiting for our turns. I thought he was one of the artists: he looked so splendid. But he was only one of the committee. I happened to tell him that I was copying a picture at the National Gallery. I make a little money that way. I cant paint much; but as it's always the same picture I can do it pretty quickly and get two or three pounds for it. It happened that he came to the National Gallery one day.

MRS HUSHABYE. One student's day. Paid sixpence to stumble about through a crowd of easels, when he might have come in next day for nothing and found the floor clear! Quite by accident?

ELLIE [*triumphantly*] No. On purpose. He liked talking to me. He knows lots of the most splendid people. Fashionable women who are all in love with him. But he ran away from them to see me at the National Gallery and persuade me to come with him for a drive round Richmond Park in a taxi.

MRS HUSHABYE. My pettikins, you have been going it. It's wonderful what you good girls can do without anyone saying a word.

ELLIE. I am not in society, Hesione. If I didnt make acquaintances in that way I shouldnt have any at all.

MRS HUSHABYE. Well, no harm if you know how to take care of yourself. May I ask his name?

ELLIE [*slowly and musically*] Marcus Darnley.

MRS HUSHABYE [*echoing the music*] Marcus Darnley! What a splendid name!

ELLIE. Oh, I'm so glad you think so. I think so too; but I was afraid it was only a silly fancy of my own.

MRS HUSHABYE. Hm! Is he one of the Aberdeen Darnleys?

ELLIE. Nobody knows. Just fancy! He was found in an antique chest—

MRS HUSHABYE. A what?

ELLIE. An antique chest, one summer morning in a rose garden, after a night of the most terrible thunderstorm.

MRS HUSHABYE. What on earth was he doing in the chest? Did he get into it because he was afraid of the lightning?

ELLIE. Oh no, no: he was a baby. The name Marcus Darnley was embroidered on his babyclothes. And five hundred pounds in gold.

MRS HUSHABYE [*looking hard at her*] Ellie!

ELLIE. The garden of the Viscount—

MRS HUSHABYE. —de Rougemont?

ELLIE [*innocently*] No: de Larochejaquelin. A French family. A vicomte. His life has been one long romance. A tiger—

MRS HUSHABYE. Slain by his own hand?

ELLIE. Oh no: nothing vulgar like that. He saved the life of the tiger from a hunting party: one of King Edward's hunting parties in India. The King was furious: that was why he never had his military services properly recognized. But he doesnt care. He is a Socialist and despises rank, and has been in three revolutions fighting on the barricades.

MRS HUSHABYE. How can you sit there telling me such lies? You, Ellie, of all people! And I thought you were a perfectly simple, straightforward, good girl.

ELLIE [*rising, dignified but very angry*] Do you mean to say you dont believe me?

MRS HUSHABYE. Of course I dont believe you. Youre inventing every word of it. Do you take me for a fool?

Ellie stares at her. Her candor is so obvious that Mrs Hushabye is puzzled.

ELLIE. Goodbye, Hesione. I'm very sorry. I see now that it sounds very improbable as I tell it. But I cant stay if you think that way about me.

MRS HUSHABYE [*catching her dress*] You shant go. I couldnt be so mistaken: I know too well what liars are like. Somebody has really told you all this.

ELLIE [*flushing*] Hesione: dont say that you dont believe him. I couldnt bear that.

MRS HUSHABYE [*soothing her*] Of course I believe him, dearest. But you should have broken it to me by degrees. [*Drawing her back to her seat*] Now tell me all about him. Are you in love with him?

ELLIE. Oh no. I'm not so foolish. I dont fall in love with people. I'm not so silly as you think.

MRS HUSHABYE. I see. Only something to think about—to give some interest and pleasure to life.

ELLIE. Just so. Thats all, really.

MRS HUSHABYE. It makes the hours go fast, doesnt it? No tedious waiting to go to sleep at nights and wondering whether you will have a bad night. How delightful it makes waking up in the morning! How much better than the happiest dream! All life transfigured! No more wishing one had an interesting book to read, because life is so much happier than any book! No desire but to be alone and not to have to talk to anyone: to be alone and just think about it.

ELLIE [*embracing her*] Hesione: you are a witch. How do you know? Oh, you are the most sympathetic woman in the world.

MRS HUSHABYE [*caressing her*] Pettikins, my pettikins: how I envy you! and how I pity you!

ELLIE. Pity me! Oh, why?

A very handsome man of fifty, with mousquetaire moustaches, wearing a rather dandified curly brimmed hat, and carrying an elaborate walking-stick, comes into the room from the hall, and stops short at sight of the women on the sofa.

ELLIE [*seeing him and rising in glad surprise*] Oh! Hesione: this is Mr Marcus Darnley.

MRS HUSHABYE [*rising*] What a lark! He is my husband.

ELLIE. But how—[*she stops suddenly; then turns pale and sways*].

MRS HUSHABYE [*catching her and sitting down with her on the sofa*] Steady, my pettikins.

THE MAN [*with a mixture of confusion and effrontery, depositing his hat and stick on the teak table*] My real name, Miss Dunn, is Hector Hushabye. I leave you to judge whether that is a name any sensitive man would care to confess to. I never use it when I can possibly help it. I have been away for nearly a month; and I had no idea you knew my wife, or that you were coming here. I am none the less delighted to find you in our little house.

ELLIE [*in great distress*] I dont know what to do. Please, may I speak to Papa? Do leave me. I cant bear it.

MRS HUSHABYE. Be off, Hector.

HECTOR. I—

MRS HUSHABYE. Quick, quick. Get out.

HECTOR. If you think it better—[*he goes out, taking his hat with him but leaving the stick on the table*].

MRS HUSHABYE [*laying Ellie down at the end of the sofa*] Now, pettikins, he is gone. Theres nobody but me. You can let yourself go. Dont try to control yourself. Have a good cry.

ELLIE [*raising her head*] Damn!

MRS HUSHABYE. Splendid! Oh, what a relief! I thought you were going to be broken-hearted. Never mind me. Damn him again.

ELLIE. I am not damning him: I am damning myself for being such a fool. [*Rising*] How could I let myself be taken in so? [*She begins *prowling to and fro, her bloom gone, looking curiously older and harder*].

MRS HUSHABYE [*cheerfully*] Why not, pettikins? Very few young women can resist Hector. I couldnt when I was your age. He is really rather splendid, you know.

ELLIE [*turning on her*] Splendid! Yes: splendid l o o k i n g, of course. But how can you love a liar?

MRS HUSHABYE. I dont know. But you can, fortunately. Otherwise there wouldnt be much love in the world.

ELLIE. But to lie like that! To be a boaster! a coward!

MRS HUSHABYE [*rising in alarm*] Pettikins: none of that, if you please. If you hint the slightest doubt of Hector's courage, he will go straight off and do the most horribly dangerous things to convince himself that he isnt a coward. He has a dreadful trick of getting out of one third-floor window and coming in at another, just to test his nerve. He has a whole drawerful of Albert Medals for saving people's lives.

ELLIE. He never told me that.

MRS HUSHABYE. He never boasts of anything he really did: he cant bear it; and it makes him shy if anyone else does. All his stories are made-up stories.

ELLIE [*coming to her*] Do you mean that he is really brave, and really has adventures, and yet tells lies about things that he never did and that never happened?

MRS HUSHABYE. Yes, pettikins, I do. People dont have their virtues and vices in sets: they have them anyhow: all mixed.

ELLIE [*staring at her thoughtfully*] Theres something odd about this house, Hesione, and even about you. I dont know why I'm talking to you so calmly. I have a horrible fear that my heart is broken, but that heartbreak is not like what I thought it must be.

MRS HUSHABYE [*fondling her*] It's only life educating you, pettikins. How do you feel about Boss Mangan now?

ELLIE [*disengaging herself with an expression of distaste*] Oh, how can you remind me of him, Hesione?

MRS HUSHABYE. Sorry, dear. I think I hear Hector coming back. You dont mind now, do you, dear?

ELLIE. Not in the least. I am quite cured.

Mazzini Dunn and Hector come in from the hall.

HECTOR [*as he opens the door and allows Mazzini to pass in*] One second more, and she would have been a dead woman!

MAZZINI. Dear! dear! what an escape! Ellie, my love: Mr Hushabye has just been telling me the most extraordinary—

ELLIE. Yes: Ive heard it [*She crosses to the other side of the room*].

HECTOR [*following her*] Not this one: I'll tell it to you after dinner. I think youll like it. The truth is, I made it up for you, and was looking forward to the pleasure of telling it to you. But in a moment of impatience at being turned out of the room, I threw it away on your father.

ELLIE [*turning at bay with her back to the carpenter's bench, scornfully self-possessed*] It was not thrown away. He believes it. I should not have believed it.

MAZZINI [*benevolently*] Ellie is very naughty, Mr Hushabye. Of course she does not really think that. [*He goes to the bookshelves, and inspects the titles of the volumes*].

Boss Mangan comes in from the hall, followed by the Captain. Mangan, carefully frock-coated as for church or for a directors meeting, is about fiftyfive, with a careworn, mistrustful expression, standing a little on an entirely imaginary dignity, with a dull complexion, straight, lustreless hair, and features so entirely commonplace that it is impossible to describe them.

CAPTAIN SHOTOVER [*to Mrs Hushabye, introducing the newcomer*] Says his name is Mangan. Not able-bodied.

MRS HUSHABYE [*graciously*] How do you do, Mr Mangan?

MANGAN [*shaking hands*] Very pleased.

CAPTAIN SHOTOVER. Dunn's lost his muscle, but recovered his nerve. Men seldom do after three attacks of delirium tremens [*he goes into the pantry*].

MRS HUSHABYE. I congratulate you, Mr Dunn.

MAZZINI [*dazed*] I am a lifelong teetotaler.

MRS HUSHABYE. You will find it far less trouble to let papa have his own way than try to explain.

MAZZINI. But three attacks of delirium tremens, really!

MRS HUSHABYE [*to Mangan*] Do you know my husband, Mr Mangan [*she indicates Hector*].

MANGAN [*going to Hector, who meets him with outstretched hand*] Very pleased. [*Turning to Ellie*] I hope, Miss Ellie, you have not found the journey down too fatiguing. [*They shake hands*].

MRS HUSHABYE. Hector: shew Mr Dunn his room.

HECTOR. Certainly. Come along, Mr Dunn. [*He takes Mazzini out*].

ELLIE. You havnt shewn me my room yet, Hesione.

MRS HUSHABYE. How stupid of me! Come along. Make yourself quite at home, Mr Mangan. Papa will entertain you. [*She calls to the Captain in the pantry*] Papa: come and explain the house to Mr Mangan.

She goes out with Ellie. The Captain comes from the pantry.

CAPTAIN SHOTOVER. Youre going to marry Dunn's daughter. Dont. Youre too old.

MANGAN [*staggered*] Well! Thats fairly blunt, Captain.

CAPTAIN SHOTOVER. It's true.

MANGAN. She doesnt think so.

CAPTAIN SHOTOVER. She does.

MANGAN. Older men than I have—

CAPTAIN SHOTOVER [*finishing the sentence for him*]—made fools of themselves. That, also, is true.

MANGAN [*asserting himself*] I dont see that this is any business of yours.

CAPTAIN SHOTOVER. It is everybody's business. The stars in their courses are shaken when such things happen.

MANGAN. I'm going to marry her all the same.

CAPTAIN SHOTOVER. How do you know?

MANGAN [*playing the strong man*] I intend to. I mean to. See? I never made up my mind to do a thing yet that I didnt bring it off. Thats the sort of man I am; and there will be a better understanding between us when you make up your mind to that, Captain.

CAPTAIN SHOTOVER. You frequent picture palaces.

MANGAN. Perhaps I do. Who told you?

CAPTAIN SHOTOVER. Talk like a man, not like a movy. You mean that you make a hundred thousand a year.

MANGAN. I dont boast. But when I meet a man that makes a hundred thousand a year, I take off my hat to that man, and stretch out my hand to him and call him brother.

CAPTAIN SHOTOVER. Then you also make a hundred thousand a year, hey?

MANGAN. No. I cant say that. Fifty thousand, perhaps.

CAPTAIN SHOTOVER. His half brother only [*he turns away from Mangan with his usual abruptness, and collects the empty tea-cups on the Chinese tray*].

MANGAN [*irritated*] See here, Captain Shotover. I dont quite understand my position here. I came here on your daughter's invitation. Am I in her house or in yours?

CAPTAIN SHOTOVER. You are beneath the dome of heaven, in the house of God. What is true within these walls is true outside them. Go out on the seas; climb the mountains; wander through the valleys. She is still too young.

MANGAN [*weakening*] But I'm very little over fifty.

CAPTAIN SHOTOVER. You are still less under sixty. Boss Mangan: you will not marry the pirate's child [*he carries the tray away into the pantry*].

MANGAN [*following him to the half door*] What pirate's child? What are you talking about?

CAPTAIN SHOTOVER [*in the pantry*] Ellie Dunn. You will not marry her.

MANGAN. Who will stop me?

CAPTAIN SHOTOVER [*emerging*] My daughter [*he makes for the door leading to the hall*].

MANGAN [*following him*] Mrs Hushabye! Do you mean to say she brought me down here to break it off?

CAPTAIN SHOTOVER [*stopping and turning on him*] I know nothing more than I have seen in her eye. She will break it off. Take my advice: marry a West Indian negress: they make excellent wives. I was married to one myself for two years.

MANGAN. Well, I am damned!

CAPTAIN SHOTOVER. I thought so. I was, too, for many years. The negress redeemed me.

MANGAN [*feebly*] This is queer. I ought to walk out of this house.

CAPTAIN SHOTOVER. Why?

MANGAN. Well, many men would be offended by your style of talking.

CAPTAIN SHOTOVER. Nonsense! It's the other sort of talking that makes quarrels. Nobody ever quarrels with me.

A gentleman, whose firstrate tailoring and frictionless manners proclaim the wellbred West Ender, comes in from the hall. He has an engaging air of being young and unmarried, but on close inspection is found to be at least over forty.

THE GENTLEMAN. Excuse my intruding in this fashion; but there is no knocker on the door; and the bell does not seem to ring.

CAPTAIN SHOTOVER. Why should there be a knocker? Why should the bell ring? The door is open.

THE GENTLEMAN. Precisely. So I ventured to come in.

CAPTAIN SHOTOVER. Quite right. I will see about a room for you [*he makes for the door*].

THE GENTLEMAN [*stopping him*] But I'm afraid you dont know who I am.

CAPTAIN SHOTOVER. Do you suppose that at my age I make distinctions between one fellowcreature and another? [*He goes out. Mangan and the newcomer stare at one another*].

MANGAN. Strange character, Captain Shotover, sir.

THE GENTLEMAN. Very.

CAPTAIN SHOTOVER [*shouting outside*] Hesione: another person has arrived and wants a room. Man about town, well dressed, fifty.

THE GENTLEMAN. Fancy Hesione's feelings! May I ask are you a member of the family?

MANGAN. No.

THE GENTLEMAN. I am. At least a connexion.

Mrs Hushabye comes back.

MRS HUSHABYE. How do you do? How good of you to come!

THE GENTLEMAN. I am very glad indeed to make your acquaintance, Hesione. [*Instead of taking her hand he kisses her. At the same moment the Captain appears in the doorway*]. You will excuse my kissing your daughter, Captain, when I tell you that—

CAPTAIN SHOTOVER. Stuff! Everyone kisses my daughter. Kiss her as much as you like [*he makes for the pantry*].

THE GENTLEMAN. Thank you. One moment, Captain. [*The Captain halts and turns. The gentleman goes to him affably*]. Do you happen to remember—but probably you dont, as it occurred many years ago—that your younger daughter married a numskull.

CAPTAIN SHOTOVER. Yes. She said she'd marry anybody to get away from this house. I should not have recognized you: your head is no longer like a walnut. Your aspect is softened. You have been boiled in bread and milk for years and years, like other married men. Poor devil! [*He disappears into the pantry*].

MRS HUSHABYE [*going past Mangan to the gentleman and scrutinizing him*] I dont believe you are Hastings Utterword.

THE GENTLEMAN. I am not.

MRS HUSHABYE. Then what business had you to kiss me?

THE GENTLEMAN. I thought I would like to. The fact is, I am Randall Utterword, the unworthy younger brother of Hastings. I was abroad diplomatizing when he was married.

LADY UTTERWORD [*dashing in*] Hesione: where is the key of the wardrobe in my room? My diamonds are in my dressing-bag: I must lock it up—[*recognizing the stranger with a shock*] Randall: how dare you?

[*She marches at him past Mrs Hushabye, who retreats and joins Mangan near the sofa*].

RANDALL. How dare I what? I am not doing anything.

LADY UTTERWORD. Who told you I was here?

RANDALL. Hastings. You had just left when I called on you at Claridge's; so I followed you down here. You are looking extremely well.

LADY UTTERWORD. Dont presume to tell me so.

MRS HUSHABYE. What is wrong with Mr Randall, Addy?

LADY UTTERWORD [*recollecting herself*] Oh, nothing. But he has no right to come bothering you and papa without being invited [*she goes to the window-seat and sits down, turning away from them ill-humoredly and looking into the garden, where Hector and Ellie are now seen strolling together*].

MRS HUSHABYE. I think you have not met Mr Mangan, Addy.

LADY UTTERWORD [*turning her head and nodding coldly to Mangan*] I beg your pardon. Randall: you have flustered me so: I made a perfect fool of myself.

MRS HUSHABYE. Lady Utterword. My sister. My y o u n g e r sister.

MANGAN [*bowing*] Pleased to meet you, Lady Utterword.

LADY UTTERWORD [*with marked interest*] Who is that gentleman walking in the garden with Miss Dunn?

MRS HUSHABYE. I dont know. She quarrelled mortally with my husband only ten minutes ago; and I didn't know anyone else had come. It must be a visitor. [*She goes to the window to look*]. Oh, it is Hector. Theyve made it up.

LADY UTTERWORD. Your husband! That handsome man?

MRS HUSHABYE. Well, why shouldnt my husband be a handsome man?

RANDALL [*joining them at the window*] One's husband never is, Ariadne [*he sits by Lady Utterword, on her right*].

MRS HUSHABYE. One's sister's husband always is, Mr Randall.

LADY UTTERWORD. Dont be vulgar, Randall. And you, Hesione, are just as bad.

Ellie and Hector come in from the garden by the starboard door. Randall rises. Ellie retires into the corner near the pantry. Hector comes forward; and Lady Utterword rises looking her very best.

MRS HUSHABYE. Hector: this is Addy.

HECTOR [*apparently surprised*] Not this lady.

LADY UTTERWORD [*smiling*] Why not?

HECTOR [*looking at her with a piercing glance of deep but respectful admiration, his moustache bristling*] I thought—[*pulling himself together*] I beg your pardon, Lady Utterword. I am extremely glad to welcome you at last under our roof [*he offers his hand with grave courtesy*].

MRS HUSHABYE. She wants to be kissed, Hector.

LADY UTTERWORD. Hesione! [*but she still smiles*].

MRS HUSHABYE. Call her Addy; and kiss her like a good brother-in-law; and have done with it. [*She leaves them to themselves*].

HECTOR. Behave yourself, Hesione. Lady Utterword is entitled not only to hospitality but to civilization.

LADY UTTERWORD [*gratefully*] Thank you, Hector. [*They shake hands cordially*].

Mazzini Dunn is seen crossing the garden from starboard to port.

CAPTAIN SHOTOVER [*coming from the pantry and addressing Ellie*] Your father has washed himself.

ELLIE [*quite self-possessed*] He often does, Captain Shotover.

CAPTAIN SHOTOVER. A strange conversion! I saw him through the pantry window.

Mazzini Dunn enters through the port window door, newly washed and brushed, and stops, smiling benevolently, between Mangan and Mrs Hushabye.

MRS HUSHABYE [*introducing*] Mr Mazzini Dunn, Lady Ut—oh, I forgot: youve met. [*Indicating Ellie*] Miss Dunn.

MAZZINI [*walking across the room to take Ellie's hand, and beaming at his own naughty irony*] I have met Miss Dunn also. She is my daughter. [*He draws her arm through his caressingly*].

MRS HUSHABYE. Of course: how stupid! Mr Utterword, my sister's-er-

RANDALL [*shaking hands agreeably*] Her brother-in-law, Mr Dunn. How do you do?

MRS HUSHABYE. This is my husband.

HECTOR. We have met, dear. Dont introduce us any more. [*He moves away to the big chair, and adds*] Wont you sit down, Lady Utterword? [*She does so very graciously*].

MRS HUSHABYE. Sorry. I hate it: it's like making people shew their tickets.

MAZZINI [*sententiously*] How little it tells us, after all! The great question is, not who we are, but what we are.

CAPTAIN SHOTOVER. Ha! What are you?

MAZZINI [*taken aback*] What am I?

CAPTAIN SHOTOVER. A thief, a pirate, and a murderer.

MAZZINI. I assure you you are mistaken.

CAPTAIN SHOTOVER. An adventurous life; but what does it end in? Respectability. A ladylike daughter. The language and appearance of a city missionary. Let it be a warning to all of you [*he goes out through the garden*].

DUNN. I hope nobody here believes that I am a thief, a pirate, or a murderer. Mrs Hushabye: will you excuse me a moment? I must really go and explain. [*He follows the Captain*].

MRS HUSHABYE [*as he goes*] It's no use. Youd really better—[*but Dunn has vanished*] We had better all go out and look for some tea. We never have regular tea; but you can always get some when you want: the servants keep it stewing all day. The kitchen veranda is the best place to ask. May I shew you? [*She goes to the starboard door*].

RANDALL [*going with her*] Thank you, I dont think I'll take any tea this afternoon. But if you will shew me the garden—?

MRS HUSHABYE. Theres nothing to see in the garden except papa's observatory, and a gravel pit with a cave where he keeps dynamite and things of that sort. However, it's pleasanter out of doors: so come along.

RANDALL. Dynamite! Isnt that rather risky?

MRS HUSHABYE. Well, we dont sit in the gravel pit when theres a thunderstorm.

LADY UTTERWORD. Thats something new. What is the dynamite for?

HECTOR. To blow up the human race if it goes too far. He is trying to discover a psychic ray that will explode all the explosives at the will of a Mahatma.

ELLIE. The Captain's tea is delicious, Mr Utterword.

MRS HUSHABYE [*stopping in the doorway*] Do you mean to say that youve had some of my father's tea? that you got round him before you were ten minutes in the house?

ELLIE. I did.

MRS HUSHABYE. You little devil! [*She goes out with Randall*].

MANGAN. Wont you come, Miss Ellie?

ELLIE. I'm too tired. I'll take a book up to my room and rest a little. [*She goes to the bookshelf*].

MANGAN. Right. You cant do better. But I'm disappointed. [*He follows Randall and Mrs Hushabye*].

Ellie, Hector, and Lady Utterword are left. Hector is close to Lady Utterword. They look at Ellie, waiting for her to go.

ELLIE [*looking at the title of a book*] Do you like stories of adventure, Lady Utterword?

LADY UTTERWORD [*patronizingly*] Of course, dear.

ELLIE. Then I'll leave you to Mr Hushabye. [*She goes out through the hall*].

HECTOR. That girl is mad about tales of adventure. The lies I have to tell her!

LADY UTTERWORD [*not interested in Ellie*] When you saw me what did you mean by saying that you thought, and then stopping short? What did you think?

HECTOR [*folding his arms and looking down at her magnetically*] May I tell you?

LADY UTTERWORD. Of course.

HECTOR. It will not sound very civil. I was on the point of saying "I thought you were a plain woman."

LADY UTTERWORD. Oh for shame, Hector! What right had you to notice whether I am plain or not?

HECTOR. Listen to me Ariadne. Until today I have seen only photographs of you; and no photograph can give the strange fascination of the daughters of that supernatural old man. There is some damnable quality in them that destroys men's moral sense, and carries them beyond honor and dishonor. You know that, dont you?

LADY UTTERWORD. Perhaps I do, Hector. But let me warn you once for all that I am a rigidly conventional woman. You may think because I'm a Shotover that I'm a Bohemian, because we are all so horribly Bohemian. But I'm not. I hate and loathe Bohemianism. No child brought up in a strict Puritan household ever suffered from Puritanism as I suffered from our Bohemianism.

HECTOR. Our children are like that. They spend their holidays in the houses of their respectable schoolfellows.

LADY UTTERWORD. I shall invite them for Christmas.

HECTOR. Their absence leaves us both without our natural chaperons.

LADY UTTERWORD. Children are certainly very inconvenient sometimes. But intelligent people can always manage, unless they are Bohemians.

HECTOR. You are no Bohemian; but you are no Puritan either: your attraction is alive and powerful. What sort of woman do you count yourself?

LADY UTTERWORD. I am a woman of the world, Hector; and I can assure you that if you will only take the trouble always to do the perfectly correct thing, and to say the perfectly correct thing, you can do just what you like. An ill-conducted, careless woman gets simply no chance. An ill-conducted, careless man is never allowed within arms length of any woman worth knowing.

HECTOR. I see. You are neither a Bohemian woman nor a Puritan woman. You are a dangerous woman.

LADY UTTERWORD. On the contrary, I am a safe woman.

HECTOR. You are a most accursedly attractive woman. Mind: I am not making love to you. I do not like being attracted. But you had better know how I feel if you are going to stay here.

LADY UTTERWORD. You are an exceedingly clever lady-killer, Hector. And terribly handsome. I am quite a good player, myself, at that game. Is it quite understood that we are only playing?

HECTOR. Quite. I am deliberately playing the fool, out of sheer worthlessness.

LADY UTTERWORD [*rising brightly*] Well, you are my brother-in-law. Hesione asked you to kiss me. [*He seizes her in his arms, and kisses her strenuously*]. Oh! that was a little more than play, brother-in-law. [*She pushes him suddenly away*]. You shall not do that again.

HECTOR. In effect, you got your claws deeper into me than I intended.

MRS HUSHABYE [*coming in from the garden*] Dont let me disturb you: I only want a cap to put on daddiest. The sun is setting; and he'll catch cold [*she makes for the door leading to the hall*].

LADY UTTERWORD. Your husband is quite charming, darling. He has actually condescended to kiss me at last. I shall go into the garden: it's cooler now [*she goes out by the port door*].

MRS HUSHABYE. Take care, dear child. I dont believe any man can kiss Addy without falling in love with her. [*She goes into the hall*].

HECTOR [*striking himself on the chest*] Fool! Goat!

Mrs Hushabye comes back with the Captain's cap.

HECTOR. Your sister is an extremely enterprising old girl. Wheres Miss Dunn?

MRS HUSHABYE. Mangan says she has gone up to her room for a nap. Addy wont let you talk to Ellie: she has marked you for her own.

HECTOR. She has the diabolical family fascination. I began making love to her automatically. What am I to do? I cant fall in love; I cant hurt a woman's feelings by telling her so when she falls in love with me. And as women are always falling in love with my moustache I get landed in all sorts of tedious and terrifying flirtations in which I'm not a bit in earnest.

MRS HUSHABYE. Oh, neither is Addy. She has never been in love in her life, though she has always been trying to fall in head over ears. She is worse than you, because you had one real go at least, with me.

HECTOR. That was a confounded madness. I cant believe that such an amazing experience is common. It has left its mark on me. I believe that is why I have never been able to repeat it.

MRS HUSHABYE [*laughing and caressing his arm*] We were frightfully in love with one another, Hector. It was such an enchanting dream that I have never been able to grudge it to you or anyone else since. I have invited all sorts of pretty women to the house on the chance of giving you another turn. But it has never come off.

HECTOR. I dont know that I want it to come off. It was damned dangerous. You fascinated me; but I loved you; so it was heaven. This sister of yours fascinates me; but I hate her; so it is hell. I shall kill her if she persists.

MRS HUSHABYE. Nothing will kill Addy: she is as strong as a horse. [*Releasing him*] Now *I* am going off to fascinate somebody.

HECTOR. The Foreign Office toff? Randall?

MRS HUSHABYE. Goodness gracious, no! Why should I fascinate him?

HECTOR. I presume you dont mean the bloated capitalist, Mangan?

MRS HUSHABYE. Hm! I think he had better be fascinated by me than by Ellie. [*She is going into the garden when the Captain comes in from it with some sticks in his hand*]. What have you got there, daddiest?

CAPTAIN SHOTOVER. Dynamite.

MRS HUSHABYE. Youve been to the gravel pit. Dont drop it about the house: theres a dear. [*She goes into the garden, where the evening light is now very red*].

HECTOR. Listen, O sage. How long dare you concentrate on a feeling without risking having it fixed in your consciousness all the rest of your life?

CAPTAIN SHOTOVER. Ninety minutes. An hour and a half. [*He goes into the pantry*].

Hector, left alone, contracts his brows, and falls into a daydream. He does not move for some time. Then he folds his arms. Then, throwing his hands behind him, and gripping one with the other, he strides tragically once to and fro. Suddenly he snatches his walking-stick from the teak table, and draws it; for it is a sword-stick. He fights a desperate duel with an imaginary antagonist, and after many vicissitudes runs him through the body up to the hilt. He sheathes his sword and throws it on the sofa, falling into another reverie as he does so. He looks straight into the eyes of an imaginary woman; seizes her by the arms; and says in a deep and thrilling tone "Do you love me!" *The Captain comes out of the pantry at this moment; and Hector, caught with his arms stretched out and his fists clenched, has to account for his attitude by going through a series of gymnastic exercises.*

CAPTAIN SHOTOVER. That sort of strength is no good. You will never be as strong as a gorilla.

HECTOR. What is the dynamite for?

CAPTAIN SHOTOVER. To kill fellows like Mangan.

HECTOR. No use. They will always be able to buy more dynamite than you.

CAPTAIN SHOTOVER. I will make a dynamite that he cannot explode.

HECTOR. And that you can, eh?

CAPTAIN SHOTOVER. Yes: when I have attained the seventh degree of concentration.

HECTOR. Whats the use of that? You never do attain it.

CAPTAIN SHOTOVER. What then is to be done? Are we to be kept for ever in the mud by these hogs to whom the universe is nothing but a machine for greasing their bristles and filling their snouts?

HECTOR. Are Mangan's bristles worse than Randall's lovelocks?

CAPTAIN SHOTOVER. We must win powers of life and death over them both. I refuse to die until I have invented the means.

HECTOR. Who are we that we should judge them?

CAPTAIN SHOTOVER. What are they that they should judge us? Yet they do, unhesitatingly. There is enmity between our seed and their seed. They know it and act on it, strangling our souls. They believe in themselves. When we believe in ourselves, we shall kill them.

HECTOR. It is the same seed. You forget that your pirate has a very nice daughter. Mangan's son may be a Plato: Randall's a Shelley. What was my father?

CAPTAIN SHOTOVER. The damndest scoundrel I ever met. [*He replaces the drawing-board; sits down at the table; and begins to mix a wash of color*].

HECTOR. Precisely. Well, dare you kill his innocent grandchildren?

CAPTAIN SHOTOVER. They are mine also.

HECTOR. Just so. We are members one of another. [*He throws himself carelessly on the sofa*]. I tell you I have often thought of this killing of human vermin. Many men have thought of it. Decent men are like Daniel in the lion's den: their survival is a miracle; and they do not always survive. We live among the Mangans and Randalls and Billy Dunns as they, poor devils, live among the disease germs and the doctors and the lawyers and the parsons and the restaurant chefs and the tradesmen and the servants and all the rest of the parasites and blackmailers. What are our terrors to theirs? Give me the power to kill them; and I'll spare them in sheer—

CAPTAIN SHOTOVER [*cutting in sharply*] Fellow feeling?

HECTOR. No. I should kill myself if I believed that. I must believe that my spark, small as it is, is divine, and that the red light over their door is hell fire. I should spare them in simple magnanimous pity.

CAPTAIN SHOTOVER. You cant spare them until you have the power to kill them. At present they have the power to kill you. There are millions of blacks over the water for them to train and let loose on us. Theyre going to do it. Theyre doing it already.

HECTOR. They are too stupid to use their power.

CAPTAIN SHOTOVER [*throwing down his brush and coming to the end of the sofa*] Do not deceive yourself: they do use it. We kill the better half of ourselves every day to propitiate them. The knowledge that these people are there to render all our aspirations barren prevents us having the aspirations. And when we are tempted to seek their destruction they bring forth demons to delude us, disguised as pretty daughters, and singers and poets and the like, for whose sake we spare them.

HECTOR [*sitting up and leaning towards him*] May not Hesione be such a demon, brought forth by you lest I should slay you?

CAPTAIN SHOTOVER. That is possible. She has used you up, and left you nothing but dreams, as some women do.

HECTOR. Vampire women, demon women.

CAPTAIN SHOTOVER. Men think the world well lost for them, and lose it accordingly. Who are the men that do things? The husbands of the shrew and of the drunkard, the men with the thorn in the flesh. [*Walking distractedly away towards the pantry*] I must think these things out. [*Turning suddenly*] But I go on with the dynamite none the less. I will discover a ray mightier than any X-ray: a mind ray that will explode the ammunition in the belt of my adversary before he can point his gun at me. And I must hurry. I am old: I have no time to waste in talk [*he is about to go into the pantry, and Hector is making for the hall, when Hesione comes back*].

MRS HUSHABYE. Daddiest: you and Hector must come and help me to entertain all these people. What on earth were you shouting about?

HECTOR [*stopping in the act of turning the doorhandle*] He is madder than usual.

MRS HUSHABYE. We all are.

HECTOR. I must change [*he resumes his door opening*].

MRS HUSHABYE. Stop, stop. Come back, both of you. Come back [*They return, reluctantly*]. Money is running short.

HECTOR. Money! Where are my April dividends?

MRS HUSHABYE. Where is the snow that fell last year?

CAPTAIN SHOTOVER. Where is all the money you had for that patent lifeboat I invented?

MRS HUSHABYE. Five hundred pounds; and I have made it last since Easter!

CAPTAIN SHOTOVER. Since Easter! Barely four months! Monstrous extravagance! I could live for seven years on £500.

MRS HUSHABYE. Not keeping open house as we do here, daddiest.

CAPTAIN SHOTOVER. Only £500 for that lifeboat! I got twelve thousand for the invention before that.

MRS HUSHABYE. Yes, dear; but that was for the ship with the magnetic keel that sucked up submarines. Living at the rate we do, you cannot afford life-saving inventions. Cant you think of something that will murder half Europe at one bang?

CAPTAIN SHOTOVER. No. I am ageing fast. My mind does not dwell on slaughter as it did when I was a boy. Why doesnt your husband invent something? He does nothing but tell lies to women.

HECTOR. Well, that is a form of invention, is it not? However, you are right: I ought to support my wife.

MRS HUSHABYE. Indeed you shall do nothing of the sort: I should never see you from breakfast to dinner. I want my husband.

HECTOR [*bitterly*] I might as well be your lapdog.

MRS HUSHABYE. Do you want to be my breadwinner, like the other poor husbands?

HECTOR. No, by thunder! What a damned creature a husband is anyhow!

MRS HUSHABYE [*to the Captain*] What about that harpoon cannon?

CAPTAIN SHOTOVER. No use. It kills whales, not men.

MRS HUSHABYE. Why not? You fire the harpoon out of a cannon. It sticks in the enemy's general; you wind him in; and there you are.

HECTOR. You are your father's daughter, Hesione.

CAPTAIN SHOTOVER. There is something in it. Not to wind in generals: they are not dangerous. But one could fire a grapnel and wind in a machine gun or even a tank. I will think it out.

MRS HUSHABYE [*squeezing the Captain's arm affectionately*] Saved!

You *are* a darling, daddiest. Now we must go back to these dreadful people and entertain them.

CAPTAIN SHOTOVER. They have had no dinner. Dont forget that.

HECTOR. Neither have I. And it is dark: it must be all hours.

MRS HUSHABYE. Oh, Guinness will produce some sort of dinner for them. The servants always take jolly good care that there is food in the house.

CAPTAIN SHOTOVER [*raising a strange wail in the darkness*] What a house! What a daughter!

MRS HUSHABYE [*raving*] What a father!

HECTOR [*following suit*] What a husband!

CAPTAIN SHOTOVER. Is there no thunder in heaven?

HECTOR. Is there no beauty, no bravery, on earth?

MRS HUSHABYE. What do men want? They have their food, their firesides, their clothes mended, and our love at the end of the day. Why are they not satisfied? Why do they envy us the pain with which we bring them into the world, and make strange dangers and torments for themselves to be even with us?

CAPTAIN SHOTOVER [*weirdly chanting*]

I builded a house for my daughters, and opened the doors thereof,
That men might come for their choosing, and their betters spring from their love;
But one of them married a numskull;

HECTOR [*taking up the rhythm*]

The other a liar wed;

MRS HUSHABYE [*completing the stanza*]

And now must she lie beside him, even as she made her bed.

LADY UTTERWORD [*calling from the garden*] Hesione! Hesione! Where are you?

HECTOR. The cat is on the tiles.

MRS HUSHABYE. Coming, darling, coming [*she goes quickly into the garden*].

The Captain goes back to his place at the table.

HECTOR [*going into the hall*] Shall I turn up the lights for you?

CAPTAIN SHOTOVER. No. Give me deeper darkness. Money is not made in the light.

ACT II

The same room, with the lights turned up and the curtains drawn. Ellie comes in, followed by Mangan. Both are dressed for dinner. She strolls to the drawing-table. He comes between the table and the wicker chair.

MANGAN. What a dinner! I dont call it a dinner: I call it a meal.

ELLIE. I am accustomed to meals, Mr Mangan, and very lucky to get them. Besides, the captain cooked some macaroni for me.

MANGAN [*shuddering liverishly*] Too rich: I cant eat such things. I suppose it's because I have to work so much with my brain. Thats the worst of being a man of business: you are always thinking, thinking, thinking. By the way, now that we are alone, may I take the opportunity to come to a little understanding with you?

ELLIE [*settling into the draughtsman's seat*] Certainly. I should like to.

MANGAN [*taken aback*] Should you? That surprises me; for I thought I noticed this afternoon that you avoided me all you could. Not for the first time either.

ELLIE. I was very tired and upset. I wasn't used to the ways of this extraordinary house. Please forgive me.

MANGAN. Oh, thats all right: I dont mind. But Captain Shotover has been talking to me about you. You and me, you know.

ELLIE [*interested*] The Captain! What did he say?

MANGAN. Well, he noticed the difference between our ages.

ELLIE. He notices everything.

MANGAN. You dont mind, then?

ELLIE. Of course I know quite well that our engagement—

MANGAN. Oh! you call it an engagement.

ELLIE. Well, isnt it?

MANGAN. Oh, yes, yes: no doubt it is if you hold to it. This is the first time youve used the word; and I didnt quite know where we stood: thats all. [*He sits down in the wicker chair; and resigns himself to allow her to lead the conversation*]. You were saying—?

ELLIE. Was I? I forget. Tell me. Do you like this part of the country? I heard you ask Mr Hushabye at dinner whether there are any nice houses to let down here.

MANGAN. I like the place. The air suits me. I shouldnt be surprised if I settled down here.

ELLIE. Nothing would please me better. The air suits me too. And I want to be near Hesione.

MANGAN [*with growing uneasiness*] The air may suit us; but the question is, should we suit one another? Have you thought about that?

ELLIE. Mr Mangan: we must be sensible, mustnt we? It's no use pretending that we are Romeo and Juliet. But we can get on very well together if we choose to make the best of it. Your kindness of heart will make it easy for me.

MANGAN [*leaning forward, with the beginning of something like deliberate unpleasantness in his voice*] Kindness of heart, eh? I ruined your father, didnt I?

ELLIE. Oh, not intentionally.

MANGAN. Yes I did. Ruined him on purpose.

ELLIE. On purpose!

MANGAN. Not out of ill-nature, you know. And youll admit that I kept a job for him when I had finished with him. But business is business; and I ruined him as a matter of business.

ELLIE. I dont understand how that can be. Are you trying to make me feel that I need not be grateful to you, so that I may choose freely?

MANGAN [*rising aggressively*] No. I mean what I say.

ELLIE. But how could it possibly do you any good to ruin my father? The money he lost was yours.

MANGAN [*with a sour laugh*] W a s mine! It i s mine, Miss Ellie, and all the money the other fellows lost too. [*He shoves his hands into his pockets and shews his teeth*]. I just smoked them out like a hive of bees. What do you say to that? A bit of a shock, eh?

ELLIE. It would have been, this morning. N o w! you cant think how little it matters. But it's quite interesting. Only, you must explain it to me. I dont understand it. [*Propping her elbows on the drawing-board and her chin on her hands, she composes herself to listen with a combination of conscious curiosity with unconscious contempt which provokes him to more and more unpleasantness, and an attempt at patronage of her ignorance*].

MANGAN. Of course you dont understand: what do y o u know about business? You just listen and learn. Your father's business was a new business; and I dont start new businesses: I let other fellows start them. They put all their money and their friends' money into starting them. They wear out their souls and bodies trying to make a success of them. Theyre what you call enthusiasts. But the first dead lift of the thing is too much for them; and they havnt enough financial experience. In a year or so they have either to let the whole show go bust, or sell out to a new lot of fellows for a few deferred ordinary shares: that is, if theyre lucky enough to get anything at all. As likely as not the very same thing happens to the new lot. They put in more money and a couple of years more work; and then perhaps t h e y have to sell out to a third lot. If it's really a big thing the third lot will have to sell out too, and leave t h e i r work and t h e i r money behind them. And thats where the real business man comes in: where I come in. But I'm cleverer than some: I dont mind dropping a little money to start the process. I took your father's measure. I saw that he had a sound idea, and that he would work himself silly for it if he got the chance. I saw that he was a child in business, and was dead certain to outrun his expenses and be in too great a hurry to wait for his market. I knew that the surest way to ruin a man who doesnt know how to handle money is to give him some. I explained my idea to some friends in the city, and they found the money; for I take no risks in ideas, even when theyre my own. Your father and the friends that ventured their money with him were no more to me than a heap of squeezed lemons. Youve been wasting your gratitude: my kind heart is all rot. I'm sick of it. When I see your father beaming at me with his moist, grateful eyes, regularly wallowing in gratitude, I sometimes feel I must tell him the truth or burst. What stops me is that I know he wouldnt believe me. He'd think it was my modesty, as you did just now. He'd think anything rather than the truth, which is that he's a blamed fool, and I am a man that knows how to take care of himself. [*He throws himself back into the big chair with large self-approval*]. Now what do you think of me, Miss Ellie?

ELLIE [*dropping her hands*] How strange! that my mother, who knew nothing at all about business, should have been quite right about you! She always said—not before papa, of course, but to us children—that you were just that sort of man.

MANGAN [*sitting up, much hurt*] Oh! did she? And yet she'd have let you marry me.

ELLIE. Well, you see, Mr Mangan, my mother married a very good man—for whatever you may think of my father as a man of business, he is the soul of goodness—and she is not at all keen on my doing the same.

MANGAN. Anyhow, you dont want to marry me now, do you?

ELLIE [*very calmly*] Oh, I think so. Why not?

MANGAN [*rising aghast*] Why not!

ELLIE. I dont see why we shouldnt get on very well together.

MANGAN. Well, but look here, you know—[*he stops, quite at a loss*].

ELLIE [*patiently*] Well?

MANGAN. Well, I thought you were rather particular about people's characters.

ELLIE. If we women were particular about men's characters, we should never get married at all, Mr Mangan.

MANGAN. A child like you talking of "we women"! What next! Youre not in earnest?

ELLIE. Yes I am. Arnt you?

MANGAN. You mean to hold me to it?

ELLIE. Do you wish to back out of it?

MANGAN. Oh no. Not exactly back out of it.

ELLIE. Well?

He has nothing to say. With a long whispered whistle, he drops into the wicker chair and stares before him like a beggared gambler. But a cunning look soon comes into his face. He leans over towards her on his right elbow, and speaks in a low steady voice.

MANGAN. Suppose I told you I was in love with another woman!

ELLIE [*echoing him*] Suppose I told you I was in love with another man!

MANGAN [*bouncing angrily out of his chair*] I'm not joking.

ELLIE. Who told you *I* was?

MANGAN. I tell you I'm serious. Youre too young to be serious; but youll have to believe me. I want to be near your friend Mrs Hushabye. I'm in love with her. Now the murder's out.

ELLIE. I want to be near your friend Mr Hushabye. I'm in love with him. [*She rises and adds with a frank air*] Now we are in one another's confidence, we shall be real friends. Thank you for telling me.

MANGAN [*almost beside himself*] Do you think I'll be made a convenience of like this?

ELLIE. Come, Mr Mangan! you made a business convenience of my father. Well, a woman's business is marriage. Why shouldnt I make a domestic convenience of you?

MANGAN. Because I dont choose, see? Because I'm not a silly gull like your father. Thats why.

ELLIE [*with serene contempt*] You are not good enough to clean my father's boots, Mr Mangan; and I am paying you a great compliment in condescending to make a convenience of you, as you call it. Of course you are free to throw over our engagement if you like; but, if you do, youll never enter Hesione's house again: I will take care of that.

MANGAN [*gasping*] You little devil, youve done me [*On the point of collapsing into the big chair again he recovers himself*] Wait a bit, though: youre not so cute as you think. You cant beat Boss Mangan as easy as that. Suppose I go straight to Mrs Hushabye and tell her that youre in love with her husband.

ELLIE. She knows it.

MANGAN. You told her!!!

ELLIE. She told me.

MANGAN [*clutching at his bursting temples*] Oh, this is a crazy house. Or else I'm going clean off my chump. Is she making a swop with you —she to have your husband and you to have hers?

ELLIE. Well, you dont want us both, do you?

MANGAN [*throwing himself into the chair distractedly*] My brain wont stand it. My head's going to split. Help! Help me to hold it. Quick: hold it: squeeze it: Save me. [*Ellie comes behind his chair; clasps his head hard for a moment; then begins to draw her hands from his forehead back to his ears*]. Thank you. [*Drowsily*] Thats very refreshing. [*Waking a little*] Dont you hypnotize me, though. Ive seen men made fools of by hypnotism.

ELLIE [*steadily*] Be quiet. Ive seen men made fools of without hypnotism.

MANGAN [*humbly*] You dont dislike touching me, I hope. You never touched me before, I noticed.

ELLIE. Not since you fell in love naturally with a grown-up nice woman, who will never expect you to make love to her. And I will never expect him to make love to me.

MANGAN. He may, though.

ELLIE [*making her passes rhythmically*] Hush. Go to sleep. Do you hear? You are to go to sleep, go to sleep, go to sleep; be quiet, deeply deeply quiet; sleep, sleep, sleep, sleep, sleep, sleep.

He falls asleep. Ellie steals away; turns the light out; and goes into the garden.

Nurse Guinness opens the door and is seen in the light which comes in from the hall.

GUINNESS [*speaking to someone outside*] Mr Mangan's not here, ducky: theres no one here. It's all dark.

MRS HUSHABYE [*without*] Try the garden. Mr Dunn and I will be in my boudoir. Shew him the way.

GUINNESS. Yes, ducky. [*She makes for the garden door in the dark; stumbles over the sleeping Mangan; and screams*] Ahoo! Oh Lord, sir! I beg your pardon, I'm sure: I didnt see you in the dark. Who is it? [*She goes back to the door and turns on the light*]. Oh, Mr Mangan, sir, I hope I havnt hurt you plumping into your lap like that. [*Coming to him*] I was looking for you, sir. Mrs Hushabye says will you please—[*noticing that he remains quite insensible*] Oh, my good Lord, I hope I havnt killed him. Sir! Mr Mangan! Sir! [*She shakes him; and he is rolling inertly off the chair on the floor when she holds him up and props him against the cushion*]. Miss Hessy! Miss Hessy! Quick, doty darling. Miss Hessy! [*Mrs Hushabye comes in from the hall, followed by Mazzini Dunn*]. Oh, Miss Hessy, Ive been and killed him.

Mazzini runs round the back of the chair to Mangan's right hand, and sees that the nurse's words are apparently only too true.

MAZZINI. What tempted you to commit such a crime, woman?

MRS HUSHABYE [*trying not to laugh*] Do you mean you did it on purpose?

GUINNESS. Now is it likely I'd kill any man on purpose. I fell over him in the dark; and I'm a pretty tidy weight. He never spoke nor moved until I shook him; and then he would have dropped dead on the floor. Isnt it tiresome?

MRS HUSHABYE [*going past the nurse to Mangan's side, and inspecting him less credulously than Mazzini*] Nonsense! he is not dead: he is only asleep. I can see him breathing.

GUINNESS. But why wont he wake?

MAZZINI [*speaking very politely into Mangan's ear*] Mangan! My dear Mangan! [*he blows into Mangan's ear*].

MRS HUSHABYE. Thats no good [*she shakes him vigorously*]. Mr Mangan: wake up. Do you hear? [*He begins to roll over*]. Oh! Nurse, nurse: he's falling: help me.

Nurse Guinness rushes to the rescue. With Mazzini's assistance, Mangan is propped safely up again.

GUINNESS [*behind the chair; bending over to test the case with her nose*] Would he be drunk, do you think, pet?

MRS HUSHABYE. Had he any of papa's rum?

MAZZINI. It cant be that: he is most abstemious. I am afraid he drank too much formerly, and has to drink too little now. You know, Mrs Hushabye, I really think he has been hypnotized.

GUINNESS. Hip no what, sir?

MAZZINI. One evening at home, after we had seen a hypnotizing performance, the children began playing at it; and Ellie stroked my head. I assure you I went off dead asleep; and they had to send for a professional to wake me up after I had slept eighteen hours. They had to carry me upstairs; and as the poor children were not very strong, they let me slip; and I rolled right down the whole flight and never woke up. [*Mrs Hushabye splutters*]. Oh, you may laugh, Mrs Hushabye; but I might have been killed.

MRS HUSHABYE. I couldnt have helped laughing even if you had been, Mr Dunn. So Ellie has hypnotized him. What fun!

MAZZINI. Oh no, no, no. It was such a terrible lesson to her: nothing would induce her to try such a thing again.

MRS HUSHABYE. Then who did it? *I* didnt.

MAZZINI. I thought perhaps the Captain might have done it unintentionally. He is so fearfully magnetic: I feel vibrations whenever he comes close to me.

GUINNESS. The Captain will get him out of it anyhow, sir: I'll back him for that. I'll go fetch him [*she makes for the pantry*].

MRS HUSHABYE. Wait a bit. [*To Mazzini*] You say he is all right for eighteen hours?

MAZZINI. Well, *I* was asleep for eighteen hours.

MRS HUSHABYE. Were you any the worse for it?

MAZZINI. I dont quite remember. They had poured brandy down my throat, you see; and—

MRS HUSHABYE. Quite. Anyhow, you survived. Nurse, darling: go and ask Miss Dunn to come to us here. Say I want to speak to her particularly. You will find her with Mr Hushabye probably.

GUINNESS. I think not ducky: Miss Addy is with him. But I'll find her and send her to you. [*She goes out into the garden*].

MRS HUSHABYE [*calling Mazzini's attention to the figure on the chair*] Now, Mr Dunn, look. Just look. Look hard. Do you still intend to sacrifice your daughter to that thing?

MAZZINI [*troubled*] You have completely upset me, Mrs Hushabye, by all you have said to me. That anyone could imagine that I—*I*, a consecrated soldier of freedom, if I may say so—could sacrifice Ellie to anybody or anyone, or that I should ever have dreamed of forcing her inclinations in any way, is a most painful blow to my—well, I suppose you would say to my good opinion of myself.

MRS HUSHABYE [*rather stolidly*] Sorry.

MAZZINI [*looking forlornly at the body*] What is your objection to poor Mangan, Mrs Hushabye? He looks all right to me. But then I am so accustomed to him.

MRS HUSHABYE. Have you no heart? Have you no sense? Look at the brute! Think of poor weak innocent Ellie in the clutches of this slavedriver, who spends his life making thousands of rough violent workmen bend to his will and sweat for him: a man accustomed to have great masses of iron beaten into shape for him by steamhammers! to fight with women and girls over a halfpenny an hour ruthlessly! a captain of industry, I think you call him, dont you? Are you going to fling your delicate, sweet, helpless child into such a beast's claws just because he will keep her in an expensive house and make her wear diamonds to shew how rich he is?

MAZZINI [*staring at her in wide-eyed amazement*] Bless you, dear Mrs Hushabye, what romantic ideas of business you have! Poor dear Mangan isnt a bit like that.

MRS HUSHABYE [*scornfully*] Poor dear Mangan indeed!

MAZZINI. But he doesnt know anything about machinery. He never goes near the men: he couldnt manage them: he is afraid of them. I never can get him to take the least interest in the works: he hardly knows more about them than you do. People are cruelly unjust to Mangan: they think he is all rugged strength just because his manners are bad.

MRS HUSHABYE. Do you mean to tell me he isnt strong enough to crush poor little Ellie?

MAZZINI. Of course it's very hard to say how any marriage will turn out; but speaking for myself, I should say that he wont have a dog's chance against Ellie. You know, Ellie has remarkable strength of character. I think it is because I taught her to like Shakespear when she was very young.

MRS HUSHABYE [*contemptuously*] Shakespear! The next thing you will tell me is that you could have made a great deal more money than Mangan. [*She retires to the sofa, and sits down at the port end of it in the worst of humors*].

MAZZINI [*following her and taking the other end*] No: I'm no good at making money. I dont care enough for it, somehow. I'm not ambitious! that must be it. Mangan is wonderful about money: he thinks of nothing else. He is so dreadfully afraid of being poor. I am always thinking of other things: even at the works I think of the things we are doing and not of what they cost. And the worst of it is, poor Mangan doesnt know what to do with his money when he gets it. He is such a baby that he doesnt know even what to eat and drink: he has ruined his liver eating and drinking the wrong things; and now he can hardly eat at all. Ellie will diet him splendidly. You will be surprised when you come to know him better: he is really the most helpless of mortals. You get quite a protective feeling towards him.

MRS HUSHABYE. Then who manages his business, pray?

MAZZINI. I do. And of course other people like me.

MRS HUSHABYE. Footling people, you mean.

MAZZINI. I suppose youd think us so.

MRS HUSHABYE. And pray why dont you do without him if youre all so much cleverer?

MAZZINI. Oh, we couldnt: we should ruin the business in a year. I've tried; and I know. We should spend too much on everything. We should improve the quality of the goods and make them too dear. We should be sentimental about the hard cases among the workpeople. But Mangan keeps us in order. He is down on us about every extra halfpenny. We could never do without him. You see, he will sit up all night thinking of how to save sixpence. Wont Ellie make him jump, though, when she takes his house in hand!

MRS HUSHABYE. Then the creature is a fraud even as a captain of industry!

MAZZINI. I am afraid all the captains of industry are what y o u call frauds, Mrs Hushabye. Of course there are some manufacturers who really do understand their own works; but they dont make as high a rate of profit as Mangan does. I assure you Mangan is quite a good fellow in his way. He means well.

MRS HUSHABYE. He doesnt look well. He is not in his first youth, is he?

MAZZINI. After all, no husband is in his first youth for very long, Mrs Hushabye. And men cant afford to marry in their first youth nowadays.

MRS HUSHABYE. Now if *I* said that, it would sound witty. Why cant y o u say it wittily? What on earth is the matter with you? Why dont you inspire everybody with confidence? with respect?

MAZZINI [*humbly*] I think that what is the matter with me is that I am poor. You dont know what that means at home. Mind: I dont say they have ever complained. Theyve all been wonderful: theyve been proud of my poverty. Theyve even joked about it quite often. But my wife has had a very poor time of it. She has been quite resigned—

MRS HUSHABYE [*shuddering involuntarily*]!!

MAZZINI. There! You see, Mrs Hushabye. I dont want Ellie to live on resignation.

MRS HUSHABYE. Do you want her to have to resign herself to living with a man she doesnt love?

MAZZINI [*wistfully*] Are you sure that would be worse than living with a man she did love, if he was a footling person?

MRS HUSHABYE [*relaxing her contemptuous attitude, quite interested in Mazzini now*] You know, I really think you must love Ellie very much; for you become quite clever when you talk about her.

MAZZINI. I didnt know I was so very stupid on other subjects.

MRS HUSHABYE. You are, sometimes.

MAZZINI [*turning his head away; for his eyes are wet*] I have learnt a good deal about myself from you, Mrs Hushabye; and I'm afraid I shall not be the happier for your plain speaking. But if you thought I needed it to make me think of Ellie's happiness you were very much mistaken.

MRS HUSHABYE [*leaning towards him kindly*] Have I been a beast?

MAZZINI [*pulling himself together*] It doesnt matter about me, Mrs Hushabye. I think you like Ellie; and that is enough for me.

MRS HUSHABYE. I'm beginning to like you a little. I perfectly loathed you at first. I thought you the most odious, self-satisfied, boresome elderly prig I ever met.

MAZZINI [*resigned, and now quite cheerful*] I daresay I am all that. I never have been a favorite with gorgeous women like you. They always frighten me.

MRS HUSHABYE [*pleased*] Am I a gorgeous woman, Mazzini? I shall fall in love with you presently.

MAZZINI [*with placid gallantry*] No you wont, Hesione. But you would be quite safe. Would you believe it that quite a lot of women have flirted with me because I am quite safe? But they get tired of me for the same reason.

MRS HUSHABYE [*mischievously*] Take care. You may not be so safe as you think.

MAZZINI. Oh yes, quite safe. You see, I have been in love really: the sort of love that only happens once. [*softly*] Thats why Ellie is such a lovely girl.

MRS HUSHABYE. Well, really, you a r e coming out. Are you quite sure you wont let me tempt you into a second grand passion?

MAZZINI. Quite. It wouldnt be natural. The fact is, you dont strike on my box, Mrs Hushabye; and I certainly dont strike on yours.

MRS HUSHABYE. I see. Your marriage was a safety match.

MAZZINI. What a very witty application of the expression I used! I should never have thought of it.

Ellie comes in from the garden, looking anything but happy.

MRS HUSHABYE [*rising*] Oh! here is Ellie at last. [*She goes behind the sofa*].

ELLIE [*on the threshold of the starboard door*] Guinness said you wanted me: you and papa.

MRS HUSHABYE. You have kept us waiting so long that it almost came to —well, never mind. Your father is a very wonderful man [*she ruffles his hair affectionately*]: the only one I ever met who could resist me when I made myself really agreeable. [*She comes to the big chair, on Mangan's left*]. Come here. I have something to shew you. [*Ellie strolls listlessly to the other side of the chair*]. Look.

ELLIE [*contemplating Mangan without interest*] I know. He is only asleep. We had a talk after dinner; and he fell asleep in the middle of it.

MRS HUSHABYE. You did it, Ellie. You put him asleep.

MAZZINI [*rising quickly and coming to the back of the chair*] Oh, I hope not. Did you, Ellie?

ELLIE [*wearily*] He asked me to.

MAZZINI. But it's dangerous. You know what happened to me.

ELLIE [*utterly indifferent*] Oh, I daresay I can wake him. If not, somebody else can.

MRS HUSHABYE. It doesnt matter, anyhow, because I have at last persuaded your father that you dont want to marry him.

ELLIE [*suddenly coming out of her listlessness, much vexed*] But why did you do that, Hesione? I do want to marry him. I fully intend to marry him.

MAZZINI. Are you quite sure, Ellie? Mrs Hushabye has made me feel that I may have been thoughtless and selfish about it.

ELLIE [*very clearly and steadily*] Papa. When Mrs Hushabye takes it on herself to explain to you what I think or dont think, shut your ears tight; and shut your eyes too. Hesione knows nothing about me: she hasnt the least notion of the sort of person I am, and never will. I promise you I wont do anything I dont want to do and mean to do for my own sake.

MAZZINI. You are quite, quite sure?

ELLIE. Quite, quite sure. Now you must go away and leave me to talk to Mrs Hushabye.

MAZZINI. But I should like to hear. Shall I be in the way?

ELLIE [*inexorable*] I had rather talk to her alone.

MAZZINI [*affectionately*] Oh, well, I know what a nuisance parents are, dear. I will be good and go. [*He goes to the garden door*]. By the way, do you remember the address of that professional who woke me up? Dont you think I had better telegraph to him.

MRS HUSHABYE [*moving towards the sofa*] It's too late to telegraph tonight.

MAZZINI. I suppose so. I do hope he'll wake up in the course of the night. [*He goes out into the garden*].

ELLIE [*turning vigorously on Hesione the moment her father is out of the room*] Hesione: what the devil do you mean by making mischief with my father about Mangan?

MRS HUSHABYE [*promptly losing her temper*] Dont you dare speak to me like that, you little minx. Remember that you are in my house.

ELLIE. Stuff! Why dont you mind your own business? What is it to you whether I choose to marry Mangan or not?

MRS HUSHABYE. Do you suppose you can bully me, you miserable little matrimonial adventurer?

ELLIE. Every woman who hasnt any money is a matrimonial adventurer. It's easy for you to talk: you have never known what it is to want money; and you can pick up men as if they were daisies. I am poor and respectable—

MRS HUSHABYE [*interrupting*] Ho! respectable! How did you pick up Mangan? How did you pick up my husband? You have the audacity to tell me that I am a—a—a—

ELLIE. A siren. So you are. You were born to lead men by the nose: if you werent, Marcus would have waited for me, perhaps.

MRS HUSHABYE [*suddenly melting and half laughing*] Oh, my poor Ellie, my pettikins, my unhappy darling! I am so sorry about Hector. But what can I do? It's not my fault: I'd give him to you if I could.

ELLIE. I dont blame you for that.

MRS HUSHABYE. What a brute I was to quarrel with you and call you names! Do kiss me and say youre not angry with me.

ELLIE [*fiercely*] Oh, dont slop and gush and be sentimental. Dont you see that unless I can be hard—as hard as nails—I shall go mad. I dont care a damn about your calling me names: do you think a woman in my situation can feel a few hard words?

MRS HUSHABYE. Poor little woman! Poor little situation!

ELLIE. I suppose you think youre being sympathetic. You are just foolish and stupid and selfish. You see me getting a smasher right in the face that kills a whole part of my life: the best part that can never come again; and you think you can help me over it by a little coaxing and kissing. When I want all the strength I can get to lean on: something iron, something stony, I dont care how cruel it is, you go all mushy and want to slobber over me. I'm not angry; I'm not unfriendly; but for God's sake do pull yourself together; and dont think that because youre on velvet and always have been, women who are in hell can take it as easily as you.

MRS HUSHABYE [*shrugging her shoulders*] Very well. [*She sits down on the sofa in her old place*]. But I warn you that when I am neither coaxing and kissing nor laughing, I am just wondering how much longer I can stand living in this cruel, damnable world. You object to the siren: well, I drop the siren. You want to rest your wounded bosom against a grindstone. Well [*folding her arms*], here is the grindstone.

ELLIE [*sitting down beside her, appeased*] Thats better: you really have the trick of falling in with everyone's mood; but you dont understand, because you are not the sort of woman for whom there is only one man and only one chance.

MRS HUSHABYE. I certainly dont understand how your marrying that object [*indicating Mangan*] will console you for not being able to marry Hector.

ELLIE. Perhaps you dont understand why I was quite a nice girl this morning, and am now neither a girl nor particularly nice.

MRS HUSHABYE. Oh yes I do. It's because you have made up your mind to do something despicable and wicked.

ELLIE. I dont think so, Hesione. I must make the best of my ruined house.

MRS HUSHABYE. Pooh! Youll get over it. Your house isnt ruined.

ELLIE. Of course I shall get over it. You dont suppose I'm going to sit down and die of a broken heart, I hope, or be an old maid living on a pittance from the Sick and Indigent Roomkeeper's Association. But my heart is broken, all the same. What I mean by that is that I know that what has happened to me with Marcus will not happen to me ever again. In the world for me there is Marcus and a lot of other men of whom one is just the same as another. Well, if I cant have love, thats no reason why I should have poverty. If Mangan has nothing else, he has money.

MRS HUSHABYE. And are there no young men with money?

ELLIE. Not within my reach. Besides, a young man would have the right to expect love from me, and would perhaps leave me when he found I could not give it to him. Rich young men can get rid of their wives, you know, pretty cheaply. But this object, as you call him, can expect nothing more from me than I am prepared to give him.

MRS HUSHABYE. He will be your owner, remember. If he buys you, he will make the bargain pay him and not you. Ask your father.

ELLIE [*rising and strolling to the chair to contemplate their subject*] You need not trouble on that score, Hesione. I have more to give Boss Mangan than he has to give me: it is I who am buying him, and at a pretty good price too, I think. Women are better at that sort of bargain than men. I have taken the Boss's measure; and ten Boss Mangans shall not prevent me doing far more as I please as his wife than I have ever been able to do as a poor girl. [*Stooping to the recumbent figure*] Shall they, Boss? I think not. [*She passes on to the drawing-table, and leans against the end of it, facing the windows*]. I shall not have to spend most of my time wondering how long my gloves will last, anyhow.

MRS HUSHABYE [*rising superbly*] Ellie: you are a wicked sordid little beast. And to think that I actually condescended to fascinate that creature there to save you from him! Well, let me tell you this: if you make this disgusting match, you will never see Hector again if I can help it.

ELLIE [*unmoved*] I nailed Mangan by telling him that if he did not marry me he should never see you again [*she lifts herself on her wrists and seats herself on the end of the table*].

MRS HUSHABYE [*recoiling*] Oh!

ELLIE. So you see I am not unprepared for your playing that trump against me. Well, you just try it: thats all. I should have made a man of Marcus, not a household pet.

MRS HUSHABYE [*flaming*] You dare!

ELLIE [*looking almost dangerous*] Set him thinking about me if you dare.

MRS HUSHABYE. Well, of all the impudent little fiends I ever met! Hector says there is a certain point at which the only answer you can give to a man who breaks all the rules is to knock him down. What would you say if I were to box your ears?

ELLIE [*calmly*] I should pull your hair.

MRS HUSHABYE [*mischievously*] That wouldnt hurt me. Perhaps it comes off at night.

ELLIE [*so taken aback that she drops off the table and runs to her*] Oh, you dont mean to say, Hesione, that your beautiful black hair is false?

MRS HUSHABYE [*patting it*] Dont tell Hector. He believes in it.

ELLIE [*groaning*] Oh! Even the hair that ensnared him false! Everything false!

MRS HUSHABYE. Pull it and try. Other women can snare men in their hair; but I can swing a baby on mine. Aha! you cant do that, Goldylocks.

ELLIE [*heartbroken*] No. You have stolen my babies.

MRS HUSHABYE. Pettikins: dont make me cry. You know, what you said about my making a household pet of him is a little true. Perhaps he ought to have waited for you. Would any other woman on earth forgive you?

ELLIE. Oh, what right had you to take him all for yourself! [*Pulling herself together*] There! You couldn't help it: neither of us could help it. He couldnt help it. No: dont say anything more: I cant bear it. Let us wake the object. [*She begins stroking Mangan's head, reversing the movement with which she put him to sleep*]. Wake up, do you hear? You are to wake up at once. Wake up, wake up, wake—

MANGAN [*bouncing out of the chair in a fury and turning on them*] Wake up! So you think Ive been asleep, do you? [*He kicks the chair violently back out of his way, and gets between them*]. You throw me into a trance so that I cant move hand or foot—I might have been buried alive! it's a mercy I wasnt—and then you think I was only asleep. If youd let me drop the two times you rolled me about, my nose would have been flattened for life against the floor. But Ive found you all out, anyhow. I know the sort of people I'm among now. Ive heard every word youve said, you and your precious father, and [*to Mrs Hushabye*] you too. So I'm an object, am I? I'm a thing, am I? I'm a fool that hasnt sense enough to feed myself properly, am I? I'm afraid of the men that would starve if it werent for the wages I give them, am I? I'm nothing but a disgusting old skinflint to be made a convenience of by designing women and fool managers of my works, am I? I'm—

MRS HUSHABYE [*with the most elegant aplomb*] Sh-sh-sh-sh-sh! Mr Mangan: you are bound in honor to obliterate from your mind all you heard while you were pretending to be asleep. It was not meant for you to hear.

MANGAN. Pretending to be asleep! Do you think if I was only pretending that I'd have sprawled there helpless, and listened to such unfairness, such lies, such injustice and plotting and backbiting and slandering of me, if I could have up and told you what I thought of you! I wonder I didnt burst.

MRS HUSHABYE [*sweetly*] You dreamt it all, Mr Mangan. We were only saying how beautifully peaceful you looked in your sleep. That was all, wasnt it, Ellie? Believe me, Mr Mangan, all those unpleasant things came into your mind in the last half second before you woke. Ellie rubbed your hair the wrong way; and the disagreeable sensation suggested a disagreeable dream.

MANGAN [*doggedly*] I believe in dreams.

MRS HUSHABYE. So do I. But they go by contraries, dont they?

MANGAN [*depths of emotion suddenly welling up in him*] I shant forget, to my dying day, that when you gave me the glad eye that time in the garden, you were making a fool of me. That was a dirty low mean thing to do. You had no right to let me come near you if I disgusted you. It isnt my fault if I'm old and havnt a moustache like a bronze candlestick as your husband has. There are things no decent woman would do to a man—like a man hitting a woman in the breast.

Hesione, utterly shamed, sits down on the sofa and covers her face with her hands. Mangan sits down also on his chair and begins to cry like a child. Ellie stares at them. Mrs Hushabye, at the distressing sound he makes, takes down her hands and looks at him. She rises and runs to him.

MRS HUSHABYE. Dont cry: I cant bear it. Have I broken your heart? I didnt know you had one. How could I?

MANGAN. I'm a man aint I?

MRS HUSHABYE [*half coaxing, half rallying, altogether tenderly*] Oh no: not what I call a man. Only a Boss: just that and nothing else. What business has a Boss with a heart?

MANGAN. Then youre not a bit sorry for what you did, nor ashamed?

MRS HUSHABYE. I was ashamed for the first time in my life when you said that about hitting a woman in the breast, and I found out what

I'd done. My very bones blushed red. Youve had your revenge, Boss. Arnt you satisfied?

MANGAN. Serve you right! Do you hear? Serve you right! Youre just cruel. Cruel.

MRS HUSHABYE. Yes: cruelty would be delicious if one could only find some sort of cruelty that didnt really hurt. By the way [*sitting down beside him on the arm of the chair*], whats your name? It's not really Boss, is it?

MANGAN [*shortly*] If you want to know, my name's Alfred.

MRS HUSHABYE [*springing up*] Alfred!! Ellie: he was christened after Tennyson!!!

MANGAN [*rising*] I was christened after my uncle, and never had a penny from him, damn him! What of it?

MRS HUSHABYE. It comes to me suddenly that you are a real person: that you had a mother, like anyone else. [*Putting her hands on his shoulders and surveying him*] Little Alf!

MANGAN. Well, you have a nerve.

MRS HUSHABYE. And you have a heart, Alfy, a whimpering little heart, but a real one. [*Releasing him suddenly*] Now run and make it up with Ellie. She has had time to think what to say to you, which is more than I had [*she goes out quickly into the garden by the port door*].

MANGAN. That woman has a pair of hands that go right through you.

ELLIE. Still in love with her, in spite of all we said about you?

MANGAN. Are all women like you two? Do they never think of anything about a man except what they can get out of him? You werent even thinking that about me. You were only thinking whether your gloves would last.

ELLIE. I shall not have to think about that when we are married.

MANGAN. And you think I am going to marry you after what I heard there!

ELLIE. You heard nothing from me that I did not tell you before.

MANGAN. Perhaps you think I cant do without you.

ELLIE. I think you would feel lonely without us all now, after coming to know us so well.

MANGAN [*with something like a yell of despair*] Am I never to have the last word?

CAPTAIN SHOTOVER [*appearing at the starboard garden door*] There is a soul in torment here. What is the matter?

MANGAN. This girl doesnt want to spend her life wondering how long her gloves will last.

CAPTAIN SHOTOVER [*passing through*] Dont wear any. I never do [*he goes into the pantry*].

LADY UTTERWORD [*appearing at the port garden door, in a handsome dinner dress*] Is anything the matter?

ELLIE. This gentleman wants to know is he never to have the last word?

LADY UTTERWORD [*coming forward to the sofa*] I should let him have it, my dear. The important thing is not to have the last word, but to have your own way.

MANGAN. She wants both.

LADY UTTERWORD. She wont get them, Mr Mangan. Providence always has the last word.

MANGAN [*desperately*] Now y o u are going to come religion over me. In this house a man's mind might as well be a football. I'm going. [*He makes for the hall, but is stopped by a hail from the Captain, who has just emerged from his pantry*].

CAPTAIN SHOTOVER. Whither away, Boss Mangan?

MANGAN. To hell out of this house: let that be enough for you and all here.

CAPTAIN SHOTOVER. You were welcome to come: you are free to go. The wide earth, the high seas, the spacious skies are waiting for you outside.

LADY UTTERWORD. But your things, Mr Mangan. Your bags, your comb and brushes, your pyjamas–

HECTOR [*who has just appeared in the port doorway in a handsome Arab costume*] Why should the escaping slave take his chains with him?

MANGAN. Thats right, Hushabye. Keep the pyjamas, my lady; and much good may they do you.

HECTOR [*advancing to Lady Utterword's left hand*] Let us all go out into the night and leave everything behind us.

MANGAN. You stay where you are, the lot of you. I want no company, especially female company.

ELLIE. Let him go. He is unhappy here. He is angry with us.

CAPTAIN SHOTOVER. Go, Boss Mangan; and when you have found the land where there is happiness and where there are no women, send me its latitude and longitude; and I will join you there.

LADY UTTERWORD. You will certainly not be comfortable without your luggage, Mr Mangan.

ELLIE [*impatient*] Go, go: why dont you go? It is a heavenly night: you can sleep on the heath. Take my waterproof to lie on: it is hanging up in the hall.

HECTOR. Breakfast at nine, unless you prefer to breakfast with the Captain at six.

ELLIE. Good night, Alfred.

HECTOR. Alfred! [*He runs back to the door and calls into the garden*] Randall: Mangan's Christian name is Alfred.

RANDALL [*appearing in the starboard doorway in evening dress*] Then Hesione wins her bet.

Mrs Hushabye appears in the port doorway. She throws her left arm round Hector's neck; draws him with her to the back of the sofa; and throws her right arm round Lady Utterword's neck.

MRS HUSHABYE. They wouldnt believe me, Alf.

They contemplate him.

MANGAN. Is there any more of you coming in to look at me, as if I was the latest thing in a menagerie.

MRS HUSHABYE. You a r e the latest thing in this menagerie.

Before Mangan can retort, a fall of furniture is heard from upstairs; then a pistol shot, and a yell of pain. The staring group breaks up in consternation.

MAZZINI'S VOICE [*from above*] Help! A burglar! Help!

HECTOR [*his eyes blazing*] A burglar!!!

MRS HUSHABYE. No, Hector: youll be shot [*but it is too late: he has dashed out past Mangan, who hastily moves towards the bookshelves out of his way*].

CAPTAIN SHOTOVER [*blowing his whistle*] All hands aloft! [*He strides out after Hector*].

LADY UTTERWORD. My diamonds! [*She follows the Captain*].

RANDALL [*rushing after her*] No, Ariadne. Let me.

ELLIE. Oh, is papa shot? [*she runs out*].

MRS HUSHABYE. Are you frightened, Alf?

MANGAN. No. It aint my house, thank God.

MRS HUSHABYE. If they catch a burglar, shall we have to go into court as witnesses, and be asked all sorts of questions about our private lives?

MANGAN. You wont be believed if you tell the truth.

Mazzini, terribly upset, with a duelling pistol in his hand, comes from the hall, and makes his way to the drawing-table.

MAZZINI. Oh, my dear Mrs Hushabye, I might have killed him [*He throws the pistol on the table and staggers round to the chair*]. I hope you wont believe I really intended to.

Hector comes in, marching an old and villainous looking man before him by the collar. He plants him in the middle of the room and releases him.

Ellie follows, and immediately runs across to the back of her father's chair, and pats his shoulders.

RANDALL [*entering with a poker*] Keep your eye on this door, Mangan. I'll look after the other [*he goes to the starboard door and stands on guard there*].

Lady Utterword comes in after Randall, and goes between Mrs Hushabye and Mangan.

Nurse Guinness brings up the rear, and waits near the door, on Mangan's left.

MRS HUSHABYE. What has happened?

MAZZINI. Your housekeeper told me there was somebody upstairs, and gave me a pistol that Mr Hushabye had been practising with. I thought it would frighten him; but it went off at a touch.

THE BURGLAR. Yes, and took the skin off my ear. Precious near took the top off my head. Why dont you have a proper revolver instead of a thing like that, that goes off if you as much as blow on it?

HECTOR. One of my duelling pistols. Sorry.

MAZZINI. He put his hands up and said it was a fair cop.

THE BURGLAR. So it was. Send for the police.

HECTOR. No, by thunder! It was not a fair cop. We were four to one.

MRS HUSHABYE. What will they do to him?

THE BURGLAR. Ten years. Beginning with solitary. Ten years off my life. I shant serve it all: I'm too old. It will see me out.

LADY UTTERWORD. You should have thought of that before you stole my diamonds.

THE BURGLAR. Well, youve got them back, lady: havnt you? Can you give me back the years of my life you are going to take from me?

MRS HUSHABYE. Oh, we cant bury a man alive for ten years for a few diamonds.

THE BURGLAR. Ten little shining diamonds! Ten long black years!

LADY UTTERWORD. Think of what it is for us to be dragged through the horrors of a criminal court, and have all our family affairs in the papers! If you were a native, and Hastings could order you a good beating and send you away, I shouldnt mind; but here in England there is no real protection for any respectable person.

THE BURGLAR. I'm too old to be giv a hiding, lady. Send for the police and have done with it. It's only just and right you should.

RANDALL [*who has relaxed his vigilance on seeing the burglar so pacifically disposed, and comes forward swinging the poker between his fingers like a well-folded umbrella*] It is neither just nor right that we should be put to a lot of inconvenience to gratify your moral enthusiasm, my friend. You had better get out, while you have the chance.

THE BURGLAR [*inexorably*] No. I must work my sin off my conscience. This has come as a sort of call to me. Let me spend the rest of my life repenting in a cell. I shall have my reward above.

MANGAN [*exasperated*] The very burglars cant behave naturally in this house.

HECTOR. My good sir: you must work out your salvation at somebody else's expense. Nobody here is going to charge you.

THE BURGLAR. Oh, you wont charge me, wont you?

HECTOR. No. I'm sorry to be inhospitable; but will you kindly leave the house?

THE BURGLAR. Right. I'll go to the police station and give myself up. [*He turns resolutely to the door; but Hector stops him*].

HECTOR. Oh no. You mustnt do that.
RANDALL. No, no. Clear out, man, cant you; and dont be a fool.
MRS HUSHABYE. Dont be so silly. Cant you repent at home?

LADY UTTERWORD. You will have to do as you are told.

THE BURGLAR. It's compounding a felony, you know.

MRS HUSHABYE. This is utterly ridiculous. Are we to be forced to prosecute this man when we dont want to?

THE BURGLAR. Am I to be robbed of my salvation to save you the trouble of spending a day at the sessions? Is that justice? Is it right? Is it fair to me?

MAZZINI [*rising and leaning across the table persuasively as if it were a pulpit desk or a shop counter*] Come, come! let me shew you how you can turn your very crimes to account. Why not set up as a locksmith? You must know more about locks than most honest men?

THE BURGLAR. Thats true, sir. But I couldnt set up as a locksmith under twenty pounds.

RANDALL. Well, you can easily steal twenty pounds. You will find it in the nearest bank.

THE BURGLAR [*horrified*] Oh what a thing for a gentleman to put into the head of a poor criminal scrambling out of the bottomless pit as it were! Oh, shame on you, sir! Oh, God forgive you! [*He throws himself into the big chair and covers his face as if in prayer*].

LADY UTTERWORD. Really, Randall!

HECTOR. It seems to me that we shall have to take up a collection for this inopportunely contrite sinner.

LADY UTTERWORD. But twenty pounds is ridiculous.

THE BURGLAR [*looking up quickly*] I shall have to buy a lot of tools, lady.

LADY UTTERWORD. Nonsense: you have your burgling kit.

THE BURGLAR. Whats a jemmy and a centrebit and an acetylene welding plant and a bunch of skeleton keys? I shall want a forge, and a smithy, and a shop, and fittings. I cant hardly do it for twenty.

HECTOR. My worthy friend, we havnt got twenty pounds.

THE BURGLAR [*now master of the situation*] You can raise it among you, cant you?

MRS HUSHABYE. Give him a sovereign, Hector; and get rid of him.

HECTOR [*giving him a pound*] There! Off with you.

THE BURGLAR [*rising and taking the money very ungratefully*] I wont promise nothing. You have more on you than a quid: all the lot of you, I mean.

LADY UTTERWORD [*vigorously*] Oh, let us prosecute him and have done with it. I have a conscience too, I hope; and I do not feel at all sure that we have any right to let him go, especially if he is going to be greedy and impertinent.

THE BURGLAR [*quickly*] All right, lady, all right. Ive no wish to be anything but agreeable. Good evening, ladies and gentlemen; and thank you kindly.

He is hurrying out when he is confronted in the doorway by Captain Shotover.

CAPTAIN SHOTOVER [*fixing the burglar with a piercing regard*] Whats this? Are there two of you?

THE BURGLAR [*falling on his knees before the Captain in abject terror*] Oh my Good Lord, what have I done? Dont tell me it's y o u r house Ive broken into, Captain Shotover.

The Captain seizes him by the collar; drags him to his feet; and leads him to the middle of the group, Hector falling back beside his wife to make way for them.

CAPTAIN SHOTOVER [*turning him towards Ellie*] Is that your daughter? [*He releases him*].

THE BURGLAR. Well, how do I know, Captain? You know the sort of life you and me has led. Any young lady of that age might be my daughter anywhere in the wide world, as you might say.

CAPTAIN SHOTOVER [*to Mazzini*] You are not Billy Dunn. This is Billy Dunn. Why have you imposed on me?

THE BURGLAR [*indignantly to Mazzini*] Have you been giving yourself out to be me? You, that nigh blew my head off! Shooting y o u r s e l f, in a manner of speaking!

MAZZINI. My dear Captain Shotover, ever since I came into this house I have done hardly anything else but assure you that I am not Mr William Dunn, but Mazzini Dunn, a very different person.

THE BURGLAR. He dont belong to my branch, Captain. Theres two sets in the family: the thinking Dunns and the drinking Dunns, each going their own ways. I'm a drinking Dunn: he's a thinking Dunn. But that didnt give him any right to shoot me.

CAPTAIN SHOTOVER. So youve turned burglar, have you?

THE BURGLAR. No, Captain: I wouldnt disgrace our old sea calling by such a thing. I am no burglar.

LADY UTTERWORD. What were you doing with my diamonds?

GUINNESS. What did you break into the house for if youre no burglar?

RANDALL. Mistook the house for your own and came in by the wrong window, eh?

THE BURGLAR. Well, it's no use my telling you a lie: I can take in most captains, but not Captain Shotover, because he sold himself to the devil in Zanzibar, and can divine water, spot gold, explode a cartridge in your pocket with a glance of his eye, and see the truth hidden in the heart of man. But I'm no burglar.

CAPTAIN SHOTOVER. Are you an honest man?

THE BURGLAR. I dont set up to be better than my fellow-creatures, and never did, as you well know, Captain. But what I do is innocent and pious. I enquire about for houses where the right sort of people live. I work it on them same as I worked it here. I break into the house; put a few spoons or diamonds in my pocket; make a noise; get caught; and take up a collection. And you wouldnt believe how hard it is to get caught when youre actually trying to. I have knocked over all the chairs in a room without a soul paying any attention to me. In the end I have had to walk out and leave the job.

RANDALL. When that happens, do you put back the spoons and diamonds?

THE BURGLAR. Well, I dont fly in the face of Providence, if thats what you want to know.

CAPTAIN SHOTOVER. Guinness: you remember this man?

GUINNESS. I should think I do, seeing I was married to him, the blackguard!

HESIONE	*exclaiming*	Married to him!
LADY UTTERWORD	*together*	Guinness!!

THE BURGLAR. It wasnt legal. Ive been married to no end of women. No use coming that over me.

CAPTAIN SHOTOVER. Take him to the forecastle [*he flings him to the door with a strength beyond his years*].

GUINNESS. I suppose you mean the kitchen. They wont have him there. Do you expect servants to keep company with thieves and all sorts?

CAPTAIN SHOTOVER. Land-thieves and water-thieves are the same flesh and blood. I'll have no boatswain on my quarter-deck. Off with you both.

THE BURGLAR. Yes, Captain. [*He goes out humbly*].

MAZZINI. Will it be safe to have him in the house like that?

GUINNESS. Why didnt you shoot him, sir? If I'd known who he was, I'd have shot him myself. [*She goes out*].

MRS HUSHABYE. Do sit down, everybody. [*She sits down on the sofa*]

They all move except Ellie. Mazzini resumes his seat. Randall sits down in the window seat near the starboard door, again making a pendulum of his poker, and studying it as Galileo might have done. Hector sits on his left, in the middle. Mangan, forgotten, sits in the port corner. Lady Utterword takes the big chair. Captain Shotover goes into the pantry in deep abstraction. They all look after him; and Lady Utterword coughs consciously.

MRS HUSHABYE. So Billy Dunn was poor nurse's little romance. I knew there had been somebody.

RANDALL. They will fight their battles over again and enjoy themselves immensely.

LADY UTTERWORD [*irritably*] You are not married; and you know nothing about it, Randall. Hold your tongue.

RANDALL. Tyrant!

MRS HUSHABYE. Well, we have had a very exciting evening. Everything will be an anticlimax after it. We'd better all go to bed.

RANDALL. Another burglar may turn up.

MAZZINI. Oh, impossible! I hope not.

RANDALL. Why not? there is more than one burglar in England.

MRS HUSHABYE. What do you say, Alf?

MANGAN [*huffily*] Oh, I dont matter. I'm forgotten. The burglar has put my nose out of joint. Shove me into a corner and have done with me.

MRS HUSHABYE [*jumping up mischievously, and going to him*] Would you like a walk on the heath, Alfred? With me?

ELLIE. Go, Mr Mangan. It will do you good. Hesione will soothe you.

MRS HUSHABYE [*slipping her arm under his and pulling him upright*] Come, Alfred. There is a moon: it's like the night in Tristan and Isolde. [*She caresses his arm and draws him to the port garden door*].

MANGAN [*writhing but yielding*] How you can have the face—the heart—[*he breaks down and is heard sobbing as she takes him out*].

LADY UTTERWORD. What an extraordinary way to behave! What is the matter with the man?

ELLIE [*in a strangely calm voice, staring into an imaginary distance*] His heart is breaking: that is all. [*The Captain appears at the pantry door, listening*]. It is a curious sensation: the sort of pain that goes mercifully beyond our powers of feeling. When your heart is broken, your boats are burned: nothing matters any more. It is the end of happiness and the beginning of peace.

LADY UTTERWORD [*suddenly rising in a rage, to the astonishment of the rest*] How dare you?

HECTOR. Good heavens! Whats the matter?

RANDALL [*in a warning whisper*] Tch—tch—tch! Steady.

ELLIE [*surprised and haughty*] I was not addressing you particularly, Lady Utterword. And I am not accustomed to be asked how dare I.

LADY UTTERWORD. Of course not. Anyone can see how badly you have been brought up.

MAZZINI. Oh, I hope not, Lady Utterword. Really!

LADY UTTERWORD. I know very well what you meant. The impudence!

ELLIE. What on earth do you mean?

CAPTAIN SHOTOVER [*advancing to the table*] She means that her heart will not break. She has been longing all her life for someone to break it. At last she has become afraid she has none to break.

LADY UTTERWORD [*flinging herself on her knees and throwing her arms round him*] Papa: dont say you think Ive no heart.

CAPTAIN SHOTOVER [*raising her with grim tenderness*] If you had no heart how could you want to have it broken, child?

HECTOR [*rising with a bound*] Lady Utterword: you are not to be trusted. You have made a scene [*he runs out into the garden through the starboard door*].

LADY UTTERWORD Oh! Hector, Hector! [*she runs out after him*].

RANDALL. Only nerves, I assure you [*He rises and follows her, waving the poker in his agitation*] Ariadne! Ariadne! For God's sake be careful. You will– [*he is gone*].

MAZZINI [*rising*] How distressing! Can I do anything, I wonder?

CAPTAIN SHOTOVER [*promptly taking his chair and setting to work at the drawing-board*] No. Go to bed. Goodnight.

MAZZINI [*bewildered*] Oh! Perhaps you are right.

ELLIE. Goodnight, dearest. [*She kisses him*].

MAZZINI. Goodnight, love. [*He makes for the door, but turns aside to the bookshelves*]. I'll just take a book [*he takes one*]. Goodnight. [*He goes out, leaving Ellie alone with the Captain*].

The Captain is intent on his drawing. Ellie, standing sentry over his chair, contemplates him for a moment.

ELLIE. Does nothing ever disturb you, Captain Shotover?

CAPTAIN SHOTOVER. Ive stood on the bridge for eighteen hours in a typhoon. Life here is stormier; but I can stand it.

ELLIE. Do you think I ought to marry Mr. Mangan?

CAPTAIN SHOTOVER [*never looking up*] One rock is as good as another to be wrecked on.

ELLIE. I am not in love with him.

CAPTAIN SHOTOVER. Who said you were?

ELLIE. You are not surprised?

CAPTAIN SHOTOVER. Surprised! At my age!

ELLIE. It seems to me quite fair. He wants me for one thing: I want him for another.

CAPTAIN SHOTOVER. Money?

ELLIE. Yes.

CAPTAIN SHOTOVER. Well, one turns the cheek: the other kisses it. One provides the cash: the other spends it.

ELLIE. Who will have the best of the bargain, I wonder?

CAPTAIN SHOTOVER. You. These fellows live in an office all day. You will have to put up with him from dinner to breakfast; but you will both be asleep most of that time. All day you will be quit of him; and you will be shopping with his money. If that is too much for you, marry a seafaring man: you will be bothered with him only three weeks in the year, perhaps.

ELLIE. That would be best of all, I suppose.

CAPTAIN SHOTOVER. It's a dangerous thing to be married right up to the hilt, like my daughter's husband. The man is at home all day, like a damned soul in hell.

ELLIE. I never thought of that before.

CAPTAIN SHOTOVER. If youre marrying for business, you cant be too businesslike.

ELLIE. Why do women always want other women's husbands?

CAPTAIN SHOTOVER. Why do horse-thieves prefer a horse that is broken-in to one that is wild?

ELLIE [*with a short laugh*] I suppose so. What a vile world it is!

CAPTAIN SHOTOVER. It doesnt concern me. I'm nearly out of it.

ELLIE. And I'm only just beginning.

CAPTAIN SHOTOVER. Yes; so look ahead.

ELLIE. Well, I think I am being very prudent.

CAPTAIN SHOTOVER. I didnt say prudent. I said look ahead.

ELLIE. Whats the difference?

CAPTAIN SHOTOVER. It's prudent to gain the whole world and lose your own soul. But dont forget that your soul sticks to you if you stick to it; but the world has a way of slipping through your fingers.

ELLIE [*wearily, leaving him and beginning to wander restlessly about the room*] I'm sorry, Captain Shotover; but it's no use talking like that to me. Old-fashioned people are no use to me. Old-fashioned people think you can have a soul without money. They think the less money you have, the more soul you have. Young people nowadays know better. A soul is a very expensive thing to keep: much more so than a motor car.

CAPTAIN SHOTOVER. Is it? How much does your soul eat?

ELLIE. Oh, a lot. It eats music and pictures and books and mountains and lakes and beautiful things to wear and nice people to be with. In this country you cant have them without lots of money: that is why our souls are so horribly starved.

CAPTAIN SHOTOVER. Mangan's soul lives on pigs' food.

ELLIE. Yes: money is thrown away on him. I suppose his soul was starved when he was young. But it will not be thrown away on me. It is just because I want to save my soul that I am marrying for money. All the women who are not fools do.

CAPTAIN SHOTOVER. There are other ways of getting money. Why dont you steal it?

ELLIE. Because I dont want to go to prison.

CAPTAIN SHOTOVER. Is that the only reason? Are you quite sure honesty has nothing to do with it?

ELLIE. Oh, you are very v e r y old-fashioned, Captain. Does any modern girl believe that the legal and illegal ways of getting money are the honest and dishonest ways? Mangan robbed my father and my father's friends. I should rob all the money back from Mangan if the police would let me. As they wont, I must get it back by marrying him.

CAPTAIN SHOTOVER. I cant argue: I'm too old: my mind is made up and finished. All I can tell you is that, old-fashioned or new-fashioned, if you sell yourself, you deal your soul a blow that all the books and pictures and concerts and scenery in the world wont heal [*he gets up suddenly and makes for the pantry*].

ELLIE [*running after him and seizing him by the sleeve*] Then why did you sell yourself to the devil in Zanzibar?

CAPTAIN SHOTOVER [*stopping, startled*] What?

ELLIE. You shall not run away before you answer. I have found out that trick of yours. If you sold yourself, why shouldnt I?

CAPTAIN SHOTOVER. I had to deal with men so degraded that they wouldnt obey me unless I swore at them and kicked them and beat them with my fists. Foolish people took young thieves off the streets; flung them into a training ship where they were taught to fear the cane instead of fearing God; and thought theyd made men and sailors of them by private subscription. I tricked these thieves into believing I'd sold myself to the devil. It saved my soul from the kicking and swearing that was damning me by inches.

ELLIE [*releasing him*] I shall pretend to sell myself to Boss Mangan to save my soul from the poverty that is damning m e by inches.

CAPTAIN SHOTOVER. Riches will damn you ten times deeper. Riches wont save even your body.

ELLIE. Old-fashioned again. We know now that the soul is the body, and the body the soul. They tell us they are different because they want to persuade us that we can keep our souls if we let them make slaves of our bodies. I am afraid you are no use to me, Captain.

CAPTAIN SHOTOVER. What did you expect? A Savior, eh? Are you old-fashioned enough to believe in that?

ELLIE. No. But I thought you were very wise, and might help me. Now I have found you out. You pretend to be busy, and think of fine things to say, and run in and out to surprise people by saying them, and get away before they can answer you.

CAPTAIN SHOTOVER. It confuses me to be answered. It discourages me. I cannot bear men and women. I h a v e to run away. I must run away now [*he tries to*].

ELLIE [*again seizing his arm*] You shall not run away from me. I can hypnotize you. You are the only person in the house I can say what I like to. I know you are fond of me. Sit down. [*She draws him to the sofa*].

CAPTAIN SHOTOVER [*yielding*] Take care: I am in my dotage. Old men are dangerous: it doesnt matter to them what is going to happen to the world.

They sit side by side on the sofa. She leans affectionately against him with her head on his shoulder and her eyes half closed.

ELLIE [*dreamily*] I should have thought nothing else mattered to old men. They cant be very interested in what is going to happen to themselves.

CAPTAIN SHOTOVER. A man's interest in the world is only the overflow from his interest in himself. When you are a child your vessel is not yet full; so you care for nothing but your own affairs. When you grow up, your vessel overflows; and you are a politician, a philospher, or an explorer and adventurer. In old age the vessel dries up: there is no overflow: you are a child again. I can give you the memories of my ancient wisdom: mere scraps and leavings; but I no longer really care for anything but my own little wants and hobbies. I sit here working out my old ideas as a means of destroying my fellow-creatures. I see my daughters and their men living foolish lives of romance and sentiment and snobbery. I see you, the younger generation, turning from their romance and sentiment and snobbery to money and comfort and hard common sense. I was ten times happier on the bridge in the typhoon, or frozen into Arctic ice for months in darkness, than you or they have ever been. You are looking for a rich husband. At your age I looked for hardship, danger, horror, and death, that I might feel the life in me more intensely. I did not let the fear of death govern my life; and my reward was, I had my life. You are going to let the fear of poverty govern your life; and your reward will be that you will eat, but you will not live.

ELLIE [*sitting up impatiently*] But what can I do? I am not a sea captain: I cant stand on bridges in typhoons, or go slaughtering seals and whales in Greenland's icy mountains. They wont let women be captains. Do you want me to be a stewardess?

CAPTAIN SHOTOVER. There are worse lives. The stewardesses could come ashore if they liked; but they sail and sail and sail.

ELLIE. What could they do ashore but marry for money? I dont want to be a stewardess: I am too bad a sailor. Think of something else for me.

CAPTAIN SHOTOVER. I cant think so long and continuously. I am too old. I must go in and out. [*He tries to rise*].

ELLIE [*pulling him back*] You shall not. You are happy here, arnt you?

CAPTAIN SHOTOVER. I tell you it's dangerous to keep me. I cant keep awake and alert.

ELLIE. What do you run away for? To sleep?

CAPTAIN SHOTOVER. No. To get a glass of rum.

ELLIE [*frightfully disillusioned*] Is t h a t it? How disgusting! Do you like being drunk?

CAPTAIN SHOTOVER. No: I dread being drunk more than anything in the world. To be drunk means to have dreams; to go soft; to be easily pleased and deceived; to fall into the clutches of women. Drink does that for you when you are young. But when you are old: very very old, like me, the dreams come by themselves. You dont know how terrible that is: you are young: you sleep at night only, and sleep soundly. But later on you will sleep in the afternoon. Later still you will sleep even in the mornings; and you will awake tired, tired of life. You will never be free from dozing and dreams: the dreams will steal upon your work every ten minutes unless you can awaken yourself with rum. I drink now to keep sober; but the dreams are conquering: rum is not what it was: I have had ten glasses since you came; and it might be so much water. Go get me another: Guinness knows where it is. You had better see for yourself the horror of an old man drinking.

ELLIE. You shall not drink. Dream. I like you to dream. You must never be in the real world when we talk together.

CAPTAIN SHOTOVER. I am too weary to resist or too weak. I am in my second childhood. I do not see you as you really are. I cant remember what I really am. I feel nothing but the accursed happiness I have dreaded all my life long: the happiness that comes as life goes, the happiness of yielding and dreaming instead of resisting and doing, the sweetness of the fruit that is going rotten.

ELLIE. You dread it almost as much as I used to dread losing my dreams and having to fight and do things. But that is all over for me: my dreams are dashed to pieces. I should like to marry a very old, very rich man. I should like to marry you. I had much rather marry you than marry Mangan. Are you very rich?

CAPTAIN SHOTOVER. No. Living from hand to mouth. And I have a wife somewhere in Jamaica: a black one. My first wife. Unless she's dead.

ELLIE. What a pity! I feel so happy with you. [*She takes his hand, almost unconsciously, and pats it*]. I thought I should never feel happy again.

CAPTAIN SHOTOVER. Why?

ELLIE. Dont you know?

CAPTAIN SHOTOVER. No.

ELLIE. Heartbreak. I fell in love with Hector, and didnt know he was married.

CAPTAIN SHOTOVER. Heartbreak? Are you one of those who are so sufficient to themselves that they are only happy when they are stripped of everything, even of hope?

ELLIE [*gripping the hand*] It seems so; for I feel now as if there was nothing I could not do, because I want nothing.

CAPTAIN SHOTOVER. Thats the only real strength. Thats genius. Thats better than rum.

ELLIE [*throwing away his hand*] Rum! Why did you spoil it?

Hector and Randall come in from the garden through the starboard door.

HECTOR. I beg your pardon. We did not know there was anyone here.

ELLIE [*rising*] That means that you want to tell Mr Randall the story about the tiger. Come, Captain: I want to talk to my father; and you had better come with me.

CAPTAIN SHOTOVER [*rising*] Nonsense! the man is in bed.

ELLIE. Aha! Ive caught you. My real father has gone to bed; but the father you gave me is in the kitchen. You knew quite well all along. Come. [*She draws him out into the garden with her through the port door*].

HECTOR. Thats an extraordinary girl. She has the Ancient Mariner on a string like a Pekinese dog.

RANDALL. Now that they have gone, shall we have a friendly chat?

HECTOR. You are in what is supposed to be my house. I am at your disposal.

Hector sits down in the draughtsman's chair, turning it to face Randall, who remains standing, leaning at his ease against the carpenter's bench.

RANDALL. I take it that we may be quite frank. I mean about Lady Utterword.

HECTOR. You may. I have nothing to be frank about. I never met her until this afternoon.

RANDALL [*straightening up*] What! But you are her sister's husband.

HECTOR. Well, if you come to that, you are her husband's brother.

RANDALL. But you seem to be on intimate terms with her.

HECTOR. So do you.

RANDALL. Yes; but I am on intimate terms with her. I have known her for years.

HECTOR. It took her years to get to the same point with you that she got to with me in five minutes, it seems.

RANDALL [*vexed*] Really, Ariadne is the limit [*he moves away huffishly towards the windows*].

HECTOR [*coolly*] She is, as I remarked to Hesione, a very enterprising woman.

RANDALL [*returning, much troubled*] You see, Hushabye, you are what women consider a good-looking man.

HECTOR. I cultivated that appearance in the days of my vanity; and Hesione insists on my keeping it up. She makes me wear these ridiculous things [*indicating his Arab costume*] because she thinks me absurd in evening dress.

RANDALL. Still, you do keep it up, old chap. Now, I assure you I have not an atom of jealousy in my disposition—

HECTOR. The question would seem to be rather whether your brother has any touch of that sort.

RANDALL. What! Hastings! Oh, dont trouble about Hastings. He has the gift of being able to work sixteen hours a day at the dullest detail, and actually likes it. That gets him to the top wherever he goes. As long as Ariadne takes care that he is fed regularly, he is only too thankful to anyone who will keep her in good humor for him.

HECTOR. And as she has all the Shotover fascination, there is plenty of competition for the job, eh?

RANDALL [*angrily*] She encourages them. Her conduct is perfectly scandalous. I assure you, my dear fellow, I havnt an atom of jealousy in my composition; but she makes herself the talk of every place she goes to by her thoughtlessness. It's nothing more: she doesnt really care for the men she keeps hanging about her; but how is the world to know that? It's not fair to Hastings. It's not fair to me.

HECTOR. Her theory is that her conduct is so correct—

RANDALL. Correct! She does nothing but make scenes from morning til night. You be careful, old chap. She will get you into trouble: that is, she would if she really cared for you.

HECTOR. Doesnt she?

RANDALL. Not a scrap. She may want your scalp to add to her collection; but her true affection has been engaged years ago. You had really better be careful.

HECTOR. Do you suffer much from this jealousy?

RANDALL. Jealousy? I jealous! My dear fellow, havnt I told you that there is not an atom of—

HECTOR. Yes. And Lady Utterword told me she never made scenes. Well, dont waste your jealousy on my moustache. Never waste jealousy on a real man: it is the imaginary hero that supplants us all in the long run. Besides, jealousy does not belong to your easy man-of-the-world pose, which you carry so well in other respects.

RANDALL. Really, Hushabye, I think a man may be allowed to be a gentleman without being accused of posing.

HECTOR. It is a pose like any other. In this house we know all the poses: our game is to find out the man under the pose. The man under your pose is apparently Ellie's favorite, Othello.

RANDALL. Some of your games in this house are damned annoying, let me tell you.

HECTOR. Yes: I have been their victim for many years. I used to writhe under them at first; but I became accustomed to them. At last I learned to play them.

RANDALL. If it's all the same to you, I had rather you didnt play them on me. You evidently dont quite understand my character, or my notions of good form.

HECTOR. Is it your notion of good form to give away Lady Utterword?

RANDALL [*a childishly plaintive note breaking into his huff*] I have not said a word against Lady Utterword. This is just the conspiracy over again.

HECTOR. What conspiracy?

RANDALL. You know very well, sir. A conspiracy to make me out to be pettish and jealous and childish and everything I am not. Everyone knows I am just the opposite.

HECTOR [*rising*] Something in the air of the house has upset you. It often does have that effect. [*He goes to the garden door and calls Lady Utterword with commanding emphasis*] Ariadne!

LADY UTTERWORD [*at some distance*] Yes.

RANDALL. What are you calling her for? I want to speak—

LADY UTTERWORD [*arriving breathless*] Yes. You really are a terribly commanding person. Whats the matter?

HECTOR. I do not know how to manage your friend Randall. No doubt you do.

LADY UTTERWORD. Randall: have you been making yourself ridiculous, as usual? I can see it in your face. Really, you are the most pettish creature.

RANDALL. You know quite well, Ariadne, that I have not an ounce of pettishness in my disposition. I have made myself perfectly pleasant here. I have remained absolutely cool and imperturbable in the face of a burglar. Imperturbability is almost too strong a point of mine. But [*putting his foot down with a stamp, and walking angrily up and down the room*] I i n s i s t on being treated with a certain consideration. I will not allow Hushabye to take liberties with me. I will not stand your encouraging people as you do.

HECTOR. The man has a rooted delusion that he is your husband.

LADY UTTERWORD. I know. He is jealous. As if he had any right to be! He compromises me everywhere. He makes scenes all over the place. Randall: I will not allow it. I simply will not allow it. You had no right to discuss me with Hector. I will not be discussed by men.

HECTOR. Be reasonable, Ariadne. Your fatal gift of beauty forces men to discuss you.

LADY UTTERWORD. Oh indeed! what about y o u r fatal gift of beauty?

HECTOR. How can I help it?

LADY UTTERWORD. You could cut off your moustache: I cant cut off my nose. I get my whole life messed up with people falling in love with me. And then Randall says I run after men.

RANDALL. I—

LADY UTTERWORD. Yes you do: you said it just now. Why cant you think of something else than women? Napoleon was quite right when he said that women are the occupation of the idle man. Well, if ever there was an idle man on earth, his name is Randall Utterword.

RANDALL. Ariad—

LADY UTTERWORD [*overwhelming him with a torrent of words*] Oh yes you are: it's no use denying it. What have you ever done? What good are you? You are as much trouble in the house as a child of three. You couldnt live without your valet.

RANDALL. This is—

LADY UTTERWORD. Laziness! You are laziness incarnate. You are selfishness itself. You are the most uninteresting man on earth. You cant even gossip about anything but yourself and your grievances and your ailments and the people who have offended you. [*Turning to Hector*] Do you know what they call him, Hector?

HECTOR } [*speaking* { Please dont tell me.
RANDALL } *together*] { I'll not stand it—

LADY UTTERWORD. Randall the Rotter: that is his name in good society.

RANDALL [*shouting*] I'll not bear it, I tell you. Will you listen to me, you infernal— [*he chokes*].

LADY UTTERWORD. Well: go on. What were you going to call me? An infernal what? Which unpleasant animal is it to be this time?

RANDALL [*foaming*] There is no animal in the world so hateful as a woman can be. You are a maddening devil. Hushabye: you will not believe me when I tell you that I have loved this demon all my life; but God knows I have paid for it [*he sits down in the draughtsman's chair, weeping*].

LADY UTTERWORD [*standing over him with triumphant contempt*] Cry-baby!

HECTOR [*gravely, coming to him*] My friend: the Shotover sisters have two strange powers over men. They can make them love; and they can make them cry. Thank your stars that you are not married to one of them.

LADY UTTERWORD [*haughtily*] And pray, Hector—

HECTOR [*suddenly catching her round the shoulders; swinging her right round him and away from Randall; and gripping her throat with the other hand*] Ariadne; if you attempt to start on me, I'll choke you: do you hear? The cat-and-mouse game with the other sex is a good game; but I can play your head off at it. [*He throws her, not at all gently, into the big chair, and proceeds, less fiercely but firmly*] It is true that Napoleon said that woman is the occupation of the idle man. But he added that she is the relaxation of the warrior. Well, *I* am the warrior. So take care.

LADY UTTERWORD [*not in the least put out, and rather pleased by his violence*] My dear Hector: I have only done what you asked me to do.

HECTOR. How do you make that out, pray?

LADY UTTERWORD. You called me in to manage Randall, didnt you? You said you couldnt manage him yourself.

HECTOR. Well, what if I did? I did not ask you to drive the man mad.

LADY UTTERWORD. He isnt mad. Thats the way to manage him. If you were a mother, youd understand.

HECTOR. Mother! What are you up to now?

LADY UTTERWORD. It's quite simple. When the children got nerves and were naughty, I smacked them just enough to give them a good cry and a healthy nervous shock. They went to sleep and were quite good afterwards. Well, I cant smack Randall: he is too big; so when he gets nerves and is naughty, I just rag him til he cries. He will be all right now. Look: he is half asleep already [*which is quite true*].

RANDALL [*waking up indignantly*] I'm not. You are most cruel, Ariadne. [*Sentimentally*] But I suppose I must forgive you, as usual [*he checks himself in the act of yawning*].

LADY UTTERWORD [*to Hector*] Is the explanation satisfactory, dread warrior?

HECTOR. Some day I shall kill you, if you go too far. I thought you were a fool.

LADY UTTERWORD [*laughing*] Everybody does, at first. But I am not such a fool as I look. [*She rises complacently*]. Now, Randall: go to bed. You will be a good boy in the morning.

RANDALL [*only very faintly rebellious*] I'll go to bed when I like. It isnt ten yet.

LADY UTTERWORD. It is long past ten. See that he goes to bed at once, Hector. [*She goes into the garden*].

HECTOR. Is there any slavery on earth viler than this slavery of men to women?

RANDALL [*rising resolutely*] I'll not speak to her tomorrow. I'll not speak to her for another week. I'll give her such a lesson. I'll go straight to bed without bidding her goodnight. [*He makes for the door leading to the hall*].

HECTOR. You are under a spell, man. Old Shotover sold himself to the devil in Zanzibar. The devil gave him a black witch for a wife; and these two demon daughters are their mystical progeny. I am tied to Hesione's apron-string; but I'm her husband; and if I did go stark staring mad about her, at least we became man and wife. But why should you let yourself be dragged about and beaten by Ariadne as a toy donkey is dragged about and beaten by a child? What do you get by it? Are you her lover?

RANDALL. You must not misunderstand me. In a higher sense–in a Platonic sense–

HECTOR. Psha! Platonic sense! She makes you her servant; and when pay-day comes round, she bilks you: that is what you mean.

RANDALL [*feebly*] Well, if I dont mind, I dont see what business it is of yours. Besides, I tell you I am going to punish her. You shall see: *I* know how to deal with women. I'm really very sleepy. Say goodnight to Mrs Hushabye for me, will you, like a good chap. Goodnight. [*He hurries out*].

HECTOR. Poor wretch! Oh women! women! women! [*He lifts his fists in invocation to heaven*] Fall. Fall and crush. [*He goes out into the garden*].

ACT III

In the garden, Hector, as he comes out through the glass door of the poop, finds Lady Utterword lying voluptuously in the hammock on the east side of the flagstaff, in the circle of light cast by the electric arc, which is like a moon in its opal globe. Beneath the head of the hammock, a campstool. On the other side of the flagstaff, on the long garden seat, Captain Shotover is asleep, with Ellie beside him, leaning affectionately against him on his right hand. On his left is a deck chair. Behind them in the gloom, Hesione is strolling about with Mangan. It is a fine still night, moonless.

LADY UTTERWORD. What a lovely night! It seems made for us.

HECTOR. The night takes no interest in us. What are we to the night? [*He sits down moodily in the deck chair*].

ELLIE [*dreamily, nestling against the Captain*] Its beauty soaks into my nerves. In the night there is peace for the old and hope for the young.

HECTOR. Is that remark your own?

ELLIE. No. Only the last thing the Captain said before he went to sleep.

CAPTAIN SHOTOVER. I'm not asleep.

HECTOR. Randall is. Also Mr Mazzini Dunn. Mangan too, probably.

MANGAN. No.

HECTOR. Oh, you are there. I thought Hesione would have sent you to bed by this time.

MRS HUSHABYE [*coming to the back of the garden seat, into the light, with Mangan*] I think I shall. He keeps telling me he has a presentiment that he is going to die. I never met a man so greedy for sympathy.

MANGAN [*plaintively*] But I have a presentiment. I really have. And you wouldnt listen.

MRS HUSHABYE. I was listening for something else. There was a sort of splendid drumming in the sky. Did none of you hear it? It came from a distance and then died away.

MANGAN. I tell you it was a train.

MRS HUSHABYE. And *I* tell you, Alf, there is no train at this hour. The last is nine fortyfive.

MANGAN. But a goods train.

MRS HUSHABYE. Not on our little line. They tack a truck on to the passenger train. What can it have been, Hector?

HECTOR. Heaven's threatening growl of disgust at us useless futile creatures. [*Fiercely*] I tell you, one of two things must happen. Either out of that darkness some new creation will come to supplant us as we have supplanted the animals, or the heavens will fall in thunder and destroy us.

LADY UTTERWORD [*in a cool instructive manner, wallowing comfortably in her hammock*] We have not supplanted the animals, Hector. Why do you ask heaven to destroy this house, which could be made quite comfortable if Hesione had any notion of how to live? Dont you know what is wrong with it?

HECTOR. We are wrong with it. There is no sense in us. We are useless, dangerous, and ought to be abolished.

LADY UTTERWORD. Nonsense! Hastings told me the very first day he came here, nearly twentyfour years ago, what is wrong with the house.

CAPTAIN SHOTOVER. What! The numskull said there was something wrong with my house!

LADY UTTERWORD. I said Hastings said it; and he is not in the least a numskull.

CAPTAIN SHOTOVER. Whats wrong with my house?

LADY UTTERWORD. Just what is wrong with a ship, papa. Wasnt it clever of Hastings to see that?

CAPTAIN SHOTOVER. The man's a fool. Theres nothing wrong with a ship.

LADY UTTERWORD. Yes there is.

MRS HUSHABYE. But what is it? Dont be aggravating, Addy.

LADY UTTERWORD. Guess.

HECTOR. Demons. Daughters of the witch of Zanzibar. Demons.

LADY UTTERWORD. Not a bit. I assure you, all this house needs to make it a sensible, healthy, pleasant house, with good appetites and sound sleep in it, is horses.

MRS HUSHABYE. Horses! What rubbish!

LADY UTTERWORD. Yes: horses. Why have we never been able to let this house? Because there are no proper stables. Go anywhere in England where there are natural, wholesome, contented, and really nice English people; and what do you always find? That the stables are the real centre of the household; and that if any visitor wants to play the piano the whole room has to be upset before it can be opened, there are so many things piled on it. I never lived until I learned to ride; and I shall never ride really well because I didnt begin as a child. There are only two classes in good society in England: the equestrian classes and the neurotic classes. It isnt mere convention: everybody can see that the people who hunt are the right people and the people who dont are the wrong ones.

CAPTAIN SHOTOVER. There is some truth in this. My ship made a man of me; and a ship is the horse of the sea.

LADY UTTERWORD. Exactly how Hastings explained your being a gentleman.

CAPTAIN SHOTOVER. Not bad for a numskull. Bring the man here with you next time: I must talk to him.

LADY UTTERWORD. Why is Randall such an obvious rotter? He is well bred; he has been at a public school and a university; he has been in the Foreign Office; he knows the best people and has lived all his life among them. Why is he so unsatisfactory, so contemptible? Why cant he get a valet to stay with him longer than a few months? Just because he is too lazy and pleasure-loving to hunt and shoot. He strums the piano, and sketches, and runs after married women, and reads literary books and poems. He actually plays the flute; but I never let him bring it into my house. If he would only—[*she is interrupted by the melancholy strains of a flute coming from an open window above. She raises herself indignantly in the hammock*]. Randall: you have not gone to bed. Have you been listening? [*The flute replies pertly:*]

How vulgar! Go to bed instantly, Randall: how dare you? [*The window is slammed down. She subsides*]. How can anyone care for such a creature!

MRS HUSHABYE. Addy: do you think Ellie ought to marry poor Alfred merely for his money?

MANGAN [*much alarmed*] Whats that? Mrs Hushabye: are my affairs to be discussed like this before everybody?

LADY UTTERWORD. I dont think Randall is listening now.

MANGAN. Everybody is listening. It isnt right.

MRS HUSHABYE. But in the dark, what does it matter? Ellie doesnt mind. Do you, Ellie?

ELLIE. Not in the least. What is your opinion, Lady Utterword? You have so much good sense.

MANGAN. But it isnt right. It– [*Mrs Hushabye puts her hand on his mouth*]. Oh, very well.

LADY UTTERWORD. How much money have you, Mr Mangan?

MANGAN. Really– No: I cant stand this.

LADY UTTERWORD. Nonsense, Mr Mangan! It all turns on your income, doesnt it?

MANGAN. Well, if you come to that, how much money has she?

ELLIE. None.

LADY UTTERWORD. You are answered, Mr Mangan. And now, as you have made Miss Dunn throw her cards on the table, you cannot refuse to shew your own.

MRS HUSHABYE. Come, Alf! out with it! How much?

MANGAN [*baited out of all prudence*] Well, if you want to know, I have no money and never had any.

MRS HUSHABYE. Alfred: you mustnt tell naughty stories.

MANGAN. I'm not telling you stories. I'm telling you the raw truth.

LADY UTTERWORD. Then what do you live on, Mr Mangan?

MANGAN. Travelling expenses. And a trifle of commission.

CAPTAIN SHOTOVER. What more have any of us but travelling expenses for our life's journey?

MRS HUSHABYE. But you have factories and capital and things?

MANGAN. People think I have. People think I'm an industrial Napoleon. Thats why Miss Ellie wants to marry me. But I tell you I have nothing.

ELLIE. Do you mean that the factories are like Marcus's tigers? That they dont exist?

MANGAN. They exist all right enough. But theyre not mine. They belong to syndicates and shareholders and all sorts of lazy good-for-nothing capitalists. I get money from such people to start the factories. I find people like Miss Dunn's father to work them, and keep a tight hand so as to make them pay. Of course I make them keep me going pretty well; but it's a dog's life; and I dont own anything.

MRS HUSHABYE. Alfred, Alfred: you are making a poor mouth of it to get out of marrying Ellie.

MANGAN. I'm telling the truth about my money for the first time in my life; and it's the first time my word has ever been doubted.

LADY UTTERWORD. How sad! Why dont you go in for politics, Mr Mangan?

MANGAN. Go in for politics! Where have you been living? I am in politics.

LADY UTTERWORD. I'm sure I beg your pardon. I never heard of you.

MANGAN. Let me tell you, Lady Utterword, that the Prime Minister of this country asked me to join the Government without even going through the nonsense of an election, as the dictator of a great public department.

LADY UTTERWORD. As a Conservative or a Liberal?

MANGAN. No such nonsense. As a practical business man. [*They all burst out laughing*]. What are you all laughing at?

MRS HUSHABYE. Oh, Alfred, Alfred!

ELLIE. You! who have to get my father to do everything for you!

MRS HUSHABYE. You! who are afraid of your own workmen!

HECTOR. You! with whom three women have been playing cat and mouse all the evening!

LADY UTTERWORD. You must have given an immense sum to the party funds, Mr Mangan.

MANGAN. Not a penny out of my pocket. The syndicate found the money: they knew how useful I should be to them in the Government.

LADY UTTERWORD. This is most interesting and unexpected, Mr Mangan. And what have your administrative achievements been, so far?

MANGAN. Achievements? Well, I dont know what you call achievements; but Ive jolly well put a stop to the games of the other fellows in the other departments. Every man of them thought he was going to save the country all by himself, and do me out of the credit and out of my chance of a title. I took good care that if they wouldnt let me do it they shouldnt do it themselves either. I may not know anything about my own machinery; but I know how to stick a ramrod into the other fellow's. And now they all look the biggest fools going.

HECTOR. And in heaven's name, what do y o u look like?

MANGAN. I look like the fellow that was too clever for all the others, dont I? If that isnt a triumph of practical business, what is?

HECTOR. Is this England, or is it a madhouse?

LADY UTTERWORD. Do you expect to save the country, Mr Mangan?

MANGAN. Well, who else will? Will your Mr Randall save it?

LADY UTTERWORD. Randall the rotter! Certainly not.

MANGAN. Will your brother-in-law save it with his moustache and his fine talk.

HECTOR. Yes, if they will let me.

MANGAN [*sneering*] Ah! Will they let you?

HECTOR. No. They prefer you.

MANGAN. Very well then, as youre in a world where I'm appreciated and youre not, youd best be civil to me, hadnt you? Who else is there but me?

LADY UTTERWORD. There is Hastings. Get rid of your ridiculous sham democracy; and give Hastings the necessary powers, and a good supply of bamboo to bring the British native to his senses: he will save the country with the greatest ease.

CAPTAIN SHOTOVER. It had better be lost. Any fool can govern with a stick in his hand. *I* could govern that way. It is not God's way. The man is a numskull.

LADY UTTERWORD. The man is worth all of you rolled into one. What do you say, Miss Dunn?

ELLIE. I think my father would do very well if people did not put upon him and cheat him and despise him because he is so good.

MANGAN [*contemptuously*] I think I see Mazzini Dunn getting into parliament or pushing his way into the Government. Weve not come to that yet, thank God! What do you say, Mrs Hushabye?

MRS HUSHABYE. Oh, *I* say it matters very little which of you governs the country so long as we govern you.

HECTOR. We? Who is we, pray?

MRS HUSHABYE. The devil's granddaughters, dear. The lovely women.

HECTOR [*raising his hands as before*] Fall, I say; and deliver us from the lures of Satan!

ELLIE. There seems to be nothing real in the world except my father and Shakespear. Marcus's tigers are false; Mr Mangan's millions are false; there is nothing really strong and true about Hesione but her beautiful black hair; and Lady Utterword's is too pretty to be real. The one thing that was left to me was the Captain's seventh degree of concentration; and that turns out to be—

CAPTAIN SHOTOVER. Rum.

LADY UTTERWORD [*placidly*] A good deal of my hair is quite genuine. The Duchess of Dithering offered me fifty guineas for this [*touching her forehead*] under the impression that it was a transformation; but it is all natural except the color.

MANGAN [*wildly*] Look here: I'm going to take off all my clothes [*he begins tearing off his coat*].

[*in consternation*]
LADY UTTERWORD. Mr Mangan!
CAPTAIN SHOTOVER. Whats that?
HECTOR. Ha! ha! Do. Do.
ELLIE. Please dont.

MRS HUSHABYE [*catching his arm and stopping him*] Alfred: for shame! Are you mad?

MANGAN. Shame! What shame is there in this house? Let's all strip stark naked. We may as well do the thing thoroughly when we're about it. Weve stripped ourselves morally naked: well, let us strip ourselves physically naked as well, and see how we like it. I tell you I cant bear this. I was brought up to be respectable. I dont mind the women dyeing their hair and the men drinking: it's human nature. But it's not human nature to tell everybody about it. Every time one of you opens your mouth I go like this [*he cowers as if to avoid a missile*] afraid of what will come next. How are we to have any self-respect if we dont keep it up that we're better than we really are?

LADY UTTERWORD. I quite sympathize with you, Mr Mangan. I have been through it all; and I know by experience that men and women are delicate plants and must be cultivated under glass. Our family habit of throwing stones in all directions and letting the air in is not only unbearably rude, but positively dangerous. Still, there is no use catching physical colds as well as moral ones; so please keep your clothes on.

MANGAN. I'll do as I like: not what you tell me. Am I a child or a grown man? I wont stand this mothering tyranny. I'll go back to the city, where I'm respected and made much of.

MRS HUSHABYE. Goodbye, Alf. Think of us sometimes in the city. Think of Ellie's youth!

ELLIE. Think of Hesione's eyes and hair!

CAPTAIN SHOTOVER. Think of this garden in which you are not a dog barking to keep the truth out!

HECTOR. Think of Lady Utterword's beauty! her good sense! her style!

LADY UTTERWORD. Flatterer. Think, Mr Mangan, whether you can really do any better for yourself elsewhere: that is the essential point, isnt it?

MANGAN [*surrendering*] All right: all right. I'm done. Have it your own way. Only let me alone. I dont know whether I'm on my head or my heels when you all start on me like this. I'll stay. I'll marry her. I'll do anything for a quiet life. Are you satisfied now?

ELLIE. No. I never really intended to make you marry me, Mr Mangan. Never in the depths of my soul. I only wanted to feel my strength: to know that you could not escape if I chose to take you.

MANGAN [*indignantly*] What! Do you mean to say you are going to throw me over after my acting so handsome?

LADY UTTERWORD. I should not be too hasty, Miss Dunn. You can throw Mr Mangan over at any time up to the last moment. Very few men in his position go bankrupt. You can live very comfortably on his reputation for immense wealth.

ELLIE. I cannot commit bigamy, Lady Utterword.

<table>
<tr><td>MRS. HUSHABYE.</td><td rowspan="4">[exclaiming all together]</td><td>Bigamy! Whatever on earth are you talking about, Ellie?</td></tr>
<tr><td>LADY UTTERWORD.</td><td>Bigamy! What do you mean, Miss Dunn?</td></tr>
<tr><td>MANGAN.</td><td>Bigamy! Do you mean to say youre married already?</td></tr>
<tr><td>HECTOR.</td><td>Bigamy! This is some enigma.</td></tr>
</table>

ELLIE. Only half an hour ago I became Captain Shotover's white wife.

MRS HUSHABYE. Ellie! What nonsense! Where?

ELLIE. In heaven, where all true marriages are made.

LADY UTTERWORD. Really, Miss Dunn! Really, papa!

MANGAN. He told me *I* was too old! And him a mummy!

HECTOR [*quoting Shelley*]

"Their altar the grassy earth outspread,
And their priest the muttering wind."

ELLIE. Yes: I, Ellie Dunn, give my broken heart and my strong sound soul to its natural captain, my spiritual husband and second father.

She draws the Captain's arm through hers, and pats his hand. The Captain remains fast asleep.

MRS HUSHABYE. Oh, thats very clever of you, pettikins. V e r y clever. Alfred: you could never have lived up to Ellie. You must be content with a little share of me.

MANGAN [*sniffing and wiping his eyes*] It isnt kind— [*his emotion chokes him*].

LADY UTTERWORD. You are well out of it, Mr Mangan. Miss Dunn is the most conceited young woman I have met since I came back to England.

MRS HUSHABYE. Oh, Ellie isnt conceited. Are you, pettikins?

ELLIE. I know my strength now, Hesione.

MANGAN. Brazen, I call you. Brazen.

MRS HUSHABYE. Tut, tut, Alfred: dont be rude. Dont you feel how lovely this marriage night is, made in heaven? Arnt you happy, you and Hector? Open your eyes: Addy and Ellie look beautiful enough to please the most fastidious man: we live and love and have not a care in the world. We women have managed all that for you. Why in the name of common sense do you go on as if you were two miserable wretches?

CAPTAIN SHOTOVER. I tell you happiness is no good. You can be happy when you are only half alive. I am happier now I am half dead than ever I was in my prime. But there is no blessing on my happiness.

ELLIE [*her face lighting up*] Life with a blessing! that is what I want. Now I know the real reason why I couldnt marry Mr Mangan: there would be no blessing on our marriage. There is a blessing on my broken heart. There is a blessing on your beauty, Hesione. There is a blessing on your father's spirit. Even on the lies of Marcus there is a blessing; but on Mr Mangan's money there is none.

MANGAN. I dont understand a word of that.

ELLIE. Neither do I. But I know it means something.

MANGAN. Dont say there was any difficulty about the blessing. I was ready to get a bishop to marry us.

MRS HUSHABYE. Isnt he a fool, pettikins?

HECTOR [*fiercely*] Do not scorn the man. We are all fools.

Mazzini, in pyjamas and a richly colored silk dressing-gown, comes from the house, on Lady Utterword's side.

MRS HUSHABYE. Oh! here comes the only man who ever resisted me. Whats the matter, Mr Dunn? Is the house on fire?

MAZZINI. Oh no: nothing's the matter; but really it's impossible to go to sleep with such an interesting conversation going on under one's window, and on such a beautiful night too. I just had to come down and join you all. What has it all been about?

MRS HUSHABYE. Oh, wonderful things, soldier of freedom.

HECTOR. For example, Mangan, as a practical business man, has tried to undress himself and has failed ignominiously; whilst you, as an idealist, have succeeded brilliantly.

MAZZINI. I hope you dont mind my being like this, Mrs Hushabye. [*He sits down on the campstool*].

MRS HUSHABYE. On the contrary, I could wish you always like that.

LADY UTTERWORD. Your daughter's match is off, Mr Dunn. It seems that

Mr Mangan, whom we all supposed to be a man of property, owns absolutely nothing.

MAZZINI. Well of course I knew that, Lady Utterword. But if people believe in him and are always giving him money, whereas they dont believe in me and never give me any, how can I ask poor Ellie to depend on what I can do for her?

MANGAN. Dont you run away with this idea that I have nothing. I—

HECTOR. Oh, dont explain. We understand. You have a couple of thousand pounds in exchequer bills, 50,000 shares worth tenpence a dozen, and half a dozen tabloids of cyanide of potassium to poison yourself with when you are found out. Thats the reality of your millions.

MAZZINI. Oh no, no, no. He is quite honest: the businesses are genuine and perfectly legal.

HECTOR [*disgusted*] Yah! Not even a great swindler!

MANGAN. So you think. But Ive been too many for some honest men, for all that.

LADY UTTERWORD. There is no pleasing you, Mr Mangan. You are determined to be neither rich nor poor, honest nor dishonest.

MANGAN. There you go again. Ever since I came into this silly house I have been made to look like a fool, though I'm as good a man in this house as in the city.

ELLIE [*musically*] Yes: this silly house, this strangely happy house, this agonizing house, this house without foundations. I shall call it Heartbreak House.

MRS HUSHABYE. Stop, Ellie; or I shall howl like an animal.

MANGAN [*breaks into a low snivelling*]!!!

MRS HUSHABYE. There! you have set Alfred off.

ELLIE. I like him best when he is howling.

CAPTAIN SHOTOVER. Silence! [*Mangan subsides into silence*]. I say, let the heart break in silence.

HECTOR. Do you accept that name for your house?

CAPTAIN SHOTOVER. It is not my house: it is only my kennel.

HECTOR. We have been too long here. We do not live in this house: we haunt it.

LADY UTTERWORD [*heart torn*] It is dreadful to think how you have been here all these years while I have gone round the world. I escaped young; but it has drawn me back. It wants to break my heart too. But it shant. I have left you and it behind. It was silly of me to come back. I felt sentimental about papa and Hesione and the old place. I felt them calling to me.

MAZZINI. But what a very natural and kindly and charming human feeling, Lady Utterword!

LADY UTTERWORD. So I thought, Mr Dunn. But I know now that it was only the last of my influenza. I found that I was not remembered and not wanted.

CAPTAIN SHOTOVER. You left because you did not want us. Was there no heartbreak in that for your father? You tore yourself up by the roots; and the ground healed up and brought forth fresh plants and forgot you. What right had you to come back and probe old wounds?

MRS HUSHABYE. You were a complete stranger to me at first, Addy; but now I feel as if you had never been away.

LADY UTTERWORD. Thank you, Hesione; but the influenza is quite cured. The place may be Heartbreak House to you, Miss Dunn, and to this gentleman from the city who seems to have so little self-control; but to me it is only a very ill-regulated and rather untidy villa without any stables.

HECTOR. Inhabited by—?

ELLIE. A crazy old sea captain and a young singer who adores him.

MRS HUSHABYE. A sluttish female, trying to stave off a double chin and an elderly spread, vainly wooing a born soldier of freedom.

MAZZINI. Oh, really, Mrs Hushabye—

MANGAN. A member of His Majesty's Government that everybody sets down as a nincompoop: dont forget him, Lady Utterword.

LADY UTTERWORD. And a very fascinating gentleman whose chief occupation is to be married to my sister.

HECTOR. All heartbroken imbeciles.

MAZZINI. Oh no. Surely, if I may say so, rather a favorable specimen of what is best in our English culture. You are very charming people, most advanced, unprejudiced, frank, humane, unconventional, democratic, free-thinking, and everything that is delightful to thoughtful people.

MRS HUSHABYE. You do us proud, Mazzini.

MAZZINI. I am not flattering, really. Where else could I feel perfectly at ease in my pyjamas? I sometimes dream that I am in very distinguished society, and suddenly I have nothing on but my pyjamas! Sometimes I havnt even pyjamas. And I always feel overwhelmed with confusion. But here, I dont mind in the least: it seems quite natural.

LADY UTTERWORD. An infallible sign that you are not now in really distinguished society, Mr Dunn. If you were in my house, you *would* feel embarrassed.

MAZZINI. I shall take particular care to keep out of your house, Lady Utterword.

LADY UTTERWORD. You will be quite wrong, Mr Dunn. I should make you very comfortable; and you would not have the trouble and anxiety of wondering whether you should wear your purple and gold or your green and crimson dressing-gown at dinner. You complicate life instead of simplifying it by doing these ridiculous things.

ELLIE. Your house is not Heartbreak House: is it, Lady Utterword?

HECTOR. Yet she breaks hearts, easy as her house is. That poor devil upstairs with his flute howls when she twists his heart, just as Mangan howls when my wife twists his.

LADY UTTERWORD. That is because Randall has nothing to do but have his heart broken. It is a change from having his head shampooed. Catch anyone breaking Hastings' heart!

CAPTAIN SHOTOVER. The numskull wins, after all.

LADY UTTERWORD. I shall go back to my numskull with the greatest satisfaction when I am tired of you all, clever as you are.

MANGAN [*huffily*] I never set up to be clever.

LADY UTTERWORD. I forgot you, Mr Mangan.

MANGAN. Well, I dont see that quite, either.

LADY UTTERWORD. You may not be clever, Mr Mangan; but you are successful.

MANGAN. But I dont want to be regarded merely as a successful man. I have an imagination like anyone else. I have a presentiment—

MRS HUSHABYE. Oh, you are impossible, Alfred. Here I am devoting myself to you; and you think of nothing but your ridiculous presentiment. You bore me. Come and talk poetry to me under the stars. [*She drags him away into the darkness*].

MANGAN [*tearfully, as he disappears*] Yes: it's all very well to make fun of me; but if you only knew—

HECTOR [*impatiently*] How is all this going to end?

MAZZINI. It wont end, Mr Hushabye. Life doesnt end: it goes on.

ELLIE. Oh, it cant go on for ever. I'm always expecting something. I dont know what it is; but life must come to a point sometime.

LADY UTTERWORD. The point for a young woman of your age is a baby.

HECTOR. Yes, but, damn it, I have the same feeling; and *I* cant have a baby.

LADY UTTERWORD. By deputy, Hector.

HECTOR. But I *have* children. All that is over and done with for me: and yet I too feel that this cant last. We sit here talking, and leave everything to Mangan and to chance and to the devil. Think of the powers of destruction that Mangan and his mutual admiration gang wield! It's madness: it's like giving a torpedo to a badly brought up child to play at earthquakes with.

MAZZINI. I know. I used often to think about that when I was young.

HECTOR. Think! Whats the good of thinking about it? Why didnt you do something?

MAZZINI. But I did. I joined societies and made speeches and wrote pamphlets. That was all I could do. But, you know, though the people in the societies thought they knew more than Mangan, most of them wouldnt have joined if they had known as much. You see they had never had any money to handle or any men to manage. Every year I expected a revolution, or some frightful smash-up: it seemed impossible that we could blunder and muddle on any longer. But nothing happened, except, of course, the usual poverty and crime and drink that we are used to. Nothing ever does happen. It's amazing how well we get along, all things considered.

LADY UTTERWORD. Perhaps somebody cleverer than you and Mr Mangan was at work all the time.

MAZZINI. Perhaps so. Though I was brought up not to believe in anything, I often feel that there is a great deal to be said for the theory of an overruling Providence, after all.

LADY UTTERWORD. Providence! I meant Hastings.

MAZZINI. Oh, I *beg* your pardon, Lady Utterword.

CAPTAIN SHOTOVER. Every drunken skipper trusts to Providence. But one of the ways of Providence with drunken skippers is to run them on the rocks.

MAZZINI. Very true, no doubt, at sea. But in politics, I assure you, they only run into jellyfish. Nothing happens.

CAPTAIN SHOTOVER. At sea nothing happens to the sea. Nothing happens to the sky. The sun comes up from the east and goes down to the west. The moon grows from a sickle to an arc lamp, and comes later and later until she is lost in the light as other things are lost in the darkness. After the typhoon, the flying-fish glitter in the sunshine like birds. It's amazing how *they* get along, all things considered. Nothing happens, except something not worth mentioning.

ELLIE. What is that, O Captain, my captain?

CAPTAIN SHOTOVER [*savagely*] Nothing but the smash of the drunken skipper's ship on the rocks, the splintering of her rotten timbers, the tearing of her rusty plates, the drowning of the crew like rats in a trap.

ELLIE. Moral: dont take rum.

CAPTAIN SHOTOVER [*vehemently*] That is a lie, child. Let a man drink ten barrels of rum a day, he is not a drunken skipper until he is a drifting skipper. Whilst he can lay his course and stand on his bridge and steer it, he is no drunkard. It is the man who lies drinking in his bunk and trusts to Providence that I call the drunken skipper, though he drank nothing but the waters of the River Jordan.

ELLIE. Splendid! And you havnt had a drop for an hour. You see you dont need it: your own spirit is not dead.

CAPTAIN SHOTOVER. Echoes: nothing but echoes. The last shot was fired years ago.

HECTOR. And this ship that we are all in? This soul's prison we call England?

CAPTAIN SHOTOVER. The captain is in his bunk, drinking bottled ditch-water; and the crew is gambling in the forecastle. She will strike and sink and split. Do you think the laws of God will be suspended in favor of England because you were born in it?

HECTOR. Well, I dont mean to be drowned like a rat in a trap. I still have the will to live. What am I to do?

CAPTAIN SHOTOVER. Do? Nothing simpler. Learn your business as an Englishman.

HECTOR. And what may my business as an Englishman be, pray?

CAPTAIN SHOTOVER. Navigation. Learn it and live; or leave it and be damned.

ELLIE. Quiet, quiet: youll tire yourself.

MAZZINI. I thought all that once, Captain; but I assure you nothing will happen.

A dull distant explosion is heard.

HECTOR [*starting up*] What was that?

CAPTAIN SHOTOVER. Something happening [*he blows his whistle*]. Breakers ahead!

The light goes out.

HECTOR [*furiously*] Who put that light out? Who dared put that light out?

NURSE GUINNESS [*running in from the house to the middle of the esplanade*] I did, sir. The police have telephoned to say we'll be summoned if we dont put that light out: it can be seen for miles.

HECTOR. It shall be seen for a hundred miles [*he dashes into the house*].

NURSE GUINNESS. The rectory is nothing but a heap of bricks, they say. Unless we can give the rector a bed he has nowhere to lay his head this night.

CAPTAIN SHOTOVER. The Church is on the rocks, breaking up. I told him it would unless it headed for God's open sea.

NURSE GUINNESS. And you are all to go down to the cellars.

CAPTAIN SHOTOVER. Go there yourself, you and all the crew. Batten down the hatches.

NURSE GUINNESS. And hide beside the coward I married! I'll go on the roof first. [*The lamp lights up again*]. There! Mr Hushabye's turned it on again.

THE BURGLAR [*hurrying in and appealing to Nurse Guinness*] Here: wheres the way to that gravel pit? The boot-boy says theres a cave in the gravel pit. Them cellars is no use. Wheres the gravel pit, Captain?

NURSE GUINNESS. Go straight on past the flagstaff until you fall into it and break your dirty neck. [*She pushes him contemptuously towards the flagstaff, and herself goes to the foot of the hammock and waits there, as it were by Ariadne's cradle*].

Another and louder explosion is heard. The burglar stops and stands trembling.

ELLIE [*rising*] That was nearer.

CAPTAIN SHOTOVER. The next one will get us. [*He rises*]. Stand by, all hands, for judgment.

THE BURGLAR. Oh my Lordy God! [*He rushes away frantically past the flagstaff into the gloom*].

MRS HUSHABYE [*emerging panting from the darkness*] Who was that running away? [*She comes to Ellie*]. Did you hear the explosions? And the sound in the sky: it's splendid: it's like an orchestra: it's like Beethoven.

ELLIE. By thunder, Hesione: it i s Beethoven.

She and Hesione throw themselves into one another's arms in wild excitement. The light increases.

MAZZINI [*anxiously*] The light is getting brighter.

NURSE GUINNESS [*looking up at the house*] It's Mr Hushabye turning on all the lights in the house and tearing down the curtains.

RANDALL [*rushing in in his pyjamas, distractedly waving a flute*] Ariadne: my soul, my precious, go down to the cellars: I beg and implore you, go down to the cellars!

LADY UTTERWORD [*quite composed in her hammock*] The governor's wife in the cellars with the servants! Really, Randall!

RANDALL. But what shall I do if you are killed?

LADY UTTERWORD. You will probably be killed, too, Randall. Now play your flute to shew that you are not afraid; and be good. Play us Keep the Home Fires Burning.

NURSE GUINNESS [*grimly*] Theyll keep the home fires burning for us: them up there.

RANDALL [*having tried to play*] My lips are trembling. I cant get a sound.

MAZZINI. I hope poor Mangan is safe.

MRS HUSHABYE. He is hiding in the cave in the gravel pit.

CAPTAIN SHOTOVER. My dynamite drew him there. It is the hand of God.

HECTOR [*returning from the house and striding across to his former place*] There is not half light enough. We should be blazing to the skies.

ELLIE [*tense with excitement*] Set fire to the house, Marcus.

MRS HUSHABYE. My house! No.

HECTOR. I thought of that; but it would not be ready in time.

CAPTAIN SHOTOVER. The judgment has come. Courage will not save you; but it will shew that your souls are still alive.

MRS HUSHABYE. Sh-sh! Listen: do you hear it now? It's magnificent.

They all turn away from the house and look up, listening.

HECTOR [*gravely*] Miss Dunn: you can do no good here. We of this house are only moths flying into the candle. You had better go down to the cellar.

ELLIE [*scornfully*] I dont think.

MAZZINI. Ellie, dear, there is no disgrace in going to the cellar. An officer would order his soldiers to take cover. Mr Hushabye is behaving like an amateur. Mangan and the burglar are acting very sensibly; and it is they who will survive.

ELLIE. Let them. I shall behave like an amateur. But why should you run any risk?

MAZZINI. Think of the risk those poor fellows up there are running!

NURSE GUINNESS. Think of them, indeed, the murdering blackguards! What next?

A terrific explosion shakes the earth. They reel back into their seats, or clutch the nearest support. They hear the falling of the shattered glass from the windows.

MAZZINI. Is anyone hurt?
HECTOR. Where did it fall?
NURSE GUINNESS [*in hideous triumph*] Right in the gravel pit: I seen it. Serve un right! I seen it [*she runs away towards the gravel pit, laughing harshly*].
HECTOR. One husband gone.
CAPTAIN SHOTOVER. Thirty pounds of good dynamite wasted.
MAZZINI. Oh, poor Mangan!
HECTOR. Are you immortal that you need pity him? Our turn next.

They wait in silence and intense expectation. Hesione and Ellie hold each other's hand tight.

A distant explosion is heard.

MRS HUSHABYE [*relaxing her grip*] Oh! they have passed us.
LADY UTTERWORD. The danger is over, Randall. Go to bed.
CAPTAIN SHOTOVER. Turn in, all hands. The ship is safe. [*He sits down and goes asleep*].
ELLIE [*disappointedly*] Safe!
HECTOR [*disgustedly*] Yes, safe. And how damnably dull the world has become again suddenly! [*He sits down*].
MAZZINI [*sitting down*] I was quite wrong, after all. It is we who have survived; and Mangan and the burglar—
HECTOR. —the two burglars—
LADY UTTERWORD. —the two practical men of business—
MAZZINI. —both gone. And the poor clergyman will have to get a new house.
MRS HUSHABYE. But what a glorious experience! I hope theyll come again tomorrow night.
ELLIE [*radiant at the prospect*] Oh, I h o p e so.

Randall at last succeeds in keeping the home fires burning on his flute.

SAINT JOAN:
A Chronicle Play

Composition begun 29 April 1923; completed 24 August 1923. First published in German translation, as *Die heilige Johanna,* in the *Neue Rundschau* (Berlin), June-September 1924. Published in English, 1924. First presented by the Theatre Guild at the Garrick Theatre, New York, on 28 December 1923.

Robert de Baudricourt *Ernest Cossart*
Steward *William M. Griffith*
Joan ("The Maid") *Winifred Lenihan*
Bertrand de Poulengey *Frank Tweed*
La Trémouille, Constable of France *Herbert Ashton*
The Archbishop of Rheims *Albert Bruning*
Court Page *Jo Mielziner*
Gilles de Rais ("Bluebeard") *Walton Butterfield*
Captain La Hire *Morris Carnovsky*
The Dauphin (later Charles VII) *Philip Leigh*
The Duchesse de la Trémouille *Elizabeth Pearré*
Dunois, Bastard of Orleans *Maurice Colbourne*
Dunois' Page *James Norris*
Richard de Beauchamp, Earl of Warwick *A. H. Van Buren*
John Bowyer Spenser Neville de Stogumber (Warwick's Chaplain) *Henry Travers*
Warwick's Page *Seth Baldwin*
Peter Cauchon, Bishop of Beauvais *Ian Maclaren*
Brother John Lemaître (The Inquisitor) *Joseph Macaulay*
John d'Estivet, Canon of Bayeux *Albert Perry*
De Courcelles, Canon of Paris *Walton Butterfield*
Brother Martin Ladvenu *Morris Carnovsky*
The Executioner *Herbert Ashton*
An English Soldier *Frank Tweed*
A Clerical Gentleman *Ernest Cossart*
Also Courtiers, Monks, Soldiers, etc.

Period—The Fifteenth Century, during the Hundred Years War. In France

Scene 1: *The Castle of Vaucouleurs. 23 February 1429*
Scene 2: *Antechamber and Throne Room at Chinon. 8 March 1429*

Scene 3: *The Bank of the River Loire near Orléans. 29 May 1429*
Scene 4: *The Earl of Warwick's Tent in the English Camp*
Scene 5: *The Ambulatory of Rheims Cathedral. 17 July 1429*
Scene 6: *A Hall in the Castle at Rouen. The Trial of Joan. 30 May 1431*
Epilogue: *Bedroom in the Château of Charles VII. June 1456*

Preface

Contents

JOAN THE ORIGINAL AND PRESUMPTUOUS

Joan of Arc, a village girl from the Vosges, was born about 1412; burnt for heresy, witchcraft, and sorcery in 1431; rehabilitated after a fashion in 1456; designated Venerable in 1904; declared Blessed in 1908; and finally canonized in 1920. She is the most notable Warrior Saint in the Christian calendar, and the queerest fish among the eccentric worthies of the Middle Ages. Though a professed and most pious Catholic, and the projector of a Crusade against the Husites, she was in fact one of the first Protestant martyrs. She was also one of the first apostles of Nationalism, and the first French practitioner of Napoleonic realism in warfare as distinguished from the sporting ransom-gambling chivalry of her time. She was the pioneer of rational dressing for women, and, like Queen Christina of Sweden two centuries later, to say nothing of Catalina de Erauso and innumerable obscure heroines who have disguised themselves as men to serve as soldiers and sailors, she refused to accept the specific woman's lot, and dressed and fought and lived as men did.

As she contrived to assert herself in all these ways with such force that she was famous throughout western Europe before she was out of her teens (indeed she never got out of them), it is hardly surprising that she was judicially burnt, ostensibly for a number of capital crimes which we no longer punish as such, but essentially for what we call unwomanly and insufferable presumption. At eighteen Joan's pretensions were beyond those of the proudest Pope or the haughtiest emperor. She claimed to be the ambassador and plenipotentiary of God, and to be, in effect, a member of the Church Triumphant whilst still in the flesh on earth. She patronized her own king, and summoned the English king to repentance and obedience to her commands. She lectured, talked down, and overruled statesmen and prelates. She poohpoohed the plans of generals, leading their troops to victory on plans of her own. She had an unbounded and quite unconcealed contempt for official opinion, judgment, and authority, and for War Office tactics and strategy. Had she been a sage and monarch in whom the most venerable hierarchy and the most illustrious dynasty converged, her pretensions and proceedings would have been as trying to the official mind as the pretensions of Caesar were to Cassius. As her actual condition was pure upstart, there were only two opinions about her. One was that she was miraculous: the other that she was unbearable.

JOAN AND SOCRATES

If Joan had been malicious, selfish, cowardly or stupid, she would have been one of the most odious persons known to history instead of one of the most attractive. If she had been old enough to know the effect she was producing on the men whom she humiliated by being right when they were wrong, and had learned to flatter and manage them, she might have lived as long as Queen Elizabeth. But she was too young and rustical and inexperienced to have any such arts. When she was thwarted by men whom she thought fools, she made no secret of her opinion of them or her impatience with their folly; and she was naïve enough to expect them to be obliged to her for setting them right and keeping them out of mischief. Now it is always hard for superior wits to understand the fury roused by their exposures of the stupidities of comparative dullards. Even Socrates, for all his age and experience, did not defend himself at his trial like a man who understood the long accumulated fury that had burst on him, and was clamoring for his death. His accuser, if born 2300 years later, might have been picked out of any first class carriage on a suburban railway during the evening or morning rush from or to the City; for he had really nothing to say except that he and his like could not endure being shewn up as idiots every time Socrates opened his mouth. Socrates, unconscious of this, was paralyzed by his sense that somehow he was missing the point of the attack. He petered out after he had established the fact that he was an old soldier and a man of honorable life, and that his accuser was a silly snob. He had no suspicion of the extent to which his mental superiority had roused fear and hatred against him in the hearts of men towards whom he was conscious of nothing but good will and good service.

CONTRAST WITH NAPOLEON

If Socrates was as innocent as this at the age of seventy, it may be imagined how innocent Joan was at the age of seventeen. Now Socrates was a man of argument, operating slowly and peacefully on men's minds, whereas Joan was a woman of action, operating with impetuous violence on their bodies. That, no doubt, is why the contemporaries of Socrates endured him so long, and why Joan was destroyed before she was fully grown. But both of them combined terrifying ability with a frankness, personal modesty, and benevolence which made the furious dislike to which they fell victims absolutely unreasonable, and therefore inapprehensible by themselves. Napoleon, also possessed of terrifying ability, but neither frank nor disinterested, had no illusions as to the nature of his popularity. When he was asked how the world would take his death, he said it would give a gasp of relief. But it is not so easy for mental giants who neither hate nor intend to injure their fellows to realize that nevertheless their fellows hate mental giants and would like to destroy them, not only enviously because the juxtaposition of a superior wounds their vanity, but quite humbly and honestly because it frightens them. Fear will drive men to any extreme; and the fear inspired by a superior being is a mystery which cannot be reasoned away. Being immeasurable it is unbearable when there is no presumption or guarantee of its benevolence and moral responsibility: in other words, when it has no official status. The legal and conventional superiority of Herod and Pilate, and of Annas and Caiaphas, inspires fear; but the fear, being a reasonable fear of measurable and avoidable consequences which seem salutary and protective, is bearable; whilst the strange superiority of Christ and the fear it inspires elicit a shriek of Crucify Him from all who cannot divine its benevolence. Socrates has to drink the hemlock, Christ to hang on the cross, and Joan to burn at the stake, whilst Napoleon, though he ends in St Helena, at least dies in his bed there; and many terrifying but quite comprehensible official scoundrels die natural deaths in all the glory of the kingdoms of this world, proving that it is far more dangerous to be a saint than to be a conqueror. Those who have been both, like Mahomet and Joan, have found that it is the conqueror who must save the saint, and that defeat and capture mean martyrdom. Joan was burnt without a hand lifted on her own side to save her. The comrades she had led to victory and the enemies she had disgraced and defeated, the French king she had crowned and the English king whose crown she had kicked into the Loire, were equally glad to be rid of her.

WAS JOAN INNOCENT OR GUILTY?

As this result could have been produced by a crapulous inferiority as well as by a sublime superiority, the question which of the two was operative in Joan's case has to be faced. It was decided against her by her contemporaries after a very careful and conscientious trial; and the reversal of the verdict twentyfive years later, in form a rehabilitation of Joan, was really only a confirmation of the validity of the coronation of Charles VII. It is the more impressive reversal by a unanimous Posterity, culminating in her canonization, that has quashed the original proceedings, and put her judges on their trial, which, so far, has been much more unfair than their trial of her. Nevertheless the rehabilitation of 1456, corrupt job as it was, really did produce evidence enough to satisfy all reasonable critics that Joan was not a common termagant, not a harlot, not a witch, not a blasphemer, no more an idolater than the Pope himself, and not ill conducted in any sense apart from her soldiering, her wearing of men's clothes, and her audacity, but on the contrary good-humored, an intact virgin, very pious, very temperate (we should call her meal of bread soaked in the common wine which is the drinking water of France ascetic), very kindly, and, though a brave and hardy soldier, unable to endure loose language or licentious conduct. She went to the stake without a stain on her character except the overweening presumption, the superbity as they called it, that led her thither. It would therefore be waste of time now to prove that the Joan of the first part of the Elizabethan chronicle play of Henry VI (supposed to have been tinkered by Shakespear) grossly libels her in its concluding scenes in deference to Jingo patriotism. The mud that was thrown at her has dropped off by this time so completely that there is no need for any modern writer to wash up after it. What is far more difficult to get rid of is the mud that is being thrown at her judges, and the whitewash which disfigures her beyond recognition. When Jingo scurrility had done its worst to her, sectarian scurrility (in this case Protestant scurrility) used her stake to beat the Roman Catholic Church and the Inquisition. The easiest way to make these institutions the villains of a melodrama was to make The Maid its heroine. That melodrama may be dismissed as rubbish. Joan got a far fairer trial from the Church and the Inquisition than any prisoner of her type and in her situation gets nowadays in any official secular court; and the decision was strictly according to law. And she was not a melodramatic heroine: that is, a physically beautiful lovelorn parasite on an equally beautiful hero, but a genius and a saint, about as completely the opposite of a melodramatic heroine as it is possible for a human being to be.

Let us be clear about the meaning of the terms. A genius is a person who, seeing farther and probing deeper than other people, has a different set of ethical valuations from theirs, and has energy enough to give effect to this extra vision and its valuations in whatever manner best suits his or her specific talents. A saint is one who having practised heroic virtues, and enjoyed revelations or powers of the order which The Church classes technically as supernatural, is eligible for canonization. If a historian is an Anti-Feminist, and does not believe women to be capable of genius in the traditional masculine departments, he will never make anything of Joan, whose genius was turned to practical account mainly in soldiering and politics. If he is Rationalist enough to deny that saints exist, and to hold that new ideas cannot come otherwise than by conscious ratiocination, he will never catch Joan's likeness. Her ideal biographer must be free from nineteenth century prejudices and biases; must understand the Middle Ages, the Roman Catholic Church, and the Holy Roman Empire much more intimately than our Whig historians have ever understood them; and must be capable of throwing off sex partialities and their romance, and regarding woman as the female of the human species, and not as a different kind of animal with specific charms and specific imbecilities.

JOAN'S GOOD LOOKS

To put the last point roughly, any book about Joan which begins by describing her as a beauty may be at once classed as a romance. Not one of Joan's comrades, in village, court, or camp, even when they were straining themselves to please the king by praising her, ever claimed that she was pretty. All the men who alluded to the matter declared most emphatically that she was unattractive sexually to a degree that seemed to them miraculous, considering that she was in the bloom of youth, and neither ugly, awkward, deformed, nor unpleasant in her person. The evident truth is that like most women of her hardy managing type she seemed neutral in the conflict of sex because men were too much afraid of her to fall in love with her. She herself was not sexless: in spite of the virginity she had vowed up to a point, and preserved to her death, she never excluded the possibility of marriage for herself. But marriage, with its preliminary of the attraction, pursuit, and capture of a husband, was not her business: she had something else to do. Byron's formula, "Man's love is of man's life a thing apart: 'tis woman's whole existence," did not apply to her any more than to George Washington or any other masculine worker on the heroic scale. Had she lived in our time, picture postcards might have been sold of her as a general: they would not have been sold of her as a sultana. Nevertheless there is one reason for crediting her with a very remarkable face. A sculptor of her time in Orleans made a statue of a helmeted young woman with a face that is unique in art in point of being evidently not an ideal face but a portrait, and yet so uncommon as to be unlike any real woman one has ever seen. It is surmised that Joan served unconsciously as the sculptor's model. There is no proof of this; but those extraordinarily spaced eyes raise so powerfully the question "If this woman be not Joan, who is she?" that I dispense with further evidence, and challenge those who disagree with me to prove a negative. It is a wonderful face, but quite neutral from the point of view of the operatic beauty fancier.

Such a fancier may perhaps be finally chilled by the prosaic fact that Joan was the defendant in a suit for breach of promise of marriage, and that she conducted her own case and won it.

JOAN'S SOCIAL POSITION

By class Joan was the daughter of a working farmer who was one of the headmen of his village, and transacted its feudal business for it with the neighboring squires and their lawyers. When the castle in which the villagers were entitled to take refuge from raids became derelict, he organized a combination of half a dozen farmers to obtain possession of it so as to occupy it when there was any danger of invasion. As a child, Joan could please herself at times with being the young lady of this castle. Her mother and brothers were able to follow and share her fortune at court without making themselves notably ridiculous. These facts leave us no excuse for the popular romance that turns every heroine into either a princess or a beggar-maid. In the somewhat similar case of Shakespear a whole inverted pyramid of wasted research has been based on the assumption that he was an illiterate laborer, in the face of the plainest evidence that his father was a man of business, and at one time a very prosperous one, married to a woman of some social pretensions. There is the same tendency to drive Joan into the position of a hired shepherd girl, though a hired shepherd girl in Domrémy would have deferred to her as the young lady of the farm.

The difference between Joan's case and Shakespear's is that Shakespear was not illiterate. He had been to school, and knew as much Latin and Greek as most university passmen retain: that is, for practical purposes, none at all. Joan was absolutely illiterate. "I do not know A from B" she said. But many princesses at that time and for long after might have said the same. Marie Antoinette, for instance, at Joan's age could not spell her own name correctly. But this does not mean that Joan was an ignorant person, or that she suffered from the diffidence and sense of social disadvantage now felt by people who cannot read or write. If she could not write letters, she could and did dictate them and attach full and indeed excessive importance to them. When she was called a shepherd lass to her face she very warmly resented it, and challenged any woman to compete with her in the household arts of the mistresses of well furnished houses. She understood the political and military situation in France much better than most of our newspaper fed university women-graduates understand the corresponding situation of their own country today. Her first convert was the neighboring commandant at Vaucouleurs; and she converted him by telling him about the defeat of the Dauphin's troops at the Battle of Herrings so long before he had official news of it that he concluded she must have had a divine revelation. This knowledge of and interest in public affairs was nothing extraordinary among farmers in a war-swept countryside. Politicians came to the door too often sword in hand to be disregarded: Joan's people could not afford to be ignorant of what was going on in the feudal world. They were not rich; and Joan worked on the farm as her father did, driving the sheep to pasture and so forth; but there is no evidence or suggestion of sordid poverty, and no reason to believe that Joan had to work as a hired servant works, or indeed to work at all when she preferred to go to confession, or dawdle about waiting for visions and listening to the church bells to hear voices in them. In short, much more of a young lady, and even of an intellectual, than most of the daughters of our petty bourgeoisie.

JOAN'S VOICES AND VISIONS

Joan's voices and visions have played many tricks with her reputation. They have been held to prove that she was mad, that she was a liar and impostor, that she was a sorceress (she was burned for this), and finally that she was a saint. They do not prove any of these things; but the variety of the conclusions reached shew how little our matter-of-fact historians know about other people's minds, or even about their own. There are people in the world whose imagination is so vivid that when they have an idea it comes to them as an audible voice, sometimes uttered by a visible figure. Criminal lunatic asylums are occupied largely by murderers who have obeyed voices. Thus a woman may hear voices telling her that she must cut her husband's throat and strangle her child as they lie asleep; and she may feel obliged to do what she is told. By a medico-legal superstition it is held in our courts that criminals whose temptations present themselves under these illusions are not responsible for their actions, and must be treated as insane. But the seers of visions and the hearers of revelations are not always criminals. The inspirations and intuitions and unconsciously reasoned conclusions of genius sometimes assume similar illusions. Socrates, Luther, Swedenborg, Blake saw visions and heard voices just as Saint Francis and Saint Joan did. If Newton's imagination had been of the same vividly dramatic kind he might have seen the ghost of Pythagoras walk into the orchard and explain why the apples were falling. Such an illusion would have invalidated neither the theory of gravitation nor Newton's general sanity. What is more, the visionary method of making the discovery would not be a whit more miraculous than the normal method. The test of sanity is not the normality of the method but the reasonableness of the discovery. If Newton had been informed by Pythagoras that the moon was made of green cheese, then Newton would have been locked up. Gravitation, being a reasoned hypothesis which fitted remarkably well into the Copernican version of the observed physical facts of the universe, established Newton's reputation for extraordinary intelligence, and would have done so no matter how fantastically he had arrived at it. Yet his theory of gravitation is not so impressive a mental feat as his astounding chronology, which establishes him as the king of mental conjurors, but a Bedlamite king whose authority no one now accepts. On the subject of the eleventh horn of the beast seen by the prophet Daniel he was more fantastic than Joan, because his imagination was not dramatic but mathematical and therefore extraordinarily susceptible to numbers: indeed if all his works were lost except his chronology we should say that he was as mad as a hatter. As it is, who dares diagnose Newton as a madman?

In the same way Joan must be judged a sane woman in spite of her voices because they never gave her any advice that might not have come to her from her mother wit exactly as gravitation came to Newton. We can all see now, especially since the late war threw so many of our women into military life, that Joan's campaigning could not have been carried on in petticoats. This was not only because she did a man's work, but because it was morally necessary that sex should be left out of the question as between her and her comrades-in-arms. She gave this reason herself when she was pressed on the subject; and the fact that this entirely reasonable necessity came to her imagination first as an order from God delivered through the mouth of Saint Catherine does not prove that she was mad. The soundness of the order proves that she was unusually sane; but its form proves that her dramatic imagination played tricks with her senses. Her policy was also quite sound: nobody disputes that the relief of Orleans, followed up by the coronation at Rheims of the Dauphin as a counterblow to the suspicions then current of his legitimacy and consequently of his title, were military and political masterstrokes that saved France. They might have been planned by Napoleon or any other illusionproof genius. They came to Joan as an instruction from her Counsel, as she called her visionary saints; but she was none the less an able leader of men for imagining her ideas in this way.

THE EVOLUTIONARY APPETITE

What then is the modern view of Joan's voices and visions and messages from God? The nineteenth century said that they were delusions, but that as she was a pretty girl, and had been abominably ill-treated and finally done to death by a superstitious rabble of medieval priests hounded on by a corrupt political bishop, it must be assumed that she was the innocent dupe of these delusions. The twentieth century finds this explanation too vapidly commonplace, and demands something more mystic. I think the twentieth century is right, because an explanation which amounts to Joan being mentally defective instead of, as she obviously was, mentally excessive, will not wash. I cannot believe, nor, if I could, could I expect all my readers to believe, as Joan did, that three ocularly visible well dressed persons, named respectively Saint Catherine, Saint Margaret, and Saint Michael, came down from heaven and gave her certain instructions with which they were charged by God for her. Not that such a belief would be more improbable or fantastic than some modern beliefs which we all swallow; but there are fashions and family habits in belief, and it happens that, my fashion being Victorian and my family habit Protestant, I find myself unable to attach any such objective validity to the form of Joan's visions.

But that there are forces at work which use individuals for purposes far transcending the purpose of keeping these individuals alive and prosperous and respectable and safe and happy in the middle station in life, which is all any good bourgeois can reasonably require, is established by the fact that men will, in the pursuit of knowledge and of social readjustments for which they will not be a penny the better, and are indeed often many pence the worse, face poverty, infamy, exile, imprisonment, dreadful hardship, and death. Even the selfish pursuit of personal power does not nerve men to the efforts and sacrifices which are eagerly made in pursuit of extensions of our power over nature, though these extensions may not touch the personal life of the seeker at any point. There is no more mystery about this appetite for knowledge and power than about the appetite for food: both are known as facts and as facts only, the difference between them being that the appetite for food is necessary to the life of the hungry man and is therefore a personal appetite, whereas the other is an appetite for evolution, and therefore a superpersonal need.

The diverse manners in which our imaginations dramatize the approach of the superpersonal forces is a problem for the psychologist, not for the historian. Only, the historian must understand that visionaries are neither impostors nor lunatics. It is one thing to say that the figure Joan recognized as St Catherine was not really St Catherine, but the dramatization by Joan's imagination of that pressure upon her of the driving force that is behind evolution which I have just called the evolutionary appetite. It is quite another to class her visions with the vision of two moons seen by a drunken person, or with Brocken spectres, echoes and the like. Saint Catherine's instructions were far too cogent for that; and the simplest French peasant who believes in apparitions of celestial personages to favored mortals is nearer to the scientific truth about Joan than the Rationalist and Materialist historians and essayists who feel obliged to set down a girl who saw saints and heard them talking to her as either crazy or mendacious. If Joan was mad, all Christendom was mad too; for people who believe devoutly in the existence of celestial personages are every whit as mad in that sense as the people who think they see them. Luther, when he threw his inkhorn at the devil, was no more mad than any other Augustinian monk: he had a more vivid imagination, and had perhaps eaten and slept less: that was all.

THE MERE ICONOGRAPHY DOES NOT MATTER

All the popular religions in the world are made apprehensible by an array of legendary personages, with an Almighty Father, and sometimes a mother and divine child, as the central figures. These are presented to the mind's eye in childhood; and the result is a hallucination which persists strongly throughout life when it has been well impressed. Thus all the thinking of the hallucinated adult about the fountain of inspiration which is continually flowing in the universe, or about the promptings of virtue and the revulsions of shame: in short, about aspiration and conscience, both of which forces are matters of fact more obvious than electro-magnetism, is thinking in terms of the celestial vision. And when in the case of exceptionally imaginative persons, especially those practising certain appropriate austerities, the hallucination extends from the mind's eye to the body's, the visionary sees Krishna or the Buddha or the Blessed Virgin or St Catherine as the case may be.

THE MODERN EDUCATION WHICH JOAN ESCAPED

It is important to everyone nowadays to understand this, because modern science is making short work of the hallucinations without regard to the vital importance of the things they symbolize. If Joan were reborn today she would be sent, first to a convent school in which she would be mildly taught to connect inspiration and conscience with St Catherine and St Michael exactly as she was in the fifteenth century, and then finished up with a very energetic training in the gospel of Saints Louis Pasteur and Paul Bert, who would tell her (possibly in visions but more probably in pamphlets) not to be a superstitious little fool, and to empty out St Catherine and the rest of the Catholic hagiology as an obsolete iconography of exploded myths. It would be rubbed into her that Galileo was a martyr, and his persecutors incorrigible ignoramuses, and that St Teresa's hormones had gone astray and left her incurably hyperpituitary or hyperadrenal or hysteroid or epileptoid or anything but asteroid. She would have been convinced by precept and experiment that baptism and receiving the body of her Lord were contemptible superstitions, and that vaccination and vivisection were enlightened practices. Behind her new Saints Louis and Paul there would be not only Science purifying Religion and being purified by it, but hypochondria, melancholia, cowardice, stupidity, cruelty, muckraking curiosity, knowledge without wisdom, and everything that the eternal soul in Nature loathes, instead of the virtues of which St Catherine was the figure head. As to the new rites, which would be the saner Joan? the one who carried little children to be baptized of water and the spirit, or the one who sent the police to force their parents to have the most villainous racial poison we know thrust into their veins? the one who told them the story of the angel and Mary, or the one who questioned them as to their experiences of the Edipus complex? the one to whom the consecrated wafer was the very body of the virtue that was her salvation, or the one who looked forward to a precise and convenient regulation of her health and her desires by a nicely calculated diet of thyroid extract, adrenalin, thymin, pituitrin, and insulin, with pick-me-ups of hormone stimulants, the blood being first carefully fortified with antibodies against all possible infections by inoculations of infected bacteria and serum from infected animals, and against old age by surgical extirpation of the reproductive ducts or weekly doses of monkey gland?

It is true that behind all these quackeries there is a certain body of genuine scientific physiology. But was there any the less a certain body of genuine psychology behind St Catherine and the Holy Ghost? And which is the healthier mind? the saintly mind or the monkey gland mind? Does not the present cry of Back to the Middle Ages, which has been incubating ever since the pre-Raphaelite movement began, mean that it is no longer our Academy pictures that are intolerable, but our credulities that have not the excuse of being superstitions, our cruelties that have not the excuse of barbarism, our persecutions that have not the excuse of religious faith, our shameless substitution of successful swindlers and scoundrels and quacks for saints as objects of worship, and our deafness and blindness to the calls and visions of the inexorable power that made us, and will destroy us if we disregard it? To Joan and her contemporaries we should appear as a drove of Gadarene swine, possessed by all the unclean spirits cast out by the faith and civilization of the Middle Ages, running violently down a steep place into a hell of high explosives. For us to set up our condition as a standard of sanity, and declare Joan mad because she never condescended to it, is to prove that we are not only lost but irredeemable. Let us then once for all drop all nonsense about Joan being cracked, and accept her as at least as sane as Florence Nightingale, who also combined a very simple iconography of religious belief with a mind so exceptionally powerful that it kept her in continual trouble with the medical and military panjandrums of her time.

FAILURES OF THE VOICES

That the voices and visions were illusory, and their wisdom all Joan's own, is shewn by the occasions on which they failed her, notably during her trial, when they assured her that she would be rescued. Here her hopes flattered her; but they were not unreasonable: her military colleague La Hire was in command of a considerable force not so very far off; and if the Armagnacs, as her party was called, had really wanted to rescue her, and had put anything like her own vigor into the enterprise, they could have attempted it with very fair chances of success. She did not understand that they were glad to be rid of her, nor that the rescue of a prisoner from the hands of the Church was a much more serious business for a medieval captain, or even a medieval king, than its mere physical difficulty as a military exploit suggested. According to her lights her expectation of a rescue was reasonable; therefore she heard Madame Saint Catherine assuring her it would happen, that being her way of finding out and making up her own mind. When it became evident that she had miscalculated: when she was led to the stake, and La Hire was not thundering at the gates of Rouen nor charging Warwick's men at arms, she threw over Saint Catherine at once, and recanted. Nothing could be more sane or practical. It was not until she discovered that she had gained nothing by her recantation but close imprisonment for life that she withdrew it, and deliberately and explicitly chose burning instead: a decision which shewed not only the extraordinary decision of her character, but also a Rationalism carried to its ultimate human test of suicide. Yet even in this the illusion persisted; and she announced her relapse as dictated to her by her voices.

JOAN A GALTONIC VISUALIZER

The most sceptical scientific reader may therefore accept as a flat fact, carrying no implication of unsoundness of mind, that Joan was what Francis Galton and other modern investigators of human faculty call a visualizer. She saw imaginary saints just as some other people see imaginary diagrams and landscapes with numbers dotted about them, and are thereby able to perform feats of memory and arithmetic impossible to non-visualizers. Visualizers will understand this at once. Non-visualizers who have never read Galton will be puzzled and incredulous. But a very little inquiry among their acquaintances will reveal to them that the mind's eye is more or less a magic lantern, and that the street is full of normally sane people who have hallucinations of all sorts which they believe to be part of the normal permanent equipment of all human beings.

JOAN'S MANLINESS AND MILITARISM

Joan's other abnormality, too common among uncommon things to be properly called a peculiarity, was her craze for soldiering and the masculine life. Her father tried to frighten her out of it by threatening to drown her if she ran away with the soldiers, and ordering her brothers to drown her if he were not on the spot. This extravagance was clearly not serious: it must have been addressed to a child young enough to imagine that he was in earnest. Joan must therefore as a child have wanted to run away and be a soldier. The awful prospect of being thrown into the Meuse and drowned by a terrible father and her big brothers kept her quiet until the father had lost his terrors and the brothers yielded to her natural leadership; and by that time she had sense enough to know that the masculine and military life was not a mere matter of running away from home. But the taste for it never left her, and was fundamental in determining her career.

If anyone doubts this, let him ask himself why a maid charged with a special mission from heaven to the Dauphin (this was how Joan saw her very able plan for retrieving the desperate situation of the uncrowned king) should not have simply gone to the court as a maid, in woman's dress, and urged her counsel upon him in a woman's way, as other women with similar missions had come to his mad father and his wise grandfather. Why did she insist on having a soldier's dress and arms and sword and horse and equipment, and on treating her escort of soldiers as comrades, sleeping side by side with them on the floor at night as if there were no difference of sex between them? It may be answered that this was the safest way of travelling through a country infested with hostile troops and bands of marauding deserters from both sides. Such an answer has no weight because it applies to all the women who travelled in France at that time, and who never dreamt of travelling otherwise than as women. But even if we accept it, how does it account for the fact that when the danger was over, and she could present herself at court in feminine attire with perfect safety and obviously with greater propriety, she presented herself in her man's dress, and instead of urging Charles, like Queen Victoria urging the War Office to send Roberts to the Transvaal, to send D'Alençon, De Rais, La Hire and the rest to the relief of Dunois at Orleans, insisted that she must go herself and lead the assault in person? Why did she give exhibitions of her dexterity in handling a lance, and of her seat as a rider? Why did she accept presents of armor and chargers and masculine surcoats, and in every action repudiate the conventional character of a woman? The simple answer to all these questions is that she was the sort of woman that wants to lead a man's life. They are to be found wherever there are armies on foot or navies on the seas, serving in male disguise, eluding detection for astonishingly long periods, and sometimes, no doubt, escaping it entirely. When they are in a position to defy public opinion they throw off all concealment. You have your Rosa Bonheur painting in male blouse and trousers, and George Sand living a man's life and almost compelling her Chopins and De Mussets to live women's lives to amuse her. Had Joan not been one of those "unwomanly women", she might have been canonized much sooner.

But it is not necessary to wear trousers and smoke big cigars to live a man's life any more than it is necessary to wear petticoats to live a woman's. There are plenty of gowned and bodiced women in ordinary civil life who manage their own affairs and other people's, including those of their menfolk, and are entirely masculine in their tastes and pursuits. There always were such women, even in the Victorian days when women had fewer legal rights than men, and our modern women magistrates, mayors, and members of Parliament were unknown. In reactionary Russia in our own century a woman soldier organized an effective regiment of amazons, which disappeared only because it was Aldershottian enough to be against the Revolution. The exemption of women from military service is founded, not on any natural inaptitude that men do not share, but on the fact that communities cannot reproduce themselves without plenty of women. Men are more largely dispensable, and are sacrificed accordingly.

WAS JOAN SUICIDAL?

These two abnormalities were the only ones that were irresistibly prepotent in Joan; and they brought her to the stake. Neither of them was peculiar to her. There was nothing peculiar about her except the vigor and scope of her mind and character, and the intensity of her vital energy. She was accused of a suicidal tendency; and it is a fact that when she attempted to escape from Beaurevoir Castle by jumping from a tower said to be sixty feet high, she took a risk beyond reason, though she recovered from the crash after a few days fasting. Her death was deliberately chosen as an alternative to life without liberty. In battle she challenged death as Wellington did at Waterloo, and as Nelson habitually did when he walked his quarter deck during his battles with all his decorations in full blaze. As neither Nelson nor Wellington nor any of those who have performed desperate feats, and preferred death to captivity, has been accused of suicidal mania, Joan need not be suspected of it. In the Beaurevoir affair there was more at stake than her freedom. She was distracted by the news that Compiègne was about to fall; and she was convinced that she could save it if only she could get free. Still, the leap was so perilous that her conscience was not quite easy about it; and she expressed this, as usual, by saying that Saint Catherine had forbidden her to do it, but forgave her afterwards for her disobedience.

JOAN SUMMED UP

We may accept and admire Joan, then, as a sane and shrewd country girl of extraordinary strength of mind and hardihood of body. Everything she did was thoroughly calculated; and though the process was so rapid that she was hardly conscious of it, and ascribed it all to her voices, she was a woman of policy and not of blind impulse. In war she was as much a realist as Napoleon: she had his eye for artillery and his knowledge of what it could do. She did not expect besieged cities to fall Jerichowise at the sound of her trumpet, but, like Wellington, adapted her methods of attack to the peculiarities of the defence; and she anticipated the Napoleonic calculation that if you only hold on long enough the other fellow will give in: for example, her final triumph at Orleans was achieved after her commander Dunois had sounded the retreat at the end of a day's fighting without a decision. She was never for a moment what so many romancers and playwrights have pretended: a romantic young lady. She was a thorough daughter of the soil in her peasantlike matter-of-factness and doggedness, and her acceptance of great lords and kings and prelates as such without idolatry or snobbery, seeing at a glance how much they were individually good for. She had the respectable countrywoman's sense of the value of public decency, and would not tolerate foul language and neglect of religious observances, nor allow disreputable women to hang about her soldiers. She had one pious ejaculation "En nom Dé!" and one meaningless oath "Par mon martin"; and this much swearing she allowed to the incorrigibly blasphemous La Hire equally with herself. The value of this prudery was so great in restoring the self-respect of the badly demoralized army that, like most of her policy, it justified itself as soundly calculated. She talked to and dealt with people of all classes, from laborers to kings, without embarrassment or affectation, and got them to do what she wanted when they were not afraid or corrupt. She could coax and she could hustle, her tongue having a soft side and a sharp edge. She was very capable: a born boss.

JOAN'S IMMATURITY AND IGNORANCE

All this, however, must be taken with one heavy qualification. She was only a girl in her teens. If we could think of her as a managing woman of fifty we should seize her type at once; for we have plenty of managing women among us of that age who illustrate perfectly the sort of person she would have become had she lived. But she, being only a lass when all is said, lacked their knowledge of men's vanities and of the weight and proportion of social forces. She knew nothing of iron hands in velvet gloves: she just used her fists. She thought political changes much easier than they are, and, like Mahomet in his innocence of any world but the tribal world, wrote letters to kings calling on them to make millennial rearrangements. Consequently it was only in the enterprises that were really simple and compassable by swift physical force, like the coronation and the Orleans campaign, that she was successful.

Her want of academic education disabled her when she had to deal with such elaborately artificial structures as the great ecclesiastical and social institutions of the Middle Ages. She had a horror of heretics without suspecting that she was herself a heresiarch, one of the precursors of a schism that rent Europe in two, and cost centuries of bloodshed that is not yet staunched. She objected to foreigners on the sensible ground that they were not in their proper place in France; but she had no notion of how this brought her into conflict with Catholicism and Feudalism, both essentially international. She worked by commonsense; and where scholarship was the only clue to institutions she was in the dark, and broke her shins against them, all the more rudely because of her enormous self-confidence, which made her the least cautious of human beings in civil affairs.

This combination of inept youth and academic ignorance with great natural capacity, push, courage, devotion, originality and oddity, fully accounts for all the facts in Joan's career, and makes her a credible historical and human phenomenon; but it clashes most discordantly both with the idolatrous romance that has grown up round her, and the belittling scepticism that reacts against that romance.

THE MAID IN LITERATURE

English readers would probably like to know how these idolizations and reactions have affected the books they are most familiar with about Joan. There is the first part of the Shakespearean, or pseudo-Shakespearean trilogy of Henry VI, in which Joan is one of the leading characters. This portrait of Joan is not more authentic than the descriptions in the London papers of George Washington in 1780, of Napoleon in 1803, of the German Crown Prince in 1915, or of Lenin in 1917. It ends in mere scurrility. The impression left by it is that the playwright, having begun by an attempt to make Joan a beautiful and romantic figure, was told by his scandalized company that English patriotism would never stand a sympathetic representation of a French conqueror of English troops, and that unless he at once introduced all the old charges against Joan of being a sorceress and a harlot, and assumed her to be guilty of all of them, his play could not be produced. As likely as not, this was what actually happened: indeed there is only one other apparent way of accounting for the sympathetic representation of Joan as a heroine culminating in her eloquent appeal to the Duke of Burgundy, followed by the blackguardly scurrility of the concluding scenes. That other way is to assume that the original play was wholly scurrilous, and that Shakespear touched up the earlier scenes. As the work belongs to a period at which he was only beginning his practice as a tinker of old works, before his own style was fully formed and hardened, it is impossible to verify this guess. His finger is not unmistakeably evident in the play, which is poor and base in its moral tone; but he may have tried to redeem it from downright infamy by shedding a momentary glamor on the figure of The Maid.

When we jump over two centuries to Schiller, we find Die Jungfrau von Orleans drowned in a witch's caldron of raging romance. Schiller's Joan has not a single point of contact with the real Joan, nor indeed with any mortal woman that ever walked this earth. There is really nothing to be said of his play but that it is not about Joan at all, and can hardly be said to pretend to be; for he makes her die on the battlefield, finding her burning unbearable. Before Schiller came Voltaire, who burlesqued Homer in a mock epic called La Pucelle. It is the fashion to dismiss this with virtuous indignation as an obscene libel;

and I certainly cannot defend it against the charge of extravagant indecorum. But its purpose was not to depict Joan, but to kill with ridicule everything that Voltaire righteously hated in the institutions and fashions of his own day. He made Joan ridiculous, but not contemptible nor (comparatively) unchaste; and as he also made Homer and St Peter and St Denis and the brave Dunois ridiculous, and the other heroines of the poem very unchaste indeed, he may be said to have let Joan off very easily. But indeed the personal adventures of the characters are so outrageous, and so Homerically free from any pretence at or even possibility of historical veracity, that those who affect to take them seriously only make themselves Pecksniffian. Samuel Butler believed The Iliad to be a burlesque of Greek Jingoism and Greek religion, written by a hostage or a slave; and La Pucelle makes Butler's theory almost convincing. Voltaire represents Agnes Sorel, the Dauphin's mistress, whom Joan never met, as a woman with a consuming passion for the chastest concubinal fidelity, whose fate it was to be continually falling into the hands of licentious foes and suffering the worst extremities of rapine. The combats in which Joan rides a flying donkey, or in which, taken unaware with no clothes on, she defends Agnes with her sword, and inflicts appropriate mutilations on her assailants, can be laughed at as they are intended to be without scruple; for no sane person could mistake them for sober history; and it may be that their ribald irreverence is more wholesome than the beglamored sentimentality of Schiller. Certainly Voltaire should not have asserted that Joan's father was a priest; but when he was out to *écraser l'infâme* (the French Church) he stuck at nothing.

So far, the literary representations of The Maid were legendary. But the publication by Quicherat in 1841 of the reports of her trial and rehabilitation placed the subject on a new footing. These entirely realistic documents created a living interest in Joan which Voltaire's mock Homerics and Schiller's romantic nonsense missed. Typical products of that interest in America and England are the histories of Joan by Mark Twain and Andrew Lang. Mark Twain was converted to downright worship of Joan directly by Quicherat. Later on, another man of genius, Anatole France, reacted against the Quicheratic wave of enthusiasm, and wrote a Life of Joan in which he attributed Joan's ideas to clerical prompting and her military success to an adroit use of her by Dunois as a *mascotte:* in short, he denied that she had any serious military or political ability. At this Andrew saw red, and went for Anatole's scalp in a rival Life of her which should be read as a corrective to the other. Lang had no difficulty in shewing that Joan's ability was not unnatural fiction to be explained away as an illusion manufactured by priests and soldiers, but a straightforward fact.

It has been lightly pleaded in explanation that Anatole France is a Parisian of the art world, into whose scheme of things the able, hardheaded, hardhanded female, though she dominates provincial France and business Paris, does not enter; whereas Lang was a Scot, and every Scot knows that the grey mare is as likely as not to be the better horse. But this explanation does not convince me. I cannot believe that Anatole France does not know what everybody knows. I wish everybody knew all that he knows. One feels antipathies at work in his book. He is not anti-Joan; but he is anti-clerical, anti-mystic, and fundamentally unable to believe that there ever was any such person as the real Joan.

Mark Twain's Joan, skirted to the ground, and with as many petticoats as Noah's wife in a toy ark, is an attempt to combine Bayard with Esther Summerson from Bleak House into an unimpeachable American school teacher in armor. Like Esther Summerson she makes her creator ridiculous, and yet, being the work of a man of genius, remains a credible human goodygoody in spite of her creator's infatuation. It is the description rather than the valuation that is wrong. Andrew Lang and Mark Twain are equally determined to make Joan a beautiful and most ladylike Victorian; but both of them recognize and insist on her capacity for leadership, though the Scots scholar is less romantic about it than the Mississippi pilot. But then Lang was, by lifelong professional habit, a critic of biographies rather than a biographer, whereas Mark Twain writes his biography frankly in the form of a romance.

PROTESTANT MISUNDERSTANDINGS OF THE MIDDLE AGES

They had, however, one disability in common. To understand Joan's history it is not enough to understand her character: you must understand her environment as well. Joan in a nineteenth-twentieth century environment is as incongruous a figure as she would appear were she to walk down Piccadilly today in her fifteenth century armor. To see her in her proper perspective you must understand Christendom and the Catholic Church, and the Holy Roman Empire and the Feudal

System, as they existed and were understood in the Middle Ages. If you confuse the Middle Ages with the Dark Ages, and are in the habit of ridiculing your aunt for wearing "medieval clothes," meaning those in vogue in the eighteen-nineties, and are quite convinced that the world has progressed enormously, both morally and mechanically, since Joan's time, then you will never understand why Joan was burnt, much less feel that you might have voted for burning her yourself if you had been a member of the court that tried her; and until you feel that you know nothing essential about her.

That the Mississippi pilot should have broken down on this misunderstanding is natural enough. Mark Twain, the Innocent Abroad, who saw the lovely churches of the Middle Ages without a throb of emotion, author of A Yankee at the Court of King Arthur, in which the heroes and heroines of medieval chivalry are guys seen through the eyes of a street arab, was clearly out of court from the beginning. Andrew Lang was better read; but, like Walter Scott, he enjoyed medieval history as a string of Border romances rather than as the record of a high European civilization based on a catholic faith. Both of them were baptized as Protestants, and impressed by all their schooling and most of their reading with the belief that Catholic bishops who burnt heretics were persecutors capable of any villainy; that all heretics were Albigensians or Husites or Jews or Protestants of the highest character; and that the Inquisition was a Chamber of Horrors invented expressly and exclusively for such burnings. Accordingly we find them representing Peter Cauchon, Bishop of Beauvais, the judge who sent Joan to the stake, as an unconscionable scoundrel, and all the questions put to her as "traps" to ensnare and destroy her. And they assume unhesitatingly that the two or three score of canons and doctors of law and divinity who sat with Cauchon as assessors, were exact reproductions of him on slightly less elevated chairs and with a different headdress.

COMPARATIVE FAIRNESS OF JOAN'S TRIAL

The truth is that Cauchon was threatened and insulted by the English for being too considerate to Joan. A recent French writer denies that Joan was burnt, and holds that Cauchon spirited her away and burnt somebody or something else in her place, and that the pretender who subsequently personated her at Orleans and elsewhere was not a pretender but the real authentic Joan. He is able to cite Cauchon's pro-Joan partiality in support of his view. As to the assessors, the objection to them is not that they were a row of uniform rascals, but that they were political partisans of Joan's enemies. This is a valid objection to all such trials; but in the absence of neutral tribunals they are unavoidable. A trial by Joan's French partisans would have been as unfair as the trial by her French opponents; and an equally mixed tribunal would have produced a deadlock. Such recent trials as those of Edith Cavell by a German tribunal and Roger Casement by an English one were open to the same objection; but they went forward to the death nevertheless, because neutral tribunals were not available. Edith, like Joan, was an arch heretic: in the middle of the war she declared before the world that "Patriotism is not enough." She nursed enemies back to health, and assisted their prisoners to escape, making it abundantly clear that she would help any fugitive or distressed person without asking whose side he was on, and acknowledging no distinction before Christ between Tommy and Jerry and Pitou the *poilu*. Well might Edith have wished that she could bring the Middle Ages back, and have fifty civilians, learned in the law or vowed to the service of God, to support two skilled judges in trying her case according to the Catholic law of Christendom, and to argue it out with her at sitting after sitting for many weeks. The modern military Inquisition was not so squeamish. It shot her out of hand; and her countrymen, seeing in this a good opportunity for lecturing the enemy on his intolerance, put up a statue to her, but took particular care not to inscribe on the pedestal "Patriotism is not enough," for which omission, and the lie it implies, they will need Edith's intercession when they are themselves brought to judgment, if any heavenly power thinks such moral cowards capable of pleading to an intelligible indictment.

The point need be no further labored. Joan was persecuted essentially as she would be persecuted today. The change from burning to hanging or shooting may strike us as a change for the better. The change from careful trial under ordinary law to recklessly summary military terrorism may strike us a change for the worse. But as far as toleration is concerned the trial and execution in Rouen in 1431 might have been an event of today; and we may charge our consciences accordingly. If Joan had to be dealt with by us in London she would be treated with no more toleration than Miss Sylvia Pankhurst, or the Peculiar People, or the parents who keep their children from the elementary school, or any of the others who cross the line we have to draw, rightly or wrongly, between the tolerable and the intolerable.

JOAN NOT TRIED AS A POLITICAL OFFENDER

Besides, Joan's trial was not, like Casement's, a national political trial. Ecclesiastical courts and the courts of the Inquisition (Joan was tried by a combination of the two) were Courts Christian: that is, international courts; and she was tried, not as a traitress, but as a heretic, blasphemer, sorceress and idolater. Her alleged offences were not political offences against England, nor against the Burgundian faction in France, but against God and against the common morality of Christendom. And although the idea we call Nationalism was so foreign to the medieval conception of Christian society that it might almost have been directly charged against Joan as an additional heresy, yet it was not so charged; and it is unreasonable to suppose that the political bias of a body of Frenchmen like the assessors would on this point have run strongly in favor of the English foreigners (even if they had been making themselves particularly agreeable in France instead of just the contrary) against a Frenchwoman who had vanquished them.

The tragic part of the trial was that Joan, like most prisoners tried for anything but the simplest breaches of the ten commandments, did not understand what they were accusing her of. She was much more like Mark Twain than like Peter Cauchon. Her attachment to the Church was very different from the Bishop's, and does not, in fact, bear close examination from his point of view. She delighted in the solaces the Church offers to sensitive souls: to her, confession and communion were luxuries beside which the vulgar pleasures of the senses were trash. Her prayers were wonderful conversations with her three saints. Her piety seemed superhuman to the formally dutiful people whose religion was only a task to them. But when the Church was not offering her her favorite luxuries, but calling on her to accept its interpretation of God's will, and to sacrifice her own, she flatly refused, and made it clear that her notion of a Catholic Church was one in which the Pope was Pope Joan. How could the Church tolerate that, when it had just destroyed Hus, and had watched the career of Wycliffe with a growing anger that would have brought him, too, to the stake, had he not died a natural death before the wrath fell on him in his grave? Neither Hus nor Wycliffe was as bluntly defiant as Joan: both were reformers of the Church like Luther; whilst Joan, like Mrs Eddy, was quite prepared to supersede St Peter as the rock on which the Church was built, and, like Mahomet, was always ready with a private revelation from God to settle every question and fit every occasion.

The enormity of Joan's pretension was proved by her own unconsciousness of it, which we call her innocence, and her friends called her simplicity. Her solutions of the problems presented to her seemed, and indeed mostly were, the plainest commonsense, and their revelation to her by her Voices was to her a simple matter of fact. How could plain commonsense and simple fact seem to her to be that hideous thing, heresy? When rival prophetesses came into the field, she was down on them at once for liars and humbugs; but she never thought of them as heretics. She was in a state of invincible ignorance as to the Church's view; and the Church could not tolerate her pretensions without either waiving its authority or giving her a place beside the Trinity during her lifetime and in her teens, which was unthinkable. Thus an irresistible force met an immovable obstacle, and developed the heat that consumed poor Joan.

Mark and Andrew would have shared her innocence and her fate had they been dealt with by the Inquisition: that is why their accounts of the trial are as absurd as hers might have been could she have written one. All that can be said for their assumption that Cauchon was a vulgar villain, and that the questions put to Joan were traps, is that it has the support of the inquiry which rehabilitated her twentyfive years later. But this rehabilitation was as corrupt as the contrary proceeding applied to Cromwell by our Restoration reactionaries. Cauchon had been dug up, and his body thrown into the common sewer. Nothing was easier than to accuse him of cozenage, and declare the whole trial void on that account. That was what everybody wanted, from Charles the Victorious, whose credit was bound up with The Maid's, to the patriotic Nationalist populace, who idolized Joan's memory. The English were gone; and a verdict in their favor would have been an outrage on the throne and on the patriotism which Joan had set on foot.

We have none of these overwhelming motives of political convenience and popularity to bias us. For us the first trial stands valid; and the rehabilitation would be negligible but for the mass of sincere testimony it produced as to Joan's engaging personal character. The question then arises: how did The Church get over the verdict at the first trial when it canonized Joan five hundred years later?

THE CHURCH UNCOMPROMISED BY ITS AMENDS

Easily enough. In the Catholic Church, far more than in law, there is no wrong without a remedy. It does not defer to Joanesque private judgment as such, the supremacy of private judgment for the individual being the quintessence of Protestantism; nevertheless it finds a place for private judgment *in excelsis* by admitting that the highest wisdom may come as a divine revelation to an individual. On sufficient evidence it will declare that individual a saint. Thus, as revelation may come by way of an enlightenment of the private judgment no less than by the words of a celestial personage appearing in a vision, a saint may be defined as a person of heroic virtue whose private judgment is privileged. Many innovating saints, notably Francis and Clare, have been in conflict with the Church during their lives, and have thus raised the question whether they were heretics or saints. Francis might have gone to the stake had he lived longer. It is therefore by no means impossible for a person to be excommunicated as a heretic, and on further consideration canonized as a saint. Excommunication by a provincial ecclesiastical court is not one of the acts for which the Church claims infallibility. Perhaps I had better inform my Protestant readers that the famous Dogma of Papal Infallibility is by far the most modest pretension of the kind in existence. Compared with our infallible democracies, our infallible medical councils, our infallible astronomers, our infallible judges, and our infallible parliaments, the Pope is on his knees in the dust confessing his ignorance before the throne of God, asking only that as to certain historical matters on which he has clearly more sources of information open to him than anyone else his decision shall be taken as final. The Church may, and perhaps some day will, canonize Galileo without compromising such infallibility as it claims for the Pope, if not without compromising the infallibility claimed for the Book of Joshua by simple souls whose rational faith in more important things has become bound up with a quite irrational faith in the chronicle of Joshua's campaigns as a treatise on physics. Therefore the Church will probably not canonize Galileo yet awhile, though it might do worse. But it has been able to canonize Joan without any compromise at all. She never doubted that the sun went round the earth: she had seen it do so too often.

Still, there was a great wrong done to Joan and to the conscience of the world by her burning. *Tout comprendre, c'est tout pardonner,* which is the Devil's sentimentality, cannot excuse it. When we have admitted that the tribunal was not only honest and legal, but exceptionally merciful in respect of sparing Joan the torture which was customary when she was obdurate as to taking the oath, and that Cauchon was far more self-disciplined and conscientious both as priest and lawyer than any English judge ever dreams of being in a political case in which his party and class prejudices are involved, the human fact remains that the burning of Joan of Arc was a horror, and that a historian who would defend it would defend anything. The final criticism of its physical side is implied in the refusal of the Marquesas islanders to be persuaded that the English did not eat Joan. Why, they ask, should anyone take the trouble to roast a human being except with that object? They cannot conceive its being a pleasure. As we have no answer for them that is not shameful to us, let us blush for our more complicated and pretentious savagery before we proceed to unravel the business further, and see what other lessons it contains for us.

CRUELTY, MODERN AND MEDIEVAL

First, let us get rid of the notion that the mere physical cruelty of the burning has any special significance. Joan was burnt just as dozens of less interesting heretics were burnt in her time. Christ, in being crucified, only shared the fate of thousands of forgotten malefactors. They have no pre-eminence in mere physical pain: much more horrible executions than theirs are on record, to say nothing of the agonies of so-called natural death at its worst.

Joan was burnt more than five hundred years ago. More than three hundred years later: that is, only about a hundred years before I was born, a woman was burnt on Stephen's Green in my native city of Dublin for coining, which was held to be treason. In my preface to the recent volume on English Prisons under Local Government, by Sidney and Beatrice Webb, I have mentioned that when I was already a grown man I saw Richard Wagner conduct two concerts, and that when Richard Wagner was a young man he saw and avoided a crowd of people hastening to see a soldier broken on the wheel by the more cruel of the two ways of carrying out that hideous method of execution. Also that the penalty of hanging, drawing, and quartering, unmentionable in its details, was abolished so recently that there are men living who have been sentenced to it. We are still flogging criminals, and clamoring for more flogging. Not even the most sensationally frightful of these atrocities inflicted on its victim the misery, degradation, and conscious waste and loss of life suffered in our modern prisons, especially the model ones, without, as far as I can see, rousing any more compunction than the burning of heretics did in the Middle Ages. We have not even the excuse of getting some fun out of our prisons as the Middle Ages did out of their stakes and wheels and gibbets. Joan herself judged this matter when she had to choose between imprisonment and the stake, and chose the stake. And thereby she deprived The Church of the plea that it was guiltless of her death, which was the work of the secular arm. The Church should have confined itself to excommunicating her. There it was within its rights: she had refused to accept its authority or comply with its conditions; and it could say with truth "You are not one of us: go forth and find the religion that suits you, or found one for yourself." It had no right to say "You may return to us now that you have recanted; but you shall stay in a dungeon all the rest of your life." Unfortunately, The Church did not believe that there was any genuine soul saving religion outside itself; and it was deeply corrupted, as all the Churches were and still are, by primitive Calibanism (in Browning's sense), or the propitiation of a dreaded deity by suffering and sacrifice. Its method was not cruelty for cruelty's sake, but cruelty for the salvation of Joan's soul. Joan, however, believed that the saving of her soul was her own business, and not that of *les gens d'église*. By using that term as she did, mistrustfully and contemptuously, she announced herself as, in germ, an anti-Clerical as thoroughgoing as Voltaire or Anatole France. Had she said in so many words "To the dustbin with the Church Militant and its blackcoated officials: I recognize only the Church Triumphant in heaven," she would hardly have put her view more plainly.

CATHOLIC ANTI-CLERICALISM

I must not leave it to be inferred here that one cannot be an anti-Clerical and a good Catholic too. All the reforming Popes have been vehement anti-Clericals, veritable scourges of the clergy. All the great Orders arose from dissatisfaction with the priests: that of the Franciscans with priestly snobbery, that of the Dominicans with priestly laziness and Laodiceanism, that of the Jesuits with priestly apathy and ignorance and indiscipline. The most bigoted Ulster Orangeman or Leicester Low Church bourgeois (as described by Mr Henry Nevinson) is a mere Gallio compared to Machiavelli, who, though no Protestant, was a fierce anti-Clerical. Any Catholic may, and many Catholics do, denounce any priest or body of priests, as lazy, drunken, idle, dissolute, and unworthy of their great Church and their functions as the pastors of their flocks of human souls. But to say that the souls of the people are no business of the Churchmen is to go a step further, a step across the Rubicon. Joan virtually took that step.

CATHOLICISM NOT YET CATHOLIC ENOUGH

And so, if we admit, as we must, that the burning of Joan was a mistake, we must broaden Catholicism sufficiently to include her in its charter. Our Churches must admit that no official organization of mortal men whose vocation does not carry with it extraordinary mental powers (and this is all that any Church Militant can in the face of fact and history pretend to be), can keep pace with the private judgment of persons of genius except when, by a very rare accident, the genius happens to be Pope, and not even then unless he is an exceedingly overbearing Pope. The Churches must learn humility as well as teach it. The Apostolic Succession cannot be secured or confined by the laying on of hands: the tongues of fire have descended on heathens and outcasts too often for that, leaving anointed Churchmen to scandalize History as worldly rascals. When the Church Militant behaves as if it were already the Church Triumphant, it makes these appalling blunders about Joan and Bruno and Galileo and the rest which make it so difficult for a Freethinker to join it; and a Church which has no place for Freethinkers: nay, which does not inculcate and encourage freethinking with a complete belief that thought, when really free, must by its own law take the path that leads to The Church's bosom, not only has no future in modern culture, but obviously has no faith in the valid science of its own tenets, and is guilty of the heresy that theology and science are two different and opposite impulses, rivals for human allegiance.

I have before me the letter of a Catholic priest. "In your play," he writes, "I see the dramatic presentation of the conflict of the Regal, sacerdotal, and Prophetical powers, in which Joan was crushed. To me it is not the victory of any one of them over the others that will bring peace and the Reign of the Saints in the Kingdom of God, but their fruitful interaction in a costly but noble state of tension." The Pope himself could not put it better; nor can I. We must accept the tension, and maintain it nobly without letting ourselves be tempted to relieve it by burning the thread. This is Joan's lesson to The Church; and its formulation by the hand of a priest emboldens me to claim that her canonization was a magnificently Catholic gesture as the canonization of a Protestant saint by the Church of Rome. But its special value and virtue cannot be apparent until it is known and understood as such. If any simple priest for whom this is too hard a saying tells me that it was not so intended, I shall remind him that the Church is in the hands of God, and not, as simple priests imagine, God in the hands of the Church; so if he answers too confidently for God's intentions he may be asked "Hast thou entered into the springs of the sea? or hast thou walked in the recesses of the deep?" And Joan's own answer is also the answer of old: "Though He slay me, yet will I trust Him; *but I will maintain my own ways before Him.*"

THE LAW OF CHANGE IS THE LAW OF GOD

When Joan maintained her own ways she claimed, like Job, that there was not only God and the Church to be considered, but the Word made Flesh: that is, the unaveraged individual, representing life possibly at its highest actual human evolution and possibly at its lowest, but never at its merely mathematical average. Now there is no deification of the democratic average in the theory of the Church: it is an avowed hierarchy in which the members are sifted until at the end of the process an individual stands supreme as the Vicar of Christ. But when the process is examined it appears that its successive steps of selection and election are of the superior by the inferior (the cardinal vice of democracy), with the result that great popes are as rare and accidental as great kings, and that it has sometimes been safer for an aspirant to the Chair and the Keys to pass as a moribund dotard than as an energetic saint. At best very few popes have been canonized, or could be without letting down the standard of sanctity set by the self-elected saints.

No other result could have been reasonably expected; for it is not possible that an official organization of the spiritual needs of millions of men and women, mostly poor and ignorant, should compete successfully in the selection of its principals with the direct choice of the Holy Ghost as it flashes with unerring aim upon the individual. Nor can any College of Cardinals pray effectively that its choice may be inspired. The conscious prayer of the inferior may be that his choice may light on a greater than himself; but the sub-conscious intention of his self-preserving individuality must be to find a trustworthy servant for his own purposes. The saints and prophets, though they may be accidentally in this or that official position or rank, are always really self-selected, like Joan. And since neither Church nor State, by the secular necessities of its constitution, can guarantee even the recognition of such self-chosen missions, there is nothing for us but to make it a point of honor to privilege heresy to the last bearable degree on the simple ground that all evolution in thought and conduct must at first appear as heresy and misconduct. In short, though all society is founded on intolerance, all improvement is founded on tolerance, or the recognition of the fact that the law of evolution is Ibsen's law of change. And as the law of God in any sense of the word which can now command a faith proof against science is a law of evolution, it follows that the law of God is a law of change, and that when the Churches set themselves against change as such, they are setting themselves against the law of God.

CREDULITY, MODERN AND MEDIEVAL

When Abernethy, the famous doctor, was asked why he indulged himself with all the habits he warned his patients against as unhealthy, he replied that his business was that of a direction post, which points out the way to a place, but does not go thither itself. He might have added that neither does it compel the traveller to go thither, nor prevent him from seeking some other way. Unfortunately our clerical direction posts always do coerce the traveller when they have the political power to do so. When the Church was a temporal as well as a spiritual power, and for long after to the full extent to which it could control or influence the temporal power, it enforced conformity by persecutions that were all the more ruthless because their intention was so excellent. Today, when the doctor has succeeded to the priest, and can do practically what he likes with parliament and the press through the blind faith in him which has succeeded to the far more critical faith in the parson, legal compulsion to take the doctor's prescription, however poisonous, is carried to an extent that would have horrified the Inquisition and staggered Archbishop Laud. Our credulity is grosser than that of the Middle Ages, because the priest had no such direct pecuniary interest in our sins as the doctor has in our diseases: he did not starve when all was well with his flock, nor prosper when they were perishing, as our private commercial doctors must. Also the medieval cleric believed that something extremely unpleasant would happen to him after death if he was unscrupulous, a belief now practically extinct among persons receiving a dogmatically materialist education. Our professional corporations are Trade Unions without souls to be damned; and they will soon drive us to remind them that they have bodies to be kicked. The Vatican was never soulless: at worst it was a political conspiracy to make the Church supreme temporally as well as spiritually. Therefore the question raised by Joan's burning is a burning question still, though the penalties involved are not so sensational. That is why I am probing it. If it were only an historical curiosity I would not waste my readers' time and my own on it for five minutes.

TOLERATION, MODERN AND MEDIEVAL

The more closely we grapple with it the more difficult it becomes. At first sight we are disposed to repeat that Joan should have been excommunicated and then left to go her own way, though she would have protested vehemently against so cruel a deprivation of her spiritual food; for confession, absolution, and the body of her Lord were first necessaries of life to her. Such a spirit as Joan's might have got over that difficulty as the Church of England got over the Bulls of Pope Leo, by making a Church of her own, and affirming it to be the temple of the true and original faith from which her persecutors had strayed. But as such a proceeding was, in the eyes of both Church and State at that time, a spreading of damnation and anarchy, its toleration involved a greater strain on faith in freedom than political and ecclesiastical human nature could bear. It is easy to say that the Church should have waited for the alleged evil results instead of assuming that they would occur, and what they would be. That sounds simple enough; but if a modern Public Health Authority were to leave people entirely to their own devices in the matter of sanitation, saying, "We have nothing to do with drainage or your views about drainage; but if you catch smallpox or typhus we will prosecute you and have you punished very severely like the authorities in Butler's Erewhon," it would either be removed to the County Asylum or reminded that A's neglect of sanitation may kill the child of B two miles off, or start an epidemic in which the most conscientious sanitarians may perish.

We must face the fact that society is founded on intolerance. There are glaring cases of the abuse of intolerance; but they are quite as characteristic of our own age as of the Middle Ages. The typical modern example and contrast is compulsory inoculation replacing what was virtually compulsory baptism. But compulsion to inoculate is objected to as a crudely unscientific and mischievous anti-sanitary quackery, not in the least because we think it wrong to compel people to protect their children from disease. Its opponents would make it a crime, and will probably succeed in doing so; and that will be just as intolerant as making it compulsory. Neither the Pasteurians nor their opponents the Sanitarians would leave parents free to bring up their children naked, though that course also has some plausible advocates. We may prate of toleration as we will; but society must always draw a line somewhere between allowable conduct and insanity or crime, in spite of the risk of mistaking sages for lunatics and saviors for blasphemers. We must persecute, even to the death; and all we can do to mitigate the danger of persecution is, first, to be very careful what we persecute, and second, to bear in mind that unless there is a large liberty to shock conventional people, and a well informed sense of the value of originality, individuality, and eccentricity, the result will be apparent stagnation covering a repression of evolutionary forces which will eventually explode with extravagant and probably destructive violence.

VARIABILITY OF TOLERATION

The degree of tolerance attainable at any moment depends on the strain under which society is maintaining its cohesion. In war, for instance, we suppress the gospels and put Quakers in prison, muzzle the newspapers, and make it a serious offence to shew a light at night. Under the strain of invasion the French Government in 1792 struck off 4000 heads, mostly on grounds that would not in time of settled peace have provoked any Government to chloroform a dog; and in 1920 the British Government slaughtered and burnt in Ireland to persecute the advocates of a constitutional change which it had presently to effect itself. Later on the Fascisti in Italy did everything that the Black and Tans did in Ireland, with some grotesquely ferocious variations, under the strain of an unskilled attempt at industrial revolution by Socialists who understood Socialism even less than Capitalists understand Capitalism. In the United States an incredibly savage persecution of Russians took place during the scare spread by the Russian Bolshevik revolution after 1917. These instances could easily be multiplied; but they are enough to shew that between a maximum of indulgent toleration and a ruthlessly intolerant Terrorism there is a scale through which toleration is continually rising or falling, and that there was not the smallest ground for the self-complacent conviction of the nineteenth century that it was more tolerant than the fifteenth, or that such an event as the execution of Joan could not possibly occur in what we call our own more enlightened times. Thousands of women, each of them a thousand times less dangerous and terrifying to our Governments than Joan was to the Government of her day, have within the last ten years been slaughtered, starved to death, burnt out of house and home, and what not that Persecution and Terror could do to them, in the course of Crusades far more tyrannically pretentious than the medieval Crusades which proposed nothing more hyperbolical than the rescue of the Holy Sepulchre from the Saracens. The Inquisition, with its English equivalent the Star Chamber, are gone in the sense that their names are now disused; but can any of the modern substitutes for the Inquisition, the Special Tribunals and Commissions, the punitive expeditions, the suspensions of the Habeas Corpus Act, the proclamations of martial law and of minor states of siege, and the rest of them, claim that their victims have as fair a trial, as well considered a body of law to govern their cases, or as conscientious a judge to insist on strict legality of procedure as Joan had from the Inquisition and from the spirit of the Middle Ages even when her country was under the heaviest strain of civil and foreign war? From us she would have had no trial and no law except a Defence of The Realm Act suspending all law; and for judge she would have had, at best, a bothered major, and at worst a promoted advocate in ermine and scarlet to whom the scruples of a trained ecclesiastic like Cauchon would seem ridiculous and ungentlemanly.

THE CONFLICT BETWEEN GENIUS AND DISCIPLINE

Having thus brought the matter home to ourselves, we may now consider the special feature of Joan's mental constitution which made her so unmanageable. What is to be done on the one hand with rulers who will not give any reason for their orders, and on the other with people who cannot understand the reasons when they are given? The government of the world, political, industrial, and domestic, has to be carried on mostly by the giving and obeying of orders under just these conditions. "Dont argue: do as you are told" has to be said not only to children and soldiers, but practically to everybody. Fortunately most people do not want to argue: they are only too glad to be saved the trouble of thinking for themselves. And the ablest and most independent thinkers are content to understand their own special department. In other departments they will unhesitatingly ask for and accept the instructions of a policeman or the advice of a tailor without demanding or desiring explanations.

Nevertheless, there must be some ground for attaching authority to an order. A child will obey its parents, a soldier his officer, a philosopher a railway porter, and a workman a foreman, all without question, because it is generally accepted that those who give the orders understand what they are about, and are duly authorized and even obliged to give them, and because, in the practical emergencies of daily life, there is no time for lessons and explanations, or for arguments as to their validity. Such obediences are as necessary to the continuous operation of our social system as the revolutions of the earth are to the succession of night and day. But they are not so spontaneous as they seem: they have to be very carefully arranged and maintained. A bishop will defer to and obey a king; but let a curate venture to give him an order, however necessary and sensible, and the bishop will forget his cloth and damn the curate's impudence. The more obedient a man is to accredited authority the more jealous he is of allowing any unauthorized person to order him about.

With all this in mind, consider the career of Joan. She was a village girl, in authority over sheep and pigs, dogs and chickens, and to some extent over her father's hired laborers when he hired any, but over no one else on earth. Outside the farm she had no authority, no prestige, no claim to the smallest deference. Yet she ordered everybody about, from her uncle to the king, the archbishop, and the military General Staff. Her uncle obeyed her like a sheep, and took her to the castle of the local commander, who, on being ordered about, tried to assert himself, but soon collapsed and obeyed. And so on up to the king, as we have seen. This would have been unbearably irritating even if her orders had been offered as rational solutions of the desperate difficulties in which her social superiors found themselves just then. But they were not so offered. Nor were they offered as the expression of Joan's arbitrary will. It was never "I say so," but always "God says so."

JOAN AS THEOCRAT

Leaders who take that line have no trouble with some people, and no end of trouble with others. They need never fear a lukewarm reception. Either they are messengers of God, or they are blasphemous impostors. In the Middle Ages the general belief in witchcraft greatly intensified this contrast, because when an apparent miracle happened (as in the case of the wind changing at Orleans) it proved the divine mission to the credulous, and proved a contract with the devil to the sceptical. All through, Joan had to depend on those who accepted her as an incarnate angel against those who added to an intense resentment of her presumption a bigoted abhorrence of her as a witch. To this abhorrence we must add the extreme irritation of those who did not believe in the voices, and regarded her as a liar and impostor. It is hard to conceive anything more infuriating to a statesman or a military commander, or to a court favorite, than to be overruled at every turn, or to be robbed of the ear of the reigning sovereign, by an impudent young upstart practising on the credulity of the populace and the vanity and silliness of an immature prince by exploiting a few of those lucky coincidences which pass as miracles with uncritical people. Not only were the envy, snobbery, and competitive ambition of the baser natures exacerbated by Joan's success, but among the friendly ones that were clever enough to be critical a quite reasonable scepticism and mistrust of her ability, founded on a fair observation of her obvious ignorance and temerity, were at work against her. And as she met all remonstrances and all criticisms, not with arguments or persuasion, but with a flat appeal to the authority of God and a claim to be in God's special confidence, she must have seemed, to all who were not infatuated by her, so insufferable that nothing but an unbroken chain of overwhelming successes in the military and political field could have saved her from the wrath that finally destroyed her.

UNBROKEN SUCCESS ESSENTIAL IN THEOCRACY

To forge such a chain she needed to be the King, the Archbishop of Rheims, the Bastard of Orleans, and herself into the bargain; and that was impossible. From the moment when she failed to stimulate Charles to follow up his coronation with a swoop on Paris she was lost. The fact that she insisted on this whilst the king and the rest timidly and foolishly thought they could square the Duke of Burgundy, and effect a combination with him against the English, made her a terrifying nuisance to them; and from that time onward she could do nothing but prowl about the battlefields waiting for some lucky chance to sweep the captains into a big move. But it was to the enemy that the chance came: she was taken prisoner by the Burgundians fighting before Compiègne, and at once discovered that she had not a friend in the political world. Had she escaped she would probably have fought on until the English were gone, and then had to shake the dust of the court off her feet, and retire to Domrémy as Garibaldi had to retire to Caprera.

MODERN DISTORTIONS OF JOAN'S HISTORY

This, I think, is all that we can now pretend to say about the prose of Joan's career. The romance of her rise, the tragedy of her execution, and the comedy of the attempts of posterity to make amends for that execution, belong to my play and not to my preface, which must be confined to a sober essay on the facts. That such an essay is badly needed can be ascertained by examining any of our standard works of reference. They give accurately enough the facts about the visit to Vaucouleurs, the annunciation to Charles at Chinon, the raising of the siege of Orleans and the subsequent battles, the coronation at Rheims, the capture at Compiègne, and the trial and execution at Rouen, with their dates and the names of the people concerned; but they all break down on the melodramatic legend of the wicked bishop and the entrapped maiden and the rest of it. It would be far less misleading if they were wrong as to the facts, and right in their view of the facts. As it is, they illustrate the too little considered truth that the fashion in which we think changes like the fashion of our clothes, and that it is difficult, if not impossible, for most people to think otherwise than in the fashion of their own period.

HISTORY ALWAYS OUT OF DATE

This, by the way, is why children are never taught contemporary history. Their history books deal with periods of which the thinking has passed out of fashion, and the circumstances no longer apply to active life. For example, they are taught history about Washington, and told lies about Lenin. In Washington's time they were told lies (the same lies) about Washington, and taught history about Cromwell. In the fifteenth and sixteenth centuries they were told lies about Joan, and by this time might very well be told the truth about her. Unfortunately the lies did not cease when the political circumstances became obsolete. The Reformation, which Joan had unconsciously anticipated, kept the questions which arose in her case burning up to our own day (you can see plenty of the burnt houses still in Ireland), with the result that Joan has remained the subject of anti-Clerical lies, of specifically Protestant lies, and of Roman Catholic evasions of her unconscious Protestantism. The truth sticks in our throats with all the sauces it is served with: it will never go down until we take it without any sauce at all.

THE REAL JOAN NOT MARVELLOUS ENOUGH FOR US

But even in its simplicity, the faith demanded by Joan is one which the anti-metaphysical temper of nineteenth century civilization, which remains powerful in England and America, and is tyrannical in France, contemptuously refuses her. We do not, like her contemporaries, rush to the opposite extreme in a recoil from her as from a witch self-sold to the devil, because we do not believe in the devil nor in the possibility of commercial contracts with him. Our credulity, though enormous, is not boundless; and our stock of it is quite used up by our mediums, clairvoyants, hand readers, slate writers, Christian Scientists, psycho-analysts, electronic vibration diviners, therapeutists of all schools registered and unregistered, astrologers, astronomers who tell us that the sun is nearly a hundred million miles away and that Betelgeuse is ten times as big as the whole universe, physicists who balance Betelgeuse by describing the incredible smallness of the atom, and a host of other marvel mongers whose credulity would have dissolved the Middle Ages in a roar of sceptical merriment. In the Middle Ages people believed that the earth was flat, for which they had at least the evidence of their senses: we believe it to be round, not because as many as one per cent of us could give the physical reasons for so quaint a belief, but because modern science has convinced us that nothing that is obvious is true, and that everything that is magical, improbable, extraordinary, gigantic, microscopic, heartless, or outrageous is scientific.

I must not, by the way, be taken as implying that the earth is flat, or that all or any of our amazing credulities are delusions or impostures. I am only defending my own age against the charge of being less imaginative than the Middle Ages. I affirm that the nineteenth century, and still more the twentieth, can knock the fifteenth into a cocked hat in point of susceptibility to marvels and miracles and saints and prophets and magicians and monsters and fairy tales of all kinds. The proportion of marvel to immediately credible statement in the latest edition of the Encyclopædia Britannica is enormously greater than in the Bible. The medieval doctors of divinity who did not pretend to settle how many angels could dance on the point of a needle cut a very poor figure as far as romantic credulity is concerned beside the modern physicists who have settled to the billionth of a millimetre every movement and position in the dance of the electrons. Not for worlds would I question the precise accuracy of these calculations or the existence of electrons (whatever they may be). The fate of Joan is a warning to me against such heresy. But why the men who believe in electrons should regard themselves as less credulous than the men who believed in angels is not apparent to me. If they refuse to believe, with the Rouen assessors of 1431, that Joan was a witch, it is not because that explanation is too marvellous, but because it is not marvellous enough.

THE STAGE LIMITS OF HISTORICAL REPRESENTATION

For the story of Joan I refer the reader to the play which follows. It contains all that need be known about her; but as it is for stage use I have had to condense into three and a half hours a series of events which in their historical happening were spread over four times as many months; for the theatre imposes unities of time and place from which Nature in her boundless wastefulness is free. Therefore the reader must not suppose that Joan really put Robert de Baudricourt in her pocket in fifteen minutes, nor that her excommunication, recantation, relapse, and death at the stake were a matter of half an hour or so. Neither do I claim more for my dramatizations of Joan's contemporaries than that some of them are probably slightly more like the originals than those imaginary portraits of all the Popes from Saint Peter onward through the Dark Ages which are still gravely exhibited in the Uffizi in Florence (or were when I was there last). My Dunois would do equally well for the Duc d'Alençon. Both left descriptions of Joan so similar that, as a man always describes himself unconsciously whenever he describes anyone else, I have inferred that these goodnatured young men were very like one another in mind; so I have lumped the twain into a single figure, thereby saving the theatre manager a salary and a suit of armor. Dunois' face, still on record at Châteaudun, is a suggestive help. But I really know no more about these men and their circle than Shakespear knew about Falconbridge and the Duke of Austria, or about Macbeth and Macduff. In view of the things they did in history, and have to do again in the play, I can only invent appropriate characters for them in Shakespear's manner.

A VOID IN THE ELIZABETHAN DRAMA

I have, however, one advantage over the Elizabethans. I write in full view of the Middle Ages, which may be said to have been rediscovered in the middle of the nineteenth century after an eclipse of about four hundred and fifty years. The Renascence of antique literature and art in the sixteenth century, and the lusty growth of Capitalism, between them buried the Middle Ages; and their resurrection is a second Renascence. Now there is not a breath of medieval atmosphere in Shakespear's histories. His John of Gaunt is like a study of the old age of Drake. Although he was a Catholic by family tradition, his figures are all intensely Protestant, individualist, sceptical, selfcentred in everything but their love affairs, and completely personal and selfish even in them. His kings are not statesmen: his cardinals have no religion: a novice can read his plays from one end to the other without learning that the world is finally governed by forces expressing themselves in religions and laws which make epochs rather than by vulgarly ambitious individuals who make rows. The divinity which shapes our ends, rough hew them how we will, is mentioned fatalistically only to be forgotten immediately like a passing vague apprehension. To Shakespear as to Mark Twain, Cauchon would have been a tyrant and a bully instead of a Catholic, and the inquisitor Lemaître would have been a Sadist instead of a lawyer. Warwick would have had no more feudal quality than his successor the King Maker has in the play of Henry VI. We should have seen them all completely satisfied that if they would only to their own selves be true they could not then be false to any man (a precept which represents the reaction against medievalism at its intensest) as if they were beings in the air, without public responsibilities of any kind. All Shakespear's characters are so: that is why they seem natural to our middle classes, who are comfortable and irresponsible at other people's expense, and are neither ashamed of that condition nor even conscious of it. Nature abhors this vacuum in Shakespear; and I have taken care to let the medieval atmosphere blow through my play freely. Those who see it performed will not mistake the startling event it records for a mere personal accident. They will have before them not only the visible and human puppets, but the Church, the Inquisition, the Feudal System, with divine inspiration always beating against their too inelastic limits: all more terrible in their dramatic force than any of the little mortal figures clanking about in plate armor or moving silently in the frocks and hoods of the order of St Dominic.

TRAGEDY, NOT MELODRAMA

There are no villains in the piece. Crime, like disease, is not interesting: it is something to be done away with by general consent, and that is all about it. It is what men do at their best, with good intentions, and what normal men and women find that they must and will do in spite of their intentions, that really concern us. The rascally bishop and the cruel inquisitor of Mark Twain and Andrew Lang are as dull as pickpockets; and they reduce Joan to the level of the even less interesting person whose pocket is picked. I have represented both of them as capable and eloquent exponents of The Church Militant and The Church Litigant, because only by doing so can I maintain my drama on the level of high tragedy and save it from becoming a mere police court sensation. A villain in a play can never be anything more than a *diabolus ex machina,* possibly a more exciting expedient than a *deus ex machina,* but both equally mechanical, and therefore interesting only as mechanism. It is, I repeat, what normally innocent people do that concerns us; and if Joan had not been burnt by normally innocent people in the energy of their righteousness her death at their hands would have no more significance than the Tokyo earthquake, which burnt a great many maidens. The tragedy of such murders is that they are not committed by murderers. They are judical murders, pious murders; and this contradiction at once brings an element of comedy into the tragedy: the angels may weep at the murder, but the gods laugh at the murderers.

THE INEVITABLE FLATTERIES OF TRAGEDY

Here then we have a reason why my drama of Saint Joan's career, though it may give the essential truth of it, gives an inexact picture of some accidental facts. It goes almost without saying that the old Jeanne d'Arc melodramas, reducing everything to a conflict of villain and hero, or in Joan's case villain and heroine, not only miss the point entirely, but falsify the characters, making Cauchon a scoundrel, Joan a prima donna, and Dunois a lover. But the writer of high tragedy and comedy, aiming at the innermost attainable truth, must needs flatter Cauchon nearly as much as the melodramatist vilifies him. Although there is, as far as I have been able to discover, nothing against Cauchon that convicts him of bad faith or exceptional severity in his judicial relations with Joan, or of as much anti-prisoner, pro-police, class and sectarian bias as we now take for granted in our own courts, yet there is hardly more warrant for classing him as a great Catholic churchman, completely proof against the passions roused by the temporal situation. Neither does the inquisitor Lemaître, in such scanty accounts of him as are now recoverable, appear quite so able a master of his duties and of the case before him as I have given him credit for being. But it is the business of the stage to make its figures more intelligible to themselves than they would be in real life; for by no other means can they be made intelligible to the audience. And in this case Cauchon and Lemaître have to make intelligible not only themselves but the Church and the Inquisition, just as Warwick has to make the feudal system intelligible, the three between them having thus to make a twentieth-century audience conscious of an epoch fundamentally different from its own. Obviously the real Cauchon, Lemaître, and Warwick could not have done this: they were part of the Middle Ages themselves, and therefore as unconscious of its peculiarities as of the atomic formula of the air they breathed. But the play would be unintelligible if I had not endowed them with enough of this consciousness to enable them to explain their attitude to the twentieth century. All I claim is that by this inevitable sacrifice of verisimilitude I have secured in the only possible way sufficient veracity to justify me in claiming that as far as I can gather from the available documentation, and from such powers of divination as I possess, the things I represent these three exponents of the drama as saying are the things they actually would have said if they had known what they were really doing. And beyond this neither drama nor history can go in my hands.

SOME WELL-MEANT PROPOSALS FOR THE IMPROVEMENT OF THE PLAY

I have to thank several critics on both sides of the Atlantic, including some whose admiration for my play is most generously enthusiastic, for their heartfelt instructions as to how it can be improved. They point out that by the excision of the epilogue and all the references to such undramatic and tedious matters as the Church, the feudal system, the Inquisition, the theory of heresy and so forth, all of which, they point out, would be ruthlessly blue pencilled by any experienced manager, the play could be considerably shortened. I think they are mistaken. The experienced knights of the blue pencil, having saved an hour and a half by disembowelling the play, would at once proceed to waste two hours in building elaborate scenery, having real water in the river Loire and a real bridge across it, and staging an obviously sham fight for possession of it, with the victorious French led by Joan on a real horse. The coronation would eclipse all previous theatrical displays, shewing, first, the procession through the streets of Rheims, and then the service in the cathedral, with special music written for both. Joan would be burnt on the stage, as Mr Matheson Lang always is in The Wandering Jew, on the principle that it does not matter in the least why a woman is burnt provided she is burnt, and people can pay to see it done. The intervals between the acts whilst these splendors were being built up and then demolished by the stage carpenters would seem eternal, to the great profit of the refreshment bars. And the weary and demoralized audience would lose their last trains and curse me for writing such inordinately long and intolerably dreary and meaningless plays. But the applause of the press would be unanimous. Nobody who knows the stage history of Shakespear will doubt that this is what would happen if I knew my business so little as to listen to these well intentioned but disastrous counsellors: indeed it probably will happen when I am no longer in control of the performing rights. So perhaps it will be as well for the public to see the play while I am still alive.

THE EPILOGUE

As to the epilogue, I could hardly be expected to stultify myself by implying that Joan's history in the world ended unhappily with her execution, instead of beginning there. It was necessary by hook or crook to shew the canonized Joan as well as the incinerated one; for many a woman has got herself burnt by carelessly whisking a muslin skirt into the drawing room fireplace, but getting canonized is a different matter, and a more important one. So I am afraid the epilogue must stand.

TO THE CRITICS, LEST THEY SHOULD FEEL IGNORED

To a professional critic (I have been one myself) theatre-going is the curse of Adam. The play is the evil he is paid to endure in the sweat of his brow; and the sooner it is over, the better. This would seem to place him in irreconcilable opposition to the paying playgoer, from whose point of view the longer the play, the more entertainment he gets for his money. It does in fact so place him, especially in the provinces, where the playgoer goes to the theatre for the sake of the play solely, and insists so effectively on a certain number of hours' entertainment that touring managers are sometimes seriously embarrassed by the brevity of the London plays they have to deal in.

For in London the critics are reinforced by a considerable body of persons who go to the theatre as many others go to church, to display their best clothes and compare them with other people's; to be in the fashion, and have something to talk about at dinner parties; to adore a pet performer; to pass the evening anywhere rather than at home: in short, for any or every reason except interest in dramatic art as such. In fashionable centres the number of irreligious people who go to church, of unmusical people who go to concerts and operas, and of undramatic people who go to the theatre, is so prodigious that sermons have been cut down to ten minutes and plays to two hours; and, even at that, congregations sit longing for the benediction and audiences for the final curtain, so that they may get away to the lunch or supper they really crave for, after arriving as late as (or later than) the hour of beginning can possibly be made for them.

Thus from the stalls and in the Press an atmosphere of hypocrisy spreads. Nobody says straight out that genuine drama is a tedious nuisance, and that to ask people to endure more than two hours of it (with two long intervals of relief) is an intolerable imposition. Nobody says "I hate classical tragedy and comedy as I hate sermons and symphonies; but I like police news and divorce news and any kind of dancing or decoration that has an aphrodisiac effect on me or on my wife or husband. And whatever superior people may pretend, I cannot associate pleasure with any sort of intellectual activity; and I dont believe anyone else can either." Such things are not said; yet nine-tenths of what is offered as criticism of the drama in the metropolitan Press of Europe and America is nothing but a muddled paraphrase of it. If it does not mean that, it means nothing.

I do not complain of this, though it complains very unreasonably of me. But I can take no more notice of it than Einstein of the people who are incapable of mathematics. I write in the classical manner for those who pay for admission to a theatre because they like classical comedy or tragedy for its own sake, and like it so much when it is good of its kind and well done that they tear themselves away from it with reluctance to catch the very latest train or omnibus that will take them home. Far from arriving late from an eight or half-past eight o'clock dinner so as to escape at least the first half-hour of the performance, they stand in queues outside the theatre doors for hours beforehand in bitingly cold weather to secure a seat. In countries where a play lasts a week, they bring baskets of provisions and sit it out. These are the patrons on whom I depend for my bread. I do not give them performances twelve hours long, because circumstances do not at present make such entertainments feasible; though a performance beginning after breakfast and ending at sunset is as possible physically and artistically in Surrey or Middlesex as in Ober-Ammergau; and an all-night sitting in a theatre would be at least as enjoyable as an all-night sitting in the House of Commons, and much more useful. But in St Joan I have done my best by going to the well-established classical limit of three and a half hours practically continuous playing, barring the one interval imposed by considerations which have nothing to do with art. I know that this is hard on the pseudo-critics and on the fashionable people whose playgoing is a hypocrisy. I cannot help feeling some compassion for them when they assure me that my play, though a great play, must fail hopelessly, because it does not begin at a quarter to nine and end at eleven. The facts are overwhelmingly against them. They forget that all men are not as they are. Still, I am sorry for them; and though I cannot for their sakes undo my work and help the people who hate the theatre to drive out the people who love it, yet I may point out to them that they have several remedies in their own hands. They can escape the first part of the play by their usual practice of arriving late. They can escape the epilogue by not waiting for it. And if the irreducible minimum thus attained is still too painful, they can stay away altogether. But I deprecate this extreme course, because it is good neither for my pocket nor for their own souls. Already a few of them, noticing that what matters is not the absolute length of time occupied by a play, but the speed with which that time passes, are discovering that the theatre, though purgatorial in its Aristotelian moments, is not necessarily always the dull place they have so often found it. What do its discomforts matter when the play makes us forget them?

AYOT ST LAWRENCE, *May 1924*

SCENE I

A fine spring morning on the river Meuse, between Lorraine and Champagne, in the year 1429 A.D., *in the castle of Vaucouleurs.*

Captain Robert de Baudricourt, a military squire, handsome and physically energetic, but with no will of his own, is disguising that defect in his usual fashion by storming terribly at his steward, a trodden worm, scanty of flesh, scanty of hair, who might be any age from 18 *to* 55, *being the sort of man whom age cannot wither because he has never bloomed.*

The two are in a sunny stone chamber on the first floor of the castle. At a plain strong oak table, seated in chair to match, the captain presents his left profile. The steward stands facing him at the other side of the table, if so deprecatory a stance as his can be called standing. The mullioned thirteenth-century window is open behind him. Near it in the corner is a turret with a narrow arched doorway leading to a winding stair which descends to the courtyard. There is a stout fourlegged stool under the table, and a wooden chest under the window.

ROBERT. No eggs! No eggs!! Thousand thunders, man, what do you mean by no eggs?

STEWARD. Sir: it is not my fault. It is the act of God.

ROBERT. Blasphemy. You tell me there are no eggs; and you blame your Maker for it.

STEWARD. Sir: what can I do? I cannot lay eggs.

ROBERT [*sarcastic*] Ha! You jest about it.

STEWARD. No, sir, God knows. We all have to go without eggs just as you have, sir. The hens will not lay.

ROBERT. Indeed! [*Rising*] Now listen to me, you.

STEWARD [*humbly*] Yes, sir.

ROBERT. What am I?

STEWARD. What are you, sir?

ROBERT [*coming at him*] Yes: what am I? Am I Robert, squire of

Baudricourt and captain of this castle of Vaucouleurs; or am I a cowboy?

STEWARD. Oh, sir, you know you are a greater man here than the king himself.

ROBERT. Precisely. And now, do you know what you are?

STEWARD. I am nobody, sir, except that I have the honor to be your steward.

ROBERT [*driving him to the wall, adjective by adjective*] You have not only the honor of being my steward, but the privilege of being the worst, most incompetent, drivelling snivelling jibbering jabbering idiot of a steward in France. [*He strides back to the table*].

STEWARD [*cowering on the chest*] Yes, sir: to a great man like you I must seem like that.

ROBERT [*turning*] My fault, I suppose. Eh?

STEWARD [*coming to him deprecatingly*] Oh, sir: you always give my most innocent words such a turn!

ROBERT. I will give your neck a turn if you dare tell me, when I ask you how many eggs there are, that you cannot lay any.

STEWARD [*protesting*] Oh sir, oh sir—

ROBERT. No: not oh sir, oh sir, but no sir, no sir. My three Barbary hens and the black are the best layers in Champagne. And you come and tell me that there are no eggs! Who stole them? Tell me that, before I kick you out through the castle gate for a liar and a seller of my goods to thieves. The milk was short yesterday, too: do not forget that.

STEWARD [*desperate*] I know, sir. I know only too well. There is no milk: there are no eggs: tomorrow there will be nothing.

ROBERT. Nothing! You will steal the lot: eh?

STEWARD. No, sir: nobody will steal anything. But there is a spell on us: we are bewitched.

ROBERT. That story is not good enough for me. Robert de Baudricourt burns witches and hangs thieves. Go. Bring me four dozen eggs and two gallons of milk here in this room before noon, or Heaven have mercy on your bones! I will teach you to make a fool of m e. [*He resumes his seat with an air of finality*].

STEWARD. Sir: I tell you there are no eggs. There will be none—not if you were to kill me for it—as long as The Maid is at the door.

ROBERT. The Maid! What maid? What are you talking about?

STEWARD. The girl from Lorraine, sir. From Domrémy.

ROBERT [*rising in fearful wrath*] Thirty thousand thunders! Fifty thousand devils! Do you mean to say that that girl, who had the impudence to ask to see me two days ago, and whom I told you to send back to her father with my orders that he was to give her a good hiding, is here still?

STEWARD. I have told her to go, sir, She wont.

ROBERT. I did not tell you to tell her to go: I told you to throw her out. You have fifty men-at-arms and a dozen lumps of able-bodied servants to carry out my orders. Are they afraid of her?

STEWARD. She is so positive, sir.

ROBERT [*seizing him by the scruff of the neck*] Positive! Now see here. I am going to throw you downstairs.

STEWARD. No, sir. Please.

ROBERT. Well, stop me by being positive. It's quite easy: any slut of a girl can do it.

STEWARD [*hanging limp in his hands*] Sir, s i r: you cannot get rid of h e r by throwing m e out. [*Robert has to let him drop. He squats on his knees on the floor, contemplating his master resignedly*]. You see, sir, you are much more positive than I am. But so is she.

ROBERT. I am stronger than you are, you fool.

STEWARD. No, sir: it isnt that: it's your strong character, sir. She is weaker than we are: she is only a slip of a girl; but we cannot make her go.

ROBERT. You parcel of curs: you are afraid of her.

STEWARD [*rising cautiously*] No, sir: we are afraid of you, but she puts courage into us. She really doesnt seem to be afraid of anything. Perhaps you could frighten her, sir.

ROBERT [*grimly*] Perhaps. Where is she now?

STEWARD. Down in the courtyard, sir, talking to the soldiers as usual She is always talking to the soldiers except when she is praying.

ROBERT. Praying! Ha! You believe she prays, you idiot. I know the sort of girl that is always talking to soldiers. She shall talk to me a bit [*He goes to the window and shouts fiercely through it*] Hallo, you there!

A GIRL'S VOICE [*bright, strong and rough*] Is it me, sir?

ROBERT. Yes, you.

THE VOICE. Be you captain?

ROBERT. Yes, damn your impudence, I be captain. Come up here. [*To the soldiers in the yard*] Shew her the way, you. And shove her along quick. [*He leaves the window, and returns to his place at the table, where he sits magisterially*].

STEWARD [*whispering*] She wants to go and be a soldier herself. She wants you to give her soldier's clothes. Armor, sir! And a sword! Actually! [*He steals behind Robert*].

Joan appears in the turret doorway. She is an able-bodied country girl of 17 or 18, respectably dressed in red, with an uncommon face: eyes very wide apart and bulging as they often do in very imaginative people, a long well-shaped nose with wide nostrils, a short upper lip, resolute but full-lipped mouth, and handsome fighting chin. She comes eagerly to the table, delighted at having penetrated to Baudricourt's presence at last, and full of hope as to the result. His scowl does not check or frighten her in the least. Her voice is normally a hearty coaxing voice, very confident, very appealing, very hard to resist.

JOAN [*bobbing a curtsey*] Good morning, captain squire. Captain: you are to give me a horse and armor and some soldiers, and send me to the Dauphin. Those are your orders from my Lord.

ROBERT [*outraged*] Orders from y o u r lord! And who the devil may your lord be? Go back to him, and tell him that I am neither duke nor peer at his orders: I am squire of Baudricourt; and I take no orders except from the king.

JOAN [*reassuringly*] Yes, squire: that is all right. My Lord is the King of Heaven.

ROBERT. Why, the girl's mad. [*To the steward*] Why didnt you tell me so, you blockhead?

STEWARD. Sir: do not anger her: give her what she wants.

JOAN [*impatient, but friendly*] They all say I am mad until I talk to them, squire. But you see that it is the will of God that you are to do what He has put into my mind.

ROBERT. It is the will of God that I shall send you back to your father with orders to put you under lock and key and thrash the madness out of you. What have you to say to that?

JOAN. You think you will, squire; but you will find it all coming quite different. You said you would not see me; but here I am.

STEWARD [*appealing*] Yes, sir. You see, sir.

ROBERT. Hold your tongue, you.

STEWARD [*abjectly*] Yes, sir.

ROBERT [*to Joan, with a sour loss of confidence*] So you are presuming on my seeing you, are you?

JOAN [*sweetly*] Yes, squire.

ROBERT [*feeling that he has lost ground, brings down his two fists squarely on the table, and inflates his chest imposingly to cure the unwelcome and only too familiar sensation*] Now listen to me. I am going to assert myself.

JOAN [*busily*] Please do, squire. The horse will cost sixteen francs. It is a good deal of money; but I can save it on the armor. I can find a soldier's armor that will fit me well enough: I am very hardy; and I do not need beautiful armor made to my measure like you wear. I shall not want many soldiers: the Dauphin will give me all I need to raise the siege of Orleans.

ROBERT [*flabbergasted*] To raise the siege of Orleans!

JOAN [*simply*] Yes, squire: that is what God is sending me to do. Three men will be enough for you to send with me if they are good men and gentle to me. They have promised to come with me. Polly and Jack and—

ROBERT. Polly!! You impudent baggage, do you dare call squire Bertrand de Poulengey Polly to my face?

JOAN. His friends call him so, squire: I did not know he had any other name. Jack—

ROBERT. That is Monsieur John of Metz, I suppose?

JOAN. Yes, squire. Jack will come willingly: he is a very kind gentleman, and gives me money to give to the poor. I think John Godsave will come, and Dick the Archer, and their servants John of Honecourt and Julian. There will be no trouble for you, squire: I have arranged it all: you have only to give the order.

ROBERT [*contemplating her in a stupor of amazement*] Well, I am damned!

JOAN [*with unruffled sweetness*] No, squire: God is very merciful; and the blessed saints Catherine and Margaret, who speak to me every day [*he gapes*], will intercede for you. You will go to paradise; and your name will be remembered for ever as my first helper.

ROBERT [*to the steward, still much bothered, but changing his tone as he pursues a new clue*] Is this true about Monsieur de Poulengey?

STEWARD [*eagerly*] Yes, sir, and about Monsieur de Metz too. They both want to go with her.

ROBERT [*thoughtful*] Mf! [*He goes to the window, and shouts into the courtyard*] Hallo! You there: send Monsieur de Poulengey to me, will you? [*He turns to Joan*] Get out; and wait in the yard.

JOAN [*smiling brightly at him*] Right, squire. [*She goes out*].

ROBERT [*to the steward*] Go with her, you, you dithering imbecile.

Stay within call; and keep your eye on her. I shall have her up here again.

STEWARD. Do so in God's name, sir. Think of those hens, the best layers in Champagne: and—

ROBERT. Think of my boot; and take your backside out of reach of it.

The steward retreats hastily and finds himself confronted in the doorway by Bertrand de Poulengey, a lymphatic French gentleman-at-arms, age 36 or thereabout, employed in the department of the provost-marshal, dreamily absent-minded, seldom speaking unless spoken to, and then slow and obstinate in reply: altogether in contrast to the self-assertive, loud-mouthed, superficially energetic, fundamentally will-less Robert. The steward makes way for him, and vanishes.

Poulengey salutes, and stands awaiting orders.

ROBERT [*genially*] It isnt service, Polly. A friendly talk. Sit down. [*He hooks the stool from under the table with his instep*].

Poulengey, relaxing, comes into the room; places the stool between the table and the window; and sits down ruminatively. Robert, half sitting on the end of the table, begins the friendly talk.

ROBERT. Now listen to me, Polly. I must talk to you like a father.

Poulengey looks up at him gravely for a moment, but says nothing.

ROBERT. It's about this girl you are interested in. Now, I have seen her. I have talked to her. First, she's mad. That doesnt matter. Second, she's not a farm wench. She's a bourgeoise. That matters a good deal. I know her class exactly. Her father came here last year to represent his village in a lawsuit: he is one of their notables. A farmer. Not a gentleman farmer: he makes money by it, and lives by it. Still, not a laborer. Not a mechanic. He might have a cousin a lawyer, or in the Church. People of this sort may be of no account socially; but they can give a lot of bother to the authorities. That is to say, to m e. Now no doubt it seems to you a very simple thing to take this girl away, humbugging her into the belief that you are taking her to the Dauphin. But if you get her into trouble, you may get m e into no end of a mess, as I am her father's lord, and responsible for her protection. So friends or no friends, Polly, hands off her.

POULENGEY [*with deliberate impressiveness*] I should as soon think of the Blessed Virgin herself in that way, as of this girl.

ROBERT [*coming off the table*] But she says you and Jack and Dick have offered to go with her. What for? You are not going to tell me that you take her crazy notion of going to the Dauphin seriously, are you?

POULENGEY [*slowly*] There is something about her. They are pretty foulmouthed and foulminded down there in the guardroom, some of them. But there hasnt been a word that has anything to do with her being a woman. They have stopped swearing before her. There is something. Something. It may be worth trying.

ROBERT. Oh, come, Polly! pull yourself together. Commonsense was never your strong point; but this is a little too much. [*He retreats disgustedly*].

POULENGEY [*unmoved*] What is the good of commonsense? If we had any commonsense we should join the Duke of Burgundy and the English king. They hold half the country, right down to the Loire. They have Paris. They have this castle: you know very well that we had to surrender it to the Duke of Bedford, and that you are only holding it on parole. The Dauphin is in Chinon, like a rat in a corner, except that he wont fight. We dont even know that he is the Dauphin: his mother says he isnt; and she ought to know. Think of that! the queen denying the legitimacy of her own son!

ROBERT. Well, she married her daughter to the English king. Can you blame the woman?

POULENGEY. I blame nobody. But thanks to her, the Dauphin is down and out; and we may as well face it. The English will take Orleans: the Bastard will not be able to stop them.

ROBERT. He beat the English the year before last at Montargis. I was with him.

POULENGEY. No matter: his men are cowed now; and he cant work miracles. And I tell you that nothing can save our side now but a miracle.

ROBERT. Miracles are all right, Polly. The only difficulty about them is that they dont happen nowadays.

POULENGEY. I used to think so. I am not so sure now. [*Rising, and moving ruminatively towards the window*] At all events this is not a time to leave any stone unturned. There is something about the girl.

ROBERT. Oh! You think the girl can work miracles, do you?

POULENGEY. I think the girl herself is a bit of a miracle. Anyhow, she is the last card left in our hand. Better play her than throw up the game. [*He wanders to the turret*].

ROBERT [*wavering*] You really think that?

POULENGEY [*turning*] Is there anything else left for us to think?

ROBERT [*going to him*] Look here, Polly. If you were in my place would you let a girl like that do you out of sixteen francs for a horse?
POULENGEY. I will pay for the horse.
ROBERT. You will!
POULENGEY. Yes: I will back my opinion.
ROBERT. You will really gamble on a forlorn hope to the tune of sixteen francs?
POULENGEY. It is not a gamble.
ROBERT. What else is it?
POULENGEY. It is a certainty. Her words and her ardent faith in God have put fire into me.
ROBERT [*giving him up*] Whew! You are as mad as she is.
POULENGEY [*obstinately*] We want a few mad people now. See where the sane ones have landed us!
ROBERT [*his irresoluteness now openly swamping his affected decisiveness*] I shall feel like a precious fool. Still, if you feel sure—?
POULENGEY. I feel sure enough to take her to Chinon—unless you stop me.
ROBERT. This is not fair. You are putting the responsibility on me.
POULENGEY. It is on you whichever way you decide.
ROBERT. Yes: thats just it. Which way am I to decide? You dont see how awkward this is for me. [*Snatching at a dilatory step with an unconscious hope that Joan will make up his mind for him*] Do you think I ought to have another talk to her?
POULENGEY [*rising*] Yes. [*He goes to the window and calls*] Joan!
JOAN'S VOICE. Will he let us go, Polly?
POULENGEY. Come up. Come in. [*Turning to Robert*] Shall I leave you with her?
ROBERT. No: stay here; and back me up.

Poulengey sits down on the chest. Robert goes back to his magisterial chair, but remains standing to inflate himself more imposingly. Joan comes in, full of good news.

JOAN. Jack will go halves for the horse.
ROBERT. Well!! [*He sits, deflated*].
POULENGEY [*gravely*] Sit down, Joan.
JOAN [*checked a little, and looking to Robert*] May I?
ROBERT. Do what you are told.

Joan curtsies and sits down on the stool between them. Robert outfaces his perplexity with his most peremptory air.

ROBERT. What is your name?

JOAN [*chattily*] They always call me Jenny in Lorraine. Here in France I am Joan. The soldiers call me The Maid.

ROBERT. What is your surname?

JOAN. Surname? What is that? My father sometimes calls himself d'Arc; but I know nothing about it. You met my father. He—

ROBERT. Yes, yes: I remember. You come from Domrémy in Lorraine, I think.

JOAN. Yes; but what does it matter? we all speak French.

ROBERT. Dont ask questions: answer them. How old are you?

JOAN. Seventeen: so they tell me. It might be nineteen. I dont remember.

ROBERT. What did you mean when you said that St Catherine and St Margaret talked to you every day?

JOAN. They do.

ROBERT. What are they like?

JOAN [*suddenly obstinate*] I will tell you nothing about that: they have not given me leave.

ROBERT. But you actually see them; and they talk to you just as I am talking to you?

JOAN. No: it is quite different. I cannot tell you: you must not talk to me about my voices.

ROBERT. How do you mean? voices?

JOAN. I hear voices telling me what to do. They come from God.

ROBERT. They come from your imagination.

JOAN. Of course. That is how the messages of God come to us.

POULENGEY. Checkmate.

ROBERT. No fear! [*To Joan*] So God says you are to raise the siege of Orleans?

JOAN. And to crown the Dauphin in Rheims Cathedral.

ROBERT [*gasping*] Crown the D——! Gosh!

JOAN. And to make the English leave France.

ROBERT [*sarcastic*] Anything else?

JOAN [*charming*] Not just at present, thank you, squire.

ROBERT. I suppose you think raising a siege is as easy as chasing a cow out of a meadow. You think soldiering is anybody's job?

JOAN. I do not think it can be very difficult if God is on your side, and you are willing to put your life in His hand. But many soldiers are very simple.

ROBERT [*grimly*] Simple! Did you ever see English soldiers fighting?

JOAN. They are only men. God made them just like us; but He gave them their own country and their own language; and it is not His will that they should come into our country and try to speak our language.

ROBERT. Who has been putting such nonsense into your head? Dont you know that soldiers are subject to their feudal lord, and that it is nothing to them or to you whether he is the duke of Burgundy or the king of England or the king of France? What has their language to do with it?

JOAN. I do not understand that a bit. We are all subject to the King of Heaven; and He gave us our countries and our languages, and meant us to keep to them. If it were not so it would be murder to kill an Englishman in battle; and you, squire, would be in great danger of hell fire. You must not think about your duty to your feudal lord, but about your duty to God.

POULENGEY. It's no use, Robert: she can choke you like that every time.

ROBERT. Can she, by Saint Dennis! We shall see. [*To Joan*] We are not talking about God: we are talking about practical affairs. I ask you again, girl, have you ever seen English soldiers fighting? Have you ever seen them plundering, burning, turning the countryside into a desert? Have you heard no tales of their Black Prince who was blacker than the devil himself, or of the English king's father?

JOAN. You must not be afraid, Robert—

ROBERT. Damn you, I am not afraid. And who gave you leave to call me Robert?

JOAN. You were called so in church in the name of our Lord. All the other names are your father's or your brother's or anybody's.

ROBERT. Tcha!

JOAN. Listen to me, squire. At Domrémy we had to fly to the next village to escape from the English soldiers. Three of them were left behind, wounded. I came to know these three poor goddams quite well. They had not half my strength.

ROBERT. Do you know why they are called goddams?

JOAN. No. Everyone calls them goddams.

ROBERT. It is because they are always calling on their God to condemn their souls to perdition. That is what goddam means in their language. How do you like it?

JOAN. God will be merciful to them; and they will act like His good children when they go back to the country He made for them, and made them for. I have heard the tales of the Black Prince. The moment he touched the soil of our country the devil entered into him and made him a black fiend. But at home, in the place made for him by

God, he was good. It is always so. If I went into England against the will of God to conquer England, and tried to live there and speak its language, the devil would enter into me; and when I was old I should shudder to remember the wickednesses I did.

ROBERT. Perhaps. But the more devil you were the better you might fight. That is why the goddams will take Orleans. And you cannot stop them, nor ten thousand like you.

JOAN. O n e thousand like me can stop them. Ten like me can stop them with God on our side. [*She rises impetuously, and goes at him, unable to sit quiet any longer*]. You do not understand, squire. Our soldiers are always beaten because they are fighting only to save their skins; and the shortest way to save your skin is to run away. Our knights are thinking only of the money they will make in ransoms: it is not kill or be killed with them, but pay or be paid. But I will teach them all to fight that the will of God may be done in France; and then they will drive the poor goddams before them like sheep. You and Polly will live to see the day when there will not be an English soldier on the soil of France; and there will be but one king there: not the feudal English king, but God's French one.

ROBERT [*to Poulengey*] This may be all rot, Polly; but the troops might swallow it, though nothing that we can say seems able to put any fight into them. Even the Dauphin might swallow it. And if she can put fight into him, she can put it into anybody.

POULENGEY. I can see no harm in trying. Can you? And there is something about the girl—

ROBERT [*turning to Joan*] Now listen you to me; and [*desperately*] dont cut in before I have time to think.

JOAN [*plumping down on the stool again, like an obedient schoolgirl*] Yes, squire.

ROBERT. Your orders are, that you are to go to Chinon under the escort of this gentleman and three of his friends.

JOAN [*radiant, clasping her hands*] Oh, squire! Your head is all circled with light, like a saint's.

POULENGEY. How is she to get into the royal presence?

ROBERT [*who has looked up for his halo rather apprehensively*] I dont know: how did she get into my presence? If the Dauphin can keep her out he is a better man than I take him for. [*Rising*] I will send her to Chinon; and she can say I sent her. Then let come what may: I can do no more.

JOAN. And the dress? I may have a soldier's dress, maynt I, squire?

ROBERT. Have what you please. I wash my hands of it.

JOAN [*wildly excited by her success*] Come, Polly. [*She dashes out*].

ROBERT [*shaking Poulengey's hand*] Goodbye, old man, I am taking a big chance. Few other men would have done it. But as you say, there is something about her.

POULENGEY. Yes: there is something about her. Goodbye. [*He goes out*].

Robert, still very doubtful whether he has not been made a fool of by a crazy female, and a social inferior to boot, scratches his head and slowly comes back from the door.

The steward runs in with a basket.

STEWARD. Sir, sir—

ROBERT. What now?

STEWARD. The hens are laying like mad, sir. Five dozen eggs!

ROBERT [*stiffens convulsively; crosses himself; and forms with his pale lips the words*] Christ in heaven! [*Aloud but breathless*] She did come from God.

SCENE II

Chinon, in Touraine. An end of the throne room in the castle, curtained off to make an antechamber. The Archbishop of Rheims, close on 50, full-fed political prelate with nothing of the ecclesiastic about him except his imposing bearing, and the Lord Chamberlain, Monseigneur de la Trémouille, a monstrous arrogant wineskin of a man, are waiting for the Dauphin. There is a door in the wall to the right of the two men. It is late in the afternoon on the 8th of March, 1429. The Archbishop stands with dignity whilst the Chamberlain, on his left, fumes about in the worst of tempers.

LA TRÉMOUILLE. What the devil does the Dauphin mean by keeping us waiting like this? I dont know how you have the patience to stand there like a stone idol.

THE ARCHBISHOP. You see, I am an archbishop; and an archbishop is a sort of idol. At any rate he has to learn to keep still and suffer fools patiently. Besides, my dear Lord Chamberlain, it is the Dauphin's royal privilege to keep you waiting, is it not?

LA TRÉMOUILLE. Dauphin be damned! saving your reverence. Do you know how much money he owes me?

THE ARCHBISHOP. Much more than he owes me, I have no doubt, because you are a much richer man. But I take it he owes you all you could afford to lend him. That is what he owes me.

LA TRÉMOUILLE. Twenty-seven thousand: that was his last haul. A cool twenty-seven thousand!

THE ARCHBISHOP. What becomes of it all? He never has a suit of clothes that I would throw to a curate.

LA TRÉMOUILLE. He dines on a chicken or a scrap of mutton. He borrows my last penny; and there is nothing to shew for it [*A page appears in the doorway*]. At last!

THE PAGE. No, my lord: it is not His Majesty. Monsieur de Rais is approaching.

LA TRÉMOUILLE. Young Bluebeard! Why announce h i m?

THE PAGE. Captain La Hire is with him. Something has happened, I think.

Gilles de Rais, a young man of 25, very smart and self-possessed, and sporting the extravagance of a little curled beard dyed blue at a clean-shaven court, comes in. He is determined to make himself agreeable, but lacks natural joyousness, and is not really pleasant. In fact when he defies the Church some eleven years later he is accused of trying to extract pleasure from horrible cruelties, and hanged. So far, however, there is no shadow of the gallows on him. He advances gaily to the Archbishop. The page withdraws.

BLUEBEARD. Your faithful lamb, Archbishop. Good day, my lord. Do you know what has happened to La Hire?

LA TRÉMOUILLE. He has sworn himself into a fit, perhaps.

BLUEBEARD. No: just the opposite. Foul Mouthed Frank, the only man in Touraine who could beat him at swearing, was told by a soldier that he shouldnt use such language when he was at the point of death.

THE ARCHBISHOP. Nor at any other point. But was Foul Mouthed Frank on the point of death?

BLUEBEARD. Yes: he has just fallen into a well and been drowned. La Hire is frightened out of his wits.

Captain La Hire comes in: a war dog with no court manners and pronounced camp ones.

BLUEBEARD. I have just been telling the Chamberlain and the Archbishop. The Archbishop says you are a lost man.

LA HIRE [*striding past Bluebeard, and planting himself between the Archbishop and La Trémouille*] This is nothing to joke about. It is worse than we thought. It was not a soldier, but an angel dressed as a soldier.

THE ARCHBISHOP
THE CHAMBERLAIN
BLUEBEARD } [*exclaiming all together*] An angel!

LA HIRE. Yes, an angel. She has made her way from Champagne with half a dozen men through the thick of everything: Burgundians, Goddams, deserters, robbers, and Lord knows who; and they never met a soul except the country folk. I know one of them: de Poulengey. He says she's an angel. If ever I utter an oath again may my soul be blasted to eternal damnation!

THE ARCHBISHOP. A very pious beginning, Captain.

Bluebeard and La Trémouille laugh at him. The page returns.

THE PAGE. His Majesty.

They stand perfunctorily at court attention. The Dauphin, aged 26, really King Charles the Seventh since the death of his father, but as yet uncrowned, comes in through the curtains with a paper in his hands. He is a poor creature physically; and the current fashion of shaving closely, and hiding every scrap of hair under the headcovering or headdress, both by women and men, makes the worst of his appearance. He has little narrow eyes, near together, a long pendulous nose that droops over his thick short upper lip, and the expression of a young dog accustomed to be kicked, yet incorrigible and irrepressible. But he is neither vulgar nor stupid; and he has a cheeky humor which enables him to hold his own in conversation. Just at present he is excited, like a child with a new toy. He comes to the Archbishop's left hand. Bluebeard and La Hire retire towards the curtains.

CHARLES. Oh, Archbishop, do you know what Robert de Baudricourt is sending me from Vaucouleurs?

THE ARCHBISHOP [*contemptuously*] I am not interested in the newest toys.

CHARLES [*indignantly*] It isnt a toy. [*Sulkily*] However, I can get on very well without your interest.

THE ARCHBISHOP. Your Highness is taking offence very unnecessarily.

CHARLES. Thank you. You are always ready with a lecture, arnt you?

LA TRÉMOUILLE [*roughly*] Enough grumbling. What have you got there?

CHARLES. What is that to you?

LA TRÉMOUILLE. It is my business to know what is passing between you and the garrison at Vaucouleurs. [*He snatches the paper from the Dauphin's hand, and begins reading it with some difficulty, following the words with his finger and spelling them out syllable by syllable.*]

CHARLES [*mortified*] You all think you can treat me as you please because I owe you money, and because I am no good at fighting. But I have the blood royal in my veins.

THE ARCHBISHOP. Even that has been questioned, your Highness. One hardly recognizes in you the grandson of Charles the Wise.

CHARLES. I want to hear no more of my grandfather. He was so wise that he used up the whole family stock of wisdom for five generations, and left me the poor fool I am, bullied and insulted by all of you.

THE ARCHBISHOP. Control yourself, sir. These outbursts of petulance are not seemly.

CHARLES. Another lecture! Thank you. What a pity it is that though you are an archbishop saints and angels dont come to see y o u!

THE ARCHBISHOP. What do you mean?

CHARLES. Aha! Ask that bully there [*pointing to La Trémouille*].

LA TRÉMOUILLE [*furious*] Hold your tongue. Do you hear?

CHARLES. Oh, I hear. You neednt shout. The whole castle can hear. Why dont you go and shout at the English, and beat them for me?

LA TRÉMOUILLE [*raising his fist*] You young—

CHARLES [*running behind the Archbishop*] Dont you raise your hand to me. It's high treason.

LA HIRE. Steady, Duke! Steady!

THE ARCHBISHOP [*resolutely*] Come, come! this will not do. My Lord Chamberlain: please! please! we must keep some sort of order. [*To the Dauphin*] And you, sir: if you cannot rule your kingdom, at least try to rule yourself.

CHARLES. Another lecture! Thank you.

LA TRÉMOUILLE [*handing the paper to the Archbishop*] Here: read the accursed thing for me. He has sent the blood boiling into my head: I cant distinguish the letters.

CHARLES [*coming back and peering round La Trémouille's left shoulder*] I will read it for you if you like. I c a n read, you know.

LA TRÉMOUILLE [*with intense contempt, not at all stung by the taunt*] Yes: reading is about all you are fit for. Can you make it out, Archbishop?

THE ARCHBISHOP. I should have expected more commonsense from De Baudricourt. He is sending some cracked country lass here—

CHARLES [*interrupting*] No: he is sending a saint: an angel. And she is coming to me: to m e, the king, and not to you, Archbishop, holy as you are. She knows the blood royal if you dont. [*He struts up to the curtains between Bluebeard and La Hire*].

THE ARCHBISHOP. You cannot be allowed to see this crazy wench.

CHARLES [*turning*] But I am the king; and I will.

LA TRÉMOUILLE [*brutally*] Then she cannot be allowed to see y o u. Now!

CHARLES. I tell you I will. I am going to put my foot down—

BLUEBEARD [*laughing at him*] Naughty! What would your wise grandfather say?

CHARLES. That just shews your ignorance, Bluebeard. My grandfather had a saint who used to float in the air when she was praying, and told him everything he wanted to know. My poor father had two saints, Marie de Maillé and the Gasque of Avignon. It is in our family; and I dont care what you say: I will have my saint too.

THE ARCHBISHOP. This creature is not a saint. She is not even a respectable woman. She does not wear women's clothes. She is dressed like a soldier, and rides round the country with soldiers. Do you suppose such a person can be admitted to your Highness's court?

LA HIRE. Stop. [*Going to the Archbishop*] Did you say a girl in armor, like a soldier?

THE ARCHBISHOP. So De Baudricourt describes her.

LA HIRE. But by all the devils in hell—Oh, God forgive me, what am I saying?—by Our Lady and all the saints, this must be the angel that struck Foul Mouthed Frank dead for swearing.

CHARLES [*triumphant*] You see! A miracle!

LA HIRE. She may strike the lot of us dead if we cross her. For Heaven's sake, Archbishop, be careful what you are doing.

THE ARCHBISHOP [*severely*] Rubbish! Nobody has been struck dead. A drunken blackguard who has been rebuked a hundred times for swearing has fallen into a well, and been drowned. A mere coincidence.

LA HIRE. I do not know what a coincidence is. I do know that the man is dead, and that she told him he was going to die.

THE ARCHBISHOP. We are all going to die, Captain.

LA HIRE [*crossing himself*] I hope not. [*He backs out of the conversation*].

BLUEBEARD. We can easily find out whether she is an angel or not. Let us arrange when she comes that I shall be the Dauphin, and see whether she will find me out.

CHARLES. Yes: I agree to that. If she cannot find the blood royal I will have nothing to do with her.

THE ARCHBISHOP. It is for the Church to make saints: let De Baudricourt mind his own business, and not dare usurp the function of his priest. I say the girl shall not be admitted.

BLUEBEARD. But, Archbishop—

THE ARCHBISHOP [*sternly*] I speak in the Church's name. [*To the Dauphin*] Do you dare say she shall?

CHARLES [*intimidated but sulky*] Oh, if you make it an excommunication matter, I have nothing more to say, of course. But you havnt read the end of the letter. De Baudricourt says she will raise the siege of Orleans, and beat the English for us.

LA TRÉMOUILLE. Rot!

CHARLES. Well, will y o u save Orleans for us, with all your bullying?

LA TRÉMOUILLE [*savagely*] Do not throw that in my face again: do you hear? I have done more fighting than you ever did or ever will. But I cannot be everywhere.

THE DAUPHIN. Well, thats something.

BLUEBEARD [*coming between the Archbishop and Charles*] You have Jack Dunois at the head of your troops in Orleans: the brave Dunois, the handsome Dunois, the wonderful invincible Dunois, the darling of all the ladies, the beautiful bastard. Is it likely that the country lass can do what he cannot do?

CHARLES. Why doesnt he raise the siege, then?

LA HIRE. The wind is against him.

BLUEBEARD. How can the wind hurt him at Orleans? It is not on the Channel.

LA HIRE. It is on the river Loire; and the English hold the bridgehead. He must ship his men across the river and upstream, if he is to take them in the rear. Well, he cannot, because there is a devil of a wind blowing the other way. He is tired of paying the priests to pray for a west wind. What he needs is a miracle. You tell me that what the girl did to Foul Mouthed Frank was no miracle. No matter: it finished Frank. If she changes the wind for Dunois, that may not be a miracle either; but it may finish the English. What harm is there in trying?

THE ARCHBISHOP [*who has read the end of the letter and become more thoughtful*] It is true that De Baudricourt seems extraordinarily impressed.

LA HIRE. De Baudricourt is a blazing ass; but he is a soldier; and if he thinks she can beat the English, all the rest of the army will think so too.

LA TRÉMOUILLE [*to the Archbishop, who is hesitating*] Oh, let them have their way. Dunois' men will give up the town in spite of him if somebody does not put some fresh spunk into them.

THE ARCHBISHOP. The Church must examine the girl before anything decisive is done about her. However, since his Highness desires it, let her attend the Court.

LA HIRE. I will find her and tell her. [*He goes out*].

CHARLES. Come with me, Bluebeard; and let us arrange so that she will not know who I am. You will pretend to be me. [*He goes out through the curtains*].

BLUEBEARD. Pretend to be that thing! Holy Michael! [*He follows the Dauphin*].

LA TRÉMOUILLE. I wonder will she pick him out!

THE ARCHBISHOP. Of course she will.

LA TRÉMOUILLE. Why? How is she to know?

THE ARCHBISHOP. She will know what everybody in Chinon knows: that the Dauphin is the meanest-looking and worst-dressed figure in the Court, and that the man with the blue beard is Gilles de Rais.

LA TRÉMOUILLE. I never thought of that.

THE ARCHBISHOP. You are not so accustomed to miracles as I am. It is part of my profession.

LA TRÉMOUILLE [*puzzled and a little scandalized*] But that would not be a miracle at all.

THE ARCHBISHOP [*calmly*] Why not?

LA TRÉMOUILLE. Well, come! what i s a miracle?

THE ARCHBISHOP. A miracle, my friend, is an event which creates faith. That is the purpose and nature of miracles. They may seem very wonderful to the people who witness them, and very simple to those who perform them. That does not matter: if they confirm or create faith they are true miracles.

LA TRÉMOUILLE. Even when they are frauds, do you mean?

THE ARCHBISHOP. Frauds deceive. An event which creates faith does not deceive: therefore it is not a fraud, but a miracle.

LA TRÉMOUILLE [*scratching his neck in his perplexity*] Well, I suppose as you are an archbishop you must be right. It seems a bit fishy to me. But I am no churchman, and dont understand these matters.

THE ARCHBISHOP. You are not a churchman; but you are a diplomatist and a soldier. Could you make our citizens pay war taxes, or our soldiers sacrifice their lives, if they knew what is really happening instead of what seems to them to be happening?

LA TRÉMOUILLE. No, by Saint Dennis: the fat would be in the fire before sundown.

THE ARCHBISHOP. Would it not be quite easy to tell them the truth?

LA TRÉMOUILLE. Man alive, they wouldnt believe it.

THE ARCHBISHOP. Just so. Well, the Church has to rule men for the good of their souls as you have to rule them for the good of their bodies. To do that, the Church must do as you do: nourish their faith by poetry.

LA TRÉMOUILLE. Poetry! I should call it humbug.

THE ARCHBISHOP. You would be wrong, my friend. Parables are not lies because they describe events that have never happened. Miracles are not frauds because they are often—I do not say always—very simple and innocent contrivances by which the priest fortifies the faith of his flock. When this girl picks out the Dauphin among his courtiers, it will not be a miracle for me, because I shall know how it has been done, and my faith will not be increased. But as for the others, if they feel the thrill of the supernatural, and forget their sinful clay in a sudden sense of the glory of God, it will be a miracle and a blessed one. And you will find that the girl herself will be more affected than anyone else. She will forget how she really picked him out. So, perhaps, will you.

LA TRÉMOUILLE. Well, I wish I were clever enough to know how much of you is God's archbishop and how much the most artful fox in Touraine. Come on, or we shall be late for the fun; and I want to see it, miracle or no miracle.

THE ARCHBISHOP [*detaining him a moment*] Do not think that I am a lover of crooked ways. There is a new spirit rising in men: we are at the dawning of a wider epoch. If I were a simple monk, and had not to rule men, I should seek peace for my spirit with Aristotle and Pythagoras rather than with the saints and their miracles.

LA TRÉMOUILLE. And who the deuce was Pythagoras?

THE ARCHBISHOP. A sage who held that the earth is round, and that it moves round the sun.

LA TRÉMOUILLE. What an utter fool! Couldnt he use his eyes?

They go out together through the curtains, which are presently withdrawn, revealing the full depth of the throne room with the Court assembled. On the right are two Chairs of State on a dais. Bluebeard is standing theatrically on the dais, playing the king, and, like the courtiers, enjoying the joke rather obviously. There is a curtained arch in the wall behind the dais; but the main door, guarded by men-at-arms, is at the other side of the room; and a clear path across is kept and lined by the courtiers. Charles is in this path in the middle of the room. La Hire is on his right. The Archbishop, on his left, has taken his place by the dais: La Trémouille at the other side of it. The Duchess de la Trémouille, pretending to be the Queen, sits in the Consort's chair, with a group of ladies in waiting close by, behind the Archbishop.

The chatter of the courtiers makes such a noise that nobody notices the appearance of the page at the door.

THE PAGE. The Duke of— [*Nobody listens*]. The Duke of— [*The chatter continues. Indignant at his failure to command a hearing, he snatches the halberd of the nearest man-at-arms, and thumps the floor with it. The chatter ceases; and everybody looks at him in silence*]. Attention! [*He restores the halberd to the man-at-arms*]. The Duke of Vendôme presents Joan the Maid to his Majesty.

CHARLES [*putting his finger on his lip*] Ssh! [*He hides behind the nearest courtier, peering out to see what happens*].

BLUEBEARD [*majestically*] Let her approach the throne.

Joan, dressed as a soldier, with her hair bobbed and hanging thickly round her face, is led in by a bashful and speechless nobleman, from whom she detaches herself to stop and look round eagerly for the Dauphin.

THE DUCHESS [*to the nearest lady in waiting*] My dear! Her Hair! [*All the ladies explode in uncontrollable laughter*].

BLUEBEARD [*trying not to laugh, and waving his hand in deprecation of their merriment*] Ssh–ssh! Ladies! Ladies!!

JOAN [*not at all embarrassed*] I wear it like this because I am a soldier. Where be Dauphin?

A titter runs through the Court as she walks to the dais.

BLUEBEARD [*condescendingly*] You are in the presence of the Dauphin.

Joan looks at him sceptically for a moment, scanning him hard up and down to make sure. Dead silence, all watching her. Fun dawns in her face.

JOAN. Coom, Bluebeard! Thou canst not fool me. Where be Dauphin?

A roar of laughter breaks out as Gilles, with a gesture of surrender, joins in the laugh, and jumps down from the dais beside La Trémouille. Joan, also on the broad grin, turns back, searching along the row of courtiers, and presently makes a dive, and drags out Charles by the arm.

JOAN [*releasing him and bobbing him a little curtsey*] Gentle little Dauphin. I am sent to you to drive the English away from Orleans and from France, and to crown you king in the cathedral at Rheims, where all true kings of France are crowned.

CHARLES [*triumphant, to the Court*] You see, all of you: she knew the blood royal. Who dare say now that I am not my father's son? [*To Joan*] But if you want me to be crowned at Rheims you must talk to the Archbishop, not to me. There he is [*he is standing behind her*]!

JOAN [*turning quickly, overwhelmed with emotion*] Oh, my lord! [*She falls on both knees before him, with bowed head, not daring to look up*] My lord: I am only a poor country girl; and you are filled with the blessedness and glory of God Himself; but you will touch me with your hands, and give me your blessing, wont you?

BLUEBEARD [*whispering to La Trémouille*] The old fox blushes.

LA TRÉMOUILLE. Another miracle!

THE ARCHBISHOP [*touched, putting his hand on her head*] Child: you are in love with religion.

JOAN [*startled: looking up at him*] Am I? I never thought of that. Is there any harm in it?

THE ARCHBISHOP. There is no harm in it, my child. But there is danger.

JOAN [*rising, with a sunflush of reckless happiness irradiating her face*] There is always danger, except in heaven. Oh, my lord, you have given me such strength, such courage. It must be a most wonderful thing to be Archbishop.

The Court smiles broadly: even titters a little.

THE ARCHBISHOP [*drawing himself up sensitively*] Gentlemen: your levity is rebuked by this maid's faith. I am, God help me, all unworthy; but your mirth is a deadly sin.

Their faces fall. Dead silence.

BLUEBEARD. My lord: we were laughing at her, not at you.

THE ARCHBISHOP. What? Not at my unworthiness but at her faith! Gilles de Rais: this maid prophesied that the blasphemer should be drowned in his sin—

JOAN [*distressed*] No!

THE ARCHBISHOP [*silencing her by a gesture*] I prophesy now that you will be hanged in yours if you do not learn when to laugh and when to pray.

BLUEBEARD. My lord: I stand rebuked. I am sorry: I can say no more. But if you prophesy that I shall be hanged, I shall never be able to resist temptation, because I shall always be telling myself that I may as well be hanged for a sheep as a lamb.

The courtiers take heart at this. There is more tittering.

JOAN [*scandalized*] You are an idle fellow, Bluebeard; and you have great impudence to answer the Archbishop.

LA HIRE [*with a huge chuckle*] Well said, lass! Well said!

JOAN [*impatiently to the Archbishop*] Oh, my lord, will you send all these silly folks away so that I may speak to the Dauphin alone?

LA HIRE [*goodhumoredly*] I can take a hint. [*He salutes; turns on his heel; and goes out*].

THE ARCHBISHOP. Come, gentlemen. The Maid comes with God's blessing, and must be obeyed.

The courtiers withdraw, some through the arch, others at the opposite side. The Archbishop marches across to the door, followed by the Duchess and La Trémouille. As the Archbishop passes Joan, she falls on her knees, and kisses the hem of his robe fervently. He shakes his head in instinctive remonstrance; gathers the robe from her; and goes out. She is left kneeling directly in the Duchess's way.

THE DUCHESS [*coldly*] Will you allow me to pass, please?

JOAN [*hastily rising, and standing back*] Beg pardon, maam, I am sure.

The Duchess passes on. Joan stares after her; then whispers to the Dauphin.

JOAN. Be that Queen?

CHARLES. No. She thinks she is.

JOAN [*again staring after the Duchess*] Oo-oo-ooh! [*Her awestruck amazement at the figure cut by the magnificently dressed lady is not wholly complimentary*].

LA TRÉMOUILLE [*very surly*] I'll trouble your Highness not to gibe at my wife. [*He goes out. The others have already gone*].

JOAN [*to the Dauphin*] Who be old Gruff-and-Grum?

CHARLES. He is the Duke de la Trémouille.

JOAN. What be his job?

CHARLES. He pretends to command the army. And whenever I find a friend I can care for, he kills him.

JOAN. Why dost let him?

CHARLES [*petulantly moving to the throne side of the room to escape from her magnetic field*] How can I prevent him? He bullies me. They all bully me.

JOAN. Art afraid?

CHARLES. Yes: I am afraid. It's no use preaching to me about it. It's all very well for these big men with their armor that is too heavy for me, and their swords that I can hardly lift, and their muscle and their shouting and their bad tempers. They like fighting: most of them are making fools of themselves all the time they are not fighting; but I am quiet and sensible; and I dont want to kill people: I only want to be left alone to enjoy myself in my own way. I never asked to be a king: it was pushed on me. So if you are going to say "Son of St Louis: gird on the sword of your ancestors, and lead us to victory" you may spare your breath to cool your porridge; for I cannot do it. I am not built that way; and there is an end of it.

JOAN [*trenchant and masterful*] Blethers! We are all like that to begin with. I shall put courage into thee.

CHARLES. But I dont want to have courage put into me. I want to sleep in a comfortable bed, and not live in continual terror of being killed or wounded. Put courage into the others, and let them have their bellyful of fighting; but let me alone.

JOAN. It's no use, Charlie: thou must face what God puts on thee. If thou fail to make thyself king, thoult be a beggar: what else art fit for? Come! Let me see thee sitting on the throne. I have looked forward to that.

CHARLES. What is the good of sitting on the throne when the other fellows give all the orders? However! [*he sits enthroned, a piteous figure*] Here is the king for you! Look your fill at the poor devil.

JOAN. Thourt not king yet, lad: thourt but Dauphin. Be not led away by them around thee. Dressing up dont fill empty noddle. I know the people: the real people that make thy bread for thee; and I tell thee they count no man king of France until the holy oil has been poured on his hair, and himself consecrated and crowned in Rheims Cathedral. And thou needs new clothes, Charlie. Why does not Queen look after thee properly?

CHARLES. We're too poor. She wants all the money we can spare to put on her own back. Besides, I like to see her beautifully dressed; and I dont care what I wear myself: I should look ugly anyhow.

JOAN. There is some good in thee, Charlie; but it is not yet a king's good.

CHARLES. We shall see. I am not such a fool as I look. I have my eyes open; and I can tell you that one good treaty is worth ten good fights. These fighting fellows lose all on the treaties that they gain on the fights. If we can only have a treaty, the English are sure to have the worst of it, because they are better at fighting than at thinking.

JOAN. If the English win, it is they that will make the treaty; and then God help poor France! Thou must fight, Charlie, whether thou will or no. I will go first to hearten thee. We must take our courage in both hands: aye, and pray for it with both hands too.

CHARLES [*descending from his throne and again crossing the room to escape from her dominating urgency*] Oh do stop talking about God and praying. I cant bear people who are always praying. Isnt it bad enough to have to do it at the proper times?

JOAN [*pitying him*] Thou poor child, thou hast never prayed in thy life. I must teach thee from the beginning.

CHARLES. I am not a child: I am a grown man and a father; and I will not be taught any more.

JOAN. Aye, you have a little son. He that will be Louis the Eleventh when you die. Would you not fight for him?

CHARLES. No: a horrid boy. He hates me. He hates everybody, selfish little beast! I dont want to be bothered with children. I dont want to be a father; and I dont want to be a son: especially a son of St Louis. I dont want to be any of these fine things you all have your heads full of: I want to be just what I am. Why cant you mind your own business, and let me mind mine?

JOAN [*again contemptuous*] Minding your own business is like minding your own body: it's the shortest way to make yourself sick. What is my business? Helping mother at home. What is thine? Petting lapdogs and sucking sugar-sticks. I call that muck. I tell thee it is God's business we are here to do: not our own. I have a message to thee from God; and thou must listen to it, though thy heart break with the terror of it.

CHARLES. I dont want a message; but can you tell me any secrets? Can you do any cures? Can you turn lead into gold, or anything of that sort?

JOAN. I can turn thee into a king, in Rheims Cathedral; and that is a miracle that will take some doing, it seems.

CHARLES. If we go to Rheims, and have a coronation, Anne will want new dresses. We cant afford them. I am all right as I am.

JOAN. As you are! And what is that? Less than my father's poorest shepherd. Thourt not lawful owner of thy own land of France till thou be consecrated.

CHARLES. But I shall not be lawful owner of my own land anyhow. Will the consecration pay off my mortgages? I have pledged my last acre to the Archbishop and that fat bully. I owe money even to Bluebeard.

JOAN [*earnestly*] Charlie: I come from the land, and have gotten my strength working on the land; and I tell thee that the land is thine to rule righteously and keep God's peace in, and not to pledge at the pawnshop as a drunken woman pledges her children's clothes. And I come from God to tell thee to kneel in the cathedral and solemnly give thy kingdom to Him for ever and ever, and become the greatest king in the world as His steward and His bailiff, His soldier and His servant. The very clay of France will become holy: her soldiers will be the soldiers of God: the rebel dukes will be rebels against God: the English will fall on their knees and beg thee let them return to their lawful homes in peace. Wilt be a poor little Judas, and betray me and Him that sent me?

CHARLES [*tempted at last*] Oh, if I only dare!

JOAN. I shall dare, dare, and dare again, in God's name! Art for or against me?

CHARLES [*excited*] I'll risk it, I warn you I shant be able to keep it up; but I'll risk it. You shall see. [*Running to the main door and shouting*] Hallo! Come back, everybody. [*To Joan, as he runs back to the arch opposite*] Mind you stand by and dont let me be bullied. [*Through the arch*] Come along, will you: the whole Court. [*He sits down in the royal chair as they all hurry in to their former places, chattering and wondering*]. Now I'm in for it; but no matter: here goes! [*To the page*] Call for silence, you little beast, will you?

THE PAGE [*snatching a halberd as before and thumping with it repeatedly*] Silence for His Majesty the King. The King speaks. [*Peremptorily*] Will you be silent there? [*Silence*].

CHARLES [*rising*] I have given the command of the army to The Maid. The Maid is to do as she likes with it. [*He descends from the dais*].

General amazement. La Hire, delighted, slaps his steel thighpiece with his gauntlet.

LA TRÉMOUILLE [*turning threateningly towards Charles*] What is this? *I* command the army.

Joan quickly puts her hand on Charles's shoulder as he instinctively recoils. Charles, with a grotesque effort culminating in an extravagant gesture, snaps his fingers in the Chamberlain's face.

JOAN. Thourt answered, old Gruff-and-Grum. [*Suddenly flashing out her sword as she divines that her moment has come*] Who is for God and His Maid? Who is for Orleans with me?

LA HIRE [*carried away, drawing also*] For God and His Maid! To Orleans!

ALL THE KNIGHTS [*following his lead with enthusiasm*] To Orleans!

Joan, radiant, falls on her knees in thanksgiving to God. They all kneel, except the Archbishop, who gives his benediction with a sign, and La Trémouille, who collapses, cursing.

SCENE III

Orlean, 29th April, 1429. Dunois, aged 26, is pacing up and down a patch of ground on the south bank of the silver Loire, commanding a long view of the river in both directions. He has had his lance stuck up with a pennon, which streams in a strong east wind. His shield with its bend sinister lies beside it. He has his commander's baton in his hand. He is well built, carrying his armor easily. His broad brow and pointed chin give him an equilaterally triangular face, already marked by active service and responsibility, with the expression of a goodnatured and capable man who has no affectations and no foolish illusions. His page is sitting on the ground, elbows on knees, cheeks on fists, idly watching the water. It is evening; and both man and boy are affected by the loveliness of the Loire.

DUNOIS [*halting for a moment to glance up at the streaming pennon and shake his head wearily before he resumes his pacing*] West wind, west wind, west wind. Strumpet: steadfast when you should be wanton, wanton when you should be steadfast. West wind on the silver Loire: what rhymes to Loire? [*He looks again at the pennon, and shakes his fist at it*] Change, curse you, change, English harlot of a wind, change. West, west, I tell you. [*With a growl he resumes his march in silence, but soon begins again*] West wind, wanton wind, wilful wind, womanish wind, false wind from over the water, will you never blow again?

THE PAGE [*bounding to his feet*] See! There! There she goes!

DUNOIS [*startled from his reverie: eagerly*] Where? Who? The Maid?

THE PAGE. No: the kingfisher. Like blue lightning. She went into that bush.

DUNOIS [*furiously disappointed*] Is that all? You infernal young idiot: I have a mind to pitch you into the river.

THE PAGE [*not afraid, knowing his man*] It looked frightfully jolly, that flash of blue. Look! There goes the other!

DUNOIS [*running eagerly to the river brim*] Where? Where?

THE PAGE [*pointing*] Passing the reeds.

DUNOIS [*delighted*] I see.

They follow the flight till the bird takes cover.

THE PAGE. You blew me up because you were not in time to see them yesterday.

DUNOIS. You knew I was expecting The Maid when you set up your yelping. I will give you something to yelp for next time.

THE PAGE. Arnt they lovely? I wish I could catch them.

DUNOIS. Let me catch you trying to trap them, and I will put you in the iron cage for a month to teach you what a cage feels like. You are an abominable boy.

THE PAGE [*laughs, and squats down as before*]!

DUNOIS [*pacing*] Blue bird, blue bird, since I am friend to thee, change thou the wind for me. No: it does not rhyme. He who has sinned for thee: thats better. No sense in it, though. [*He finds himself close to the page*] You abominable boy! [*He turns away from him*] Mary in the blue snood, kingfisher color: will you grudge me a west wind?

A SENTRY'S VOICE WESTWARD. Halt! Who goes there?

JOAN'S VOICE. The Maid.

DUNOIS. Let her pass. Hither, Maid! To me!

Joan, in splendid armor, rushes in in a blazing rage. The wind drops; and the pennon flaps idly down the lance; but Dunois is too much occupied with Joan to notice it.

JOAN [*bluntly*] Be you Bastard of Orleans?

DUNOIS [*cool and stern, pointing to his shield*] You see the bend sinister. Are you Joan the Maid?

JOAN. Sure.

DUNOIS. Where are your troops?

JOAN. Miles behind. They have cheated me. They have brought me to the wrong side of the river.

DUNOIS. I told them to.

JOAN. Why did you? The English are on the other side!

DUNOIS. The English are on both sides.

JOAN. But Orleans is on the other side. We must fight the English there. How can we cross the river?

DUNOIS [*grimly*] There is a bridge.

JOAN. In God's name, then, let us cross the bridge, and fall on them.

DUNOIS. It seems simple; but it cannot be done.

JOAN. Who says so?

DUNOIS. I say so; and older and wiser heads than mine are of the same opinion.

JOAN [*roundly*] Then your older and wiser heads are fat-heads: they have made a fool of you; and now they want to make a fool of me too, bringing me to the wrong side of the river. Do you not know that I bring you better help than ever came to any general or any town?

DUNOIS [*smiling patiently*] Your own?

JOAN. No: the help and the counsel of the King of Heaven. Which is the way to the bridge?

DUNOIS. You are impatient, Maid.

JOAN. Is this a time for patience? Our enemy is at our gates; and here we stand doing nothing. Oh, why are you not fighting? Listen to me: I will deliver you from fear. I–

DUNOIS [*laughing heartily, and waving her off*] No, no, my girl: if you delivered me from fear I should be a good knight for a story book, but a very bad commander of the army. Come! let me begin to make a soldier of you. [*He takes her to the water's edge*]. Do you see those two forts at this end of the bridge? the big ones?

JOAN. Yes. Are they ours or the goddams'?

DUNOIS. Be quiet, and listen to me. If I were in either of those forts with only ten men I could hold it against an army. The English have more than ten times ten goddams in those forts to hold them against us.

JOAN. They cannot hold them against God. God did not give them the land under those forts: they stole it from Him. He gave it to us. I will take those forts.

DUNOIS. Single-handed?

JOAN. Our men will take them. I will lead them.

DUNOIS. Not a man will follow you.

JOAN. I will not look back to see whether anyone is following me.

DUNOIS [*recognizing her mettle, and clapping her heartily on the shoulder*] Good. You have the makings of a soldier in you. You are in love with war.

JOAN [*startled*] Oh! And the Archbishop said I was in love with religion.

DUNOIS. I, God forgive me, am a little in love with war myself, the ugly devil! I am like a man with two wives. Do you want to be like a woman with two husbands?

JOAN [*matter-of-fact*] I will never take a husband. A man in Toul took an action against me for breach of promise; but I never promised him. I am a soldier: I do not want to be thought of as a woman. I will not dress as a woman. I do not care for the things women care for. They dream of lovers, and of money. I dream of leading a charge, and of placing the big guns. You soldiers do not know how to use the big guns: you think you can win battles with a great noise and smoke.

DUNOIS [*with a shrug*] True. Half the time the artillery is more trouble than it is worth.

JOAN. Aye, lad; but you cannot fight stone walls with horses: you must have guns, and much bigger guns too.

DUNOIS [*grinning at her familiarity, and echoing it*] Aye, lass; but a good heart and a stout ladder will get over the stoniest wall.

JOAN. I will be first up the ladder when we reach the fort, Bastard. I dare you to follow me.

DUNOIS. You must not dare a staff officer, Joan: only company officers are allowed to indulge in displays of personal courage. Besides, you must know that I welcome you as a saint, not as a soldier. I have daredevils enough at my call, if they could help me.

JOAN. I am not a daredevil: I am a servant of God. My sword is sacred: I found it behind the altar in the church of St Catherine, where God hid it for me; and I may not strike a blow with it. My heart is full of courage, not of anger. I will lead; and your men will follow: that is all I can do. But I must do it: you shall not stop me.

DUNOIS. All in good time. Our men cannot take those forts by a sally across the bridge. They must come by water, and take the English in the rear on this side.

JOAN [*her military sense asserting itself*] Then make rafts and put big guns on them; and let your men cross to us.

DUNOIS. The rafts are ready; and the men are embarked. But they must wait for God.

JOAN. What do you mean? God is waiting for them.

DUNOIS. Let Him send us a wind then. My boats are downstream: they cannot come up against both wind and current. We must wait until God changes the wind. Come: let me take you to the church.

JOAN. No. I love church; but the English will not yield to prayers: they understand nothing but hard knocks and slashes. I will not go to church until we have beaten them.

DUNOIS. You must: I have business for you there.

JOAN. What business?

DUNOIS. To pray for a west wind. I have prayed; and I have given two silver candlesticks; but my prayers are not answered. Yours may be: you are young and innocent.

JOAN. Oh yes: you are right. I will pray: I will tell St Catherine: she will make God give me a west wind. Quick: shew me the way to the church.

THE PAGE [*sneezes violently*] At-cha!!!

JOAN. God bless you, child! Coom, Bastard.

They go out. The page rises to follow. He picks up the shield, and is taking the spear as well when he notices the pennon, which is now streaming eastward.

THE PAGE [*dropping the shield and calling excitedly after them*] Seigneur! Seigneur! Mademoiselle!

DUNOIS [*running back*] What is it? The kingfisher? [*He looks eagerly for it up the river*].

JOAN [*joining them*] Oh, a kingfisher! Where?

THE PAGE. No: the wind, the wind, the wind [*pointing to the pennon*]: that is what made me sneeze.

DUNOIS [*looking at the pennon*] The wind has changed. [*He crosses himself*] God has spoken. [*Kneeling and handing his baton to Joan*] You command the king's army. I am your soldier.

THE PAGE [*looking down the river*] The boats have put off. They are ripping upstream like anything.

DUNOIS [*rising*] Now for the forts. You dared me to follow. Dare you lead?

JOAN [*bursting into tears and flinging her arms round Dunois, kissing him on both cheeks*] Dunois, dear comrade in arms, help me. My eyes are blinded with tears. Set my foot on the ladder, and say "Up, Joan."

DUNOIS [*dragging her out*] Never mind the tears: make for the flash of the guns.

JOAN [*in a blaze of courage*] Ah!

DUNOIS [*dragging her along with him*] For God and Saint Dennis!

THE PAGE [*shrilly*] The Maid! The Maid! God and The Maid! Hurray-ay-ay! [*He snatches up the shield and lance, and capers out after them, mad with excitement*].

SCENE IV

A tent in the English camp. A bullnecked English chaplain of 50 is sitting on a stool at a table, hard at work writing. At the other side of the table an imposing nobleman, aged 46, is seated in a handsome chair turning over the leaves of an illuminated Book of Hours. The nobleman is enjoying himself: the chaplain is struggling with suppressed wrath. There is an unoccupied leather stool on the nobleman's left. The table is on his right.

THE NOBLEMAN. Now this is what I call workmanship. There is nothing on earth more exquisite than a bonny book, with well-placed columns of rich black writing in beautiful borders, and illuminated pictures cunningly inset. But nowadays, instead of looking at books, people read them. A book might as well be one of those orders for bacon and bran that you are scribbling.

THE CHAPLAIN. I must say, my lord, you take our situation very coolly. Very coolly indeed.

THE NOBLEMAN [*supercilious*] What is the matter?

THE CHAPLAIN. The matter, my lord, is that we English have been defeated.

THE NOBLEMAN. That happens, you know. It is only in history books and ballads that the enemy is always defeated.

THE CHAPLAIN. But we are being defeated over and over again. First, Orleans—

THE NOBLEMAN [*poohpoohing*] Oh, Orleans!

THE CHAPLAIN. I know what you are going to say, my lord: that was a clear case of witchcraft and sorcery. But we are still being defeated. Jargeau, Meung, Beaugency, just like Orleans. And now we have been butchered at Patay, and Sir John Talbot taken prisoner. [*He throws down his pen, almost in tears*] I feel it, my lord: I feel it very deeply. I cannot bear to see my countrymen defeated by a parcel of foreigners.

THE NOBLEMAN. Oh! you are an Englishman, are you?

THE CHAPLAIN. Certainly not, my lord: I am a gentleman. Still, like your lordship, I was born in England; and it makes a difference.

THE NOBLEMAN. You are attached to the soil, eh?

THE CHAPLAIN. It pleases your lordship to be satirical at my expense: your greatness privileges you to be so with impunity. But your lordship knows very well that I am not attached to the soil in a vulgar manner, like a serf. Still, I have a feeling about it; [*with growing agitation*] and I am not ashamed of it; and [*rising wildly*] by God, if this goes on any longer I will fling my cassock to the devil, and take arms myself, and strangle the accursed witch with my own hands.

THE NOBLEMAN [*laughing at him goodnaturedly*] So you shall, chaplain: so you shall, if we can do nothing better. But not yet, not quite yet.

The Chaplain resumes his seat very sulkily.

THE NOBLEMAN [*airily*] I should not care very much about the witch—you see, I have made my pilgrimage to the Holy Land; and the Heavenly Powers, for their own credit, can hardly allow m e to be worsted by a village sorceress—but the Bastard of Orleans is a harder nut to crack; and as he has been to the Holy Land too, honors are easy between us as far as that goes.

THE CHAPLAIN. He is only a Frenchman, my lord.

THE NOBLEMAN. A Frenchman! Where did you pick up that expression? Are these Burgundians and Bretons and Picards and Gascons beginning to call themselves Frenchmen, just as our fellows are beginning to call themselves Englishmen? They actually talk of France and England as their countries. T h e i r s, if you please! What is to become of me and you if that way of thinking comes into fashion?

THE CHAPLAIN. Why, my lord? Can it hurt us?

THE NOBLEMAN. Men cannot serve two masters. If this cant of serving their country once takes hold of them, goodbye to the authority of their feudal lords, and goodbye to the authority of the Church. That is, goodbye to you and me.

THE CHAPLAIN. I hope I am a faithful servant of the Church; and there are only six cousins between me and the barony of Stogumber, which was created by the Conqueror. But is that any reason why I should stand by and see Englishmen beaten by a French bastard and a witch from Lousy Champagne?

THE NOBLEMAN. Easy, man, easy: we shall burn the witch and beat the bastard all in good time. Indeed I am waiting at present for the Bishop of Beauvais, to arrange the burning with him. He has been turned out of his diocese by her faction.

THE CHAPLAIN. You have first to catch her, my lord.

THE NOBLEMAN. Or buy her. I will offer a king's ransom.
THE CHAPLAIN. A king's ransom! For that slut!
THE NOBLEMAN. One has to leave a margin. Some of Charles's people will sell her to the Burgundians; the Burgundians will sell her to us; and there will probably be three or four middlemen who will expect their little commissions.
THE CHAPLAIN. Monstrous. It is all those scoundrels of Jews: they get in every time money changes hands. I would not leave a Jew alive in Christendom if I had my way.
THE NOBLEMAN. Why not? The Jews generally give value. They make you pay; but they deliver the goods. In my experience the men who want something for nothing are invariably Christians.

A page appears.

THE PAGE. The Right Reverend the Bishop of Beauvais: Monseigneur Cauchon.

Cauchon, aged about 60, comes in. The page withdraws. The two Englishmen rise.

THE NOBLEMAN [*with effusive courtesy*] My dear Bishop, how good of you to come! Allow me to introduce myself: Richard de Beauchamp, Earl of Warwick, at your service.
CAUCHON. Your lordship's fame is well known to me.
WARWICK. This reverend cleric is Master John de Stogumber.
THE CHAPLAIN [*glibly*] John Bowyer Spenser Neville de Stogumber, at your service, my lord: Bachelor of Theology, and Keeper of the Private Seal to His Eminence the Cardinal of Winchester.
WARWICK [*to Cauchon*] You call him the Cardinal of England, I believe. Our king's uncle.
CAUCHON. Messire John de Stogumber: I am always the very good friend of His Eminence. [*He extends his hand to the chaplain, who kisses his ring*].
WARWICK. Do me the honor to be seated. [*He gives Cauchon his chair, placing it at the head of the table*].

Cauchon accepts the place of honor with a grave inclination. Warwick fetches the leather stool carelessly, and sits in his former place. The chaplain goes back to his chair.

Though Warwick has taken second place in calculated deference to the Bishop, he assumes the lead in opening the proceedings as a matter of course. He is still cordial and expansive; but there is a new note in his voice which means that he is coming to business.

WARWICK. Well, my Lord Bishop, you find us in one of our unlucky moments. Charles is to be crowned at Rheims, practically by the young woman from Lorraine; and—I must not deceive you, nor flatter your hopes—we cannot prevent it. I suppose it will make a great difference to Charles's position.

CAUCHON. Undoubtedly. It is a masterstroke of The Maid's.

THE CHAPLAIN [*again agitated*] We were not fairly beaten, my lord. No Englishman is ever fairly beaten.

Cauchon raises his eyebrow slightly, then quickly composes his face.

WARWICK. Our friend here takes the view that the young woman is a sorceress. It would, I presume, be the duty of your reverend lordship to denounce her to the Inquisition, and have her burnt for that offence.

CAUCHON. If she were captured in my diocese: yes.

WARWICK [*feeling that they are getting on capitally*] Just so. Now I suppose there can be no reasonable doubt that she i s a sorceress.

THE CHAPLAIN. Not the least. An arrant witch.

WARWICK [*gently reproving the interruption*] We are asking for the Bishop's opinion, Messire John.

CAUCHON. We shall have to consider not merely our own opinions here, but the opinions—the prejudices, if you like—of a French court.

WARWICK [*correcting*] A Catholic court, my lord.

CAUCHON. Catholic courts are composed of mortal men, like other courts, however sacred their function and inspiration may be. And if the men are Frenchmen, as the modern fashion calls them, I am afraid the bare fact that an English army has been defeated by a French one will not convince them that there is any sorcery in the matter.

THE CHAPLAIN. What! Not when the famous Sir John Talbot himself has been defeated and actually taken prisoner by a drab from the ditches of Lorraine!

CAUCHON. Sir John Talbot, we all know, is a fierce and formidable soldier, Messire; but I have yet to learn that he is an able general. And though it pleases you to say that he has been defeated by this girl, some of us may be disposed to give a little of the credit to Dunois.

THE CHAPLAIN [*contemptuously*] The Bastard of Orleans!

CAUCHON. Let me remind—

WARWICK [*interposing*] I know what you are going to say, my lord. Dunois defeated m e at Montargis.

CAUCHON [*bowing*] I take that as evidence that the Seigneur Dunois is a very able commander indeed.

WARWICK. Your lordship is the flower of courtesy. I admit, on our side, that Talbot is a mere fighting animal, and that it probably served him right to be taken at Patay.

THE CHAPLAIN [*chafing*] My lord: at Orleans this woman had her throat pierced by an English arrow, and was seen to cry like a child from the pain of it. It was a death wound; yet she fought all day; and when our men had repulsed all her attacks like true Englishmen, she walked alone to the wall of our fort with a white banner in her hand; and our men were paralyzed, and could neither shoot nor strike whilst the French fell on them and drove them on to the bridge, which immediately burst into flames and crumbled under them, letting them down into the river, where they were drowned in heaps. Was this your bastard's generalship? or were those flames the flames of hell, conjured up by witchcraft?

WARWICK. You will forgive Messire John's vehemence, my lord; but he has put our case. Dunois is a great captain, we admit; but why could he do nothing until the witch came?

CAUCHON. I do not say that there were no supernatural powers on her side. But the names on that white banner were not the names of Satan and Beelzebub, but the blessed names of our Lord and His holy mother. And your commander who was drowned—Clahz-da I think you call him—

WARWICK. Glasdale. Sir William Glasdale.

CAUCHON. Glass-dell, thank you. He was no saint; and many of our people think that he was drowned for his blasphemies against The Maid.

WARWICK [*beginning to look very dubious*] Well, what are we to infer from all this, my lord? Has The Maid converted you?

CAUCHON. If she had, my lord, I should have known better than to have trusted myself here within your grasp.

WARWICK [*blandly deprecating*] Oh! oh! My lord!

CAUCHON. If the devil is making use of this girl—and I believe he is—

WARWICK [*reassured*] Ah! You hear, Messire John? I knew your lordship would not fail us. Pardon my interruption. Proceed.

CAUCHON. If it be so, the devil has longer views than you give him credit for.

WARWICK. Indeed? In what way? Listen to this, Messire John.

CAUCHON. If the devil wanted to damn a country girl, do you think so easy a task would cost him the winning of half a dozen battles? No, my lord: any trumpery imp could do that much if the girl could be damned at all. The Prince of Darkness does not condescend to such cheap drudgery. When he strikes, he strikes at the Catholic Church, whose realm is the whole spiritual world. When he damns, he damns the souls of the entire human race. Against that dreadful design The Church stands ever on guard. And it is as one of the instruments of that design that I see this girl. She is inspired, but diabolically inspired.

THE CHAPLAIN. I told you she was a witch.

CAUCHON [*fiercely*] She is not a witch. She is a heretic.

THE CHAPLAIN. What difference does that make?

CAUCHON. You, a priest, ask me that! You English are strangely blunt in the mind. All these things that you call witchcraft are capable of a natural explanation. The woman's miracles would not impose on a rabbit: she does not claim them as miracles herself. What do her victories prove but that she has a better head on her shoulders than your swearing Glass-dells and mad bull Talbots, and that the courage of faith, even though it be a false faith, will always outstay the courage of wrath?

THE CHAPLAIN [*hardly able to believe his ears*] Does your lordship compare Sir John Talbot, three times Governor of Ireland, to a mad bull?!!!

WARWICK. It would not be seemly for you to do so, Messire John, as you are still six removes from a barony. But as I am an earl, and Talbot is only a knight, I may make bold to accept the comparison. [*To the Bishop*] My lord: I wipe the slate as far as the witchcraft goes. None the less, we must burn the woman.

CAUCHON. I cannot burn her. The Church cannot take life. And my first duty is to seek this girl's salvation.

WARWICK. No doubt. But you do burn people occasionally.

CAUCHON. No. When The Church cuts off an obstinate heretic as a dead branch from the tree of life, the heretic is handed over to the secular arm. The Church has no part in what the secular arm may see fit to do.

WARWICK. Precisely. And I shall be the secular arm in this case. Well, my lord, hand over your dead branch; and I will see that the fire is ready for it. If you will answer for The Church's part, I will answer for the secular part.

CAUCHON [*with smouldering anger*] I can answer for nothing. You great lords are too prone to treat The Church as a mere political convenience.

WARWICK [*smiling and propitiatory*] Not in England, I assure you.

CAUCHON. In England more than anywhere else. No, my lord: the soul of this village girl is of equal value with yours or your king's before the throne of God; and my first duty is to save it. I will not suffer your lordship to smile at me as if I were repeating a meaningless form of words, and it were well understood between us that I should betray the girl to you. I am no mere political bishop: my faith is to me what your honor is to you; and if there be a loophole through which this baptized child of God can creep to her salvation, I shall guide her to it.

THE CHAPLAIN [*rising in a fury*] You are a traitor.

CAUCHON [*springing up*] You lie, priest. [*Trembling with rage*] If you dare do what this woman has done—set your country above the holy Catholic Church—you shall go to the fire with her.

THE CHAPLAIN. My lord: I—I went too far. I—[*he sits down with a submissive gesture*].

WARWICK [*who has risen apprehensively*] My Lord: I apologize to you for the word used by Messire John de Stogumber. It does not mean in England what it does in France. In your language traitor means betrayer: one who is perfidious, treacherous, unfaithful, disloyal. In our country it means simply one who is not wholly devoted to our English interests.

CAUCHON. I am sorry: I did not understand. [*He subsides into his chair with dignity*].

WARWICK [*resuming his seat, much relieved*] I must apologize on my own account if I have seemed to take the burning of this poor girl too lightly. When one has seen whole countrysides burnt over and over again as mere items in military routine, one has to grow a very thick skin. Otherwise one might go mad: at all events, I should. May I venture to assume that your lordship also, having to see so many heretics burned from time to time, is compelled to take—shall I say a professional view of what would otherwise be a very horrible incident?

CAUCHON. Yes: it is a very painful duty: even, as you say, a horrible one. But in comparison with the horror of heresy it is less than nothing. I am not thinking of this girl's body, which will suffer for a few moments only, and which must in any event die in some more or less painful manner, but of her soul, which may suffer to all eternity.

WARWICK. Just so; and God grant that her soul may be saved! But the practical problem would seem to be how to save her soul without saving her body. For we must face it, my lord: if this cult of The Maid goes on, our cause is lost.

THE CHAPLAIN [*his voice broken like that of a man who has been crying*] May I speak, my lord?
WARWICK. Really, Messire John, I had rather you did not, unless you can keep your temper.
THE CHAPLAIN. It is only this. I speak under correction; but The Maid is full of deceit: she pretends to be devout. Her prayers and confessions are endless. How can she be accused of heresy when she neglects no observance of a faithful daughter of The Church?
CAUCHON [*flaming up*] A faithful daughter of The Church! The Pope himself at his proudest dare not presume as this woman presumes. She acts as if she herself were The Church. She brings the message of God to Charles; and The Church must stand aside. She will crown him in the cathedral of Rheims: she, not The Church! She sends letters to the king of England giving him God's command through her to return to his island on pain of God's vengeance, which she will execute. Let me tell you that the writing of such letters was the practice of the accursed Mahomet, the anti-Christ. Has she ever in all her utterances said one word of The Church? Never. It is always God and herself.
WARWICK. What can you expect? A beggar on horseback! Her head is turned.
CAUCHON. Who has turned it? The devil. And for a mighty purpose. He is spreading this heresy everywhere. The man Hus, burnt only thirteen years ago at Constance, infected all Bohemia with it. A man named WcLeef, himself an anointed priest, spread the pestilence in England; and to your shame you let him die in his bed. We have such people here in France too: I know the breed. It is cancerous: if it be not cut out, stamped out, burnt out, it will not stop until it has brought the whole body of human society into sin and corruption, into waste and ruin. By it an Arab camel driver drove Christ and His Church out of Jerusalem, and ravaged his way west like a wild beast until at last there stood only the Pyrenees and God's mercy between France and damnation. Yet what did the camel driver do at the beginning more than this shepherd girl is doing? He had his voices from the angel Gabriel: she has her voices from St Catherine and St Margaret and the Blessed Michael. He declared himself the messenger of God, and wrote in God's name to the kings of the earth. Her letters to them are going forth daily. It is not the Mother of God now to whom we must look for intercession, but to Joan the Maid. What will the world be like when The Church's accumulated wisdom and knowledge and ex-

perience, its councils of learned, venerable pious men, are thrust into the kennel by every ignorant laborer or dairymaid whom the devil can puff up with the monstrous self-conceit of being directly inspired from heaven? It will be a world of blood, of fury, of devastation, of each man striving for his own hand: in the end a world wrecked back into barbarism. For now you have only Mahomet and his dupes, and the Maid and her dupes; but what will it be when every girl thinks herself a Joan and every man a Mahomet? I shudder to the very marrow of my bones when I think of it. I have fought it all my life; and I will fight it to the end. Let all this woman's sins be forgiven her except only this sin; for it is the sin against the Holy Ghost; and if she does not recant in the dust before the world, and submit herself to the last inch of her soul to her Church, to the fire she shall go if she once falls into my hand.

WARWICK [*unimpressed*] You feel strongly about it, naturally.

CAUCHON. Do not you?

WARWICK. I am a soldier, not a churchman. As a pilgrim I saw something of the Mahometans. They were not so ill-bred as I had been led to believe. In some respects their conduct compared favorably with ours.

CAUCHON [*displeased*] I have noticed this before. Men go to the East to convert the infidels. And the infidels pervert them. The Crusader comes back more than half a Saracen. Not to mention that all Englishmen are born heretics.

THE CHAPLAIN. Englishmen heretics!!! [*Appealing to Warwick*] My lord: must we endure this? His lordship is beside himself. How can what an Englishman believes be heresy? It is a contradiction in terms.

CAUCHON. I absolve you, Messire de Stogumber, on the ground of invincible ignorance. The thick air of your country does not breed theologians.

WARWICK. You would not say so if you heard us quarrelling about religion, my lord! I am sorry you think I must be either a heretic or a blockhead because, as a travelled man, I know that the followers of Mahomet profess great respect for our Lord, and are more ready to forgive St Peter for being a fisherman than your lordship is to forgive Mahomet for being a camel driver. But at least we can proceed in this matter without bigotry.

CAUCHON. When men call the zeal of the Christian Church bigotry I know what to think.

WARWICK. They are only east and west views of the same thing.

CAUCHON [*bitterly ironical*] Only east and west! Only!!

WARWICK. Oh, my Lord Bishop, I am not gainsaying you. You will carry The Church with you; but you have to carry the nobles also. To my mind there is a stronger case against The Maid than the one you have so forcibly put. Frankly, I am not afraid of this girl becoming another Mahomet, and superseding The Church by a great heresy. I think you exaggerate that risk. But have you noticed that in these letters of hers, she proposes to all the kings of Europe, as she has already pressed on Charles, a transaction which would wreck the whole social structure of Christendom?

CAUCHON. Wreck The Church. I tell you so.

WARWICK [*whose patience is wearing out*] My lord: pray get The Church out of your head for a moment; and remember that there are temporal institutions in the world as well as spiritual ones. I and my peers represent the feudal aristocracy as you represent The Church. We are the temporal power. Well, do you not see how this girl's idea strikes at us?

CAUCHON. How does her idea strike at you, except as it strikes at all of us, through The Church?

WARWICK. Her idea is that the kings should give their realms to God, and then reign as God's bailiffs.

CAUCHON [*not interested*] Quite sound theologically, my lord. But the king will hardly care, provided he reign. It is an abstract idea: a mere form of words.

WARWICK. By no means. It is a cunning device to supersede the aristocracy, and make the king sole and absolute autocrat. Instead of the king being merely the first among his peers, he becomes their master. That we cannot suffer: we call no man master. Nominally we hold our lands and dignities from the king, because there must be a keystone to the arch of human society; but we hold our lands in our own hands, and defend them with our own swords and those of our own tenants. Now by The Maid's doctrine the king will take our lands—o u r lands!—and make them a present to God; and God will then vest them wholly in the king.

CAUCHON. Need you fear that? You are the makers of kings after all. York or Lancaster in England, Lancaster or Valois in France: they reign according to your pleasure.

WARWICK. Yes; but only as long as the people follow their feudal lords, and know the king only as a travelling show, owning nothing but the highway that belongs to everybody. If the people's thoughts and hearts were turned to the king, and their lords became only the king's servants in their eyes, the king could break us across his knee one by one; and then what should we be but liveried courtiers in his halls?

CAUCHON. Still you need not fear, my lord. Some men are born kings; and some are born statesmen. The two are seldom the same. Where would the king find counsellors to plan and carry out such a policy for him?

WARWICK [*with a not too friendly smile*] Perhaps in the Church, my lord.

Cauchon, with an equally sour smile, shrugs his shoulders, and does not contradict him.

WARWICK. Strike down the barons; and the cardinals will have it all their own way.

CAUCHON [*conciliatory, dropping his polemical tone*] My lord: we shall not defeat The Maid if we strive against one another. I know well that there is a Will to Power in the world. I know that while it lasts there will be a struggle between the Emperor and the Pope, between the dukes and the political cardinals, between the barons and the kings. The devil divides us and governs. I see you are no friend to The Church: you are an earl first and last, as I am a churchman first and last. But can we not sink our differences in the face of a common enemy? I see now that what is in your mind is not that this girl has never once mentioned The Church, and thinks only of God and herself, but that she has never once mentioned the peerage, and thinks only of the king and herself.

WARWICK. Quite so. These two ideas of hers are the same idea at bottom. It goes deep, my lord. It is the protest of the individual soul against the interference of priest or peer between the private man and his God. I should call it Protestantism if I had to find a name for it.

CAUCHON [*looking hard at him*] You understand it wonderfully well, my lord. Scratch an Englishman, and find a Protestant.

WARWICK [*playing the pink of courtesy*] I think you are not entirely void of sympathy with The Maid's secular heresy, my lord. I leave you to find a name for it.

CAUCHON. You mistake me, my lord. I have no sympathy with her political presumptions. But as a priest I have gained a knowledge of the minds of the common people; and there you will find yet another most dangerous idea. I can express it only by such phrases as France for the French, England for the English, Italy for the Italians, Spain for the

Spanish, and so forth. It is sometimes so narrow and bitter in country folk that it surprises me that this country girl can rise above the idea of her village for its villagers. But she can. She does. When she threatens to drive the English from the soil of France she is undoubtedly thinking of the whole extent of country in which French is spoken. To her the French-speaking people are what the Holy Scriptures describe as a nation. Call this side of her heresy Nationalism if you will: I can find you no better name for it. I can only tell you that it is essentially anti-Catholic and anti-Christian; for the Catholic Church knows only one realm, and that is the realm of Christ's kingdom. Divide that kingdom into nations, and you dethrone Christ. Dethrone Christ, and who will stand between our throats and the sword? The world will perish in a welter of war.

WARWICK. Well, if you will burn the Protestant, I will burn the Nationalist, though perhaps I shall not carry Messire John with me there. England for the English will appeal to him.

THE CHAPLAIN. Certainly England for the English goes without saying: it is the simple law of nature. But this woman denies to England her legitimate conquests, given her by God because of her peculiar fitness to rule over less civilized races for their own good. I do not understand what your lordships mean by Protestant and Nationalist: you are too learned and subtle for a poor clerk like myself. But I know as a matter of plain commonsense that the woman is a rebel; and that is enough for me. She rebels against Nature by wearing man's clothes, and fighting. She rebels against The Church by usurping the divine authority of the Pope. She rebels against God by her damnable league with Satan and his evil spirits against our Army. And all these rebellions are only excuses for her great rebellion against England. That is not to be endured. Let her perish. Let her burn. Let her not infect the whole flock. It is expedient that one woman die for the people.

WARWICK [*rising*] My lord: we seem to be agreed.

CAUCHON [*rising also, but in protest*] I will not imperil my soul. I will uphold the justice of the Church. I will strive to the utmost for this woman's salvation.

WARWICK. I am sorry for the poor girl. I hate these severities. I will spare her if I can.

THE CHAPLAIN [*implacably*] I would burn her with my own hands.

CAUCHON [*blessing him*] Sancta simplicitas!

SCENE V

The ambulatory in the cathedral of Rheims, near the door of the vestry. A pillar bears one of the stations of the cross. The organ is playing the people out of the nave after the coronation. Joan is kneeling in prayer before the station. She is beautifully dressed, but still in male attire. The organ ceases as Dunois, also splendidly arrayed, comes into the ambulatory from the vestry.

DUNOIS. Come, Joan! you have had enough praying. After that fit of crying you will catch a chill if you stay here any longer. It is all over: the cathedral is empty; and the streets are full. They are calling for The Maid. We have told them you are staying here alone to pray; but they want to see you again.

JOAN. No: let the king have all the glory.

DUNOIS. He only spoils the show, poor devil. No, Joan: you have crowned him; and you must go through with it.

JOAN [*shakes her head reluctantly*].

DUNOIS [*raising her*] Come come! it will be over in a couple of hours. It's better than the bridge at Orleans: eh?

JOAN. Oh, dear Dunois, how I wish it were the bridge at Orleans again! We l i v e d at that bridge.

DUNOIS. Yes, faith, and died too: some of us.

JOAN. Isnt it strange, Jack? I am such a coward: I am frightened beyond words before a battle; but it is so dull afterwards when there is no danger: oh, so dull! dull! dull!

DUNOIS. You must learn to be abstemious in war, just as you are in your food and drink, my little saint.

JOAN. Dear Jack: I think you like me as a soldier likes his comrade.

DUNOIS. You need it, poor innocent child of God. You have not many friends at court.

JOAN. Why do all these courtiers and knights and churchmen hate me? What have I done to them? I have asked nothing for myself except that my village shall not be taxed; for we cannot afford war taxes. I have brought them luck and victory: I have set them right when they were doing all sorts of stupid things: I have crowned Charles and made him a real king; and all the honors he is handing out have gone to them. Then why do they not love me?

DUNOIS [*rallying her*] Sim-ple-ton! Do you expect stupid people to love you for shewing them up? Do blundering old military dug-outs love the successful young captains who supersede them? Do ambitious politicians love the climbers who take the front seats from them? Do archbishops enjoy being played off their own altars, even by saints? Why, I should be jealous of you myself if I were ambitious enough.

JOAN. You are the pick of the basket here, Jack: the only friend I have among all these nobles. I'll wager your mother was from the country. I will go back to the farm when I have taken Paris.

DUNOIS. I am not so sure that they will let you take Paris.

JOAN [*startled*] What!

DUNOIS. I should have taken it myself before this if they had all been sound about it. Some of them would rather Paris took you, I think. So take care.

JOAN. Jack: the world is too wicked for me. If the goddams and the Burgundians do not make an end of me, the French will. Only for my voices I should lose all heart. That is why I had to steal away to pray here alone after the coronation. I'll tell you something, Jack. It is in the bells I hear my voices. Not to-day, when they all rang: that was nothing but jangling. But here in this corner, where the bells come down from heaven, and the echoes linger, or in the fields, where they come from a distance through the quiet of the countryside, my voices are in them. [*The cathedral clock chimes the quarter*] Hark! [*She becomes rapt*] Do you hear? "Dear-child-of-God": just what you said. At the half-hour they will say "Be-brave-go-on." At the three-quarters they will say "I-am-thy-Help." But it is at the hour, when the great bell goes after "God-will-save-France": it is then that St Margaret and St Catherine and sometimes even the blessed Michael will say things that I cannot tell beforehand. Then, oh then—

DUNOIS [*interrupting her kindly but not sympathetically*] Then, Joan, we shall hear whatever we fancy in the booming of the bell. You make me uneasy when you talk about your voices: I should think you were a bit cracked if I hadnt noticed that you give me very sensible reasons for what you do, though I hear you telling others you are only obeying Madame Saint Catherine.

JOAN [*crossly*] Well, I have to find reasons for you, because you do not believe in my voices. But the voices come first; and I find the reasons after: whatever you may choose to believe.

DUNOIS. Are you angry, Joan?

JOAN. Yes. [*Smiling*] No: not with you. I wish you were one of the village babies.

DUNOIS. Why?

JOAN. I could nurse you for awhile.

DUNOIS. You are a bit of a woman after all.

JOAN. No: not a bit: I am a soldier and nothing else. Soldiers always nurse children when they get a chance.

DUNOIS. That is true. [*He laughs*].

King Charles, with Bluebeard on his left and La Hire on his right, comes from the vestry, where he has been disrobing. Joan shrinks away behind the pillar. Dunois is left between Charles and La Hire.

DUNOIS. Well, your Majesty is an anointed king at last. How do you like it?

CHARLES. I would not go through it again to be emperor of the sun and moon. The weight of those robes! I thought I should have dropped when they loaded that crown on to me. And the famous holy oil they talked so much about was rancid: phew! The Archbishop must be nearly dead: his robes must have weighed a ton: they are stripping him still in the vestry.

DUNOIS [*drily*] Your majesty should wear armor oftener. That would accustom you to heavy dressing.

CHARLES. Yes: the old jibe! Well, I am not going to wear armor: fighting is not my job. Where is The Maid?

JOAN [*coming forward between Charles and Bluebeard, and falling on her knee*] Sire: I have made you king: my work is done. I am going back to my father's farm.

CHARLES [*surprised, but relieved*] Oh, are you? Well, that will be very nice.

Joan rises, deeply discouraged.

CHARLES [*continuing heedlessly*] A healthy life, you know.

DUNOIS. But a dull one.

BLUEBEARD. You will find the petticoats tripping you up after leaving them off for so long.

LA HIRE. You will miss the fighting. It's a bad habit, but a grand one, and the hardest of all to break yourself of.

CHARLES [*anxiously*] Still, we dont want you to stay if you would really rather go home.

JOAN [*bitterly*] I know well that none of you will be sorry to see me go. [*She turns her shoulder to Charles and walks past him to the more congenial neighbourhood of Dunois and La Hire*].

LA HIRE. Well, I shall be able to swear when I want to. But I shall miss you at times.

JOAN. La Hire: in spite of all your sins and swears we shall meet in heaven; for I love you as I love Pitou, my old sheep dog. Pitou could kill a wolf. You will kill the English wolves until they go back to their country and become good dogs of God, will you not?

LA HIRE. You and I together: yes.

JOAN. No: I shall last only a year from the beginning.

ALL THE OTHERS. What!

JOAN. I know it somehow.

DUNOIS. Nonsense!

JOAN. Jack: do you think you will be able to drive them out?

DUNOIS [*with quiet conviction*] Yes: I shall drive them out. They beat us because we thought battles were tournaments and ransom markets. We played the fool while the goddams took war seriously. But I have learnt my lesson, and taken their measure. They have no roots here. I have beaten them before; and I shall beat them again.

JOAN. You will not be cruel to them, Jack?

DUNOIS. The goddams will not yield to tender handling. We did not begin it.

JOAN [*suddenly*] Jack: before I go home, let us take Paris.

CHARLES [*terrified*] Oh no no. We shall lose everything we have gained. Oh dont let us have any more fighting. We can make a very good treaty with the Duke of Burgundy.

JOAN. Treaty! [*She stamps with impatience*].

CHARLES. Well, why not, now that I am crowned and anointed? Oh, that oil!

The Archbishop comes from the vestry, and joins the group between Charles and Bluebeard.

CHARLES. Archbishop: The Maid wants to start fighting again.

THE ARCHBISHOP. Have we ceased fighting, then? Are we at peace?

CHARLES. No: I suppose not; but let us be content with what we have done. Let us make a treaty. Our luck is too good to last; and now is our chance to stop before it turns.

JOAN. Luck! God has fought for us; and you call it luck! And you would stop while there are still Englishmen on this holy earth of dear France!

THE ARCHBISHOP [*sternly*] Maid: the king addressed himself to me, not to you. You forget yourself. You very often forget yourself.

JOAN [*unabashed, and rather roughly*] Then speak, you; and tell him that it is not God's will that he should take his hand from the plough.

THE ARCHBISHOP. If I am not so glib with the name of God as you are, it is because I interpret His will with the authority of the Church and of my sacred office. When you first came you respected it, and would not have dared to speak as you are now speaking. You came clothed with the virtue of humility; and because God blessed your enterprises accordingly, you have stained yourself with the sin of pride. The old Greek tragedy is rising among us. It is the chastisement of hubris.

CHARLES. Yes: she thinks she knows better than everyone else.

JOAN [*distressed, but naïvely incapable of seeing the effect she is producing*] But I d o know better than any of you seem to. And I am not proud: I never speak unless I know I am right.

BLUEBEARD } [*exclaiming* { Ha ha!
CHARLES } *together*] { Just so.

THE ARCHBISHOP. How do you know you are right?

JOAN. I always know. My voices—

CHARLES. Oh, your voices, your voices. Why dont the voices come to me? I am king, not you.

JOAN. They do come to you; but you do not hear them. You have not sat in the field in the evening listening for them. When the angelus rings you cross yourself and have done with it; but if you prayed from your heart, and listened to the thrilling of the bells in the air after they stop ringing, you would hear the voices as well as I do. [*Turning brusquely from him*] But what voices do you need to tell you what the blacksmith can tell you: that you must strike while the iron is hot? I tell you we must make a dash at Compiègne and relieve it as we relieved Orleans. Then Paris will open its gates; or if not, we will break through them. What is your crown worth without your capital?

LA HIRE. That is what I say too. We shall go through them like a red hot shot through a pound of butter. What do you say, Bastard?

DUNOIS. If our cannon balls were all as hot as your head, and we had enough of them, we should conquer the earth, no doubt. Pluck and impetuosity are good servants in war, but bad masters: they have delivered us into the hands of the English every time we have trusted to them. We never know when we are beaten: that is our great fault.

JOAN. You never know when you are victorious: that is a worse fault. I shall have to make you carry looking-glasses in battle to convince you that the English have not cut off all your noses. You would have been besieged in Orleans still, you and your councils of war, if I had not made you attack. You should always attack; and if you only hold on long enough the enemy will stop first. You dont know how to begin a battle; and you dont know how to use your cannons. And I do.

She squats down on the flags with crossed ankles, pouting.

DUNOIS. I know what you think of us, General Joan.

JOAN. Never mind that, Jack. Tell them what you think of me.

DUNOIS. I think that God was on your side; for I have not forgotten how the wind changed, and how our hearts changed when you came; and by my faith I shall never deny that it was in your sign that we conquered. But I tell you as a soldier that God is no man's daily drudge, and no maid's either. If you are worthy of it He will sometimes snatch you out of the jaws of death and set you on your feet again; but that is all: once on your feet you must fight with all your might and all your craft. For He has to be fair to your enemy too: dont forget that. Well, He set us on our feet through you at Orleans; and the glory of it has carried us through a few good battles here to the coronation. But if we presume on it further, and trust to God to do the work we should do ourselves, we shall be defeated; and serve us right!

JOAN. But—

DUNOIS. Sh! I have not finished. Do not think, any of you, that these victories of ours were won without generalship. King Charles: you have said no word in your proclamations of my part in this campaign; and I make no complaint of that; for the people will run after The Maid and her miracles and not after the Bastard's hard work finding troops for her and feeding them. But I know exactly how much God did for us through The Maid, and how much He left me to do by my own wits; and I tell you that your little hour of miracles is over, and that from this time on he who plays the war game best will win—if the luck is on his side.

JOAN. Ah! if, if, if, if! If ifs and ans were pots and pans there'd be no need of tinkers. [*Rising impetuously*] I tell you, Bastard, your art of war is no use, because your knights are no good for real fighting. War is only a game to them, like tennis and all their other games: they make rules as to what is fair and what is not fair, and heap armor on themselves and on their poor horses to keep out the arrows; and when they fall they cant get up, and have to wait for their squires to come and lift them to arrange about the ransom with the man that has poked them off their horse. Cant you see that all the like of that is gone by and done with? What use is armor against gunpowder? And if it was, do you think men that are fighting for France and for God will stop to bargain about ransoms, as half your knights live by doing? No: they will fight to win; and they will give up their lives out of their own hand into the hand of God when they go into battle, as I do. Common folks understand this. They cannot afford armor and cannot pay ransoms; but they followed me half naked into the moat and up the ladder and over the wall. With them it is my life or thine, and God defend the right! You may shake your head, Jack; and Bluebeard may twirl his billygoat's beard and cock his nose at me; but remember the day your knights and captains refused to follow me to attack the English at Orleans! You locked the gates to keep me in; and it was the townsfolk and the common people that followed me, and forced the gate, and shewed you the way to fight in earnest.

BLUEBEARD [*offended*] Not content with being Pope Joan, you must be Caesar and Alexander as well.

THE ARCHBISHOP. Pride will have a fall, Joan.

JOAN. Oh, never mind whether it is pride or not: is it true? is it commonsense?

LA HIRE. It is true. Half of us are afraid of having our handsome noses broken; and the other half are out for paying off their mortgages. Let her have her way, Dunois: she does not know everything; but she has got hold of the right end of the stick. Fighting is not what it was; and those who know least about it often make the best job of it.

DUNOIS. I know all that. I do not fight in the old way: I have learnt the lesson of Agincourt, of Poitiers and Crecy. I know how many lives any move of mine will cost; and if the move is worth the cost I make it and pay the cost. But Joan never counts the cost at all: she goes ahead and trusts to God: she thinks she has God in her pocket. Up to now she has had the numbers on her side; and she has won. But I know Joan; and I see that some day she will go ahead when she has only ten men to do the work of a hundred. And then she will find that God is on the side of the big battalions. She will be taken by the enemy. And the lucky man that makes the capture will receive sixteen thousand pounds from the Earl of Ouareek.

JOAN [*flattered*] Sixteen thousand pounds! Eh, laddie, have they offered that for me? There cannot be so much money in the world.

DUNOIS. There is, in England. And now tell me, all of you, which of you will lift a finger to save Joan once the English have got her? I speak first, for the army. The day after she has been dragged from her horse by a goddam or a Burgundian, and he is not struck dead: the day after she is locked in a dungeon, and the bars and bolts do not fly open at the touch of St Peter's angel: the day when the enemy finds out that she is as vulnerable as I am and not a bit more invincible, she will not be worth the life of a single soldier to us; and I will not risk that life, much as I cherish her as a companion-in-arms.

JOAN. I dont blame you, Jack: you are right. I am not worth one soldier's life if God lets me be beaten; but France may think me worth my ransom after what God has done for her through me.

CHARLES. I tell you I have no money; and this coronation, which is all your fault, has cost me the last farthing I can borrow.

JOAN. The Church is richer than you. I put my trust in the Church.

THE ARCHBISHOP. Woman: they will drag you through the streets, and burn you as a witch.

JOAN [*running to him*] Oh, my lord, do not say that. It is impossible. I a witch!

THE ARCHBISHOP. Peter Cauchon knows his business. The University of Paris has burnt a woman for saying that what you have done was well done, and according to God.

JOAN [*bewildered*] But why? What sense is there in it? What I have done is according to God. They could not burn a woman for speaking the truth.

THE ARCHBISHOP. They did.

JOAN. But you know that she was speaking the truth. You would not let them burn me.

THE ARCHBISHOP. How could I prevent them?

JOAN. You would speak in the name of the Church. You are a great prince of the Church. I would go anywhere with your blessing to protect me.

THE ARCHBISHOP. I have no blessing for you while you are proud and disobedient.

JOAN. Oh, why will you go on saying things like that? I am not proud and disobedient. I am a poor girl, and so ignorant that I do not know A from B. How could I be proud? And how can you say that I am disobedient when I always obey my voices, because they come from God.

THE ARCHBISHOP. The voice of God on earth is the voice of the Church Militant; and all the voices that come to you are the echoes of your own wilfulness.

JOAN. It is not true.

THE ARCHBISHOP [*flushing angrily*] You tell the Archbishop in his cathedral that he lies; and yet you say you are not proud and disobedient.

JOAN. I never said you lied. It was you that as good as said my voices lied. When have they ever lied? If you will not believe in them: even if they are only the echoes of my own commonsense, are they not always right? and are not your earthly counsels always wrong?

THE ARCHBISHOP [*indignantly*] It is waste of time admonishing you.

CHARLES. It always comes back to the same thing. She is right; and everyone else is wrong.

THE ARCHBISHOP. Take this as your last warning. If you perish through setting your private judgment above the instructions of your spiritual directors, the Church disowns you, and leaves you to whatever fate your presumption may bring upon you. The Bastard has told you that if you persist in setting up your military conceit above the counsels of your commanders—

DUNOIS [*interposing*] To put it quite exactly, if you attempt to relieve the garrison in Compiègne without the same superiority in numbers you had at Orleans—

THE ARCHBISHOP. The army will disown you, and will not rescue you. And His Majesty the King has told you that the throne has not the means of ransoming you.

CHARLES. Not a penny.

THE ARCHBISHOP. You stand alone: absolutely alone, trusting to your own conceit, your own ignorance, your own headstrong presumption, your own impiety in hiding all these sins under the cloak of a trust in God. When you pass through these doors into the sunlight, the crowd will cheer you. They will bring you their little children and their invalids to heal: they will kiss your hands and feet, and do what they can, poor simple souls, to turn your head, and madden you with the self-confidence that is leading you to your destruction. But you will be none the less alone: they cannot save you. We and we only can stand between you and the stake at which our enemies have burnt that wretched woman in Paris.

JOAN [*her eyes skyward*] I have better friends and better counsel than yours.

THE ARCHBISHOP. I see that I am speaking in vain to a hardened heart. You reject our protection, and are determined to turn us all against you. In future, then, fend for yourself; and if you fail, God have mercy on your soul.

DUNOIS. That is the truth, Joan. Heed it.

JOAN. Where would you all have been now if I had heeded that sort of truth? There is no help, no counsel, in any of you. Yes: I am alone on earth: I have always been alone. My father told my brothers to drown me if I would not stay to mind his sheep while France was bleeding to death: France might perish if only our lambs were safe. I thought France would have friends at the court of the king of France; and I find only wolves fighting for pieces of her poor torn body. I thought God would have friends everywhere, because He is the friend of everyone; and in my innocence I believed that you who now cast me out would be like strong towers to keep harm from me. But I am wiser now; and nobody is any the worse for being wiser. Do not think you can frighten me by telling me that I am alone. France is alone; and God is alone; and what is my loneliness before the loneliness of my country and my God? I see now that the loneliness of God is His strength: what would He be if He listened to your jealous little counsels? Well, my loneliness shall be my strength too; it is better to be alone with God: His friendship will not fail me, nor His counsel, nor His love. In His strength I will dare, and dare, and dare, until I die. I will go out now to the common people, and let the love in their eyes comfort me for the hate in yours. You will all be glad to see me burnt; but if I go through the fire I shall go through it to their hearts for ever and ever. And so, God be with me!

She goes from them. They stare after her in glum silence for a moment. Then Gilles de Rais twirls his beard.

BLUEBEARD. You know, the woman is quite impossible. I dont dislike her, really; but what are you to do with such a character?

DUNOIS. As God is my judge, if she fell into the Loire I would jump in in full armor to fish her out. But if she plays the fool at Compiègne, and gets caught, I must leave her to her doom.

LA HIRE. Then you had better chain me up; for I could follow her to hell when the spirit rises in her like that.

THE ARCHBISHOP. She disturbs my judgment too: there is a dangerous power in her outbursts. But the pit is open at her feet, and for good or evil we cannot turn her from it.

CHARLES. If only she would keep quiet, or go home!

They follow her dispiritedly.

SCENE VI

Rouen, 30th May 1431. A great stone hall in the castle, arranged for a trial-at-law, but not a trial-by-jury, the court being the Bishop's court with the Inquisition participating: hence there are two raised chairs side by side for the Bishop and the Inquisitor as judges. Rows of chairs radiating from them at an obtuse angle are for the canons, the doctors of law and theology, and the Dominican monks, who act as assessors. In the angle is a table for the scribes, with stools. There is also a heavy rough wooden stool for the prisoner. All these are at the inner end of the hall. The further end is open to the courtyard through a row of arches. The court is shielded from the weather by screens and curtains.

Looking down the great hall from the middle of the inner end, the judicial chairs and scribes' table are to the right. The prisoner's stool is to the left. There are arched doors right and left. It is a fine sunshiny May morning.

Warwick comes in through the arched doorway on the judges' side, followed by his page.

THE PAGE [*pertly*] I suppose your lordship is aware that we have no business here. This is an ecclesiastical court; and we are only the secular arm.

WARWICK. I am aware of that fact. Will it please your impudence to find the Bishop of Beauvais for me, and give him a hint that he can have a word with me here before the trial, if he wishes?

THE PAGE [*going*] Yes, my lord.

WARWICK. And mind you behave yourself. Do not address him as Pious Peter.

THE PAGE. No, my lord. I shall be kind to him, because, when The Maid is brought in, Pious Peter will have to pick a peck of pickled pepper.

Cauchon enters through the same door with a Dominican monk and a canon, the latter carrying a brief.

THE PAGE. The Right Reverend his lordship the Bishop of Beauvais. And two other reverend gentlemen.
WARWICK. Get out; and see that we are not interrupted.
THE PAGE. Right, my lord [*he vanishes airily*].
CAUCHON. I wish your lordship good-morrow.
WARWICK. Good-morrow to your lordship. Have I had the pleasure of meeting your friends before? I think not.
CAUCHON [*introducing the monk, who is on his right*] This, my lord, is Brother John Lemaître, of the order of St Dominic. He is acting as deputy for the Chief Inquisitor into the evil of heresy in France. Brother John: the Earl of Warwick.
WARWICK. Your Reverence is most welcome. We have no Inquisitor in England, unfortunately; though we miss him greatly, especially on occasions like the present.

The Inquisitor smiles patiently, and bows. He is a mild elderly gentleman, but he has evident reserves of authority and firmness.

CAUCHON [*introducing the Canon, who is on his left*] This gentleman is Canon John D'Estivet, of the Chapter of Bayeux. He is acting as Promoter.
WARWICK. Promoter?
CAUCHON. Prosecutor, you would call him in civil law.
WARWICK. Ah! prosecutor. Quite, quite. I am very glad to make your acquaintance, Canon D'Estivet.

D'Estivet bows. [He is on the young side of middle age, well mannered, but vulpine beneath his veneer].

WARWICK. May I ask what stage the proceedings have reached? It is now more than nine months since The Maid was captured at Compiègne by the Burgundians. It is fully four months since I bought her from the Burgundians for a very handsome sum, solely that she might be brought to justice. It is very nearly three months since I delivered her up to you, my Lord Bishop, as a person suspected of heresy. May I suggest that you are taking a rather unconscionable time to make up your minds about a very plain case? Is this trial never going to end?
THE INQUISITOR [*smiling*] It has not yet begun, my lord.
WARWICK. Not yet begun! Why, you have been at it eleven weeks!
CAUCHON. We have not been idle, my lord. We have held fifteen examinations of The Maid: six public and nine private.
THE INQUISITOR [*always patiently smiling*] You see, my lord, I have been present at only two of these examinations. They were proceed-

ings of the Bishop's court solely, and not of the Holy Office. I have only just decided to associate myself—that is, to associate the Holy Inquisition—with the Bishop's court. I did not at first think that this was a case of heresy at all. I regarded it as a political case, and The Maid as a prisoner of war. But having now been present at two of the examinations, I must admit that this seems to be one of the gravest cases of heresy within my experience. Therefore everything is now in order, and we proceed to trial this morning. [*He moves towards the judicial chairs*].

CAUCHON. This moment, if your lordship's convenience allows.

WARWICK [*graciously*] Well, that is good news, gentlemen. I will not attempt to conceal from you that our patience was becoming strained.

CAUCHON. So I gathered from the threats of your soldiers to drown those of our people who favor The Maid.

WARWICK. Dear me! At all events their intentions were friendly to y o u, my lord.

CAUCHON [*sternly*] I hope not. I am determined that the woman shall have a fair hearing. The justice of the Church is not a mockery, my lord.

THE INQUISITOR [*returning*] Never has there been a fairer examination within my experience, my lord. The Maid needs no lawyers to take her part: she will be tried by her most faithful friends, all ardently desirous to save her soul from perdition.

D'ESTIVET. Sir: I am the Promoter; and it has been my painful duty to present the case against the girl; but believe me, I would throw up my case today and hasten to her defence if I did not know that men far my superiors in learning and piety, in eloquence and persuasiveness, have been sent to reason with her, to explain to her the danger she is running, and the ease with which she may avoid it. [*Suddenly bursting into forensic eloquence, to the disgust of Cauchon and the Inquisitor, who have listened to him so far with patronizing approval*] Men have dared to say that we are acting from hate; but God is our witness that they lie. Have we tortured her? No. Have we ceased to exhort her; to implore her to have pity on herself; to come to the bosom of her Church as an erring but beloved child? Have we—

CAUCHON [*interrupting drily*] Take care, Canon. All that you say is true; but if you make his lordship believe it I will not answer for your life, and hardly for my own.

WARWICK [*deprecating, but by no means denying*] Oh, my lord, you are very hard on us poor English. But we certainly do not share your pious desire to save The Maid: in fact I tell you now plainly that her death is a political necessity which I regret but cannot help. If the Church lets her go—

CAUCHON [*with fierce and menacing pride*] If the Church lets her go, woe to the man, were he the Emperor himself, who dares lay a finger on her! The Church is not subject to political necessity, my lord.

THE INQUISITOR [*interposing smoothly*] You need have no anxiety about the result, my lord. You have an invincible ally in the matter: one who is far more determined than you that she shall burn.

WARWICK. And who is this very convenient partisan, may I ask?

THE INQUISITOR. The Maid herself. Unless you put a gag in her mouth you cannot prevent her from convicting herself ten times over every time she opens it.

D'ESTIVET. That is perfectly true, my lord. My hair bristles on my head when I hear so young a creature utter such blasphemies.

WARWICK. Well, by all means do your best for her if you are quite sure it will be of no avail. [*Looking hard at Cauchon*] I should be sorry to have to act without the blessing of the Church.

CAUCHON [*with a mixture of cynical admiration and contempt*] And yet they say Englishmen are hypocrites! You play for your side, my lord, even at the peril of your soul. I cannot but admire such devotion; but I dare not go so far myself. I fear damnation.

WARWICK. If we feared anything we could never govern England, my lord. Shall I send your people in to you?

CAUCHON. Yes: it will be very good of your lordship to withdraw and allow the court to assemble.

Warwick turns on his heel, and goes out through the courtyard. Cauchon takes one of the judicial seats; and D'Estivet sits at the scribes' table, studying his brief.

CAUCHON [*casually, as he makes himself comfortable*] What scoundrels these English nobles are!

THE INQUISITOR [*taking the other judicial chair on Cauchon's left*] All secular power makes men scoundrels. They are not trained for the work; and they have not the Apostolic Succession. Our own nobles are just as bad.

The Bishop's assessors hurry into the hall, headed by Chaplain de Stogumber and Canon de Courcelles, a young priest of 30. The scribes sit at the table, leaving a chair vacant opposite D'Estivet. Some of the assessors take their seats: others stand chatting, waiting for the pro-

ceedings to begin formally. De Stogumber, aggrieved and obstinate, will not take his seat: neither will the Canon, who stands on his right.

CAUCHON. Good morning, Master de Stogumber. [*To the Inquisitor*] Chaplain to the Cardinal of England.

THE CHAPLAIN [*correcting him*] Of Winchester, my lord. I have to make a protest, my lord.

CAUCHON. You make a great many.

THE CHAPLAIN. I am not without support, my lord. Here is Master de Courcelles, Canon of Paris, who associates himself with me in my protest.

CAUCHON. Well, what is the matter?

THE CHAPLAIN [*sulkily*] Speak you, Master de Courcelles, since I do not seem to enjoy his lordship's confidence. [*He sits down in dudgeon next to Cauchon, on his right*].

COURCELLES. My lord: we have been at great pains to draw up an indictment of The Maid on sixty-four counts. We are now told that they have been reduced, without consulting us.

THE INQUISITOR. Master de Courcelles: I am the culprit. I am overwhelmed with admiration for the zeal displayed in your sixty-four counts; but in accusing a heretic, as in other things, enough is enough. Also you must remember that all the members of the court are not so subtle and profound as you, and that some of your very great learning might appear to them to be very great nonsense. Therefore I have thought it well to have your sixty-four articles cut down to twelve—

COURCELLES [*thunderstruck*] Twelve!!!

THE INQUISITOR. Twelve will, believe me, be quite enough for your purpose.

THE CHAPLAIN. But some of the most important points have been reduced almost to nothing. For instance, The Maid has actually declared that the blessed saints Margaret and Catherine, and the holy Archangel Michael, spoke to her in French. That is a vital point.

THE INQUISITOR. You think, doubtless, that they should have spoken in Latin?

CAUCHON. No: he thinks they should have spoken in English.

THE CHAPLAIN. Naturally, my lord.

THE INQUISITOR. Well, as we are all here agreed, I think, that these voices of The Maid are the voices of evil spirits tempting her to her damnation, it would not be very courteous to you, Master de Stogumber, or to the King of England, to assume that English is the devil's native language. So let it pass. The matter is not wholly omitted from the twelve articles. Pray take your places, gentlemen; and let us proceed to business.

All who have not taken their seats, do so.

THE CHAPLAIN. Well, I protest. That is all.

COURCELLES. I think it hard that all our work should go for nothing. It is only another example of the diabolical influence which this woman exercises over the court. [*He takes his chair, which is on the Chaplain's right*].

CAUCHON. Do you suggest that I am under diabolical influence?

COURCELLES. I suggest nothing, my lord. But it seems to me that there is a conspiracy here to hush up the fact that The Maid stole the Bishop of Senlis's horse.

CAUCHON [*keeping his temper with difficulty*] This is not a police court. Are we to waste our time on such rubbish?

COURCELLES [*rising, shocked*] My lord: do you call the Bishop's horse rubbish?

THE INQUISITOR [*blandly*] Master de Courcelles: The Maid alleges that she paid handsomely for the Bishop's horse, and that if he did not get the money the fault was not hers. As that may be true, the point is one on which The Maid may well be acquitted.

COURCELLES. Yes, if it were an ordinary horse. But the Bishop's horse! how can she be acquitted for that? [*He sits down again, bewildered and discouraged*].

THE INQUISITOR. I submit to you, with great respect, that if we persist in trying The Maid on trumpery issues on which we may have to declare her innocent, she may escape us on the great main issue of heresy, on which she seems so far to insist on her own guilt. I will ask you, therefore, to say nothing, when The Maid is brought before us, of these stealings of horses, and dancings round fairy trees with the village children, and prayings at haunted wells, and a dozen other things which you were diligently inquiring into until my arrival. There is not a village girl in France against whom you could not prove such things: they all dance round haunted trees, and pray at magic wells Some of them would steal the Pope's horse if they got the chance Heresy, gentlemen, heresy is the charge we have to try. The detection and suppression of heresy is my peculiar business: I am here as an inquisitor, not as an ordinary magistrate. Stick to the heresy, gentlemen, and leave the other matters alone.

CAUCHON. I may say that we have sent to the girl's village to make inquiries about her? and there is practically nothing serious against her.

THE CHAPLAIN	[*rising and clamoring together*]	Nothing serious, my lord—
COURCELLES		What! The fairy tree not—

CAUCHON [*out of patience*] Be silent, gentlemen; or speak one at a time.

Courcelles collapses into his chair, intimidated.

THE CHAPLAIN [*sulkily resuming his seat*] That is what The Maid said to us last Friday.

CAUCHON. I wish you had followed her counsel, sir. When I say nothing serious, I mean nothing that men of sufficiently large mind to conduct an inquiry like this would consider serious. I agree with my colleague the Inquisitor that it is on the count of heresy that we must proceed.

LADVENU [*a young but ascetically fine-drawn Dominican who is sitting next Courcelles, on his right*] But is there any great harm in the girl's heresy? Is it not merely her simplicity? Many saints have said as much as Joan.

THE INQUISITOR [*dropping his blandness and speaking very gravely*] Brother Martin: if you had seen what I have seen of heresy, you would not think it a light thing even in its most apparently harmless and even lovable and pious origins. Heresy begins with people who are to all appearance better than their neighbors. A gentle and pious girl, or a young man who has obeyed the command of our Lord by giving all his riches to the poor, and putting on the garb of poverty, the life of austerity, and the rule of humility and charity, may be the founder of a heresy that will wreck both Church and Empire if not ruthlessly stamped out in time. The records of the holy Inquisition are full of histories we dare not give to the world, because they are beyond the belief of honest men and innocent women; yet they all began with saintly simpletons. I have seen this again and again. Mark what I say: the woman who quarrels with her clothes, and puts on the dress of a man, is like the man who throws off his fur gown and dresses like John the Baptist: they are followed, as surely as the night follows the day, by bands of wild women and men who refuse to wear any clothes at all. When maids will neither marry nor take regular vows, and men reject marriage and exalt their lusts into divine inspirations, then, as surely as the summer follows the spring, they begin with polygamy, and end by incest. Heresy at first seems innocent and even laudable; but it ends in such a monstrous horror of unnatural wickedness that the most tender-hearted among you, if you saw it at work as I have seen it, would clamor against the mercy of the Church in dealing with it. For two hundred years the Holy Office has striven with these diabolical madnesses; and it knows that they begin always by vain and ignorant persons setting up their own judgment against the Church, and taking it upon themselves to be the interpreters of God's will. You must not fall into the common error of mistaking these simpletons for liars and hypocrites. They believe honestly and sincerely that their diabolical inspiration is divine. Therefore you must be on your guard against your natural compassion. You are all, I hope, merciful men: how else could you have devoted your lives to the service of our gentle Savior? You are going to see before you a young girl, pious and chaste; for I must tell you, gentlemen, that the things said of her by our English friends are supported by no evidence, whilst there is abundant testimony that her excesses have been excesses of religion and charity and not of worldliness and wantonness. This girl is not one of those whose hard features are the sign of hard hearts, and whose brazen looks and lewd demeanor condemn them before they are accused. The devilish pride that has led her into her present peril has left no mark on her countenance. Strange as it may seem to you, it has even left no mark on her character outside those special matters in which she is proud; so that you will see a diabolical pride and a natural humility seated side by side in the selfsame soul. Therefore be on your guard. God forbid that I should tell you to harden your hearts; for her punishment if we condemn her will be so cruel that we should forfeit our own hope of divine mercy were there one grain of malice against her in our hearts. But if you hate cruelty—and if any man here does not hate it I command him on his soul's salvation to quit this holy court—I say, if you hate cruelty, remember that nothing is so cruel in its consequences as the toleration of heresy. Remember also that no court of law can be so cruel as the common people are to those whom they suspect of heresy. The heretic in the hands of the Holy Office is safe from violence, is assured of a fair trial, and cannot suffer death, even when guilty, if repentance follows sin. Innumerable lives of heretics have been saved because the Holy Office has taken them out of the hands of the people, and because the people have yielded them up, knowing that the Holy Office would deal with them. Before the Holy Inquisition existed, and even now when its officers are not within reach, the unfortunate wretch suspected of heresy, perhaps quite ignorantly and unjustly, is stoned, torn in pieces, drowned, burned in his house with all his innocent children, without a trial, unshriven, unburied save as a dog is buried: all of them deeds hateful to God and most cruel to man. Gentlemen: I am compassionate by nature as well as by my profession; and though the work I have to do may seem cruel to those who do not know how much more cruel it would be to leave it undone, I would go to the stake myself sooner than do it if I did not know its righteousness, its necessity, its essential mercy. I ask you to address yourself to this trial in that conviction. Anger is a bad counsellor: cast out anger. Pity is sometimes worse: cast out pity. But do not cast out mercy. Remember only that justice comes first. Have you anything to say, my lord, before we proceed to trial?

CAUCHON. You have spoken for me, and spoken better than I could. I do not see how any sane man could disagree with a word that has fallen from you. But this I will add. The crude heresies of which you have told us are horrible; but their horror is like that of the black death: they rage for a while and then die out, because sound and sensible men will not under any incitement be reconciled to nakedness and incest and polygamy and the like. But we are confronted today throughout Europe with a heresy that is spreading among men not weak in mind nor diseased in brain: nay, the stronger the mind, the more obstinate the heretic. It is neither discredited by fantastic extremes nor corrupted by the common lusts of the flesh; but it, too, sets up the private judgment of the single erring mortal against the considered wisdom and experience of the Church. The mighty structure of Catholic Christendom will never be shaken by naked madmen or by the sins of Moab and Ammon. But it may be betrayed from within, and brought to barbarous ruin and desolation, by this arch heresy which the English Commander calls Protestantism.

THE ASSESSORS [*whispering*] Protestantism! What was that? What does the Bishop mean? Is it a new heresy? The English Commander, he said. Did y o u ever hear of Protestantism? etc., etc.

CAUCHON [*continuing*] And that reminds me. What provision has the Earl of Warwick made for the defence of the secular arm should The Maid prove obdurate, and the people be moved to pity her?

THE CHAPLAIN. Have no fear on that score, my lord. The noble earl has eight hundred men-at-arms at the gates. She will not slip through our English fingers even if the whole city be on her side.

CAUCHON [*revolted*] Will you not add, God grant that she repent and purge her sin?

THE CHAPLAIN. That does not seem to me to be consistent; but of course I agree with your lordship.

CAUCHON [*giving him up with a shrug of contempt*] The court sits.

THE INQUISITOR. Let the accused be brought in.

LADVENU [*calling*] The accused. Let her be brought in.

Joan, chained by the ankles, is brought in through the arched door behind the prisoner's stool by a guard of English soldiers. With them is the Executioner and his assistants. They lead her to the prisoner's stool, and place themselves behind it after taking off her chain. She wears a page's black suit. Her long imprisonment and the strain of the examinations which have preceded the trial have left their mark on her; but her vitality still holds: she confronts the court unabashed, without a trace of the awe which their formal solemnity seems to require for the complete success of its impressiveness.

THE INQUISITOR [*kindly*] Sit down, Joan. [*She sits on the prisoner's stool*]. You look very pale today. Are you not well?

JOAN. Thank you kindly: I am well enough. But the Bishop sent me some carp; and it made me ill.

CAUCHON. I am sorry. I told them to see that it was fresh.

JOAN. You meant to be good to me, I know; but it is a fish that does not agree with me. The English thought you were trying to poison me—

CAUCHON } [*together*] { What!
THE CHAPLAIN } { No, my lord.

JOAN [*continuing*] They are determined that I shall be burnt as a witch; and they sent their doctor to cure me; but he was forbidden to bleed me because the silly people believe that a witch's witchery leaves her if she is bled; so he only called me filthy names. Why do you leave me in the hands of the English? I should be in the hands of the Church. And why must I be chained by the feet to a log of wood? Are you afraid I will fly away?

D'ESTIVET [*harshly*] Woman: it is not for you to question the court: it is for us to question you.

COURCELLES. When you were left unchained, did you not try to escape by jumping from a tower sixty feet high? If you cannot fly like a witch, how is it that you are still alive?

JOAN. I suppose because the tower was not so high then. It has grown higher every day since you began asking me questions about it.

D'ESTIVET. Why did you jump from the tower?

JOAN. How do you know that I jumped?

D'ESTIVET. You were found lying in the moat. Why did you leave the tower?

JOAN. Why would anybody leave a prison if they could get out?

D'ESTIVET. You tried to escape?

JOAN. Of course I did; and not for the first time either. If you leave the door of the cage open the bird will fly out.

D'ESTIVET [*rising*] That is a confession of heresy. I call the attention of the court to it.

JOAN. Heresy, he calls it! Am I a heretic because I try to escape from prison?

D'ESTIVET. Assuredly, if you are in the hands of the Church, and you wilfully take yourself out of its hands, you are deserting the Church; and that is heresy.

JOAN. It is great nonsense. Nobody could be such a fool as to think that.

D'ESTIVET. You hear, my lord, how I am reviled in the execution of my duty by this woman. [*He sits down indignantly*].

CAUCHON. I have warned you before, Joan, that you are doing yourself no good by these pert answers.

JOAN. But you will not talk sense to me. I am reasonable if you will be reasonable.

THE INQUISITOR [*interposing*] This is not yet in order. You forget, Master Promoter, that the proceedings have not been formally opened. The time for questions is after she has sworn on the Gospels to tell us the whole truth.

JOAN. You say this to me every time. I have said again and again that I will tell you all that concerns this trial. But I cannot tell you the whole truth: God does not allow the whole truth to be told. You do not understand it when I tell it. It is an old saying that he who tells too much truth is sure to be hanged. I am weary of this argument: we have been over it nine times already. I have sworn as much as I will swear; and I will swear no more.

COURCELLES. My lord: she should be put to the torture.

THE INQUISITOR. You hear, Joan? That is what happens to the obdurate. Think before you answer. Has she been shewn the instruments?

THE EXECUTIONER. They are ready, my lord. She has seen them.

JOAN. If you tear me limb from limb until you separate my soul from my body you will get nothing out of me beyond what I have told you. What more is there to tell that you could understand? Besides, I cannot bear to be hurt; and if you hurt me I will say anything you like to stop the pain. But I will take it all back afterwards; so what is the use of it?

LADVENU. There is much in that. We should proceed mercifully.

COURCELLES. But the torture is customary.

THE INQUISITOR. It must not be applied wantonly. If the accused will confess voluntarily, then its use cannot be justified.

COURCELLES. But this is unusual and irregular. She refuses to take the oath.

LADVENU [*disgusted*] Do you want to torture the girl for the mere pleasure of it?

COURCELLES [*bewildered*] But it is not a pleasure. It is the law. It is customary. It is always done.

THE INQUISITOR. That is not so, Master, except when the inquiries are carried on by people who do not know their legal business.

COURCELLES. But the woman is a heretic. I assure you it is always done.

CAUCHON [*decisively*] It will not be done today if it is not necessary. Let there be an end of this. I will not have it said that we proceeded on forced confessions. We have sent our best preachers and doctors to this woman to exhort and implore her to save her soul and body from the fire: we shall not now send the executioner to thrust her into it.

COURCELLES. Your lordship is merciful, of course. But it is a great responsibility to depart from the usual practice.

JOAN. Thou art a rare noodle, Master. Do what was done last time is thy rule, eh?

COURCELLES [*rising*] Thou wanton: dost thou dare call me noodle?

THE INQUISITOR. Patience, Master, patience: I fear you will soon be only too terribly avenged.

COURCELLES [*mutters*] Noodle indeed! [*He sits down, much discontented*].

THE INQUISITOR. Meanwhile, let us not be moved by the rough side of a shepherd lass's tongue.

JOAN. Nay: I am no shepherd lass, though I have helped with the sheep like anyone else. I will do a lady's work in the house—spin or weave—against any woman in Rouen.

THE INQUISITOR. This is not a time for vanity, Joan. You stand in great peril.

JOAN. I know it: have I not been punished for my vanity? If I had not worn my cloth of gold surcoat in battle like a fool, that Burgundian soldier would never have pulled me backwards off my horse; and I should not have been here.

THE CHAPLAIN. If you are so clever at woman's work why do you not stay at home and do it?

JOAN. There are plenty of other women to do it; but there is nobody to do my work.

CAUCHON. Come! we are wasting time on trifles. Joan: I am going to put a most solemn question to you. Take care how you answer; for your life and salvation are at stake on it. Will you for all you have said and done, be it good or bad, accept the judgment of God's Church on earth? More especially as to the acts and words that are imputed to you in this trial by the Promoter here, will you submit your case to the inspired interpretation of the Church Militant?

JOAN. I am a faithful child of the Church. I will obey the Church—

CAUCHON [*hopefully leaning forward*] You will?

JOAN. —provided it does not command anything impossible.

Cauchon sinks back in his chair with a heavy sigh. The Inquisitor purses his lips and frowns. Ladvenu shakes his head pitifully.

D'ESTIVET. She imputes to the Church the error and folly of commanding the impossible.

JOAN. If you command me to declare that all that I have done and said, and all the visions and revelations I have had, were not from God, then that is impossible: I will not declare it for anything in the world. What God made me do I will never go back on; and what He has commanded or shall command I will not fail to do in spite of any man alive. That is what I mean by impossible. And in case the Church should bid me do anything contrary to the command I have from God, I will not consent to it, no matter what it may be.

THE ASSESSORS [*shocked and indignant*] Oh! The Church contrary to God! What do you say now? Flat heresy. This is beyond everything, etc., etc.

D'ESTIVET [*throwing down his brief*] My lord: do you need anything more than this?

CAUCHON. Woman: you have said enough to burn ten heretics. Will you not be warned? Will you not understand?

THE INQUISITOR. If the Church Militant tells you that your revelations and visions are sent by the devil to tempt you to your damnation, will you not believe that the Church is wiser than you?

JOAN. I believe that God is wiser than I; and it is His commands that I will do. All the things that you call my crimes have come to me by the command of God. I say that I have done them by the order of God: it is impossible for me to say anything else. If any Churchman says the contrary I shall not mind him: I shall mind God alone, whose command I always follow.

LADVENU [*pleading with her urgently*] You do not know what you are saying, child. Do you want to kill yourself? Listen. Do you not believe that you are subject to the Church of God on earth?

JOAN. Yes. When have I ever denied it?

LADVENU. Good. That means, does it not, that you are subject to our Lord the Pope, to the cardinals, the archbishops, and the bishops for whom his lordship stands here today?

JOAN. God must be served first.

D'ESTIVET. Then your voices command you not to submit yourself to the Church Militant?

JOAN. My voices do not tell me to disobey the Church; but God must be served first.

CAUCHON. And you, and not the Church, are to be the judge?

JOAN. What other judgment can I judge by but my own?

THE ASSESSORS [*scandalized*] Oh! [*They cannot find words*].

CAUCHON. Out of your own mouth you have condemned yourself. We have striven for your salvation to the verge of sinning ourselves: we have opened the door to you again and again; and you have shut it in our faces and in the face of God. Dare you pretend, after what you have said, that you are in a state of grace?

JOAN. If I am not, may God bring me to it: if I am, may God keep me in it!

LADVENU. That is a very good reply, my lord.

COURCELLES. Were you in a state of grace when you stole the Bishop's horse?

CAUCHON [*rising in a fury*] Oh, devil take the Bishop's horse and you too! We are here to try a case of heresy; and no sooner do we come to the root of the matter than we are thrown back by idiots who understand nothing but horses. [*Trembling with rage, he forces himself to sit down*].

THE INQUISITOR. Gentlemen, gentlemen: in clinging to these small issues you are The Maid's best advocates. I am not surprised that his lordship has lost patience with you. What does the Promoter say? Does he press these trumpery matters?

D'ESTIVET. I am bound by my office to press everything; but when the woman confesses a heresy that must bring upon her the doom of excommunication, of what consequence is it that she has been guilty also of offences which expose her to minor penances? I share the impatience of his lordship as to these minor charges. Only, with great respect, I must emphasize the gravity of two very horrible and blasphemous crimes which she does not deny. First, she has intercourse with evil spirits, and is therefore a sorceress. Second, she wears men's clothes, which is indecent, unnatural, and abominable; and in spite of our most earnest remonstrances and entreaties, she will not change them even to receive the sacrament.

JOAN. Is the blessed St Catherine an evil spirit? Is St Margaret? Is Michael the Archangel?

COURCELLES. How do you know that the spirit which appears to you is an archangel? Does he not appear to you as a naked man?

JOAN. Do you think God cannot afford clothes for him?

The assessors cannot help smiling, especially as the joke is against Courcelles.

LADVENU. Well answered, Joan.

THE INQUISITOR. It is, in effect, well answered. But no evil spirit would be so simple as to appear to a young girl in a guise that would scandalize her when he meant her to take him for a messenger from the Most High? Joan: the Church instructs you that these apparitions are demons seeking your soul's perdition. Do you accept the instruction of the Church?

JOAN. I accept the messenger of God. How could any faithful believer in the Church refuse him?

CAUCHON. Wretched woman: again I ask you, do you know what you are saying?

THE INQUISITOR. You wrestle in vain with the devil for her soul, my lord: she will not be saved. Now as to this matter of the man's dress. For the last time, will you put off that impudent attire, and dress as becomes your sex?

JOAN. I will not.

D'ESTIVET [*pouncing*] The sin of disobedience, my lord.

JOAN [*distressed*] But my voices tell me I must dress as a soldier.

LADVENU. Joan, Joan: does not that prove to you that the voices are the voices of evil spirits? Can you suggest to us one good reason why an angel of God should give you such shameless advice?

JOAN. Why, yes: what can be plainer commonsense? I was a soldier living among soldiers. I am a prisoner guarded by soldiers. If I were to dress as a woman they would think of me as a woman; and then what would become of me? If I dress as a soldier they think of me as a soldier, and I can live with them as I do at home with my brothers. That is why St Catherine tells me I must not dress as a woman until she gives me leave.

COURCELLES. When will she give you leave?

JOAN. When you take me out of the hands of the English soldiers. I have told you that I should be in the hands of the Church, and not left night and day with four soldiers of the Earl of Warwick. Do you want me to live with them in petticoats?

LADVENU. My lord: what she says is, God knows, very wrong and shocking; but there is a grain of worldly sense in it such as might impose on a simple village maiden.

JOAN. If we were as simple in the village as you are in your courts and palaces, there would soon be no wheat to make bread for you.

CAUCHON. That is the thanks you get for trying to save her, Brother Martin.

LADVENU. Joan: we are all trying to save you. His lordship is trying to save you. The Inquisitor could not be more just to you if you were his own daughter. But you are blinded by a terrible pride of self-sufficiency.

JOAN. Why do you say that? I have said nothing wrong. I cannot understand.

THE INQUISITOR. The blessed St Athanasius has laid it down in his creed that those who cannot understand are damned. It is not enough to be simple. It is not enough even to be what simple people call good. The simplicity of a darkened mind is no better than the simplicity of a beast.

JOAN. There is great wisdom in the simplicity of a beast, let me tell you; and sometimes great foolishness in the wisdom of scholars.

LADVENU. We know that, Joan: we are not so foolish as you think us. Try to resist the temptation to make pert replies to us. Do you see that man who stands behind you [*he indicates the Executioner*]?

JOAN [*turning and looking at the man*] Your torturer? But the Bishop said I was not to be tortured.

LADVENU. You are not to be tortured because you have confessed everything that is necessary to your condemnation. That man is not only the torturer: he is also the Executioner. Executioner: let The Maid hear your answers to my questions. Are you prepared for the burning of a heretic this day?

THE EXECUTIONER. Yes, Master.

LADVENU. Is the stake ready?

THE EXECUTIONER. It is. In the market-place. The English have built it too high for me to get near her and make the death easier. It will be a cruel death.

JOAN [*horrified*] But you are not going to burn me now?

THE INQUISITOR. You realize it at last.

LADVENU. There are eight hundred English soldiers waiting to take you to the market-place the moment the sentence of excommunication has passed the lips of your judges. You are within a few short moments of that doom.

JOAN [*looking round desperately for rescue*] Oh God!

LADVENU. Do not despair, Joan. The Church is merciful. You can save yourself.

JOAN [*hopefully*] Yes: my voices promised me I should not be burnt. St Catherine bade me be bold.

CAUCHON. Woman: are you quite mad? Do you not yet see that your voices have deceived you?

JOAN. Oh no: that is impossible.

CAUCHON. Impossible! They have led you straight to your excommunication, and to the stake which is there waiting for you.

LADVENU. [*pressing the point hard*] Have they kept a single promise to you since you were taken at Compiègne? The devil has betrayed you. The Church holds out its arms to you.

JOAN [*despairing*] Oh, it is true: it is true: my voices have deceived me. I have been mocked by devils: my faith is broken. I have dared and dared; but only a fool will walk into a fire: God, who gave me my commonsense, cannot will me to do that.

LADVENU. Now God be praised that He has saved you at the eleventh hour! [*He hurries to the vacant seat at the scribes' table, and snatches a sheet of paper, on which he sets to work writing eagerly*].

CAUCHON. Amen!

JOAN. What must I do?

CAUCHON. You must sign a solemn recantation of your heresy.

JOAN. Sign? That means to write my name. I cannot write.

CAUCHON. You have signed many letters before.

JOAN. Yes; but someone held my hand and guided the pen. I can make my mark.

THE CHAPLAIN [*who has been listening with growing alarm and indignation*] My lord: do you mean that you are going to allow this woman to escape us?

THE INQUISITOR. The law must take its course, Master de Stogumber. And you know the law.

THE CHAPLAIN [*rising, purple with fury*] I know that there is no faith in a Frenchman [*Tumult, which he shouts down*]. I know what my lord the Cardinal of Winchester will say when he hears of this. I know what the Earl of Warwick will do when he learns that you intend to betray him. There are eight hundred men at the gate who will see that this abominable witch is burnt in spite of your teeth.

THE ASSESSORS [*meanwhile*] What is this? What did he say? He accuses us of treachery! This is past bearing. No faith in a Frenchman! Did you hear that? This is an intolerable fellow. Who is he? Is this what English Churchmen are like? He must be mad or drunk, etc., etc.

THE INQUISITOR [*rising*] Silence, pray! Gentlemen: pray silence! Master Chaplain: bethink you a moment of your holy office: of what you are, and where you are. I direct you to sit down.

THE CHAPLAIN [*folding his arms doggedly, his face working convulsively*] I will NOT sit down.

CAUCHON. Master Inquisitor: this man has called me a traitor to my face before now.

THE CHAPLAIN. So you are a traitor. You are all traitors. You have been doing nothing but begging this damnable witch on your knees to recant all through this trial.

THE INQUISITOR [*placidly resuming his seat*] If you will not sit, you must stand: that is all.

THE CHAPLAIN. I will NOT stand [*he flings himself back into his chair*].

LADVENU [*rising with the paper in his hand*] My lord: here is the form of recantation for The Maid to sign.

CAUCHON. Read it to her.

JOAN. Do not trouble. I will sign it.

THE INQUISITOR. Woman: you must know what you are putting your hand to. Read it to her, Brother Martin. And let all be silent.

LADVENU [*reading quietly*] "I, Joan, commonly called The Maid, a miserable sinner, do confess that I have most grievously sinned in the following articles. I have pretended to have revelations from God and the angels and the blessed saints, and perversely rejected the Church's warnings that these were temptations by demons. I have blasphemed abominably by wearing an immodest dress, contrary to the Holy Scripture and the canons of the Church. Also I have clipped my hair in the style of a man, and, against all the duties which have made my sex specially acceptable in heaven, have taken up the sword, even to the shedding of human blood, inciting men to slay each other, invoking evil spirits to delude them, and stubbornly and most blasphemously imputing these sins to Almighty God. I confess to the sin of sedition, to the sin of idolatry, to the sin of disobedience, to the sin of pride, and to the sin of heresy. All of which sins I now renounce and abjure and depart from, humbly thanking you Doctors and Masters who have brought me back to the truth and into the grace of our Lord. And I will never return to my errors, but will remain in communion with our Holy Church and in obedience to our Holy Father the Pope of Rome. All this I swear by God Almighty and the Holy Gospels, in witness whereto I sign my name to this recantation."

THE INQUISITOR. You understand this, Joan?

JOAN [*listless*] It is plain enough, sir.

THE INQUISITOR. And it is true?

JOAN. It may be true. If it were not true, the fire would not be ready for me in the market-place.

LADVENU [*taking up his pen and a book, and going to her quickly lest she should compromise herself again*] Come, child: let me guide your hand. Take the pen. [*She does so; and they begin to write, using the book as a desk*] J. E. H. A. N. E. So. Now make your mark by yourself.

JOAN [*makes her mark, and gives him back the pen, tormented by the rebellion of her soul against her mind and body*] There!

LADVENU [*replacing the pen on the table, and handing the recantation to Cauchon with a reverence*] Praise be to God, my brother, the lamb has returned to the flock; and the shepherd rejoices in her more than in ninety and nine just persons. [*He returns to his seat*].

THE INQUISITOR [*taking the paper from Cauchon*] We declare thee by this act set free from the danger of excommunication in which thou stoodest. [*He throws the paper down to the table*].

JOAN. I thank you.

THE INQUISITOR. But because thou hast sinned most presumptuously against God and the Holy Church, and that thou mayst repent thy errors in solitary contemplation, and be shielded from all temptation to return to them, we, for the good of thy soul, and for a penance that may wipe out thy sins and bring thee finally unspotted to the throne of grace, do condemn thee to eat the bread of sorrow and drink the water of affliction to the end of thy earthly days in perpetual imprisonment.

JOAN [*rising in consternation and terrible anger*] Perpetual imprisonment! Am I not then to be set free?
LADVENU [*mildly shocked*] Set free, child, after such wickedness as yours! What are you dreaming of?
JOAN. Give me that writing. [*She rushes to the table; snatches up the paper; and tears it into fragments*] Light your fire: do you think I dread it as much as the life of a rat in a hole? My voices were right.
LADVENU. Joan! Joan!
JOAN. Yes: they told me you were fools [*the word gives great offence*], and that I was not to listen to your fine words nor trust to your charity. You promised me my life; but you lied [*indignant exclamations*]. You think that life is nothing but not being stone dead. It is not the bread and water I fear: I can live on bread: when have I asked for more? It is no hardship to drink water if the water be clean. Bread has no sorrow for me, and water no affliction. But to shut me from the light of the sky and the sight of the fields and flowers; to chain my feet so that I can never again ride with the soldiers nor climb the hills; to make me breathe foul damp darkness, and keep from me everything that brings me back to the love of God when your wickedness and foolishness tempt me to hate Him: all this is worse than the furnace in the Bible that was heated seven times. I could do without my warhorse; I could drag about in a skirt; I could let the banners and the trumpets and the knights and soldiers pass me and leave me behind as they leave the other women, if only I could still hear the wind in the trees, the larks in the sunshine, the young lambs crying through the healthy frost, and the blessed blessed church bells that send my angel voices floating to me on the wind. But without these things I cannot live; and by your wanting to take them away from me, or from any human creature, I know that your counsel is of the devil, and that mine is of God.
THE ASSESSORS [*in great commotion*] Blasphemy! blasphemy! She is possessed. She said our counsel was of the devil. And hers of God. Monstrous! The devil is in our midst, etc., etc.
D'ESTIVET [*shouting above the din*] She is a relapsed heretic, obstinate, incorrigible, and altogether unworthy of the mercy we have shewn her. I call for her excommunication.
THE CHAPLAIN [*to the Executioner*] Light your fire, man. To the stake with her.

The Executioner and his assistants hurry out through the courtyard.

LADVENU. You wicked girl: if your counsel were of God would He not deliver you?

JOAN. His ways are not your ways. He wills that I go through the fire to His bosom; for I am His child, and you are not fit that I should live among you. That is my last word to you.

The soldiers seize her.

CAUCHON [*rising*] Not yet.

They wait. There is a dead silence. Cauchon turns to the Inquisitor with an inquiring look. The Inquisitor nods affirmatively. They rise solemnly, and intone the sentence antiphonally.

CAUCHON. We decree that thou art a relapsed heretic.

THE INQUISITOR. Cast out from the unity of the Church.

CAUCHON. Sundered from her body.

THE INQUISITOR. Infected with the leprosy of heresy.

CAUCHON. A member of Satan.

THE INQUISITOR. We declare that thou must be excommunicate.

CAUCHON. And now we do cast thee out, segregate thee, and abandon thee to the secular power.

THE INQUISITOR. Admonishing the same secular power that it moderate its judgment of thee in respect of death and division of the limbs. [*He resumes his seat*].

CAUCHON. And if any true sign of penitence appear in thee, to permit our Brother Martin to administer to thee the sacrament of penance.

THE CHAPLAIN. Into the fire with the witch [*he rushes at her, and helps the soldiers to push her out*].

Joan is taken away through the courtyard. The assessors rise in disorder, and follow the soldiers, except Ladvenu, who has hidden his face in his hands.

CAUCHON [*rising again in the act of sitting down*] No, no: this is irregular. The representative of the secular arm should be here to receive her from us.

THE INQUISITOR [*also on his feet again*] That man is an incorrigible fool.

CAUCHON. Brother Martin: see that everything is done in order.

LADVENU. My place is at her side, my lord. You must exercise your own authority. [*He hurries out*].

CAUCHON. These English are impossible: they will thrust her straight into the fire. Look!

He points to the courtyard, in which the glow and flicker of fire can now be seen reddening the May daylight. Only the Bishop and Inquisitor are left in the court.

CAUCHON [*turning to go*] We must stop that.

THE INQUISITOR [*calmly*] Yes; but not too fast, my lord.

CAUCHON [*halting*] But there is not a moment to lose.

THE INQUISITOR. We have proceeded in perfect order. If the English choose to put themselves in the wrong, it is not our business to put them in the right. A flaw in the procedure may be useful later on: one never knows. And the sooner it is over, the better for that poor girl.

CAUCHON [*relaxing*] That is true. But I suppose we must see this dreadful thing through.

THE INQUISITOR. One gets used to it. Habit is everything. I am accustomed to the fire: it is soon over. But it is a terrible thing to see a young and innocent creature crushed between these mighty forces, the Church and the Law.

CAUCHON. You call her innocent!

THE INQUISITOR. Oh, quite innocent. What does she know of the Church and the Law? She did not understand a word we were saying. It is the ignorant who suffer. Come, or we shall be late for the end.

CAUCHON [*going with him*] I shall not be sorry if we are: I am not so accustomed as you.

They are going out when Warwick comes in, meeting them.

WARWICK. Oh, I am intruding. I thought it was all over. [*He makes a feint of retiring*].

CAUCHON. Do not go, my lord. It is all over.

THE INQUISITOR. The execution is not in our hands, my lord; but it is desirable that we should witness the end. So by your leave— [*He bows, and goes out through the courtyard*].

CAUCHON. There is some doubt whether your people have observed the forms of law, my lord.

WARWICK. I am told that there is some doubt whether your authority runs in this city, my lord. It is not in your diocese. However, if you will answer for that I will answer for the rest.

CAUCHON. It is to God that we both must answer. Good morning, my lord.

WARWICK. My lord: good morning.

They look at one another for a moment with unconcealed hostility. Then Cauchon follows the Inquisitor out. Warwick looks round. Finding himself alone, he calls for attendance.

WARWICK. Hallo: some attendance here! [*Silence*]. Hallo, there! [*Silence*]. Hallo! Brian, you young blackguard, where are you? [*Silence*]. Guard! [*Silence*]. They have all gone to see the burning: even that child.

The silence is broken by someone frantically howling and sobbing.

WARWICK. What in the devil's name—?

The Chaplain staggers in from the courtyard like a demented creature, his face streaming with tears, making the piteous sounds that Warwick has heard. He stumbles to the prisoner's stool, and throws himself upon it with heartrending sobs.

WARWICK [*going to him and patting him on the shoulder*] What is it, Master John? What is the matter?

THE CHAPLAIN [*clutching at his hands*] My lord, my lord: for Christ's sake pray for my wretched guilty soul.

WARWICK [*soothing him*] Yes, yes: of course I will. Calmly, gently—

THE CHAPLAIN [*blubbering miserably*] I am not a bad man, my lord.

WARWICK. No, no: not at all.

THE CHAPLAIN. I meant no harm. I did not know what it would be like.

WARWICK [*hardening*] Oh! You saw it, then?

THE CHAPLAIN. I did not know what I was doing. I am a hot-headed fool; and I shall be damned to all eternity for it.

WARWICK. Nonsense! Very distressing, no doubt; but it was not your doing.

THE CHAPLAIN [*lamentably*] I let them do it. If I had known, I would have torn her from their hands. You dont know: you havnt seen: it is so easy to talk when you dont know. You madden yourself with words: you damn yourself because it feels grand to throw oil on the flaming hell of your own temper. But when it is brought home to you; when you see the thing you have done; when it is blinding your eyes, stifling your nostrils, tearing your heart, then—then—[*Falling on his knees*] O God, take away this sight from me! O Christ, deliver me from this fire that is consuming me! She cried to Thee in the midst of it: Jesus! Jesus! Jesus! She is in Thy bosom; and I am in hell for evermore.

WARWICK [*summarily hauling him to his feet*] Come come, man! you must pull yourself together. We shall have the whole town talking of this. [*He throws him not too gently into a chair at the table*] If you have not the nerve to see these things, why do you not do as I do, and stay away?

THE CHAPLAIN [*bewildered and submissive*] She asked for a cross. A soldier gave her two sticks tied together. Thank God he was an Englishman! I might have done it; but I did not: I am a coward, a mad dog, a fool. But he was an Englishman too.

WARWICK. The fool! they will burn him too if the priests get hold of him.

THE CHAPLAIN [*shaken with a convulsion*] Some of the people laughed at her. They would have laughed at Christ. They were French people, my lord: I know they were French.

WARWICK. Hush! someone is coming. Control yourself.

Ladvenu comes back through the courtyard to Warwick's right hand, carrying a bishop's cross which he has taken from a church. He is very grave and composed.

WARWICK. I am informed that it is all over, Brother Martin.

LADVENU [*enigmatically*] We do not know, my lord. It may have only just begun.

WARWICK. What does that mean, exactly?

LADVENU. I took this cross from the church for her that she might see it to the last: she had only two sticks that she put into her bosom. When the fire crept round us, and she saw that if I held the cross before her I should be burnt myself, she warned me to get down and save myself. My lord: a girl who could think of another's danger in such a moment was not inspired by the devil. When I had to snatch the cross from her sight, she looked up to heaven. And I do not believe that the heavens were empty. I firmly believe that her Savior appeared to her then in His tenderest glory. She called to Him and died. This is not the end for her, but the beginning.

WARWICK. I am afraid it will have a bad effect on the people.

LADVENU. It had, my lord, on some of them. I heard laughter. Forgive me for saying that I hope and believe it was English laughter.

THE CHAPLAIN [*rising frantically*] No: it was not. There was only one Englishman there that disgraced his country; and that was the mad dog, de Stogumber. [*He rushes wildly out, shrieking*] Let them torture him. Let them burn him. I will go pray among her ashes. I am no better than Judas: I will hang myself.

WARWICK. Quick, Brother Martin: follow him: he will do himself some mischief. After him, quick.

Ladvenu hurries out, Warwick urging him. The Executioner comes in by the door behind the judges' chairs; and Warwick, returning, finds himself face to face with him.

WARWICK. Well, fellow: who are you?
THE EXECUTIONER [*with dignity*] I am not addressed as fellow, my lord. I am the Master Executioner of Rouen: it is a highly skilled mystery. I am come to tell your lordship that your orders have been obeyed.
WARWICK. I crave your pardon, Master Executioner; and I will see that you lose nothing by having no relics to sell. I have your word, have I, that nothing remains, not a bone, not a nail, not a hair?
THE EXECUTIONER. Her heart would not burn, my lord; but everything that was left is at the bottom of the river. You have heard the last of her.
WARWICK [*with a wry smile, thinking of what Ladvenu said*] The last of her? Hm! I wonder!

EPILOGUE

A restless fitfully windy night in June 1456, full of summer lightning after many days of heat. King Charles the Seventh of France, formerly Joan's Dauphin, now Charles the Victorious, aged 51, is in bed in one of his royal chateaux. The bed, raised on a dais of two steps, is towards the side of the room so as to avoid blocking a tall lancet window in the middle. Its canopy bears the royal arms in embroidery. Except for the canopy and the huge down pillows there is nothing to distinguish it from a broad settee with bed-clothes and a valance. Thus its occupant is in full view from the foot.

Charles is not asleep: he is reading in bed, or rather looking at the pictures in Fouquet's Boccaccio with his knees doubled up to make a reading desk. Beside the bed on his left is a little table with a picture of the Virgin, lighted by candles of painted wax. The walls are hung from ceiling to floor with painted curtains which stir at times in the draughts. At first glance the prevailing yellow and red in these hanging pictures is somewhat flamelike when the folds breathe in the wind.

The door is on Charles's left, but in front of him close to the corner farthest from him. A large watchman's rattle, handsomely designed and gaily painted, is in the bed under his hand.

Charles turns a leaf. A distant clock strikes the half-hour softly. Charles shuts the book with a clap; throws it aside; snatches up the rattle; and whirls it energetically, making a deafening clatter. Ladvenu enters, 25 years older, strange and stark in bearing, and still car-

rying the cross from Rouen. Charles evidently does not expect him; for he springs out of bed on the farther side from the door.

CHARLES. Who are you? Where is my gentleman of the bedchamber? What do you want?
LADVENU [*solemnly*] I bring you glad tidings of great joy. Rejoice, O king; for the taint is removed from your blood, and the stain from your crown. Justice, long delayed, is at last triumphant.
CHARLES. What are you talking about? Who are you?
LADVENU. I am Brother Martin.
CHARLES. And who, saving your reverence, may Brother Martin be?
LADVENU. I held this cross when The Maid perished in the fire. Twenty-five years have passed since then: nearly ten thousand days. And on every one of those days I have prayed God to justify His daughter on earth as she is justified in heaven.
CHARLES [*reassured, sitting down on the foot of the bed*] Oh, I remember now. I have heard of you. You have a bee in your bonnet about The Maid. Have you been at the inquiry?
LADVENU. I have given my testimony.
CHARLES. Is it over?
LADVENU. It is over.
CHARLES. Satisfactorily?
LADVENU. The ways of God are very strange.
CHARLES. How so?
LADVENU. At the trial which sent a saint to the stake as a heretic and a sorceress, the truth was told; the law was upheld; mercy was shewn beyond all custom; no wrong was done but the final and dreadful wrong of the lying sentence and the pitiless fire. At this inquiry from which I have just come, there was shameless perjury, courtly corruption, calumny of the dead who did their duty according to their lights, cowardly evasion of the issue, testimony made of idle tales that could not impose on a ploughboy. Yet out of this insult to justice, this defamation of the Church, this orgy of lying and foolishness, the truth is set in the noonday sun on the hilltop; the white robe of innocence is cleansed from the smirch of the burning faggots; the holy life is sanctified; the true heart that lived through the flame is consecrated; a great lie is silenced for ever; and a great wrong is set right before all men.
CHARLES. My friend: provided they can no longer say that I was

crowned by a witch and a heretic, I shall not fuss about how the trick has been done. Joan would not have fussed about it if it came all right in the end: she was not that sort: I knew her. Is her rehabilitation complete? I made it pretty clear that there was to be no nonsense about it.

LADVENU. It is solemnly declared that her judges were full of corruption, cozenage, fraud, and malice. Four falsehoods.

CHARLES. Never mind the falsehoods: her judges are dead.

LADVENU. The sentence on her is broken, annulled, annihilated, set aside as non-existent, without value or effect.

CHARLES. Good. Nobody can challenge my consecration now, can they?

LADVENU. Not Charlemagne nor King David himself was more sacredly crowned.

CHARLES [*rising*] Excellent. Think of what that means to me!

LADVENU. I think of what it means to her!

CHARLES. You cannot. None of us ever knew what anything meant to her. She was like nobody else; and she must take care of herself wherever she is; for *I* cannot take care of her; and neither can you, whatever you may think: you are not big enough. But I will tell you this about her. If you could bring her back to life, they would burn her again within six months, for all their present adoration of her. And you would hold up the cross, too, just the same. So [*crossing himself*] let her rest; and let you and I mind our own business, and not meddle with hers.

LADVENU. God forbid that I should have no share in her, nor she in me! [*He turns and strides out as he came, saying*] Henceforth my path will not lie through palaces, nor my conversation be with kings.

CHARLES [*following him towards the door, and shouting after him*] Much good may it do you, holy man! [*He returns to the middle of the chamber, where he halts, and says quizzically to himself*] That was a funny chap. How did he get in? Where are my people? [*He goes impatiently to the bed, and swings the rattle. A rush of wind through the open door sets the walls swaying agitatedly. The candles go out. He calls in the darkness*] Hallo! Someone come and shut the windows: everything is being blown all over the place. [*A flash of summer lightning shews up the lancet window. A figure is seen in silhouette against it*] Who is there? Who is that? Help! Murder! [*Thunder. He jumps into bed, and hides under the clothes*].

JOAN'S VOICE. Easy, Charlie, easy. What art making all that noise for?

No one can hear thee. Thourt asleep. [*She is dimly seen in a pallid greenish light by the bedside*].

CHARLES [*peeping out*] Joan! Are you a ghost, Joan?

JOAN. Hardly even that, lad. Can a poor burnt-up lass have a ghost? I am but a dream that thourt dreaming. [*The light increases: they become plainly visible as he sits up*] Thou looks older, lad.

CHARLES. I am older. Am I really asleep?

JOAN. Fallen asleep over thy silly book.

CHARLES. That's funny.

JOAN. Not so funny as that I am dead, is it?

CHARLES. Are you really dead?

JOAN. As dead as anybody ever is, laddie. I am out of the body.

CHARLES. Just fancy! Did it hurt much?

JOAN. Did what hurt much?

CHARLES. Being burnt.

JOAN. Oh, that! I cannot remember very well. I think it did at first; but then it all got mixed up; and I was not in my right mind until I was free of the body. But do not thou go handling fire and thinking it will not hurt thee. How hast been ever since?

CHARLES. Oh, not so bad. Do you know, I actually lead my army out and win battles? Down into the moat up to my waist in mud and blood. Up the ladders with the stones and hot pitch raining down. Like you.

JOAN. No! Did I make a man of thee after all, Charlie?

CHARLES. I am Charles the Victorious now. I had to be brave because you were. Agnes put a little pluck into me too.

JOAN. Agnes! Who was Agnes?

CHARLES. Agnes Sorel. A woman I fell in love with. I dream of her often. I never dreamed of you before.

JOAN. Is she dead, like me?

CHARLES. Yes. But she was not like you. She was very beautiful.

JOAN [*laughing heartily*] Ha ha! I was no beauty: I was always a rough one: a regular soldier. I might almost as well have been a man. Pity I wasnt: I should not have bothered you all so much then. But my head was in the skies; and the glory of God was upon me; and, man or woman, I should have bothered you as long as your noses were in the mud. Now tell me what has happened since you wise men knew no better than to make a heap of cinders of me?

CHARLES. Your mother and brothers have sued the courts to have your case tried over again. And the courts have declared that your judges were full of corruption and cozenage, fraud and malice.

JOAN. Not they. They were as honest a lot of poor fools as ever burned their betters.

CHARLES. The sentence on you is broken, annihilated, annulled: null, non-existent, without value or effect.

JOAN. I was burned, all the same. Can they unburn me?

CHARLES. If they could, they would think twice before they did it. But they have decreed that a beautiful cross be placed where the stake stood, for your perpetual memory and for your salvation.

JOAN. It is the memory and the salvation that sanctify the cross, not the cross that sanctifies the memory and the salvation. [*She turns away, forgetting him*] I shall outlast that cross. I shall be remembered when men will have forgotten where Rouen stood.

CHARLES. There you go with your self-conceit, the same as ever! I think you might say a word of thanks to me for having had justice done at last.

CAUCHON [*appearing at the window between them*] Liar!

CHARLES. Thank you.

JOAN. Why, if it isnt Peter Cauchon! How are you, Peter? What luck have you had since you burned me?

CAUCHON. None. I arraign the justice of Man. It is not the justice of God.

JOAN. Still dreaming of justice, Peter? See what justice came to with me! But what has happened to thee? Art dead or alive?

CAUCHON. Dead. Dishonored. They pursued me beyond the grave. They excommunicated my dead body: they dug it up and flung it into the common sewer.

JOAN. Your dead body did not feel the spade and the sewer as my live body felt the fire.

CAUCHON. But this thing that they have done against me hurts justice; destroys faith; saps the foundation of the Church. The solid earth sways like the treacherous sea beneath the feet of men and spirits alike when the innocent are slain in the name of law, and their wrongs are undone by slandering the pure of heart.

JOAN. Well, well, Peter, I hope men will be the better for remembering me; and they would not remember me so well if you had not burned me.

CAUCHON. They will be the worse for remembering *me*: they will see in me evil triumphing over good, falsehood over truth, cruelty over mercy, hell over heaven. Their courage will rise as they think of you, only to faint as they think of me. Yet God is my witness I was just: I was merciful: I was faithful to my light: I could do no other than I did.

CHARLES [*scrambling out of the sheets and enthroning himself on the side of the bed*] Yes: it is always you good men that do the big mischiefs. Look at me! I am not Charles the Good, nor Charles the Wise, not Charles the Bold. Joan's worshippers may even call me Charles the Coward because I did not pull her out of the fire. But I have done less harm than any of you. You people with your heads in the sky spend all your time trying to turn the world upside down; but I take the world as it is, and say that top-side-up is right-side-up; and I keep my nose pretty close to the ground. And I ask you, what king of France has done better, or been a better fellow in his little way?

JOAN. Art really king of France, Charlie? Be the English gone?

DUNOIS [*coming through the tapestry on Joan's left, the candles relighting themselves at the same moment, and illuminating his armor and surcoat cheerfully*] I have kept my word: the English are gone.

JOAN. Praised be God! now is fair France a province in heaven. Tell me all about the fighting, Jack. Was it thou that led them? Wert thou God's captain to thy death?

DUNOIS. I am not dead. My body is very comfortably asleep in my bed at Chateaudun; but my spirit is called here by yours.

JOAN. And you fought them *my* way, Jack: eh? Not the old way, chaffering for ransoms; but The Maid's way: staking life against death, with the heart high and humble and void of malice, and nothing counting under God but France free and French. Was it my way, Jack?

DUNOIS. Faith, it was any way that would win. But the way that won was always your way. I give you best, lassie. I wrote a fine letter to set you right at the new trial. Perhaps I should never have let the priests burn you; but I was busy fighting; and it was the Church's business, not mine. There was no use in both of us being burned, was there?

CAUCHON. Ay! put the blame on the priests. But I, who am beyond praise and blame, tell you that the world is saved neither by its priests nor its soldiers, but by God and His Saints. The Church Militant sent this woman to the fire; but even as she burned, the flames whitened into the radiance of the Church Triumphant.

The clock strikes the third quarter. A rough male voice is heard trolling an improvised tune.

Rum tum trumpledum,
Bacon fat and rumpledum,
Old Saint mumpledum,
Pull his tail and stumpledum
O my Ma–ry Ann!

A ruffianly English soldier comes through the curtains and marches between Dunois and Joan.

DUNOIS. What villainous troubadour taught you that doggrel?

THE SOLDIER. No troubadour. We made it up ourselves as we marched. We were not gentlefolks and troubadours. Music straight out of the heart of the people, as you might say. Rum tum trumpledum, Bacon fat and rumpledum, Old Saint mumpledum, Pull his tail and stumpledum: that dont mean anything, you know; but it keeps you marching. Your servant, ladies and gentlemen. Who asked for a saint?

JOAN. Be you a saint?

THE SOLDIER. Yes, lady, straight from hell.

DUNOIS. A saint, and from hell!

THE SOLDIER. Yes, noble captain: I have a day off. Every year, you know. Thats my allowance for my one good action.

CAUCHON. Wretch! In all the years of your life did you do only one good action?

THE SOLDIER. I never thought about it: it came natural like. But they scored it up for me.

CHARLES. What was it?

THE SOLDIER. Why, the silliest thing you ever heard of. I—

JOAN [*interrupting him by strolling across to the bed, where she sits beside Charles*] He tied two sticks together, and gave them to a poor lass that was going to be burned.

THE SOLDIER. Right. Who told you that?

JOAN. Never mind. Would you know her if you saw her again?

THE SOLDIER. Not I. There are so many girls! and they all expect you to remember them as if there was only one in the world. This one must have been a prime sort; for I have a day off every year for her; and so, until twelve o'clock punctually, I am a saint, at your service, noble lords and lovely ladies.

CHARLES. And after twelve?

THE SOLDIER. After twelve, back to the only place fit for the likes of me.

JOAN [*rising*] Back there! You! that gave the lass the cross!

THE SOLDIER [*excusing his unsoldierly conduct*] Well, she asked for it; and they were going to burn her. She had as good a right to a cross as they had; and they had dozens of them. It was her funeral, not theirs. Where was the harm in it?

JOAN. Man: I am not reproaching you. But I cannot bear to think of you in torment.

THE SOLDIER [*cheerfully*] No great torment, lady. You see I was used to worse.

CHARLES. What! worse than hell?

THE SOLDIER. Fifteen years' service in the French wars. Hell was a treat after that.

Joan throws up her arms, and takes refuge from despair of humanity before the picture of the Virgin.

THE SOLDIER [*continuing*]—Suits me somehow. The day off was dull at first, like a wet Sunday. I dont mind it so much now. They tell me I can have as many as I like as soon as I want them.

CHARLES. What is hell like?

THE SOLDIER. You wont find it so bad, sir. Jolly. Like as if you were always drunk without the trouble and expense of drinking. Tip top company too: emperors and popes and kings and all sorts. They chip me about giving that young judy the cross; but I dont care: I stand up to them proper, and tell them that if she hadnt a better right to it than they, she'd be where they are. That dumbfounds them, that does. All they can do is gnash their teeth, hell fashion; and I just laugh, and go off singing the old chanty: Rum tum trumple— Hullo! Who's that knocking at the door?

They listen. A long gentle knocking is heard.

CHARLES. Come in.

The door opens; and an old priest, white-haired, bent, with a silly but benevolent smile, comes in and trots over to Joan.

THE NEWCOMER. Excuse me, gentle lords and ladies. Do not let me disturb you. Only a poor old harmless English rector. Formerly chaplain to the cardinal: to my lord of Winchester. John de Stogumber, at your service. [*He looks at them inquiringly*] Did you say anything? I am a little deaf, unfortunately. Also a little—well, not always in my right mind, perhaps; but still, it is a small village with a few simple people. I suffice: I suffice: they love me there; and I am able to do a little good. I am well connected, you see; and they indulge me.

JOAN. Poor old John! What brought thee to this state?

DE STOGUMBER. I tell my folks they must be very careful. I say to them, "If you only saw what you think about you would think quite differently about it. It would give you a great shock. Oh, a great shock." And they all say "Yes, parson: we all know you are a kind man, and would not harm a fly." That is a great comfort to me. For I am not cruel by nature, you know.

THE SOLDIER. Who said you were?

DE STOGUMBER. Well, you see, I did a very cruel thing once because I did not know what cruelty was like. I had not seen it, you know. That is the great thing: you must see it. And then you are redeemed and saved.

CAUCHON. Were not the sufferings of our Lord Christ enough for you?

DE STOGUMBER. No. Oh no: not at all. I had seen them in pictures, and read of them in books, and been greatly moved by them, as I thought. But it was no use: it was not our Lord that redeemed me, but a young woman whom I saw actually burned to death. It was dreadful: oh, most dreadful. But it saved me. I have been a different man ever since, though a little astray in my wits sometimes.

CAUCHON. Must then a Christ perish in torment in every age to save those that have no imagination?

JOAN. Well, if I saved all those he would have been cruel to if he had not been cruel to me, I was not burnt for nothing, was I?

DE STOGUMBER. Oh no; it was not you. My sight is bad: I cannot distinguish your features: but you are not she: oh no: she was burned to a cinder: dead and gone, dead and gone.

THE EXECUTIONER [*stepping from behind the bed curtains on Charles's right, the bed being between them*] She is more alive than you, old man. Her heart would not burn; and it would not drown. I was a master at my craft: better than the master of Paris, better than the master of Toulouse; but I could not kill The Maid. She is up and alive everywhere.

THE EARL OF WARWICK [*sallying from the bed curtains on the other side, and coming to Joan's left hand*] Madam: my congratulations on your rehabilitation. I feel that I owe you an apology.

JOAN. Oh, please dont mention it.

WARWICK [*pleasantly*] The burning was purely political. There was no personal feeling against you, I assure you.

JOAN. I bear no malice, my lord.

WARWICK. Just so. Very kind of you to meet me in that way: a touch of true breeding. But I must insist on apologizing very amply. The truth is, these political necessities sometimes turn out to be political mistakes; and this one was a veritable howler; for your spirit conquered us, madam, in spite of our faggots. History will remember me for your sake, though the incidents of the connection were perhaps a little unfortunate.

JOAN. Ay, perhaps just a little, you funny man.

WARWICK. Still, when they make you a saint, you will owe your halo to me, just as this lucky monarch owes his crown to you.

JOAN [*turning from him*] I shall owe nothing to any man: I owe everything to the spirit of God that was within me. But fancy me a saint! What would St Catherine and St Margaret say if the farm girl was cocked up beside them!

A clerical-looking gentleman in black frockcoat and trousers, and tall hat, in the fashion of the year 1920, suddenly appears before them in the corner on their right. They all stare at him. Then they burst into uncontrollable laughter.

THE GENTLEMAN. Why this mirth, gentlemen?

WARWICK. I congratulate you on having invented a most extraordinarily comic dress.

THE GENTLEMAN. I do not understand. You are all in fancy dress: I am properly dressed.

DUNOIS. All dress is fancy dress, is it not, except our natural skins?

THE GENTLEMAN. Pardon me: I am here on serious business, and cannot engage in frivolous discussions. [*He takes out a paper, and assumes a dry official manner*]. I am sent to announce to you that Joan of Arc, formerly known as The Maid, having been the subject of an inquiry instituted by the Bishop of Orleans—

JOAN [*interrupting*] Ah! They remember me still in Orleans.

THE GENTLEMAN [*emphatically, to mark his indignation at the interruption*]—by the Bishop of Orleans into the claim of the said Joan of Arc to be canonized as a saint—

JOAN [*again interrupting*] But I never made any such claim.

THE GENTLEMAN [*as before*]—the Church has examined the claim exhaustively in the usual course, and, having admitted the said Joan successively to the ranks of Venerable and Blessed,—

JOAN [*chuckling*] Me venerable!

THE GENTLEMAN.—has finally declared her to have been endowed with heroic virtues and favored with private revelations, and calls the said Venerable and Blessed Joan to the communion of the Church Triumphant as Saint Joan.

JOAN [*rapt*] Saint Joan!

THE GENTLEMAN. On every thirtieth day of May, being the anniversary of the death of the said most blessed daughter of God, there shall in every Catholic church to the end of time be celebrated a special office in commemoration of her; and it shall be lawful to dedicate a special chapel to her, and to place her image on its altar in every such church. And it shall be lawful and laudable for the faithful to kneel and address their prayers through her to the Mercy Seat.

JOAN. Oh no. It is for the saint to kneel. [*She falls on her knees, still rapt*].

THE GENTLEMAN [*putting up his paper, and retiring beside the Executioner*] In Basilica Vaticana, the sixteenth day of May, nineteen hundred and twenty.

DUNOIS [*raising Joan*] Half an hour to burn you, dear Saint: and four centuries to find out the truth about you!

DE STOGUMBER. Sir: I was chaplain to the Cardinal of Winchester once. They always would call him the Cardinal of England. It would be a great comfort to me and to my master to see a fair statue to The Maid in Winchester Cathedral. Will they put one there, do you think?

THE GENTLEMAN. As the building is temporarily in the hands of the Anglican heresy, I cannot answer for that.

A vision of the statue in Winchester Cathedral is seen through the window.

DE STOGUMBER. Oh look! look! that is Winchester.

JOAN. Is that meant to be me? I was stiffer on my feet.

The vision fades.

THE GENTLEMAN. I have been requested by the temporal authorities of France to mention that the multiplication of public statues to The Maid threatens to become an obstruction to traffic. I do so as a matter of courtesy to the said authorities, but must point out on behalf of the

Church that The Maid's horse is no greater obstruction to traffic than any other horse.

JOAN. Eh! I am glad they have not forgotten my horse.

A vision of the statue before Rheims Cathedral appears.

JOAN. Is that funny little thing me too?

CHARLES. That is Rheims Cathedral where you had me crowned. It must be you.

JOAN. Who has broken my sword? My sword was never broken. It is the sword of France.

DUNOIS. Never mind. Swords can be mended. Your soul is unbroken; and you are the soul of France.

The vision fades. The Archbishop and the Inquisitor are now seen on the right and left of Cauchon.

JOAN. My sword shall conquer yet: the sword that never struck a blow. Though men destroyed my body, yet in my soul I have seen God.

CAUCHON [*kneeling to her*] The girls in the field praise thee; for thou hast raised their eyes; and they see that there is nothing between them and heaven.

DUNOIS [*kneeling to her*] The dying soldiers praise thee, because thou art a shield of glory between them and the judgment.

THE ARCHBISHOP [*kneeling to her*] The princes of the Church praise thee, because thou hast redeemed the faith their worldlinesses have dragged through the mire.

WARWICK [*kneeling to her*] The cunning counsellors praise thee, because thou hast cut the knots in which they have tied their own souls.

DE STOGUMBER [*kneeling to her*] The foolish old men on their deathbeds praise thee, because their sins against thee are turned into blessings.

THE INQUISITOR [*kneeling to her*] The judges in the blindness and bondage of the law praise thee, because thou hast vindicated the vision and the freedom of the living soul.

THE SOLDIER [*kneeling to her*] The wicked out of hell praise thee, because thou hast shewn them that the fire that is not quenched is a holy fire.

THE EXECUTIONER [*kneeling to her*] The tormentors and executioners praise thee, because thou hast shewn that their hands are guiltless of the death of the soul.

CHARLES [*kneeling to her*] The unpretending praise thee, because thou hast taken upon thyself the heroic burdens that are too heavy for them.

JOAN. Woe unto me when all men praise me! I bid you remember that I am a saint, and that saints can work miracles. And now tell me: shall I rise from the dead, and come back to you a living woman?

A sudden darkness blots out the walls of the room as they all spring to their feet in consternation. Only the figures and the bed remain visible.

JOAN. What! Must I burn again? Are none of you ready to receive me?

CAUCHON. The heretic is always better dead. And mortal eyes cannot distinguish the saint from the heretic. Spare them. [*He goes out as he came*].

DUNOIS. Forgive us, Joan: we are not yet good enough for you. I shall go back to my bed. [*He also goes*].

WARWICK. We sincerely regret our little mistake; but political necessities, though occasionally erroneous, are still imperative; so if you will be good enough to excuse me— [*He steals discreetly away*].

THE ARCHBISHOP. Your return would not make me the man you once thought me. The utmost I can say is that though I dare not bless you, I hope I may one day enter into your blessedness. Meanwhile, however— [*He goes*].

THE INQUISITOR. I who am of the dead, testified that day that you were innocent. But I do not see how The Inquisition could possibly be dispensed with under existing circumstances. Therefore— [*He goes*].

DE STOGUMBER. Oh, do not come back: you must not come back. I must die in peace. Give us peace in our time, O Lord! [*He goes*].

THE GENTLEMAN. The possibility of your resurrection was not contemplated in the recent proceedings for your canonization. I must return to Rome for fresh instructions. [*He bows formally, and withdraws*].

THE EXECUTIONER. As a master in my profession I have to consider its interests. And, after all, my first duty is to my wife and children. I must have time to think over this. [*He goes*].

CHARLES. Poor old Joan! They have all run away from you except this blackguard who has to go back to hell at twelve o'clock. And what can I do but follow Jack Dunois' example, and go back to bed too? [*He does so*].

JOAN [*sadly*] Goodnight, Charlie.

CHARLES [*mumbling in his pillows*] Goo ni. [*He sleeps. The darkness envelops the bed*].

JOAN [*to the soldier*] And you, my one faithful? What comfort have you for Saint Joan?

THE SOLDIER. Well, what do they all amount to, these kings and captains and bishops and lawyers and such like? They just leave you in the ditch to bleed to death; and the next thing is, you meet them down there, for all the airs they give themselves. What I say is, you have as good a right to your notions as they have to theirs, and perhaps better. [*Settling himself for a lecture on the subject*] You see, it's like this. If— [*the first stroke of midnight is heard softly from a distant bell*]. Excuse me: a pressing appointment— [*He goes on tiptoe*].

The last remaining rays of light gather into a white radiance descending on Joan. The hour continues to strike.

JOAN. O God that madest this beautiful earth, when will it be ready to receive Thy saints? How long, O Lord, how long?